A Dictionary of

Literature in the English Language

From Chaucer to 1940

A Dictionary of

Literature in the English Language

From Chaucer to 1940

VOLUME 2

(Title–Author Index)

Compiled and Edited by *ROBIN MYERS*
for the *NATIONAL BOOK LEAGUE*

PERGAMON PRESS
OXFORD · NEW YORK · TORONTO
SYDNEY · BRAUNSCHWEIG

Pergamon Press Ltd., Headington Hill Hall, Oxford

Pergamon Press Inc., Maxwell House, Fairview Park, Elmsford, New York 10523

Pergamon of Canada Ltd., 207 Queen's Quay West, Toronto 1

Pergamon Press (Aust.) Pty. Ltd., 19a Boundary Street,
Rushcutters Bay, N.S.W. 2011, Australia

Vieweg & Sohn GmbH, Burgplatz 1, Braunschweig

First edition 1970

Library of Congress Catalog Card No. 68–18529

PRINTED IN GERMANY
08 016 142 1   VOL 2
08 016 143 X   SET

Contents

Preface to volume 1

THE aim of the present work is to provide in a single volume, bibliographical and biographical details of some 3500 authors who have used English as their medium throughout the world over a period of 600 years, together with reference to other bibliographical studies. I thought to begin with Chaucer, Gower and their contemporaries as being the first to use a language that we can recognise as English; although a handful of thirteenth century writers are also included. There are several reasons for choosing to end with those authors who began to publish before 1940. First, there was the difficulty of evaluating contemporary literature, working without the aid of definitive histories, and it was thought better to wait until the period could be seen in perspective. Moreover, to have included all the important writers throughout the world who have begun writing in English in the last 28 years would have too greatly enlarged the scope of the work I had in mind. But the main consideration was that, after that date, adequate national bibliographies exist to which librarians and scholars can have easy access. The date 1940 is arbitrary, as must be any one date, and the user will find examples of authors included because their first book was published in 1939 while others miss inclusion by one year.

The work was originally submitted to the publishers in February 1966 and this was intended to be the latest publication date given of works by living authors. However, revision in proof during 1967 allowed me to bring a certain number of British authors up to date at that point. But it was decided not to delay publication by making a thorough-going search for recently published work by living, or for new editions of the older authors. More could have been achieved had time permitted, on this and other aspects, but above all it was necessary to bring the work to a close before much became out of date.

The definition of literature is a wide one. It includes not only the great poets, dramatists and novelists, but also such writers as might be considered to form part of the literary history of their time, together with select examples of such semi-literary genres as the detective story and the romantic novel, too numerous and too ephemeral to be fully documented in a work of this nature. Certain non-literary writers, too, scientists, historians, economists, lawyers and statesmen, who have much influenced the thought of their day, or who have written excellently, have an undoubted place in literary history and are included in the dictionary. The user will find a selection of these peripheral literary figures who are often the very ones that the librarian finds most in demand.

A distinction has been made, where feasible, between an author's literary and non-literary or technical writings. The latter, if of sufficient importance, are generally mentioned in the biographical notes but without details of publication. I have attempted consistency to this principle, but each case has had to be individually considered in defining what is literary and what is not. Translations, editions, works in languages other than English, unpublished plays and the like, are dealt with in the same way, namely placed in the biographical notes; except insofar as certain celebrated editions, such as Johnson's edition of Shakespeare, or translations, such as Florio's Montaigne, are treated as creative writing in English. Important editors and translators who only produced editions or translations were to have been given a biographical entry without appending a list of works. But it has not been found possible to abide by this principle throughout. Major periodicals and newspapers, certain literary groups and movements and literary prizes referred to in the biographical notes are to be found as separate entries.

I have employed an alphabetical arrangement. The last name on the title page is the one which an author will be found under, even though this may give rise to incorrect forms where the writer's last name is not a surname in the European sense. Pseudonyms are generally cross-referenced to the author's real name, although in certain cases the entry will be found under pseudonym where this is better known. The biographical notes which precede each list of works relate the circumstances of the author's life without attempting critical assessment.

Each entry consists of full name and title, dates, biographical note and a list of bibliographical sources used in compilation or suggested for further study, arranged alphabetically under the author of the bibliography. Then follows a list of the first editions of separately published literary works in chronological order. Most of the lists are arranged under the head of collected or complete works, both the first and one or more later standard editions, where such exist, being itemised, followed by separately published works, where possible sub-divided into categories such as novels, plays, poems, published correspondence. Chronology is observed within each sub-section.

Piracies, including the "bad" quartos of Shakespeare, spurious and supposititious works, selections, unpublished plays, manuscripts, single broadsheets, works of which only one copy is known, and work published only in periodical form, are for the most part omitted. In the case of those nineteenth-century novels first published in parts or serially in a magazine, both the serial date and that of first issue in book form are given. In the case of plays, such as those by W. S. Gilbert, which were not published at the same time or in the same order as they were first performed, order and date of publication is given. And finally, in the case of those few authors who lived before the age of printing and where the supposed order of composition is very different from that of first printing, once again it has been decided to conform to the rule of first publication date. Bibliographers who have spent a lifetime of study on one particular author know how difficult it is to be conclusive about the identity and date of a first edition. In dealing with controversies I have checked entries with the aid of catalogues of the major national libraries, first and foremost the *British Museum General Catalogue*, the *Library of Congress Catalog*, and single-author bibliographies before completing the editing of an entry. In common with other compilers of bibliographies I have favourite reference books and short cuts to information, and on this point I must record my personal gratitude to the teams of scholars who laboured over long years to compile *The Cambridge Bibliography of English Literature*, without whose work my task would have been infinitely more difficult.

The publishers invited extensive revision in proof and this afforded opportunities to include fresh suggestions. In a work of this character, by the nature of the selection process involved, the more was offered the more controversy inevitably arose regarding what to include or exclude, how much biographical detail was appropriate, and whether some later editions were important enough to justify abandoning the general rule of listing only first editions of single works. A case in point was Sir J.G. Frazer's *Golden Bough*, whose first two-volume edition is dwarfed in importance by the later, 13 volume edition. There was, moreover, some conflict between what would be useful to working librarians and what to scholars and teachers of literature.

The observance of strict consistency of approach throughout presented increasing problems. The instance of Daniel Defoe may be cited as an author whose works are so numerous, and are so well listed in *The Cambridge Bibliography of English Literature* and other works of reference as to justify the inclusion here of a limited number of titles. In contrast the writings of the detective novelist John Dickson Carr have been given detailed treatment since they are of great interest to librarians whose need for comprehensive lists of titles cannot be met elsewhere. Uniformity of approach has thus been relinquished in special circumstances.

Suggestions are invited for the inclusion or exclusion of certain authors, titles and editions in the hope of incorporating these in a possible future edition.

Library of the National Book League   ROBIN MYERS

Addendum

This index volume of the sixty thousand titles found under author in volume 1 was derived from a card index prepared during the initial compilation. Because of its potential value to librarians and students this index was carefully revised and is here presented as a complete title–author index which, we believe, is a unique feature in a work of this kind.

Acknowledgements

THE editor is indebted to many for help and advice in compiling the following work and is particularly grateful to the following for their assistance:

Mr. Walter Allen; Mr. Robert Armstrong; Sardar S. Balasubrabramyan; Miss Judith Baskin; Professor Edmund Blunden; Mr. Dan Davin; Professor Brian Elliott; Mr. K. B. Gardner; Mr. D. B. Gibson; Mr. Ian Goonetilleke; Professor Douglas Grant; Mr. C. A. Gunawardena; Mr. K. E. Ingram; Professor K. R. Srinivasa Iyengar; Professor Eldred Jones; Miss Anne Laycock; Professor E. F. C. Lludowyk; Mr. David Overton; Mr. T. G. Rosenthal; Mr. Andrew Salkey; Sardar Khushwant Singh; Professor A. J. M. Smith; Miss R. South; Miss Thorn; Mr. J. C. Trewin; Mr. D. H. Varley; Mr. K. D. C. Vernon; Mr. Susanaga Weeraperuma; Miss G. M. Wiles; Mr. Ian Willison; Miss Margaret Yu.

Special thanks go to Mr. J. E. Morpurgo, Director-General of the National Book League, and to Miss Margaret Lindesay Clarke, without whose constant help and encouragement this work would not have been completed, let alone undertaken, and to Mr. Douglas Hamer and Mr. W. B. Stevenson who have undertaken the correction of large sections of the text in proof.

Alphabetical list of titles

A

A.B.: Smith, Pauline
A.B.C. murders, The: Christie, Agatha
A.B.C. of atoms: Russell, Bertrand
A.B.C. of economics: Pound, Ezra
A.B.C. of reading: Pound, Ezra
A.B.C. of relativity: Russell, Bertrand
A.B.C. of the theatre: Wolfe, Humbert
A.B.C. song book, The: Hassall, Christopher
A.E.F., The: Broun, Heywood
A.E.H.: Housman, Laurence
A.R.P.: Haldane, J.B.S.
A.W. Pollard: a memoir: Wilson, J.D.
A l'Abri: Willis, N.P.
A propos of Lady Chatterley's lover: Lawrence, D.H.
A si quis: Wither, George
A to Z: †Novello, Ivor
Aaron: Davies, Rhys
Aaron in the wildwoods: Harris, Joel Chandler
Aaron the Jew: Farjeon, B.L.
Aaron's rod: Lawrence, D.H.
Abacus and the rose, The: Bronowski, J.
Abaddon, the spirit of destruction: Fairfield, S.L.
Abaft the funnel: Kipling, Rudyard
Abandoned: Russell, W.C.
Abandoned, The: Gallico, Paul
Abandoned farm, The: Holmes, M.J.
Abba: Underhill, Evelyn
Abbess, The: Trollope, Frances
Abbess of Vlaye, The: Weyman, Stanley

Abbey by the sea, The: Molesworth, Mrs.
Abbeychurch: Yonge, C.M.
Abbot, The: Scott, Sir Walter
Abbot's heel: †Bell, Neil
Abbots Verney: Macaulay, Rose
Abby Aldrich Rockefeller: Chase, M.E.
Abdallah and Labat: Montgomery, James
Abdelazar: Behn, Mrs. Afra
Abe Lincoln and Nancy Hawks: Hubbard, Elbert
Abe Lincoln grows up: Sandburg, Carl
Abe Lincoln in Illinois: Sherwood, R.E.
Abeokuta and the Cameroon Mountains: Burton, Sir Richard Francis
Ability to kill, The: Ambler, Eric
Abimlech: Smart, Christopher
Abinger harvest: Forster, E.M.
Abode of love: (†Joseph Shearing) †Bowen, Marjorie
Abolishing of death, The: †King, Basil
Abolition of man: Lewis, C.S.
Abolition of slavery, The: Garrison, W.L.
Abolition of the Poor Law, The: Webb, Beatrice
About education: Joad, C.E.M.
About hymns: Bridges, Robert
About Ireland: Linton, Eliza
About Kingsmill: Pearson, Hesketh
About Levy: Calder-Marshall, Arthur
About money and other things: Craik, Mrs. Dinah Maria
About old story-tellers: Mitchell, D.G.

About ourselves: Wood, Ellen
About Paris: Davis, Richard Harding
About Ulster: Linton, Eliza
About women: Sutro, Alfred
About Zionism: Einstein, Albert
Above all else: Shiel, M.P.
Above all nations: Brittain, Vera
Above suspicion: Riddell, Mrs. J.H.
Above the dark circus: Walpole, Sir Hugh
Above your heads: Niven, F.J.
Abracadabra: Galsworthy, John
Abraham: Woolley, Sir Leonard
Abraham Aesop: Newbery, John
Abraham Lincoln: Brogan, Sir Denis
Abraham Lincoln: Drinkwater, John
Abraham Lincoln: Whitlock, Brand
Abraham Lincoln: an Horatian ode: Stoddard, R.H.
Abraham Lincoln, the prairie years: Sandburg, Carl
Abraham Lincoln, the war years: Sandburg, Carl
Abraham's bosom: †King, Basil
Abridgement of Blackstone's Commentaries, An: Warren, Samuel
Abridgement of the history of England from the invasion of Julius Caesar to the death of George II, An: Goldsmith, Oliver
Abridgement of the life and times of Anthony à Wood: Powys, Llewelyn
Abridgement of The light of nature pursued, by Abraham Tucker, An: Hazlitt, William

Absalom: Moore, T.S.

Absalom, Absalom!: Faulkner, William

Absalom and Achitophel: Dryden, John

Absalom Senior: Settle, Elkanah

Absent in the spring: Christie, Agatha

Absent man, The: Bickerstaffe, Isaac

Absentee, The: Edgeworth, Maria

Absentee, The: Strong, L.A.G.

Absentee ownership and business enterprise in recent times: Veblen, T.B.

Absenteeism: Morgan, *Lady* Sydney

Absent-minded beggar, The: Kipling, Rudyard

Absolutely Bob Brown: Stein, Gertrude

Abstract of the lawes of New England, An: Cotton, John

Abu Hassan: Chattopadhyaya, Harindranath

Abu Hassan: (†Geoffrey Crayon), Irving, Washington

Abuses of conscience, The: Sterne, Laurence

Abuses stript, and whipt: Wither, George

Abydos I: Petrie, *Sir* William Flinders

Abydos II: Petrie, *Sir* William Flinders

Abysmal brute, The: London, Jack

Academies of art, past and present: Pevsner, Nikolaus

Acadian exiles, The: Doughty, *Sir* A.G.

Acanthus and wild grape: Call, F.O.

Accedence commend't grammar: Milton, John

Acceptable sacrifice, The: Bunyan, John

Acceptance world, The: Powell, Anthony

Accepted addresses: Sala, G.A.H.

Accepting the universe: Burroughs, John

Accidence, An: Smith, John

Accident: Bennett, Arnold

Accidents of an antiquary's life: Hogarth, David George

Accolade: Williams, Emlyn

Accolade, The: Sidgwick, Ethel

Accolon of Gaul: Cawein, Madison

Accomplished Irish antiquary: Croker, Thomas Crofton

Accomplished preacher, The: Blackmore, R.D.

Accomplished singer, The: Mather, Cotton

According to Gibson: Mackail, Denis

According to plan: Peach, L. du Garde

Account of a journey into Wales: Lyttelton, George *Baron*

Account of a voyage round the world, An: Cook, James

Account of Christian slavery in Algiers, An: Hone, William

Account of Clopton Hall, Warwickshire: Gaskell, Elizabeth Cleghorn

Account of Corsica, An: Boswell, James

Account of French painting, An: Bell, Clive

Account of negotiations in London: Franklin, Benjamin

Account of New South Wales and state of the convicts: Dyer, George

Account of the battle of Chateauguay, An: Lighthall, W.D.

Account of the Coronation of George III: Scott, *Sir* Walter

Account of the English dramatick poets, An: Langbaine, Gerard

Account of the European settlements in America, An: Burke, Edmund

Account of the fish pool, An: Steele, *Sir* Richard

Account of the giants lately discovered, An: Walpole, Horace

Account of the Grand Federal Procession: Hopkinson, Francis

Account of the growth of Popery and arbitrary government in England, An: Marvell, Andrew

Account of the incidents from which the title and part of the story of Shakespeare's Tempest were derived, An: Malone, Edmund

Account of the late Dr. John Morgan, An: Rush, Benjamin

Account of the life and character of Christopher Ludwick, An: Rush, Benjamin

Account of the life and writings of Sir Thomas Craig, An: Tytler, P.F.

Account of the life of Dr. Samuel Johnson, from his birth to his eleventh year, An: Johnson, Samuel

Account of the life of John Philip Barretier, An: Johnson, Samuel

Account of the life of Mr. Richard Savage, An: Johnson, Samuel

Account of the life of the late Reverend Mr. David Brainerd, An: Edwards, Jonathan

Account of the lock-out of engineers: Hughes, Thomas

Account of the loyal Mohomedans of India, An: Ahmad Khan, *Sir* Saiyid

Account of the manners and customs of modern Egyptians, An: Lane, Edward William

Account of the manners of the German inhabitants of Pennsylvania, An: Rush, Benjamin

Account of the new north wing and recent additions to University College, London, An: Morley, Henry

Account of the new Pennsylvania fire-places, An: Franklin, Benjamin

Account of the riots in London, An: Hone, William

Account of the seminary that will be opened on Monday the fourth day of August at Epsom in Surrey, An: Godwin, William

Account of the statues, pictures and temples in Greece, An: Price, *Sir* Uvedale

Account of the trial of J. Thurtell and J. Hunt: Egan, Pierce

Account rendered: Benson, E.F.

Account rendered: Brittain, Vera

Accurate catalogue of the paintings in the King of Spain's palace at Madrid, An: Cumberland, Richard

Accuser, The: †Field, Michael

Accusing ghost, The: Noyes, Alfred

Ace, The: Malleson, Miles

Ace of clubs: Coward, Noel

Acetaria: Evelyn, John

Achievement in American poetry: Bogan, Louise

Achievement in feeding Britain: Bullett, Gerald

Achilles: Gay, John

Achilles and the twins: Bates, H.E.

Achilles had a heel: Flavin, Martin

Achilles in Scyros: Bridges, Robert

Acid drops: Jennings, Gertrude

Acis and Galatea: Gay, John

Acis in Oxford: Finch, R.D.C.

Ackymals, The: Williamson, Henry

Acorn-planter, The: London, Jack

Acquaintance with description, An: Stein, Gertrude

Acquisitive society, The: Tawney, R.H.

Acquittal: Simpson, H. de G.

Acre of grass, An: (†Michael Innes), Stewart, J.I.M.

Acres and pains: Perelman, S.J.

Across my path: Edgar, O.P.

Across Spoon River: Masters, E.L.

Across the black waters: Anand, M.R.

Across the board on tomorrow morning: Saroyan, William

Across the frontiers: Gibbs, Philip Hamilton

Across the plains: Stevenson, R.L.

Across the river and into the trees: Hemingway, Ernest

Across the wide Missouri: De Voto, Bernard

Across the years: Porter, E.H.

Act five: MacLeish, Archibald

Act for the better ordering and regulating ... for military purposes, An: Franklin, Benjamin

Act in a backwater, An: Benson, E.F.

Act of faith: Shaw, Irwin

Actaeon: Erskine, John

Acte: Durrell, L.G.

Actes and monuments: Foxe, John

Acting charades: Mayhew, Henry

Acting edition of Ariadne, The: Milne, A.A.

Acting edition of Mr. Pim passes by, The: Milne, A.A.

Action: Montague, C.E.

Action and passion: Wren, P.C.

Action and the word, The: Matthews, J.B.

Action at Aquila: Allen, Hervey

Action front: Ewart, E.A.

Actions and reactions: Kipling, Rudyard

Active service: Crane, Stephen

Actor, The: Vachell, H.A.

Actor, The: Winter, William

Actor and his audience, The: Darlington, W.A.

Actor manager, The: Merrick, Leonard

Actor visits China, An: Malleson, Miles

Actors and actresses of Great Britain and the United States: Matthews, J.B.

Actor's blood: Hecht, Ben

Acts of darkness: Bishop, John Peale

Acts of Saint Peter, The: Bottomley, Gordon

Ad multos annos: Morgan, H.J.

Ad vesperum: Carman, Bliss

Ada Rehan: Winter, William

Ada Reis: Lamb, *Lady* Caroline

Adagio in blue: Moore, T.I.

Adam: Lewisohn, Ludwig

Adam and Eve: Murry, John Middlebon

Adam & Eve & pinch me: Coppard, A.E.

Adam & Eve & the city: Williams, W.C.

Adam and Eve, though he knew better: Erskine, John

Adam and the serpent: Fisher, V.A.

Adam Bede: †Eliot, George

Adam Brown: Smith, Horatio

Adam cast forth: Doughty, Charles Montagu

Adam Grainger: Wood, Ellen

Adam in moonshine: Priestley, J.B.

Adam Johnstone's son: Crawford, Francis Marion

Adam Lindsay Gordon and his friends: Sladen, D.B.W.

Adam of a new world: Lindsay, Jack

Adam the gardener: Clarke, Charles Cowden

Adam unparadised: Bottrall, Ronald

Adamastor: Campbell, Roy

Adam's breed: Hall, M.R.

Adams family, The: Adams, J.T.

Adam's opera: †Dane, Clemence

Adam's orchard: †Grand, Sarah

Adam's rest: Millin, Sarah Gertrude

Adam's rib: Graves, Robert

Adaptation of external nature to the moral and intellectual constitution of man: Chalmers, Thomas

Adaptation of Faust: Parker, *Sir* H.G.

Adder, The: Abercrombie, Lascelles

Adding machine, The: Rice, Elmer

Additional dialogue of the dead, An: Lyttelton, George *Baron*

Additions and corrections to Sir John Fortescue's edition of the correspondence of King George III: Namier, *Sir* L.B.

Address at the unveiling of the statue of Washington, An: Curtis, George William

Address by way of a last statutory public lecture, An: Stubbs, William

Address by way of inaugural lecture, An: Stubbs, William

Address delivered at the eightieth commencement, An: Van Doren, Mark

Address delivered before the senior class in Divinity College, Cambridge, An: Emerson, Ralph Waldo

Address delivered in St. Andrews Hall: Mackenzie, *Sir* C.

Address delivered in the Court House in Concord, Massachusetts, An: Emerson, Ralph Waldo

Address; National Civil Service Reform League: Curtis, G.W.

Address occasioned by the death of General Lingan, An: Custis, G.W.P.

Address of Congress to the inhabitants of the province of Quebec: Dickinson, John

Address of Congress to the several States on the present situation of affairs: Dickinson, John

Address of John Dryden, Laureat to His Highness the Prince of Orange, The: Shadwell, Thomas

Address of thanks from the Society of rakes, An: Ramsay, Allan

Address on Henry Lawson: Brereton, John Le G.

Address on the collection of paintings of the English pre-Raphaelite school, An: Morris, William

Address on the occasion of reading the Declaration of Independence, An: Adams, John Quincy

Address on the occasion of the presentation of a testimonial of his services to the cause of co-operation: Hughes, Thomas

Address on the past, present, and eventual relations of the United States to France, An: Dickinson, John

Address prepared for the annual meeting of the New York Civil-Service Reform Association: Curtis, G.W.

Address read at a meeting of merchants to consider non-importation, An: Dickinson, John

Address to be spoken at the opening of Drury Lane Theatre, An: †Pindar, Peter

Address to the anthropological department of the British Association: Galton, *Sir* Francis

Address to the committee of correspondence in Barbados, An: Dickinson, John

Address ... to the French delegation, on their visit to the torpedo station: Calvert, G.H.

Address to the graduates of the Yonkers High School, An: Bangs, John Kendrick

Address to the Irish people, An: Shelley, P.B.

Address to the people of the United States on the importance of encouraging agriculture and domestic manufactures, An: Custis, G.W.P.

Address to the people on the death of the Princess Charlotte, An: Shelley, P.B.

Address to the public, on the treatment which the editor of The history of Sir Charles Grandison has met with, An: Richardson, Samuel

Address unknown: Phillpotts, Eden

Address upon the life and services, of Edward Everett, An: Dana, R.H. *junior*

Address, vindicating the right of women to the elective franchise, An: Curtis, G.W.

Addresses delivered at Manchester, Leeds and Birmingham: Stanhope, P.H. *Earl*

Addresses in America: Galsworthy, John

Addresses on general subjects connected with English literature: Blunden, Edmund

Addresses on the triumph of liberty in France: Wirt, William

Addresses to Cardinal Newman, with his replies: Newman, J.H.

Addresses to the literary societies of Rutgers College: Wirt, William

Addresses with prayers and original hymns for the use of families: Martineau, Harriet

Adela Cathcart: Macdonald, George

Adelaide: Pye, H.J.

Adèle: Kavanagh, Julia

Adèle and Co.: †Yates, Dornford

Adelgitha: Lewis, Matthew Gregory

Adeline Mowbray: Opie, Amelia

Adelmorn the outlaw: Lewis, Matthew Gregory

Adirondack cycle: Untermeyer, Louis

Adjectives and other words: Weekley, Ernest

Adjectives from proper names: Chapman, R.W.

Admetus: Lazarus, Emma

Administration and politics of Tokyo, The: Beard, C.A.

Administration of war production, The: Hughes, R.A.W.

Administrator, The: Macneice, Louis

Admirable Bashville, The: Shaw, G.B.

Admirable Carfew: Wallace, Edgar

Admirable Crichton, The: Barrie, J.M.

Admiral, The: Sladen, D.B.W.

Admiral Arthur Philip, founder of New South Wales, 1738–1814: Mackaness, George

Admiral Eddy: †Onions, Oliver

Admiral Guinea: Henley, W.E.

Admiral Guinea: Stevenson, R.L.

Admiral Hornblower: Forester, C.S.

Admiral Hosier's ghost: Glover, Richard

Admiral of the Ocean Sea: Morison, S.E.

Admiral Peters: Jacobs, W.W.

Admiral Philip: †Becke, Louis

Admirals all: (†Ian Hay), Beith, *Sir* John Hay

Admirals all: Newbolt, *Sir* Henry

Admiral's million: Divine, A.D.

Adobe walls: Burnett, W.R.

Adonai, the pilgrim of eternity: Lippard, George

Adonais: Shelley, P.B.

Adonis and the alphabet: Huxley, Aldous

Adonis, Attis, Osiris, studies in the history of Oriental religion: Frazer, *Sir* James

Adopted, The: McFee, William

Adopted daughter, The: Fawcett, Edgar

Adra: James, George Payne Rainsford

Adrea: Belasco, David

Adriaen Block, skipper, trader, explorer: Van Loon, Hendrik

Adrian: James, George Payne Rainsford

Adrian Glynde: Armstrong, M.D.

Adrian Rome: Dowson, Ernest Christopher

Adrienne Toner: Sedgwick, A.D.

A drift on an ice-pan: Grenfell, *Sir* Wilfred

Advance agent: De Voto, Bernard

Advance Australia—where?: Penton, B.C.

Advance of Harriet, The: Bottome, Phyllis

Advance under fire: Murray, George

Advanced English grammar, with exercises, An: Kittredge, G.L.

Advanced English reader, An: Craigie, *Sir* William Alexander

Advanced English syntax: Onions, C.T.

Advanced French composition: Onions, C.T.

Advancement and reformation of modern poetry, The: Dennis, John

Advancing science: Lodge, *Sir* Oliver

Advantages propos'd by repealing the Sacramental test, The: Swift, Jonathan

Advent sermons: Church, Richard William

Adventure: London, Jack

Adventure of criticism, The: Iyengar, K.R. Srinivasa

Adventure of hare, The: Uttley, Alison

Adventure of life, The: Grenfell, *Sir* Wilfred

Adventure of living, The: Strachey, John St.Loe

Adventure of my freshman, The: Davis, R. H.

Adventure of the Christmas pudding, The: Christie, Agatha

Adventure of the Orient Express, The: Derleth, A.W.

Adventure of Wrangel Island, The: Stefansson, V.

Adventure story: Rattigan, Terence

Adventurer, The: Hawkesworth, John

Adventurer in Spain, The: Crockett, S.R.

Adventurer of the North, An: Parker, *Sir* H.G.

Adventurers of Oregon: Skinner, C.L.

Adventures: Cruden, Alexander

Adventures among birds: Hudson, W. H.

Adventures among books: Lang, Andrew

Adventures and enthusiasms: Lucas, E.V.

Adventures and misgivings: Lucas, E.V.

Adventures in Borneo: Gore, Catherine

Adventures in contentment: Baker, Ray Stannard

Adventures in criticism: (†Q), Quiller-Couch, *Sir* A.

Adventures in error: Stefansson, V.

Adventures in fishing: Grey, Zane

Adventures in friendship: Baker, Ray Stannard

Adventures in genius: Durant, W.J.

Adventures in journalism: Gibbs, *Sir* Philip

Adventures in living dangerously: Golding, Louis

Adventures in religion: †King, Basil

Adventures in solitude: Baker, Ray Stannard

Adventures in the skin trade: Thomas, Dylan

Adventures in Thule: Black, William

Adventures in two worlds: Cronin, A. J.

Adventures in understanding: Baker, Ray Stannard

Adventures of a Brownie, The: Craik, *Mrs.* Dinah Maria

Adventures of a modest man, The: Chambers, R.W.

Adventures of a novelist: Atherton, Gertrude Franklin

Adventures of a supercargo: †Becke, Louis

Adventures of a widow, The: Fawcett, Edgar

Adventures of a young man: Dos Passos, John

Adventures of a younger son, The: Trelawny, E.J.

Adventures of an aide-de-camp: Grant, James

Adventures of an attorney in search of practice: Warren, Samuel

Adventures of Ann, The: Freeman, Mary

Adventures of Aron Rod, The: Oppenheim, E. Phillips

Adventures of Billy Topsail, The: Duncan, Norman

Adventures of Bobby Orde, The: White, S.E.

Adventures of Brusanus, Prince of Hungaria, The: Rich, Barnabe

Adventures of Captain Horn, The: Stockton, F.R.

Adventures of Colonel Gracchus Vanderbomb: Jones, J.B.

Adventures of Covent Garden, The: Farquhar, George

Adventures of D.G.: Baker, Ray Stannard

Adventures of David Simple, The: Fielding, Sarah

Adventures of David Vane and David Crane, The: Trowbridge, J.T.

Adventures of detective Barney, The: O'Higgins, H.J.

Adventures of Elizabeth in Reugen, The: Russell, E.M.

Adventures of Eovaii, Princess of Ijaveo, The: Haywood, *Mrs.* Eliza

Adventures of Ernest Alembert, The: Brontë, Charlotte

Adventures of Ernest Bliss, The: Oppenheim, E. Phillips

Adventures of Ferdinand Count Fathom, The: Smollett, Tobias

Adventures of François, The: Mitchell, S.W.

Adventures of Gerard: Doyle, Sir Arthur Conan

Adventures of Hajji Baba of Ispahan, The: Morier, J.J.

Adventures of Hajji Baba of Ispahan in England, The: Morier, J.J.

Adventures of Harry Revel, The: (†Q), Quiller-Couch, Sir A.

Adventures of Harry Richmond, The: Meredith, George

Adventures of Heine, the spy, The: Wallace, Edgar

Adventures of Hiram Holliday: Gallico, Paul

Adventures of Huckleberry Finn, The: (†Mark Twain), Clemens, S.L.

Adventures of Hugh Trevor, The: Holcroft, Thomas

Adventures of ideas: Whitehead, A.N.

Adventures of Isobel, The: Nash, Ogden

Adventures of Jimmy Dale, The: Packard, F.L.

Adventures of John Timothy Homespun in Switzerland: Kemble, Frances Anne

Adventures of Johnny Walker, tramp, The: Davies, W.H.

Adventures of Kimble Bent, The: Cowan, James

Adventures of little Downy: Traill, C.P.

Adventures of Louis Blake, The: †Becke, Louis

Adventures of Martin Hewitt: Morrison, Arthur

Adventures of Miss Volney, The: Wilcox, Ella Wheeler

Adventures of Mr. Joseph P. Clay, The: Oppenheim, E. Phillips

Adventures of Mr. Verdant Green, The: †Bede, Cuthbert

Adventures of no ordinary rabbit: Uttley, Alison

Adventures of Odysseus and the tale of Troy, The: Colum, Padraic

Adventures of Peregrine Pickle, The: Smollett, Tobias

Adventures of Peter and Judy in Bunnyland, The: Uttley, Alison

Adventures of Philip on his way through the world, The: Thackeray, W.M.

Adventures of Rob Roy: Grant, James

Adventures of Robin Day, The: Bird, Robert Montgomery

Adventures of Roderick Random, The: Smollett, Tobias

Adventures of Sajo and her beaver people, The: (†Grey Owl), Belaney, G.S.

Adventures of Sally, The: Wodehouse, P.G.

Adventures of Sam Pig: Uttley, Alison

Adventures of Sam Spade, The: Hammett, S.D.

Adventures of Seumas Beg, The: Stephens, James

Adventures of Sherlock Holmes, The: Doyle, Sir Arthur Conan

Adventures of Sir Launcelot Greaves, The: Smollett, Tobias

Adventures of the black girl in her search for God, The: Shaw, G.B.

Adventures of the far North: Leacock, Stephen

Adventures of the Sandboys family: Mayhew, Henry

Adventures of the Scarlet Pimpernel: Orczy, Baroness

Adventures of the young soldier in search of the better world, The: Joad, C.E.M.

Adventures of Thomas Jefferson Snodgrass, The: (†Mark Twain), Clemens, S.L.

Adventures of Tim Rabbit: Uttley, Alison

Adventures of Timothy Peacock, Esq, The: Thompson, D.P.

Adventures of Tom Bombadil, The: Tolkien, J.R.R.

Adventures of Tom Leigh, The: Bentley, Phyllis

Adventures of Tom Sawyer, The: (†Mark Twain), Clemens, S.L.

Adventures of Tom Spicer, who advertised for a wife, The: Morier, J.J.

Adventures of Tommy, The: Wells, H.G.

Adventures of two chairs, The: Mackenzie, Sir C.

Adventures of Ulysses, The: Lamb, Charles

Adventures of war with cross and crescent: Gibbs, Sir Philip

Adventures of Wesley Jackson, The: Saroyan, William

Adventures of Will Wizard, The: Ingraham, J.H.

Adventures while preaching the gospel of beauty: Lindsay, N.V.

Adventuring among words: Partridge, E.H.

Adventurous love: Cannan, Gilbert

Adversary, The: Young, A.J.

Advertisement touching an Holy warre: Bacon, Francis

Advertisements for the unexperienced planters of New-England, or any where: Smith, John

Advertising and advertisements: Hubbard, Elbert

Advertising April: Farjeon, Herbert

Advice: Bodenheim, Maxwell

Advice: Smollett, Tobias

Advice limited: Oppenheim, E. Phillips

Advice to a lady: Lyttelton, George Baron

Advice to a son: Osborne, Francis

Advice to a young man on choosing a mistress: Franklin, Benjamin

Advice to a young tradesman: Franklin, Benjamin

Advice to Julia: Luttrell, Henry

Advice to the future Laureat: †Pindar, Peter

Advice to the officers of the British Army: Grose, Francis

Advice to the poets: Blackmore, R.D.

Advice to the poets: Hill, Aaron

Advice to the priviledged orders in the several states of Europe: Barlow, Joel

Advice to unmarried ladies: Richardson, Samuel

Advice to young men: Cobbett, William

Advisory Ben: Lucas, E.V.

Advocate, The: Heavysege, Charles

Advocateship of Jesus Christ, The: Bunyan, John

Adzuma: Arnold, Edwin

Aedes Walpolianae: Walpole, Horace

Aegean memories: Mackenzie, *Sir* Compton

Aeneid of Virgil, The: Mackail, J.W.

Aeneids of Virgil, The: Morris, William

Aeriphorion: Pye, H.J.

Aerius redivivus: Heylyn, Peter

Aerodrome, The: Warner, Rex

Aëromancy: Woods, M.L.

Aeschylus, creator of tragedy: Murray, George

Aeschylus. Prometheus bound: Murray, George

Aeschylus. The: Oresteia Murray, George

Aeschylus. The suppliant women: Murray, George

Aesop: Vanbrugh, *Sir* John

Aesop. Fables (trn.): Caxton, William

Aesop's fables: Philipot, Thomas

Aesop's fables: Richardson, Samuel

Aesthetes, The: Turner, W.J.R.

Aesthetic criticism in Canada: Logan, J.D.

Aesthetics: Mumford, Lewis

Aesthetics and history in the visual arts: Berenson, Bernhard

Afar in the desert: Pringle, Thomas

Afar in the forest: Traill, C.P.

Affable stranger, The: McArthur, Peter

Affair, The: Snow, C.P.

Affair at Aliquid, The: Cole, G.D.H.

Affair at Little Wokeham, The: Crofts, F.W.

Affair of dishonour, An: De Morgan, W.F.

Affair of honour, An: Nabokov, Vladimir

Affairs of men: †Bowen, Marjorie

Affectionate regards: Ridge, W.Pett

Affectionate shepheard, The: Barnfield, Richard

Affectionately Eve: Sinclair, Upton

Affinities: Praed, *Mrs.* C.

Affinities: Rinehart, Mary Roberts

Affirmations: Ellis, Henry Havelock

Afield and afloat: Stockton, F.R.

Afloat and ashore: Cooper, James Fenimore

Afloat and ashore: Hale, E.E.

Afloat in the forest: Reid, T.M.

Afoot in England: Hudson, W.H.

Afoot in Ultima Thule: MacMechan, A.M.

Aforetime: Moore, T.S.

Africa: Cripps, A.S.

Africa for Africans, An: Cripps, A.S.

Africa in the world democracy: Johnson, J.W.

Africa view: Huxley, *Sir* Julian

African camp fires: White, S.E.

African colony, The: Buchan, John

African giant, The: Cloete, E.F.S.G.

African millionaire, An: Allen, Grant

African poison murders, The: Huxley, Elspeth J.

African portraits: Cloete, E.F.S.G.

African Queen, The: Forester, C.S.

African sketches: Pringle, Thomas

African tragedy, An: Dhlomo, R.R.R.

African tragedy: Graham, Stephen

African witch, The: Cary, Joyce

African year, An: Gouldsbury, H.C.

Africans, The: Colman, George, *the younger*

Africans all: Cripps, A.S.

Afrikander: Reitz, Deneys

Afro-Asian states and their problems, The: Panikkar, K.M.

After all: Angell, *Sir* Norman

After all: Day, C.S.

After all: Van Druten, J.W.

After all, not to create only: Whitman, Walt

After breakfast: Sala, G.A.H.

After breakfast book, The: †Armstrong, Anthony

After dark: Collins, William Wilkie

After democracy: Wells, H.G.

After dinner philosophy: Joad, C.E.M.

After glow: Rubenstein, Harold F.

After house, The: Rinehart, Mary Roberts

After London: Jefferies, Richard

After many a summer: Huxley, Aldous

After 1903—what?: Benchley, Robert

After October: Ackland, Rodney

After office hours: Yates, E.H.

After Paradise: (†Owen Meredith), Lytton, E.R.B., *Earl*

After strange gods: Eliot, T.S.

After such pleasures: Parker, Dorothy

After sunset: Sterling, George

After the ball: Coward, Noel

After the dance: Rattigan, Terence

After the death of Don Juan: Warner, Sylvia Townsend

After the deluge: Woolf, Leonard

After the funeral: Christie, Agatha

After the genteel tradition: Cowley, Malcolm

After the thirties: Lindsay, Jack

After the verdict: Hichens, R.S.

After the war: Dickinson, Goldsworthy Lowes

After the war: Jennings, Gertrude

After thirty years: Saroyan, William

After two thousand years, a dialogue between Plato and a modern young man: Dickinson, Goldsworthy Lowes

Afterglow, The: Hichens, R.S.

Afterglow: Lathrop, G.P.

Aftermath: Allen, James Lane

Aftermath: Frazer, *Sir* James

Aftermath: Longfellow, H.W.

Aftermath: Trevelyan, R.C.

Afternoon landscape, The: Higginson, T.W.

Afternoon men: Powell, Anthony

Afternoon neighbours: Garland, Hamlin

Afternoon of a pawnbroker: Fearing, Kenneth

Afternoon of an author: Fitzgerald, F.Scott

Afternoons in Utopia: Leacock, Stephen

Afterthought: Bowen, E.D.C.

After-war settlement and employment of ex-servicemen, The: Haggard, *Sir* Henry Rider

After-whiles: Riley, J.W.

Again Sanders: Wallace, Edgar

Again the ringer: Wallace, Edgar

Again the three just men: Wallace, Edgar

Against heavy odds: Boyesen, H.H.

Against the cold: Bynner, Witter

Against the sky: Bercovici, Konrad

Against the tide: Bedford-Jones, Henry

Against this age: Bodenheim, Maxwell

Against whom?: Bottome, Phyllis

Against wind and tide: Moulton, E.L.

Against women inconstant: Chaucer, Geoffrey

Agamemnon: Fitzgerald, Edward

Agamemnon: Thomson, James

Agamemnon of Aeschylus, The: Macneice, Louis

Agamemnon of Aeschylus, The: Murray, Gilbert

Agate lamp, The: Gore-Booth, E.S.

Agate's folly: Agate, J.E.

Agatha: †Eliot, George

Agatha's husband: Craik, *Mrs.* Dinah Maria

Agathonia: Gore, Catherine

Age, The: Bailey, P.J.

Age of anxiety, The: Auden, W.H.

Age of benevolence, The: Wilcox, Carlos

Age of bronze, The: Byron, G.G. *Lord*

Age of Catherine de Medici, The: Neale, J.E.

Age of Chaucer, The: (†Q), Quiller-Couch, *Sir* A.

Age of chivalry, The: Bryant, *Sir* Arthur

Age of confidence, The: Canby, Henry Seidel

Age of consent: Lindsay, Norman

Age of Dryden, The: Garnett, Richard

Age of elegance, The: Bryant, *Sir* Arthur

Age of innocence, The: Wharton, Edith

Age of Jackson, The: Schlesinger, Arthur

Age of reason, The: Gibbs, *Sir* Philip

Age of reason, The: Nicolson, *Sir* Harold

Age of reason being an investigation of true and fabulous theology, The: Paine, Thomas

Age of Roosevelt, The: Schlesinger, Arthur

Age of scandal, The: White, T.H.

Age of Shakespeare, The: Swinburne, A.C.

Age of thunder: Prokosch, Frederic

Age of the dragon, The: Lehmann, John

Age of Voltaire, The: Durant, W.J.

Age of youth, The: Maltby, H.F.

Age reviewed, The: Montgomery, Robert

Aged poor in England and Wales, The: Booth, Charles

Agents and patients: Powell, Anthony

Ages ago: Gilbert, W.S.

Agincourt: James, George Payne Rainsford

Agis: Home, John

Aglaura: Suckling, *Sir* John

Aglavaine and Selysette (trn.): Sutro, Alfred

Agnes: Oliphant, Margaret

Agnes: Reynolds, G.

Agnes de Mansfeldt: Gratton, Thomas Colley

Agnes de Tracy: Neale, J.M.

Agnes Evelyn: Reynolds, G.

Agnes Grey: Brontë, Anne

Agnes Hopetoun's schools and holidays: Oliphant, Margaret

Agnes Irwin: Repplier, Agnes

Agnes of Sorrento: Stowe, Hariet Beecher

Agnes Sorrel: James, George Payne Rainsford

Agnes Strickland: biographer of the queens of England: Pope-Hennessy, *Dame* Una

Agnes Surriage: Bynner, Edwin Lassetter

Agnosticism: Fawcett, Edgar

Agnostic's apology, An: Stephen, *Sir* Leslie

Agonists, The: Hewlett, M.H.

Agrarian problem in the sixteenth century, The: Tawney, R.H.

Agreeable surprise, The: O'Keeffe, John

Agrippa's daughter: Fast, Howard M.

Ah king: Maugham, Somerset

Ah! wilderness! O'Neill, Eugene

Ahalya Baee: Baillie, Joanna

A'hunting of the deer: Warner, C.D.

Aideen's grave: Fergusson, *Sir* Samuel

Aids to reflection in the formation of a manly character: Coleridge, Samuel Taylor

Aim of Indian art, The: Coomaraswamy, A.K.

Aims of education, The: Whitehead, A.N.

Air men o'war: Ewart, E.A.

Air Ministry, Room 28: Frankau, Gilbert

Air raid: MacLeish, Archibald

Air-conditioned nightmare, The: Miller, Henry

Airing in a closed carriage: (†Joseph Shearing), †Bowen, Marjorie

Airs—for the hautbois and other instruments: Andrade, E.N. da Costa

Airs from Arcady: Bunner, Henry Cuyler

Airship, The: †Caudwell, Christopher

Air-storming: Van Loon, Hendrik

Airways, inc.: Dos Passos, John

Aissa saved: Cary, Joyce

Akaroa: Baughan, B.E.

Akbar's dream: Tennyson, Alfred *Lord*

Akra the slave: Gibson, Wilfred

Al Aaraaf: Poe, Edgar Allan

Alabama: Thomas, Augustus

Alabaster box, An: Freeman, Mary Wilkins

Alabaster box, The: Alen, James Lane

Aladdin: Ransome, A.M.

Aladdin and the Boss Cockie: Bedford, Randolph

Aladdin in London: Hume, F.W.

Aladdin, or the wonderful lamp: Braddon, Mary Elizabeth

Aladdin's cave: Jennings, Gertrude

Aladore: Newbolt, *Sir* Henry

Alalakh: Woolley, *Sir* Leonard

Alan: Benson, E.F.

Alanna autumnal: Barker, George

Alaric at Rome: Arnold, Matthew

Alaric Spenceley: Riddell, *Mrs.* J.H.

Alarm-bell of Atri: The, Longfellow, H.W.

Alarms and discursions: Chesterton, G.K.

Alarms and diversions: Thurber, James

Alarum against usurers, An: Lodge, Thomas

Alarums and excursions: Agate, J.E.

Alas!: Broughton, Rhoda

Alas that spring!: †Mordaunt, Elinor

Alaska: Dole, N.H.

Alastor: Shelley, P.B.

Albania and Epirus: Reeves, W.P.

Albany depot, The: Howells, W.D.

Albert Dürer: Moore, T.S.

Albert Durrant Watson: Pierce, Lorne

Albert Gates: Brighouse, Harold

Albert goes through: Priestley, J.B.

Albert Kahn travelling fellowships: Dickinson, Goldsworthy Lowes

Albert Lunel: Brougham, Henry Peter

Albert of Belgium: Cammaerts, Emile

Albert the good: Bolitho, H.H.

Alberto Sani, an artist out of his time: Berenson, Bernhard

Albigenses, The: Maturin, C.R.

Albina, Countess Raymond: Cowley, *Mrs.* Hannah

Albion and Albanius: Dryden, John

Albions England: Warner, William

Albrecht Dürer: his life and works: Scott, W.B.

Album, The: Rinehart, Mary Roberts

Album verses: Davin, N.F.

Album verses: Lamb, Charles

Albumazar: Tomkis, Thomas

Albyn: †McDiarmid, Hugh

Alcatraz: †Brand, Max

Alcestis: Todhunter, John

Alcestis of Euripides, The: Murray, Gilbert

Alchemist, The: Jonson, Ben

Alchemy: Hillyer, Robert

Alcibiades: Otway, Thomas

Alcida: Greene, Robert

Alciphron: Berkeley, George

Alciphron: Moore, Thomas

Alcuin: Brown, Charles Brockden

Alcyone: Lampman, Archibald

Alcyone: Phillpotts, Eden

Aldebaran: Mulgan, A.E.

Alden case, The: Bridges, Roy

Alderman's son, The: Bullett, Gerald

Alec Forbes of Howglen: MacDonald, George

Alert, The: Gibson, Wilfred

Aletta: Mitford, Bertram

Alexander: Bercovici, Konrad

Alexander: Dunsany, E.J.M.D.P.

Alexander and three small plays: Dunsany, E.J.M.D.P.

Alexander Dyce: Forster, John

Alexander Hamilton: Hubbard, Elbert

Alexander of Yugoslavia: Graham, Stephen

Alexander Pope: Dobrée, Bonamy

Alexander Pope: Sitwell, Edith

Alexander Pope: Stephen, *Sir* Leslie

Alexander the Great: De Vere, Aubrey Thomas

Alexander was great: Stringer, A.J.A.

Alexander's bridge: Cather, Willa

Alexander's feast: Dryden, John

Alexander's path: Stark, F.M.

Alexandria: Forster, E.M.

Alexandria and her schools: Kingsley, Charles

Alexandria quartet, The: Durrell, Lawrence

Alfonso, King of Castile: Lewis, Matthew Gregory

Alfred: Besant, *Sir* Walter

Alfred: Blackmore, R.S.

Alfred: Home, John

Alfred: O'Keeffe, John

Alfred: Pye, H.J.

Alfred: Reynolds, G.

Alfred: Thomson, James

Alfred: a masque: Mallet, David

Alfred Adler: Bottome, Phyllis

Alfred de Rosanne: Reynolds, G.

Alfred Hagart's household: Smith, Alexander

Alfred, Lord Tennyson and William Kirby: Kirby, William

Alfred, Lord Tennyson and William Kirby: Pierce, Lorne

Alfred Mond, the first Lord Melchett: Bolitho, H.H.

Alfred Tennyson: Benson, A.C.

Alfred Tennyson: Browning, Elizabeth Barrett

Alfred Tennyson: Lang, Andrew

Alfred the Great: Clarke, Marcus

Alfred the Great: Gustafson, Ralph

Alfred the Great: Hughes, Thomas

Alfred the Great: Monkhouse, A.N.

Alf's button (novel and play): Darlington, W.A.

Alf's carpet: Darlington, W.A.

Alf's new button: Darlington, W.A.

Algerine captive, The: Tyler, Royall

Algonquin maiden, An: Adam, G.M.

Alhambra, The: (†Geoffrey Crayon), Irving, Washington

Ali Baba and other stories retold from the Arabian nights: Housman, Laurence

Ali the lion: Plomer, W.C.F.

Alias Walt Whitman: O'Higgins, H.J.

Alibi: Christie, Agatha

Alice: (†E.V.Cunningham) Fast, Howard M.

Alice: Lytton, E.G.E.B. *1st Baron*

Alice Adams: Tarkington, Booth

Alice and a family: Ervine, St. John

Alice, and The lost novel: Anderson, Sherwood

Alice and Thomas and Jane: Bagnold, Enid

Alice in Blunderland: Bangs, John Kendrick

Alice in Ganderland: Housman, Laurence

Alice in Wonderland: †Dane, Clemence

Alice Learmont: Craik, *Mrs.* Dinah Maria

Alice Lorraine: Blackmore, R.D.

Alice May, and Bruising Bill: Ingraham, J.H.

Alice Meynell: Meynell, Viola

Alice of Monmouth: an idyl of the Great War: Stedman, E.C.

Alice of old Vincennes: Thompson, Maurice

Alice Ray: a romance in rhyme: Hale, S.J.B.

Alice Stanley: Hall, Anna Maria

Alice-for-short: De Morgan, W.F.

Alice's adventures in Wonderland: †Carroll, Lewis

Alicia Deane: Timms, E.V.

Alide: an episode in Goethe's life: Lazarus, Emma

Alien corn: Howard, S.C.

Alien guest: Webster, M.M.

Aliens: McFee, William

Alisa Page: Chambers, R.W.

Alison's house: Glaspell, Susan

All aboard for Ararat: Wells, H.G.

All about me: Drinkwater, John

All about ships: †Taffrail

All about women, essays and parodies: Gould, Gerald

All alone, the life and private history of Emily Jane Brontë: Wilson, Romer

All along the river: Braddon, Mary Elizabeth

All at sea: Sitwell, *Sir* Osbert

All expenses paid: Gale, Norman R.

All experience: Mannin, Ethel

All fall down: Strong, L.A.G.

All fooles: Chapman, George

All fools: Pickthall, M.W.

All Fools Day: Brown, A.A.

All for Jesus: Faber, Frederick William

All for love: Dryden, John

All for love: Southey, Robert

All for the love of a lady: Maltby, H.F.

All glorious within: Marshall, Bruce

All God's chillun got wings: O'Neill, Eugene

All hallows' Eve: Williams, Charles

All hands: Tomlinson, H.M.

All I could never be: Nichols, J.B.

All I survey: Chesterton, G.K.

All in a bustle: Lathom, Francis

All in a garden fair: Besant, *Sir* Walter

All in a lifetime: Allen, Walter Ernest

All in a maze: †George, Daniel

All in all: Marston, P.B.

All in good time: Stern, G.B.

All in the dark: Le Fanu, Joseph Sheridan

All in the day's work: Tarbell, Ida

All in the wrong: Murphy, Arthur

All is grist: Chesterton, G.K.

All is not gold that glitters: Hall, Anna Maria

All manner of folk: Jackson, Holbrook

All men are brothers: Anand, M.R.

All men are enemies: Aldington, Richard

All men come to the hills: Mais, Roger

All my days: †Bell, Neil

All my yesterdays: Karaka, D.F.

All night long: Caldwell, Erskine Preston

All night sitting: Royde-Smith, Naomi

All of a piece: Lucas, E.V.

All on the Irish shore: Somerville, E.

All on the never-never: Lindsay, Jack

All or nothing: Beresford, John Davys

All or nothing: Powys, J.C.

All our yesterdays: Tomlinson, H.M.

All out on the road to Smolensk: Caldwell, Erskine Preston

All over forty: Sheldon, C.M.

All over the place: Mackenzie, *Sir* Compton

All Ovids elegies: Marlowe, Christopher

All passion spent: Sackville-West, V.

All quiet on the western front: Morley, C.D.

All religions are one: Blake, William

All right, Mr. Roosevelt: Leacock, S.B.

All roads lead to Calvary: Jerome, Jerome K.

All roads lead to Rome: Clune, Frank

All Saints Day: Kingsley, Charles

All sorts and conditions of men: Besant, *Sir* Walter

All souls' night: Walpole, *Sir* Hugh

All star cast: Royde-Smith, Naomi

All summer in a day: Sitwell, Sacheverell

All that fall: Beckett, Samuel

All that matters: Trench, F.H.

All that swagger: Franklin, Miles

All the blocks!: Ireland, William Henry

All the comforts of home: Gillette, William

All the conspirators: Isherwood, C.

All the day long: Spring, Howard

All the days of my life: Barr, A.E.H.

All the days of my life: Mais, S.P.B.

All the dogs of my life: Russell, E.M.

All the King's horses: Widdemer, Margaret

All the king's men: Warren, Robert Penn

All the Mowgli stories: Kipling, Rudyard

All the papers: Lucas, E.V.

All the proud tribesmen: Tennant, Kylie

All the sad young men: Fitzgerald, F.Scott

All the trumpets sounded: Hardy, W.G.

All the voyages round the world: Galt, John

All the works of Epictetus: Carter, *Mrs.* Elizabeth

All the world: Sheldon, C.M.

All the world over: Lucas, E.V.

All the world wondered: Merrick, Leonard

All the year round: Coates, R.M.

All the young men: La Farge, Oliver

All things are possible: Rubenstein, Harold F.

All things considered: Chesterton, G.K.

Alla giornata: Bury, *Lady* C.S.M.

Alladine and Palomides (trn.): Sutro, Alfred

Allahakbarrie book of Broadway Cricket for 1899, The: Barrie, J.M.

Allahakbarries C(ricket) C(lub): Barrie, *Sir* J.M.

Allan and the Ice Gods: Haggard, *Sir* Henry Rider

Allan Quatermain: Haggard, *Sir* Henry Rider

Allan's wife: Haggard, *Sir* Henry Rider

Allarme to England, fore-shewing what perilles are procured, where the people live without regard of martiall lawe: Rich, Barnabe

Allegory of love, The: Lewis, C.S.

Allen Adair: Mander, Jane

Allen Prescott: Sedgwick, *Mrs.* S.A.L.

Allenby: Wavell, A.P., *1st Earl*

Allenby in Egypt: Wavell, A.P., *1st Earl*

Allerton and Dreux: Ingelow, Jean

Alley of flashing spears, An: Byrne, Donn

All-fellows: Housman, Laurence

Alliance between church and state, The: Warburton, William

Allinghams, The: Sinclair, May

Allotments: Jennings, Gertrude

All's well that ends well: Shakespeare, William

Allusions in Lothair, The: Smith, Goldwin

Alma: Trench, R.C.

Alma mater: Canby, Henry Seidel

Alma Venus!: O'Dowd, B.P.

Almada Hill: Mickle, William Julius

Almain: Ashton, Helen

Almanac of Independence and Freedom for the year 1860, An: Mackenzie, W.L.

Almanac of sports: Kipling, Rudyard

Almayer's folly: Conrad, Joseph

Almeyda, Queen of Granada: Lee, Sophia

Almond, wild almond: Broster, D.K.

Almoran and Hamet: Hawkesworth, John

Almost perfect state, The: Marquis, Don

Almyna: *Mrs.* Manley

Alnwick Castle: Halleck, Fitz-Greene

Aloe, The: Mansfield, Katherine

Alone: Douglas, Norman

Alone in London: †Stretton, Hesba

Alone on a wide wide sea: Russell, W.C.

Along the Castlereagh: Stephens, A.G.

Along the Illinois: Masters, E.L.

Along the road: Benson, A.C.

Along the road: Huxley, Aldous

Along the road to Frome: Hollis, Christopher

Along the trail: Hovey, Richard

Along this way: Johnson, J.W.

Alonzo: Home, John

Alpha and Omega: †Bell, Neil

Alphabet for Joanna: Gregory, Horace

Alphabet of elegies, upon the death of doctor Ailmer, An: Quarles, Francis

Alphabet of wine, An: Postgate, Raymond

Alphabet-cipher, The: †Carroll, Lewis

Alphabetical index to the New Testament, An: Allibone, S.A.

Alphabetical order: †George, Daniel

Alpine roses: Boyesen, H.H.

Alps and sanctuaries of Piedmont and the Canton Ticino: Butler, Samuel

Already walks tomorrow: Street, A.G.

Also ran: Mais, S.P.B.

Altar, The: Williams, Isaac

Altar and pew: Betjeman, John

Altar fire, The: Benson, A.C.

Altar in the fields, An: Lewisohn, Ludwig

Altar of flowers: Isvaran, M.S.

Altar of freedom, The: Rinehart, Mary Roberts

Altar stairs, The: †Lancaster, G.B.

Altar steps, The: Mackenzie, *Sir* Compton

Altar-piece, The: Royde-Smith, Naomi

Altdorfer: Moore, T.S.
Altemira: Boyle, Roger
Alterations strange: Taylor, John
Alternative, The: McCutcheon, G.B.
Althea: Lee, Vernon
Althea: Masters, E.L.
Altiora Peto: Oliphant, Laurence
Alton Locke: Kingley, Charles
Altruist, An: †Ouida
Al'Ubaid: Woolley, Sir Leonard
Always the land: Engle, Paul
Always the young strangers: Sandburg, Carl
Always young and fair: Richter, Conrad
Alwyn: Holcroft, Thomas
Alzira: Hill, Aaron
Alzuna: Murphy, Arthur
Am I my brother's keeper?: Coomaraswamy, A.K.
Amabel Channice: Sedgwick, A.D.
Amaco: Flavin, Martin
Amaranth: Robinson, E.A.
Amaryllis at the fair: Jefferies, Richard
Amarynthus, the nympholept: Smith, Horatio
Amateur benefit, The: Howard, B.C.
Amateur cracksman, The: Hornung, E.W.
Amateur emigrant, The: Stevenson, R.L.
Amateur emigrant from the Clyde to Sandy Hook, The: Stevenson, R.L.
Amateur garden, The: Cable, George Washington
Amateur gentleman, The: Farnol, J.J.
Amateur poacher, The: Jefferies, Richard
Amazed evangelist, The: †Bridie, James
Amazing adventures: Baring-Gould, Sabine
Amazing adventures of Letitia Carberry, The: Rinehart, Mary Roberts
Amazing interlude, The: Rinehart, Mary Roberts
Amazing judgement, The: Oppenheim, E. Phillips

Amazing marriage, The: Meredith, George
Amazing monument: Brown, Ivor
Amazing partnership, The: Oppenheim, E. Phillips
Amazing summer, The: Gibbs, P.H.
Amazing theatre, The: Agate, J.E.
Amazing years, The: Ridge, W. Pett
Amazoniad, The: Croker, John Wilson
Amazons, The: Pinero, Sir A.W.
Ambarvalia: Clough, Arthur Hugh
Ambassador, The: †Hobbes, John Oliver
Ambassadors, The: James, Henry
Ambassador's wife, The: Gibbs, Sir Philip
Ambassador's wife, The: Gore, Catherine
Ambedkar refuted: Rajagopalachari, Chakravati
Amber gods, The: Spofford, Harriet
Amber-riders, The: Dalton, A.C.
Ambition: Davies, W.H.
Ambitious man, An: Wilcox, Ella Wheeler
Ambitious slave, The: Settle, Elkanah
Ambitious step-mother, The: Rowe, Nicholas
Amblers, The: Farjeon, B.L.
Ambleside Roman Fort: Collingwood, R.G.
Amboyna: Dryden, John
Ambrose Bierce: Starrett, Vincent
Ambrose Fecit; or, the Peer and the printer: English, Thomas Dunn
Ambrose Holt and family: Glaspell, Susan
Ambrose Loverdale, diplomat: Oppenheim, E. Phillips
Ambush: Read, Sir Herbert
Ambush of young days: Uttley, Alison
Amelia: Carey, Henry
Amelia: Cumberland, Richard
Amelia: Fielding, Henry

Amelia: Patmore, Conventry
Ameliaranne and the magic ring: Farjeon, Eleanor
Ameliaranne's price packet: Farjeon, Eleanor
Ameliaranne's washing day: Farjeon, Eleanor
Ameliorator, The: Lucas, E.V.
Amendments of Mr. Collier's false and imperfect citations: Congreve, William
Amends for ladies: Field, Nathaniel
Amenities of literature: D'Israeli, Isaac
Amenophis: Palgrave, F.T.
America: Benét, Stephen Vincent
America: Blake, William
America: Chambers, R.W.
America: Van Loon, Hendrik
America: a re-appraisal: Stearns, H.E.
America and cosmic man: Lewis, P. Wyndham
America and her commentators: with a critical sketch of travel in the United States: Tuckerman, H.T.
America and the refugees: Adamic, Louis
America and the young intellectual: Stearns, H.E.
America at last: White, T.H.
America comes across: (†Ian Hay), Beith, Sir John Hay
America, give me a chance! Bok, E.W.
America hispana: Frank, Waldo
America in literature: Woodberry, G.E.
America in mid-passage: Beard, C.A. and M.
America in Spitsbergen: Dole, N.H.
America in the modern world: Brogan, Sir Denis
America is worth saving: Dreiser, Theodore
America now: Stearns, H.E.
America. Our national hymn: Smith, S.F.
America revisited: Sala, G.A.H.
America South: Beals, Carleton
America speaks: Gibbs, Sir Philip
America, story of a free nation: Commager, H. S.

America strikes back: Myers, Gustavus

America: the story of a free people: Commager, H.S.

America to-day: Archer, William

America was promises: Mac-Leish, Archibald

American, The: Adams, J.T.

American, The: Fast, Howard M.

American, The: James, Henry

American addresses: Huxley, T.H.

American adventure by land and sea: Sargent, Epes

American and allied ideals: Sherman, S.P.

American and British literature since 1890: Van Doren, Carl and Mark

American angler in Australia, An: Grey, Zane

American architecture: Wright, Frank Lhoyd

American as reformer, The: Schlesinger, A.M.

American aspects: Brogan, *Sir* Denis

American authors and British pirates: Matthews, J.B.

American ballads: English, Thomas Dunn

American baron, The: De Mille, James

American basin, The: Mair, Charles

American beauty: Ferber, Edna

American biography: Belknap, Jeremy

American cause, The: MacLeish, Archibald

American cavalier, The: Read, O.P.

American character: Erskine, John

American character: Matthews, J.B.

American child: Engle, Paul

American citizen: Boyle, Kay

American citizenship: Beard, C.A. and M.

American city government: Beard, C.A.

American claimant, The: (†Mark Twain), Clemens, S.L.

American comedies: Paulding, J.K.

American composition and rhetoric: Davidson, Donald

American consecration hymn: Mackaye, Percy

American contributions to the strategy of World War II: Morison, S.E.

American county fair, The: Anderson, Sherwood

American credo, The: Mencken, H.L.

American credo, The: Nathan, G.J.

American credos: Chase, Stuart

American criticism: Foerster, Norman

American cyclopaedia, The: Ripley, George

American democracy, The: Laski, Harold

American democracy in theory and practice: Carr, J.D.

American Democrat, The: Cooper, James Fenimore

American diary of a Japanese girl, The: Noguchi, Yone

American dictionary of the English language, An: Webster, Noah

American drama since 1918, The: Krutch, J.W.

American dream girl, An: Farrell, James

American earth: Beals, Carleton

American earth: Caldwell, Erskine Preston

American earthquake, The: Wilson, Edmund

American estimates: Canby, Henry Seidel

American fear of literature, The: Lewis, H.S.

American foreign policy and the blessings of liberty: Bemis, S.F.

American foreign policy in the making, 1932–40: Beard, C.A.

American foundation for the blind, 1923–38: Keller, Helen

American game in its seasons: Herbert, H.W.

American genius, The: Sitwell, Edith

American girl in London, An: Duncan, S.J.

American government and politics: Beard, C.A.

American gun mystery: †Queen, Ellery

American heartwood: Peattie, D.C.

American heresy: Hollis, Christopher

American ideal, The: Bryant, *Sir* Arthur

American illustrators: Smith, F.H.

American images of Spanish California: Hart, James D.

American immortals, The: Eggleston, G.C.

American in New York, The: Read, O.P.

American Indian: La Farge, Oliver

American inquisitors: Lippmann, Walter

American Jew, The: Lewisohn, Ludwig

American jitters, The: Wilson, Edmund

American labor movement, The: Beard, Mary

American lands and letters: Mitchell, D.G.

American landscape: Rice, Elmer

American language, The: Mencken, H.L.

American leviathan, The: Beard, C.A.

American liberty: Freneau, Philip

American literature: Matthews, J.B.

American literature, an introduction: Van Doren, Carl

American literature and the American language: Eliot, T.S.

American literature at the crossroads: Calverton, V.F.

American lounger, The: Ingraham, J.H.

American memoirs: Canby, Henry Seidel

American mind, The: Commager, H.S.

American mind in action, The: O'Higgins, H.J.

American newspaper, The: Warner, C.D.

American notebooks, The: Hawthorne, Nathaniel

American notes: Kipling, Rudyard

American notes for general circulation: Dickens, Charles

American novel, The: Van Doren, Carl

American of the future, The: Matthews, J.B.

American outpost: Sinclair, Upton

American party battle, The: Beard, C.A.

American patrician, An: Lewis, A.H.

American pioneer in science: Baker, R.S.

American poems and others: Squire, *Sir* John

American poetry: Shapiro, Karl

American political ideas: Fiske, John

American political system, The: Brogan, *Sir* Denis

American politician, An: Crawford, Francis Marion

American portraits: Bradford, Gamaliel

American portraits: Canfield, Dorothy

American presidency, The: Laski, Harold

American primer, An: Whitman, Walt

American principles: Adams, J.Q.

American prisoner, The: Phillpotts, Eden

American problem, The: Brogan, *Sir* Denis

American prose masters: Brownell, William C.

American push: Fawcett, Edgar

American Republic, The: Brownson, Orestes

American revolution, The: Fiske, John

American revolution, The: Trevelyan, *Sir* G.O.

American rhythm, The: Austin, Mary

American scene, The: James, Henry

American scenery: Willis, N.P.

American scholar, The: Foerster, Norman

American scriptures: Van Doren, Carl

American Secretaries of State and their diplomacy, The: Bemis, S.F.

American selection of lessons in reading and speaking, An: Webster, Noah

American Senator, The: Trollope, Anthony

American social science association: Curtis, George William

American song: Engle, Paul

American songbag: Sandburg, Carl

American soundings: Strachey, John St. Loe

American spelling book, The: Webster, Noah

American State University: its relation to democracy, The: Foerster, Norman

American story, The: MacLeish, Archibald

American taste: Mumford, Lewis

American theatre-poets: Mackaye, Percy

American themes: Brogan, *Sir* Denis

American Times, The: Odell, Jonathan

American tragedy, An: Dreiser, Theodore

American triptych: three John Sedge novels: Buck, Pearl

American troops and the British community, The: Mead, Margaret

American Unitarian biography: Ware, William

American unity and Asia: Buck, Pearl

American vignettes, 1860–65: Drinkwater, John

American village, The: Freneau, Philip

American visitor, An: Cary, Joyce

American war ballads and lyrics: Eggleston, George Cary

American way, The: Kaufman, G.S.

American wives and English husbands: Atherton, Gertrude Franklin

American woman's home, The: Stowe, Harriet Beecher

American Wonderland: Leslie, *Sir* J.R. Shane

American writers: Neal, John

Americanisms and Britticisms: Matthews, J.B.

Americanization of Edward Bok, The: Bok, E.W.

Americans: Riding, Laura

Americans: Sherman, S.P.

Americans and others: Repplier, Agnes

Americans at home, The: Haliburton, T.C.

Americans in England: Rowson, S.H.

"Americanus" letters: Hamilton, Alexander

America's coming-of-age: Brooks, Van Wyck

America's dilemma: Angell, *Sir* Norman

America's opportunity: Adams, J.T.

America's Paul Revere: Forbes, Esther

America's Robert E. Lee: Commager, H.S.

America's tragedy: Adams, J.T.

Ames Judd: Mitchell, J.A.

Amiable Charles, The: Richards, Grant

Amicable parting: Kaufman, G.S.

Among my books: Harrison, Frederic

Among my books: Lowell, J.R.

Among the brigands: De Mille, James

Among the camps: Page, T.N.

Among the Canadian Alps: Burpee, Lawrence J.

Among the Cape Kafirs: Glanville, Ernest

Among the Elgin watchmakers: Eggleston, Edward

Among the hills: Whittier, J.G.

Among the Isles of Shoals: Thaxter, C.L.

Among the lost people: Aiken, Conrad

Among the millet: Lampman, Archibald

Amorel of Lyonesse: Besant, *Sir* Walter

Amores: Lawrence, D.H.

Amores Britannici: Oldmixon, John

Amoretti: Spenser, Edmund

Amoris victima: Symons, Arthur

Amorous bigotte, The: Shadwell, Thomas

Amorous miser, The: Motteux, P.A.

Amorous prince, The: Behn, *Mrs*. Afra

Amorous widow, The: Betterton, Thomas

Amos Kilbright: Stockton, F.R.

Amphitryon: Dryden, John

Amphitryon: Hawkesworth, John

Ample proposition, The: Lehmann, J.F.

Amulet, The: †Craddock, C.E.

Amulets: Petrie, *Sir* William Flinders

Amurath to Amurath: Bell, Gertrude

Amusement: Pye, H.J.

Amusements of Khan Kharuda, The: Dunsany, E.J.M.D.P.

Amusements of leisure hours: Skinner, John

Amusements serious and comical: Brown, Thomas

Amy Lowell; portrait of the poet in her time: Gregory, Horace

Amygdala Britannica, almonds for parrets: Wither, George

Amymone: Linton, Eliza

Amyntas: Hunt, Leigh

Amyntor and Theodora: Mallet, David

An acre of grass: (†Michael Innes), Stewart, J.I.M.

Analecta: Wodrow, Robert

Analects of Confucius, The: Waley, Arthur

Analysis of matter, The: Russell, Bertrand

Analysis of mind, The: Russell, Bertrand

Analysis of the hunting field, The: Surtees, R.S.

Analysis of the influence of natural religion upon the temporal happiness of mankind, by Philip Beauchamp, The: Bentham, Jeremy

Analysis of the phenomena of the human mind: Mill, James

Analysis of the sexual impulse: Ellis, Henry Havelock

Analyst, The: Berkeley, George

Anarchiad, The: Barlow, Joel

Anarchiad, The: Connecticut Wits

Anarchism is not enough: Riding, Laura

Anarchy or hierarchy: Madariaga, Salvador de

Anastasius: Hope, Thomas

Anatol: Barker, Harley Granville

Anatomie of absurditie, The: Nash, Thomas

Anatomist, The: †Bridie, James

Anatomy of an equivalent, The: Savile, George

Anatomy of art, The: Read, *Sir* Herbert

Anatomy of bibliomania, The: Jackson, Holbrook

Anatomy of frustration, The: Wells, H.G.

Anatomy of love, The: †George, Daniel

Anatomy of melancholy, The: Burton, Robert

Anatomy of negation, The: Saltus, E.E.

Anatomy of nonsense, The: Winters, Yvor

Anatomy of play, The: Denham, *Sir* John

Anatomy of satire, The: Vulliamy, C.E.

Anatomy of society, The: Cannan, Gilbert

Anatomy of spirit, The: Lindsay, Jack

Anatomy of the body of man, The: Culpeper, Nicolas

Anatomy of the world, An: Donne, John

Anatomy of tobacco, The: †Machen, Arthur

Anatomy of villainy, The: Balchin, Nigel

Ancestors: Atherton, Gertrude Franklin

Ancestors and friends: Lehmann, John

Anchor of civilization, The: Murray, George

Anchors to windward: White, S.E.

Anciens and modernes: Picasso: Stein, Gertrude

Ancient Allan, The: Haggard, *Sir* Henry Rider

Ancient and modern Italy compared: Thomson, James

Ancient ballads and legends of Hindustan: Dutt, Toru

Ancient classics in a modern democracy, The: Morison, S.E.

Ancient cures, charms, and usages of Ireland: Wilde, *Lady* J.F.

Ancient earthworks at Casterbridge: Hardy, Thomas

Ancient East, The: Hogarth, David George

Ancient Egypt (trn.): Sutro, Alfred

Ancient Egypt the light of the world: Massey, Gerald

Ancient Egyptian legends: Murray, Margaret

Ancient English metrical romances: Ritson, Joseph

Ancient Gaza: Petrie, *Sir* William Flinders

Ancient Greek literature: Bowra, *Sir* Maurice

Ancient hymns for children: Williams, Isaac

Ancient India: Rothenstein, *Sir* William

Ancient law, The: Glasgow, Ellen Anderson

Ancient legends, mystic charms, and superstitions of Ireland: Wilde, *Lady* J.F.

Ancient lights: Ford, Ford Madox

Ancient lights: Percy, Edward

Ancient man, the beginning of civilizations: Van Loon, Hendrik

Ancient mysteries described, The: Hone, William

Ancient poetry and romances of Spain: Bowring, *Sir* John

Ancient races of Ireland, The: Wilde, *Sir* William Robert Wills

Ancient records of Egypt: Breadsted, J.H.

Ancient regime, The: James, George Payne Rainsford

Ancient sea-margins: Chambers, Robert

Ancient Scotish poems: Douglas, Gawin

Ancient songs, chiefly on Moorish subjects: Percy, Thomas

Ancient songs from the time of King Henry the third to the Revolution: Ritson, Joseph

Ancient spell, An: Carleton, William (Mc Kendree)

Ancient times: Breasted, J.H.

Ancient topography of London: Smith, J.T.

Ancient types of man: Keith, *Sir* Arthur

Ancient weights and measures: Petrie, *Sir* William

Ancient wings: Chattopadhyaya, Harindranath

Ancient wisdom, The: Besant, *Mrs.* Annie

Ancrene Wisse: Tolkien, J.R.R.

And all that beauty: Bridges, Roy

And another thing: Spring, Howard

And Berry came too: †Yates, Dornford

And call it accident: Lowndes, M.A.

And did he stop and speak to you? Stern, G.B.

And died so? Gielgud, Val

And even now: Beerbohm, *Sir* Max

And five were foolish: †Yates, Dornford

And from that day: Sullivan, Alan

And gazelles leaping: Ghose, S.N.

And I dance, my own child: Farjeon, Eleanor

And in the hanging gardens: Aiken, Conrad

And in the human heart: Aiken, Conrad

And keep your powder dry: Mead, Margaret

And long remember: Canfield, Dorothy

And looke forward, upon this yeare, 1630: Dekker, Thomas

And most of all man: Mais, Roger

And no man's wit: Macaulay, *Dame* Rose

And no quarter: Walsh, Maurice

And not to yield: Villiers, A.J.

And now goodbye: Hilton, James

—and other poets: Untermeyer, Louis

And so to America: (†Beresford Russell), Roberts, C.E.M.

And so to Bath: (†Beresford Russell), Roberts, C.E.M.

And so to murder: †Carter Dickson

And so to Rome: (†Beresford Russell), Roberts, C.E.M.

And still I cheat the gallows: Oppenheim, E. Phillips

And the third day: Grierson, *Sir* Herbert

And then?: †Mordaunt, Elinor

And then you wish: Van Druten, J.W.

And there were giants: Marshall, Bruce

And they lived happily ever after: Nicholson, Meredith

And we go on: Bird, W.R.

And you, Thoreau!: Derleth, A.W.

Anderby Wold: Holtby, Winifred

Anderson Crow: McCutcheon, G.B.

Andersonville: Kantor, Mackinlay

Andiron tales: Bangs, John Kendrick

Andrea Caslin: Mann, Leonard

Andrea of Hungary, and Giovanna of Naples: Landor, Walter Savage

Andrew Marvell: Birrell, Augustine

Andrew Marvell: Sackville-West, V.

Androcles and the lion: Shaw, G.B.

Andromache: Murray, Gilbert

Andromeda: Buchanan, R.W.

Andromeda: Kingsley, Charles

Andromeda liberata: Chapman, George

Andronicus: Fuller, Thomas

Andronicus Comnenius: Wilson, John

Andy breaks trail: Skinner, C.L.

Andy O'Hara: De Mille, James

Andy's trip to the west, together with a life of its hero: (†Petroleum V. Nasby), Locke, David Ross

Ane dialog betuix experience and ane courteour: Lindsay, *Sir* David

Ane satyre of the thrie estaits: Lindsay, *Sir* David

Anecdotes and traditions illustrative of early English history and literature: Thoms, W.J.

Anecdotes, biographical and literary, of William Bowyer, printer: Nichols, John

Anecdotes of Aurangzib: Sarkar, Y.J.

Anecdotes of eminent painters in Spain: Cumberland, Richard

Anecdotes of Mr. Hogarth: Nichols, John

Anecdotes of painting in England: Walpole, Horace

Anecdotes of the Delborough family: Gunnings, *Mrs.* Susannah

Anecdotes of the late Samuel Johnson, LL.D. during the last twenty years of his life: Thrale, *Mrs.* H.L.

Anecdotes of the turf, the chase, the ring and the stage: Egan, Pierce

Anecdotes told me by Lady Denbigh: Walpole, Horace

Anelida and Arcite: Chaucer, Geoffrey

Angel: Heyward, DuBose

Angel and the author and others, The: Jerome, Jerome K.

Angel Arms: Fearing, Kenneth

Angel, Esq.: Wallace, Edgar

Angel in the corner, The: Dickens, Monica

Angel in the house, The: Patmore, Coventry

Angel in the house, The: Phillpotts, Eden

Angel intrudes, The: Dell, Floyd

Angel is my watermark, The: Miller, Henry

Angel of pain, The: Benson, E.F.

Angel of terror, The: Wallace, Edgar

Angel of the world, The: Croly, George

Angel Pavement: Priestley, J.B.

Angel that troubled the water, The: Wilder, Thornton

Angel world, The: Bailey, Philip James

Angela comes home: Widdemer, Margaret

Angeline: Calvert, George Henry

Angelo: Jewsbury, Geraldine Endsor

Angelo: Reade, Charles

Angelographia: Mather, Increase

Angel's adventure: Hannay, J.O.

Angels and earthly creatures: Wylie, Elinor

Angels and ministers: Housman, Laurence

Angels of Mons, The: †Machen, Arthur

Angels' shoes: Pickthall, M.L.C.

Angler, The: Ireland, William Henry

Anglers' moon: Walmsley, Leo

Anglican cobwebs: Knox, R.A.

Angling sketches: Lang, Andrew

Anglo-American future, The: Gardiner, A.G.

Anglo-Catholic, The: Leslie, Sir J.R.Shane

Anglo-Catholicism: Kaye-Smith, S.

Anglo-Irish of the nineteenth century, The: Banim, John

Anglorum Feriae: Peele, George

Anglo-Saxon primer, An: Sweet, Henry

Anglo-Saxon, Viking and Norman times: Quennell, Marjorie

Anglo-Saxony: Lewis, P.Wyndham

Angola in flames: Panikkar, K.M.

Angry dust: Isvaran, M.S.

Angry wife: Buck, Pearl

Anima magica abscondita: Vaughan, Thomas

Anima poetae: Coleridge, Samuel Taylor

Anima semplicetta: Hewlett, M.H.

Animadversion upon Dr. Sherlock's book entituled a vindication of the holy and everblessed Trinity: South, Robert

Animadversions on a pretended account of Danmark: King, William

Animadversions upon the remonstrant's defence, against Smectymnuus: Milton, John

Animal biology: Haldane, J.B.S.

Animal biology: Huxley, Sir Julian

Animal farm: †Orwell, George

Animal heroes: Seton-Thompson, E.

Animal kingdom, The: Barry, Philip

Animal magnetism: Inchbald, Mrs. Elizabeth

Animal stories: De La Mare, Walter

Animal stories: Kipling, Rudyard

Animal, vegetable, mineral: Deutsch, Babette

Animals all: Lucas, E.V.

Animals and other people: Bromfield, Louis

Animals Noah forgot, The: †The Banjo, Paterson, A.B.

Animi Figura: Symonds, J.A.

Animula: Eliot, T.S.

Animula Vagula: Bacon, Leonard

Ankle deep: Thirkell, Angela

Ann and her mother: Buchan, Anna

Ann and Peter in Austria: Mannin, Ethel

Ann and Peter in Japan: Mannin, Ethel

Ann and Peter in Sweden: Mannin, Ethel

Ann at High Wood Hall: Graves, Robert

Ann Lee's: Bowen, E.D.C.

Ann Leslie: Ball, Anna Maria

Ann Morgan's love: Munby, A.J.

Ann Veronica: Gow, Ronald

Ann Veronica: Wells, H.G.

Ann Vickers: Lewis, H.S.

Anna: Collins, Norman

Anna Christie: O'Neill, Eugene

Anna Comnena: Mitchison, Naomi

Anna Fitzalan: Steen, Marguerite

Anna Livia Plurabelle: Joyce, James

Anna of the five towns: Bennett, Arnold

Anna ruina: †Field, Michael

Anna the adventuress: Oppenheim, E.Phillipps

Annajanska, the Bolshevik Empress: Shaw, G.B.

Annals of a publishing house: Oliphant, Margaret

Annals of a quiet neighbourhood: Macdonald, George

Annals of an Old Manor House, Sutton Place, Guildford: Harrison, Frederic

Annals of innocence and experience: Read, Sir Herbert

Annals of Laycock Abbey: Bowles, William Lisle

Annals of New Zealand literature: Anderson, J.C.

Annals of Niagara: Kirby, William

Annals of Quodlibet, The: Kennedy, J.P.

Annals of rural Bengal, The: Hunter, Sir William Wilson

Annals of St. Paul's Cathedral: Milman, H.H.

Annals of the first four years of the reign of Queen Elizabeth (of which The Beginning is a part): Hayward, Sir John

Annals of the five senses: †McDiarmid, Hugh

Annals of the Parish, or the chronicle of Dalmailing: Galt, John

Annals of virgin saints: Neale, J.M.

Annan Water: Buchanan, R.W.

Anne: Woolson, C.F.

Anne Blake: Marston, J.W.

Anne Boleyn: Beck, Mrs. Lily

Anne Boleyn: Boker, George Henry

Anne Boleyn: Milman, H.H.

Anne Boleyn to Henry the Eighth: Whitehead, William

Anne Hereford: Wood, Ellen

Anne of Avonlea: Montgomery, L.M.

Anne of Geierstein: Scott, Sir Walter

Anne of Green Gables: Montgomery, L.M.

Anne of Ingleside: Montgomery, L.M.

Anne of the barricades: Crockett, S.R.

Anne of the island: Montgomery, L.M.

Anne of the thousand days: Anderson, Maxwell

Anne of Windy Poplars: Montgomery, L.M.

Anne St. Ives: Holcroft, Thomas

Anne Severn and the Fieldings: Sinclair, May

Anne's animals: (†Elzevir), Murdoch, *Sir* W.L.F.

Anne's bridge: Chambers, R.W.

Anne's house of dreams: Montgomery, L.M.

Anne's terrible good nature: Lucas, E.V.

Annette and Bennett: Cannan, Gilbert

Annexation of Texas, The: Clarke, J.F.

Anni mirabiles, 1921–5: Blackmur, R.P.

Annie Kilburn: Howells, W.D.

Anniversary ode for his Majesty's birthday, The: Tate, Nahum

Anniversary of St. Andrew's Church, Niagara: Carnochan, Janet

Anniversary poem: Fields, James Thomas

Anno Domini 2000: Vogel, *Sir* Julius

Annual address of the carriers of the Newark Daily Advertiser, to its patrons: Herbert, H.W.

Annual register, The: Burke, Edmund

Annual Shakespeare lecture, British Academy: Spurgeon, Caroline

Annus domini: a prayer for each day of the year: Rossetti, C.G.

Anonymity: Forster, E.M.

Another book on the theatre: Nathan, G.J.

Another day: Farnol, J.J.

Another Englishwoman's love letters: Pain, B.E.O.

Another future of poetry: Graves, Robert

Another kind of blacklist: Levin, Meyer

Another letter to Lord Chesterfield: Morley, C.D.

Another little drink: †Cheyney, Peter

Another love story: †Lonsdale, Frederick

Another man's wife: Lowndes, M.A.

Another ministerial defeat: Hone, William

Another Pamela: Sinclair, Upton

Another part of the forest: Stern, G.B.

Another part of the wood: Mackail, Denis

Another sheaf: Galsworthy, John

Another time: Auden, W.H.

Another window seat: Mottram, R.H.

Another world than this: Nicolson, Hon. *Sir* Harold

Another year: Sherriff, R.C.

Another's burden: Payn, James

Anster Fair: Tennant, William

Answer, the Jew and the world, The: Lewisohn, Ludwig

Answer to a book, which will be publish'd next week, An: King, William

Answer to a letter sent from Mr. Coddington, An: Williams, Roger

Answer to a paper called A memorial of the poor inhabitants, tradesmen and labourers of the Kingdom of Ireland, An: Swift, Jonathan

Answer to a scurrilous pamphlet, lately printed, intituled a letter from Monsieur de Cros, to the Lord —, An: Temple, *Sir* William

Answer to certain calumnies in the late Governor Macquaries pamphlet, An: Marsden, Samuel

Answer to Dr. D—y's fable of the pheasant and the lark, An: Swift, Jonathan

Answer to Pain's Rights of man, An: Adams, J.Q.

Answer to the animadversions on the history of the rights of princes, An: Burnet, Gilbert

Answer to the articles of the commoners of Devonsheir and Cornwall, An: Udall, Nicholas

Answer to the first part of a certaine conference, concerning succession, An: Hayward, *Sir* John

Answer unto a crafty and sophistical cavillation devised by Stephen Gardiner, An: Cranmer, Thomas

Answere unto Sir T. More's dialogue, An: Tyndale, William

Answers: Murdoch, *Sir* W.L.F.

Antaeopolis: Petrie, *Sir* William Flinders

Antar and Zara: De Vere, Aubrey Thomas

Antecedents of post-war Europe, The: Steed, H.W.

Antechamber, The: Tennyson, Alfred *Lord*

Antediluvians: McHenry, James

Ante-room, The: O'Brien, Kate

Anteros: Lawrence, George Alfred

Anthedon, Sinai: Petrie, *Sir* William Flinders

Antheil and the treatise on harmony: Pound, Ezra

Anthologia anthropologica: Frazer, *Sir* James

Anthology of Catholic poets, An: Leslie, *Sir* J.R. Shane

Anthology of nineties verse, An: Symons, A.J.A.

Anthony Adverse: Allen, Hervey

Anthony and Anna: Ervine, St. John

Anthony Comstock: Leech, M.K. and Heywood Broun

Anthony in wonderland: Hoffe, Monckton

Anthony John: Jerome, Jerome K.

Anthony Lyveden: †Yates, Dornford

Anthony Trollope: Walpole, *Sir* Hugh

Anthony Trollope: a new judgment: Bowen, E.D.C.

Anthony Wilding: Sabatini, R.

Anthropologists and what they do: Mead, Margaret

Anthropology, a human science: Mead, Margaret

Anthropos: Cummings, E.E.

Anthroposophia theomagica: Vaughan, Thomas

Anti woo: Potter, Stephen

Antic hay: Huxley, Aldous

Anticipations of the reaction of mechanical and scientific progress upon human life and thought: Wells, H.G.

Anti-Diabo-Lady: Combe, William

Antidote: (†Sinclair Murray), Sullivan, Alan

Antidote, The: Steele, *Sir* Richard

Antidote against atheism, An: More, Henry

Antidote to venom: Crofts, F.W.

Antient metaphysics: Monboddo, *Lord*

Antigua Penny Puce: Graves, Robert

Anti-matrimony: Mackaye, Percy

Antinomianism in the Colony of Massachusetts Bay, 1636–8: Adams, C.F.

Antiochus: Mottley, John

Anti-Pamela: Haywood, *Mrs.* Eliza

Antiphon, The: Barnes, Djuna

Antiquamania: Roberts, Kenneth

Antiquarian prejudice: Betjeman, John

Antiquarian ramble in the streets of London, An: Smith, J.T.

Antiquarian repository, The: Grose, Francis

Antiquarian researches in Illyricum: Evans, *Sir* Arthur

Antiquary, The: Marmion, Shackerley

Antiquary, The: Scott, *Sir* Walter

Antiquities of England and Wales, The: Grose, Francis

Antiquities of Ireland, The: Grose, Francis

Antiquities of Scotland, The: Grose, Francis

Antiquities of the county of Meath: Grose, Francis

Antiquities of Warwickshire illustrated: Dugdale, *Sir* William

Antiquities of Westminster: Smith, J.T.

Antiquity of man: Keith, *Sir* Arthur

Anti-slavery catechism: Child, Lydia Maria

Anti-slavery days: Clarke, J.F.

Anti-Suffragist anxieties: Russell, Bertrand

Anti-Thelyphthora: Cowper, William

Antoinette de Mirecourt: Leprohon, R.E.

Antonia: Jacob, Naomi

Antonia: Meynell, Viola

Antonina: Collins, William Wilkie

Antonio: Godwin, William

Antonio galvam: Hakluyt, Richard

Antonios revenge: Marston, John

Antony and Cleopatra: Sedley, *Sir* Charles

Antony and Cleopatra: Shakespeare, William

Antony and Octavius: Landor, Walter Savage

Antony Brade: a story of a school: Lowell, Robert

Ants: Huxley, *Sir* Julian

Antwerp: Ford, Ford Madox

Anus mirabilis: Dryden, John

Anvil, The: Binyon, Laurence

Anxious days, The: Gibbs, *Sir* Philip

Any day now: Derleth, A.W.

Any thing for a quiet life: Middleton, Thomas

Anyta: Calvert, George Henry

Anything for a change: Brooks, C.W.S.

Anything goes: Wodehouse, P.G.

Anzac muster, An: Blocksidge, C.W.

Aotrou and Itroun: Tolkien, J.R.R.

Apache gold and Yaqui silver: Dobie, J.F.

Apaches of New York, The: Lewis, A.H.

Apartment in Athens: Wescott, Glenway

Ape and essence: Huxley, Aldous

Ape in me, The: Skinner, C.O.

Apes, The: Phillpotts, Eden

Apes and angels: Priestley, J.B.

Apes of God, The: Lewis, P. Wyndham

Aphorisms of Sir Philip Sidney with remarks: Porter, Jane

Aphra Benn: Sackville-West, V.

Aphrodite against Artemis: Moore, T.S.

Aphrodite in Aulis: Moore, George

Apocalypse: Lawrence, D.H.

Apocryphal New Testament, The: Hone, William

Apollinarianism: Raven, C.E.

Apollo and the seaman: Trench, F.H.

Apollo in Australia: Bayldon, Arthur

Apollo in Diloeryum: Sassoon, Siegfried

Apollo's edict: Swift, Jonathan

Apologetic postscript to ode upon ode, An: †Pindar, Peter

Apologia pro sua preoccupatione: Morley, C.D.

Apologia pro vita sua: Newman, J.H.

Apologie for his voyage to Guiana: Ralegh, *Sir* Walter

Apologies to the Iroquois: Wilson, Edmund

Apology, The: Churchill, Charles

Apology against a pamphlet call'd A modest confutation of the animadversions upon the remonstrant against Smectymnuus: Milton, John

Apology for actors, An: Heywood, Thomas

Apology for bad dreams: Jeffers, J.R.

Apology for Boccaccio, An: Morley, C.D.

Apology for dancing: Heppenstall, J.R.

Apology for heroism: Anand, M.R.

Apology for Lollard doctrines: Wycliffe, John

Apology for princes, An: Young, Edward

Apology for printers, An: Franklin, Benjamin

Apology for the conduct of Mr. Charles Macklin, comedian, An: Macklin, Charles

Apology for the life of Mrs. Shamela Andrews, An: Fielding, Henry

Apology for the Royal Party, An: Evelyn, John

Apology of Arthur Rimbaud, The: Sackville-West, Edward

Apology to the Lady C-R-T, An: Swift, Jonathan

Apologye of syr T. More knyght, The: More, *Sir* Thomas

Apophthages new and old: Bacon, Francis

Apostate: Reid, Forrest

Apostle, The: Moore, George

Apostle of personal harmonizing, An: Carman, Bliss

Apostle of the north, An: Cody, H.A.

Apostolical succession in the Church of England, The: Stubbs, William

Apostrophe to the skylark: Stoddard, C.W.

Apparition, The: Eberhart, Richard

Appartement in Brussels: Mickle, A.D.

Appeal for the Indians, An: Child, Lydia Maria

Appeal from the new to the old Whigs, An: Burke, Edmund

Appeal in behalf of the Negro slaves: Wilberforce, William

Appeal in favor of that class of American called Africans, An: Child, Lydia Maria

Appeal to Caesar, An: Tourgée, A.W.

Appeal to honour and justice tho' it be of his worst enemies, An: Defoe, Daniel

Appeal to the British nation, An: Gourlay, R.F.

Appeal to womanhood throughout the world: Howe, Julia Word

Appearance and reality: Bradley, F.H.

Appearance is against them: Inchbald, *Mrs.* Elizabeth

Appearance of an apparition to James Sympson: Hone, William

Appearances, being notes of travel: Dickinson, Goldsworthy Lowes

Appeasement: Hannay, J.O.

Appendix to the notes on Virginia, An: Jefferson, Thomas

Appendix to the Patriot: Anstey, Christopher

Appius and Virginia: Betterton, Thomas

Appius and Virginia: Dennis, John

Appius and Virginia: Webster, John

Apple acre: Bell, Adrian

Apple and Percival: †Armstrong, Anthony

Apple cart, The: Shaw, G.B.

Apple disdained, The: Mottram, R.H.

Apple of Concord: Church, Richard

Apple of happiness, The: Turner, E.S.

Apple of the eye, The: Wescott, Glenway

Apple stand, The: Herbert, H.W.

Apple tree, The: Du Maurier, Daphne

Apple trees, The: Walpole, *Sir* Hugh

Appleby on Ararat: (†Michael Innes), Stewart, J.I.M.

Appleby talks again: (†Michael Innes), Stewart, J.I.M.

Appleby's end: (†Michael Innes), Stewart, J.I.M.

Apple-Georgie farm: Thompson, Flora

Apple-pye: King, William

Apples be ripe: Powys, Llewelyn

Apples by ocean: Coffin, Robert

Apples of gold: Deeping, Warwick

Apple-tree, The: Brighouse, Harold

Appley Dapply's nursery rhymes: Potter, Helen Beatrix

Application of redemption, The: Hooker, Thomas

Appointment, The: Reynolds, G.

Appointment in Samarra: O'Hara, J.H.

Appointment with death: Christie, Agatha

Appreciation of architecture, The: Byron, Robert

Appreciation of literature, The: Woodberry, G.E.

Appreciation of poetry: Moll, E.G.

Appreciation of Voltaire's Zadig, The: Garnett, David

Appreciations: Pater, Walter

Appreciations and criticisms of the works of Charles Dickens: Chesterton, G.K.

Apprentice, The: Murphy, Arthur

Apprentice, by Mr. Murphy, The: Smart, Christopher

Apprentices advice to the XII Bishops, The: Taylor, John

Approach to Hamlet, An: Knights, L.C.

Approach to literature, An: Brooks, Cleanth

Approach to literature, An: Warren, Robert Penn

Approach to modern physics, An: Andrade, E.N. da Costa

Approach to Shakespeare, The: Mackail, J.W.

Approach to the New Testament, The: Moffat, James

Approaches to American social history: De Voto, Bernard

April—a fable of love: Fisher, V.A.

April airs: Carman, Bliss

April alibi, An: Carman, Bliss

April baby's book of tunes, The: Russell, E.M.

April clouds: Malleson, Miles

April elegy, An: Ficke, Arthur Davison

April fire: Mackaye, Percy

April fools: Mackenzie, *Sir* Compton

April hopes: Howells, W.D.

April lady: Heyer, Georgette

April morning: Fast, Howard M.

April twilights: Cather, Willa

April was when it began: Benefield, Barry

April's lonely soldier: Mais, S. P.B.

Apropos of Dolores: Wells, H.G

Aqua-Musae: Taylor, John

Aquarium: Acton, Harold

Ara vos prec: Eliot, T.S.

Arab war, The: Bell, Gertrude

Arabella: Heyer, Georgette

Arabella Stuart: James, George Payne Rainsford

Arabesque: Tietjens, E.S.

Arabesque and honeycomb: Sitwell, Sacheverell

Arabia: Hogarth, David George

Arabia infelix: Huxley, Aldous

Arabian nights, The: Burton, *Sir* Richard

Arabian nights murder, The: Carr, J.D.

Arabian tale, An: Beckford, William

Arabic-English Lexicon, An: Lane, Edward William

Arable holdings: Higgins, F.R.

Arabs and Palestine, The: Einstein, Albert

Arab's ride to Cairo, The: Whyte-Melville, G.J.

Arachne: Phillpotts, Eden

Aran Islands, The: Synge, J.M.

Aratra Pentelici: Ruskin, John

Arawata Bill: Glover, Denis

Araygnement of Paris, a pastorall, The: Peele, George

Arbasto: Greene, Robert

Arbitration and international politics: Bourne, R.S.

Arbour of amorous devises, The: Breton, Nicholas

Arbour of refuge, The: Cannan, Gilbert

Arc de Triomphe: Hassall, Christopher

Arc de Triomphe: †Novello, Ivor

Arcadian adventures with the idle rich: Leacock, Stephen

Arcana Gallica: Oldmixon, John

Arch of Constantine, The: Berenson, Bernhard

Archaeology of Middlesex and London: Vulliamy, C.E.

Archaeology of Roman Britain, The: Collingwood, R.G.

Archaia: Dawson, *Sir* J.W.

Archaic Artemisia of Ephesus, The: Hogarth, David George

Archaica: Brydges, *Sir* Samuel Egerton

Arches of the years, The: Sutherland, H.G.

Archibald Henderson: Markham, Edwin

Archie McKenzie: Oxley, J.M. J.M.

Archie of Athabasca: Oxley, J.M.

Architecture: Mumford, Lewis

Architecture and history: Morris, William

Architecture and modern life: Wright, Frank Woyd

Architecture and sculpture: Gill, Eric

Architecture, industry and wealth: Morris, William

Architecture of truth: Heppenstall, Rayner

Archy and Mehitabel: Marquis, Don

Archy does his part: Marquis, Don

Archy Moore, the white slave: Hildreth, Richard

Archys life of Mehitabel: Marquis, Don

Arctic adventures by sea and land: Sargent, Epes

Arctic convoy: †Taffrail

Arctic in fact and fable, The: Stefansson, V.

Arctic ox, The: Moore, M.C.

Arctic prairies, The: Seton-Thompson, E.

Arcturus adventure, The: Beebe, William

Ardath: †Corelli, Marie

Arden and Avon: Mais, S.P.B.

Arden of Feversham: Lillo, George

Ardis Claverden: Stockton, F.R.

Are all men alike?: Stringer, A.J.A.

Are armies needed any longer?: Wells, H.G.

Are our pearls real?: Murray, George

Are radicals crazy?: Chase, Stuart

Are they the same at home?: Nichols, J.B.

Are you hungry, are you cold: Bemelmans, Ludwig

Areika, Karanog, Karanog: the town, Buhen: Woolley, *Sir* Leonard

Aren't we all?: †Lonsdale, Frederick

Areopagitica: Milton, John

Arethusa: Crawford, Francis Marion

Areytos: Simms, W.G.

Arfon: Davies, Rhys

Argalus and Parthenia: Glapthorne, Henry

Argalus and Parthenia: Quarles, Francis

Argentine tango: Guedalla, Philip

Argonaut and Juggernaut: Sitwell, *Sir* Osbert

Argonauts of North Liberty, The: Harte, Bret

Argument drawn from the circumstances of Christ's death, for the truth of religion, An: Young, Edward

Argument for an extension of the Franchise, An: White, W.H.

Argument proving that the present Mohocks and Hawkubites are the Gog and Magog mention'd in the Revelations, An: Gay, John

Arguments to manifest the advantages of a good fleet: Ralegh, *Sir* Walter

Argyll's Highlands, or MacCailein Mor and the Lords of Lorne: †Bede, Cuthbert

Aria and finale: Hanley, James

Aria de capo: Millay, E. St. Vincent

Ariadne: Lucas, F.L.

Ariadne: Milne, A.A.

Ariadne: †Ouida

Ariadne and the bull: Farjeon, Eleanor

Ariadne Florentina: Ruskin, John

Ariadne in Mantua: †Lee, Vernon

Arians of the fourth century, The: Newman, J.H.

Arise to conquer: Strachey, John

Arising out of that: Vachell, H.A.

Aristide case, The: Jameson, Storm

Aristocracy and justice: More, P.E.

Aristocrat, The: Pye, H.J.

Aristocratic journey, The: Pope-Hennessy, *Dame* Una

Aristocratic West, The: Gerould, Katharine

Aristocrats, The: Atherton, Gertrude

Aristophanes: Murray, Gilbert

Aristophanes and the war party: Murray, Gilbert

Aristophanes' apology: Browning, Robert

Aristotle: Lewes, George Henry

Arizona: Thomas, Augustus

Arizona Ames: Grey, Zane

Arizona nights: White, S.E.

Arizonian: †Miller, Joaquin

Ark and the alphabet: Crane, Nathalia

Arkansas: Fletcher, John Gould

Arkansas planter, An: Read, O.P.

Arkham House: the first twenty years, 1939–59: Derleth, A.W.

Arm of gold, The: †Connor, Ralph

Armadale: Collins, William Wilkie

Armageddon: Phillips, Stephen

Armageddon: Ransom, J.C.

Armand Durand: Leprohon, R.E.

Armazindy: Riley, J.W.

Armchair at the inn, The: Smith, F.H.

Armed muse, The: Palmer, H.E.

Arminell: Baring-Gould, Sabine

Arminian Magazine, The: Wesley, John

Arminius: Knight, Charles

Arminius: Murphy, Arthur

Armistice and other memories: Mottram, R.H.

Armour for Aphrodite: Moore, T.S.

Armour wherein he trusted: Webb, Mary

Armourrer, The: Cumberland, Richard

Armoury in our halls, The: Pierce, Lorne

Arms and the covenant: Churchill, *Sir* Winston

Arms and the man: Shaw, G.B.

Arms and the men: (†Ian Hay), Beith, *Sir* John Hay

Army doctor's romance, An: Allen, Grant

Army life in a black regiment: Higginson, T.W.

Army of a dream, The: Kipling, Rudyard

Army's first fifteen months of the war, The: Yeats-Brown, F.C.C.

Arnold: Ingraham, J.H.

Arnold and André: Calvert, George Henry

Arnold and Talleyrand: Carleton, William (McKendree)

Arnold Bennett: Allen, Walter Ernest

Arnold Bennett himself: †West, Rebecca

Arnold Waterlow: Sinclair, May

Arnold's travelling journals: Arnold, Thomas

Around about America: Caldwell, Erskine Preston

Around Australia: (†Donald Barr), Barrett, C.L.

Around home: McArthur, Peter

Around old Chester: Deland, Margaret

Around the corner: Flavin, Martin

Around the world in New York: Bercovici, Konrad

Around the world with the alphabet: Van Loon, Hendrik

Around the year: Wilcox, E.W.

Around theatres: Beerbohm, *Sir* Max

Arouse and beware: Kantor, Mac Kinlay

Arrah Neil: James, George Payne Rainsford

Arrant thiefe, An: Taylor, John

Arras of youth: †Onions, Oliver

Arristippus: Randolph, Thomas

Arrogant history of White Ben, The: †Dane, Clemence

Arrow, The: Morley, C.D.

Arrow against profane and promiscuous dancing, An: Mather, Increase

Arrow of gold, The: Conrad, Joseph

Arrow of gold, The: Ingraham, J.H.

Arrows of longing: †Maurice, Furnley

Arrows of the chace: Ruskin, John

Arrowsmith: Lewis, H.S.

Ars recte vivendi: Curtis, G.W.

Arsinoe, Queen of Cyprus: Motteux, P.A.

Art: Bell, Clive

Art anatomy of animals: Seton-Thompson, E.

Art and beauty of the earth: Morris, William

Art and craft of letters, The: Drinkwater, John

Art and craft to know well to die (trn.): Caxton, William

Art and industry: Read, *Sir* Herbert

Art and its producers: Morris, William

Art and life: Moore, T.S.

Art and love: Gill, Eric

Art and manufacture: Gill, Eric

Art and Mrs. Bottle: Levy, Benn

Art and prudence: Gill, Eric

Art and reality: Cary, Joyce

Art and society: Read, *Sir* Herbert

Art and Swadeshi: Coomaraswamy, A.K.

Art and technics: Mumford, Lewis

Art and the evolution of Man: Read, *Sir* Herbert

Art and the life of action: Eastman, Max

Art and the Reformation: Coulton, G.G.

Art and the state: Drinkwater, John

Art decoration applied to furniture: Spofford, H.E.

Art here: Turnbull, S.C.P.

Art in Australia: McCrae, Hugh

Art Maguire: Carleton, William

Art now: Read, *Sir* Herbert

Art of acting, The: Hill, Aaron

Art of adventure, The: Linklater, Eric

Art of archerie, The: Markham, Gervase

Art of being alive, The: Wilcox, E.W.

Art of being ruled, The: Lewis, P.Wyndham

Art of book-collecting, The: Mackaness, George

Art of cookery, The: King, William

Art of dancing, The: Jenyns, Soame

Art of dining, The: Hayward, Abraham

Art of directing plays, The: †Dane, Clemence

Art of drawing with the pen, and limning in water colours, The: Peacham, Henry

Art of dying, The: Lucas, F.L.

Art of England, The: Ruskin, John

Art of feminine beauty, The: Rubenstein, Harold F.

Art of fiction, The: Besant, *Sir* Walter

Art of fiction, The: Kipling, Rudyard

Art of Geoffrey Chaucer, The: Lowes, J.L.

Art of growing old, The: Powys, John Cowper

Art of happiness, The: Powys, John Cowper

Art of health, The: Sinclair, Upton

Art of James Branch Cabell, The: Walpole, *Sir* Hugh

Art of letters, The: Lynd, Robert

Art of living, The: Grant, Robert

Art of living, The: Lucas, F.L.

Art of living in London, The: Peacham, Henry

Art of love, The: Hopkins, Charles

Art of playwriting, The: Crothers, Rachel

Art of pleasing, The: Chesterfield, *4th Earl of*

Art of poetry, The: Ker, W.P.

Art of politicks, The: Bramston, James

Art of preserving health, The: Armstrong, John

Art of procuring pleasant dreams: Franklin, Benjamin

Art of Rupert Bunny, The: Turnbull, S.C.P.

Art of sculpture, The: Read, *Sir* Herbert

Art of seeing, The: Huxley, Aldous

Art of swimming: Franklin, Benjamin

Art of the Australian aborigine: (†Donald Barr), Barrett, C.L.

Art of the dramatist, The: Priestley, J.B.

Art of the moving picture, The: Lindsay, N.V.

Art of the night: Nathan, G.J.

Art of the novel from 1700 to the present time, The: Edgar, O.P.

Art of the playwright, The: Percy, Edward

Art of the theatre, The: Craig, *Sir* Gordon

Art of the Vieux Colombier, The: Frank, Waldo

Art of theatre: †O'Connor, Frank

Art of Thomas Hardy, The: Johnson, Lionel Pigot

Art treasures of the British Museum: Grigson, Geoffrey

Arte of English poesie, The: Puttenham, R.

Arte of rhetorique, The: Wilson, Thomas

Artemis and Actaeon: Wharton, Edith

Artemision: Hewlett, M.H.

†Artemus Ward among the Fenians: Browne, Charles Farrar

†Artemus Ward; his book with many comic illustrations: Browne, Charles Farrar

†Artemus Ward; his travels: Browne, Charles Farrar

†Artemus Ward in London: Browne, Charles Farrar

†Artemus Ward's panorama: Browne, Charles Farrar

Arthur: Binyon, Laurence

Arthur and Gorlagon: Kittredge, G.L.

Arthur and his times: Lindsay, Jack

Arthur Arundel: Smith, Horatio

Arthur Blane: Grant, James

Arthur Bonnicastle: Holland, J.G.

Arthur Coningsby: Sterling, John

Arthur Denwood: Ingraham, J.H.

Arthur Fitz Albini: Brydges, *Sir* Samuel Egerton

Arthur Griffin, journalist and statesman: Stephens, James

Arthur Griffith: Colum, Padraic

Arthur Machen: Starrett, Vincent

Arthur Mervyn: Brown, Charles Brockden

Arthur of Britain: Chambers, E.K.

Arthur O'Leary: Lever, C.J.

Arthur's Pass and the Otira Gorge: Baughan, B.E.

Articles of belief and acts of religion: Franklin, Benjamin

Articles of charge of high crimes and misdemeanours, against Warren Hastings, Esq.: Burke, Edmund

Articles of confederation: Franklin, Benjamin

Articles of faith: Housman, Laurence

Artificial princess, The: Firbank, Ronald

Artist, An: Jeffers, J.R.

Artist, The: Mencken, H.L.

Artist, The: Milne, A.A.

Artist and his public, The: Newton, Eric

Artist in the family, An: Millin, Sarah Gertrude

Artist-life: Tuckerman, H.T.

Artists in crime: Marsh, Ngaio Edith

Artists in uniform, a study of literature and bureaucratism: Eastman, Max

Artist's life, The: †Hobbes, John Oliver

Artists of the 1890's, The: Rothenstein, *Sir* John

Artist's proof, An: Austin, Alfred

Artless tales: Porter, A.M.

Art-nonsense and other essays: Gill, Eric

Arts, The: Van Loon, Hendrik

Arts and crafts in Egypt: Petrie, *Sir* William Flinders

Arts and crafts of India and Ceylon: Coomaraswamy, A.K.

Arts of logick and rhetorick, The: Oldmixon, John

Arts of man, The: Newton, Eric

Arts of mankind, The: Van Loon, H.W.

Arts under Socialism, The: Priestley, J.B.

Arundel: Benson, E. F.

Arundel: Cumberland, Richard

Arundel: Roberts, Kenneth

Arvat: Myers, L.H.

As a man I was: Oppenheim, E.Phillips

As a man thinks: Thomas, Augustus

As a strong bird on pinions free: Whitman, Walt

As a thief in the night: Marshall, Bruce

As a watch in the night: Praed, Mrs. C.

As Berry and I were saying: †Yates, Dornford

As God made them: Bradford, Gamaliel

As good as gold: Housman, Laurence

As good as a comedy: Simms, W.G.

As husbands go: Crothers, Rachel

As I lay dying: Faulkner, William

As I remember it: Cabell, James Branch

As I was going down Sackville Street: Gogarty, Oliver St. John

As I was saying: Chesterton, G.K.

As it is in heaven: Larcom, Lucy

As it was in the beginning: Deamer, Dulcie

As it was in the beginning: †Miller, Joaquin

As it was in the beginning: Mitchison, Naomi

As long as the grass shall grow: La Farge, Oliver

As music and splendour: O'Brien, Kate

As once we were: Hutchinson, Arthur

As other men are: †Yates, Dornford

As others hear us: †Delafield, E.M.

As others see us: Pickthall, M.W.

As the bee sucks: Lucas, E.V.

As the sparks fly upward: Sigerson, Dora

As the sun shines: Williamson, Henry

As the wind blows: Phillpotts, Eden

As their friends saw them: Dobrée, Bonamy

As we are: Benson, E. F.

As we are and as we may be: Besant, Sir Walter

As we go: Warner, C.D.

As we were: Benson, E. F.

As we were saying: Warner, C.D.

As you like it: Shakespeare, William

Ascent of Elijah, The: Praed, W.M.

Ascent of F.6, The: Auden, W.H.and Isherwood, Christopher

Ascent of man, The: Milne, A. A.

Ascent to Avernus: Mickle, A. D.

Ash Wednesday: Eliot, T. S.

Ash Wednesday: Erskine, John

Ashby Manor: Allingham, William

Ashenden: Maugham, Somerset

Ashes of empire: Chambers, R.W.

Ashes of Hiroshima: Clune, Frank

Ashley: Wood, Ellen

Ashley Library, The: Wise, T.J.

Ashtaroth: Gordon, A.L.

Asia and Western dominance: Panikkar, K.M.

Asia and Western dominions: Panikkar, K.M.

Asiatic art: Coomaraswamy, A.K.

Asiatic studies, religious and social: Lyall, Sir Alfred

Asiatics, The: Prokosch, Frederic

Ask a policeman: Sayers, Dorothy

Ask Dad: Wodehouse, P.G.

Ask for King Billy: Treece, Henry

Ask for Ronald Standish: †Sapper

Ask Mamma: Surtees, R. S.

Ask me no more: Frankau, Pamela

Ask me tomorrow: Cozzens, James Gould

Ask Miss Mott: Oppenheim, E.Phillips

Ask your mama: Hughes, J.L.

Asloan manuscript, The: Craigie, Sir William

Asmodeus at large: Lytton, E.G.E.B., 1st baron

Asolando: Browning, Robert

Aspasia: Vulliamy, C.E.

Aspects and impressions: Gosse, Sir Edmund

Aspects of Egypt: Mannin, Ethel

Aspects of fiction: Matthews, J. B.

Aspects of literature: Murry, John Middleton

Aspects of love: Garnett, David

Aspects of modern Oxford: Godley, A. D.

Aspects of modern poetry: Sitwell, Edith

Aspects of the novel: Forster, E. M.

Aspects of the social history of America: Canby, Henry Seidel

Aspen Court: Brooks, Charles William Shirley

Aspern papers, The: James, Henry

Asphalt jungle: Burnett, W.R.

Asphodel: Braddon, Mary Elizabeth

Aspidistra in Babylon, An: Bates, H.E.

Aspidistras: Temple, Joan

Aspirant, The: Dreiser, Theodore

Assassin, The: O'Flaherty, Liam

Assassin, The: Shaw, Irwin

Assassins, The: Prokosch, Frederic

Assaying of Brabantius: Sherrington, Sir Charles

Assemble of gods, The: Lydgate, John

Assembly: O'Hara, J.H.

Assessments and anticipations: Inge, W.R.

Assignation, The: Dryden, John

Associate hermits, The: Stockton, F.R.

Associating with Shakespeare: Barker, Harley Granville

Assorted articles: Lawrence, D.H.

Assyrian, The: Saroyan, William

Astonishing history of Troy Town, The: Quiller-Couch, *Sir* A.

Astonishing island, The: Holtby, Winifred

Astonishment!!!: Lathom, Francis

Astoria: (†Geoffrey Crayon), Irving, Washington

Astounding crime on Torrington Road, The: Gillette, William

Astraea: the balance of illusions: Holmes, O.W.

Astraea Redux: Dryden, John

Astrologer's day, An: Narayan, R.K.

Astronomical knowledge of the Maori, genuine and empirical, The: Best, Elsdon

Astrophel: Swinburne, A.C.

At all costs: Aldington, Richard

At bay: Hanley, James

At Bertram's hotel: Christie, Agatha

At Christmas: O'Sullivan, Seumas

At close range: Smith, F.H.

At dawn and dusk: Daley, Victor

At eventide: O'Hara, J.B.

At fault: Chopin, Kate

At first sight: Monsarrat, Nicholas

At half-past eight: Agate, J.E.

At Heaven's gate: Warren, Robert Penn

At her mercy: Payn, James

At his gates: Oliphant, Margaret

At home and abroad: Fuller, Margaret

At home and abroad: Kennedy, J.P.

At home and abroad: Taylor, Bayard

At Lady Molly's: Powell, Anthony

At large: Benson, A.C.

At large: Hornung, E.W.

At last: A Christmas in the West Indies: Kingsley, Charles

At liberty: Thomas, Augustus

At Long Bay: Euroclydon: Kendall, Henry

At love's extremes: Thompson, Maurice

At market value: Allen, Grant

At Michaelmas: Carman, Bliss

At midnight: Cambridge, Ada

At Miss Lamblion's: Rowe, Richard

At Mrs. Beam's: Munro, C.K.

At my heart's core: Davies, Robertson

At night in a hospital: Linton, Eliza

At odds: Tautphoeus, Jemima *Baroness*

At Prior Park: Dobson, Henry Austin

At Scarboro' Beach: Scott, D.C.

At school with Rachel: Brazil, Angela

At sea: Calder-Marshall, Arthur

At sundown: Whittier, J.G.

At sundown, the tiger ...: Mannin, Ethel

At sunset: Howe, Julia Ward

At Sunwich Port: Jacobs, W.W.

At the back of the north wind: Macdonald, George

At the beautiful, gate: Larcom, Lucy

At the Blue Moon again: Lewis, D.B. Wyndham

At the Casa Napoleon: Janvier, T.A.

At the door of the gate: Reid, Forrest

At the feet of the master: Krishnamurti, Jiddu

At the foot of the rainbow: Stratton-Porter, Gene

At the gate of the convent: Austin, Alfred

At the gateways of the day: Colum, Padraic

At the Grand hôtel du Paradis: Janvier, T.A.

At the Green Goose: Lewis, D.B. Wyndham

At the holy well: Piatt, J.J.

At the house of Mrs. Kinfoot: Sitwell, *Sir* Osbert

At the Long Sault: Lampman, Archibald

At the mercy of Tiberius: Evans, Augusta Jane

At the ribbon counter: Jennings, Gertrude

At the shrine: Clarke, G.H.

At the shrine of St. Charles: Lucas, E.V.

At the sign of the Blue Moon: Lewis, D.B. Wyndham

At the sign of the dove: Lucas, E.V.

At the sign of the grid: Vachell, H.A.

At the sign of the lame dog: Mottram, R.H.

At the sign of the silver flagon: Farjeon, B.L.

At the sign of the thistle: †McDiarmid, Hugh

At the sign of the unicorn: †Bell, Neil

At the Villa Rose: Mason, A.E.W.

At the wind's will: Moulton, E.L.

At the zoo: Huxley, *Sir* Julian

At your service: Bemelmans, Ludwig

Atala and René: Heppenstall, J.R.

Atalanta in Calydon: Swinburne, A.C.

Atalanta in the South: Elliott, M.H.

Atalantis: Simms, W.G.

Atareta: Grace, A.A.

Athalie: Chambers, R.W.

Atheism and the value of life: Mallock, W.H.

Atheist, The: Otway, Thomas

Atheist's tragedie, The: Tourneur, Cyril

Athelings, The: Oliphant, Margaret

Athelwold: Hill, Aaron

Athenae Oxonienses: Wood, Anthony à

Atheniad, The: Glover, Richard

Athenian captive, The: Talfourd, *Sir* T.N.

Athens: Praed, W.M.

Athens: (†Q), Quiller-Couch, *Sir* Arthur

Athens: its rise and fall: Lytton, E.G.E.B., *1st Baron*

Atherton: Mitford, Mary Russel

Athos: treasures and men: Byron, Robert

Athribis: Petrie, *Sir* William Flinders

Atlantic battle won, May 1943–May 1945, The: Morison, S.E.

Atlantic crossings: Knight, G.W.

Atlantic essays: Higginson, T.W.

Atlantic meeting: Morton, H.V.

Atlantic ordeal: Huxley, Elspeth J.

Atlantic tragedy, An: Russell, W.C.

Atlantis: Donnelly, Ignatius Loyola

Atlantis: Powys, John Cowper

Atlas of American history: Adams, J.T.

Atmosphere of horses: Derleth, A.W.

Atmospherics: Dunsany, E.J.M.D.P.

Atom and its energy, The: Andrade, E.N. da Costa

Atom of Spithead: (†David Divine), Divine, A.D.

Atom of delight, The: Gunn, Neil M.

Atomic age, The: Russell, Bertrand

Atomic structure of minerals: Bragg, Sir Laurence

Atomic war—the way out: Mumford, Lewis

Atomicity and quanta: Jeans, Sir James

Atoms and rays: Lodge, Sir Oliver

Atonement of Leam Dundas, The: Linton, Eliza

Atrocities of justice under British rule in Egypt: Blunt, Wilfred

Attaché, The: Haliburton, T.C.

Attack, The: Tawney, R.H.

Attack on Leviathan, The: Davison, D.G.

Attack on St. Winefride's well, The: (†Baron Corvo), Rolfe, Frederick

Attempt to ascertain the order in which the plays attributed to Shakespeare were written, An: Malone, Edmund

Attempt to shew the folly and danger of Methodism, An: Hunt, Leigh

Attempts at General Union: Cole, G.D.H.

Attention! Webster, Noah

Attic room, An: Coffin, Robert

Attila: Binyon, Laurence

Attila: James, George Payne Rainsford

Attila, my Attila!: †Field, Michael

Attitudes and avowals: Le Gallienne, Richard

Attitudes toward history: Burke, Kenneth

Attractive man, The: Trollope, Frances

Attractive way, The: Grenfell, Sir Wilfred

Atys and Adrastus: Whitehead, William

Aubert Dubayet: Gayarré, C.E.A.

Aubrey Beardsley: Symons, Arthur

Auchinleck: Connell, John

Auckland: Cowan, James

Auction, The: Combe, William

Auction block, The: Beach, R.E.

Audible silence: Whistler, Laurence

Audrey Craven: Sinclair, May

Augs, The: Stern, G.B.

Auguries: Binyon, Laurence

August folly: Thirkell, Angela

Augustan books of poetry, The: Frost, Robert

Augustan studies: Tillotson, Geoffrey

Auguste Comte and Positivism: Mill, John Stuart

Augustus: Buchan, John

Augustus Britannicus, The: Phillips, John

Augustus does his bit: Shaw, G.B.

Augustus John: Rothenstein, Sir John

Auld Lang Syne: Kipling, Rudyard

Auld Lang Syne: Russell, W.C.

Auld licht idylls: Barrie, Sir J.M.

Auld licht manse, An: Barrie, Sir J.M.

Auld Reekie: Fergusson, Robert

Auld Robin Gray: Barnard, Lady Anne

Auld shop and the new, The: Lawson, Henry

Aunt Beardie: (†Joseph Shearing), †Bowen, Marjorie

Aunt Becky began it: Montgomery, L.M.

Aunt Caroline's present: Hale, E.E.

Aunt Jeannie: Benson, E.F.

Aunt Jo's scrap bag: Alcott, Louisa May

Aunt Judy's letters: Gatty, Margaret

Aunt Judy's tales: Gatty, Mrs. Margaret

Aunt Kipp: Alcott, Louisa May

Aunt Polly's story of mankind: Stewart, D.O.

Aunt Sarah and the war: Meynell, Wilfred

Aunt's story, The: White, Patrick

Aurelian: Ware, William

Aurélie: Hardy, A.S.

Aureng-Zebe: Dryden, John

Auriol: Ainsworth, William Harrison

Aurora: Alexander, William

Aurora Australis: Lang, J.D.

Aurora Borealis, The: Dunsany, E.J.M.D.P.

Aurora Floyd: Braddon, Mary Elizabeth

Aurora la Cujiñi: Cunninghame Graham, Robert

Aurora Leigh: Browning, Elizabeth Barrett

Aurora Leigh: Swinburne, A.C.

Auroras of autumn, The: Stevens, Wallace

Auspicante Jehova: Breton, Nicholas

Austin Elliott: Kingsley, Henry

Austin Friars: Riddell, Mrs. J.H.

Austin Phelps: Ward, E.S.

Australaise, The: Dennis, C.M.J.

Australasia: Gibbs, Sir Philip

Australasia: Praed, W.M.

Australasia: Wentworth, W.C.

Australia: Woolls, William

Australia and New Zealand: Trollope, Anthony

Australia Felix: †Richardson, H.H.

Australia: her story: Tennant, Kylie

Australia, human and economic: Jose, A.W.

Australia in pictures: (†Donald Barr), Barrett, C.L.

Australia, land of contrasts: Hill, Ernestine

Australia: my country: (†Donald Barr), Barrett, C.L.

Australia to England: Blocksidge, C.W.

Australia to England: Farrell, John

Australian, The: Ogilvie, W.H.

Australian animal book, An: (†Donald Barr), Barrett, C.L.

Australian bird life: (†Donald Barr), Barrett, C.L.

Australian birds: (†Donald Barr), Barrett, C.L.

Australian byways: Duncan, Norman

Australian caves, cliffs and waterfalls: (†Donald Barr), Barrett, C.L.

Australian citizen, The: (†Elzevir), Murdoch, *Sir* W.L.F.

Australian Crusoes, The: Rowcroft, Charles

Australian dream, The: Mudie, I.M.

Australian essays: Adams, Francis

Australian facts and prospects: Horne, Richard Henry

Australian flower masque, The: Stephens, A.G.

Australian girl, An: Martin, C.E.

Australian heroine, An: Praed, *Mrs*. C.

Australian life: Adams, Francis

Australian life: black and white: Praed, *Mrs*. C.

Australian literature: Miller, E.M.

Australian literature: a summary: Green, H.M.

Australian lyrics: Sladen, D.B.W.

Australian national anthem, An: Stephens, A.G.

Australian nature wonders (†Donald Barr), Barrett C.L.

Australian outback: (†Donald Barr), Barrett, C.L.

Australian outline: Barnard, M.

Australian poems: O'Reilly, D.P.

Australian Rip Van Winkle, An: Hay, William

Australian spring: Spence, C.H.

Australian summer: Cardus, Neville

Australian tales: Clarke, Marcus

Australian tales: Lawson, Henry

Australian wild flower book, An: (†Donald Barr), Barrett, C.L.

Australian wild life: (†Donald Barr), Barrett, C.L.

Australians, The: Adams, Arthur H.

Australians, The: Adams, Francis

Australia's coral realm: (†Donald Barr), Barrett, C.L.

Australia's first preacher: Richard Johnson: Bonwick, James

Australia's inland wonders: (†Donald Barr), Barrett, C.L.

Austria: Gibbon, Monk

Austrian holiday: Mais, S.P.B.

Authentic account of the Royal Marriage, An: Hone, William

Authentic anecdotes of American slavery: Child, Lydia Maria

Authentic anecdotes of Old Zack: Melville, Herman

Author, The: Churchill, Charles

Author and curator: Fortescue, *Sir* John William

Author hero of the American revolution, The: Lippard, George

Author hunting: Richards, Grant

Author unknown: †Dane, Clemence

Author unknown: Simpson, H. de G.

Authoress of the Odyssey, The: Butler, Samuel

Authority and archaeology: Hogarth, David George

Authority and the individual: Russell, Bertrand

Authority in the modern state: Laski, Harold

Authors and the book trade: Swinnerton, Frank

Author's apology, The: Bangs, John Kendrick

Author's craft, The: Bennett, Arnold

Author's daughter, The: Spence, C.H.

Authors dead and living: Lucas, F.L.

Author's farce, The: Fielding, Henry

Authors I never met: Swinnerton, F.A.

Authorship: Neal, John

Authorship: Strong, L.A.G.

Autobiographia: Whitman, Walt

Autobiographic memoirs: Harrison, Frederic

Autobiography and other essays, An: Trevelyan, G.M.

Autobiography of a cad: Macdonell, A.G.

Autobiography of a play, The: Howard, B.C.

Autobiography of a quack, The: Mitchell, S.W.

Autobiography of a slander: Lyall, Edna

Autobiography of a super-tramp, The: Davies, W.H.

Autobiography of a truth, The: Lyall, Edna

Autobiography of Alice B. Toklas, The: Stein, Gertrude

Autobiography of an actress: Ritchie, *Mrs*.

Autobiography of an attitude, The: Nathan, G.J.

Autobiography of an ex-colored man, The: Johnson, J.W.

Autobiography of Benvenuto Cellini: Symonds, J.A.

Autobiography of Count Carlo Gozzi, The: Symonds, J.A.

Autobiography of Christopher Kirkland, The: Linton, Eliza

Autobiography of Cornelis Blake, The: †Preedy, George

Autobiography of Jack Ketch, The: Whitehead, Charles

Autobiography of Leigh Hunt, The: Hunt, Leigh

Autobiography of Mark Rutherford, dissenting Minister, The: †Rutherford, Mark

Autobiography of Mary Countess of Warwick: Croker, Thomas Crofton

Autobiography of Methuselah, The: Bangs, John Kendrick

Autobiography of the devil, The: Read, O.P.

Autobiography of Valentine Duval: Manning, Anne

Autobiography of William Russell, An: Thomas, F.W.

Autobiography of Wolfe Tone, The: O'Faolain, Sean

Autobiography with a difference: Mottram, R.H.

Autocracy of Mr. Parham, The: Wells, H.G.

Autocrat of the breakfast-table, The: Holmes, Oliver Wendell

Autograph letters: Stevenson, R.L.

Autolycus in limbo: Starrett, Vincent

Autumn: Kennedy, Margaret

Autumn: Thoreau, H.D.

Autumn crocus: Smith, Dodie

Autumn crocuses: Sedgwick, A.D.

Autumn garden, The: Gosse, Sir Edmund

Autumn journal: Macneice, Louis

Autumn midnight: Cornford, Francis

Autumn sequel: Macneice, Louis

Autumn sheaf, The: Ricketson, Daniel

Autumnal excursion, The: Pringle, Thomas

Avalanche, The: Atherton, Gertrude

Avalanche: Boyle, Kay

Avalanche: Nichols, J.B.

Avalanche, The: Poole, Ernest

Avarice House: Green, Julian

Avatars, The: Russell, G.W.

Avatars of Vayu: Rao, Raja

Ave Caesar: Rowlands, Samuel

Ave Roma immortalis: Crawford, Francis Marion

Avel Allnutt: Morier, J.J.

Avenger, The: Oppenheim, E. Phillips

Avenger, The: Wallace, Edgar

Avenging brother, The: Ingraham, J.H.

Avenue of stone, An: Johnson, Pamela H.

Avenue of the allies and victory, The: Noyes, Alfred

Avenues of history: Namier, Sir Lewis

Average man, An: Grant, Robert

Average woman, The: Balestier, C.W.

Averil: Vachell, H.A.

Averno: Mitford, Bertram

Avery: Ward, E.S.

Avery Glibun: Newell, R.H.

Avillion: Craik, Mrs. Dinah Maria

Avolio: a legend of the Island of Cos: Hayne, P.H.

Avon's harvest: Robinson, E.A.

Avowals: Moore, George

Avowals and denials: Chesterton, G.K.

Avril: Belloc, Hilaire

Awake and release: Bromfield, Louis

Awake and sing: Odets, Clifford

Awakening: Galsworthy, John

Awakening, The: Benson, Stella

Awakening, The: Chopin, Kate

Awakening, The: Marquis, Don

Awakening of America, The: Calverton, V.F.

Awakening of Helena Richie, The: Deland, Margaret

Awakening of Japan, The: †Okakura, Tenshin

Away from it all: Gielgud, Val

Awful occasions: Knox, E.V.

Awfully big adventure: †Bartimeus

Awkwardage, The: James, Henry

Axel's castle: Wilson, Edmund

Ayala's angel: Trollope, Anthony

Ayes and the noes, The: Hollis, Christopher

Ayes have it, The: Herbert, Sir A.P.

Ayesha, the maid of Kars: Morier, J.J.

Ayesha; the return of She: Haggard, Sir Henry Rider

Aylmer's field: Tennyson, Alfred Lord

Aylwin: Watts-Dunton, W.T.

Aylwins, The: (†Michael Innes), Stewart, J.I.M.

Ayodhye canto of the Ramayana as told by Kamban, The: Rajagopalachari, Chakravati

Ayrshire idylls: Munro, Neil

Ayrshire legatees, The: Galt, John

Ayuli: Binyon, Laurence

Azaïs: Maltby, H.F.

Azaria and Hushai: Pordage, Samuel

Azarin: an episode: Spofford, H.E.

Azarias: Brown, Thomas

Azemia: Beckford, William

Azeth the Egyptian: Linton, Eliza

Aztec treasure house, The: Janvier, T.A.

Aztec treasure house for boys, The: Janvier, T.A.

Azure hand, The: Crockett, S.R.

B

B-Berry and I look back: †Yates, Dornford

B.F.'s daughter: Marquand, J.P.

B.M. Malabani: rambles with a pilgrim reformer: Singh, Jogendra

BR's secret passion: Morley, C.D.

B. Taylor's Opuscula: Taylor, Jeremy

Baa, baa, black sheep: (†Ian Hay), Beith, Sir John Hay

Baa, baa, black sheep: Wodehouse, P.G.

Bab, a sub-deb: Rinehart, Mary Roberts

Bab ballads, The: Gilbert, Sir W. S.

Babbitt: Lewis, H.S.

Babbitt Warren, The: Joad, C.E.M.

Babbling April: Greene, Graham

Babe, The: Benson, E.F.

Babel: Cournos, John

Babe's bed, The: Wescott, Glenway

Babes in the Bush: †Boldrewood, Rolf

Babes in the darkling wood: Wells, H.G.

Babes in the wood: Arlen, Michael

Babes in the wood: †Bridie, James

Babes in the wood, The: De Mille, James

Babler, The: Kelly, Hugh

Baboo Jabberjee, B.A.: †Anstey, F.

Babs the impossible: †Grand, Sarah

Baby Grand: Long, J.L.

Baby of the future, The: Traill, H.D.

Baby sitters, The: Pertwee, Roland

Babylon: (†Cecil Power), Allen, Grant

Babylonica: Benson, A.C.

Babyons, The: †Dane, Clemence

Bacchante and the nun, The: Hichens, R.S.

Bacchus festival: Jordan, Thomas

Bachelor, The: Gibbons, Stella

Bachelor, The: Malleson, Miles

Bachelor—of arts: Erskine, John

Bachelor of arts, The: Narayan, R.K.

Bachelor's Christmas, The: Grant, Robert

Bachelor's club, The: Zangwill, Israel

Bachelors get lonely: (†A.A. Fair), Gardner, Erle Stanley

Bachelor's wife, The: Galt, John

Back: Green, Henry

Back again: Mackail, Denis

Back at our selection: †Rudd, Steele

Back o' the moon: †Onions, Oliver

Back of beyond: White, S.E.

Back of the book, The: Leech, M.K.

Back seat, The: Stern, G.B.

Back street new worlds: Huxley, Elspeth J.

Back talk: Weidman, Jerome

Back to Adam: Brighouse, Harold

Back to back: Hale, E.E.

Back to Bool Bool: (†Brent of Bin Bin), Franklin, Miles

Back to humanity: Raymond, Ernest

Back to life: Gibbs, Sir Philip

Back to Methuselah: Shaw, G.B.

Back to virtue, Betty: Widdemer, Margaret

Backblock ballads and other verses: Dennis, C.M.J.

Background for Caroline, A: Ashton, Helen

Background for Domenico Scarlatti, A: Sitwell, Sacheverell

Background in Tennessee: Scott, Evelyn

Background of English literature, The: Grierson, Sir Herbert

Background of war: MacLeish, Archibald

Background with chorus: Swinnerton, Frank

Backlog studies: Warner, C.D.

Backslider, The: Allen, Grant

Back-trailers from the middle border: Garland, Hamlin

Backward glance, A: Wharton, Edith

Backward look, The: †O'Connor, Frank

Backward sun, The: Spender, Stephen

Backwater: Richardson, D.M.

Backwater: Stribling, T.S.

Backwater of life, The: Payn, James

Backwoods of Canada, The: Traill, C.P.

Backwoodsman, The: Paulding, J.K.

Bacon: Church, Richard William

Bacon: Williams, Charles

Bad child's book of beasts, The: Belloc, Hilair

Bad day for Martha: Farjeon, Eleanor

Bad manners: Agate, J.E.

Bad parents' garden of verse, The: Nash, Ogden

Bad seed, The: Anderson, Maxwell

Bad times, The: Hannay, J.O.

Baddeck: Warner, C.D.

Baddington peerage, The: Sala, G.A.H.

Badger's Green: Sherriff, R.C.

Badon parchments: Masefield, John

Baffling the blockade: Oxley, J.M.

Bag Nodle's feast: Hone, William

Bagatelle: †Preedy, George

Bagdad sketches: Stark, F.M.

Bagpipe ballads: Munro, Neil

Bahrein and Hemamieh: Petrie, Sir William Flinders

Baikie Charivari, The: †Bridie, James

Bail jumper, The: Stead, R.J.C.

Baked meats of the funeral: Halpine, C.G.

Baker's cart, The: Bullett, Gerald

Baker's dozen of emblems, A: Benét, William Rose

Balaam and his friends: Harris, Joel Chandler

Balade moral of gode counsayle: Gower, John

Balade of compleint, A: Chaucer, Geoffrey

Balaustion's adventure: Browning, Robert

Balconinny, The: Priestley, J.B.

Balcony, The: Bell, Adrian

Balcony, A: Royde-Smith, Naomi

Balcony stories: King, G.E.

Balder: Dobell, Sydney Thompson

Balder the beautiful: Buchanan, R.W.

Balder the beautiful: Frazer, Sir James

Baldwin: Barham, Richard Harris

Baldwin, LaFontaine, Hincks: responsible government: Leacock, Stephen

Baldwin: †Lee, Vernon

Bale marked circle X, The: Eggleston, G.C.

Baled hay: (†Bill Nye), Nye, E.W.

Balisand: Hergesheimer, Joseph

Balkan Monastery: Graham, Stephen

Balkan pivot, The: Beard, C.A.

Balkan princes, The: †Lonsdale, Frederick

Balkans, The: Hogarth, David George

Ball, The: Shirley, James

Ball and the cross, The: Chesterton, G.K.

Ballad and lyrical poems: Neilson, J.S.

Ballad and the source, The: Lehmann, R.N.

Ballad of a nun: Davidson, John

Ballad of Babe Christabel, The: Massey, Gerald

Ballad of Babie Bell, The: Aldrich, Thomas Bailey

Ballad of Bulgarie, The: Swinburne, A.C.

Ballad of Christmas, A: De La Mare, Walter

Ballad of dead men's bay: Swinburne, A.C.

Ballad of Flatfoot Fred, The: Mickle, A.D.

Ballad of Jan van Hunks, The: Rossetti, D.G.

Ballad of love, A: Prokosch, Frederic

Ballad of Mary the mother, The: Buchanan, R.W.

Ballad of New York, The: Morley, C.D.

Ballad of Reading Gaol, The: Wilde, Oscar

Ballad of St. Barbara, The: Chesterton, G.K.

Ballad of the brown girl, The: Cullen, Countée

Ballad of the Duke's mercy, The: Benét, Stephen Vincent

Ballad of "The Gloster" and "The Goeben", A: Hewlett, Maurice

Ballad of the harp-weaver, The: Millay, E. St. Vincent

Ballad of the white horse, The: Chesterton, G.K.

Ballad of William Sycamore, The: Benét, Stephen

Ballad romances: Horne, Richard Henry

Ballade of slow decay: Durrell, Lawrence

Ballade of the day's run: Morley, C.D.

Ballade of the scottysshe kynge, A: Skelton, John

Ballade of truthful Charles, The: Swinburne, A.C.

Ballade tragique: Beerbohm, Sir Max

Ballade, wrotten on the feastynge and merrimentes of Easter Maunday, laste paste, A: Ireland, William Henry

Ballades and verses vain: Lang, Andrew

Ballades from the hidden way: Cabell, James Branch

Ballads: Ainsworth, William Harrison

Ballads about authors: Spofford, H.E.

Ballads and barrack-room ballads: Kipling, Rudyard

Ballads and lyrics: Nesbit, Edith

Ballads and lyrics of Old France: Lang, Andrew

Ballads and lyrics of socialism, 1883–1903: Nesbit, Edith

Ballads and metrical sketches: Warren, J.B.L.

Ballads and poems of tragic life: Meredith, George

Ballads and songs: Mallet, David

Ballads and stories from Tun-Huang: Waley, Arthur

Ballads and verses of the spiritual life: Nesbit, Edith

Ballads for broadbrows: Herbert, Sir A.P.

Ballads for sale: Lowell, Amy

Ballads, in imitation of the ancient: Ireland, William Henry

Ballads of a bohemian: Service, Robert

Ballads of a Cheechako: Service, Robert

Ballads of B.C.: Gibbon, J.M.

Ballads of Irish Chivalry: Joyce, Robert Dwyer

Ballads of life: Buchanan, R.W.

Ballads of lost haven: Carman, Bliss

Ballads of Robin Hood: Hunt, Leigh

Ballads of square-toed Americans: Coffin, Robert

Ballads of the border: Allen, Hervey

Ballads of the English Border: Swinburne, A.C.

Ballads of valor and victory: Scollard, Clinton

Ballads, patriotic and romantic: Scollard, Clinton

Ballads, poems and Lyrics: Maccorthy, Denis

Ballads, Romances and Songs: Joyce, Robert Dwyer

Ballads to sell: Carman, Bliss

Ballantyne-Humbug handled, The: Lockhart, John Gibson

Ballerina: Ackland, Rodney

Ballet of the Nations, The: †Lee, Vernon

Balliols, The: Waugh, Alec

Balloon: Colum, Padraic

Ballot: Smith, Sydney

Balls, and another book for suppression: Aldington, Richard

Ballyfarland's Festival: Ervine, St. John

Balmoral: Brown, Ivor

Balzac: Saltus, E.E.

Ban and arrière ban: Lang, Andrew

Banana bottom: McKay, Claude

Banana gold: Beals, Carleton

Banbrytarna: †Lancaster, G.B.

Band of angels: Warren, Robert Penn

Bandit of the Rhine: Thomas, E.H.

Bandolero, The: Reid, T.M.

Bang you're dead: Treece, Henry

Banished Briton and Neptunian, The: Gourlay, R.F.

Banishment of Cicero, The: Cumberland, Richard

Banjo: McKay, Claude

Bank audit, The: Marshall, Bruce

Bank director's son, The: Lippard, George

Bank manager, The: Oppenheim, E. Phillips

Bank thrown down, The: Swift, Jonathan

Banker of Bankersville, A: Thompson, Maurice

Banker's daughter, The:Howard, B.C.

Banker's daughter, The: Reynolds, G.

Banker's wife, The: Gore, Catherine

Bankette of sapience, The:Elyot, *Sir* Thomas

Bankim-Tilak-Dayananda: Ghose, Sri Aurobindo

Bank-restriction barometer, The: Hone, William

Bankrupt, The: Boker, G.H.

Bankruptcy of marriage, The: Calverton, V.F.

Banks, banking and paper currencies: Hildreth, Richard

Banks for the people, The: Strachey, John

Banks of Wye, The: Bloomfield, Robert

Banned broadcast, A: Haldane, J.B.S.

Banner of blue, The: Crockett, S.R.

Banner of the bull, The: Sabatini, R.

Banners: Deutsch, Babette

Banners in the dawn: Starrett, Vincent

Bannertail: Seton-Thompson, E.

Bannerton's agency: Ridge, W. Pett

Banquet, The: Mottram, R.H.

Banquet for gentlemen and ladies, A: Motteux, P.A.

Banquet of daintie conceits, A: Munday, Anthony

Banshee, The: Todhunter, John

Banshee's warning, The:Riddell, *Mrs.* J.H.

Bantam V.C., The: Brighouse, Harold

Banter: Sala, G.A.H.

Baptist Lake: Davidson, John

Baptistery, The: Williams, Isaac

Bar and the courts of the Province of Upper Canada or Ontario, The: Riddell, W. Robert

Bar of shadow, A: Van der Post, L.J.

Bar, stage and platform: Merivale, H.C.

Barabbas: †Corelli, Marie

Barb of an arrow, The: Bridges, Roy

Barbaloot: Muir, D.C.A.

Barbara Frietchie, the Frederick girl: Fitch, Clyde William

Barbara on her own: Wallace, Edgar

Barbara Rebell: Lowndes, M.A.

Barbarian stories: Mitchison, Naomi

Barbarians: Chambers, R.W.

Barbarians at the gate: Woolf, Leonard

Barbarism of Berlin, The: Chesterton, G.K.

Barbarous Britishers,The:Traill, H.D.

Barbary sheep: Hichens, Robert

Barber Cox and the cutting of his comb: Thackeray, W.M.

Barberry Bush, The: Coolidge, Susan

Barber's clock, The: Lucas, E.V.

Barber's trade union, The: Anand, M.R.

Barbour's Bruce: Barbour, J.

Barcellona: Farquhar, George

Barchester pilgrimage: Knox, R.A.

Barchester Towers: Trollope, Anthony

Bardelys the magnificent (novel and play): Sabatini, R.

Bare hills, The: Winters, Yvor

Bare souls: Bradford, Gamaliel

Barefoot in Athens: Anderson, Maxwell

Barefoot saint, The: Benét, Stephen Vincent

Bare-knuckle breed, The: Golding, Louis

Bargain, The: Malleson, Miles

Bargain basement: (†Beresford Russell), Roberts, C.E.M.

Barham Downs: Bage, Robert

Barker's luck: Harte, Bret

Barlamb's ballad book, A: Underhill, Evelyn

Barlasch of the Guard: †Merriman, Seton

Barmy in wonderland: Wodehouse, P.G.

Barn, The: Blunden, Edmund

Barnaby Rudge: Dickens, Charles

Barnabys in America, The: Trollope, Frances

Barney the Baron: Lover, Samuel

Barns: Morley, C.D.

Baron Rudolph: Belasco, David

Baronage of England, The: Dugdale, *Sir* William

Baroness of New York, The: †Miller, Joaquin

Baronet and the butterfly, The: Whistler, James McNeill

Baronettage of England, The: Collins, Arthur

Baron's hostage, The: Trease, Geoffrey

Barons of the Potomack and the Rappahannock: Conway, Moncure Daniel

Barony, The: Porter, A.M.

Baroque architecture of Leipzig, The: Pevsner, Nikolaus

Barrack-room ballads: Kipling, Rudyard

Barren fig-tree, The: Bunyan, John

Barren ground: Glasgow, Ellen

Barren honour: Lawrence, George Alfred

Barren metal: Jacob, Naomi

Barren tree, The: Griffith, Llewelyn

Barretts of Wimpole Street, The: Besier, Rudolf

Barricades, The: Toynbee, T.P.

Barrie: the story of J.M.B.: Mackail, Denis

Barrier, The: Beach, R.E.

Barriers are down, The: Lindsay, Jack

Barriers burned away: Roe, E.P.

Barrington: Lever, C.J.

Bar-room ballads: Service, Robert

Barry Lyndon: Thackeray, W.M.

Barford Abbey: Gunning, *Mrs.* Susannah

Bartholomew fair: Jonson, Ben

Barty Crusoe and his man Saturday: Burnett, Frances Hodgson

Barty's star: Gale, Norman R.

Barwon ballads: (†C), Cuthbertson, J.L.

Barwon ballads and school verses: (†C), Cuthbertson, J.L.

Bas Bleu, The: More, Hannah

Baseless biography: Bentley, E.C.

Baseless fabric, The: Simpson, H.de G.

Basement room, The: Greene, Graham

Bases of artistic creation, The: Anderson, Maxwell

Bases of Yoga: Ghose, Sri Aurobindo

Bashful lover, The: Massinger, Philip

Basic English and its uses: Richards, I.A.

Basic history of the United States, A: Beard, C.A. and M.

Basic principles of fiction writing: Widdemer, Margaret

Basic problem of democracy, The: Lippmann, Walter

Basic rules of reason: Richards, I.A.

Basil: Collins, William Wilkie

Basil and Annette: Farjeon, B.L.

Basil Netherby: Benson, A.C.

Basil Seal rides again: Waugh, Evelyn

Basilicon Doron: James VI of Scotland

Basilissa: Masefield, John

Basis of freedom: Miller, E.M.

Basis of sensation, The: Adrian, E.D. *1st Baron*

Basket woman, The: Austin, Mary

Basque people: Canfield, Dorothy

Bassett: Gibbons, Stella

Bastard, The: Caldwell, Erskine Preston

Bastille, The: Brooke, Rupert

Bat, The: Rinehart, Mary Roberts

Bat that flits, The: Collins, Norman

Batavian anthology: Bowring, *Sir* John

Bateman household, The: Payn, James

Bath: Mee, Arthur

Bath: Sitwell, Edith

Bath, its beauties and amusements: Ellis, George

Bath, its history and social tradition: Falkner, John Meade

Bath tangle: Heyer, Georgette

Bath waters: Baring-Gould, Sabine

Bathroom door, The: Jennings, Gertrude

Battaile of Agincourt, The: Drayton, Michael

Battel, The: Ramsay, Allan

Battell of Alcazar, fought in Barbarie, The: Peele, George

Battle: Gibson, Wilfred

Battle continues, The: †McDiarmid, Hugh

Battle for the rock: Schull, J.J.

Battle ground, a history of Syria to 1187 A.D., The: Belloc, Hilaire

Battle hymn of the Republic, The: Howe, Julia Ward

Battle in Greece, A: Crane, Stephen

Battle of Basinghall Street: Oppenheim, E.Phillips

Battle of Borodino, The: Fairfield, S.L.

Battle of Britain, The: Saunders, H.A. St. George

Battle of Bull Run, The: Stedman, E.C.

Battle of Bunkers-Hill, The: Brackenridge, Hugh Henry

Battle of College Point, The: Bangs, John Kendrick

Battle of Dorking, The: Chesney, *Sir* George Tomkyns

Battle of Hastings, The: Cumberland, Richard

Battle of Hexham, The: Colman, George, *the younger*

Battle of Kadesh, The: Breasted, J.H.

Battle of Largs, The: Galt, John

Battle of life, The: Dickens, Charles

Battle of Marathon, The: Browning, Elizabeth Barrett

Battle of Niagara, The: Neal, John

Battle of Ramillia, The: Dennis, John

Battle of Talavera, The: Croker, John Wilson

Battle of the Atlantic: †Taffrail

Battle of the books, The: Swift, Jonathan

Battle of the frogs and mice, The: Barlow, Jane

Battle of the kegs, The: Hopkinson, Francis

Battle of the professor, The: Traill, H.D.

Battle of the safes, The: Sala, G.A.H.

Battle of the Somme, The: Masefield, John

Battle of the strong, The: Parker, *Sir* H.G.

Battle of the Thames, The: Herbert, *Sir* A.P.

Battle of the Villa Fiorita, The: Godden, Rumer

Battle of the Wazzir, The: Dennis, C.M.J.

Battle pieces: Melville, Herman

Battle summer, The: Mitchell, D.G.

Battle within, The: Gibbs, Sir Philip

Battle-day of Germantown, The: Lippard, George

Battle-door for teachers and professors to learn singular and plural, A: Fox, George

Battlefields: Gilmore, Mary

Battle-ground, The: Glasgow, Ellen

Battlers, The: Tennant, Kylie

Battles of the Somme, The: Gibbs, *Sir* Philip

Battles royal down north: Duncan, Norman

Bauble shop, The: Jones, Henry Arthur

Baucis and Philemon: Swift, Jonathan

Baudelaire and the symbolist: Quennell, P.C.

Bavarian story: Mannin, Ethel

Bawling brotherhood, The: Housman, Laurence

Bay: Lawrence, D.H.

Bay, The: Strong, L.A.G.

Bay and Padie Book, The: †Maurice, Furnley

Bay area façades: Wright, F.L.

Bay colony, The: Fisher, H.A.L.

Bay leaves: Smith, Goldwin

Bay of Seven Islands, The: Whittier, J.G.

Bayard from Bengal, A: †Anstey, F.

Bayard Taylor: Longfellow, H.W.

Bayete! Hail to the King: Nicholls, G.H.

Bayi Brabhou: Ghose, Sri Aurobindo

Bayonets to Lhasa: Fleming, Peter

Bayou folk: Chopin, Kate

Bay-path, The: Holland, J.G.

Bay-tree country: Cripps, A.S.

Bazaar, The: Armstrong, M.D.

Be angry at the sun: Jeffers, J.R.

Be music, night: Patchen, Kenneth

Be yourself: Gershwin, Ira

Beachcomber, The: McFee, William

Beachy Head: Smith, Charlotte

Beacon, The: Phillpotts, Eden

Beadle, The: Smith, Pauline

Beads of Tasmar, The: Barr, A.E.H.

Bealby, a holiday: Wells, H.G.

Beany-Eye: Garnett, David

Bear, The: Faulkner, William

Bear dances, The: Lucas, F.L.

Bear fell free, The: Greene, Graham

Bears of Blue River, The: Major, Charles

Beasley's Christmas party: Tarkington, Booth

Beast, The: O'Higgins, H.J.

Beast in me and other animals, The: Thurber, James

Beast in view: Rukeyser, Muriel

Beast must die, The: Day-Lewis, Cecil

Beastly pride: Baker, Elizabeth

Beasts and saints: Waddell, H.J.

Beasts and super-beasts: (†Saki), Munro, H.H.

Beasts at law: Woodworth, Samuel

Beasts confession to the priest, The: Swift, Jonathan

Beat drum, beat hart: Wingfield, Shiela

Beat to quarters: Forester, C.S.

Beaten paths and those who trod them: Gratton, Thomas Colley

Beating wings: Chambers, R.W.

Beatrice: Haggard, Sir Henry Rider

Beatrice: Kavanagh, Julia

Beatrice: McFarlane, John E. Clare

Beatrice: Noel, R.B.W.

Beatrice, the goldsmith's daughter: Ingraham, J.H.

Beatrice Tyldesley: Ainsworth, William H.

Beatrice Webb: a memoir: Cole, M.I.

Beatrice Webb, 1858–1943: Tawney, R.H.

Beau Austin: Henley, W.E.

Beau Austin: Stevenson, R.L.

Beau Brocade: Orczy, Baroness

Beau Brummel: Fitch, Clyde William

Beau Brummell: Woolf, Virginia

Beau Geste: Wren, P.C.

Beau Ideal: Wren, P.C.

Beau Nash, or Bath in the eighteenth century: Ainsworth, William H.

Beau Nash, the king of Bath: Jerrold, Douglas

Beau Sabreur: Wren, P.C.

Beauchamp: James, George Payne Rainsford

Beauchampe: Simms, W.G.

Beauchamp's career: Meredith, George

Beaumaroy home from the wars: (†Anthony Hope), Hawkins, Anthony Hope

Beauregard: the great Creole: Basso, Hamilton

Beauteous terrorist, The: Parkes, Sir Henry

Beauties, The: Walpole, Horace

Beauties and furies, The: Stead, C.E.

Beauties of English Poetry, The: †Pindar, Peter

Beauties of the Boyne and the Blackwater, The: Wilde, Sir William

Beauties of the country: Miller, Thomas

Beautiful, The: †Lee, Vernon

Beautiful and the damned, The: Fitzgerald, F.Scott

Beautiful end: Holme, Constance

Beautiful lady, The: Tarkington, Booth

Beautiful land of Nod, The: Wilcox, Ella Wheeler

Beautiful lie of Rome, The: Le Gallienne, Richard

Beautiful Mrs. Blain, The: Hoffe, Monckton

Beautiful people, The: Saroyan, William

Beautiful Queen of Leix, The: Griffin, Gerald

Beautiful rebel, A: Campbell, W.W.

Beautiful rebel, A: Glanville, Ernest

Beautiful Wales: Thomas, E.E.P.

Beautiful wretch, The: Black, William

Beautiful years, The: Williamson, Henry

Beautiful young nymph going to bed, A: Swift, Jonathan

Beauty: Pye, H.J.

Beauty and life: Scott, D.C.

Beauty and Nick: Gibbs, Sir Philip Hamilton

Beauty and the barge: Jacobs, W.W.

Beauty and the beast: Lamb, Charles

Beauty and the beast and tales of home: Taylor, Bayard

Beauty and the Jacobin (novel and play): Tarkington, Booth

Beauty and ugliness: †Lee, Vernon

Beauty for ashes: Virtue, Vivian L.

Beauty, history, romance and mystery of the Canadian lake region, The: Campbell, W.W.

Beauty imposes: Neilson, J.S.

Beauty in distress: Motteux, P.A.

Beauty looks after herself: Gill, Eric

Beauty of the dead, The: Bates, H.E.

Beauty of women, The: Bax, Clifford

Beauty part: Perelman, S.J.

Beauty prize, The: Wodehouse, P.G.

Beauty spot, The: Coppard, A.E.

Beauty stone, The: Pinero, *Sir* A.W.

Beauty the pilgrim: Gould, Gerald

Beauvallet: Heyer, Georgette

Beaux stratagem, The: Farquhar, George

Beaver kings and cabins: Skinner, C.L.

Because it is: Patchen, Kenneth

Because of these things: †Bowen, Marjorie

Bechuana proverbs with literal translations and their European equivalents: Plaatje, S.T.

Becket: Belloc, Hilaire

Becket: Tennyson, Alfred *Lord*

Beckford and Beckfordism: Sitwell, Sacheverell

Beckoning hand, The: Allen, Grant

Beckoning lady, The: Allingham, Margery

Beckoning shore, The: Timms, E.V.

Beckonings for everyday: Larcom, Lucy

Becky Landers: Skinner, C.L.

Becky Sharp: Hichens, R.S.

Becoming: Phillpotts, Eden

Bed of feathers, A: Davies, Rhys

Bed of roses, A: Jones, Henry Arthur

Bed rock: Phillpotts, Eden

Bedford-Row Conspiracy, The: Thackeray, W.M.

Bedouins: Huneker, J.G.

Bedroom and boudoir, The: Barker, M.A.

Bedroom suite: Morley, C.D.

Bedside manners: Behrman, S.N.

Bedtime stories: Moulton, E.L.

Bee man of Orn, The: Stockton, F.R.

Beechen tree, The: Thomas, F.W.

Beechen vigil: Day-Lewis, Cecil

Beelzebub: Trevelyan, R.C.

Beerbohm tree: Pearson, Hesketh

Bees and honey: Maltby, H.F.

Bees on the boat deck: Priestley, J.B.

Beethoven: Pryce-Jones, Alan

Beethoven, the search for reality: Turner, W.J.R.

Befo' de war: Page, T.N.

Before Adam: London, Jack

Before and after Independence: Nehru, Jawaharlal

Before dawn: Hoffe, Monckton

Before dawn: Monro, H.E.

Before daybreak: Bottomley, Gordon

Before disaster: Winters, Yvor

Before lunch: Thirkell, Angela

Before March: MacLeish, Archibald

Before marching and after: Hardy, Thomas

Before midnight: †Mordaunt, Elinor

Before sunset: Malleson, Miles

Before the bombardment: Sitwell, *Sir* Osbert

Before the brave: Patchen, Kenneth

Before breakfast: O'Neill, Eugene

Before the crossing: Jameson, Storm

Before the curfew: Holmes, O.W.

Before the dawn: Fausset, Hugh

Before the flowers of friendship faded friendship faded: Stein, Gertrude

Before the gringo came, Atherton: Gertrude

Before the party: Ackland, Rodney

Before you go: Weidman, Jerome

Beggar, The: Mason, R.A.K.

Beggar on horseback: Connelly, Marc

Beggar on horseback: Kaufman, G.S.

Beggars: Davies, W.H.

Beggars bush, The: Beaumont, Francis and Fletcher, John

Beggar's daughter of Bethnal Green, The: Knowles, James Sheridan

Beggars' gold: Poole, Ernest

Beggars' horses: Wren, P.C.

Beggars on horseback: Somerville, E.

Beggar's opera, The: Gay, John

Beggar's opera-tion, The: Stewart, George

Begg'd at court: Knight, Charles

Begin here: Sayers, Dorothy

Beginner, A: Broughton, Rhoda

Beginners of a nation, The: Eggleston, Edward

Beginning, A: De la Mare, Walter

Beginning again: Woolf, Leonard

Beginning and the end: Jeffers, J.R.

Beginning of wisdom, The: Benét, Stephen Vincent

Beginning on the short story, A: Williams, W.C.

Beginnings of New England, The: †Fiske, John

Beginnings of the American people: Becker, C.L.

Beginnings of the Middle Ages, The: Church, Richard William

Begum's daughter, The: Bynner, Edwin Lassetter

Behind the arras: Carman, Bliss

Behind the beyond: Leacock, Stephen

Behind the crimson blind: †Carter Dickson

Behind the curtain: Gibbs, *Sir* Philip

Behind the fleets: †Divine, David

Behind the green curtains: O'Casey, Sean

Behind the lines: Milne, A.A.

Behind the log: Pratt, E.J.

Behind the mountains: La Farge, Oliver

Behind the throne: Brighouse, Harold

Behind the veil: De Mille, James

Behind the veil: Noel, R.B.W.

Behind time: Lathrop, G.P.

Behold, here's poison: Heyer, Georgette

Behold, the bridegroom—: Kelly, G.E.

Behold the judge: Brophy, John

Behold this dreamer: De La Mare, Walter

Behold trouble: Hicks, Granville

Behold, we live: Van Druten, J.W.

Behold your king: Mitchison, Naomi

Being a boy: Warner, C.D.

'Bel of Prairie Eden: Lippard, George

Belated reckoning, The: Bottome, Phyllis

Belcaro: †Lee, Vernon

Beleaguered city, A: Oliphant, Margaret

Belfast: Manning, Anne

Belford Regis: Mitford, Russell

Belfry of Bruges, The: Longfellow, H.W.

Belgian Christmas eve, A: Noyes, Alfred

Belgium: Ensor, Sir R.C.K.

Belgium: a personal record: Whitlock, Brand

Belgium and Western Germany in 1833: Trollope, Frances

Belgium, from the Roman invasion to the present day: Cammaerts, Emile

Belief and action: an everyday philosophy: Samuel, Herbert, 1st Viscount

Belief in immortality and the worship of the dead, The: Frazer, Sir James

Belief of Catholics, The: Knox, R.A.

Believe as you list: Croker, Thomas Crofton

Believe as you list: Massinger, Philip

Belinda: Belloc, Hilaire

Belinda: Broughton, Rhoda

Belinda: Edgeworth, Maria

Belinda: Milne, A.A.

Belinda Grove: Ashton, Helen

Bell Harry: Hassall, Christopher

Bell in the fog, The: Atherton, Gertrude

Bell of St. Paul's, The: Besant, Sir Walter

Bella Donna: Hichens, Robert

Bellamira: Sedley, Sir Charles

Bellamy: †Mordaunt, Elinor

Bellarion: Sabatini, R.

Belle of a season, The: Blessington, Marguerite

Belle of Bowling Green, The: Barr, A.E.H.

Belle of Toorak: Peccavi, Hornung, E.W.

Bellerophôn: †Field, Michael

Belles of Broadway, The: Clarke, Macdonald

Belle's stratagem, The: Cowley, Mrs. Hannah

Bell-founder, The: MacCarthy, Denis

Bellman's petition, The: Hume, David

Bell-ringer of Angel's, The: Harte, Bret

Bells, The: Aldrich, Thomas Bailey

Bells and bees: Esson, T.L.B.

Bells and grass: De La Mare, Walter

Bells and pomegranates: Browning, Robert

Bells of Bethlehem, The: Fields, J.T.

Bells of Christmas, The: Young, E.R.

Bells of Kirby Wiske, The: Kirby, William

Bells of Old Quebec, The: Dollard, J.B.

Bells of peace, The: Galsworthy, John

Bells of Rye, The: Church, Richard

Bells of Shoreditch, The: Sidgwick, Ethel

Bells of the city, The: Tennant, Kylie

Bellum Presbyteriale: Stevenson, Matthew

Belman of London, The: Dekker, Thomas

Beloved adventure, The: Wheelock, J.H.

Beloved community, The: Pierce, Lorne

Beloved physician, The: Jacob, Naomi

Beloved stranger, The: Bynner, Witter

Beloved traitor, The: Packard, F.L.

Below and on top: Dyson, E.G.

Below London Bridge: Tomlinson, H.M.

Below suspicion: Carr, J.D.

Below the salt: Costain, T.B.

Belphegor: Wilson, John

Belshazzar: Haggard, Sir Henry Rider

Belshazzar: Milman, H.H.

Beltane the Smith: Farnol, J.J.

Belton estate, The: Trollope, Anthony

Bel-vedere: Bodenham, John

Ben Brace: the last of Nelson's Agamemnons: Chamier, Frederick

Ben Hall the bushranger: Clune, Frank

Ben Hur: a tale of the Christ: Wallace, Lew

Ben Jonson: Palmer, J.L.

Ben Jonson and King James: Linklater, Eric

Ben Lilly legend, The: Dobie, J.F.

Ben Nazir the Saracen: Gratton, Thomas Colley

Ben Nevis goes east: Mackenzie, Sir Compton

Benchley beside himself: Benchley, Robert

Benchley—or else: Benchley, Robert

Bend sinister: Nabokov, Vladimir

Bending of the bough, The: Moore, George

Bending sickle, The: Bullett, Gerald

Bendish: Hewlett, M.H.

Beneath tropic seas: Beebe, William

Benedict Kavanaugh: Hannay, J.O.

Benefactor, The: Ford, Ford Madox

Benefactors of the Medical School of Harvard University, The: Holmes, Oliver Wendell

Benefactress, The: Russell, E.M.

Benefit of the doubt, The: Pinero, Sir A.W.

Benefits forgot: Balestier, C.W.

Benefits forgot: Stern, G.B.

Benevolent epistle to Sylvanus Urban alias Master John Nichols, printer, A: †Pindar, Peter

Bengal journey: Godden, Rumer

Bengal Nawabs: Sarkar, Y.J.

Ben-Gurion's Israel: Appel, Benjamin

Benighted: Priestley, J.B.

Benita: Haggard, Sir Henry Rider

Benjamin Constant: Nicolson, Hon. Sir Harold

Benjamin Disraeli: Meynell, Wilfred

Benjamin Franklin: Becker, C.L.

Benjamin Franklin: More, P.E.

Benjamin Franklin: Van Doren, Carl

Benno and some of the push: Dyson, E.G.

Benoni: Munby, A.J.

Bent twig, The: Canfield, Dorothy

Bentinck's tutor: Payn, James

Beowulf: the monsters and the critics: Tolkien, J.R.R.

Beppo: Byron, George Gordon *Lord*

Beppo and Beth: Wilson, Edmund

Berenice: Oppenheim, E.Phillips

Berenice, by Jean Racine (trn.): Masefield, John

Berg, The: Raymond, Ernest

Beric the Briton: Henty, G.E.

Berkeley: Ingraham, J.H.

Berkeley Square: Squire, *Sir* John

Berkshire mystery, The: Cole, G.D.H.

Berlin: Hergesheimer, Joseph

Berlioz: Turner, W.J.R.

Berna Boyle: Riddell, *Mrs.* J.H.

Bernadette: Stern, G.B.

Bernal Diaz del Castillo: Cunninghame Graham, Robert

Bernard Barton and his friends: Lucas, E.V.

Bernard Clare: Farrell, James

Bernard Palissy, the potter: Morley, Henry

Bernard Shaw: Ervine, St.John

Bernard Shaw: Jackson, Holbrook

Bernard Shaw: Pearson, Hesketh

Bernard Shaw: his life, work and friends: Ervine, St. John

Bernard Shaw in Heaven: Rubenstein, Harold F.

Bernard Shaw in his time: Brown, Ivor

Bernardine: Chase, M.C.

Bernice: Glaspell, Susan

Bernicia: Barr, A.E.H.

Berry and Co.: †Yates, Dornford

Berry scene, The: †Yates, Dornford

Bert: Phillpotts, Eden

Bert Lloyd's boyhood: Oxley, J.M.

Bertram: Brydges, *Sir* Samuel Egerton

Bertram: Maturin, C.R.

Bertram Cope's year: Fuller, Henry Blake

Bertrams, The: Trollope, Anthony

Bertrand: Ingraham, J.H.

Bertrand de la Croix: James, George Payne Rainsford

Bertrand of Brittany: Deeping, Warwick

Bert's girl: Baker, Elizabeth

Beside a Norman tower: De la Roche, Mazo

Beside Galilee: Bolitho, H.H.

Beside still waters: Benson, A.C.

Besieging city, The: Mander, Jane

Bess of the woods: Deeping, Warwick

Bessie: Kavanagh, Julia

Bessie's fortune: Holmes, M.J.

Bessy Rane: Wood, Ellen

Bessy Wells: Wood, Ellen

Bessy's money: Manning, Anne

Best in their kind, The: Mais, S.P.B.

Best laid plans, The: Ford, Paul Leicester

Best laid schemes: Nicholson, Meredith

Best of a bad job, The: Duncan, Norman

Best of England, The: Vachell, H.A.

Best of husbands, The: Payn, James

Best of Simple: Hughes, J.L.

Best of times, The: Bemelmans, Ludwig

Best of two worlds, The: Krutch, J.W.

Best people, The: †Lonsdale, Frederick

Beth: Williams, Emlyn

Beth book, The: †Grand, Sarah

Bethel Merriday: Lewis, H.S.

Bethlehem: Carman, Bliss

Bethlehem: Faber, Frederick William

Bethlehem: Housman, Laurence

Bethpelet I: Petrie, *Sir* William Flinders

Betrayal, The: Hartley, L.P.

Betrayal, The: Oppenheim, E. Phillips

Betrayal in India: Karaka, D.F.

Betrayal of Christ by the churches, The: Murry, John Middleton

Betrayal of John Fordham, The: Farjeon, B.L.

Betrayed spring: Lindsay, Jack

Betraying of Christ, The: Rowlands, Samuel

Betrothal, The: Boker, G.H.

Betrothal ring of Mary Queen of Scots: †Bede, Cuthbert

Betrothed of Wyoming, The: McHenry, James

Betsey and I are out: Carleton, William (McKendree)

Betsy Lee: Brown, Thomas Edward

Better dead: Barrie, *Sir* J.M.

Better man, The: Chambers, R.W.

Better sky, A: Herbert, *Sir* A.P.

Better sort, The: James, Henry

Better writing: Canby, Henry Seidel

Betty: †Lonsdale, Frederick

Betty and Co.: Turner, E.S.

Betty book, The: White, S.E.

Betty Wayside: Stone, Louis

Betty Zane: Grey, Zane

Betty's bright idea, etc.: Stowe, Harriet Beecher

Between doubting and daring: Barlow, Jane

Between earth and sky: Bercovici, Konrad

Between earth and sky: Thomson, E.W.

Between fairs: Gibson, Wilfred

Between friends: Cabell, James Bronch

Between friends: Chambers, R.W.

Between Niger and Nile: Toynbee, A.J.

Between Oxus and Jumna: Toynbee, A.J.

Between St. Denis and St. George: Ford, Ford Madox

Between sun and sand: Scully, W.C.

Between tears and laughter: Lin Yu-T'ang

Between the acts: Woolf, Virginia

Between the dark and the daylight: Howells, W.D.

Between the lights: Lawson, Will

Between the lights: MacKay, I.E.

Between the lines: Ewart, E.A.

Between the lines: Tomlinson, H.M.

Between the soup and the savoury: Jennings, Gertrude

Between the tides: Fausset, Hugh

Between the tides: Hanley, James

Between two loves: Barr, A.E.H.

Between two masters: Bradford, Gamaliel

Between two stools: Broughton, Rhoda

Between two worlds: Murry, John Middleton

Between two worlds: Rice, Elmer

Between two worlds: Sinclair, Upton

Between whiles: Jackson, H.H.

Betwixt the forelands: Russell, W.C.

Beulah: Evans, Augusta Jane

Beulah land: Davis, H.L.

Beverley Nichols' Cats ABC: Nichols, J.B.

Beverley Nichols' Cats XYZ: Nichols, J.B.

Beverly of Graustark: McCutcheon, G.B.

Bevis: Davies, H.H.

Bevis: Jefferies, Richard

Beware of parents: Nathan, G.J.

Beware the cuckoo: Moll, E.G.

Bewilderment: Scott, Evelyn

Bewitched lamp, The: Molesworth, Mrs.

Beyond: Galsworthy, John

Beyond control: Beach, R.E.

Beyond criticism: Shapiro, Karl

Beyond culture: Trilling, Lionel

Beyond desire: Anderson, Sherwood

Beyond Dover: Gielgud, Val

Beyond Euphrates: Stark, F.M.

Beyond life: Cabell, James Branch

Beyond personality: Lewis, C.S.

Beyond physics: Lodge, Sir Oliver

Beyond terror: Lindsay, Jack

Beyond the Alps: Coates, R.M.

Beyond the black stump: †Shute, Nevil

Beyond the borderline of life: Myers, Gustavus

Beyond the breakers: Holcroft, M.H.

Beyond the breakers: Sterling, George

Beyond the Chindwin: Fergusson, Sir Bernard

Beyond the city: Doyle, Sir Arthur Conan

Beyond the desert: Noyes, Alfred

Beyond the desert: Rhodes, E.M.

Beyond the dreams of avarice: Besant, Sir Walter

Beyond the gates: Ward, E.S.

Beyond the hills of dream: Campbell, W.W.

Beyond the horizon: O'Neill, Eugene

Beyond the marshes: †Connor, Ralph

Beyond the Mexique Bay: Huxley, Aldous

Beyond the rocks: Glyn, Elinor

Beyond these voices: Braddon, Mary Elizabeth

Beyond this limit: Mitchison, Naomi

Beyond this place: Cronin, A.J.

Bhagavad Gita: Munshi, K.M.

Bhagavad Gita abridged and explained: Rajagopalachari, Chakravati

Bianca: Dutt, Toru

Bianca Visconti: Willis, N.P.

Bias of communication: Innis, H.A.

Biathanatos: Donne, John

Bib ballads: Lardner, Ring

Bibi: Cunninghame Graham, Robert

Bible and common sense, The: †King, Basil

Bible and the common reader, The: Chase, M.E.

Bible characters: Reade, Charles

Bible in Scotland, The: Macphail, Sir Andrew

Bible in Scots literature, The: Moffat, James

Bible in Spain, The: Borrow, George

Bible in Spain, The: Ford, Richard

Bible letters for children: Barton, Bernard

Bible rhymes on the names of all the books of the Old and New Testaments: More, Hannah

Bible tragedies: Horne, Richard Henry

Biblical pictures: Grahame, James

Bibliographer's manual of English literature, The: Lowndes, William Thomas

Bibliographica: Pollard, A.W.

Bibliographical and critical account of the rarest books in the English language, A: Collier, J.P.

Bibliographical and textual problems of the English Miracle Cycles: Greg, W.W.

Bibliographical, antiquarian and picturesque tour in France and Germany, A: Dibdin, Thomas Frognall

Bibliographical, antiquarian and picturesque tour in the northern counties of England and in Scotland: Dibdin, Thomas Frognall

Bibliographical decameron, The: Dibdin, Thomas Frognall

Bibliography: Dibdin, Thomas Frognall

Bibliography—a retrospect: Greg, W.W.

Bibliography for teachers of history, A: Power, Eileen

Bibliography of books and articles relating to children's reading, A: Widdemer, Margaret

Bibliography of Byron, The: Wise, T.J.

Bibliography of Canadian fiction, A: Burpee, Lawrence J.

Bibliography of Coleridge, The: Wise, T.J.

Bibliography of Joseph Conrad, The: Wise, T.J.

Bibliography of Landor, The: Wise, T.J.

Bibliography of Michael Drayton: Tillotson, Geoffrey

Bibliography of Robert and E.E.Browning,The: Wise,T.J.

Bibliography of Ruskin, The: Wise, T.J.

Bibliography of the Brontës, The: Wise, T.J.

Bibliography of the English printed drama to the Restoration, A: Greg, W.W.

Bibliography of Swinburne, The: Wise, T.J.

Bibliography of Tennyson, The: Wise, T. J.

Bibliography of Wordsworth, The: Wise, T.J.

Bibliomania, The: Dibdin, Thomas Frognall

Bibliophobia: Dibdin, Thomas Frognall

Bibliotheca Canadiensis: Morgan, H.J.

Bicycle of Cathay, A: Stockton, F.R.

Bicycle rider in Beverly Hills, The: Saroyan, William

Bicyclers, The: Bangs, John Kendrick

Bid me to live: (†D.H.) Doolittle, Hilda

Bidden quest, The: Anthony, Frank S.

Bidden to the feast: Jones, Jack

Biddy Woodhull: Ingraham, J.H.

Biding his time: Trowbridge, J.T.

Bien venu: Davies, John

Big barn, The: Edmonds, W.D.

Big bear of Arkansas, The: Thorpe, T.B.

Big Ben: Herbert, Sir A.P.

Big Ben alibi, The: (†Neil Gordon), A.G.Macdonell

Big bow mystery, The: Zangwill, Israel

Big brother: Beach, R.E.

Big brother series, The: Eggleston, G.C.

Big business: Hutchinson, Arthur

Big business in a democracy: Adams, J. T.

Big business murder: Cole, G.D.H.

Big clock, The: Fearing, Kenneth

Big drum, The, Pinero, Sir A.W.

Big fellow, The: †O'Connor, Frank

Big fellow, The: Palmer, E.V.

Big fish: †Beeding, Francis

Big foot: Wallace, Edgar

Big four, The: Christie, Agatha

Big four, The: Wallace, Edgar

Big heart, The: Anand, M.R.

Big house, The: Mitchison, Naomi

Big house of Inver, The: Somerville, E.

Big It, The: Guthrie, A.B.

Big knife, The: Odets, Clifford

Big laugh, The: O'Hara, J.H.

Big man, The: Strong, L.A.G.

Big man, a fast man, A: Appel, Benjamin

Big Matt: Whitlock, Brand

Big money, The: Dos Passos, John

Big money: Wodehouse, P.G.

Big O and Sir Glory: Cobbett, William

Big sea, The: Hughes, J.L.

Big shot, The: Hergesheimer, Joseph

Big shot, The: Packard, F.L.

Big Six, The: Ransome, Arthur

Big sky, The: Guthrie, A.B.

Big sleep, The: Chandler, Raymond

Big Sur and the oranges of Hieronymus: Miller, Henry

Big town, The: Lardner, Ring

Big tree of Bunlahy, The: Colum, Padraic

Big wave: Buck, Pearl

Big woods: Faulkner, William

Biglow papers, The: Lowell, J.R.

Big-timer, The: Hughes, J.L.

Bihar and Orissa during the fall of the Mughul empire: Sarkar, Y.J.

Bikey the skicycle and other tales of Jimmieboy: Bangs, John Kendrick

Bill Arp's scrap book: †Arp, Bill

Bill for the better promotion of oppression on the Sabbath Day, A: Peacock, Thomas Love

Bill of divorcement, A: †Dane, Clemence

Bill Porter: Sinclair, Upton

Bill the bachelor: Mackail,Denis

Bill the conqueror: Wodehouse, P.G.

Bill the whaler: Lawson, Will

Billeted: Harwood, H.M.

Billow and the rock, The: Martineau, Harriet

Bill's idees: Stephens, A.G.

Billy Bluegum: Dyson, E.G.

Billy Budd: Forster, E.M.

Billy Budd: Melville, Herman

Billy Pagan, mining engineer: Bedford, Randolph

Billy, the maverick: Scott, Evelyn

Billy Topsail and company: Duncan, Norman

Billy Topsail, M.D.: Duncan, Norman

Billy-Boy: Long, J.L.

Billy's hero: Pickthall, M.L.C.

Biltmore Oswald: Smith, Thorne

Bimbi: †Ouida

Bimbo, the pirate: Tarkington, Booth

Binding of the beast, The: Sterling, George

Bindon Parva: Hannay, J.O.

Binkie and Bell dolls: Widdemer, Margaret

Binko's blues: Merivale, H.C.

Binodini: Tagore, Sir Rabindranath

Biochemistry of genetics, The: Haldane, J.B.S.

Biographer's notebook, A: Bolitho, H.H.

Biographia Borealis: Coleridge, Hartley

Biographica Britannica Literaria: Wright, Thomas

Biographica literaria: Coleridge, Samuel Taylor

Biographical and critical essays: Hayward, Abraham

Biographical and critical miscellanies: Prescott, W.H.

Biographical annual, The: Griswold, R.W.

Biographical dictionary, A: Strutt, Joseph

Biographical dictionary of eminent Scotsmen, A: Chambers, Robert

Biographical history of philosophy, A: Lewes, George Henry

Biographical memoir of Daniel Boone: Flint, Timothy

Biographical memoir of John Leyden, M.D.: Scott, *Sir* Walter

Biographical memoirs of extraordinary painters: Beckford, William

Biographical memoirs of Richard Gough: Nichols, John

Biographical mirrour, The: Malone, Edmund

Biographical note: and a day at Beaver Lodge, A: (†Grey Owl), Belaney, G.S.

Biographical notes, 1877–1947: Greg, W.W.

Biographical notes on the writings of Robert Louis Stevenson: Gosse, *Sir* Edmund

Biographical plays: Peach, Lawrence du Garde

Biographical sketch of James Edward Root: Hale, E.E.

Biographical sketch of James McGill: Dawson, *Sir* J.W.

Biographical sketch of Lin Yutang, A: Buck, Pearl

Biographical sketch of Thomas Campbell: (†Geoffrey Crayon), Irving, Washington

Biographical sketches: Hare, A.J.C.

Biographical sketches: Martineau, Harriet

Biographical sketches of great and good men: Child, Lydia Maria

Biographical stories for children: Hawthorne, Nathaniel

Biographical studies: Bagehot, Walter

Biographies of Lady Russell and Madame Guyon, The: Child, Lydia Maria

Biographies of Madame de Staël and Madame Roland, The: Child, Lydia Maria

Biographies of the great and good: Sigourney, L.H.

Biography. A National Book League Reader's Guide: Trevelyan, G.M.

Biography and poetical remains of the Late Margaret Miller Davidson: (†Geoffrey Crayon), Irving, Washington

Biography and the human heart: Bradford, Gamaliel

Biography for beginners: Bentley, E.C.

Biography for the use of schools: Webster, Noah

Biography of a grizzly: Seton-Thompson, E.

Biography of a silver-fox: Seton-Thompson, E.

Biography of an arctic fox: Seton-Thompson, E.

Biography of an atom: Bronowski, J.

Biography of James G. Blaine: Dodge, May Abigail

Biological aspects of cancer: Huxley, *Sir* Julian

Birch bark roll of the Woodcraft Indians: Seton-Thompson, E.

Birches: Frost, Robert

Bird alone: O'Faolain, Sean

Bird and bough: Burroughs, John

Bird haunts and bird behaviour: Raven, C.E.

Bird in a cage, The: Shirley, James

Bird in hand: Housman, Laurence

Bird its form and function, The: Beebe, William

Bird life on island and shore: Guthrie-Smith, W.H.

Bird of dawning, The: Masefield, John

Bird of paradise, The: Davies, W.H.

Bird of paradise, The: Oppenheim, E.Phillips

Bird of time, The: Naidu, Sarojini

Bird in hand: Drinkwater, John

Bird song: Anderson, J.C.

Bird store man, The: Duncan, Norman

Bird-cage, The: Young, A.J.

Birdcatcher, The: Armstrong, M.D.

Birdman, The: (†Donald Barr), Barrett, C.L.

Birds, The: Squire, *Sir* John

Birds and beasts of Greek anthology: Douglas, Norman

Birds and man: Hudson, W.H.

Birds and poets: Burroughs, John

Birds, beasts and flowers: Lawrence, D.H.

Birds' Christmas carol, The: Wiggin, K.D.

Birds fall down, The: †West, Rebecca

Birds in a village: Hudson, W.H.

Birds in London: Hudson, W.H.

Birds in town and village: Hudson, W. H.

Birds' nest: Robinson, E.S.L.

Birds of America from original drawings, The: Audubon, John James

Birds of La Plata: Hudson, W.H.

Birds of Manitoba: Seton-Thompson, E.

Birds of Parnassus, The: Nichols, John

Birds of prey: Braddon, Mary Elizabeth

Birds of prey: Robertson, T.W.

Birds of Scotland, The: Grahame, James

Birds of the Bible: Stratton-Porter, Gene

Birds of the sea shore: Massingham, Harold

Birds of the water, wood and waste: Guthrie-Smith, W.H.

Birdsville track, The: Stewart, D.A.

Bird-watching and bird behaviour: Huxley, *Sir* Julian

Birket Foster's pictures of English Landscape: Taylor, Tom

Birlinn of Clanranald, The: †McDiarmid, Hugh

Birmingham: Mee, Arthur

Birmingham bus, The: Hannay, J.O.

Birth: Gale, Zona

Birth: Robertson, T.W.

Birth control: Gill, Eric

Birth of a nation, The: Dixon, Thomas

Birth of a world: Frank, Waldo

Birth of Arthur, The: Tennyson, Alfred *Lord*

Birth of Galahad, The: Hovey, Richard

Birth of man, The: Anand, M.R.

Birth of manly virtue, The: Swift, Jonathan

Birth of Merlin, The: Rowley, William

Birth of song, The: Davies, W.H.

Birth of Parsival, The: Trevelyan, R.C.

Birth of Roland, The: Hewlett, Maurice

Birth of the muse, The: Congreve, William

Birth of the opal, The: Wilcox, Ella Wheeler

Birth of the war god, The: Ghose, Sri Aurobindo

Birth of Western painting, The: Byron, Robert

Birth through death: Watson, A.D.

Birthday: Ackland, Rodney

Birth-day, The: O'Keeffe, John

Birthday, The: Southey, C.A.

Birthday in fairy-land, The: Higginson, T.W.

Birthday party: Milne, A.A.

Birthday tribute (in verse) addressed to the Princess Alexandrina Victoria, on attaining her eighteenth year, A: Landon, Letitia Elizabeth Maclean

Birthday verses at sixty-four: Barton, Bernard

Birthmark, The: Sullivan, Alan

Birthright, The: Gore, Catherine

Birthright: Stribling, T.S.

Birthright church, The: Judd, Sylvester

Births, deaths, and marriages: Hook, Theodore Edward

Biscuits and grog: Hannay, James

Bishop and the boogerman, The: Harris, Joel Chandler

Bishop Bonner's ghost: More, Hannah

Bishop of Hell, The: †Bowen, Marjorie

Bishop Percy's Folio MS: Percy, Thomas

Bishoprick garland, The: Ritson, Joseph

Bishop's apron, The: Maugham, Somerset

Bishop's bonfire, The: O'Casey, Sean

Bishop's granddaughter, The: Grant, Robert

Bishop's jaegers, The: Smith, Thorne

Bishop's night out: Phillpotts, Eden

Bishop's secret, The: Hume, F.W.

Bit o' writin', The: Banim, Michael and John

Bit o' love, A: Galsworthy, John

Bit of old China, A: Stoddard, C.W.

Bit of war, A: Brighouse, Harold

Biter, The: Rowe, Nicholas

Bits and pieces: Masterman, Sir J.C.

Bits of gossip: Davis, R.B.H.

Bits of Old Chelsea: Johnson, Lionel Pigot

Bits of talk about home matters: Jackson, H.H.

Bits of talk, in verse and prose, for young folks: Jackson, H.H.

Bits of travel: Jackson, H.H.

Bits of travel at home: Jackson, H.H.

Bitter creek: Boyd, James

Bitter end, The: Brophy, John

Bitter ground: Burnett, W.R.

Bitter lemons: Durrell, Lawrence

Bitter lotus: Bromfield, Louis

Bitter season, The: Coates, R.M.

Bitter sweet: Coward, Noel

Bitterns, The: Wescott, Glenway

Bitter-sweet: Holland, J.G.

Bittersweet: Richards, Grant

Bivouac, The: Maxwell, W.H.

Black, The: Wallace, Edgar

Black abbot, The: Wallace, Edgar

Black and white: Collins, William Wilkie

Black and white: Flavin, Martin

Black armour: a book of poems: Wylie, Elinor

Black Arrow, The: Stevenson, R.L.

Black arrows, The: †Beeding, Francis

Black Avons, The: Wallace, Edgar

Black banner abroad: Trease, Geoffrey

Black banner players: Trease, Geoffrey

Black Bartlemy's treasure: Farnol, J.J.

Black Beauty: Sewell, Anna

Black beech and honeydew: Marsh, Ngaio Edith

Black beetles in amber: Bierce, Ambrose

Black book, The: Durrell, Lawrence

Black book, The: Royall, A.N.

Black box, The: Oppenheim, E. Phillips

Black box, The: Shiel, M.P.

Black box of Roome opened, The: Heywood, Thomas

Black boxer, The: Bates, H.E.

Black boy: Wright, Richard

Black bryony: Powys, T.F.

Black bull, The: Bedford-Jones, Henry

Black but comely: Whyte-Melville, G.J.

Black cargo, The: Marquand, J.P.

Black cat, The: Todhunter, John

Black Christ, The: Cullen, Countée

Black clown, The: Hughes, J.L.

Black coffee: Christie, Agatha

Black crusade: Mitchell, Mary

Black diamond, The: Young, Francis Brett

Black diamonds: Lawson, Will

Black dog, The: Coppard, A.E.

Black dog mystery, The: †Queen, Ellery

Black donkey, The: Bell, Adrian

Black Douglas, The: Crockett, S.R.

Black drop, The: Brown, Alice

Black 'Ell: Malleson, Miles

Black eye, The: †Bridie, James

Black-eyed Susan: Jerrold, Douglas

Black fauns: Mendes, Alfred

Black flame, The: Dubois, William

Black frailty: Golding, Louis

Black gallantry: Gielgud, Val

Black gin, The: Stephens, J.B.

Black girl, The: Shaw, G.B.

Black heart and white heart: Haggard, Sir H. Rider

Black hood, The: Dixon, Thomas

Black horse, The: Palmer, E.V.

Black horse pit: Rhys, Ernest

Black house, The: Bridges, Roy

Black huntsmen, The: Layton, Irving

Black ice: Tourgée, A.W.

Black is my truelove's hair: Roberst, E.M.

Black is white: McCutcheon, G.B.

Black ivory: Collins, Norman

Black lace: Salverson, J.G.

Black lamb and grey falcon: †West, Rebecca

Black laughter: Powys, Llewelyn

Black laurel, The: Jameson, Storm

Black lightning: Cusack, E.D.

Black lightning: Mais, Roger

Black Lion inn, The: Lewis, A.H.

Black magic: †Bowen, Marjorie

Black magic: Roberts, Kenneth

Black man, The: Payne, J.H.

Black man, white maiden: †Preedy, George

Black Manhattan: Johnson, J.W.

Black man's lament, The: Opie, Amelia

Black mask, The: Hornung, E.W.

Black mesa: Grey, Zane

Black mischief: Waugh, Evelyn

Black moth, The: Heyer, Georgette

Black narcissus: Godden, Rumer

Black nativity: Hughes, J.L.

Black night, red morning: Trease, Geoffrey

Black opal, The: Prichard, K.S.

Black oxen: Atherton, Gertrude

Blank panther, The: Wheelock, J.H.

Black parade: Jones, Jack

Black plumes: Allingham, Margery

Black poodle and other tales, The: †Anstey, F.

Black power: a record of reactions in a land of pathos: Wright, Richard

Black Prince, The: Boyle, Roger

Black Prince and other poems, The: Baring, Maurice

Black prophet, The: Carleton, William

Black Ralph: Ingraham, J.H.

Black reconstruction: Dubois, William

Black riders, The: Crane, Stephen

Black river: Beals, Carleton

Black robe, The: Collins, William Wilkie

Black rock: †Connor, Ralph

Black rock, The: Fletcher, John Gould

Black rose, The: Costain, T.B.

Black roses: Young, Francis Brett

Black seasons, The: Treece, Henry

Black sheep, The: †Bell, Neil

Black sheep, The: Heyer, Georgette

Black sheep: Rice, Elmer

Black sheep: Yates, E.H.

Black shilling, The: Barr, A.E.H.

Black soul, The: O'Flaherty, Liam

Black spaniel, The: Hichens, Robert

Black Sparta: Mitchison, Naomi

Black spectacles: Carr, J.D.

Black spider: Mais, S.P.B.

Black spring: Miller, Henry

Black squire, The: Vachell, H.A.

Black sun, The: Abbas, K.A.

Black swan, The: Sabatini, R.

Black tragedy: (†Hugh Bohun), Cronin, B.C.

Black Venus, The: Davies, Rhys

Black war: Turnbull, S.C.P.

Black Watch, The: Picken, Andrew

Black Watch and the King's enemies, The: Fergusson, Sir Bernard

Black watcher, The: Oppenheim, E. Phillips

Black, white and brindled: Phillpotts, Eden

Blackbeard: Green, Paul

Blackberry winter: Warren, Robert Penn

Blackcock's Feather: Walsh, Maurice

Blackdell's print shorthand: Blackburn, Douglas

Blacke booke, The: Middleton, Thomas

Blacke bookes messenger, The: Greene, Robert

Blacke rod, The: Dekker, Thomas

Blackfellows: the story of Australia's native race: (†Donald Barr), Barrett, C.L.

Blackfellows of Australia: (†Donald Barr), Barrett, C.L.

Blackguard: Bodenheim, Maxwell

Blackerchief Dick: Allingham, Margery

Blackman's wood: Oppenheim, E. Phillips

Blackout book, The: Mee, Arthur

Black-out in Gretley: Priestley, J.B.

Blacksheep! Blacksheep! Nicholson, Meredith

Blackthorn winter: Beresford, J.D.

Blackwater Chronicle, The: Kennedy, J.P.

Blackwood v. Carlyle: Hannay, James

Blade-o'-grass: Farjeon, B.L.

Blades: McCutcheon, G.B.

Bladys of the Stewponey: Baring-Gould, Sabine

Blaine vs. Cleveland: Eggleston, Edward

Blake's poetical sketches: Lindsay, Jack

Blameless prince, The: Stedman, E.C.

Blanchardin and Eglantine (trn.): Caxton, William

Blanche: Molesworth, Mrs.

Blanche Fury: (†Joseph Shearing), †Bowen, Marjorie

Blanche, Lady Falaise: Shorthouse, J.H.

Blanche of Brandywine: Lippard, George

Blanche of Castile: Mitford, Mary Russell

Blanche of Navarre: James, George Payne Rainsford

Blanche Talbot: Ingraham, J.H.

Blandings Castle: Wodehouse, P.G.

Blanid: Joyce, Robert Dwyer

Blank cheque, The: †Carroll, Lewis

Blank verse: Lamb, Charles

Blank verse: Symonds, J.A.

Blank verse pastels: Scollard, Clinton

Blanket of the dark, The: Buchan, John

Blanket to cover a set of sheets: Morley, C.D.

Blantyre-alien: Sullivan, Alan

Blasting and bombardiering: Lewis, P. Wyndham

Blatchington tangle, The: Cole, G.D.H.

Blaze of noon, The: Heppenstall, Rayner

Blazed trail, The: White, S.E.

Blazed trail stories: White, S.E.

Bleak House: Dickens, Charles

Bleat upon bleat: †Maurice, Furnley

Blencarrow: MacKay, I.E.

Blenheim: Lyttelton, George *Baron*

Blenheim: Philips, John

Bless the bride: Herbert, *Sir* A.P.

Blessed are the rich: Agate, J.E.

Blessed Edmund Campion: Guiney, L.I.

Blessed Sacrament, The: Faber, Frederick William

Blessing, The: Mitford, Nancy

Blessing of Pan, The: Dunsany, E.J.M.D.P.

Blessington D'Orsay: a masquerade: Sadleir, Michael

Blessington's folly: Roberts,T.G.

Blest and the centenary of Shelley: Swinburne, A.C.

Bletheroe: Munro, C.K.

Blind: Poole, Ernest

Blind Allan: Wilson, John

Blind alleys: Eggleston, G.C.

Blind barber, The: Carr, J.D.

Blind bow-boy, The: Van Vechten, Carl

Blind children: Zangwill, Israel

Blind corner: †Yates, Dornford

Blind fireworks: Macneice, Louis

Blind love: Collins, William Wilkie

Blind love: Housman, Laurence

Blind man's buff: Johnston, W.D.

Blind man's ditch: Allen, Walter Ernest

Blind man's house: The, Walpole, *Sir* Hugh

Blind man's year: Deeping, Warwick

Blind men's flowers are green: Heppenstall, Rayner

Blind Raptery: Byrne, Donn

Blind Thamyris: Moore, T.S.

Blind-beggar of Bednal-Green, The: Chettle, Henry

Blind-beggar of Bednal-Green, The: Day, John

Blinde begger of Alexandria, The: Chapman, George

Blindman, The: Allen, Hervey

Blindman's world, The:Bellamy, Edward

Blindness: Green, Henry

Blindness: Seward, Anna

Blinds down: Vachell, H.A.

Blinkers: Vachell, H.A.

Bliss: Mansfield, Katherine

Bliss Carman and the literary currents and influences of his time: Cappon, James

Blithe spirit: Coward, Noel

Blithedale romance, The: Hawthorne, Nathaniel

Blitz kids: †Mordaunt, Elinor

Blix: †Norris, Frank

Blondel Parva: Payn, James

Blood and stones: Abbas, K.A.

Blood of stones: Chattopadhyaya, Harindranath

Blood of the martyrs, The: Mitchison, Naomi

Blood of the prophets, The: (†Dexter Wallace), Masters, E.L.

Blood on the dining room floor: Stein, Gertrude

Blood relations: Gibbs, *Sir* Philip

Blood royal: Allen, Grant

Blood royal: †Yates, Dornford

Blood white rose: Farjeon, B.L.

Bloodhunt: Gunn, Neil M.

Bloodstock: Irwin, Margaret

Bloody brother, The: Fletcher, John

Bloody chasm, The: De Forest, John William

Bloody tenent yet more bloody, The: Williams, Roger

Bloody wood, The: (†Michael Innes), Stewart, J.I.M.

Bloom o' the heather, The: Crockett, S.R.

Blooms of the berry: Cawein, Madison

Blossom time: Ackland, Rodney

Blossoming bough, The: Mannin, Ethel

Blossoms: Miller, Thomas

Blot, The: Stringer, A.J.A.

Blot in the scutcheon, A: Browning, Robert

Blotting book, The:Benson, E.F.

Bloudy tenent, The: Cotton, John

Bloudy tenent of persecution, for cause of conscience, discussed, The: Williams, Roger

Blow for balloons: Turner, W.J.R.

Blow hot—blow cold: Mayhew, Augustus Septimus

Blow wind—come wrack: Child, P.A.

Blown leaves: Peattie, D.C.

Blue and red: Ewing, *Mrs.* Juliana Horatia

Blue and the gray, The: Commager, H.S.

Blue and the gray, The: Morley, C.D.

Blue angels and whales: Gibbings, Robert

Blue baby, The: Molesworth, *Mrs.*

Blue beard: Colman, George *the younger*

Blue belles of England, The: Trollope, Frances

Blue bloods of Botany Bay: Mackaness, George

Blue castle, The: Montgomery, L.M.

Blue coast caravan: Davison, F.D.

Blue comet, The:Phillpotts,Eden

Blue Danube, The: Bemelmans, Ludwig

Blue days and grey days: Lavater, Louis

Blue days at sea: Morton, H.V.

Blue devils: Colman, George *the younger*

Blue door, The: Starrett, Vincent

Blue eyes and grey: Orczy, *Baroness*

Blue fairy book, The: Lang, Andrew

Blue feathers: Knox, E.V.

Blue flag and cloth of gold: Warner, A.B.

Blue girls, The: Masefield, John

Blue grass and rhododendron: Fox, John

Blue hand, The: Wallace, Edgar

Blue homespun: Call, F.O.

Blue interval: Moll, E.G.

Blue jade sceptre, The: Ficke, A.D.

Blue Jay: †Brand, Max

Blue Juniata: Cowley, Malcolm

Blue lion, The: Lynd, Robert

Blue Mazurka, The: Hoffe, Monckton

Blue moon, The: Housman, Laurence

Blue north: Drake-Brockman, H.

Blue pavilions, The: (†Q), Quiller-Couch, *Sir* A.

Blue Peter: Herbert, *Sir* A.P.

Blue plate special: Runyon, Damon

Blue propellor, The: Layton, Irving

Blue Rhine, Black Forest, a hand- and day-book: Untermeyer, Louis

Blue rose, A: Royde-Smith, Naomi

Blue rum: Scott, Evelyn

Blue Star Line: †Taffrail

Blue voyage: Aiken, Conrad

Blue water: Wallace, F.W.

Bluebeard: Wiggin, K.D.

Bluebeard's ghost: Thackeray, W.M.

Blue-bird weather: Chambers, R.W.

Blue-eyed boy, The: Mannin, Ethel

Blue-grass region of Kentucky, The: Allen, James Lane

Blueskin's ballad: Gay, John

Blue-skin's ballad, Swift, Jonathan

Bluestone: Turnbull, S.C.P.

Bluestone quarry: Munro, C.K.

Bluff stakes: Cronin, B.C.

Blunt instrument, A: Heyer, Georgette

Blunted sword, The: †Divine, David

Blurt Master-Constable: Middleton, Thomas

Blythe mountain, Vermont: Morley, C.D.

Boadicea: Binyon, Laurence

Boadicea: Glover, Richard

Boadicea Queen of Britain: Hopkins, Charles

Boanerges: Mather, Cotton

Board walk, The: Widdemer, Margaret

Boarding house blues: Farrell, J.T.

Boarding out: Hale, S.J.B.

Boarding school, The: Foster, Hannah

Boarding schools, The: Payne, J.H.

Boat, The: Hartley, L.P.

Boat of longing, The: Rölvaag, O.E.

Boatswain's mate, The: Jacobs, W.W.

Boaz and Ruth: Young, A.J.

Bob: the story of our mockingbird: Lanier, Sidney

Bobbie settles down: Jennings, Gertrude

Bobby Bocker: Street, A.G.

Body and raiment: Tietjens, E.S.

Body and soul: Bennett, Arnold

Body and soul: Brophy, John

Body found stabbed, A: (†Neil Gordon), Macdonell, A.G.

Body in the boudoir: Vulliamy, C.E.

Body in the library, The: Christie, Agatha

Body in the silo, The: Knox, R.A.

Body of his desire, The: Praed, *Mrs*. C.

Body of this death: Bogan, Louise

Body of waking: Rukeyser, Muriel

Body's imperfection, The: Strong, L.A.G.

Body-snatcher, The: Stevenson, R.L.

Boeotian, The: Ainsworth, William Harrison

Boethius, De consolatione philosophiae: Chaucer, Geoffrey

Bog myrtle and peat: Thompson, Flora

Bog-land studies: Barlow, Jane

Bogle Corbet: Galt, John

Bog-myrtle and peat: Crockett, S.R.

Boiled owl, The: Housman, Laurence

Boke named the Governour, The: Elyot, *Sir* Thomas

Boke of Codrus and Mynalcas, The: Barclay, Alexander

Bolanyo: Read, O.P.

Bold stroke for a husband, A: Cowley, *Mrs*. Hannah

Bolingbroke: Collins, John Churton

Bolivar: Madariaga, Salvador de

Bolo book, The: Cole, M.I. and Cole, G.D.H.

Bolshevik theory, The: Postgate, Raymond

Bolshevism and the West: Russell, Bertrand

Bolted door, The: Molesworth, *Mrs*.

Bolts of melody: Dickinson, Emily Elizabeth

Bomb, The: Harris, James Thomas

Bombard: Treece, Henry

Bombardment of Algiers, The: Moir, D.M.

Bombastes in the Shades: Binyon, Laurence

Bomber gipsy, The: Herbert, *Sir* A.P.

Bombs away: Steinbeck, John

Bombshell, The: Gielgud, Val

Bon ton: Garrick, David

Bonadventure, The: Blunden, Edmund

Bonanza: Campion, Sarah

Bonanza: Turnbull, S.C.P.

Bonapartism: Fisher, H.A.L.

Bonaventure: Cable, George Washington

Bond, The: Gore, Catherine

Bond of wedlock, The: Praed, *Mrs*. C.

Bond Street story, The: Collins, Norman

Bond-man, The: Betterton, Thomas

Bondman, The: Caine, *Sir* Thomas Henry Hall

Bond-man, The: Massinger, Philip

Bonduca: Beaumont, Francis

Bone rules: Tabb, J.B.

Bones: Wallace, Edgar

Bones and I:Whyte-Melville,G.J.

Bones at Rothwell, The: Whyte-Melville, G.J.

Bones in London: Wallace, Edgar

Bones of contention: †O'Connor, Frank

Bones of the river: Wallace, Edgar

Bonfield: Ingraham, J.H.

Bonfire: Canfield, Dorothy

Boni ominis votum: Wither, George

Bonifacius: Mather, Cotton

Bonnet and shawl: Guedalla, Philip

Bonnet over the windmill:Smith, Dodie

Bonney family, The: Suckow, Ruth

Bonnie Prince Charlie: Doughty, *Sir* A.G.

Bony and Ban: Catherwood, Mary

Boobs in the woods: Denison, Merrill

Book about Longfellow, A: McIlwraith, J.N.

Book about myself, A: Dreiser, Theodore

Book about Shakespeare, A: McIlwraith, J.M.

Book about the theater, A: Matthews, J.B.

Book and child: Engle, Paul

Book and heart: Higginson, T.W.

Book bag, The: Maugham, Somerset

Book collector: a general survey of the pursuit, The: Hazlitt, William Carew

Book concluding with As a wife has a cow, A: Stein, Gertrude

Book for a rainy day, A: Smith, J.T.

Book for bookmen, A: Drinkwater, John

Book for boys and girls, A: Bunyan, John

Book for girls, The: Sigourney, L.H.

Book for kids, A:Dennis, C.M.J.

Book for the hammock, A: Russell, W.C.

Book front: Calder-Marshall, Arthur

Book here: Ridge, W. Pett

Book of a naturalist, The: Hudson, W.H.

Book of acrostics, A: Knox, R.A.

Book of Ahania, The: Blake, William

Book of all-power, The: Wallace, Edgar

Book of Americans, A: Benét, Stephen Vincent

Book of anecdotes, A: †George, Daniel

Book of animal tales, The: (Stephen Southwold) †Bell, Neill

Book of authors, The: Russell, W.C.

Book of ballads, The: Aytoun, William Edmondstone

Book of ballads, A: Herbert, *Sir* A.P.

Book of Barra, The: Mackenzie, *Sir* Compton

Book of bays: Beebe, William

Book of beasts, The: White, T.H.

Book of beauty, The: Green, H.M.

Book of both sorts, A: Masefield, John

Book of Brittany, A: Baring-Gould, Sabine

Book of burlesques, A: Mencken, H.L.

Book of business, The:Hubbard, Elbert

Book of caricatures, A: Beerbohm, *Sir* Max

Book of characters, A: †George, Daniel

Book of Dan, The: †Rudd, Steele

Book of Dartmoor, A: Baring-Gould, Sabine

Book of days, The: Chambers, Robert

Book of discoveries, A: Masefield, John

Book of dragons, The: Nesbit, Edith

Book of dreams and ghosts,The: Lang, Andrew

Book of earth, The: Noyes, Alfred

Book of eloquence, The: Warner, C.D.

Book of emblems, A: Gatty, Margaret

Book of everlasting things: Mee, Arthur

Book of fairy tales, A: Baring-Gould, Sabine

Book of fallacies: Bentham,Jeremy

Book of folk lore, A: Baring-Gould, Sabine

Book of ghosts, A: Baring-Gould, Sabine

Book of gold, A: Piatt, J.J.

Book of gold, The: Trowbridge, J.T.

Book of golden deeds of all times and all lands, A: Yonge, C.M.

Book of good hunting, The: Newbolt, *Sir* Henry

Book of good manners, The (trn.): Caxton, William

Book of hours, A: Peattie, D.C.

Book of Ireland, The: †O'Connor, Frank

Book of Joad,The: Joad,C.E.M.

Book of Job, The: Croly, George

Book of joyous children, The: Riley, J.W.

Book of life, mind and body,The: Sinclair, Upton

Book of Los, The: Blake, William

Book of love, The: Sinclair, Upton

Book of lyrics: Bynner, Witter

Book of lyrics: Coward, Noel

Book of miracles, A: Hecht, Ben

Book of moments: Burke, Kenneth

Book of months: Benson, E.F.

Book of music, A: Gilder, R.W.

Book of my lady, The: Simms, W.G.

Book of naturalists: Ed. Beebe, William

Book of nature, The: Fletcher, John Gould

Book of nonsense, A: Lear, Edward

Book of North Wales, A: Baring-Gould, Sabine

Book of nursery songs and rhymes, A: Baring-Gould, Sabine

Book of Orm, The: Buchanan, R.W.

Book of poems, Al que quiere!, A: Williams, W.C.

Book of prefaces, A: Mencken, H.L.

Book of quatrains, A: Gale, Norman R.

Book of quotations, A: Samuel, Herbert *1st Viscount*

Book of repulsive women, The: Barnes, Djuna

Book of romances, lyrics and songs, A: Taylor, Bayard

Book of roses, The: Parkman, Francis

Book of Russian verse, A: Bowra, *Sir* Maurice

Book of Saint Nicholas, The: Paulding, J.K.

Book of Saints and wonders, A: Gregory, *Lady* Augusta

Book of shops, The: Lucas, E.V.

Book of Simon, The: Hutchinson, Arthur

Book of snobs: Thackeray, W.M.

Book of songs, The: Waley, Arthur

Book of sonnets, A: O'Hara, J.B.

Book of South Wales, A: Baring-Gould, Sabine

Book of strife, A: Macdonald, George

Book of sundials, The: Gatty, Margaret

Book of table talk, The: Russell, W.C.

Book of tea, The: †Okakura, Tenshin

Book of the American Indian, The: Garland, Hamlin

Book of the artists: Tuckerman, H.T.

Book of the Bayeux tapestry, The: Belloc, Hilaire

Book of the beginnings, A: Massey, Gerald

Book of the blue sea, The: Newbolt, *Sir* Henry

Book of the boudoir, The: Morgan, *Lady* Sydney

Book of the Cevennes, A: Baring-Gould, Sabine

Book of the Church, The: Southey, Robert

Book of the court, The: Thoms, W.J.

Book of the dead, The: Boker, George Henry

Book of the Duchesse: Chaucer, Geoffrey

Book of the East, The: Stoddard, R.H.

Book of the flag: Mee, Arthur

Book of the Grenvilles, The: Newbolt, *Sir* Henry

Book of the happy warrior, The: Newbolt, *Sir* Henry

Book of the long trail, The: Newbolt, *Sir* Henry

Book of the new moral world, The: Owen, Robert

Book of the pilgrimage of Hadrian's wall, The: Collingwood, R.G.

Book of the Pyrenees, A: Baring-Gould, Sabine

Book of the Rhine, A: Baring-Gould, Sabine

Book of the Rhymers' Club, The: Dowson, Ernest Christopher

Book of the Riviera, A: Baring-Gould, Sabine

Book of the sea, The: De Selincourt, Aubrey

Book of the sword, The: Burton, *Sir* Richard

Book of the Thin Red Line, The: Newbolt, *Sir* Henry

Book of the West, A: Baring-Gould, Sabine

Book of the winter, A: Sitwell, Edith

Book of the (World's) fair, The: Bancroft, Hubert Howe

Book of Thel, The: Blake, William

Book of this and that, The: Lynd, Robert

Book of Tish, The: Rinehart, Mary Roberts

Book of towers, A: Sitwell, Sacheverell

Book of twenty songs, A: Symons, Arthur

Book of uncles: Coffin, Robert

Book of verses, A: Henley, W.E.

Book of verses, A: Masters, E.L.

Book of were wolves, The: Baring-Gould, Sabine

Book of wonder, The: Dunsany, E.J.M.D.P.

Book of Woodcraft and Indian lore, The: Seton-Thompson, E.

Book of words, A: Kipling, Rudyard

Book parade: Spring, Howard

Book without a name, The: Morgan, *Lady* Sydney

Book without a title, A: Nathan, G.J.

Book-bills of Narcissus, The: Le Gallienne, Richard

Bookbindings old and new: Matthews, J.B.

Booke of ayres, The: Campion, Thomas

Booke of faulconrie or hauking, The: Turberville, George

Booke of martyrs, The: Taylor, John

Booke of the travaile and lief of me, Thomas Hoby, A: Hoby, Thomas

Book-hunter, The: Burton, John Hill

Bookman's budget, A: Dobson, Henry Austin

Bookman's holiday: Jackson, Holbrook

Bookman's holiday: Starrett, Vincent

Bookman's London, The: Swinnerton, Frank

Bookmark, The: Joad, C.E.M.

Books about books: Pollard, A.W.

Books alive: Starrett, Vincent

Books and authors: Lynd, Robert

Books and bookmen: Lang, Andrew

Books and bookmen: Lawlor, P.A.

Books and characters, French and English: Strachey, Lytton

Books and libraries: Lowell, J.R.

Books and men: Repplier, Agnes

Books and persons: Bennett, Arnold

Books and play-books: Matthews, J.B.

Books and plays: Monkhouse, A.N.

Books and the people: Cole, M.I.

Books and theatres: Craig, *Sir* Gordon

Books and their writers: Mais, S.P.B.

Books and you: Maugham, Somerset

Books in general: Pritchett, V.S.

Books in general: (†Solomon Eagle), *Sir* J.C. Squire

Books in my life, The: Miller, Henry

Books of Bart, The: Wallace, Edgar

Books of crowns and cottages: Coffin, Robert

Books of Psalms, The: Moffat, James

Books of the prophets, The: Moffat, James

Books of visions: Jones, J.B.

Books on the table: Gosse, *Sir* Edmund

Books once were men: McCutcheon, G.B.

Books reviewed: Squire, *Sir* John

Booksellers' author, A: Morley, C.D.

Bookseller's breviary, A: Morley, C.D.

Boomerang: Simpson, H.de G.

Booming of Acre Hill, The: Bangs, John Kendrick

Boon: Wells, H.G.

Boon Island: Roberts, Kenneth

Boons and blessings: Hall, Anna Maria

Boots and the north wind: Sidgwick, Ethel

Border and Bastille: Lawrence, George Alfred

Border antiquities of England and Scotland, The: Scott, *Sir* Walter

Border ballads: Swinburne, A.C.

Border Beagles: Simms, W.G.

Border garland, A: Hogg, James

Border Legion, The: Grey, Zane

Border lines of knowledge in medical science: Holmes, Oliver Wendell

Border river: Bailey, A.G.

Border scourge, A: Mitford, Bertram

Border shepherdess, A: Barr, A.E.H.

Border states, their power and duty in the present disordered condition of the country, The: Kennedy, J.P.

Border war: Jones, J.B.

Borderers, The: Wordsworth, William

Borderlands: Gibson, Wilfred

Borgia: †Field, Michael

Borgia: Gale, Zona

Borgia Testament, The: Balchin, Nigel

Boris Godunov: Graham, Stephen

Born at sea: Frankau, Pamela

Born genius, A: O'Faolain, Sean

Born in a beer garden: Morley, C.D.

Born in exile: Gissing, George

Born 1925: Brittain, Vera

Born to serve: Sheldon, C.M.

Born with a golden spoon: Parker, *Sir* H.G.

Borough, The: Crabbe, George

Borough politics: Marston, J.W.

Boroughmonger, The: Mottram, R.H.

Bosambo of the river: Wallace, Edgar

Boscobel: Ainsworth, Harrison

Bosom friends: Brazil, Angela

Boss, and how he came to rule New York, The: Lewis, A.H.

Boss of Killara, The: Palmer, E.V.

Boss of Taroomba, The: Hornung, E.W.

Boston: Sinclair, Upton

Boston book, The: Forbes, Esther

Bostonians, The: James, Henry

Boswell of Baghdad, A: Lucas, E.V.

Boswelliana: Boswell, James

Bosworth Field: Beaumont, *Sir* John

Botanic garden, The: Darwin, Erasmus

Botany Bay: Hall, J.N. and Nordhoff, C.B.

Botany Bay: Lang, J.

Both sides of the road: Lynd, Robert

Both your houses: Anderson, Maxwell

Both your houses: Gibbs, *Sir* Philip

Bothie of Toper-na-Fuosich,The: Clough, Arthur Hugh

Bothwell: Aytoun, W.E.

Bothwell: Grant, James

Bothwell: Swinburne, A.C.

Bottle, The: Cobbold, Richard

Bottle's path, The: Powys, T.F.

Bottoms up: Nathan, G.J.

Bottoms up!: Skinner, C.O.

Bound east for Cardiff: O'Neill, Eugene

Bound for Callao: Lawson, Will

Bound in honor: Trowbridge, J.T.

Bound together: Mitchell, D.G.

Boundless water: †Bowen, Marjorie

Bounty of earth: Peattie, D.C.

Bounty of Sweden, The: Yeats, W.B.

Bouquet: Stern, G.B.

Bourbons of Naples, The: Acton, Harold

Bow of orange ribbon, The: Barr, A.E.H.

B.O.W.C., The: De Mille, James

Bowden Hill: Bowles, William Lisle

Bowen's Court: Bowen, E.D.C.

Bowler hat: Mottram, R.H.

Bowmen, The: †Machen, Arthur

Bows against the Barons: Trease, Geoffrey

Bowstring murders, The: †Carter Dickson

Box and cox: Morton, J.M.

Box of delights, A: Masefield, John

Box office murders, The: Crofts, F.W.

Box tunnel, The: Reade, Charles

Boxiana: Egan, Pierce

Box-lobby challenge, The: Cumberland, Richard

Boxwood: Warner, Sylvia Townsend

Boy: †Corelli, Marie

Boy: Hanley, James

Boy and his room, A: Nash, Ogden

Boy apprenticed to an enchanter, The: Colum, Padraic

Boy castaways, The: †Taffrail

Boy comes home, The: Milne, A.A.

Boy for the ages, A: Bacheller, Irving

Boy grew older, The: Broun, Heywood

Boy hunters, The: Reid, T.M.

Boy I left behind me, The: Leacock, Stephen

Boy in Eirinn, A: Colum, Padraic

Boy in grey, The: Kingsley, Henry

Boy in the bush, The: Lawrence, D.H.

Boy in the Bush, The: Rowe, Richard

Boy in the dark, The: Kantor, MacKinlay

Boy in the house, A: De la Roche, Mazo

Boy in the wind: Dillon, George

Boy is a boy, A: Nash, Ogden

Boy life on the prairie: Garland, Hamlin

Boy named John, A: Cournos, John

Boy of Mount Rhigi, The: Sedgwick, C.M.

Boy of stories, A: Warner, A.B.

Boy of the desert: Tietjens, E.S.

Boy of the South Seas: Tietjens, E.S.

Boy on a dolphin: †Divine, David

Boy on horseback: Steffens, Lincoln

Boy Scout, The: Davis, Richard Harding

Boy Scout's life of Lincoln: Tarbell, Ida

Boy slaves, The: Reid, T.M.

Boy tar, The: Reid, T.M.

Boy tramps, The: Oxley, J.M.

Boy who knew what the birds said, The: Colum, Padraic

Boy with a cart, The: Fry, Christopher

Boy with a trumpet: Davies, Rhys

Boyds of Black River, The: Edmonds, W.D.

Boyd's shop: Ervine, St. John

Boyhood in Norway: Boyesen, H.H.

Boyhood of Christ, The: Wallace, Lew

Boyhood of Martin Luther, The: Mayhew, Henry

Boyne Water, The: Banim, John

Boys: Barker, M.A.

Boys and girls and gods: Mitchison, Naomi

Boys and girls of history: Power, Eileen

Boys and girls together: Saroyan, William

Boys and I, The: Molesworth, *Mrs.*

Boy's book of battle-lyrics, The: English, Thomas Dunn

Boys' book of inventions, The: Baker, R.S.

Boy's book of rhyme, A: Scollard, Clinton

Boys' book of the Commonwealth: Monsarrat, Nicholas

Boys' book of the sea: Monsarrat, Nicholas

Boy's books, then and now: 1818 to 1881, A: Scadding, Henry

Boys' heroes: Hale, E.E.

Boys in the back room, The: Wilson, Edmund

Boy's marriage, A: De Selincourt, Hugh

Boys of Brimstone Court, The: Ward, E.S.

Boys of Grand Pré School, The: De Mille, James

Boys of the Old Glee Club, The: Riley, J.W.

Boy's reading-book, The: Sigourney, L.H.

Boys' second book of inventions: Baker, R.S.

Boys—then and now: White, W.A.

Boy's town, A: Howells, W.D.

Boy's voyage round the world, A: Smiles, Samuel

Boy's way, A: Derleth, A.W.

Boy's will, A: Frost, Robert

Bozzy and Piozzi: †Pindar, Peter

Bracebridge Hall: (†Geoffrey Crayon), Irving, Washington

Bracelet, The: Hichens, Robert

Bracelet, The: Sutro, Alfred

Bracken: Cronin, B.C.

Bracknels, The: Reid, Forrest

Bragonar: Calvert, George Henry

Brahminism: Lyall, *Sir* Alfred C.

Brahmo Somaj, The: Sen, Keshub Chunder

Brain capacity and intelligence: Miller, E.M.

Brain Guy: Appel, Benjamin

Brain of India, The: Ghose, Sri Aurobindo

Brains: Flavin, Martin

Brakespeare: Lawrence, George Alfred

Brambletye House: Smith, Horatio

Bramleighs of Bishop's Folly, The: Lever, C.J.

Bramo Somaj, The: Sena, Kesava Chandra

Branch of Abingdon: Cabell, J.B.

Branch of hawthorn tree, The: Gibbon, Monk

Branch of May, A: Reese, L.W.

Branches of Adam: Fletcher, John Gould

Branchiana: Cabell, J.B.

Brandons, The: Thirkell, Angela

Brangane: †Mills, Martin

Bransford in Arcadia: Rhodes, E.M.

Brant and Red Jacket: Eggleston, Edward

Branwen: Griffith, Llewelyn

Brass ankle: Heyward, DuBose

Brass bottle, The: †Anstey, F.

Brass check, The: Sinclair, Upton

Brass ring, The: Baring, Maurice

Brass-knuckle crusade: Beals, Carleton

Brat Farrar: (†Josephine Tey), Mackintosh, Elizabeth

Brave day, hideous night: Rothenstein, *Sir* John

Brave days, The: Munro, Neil

Brave employments: †Bowen, Marjorie

Brave Island: Spittel, R.L.

Brave lady, A: Craik, *Mrs.* Dinah Maria

Brave Mardi Gras: Roberts, W. Adolphe

Brave new victuals: Huxley, Elspeth J.

Brave new world: Huxley, Aldous

Brave new world revisited: Huxley, Aldous

Brave old woman: Farjeon, Eleanor

Bravery of earth, A: Eberhart, Richard

Bravo, The: Cooper, James Fenimore

Bravo!: Ferber, Edna

Bravo of London: Bramah, E.

Brazen age, The: Heywood, Thomas

Brazen head, The: Powys, John Cowper

Brazen lyre, The: Knox, E.V.

Brazenhead the Great: Hewlett, Maurice

Brazil on the move: Dos Passos, John

Brazilian adventure: Fleming, Peter

Brazilian daughter: Holcroft, M.H.

Brazilian mystic, A: Cunninghame Graham, Robert

Breach of promise, A: Robertson, T.W.

Breachley, black sheep: †Becke, Louis

Bread and a sword: Scott, Evelyn

Bread and cheese and kisses: Farjeon, B.L.

Bread and oranges: Warner, S.B.

Bread and power: Brown, E.T.

Bread and roses: Mannin, Ethel

Bread of deceit: Lowndes, M.A.

Bread of idleness, The: Masters, E.L.

Bread or stone: Knox, R.A.

Bread upon the waters: Craik, *Mrs.* Dinah Maria

Breadwinner, The: Maugham, Somerset

Break of day, The: †King, Basil

Break the heart's anger: Engle, Paul

Breakaway: †Novello, Ivor

Breakdown of money: Hollis, Christopher

Breaker of laws, A: Ridge, W.P.

Breakers and granite: Fletcher, John Gould

Breakfast at eight: Gow, Ronald

Breakfast in bed: Sala, G.A.H.

Breakfast with the Nikolides: Godden, Rumer

Breaking a butterfly: Jones, Henry Arthur

Breaking a butterfly: Lawrence, George Alfred

Breaking covert: Mais, S.P.B.

Breaking into the movies: Loos, Anita

Breaking of bonds, The: Ficke, Arthur Davison

Breaking point, The: Du Maurier, Daphne

Breaking point, The: Garnett, Edward

Breaking point, The: Rinehart, Mary Roberts

Breaking the record: †Connor, Ralph

Breaking wave, The: †Shute, Nevil

Breakspear in Gascony: Linklater, Eric

Breath of air, A: Godden, Rumer

Breath of life, The: Burroughs, John

Breath of life, The: Catlin, George

Breathe upon these: Lewisohn, Ludwig

Breathe upon these slain: Scott, Evelyn

Brébeuf and his brethren: Pratt, E.J.

Bred in the bone: Page, T.N.

Bred in the bone: Phillpotts, Eden

Bredon and sons: †Bell, Neil

Breefe and true reporte of the execution of certaine traytours, A: Munday, Anthony

Breefe aunswer made unto two seditious pamphlets, A: Munday, Anthony

Breefe discourse of the taking of Edmund Campion, A: Munday, Anthony

Breeze of morning, A: Morgan, C.L.

Breezy morning, A: Phillpotts, Eden

Breezy song, Do you fear the wind? A: Garland, Hamlin

Brendle: Pickthall, M.W.

Brethren, The: Haggard, *Sir* Henry Rider

Brevia: Helps, *Sir* Arthur

Brewsie and Willie: Stein, Gertrude

Brewster's millions: McCutcheon, G.B.

Brian Boroihme: Knowles, James Sheridan

Brian O'Linn: Maxwell, W.H.

Brian Westby: Reid, Forrest

Briary-bush, The: Dell, Floyd

Brick moon, The: Hale, E.E.

Brickfield, The: Hartley, L.P.

Bricks and mortar: Ashton, Helen

Bricks between, The: Iyengar, V.V.Srinivasa

Bricks without straw: Tourgée, A.W.

Bridal of Borthwick, The: Moir, D.M.

Bridal of the Isles, The: Knight, Charles

Bridal of Triermain, The: Scott, *Sir* Walter

Bridal of Vaumond, The: Sands, R.C.

Bridal pond: Gale, Zona

Bride, The: Baillie, Joanna

Bride, The: Irwin, Margaret

Bride, The: Jennings, Gertrude

Bride, The: Powys, T.F.

Bride, The: Rowlands, Samuel

Bride comes to Evensford, The: Bates, H.E.

Bride for the unicorn, A: Johnston, W.D.

Bride from the Bush, A: Hornung, E.W.

Bride from the desert, A: Allen, Grant

Bride of Abydos, The: Byron, George Gordon *Lord*

Bride of Dionysus, The: Trevelyan, R.C.

Bride of Fort Edward, The: Bacon, Delia Salter

Bride of Genoa, The: Sargent, Epes

Bride of Huitzil, The: Allen, Hervey

Bride of Landeck, The: James, George Payne Rainsford

Bride of Ludgate, The: Jerrold, Douglas

Bride of Newgate, The: Carr, J.D.

Bride of the mistletoe, The: Allen, James Lane

Bride of the plains, A: Orczy, *Baroness*

Bride of the rivers, The: Mackay, Jessie

Bride roses: Howells, W.D.

Bridegroom and bride: Knox, R.A.

Bridegroom cometh, The: Frank, Waldo

Bridegroom's body, The: Boyle, Kay

Brides' tragedy, The: Beddoes, T.L.

Bride's tragedy, The: Swinburne, A.C.

Brideshead revisited: Waugh, Evelyn

Bridewater: Tarkington, Booth

Bridge, The: Crane, Hart

Bridge, The: Frankau, Pamela

Bridge, The: O'Brien, Kate

Bridge, The: Pickthall, M.L.C.

Bridge, The: Pitter, Ruth

Bridge, The: Poole, Ernest

Bridge, The: Royde-Smith, Naomi

Bridge at Andau, The: Michener, J.A.

Bridge for passing, A: Buck, Pearl

Bridge of fire, The: Flecker, James Elroy

Bridge of San Luis Rey, The: Wilder, Thornton

Bridge of Sighs: Pertwee, Roland

Bridge of the Brocade Sash travels and observations in Japan: Sitwell, Sacheverell

Bridgehead: Frank, Waldo

Bridges at Toko-ri, The: Michener, J.A.

Bridges of binding, The: Benchley, Robert

Bridget Malwyn: Boyd, Martin

Bridling of Pegasus, The: Austin, Alfred

Brief account concerning several of the agents of New-England, A: Mather, Increase

Brief account of the origin of the Eragny press, A: Moore, T.S.

Brief and impartial history of the life and actions of Andrew Jackson, A: Snelling, W.J.

Brief candles: Binyon, Laurence

Brief candles: Huxley, Aldous

Brief character of the Low-Countries under the States, A: Feltham, Owen

Brief chronicles: Agate, J.E.

Brief chronicles: Winter, William

Brief discourse concerning the unlawfulness of the Common-Prayer-Worship, A: Mather, Increase

Brief discourse of the powers of the Peers and Commons, A: Selden, John

Brief discourse touching the office of Lord Chancellor: Selden, John

Brief diversions: Priestley, J.B.

Brief exposition ... of Canticles, A: Cotton, John

Brief hand-list of books, manuscripts, etc. illustrative of the life and writings of Shakespeare, collected between the years 1842 and 1859, A: Halliwell, James Orchard

Brief history of ancient and modern Bengal, A: Dutt, R.C.

Brief history of epidemic and pestilential diseases, A: Webster, Noah

Brief history of Moscovia, A: Milton, John

Brief history of the Indian people, A: Hunter, *Sir* William Wilson

Brief history of the Royal Society, A: Andrade, E.N. da Costa

Brief history of the times, A: L'Estrange, *Sir* Roger

Brief history of the warr with the Indians in New-England, A: Mather, Increase

Brief hour of François Villon, The: Erskine, John

Brief light: Lindsay, Jack

Brief memoir of Mr. Thackeray, A: Hannay, James

Brief memoirs: Nichols, John

Brief moment: Behrman, S.N.

Brief notes upon a late sermon, titl'd, The fear of God and the King: Milton, John

Brief orisons: Isvaran, M.S.

Brief reflections relative to the emigrant French clergy: Burney, Frances

Brief relation to the State of New England, A: Mather, Increase

Brief remarks on the defence of the Halifax libel on the British-American colonies: Otis, James

Brief survey of printing, history and practice, A: Jackson, Holbrook

Brief view of errors and obscurities in the common version of the Scriptures, A: Webster, Noah

Brief voices: Mannin, Ethel

Brief waters· Moll, E.G.

Brief words: Soutar, William

Briefe chronicle, of the successe of times, A: Munday, Anthony

Briefe exposition ... of Ecclesiastes, A: Cotton, John

Briefe exposition of the whole Book of Canticles, A: Cotton, John

Briefe of the art of rhetorique, A: Hobbes, Thomas

Briefe view of the state of the Church of England, A: Harington, *Sir* John

Brier Cliff: Morris, G.P.

Brieux: Shaw, G.B.

Brigand, The: Wallace, Edgar

Brigantine, The: Ingraham, J.H.

Brigitte Bardot MP.: Herbert, *Sir* A.P.

Bright ambush: Wurdemann, Audrey

Bright day: Priestley, J.B.

Bright doom, The: Wheelock, J.H.

Bright feather fading: Bowes-Lyon, Lilian

Bright island, The: Bennett, Arnold

Bright islands, The: Colum, Padraic

Bright journey: Derleth, A.W.

Bright lexicon, The: Peattie, D.C.

Bright messenger, The: Blackwood, Algernon

Bright metal: Stribling, T.S.

Bright pavilions, The: Walpole, *Sir* Hugh

Bright safety, The: Ercole, Velia

Bright shadow: Priestley, J.B.

Bright shawl, The: Hergesheimer, Joseph

Bright star: Barry, Philip

Brightmans predictions and prophesies: Heywood, Thomas

Brightness: Jenkins, Elizabeth

Brighton: Sitwell, *Sir* Osbert

Brighton as I have known it: Sala, G.A.H.

Brighton rock: Greene, Graham

Brigid and the cub: Turner, E.S.

Brimming cup, The: Canfield, Dorothy

Brimstone and chill: Beals, Carleton

Bring back the bells: Herbert, *Sir* A.P.

Bring back the days: Hutchinson, Arthur

Bring! Bring!: Aiken, Conrad

Bring on the girls: Wodehouse, P.G.

Bring the monkey: Franklin, Miles

Bringing Jazz: Bodenheim, Maxwell

Briseis: Black, William

Britain: Thomson, James

Britain and West Africa: Cary, Joyce

Britain calling: Mais, S.P.B.

Britain in India: Masani, *Sir* R.P.

Britain in the world front: Dutt, R.P.

Britain's crisis of empire: Dutt, R.P.

Britain's genius: Anstey, Christopher

Britain's happiness: Motteux, P.A.

Britain's Home Guard: Brophy, John

Britain's remembrancer: Wither, George

Britannia: Thomson, James

Britannia, a masque: Mallet, David

Britannia and Batavia: Lillo, George

Britannia Mews: Sharp, Margery

Britannia Rediviva: Dryden, John

Britannia 1651–1951: Mais, S.P.B.

Britannia triumphans: Dennis, John

Britannia victrix: Bridges, Robert

Britannia's pastorals: Browne, William

Britannia's prayer for the queen: Tate, Nahum

British Academy, The: Santayana, George

British airways: †Caudwell, Christopher

British and foreign ribbons: †Taffrail

British appeals, with Gods mercifull replies: Wither, George

British architects and craftsmen: Sitwell, Sacheverell

British art since 1900: Rothenstein, *Sir* John

British artists and the war: Rothenstein, *Sir* John

British barbarians, The: Allen, Grant

British battles of destiny: Ewart, E.A.

British battles on land and sea: Grant, James

British bibliographer, The: Brydges, *Sir* Samuel Egerton

British birds: Hudson, William Henry

British campaign in France and Flanders, The: Doyle, *Sir* Arthur Conan

British Civil Service, 1854–1954, The: Griffith, Llewelyn

British colonies: Bonwick, James

British Commonwealth, The: Underhill, F.H.

British Commonwealth series: South Africa: Millin, S.G.

British drama: Nicoll, J.R.A.

British Empire in America, The: Oldmixon, John

British Georgics: Grahame, James

British history in the nineteenth century, 1782–1901: Trevelyan, G.M.

British labour movement, The: Cole, G.D.H.

British labour movement, The: Tawney, R.H.

British librarian, The: Oldys, William

British Muse, The: Oldys, William

British nationalism and the League of Nations: Wells, H.G.

British novelists and their styles: Masson, David

British painting: Newton, Eric

British passport: Brighouse, Harold

British Phillipic, A: Akenside, Mark

British pictures and their painters: Lucas, E.V.

British portrait painters and engravers of the eighteenth century; Kneller to Reynolds: Gosse, *Sir* Edmund

British ports and harbours: Walmsley, Leo

British prison-ship, The: Freneau, Philip

British public and the General Strike, The: Martin, B.K.

British radio drama, 1922–1956, a survey: Gielgud, Val

British school, The: Lucas, E.V.

British sculpture, 1944–46: Newton, Eric

British Seas, The: Russell, W.C.

British seaweeds: Gatty, Margaret

British social services: Cole, G.D.H.

British stamps: Hamilton, Patrick

British subjects' answer to the Pretender's declaration, The: Steele, *Sir* Richard

British synonymy: Thrale, *Mrs*. H.L.

British talent: Smith, Dodie

British trade and industry, past and future: Cole, G. D. H.

British trade unionism: Cole, G. D. H.

British trade unionism today: Cole, G. D. H.

British way in warfare, The: Liddell Hart, B.

British wolf hunters, The: Miller, Thomas

British women go to war: Priestley, J. B.

British working class movements: Cole, G. D. H.

British working class politics, 1832–1914: Cole, G. D. H.

British zoology: Pennant, Thomas

Britisher on Broadway: †Armstrong, Anthony

Briton, The: Philips, Ambrose

Brittain's Ida: Fletcher, Phineas

Brittania's honor: Dekker, Thomas

Brittany: Baring-Gould, Sabine

Brittle: Shaw, Irwin

Brittle heaven, A: Deutch, Babette

Brittons bowre of delights: Breton, Nicholas

Broad arrow, The: Leakey, C. W.

Broad grins: Colman, George, *the younger*

Broad highway, The: Farnol, J. J.

Broadcast minds: Knox, R. A.

Broadcast sketches: Peach, Lawrence du Garde

Broads, The: Mottram, R. H.

Brockhouse: Mackenzie, *Sir* Compton

Broke: Hughes, J. L.

Broken barriers: Nicholson, Meredith

Broken battalions, The: Hayne, P. H.

Broken cistern, The: Dobrée, Bonamy

Broken column, The: Levin, Harry

Broken dishes: Flavin, Martin

Broken gate, The: Hough, Emerson

Broken glory: Gore-Booth, E. S.

Broken halo, The: Barclay, F. L.

Broken heart, The: Ford, John

Broken hearts: Gilbert, *Sir* W. S.

Broken journey, A: Callaghan, M. E.

Broken jug, The: Dukes, Ashley

Broken lights: Cobbe, Frances Power

Broken marriage, The: †Sinclair Murray

Broken men: Gielgud, Val

Broken music: Bottome, Phyllis

Broken necks: Hecht, Ben

Broken pledges: Gibbs, *Sir* Philip

Broken record: Campbell, Roy

Broken road, The: Mason, A. E. W.

Broken snare, The: Lewisohn, Ludwig

Broken soil: Colum, Padraic

Broken span, The: Williams, W. C.

Broken ties: Tagore, *Sir* R.

Broken to harness: Yates, E. H.

Broken walls of Jerusalem, The: Warner, S. B.

Broken water: Hanley, James

Broken waters: Packard, F. L.

Broken wing, The: Naidu, Sarojini

Broker of Bogota, A: Bird, R. M.

Bromley neighborhood: Brown, Alice

Brontës, The: Bentley, Phyllis

Brontës, The: †Delafield, E. M.

Brontës: life and letters, The: Shorter, C. K.

Bronze Age, The: Woolley, *Sir* Leonard

Bronze eagle, The: Orczy, *Baroness*

Bronze statue: Reynolds, G.

Bronze sword, The: Treece, Henry

Bronze Venus, The: Phillpotts, Eden

Brood House: McCutcheon, G. B.

Brood of ducklings, A: Swinnerton, Frank

Brooding earth, The: Cripps, A. S.

Brook, The: Tennyson, Alfred *Lord*

Brook Evans: Glaspell, Susan

Brook Kerith, The: Moore, George

Brookes of Bridlemere, The: Whyte-Melville, G. J.

Brooklyn murders, The: Cole, G. D. H.

Broom squire, The: Baring-Gould, Sabine

Broom squires, The: Phillpotts, Eden

Broome stages: †Dane, Clemence

Broomsticks: De La Mare, Walter

Brother Alfred: Wodehouse, P. G.

Brother beast: Phillpotts, Eden

Brother Blackfoot: Sullivan, Alan

Brother Copas: (†Q), Quiller-Couch, *Sir* A.

Brother Eskimo: Sullivan, Alan

Brother Fabian's manuscripts: Evans, Sebastian

Brother Jacob: †Eliot, George

Brother Jonathan: Neal, John

Brother man: Mais, Roger

Brother man: Phillpotts, Eden

Brother of Daphne, The: †Yates, Dornford

Brother of the shadow, The: Praed, *Mrs.* C.

Brother Peter to Brother Tom (Warton): †Pindar, Peter

Brother Saul: Byrne, Donn

Brother to dragons: Warren, Robert Penn

Brotherhood of man, The: Roberts, Kenneth

Brotherhood of men: Eberhart, Richard

Brotherly love: Swift, Jonathan

Brothers, The: Cumberland, Richard

Brothers, The: Herbert, H. W.

Brothers, The: Shirley, James

Brothers, The: Strong, L. A. G.

Brothers, The: Swinburne, A. C.

Brothers: Vachell, H. A.

Brothers, The: Wells, H. G.

Brothers, The: Young, Edward

Brothers and sisters: Compton-Burnett, Ivy

Brothers in arms: Denison, Merrill

Brothers in arms: Niven, F. J.

Brothers of no kin: Richter, Conrad

Brothers of peril: Roberts, T. G.

Brothers of pity: Ewing, *Mrs*, Juliana Horatia

Brothers on the trail: †Brand, Max

Brothers Sackville, The: Cole. G. D. H.

Brought forward: Cunninghame Graham, Robert Bontine

Brown bread from a colonial oven: Baughan, B.E.

Brown decades, The: Mumford, Lewis

Brown earth and bunch grass: Stephen, A.M.

Brown fairy book, The: Lang, Andrew

Brown heath and blue bells: Winter, William

Brown man's burden: Finlayson, Roderick

Brown man's servant, The: Jacobs, W.W.

Brown on resolution: Forester, C.S.

Brown owl, The: (Hueffer) Ford, Ford Madox

Brown owl, A: Tomlinson, H.M.

Brown smock; Allen, C.R.

Brown studies: Brown, Ivor

Brown waters: Blake, W.H.

Brownies, The: Ewing, *Mrs*. Juliana Horatia

Brownies and bogles: Guiney, L.I.

Browning as a philosopher: Masters, E.L.

Browning version, The: Rattigan, Terence

Browning's centenary: Gosse, *Sir* Edmund

Brownlows, The: Oliphant, Margaret

Brownstone Eclogues: Aiken, Conrad

Bruce: Davidson, John

Bruce, The: Skeat, W.W.

Bruin: Reid, T.M.

Bruised wings: Mannin, Ethel

Brumby Innes: Prichard, K.S.

Brunel's tower: Phillpotts, Eden

Brushwood: Read, T.B.

Brushwood boy, The: Kipling, Rudyard

Brute, The: (†James James), Adams, Arthur M.

Brutus: Payne, J.H.

Brutus of Alba: Tate, Nahum

Brutus Ultor: †Field, Michael

Bryan Cooper: Robinson, E.S.L.

Brynhild: Wells, H.G.

Bubble, The: Bullett, Gerald

Bubble, The: Swift, Jonathan

Bubble and Squeak: Jennings, Gertrude

Bubble moon, The: Bridges, Roy

Bubble reputation: Wren, P.C.

Bubbles of Canada, The: Haliburton, T.C.

Buccaneer, The: Hall, Anna Maria

Buccaneers, The: Wharton, Edith

Buccaneers and pirates of our coasts: Stockton, F.R.

Buchanan ballads, old and new: Buchanan, R.W.

Buck in the snow, The: Millay, E. St. Vincent

Buckingham restor'd: Sheffield, John

Buckinghamshire: Uttley, Alison

Buckskin baronet: Widdemer, Margaret

Bucolic comedies: Sitwell, Edith

Bud: Munro, Neil

Buddha, The: Bax, Clifford

Buddha and his teachings, The: Malalasekara, Gunapala

Buddha and the gospel of Buddhism: Coomaraswamy, A.K.

Buddhism and the race question: Malalasekara, Gunapala

Budding morrow, The: Bell, Adrian

Buddington peerage, The: Sala, G.A.H.

Buds of May: Seymour, B.K.

Buffalo Grove, Ill.: Burroughs, John

Buffalo wind, The: Seton-Thompson, E.

Buffets and rewards: Mais, S.P.B.

Bugle of the Black Sea: Blackmore, R.D.

Bugles in the night: Benefield, Barry

Builder of bridges, The: Sutro, Alfred

Builder of ships, A: Sheldon, C.M.

Builders, The: Glasgow, Ellen

Builders and pioneers of Australia: (†Ishmael Dare), Jose, A.W.

Builders' history, The: Postgate, Raymond

Builders of Bay colony: Morison, S.E.

Building a house with a teacup: Hall, Anna Maria

Building and planning: Cole, G.D.H.

Building eras in religion: Bushnell, Horace

Building of Britain, The: Newbolt, *Sir* Henry

Building of Jalna, The: De la Roche, Mazo

Building of the City Beautiful, The: †Miller, Joaquin

Building the British empire: Adams, J.T.

Buildings of England, The: Pevsner, Nikolaus

Build-up, The: Williams, W.C.

Bull, The: Hodgson, Ralph

Bull calf, The: Layton, Irving

Bull calves, The: Mitchison, Naomi

Bulldog Drummond: †Sapper

Bulldog Drummond at bay: †Sapper

Bulldog Drummond hits out: †Sapper

Bulldog Drummond strikes back: †Sapper

Bulldog Drummond's third round: †Sapper

Bullfinch, The: †Ouida

Bullinger bound: Bacon, Leonard

Bullion: Webster, E.C.

Bullivant and the lambs: Compton-Burnett, Ivy

Bulls of Parral: Steen, Marguerite

Bully Hayes, buccaneer: †Becke, Louis

Buln-Buln and the Brolga, The: †Collins, Tom

Bulpington of Blup, The: Wells, H.G.

Bulwark, The: Dreiser, Theodore

Bulwer and his wife, 1803–1836: Sadleir, Michael

Bulwer as a man and a novelist: Landon, Letitia Elizabeth Maclean

Bumphrey's: Mottram, R.H.

Bunch grass: Vachell, H.A.

Bunch of errors, The: Madariaga, Salvador de

Bunch of old letters, A: Nehru, J.

Bundle of ballads, A: Lawrence, George Alfred

Bundle of letters, A: James, Henry

Bundle of life, A: †Hobbes, John Oliver

Bunthorne abroad: Bengough, J.W.

Buntling Ball, The: Fawcett, Edgar

Bunyip and other mythical monsters and legends, The: (†Donald Barr), Barrett, C.L.

Buoyant billions: Shaw, G.B.

Burd Margaret: Swinburne, A.C.

Burden of a woman, The: Pryce, Richard

Bureau de change, The: Dunsany, E.J.M.D.P.

Bureau of literary control: Morley, C.D.

Burges letters, The: Lyall, Edna

Burgher Quixote, A: Blackburn, Douglas

Burglar, The: Thomas, Augustus

Burglar of the zodiac, The: Benét, William Rose

Burglar-bracelets, The: Carleton, William (McKendree)

Burglars in Bucks: Cole, G.D.H.

Burglars in Paradise: Ward, E.S.

Burglars must die: Oppenheim, E. Phillips

Burgoyne's surrender: Curtis, George William

Burial of John Brown, The: Channing, William Ellery

Burial of Sir John Moore, The: Wolfe, Charles

Burial of the guns, The: Page, T.N.

Buried alive: Bennett, Arnold

Buried Caesars: Starrett, Vincent

Buried day, The: Day-Lewis, Cecil

Buried stream, The: Bowes-Lyon, Lilian

Buried temple (trn.): Sutro, Alfred

Buried treasure, A: Roberts, E.M.

Burke's steerage: White, T.H.

Burlesque upon burlesque: Cotton, Charles

Burmese days: †Orwell, George

Burning and melting: Coomaraswamy, A.K.

Burning bright: Steinbeck, John

Burning bush: Untermeyer, Louis

Burning cactus, The: Spender, Stephen

Burning city: Benét, Stephen Vincent

Burning court, The: Carr, J.D.

Burning daylight: London, Jack

Burning glass, The: †Bowen, Marjorie

Burning glass, The: De La Mare, Walter

Burning glass, The: Morgan, Charles

Burning man, The: Millin, Sarah Gertrude

Burning Marl, The: Brereton, John Le G.

Burning mountain, The: Fletcher, John Gould

Burning oracle, The: Knight, G.W.

Burning spear, The: Galsworthy, John

Burning wheel, The: Huxley, Aldous

Burns into English: Seymour, W.K.

Burns, life, genius, achievement: Henley, W.E.

Burns today and tomorrow: †McDiarmid, Hugh

Burnt million, The: Payn, James

Burnt Norton: Eliot, T.S.

Burnt offering, The: Duncan, S.J.

Burnt ones, The: White, Patrick

Burnt out: Yonge, C.M.

Burnt out case, A: Greene, Graham

Burr Oaks: Eberhart, Richard

Burton: Ingraham, J.H.

Bury the dead: Shaw, Irwin

Bury-Fair: Shadwell, Thomas

Bush, The: O'Dowd, B.P.

Bush ballads and galloping rhymes: Gordon, A.L.

Bush boys, The: Reid, T.M.

Bush friends in Tasmania: Meredith, L.A.

Bush holiday: Collins, Dale

Bush ramblers, The: (†Donald Barr), Barrett, C.L.

Bush verses: Lawson, Will

Bush voyage: Collins, Dale

Bushido: Nitobe, Inazo

Bushland babies: (†Donald Barr), Barrett, C.L.

Bushman and buccaneer: (†The Breaker), Morant, Harry H.

Bushranger of Van Diemen's land, The: Rowcroft, Charles

Bushrangers, The: Harpur, Charles

Bushrangers, The: Tennant, Kylie

Bushranging silhouettes: Cronin, B.C.

Bushwhackers, The: †Craddock, C.E.

Business and politics under James I: Tawney, R.H.

Business for pleasure: Balchin, Nigel

Business necessity, A: Hubbard, Elbert

Business of life, The: Chambers, R.W.

Business of pleasure, The: Yates, E.H.

Business of the Supreme Court, The: Frankfurter, Felix

Busiris, King of Egypt: Young, Edward

Busman's honeymoon (novel and play): Sayers, Dorothy

Bussy D'Ambois: Chapman, George

Bustling hours, The: Ridge, W.Pett

Busy man's Bible and how to study and teach it, The: Cable, George Washington

Busybody Land: Housman, Laurence

Busybody papers: Franklin, Benjamin

But for the grace of God: †Lonsdale, Frederick

But for whom Charlie: Behrman, S.N.

But gentlemen marry brunettes: Loos, Anita

But however: Mayhew, Henry

But it still goes on: Graves, Robert

But look the morn: Kantor, Mackinlay

But not for love: Seymour, B.K.

But not yet slain: Appel, Benjamin

But soft, we are observed: Belloc, Hilaire

But the earth abideth: Soutar, William

But yet a woman: Hardy, A.S.

Butchers broom: Gunn, Neil M.

Butler in Bohemia, The: Nesbit, Edith

Butleriana (compiled by A.T. Bartholomew): Butler, Samuel

Butter and egg man, The: Kaufman, G.S.

Buttercups and daisies: Mackenzie, *Sir* Compton

Buttered side down: Ferber, Edna

Butterfield 8: O'Hara, J.H.

Butterfly, The: Armstrong, M.D.

Butterfly, The: Cain, J.M.

Butterfly house, The: Freeman, Mary Wilkins

Butterfly man, The: McCutcheon, G.B.

Buttons and design scarabs: Petrie, *Sir* William Flinders

Button's Inn: Tourgée, A.W.

Buxton the liberator: Mottram, R.H.

Buxell: Besier, Rudolf

Buy a broom: Phillpotts, Eden

Buyer's market, A: Powell, Anthony

Buzz, buzz: Agate, J.E.

Buzzards, The: Armstrong, M.D.

By auction: Mackail, Denis

By Avon river: (†H.D.), Doolittle, Hilda

By blow and kiss: Ewart, E.A.

By Canadian streams: Burpee, Lawrence J.

By Celia's arbour: Besant, *Sir* Walter and James Rice

By His Excellency's command: Bridges, Roy

By land and sea: Morison, S.E.

By love possessed: Cozzens, James Gould

By mountain tracks: Bridges, Roy

By oak and thorn: Brown, Alice

By proxy: Payn, James

By reef and palm: †Becke, Louis

By right of conquest: Henty, George Alfred

By rock and pool on an Austral shore: †Becke, Louis

By shore and sedge: Harte, Bret

By star and compass: Wallace, W.S.

By still waters: Russell, G.W.

By sundown shores: †Macleod, Fiona

By the aurelian wall: Carman, Bliss

By the Eternal: Read, O.P.

By the gods beloved: Orczy, *Baroness*

By the Ionian Sea: Gissing, George

By the light of the soul: Freeman, Mary

By the waters of Babylon: Lazarus, Emma

By the way: Allingham, William

By the way book: Wodehouse, P.G.

By their fruits: Praed, *Mrs.* C.

By underground: Blackwood, Algernon

By Veldt and Kopje: Scully, W.C.

By way of Cape Horn: Villiers, A.J.

By way of introduction: Milne, A.A.

Byeways: Hichens, Robert

Bye-words: Yonge, C.M.

Bylow Hill: Cable, George Washington

By-road: Bell, Adrian

Byron: Quennell, P.C.

Byron: Read, *Sir* Herbert

Byron: Vulliamy, C.E.

Byron in Italy: Quennell, P.C.

Byron on Wordsworth: Scott, D.C.

Byron, the last journey, April 1823–April 1824: Nicolson, Hon. *Sir* Harold

Byron, the years of fame: Quennell, P.C.

Byron's dramatic prose: Knight, G.W.

Bystander, The: Dibdin, Charles

By-ways and bird notes: Thompson, Maurice

By-ways of Europe: Taylor, Bayard

Byzantine achievement, The: Byron, Robert

Byzantine civilization: Runciman, *Sir* Steven

Byzantium: Poole, John

Byzantium into Europe: Lindsay, Jack

C

C.: Baring, Maurice

C.E. Montague: Elton, Oliver

C.M.Doughty: a memoir: Hogarth, David George

C.R.W.Nevinson: Sitwell, *Sir* Osbert

Cabala, The: Wilder, Thornton

Cabaret girl, The: Wodehouse, P.G.

Cabbage patch, The: Langley, Noel

Cabbages and kings: †Henry, O.

Cabin, The: White, S.E.

Cabinet Cyclopaedia, The: James, George Payne Rainsford

Cabinet minister, The: Gore, Catherine

Cabinet minister, The: Pinero, *Sir* A.W.

Cabinet of gems, A: Macdonald, George

Cabinet portraits, Reid: *Sir* Thomas Wemyss

Cabinet-council, The: Ralegh, *Sir* Walter

Cabiro: Calvert, George Henry

Cabman's cat, The: Hall, Anna Maria

Cactus: Mannin, Ethel

Cadences: Flint, F.S.

Cadenus and Vanessa: Swift, Jonathan

Cadmus Henry: Edmonds, W. D.

Caelica: Greville, *Sir* Fulke

Caesar Borgia; son of Pope Alexander the Sixth: Lee, Nathaniel

Caesar and Cleopatra: Shaw, G.B.

Caesar in Aegypt: Cibber, Colley

Caesar in Egypt: Adams, Francis

Caesar is dead: Lindsay, Jack

Caesar remembers: Seymour, W.K.

Caesar's column: Donnelly, Ignatius Loyola

Caesar's Gallic war: Livingstone, *Sir* Richard

Caesar's wife: Maugham, Somerset

Café Royal, The: Symons, Arthur

Cage at Cranford, The: Gaskell, Elizabeth

Cage bird, The: Young, *Mrs.* Francis Brett

Cage me a peacock: Langley, Noel

Caged birds: Mais, S.P.B.

Caged eagle, The: Sterling, George

Cagot's hut and the conscript's bride, The: Gratton, Thomas Colley

Cain: Lodge, G.C.

Cain: Ridler, A.B.

Cairngorm mountains, The: Burton, John Hill

Caius Gracchus: Knowles, James Sheridan

Cake, an indulgence: Bynner, Witter

Cakes and ale: Jerrold, Douglas

Cakes and ale: Maugham, Somerset

Cakes for your birthday: Vulliamy, C.E.

Cakes upon the waters: Akins, Zoë

Calais to Dover: Jennings, Gertrude

Calamiterror: Barker, George

Calamities of authors: D'Israeli, Isaac

Calamity Town: †Queen, Ellery

Calavar: Bird, Robert Montgomery

Calaynos: Boker, George Henry

Calculus of variants, The: Greg, W.W.

Caleb Field: Oliphant, *Mrs.* Margaret

Caleb Stone's death watch: Flavin, Martin

Caleb Stukely: Phillips, Samuel

Caleb West, master diver: Smith, F.H.

Caledonia: Defoe, Daniel

Calendar, The: Wallace, Edgar

Calendar for 1931: Beerbohm, *Sir* Max

Calendar of crime: †Queen, Ellery

Calendar of saints for unbelievers, A: Wescott, Glenway

Calendar of sin, A: Scott, Evelyn

Calendar of the Shakespearean rarities, A: Halliwell, James Orchard

Calends of Cairo, The: Mitchell, J.L.

Caliban by the yellow sands: Mackaye, Percy

Caliban in Grub Street: Knox, R.A.

Caliban's guide to letters: Belloc, Hilaire

Calico pie: Vulliamy, C.E.

Calico shoes: Farrell, James

Calicut lends a hand: De Selincourt, Aubrey

California: Atherton, Gertrude

California: Austin, Mary

California: Royce, Josiah

California and Oregon trail, The: Parkman, Francis

California Inter Pocula: Bancroft, Hubert Howe

California pastorals: Bancroft, Hubert Howe

California the wonderful: Markham, Edwin

California trail, The: Bedford-Jones, Henry

Californians: Jeffers, J.R.

Caliph's design: architects! Where is your vortex?: Lewis, P. Wyndham

Calisto and Melebea: Rastell, John

Call, A: (Hueffer), Ford, Ford Madox

Call and claims of natural beauty, The: Trevelyan, G.M.

Call from Heaven, A: Mather, Increase

Call from the past, The: Merrick, Leonard

Call home, The: Courage, J.F.

Call home the heart: †Dane, Clemence

Call it a day: Smith, Dodie

Call it experience: Caldwell, Erskine Preston

Call my people home: Livesay, Dorothy

Call of England, The: Morton, H.V.

Call of the blood, The: Hichens, Robert

Call of the canyon, The: Grey, Zane

Call of the carillon, The: Dalton, A.C.

Call of the south, The: †Becke, Louis

Call of the wild, The: London, Jack

Call to arms, A: Haggard, *Sir* Henry Rider

Call to arms: Trease, Geoffrey

Call to my countrywomen, A: Dodge, May Abigail

Call to, the nation: Kipling, Rudyard

Call to National Service, A: Hardy, Thomas

Call to the swan: Strong, L.A.G.

Call the witnesses: Mee, Arthur

Called back: Gibbs, *Sir* Philip

Called to be Saints: Rossetti, Christina

Calling adventures! Marriott, Anne

Calling again: Mais, S.P.B.

Calling for a spade: Church, Richard

Calling of Dan Matthews, The: Wright, H.B.

Callinicus: Haldane, J.B.S.

Callirrhoë: †Field, Michael

Callista: a sketch of the third ▷ century: Newman, J.H.

Calls across the sea: Slater, F.C.

Calm October: Church, Richard

Calvary: Mackenzie, *Sir* Compton

Calvary or the death of Christ: Cumberland, Richard

Calvin Coolidge: White, W.A.

Calypso: Cumberland, Richard

Calypso: O'Hara, J.B.

Camaralzaman: James, George Payne Rainsford

Camberley triangle, The: Milne, A.A.

Camberwell beauty, The: Golding, Louis

Camberwell miracle, The: Beresford, J.D.

Cambric mask, The: Chambers, R.W.

Cambridge Blue: Campion, Sarah

Cambridge book of poetry for young people, The: Grahame, Kenneth

Cambridge Dionysia, The: Trevelyan, *Sir* G.O.

Cambridge school of art: Ruskin, John

Cambyses King of Persia: Settle, Elkanah

Camelion's dish: Pertwee, Roland

Cameo Kirby: Tarkington, Booth

Cameos: †Corelli, Marie

Cameos: Wilcox, Ella Wheeler

Cameos from English history: Yonge, C.M.

Camera fiend, The: Hornung, E.W.

Camera obscura: Bolitho, William

Camera obscura: Nabokov, Vladimir

Camerado!: Mackaye, Percy

Cameron Hill: Flavin, Martin

Cameron pride, The: Holmes, M.J.

Cameronians, The: Grant, James

Camford visitation, The: Wells, H.G.

Camilla: Burney, Frances

Camillus: Hill, Aaron

Camillus letters: Hamilton, Alexander

Camoens: Burton, *Sir* Richard

Camp, The: Palmer, E.V.

Camp, The: Sheridan, Richard Brinsley

Camp and trail: White, S.E.

Camp at Wandinong, The: Turner, E.S.

Camp doctor, The: Young, E.R.

Camp venture: Eggleston, G.C.

Campaign, The: Addison, Joseph

Campaign in Greece and Crete, The: Garnett, David

Campaign of 1812 and the retreat from Moscow, The: Belloc, Hilaire

Camp-bell: Munday, Anthony

Campbell Meeker: Markham, Edwin

Camping in the Sahara: Hull, E.M.

Camping with President Roosevelt: Burroughs, John

Campo-Musae: Wither, George

Campus sonnets: Moll, E.G.

Can all this grandeur perish?: Farrell, James

Can governments cure unemployment?: Angell, *Sir* Norman

Can Grande's castle: Lowell, Amy

Can I be a Christian?: Hannay, J.O.

Can ladies kill?: †Cheyney, Peter

Can Parliament survive?: Hollis, Christopher

Can prayer be answered?: Austin, Mary

Can such things be?: Bierce, Ambrose

Can Wales unite?: Griffith, Llewelyn

Can women be gentlemen?: Atherton, Gertrude Franklin

Can wrong be right?: Hall, Anna Maria

Can you forgive her?: Trollope, Anthony

Canada: Campbell, W.W.

Canada: Herbin, J.F.

Canada, a modern nation: Lighthall, W.D.

Canada, an American nation: Dafoe, J.W.

Canada, and Corn-laws: Gourlay, R.F.

Canada and the American revolution: Wrong, G.M.

Canada and the Canadian question: Smith, Goldwin

Canada and the Canadians in 1846: Bonnycastle, *Sir* R.

Canada and the United States: Scott, F.R.

Canada, as it was, and may be: Bonnycastle, *Sir* R.H.

Canada at Dieppe: Bourinot, A.S.

Canada coast-to-coast, Castle Garac: Monsarrat, Nicholas

Canada in song: Gibbon, J.M.

Canada to Iceland: Kirkconnell, Watson

Canada to-day: Scott, F.R.

Canada under the administration of the Earl of Dufferin: Stewart, George

Canada west: Niven, F.J.

Canadas as they at present commend themselves to the enterprise of emigrants, colonists and capitalists, The: Galt, John

Canadas as they at present commend themselves to the enterprise of emigrants, colonists, and capitalists, The: Picken, Andrew

Canadas in 1841, The: Bonnycastle, *Sir* R.H.

Canadian Archives and its activities, The: Doughty, *Sir* A.G.

Canadian boat-song, A: Moore, Thomas

Canadian born: Johnson, E.P.

Canadian born: Ward, M.A.

Canadian brothers, The: Richardson, John

Canadian cadences: Gibbon, J.M.

Canadian calendar, A: Gibbon, J.M.

Canadian calendar, A: Sherman, F.J.

Canadian crusoes, The: Traill, C.P.

Canadian emigrant housekeeper's guide, The: Traill, C.P.

Canadian essays, critical and historical: O'Hagan, Thomas

Canadian Forces in the war, The: Underhill, F.H.

Canadian headmaster, A: Kirkconnell, Watson

Canadian heroines: LeMoine, Sir J.M.

Canadian idylls: Kirby, William

Canadian life in town and country: Burpee, Lawrence J.

Canadian life in town and country: Morgan, H.J.

Canadian manor and its seigneurs, A: Wrong, G.M.

Canadian mosaic: Gibbon, J.M.

Canadian nation, A: Pierce, Lorne

Canadian novels and novelists: Burpee, Lawrence

Canadian North-West, The: Adam, G.M.

Canadian people, A: Pierce, Lorne

Canadian peoples, The: Sandwell, B.K.

Canadian poems: Dudek, Louis

Canadian poets of the Great War: Lighthall, W.D.

Canadian scenery illustrated: Willis, N.P.

Canadian settler's guide, The: Traill, C.P.

Canadian student, The: Dawson, Sir J.W.

Canadian wild flowers: Traill, C.P.

Canadians all: Kirkconnell, Watson

Canal reminiscences: Bagby, George William

Canaries sometimes sing: †Lonsdale, Frederick

Cancels: Chapman, Robert William

Candelabra: Galsworthy, John

Candid appeal to public confidence, A: Moore, Thomas

Candid cuckoo, The: Gale, Norman R.

Candid examination of the reasons for depriving the East India Company of its Charter, A: Mickle, William Julius

Candid reminiscences: Sinclair, Upton

Candida: Shaw, G.B.

Candidate, The: Churchill, Charles

Candidate, The: Crabbe, George

Candidate for truth, A: Beresford, J.D.

Candidate for truth: Cournos, John

Candle for St. Jude: Godden, Rumer

Candle in the cabin, The: Lindsay, N.V.

Candle in the wilderness: Bacheller, Irving

Candle in the wind: Anderson, Maxwell

Candle of vision, The: Russell, G.W.

Candleford Green: Thompson, Flora

Candlelight: Wodehouse, P.G.

Candlelight tales: Uttley, Alison

Candour in English fiction: Hardy, Thomas

Candy floss: Godden, Rumer

Cannery Row: Steinbeck, John

Cannibal catechism, The: Swinburne, A.C.

Canning wonder, The: †Machen, Arthur

Canoe and the saddle, The: Winthrop, Theodore

Canoe route between Fort William, Lake Superior, and Fort Garry, Red River, The: Hind, H.Y.

Canolles: Cooke, John Esten

Canon, The: Benson, A.C.

Canon Charles Kingsley: Pope-Hennessy, Dame Una

Canon to the right of them: Marshall, Bruce

Canonbury House: Reynolds, G.

Canons of giant art: Sitwell, Sacheverell

Canon's ward, The: Payn, James

Canopic jar, A: Speyer, Mrs. Leonora

Can's and can'ts: Cecil, Lord David

Cantab., The: Leslie, Sir J.R. Shane

Cantab., The: Robertson, T.W.

Cantata written expressly for the opening ceremony of the Sydney International Exhibition: Kendall, Henry

Cantelman's spring mate: Lewis, P. Wyndham

Canterbury: Mee, Arthur

Canterbury Pilgrims, The: Mackaye, Percy

Canterbury Tales: Chaucer, Geoffrey

Canterbury tales, The: Lee, Harriet

Canterbury tales, The: Lee, Sophia

Canterbury tales of Chaucer, The: Tyrwhitt, Thomas

Canterbury Tales (prologue): Caxton, William

Canticle of Pan, A: Bynner, Witter

Canticle of praise, A: Bynner, Witter

Canticle of the rose, The: Sitwell, Edith

Canting academy, The: Head, Richard

Cantos (1–84), The: Pound, Ezra

Cantos LII–LXXI: Pound, Ezra

Canute the Great: †Field, Michael

Canzoni: Pound, Ezra

Cap, The: †Pindar, Peter

Cap of youth, The: Jacob, Naomi

Cape Cod: Thoreau, H.D.

Cape Cod lighter, The: O'Hara, J.H.

Cape St. Vincent: Sheridan, Richard Brinsley

Capel Sion: Evans, Caradoc

Capell's Shakespeariana: Greg, W.W.

Caper sauce: Mais, S.P.B.

Capes of freedom: Abbas, K.A.

Capful of wind: De Selincourt, Aubrey

Caprice: Firbank, Ronald

Capricornia: Herbert, A.F.X.

Capsina, The: Benson, E.F.

Captain Abby and Captain John: Coffin, Robert

Captain Archer's daughter: Deland, Margaret

Captain Banner: †Preedy, George

Captain Bayonet and others: †Armstrong, Anthony

Captain Blood: Sabatini, R.

Captain Bottell: Hanley, James

Captain Brassbound's conversion: Shaw, G.B.

Captain Caution: Roberts, Kenneth

Captain Chap: Stockton, F.R.

Captain comes home, The: Ashton, Helen

Captain Cook: Besant, *Sir* Walter

Captain Craig: Robinson, E.A.

Captain Cub: Turner, E.S.

Captain Cut-throat: Carr, J.D.

Captain Dieppe: (†Anthony Hope), Hawkins, Anthony Hope

Captain Digby Grand: Whyte-Melville, G.J.

Captain Drew on leave: Davies, H.H.

Captain Fanny: Russell, W.C.

Captain from Connecticut, The: Forester, C.S.

Captain Fury: Skinner, C.O.

Captain Hornblower, R.N.: Forester, C.S.

Captain in the ranks, A: Eggleston, G.C.

Captain Java: Beck, *Mrs.* Lily

Captain Jinks of the Horse Marines: Fitch, Clyde William

Captain John Smith: Warner, C.D.

Captain Kyd: Ingraham, J.H.

Captain Kyd: Jones, J.S.

Captain Lightfoot: Burnett, W.R.

Captain Love: Roberts, T.G.

Captain Macdonald: Lang, J.

Captain Macedoine's daughter: McFee, William

Captain Macklin: Davis, Richard Harding

Captain Margaret: Masefield, John

Captain Moonlight: Mannin, Ethel

Captain Nicholas: Walpole, *Sir* Hugh

Captain of Company K.: The, Kirkland, Joseph

Captain of industry, A: Sinclair, Upton

Captain of Raleigh's, A: Roberts, T.G.

Captain of souls: Wallace, Edgar

Captain of the Gray-horse troop, The: Garland, Hamlin

Captain of the Guard, The: Grant, James

Captain of the Polestar, The: Doyle, *Sir* Arthur Conan

Captain of the Vulture: Braddon, Mary Elizabeth

Captain O'Sullivan: Maxwell, W.H.

Captain Patch: Powys, T.F.

Captain Peggy: Brazil, Angela

Captain Quadring: Hay, William

Captain Salvation: Wallace, F.W.

Captain Sam: Eggleston, G.C.

Captain Shapely: Brighouse, Harold

Captain Starlight: reckless rascal of robbery under arms: Clune, Frank

Captain Swing: Young, Francis Brett

Captain Sword and Captain Pen: Hunt, Leigh

Captain Tatham of Tatham Island: Wallace, Edgar

Captain Thomas A. Scott: Smith, F.H.

Captains all: Jacobs, W.W.

Captains Courageous: Kipling, Rudyard

Captain's curio, The: Phillpotts, Eden

Captain's lady, The: Broster, D.K.

Captain's lamp, The: Collins, Norman

Captains of the old world, The: Herbert, H.W.

Captains of the Roman Republic, The: Herbert, H.W.

Captain's romance, The: Read, O.P.

Captain's room, The: Besant, *Sir* Walter

Captain's tiger, The: Weidman, Jerome

Captain's toll gate, The: Stockton, F.R.

Captain's woman, The: †Bell, Neil

Captive, The: Bickerstaffe, Isaac

Captive: Bottome, Phyllis

Captive and the free, The: Cary, Joyce

Captive flames: Knox, R.A.

Captive island, The: Derleth A.W.

Captive lady, The: Dutt, M.M.

Captive lion, The: Davies, W.H.

Captive of Gippsland, The: Turner, H.G.

Captive of the Sahara: Hull, E.M.

Captive shrew, The: Huxley, *Sir* Julian

Captives, The: Gay, John

Captives, The: Heywood, Thomas

Captives, The: Walpole, *Sir* Hugh

Captives of the desert: Grey, Zane

Capt'n Davy's honeymoon: Caine, *Sir* Thomas Henry Hall

Capture, death and burial of J. Wilkes Booth: Baker, Ray Stannard

Captures: Galsworthy, John

Capturing the Bushrangers: Stephens, A.G.

Car of Croesus, The: Poole, Ernest

Caravaggio, his incongruity and his fame: Berenson, Bernhard

Caravan: Bynner, Witter

Caravan: Galsworthy, John

Caravan mystery, The: Hume, F.W.

Caravaners, The: Russell, E.M.

Caravans: Michener, James

Carchemish: Lawrence, T.E.

Carchemish: Woolley, *Sir* Leonard

Carchemish I: Hogarth, David George

Card, The: Bennett, Arnold

Card Castle: Waugh, Alec

Cardboard Castle: Wren, P.C.

Card-drawing: Griffin, Gerald

Cardigan: Chambers, R.W.

Cardinal, The: Shirley, James

Cardinal Beaton: Tennant, William

Cardinal Newman: Hutton, Richard Holt

Cardinal Pole: Ainsworth, Harrison

Cardinal Prefect of Propaganda, The: (†Baron Corvo), Rolfe, Frederick

Cards of fortune, The: Bridges, Roy

Cards on the table: Christie, Agatha

Cards, with Uncle Tom: Sherriff, R.C.

Career in C Major: Cain, J.M.

Career of Katherine Bush, The: Glyn, Elinor

Careful and strict enquiry into ... freedom of will, A: Edwards, Jonathan

Careless clock, The: Van Doren, Mark

Careless husband, The: Cibber, Colley

Careless rapture: Hassall, Christopher

Careless rapture: †Novello, Ivor

Careless shepherdess, The: Goffe, Thomas

Caribbean cruise holiday: Mais, S.P.B.

Caribbean interlude: Davison, F.D.

Caribbean mystery, The: Christie, Agatha

Cariboo Road, The: Sullivan, Alan

Caricature history of Canadian politics, A: Bengough, J.W.

Caricatures of twenty-five gentlemen: Beerbohm, *Sir* Max

Caridorf: Bird, R.M.

Carillon poem, The: Brereton, John Le G.

Carita: Oliphant, Margaret

Carl Werner: Simms, W.G.

Carletons, The: Grant, Robert

Carlotta: Aldrich, Thomas Bailey

Carlton Club, The: Petrie, *Sir* Charles

Carlton House fete: †Pindar, Peter

Carlyle: Garnett, Richard

Carlyle and Hitler: Grierson, *Sir* Herbert

Carlyle personally and in his writings: Masson, David

Carlyle's laugh: Higginson, T.W.

Carlyon sahib: Murray, George

Carlyon's year: Payn, James

Carmelite, The: Cumberland, Richard

Carmen: Bangs, John Kendrick

Carmen and coal-heavers: Miller, Thomas

Carmen Eucharisticon: a private thank-oblation: Wither, George

Carmen expostulatorium: Wither, George

Carmen Nuptiale: Massey, Gerald

Carmen Saeculare, for the year 1700: Prior, Matthew

Carmen Seculare: Combe, William

Carmen Seculare for the year 1800: Pye, H.J.

Carmina Argentea: Chambers, *Sir* Edmund

Carmina Minima: Clarke, Charles Cowden

Carminetta: Hoffe, Monckton

Carnac: Parker, *Sir* H.G.

Carnac Sahib: Jones, Henry Arthur

Carnac's folly: Parker, *Sir* H.G.

Carnations in winter: Carman, Bliss

Carnegie works at Pittsburgh, The: Dreiser, Theodore

Carnival: Mackenzie, *Sir* Compton

Carnival, The: Prokosch, Frederic

Carnival king, The: Treece, Henry

Carnival of Florence, The: †Bowen, Marjorie

Carol of the fir tree, The: Noyes, Alfred

Carolina cavalier, A: Eggleston, G.C.

Carolina chansons: Allen, Hervey

Carolina chansons: Heyward, DuBose

Caroline Archer: Ingraham, J.H.

Caroline of Brunswick: Reynolds, G.

Caroline of England: Quennell, P.C.

Caroline Terrace: Deeping, Warwick

Carolinian, The: Sabatini, R.

Carols for Christmas Tide: Neale, J.M.

Carols for Easter Tide: Neale, J.M.

Carols of Christmastide from Africa: Cripps, A.S.

Carpet-bagger, The: Read, O.P.

Carpet slippers: Darlington, W.A.

Carr, being the biography of Philip Joseph Carr: Bentley, Phyllis

Carrie and Cleopatra: Bates, H.E.

Carrier pigeon, The: Phillpotts, Eden

Carrots: Molesworth, *Mrs.*

Carry on Jeeves: Wodehouse, P.G.

Carrying on: (†Ian Hay), Beith, *Sir* John Hay

Carry-over: Suckow, Ruth

Cartagena and the banks of the Sinú: Cunninghame Graham, Robert

Carter and other people: Marquis, Don

Carter Quaterman: Baker, W.M.

Carthage and Tunis: Sladen, D.B.W.

Cartoons: Beerbohm, *Sir* Max

Cartoons of the campaign: Bengough, J.W.

Carts and candlesticks: Uttley, Alison

Carved lions, The: Molesworth, *Mrs.*

Carving a statue: Greene, Graham

Casa Braccio: Crawford, Francis Marion

Casa Guidi windows: Browning, Elizabeth Barrett

Casanova's Chinese Restaurant: Powell, Anthony

Casanova's women, eleven months of the year: Erskine, John

Cascando: Beckett, Samuel

Case book of Jimmy Lavender, The: Starrett, Vincent

Case for African freedom, The: Cary, Joyce

Case for compulsory service, The: Coulton, G. G.

Case for faith-healing, The: Beresford, J. D.

Case for India, The: Durant, W. J.

Case for industrial partnership, The: Cole, G. D. H.

Case for Mrs. Heydon, The: Bridges, Roy

Case for spirit photography: Doyle, *Sir* Arthur Conan

Case for the return of Sir Hugh Lane's pictures to Dublin: Gregory, *Lady* Augusta

Case for the shorter work day, The: Frankfurter, Felix

Case in camera, A: †Onions, Oliver

Case is alterd, The: Jonson, Ben

Case is altered, The: Plomer, W. C. F.

Case of Bouck White, The: Morley, C. D.

Case of Charles Macklin, comedian, The: Macklin, Charles

Case of conscience, A: Armstrong, N. D.

Case of conscience resolved, A: Bunyan, John

Case of Dunkirk faithfully stated, and impartially considered, The: Bolingbroke, Henry St. John

Case of Elijah, The: Sterne, Laurence

Case of Elizabeth Fenning, The: Hone, William

Case of General Ople and Lady Camper, The: Meredith, George

Case of human bondage, A: Nichols, Beverley

Case of Jennie Brice, The: Rinehart, M. R.

Case of Lady Camber, The: Vachell, H. A.

Case of Mr. Crump, The: Lewisohn, Ludwig

Case of Mr. Lucraft, The: Besant, *Sir* Walter and James Rice

Case of Richard Meynell, The: Ward, M. A.

Case of Sonia Wayward: (†Michael Innes), Stewart, J. I. M.

Case of the abominable snowman, The: Day-Lewis, Cecil

Case of the amorous aunt, The: Gardner, Erle Stanley

Case of the bigamous spouse, The: Gardner, Erle Stanley

Case of the blonde bonanza, The: Gardner, Erle Stanley

Case of the buried clock, The: Gardner, Erle Stanley

Case of the calendar girl, The: Gardner, Erle Stanley

Case of the caretaker's cat, The: Gardner, Erle Stanley

Case of the constant suicides, The: Carr, J. D.

Case of the counterfeit eye, The: Gardner, Erle Stanley

Case of the curious bride, The: Gardner, Erle Stanley

Case of the daring decoy, The: Gardner, Erle Stanley

Case of the dubious bridegroom, The: Gardner, Erle Stanley

Case of the fiery fingers, The: Gardner, Erle Stanley

Case of the four friends, The: Masterman, *Sir* J. C.

Case of the frightened lady, The: Wallace, Edgar

Case of the glamorous ghost, The: Gardner, Erle Stanley

Case of the golddigger's purse, The: Gardner, Erle Stanley

Case of the hesitant hostess, The: Gardner, Erle Stanley

Case of the ice-cold hands, The: Gardner, Erle Stanley

Case of the journeying, boy, The: (†Michael Innes), Stewart, J. I. M.

Case of the late pig, The: Allingham, Margery Louise

Case of the lucky loser, The: Gardner, Erle Stanley

Case of the mischievous doll, The: Gardner, Erle Stanley

Case of the mythical monkeys, The: Gardner, Erle Stanley

Case of the nervous accomplice, The: Gardner, Erle Stanley

Case of the perjured parrot, The: Gardner, Erle Stanley

Case of the rebellious Susan, The: Jones, Henry Arthur

Case of the reluctant model, The: Gardner, Erle Stanley

Case of the Roman Catholics of Ireland, The: Brooke, Henry

Case of the screaming woman, The: Gardner, Erle Stanley

Case of the silent partner, The: Gardner, Erle Stanley

Case of the spurious spinster, The: Gardner, Erle Stanley

Case of the step-daughter's secret, The: Gardner, Erle Stanley

Case of the stuttering bishop, The: Gardner, Erle Stanley

Case of the sulky girl, The: Gardner, Erle Stanley

Case of the sunbather's diary, The: Gardner, Erle Stanley

Case of the terrified typist, The: Gardner, Erle Stanley

Case of the velvet claws, The: Gardner, Erle Stanley

Case-book of Sherlock Holmes, The: Doyle, *Sir* Arthur Conan

Casebook of Solar Pons, The: Derleth, A. W.

Casement, The: Swinnerton, Frank

Cases of conscience: Mather, Increase

Cashel Byron's profession: Shaw, G. B.

Casimir Maremma: Helps, *Sir* Arthur

Cask, The: Crofts, F. W.

Casket of fate, The: Osgood, F. S.

Casper: Warner, A. B.

Cass Timberlane: Lewis, H. S.

Cassandra at the wedding: Baker, Dorothy

Cassell's history of the war in the Soudan: Grant, James

Cassell's illustrated history of India: Grant, James

Cassell's Library of English literature: Morley, Henry

Cassell's old and new Edinburgh: Grant, James

Cassique of Accabee, The: Simms, W. G.

Cassique of Kiawah, The: Simms, W.G.

Cast over the water given gratis to William Fennor, the rimer from London, A: Taylor, John

Castara: Habington, William

Castaway: Cozzens, James Gould

Castaway: Yates, E.H.

Castaways, The: Jacobs, W.W.

Castaways, The: Reid, T.M.

Caste: Robertson, T.W.

Caste and democracy: Panikkar, K.M.

Caste and outcast: Mukherji, D.G.

Castel of helth, The: Elyot, *Sir* Thomas

Castell of labour, The: Barclay, Alexander

Castell of labour, The: Pollard, A.W.

Castiglione: The Courtyer: Hoby, Thomas

Castilian, The: Talfourd, *Sir* T.N.

Casting away of Mrs. Lecks and Mrs. Aleshine, The: Stockton, F.R.

Castle builders, The: Yonge, C.M.

Castle Conquer: Colum, Padraic

Castle Corner: Cary, Joyce

Castle Craneycrow: McCutcheon, G.B.

Castle Dismal: Simms, W.G.

Castle Dor: Du Maurier, Daphne

Castle Gay: Buchan, John

Castle in Spain, A: De Mille, James

Castle Inn, The: Weyman, Stanley

Castle island: Mottram, R.H.

Castle Nowhere: Lake County sketches: Woolson, C.F.

Castle Number Nine: Bemelmans, Ludwig

Castle of Andalusia, The: O'Keeffe, John

Castle of Ehrenstein, The: James, George Payne Rainsford

Castle of Indolence, The: Thomson, James

Castle of Ollada, The: Lathom, Francis

Castle of Otranto, The: Walpole, Horace

Castle Rackrent: Edgeworth, Maria

Castle Richmond: Trollope, Anthony

Castle Skull: Carr, J.D.

Castle spectre, The: Lewis, Matthew Gregory

Castle wafer: Wood, Ellen

Castle Warlock: Macdonald, George

Castleford case, The: Browne, Frances

Castles and kings: Treece, Henry

Castles in Spain: Galsworthy, John

Castles in the air: Gore, Catherine

Castles in the air: Orczy, *Baroness*

Castles of Athlin and Dunbayne, The: Radcliffe, *Mrs.* Ann

Castles of England: Peach, L. Du Garde

Casual commentary, A: Macaulay, *Dame* Rose

Casual ward: Godley, Alfred Denis

Casuals of the sea: McFee, William

Casuarina tree, The: Maugham, Somerset

Cat: Gielgud, Val

Cat, The: Repplier, Agnes

Cat among the pigeons: Christie, Agatha

Cat and the moon, The: Yeats, W.B.

Cat book, A: Lucas, E.V.

Cat burglar, The: Wallace, Edgar

Cat jumps, The: Bowen, E.D.C.

Cat of Bybastes, The: Henty, George Alfred

Cat of many tails: †Queen, Ellery

Cat stories: Jackson, H.H.

Cat that jumped out of the story, The: Hecht, Ben

Catacrok: Graves, Robert

Catalan circus: †Onions, Oliver

Catalina: Maugham, Somerset

Cataline his conspiracy: Jonson, Ben

Catalogue, bibliographical and critical, A: Collier, J.P.

Catalogue of all the English Stage Playes: Kirkman, Francis

Catalogue of books of the first printers: Pollard, A.W.

Catalogue of drawings illustrating the life of Gen. Washington, and of colonial life, A: Pyle, Howard

Catalogue of early printed books in the possession of J.P. Morgan: Pollard, A.W.

Catalogue of English poetry exhibition: Hayward, J.D.

Catalogue of Italian sculpture in the Victoria and Albert Museum: Pope-Hennessy, J.W.

Catalogue of pictures by the French and Dutch romanticists of this century, with an introduction and biographical notes of artists: Henley, W.E.

Catalogue of Swift exhibition: Hayward, J.D.

Catalogue of the contents of the museum of the Royal Irish Academy: Wilde, *Sir* William Robert Wills

Catalogue of the entire private library of the late Rev. Rufus W. Griswold: Griswold, R.W.

Catalogue of the Indian collections in the Museum of Fine Arts, Boston: Coomaraswamy, A.K.

Catalogue of the Italian paintings in the J.G. Johnson collection: Berenson, Bernhard

Catalogue of the Italian paintings in the Widener and Friedsam collections: Berenson, Bernhard

Catalogue of the library of the House of Lords: Gosse, *Sir* Edmund

Catalogue of the Royal and Noble authors of England, A: Walpole, Horace

Catch him who can: Hook, T.E.

Catchwords and claptrap: Macaulay, *Dame* Rose

Catechism of education: Mackenzie, W.L.

Catechismus: Cranmer, T.

Catguts: Isvaran, M.S.

Catharine Furze: †Rutherford, Mark

Catharos: Lodge, T.

Cathedral, The: Lowell, J.R.

Cathedral, The: Walpole, *Sir* Hugh

Cathedral, The: Williams, Isaac

Cathedral and University Sermons: Church, Richard William

Cathedral carol service: Walpole, *Sir* Hugh

Cathedral courtship, A: Wiggin, K.D.

Cathedral singer, A: Allen, James Lane

Catherine: Ensor, *Sir* R.C.K.

Catherine: Thackeray, W.M.

Catherine Carter: Johnson, Pamela H.

Catherine Douglas: Helps, *Sir* Arthur

Catherine Foster: Bates, H.E.

Catherine herself: Hilton, James

Catherine Volman: Reynolds, G.

Cathleen in Houlihan: Yeats, W.B.

Catholic Church and conversion, The: Chesterton, G.K.

Catholic claims: Smith, Sydney

Catholic faith, The: More, P.E.

Catholic tales: Sayers, Dorothy

Catholicism and Scotland: Mackenzie, *Sir* Compton

Catholick poet (Pope), The: Oldmixon, John

Catholicke conference betweene Syr Tady Macmareall and Patricke Plaine, A: Rich, Barnabe

Catiline: Croly, George

Catiline his conspiracy: Jonson, Ben

Cat-in-the-manger: Bentley, Phyllis

Catmint: Mackenzie, *Sir* Compton

Cato: Addison, Joseph

Cato Major: Denham, *Sir* John

Catriona: Stevenson, R.L.

Cats and Rosemary, The: Swinnerton, Frank

Cat's claws: Jennings, Gertrude

Cat's company: Mackenzie, *Sir* Compton

Cat's cradle: Baring, Maurice

Cat's cradle: De Selincourt, Aubrey

Cat's-cradle book, The: Warner, Sylvia Townsend

Cats in colour: Smith, Stevie

Catterpillers of this nation anatomized, The: Head, Richard

Cattle brands: Adams, Andy

Caught: Green, Henry

Caught wet: Crothers, Rachel

Causation and its application to history: Cohen, M.R.

Cause, The: Binyon, Laurence

Cause allegorically stated, A: Wither, George

Cause for alarm: Ambler, Eric

Cause for freedom, The: Hughes, Thomas

Causes and consequences of the affair of Harper's ferry: Clarke, J.F.

Causes of evolution, The: Haldane, J.B.S.

Causes of international war: Dickinson, Goldsworthy Lowes

Causes of the American discontent before 1768: Franklin, Benjamin

Causes of the French revolution, The: Russell, *Lord* John

Causes of the rise and success of Arianism: Newman, J.H.

Caution to stir up to watch against sin, A: Bunyan, John

Cautionary tales: Belloc, Hilaire

Cautionary verses: Belloc, Hilaire

Cautious amorist, The: Lindsay, Norman

Cavalcade: Coward, Noel

Cavalcade of kings, A: Farjeon, Eleanor

Cavalier, The: Cable, George Washington

Cavalier, The: James, G.P.R.

Cavalier, The: Whitehead, Charles

Cavalier of Tennessee, The: Nicholson, Meredith

Cavalier of Virginia, A: Roberts, T.G.

Cavalier's cup, The: †Carter Dickson

Cavaliers of England, The: Herbert, H.W.

Cavaliers of fortune, The: Grant, James

Cavaliers of Virginia, The: Caruthers, W.A.

Cavanagh, forest ranger: Garland, Hamlin

Cave, The: Church, Richard

Cave, The: Warren, Robert Penn

Cave dwellers, The: Saroyan, William

Cave of illusion, The: Sutro, Alfred

Cave of poverty, The: Theobald, Lewis

Caveat of warening for commen cursetors vulgarly called vagabones, A: Harman, Thomas

Cavelarice: Markham, Gervase

Cavender's house: Robinson, E.A.

Caviare: Richards, Grant

Caw-caw ballads: MacDonald, W.P.

Cawdor: Jeffers, J.R.

Cawnpore: Trevelyan, *Sir* G.O.

Caxton Press, The: Lawlor, P.A.

Caxtoniana: Lyttón, E.G.E.B. *1st baron*

Caxtons, The: Lytton, E.G.E.B. *1st baron*

Cecil: Gore, Catherine

Cecil a peer: Gore, Catherine

Cecil Castlemaine's Gage: †Ouida

Cecil Dreeme: Winthrop, Theodore

Cecil Lawson: a memoir: Gosse, *Sir* Edmund

Cecil Rhodes: Plomer, W.C.F.

Cécile: Lucas, F.L.

Cecilia: Burney, Fanny

Cecilia: Crawford, Francis Marion

Cecilia: Monkhouse, A.N.

Cecilia Gonzaga: Trevelyan, R.C.

Cecilia's lovers: Barr, A.E.H.

Cecily Parsley's nursery rhymes: Potter, Helen Beatrix

Cecil's trust: Payn, James

Cefalu: Durrell, Lawrence

Celebrated jumping frog of Calaveras County, The: (†Mark Twain), Clemens, S.L.

Celebrated letter from Samuel Johnson, LL.D. to Philip Dormer Stanhope, Earl of Chesterfield, The: Johnson, *Dr*. Samuel

Celebrated speeches of Ajax and Ulysses, The: Hill, Aaron

Celebration: †Pindar, Peter

Celebrities and simple souls: Sutro, Alfred

Celebrities at home: Yates, E.H.

Celebrity, The: Churchill, Winston

Celeste: †Hudson, Stephen

Celestial city, The: Orczy, *Baroness*

Celestial cycle, The: Kirkconnell, Watson

Celestial omnibus, The: Forster, E.M.

Celestial passion, The: Gilder, R.W.

Celestial rail-road, The: Hawthorne, Nathaniel

Celestina: Dukes, Ashley

Celestina: Smith, Charlotte

Celibates: Moore, George

Celibates' club, The: Zangwill, Israel

Celluloid mistress, The: Ackland, Rodney

Celt and Saxon: Meredith, George

Celt, the Roman and the Saxon, The: Wright, Thomas

Celtic bards, chiefs and kings: Borrow, George

Celtic stories: Thomas, E.E.P.

Celtic twilight, The: Yeats, W.B.

Celt's paradise, The: Banim, John

Cenci, The: Shelley, P.B.

Censor and the theatre, The: Palmer, J.L.

Censored! Penton, B.C.

Censura literaria: Brydges, *Sir* Samuel Egerton

Censure of a loyall subject, The: Whetstone, George

Census and slavery, The: Bushnell, Horace

Census of Shakespeare Quartos, A: Pollard, A.W.

Centaur, The: Blackwood, Algernon

Centaur not fabulous, The: Young, Edward

Centaur's booty, The: Moore, T.S.

Centenary at Jalna: De la Roche, Mazo

Centenary history of the South Place Society: Conway, Moncure Daniel

Centenary of Haliburton's "Nova-Scotia", The: MacMechan, A.M.

Centenary of Moore, The: MacCarthy, Denis Florence

Centennial meditation of Columbia, 1776–1876, The: Lanier, Sidney

Centennial Ode, A: Halloran, Henry

Centennial oration: Curtis, George William

Centennial St. Andrew's, Niagara, 1794–1894: Carnochan, Janet

Centennial, St. Mark's (Episcopal) Church, Niagara, 1792–1892: Carnochan, Janet

Centeola: Thompson, D.P.

Central Australia: (†Donald Barr), Barrett, C.L.

Central government: Traill, H.D.

Central Italian painters of the Italian art: Berenson, Bernhard

Central Italian painters of the Renaissance, The: Berenson, Bernhard

Centuries of Santa Fe, The: Horgan, Paul

Century, The: Morley, C.D.

Century at Chignecto, A: Bird, W.R.

Century has roots, A: Finch, R.D.C.

Century of British monarchy, A: Bolitho, H.H.

Century of candymaking, A: Untermeyer, Louis

Century of co-operation, A: Cole, G.D.H.

Century of dishonor, A: Jackson, H.H.

Century of revolution, 1789–1920, A: Kennedy, Margaret

Century of roundels, A: Swinburne, A.C.

Century of science, A: Fiske, John

Century's progress in physics, A: Lodge, *Sir* O.J.

Cerberus: Dudek, Louis

Cerberus: Layton, Irving

Cerealia: An imitation of Milton: Philips, John

Ceremonial institutions: Spencer, Herbert

Ceremony of innocence: Webster, E.C.

Ceres' runaway: Meynell, Alice

Cerise, a tale of the last century: Whyte-Melville, G.J.

Certain delightful English towns: Howells, W.D.

Certain hour, The: Cabell, James Branch

Certain man, A: †Onions, Oliver

Certain measure: An interpretation of prose fiction, A: Glasgow, Ellen

Certain miscellany tracts: Browne, *Sir* Thomas

Certain most Godly letters of such true saintes as gave their lyves: Coverdale, Miles

Certain people: Wharton, Edith

Certain people of importance: Gardiner, A.G.

Certain personal matters: Wells, H.G.

Certain rich man, A: White, W.A.

Certain select cases resolved: Shepard, Thomas

Certain star, The: Bottome, Phyllis

Certain travailles of an uncertain journey, The: Taylor, John

Certain women: Caldwell, Erskine Preston

Certayne psalmes chosen out of the psalter of David: Wyatt, *Sir* Thomas

Cesare Borgia: Symons, Arthur

Cestus of Aglaia, The: Ruskin, John

Cetewayo and his white neighbours: Haggard, *Sir* Henry Rider

Ceylon: an account of the island, physical, historical and topographical: Tennent, *Sir* J.E.

Ceylon and the Hollanders, 1658–1796: Pierus, P.E.

Ceylon and the Portuguese, 1505–1658: Pierus, P.E.

Ceylon: the Portuguese era: Pierus, P.E.

Chace, The: Somerville, William

Chad Hanna: Edmonds, W.D.

Chafing dish party, A: Bangs, John Kendrick

Chain of lilies: Rands, W.B.

Chain of philosophical reflexions and inquiries concerning the virtues of tar-water, A: Berkeley, George

Chainbearer, The: Cooper, James Fenimore

Chains: Baker, Elizabeth

Chains: Dreiser, Theodore

Chair on the Boulevard, The: Merrick, Leonard

Chalcographimania, Ireland: William Henry

Chalice and the sword, The: Raymond, Ernest

Chalk face: Frank, Waldo

Chalk Garden, The: Bagnold, Enid

Chalk stream killing, A: Pertwee, Roland

Challenge, The: Bottome, Phyllis

Challenge: Gibson, Wilfred

Challenge: Sackville-West, V.

Challenge: †Sapper

Challenge: Untermeyer, Louis

Challenge at tilt, A: Jonson, Ben

Challenge for beautie, A: Heywood, Thomas

Challenge of Schweitzer, The: Murry, John Middleton

Challenge of the Brontës, The: Gosse, Sir Edmund

Challenge of the dead, The: Graham, Stephen

Challenge of waste, The: Chase, Stuart

Challenge to Clarissa: †Delafield, E.M.

Challenge to schools: Calder-Marshall, Arthur

Challenge to Sirius, The: Kaye-Smith, S.

Challenge to the church, A: Temple, William

Challenge to the reader: †Queen, Ellery

Challenge to time and death: Brown, A.A.

Challenge to Venus: Morgan, C.L.

Challoners, The: Benson, E.F.

Chamber music: Joyce, James

Chambers of imagery: Bottomley, Gordon

Chaminuka, the man whom God taught: Cripps, A.S.

Champagne Charley: Thomas, Augustus

Champion, The: †Craddock, C.E.

Champion, The: Fielding, Henry

Champion from far away, The: Hecht, Ben

Champion of virtue, The: Reeve, Clara

Champions of freedom, The: Woodworth, Samuel

Champlain: Dawson, S.E.

Champlain and D'Arontal: Kingston, G.A.

Champlain Road, The: McDowell, F.D.

Chance: Conrad, Joseph

Chance acquaintance, A: Howells, W.D.

Chance acquaintances: Van Druten, J.W.

Chance for himself, A: Trowbridge, J.T.

Chance of a lifetime: Greenwood, Walter

Chance the idol: Jones, Henry Arthur

Chances, The: Beaumont, Francis

Chances, The: Buckingham, G.V.

Chandala woman, A: De Zilwa, Lucien

Chandos: †Ouida

Change at Maythorne: Trease, Geoffrey

Change for a halfpenny: Lucas, E.V.

Change for a shilling: Mayhew, Horace

Change for the worse, A: Bridie, James

Change in the Cabinet, A: Belloc, Hilaire

Change of air, A: Gerould, Katharine

Change of air, A: Hawkins, Anthony Hope

Change partners: Vachell, H.A.

Changed man, A: Hardy, Thomas

Changeling, The: Besant, Sir Walter

Changeling: Byrne, Donn

Changeling, The: Jacobs, W.W.

Changeling, The: Middleton, Thomas

Changeling, The: Phillpotts, Eden

Changes: Shirley, James

Changes in the scientific outlook: Lodge, Sir Oliver

Changing concepts of time: Innis, H.A.

Changing political economy as it affects women, A: Beard, Mary

Changing Russia: Graham, Stephen

Changing scene, The: Calder-Marshall, Arthur

Changing West, The: White, W.A.

Changing winds: Ervine, St. John

Channay syndicate, The: Oppenheim, E. Phillips

Channel islands, The: Mais, S.P.B.

Channel passage, A: Swinburne, A.C.

Channel shore, The: Bruce, Charles

Channel shore, The: De Selincourt, Aubrey

Channings, The: Wood, Ellen

Chant of doom, A: Brennan, C.J.

Chant of Mammonism, A: McArthur, Peter

Chant of the celestial sailors, The: Pater, Walter

Chantemerle: Broster, D.K.

Chantry House: Yonge, C.M.

Chants for the Boer: †Miller, Joaquin

Chaos and order in industry: Cole, G.D.H.

Chaos is come again: Morton, J.M.

Chaos, This: Acton, Harold

Chapbook, The: Fletcher, John Gould

Chapel of the hermits, The: Whittier, J.G.

Chaplain of the Fleet, The: Besant, *Sir* Walter and James Rice

Chapman of rhymes, The: Priestley, J.B.

Chapman, with illustrative passages: Ellis, Henry Havelock

Chapter and introduction to the English Countryside: Massingham, Harold

Chapter from the book called the ingenious gentleman Don Quixote de la Mancha, A: †Machen, Arthur

Chapter of accidents, The: Lee, Sophia

Chapters for the orthodox: Marquis, Don

Chapters from a life: Ward, E.S.

Chapters of Erie: Adams, C.F. and Henry Brooks Adams

Chapters of life: Petrie, *Sir* Charles

Chapters on churchyards: Southey, C.A.

Character: Smiles, Samuel

Character and comedy: Lucas, E.V.

Character and conduct of Cicero considered, The: Cibber, Colley

Character and motive in Shakespeare: (†Michael Innes) Stewart, J.I.M.

Character and opinion in the United States: Santayana, George

Character and opinions of Dr. Johnson, The: Swinburne, A.C.

Character and portraits of Washington, The: Tuckerman, H.T.

Character building: Washington, B.T.

Character of a Popish Successor, The: Phillips, John

Character of a trimmer, The: Savile, George

Character of Charles II, The: Sheffield, John

Character of England, A: Evelyn, John

Character of George Washington, The: Cross, W.L.

Character of Holland, The: Marvell, Andrew

Character of King Charles the Second, A: Savile, George

Character of the late Viscount Sackville, The: Cumberland, Richard

Character of women, The: Cobbold, Richard

Character sketches: Riley, J.W.

Characteristic sketches of Ireland and the Irish: Hall, Anna Maria

Characteristic sketches of Ireland and the Irish: Lover, Samuel

Characteristicks of men, manners, opinions, times: Shaftesbury, Anthony *3rd Earl of*

Characteristics: Mitchell, S.W.

Characteristics: in the manner of Rochefoucault's maxims: Hazlitt, William

Characteristics of literature: Tuckerman, H.T.

Characters and commentaries: Strachey, Lytton

Characters and criticisms: Hannay, James

Characters and events: Dewey, John

Characters of Shakespear's plays: Hazlitt, William

Characters of the most celebrated painters of Italy: Reynolds, *Sir* Joshua

Characters of the Reformation: Belloc, Hilaire

Characters of two royal masques, The: Jonson, Ben

Characters of vertue and vice: Tate, Nahum

Characters of vertues and vices: Hall, Joseph

Characters upon essaies morall, and divine: Breton, Nicholas

Charcoal sketches: Neal, J.C.

Charcoals of new and old New York: Smith, F.H.

Chardin: De La Mare, Walter

Chardin and Vigée-Lebrun: Lucas, E.V.

Charge delivered to the Grand Jury, A: Fielding, Henry

Charge fulfilled, A: Molesworth, *Mrs.*

Charge of the Light Brigade, The: Tennyson, Alfred *Lord*

Charge to the poets, A: Whitehead, William

Charing Cross: Robert, C.E.M.

Chariot of fire, The: De Voto, Bernard

Chariot of fire, A: Ward, E.S.

Chariot of wrath: Knight, G.W.

Chariots: Bynner, Witter

Charis sees it through: Widdemer, Margaret

Charity: Cunninghame Graham, Robert

Charity: Gilbert, *Sir* W.S.

Charity and its fruits: Edwards, Jonathan

Charity Ball, The: Belasco, David

Charity school spelling book, The: Trimmer, *Mrs.* Sarah

Charlemont: Simms, W.G.

Charles and Mary: Temple, Joan

Charles Baudelaire: Symons, Arthur

Charles Blackford: Ingraham, J.H.

Charles Chesterfield: Trollope, Frances

Charles Darwin: Allen, Grant

Charles Dickens: Chesterton, G.K.

Charles Dickens: Gissing, George

Charles Dickens: Pope-Hennessy, *Dame* Una

Charles Dickens: Sala, G.A.H.

Charles Dickens: Swinburne, A.C.

Charles Dickens: a pictorial biography: Priestley, J.B.

Charles Dickens and other 'Spirits of the Age': Browning, Elizabeth Barrett

Charles Dickens and other Victorians: (†Q), Quiller-Couch, *Sir* A.

Charles Dickens, his life and work: Leacock, Steffen

Charles Elwood: Brownson, Orestes

Charles Francis Adams the first: Adams, C.F.

Charles Frohman: Barrie, *Sir* J.M.

Charles G.D. Roberts: Cappon, James

Charles Heavysege: Burpee, Lawrence J.

Charles James Fox: Drinkwater, John

Charles Kingsley: Vulliamy, C.E.

Charles Lamb: Blunden, Edmund

Charles Lamb: Brown, Alice

Charles Lamb: Moxon, Edward

Charles Lamb: a memoir: Proctor, B.W.

Charles Lamb and his contemporaries: Blunden, Edmund

Charles O'Malley, the Irish Dragoon: Lever, C.J.

Charles Ricketts, R.A.: Moore, T.S.

Charles Scribner's sons present Ring W. Lardner in the golden honeymoon and haircut: Lardner, Ring

Charles Sumner: Curtis, G.W.

Charles the First: Mitford, Mary Russell

Charles I and Cromwell: Young, G.M.

Charles the first: King of England: Belloc, Hilaire

Charles the Great (trn.): Caxton, William

Charles II: Hayward, J.D.

Charles the Second: Payne, J.H.

Charles II: Pearson, Hesketh

Charles Tyrell: James, G.P.R.

Charleston and her satirists: Simms, W.G.

Charley is my darling: Cary, Joyce

Charlotte: a tale of truth: Rowson, S.H.

Charlotte Brontë: Benson, E.F.

Charlotte Brontë: Reid, *Sir* Thomas Wemyss

Charlotte Brontë and her circle: Shorter, C.K.

Charlotte Brontë and her sisters: Shorter, C.K.

Charlotte Temple: a tale of truth: Rowson, S.H.

Charlotte von Stein: Calvert, George Henry

Charlotte's daughter: Rowson, S.H.

Charlotte's inheritance: Braddon, Mary Elizabeth

Charlotte's row: Bates, H.E.

Charlotte's web: White, E.B.

Charm, The: Besant, *Sir* Walter and W. Pollock

Charm of birds, The: Grey of Fallodon, Edward *Lord*

Charm of Hobart, The: Turnbull, S.C.P.

Charm of words, A: Partridge, Eric

Charmian Lady Vibart: Farnol, J.J.

Charms of fancy, The: Alsop, Richard

Charnel rose, The: Aiken, Conrad

Chart for rough water: Frank, Waldo

Charter, The: Williams, H.M.

Charter for ramblers, A: Joad, C.E.M.

Chartism: Carlyle, Thomas

Chartist portraits: Cole, G.D.H.

Charwoman's daughter, The: Stephens, James

Charwoman's shadow, The: Dunsany, E.J.M.D.P. *Lord*

Chase of Saint-Castin, The: Catherwood, Mary

Chase of the Leviathan, The: Reid, T.M.

Chase of the meteor, The: Bynner, Edwin Lassetter

Chast and lost lovers, Arcadius and Sepha, The: Bosworth, William

Chast mayd in Cheape-side, A: Middleton, Thomas

Chaste Diana, The: Beck, *Mrs.* Lily

Chaste wanton, The: Williams, Charles

Chaste wife, The: Swinnerton, Frank

Chastelard: Swinburne, A.C.

Chateau D'Or: Holmes, M.J.

Chateau-Bigot: history and romance: LeMoine, *Sir* J.M.

Chatelaine, The: Raymond, Ernest

Chatelaine of La Trinité, The: Fuller, Henry Blake

Chatham: Harrison, Frederic

Chats by the fireside: O'Hagan, Thomas

Chats on Japanese prints: Ficke, Arthur Davison

Chaturanga: Tagore, *Sir* R.

Chaucer: Chesterton, G.K.

Chaucer: Masefield, John

Chaucer and his England: Coulton, G.G.

Chaucer and his poetry: Kittredge, G.L.

Chaucer as a philologist: Tolkien, J.R.R.

Chaucer Primer: Pollard, A.W.

Chaucer to "B.V.": Blunden, Edmund

Chaucer's England: Rands, W.B.

Chaunt of the Cholera: Banim, John and Michael Banim

Cheap and good husbandry: Markham, Gervase

Cheap books and good books: Matthews, J.B.

Cheap clothes and nasty: Kingsley, Charles

Cheap Jack Zita: Baring-Gould, Sabine

Cheap sugar means cheap slaves: Higgins, Matthew James

Cheat-the-boys: Phillpotts, Eden

Cheating the kidnappers: Kaufman, G.S.

Cheats, The: †Bowen, Marjorie

Cheats, The: Wilson, John

Check to your king: †Hyde, Robin

Checked love affair, A: Ford, Paul Leicester

Checkmate: Le Fanu, Joseph Sheridan

Checkov. The Taylorian lecture: Elton, Oliver

Chedworth: Sherriff, R.C.

Cheefoo: Coppard, A.E.

Cheerful by request: Ferber, Edna

Cheerful yesterdays: Higginson, T.W.

Cheerfulness breaks in: Thirkell, Angela

Cheery soul, The: White, Patrick

Cheery way, The: Bangs, John Kendrick

Cheiron: Trevelyan, R.C.

Chekov, Synge, Yeats and Pirandello: Lucas, F.L.

Chelbury Abbey: Mackail, Denis

Chelsea buns: Coward, Noel

Chelsea cherub, The: Roberts, C.E.M.

Chelsea pensioner, The: Dibdin, Charles

Chelsea rooming house: Gregory, H.V.

Chenies: †Taffrail

Chequer board, The: †Shute, Nevil

Cherrie and the slaye, The: Montgomerie, Alexander

Cherry: Tarkington, Booth

Cherry and Violet: Manning, Anne

Cherry gambol: Phillpotts, Eden

Cherry riband, The: Crockett, S.R.

Cherry ripe: Coppard, A.E.

Cherry tree, The: Bell, Adrian

Cherry tree, The: Grigson, Geoffrey

Cherry-stones: Phillpotts, Eden

Cherrystones: Farjeon, Eleanor

Cherwell water-lily, The: Faber, Frederick William

Cheshire chivalry: Warburton, R.E.E.

Cheskian (i.e. Czech) anthology: Bowring, Sir John

Chester: Mee, Arthur

Chester play studies: Greg, W.W.

Chestnut squirrel: Commager, H.S.

Chetwynd Calverley: Ainsworth, William Harrison

Chevaleer, The: Jones, Henry Arthur

Chevalier of Pensieri-vani, The: Fuller, Henry Blake

Chevaliers of France, The: Herbert, H.W.

Cheyne of Essilmont, The: Grant, James

Chez Pavan: Llewellyn, Richard

Chianti flask, The: Lowndes, M.A.

Chicago: city on the make: Algren, Nelson

Chicago Massacre of 1812, The: Kirkland, Joseph

Chicago poems: Sandburg, Carl

Chichester concert: Armstrong, M.D.

Chick: Wallace, Edgar

Chicken inspector: Perelman, S.J.

Chickens feed capons: Lyttelton, George Baron

Chicken-wagon family, The: Benefield, Barry

Chidiock Tichbourne: Clarke, Marcus

Chief factor, The: Parker, Sir H.G.

Chief of the herd, The: Mukherji, D.G.

Chief of the ranges, The: Cody, H.A.

Child, The: Tagore, Sir R.

Child and the book, The: Morley, C.D.

Child Christopher and Goldilind the Fair: Morris, William

Child is born, A: Newbolt, Sir Henry

Child king, The: †Fairless, Michael

Child lovers: Davies, William Henry

Child man: Pinero, Sir A.W.

Child of chequer'd fortune: †Preedy, George

Child of divorce, The: Cammaerts, Emile

Child of God, The: O'Flaherty, Liam

Child of misfortune: Day-Lewis, Cecil

Child of my sorrow: †Bell, Neil

Child of nature, A: Buchanan, R.W.

Child of nature, The: Inchbald, Mrs.

Child of Norman's End: Raymond, Ernest

Child of Queen Victoria, The: Plomer, W.C.F.

Child of storm: Haggard, Sir Henry Rider

Child of the age, A: Adams, Francis

Child of the Amazons: Eastman, Max

Child of the century: Hecht, Ben

Child of the dawn, The: Benson, A.C.

Child of the Jago, A: Morrison, Arthur

Child of the Revolution, A: Orczy, Baroness

Child of the sea: Lewis, S.A.

Child Royal: Broster, D.K.

Child verse: Tabb, J.B.

Child who never grew: Buck, Pearl

Child wife, The: Reid, T.M.

Child world: Dodge, May Abigail

Childe Harold's pilgrimage: Byron, George Gordon Lord

Childermass, The: Lewis, P. Wyndham

Childhood: Meynell, Alice

Childhood in Brittany eighty years ago, A: Sedgwick, A.D.

Childhood in contemporary cultures: Mead, Margaret

Childhood of Christ as seen by the Primitive Masters, The: Cammaerts, Emile

Childhood songs: Larcom, Lucy

Child-life in colonial days: Earle, A.M.

Children, The: Fast, Howard M.

Children, The: Meynell, Alice

Children, The: Wharton, Edith

Children and older people: Suckow, Ruth

Children and others: Cozzens, J.G.

Children and the machine age: Dell, Floyd

Children, can you answer this?: Hannay, J.O.

Children from their games: Shaw, Irwin

Children grow up, The: Seymour, B.K.

Children in bondage: Markham, Edwin

Children in the wood, The: Morton, Thomas

Children in the woods: Royde-Smith, Naomi

Children of Gibeon: Besant, Sir Walter

Children of God: Fisher, V.A.

Children of love: Monro, H.E.

Children of men: Phillpotts, Eden

Children of no man's land: Stern, G.B.

Children of Odin, The: Colum, Padraic

Children of poor: Lee, J.A.

Children of romance: Scollard, Clinton

Children of Shallowford, The: Williamson, Henry

Children of the age: Griffith, Hubert

Children of the Archbishop: Collins, Norman

Children of the Bush: Lawson, Henry

Children of the castle, The: Molesworth, *Mrs.*

Children of the dark people: Davison, F.D.

Children of the Earth: Brown, Alice

Children of the earth: Mannin, Ethel

Children of the frost: London, Jack

Children of the Ghetto: Zangwill, Israel

Children of the king, The: Crawford, Francis Marion

Children of the market place: Masters, E.L.

Children of the mist: Phillpotts, Eden

Children of the moon: Flavin, Martin

Children of the New Forest, The: Marryatt, Frederick

Children of the night, The: Robinson, E.A.

Children of the Nile, The: Pickthall, M.W.

Children of the old masters: Meynell, Alice

Children of the pool, The: †Machen, Arthur

Children of the slaves: Graham, Stephen

Children of the soil: Vachell, H.A.

Children of the tempest: Munro, Neil

Children of the valley, The: Spofford, H.E.

Children of the wind: Shiel, M.P.

Children of to-morrow: (†Macleod, Fiona), Sharp, William

Children out of doors, The: Piatt, J.J.

Children sing in the far West: Austin, Mary

Children who followed the piper, The: Colum, Padraic

Children's bells: Farjeon, Eleanor

Children's Bible, The: Mee, Arthur

Children's Bunyan, The: Mee, Arthur

Children's crusade, The: Treece, Henry

Children's gems, The: Child, Lydia Maria

Children's hour, The: Mee, Arthur

Children's hour, The: Molsworth, *Mrs.*

Children's play hour books, The: (Stephen Southwold), †Bell, Neil

Children's poetry: Craik, *Mrs.* Dinah M.

Children's rights: Wiggin, K.D.

Children's song, The: Kipling, Rudyard

Children's song of welcome to Prince Alfred, The: Meredith, L.A.

Children's summer, The: Kaye-Smith, S.

Children's tales—from the Russian Ballets: Sitwell, Edith

Children's treasury of English song, The: Palgrave, F.T.

Child's day, A: De La Mare, Walter

Child's dream of a star, A: Dickens, Charles

Child's garden of verses, A: Stevenson, R.L.

Child's history of England, A: Dickens, Charles

Child's history of Scotland, A: Oliphant, Margaret

Child's journey with Dickens, A: Wiggin, K.D.

Child-songs: Tennyson, Alfred *Lord*

Child's reminiscence, A: Whitman, Walt

Child's story of the world, A: Peattie, D.C.

Child-world, A: Riley, J.W.

Chills and fever: Ransom, J.C.

Chilmark miscellany: Brooks, Van Wyck

Chiltern country: Massingham, Harold

Chimes, The: Dickens, Charles

Chimes: Herrick, Robert

Chimney corner graduates: Allen, James Lane

Chimney-corner, The: Stowe, H.B.

Chimneysmoke: Morley, C.D.

Chimney-sweeper's friend, The: Montgomery, James

China: De Quincey, Thomas

China: Tietjens, E.S.

China and black and white: Buck, Pearl

China coast love song: Akins, Zoë

China collecting in America: Earle, A.M.

China court: Godden, Rumer

China dances: Mason, R.A.K.

China flight: Buck, Pearl

China governess, The: Allingham, Margery

China shop, The: Stern, G.B.

China, Spain and the war: Nehru, Jawaharlal

China's own critics: Lin Yu-T'ang

Chinatown family: Lin Yu-T'ang

Chinese children next door: Buck, Pearl

Chinese crackers: Seymour, W.K.

Chinese ideals of life: Lin Yu-T'ang

Chinese lantern, The: Housman, Laurence

Chinese Morrison: Clune, Frank

Chinese nightingale, The: Lindsay, N.V.

Chinese orange mystery, The: †Queen, Ellery

Chinese prime minister, The: Bagnold, Enid

Chinese puzzle: Godden, Rumer

Chinese puzzle, The: Ransome, A.M.

Chinese white: Gielgud, Val

Chinese women speak: Cusack, E.D.

Chinese written character as a medium for poetry, The: Fenollosa, E.F.

Chink in the armour, The: Lowndes, M.A.

Chinkie's flat: †Becke, Louis

Chinook days: MacInnes, T.R.E.

Chip: Untermeyer, Louis

Chip and the block, The: †Delafield, E.M.

Chippendales, The: Grant, Robert

Chippinge: Weyman, Stanley

Chips, fragments and vestiges: Dodge, M.A.

Chita: a story of last island: Hearn, Lafcadio

Chitra: Tagore, *Sir* R.

Chitrangada: Ghose, Sri Aurobindo

Chivalry: Cabell, James Branch

Chivalry: Sabatini, R.

Chivalry of the sea, The: Bridges, Robert

Chloe Marr: Milne, A.A.

Choëphoroe (Libation-bearers) of Aeschylus, The: Murray, Gilbert

Chlorinda: Jonson, Ben

Choice, The: Monkhouse, A.N.

Choice, The: Shelley, Mary

Choice, The: Sutro, Alfred

Choice before us, The: Dickinson, Goldsworthy Lowes

Choice, chance and change: Breton, Nicholas

Choice of books and other literary pieces, The: Harrison, Frederic

Choice of emblemes, A: Whitney, Geoffrey

Choice of songs: Kipling, Rudyard

Choice of times: Lindsay, Jack

Choice or chance: Blunden, Edmund

Choir invisible, The: Allen, James Lane

Choise of valentines, The: Nash, Thomas

Choleric fathers, The: Holcroft, Thomas

Choleric man, The: Cumberland, Richard

Choosing a mast: Campbell, Roy

Chopin: the man and his music: Huneker, J.G.

Choral symphony: Jones, Jack

Chords of the zither: Scollard, Clinton

Chore-boy of Camp Kippewa, The: Oxley, J.M.

Choric plays: Bottomley, Gordon

Chorle and the birde, The: Lydgate, John

Chorus, The: Lynd, Sylvia

Chorus ending, A: Raymond, Ernest

Chorus for survival: Gregory, H.V.

Chorus of clowns: Phillpotts, Eden

Chorus of the newly dead: Muir, Edwin

Chosen country: Dos Passos, John

Chosen few, A: Stockton, F.R.

Chosen people: †Seaforth, Mackenzie

Chosen peoples: Hebraic ideal versus the Teutonic: Zangwill, Israel

Chosen words: Brown, Ivor

Chrestomathia: Bentham, Jeremy

Chris Brennan: Stephens, A.G.

Chris Gascoyne. An experiment in solitude: Benson, A.C.

Chris of all sorts: Baring-Gould, Sabine

Christ: Austin, Mary

Christ and his salvation: Bushnell, Horace

Christ and modern education: Raven, C.E.

Christ and Nietzsche: Knight, G.W.

Christ and the way to peace: Temple, William

Christ Church servitors in 1853 by one of them: Brown, Thomas Edward

Christ in China: Ficke, A.D.

Christ in Hades: Phillips, Stephen

Christ in His Church: Temple, William

Christ in Italy: Austin, Mary

Christ in the cupboard: Powys, T.F.

Christ in theology: Bushnell, Horace

Christ of the New Testament, The: More, P.E.

Christ, St. Francis and to-day: Coulton, G.G.

Christ the fountaine of life: Cotton, John

Christ the hunter: Lehmann, J.F.

Christ the Word: More, P.E.

Christ upon the waters: Newman, J.H.

Christ was born on Christmas Day: Neale, J.M.

Christabel: Coleridge, S.T.

Christabel and the poems of S.T. Coleridge: Swinburne, A.C.

Christchurch: Coffin, Robert

Christchurch: Cowan, James

Christendom in Dublin: Chesterton, G.K.

Christening, The: Jennings, Gertrude

Christenings make not Christians: Williams, Roger

Christie Johnson: Reade, Charles

Christian, The: Caine, *Sir* T.H. Hall

Christian and civic economy of large towns, The: Chalmers, Thomas

Christian behaviour: Bunyan, John

Christian behaviour: Lewis, C.S.

Christian captives, The: Bridges, Robert

Christian democracy: Temple, William

Christian doctrine of forgiveness of sin, The: Clarke, J.F.

Christian doctrine of prayer, The: Clarke, J.F.

Christian ethicks: Traherne, Thomas

Christian ethics and modern problems: Inge, W.R.

Christian faith and life: Temple, William

Christian healing: Eddy, M.B.

Christian hero, The: Lillo, George

Christian hero, The: Steele, *Sir* Richard

Christian hope of eternal life: Temple, W.

Christian indeed, The: Johnson, Samuel

Christian keepsake, The: Sigourney, L.H.

Christian life: Arnold, T.

Christian life, The: Montgomery, Robert

Christian life: its hopes, its fears, and its close: Arnold, Thomas

Christian morals: Browne, *Sir* Thomas

Christian morals: More, Hannah

Christian mysticism: Inge, W.R.

Christian mysticism: More, P.E.

Christian philosopher, The: Mather, Cotton

Christian physiologist, The: Griffin, Gerald

Christian poet, The: Montgomery, James

Christian psalmist, The: Montgomery, James

Christian Quaker and his divine Testimony stated and vindicated, The: Penn, William

Christian Renaissance: Knight, G.W.

Christian scholar, The: Williams, Isaac

Christian science: (†Mark Twain), Clemens, S.C.

Christian science versus pantheism: Eddy, M.B.

Christian seasons, The: Williams, Isaac

Christian socialism: Raven, C.E.

Christian Year, The: Keble, John

Christianism: Hunt, Leigh

Christianity among the religions of the world: Toynbee, Arnold

Christianity and art: Gill, Eric

Christianity and culture: Eliot, T.S.

Christianity and culture in our time: Pierce, Lorne

Christianity and history: Butterfield, Herbert

Christianity and idealism: Watson, John

Christianity and problems of today: More, P.E.

Christianity and social order: Temple, William

Christianity and the machine age: Gill, Eric

Christianity and the State: Temple, William

Christianity, diplomacy and war: Butterfield, Herbert

Christianity in Ceylon: Tennent, *Sir* J.E.

Christianity in European history: Butterfield, Herbert

Christianity in thought and practice: Temple, William

Christianity or chaos: Mannin, Ethel

Christian's mistake: Craik, *Mrs.* Dinah

Christians only: Broun, Heywood

Christians two chiefe lessons, The: Hooker, Thomas

Christies, The: Ervine, St. John

Christina Alberta's father: Wells, H.G.

Christina Chard: Praed, *Mrs.* C.

Christina, the maid of the South Seas: Mitford, Mary Russell

Christina's fairy book: (Hueffer), Ford, Ford Madox

Christine: Green, Julian

Christine: Read, T.B.

Christine, a Fife fisher girl: Barr, A.E.H.

Christmas: Gale, Zona

Christmas: Moxon, Edward

Christmas angel: Farjeon, B.L.

Christmas at Candleshoe: (†Michael Innes), Stewart, J.I.M.

Christmas at Cold Comfort Farm: Gibbons, Stella

Christmas at Thompson Hall: Trollope, Anthony

Christmas bells: Cawein, Madison

Christmas book, A: Lewis, D.B. Wyndham

Christmas books: Thackeray, W.M.

Christmas cake in four quarters, A: Barker, M.A.

Christmas card to Woodrow Wilson, A: Morley, C.D.

Christmas Carol, A: Dickens, Charles

Christmas carol, A: Gaskell, *Mrs.* Elizabeth

Christmas carol for all good soldiers and sailors, A: Dalton, A.C.

Christmas Carolles: Skelton, John

Christmas carols: Van Loon, Hendrik

Christmas child, A: Molesworth, *Mrs.*

Christmas debates of the island of Ceylon, The: Lorenz, C.A.

Christmas epithalamium: Allen, Hervey

Christmas eve: Hecht, Ben

Christmas Eve: Tennant, Kylie

Christmas Eve and Christmas Day: Hale, E.E.

Christmas Eve and Easter-day: Browning, Robert

Christmas Eve at St. Kavins: Carman, Bliss

Christmas Eve at Swamp's End: Duncan, Norman

Christmas Eve at Topmost Tickle: Duncan, Norman

Christmas eve on lonesome: Fox, John

Christmas every day: Howells, W.D.

Christmas festivities: Poole, John

Christmas font, The: Holmes, M.J.

Christmas formula: Benson, Stella

Christmas garland woven by Max Beerbohm, A: Beerbohm, *Sir* Max

Christmas greeting of various thoughts, A: †Corelli, Marie

Christmas hamper, A: Lemon, Mark

Christmas herald, The: Allen, Hervey

Christmas holiday: Maugham, Somerset

Christmas holiday mystery, The: Trease, Geoffrey

Christmas hymn, 1914: Squire, *Sir* J.C.

Christmas in California: a poem: Sill, E.R.

Christmas in Maine: Coffin, Robert

Christmas in Narragansett: Hale, E.E.

Christmas in Matabeleland: Cloete, E.F.S.G.

Christmas Kalends of Provence, The: Janvier, T.A.

Christmas kangaroo, The: Mudie, I.M.

Christmas miniature: Buck, Pearl

Christmas night in the quarters: Russell, Irwin

Christmas, 1922: Drinkwater, John

Christmas poems: Drinkwater, John

Christmas posy, A: Molesworth, *Mrs.*

Christmas pudding: Mitford, Nancy

Christmas rose and leaf: Cawein, Madison

Christmas roses: Sedgwick, A.D.

Christmas salute, A: Morley, C.D.

Christmas songs: Van Loon, Hendrik

Christmas stocking, The: Warner, S.B.

Christmas stories: Farjeon, B.L.

Christmas stories: Holmes, M.J.

Christmas story: Mencken, H.L.

Christmas story, A: Porter, K.A.

Christmas tale, A: Garrick, David

Christmas that almost wasn't, The: Nash, Ogden

Christmas tobacco, The: Morley, C.D.

Christmas tree: Cummings, E.E.

Christmas tree, A: Dickens, Charles

Christmas trees: Frost, Robert

Christmas wreath, A: Gilder, R.W.

Christmas-tree land: Molesworth, *Mrs.*

Christobel: Logan, J.D.

Christopher: Barr, A.E.H.

Christopher: Pryce, Richard

Christopher, a study in human personality: Lodge, *Sir* Oliver

Christopher and Columbus: Russell, E.M.

Christopher Brennan: Green, H.M.

Christopher Columbus: Macneice, Louis

Christopher Columbus: Madariaga, Salvador de

Christopher Columbus, mariner: Morison, S.E.

Christopher Marlowe: Swinburne, A.C.

Christopher Strong: Frankau, Gilbert

Christopher Wood: Newton, Eric

Christowell: Blackmore, R.D.

Christ's comet: Hassall, Christopher

Christ's company: Dixon, Richard Watson

Christ's Hospital: Blunden, Edmund

Christ's Hospital book, The: Blunden, Edmund

Christ's Kirk on the green: James I

Christ's Kirk on the green: Ramsay, Allan

Christ's passion: Sandys, George

Christs teares over Jerusalem: Nash, Thomas

Christs victorie: Fletcher, Giles *the younger*

Christ's yoke an easy yoke, and yet, the gate to Heaven a strait gate: Taylor, Jeremy

Christus: Longfellow, H.W.

Christus veritas: Temple, William

Chronicle historie of Perkin Warbeck, The: Ford, John

Chronicle of a century, 1829–1929, The: Pierce, Lorne

Chronicle of a pilgrimage, The: Monro, H.E.

Chronicle of Clemendy, The: †Machen, Arthur

Chronicle of Count Antonio, The: (†Anthony Hope), Hawkins, Anthony Hope

Chronicle of England, The: Strutt, Joseph

Chronicle of English literature, A: Mais, S.P.B.

Chronicle of Ethelfled: Manning, Anne

Chronicle of fortunes of Richard Mahoney, The: †Richardson, H.H.

Chronicle of Queen Fredegond, The: Swinburne, A.C.

Chronicle of the conquest of Granada, A: (†Geoffrey Crayon), Irving, Washington

Chronicles and characters: (†Owen Meredith), Lytton, E.R.B., *Earl*

Chronicles of a cosy nook: Hall, Anna Maria

Chronicles of a schoolroom: Hall, Anna Maria

Chronicles of Aunt Minervy Ann, The: Harris, Joel Chandler

Chronicles of Avonlea: Montgomery, L.M.

Chronicles of Canada: Gourlay, R.F.

Chronicles of Captain Blood, The: Sabatini, R.

Chronicles of Clovernook, The: Jerrold, Douglas

Chronicles of Clovis, The: (†Saki), Munro, H.H.

Chronicles of Cooperstown, The: Cooper, James Fenimore

Chronicles of early Melbourne, 1835–52: Finn, Edmund

Chronicles of England, The: Stow, John

Chronicles of Golden Friars: Le Fanu, Joseph Sheridan

Chronicles of Martin Hewitt: Morrison, Arthur

Chronicles of Melhampton: Oppenheim, E. Phillips

Chronicles of Merry England: Manning, Anne

Chronicles of Rodriguez, The: Dunsany, E.J.M.D.P. *Lord*

Chronicles of St. Tid, The: Phillpotts, Eden

Chronicles of the builders of the Commonwealth: Bancroft, Hubert Howe

Chronicles of the Canongate: Scott, *Sir* Walter

Chronicles of the City of Gotham from the papers of a retired common councilman: Paulding, J.K.

Chronicles of the Fleet Street prison: Rowcroft, Charles

Chronicles of the House of Borgia: (†Baron Corvo), Rolfe, Frederick

Chronicles of the Imp, The: Farnol, J.J.

Chronicles of the St. Lawrence, The: LeMoine, *Sir* J.M.

Chronology of ancient kingdoms, The: Newton, *Sir* Isaac

Chruso-thriambos: Munday, Anthony

Chrysal: Johnstone, Charles

Chrysanaleia: the golden fishing: Munday, Anthony

Chrysold: Jones, H.A.

Chungking diary: Karaka, D.F.

Church, The: Judd, Sylvester

Church and its teaching today, The: Temple, William

Church and nation: Temple, William

Church and social progress, The: †Bowen, Marjorie

Church and state: Haggard, *Sir* H.Rider

Church and the age, The: Inge, W.R.

Church and war, The: Underhill, Evelyn

Church in a series of discourses, The: Judd, Sylvester

Church in bondage, The: Knox, R.A.

Church in the world, The: Inge, W.R.

Church looks forward, The: Temple, William

Church manual of the first Church of Christ Scientist: Eddy, M.B.

Church mouse, The: Levy, Benn W.

Church of Englandism and its catechism examined: Bentham, Jeremy

Church of the Fathers, The: Newman, J.H.

Church on earth, The: Knox, R.A.

Church reform and defence: Hughes, Thomas

Churches quarrel espoused, The: Wise, John

Churches resurrection, The: Cotton, John

Church-history of Britain, The: Fuller, Thomas

Churchill: Rubenstein, Harold F.

Church-membership of children, The: Shepard, Thomas

Chute, The: Halper, Albert

Chymists key, The: Vaughan, Thomas

Cicadas, The: Huxley, Aldous

Cicely: †Graham, Ennis (Molesworth, *Mrs.*)

Cicero, a tragedy of ancient Rome: Sinclair, Upton

Ciceronis Amor: Greene, Robert

Cigarette peril of youth, The: Mee, Arthur

Cigarette-maker's romance, A: Crawford, F.Marion

Cimarron: Ferber, Edna

Cinder Thursday: Palmer, H.E.

Cinderella: Crockett, S.R.

Cinderella: Davis, Richard Harding

Cinderella: Whitman, S.H.

Cinderella in the South: Cripps, A.S.

Cinderella of Skookum Creek: Niven, F.J.

Cinderella's daughter and other sequels and consequences: Erskine, John

Cine of Simbah, The: Macphail, *Sir* Andrew

Cinna the poet: Allen, C.R.

Cinnamon and Angelica: Murry, John Middleton

Cinnamon seed: Basso, Hamilton

Cinque ports, The: (Hueffer), Ford, Ford Madox

CIOPW: Cummings, E.E.

Cipher in the plays, The: Donnelly, Ignatius Loyola

Ciprina: Reynolds, G.

Circe: Bax, Clifford

Circe's garden: Gouldsbury, H.C.

Circé's island: Phillpotts, Eden

Circle, The: Maugham, Somerset

Circle in the water, The: †Bowen, Marjorie

Circle of affection, The: Scott, D.C.

Circling hearths, The: Quinn, R.J.

Circuit rider, The: Eggleston, Edward

Circular billiards: †Carroll, Lewis

Circular respecting memorial studies of St. Mark's Venice: Ruskin, John

Circular saws: Wolfe, Humbert

Circular staircase, The: Rinehart, Mary Roberts

Circum praecordia: Parsons, T.W.

Circumstances: Mitchell, S.W.

Circumstances alter cases: Asche, I.G.

Circumstantial evidence: Wallace, Edgar

Circus, The: Kilmer, Joyce

Circus in the attic, The: Warren, R.P.

Cistercian Saints of England, The: Newman, J.H.

Citadel, The: Cronin, A.J.

Citation and examination of William Shakespeare: Landor, Walter Savage

Cities: Symons, Arthur

Cities advocate, The: Bolton, Edmund

Cities and men: Lewisohn, Ludwig

Cities and sea-coasts and islands: Symons, Arthur

Cities and their stories: Power, Eileen

Cities of Central Italy: Hare, A.J.C.

Cities of Italy: Symons, Arthur

Cities of Northern and Central Italy: Hare, A.J.C.

Cities of Northern Italy: Hare, A.J.C.

Cities of refuge: Gibbs, *Sir* Philip

Cities of Southern Italy and Sicily: Hare, A.J.C.

Cities of the plain, The: Fairfield, S.L.

Cities, plains and people: Durrell, Lawrence

Cities under the sea, The: Timms, E.V.

Citizen, The: Murphy, Arthur

Citizen and Churchman: Temple, William

Citizen of New Salem: Horgan, Paul

Citizen of the world, The: Goldsmith, Oliver

Citizen Tom Paine: Fast, Howard M.

Citizens: Levin, Meyer

Citizens in war and after: Spender, Stephen

Citt and bumpkin: L'Estrange, *Sir* Roger

City, The: Fitch, Clyde

City and suburb: †Trafford, F.G.

City and the dream, The: Raymond, Ernest

City ballads: Carleton, William (McKendree)

City block: Frank, Waldo

City development: Mumford, Lewis

City festivals: Carleton, William (McKendree)

City flag, The: Erskine, John

City in dawn: Allen, Hervey

City in history, The: Mumford, Lewis

City legends: Carleton, William (McKendree)

City looking glass, The: Bird, R.M.

City of Colombo, 1505–1656, The: Perera, Simon

City of comrades, The: †King, Basil

City of departures: Brophy, John

City of dreadful night, The: Kipling, Rudyard

City of dreadful night, The: Thomson, James

City of dream, The: Buchanan, Robert

City of fear, The: Frankau, Gilbert

City of gold, The: Young, Francis Brett

City of illusion, The: Fisher, V.A.

City of libertines, The: Hardy, W.G.

City of masks, The: McCutcheon, G.B.

City of peril, The: Stringer, A.J.A.

City of pleasure, The: Bennett, Arnold

City of refuge, The: Besant, *Sir* Walter

City of Riddle-mee-ree, The: Cross, Zora

City of saints: Burton, *Sir* Richard

City of the Aten, The: Woolley, *Sir* Leonard

City of the plague, The: Wilson, John

City of the silent, The: Simms, W.G.

City of the soul, The: Douglas, *Lord* Alfred

City of the Strait, The: Mulgan, A.E.

City poems: Smith, Alexander

City room and the school room, The: Broun, Heywood

City-dames' petition in the behalfe of the Cavaliers, The: Nevile, Henry

City-heiress, The: Behn, *Mrs.* Afra

City-madam, The: Massinger, Philip

City-ramble, The: Settle, Elkanah

Civic improvement in the little towns: Gale, Zona

Civic patriotism: Gilder, R.W.

Civic theatre, The: Mackaye, Percy

Civil contract, A: Heyer, Georgette

Civil government in the United States: Fiske, John

Civil journey: Jameson, Storm

Civil Service as a profession, The: Trollope, Anthony

Civil Service handbook of English literature, The: Dobson, Henry Austin

Civil services, history and problems: Panikkar, K.M.

Civil war: Dukes, Ashley

Civil war: O'Flaherty, Liam

Civil war in England: Lindsay, Jack

Civile wares: Daniel, Samuel

Civilian into soldier: Lee, J.A.

Civilisation: Bell, Clive

Civilisation before Christianity: Church, Richard William

Civilisation on trial: Toynbee, Arnold

Civilized America: Gratton, Thomas Colley

Civilization in the Buddhist Age, B.C. 320 to A.D. 500: Dutt, R.C.

Civilization without delusion: Clarke, Marcus

Civil-Service reform under the present national administration: Curtis, George William

Civitatis amor: Middleton, Thomas

Claim jumpers, The: White, S.E.

Claims of labour, The: Helps, *Sir* Arthur

Claire Ambler: Tarkington, Booth

Clairvoyante, The: Farjeon, B.L.

Clandestine marriage, The: Colman, George, *the elder*

Clandestine marriage, The: Garrick, David

Clansman, The: Dixon, Thomas

Clara Barron: O'Higgins, H.J.

Clara Hopgood: †Rutherford, Mark

Clara Howard: Brown, C.B.

Clara Morison: Spence, C.H.

Clara Vaughan: Blackmore, R.D.

Clare Drummer: Pritchett, V.S.

Clarel: Melville, Herman

Clarence: Harte, Bret

Clarence: Sedgwick, C.M.

Clarence: Tarkington, Booth

Clarence Fitz-Clarence: Leprohon, R.E.

Clarence King memoirs: Adams, H.B.

Claret drinkers song, The: Oldham, John

Claret-cup, A: Hannay, James

Clari: Payne, J.H.

Clarice: Gillette, William

Clarionet, The: Carleton, William

Clarissa: Richardson, Samuel

Clark Gifford's body: Fearing, Kenneth

Clarke Papers, The: Firth, *Sir* Charles

Clark's field: Herrick, Robert

Clarkton: Fast, Howard M.

Clash, The: Jameson, Storm

Clash by night: Odets, Clifford

Class poems: Lowell, J.R.

Classic Americans: Canby, H.S.

Classical dictionary of the vulgar tongue, A: Grose, Francis

Classical influences in Renaissance literature: Bush, Douglas

Classical studies: Mackail, J.W.

Classical tradition in poetry, The: Murray, Gilbert

Classics and commercials: Wilson, Edmund

Classics and national life, The: Livingstone, Sir Richard

Classics and the man of letters, The: Eliot, T.S.

Classification of insects from embryological data, The: Agassis, J.L.R.

Classification of the sciences, The: Spencer, Herbert

Claud Lovat Fraser: Drinkwater, John

Claude the Colpasteur: Manning, Anne

Claudelle English: Caldwell, Erskine Preston

Claudius the god: Graves, Robert

Claudius the God and his wife Messalina: Graves, Robert

Claverhouse: Mackintosh, Elizabeth

Claverings, The: Trollope, Anthony

Claw and fang: Glanville, Ernest

Clayhanger: Bennett, Arnold

Clean heart, The: Hutchinson, Arthur

Clean sweep, A: Housman, Laurence

Clean wind blowing, A: Ogilvie, W.H.

Clear horizon: Richardson, D.M.

Clear state of the case of Elizabeth Canning: Fielding, Henry

Clear sun-shine of the Gospel, The: Shepard, Thomas

Clear water stream, The: Williamson, Henry

Cleared: Kipling, Rudyard

Cleft stick, The: Greenwood, Walter

Cleg Kelly, Arab of the city: Crockett, S.R.

Clem Voroshilov, the red marshall: Trease, Geoffrey

Clement Marot: Morley, Henry

Clementina: Kelly, Hugh

Clementina: Mason, A.E.W.

Cleo: Beresford, J.D.

Cleomenes, the Spartan heroe: Dryden, John

Cleopatra: Haggard, Sir Henry Rider

Cleopatra in Judaea: Symons, Arthur

Clergyman's daughter, A: †Orwell, George

Clergyman's wife, The: Ritchie, Mrs. A.C.M.

Clergymen of the Church of England: Trollope, Anthony

Clerical error, A: Jones, H.A.

Clerical error: Vulliamy, C.E.

Clerihews complete: Bentley, E.C.

Clever one, The: Wallace, Edgar

Clever stories of many nations rendered in rhyme: Saxe, J.G.

Clever wife, A: Ridge, W. Pett

Clever woman of the family, The: Yonge, C.M.

Cleverest woman in the world, The: Stringer, A.J.A.

Cleverness: Hall, Anna Maria

Clicking of Cuthbert, The: Wodehouse, P.G.

Clif, the naval cadet: Sinclair, Upton

Cliff castles and cave dwellings of Europe: Baring-Gould, S.

Cliff climbers, The: Reid, T.M.

Cliff to the islands, The: Machar, A.M.

Cliff-dwellers, The: Fuller, H.B.

Clifford Sifton in relation to his times: Dafoe, J.W.

Cliffs, The: Doughty, C.M.

Clifton: Combe, William

Clifton Chapel: Newbolt, Sir Henry

Clifton Grove: White, H.K.

Climate and health in Australasia: Bonwick, James

Climate and health in South Africa: Bonwick, James

Climate of love, The: Gibbon, Monk

Climber, The: Benson, E.F.

Climbers, The: Fitch, Clyde William

Climenson, E.J. Elizabeth Montagu, the Queen of the Blue-Stockings: Montagu, Mrs. E.

Clinical applications of hypnosis in dentistry: Shaw, Irwin

Clinton Bradshaw: Thomas, F.W.

Clio, The: Myers, L.H.

Clio: Percival, J.G.

Clio: Trevelyan, G.M.

Clio's protest: Sheridan, Richard Brinsky

Clipper-yacht, The: Ingraham, J.H.

Clippings from Denver Tribune: Field, Eugene

Clive Weston's wedding anniversary: Leprohon, R.E.

Cloak of friendship, The: Housman, Laurence

Clock goes round, The: Brighouse, Harold

Clockmaker, The: Haliburton, T.C.

Clocks, The: Christie, Agatha

Clocks of Rondaine, The: Stockton, F.R.

Cloister and the hearth, The: Reade, Charles

Clondesley: Godwin, William

Clontarf: Dollard, J.B.

Clorinda walks in heaven: Coppard, A.E.

Close chaplet, The: Riding, Laura

Close harmony: Parker, Dorothy

Close harmony: Rice, Elmer

Close of play: Cardus, Neville

Close of play: Gale, Norman R.

Close of the Middle Ages, The: Lodge, Sir Richard

Close quarters: Thirkell, Angela

Close the book: Glaspell, Susan

Closed city (Leningrad), The: Pope-Hennessy, Dame Una

Closed garden, The: Green, Julian

Closed harbour, The: Hanley, James

Closed or open shop? The: Hubbard, Elbert

Closer union: Schreiner, O.E.A.

Closing scene, The: Read, T.B.

Cloth of gold: Aldrich, Thomas Bailey

Cloth of the tempest: Patchen, Kenneth

Clothes: Gill, Eric

Clothing without cloth: Gill, Eric

Cloud: Bridges, Roy

Cloud above the green, The: Gibbs, *Sir* Philip

Cloud across the sun, A: Wingfield, Shiela

Cloud and silver: Lucas, E.V.

Cloud and the silver lining, The: Cammaerts, Emile

Cloud Castle: Thomas, E.E.P.

Cloud cuckoo land: Mitchison, Naomi

Cloud Howe: †Gibbon, L.G.

Clouded hours, The: Percy, Edward

Cloudless May: Jameson, Storm

Clouds, The: Doughty, C.M.

Clouds, The: Gale, Zona

Clouds, Aigeltinger, Russia, etc., The: Williams, W.C.

Clouds and sunshine and art: Reade, Charles

Clouds of witness: Sayers, Dorothy

Clovelly verses: Prichard, K.S.

Cloven foot, The: Braddon, M.E

Cloven foot, The: (†Orpheus C. Kerr), Newell, R.H.

Clover: Coolidge, Susan

Clown of Stratford, The: Squire, *Sir* J.C.

Clown's houses: Sitwell, Edith

Club of queer trades, The: Chesterton, G.K.

Club-book, The: Galt, John

Clue from the stars, A: Phillpotts, Eden

Clue of darkness: Lindsay, Jack

Clue of the new pin, The: Wallace, Edgar

Clue of the silver key, The: Wallace, Edgar

Clue of the twisted candle, The: Wallace, Edgar

Clues of the Caribbees: Stribling, T.S.

Clumber pup: Farjeon, Eleanor

Clung: †Brand, Max

Cluny Brown: Sharp, Margery

Cluny MacPherson: Barr, A.E.H.

Cluster of grapes, A: Mais, S.P.B.

Clutterbuck: Levy, Benn W.

Clyde mystery, The: Lang, Andrew

Clyde: river and firth, The: Munro, Neil

Clyffards of Clyffe, The: Payn, James

Clytemnestra: (†Owen Meredith), Lytton, E.R.B., *Earl*

Coalition, The: Graves, Richard

Coast calendar: Coffin, Robert

Coast of adventure: untamed North Australia: (†Donald Barr), Barrett, C.L.

Coast of Bohemia, The: Howells, W.D.

Coast of Bohemia, The: Page, T.N.

Coast of incense, The: Stark, F.M.

Coast of pleasure, The: Richards, Grant

Coastguard's secret, The: Hichens, Robert

Coastlanders, The: Cronin, B.C.

Coat of arms, The: Wallace, Edgar

Coat of many colours, A: Read, *Sir* Herbert

Coat without seam, The: Baring, Maurice

Cobbler's dream: Dickens, Monica

Cobbler's shop, The: Uttley, Alison

Cobler, The: Dibdin, Charles

Cobwebs: Bierce, Ambrose

Cobwebs from an empty shell: Bierce, Ambrose

Cobwebs of criticism: Caine, *Sir* T.H. Hall

Cochise of Arizona: La Farge, Oliver

Cochran's 1930 revue: Nichols, J.B.

Cock Lane and common-sense: Lang, Andrew

Cock pit: Cozzens, James Gould

Cock Robin: Barry, Philip

Cock Robin: Rice, Elmer

Cockadoodle dandy: O'Casey, Sean

Cockcrow: †Onions, Oliver

Cockleshell, The: Lynd, Robert

Cocks and hens: Munro, C.K.

Cocktail party, The: Eliot, T.S.

Cocktail time: Wodehouse, P.G.

Coconut Island: Gibbings, Robert

Cod fisheries, The: Innis, H.A.

Cod head, The: Williams, W.C.

Codd's last case: Herbert, *Sir* A.P.

Code of a herdsman, The: Lewis, P.Wyndham

Code of the West: Grey, Zane

Code of the Woosters, The: Wodehouse, P.G.

Codification proposals: Bentham, Jeremy

Coelebs in search of a wife: More, Hannah

Coelum Britannicum: Carew, Thomas

Coffee and repartee: Bangs, John Kendrick

Coffins for two: Starrett, Vincent

Coin collector, The: Hazlitt, William Carew

Coinage of the European Continent, The: Hazlitt, William Carew

Coincidence: Brighouse, Harold

Cola monti: Craik, *Mrs.* Dinah

Colasterion: Milton, John

Cold Comfort Farm: Gibbons, Stella

Cold Cotswolds, The: Masefield, John

Cold green element, The: Layton, Irving

Cold harbour: Young, Francis Brett

Cold steel: Shiel, M.P.

Cold table: a book of recipes, The: Simpson, H. de G.

Cold tongue: Glover, Denis

Cold war, a study in U.S. foreign policy, The: Lippmann, Walter

Cold war and the income tax, The: Wilson, Edmund

Cold wind and the warm, The: Behrman, S.N.

Colde tearme, The: Taylor, John

Coldknuckles: Gibson, Wilfred

Coleridge: Garnett, Richard

Coleridge: Traill, H.D.

Coleridge and S.T.C.: Potter, Stephen

Coleridge as critic: Read, *Sir* Herbert

Coleridge on imagination: Richards, I.A.

Coleridge, Shelley, Goethe: Calvert, George Henry

Coleridge's fellow-Grecian: Blunden, Edmund

Coleridge's miscellaneous criticism: Coleridge, S. T.

Coleridge's Shakespearean criticism: Coleridge, S. T.

Colin: Benson, E.F.

Colin Clout's calendar: Allen, Grant

Colin Clouts come home againe: Spenser, Edmund

Colin II: Benson, E.F.

Colin's mistakes: written in imitation of Spenser's style: Prior, Matthew

Collaborators, The: (†Q), Quiller-Couch, Sir A.

Collected dog stories: Kipling, Rudyard

Collected parodies: Squire, Sir J.C.

Collected poems: Seymour, W.K.

Collected sporting verse: Ogilvie, W.H.

Collected stories: Faulkner, William

Collected works Earl of Rochester: Hayward, J.D.

Collection of aphorisms, A: More, Henry

Collection of curious discourses by eminent antiquaries, A: Hearne, Thomas

Collection of curious travels and voyages, A: Ray, John

Collection of emblemes, A: Wither, George

Collection ot English proverbs: Ray, John

Collection of English words not generally used, A: Ray, John

Collection of epigrams, A: Oldys, William

Collection of epistles, A: Fox, George

Collection of essays and fugitive writings on moral, historical, political and literary subjects, A: Webster, Noah

Collection of offices or forms of prayer, A: Taylor, Jeremy

Collection of original poems, by Scotch gentlemen, A: Boswell, James

Collection of polemical and moral discourses, A: Taylor, Jeremy

Collection of political tracts, A: Bolingbroke, Henry St. John

Collection of psalm tunes, A: Hopkinson, Francis

Collection of the historie of England: Daniel, Samuel

Collection of the writings hitherto extant, A: Ward, Edward

Collection two: †O'Connor, Frank

Collections and notes: Hazlitt, William Carew

Collections of the Massachusetts Historical Society: Belknap, Jeremy

Collections upon the lives of the reformers and most eminent ministers of the Church of Scotland: Wodrow, Robert

Collector, The: Tuckerman, H.T.

Collector's craft, The: †Machen, Arthur

Collector's whatnot, The: Roberts, Kenneth

College and nation: Carleton, William (McKendree)

College Bible: Foerster, Norman

College days: Leacock, Stephen

College education: Calvert, G.H.

College sons and college fathers: Canby, H.S.

Collegians, The: Griffin, Gerald

Collier's Friday night, A: Lawrence, D.H.

Collingwood: Russell, W.C.

Collins's guide to English parish churches: Betjeman, John

Colloquial element in English poetry, The: Day Lewis, C.

Colloquial language in literature: Abercrombie, Lascelles

Colloquies of Edward Osborne, The: Manning, Anne

Colne Valley cloth: Bentley, Phyllis

Coloman: Percy, Edward

Colombe's birthday: Browning, Robert

Colombine: McCrae, Hugh

Colonel Carter of Cartersville: Smith, F.H.

Colonel Carter's Christmas: Smith, F.H.

Colonel Clipsham's calendar: Hale, E.E.

Colonel Dunwoodie, millionaire: Baker, W.M.

Colonel George of Mount Vernon: Thomas, Augustus

Colonel Guiney and the Ninth Massachusetts: Guiney, L.I.

Colonel Julian: Bates, H.E.

Colonel Lawrence: the man behind the legend: Liddell Hart, B.

Colonel Pluckett: Sullivan, Alan

Colonel Quaritch, V.C.: Haggard, Sir Henry Rider

Colonel Satan: Tarkington, Booth

Col. Smith: Mason, A.E.W.

Colonel Starbottle's client: Harte, Bret

Colonel Thorpe's scenes in Arkansas: Thorpe, T.B.

Colonel Wotherspoon: †Bridie, James

Colonel's daughter, The: Aldington, Richard

Colonel's dream, The: Chestnutt, C.W.

Colonial dames and good wives: Earle, A.M.

Colonial days in Old New York: Earle, A.M.

Colonial memories: Barker, M.A.

Colonial merchants and the American revolution, The: Schlesinger, A.M.

Colonial mind, The: Parrington, V.L.

Colonial reformer, A: †Boldrewood, Rolf

Colonization of the New World: Fiske, John

Color: Cullen, Countée

Color and democracy: colonies and peace: Dubois, William

Color curtain, a report on the Bandung Conference: Wright, Richard

Color of a great city, The: Dreiser, Theodore

Color studies: Janvier, T.A.

Çolorado: Bromfield, Louis

Colorado, a summer trip: Taylor, Bayard

Colored soldier, The: Hughes, J.L.

Colors of life: Eastman, Max

Colossal idea, A: Gilbert, *Sir* W.S.

Colossus, The: Read, O.P.

Colossus of Arcadia, The: Oppenheim, E. Phillips

Colossus of Maroussi, The: Miller, Henry

Colour blind: Mais, S.P.B.

Colour in composition: Baring-Gould, S.

Colour of life, The: Meynell, Alice

Colour scheme: Marsh, Ngaio Edith

Colour sense, The: Allen, Grant

Colour studies in Paris: Symons, Arthur

Coloured countries, The: Waugh, Alec

Coloured garden: Chattopadhyaya, H.

Coloured lands, The: Chesterton, G.K.

Coloured spectacles: Niven, F.J.

Colours of a great city: Ghose, S.N.

Colours of the day, The: Rukeyser, Muriel

Columbian daughter, The: Rowson, S.H.

Columbine: Mackenzie, *Sir* Compton

Columbine: Meynell, Viola

Columbus: Ensor, *Sir* R.C.K.

Columbus: Morton, Thomas

Columbus: Sabatini, R.

Columbus and the New World: Derleth, A.W.

Columbus and the Spanish discovery of America: Adams, C.F.

Columella: Graves, Richard

Column of dust, The: Underhill, Evelyn

Colville of the Guards: Grant, James

Colvins and their friends, The: Lucas, E.V.

Combat betweene conscience and

covetousnesse, in the minde of man, The: Barnfield, Richard

Combat of the Thirty from a Breton lay of the fourteenth century, The: Ainsworth, William Harrison

Combat report: Bolitho, H.H.

Comber cove: MacDonald, W.P.

Combined maze, The: Sinclair, May

Come and get it: Ferber, Edna

Come and see: Meynell, Wilfred

Come a-singing! Barbeau, C.M.

Come back, Paul: Rukeyser, Muriel

Come back to Erin: O'Faolain, Sean

Come Christmas: Farjeon, Eleanor

Come forth: Ward, E.S.

Come hither: De la Mare, Walter

Come home at last: Lindsay, Jack

Come in spinner: Cusack, E.D.

Come, live with me and be my love: Buchanan, R.W.

Come love, come death: Mais, S.P.B.

Come my beloved: Buck, Pearl

Come, night: end, day!: Jones, Jack

Come of age: †Dane, Clemence

Come on, The: Rhodes, E.M.

Come on Buck: Read, O.P.

Come on Jeeves: Wodehouse, P.G.

Come tell me how you live: Christie, Agatha

Come to the ball: Herbert, *Sir* A.P.

Come to the bower: Mottram, R.H.

Come to think of it: Chesterton, G.K.

Come true: De la Roche, Mazo

Come unto these yellow sands: Woods, M.L.

Come with me: Kennedy, Margaret

Comedians, The: Greene, Graham

Comedians all: Nathan, G.J.

Comedie of errors, The: Shakespeare, William

Comedies and tragedies: Beau-

mont, Francis and John Fletcher

Comedies of courtship: Hawkins, A.H.

Comediettas and farces: Morton, J.M.

Comedy: Palmer, J.L.

Comedy and conscience after the restoration: Krutch, J.W.

Comedy and tragedy: Gilbert, *Sir* W.S.

Comedy of conscience, A: Mitchell, S.W.

Comedy of good and evil, A: Hughes, R.A.W.

Comedy of manners, The: Palmer, J.L.

Comedy of masks, A: Dowson, E.C.

Comedy of terrors, A: De Mille, James

Comedy of terrors: (†Michael Innes), Stewart, J.I.M.

Comedy royal, A: Phillpotts, Eden

Comes the reckoning: Lockhart, *Sir* Robert

Comet, The: Beddoes, T.L.

Cometh up as a flower: Broughton, Rhoda

Comfort: Stewart, D.O.

Comfort of lovers: Hawes, Stephen

Comfort of the hills, The: Mitchell, S.W.

Comfort Pease and her gold ring: Freeman, Mary

Comfortless memory: Baring, Maurice

Comic almanack, The: Mayhew, Augustus Septimus

Comic almanack for 1848, The: Mayhew, Horace

Comic alphabets: Partridge, Eric

Comic artist, The: Glaspell, Susan

Comic dramas: Edgeworth, Maria

Comic tales and sketches: Thackeray, W.M.

Comical gallant, The: Dennis, John

Comical lovers, The: Cibber, Colley

Comical revenge, The: Etherege or Etheredge, *Sir* George

Comicall historie of Alphonsus King of Aragon, The: Greene, Robert

Coming and going: Gibson, Wilfred

Coming campaign, The: Oliphant, Laurence

Coming down the Seine: Gibbings, Robert

Coming down the Wye: Gibbings, Robert

Coming forth by day, The: Hillyer, Robert

Coming forth by day of Osiris Jones, The: Aiken, Conrad

Coming of age: Deutsch, Babette

Coming of age in Samoa: Mead, Margaret

Coming of Bill, The: Wodehouse P.G.

Coming of Christ, The: Masefield, John

Coming of Gabrielle, The: Moore, George

Coming of love, The: Watts-Dunton, W.T.

Coming of the fairies, The: Doyle, *Sir* Arthur Conan

Coming of the Lord, The: Millin, Sarah Gertrude

Coming of the musket, The: Finlayson, Roderick

Coming of the pakeha: Finlayson, Roderick

Coming out: Porter, A.M. and Jane Porter

Coming race, The: Lytton, Bulwer *Lord*

Coming revolution in Great Britain, The: Gould, Gerald

Coming struggle for Latin-America, The: Beals, Carleton

Coming struggle for power, The: Strachey, John

Coming terror, The: Buchanan, R.W.

Coming tests with Russia, The: Lippmann, Walter

Coming to London: Lehmann, John

Coming up for air: †Orwell, George

Coming up the road: Bacheller, Irving

Command: McFee, William

Command in the morning: Buck, Pearl

Command is forward, The: Woollcott, A.H.

Commandant, The: Glanville, Ernest

Commando: Reitz, Deneys

Commemorative ode for the opening of Parliament at Canberra: Stephens, A.G.

Commemorative tribute, to Francis Hopkinson Smith: Thomas, Augustus

Commemorative tribute to Henry Adams: More, P.E.

Commemorative tribute to James Ford Rhodes: Grant, Robert

Commemorative tribute to James Whitcomb Riley: Garland, Hamlin

Commemorative tribute to Sherman: Garland, Hamlin

Commemorative tributes to: Beveridge: Tarkington, Booth

Commencement address: Canfield, Dorothy

Commentaries of Caesar, The: Trollope, Anthony

Commentaries on living: Krishnamurti, Jiddu

Commentaries on the life and reign of Charles the First, king of England: D'Israeli, Isaac

Commentary, A: Galsworthy, John

Commentary of the psalms, A: Neale, J.M.

Commentary on Macaulay's history of England, A: Firth, *Sir* Charles

Commentary on memoirs of Mr. Fox: Landor, Walter Savage

Commentary on Mr. Pope's essay on Man, A: Warburton, William

Commentary on the Gospels, A: Knox, R.A.

Commentary on the writing of Henrik Ibsen, A: Boyesen, H.H.

Comments: Nicolson, Hon. *Sir* Harold

Comments of Juniper, The: Housman, Laurence

Comments on birth control: Mitchison, Naomi

Comments on the commentators of Shakespeare: Pye, H.J.

Commerce of Boston, The: Morison, S.E.

Commerce of the Prairies: Gregg, Josiah

Commercial empire of the St. Lawrence, The: Creighton, D.G.

Commercium: Macartney, Frederick

Commiserating epistle to James Lowther, Earl of Lonsdale, A: †Pindar, Peter

Commissioner, The: James, George Payne Rainsford

Committed to his charge: Lizars, K.M. and Robina Lizars

Committees: Bentley, Phyllis

Commodore, The: Forester, C.S.

Commodore Hornblower: Forester, C.S.

Commodus: Wallace, Lew

Common adventures: †O'Sullivan, Seumas

Common asphodel, The: Graves, Robert

Common chord, The: †O'Connor, Frank

Common day, The: (Stephen Southwold), †Bell, Neil

Common enemy, A: Beresford, J.D.

Common faith, A: Dewey, John

Common glory, The: Green, Paul

Common heart, The: Horgan, Paul

Common law, The: Chambers, R.W.

Common lot, The: Herrick, Robert

Common misquotations: Pearson, Hesketh

Common people, The: Cole, G.D.H.

Common people, 1746–1946, The: Postgate, Raymond

Common pursuit, The: Leavis, F.R.

Common Reader, The: Woolf, Virginia

Common sense about drama: Strong, L.A.G.

Common sense about India: Panikkar, K.M.

Common sense about poetry: Strong, L.A.G.

Common sense about the war: Shaw, G.B.

Common sense about women: Higginson, T.W.

Common sense and nuclear warfare: Russell, Bertrand

Common sense ethics, Joad: C.E.M.

Common sense in religion: Clarke, J.F.

Common sense of municipal trading, The: Shaw, G.B.

Common sense of science, The: Bronowski, J.

Common sense of war and peace, The: Wells, H.G.

Common sense theology: Joad, C.E.M.

Common touch, The: Agate, J.E.

Common way, The: Deland, Margaret

Common wayside flowers: Miller, Thomas

Common Weal, The: Fisher, H.A.L.

Common whore with all these graces grac'd, A: Taylor, John

Commonplace: Rossetti, C.G.

Commonsense and morality: Mannin, Ethel

Commonsense and the adolescent: Mannin, Ethel

Commonsense and the child: Mannin, Ethel

Commonsense of world peace, The: Wells, H.G.

Commonweal, The: Swinburne, A.C.

Commonwealth at war, The: Pollard, A.F.

Communication to my friends, A: Moore, George

Communication trench, The: Bird, W.R.

Communication versus expression in art: Abercrombie, Lascelles

Communism: Burton, J.H.

Communism: Laski, Harold

Communist world and ours: Lippmann, Walter

Community drama: Mackaye, Percy

Community farm: Murry, John Middleton

Companion to Mr. Wells' outline of history, A: Belloc, Hilaire

Companion to Shakespeare studies, The: Barker, Harley Granville

Companion to the guide and a guide to the companion, A: Warton, Thomas

Companion to the heart of the Andes, A: Winthrop, Theodore

Companion to the Iliad: Leaf, Walter

Companion to the railway edition of Lord Campbell's life of Bacon: Spedding, James

Companions, The: Dixon, Thomas

Companions of fortune: Trease, Geoffrey

Companions of my solitude: Helps, Sir Arthur

Companions of Pickle, The: Lang, Andrew

Companions on the trail: Garland, Hamlin

Company I've kept, The: †McDiarmid, Hugh

Company parade: Jameson, Storm

Comparative dictionary of the languages of India and Asia: Hunter, Sir W.W.

Comparative view of the new plan of education, A: Trimmer, Mrs. Sarah

Comparing notes: a dialogue across a generation: Toynbee, Arnold and Philip Toynbee

Compassion: Hardy, Thomas

Compendious introduction unto the pistle to the Romayns, A: Tyndale, William

Compendious lexicon of the Hebrew language: Moore, C.C.

Compendium dictionary of the English language, A: Webster, Noah

Competition v. co-operation: Lodge, Sir Oliver

Competition wallah, The: Trevelyan, Sir G.O.

Complaint, The: Young, Edward

Complaint of Henry Duke of Buckingham, The: Sackville, Thomas

Complaint of M. Tenterhooke, the projector, The: Taylor, John

Complaint of Mary, The: Lydgate, John

Complaint of poetrie, for the death of liberalitie, The: Barnfield, Richard

Complaint of the Black Knight, The: Lydgate, John

Complaints: Spenser, Edmund

Complaints of the poor people of England, The: Dyer, George

Complaisant lover, The: Greene, Graham

Complaynt d'amours: Chaucer, Geoffrey

Complaynte and testament of a popinjay which lyeth sore wounded, The: Lindsay, Sir David

Compleat angler, The: Cotton, Charles

Compleat angler, The: Walton, Izaak

Compleat bachelor, The: †Onions, Oliver

Compleat gamester, The: Cotton, Charles

Compleat gentleman, The: Peacham, Henry

Compleat husbandman, The: Markham, Gervase

Compleat view of the manners, customs, arms, habits, etc. of the inhabitants of England, A: Strutt, Joseph

Compleat wangler, The: Maltby, H.F.

Compleint to his Lady: Chaucer, Geoffrey

Complete catalogue of all the dramatic pieces in the English language, A: Cave, Edward

Complete collection of genteel and ingenious conversation, A: Swift, Jonathan

Complete concordance to the Holy Scriptures, A: Cruden, Alexander

Complete correspondence and works of Charles Lamb, The: Sala, G.A.H.

Complete English tradesman, The: Defoe, Daniel

Complete farriar, The: Markham, Gervase

Complete guide to the lakes: Martineau, Harriet

Complete history of England, A: Smollett, Tobias

Complete history of the Bastable family, The: Nesbit, Edith

Complete history of the English stage, A: Dibdin, Charles

Complete human boy, The: Phillpotts, Eden

Complete key to the last new farce, The what d'ye call it, A: Theobald, Lewis

Complete life: Erskine, John

Complete manual for the young sportsmen, The: Herbert, H.W.

Complete me and Gus, The: Anthony, Frank S.

Complete nonsense of Edward Lear, The: Jackson, Holbrook

Complete view of the dress and habits of the people of England, A: Strutt, Joseph

Complete works of Artemus Ward: (†Eli Perkins), Landon, Melville

Complete works of Geoffrey Chaucer, The: Skeat, W.W.

Complex vision, The: Powys, John Cowper

Compleynt of Venus and Mars: Chaucer, Geoffrey

Compleynt to his Purs: Chaucer, Geoffrey

Compleynt unto pite: Chaucer, Geoffrey

Complimentary epistle to James Bruce, Esq., A: †Pindar, Peter

Composition of rhetoric for schools: Herrick, Robert

Composition as explanation: Stein, Gertrude

Compromise: Gow, Ronald

Compromise of the King of the Golden Isles, The: Dunsany, Lord E.J.M.D.P.

Compromises: Repplier, Agnes

Compton Friars: Manning, Anne

Compulsion: Levin, Meyer

Comrade, O Comrade: Mannin, Ethel

Comrades: Dixon, Thomas

Comrades: Ward, E.S.

Comrades for the Charter: Trease, Geoffrey

Comrades of the trails: Roberts, T.G.

Comte, Mill and Spencer: Watson, John

Comte's philosophy of the sciences: Lewes, George Henry

Conan Doyle: Pearson, Hesketh

Conceited doll, The: Mackenzie, Sir Compton

Conceited letters newlie laid open: Breton, Nicholas

Conceived in liberty (Hunger no more): Fast, Howard M.

Concentrated New England: Roberts, Kenneth

Concept of a person, The: Ayer, A.J.

Concept of freedom, The: †Caudwell, Christopher

Concept of nature, The: Whitehead, A.N.

Conception of God, The: Royce, Josiah

Conception of immortality, The: Royce, Josiah

Concerning a vow: Broughton, Rhoda

Concerning a woman of sin: Hecht, Ben

Concerning all of us: Higginson, T.W.

Concerning man's origin: Keith, Sir Arthur

Concerning men: Craik, Mrs. Dianah

Concerning Peter Jackson and others: Frankau, Gilbert

Concerning slang: Hubbard, Elbert

Concerning Spencer: Digby, Sir Kenelm

Concerning spiritualism: Massey, Gerald

Concerning the eccentricities of Cardinal Pirelli: Firbank, Ronald

Concerning the inner life: Underhill, Evelyn

Concerning the nature of things: Bragg, Sir W.H.

Concerning the oldest English literature: MacMechan, A.M.

Concerning the relations of Great Britain, Spain and Portugal: Wordsworth, William

Concessions: (Sydney Schiff), †Hudson, Stephen

Conchologist's first book, The: Poe, Edgar Allen

Concise account of North America, A: Rogers, Robert

Concise American competition and rhetoric: Davidson, Donald

Concise English grammar with exercises, A: Kittredge, G.L.

Concise etymological dictionary: Weekley, Ernest

Concise etymological dictionary of the English language, A: Skeat, W.W.

Concise history of modern painting, A: Read, Sir Herbert

Concise history of modern sculpture, A: Read, Sir Herbert

Concise Oxford dictionary of current English: Fowler, H.W.

Concise usage and abusage, The: Partridge, Eric

Concluding: Green, Henry

Concord days: Alcott, A.B.

Concord lectures on philosophy: Alcott, A.B.

Concord rebel, a life of Henry D. Thoreau: Derleth, A.W.

Concubine, The: Mickle, W.J.

Condemned, The: Fausset, Hugh

Condemned playground, The: Connolly, Cyril

Condensed geography and history of the western states, A: Flint, Timothy

Condensed novels: Harte, Bret

Condition of Britain, The: Cole, G.D.H.

Condition of labor, The: George, Henry

Condition of man, The: Mumford, Lewis

Conditional justification of war, A: Temple, William

Condor and the cows, The: Isherwood, Christopher

Conduct is fate: Bury, *Lady* C.S.M.

Conduct of life, The: Mumford, Lewis

Conduct of the Allies, The: Swift, Jonathan

Confederacy, The: Green, Paul

Confederacy, The: Vanbrugh, *Sir* John

Confederate portraits: Bradford, Gamaliel

Confederates, The: Harwood, H.M.

Confederation considered in relation to the interests of the Empire: Howe, Joseph

Conference, The: Churchill, Charles

Conference at Cold Comfort Farm: Gibbons, Stella

Confessio Amantis (trn.): Caxton, William

Confessio Amantis: Gower, John

Confessio amantis: Logan, J.D.

Confessio juvenis: Hughes, R.A.W.

Confession, The: Rinehart, Mary Roberts

Confession: Simms, W.G.

Confession of my faith, A: Bunyan, John

Confessional: Harris, J.T.

Confessions: Symons, Arthur

Confessions and impressions: Mannin, Ethel

Confessions of a beachcomber, The: Banfield, E.J.

Confessions of a collector, The: Hazlitt, William Carew

Confessions of a detective: Lewis, A.H.

Confessions of a frivolous girl, The: Grant, Robert

Confessions of a journalist: Lawlor, P.A.

Confessions of a justified sinner: Hogg, James

Confessions of a loafer, The: Turner, H.G.

Confessions of a story writer: Gallico, Paul

Confessions of a thug: Taylor, P.M.

Confessions of a Unionist: Stevenson, R.L.

Confessions of a water patient: Lytton, E.G.E.B. *Ist baron*

Confessions of a wife: Ward, E.S.

Confessions of a young man: Moore, George

Confessions of Alphonse: Pain, B.E.O.

Confessions of an elderly gentleman, The: Blessington, Marguerite

Confessions of an elderly lady, The: Blessington, Marguerite

Confessions of an English opium eater: De Quincey, Thomas

Confessions of an Etonian, The: Rowcroft, Charles

Confessions of an immigrant's daughter: Salverson, L.G.

Confessions of an inquiring spirit: Coleridge, S.T.

Confessions of Claude, The: Fawcett, Edgar

Confessions of Con Cregan, the Irish Gil Blas: Lever, C.J.

Confessions of Fitz-Boodle, The: Thackeray, W.M.

Confessions of Harry Lorrequer, The: Lever, C.J.

Confessions of two brothers: Powys, John Cowper and L.C. Powys

Confidence: James, Henry

Confidence-man, The: Melville, Herman

Confident morning: Gielgud, Val

Confident tomorrow, A: Matthews, J.B.

Confident years, The: Brooks, Van Wyck

Confidential agent, The: Greene, Graham

Confidential agent, A: Payn, James

Confidential clerk, The: Eliot, T.S.

Conflict, The: Braddon, M.E.

Conflict: Malleson, Miles

Conflict, The: Phillips, D.G.

Conflict: Soutar, William

Conflict: Timms, E.V.

Conflict of European and Eastern Algonkian cultures, 1504–1700, The: Baily, A.G.

Conflicts: Namier, *Sir* Lewis

Conflicts in American public opinion: White, W.A.

Confounding of Camelia, The: Sedgwick, D.A.

Confucius saw Nancy: Lin Yu-T'ang

Confusion: Cozzens, J.G.

Confutacyon of Tyndales answere, The: More, *Sir* Thomas

Confutation of unwritten verities, A: Cranmer, Thomas

Congal: Fergusson, *Sir* Samuel

Congo, The: Lindsay, N.V.

Congo and coasts of Africa, The: Davis, R.H.

Congo song: Cloete, E.F.S.G.

Congratulatory poem on his Highness the Prince of Orange his coming into England, A: Shadwell, Thomas

Congratulatory poem on the new Parliament, A: Tate, Nahum

Congratulatory poem to her sacred Majesty Queen Mary, A: Behn, *Mrs.* Afra

Congratulatory poem to Prince George of Denmark, A: Tate, Nahum

Congratulatory poem to the most illustrious Queen Mary upon her arrival in England, A: Shadwell, Thomas

Congress canvassed, The: Seabury, Samuel

Congress of Vienna, The: Nicolson, Hon. *Sir* Harold

Congressional government: Wilson, Woodrow

Coningsby: Brydges, *Sir* S.E.

Coningsby: Disraeli, Benjamin

Coniston: Churchill, Winston

Conjectures on original composition in a letter to the author of Sir Charles Grandison: Young, Edward

Conjure woman, The: Chestnutt, C.W.

Conjuror's house: White, S.E.

Connecticut Yankee: Cross, W.L.

Connecticut Yankee in King Arthur's Court, A: (†Mark Twain), Clemens, S.L.

Connecticut's part in the Federal Constitution: Fiske, John

Connecting door, The: Heppenstall, Rayner

Connemara journal: Mannin, Ethel

Connexions between Ancient Egypt and Russia: Murray, Margaret

Connoisseur, The: Colman, George, *the elder*

Connoisseur, The: De la Mare, Walter

Connoisseur's case, A: (†Michael Innes), Stewart, J.I.M.

Conquer: Masefield, John

Conquered, The: Mitchison, Naomi

Conquering hero, The: Gibbon, J.M.

Conquering hero, The: Monkhouse, A.N.

Conqueror, The: Atherton, Gertrude

Conqueror, The: Heyer, Georgette

Conquerors, The: †Hyde, Robin

Conquerors of the New World and their bondsmen; the events which led to Negro slavery, The: Helps, *Sir* Arthur

Conquest, The: Bedford-Jones, Henry

Conquest of Canaan, The: Tarkington, Booth

Conquest of China, The: Settle, Elkanah

Conquest of civilisation, The: Breasted, J.H.

Conquest of death, The: Murry, John Middleton

Conquest of fear, The: †King, Basil

Conquest of Granada by the Spaniards, The: Dryden, John

Conquest of happiness, The: Russell, Bertrand

Conquest of New France, The: Wrong, G.M.

Conquest of New Granada, The: Cunninghame Graham, Robert

Conquest of Scinde, The: Napier, *Sir* W.F.P.

Conquest of the earth, The: Mitchell, J.L.

Conquest of the Maya, The: Mitchell, J.L.

Conquest of the river Plate, The: Cunninghame Graham, Robert Bontine

Conquest of time, The: Wells, H.G.

Conquista of Queyroz, The: Perera, Simon

Conquistador: Gerould, Katharine

Conquistador: MacLeish, Archibald

Conquistador, American fantasia: Guedalla, Philip

Conquistadors in North American history: Horgan, Paul

Conrad and the reporters: Morley, C.D.

Conrad in quest of his youth: Merrick, Leonard

Conscience of the rich, The: Snow, C.P.

Conscientious stranger, The: Clarke, Marcus

Conscious lovers, The: Steele, *Sir* Richard

Consciousness and unconsciousness: Lewes, George Henry

Conscript mother, The: Herrick, Robert

Consecration of churches, The: Hannay, J.O.

Consequences: †Delafield, E.M.

Consequences: Rubenstein, Harold, F.

Conservation of wild life in Central and East Africa: Huxley, *Sir* Julian

Consider her ways: Grove, F.P.

Consider your verdict: Derleth, A.W.

Consideration of Thackeray, A: Saintsbury, George

Consideration on the best means of affording immediate relief to the operative classes in the manufacturing districts: Ainsworth, Harrison

Considerations and proposals in order to the regulation of the press: L'Estrange, *Sir* Roger

Considerations on behalf of the colonists, in a letter to a noble lord: Otis, James

Considerations on pure wisdom and human policy: Woolman, John

Considerations on representative government: Mill, John Stuart

Considerations on the copyright question addressed to an American friend: Collins, Wilkie

Considerations on the currency and banking systems of the United States: Gallatin, Albert

Considerations on the injustice and impolicy of punishing murder by death: Rush, Benjamin

Considerations on the true harmony of mankind: Woolman, John

Considerations touching the likeliest means to remove hirelings out of the Church: Milton, John

Considerations upon two bills sent down from the R— H— the H— of L— to the H—ble H— of C— relating to the clergy of I******d: Swift, Jonathan

Consolate giantess, A: Janvier, T.A.

Consolatory poem to Lord Cutts, A: Tate, Nahum

Consort, The: Duncan, S.J.

Conspiracie, and tragedie of Charles Duke of Byron, Marshall of France, The: Chapman, George

Conspiracy of kings, The: Barlow, Joel

Conspirators, The: Chambers, R.W.

Conspirators: Oppenheim, E.Phillips

Conspirators, The: Prokosch, Frederic

Constab ballads: McKay, Claude

Constable de Bourbon, The: Ainsworth, Harrison

Constable of France, The: Grant James

Astable of the Tower, The: Coninsworth, Harrison

Constance Herbert: Jewsbury, George

Constance Markievicz: a biography: O'Faolain, Sean

Constance Trescot: Mitchell, Somerset

Constancia herself: Widdemer, Margaret

Constant couple, The: Farquhar, George

Constant image, The: Davenport, Marcia

Constant, maid, The: Shirley, James

Constant nymph, The: Kennedy, Margaret

Constant wife, The: Maugham, Somerset

Constantine the Great: Lee, Nathaniel

Constantinople: Crawford, Francis Marion

Constitution for the Socialist commonwealth of Great Britain, A: Webb, Beatrice and Sidney Webb

Constitutional code for the use of all nations and all governments professing liberal opinions: Bentham, Jeremy

Constitutional government in the United States: Wilson, Woodrow

Constitutional history of England from the accession of Henry VII to the death of George II, The: Hallam, Henry

Constitutional history of England, its origin and development, The: Stubbs, William

Constitutional law and history of New Zealand: Hight, James

Constitutional point, A: Thomas, Augustus

Constitutions of the museum Minervae, The: Kynaston, Sir Francis

Constrained attitudes: Colby, F.M.

Constructive theme writing: Chase, M.E.

Consul, The: Davis, R.H.

Consumers' co-operative movement, The: Webb, Beatrice and Sidney Webb

Contango: Hilton, James

Contarini Fleming: Disraeli, Benjamin

Contemplations: Bradstreet, Anne

Contemplations: Hubbard, Elbert

Contemplations of God in the Kosmos: Agassis, J.L.R.

Contemplations upon the principall passages of the holy story: Hall, Joseph

Contemplatist, The: Cunningham, John

Contemporaries: Higginson, T.W.

Contemporaries: Rothenstein, Sir William

Contemporaries and snobs: Riding, Laura

Contemporaries of Shakespeare, The: Swinburne, A.C.

Contemporary American authors: Squire, Sir J.C.

Contemporary American history, 1877–1913: Beard, C.A.

Contemporary American novelists, 1900–1920: Van Doren, Carl

Contemporary British art: Read, Sir Herbert

Contemporary capitalism: Strachey, John

Contemporary fiction and the high school teacher of English: Van Doren, Carl

Contemporary portraits: Marris, J.T.

Contemporary Scottish studies: †McDiarmid, Hugh

Contemporary techniques of poetry: Graves, Robert

Contemporary theatre, The: Agate, J.E.

Content: Ramsay, Allen

Contention for honour and riches, A: Shirley, James

Contention of Ajax and Ulysses, The: Shirley, James

Contexts of criticism: Levin, Harry

Continental, The: Paulding, J.K.

Continental coach holiday: Mais, S.P.B.

Continental Op, The: Hammett, S.D.

Continual dew: Betjeman, John

Continuation of Early lessons: Edgeworth, Maria

Continuation of Lingard's history: Belloc, Hilaire

Continuation of the complete history of England: Smollett, Tobias

Continue: freight of dreams: Devaney, J.M.

Continuities in cultural evolution: Mead, Margaret

Continuity: Lodge, Sir Oliver

Continuity of literature, The: Gosse, Sir Edmund

Contraband: Whyte-Melville, G.J.

Contraband war: Shiel, M.P.

Contrary experience, The: Read, Sir Herbert

Contrast, The: Glyn, Elinor

Contrast, The: Hildreth, Richard

Contrast, The: Tyler, Royall

Contrast (between Europe and America), The: Belloc, Hilaire

Contribution of ancient Greece to modern life, The: Dickinson, G.L.

Contribution to the Greenock calamity fund, A: Galt, John

Contributions to early English literature: Halliwell, J.O.

Contributions to Oriental literature: D'Alwis, James

Contributions to the Cambridge Modern History: Fisher, H.A.L.

Contributions to the Galaxy, 1868–1871: Clemens, S.L.

Contributions to the Edinburgh Review: Francis, Lord Jeffrey

Contributions to the natural history of the United States of America: Agassis, J.L.R.

Contrivances, The: Carey, Henry

Control of life: Sutherland, H.G.

Controversie concerning liberty of conscience in matters of religion, The: Cotton, John

Convalescent, The: Willis, N.P.

Convenient army, The: Heyer, Georgette

Convent, The: Winter, William

Convention and revolt in poetry: Lowes, J.L.

Convention Bill, The: †Pindar, Peter

Convercyon of swerers, The: Hawes, Stephen

Convergence of the twain, The: Hardy, Thomas

Conversation: Aiken, Conrad

Conversation: Lloyd, Evan

Conversation, The: Prior, Matthew

Conversation at midnight: Millay, E.St.Vincent

Conversation between His most Sacred Majesty George III and Samuel Johnson, LL.D., A: Boswell, James

Conversation piece: Coward, Noel

Conversation pieces: Sitwell, Sacheverell

Conversation with a cat, A: Belloc, Hilaire

Conversation with an angel, A: Belloc, Hilaire

Conversation with Max: Behrman, S.N.

Conversational pitcher, A: Fields, J.T.

Conversations: Brontë, Charlotte

Conversations and journals in Egypt and Malta: Senior, N.W.

Conversations in a studio: Story, W.W.

Conversations in Ebury Street: Moore, George

Conversations in Rome: Channing, W.E.

Conversations introducing poetry for the use of children: Smith, Charlotte

Conversations of Ben Jonson: Drummond of Hawthornden, William

Conversations of Dr. Johnson, The: Postgate, Raymond

Conversations of James Northcote, Esq.: Hazlitt, William

Conversations of Lord Byron with the Countess of Blessington: Blessington, Marguerite

Conversations of the Burman mission: Hale, S.J.B.

Conversations of the dead: Ghose, Sir Aurobindo

Conversations on some of the old poets: Lowell, J.R.

Conversations on war and general culture: Helps, Sir Arthur

Conversations with distinguished persons during the Second Empire, from 1860–1863: Senior, N.W.

Conversations with Thiers, Guizot and other distinguished persons during the second Empire: Senior, N.W.

Conversion of Winckelmann, The: Austin, Alfred

Convert, The: Brownson, Orestes

Converts: Brighouse, Harold

Convict, The: James, G.P.R.

Convict once: Stephens, J.B.

Convict ship, The: Russell, W.C.

Convict ships and sailors: Villiers, A.J.

Conviction of survival: Lodge, Sir Oliver

Convictions of a grandfather, The: Grant, Robert

Convict's appeal, The: Barton, Bernard

Conway from her foundation to the present day, The: Masefield, John

Cook and the anchor, The: Le Fanu, J.S.

Cool million, A: †West, Nathaniel

Cool thoughts: Franklin, Benjamin

Coole: Gregory, Lady Augusta

Coolie: Anand, M.R.

Coombe Ellen: Bowles, W.L.

Coonardo, the well in the shadow: Prichard, K.S.

Co-op, a novel of living together: Sinclair, Upton

Co-operation and competition among primitive peoples: Mead, Margaret

Co-operation and nationality: Russell, G.W.

Co-operation and the future of industry: Woolf, Leonard

Co-operative century: Peach, L.du Garde

Co-operative faith and practice: Hughes, Thomas

Co-operative movement in a socialist society, The: Cole, G.D.H.

Co-operative movement in Great Britain, The: Webb, Beatrice

Co-operative production: Hughes, Thomas

Cooper's crossing: Street, A.G.

Coopers Hill: Denham, Sir John

Coot Club: Ransome, A.M.

Cophetua: Drinkwater, John

Copie of a letter written upon occasion to the Earle of Pembrooke, The: Massinger, Philip

Copper disc, The: Stead, R.J.C.

Copper pot, The: La Farge, Oliver

Copper streak trail: Rhodes, E.M.

Copper sun: Cullen, Countée

Copperhead, The: Frederic, Harold

Copperhead, The: Thomas, Augustus

Coppy of a letter written to the Lower House of Parliament, The: Suckling, Sir John

Coptic reading-book: Murray, Margaret

Copy-cat, The: Freeman, M.W.

Copyright in books: Dawson, S.E.

Coquette, The: Foster, Hannah

Coquette: Swinnerton, Frank

Coral: Mackenzie, Sir Compton

Coral island, The: Ballantyne, R.M.

Coral island: Reynolds, G.

Coral sea, The: Villiers, A.J.

Corals, sea songs: Nesbit, Edith

Corbells at war, The: Mottram, R.H.

Cord and creese: De Mille, James

Cord of steel: Costain, T.B.

Corderius Americanus: Mather, Cotton

Cords of vanity, The: Cabell, John Branch

Corduroy: Bell, Adrian

Corinth House: Johnson, Pamela H.

Corinthian, The: Heyer, Georgette

Coriolanus: Shakespeare, William

Coriolanus: Thomson, James

Corleone: Crawford, Francis Marion

Corn: Engle, Paul

Corn: Suckow, Ruth

Corn in Egypt: Deeping, Warwick

Corn is green, The: Williams, Emlyn

Corn king and spring queen, The: Mitchison, Naomi

Corneille and Racine in England: Canfield, Dorothy

Cornelian: Acton, Harold

Cornelius: Priestley, J.B.

Cornelius Agrippa von Nettesheim: Morley, Henry

Cornelius Krieghoff: Barbeau, C.M.

Cornelius O'Dowd upon men, women and other things in general: Lever, C.J.

Cornell University: founders and the founding: Becker, C.L.

Corner book, A: Rowe, Richard

Corner that held them, The: Warner, Sylvia

Cornered poets: Housman, Laurence

Cornerstones, The: Linklater, Eric

Cornflower, The: Blewett, Jean

Cornhuskers: Sandburg, Carl

Cornish ballads: Hawker, Robert Stephen

Cornish characters and strange events: Baring-Gould, Sabine

Cornish droll, A: Phillpotts, Eden

Cornish heroic song for Valda Trevlyn: †McDiarmid, Hugh

Cornish interlude: Sullivan, Alan

Cornish riviera, The: Mais, S.P.B.

Corn-law rhymes: Elliott, Ebenezer

Cornwall: Betjeman, John

Cornwall illustrated: Betjeman, John

Coronado's children: Dobie, J.F.

Coronal, The: Child, Lydia Maria

Coronation, The: Beaumont, Francis and John Fletcher

Coronation: Gallico, Paul

Coronation, The: Shirley, James

Coronation ode: Benson, A.C.

Coronation ode: Carman, Bliss

Coronation ode and retrospect, A: Lawson, Henry

Coronation summer: Thirkell, Angela

Coronation time at Mrs. Beams: Munro, C.K.

Coroner's pidgin: Allingham, Margery Louise

Corporal Bess: Edmonds, W.D.

Corporal Cameron of the North West Mounted Police: †Connor, Ralph

Corporal Cat: Flavin, Martin

Corporal of the Guard, The: Raymond, Ernest

Corporal Sam: (†Q), Quiller-Couch, Sir A.

Corporal tune: Strong, L.A.G.

Corporal Wanzi: Brownlee, Frank

Corporate traditions and national rights: Martineau, Harriet

Corpse in canonicals: Cole. G.D.H.

Corpse in the waxworks: Carr, J.D.

Corpse with the sunburned face, The: †Caudwell, Christopher

Corpus of the Bronze Age pottery of Malta: Murray, Margaret

Corpus of Palestinian pottery: Petrie, Sir William Flindes

Corpus of prehistoric pottery: Petrie, Sir William Flindes

Corrected impressions: Saintsbury, George

Correggio: Moore, T.S.

Correspondence and conversations with A. de Tocqueville: Senior, N.W.

Correspondence and documents relative to the attempt to negotiate for the release of the American captives at Algiers: Noah, M.M.

Correspondence of John Hughes and Mr. Addison: Addison, Joseph

Correspondence of John Locke and Edward Clarke, The: Locke, John

Correspondence of Lewis the Sixteenth, The: Williams, H.M.

Correspondence, submitted to Parliament: Richardson, John

Correspondence with his sister: Disraeli, Benjamin

Corridor of Venus: †Bell, Neil

Corridors of power: Snow, C.P.

Corroboree to the sun: Mudie, I.M.

Corruption and intolerance: Moore, Thomas

Corsair, The: Byron, George Gordon *Lord*

Corsair of Casco Bay, The: Ingraham, J.H.

Corse de Leon: James, George Payne Rainsford

Corsica: Barbauld, Anna Letitia

Cortelyou feud, The: Ford, Paul Leicester

Coryats crudities, hastily gobled up in the five moneths travells: Coryate, Thomas

Corydon: Carman, Bliss

Coryston family, The: Ward, M.A.

Cosmic aspect of the outer consciousness, The: Lighthall, W.D.

Cosmic religion: Einstein, Albert

Cosmo de' Medici: Horne, Richard Henry

Cosmographie in four bookes, containing the horographie and historie of the whole world: Heylyn, Peter

Cosmological eye, The: Miller, Henry

Cosmopolitans: Maugham, Somerset

Cost, The: Phillips, D.G.

Cost of it, The: †Mordaunt, Elinor

Cost price: †Yates, Dornford

Costa's daughter: Bercovici, Konrad

Costume by Eros: Aiken, Conrad

Costume of colonial times: Earle, A.M.

Costume of the ancients, The: Hope, Thomas

Costume plays: Brighouse, Harold

Cosy corner stories: Molesworth, *Mrs.*

Cosy room, The: †Machen, Arthur

Cot and cradle stories: Traill, C.P.

Cote d'Or: Tomlinson, H.M.

Côté, the wood carver: Barbeau, C.M.

Cotillion: Heyer, Georgette

Cotswold characters: Drinkwater, John

Cotswold country: Massingham, Harold

Cotswold honey: Young, Francis Brett

Cotswolds, The: Massingham, Harold

Cottage history of England, The: Manning, Anne

Cottage into house: †Armstrong, Anthony

Cotton Mather's election into the Royal Society: Kittredge, G.L.

Cotton Mather's scientific communications to the Royal Society: Kittredge, G.L.

Cotton-woolleena: Housman, Laurence

Couching at the door: Broster, D.K.

Council of industry, A: Guedalla, Philip

Council of Justice, The: Wallace, Edgar

Councils and ecclesiastical documents relating to Great Britain and Ireland: Stubbs, William and A.W. Haddan

Counsellor-at-law: Rice, Elmer

Count Arezzi, The: Landor, Robert Eyres

Count Belisarius: Graves, Robert

Count Bruga: Hecht, Ben

Count Chrisoval: Reynolds, G.

Count Falcon of the Eyrie: Scollard, Clinton

Count Filippo: Heavysege, Charles

Count Frontenac and New France under Louis XIV: Parkman, Francis

Count Hannibal: Weyman, Stanley

Count Julian: Calvert, George Henry

Count Julian: Landor, Walter Savage

Count Julian: Simms, W.G.

Count Königsmark: Chamier, Frederick

Count Stefan: Coppard, A.E.

Count X: Vachell, H.A.

Count your blessings: Davies, Rhys

Count your dead: they are alive: Lewis, P. Wyndham

Count your enemies and economise your expenditure: Bagehot, Walter

Counter attack from the East: Joad, C.E.M.

Counter blaste to tobacco, A: James VI of Scotland

Counter-attack: Sassoon, Siegfried

Counter-currents: Repplier, Agnes

Counterfeit Bridegroom, The: Betterton, Thomas

Counterfeit lady unveiled, The: Kirkman, Francis

Counterfeit presentment, A: Howells, W.D.

Counterpoint murder: Cole, G.D.H.

Counter-remarks to Mr. Dudley Montagu Perceval's remarks upon passages in Colonel Napier's fourth volume: Napier, *Sir* W.F.P.

Counter-statement: Burke, Kenneth

Countess, The: Fay, Theodore Sedgwick

Countess Eve, The: Shorthouse, J.H.

Countess Fanny, The: †Bowen, Marjorie

Countess Glika: Deeping, Warwick

Countess Ida, The: Fay, Theodore Sedgwick

Countess Kate: Yonge, C.M.

Countess Kathleen, The: Yeats, W.B.

Countess of Albany, The: Lee, Vernon

Countess of Dellwyn, The: Fielding, Sarah

Countess of Lascelles, The: Reynolds, G.

Countess of Lowndes Square: Benson, E.F.

Countess of Pembrook's passion, The: Breton, Nicholas

Countess of Pembrokes Arcadia, The: Sidney, *Sir* Philip

Countrey contentments: Markham, Gervase

Countries of the mind: Murry, John Middleton

Country: Massingham, Harold

Country, The: Thomas, E.E.P.

Country bunny and the little gold shoes, The: Heyward, DuBose

Country by-ways: Jewett, S.O.

Country calendar: Street, A.G.

Country child, The: Uttley, Alison

Country comets: Day Lewis, Cecil

Country cousin, The: Tarkington, Booth

Country days: Street, A.G.

Country doctor, A: Jewett, S.O.

Country gentleman and his family, A: Oliphant, Margaret

Country girl, The: Odets, Clifford

Country growth: Derleth, A.W.

Country hoard: Uttley, Alison

Country house, A: Teasdale, Sara

Country house, The: Galsworthy, John

Country house, The: Vanbrugh, *Sir* John

Country house party, The: Sigerson, Dora

Country housewife's garden, The: Markham, Gervase

Country I come from, The: Lawson, Henry

Country lieutenancies and the army, The: Fortescue, *Sir* John

Country living and country thinking: Dodge, May Abigail

Country muse, A: Gale, Norman R.

Country neighbors: Brown, Alice

Country notes: Sackville-West, V.

Country notes in wartime: Sackville-West, V.

Country of the blind, The: Wells, H.G.

Country of the hawk, The: Derleth, A.W.

Country of the pointed firs, The: Jewett, S.O.

Country of the sea: Mannin, Ethel

Country of white clover, The: Bates, H.E.

Country people: Suckow, Ruth

Country poems: Derleth, A.W.

Country quarters: Blessington, Marguerite

Country relics: Massingham, Harold

Country road, The: Brown, Alice

Country sentiment: Graves, Robert

Country stories: Mitford, Mary Russell

Country tales: Bates, H.E.

Country things: Uttley, Alison

Country town, The: Courthorpe, William John

Country window, A: Church, Richard

Country year, The: Van Doren, Mark

Countrymans recreations, The: Markham, Gervase

Countryman's journal: Derleth, A.W.

Countryman's journal, A: Massingham, Harold

Countryman's year: Baker, Ray Stannard

Country-wife, The: Wycherley, William

County Chronicle: Thirkell, Angela

County family, A: Payn, James

Coupon bonds (stories and play): Trowbridge, J.T.

Courage in politics: Patmore, Coventry

Courageous women: Montgomery, L.M.

Couragios Turke, The: Goffe, Thomas

Course of empire: De Voto, Bernard

Course of English Literature, A: Hannay, James

Course of lectures on oratory and criticism, A: Priestley, Joseph

Course of lectures on the theory of language, A: Priestley, Joseph

Course of sermons for all the sundaies of the year, A: Taylor, Jeremy

Course of true love never did run smooth, The: Aldrich, Thomas Bailey

Course of true love never did run smooth, The: Reade, Charles

Court and country, The: Breton, Nicholas

Court and the castle, The: †West, Rebecca

Court legacy, The: Manley, Mrs.

Court Netherleigh: Wood, Ellen

Court of Atlantis, The: Oldmixon, John

Court of Boyville, The: White, W.A.

Court of death, The: Dennis, John

Court of fancy, The: Godfrey, Thomas

Court of love, The: Brown, Alice

Court poets of Iran and India: Masani, Sir R.P.

Court Royal: Baring-Gould, Sabine

Court secret, The: Shirley, James

Court theatre 1904–1907, The: MacCarthy, Sir Desmond

Courtenay of Warbreddon: Bray, Anna Eliza

Court-house square: Basso, Hamilton

Courtier of the days of Charles II, The: Gore, Catherine

Courting of Dinah Shadd, The: Kipling, Rudyard

Courting of Susie Brown: Caldwell, Erskine Preston

Courtland: Cobbold, Richard

Courtly controversie betweene loove and learning, A: Munday, Anthony

Courtly masque, A: Middleton, Thomas

Courtmartialed: (†Ensign Clarke Fitch), Sinclair, Upton

Courts and judges in France, Germany and England: Ensor, Sir R.C.K.

Courts of idleness, The: †Yates, Dornford

Courts of the morning, The: Buchan, John

Courtship of Miles Standish, The: Longfellow, H.W.

Courtship of Morrice Buckler, The: Mason, A.E.W.

Cousin Christopher: (†Ian Hay), Beith, Sir John Hay

Cousin Cinderella: Duncan, S.J.

Cousin from Fiji: Lindsay, Norman

Cousin Henry: Trollope, Anthony

Cousin Honoré: Jameson, Storm

Cousin Kate: Davies, H.H.

Cousin Mary: Oliphant, Margaret

Cousin Maude and Rosamond: Holmes, M.J.

Cousin Muriel: †Dane, Clemence

Cousin Philip: Ward, M.A.

Cousin Phillis: Gaskell, Mrs. Elizabeth

Covenant of Gods free grace, The: Cotton, John

Covenant of grace, The: Cotton, John

Covenant of grace opened, The: Hooker, Thomas

Covent Garden journal, The: Fielding, Henry

Covent-Garden tragedy, The: Fielding, Henry

Coventry Patmore: Gosse, Sir Edmund

Cover his face: †Bell, Neil

Covered wagon, The: Hough, Emerson

Covering end: James, Henry

Cow of the barricades, The: Rao, Raja

Cow people: Dobie, J.F.

Cowpuncher, The: Stead, R.J.C.

Cow with golden horns, The: Freeman, Mary

Cowardice Court: McCutcheon, G.B.

Cowboy and the lady, The: Fitch, Clyde William
Cowferry Isle: Percy, Edward
Cowled lover, The: Bird, Robert Montgomery
Cowper: Smith, Goldwin
Cow's in the corn, The: Frost, Robert
Cox's diary: Thackeray, W. M.
Cozy lion, The: Burnett, Frances Hodgson
Crab apple jelly: †O'Connor, Frank
Crabapple tree, The: Church, Richard
Crabbed youth and age: Robinson, E. S. L.
Crabtree affair, The: (†Michael Innes), Stewart, J. I. M.
Crack-up, The: Fitzgerald, F. Scott
Cradle of God, The: Powys, L. C.
Cradle of life: Adamic, Louis
Cradle of New France, The: Doughty, Sir A. G.
Cradle of the clouds: Ghose, S. N.
Cradock Nowell: Blackmore, Sir R. D.
Craft of fiction, The: Lubbock, Percy
Craft of letters in England, The: Lehmann, John
Craft of verse, The: Wolfe, Humbert
Craftsman, The: Mottley, John
Craftsmanship and science: Bragg, Sir W. H.
Craigavon: Ulsterman: Ervine, St. John
Craigcrook Castle: Massey, Gerald
Craig's wife: Kelly, G. E.
Cranford: Gaskell, Mrs. Elizabeth
Cranks and commonsense: Malleson, Miles
Cranmer: Belloc, Hilaire
Cranmer: Dibdin, Thomas Frognall
Craque-o-doom: Catherwood, Mary
Crater, The: Cooper, James Fenimore
Craven House: Hamilton, Patrick

Crayon miscellany, The: (†Geoffrey Crayon) Irving, Washington
Crazy fool, The: Stewart, D. O.
Crazy hunter: Boyle, Kay
Crazy Jane: Lewis, Matthew Gregory
Crazy like a fox: Perelman, S. J.
Crazy man: Bodenheim, Maxwell
Crazy pavements: Nichols, Beverley
Crazy tales: Stevenson, J. H.
Cream: Reade, Charles
Cream of his thoughts: Cole, E. W.
Cream of the jest, The: Cabell, James Branch
Creation: Blackmore, Sir R. D.
Creation, The: Hill, Aaron
Creation and evolution in primitive cosmogonies: Frazer, Sir James
Creation of character in literature, The: Galsworthy, John
Creative art of life, The: Munshi, K. M.
Creative criticism: Spingarn, J. E.
Creative development and evolution: Dawson, Sir J. W.
Creative effort: Lindsay, Norman
Creative element, The: Spender, Stephen
Creative experiment, The: Bowra, Sir Maurice
Creative life, The: Lewisohn, Ludwig
Creative man: Samuel, Herbert 1st Viscount
Creative problems in New Zealand: Holcroft, M. H.
Creative unity: Tagore, Sir R.
Creator and the creature, The: Faber, Frederick William
Creator Spirit, The: Raven, C. E.
Creators, The: Sinclair, May
Creatures: Colum, Padraic
Creatures of circumstance: Maugham, Somerset
Creatures of impulse: Gilbert, Sir W. S.
Credo: White, S. E.

Credo and curios: Thurber, James
Creed in slow motion, The: Knox, R. A.
Creed of a novelist, The: Mencken, H. L.
Creed of Christendom, The: Greg, W. R.
Creed or chaos? Sayers, Dorothy
Creel of Irish stories, A: Barlow, Jane
Creeping Jenny: Wiggin, K. D.
Creeping Siamese, The: Hammet, S. D.
Creeve Roe: Daley, Victor
Creole, The: Brooks, C. W. S.
Creole dusk: Roberts, W. Adolphe
Creole families of New Orleans: King, G. E.
Creoles of history, The: Gayarré, C. E. A.
Creoles of Louisiana, The: Cable, George Washington
Crescendo: Bentley, Phyllis
Crescendo: Mannin, Ethel
Crescent and iron cross: Benson, E. F.
Crescent moon, The: Tagore, Sir R.
Crescent moon, The: Young, Francis Brett
Cressage: Benson, A. C.
Cressida: Lowndes, M. A.
Cressida's first lover: Lindsay, Jack
Cressy: Harte, Bret
Crest of the wave: Hassall, Christopher
Crest on the silver, The: Grigson, Geoffrey
Cretan pictographs and Prae-Phoenician script: Evans, Sir Arthur
Crëusa, Queen of Athens: Whitehead, William
Crew of the Anaconda, The: Macdonell, A. G.
Crewe train: Macaulay, Dame R.
Crichton: Ainsworth, Harrison
Cricket: Cardus, Neville
Cricket all the year: Cardus, Neville
Cricket bag: Farjeon, Herbert

Cricket country: Blunden, Edmund

Cricket in heaven: Bullett, Gerald

Cricket match, The: De Selincourt, Hugh

Cricket of palmy days, The: Thomas, Augustus

Cricket on the hearth, The: Dickens, Charles

Cricket songs: Gale, Norman R.

Cricketer's book, A: Cardus, Neville

Crier by night, The: Bottomley, Gordon

Cries of London, The: Smith, J.T.

Cries of New York, The: Osgood, F.S.

Crilley: Hanley, James

Crime against Cania, A: Calder-Marshall, Arthur

Crime and criminals: Darrow, C.S.

Crime at Black Dudley, The: Allingham, Margery

Crime at Guildford: Crofts, F.W.

Crime at Vanderlynden's, The: Mottram, R.H.

Crime considered: Taylor, *Sir* Henry

Crime doctor, The: Hornung, E.W.

Crime in Kensington: †Caudwell, Christopher

Crime in the Whistler room, The: Wilson, Edmund

Crime: its cause and its treatment: Darrow, C.S.

Crime of Cuba, The: Beals, Carleton

Crime of Laura Sarelle, The: (†Joseph Shearing), †Bowen, Marjorie

Crime of the Congo, The: Doyle, *Sir* Arthur Conan

Crime of the crystal, The: Hume, F.W.

Crimea: the campaign of 1854–5: Vulliamy, C.E.

Crimes of charity: Bercovici, Konrad

Crimes of England, The: Chesterton, G.K.

Crimes of old London: †Bowen, Marjorie

Crimes of the "Times", The: Sinclair, Upton

Criminal, The: Ellis, Henry Havelock

Criminal at large: Wallace, Edgar

Criminal case, A: Swinburne, A.C.

Criminal code, The: Flavin, Martin

Criminal introduction, A: Peach, L. du Garde

Criminal prisons of London, The: Mayhew, Henry

Crimson circle, The: Wallace, Edgar

Crimson fairy book, The: Lang, Andrew

Crimson gardenia, The: Beach, R.E.

Crimson house, The: Carman, Bliss

Crimson sign, The: Cody, H.A.

Crimson tide, The: Chambers, R.W.

Cripple in black, The: Timms, E.V.

Cripps the carrier: Blackmore, *Sir* R.D.

Crisis, The: Churchill, Winston

Crisis: Hassall, Christopher

Crisis, The: Owen, Robert

Crisis, The: Steele, *Sir* Richard

Crisis and the constitution, The: Laski, Harold

Crisis in heaven: Linklater, Eric

Crisis in physics: †Caudwell, Christopher

Crisis in Russia, The: Ransome, A.M.

Crisis of Britain and the British empire: Dutt, R.P.

Crisis of our civilization, The: Belloc, Hilaire

Crisis of property, The: Steele, *Sir* Richard

Crisis of the film, The: Fletcher, John Gould

Crisis, what it is, how it arose, what to do, The: Cole, G.D.H.

Crispus: Guthrie-Smith, W.H.

Criss cross: Crothers, Rachel

Cristina and I: Stringer, A.J.A.

Criterion, The: Tuckerman, H.T.

Critic, The: Sheridan, R.B.

Critic and the drama, The: Nathan, G.J.

Critic in judgment, The: Murry, John Middleton

Critical and historical essays: Macaulay, *Baron* T.B.

Critical annotations: Coleridge, S.T.

Critical approaches to literature: Daiches, David

Critical attitude, The: Ford, Ford Madox

Critical dictionary of English literature, A: Allibone, S.A.

Critical essay on the life and works of George Tinworth, A: Gosse, *Sir* Edmund

Critical essays: †Orwell, George

Critical essays on the performers of the London theatres: Hunt, Leigh

Critical exposition of the philosophy of Leibniz, A: Russell, Bertrand

Critical fable, A: Lowell, Amy

Critical history of England, ecclesiastical and civil, The: Oldmixon, John

Critical history of English literature, A: Daiches, David

Critical history of English poetry: Grierson, *Sir* H.J.C.

Critical Kit-Kats: Gosse, *Sir* Edmund

Critical medley, A: Partridge, Eric

Critical miscellanies: Morley, John

Critical observations on the sixth book of the Aeneid: Gibbon, Edward

Critical period of America, The: Fiske, John

Critical reflections on the old English dramatick writers: Colman, George, *the elder*

Critical strictures on the new tragedy of Elvira: Boswell, James, and others

Critical studies of the works of Charles Dickens: Gissing, George

Critical thoughts in critical days: Lucas, F.L.

Critical woodcuts: Sherman, S.P.

Criticism: Brownell, W.C.

Criticism: MacCarthy, *Sir* Desmond

Criticism: Whitman, Walt

Criticism and creation: Grierson, *Sir* Herbert

Criticism and fiction: Howells, W.D.

Criticism and the nineteenth century: Tillotson, Geoffrey

Criticism in America: Babbitt, Irving

Criticism in America, its function and status: Sherman, S.P.

Criticism of poetry, The: Lucas, F.L.

Criticisms on contemporary thought and thinkers: Hutton, R.H.

Critics, The: Ervine, St. John

Critic's London diary: Martin, B.K.

Critique of logical positivism, A: Joad, C.E.M.

Critiques and addresses: Huxley, T.H.

Crito: Spence, Joseph

Crittenden: Fox, John

Crock of gold, The: Baring-Gould, S.

Crock of gold, The: Stephens, James

Crockford-House: Luttrell, Henry

Crocus: †Bell, Neil

Crome yellow: Huxley, Aldous

Cromlech on houth, The: Fergusson, *Sir* Samuel

Cromptons, The: Holmes, M.J.

Cromwell: Arnold, Matthew

Cromwell: Belloc, Hilaire

Cromwell: Drinkwater, John

Cromwell: Herbert, H.W.

Cromwell's army: Firth, *Sir* Charles

Croniklis of Scotland with the cosmography and dyscription thairof: Bellenden, John

Cronulla: Palmer, E.V.

Crook in the furrow, A: Street, A.G.

Crookback's crown: Bottomley, Gordon

Crooked coronet, The: Arlen, Michael

Crooked Friday, The: Hoffe, Monckton

Crooked furrow, The: Farnol, J.J.

Crooked hinge, The: Carr, J.D.

Crooked horn: †Brand, Max

Crooked house: Christie, Agatha

Crooked mile, The: De Voto, Bernard

Crooked mile, A: †Onions, Oliver

Crooked sixpence, The: Bramston, James

Crooked stick, The: †Boldrewood, Rolf

Crooked trails: Remington, Frederic

Crooked world, The: Cole, G.D.H.

Crooks' Christmas: Peach, L.du Garde

Crooks in the sunshine: Oppenheim, E.Phillips

Croquet: Reid, T.M.

Croquet castles for five players: †Carroll, Lewis

Croquet player, The: Wells, H.G.

Cross and coronet: Clarke, Macdonald

Cross and the hammer, The: Bedford-Jones, H.

Cross corner: Warner, A.B.

Cross Creek cookery: Rawlings, Marjorie

Cross currents: Porter, E.H.

Cross of peace, The: Gibbs, *Sir* Philip

Cross Patch: Coolidge, Susan

Cross purposes, and the shadows: Macdonald, George

Cross roads: Chattopadhyaya, H.

Cross roads: Flavin, Martin

Cross roads, The: Robinson, E.S.L.

Cross roads in Ireland: Colum, Padraic

Cross section of English printing, A: Jackson, Holbrook

Cross winds: †Mordaunt, Elinor

Cross-currents: Widdemer, Margaret

Cross-currents in Europe today: Beard, C.A.

Cross-currents in the literature of the seventeenth century: Grierson, *Sir* Herbert

Crossing, The: Churchill, Winston

Crossing of proverbs: Breton, Nicholas

Crossings: De la Mare, Walter

Cross-in-hand farm: Meynell, Viola

Crotchet Castle: Peacock, Thomas Love

Crotchets in the air: Poole, John

Crotty Shinkwin: Coppard A.E.

Crowded out: Harrison, S.F.

Crowded street, The: Holtby, Winifred

Crown and the establishment, The: Martin, B.K.

Crown for our queen, A: Ryan, A.J.

Crwon of Empire, The: Evans, G.E.

Crown of empire, The: Quinn, R.J.

Crown of life, The: Gissing, George

Crown of life, The: Knight, G.W.

Crown of violet: Trease, Geoffrey

Crown of wild myrtle, A: Bates, H.E.

Crown of wild olive, The: Ruskin, John

Crowned lovers, The: Beck, *Mrs.* Lily

Crowning privilege, The: Graves, Robert

Crowning years, The: Scollard, Clinton

Crowns and sceptres: †Bowen, Marjorie

Crow's nest, The: Day, C.S.

Croxley Master, The: Doyle, *Sir* Arthur Conan

Crozart story, The: Fearing, Kenneth

Crucial instances: Wharton, Edith

Crucible, The: †Sinclair Murray

Crucifixion of Philip Strong, The: Sheldon, C.M.

Crude criminology: Shaw, G.B.

Cruel sea, The: Monsarrat, Nicholas

Cruel solstice, The: Keyes, Sydney

Cruise of the Albatross, The: Allen, Grant

Cruise of the Conrad: Villiers, A.J.

Cruise of the Corwin, The: Muir, John

Cruise of the Dazzler, The: London, Jack

Cruise of the dry dock, The: Stribling, T.S.

Cruise of the Jasper B, The: Marquis, Don

Cruise of the Midge, The: Scott, Michael

Cruise of the Mystery, The: Thaxter, C.L.

Cruise of the Nona, The: Belloc, Hilaire

Cruise of the Shining Light, The: Duncan, Norman

Cruise of the Snark, The: London, Jack

Cruise of the training ship, The: (†Ensign Clarke Fitch), Sinclair, Upton

Cruise under the crescent, A: Stoddard, C.W.

Cruiser of the mist, The: Ingraham, J.H.

Cruises and cargoes: Jacobs, W.W.

Crumbling idols: Garland, Hamlin

Crump folk going home: Holme, Constance

Crusade, The: Belloc, Hilaire

Crusade: Byrne, Donn

Crusade, The: Galt, John

Crusade of the Excelsior, The: Harte, Bret

Crusader castles: Lawrence, T.E.

Crusaders, The: Jones, H.A.

Crusaders for freedom: Commager, H.S.

Crusader's key: Linklater, Eric

Crusader's tomb: Cronin, A.J.

Crusades, The: Treece, Henry

Crusades, commerce and adventure: Coulton, G.G.

Crusoe in New York: Hale, E.E.

Crux Ansata: Wells, H.G.

Cry, The: Fielding, Sarah

Cry havoc: Nichols, Beverley

Cryptogram, The: De Mille, James

Crystal age, A: Hudson, W.H.

Crystal and the sphinx, The: Sladen, D.B.W.

Crystal box, The: Walpole, *Sir* Hugh

Crystal cabinet: Gregory, Horace

Crystal cup, The: Atherton, Gertrude

Crystal heart, The: Bottome, Phyllis

Crystalline state, The: Bragg, *Sir* Lawrence

Cub, The: Turner, E.S.

Cub at Newmarket, The: Boswell, James

Cuba in war time: Davis, R.H.

Cuba libre: Kantor, Mackinlay

Cuba, prophetic island: Frank, Waldo

Cuban and Porto Rican campaigns, The: Davis, R.H.

Cuckolds-Haven: Tate, Nahum

Cuckoo cherry-tree: Uttley, Alison

Cuckoo clock: Molesworth, *Mrs*.

Cuckoo clock, The: Young, A.J.

Cuckoo in June: Uttley, Alison

Cuckoo in the dell: Langley, Noel

Cuckoo in the nest, The: Oliphant, Margaret

Cuckoo songs: Tynan, Katherine

Cuckooz contrey: Sleesor, Kenneth

Cudjo's cave: Trowbridge, J.T.

Cue for treason: Trease, Geoffrey

Culpepers school of physick: Culpeper, Nicolas

Culprit Fay, The: Drake, Joseph Rodman

Cult of power, The: Warner, Rex

Cultivation of Christmas trees, The: Eliot, T.S.

Cultural discontinuities and personality transformation: Mead, Margaret

Culture: Pound, Ezra

Culture and anarchy: Arnold, Matthew

Culture and environment: Leavis, F.R.

Culture and the coming peril: Chesterton, G.K.

Culture of cities, The: Mumford, Lewis

Culture's garland: Field, Eugene

Cumberland vendetta, A: Fox, John

Cumner's son and other South Sea folk: Parker, *Sir* H.G.

Cunning Murrell: Morrison, Arthur

Cunningham Grahame: †McDiarmid, Hugh

Cunning-man, The: Burney, *Dr.* Charles

Cup and the falcon, The: Tennyson, Alfred *Lord*

Cup of comus, The: Cawein, Madison

Cup of fury, The: Sinclair, Upton

Cup of gold: Steinbeck, John

Cup of happiness, A: Phillpotts, Eden

Cup of paint, The: Lindsay, N.V.

Cup of sky, A: Peattie, D.C.

Cup of tea for Mr. Thorgill, A: Jameson, Storm

Cup of youth, The: Mitchell, S.W.

Cupid and commonsense: Bennett, Arnold

Cupid and death: Shirley, James

Cupid and Hymen: Carey, Henry

Cupid and Mars: Ackland, Rodney

Cupid and Psyche: Levy, Benn W.

Cupid and the jacaranda: Sitwell, Sacheverell

Cupid, Death, and Psyche: Beddoes, T.L.

Cupid in Clapham: Baker, Elizabeth

Cupids revenge: Fletcher, John

Cups, wands and swords: Simpson, H. de G.

Curate, The: Lloyd, Evan

Curate in Bohemia, A: Lindsay, Norman

Curate in charge, The: Oliphant, Margaret

Curate of Cranston, The: †Bede, Cuthbert

Curate of Lawood, The: Riddell, *Mrs*. J.H.

Cure for a cuckold, A: Webster, John

Cure for love, The: Greenwood, Walter

Cure for love, A: Wells, H.G.

Cure for the heart-ache, A: Morton, Thomas

Cure for unemployment, A: O'Flaherty, Liam

Cure of flesh, A: Cozzens, J.G.

Cure of souls, A: Sinclair, May

Curfew at dawn: Mannin, Ethel

Curial, The (trn.): Caxton, William

Curiosissima curatoria: †Carroll, Lewis

Curiosities: Pain, B.E.O.

Curiosities of literature: D'Israeli, Isaac

Curiosities of the Olden Times: Baring-Gould, Sabine

Curiosity: Lathom, Francis

Curious career of Roderick Campbell, The: McIlwraith, J.N.

Curious dance round a curious tree, A: Dickens, Charles

Curious facts of old colonial days: Bonwick, James

Curious happenings: †Bowen, Marjorie

Curious happenings to the Rooke Legatees: Oppenheim, E.Phillips

Curious maid, The: Prior, Matthew

Curious myths of the Middle Ages: Baring-Gould, S.

Curious punishments of bygone days: Earle, A.M.

Curious relations: Plomer, W. C.F.

Curious republic of Gondour and other whimsical sketches: (†Mark Twain), Clemens, S.L.

Curious traveller, The: Massingham, Harold

Curlew river: Plomer, W.C.F.

Curly Locks: Coolidge, Susan

Currency and railways: Rowcroft, Charles

Currency lass, The: Devaney, J.M.

Current of war, The: Liddell Hart, B.

Currents and counter-currents in medical science: Holmes, Oliver Wendell

Curries and other Indian dishes: Anand, M.R.

Curry and rice: Brown, E.T.

Curse at farewell, The: Tagore, *Sir* R.

Curse of Clement Waynflete, The: Mitford, Bertram

Curse of Kehama, The: Southey, Robert

Curse of Minerva, The: Byron, George Gordon, *Lord Byron*

Curse of the black lady, The: Gratton, T.C.

Curse of the bronze lamp, The: †Carter Dickson

Curse of the Nile, The: Sladen, D.B.W.

Curse of the wise woman, The: Dunsany, E.J.M.D.P. *Lord*

Cursory criticism on the edition of Shakespeare published by Edmond Malone: Ritson, Joseph

Cursory reflections on political and commercial topics: Galt, John

Cursory remarks on the northern parts of Europe: Wraxall, *Sir* Nathaniel

Cursory rhymes: Wolfe, Humbert

Curtain raisers: Phillpotts, Eden

Curtain up: Robinson, E.S.L.

Curtaine lecture: as it is read by a countrey farmers wife to her good man, A: Heywood, Thomas

Curtains of yesterday, The: Gibbs, *Sir* Philip

Curtmantle: Fry, Christopher

Curve and the tusk, The: Cloete, E.F.S.G.

Curzon, the last phase, 1919–1925: Nicolson, *Sir* Harold

Custard the dragon: Nash, Ogden

Custer: Wilcox, Ella Wheeler

Custody of the child: †Bell, Neil

Custody of the child, The: Gibbs, *Sir* Philip

Custom and myth: Lang, Andrew

Custom of the country, The: Beaumont, Francis

Custom of the country, The: Wharton, Edith

Customs and fashions in Old New England: Earle, A.M.

Cut and come again: Bates, H.E.

Cut by the county: Braddon, Mary Elizabeth

Cut flowers: †Onions, Oliver

Cut from Mulga: Moll, E.G.

Cutie: Hecht, Ben

Cutter of Coleman-street: Cowley, Abraham

Cutting of an agate, The: Yeats, W.B.

Cutty Sark, The: Villiers, A.J.

Cycle: Bynner, Witter

Cycle of spring: Tagore, *Sir* R.

Cycle of the North, The: Sullivan, Alan

Cyclone: Narayan, R.K.

Cyclone: Palmer, E.V.

Cyclone Carry; the story of Carry Nation: Beals, Carleton

Cyclopaedia of modern travel: Taylor, Bayard

Cyder: Philips, John

Cyder feast, The: Sitwell, Sacheverell

Cymbeline, King of Britaine: Shakespeare, William

Cymbelinere finished: Shaw, G.B.

Cymon a dramatic romance: Garrick, David

Cynara: Harwood, H.M.

Cynic's word book, The: Bierce, Ambrose

Cynthia: Barnfield, Richard

Cynthia: Davies, H.H.

Cynthia: Merrick, Leonard

Cynthia's revels: Jonson, Ben

Cypher K: †Taffrail

Cyrano: Bedford-Jones, Henry

Cyrilla: Tautphoeus, *Baroness*

Cytherea: Hergesheimer, Joseph

Czarina's story, A: Pope-Hennessy, *Dame* Una

D

D. Co.: Malleson, Miles

D. G. Rossetti: Ford, Ford Madox

D. G. Rossetti: †Macleod, Fiona

D. G. Rossetti: his family letters, with a memoir: Rossetti, W. M.

D. H. Lawrence: Aldington, Richard

D. H. Lawrence: Leavis, F. R.

D. H. Lawrence: Potter, Stephen

D. H. Lawrence: †West, Rebecca

D. H. Lawrence and Maurice Magnus: Douglas, Norman

D. H. Lawrence: novelist: Leavis, F. R.

D. L. Moody: Bradford, Gamaliel

Dacotah: Anderson, Maxwell

Dacre of the south: Gore, Catherine

Dad in politics: †Rudd, Steele

Dadabhai Naoroji: the grand old man of India: Masani, *Sir* R. P.

Daddy Dacre's School: Hall, Anna Maria

Daddy Darwin's dovecot: Ewing, *Mrs.* Juliana Horatia

Daddy Jake the runaway: Harris, Joel Chandler

Daedalus: Haldane, J. B. S.

Daemon of the world, The: Shelley, P. B.

Daemonologie: James VI of Scotland

Daffodil affair: (†Michael Innes), Stewart, J. I. M.

Daffodil fields, The: Masefield, John

Daffodil murderer, The: Sassoon, Siegfried

Daffodil mystery, The: Wallace, Edgar

Daffodil sky, The: Bates, H. E.

Daft days, The: Munro, Neil

Dagger of the mind, The: Fearing, Kenneth

Daily bread: Gibson, Wilfred

Daily bread: Hale, E. E.

Daily counsellor, The: Sigourney, L. H.

Daily life and origin of the Tasmanians: Bonwick, James

Daily life in Roman Egypt: Lindsay, Jack

Dain curse, The: Hammett, S. D.

D'air devil: Clune, Frank

Daisies and buttercups: Riddell, *Mrs.* J. H.

Daisy: Warner, S. B.

Daisy and Daphne: Macaulay, *Dame* R.

Daisy Burns: Kavanagh, Julia

Daisy chain, The: Yonge, C. M.

Daisy Matthews: Davies, Rhys

Daisy Mayme: Kelly, G. E.

Daisy Miller: James, Henry

Daisy Plains: Warner, S. B.

Daisy Thornton and Jessie Graham: Holmes, M. J.

Daisy's aunt: Benson, E. F.

Daisy's first winter: Stowe, Harriet Beecher

Daisy's necklace: Aldrich, Thomas

Dalhousie University and Canadian literature: Logan, J. D.

Dallas Galbraith: Davis, Rebecca

Daltons, The: Lever, C. T.

Dam busters, The: Sherriff, R. C.

Damaged souls: Bradford, Gamaliel

Damascus gate: Raymond, Ernest

Damask cheek, The: Van Druten, John

Damen's ghost: Bynner, E. L.

Dames don't care: †Cheyney, Peter

Damn! a book of calumny: Mencken, H. L.

Damnable opinions: Powys, L. C.

Damnation of Theron Ware, The: Frederic, Harold

Damon and Phillida: Cibber, Colley

Damon and Pythias: Banim, John

Damozel Blanche and other fairy tales: Baring, Maurice

Damsel and the sage, The: Glyn, Elinor

Damsel in distress, A: (†Ian Hay), Beith, *Sir* John Hay

Damsel in distress, A: Wodehouse, P. G.

Damsel of Darien, The: Simms, W. G.

Dan Barry's daughter: †Brand, Max

Dan Russell the fox: Somerville, E.

Danaë: Moore, T. S.

Dance goes on, The: Golding, Louis

Dance, little gentleman: Frankau, Gilbert

Dance macabre: Lydgate, John

Dance of death, The: Auden, W. H.

Dance of death, The: Bierce, Ambrose

Dance of death, The: Blackwood, Algernon

Dance of fire: Ridge, Lola

Dance of life, The: Bierce, Ambrose

Dance of life, The: Combe, William

Dance of life, The: Ellis, Henry Havelock

Dance of Siva, The: Coomaraswamy, A. K.

Dance of the months: Phillpotts, Eden

Dance of the quick and the dead: Sitwell, Sacheverell

Dance of the seasons: Holcroft, M. H.

Dance of the years: Alligham, Margery

Dance of unskilled labor, The: Lindsay, N. V.

Dance with no music: Ackland, Rodney

Dance without music: †Cheyney, Peter

Dancers in mourning: Allingham, Margery

Dancing bear, The: †Bridie, James

Dancing feather, The: Ingraham, J.H.

Dancing floor, The: Buchan, John

Dancing girl, The: Jones, H.A.

Dancing mad: Davies, W.H.

Dancing school with the adventures of the Easter holydays, The: Ward, Edward

Dancing years, The: Hassall, Christopher

Dancing years, The: †Novello, Ivor

Dandelion clocks: Ewing, *Mrs.* Juliana Horatia

Dandelion days: Williamson, Henry

Dandy Dick: Pinero, *Sir* A.W.

Danesbury House: Wood, Ellen

Danger: Doyle, *Sir* Arthur Conan

Danger: Hughes, R.A.W.

Danger: Poole, Ernest

Danger mark, The: Chambers, R.W.

Danger of desertion, The: Hooker, Thomas

Danger of priestcraft to religion and government, The: Dennis, John

Danger of writing verse, The: Whitehead, William

Danger signal: Bottome, Phyllis

Danger under the moon: Walsh, Maurice

Dangerous ages: Macaulay, *Dame* Rose

Dangerous corner: Priestley, J.B.

Dangerous curves: †Cheyney, Peter

Dangerous days: Rinehart, Mary Roberts

Dangerous guest, The: Browne, Frances

Dangerous maid, A: Gershwin, Ira

Dangerous places, The: Golding, Louis

Dangerous woman, A: Farrell, James

Dangerous years, The: Church, Richard

Dangerous years, The: Frankau, Gilbert

Dangers of half-preparedness, The: Angell, *Sir* Norman

Dangers of obedience, The: Laski, Harold

Daniel: Blackmore, R.D.

Daniel Airlie: Hichens, Robert

Daniel Boone, wilderness scout: White, S.E.

Daniel De Foe and Charles Churchill: Forster, John

Daniel Deronda: †Eliot, George

Daniel jazz, The: Lindsay, N.V.

Daniel Sweetland: Phillpotts, Eden

Daniel the prophet: Pusey, E.B.

Danites in the Sierras, The: †Miller, Joaquin

Dan'l Druce, blacksmith: Gilbert, *Sir* W.S.

Danny's own story: Marquis, Don

Dante: Eliot, T.S.

Dante and his convito: Rossetti, W.M.

Dante and his influence: Page, T.N.

Dante Gabriel Rossetti: Symons, Arthur

Dante Gabriel Rossetti as designer and writer: Rossetti, W.M.

Danton: Belloc, Hilaire

Danvers Jewels, The: Cholmondeley, Mary

Danvis pioneer, A: Robinson, R.E.

Daphnaïda: Spenser, Edmund

Daphne: McFarlane, John E. Clare

Daphne: Tennyson, Frederick

Daphne Adeane: Baring, Maurice

Daphne and Amintor: Bickerstaffe, Isaac

Daphne Bruno I: Raymond, Ernest

Daphne Bruno II: Raymond, Ernest

Daphne in Fitzroy Street: Nesbit, Edith

Daphne Laureole: †Bridie, James

Daphne or Marriage à la mode: Ward, M.A.

Daphne's fishing: Hannay, J.O.

Daphnis and Cloe: Gay, John

Darby and Joan: Baring, Maurice

D'Archeville: Mottram, R.H.

Daring young man on the flying trapeze, The: Saroyan, William

Darius Codomannus: Brontë, Charlotte

Darius Green and his flying machine: Trowbridge, J.T.

Dark Ages, The: Ker, W.P.

Dark Ann: †Bowen, Marjorie

Dark Bahama: †Cheyney, Peter

Dark breed, The: Higgins, F.R.

Dark Bridwell: Fisher, V.A.

Dark cavalier, The: Widdemer, Margaret

Dark cloud, The: Boyd, Thomas

Dark command, The: Burnett, W.R.

Dark daughters, The: Davies, Rhys

Dark days: Robinson, E.S.L.

Dark duet: †Cheyney, Peter

Dark eye in Africa, The: Van der Post, L.J.

Dark eyes of London, The: Wallace, Edgar

Dark fire, The: †Mordaunt, Elinor

Dark fire, The: Turner, W.J.R.

Dark fleece, The: Hergesheimer, Joseph

Dark flower, The: Galsworthy, John

Dark folk: Slater, F.C.

Dark forest, The: Mannin, Ethel

Dark forest, The: Walpole, *Sir* Hugh

Dark frontier, The: Ambler, Eric

Dark gentleman, The: Stern, G.B.

Dark hazard: Burnett, W.R.

Dark hero: †Cheyney, Peter

Dark Hester: Sedgwick, A.D.

Dark horse, The: Grant, Robert

Dark horses: Phillpotts, Eden

Dark hours, The: Marquis, Don

Dark house, The: Deeping, Warwick

Dark huntsman, The: Heavysege, Charles

Dark interlude: †Cheyney, Peter

Dark interlude: Timms, E.V.

Dark is light enough, The: Fry, Christopher

Dark island, The: Sackville-West, V.

Dark island, The: Treece, Henry

Dark journey, The: Green, Julian

Dark kingdom, The: Patchen, Kenneth

Dark lady of the sonnets, The: Shaw, G.B.

Dark ladies: Brown, I.J.C.

Dark lady of Doona, The: Maxwell, W.H.

Dark lantern, A: Wither, George

Dark lantern, The: Williamson, Henry

Dark laughter: Anderson, Sherwood

Dark mile, The: Broster, D.K.

Dark moon: Divine, A.D.

Dark mother, The: Frank, Waldo

Dark night, The: Sinclair, May

Dark night's work, A: Gaskell, E.C.

Dark o' the moon, The: Crockett, S.R.

Dark of summer, The: Linklater, Eric

Dark of the moon: Teasdale, Sara

Dark outlaw: Clune, Frank

Dark page, The: †Bell, Neil

Dark princess: Dubois, William

Dark river, The: Ackland, Rodney

Dark river, The: Hall, J.N. and C.B. Nordhoff

Dark river, The: Millin, Sarah Gertrude

Dark road: Devaney, J.M.

Dark room, The: Narayan, R.K.

Dark Rosaleen: †Bowen, Marjorie

Dark Rosaleen: Mangan, J.C.

Dark scenes of history: James, G.P.R.

Dark soil: Stringer, A.J.A.

Dark stain: Appel, Benjamin

Dark star, The: Chambers, R.W.

Dark street, The: †Cheyney, Peter

Dark summer: Bogan, Louise

Dark tapestry: Mitchell, Mary

Dark thread, The: †Boake, Capel

Dark tide, The: Brittain, Vera

Dark tower, The: Bottome, Phyllis

Dark tower, The: Kaufman, G.S.

Dark tower, The: Macneice, Louis

Dark tower, The: Mickle, A.D.

Dark tower, The: Woollcott, A.H.

Dark tower, The: Young, Francis Brett

Dark traveler: Johnson, Josephine

Dark wanton: †Cheyney, Peter

Dark weaver, The: Salverson, L.G.

Dark weeping: Russell, G.W.

Dark well, The: Chattopadhyaya, H.

Dark wind, The: Turner, W.J.R.

Dark windows: Ercole, Velia

Dark wing, The: Stringer, A.J.A.

Dark world of animals: Farjeon, Eleanor

Dark youth: Hughes, J.L.

Darkened rooms: Gibbs, Sir Philip

Darkening green, The: Mackenzie, Sir Compton

Dark-eyed Lady: Coppard, A.E.

Darkie and Co.: Spring, Howard

Darkness: O'Flaherty, Liam

Darkness and day: Compton-Burnett, Ivy

Darkness and daylight: Holmes, M.J.

Darkness and the dawn: Caostin, T.B.

Darkness and the deep: Fisher, V.A.

Darkness at Pemberley: White, T.H.

Darkness falls from the air: Balchin, Nigel

Darkness my bride: Mannin, Ethel

Darkness visible: Hook, T.E.

Darkwater: Dubois, William

Darley steps: Allen, C.R.

Darling buds of May, The: Bates, H.E.

Darling of her heart, The: Davies, Rhys

Darling of the gods, The: Belasco, David

Darling Tom: Strong, L.A.G.

Darlinghurst nights and morning glories: Slessor, Kenneth

Darnley: James, G.P.R.

Darrel of the Blessed Isles: Bacheller, Irving

D'Artagnan: Bedford-Jones, Henry

D'Artagnan's letter: Bedford-Jones, Henry

Dartmoor: Hemans, Mrs. Felicia

Dartmoor idylls: Baring-Gould, S.

Dartmoor village, A: Phillpotts, Eden

Dartmouth lyrics: Hovey, Richard

Darwin: Bradford, Gamaliel

Darwin and his world: Huxley, Sir Julian and H.D.B. Kettlewell

Darwin revalued: Keith, Sir Arthur

Darwinism: Fiske, John

Darwinism: Wallace, A.R.

Darwinism and its critics: Keith, Sir Arthur

Darwinism in morals: Cobbe, Frances Power

Dash of the day, The: Lathom, Francis

Dashes at life with a free pencil: Willis, N.P.

Dashing dragoon, A: Reid, T.M.

Dashwoods, The: †Rudd, Steele

Date of Chaucer's Troilus and other Chaucer matters, The: Kittredge, G.L.

Date with a duchess, A: Calder-Marshall, Arthur

Dauber: Masefield, John

Daughter of Anderson Crow, The: McCutcheon, G.B.

Daughter of Astrea, A: Oppenheim, E. Phillips

Daughter of Bugle Ann, The: Kantor, Mackinlay

Daughter of Fife, A: Barr, A.E.H.

Daughter of France: Sackville-West, V.

Daughter of Heth, A: Black, William

Daughter of India: Fyzee Rahamin, S.

Daughter of New France, A: Doughty, *Sir* A.G.

Daughter of silence, A: Fawcett, Edgar

Daughter of the fields, A: Tynan, Katherine

Daughter of the Incas, A: Deamer, Dulcie

Daughter of the Marionis, A: Oppenheim, E. Phillips

Daughter of the Medici, A: Byrne, Donn

Daughter of the middle border, A: Garland, Hamlin

Daughter of the morning, A: De Selincourt, Hugh

Daughter of the morning, A: Gale, Zona

Daughter of the Pangaran, The: †Divine, David

Daughter of the Philistines, A: Boyesen, H.H.

Daughter of the snows, A: London, Jack

Daughter of the south, A: Eggleston, G.C.

Daughter of the stars, The: Brooks, C.W.S.

Daughter of the storage, The: Howells, W.D.

Daughter of time, The: (†Josephine Tey), Mackintosh, Elizabeth

Daughter of to-day, A: Duncan, S.J.

Daughter of the vine, A: Atherton, Gertrude

Daughter to Philip: Seymour, B.K.

Daughters and sons: Compton-Burnett, Ivy

Daughters of Babylon, The: Hichens, Robert

Daughters of dawn: Carman, Bliss

Daughters of Eve: Bradford, Gamaliel

Daughters of Mrs. Peacock, The: Bullett, Gerald

Daughters of Pola, The: Neale, J.M.

Daughters of Queen Victoria: Benson, E.F.

Daughters of the night, The: Wallace, Edgar

Daughters of the rich: Saltus, E.E.

Daughters of the Seven Mile: Cross, Zora

Daumier: Sadleir, Michael

Davenport Dunn: Lever, C.J.

David: Birney, Earle

David: Cooper, Alfred Duff

David: Kingsley, Charles

David: Lawrence, D.H.

David: Royde-Smith, Naomi

David and destiny: (†Ian Hay), Beith, *Sir* John Hay

David and Diana: Roberts, C.E.M.

David Blaize: Benson, E.F.

David Elginbrod: Macdonald, George

David Garrick: Robertson, T.W.

David go back: Connell, John

David Gray: Buchanan, R.W.

David Harum: Westcott, E.N.

David of King's: Benson, E.F.

David Penstephen: Pryce, Richard

David Williams, founder of the Royal Literary Fund: Lucas, E.V.

David's Day: Mackail, Denis

Davids hainous sin: Fuller, Thomas

Dawk bungalow, The: Trevelyan, *Sir* G.O.

Dawn: Bacheller, Irving

Dawn: Haggard, *Sir* Henry Rider

Dawn: Porter, E.H.

Dawn approaching noon: Chattopadhyaya, H.

Dawn Ginsbergh's revenge: Perelman, S.J.

Dawn in Britain, The: Doughty, C.M.

Dawn in Lyonesse: Chase, M.E.

Dawn in Russia: Frank, Waldo

Dawn island: Martineau, Harriet

Dawn of a to-morrow, The: Burnett, Frances Hodgson

Dawn of Canadian history, The: Leacock, Stephen

Dawn of conscience, The: Breasted, J.H.

Dawn of liberation, The: Churchill, *Sir* Winston

Dawn O'Hara, the girl who laughed: Ferber, Edna

Dawning lights: Cobbe, Frances Power

Dawn's left hand: Richardson, D.M.

Dawnward?: O'Dowd, B.P.

Dawson pedigree, The: Sayers, Dorothy

Day, A: Armstrong, John

Day: Cunningham, John

Day after tomorrow, The: Gibbs, *Sir* Philip

Day and night: Livesay, Dorothy

Day and night songs: Allingham, William

Day and night stories: Blackwood, Algernon

Day at Castrogiovanni, A: Woodberry, G.E.

Day at Laguerre's and other days, A: Smith, F.H.

Day before, The: Tomlinson, H.M.

Day before yesterday, The: Moffat, James

Day by day: Green, Paul

Day by the fire, A: Hunt, Leigh

Day in the Autumn, A: Barton, Bernard

Day in Turkey, A: Cowley, *Mrs.* Hannah

Day is wooing: Caldwell, Erskine Preston

Day Jean-Pierre was pignapped, The: Gallico, Paul

Day Jean-Pierre went round the world, The: Gallico, Paul

Day of atonement: Golding, Louis

Day of deliverance: Benét, William Rose

Day of doom, The: Wigglesworth, Michael

Day of fate, A: Roe, E.P.

Day of fire: Bacon, Leonard

Day of glory, The: Bates, H.E.

Day of glory, The: Canfield, Dorothy

Day of his youth, The: Brown, Alice

Day of pleasant bread, A: Baker, Ray Stannard

Day of small things, The: Buchan, Anna

Day of small things, The: Manning, Anne

Day of the beast, The: Grey, Zane

Day of the dog, The: Lucas, E.V.

Day of the dog, The: McCutcheon, G.B.

Day of the locust, The: †West, Nathaniel

Day of the tortoise, The: Bates, H.E.

Day of their wedding, The: Howells, W.D.

Day of trial, The: Griffin, Gerald

Day of uniting, The: Wallace, Edgar

Day of wrath: Child, P.A.

Day off, A: Jameson, Storm

Day the guinea pig talked, The: Gallico, Paul

Day the money stopped, The: Anderson, Maxwell

Day they robbed the Bank of England, The: Brophy, John

Day will come, The: Braddon, Mary Elizabeth

Day will dawn, The: Rattigan, Terence

Daybreak, Palmer, E.V.

Day-breaking, The: Shepard, Thomas

Day-dream, The: Tennyson, Alfred *Lord*

Daylight and Champaigne: Young, G.M.

Daylight on Saturday: Priestley, J.B.

Day's alarm, The: Dehn, Paul

Days and dreams: Cawein, Madison

Days and hours: Tennyson, Frederick

Days and nights: Symons, Arthur

Days before Lent: Basso, Hamilton

Days departed: Bowles, William Lisle

Days dividing, The: †Bell, Neil

Day's end and other stories: Bates, H.E.

Days gone by, The: Riley, J.W.

Days in the sun: Cardus, Neville

Days near Paris: Hare, A.J.C.

Days near Rome: Hare, A.J.C.

Days of Bruce, The: Aguilar, Grace

Days of disillusion: Cobb, C.F.

Days of Hogarth, The: Reynolds, G.

Days of my life, The: Haggard, *Sir* Henry Rider

Days of my life, The: Oliphant, Margaret

Days of the Phoenix: Brooks, Van Wyck

Days of their youth, The: Sullivan, Alan

Days of used to be, The: Cawein, Madison

Days of yore, The: Cumberland, Richard

Days play, The: Milne, A.A.

Day's pleasure, A: Howells, W.D.

Day's ride, A: Lever, C.J.

Days to remember: Newbolt, *Sir* Henry

Days without end: O'Neill, Eugene

Day's work: Kipling, Rudyard

Dazzle: Mottram, R.H.

Dazzled not blinded: Robertson, T.W.

De Amore Amicorum: Guiney, L.I.

De Bello Germanico: Blunden, Edmund

De Clifford: Ward, Robert Plumer

De consolatione philosophiae: Chaucer, Geoffrey

De corpore politico: Hobbes, Thomas

De curia sapientiae: Lydgate, John

De flagello myrteo: Garnett, Richard

De Foix: Bray, Anna Eliza

De Forests of Avesnes, The: De Forest, John William

De haeretico comburendo: Trevelyan, G.M.

De libris: Dobson, H.A.

De L'orme: James, G.P.R.

De omnibus, by the conductor: Pain, B.E.O.

De profundis: Dickinson, Goldsworthy Lowes

De profundis: Wilde, Oscar

De Quincey: Masson, David

De Regimine Principum: Hoccleve (*or* Occleve), Thomas

De senectute: more last words: Harrison, Frederic

De Soto and his men in the land of Florida: King, G.E.

De Valera: O'Faolain, Sean

De Vere: Ward, Robert Plumer

Deacon, The: Jones, H.A.

Deacon Brodie: Henley, W.E.

Deacon Brodie: Stevenson, R.L.

Deacon Herbert's Bible-class: Clarke, J.F.

Deacon's week, The: Cooke, Rose Terry

Dead alive, The: O'Keeffe, John

Dead centre: Calder-Marshall, Arthur

Dead end: Kingsley, Sidney

Dead king, The: Kipling, Rudyard

Dead love has chains: Braddon, Mary Elizabeth

Dead man inside: Starrett, Vincent

Dead man leading: Pritchett, V.S.

Dead man over all: Allen, Walter Ernest

Dead man's folly: Christie, Agatha

Dead man's knock, The: Carr, J.D.

Dead man's plack, and An old thorn: Hudson, W.H.

Dead man's rock: (†Q), Quiller-Couch, *Sir* A.

Dead man's shoes: (†Michael Innes), Stewart, J.I.M.

Dead man's watch: Cole, G.D.H.

Dead men tell no tales: Hornung, E.W.

Dead men tell no tales, but live men do: Sala, G.A.H.

Dead men's bells: Nixen, F.J.

Dead men's gold: Bridges, Roy

Dead men's shoes: Braddon, Mary Elizabeth

Dead Mr. Nixon: White, T.H.

Dead Ned: Masefield, John

Dead or alive: †Brand, Max

Dead reckoning: Fearing Kenneth

Dead Sea fruit: Braddon, Mary Elizabeth

Dead seagull, The: Barker, George

Dead secret, The: Collins, William Wilkie

Dead student, The: Carleton, William (Mc Kendree)

Dead tearme, The: Dekker, Thomas

Dead timber: Esson, T.L.B.

Dead towns and living men: Woolley, *Sir* Leonard

Dead tryst, The: Grant, James

Dead water: Marsh, Ngaio Edith

Dead yellow women: Hammett, S.D.

Deadlock: Richardson, D.M.

Deadly friend, The: Wescott, Glenway

Deadly joker, The: Day-Lewis, C.

Deadly poison: Pertwee, Roland

Deal in wheat, A: †Norris, Frank

Deal with the devil, A: Phill-potts, Eden

Dealing in futures: Brighouse, Harold

Dealings with the fairies: Mac-donald, George

Dealings with the firm of Dombey and son: Dickens, Charles

Deals: Pain, B.E.O.

Dean's daughter, The: Gore, Catherine

Dean's elbow, The: Mason, A.E.W.

Dear baby: Saroyan, William

Dear departed, The: Houghton, W.S.

Dear Faustina: Broughton, Rhoda

Dear Irish girl, The: Tynan, Katherine

Dear Judas: Jeffers, J.R.

Dear life: Bates, H.E.

Dear lovely death: Hughes, J.L.

Dear octopus: Smith, Dodie

Dear old Templeton: Brown, Alice

Dearly beloved of Benjamin Cobb, The: †Dane, Clemence

Death: Montgomery, Robert

Death and afterwards: Arnold, Edwin

Death and birth of David Markand, The: Frank, Waldo

Death and taxes: Parker, Dorothy

Death and the dancing footman: Marsh, Ngaio Edith

Death as an extra: Gielgud, Val

Death at Broadcasting House: Gielgud, Val

Death at the bar: Marsh, Ngaio Edith

Death at the "Dolphin": Marsh, Ngaio Edith

Death at the president's lodging: (†Michael Innes), Stewart, J.I.M.

Death by design: Derleth, A.W.

Death comes as the end: Christie, Agatha

Death comes to the Archbishop: Cather, Willa

Death in a white tie: Marsh, Ngaio Edith

Death in Budapest: Gielgud, Val

Death in disguise: a temperance poem: Clarke, Macdonald

Death in ecstasy: Marsh, Ngaio Edith

Death in five boxes: †Carter Dickson

Death in the afternoon: Hemingway, Ernest

Death in the clouds: Christie, Agatha

Death in the quarry: Cole, G.D.H.

Death in the stocks: Heyer, Georgette

Death in the sun: Cole, G.D.H.

Death in the woods: Anderson, Sherwood

Death it is: †Mordaunt, Elinor

Death of a bride: Cole, G.D.H.

Death of a fool: Marsh, Ngaio Edith

Death of a gentleman: Hollis, Christopher

Death of a ghost: Allingham, Margery

Death of a God: Sitwell, *Sir* Osbert

Death of a hero: Aldington, Richard

Death of a hero: Anand, M.R.

Death of a highbrow: Swinnerton, Frank

Death of a man: Boyle, Kay

Death of a millionaire, The: Cole, G.D.H.

Death of a peer: Marsh, Ngaio Edith

Death of a queen: †Caudwell, Christopher

Death of a star, The: Cole, G.D.H.

Death of a train: Crofts, F.W.

Death of Adam, The: Binyon, Laurence

Death of Agrippina, The: Symons, Arthur

Death of Alkibiades, The: Adams, Francis

Death of an airman: †Caudwell, Christopher

Death of an Aryan: Huxley, Elspeth J.

Death of Dickie Draper, The: Weidman, Jerome

Death of Eli, The: Young, A.J.

Death of Fionavar, The: Gore-Booth, E.S.

Death of General Montgomery, The: Brackenridge, Hugh

Death of good fortune, The: Williams, Charles

Death of Leander, The: Drinkwater, John

Death of man, The: Trevelyan, R.C.

Death of Marlowe, The: Horne, Richard

Death of Maurice, The: Pain, B.E.O.

Death of Noble Godavary and Gottfried Künstler, The: Sackville-West, V.

Death of Oenone, The: Tennyson, Alfred *Lord*

Death of Orpheus, The: Housman, Laurence

Death of poetry: Crane, Nathalia

Death of Robert, Earle of Huntington, The: Chettle, Henry

Death of Robert, Earle of Huntington, The: Munday, Anthony

Death of Sir John Franklin, The: Swinburne, A.C.

Death of society, The: Wilson, Romer

Death of Socrates, The: Housman, Laurence

Death of Synge, The: Yeats, W.B.

Death of Tintagiles, The (trn.): Sutro, Alfred

Death of the Duke of Clarence and Avondale, The: Tennyson, Alfred *Lord*

Death of the heart, The: Bowen, E.D.C.

Death of the hero, The: Lindsay, Jack

Death of the lion, The: James, Henry

Death of the moth, The: Woolf, Virginia

Death of yesterday, The: Graham, Stephen

Death on a quiet day: (†Michael Innes), Stewart, J.I.M.

Death on the left: Connell, John

Death on the Nile: Christie, Agatha

Death on the way: Crofts, F.W.

Death rocks the cradle: (†Paul Martens), †Bell, Neil

Death ship, The: Russell, W.C.

Death shot, The: Reid, T.M.

Death to slow music: Nichols, Beverley

Death to the French: Forester, C.S.

Death turns the tables: Carr, J.D.

Death under sail: Snow, C.P.

Death walks in Eastrepps:†Beeding, Francis

Death watch: Carr, J.D.

Death-ride, The: Marston, J.W.

Deaths and entrances: Thomas, Dylan

Death's duell: Donne, John

Death's jest-book: Beddoes, T.L.

Debate continues, The: Campbell, Margaret

Debate! Is modern marriage a failure?: Powys, John Cowper

Debate! Is modern marriage a failure?: Russell, Bertrand

Debate, Resolved: That the soviet form of government is applicable to western civilization: Russell, Bertrand

Debateable ground: Stern, G.B.

Debates in Parliament: Johnson, Samuel

Debauchee, The: Behn, *Mrs.* Afra

Debit account, The: †Onions, Oliver

Debits and credits: Kipling, Rudyard

Debonair: Stern, G.B.

Deborah: Abercrombie, Lascelles

Deborah's diary: Manning, Anne

Debt discharged, A: Wallace, Edgar

Debtor, The: Freeman, M.W.

Debtor's prison, The: Green, Asa

Débutante, The: Gore, Catherine

Debutantes: Devaney, J.M.

Decadence: Balfour, A.J.

Decadence, a philosophical enquiry: Joad, C.E.M.

Decay of capitalist civilisation: Webb, Beatrice and Sidney Webb

December love: Hichens, Robert

December lyrics: Campbell, W.W.

December roses: Praed, *Mrs.* C.

December tales: Ainsworth, Harrison

Decennium Luctuosum: Mather, Cotton

Decent birth, A: Saroyan, William

Decision: Boyle, Kay

Decision of the court, The: Matthews, J.B.

Decisive wars of history, The: Liddell Hart, B.

Decius and Paulina: Theobald, Lewis

Deck-chair stories: Pryce, Richard

Declaration by the representatives of the United Colonies, A: Dickinson, John

Declaration of independence, The: Becker, C.L.

Declaration of Independence, The: Jefferson, Thomas

Declaration of rights: Shelley, P.B.

Declaration of the gentlemen, The: Mather, Cotton

Déclassée: Akins, Zoë

Decline and fall: Waugh, Evelyn

Decline and fall of a British matron, The: Mitchell, Mary

Decline and fall of Keewatin, The: Bengough, J.W.

Decline and fall of the Roman Empire, The: Gibbon, Edward

Decline and fall of the Romantic ideal, The: Lucas, F.L.

Decline of merry England, The: Jameson, Storm

Decoration of houses, The: Wharton, Edith

Decorations in verse and prose: Dowson, E.C.

Decorative art: Petrie, *Sir* William Flinders

Decorative arts, The: Morris, William

Decorative patterns: Petrie, *Sir* William Flinders

Decorative plaques: Freeman, M.W.

Decoy, The: Beresford, J.D.

Dede of pittie, The: Blunden, Edmund

Dedicated: †Field, Michael

Dedication for a bookseller's window: Morley, C.D.

Dedication of the beech-tree, The: Hill, Aaron

Deed without a name, A: Phillpotts, Eden

Deeds that held the Empire: Divine, A.D.

Deemster, The: Caine, *Sir* Thomas

Deep blue sea, The: Rattigan, Terence

Deep down: Ballantyne, R.M.

Deep Moat Grange: Crockett, S.R.

Deep sea: Young, Francis Brett

Deep waters: Jacobs, W.W.

Deepening stream, The: Canfield, Dorothy

Deepening stream: Holcroft, M.H.

Deephaven: Jewett, S.O.

Deer at our house: Caldwell, Erskine Preston

Deerbrook: Martineau, Harriet

Deerslayer, The: Cooper, James Fenimore

Deerstalkers, The: Herbert, H.W.

Defeat: Galsworthy, John

Defeat for death: Abbas, K.A.

Defeat of the confederacy: Commager, H.S.

Defeat of youth, The: Huxley, Aldous

Defeat or victory: Mee, Arthur

Defeated, The: Lewisohn, Ludwig

Defective Santa Claus, A: Riley, J.W.

Defence, The: Nabokov, Vladimir

Defence and the English-speaking rôle: Angell, *Sir* Norman

Defence of a philosophic doubt, A: Balfour, A.J.

Defence of an essay of dramatique poesie, A: Dryden, John

Defence of Britain, The: Liddell Hart, B.

Defence of Calais: Linklater, Eric

Defence of Christian science: Eddy, M.B.

Defence of classical education, A: Livingstone, *Sir* Richard

Defence of cosmetics, A: Beerbohm, *Sir* Max

Defence of democracy, The: Murray, John Middleton

Defence of dramatick poetry, A: Settle, Elkanah

Defence of free-thinking in mathematics, A: Berkeley, George

Defence of good women, The: Elyot, *Sir* Thomas

Defence of Guenevere, The: Morris, William

Defence of idealism, A: Sinclair, May

Defence of ignorance, A: Morley, Henry

Defence of Mr. John Cotton, A: Cotton, John

Defence of nonsense: Chesterton, G.K.

Defence of poesie, The: Sidney, *Sir* Philip

Defence of poetry, A: D'Israeli, Isaac

Defence of poetry, music, and stage plays, A: Lodge, Thomas

Defence of the answer, A: Shepard, Thomas

Defence of the character of Thomas Jefferson: Tucker, George

Defence of the doctrine of justification, by faith in Jesus Christ, A: Bunyan, John

Defence of the Empire, The: Angell, *Sir* Norman

Defence of the Reformation: Coulton, G.G.

Defence of the short view of the profaneness and immorality of the English stage, A: Collier, Jeremy

Defence of the treaty of amity, commerce, and navigation, A: Hamilton, Alexander

Defence of the true and Catholike doctrine of the Sacrament, A: Cranmer, Thomas

Defence of the West: Liddell Hart, B.

Defence of the Whigs, A: Kennedy, J.P.

Defence of usury: Bentham, Jeremy

Defendant, The: Chesterton, G.K.

Defender of the faith: †Bowen, Marjorie

Defense of Circe, A: Porter, K.A.

Defense of Sir Foppling Flutter, A: Dennis, John

Definite object, The: Farnol, J.J.

Definitions: Canby, H.S.

Deformed transformed, The: Byron, George Gordon, *Lord*

Defy the foul fiend: Collier, John

Degarmo's wife: Phillips, D.G.

Degradation of the democratic dogma, The: Adams, H.B.

Deirdre: Fergusson, *Sir* Samuel

Deirdre: Field, Michael

Deirdrè: Joyce, R.D.

Deirdre: Russell, G.W.

Deirdre: Stephens, James

Deirdre: Yeats, W.B.

Deirdre of the sorrows: Synge, J.M.

Deirdre wed: Trench, F.H.

Delaware: James, G.P.R.

Delectable Duchy, The: (†Q), Quiller-Couch, *Sir* A.

Delectable mountains, The: Mann, Leonard

Delhi affairs (1761–88): Sarkar, Y.J.

Delia: Daniel, Samuel

Delia Blanchflower: Ward, M.A.

Delicate, dainty, damnable dialogue between the devill and a Jesuite, A: Taylor, John

Delicate diet, for daintie mouth de Droonkardes, A: Gascoigne, George

Delicate fire, The: Mitchison, Naomi

Delicate monster: Jameson, Storm

Delicate situation, The: Royde-Smith, Naomi

Delight: De la Roche, Mazo

Delight: Phillpotts, Eden

Delight in books: Mais, S.P.B.

Delight of great books, The: Erskine, John

Delights: Priestley, J.B.

Delights of dictatorship, The: Lucas, F.L.

Delilah upside down: Marshall, Bruce

Deliver my darling: Temple, Joan

Deliverance, The: Glasgow, E.A.G.

Deliverance, A: Monkhouse, A.N.

Deliverance: Strong, L.A.G.

Delmour: Lytton, E.G.E.B., *1st Baron*

Deloraine: Godwin, William

Deluge, The: Phillips, D.G.

Deluge, The: Trevelyan, R.C.

Demagogue, The: Falconer, William

Demagogue, The: †Nasby, Petroleum V.

Demeter: Bridges, Robert

Demeter: Tennyson, Alfred *Lord*

Demeter's daughter: Phillpotts, Eden

Demi-gods, The: Stephens, James

Democracy: Adams, H.B.

Democracy: Lowell, J.R.

Democracy and education: Dewey, John

Democracy and ideals, a definition: Erskine, John

Democracy and leadership: Babbitt, Irving

Democracy and liberty: Lecky, W.E.H.

Democracy and social ethics: Addams, Jane

Democracy and the arts: Brooke, Rupert

Democracy, education and the new dispensation: Logan, J.D.

Democracy in crisis: Laski, Harold

Democracy in industry: Cole, G.D.H.

Democracy, its claims and perils: Temple, William

Democracy marches: Huxley, Sir Julian

Democracy today: Grey of Fallodon, Edward Lord

Democracy under pressure: Chase, Stuart

Democracy under revision: Wells, H.G.

Democracy versus liberty?: Madariaga, Salvador de

Democrat, The: Pye, H.J.

Democrat dies, A: Frankau, Pamela

Democratiad, The: Hopkins, Lemuel

Democratic distinction in America: Brownell, William C.

Democratic John Bunyan, The: †Nasby, Petroleum V.

Democratic sonnets: Rossetti, W.M.

Democratic vistas: Whitman, Walt

Democritus: Gould, Gerald

Democritus: Rowlands, Samuel

Democritus Platonissans: More, Henry

Demon in the house, The: Thirkell, Angela

Demon killer, The: Clune, Frank

Demon lady, The: Whittier, J.G.

Demon lover, The: Bowen, E.D.C.

Demon of destiny, The: Galt, John

Demon of the absolute, The: More, P.E.

Demon trapper of Umbabog, The: Thompson, D.P.

Demoniac, The: Besant, Sir Walter

Demoniacs, The: Carr, J.D.

Demonogy and Devil lore: Conway, M.D.

Demonstrated survival: Lodge, Sir Oliver

Demophon: Reid, Forrest

Demoralizing marriage, A: Fawcett, Edgar

Demos: Gissing, George

Demos the Emperor: Sitwell, Sir Osbert

Dendereh: Petrie, Sir William

Dene Hollow: Wood, Ellen

Denis Dent: Hornung, E.W.

Denis Duval: Thackeray, W.M.

Denis O'Shaughnessy going to Maynooth: Carleton, William

Denmark: Sitwell, Sacheverell

Dennison Grant: Stead, R.J.C.

Denounced, The: Banim, John

Denvis folks: Robinson, R.E.

Denzil Quarrier: Gissing, George

Deontology or science of morality: Bentham, Jeremy

Department of queer complaints, The: †Carter Dickson

Departmental ditties: barrackroom ballads: Kipling, Rudyard

Departure: Campbell, W.W.

Departure: Fast, Howard M.

Depends what you mean by love: Monsarrat, Nicholas

Deplorable state of New-England, The: Mather, Cotton

Depression island: Sinclair, Upton

Depths of prosperity, The: Bottome, Phyllis

Deputy was king, A: Stern, G.B.

Der eggsberiences ov Hans Schwartz:(†Garryowen),Finn, Edmund

Der Tag: Barrie, Sir J.M.

Derby Barnes, trader: Skinner, C.L.

Derby day: Herbert, Sir A.P.

Derelict, The: Bottome, Phyllis

Derelict, The: Nordhoff, C.B.

Derelicts: McFee, William

Dermot Mac Morrogh: Adams, J.Q.

Dermot O'Brien: Herbert, H.W.

Derrick Vaughan, novelist: Lyall, Edna

Derval Hampton: Grant, James

Descendant, The: Glasgow, E.A.G.

Descensus Astraeae: Peele, George

Descent into hell: Williams, Charles

Descent of liberty, The: Hunt, Leigh

Descent of man, The: Darwin, Charles

Descent of man, The: Wharton, Edith

Descent of property in the Old Kingdom: Murray, Margaret

Descent of the dove, The: Williams, Charles

Descent to the dead: Jeffers, J.R.

Description of a maske, The: Campion, Thomas

Description of a new world, called the blazing worlde: Newcastle, Margaret, Duchess

Description of Britain, The (trn.): Caxton, William

Description of Mr. D(ryden)'s funeral, A: Brown, Thomas

Description of New England, A: Smith, John

Description of the city, colleges and cathedral of Winchester, A: Warton, Thomas

Description of the collegegreen club: Brooke, Henry

Description of the masque celebrating the marriage of Viscount Haddington, The: Jonson, Ben

Description of the part of Devonshire bordering on the Tamar and Tavy: Bray, A.E.

Description of the regalia of Scotland: Scott, Sir Walter

Description of the scenery of the Lakes in the North of England, A: Wordsworth, William

Description of the Wordsworth and Coleridge MSS, A: White, W.H.

Descriptive catalogue of Sanskrit, Pali and Singhalese literary works of Ceylon, A: D'Alwis, James

Descriptive sketches. In verse: Wordsworth, William

Descriptive sociology: Spencer, Herbert

Descriptive sociology of Ancient Egypt: Petrie, *Sir* William Flinders

Desert: Armstrong, M.D.

Desert, The: Colum, Padraic

Desert and the sown, The: Bell, Gertrude

Desert fathers, The: Waddell, H.J.

Desert gold: Grey, Zane

Desert healer, The: Hull, E.M.

Desert highway: Priestley, J.B.

Desert home, The: Reid, T.M.

Desert island, The: Murphy, Arthur

Desert music, The: Williams, W.C.

Desert of wheat, The: Grey, Zane

Desert poems: Wellesley, D.V.

Desert year, The: Krutch, J.W.

Deserted bride, The: Morris, G.P.

Deserted city, The: Sherman, F.J.

Deserted daughter, The: Holcroft, Thomas

Deserted house: Wellesley, D.V.

Deserted parks, The: †Carroll, Lewis

Deserted village, The: Goldsmith, Oliver

Deserter, The: Abercrombie, Lascelles

Deserter: Aldington, Richard

Deserter, The: Dibdin, Charles

Deserter, The: Frederic, Harold

Deserts of Southern France, The: Baring-Gould, Sabine

Deshasheh: Petrie, *Sir* William Flinders

Desiderio: Baring, Maurice

Design for living: Coward, Noel

Design for living: Hecht, Ben

Designs of modern costumes: Hope, Thomas

Desire and pursuit of the whole, The: (†Baron Corvo), Rolfe, Frederick

Desire of content: Courage, F.J.

Desire of the moth, The: Rhodes, E.M.

Desire to please, The: Nicolson, Hon. *Sir* Harold

Desire under the elms: O'Neill, Eugene

Desires and devices: Simpson, H. de G.

Desmond: Smith, Charlotte

Desolate house, The: Simpson, H. de G.

Desolate splendour: Sadleir, Michael

Desolate star, The: †Hyde, Robin

Despair: Nabokov, Vladimir

Despatch rider, The: Glanville, Ernest

Desperate journey: Treece, Henry

Desperate lovers, The: Sutro, Alfred

Desperate pursuit: †Bell, Neil

Desperate remedies: Hardy, Thomas

Despoiling Venus: Lindsay, Jack

Despot of Broomsedge Cove, The: †Craddock, C.E.

Despotism: D'Israeli, Isaac

Despotism in America: Hildreth, Richard

Destination: Reeve, Clara

Destination unknown: Christie, Agatha

Destiny Bay: Byrne, Donn

Destiny of man viewed in the light of his origin, The: Fiske, John

Destiny, or the chief's daughter: Ferrier, Susan

Destroyer, The: Poole, Ernest

Destroyer's war: Divine, A.D.

Destroying victor: Beals, Carleton

Destruction: Glyn, Elinor

Destruction of Gotham, The: †Miller, Joaquin

Destruction of Troy, The: Denham, *Sir* John

Destructive element, The: Spender, Stephen

Destry rides again: †Brand, Max

Desultoria: Brydges, *Sir* Samuel Egerton

Desultory man, The: James, G.P.R.

Desultory thoughts and reflections: Blessington, Marguerite

Detection unlimited: Heyer, Georgette

Detective short story, The: †Queen, Ellery

Detective story: Kingsley, Sidney

Detectives of the dales: Trease, Geoffrey

Determinism and physics: Russell, Bertrand

Deterrent or defence: Liddell Hart, B.

Dethronements: Housman, Laurence

Detraction displayed: Opie, Amelia

Deucalion: Ruskin, John

Deuce is in him, The: Colman, George, *the elder*

Deus justificatus: Taylor, Jeremy

Devastator, The: Stringer, A.J.A.

Devastators, The: Cambridge, Ada

Development hypothesis, The: Spencer, Herbert

Development of English biography, The: Nicolson, Hon. *Sir* Harold

Development of English prose between 1918 and 1939: Forster, E.M.

Development of European polity, The: Sidgwick, Henry

Development of metaphysics in Persia, The: Iqbal, *Sir* Muhammad

Development of modern France, 1870–1939, The: Brogan, *Sir* Denis

Development of Parliament during the nineteenth century, The: Dickinson, G.L.

Development of piano music, The: Huneker, J.G.

Development of religion and thought in Ancient Egypt: Breasted, J.H.

Development of Sumerian art, The: Woolley, *Sir* Leonard

Development of the drama, The: Matthews, J.B.

Development of the English novel: Cross, W.L.

Development of the theatre, The: Nicoll, J.R.A.

Development of theology as illustrated in English poetry from 1780–1830, The: Brooke, Stopford A.

Devereux: Lytton, E.G.E.B., *1st Baron*

Devia Cypria: Hogarth, D.G.

Device of the pageant borne before Woolstone Dixi Lord Maior of the Citie of London, The: Peele, George

Devil, The: Levy, Benn W.

Devil and all, The: Collier, John

Devil and Daniel Webster, The: Benét, S.V.

Devil and the deep sea, The: Broughton, Rhoda

Devil and the lady, The: Tennyson, Alfred *Lord*

Devil came from Dublin, The: Carroll, P.V.

Devil for his niece, The: †Bridie, James

Devil in paradise, A: Miller, Henry

Devil in the desert, The: Horgan, Paul

Devil in velvet, The: Carr, J.D.

Devil is an ass, The: Jonson, Ben

Devil is an Englishman, The: Cournos, John

Devil man, The: Wallace, Edgar

Devil passes, The: Levy, Benn W.

Devil snared, The: †Preedy, George

Devil takes a holiday, The: Noyes, Alfred

Devil takes the chair, The: Cammaerts, Emile

Devil theory of war, The: Beard, C.A.

Devil to pay, The (film): †Lonsdale, Frederick

Devil to pay: †Queen, Ellery

Devil to pay, The: Sayers, Dorothy

Devil we know, The: Frankau, Pamela

Devil Wilkes, The: Postgate, Raymond

Devil's case, The: Buchanan, R.W.

Devil's charter, The: McKerrow, R.B.

Devil's cub: Heyer, Georgette

Devil's dictionary, The: Bierce, Ambrose

Devil's die, The: Allen, Grant

Devil's disciple, The: Shaw, G.B.

Devil's due, The: Swinburne, A.C.

Devil's Dyke: Hassall, Christopher

Devil's highway, The: Wright, H.B.

Devil's in the news, The: Linklater, Eric

Devil's jig, The: †Paye, Robert

Devils law-case, The: Webster, John

Devil's mantle, The: Packard, F.L.

Devil's motor, The: †Corelli, Marie

Devils of Loudun, The: Huxley, Aldous

Devil's own dear son, The: Cabell, James Branch

Devil's paw, The: Oppenheim, E. Phillips

Devil's saint, The: Deamer, Dulcie

Devil's walk, The: Coleridge, S.T.

Devil's walk, The: Shelley, P.B.

Devil's walk, The: Southey, Robert

Devious ways: Cannan, Gilbert

Devlin the barber: Farjeon, B.L.

Devon: Betjeman, John

Devon holiday, The: Williamson, Henry

Devonshire characters and strange events: Baring-Gould, Sabine

Devonshire cream: Phillpotts, Eden

Devota: Evans, *Sir* Arthur

Devoted, The: Bury, *Lady* C.S.M.

Devoted Sparkes: Ridge, W. Pett

Devotee, The: Cholmondeley, Mary

Devotional commentary on the Gospel narrative: Williams, Isaac

Devotional exercises for the use of young persons: Martineau, Harriet

Devotionarie book, A: Evelyn, John

Devotions upon emergent occasions: Donne, John

Devouring love: Tagore, *Sir* R.

Dew and bronze: Coffin, Robert

Dew and mildew: Wren, P.C.

Dew of the sea: Vachell, H.A.

Dew of their youth: Crockett, S.R.

Dewdrops: Kennedy, Margaret

Dew-drops of the nineteenth century: Smith, Seba

Dewed petals: Macartney, Frederick

Dewer rides: Strong, L.A.G.

Dew-pond, The: Powys, T.F.

Dewy morn, The: Jefferies, Richard

Diabo-lady, or a match in Hell, The: Combe, William

Diaboliad, The: Combe, William

Diabolical principle and the dithyrambic spectator, The: Lewis, P. Wyndham

Diabolus amans: Davidson, John

Diall of princes, The: North, *Sir* Thomas

Dialoge of comfort against tribulacion, A: More, *Sir* Thomas

Dialogue, A: Bradford, William

Dialogue: (†Anthony Hope), Hawkins, Anthony Hope

Dialogue at Christmas: Drinkwater, John

Dialogue between a philosopher and a student of the common laws of England, A: Hobbes, Thomas

Dialogue between Franklin and the gout: Franklin, Benjamin

Dialogue between master and clerk: Trevisa, John of

Dialogue between Philocles and Horatio, A: Franklin, Benjamin

Dialogue between the Devil, the Pope, and the Pretender, A: Fielding, Henry

Dialogue between X, Y and Z, A: Franklin, Benjamin

Dialogue full of pithe and pleasure, A: Breton, Nicholas

Dialogue in the shades, A: Combe, William

Dialogue on the distinct characters of the picturesque and the beautiful: Price, *Sir* Uvedale

Dialogue upon the gardens of Viscount Cobham, at Stowe, A: Gilpin, William

Dialogues and monologues: Wolfe, Humbert

Dialogues concerning natural religion: Hume, David

Dialogues in limbo: Santayana, George

Dialogues of Archibald MacLeish and Mark Van Doren, The: MacLeish, Archibald

Dialogues of the dead: King, William

Dialogues of the dead: Lyttelton, George *Baron*

Dialstone Lane: Jacobs, W.W.

Diamond and the pearl, The: Gore, Catherine

Diamond coast: Divine, A.D.

Diamond dust: Cook, Eliza

Diamond Jubilee, The: Morris, *Sir* Lewis

Diamond rock: Oxley, J.M.

Diamond seekers, The: Glanville, Ernest

Diamond thieves, The: Stringer, A.J.A.

Diana: Constable, Henry

Diana: Warner, S.B.

Diana Mallory: Ward, M.A.

Diana of Quebec, A:McIlwraith, J.N.

Diana of the Crossways: Meredith, George

Diana Stair: Dell, Floyd

Diana Tempest: Cholmondeley, Mary

Diana Trelawny: Oliphant, Margaret

Diana's crescent: Manning, Anne

Diana's hunting:Buchanan,R.W.

Diane and her friends: Hardy, A.S.

Diaries and letters. 1930–39: Nicolson, *Hon. Sir* Harold

Diaries and letters. 1939–45: Nicolson, *Hon. Sir* Harold

Diary, The: Lawrence, T.E.

Diary, 1556–1601: Melville, James

Diary and letters of Madame d'Arblay, 1778–1840, The: Burney, Frances

Diary and notes of Horace Templeton: Lever, C.J.

Diary. (by Lady C Bury) Illustrative of the times of George IV: Galt, John

Diary in America, with remarks on its institutions, A: Marryatt, Frederick

Diary in Ceylon: Sen, Keshub Chunder

Diary in England, 1870: Sena, Kesava Chandra

Diary in Madras and Bombay: Sen, Keshub Chunder

Diary of a baby, The: Pain, B.E.O.

Diary of a blasé, The: Marryatt, Frederick

Diary of a citizen in war time: Mais, S.P.B.

Diary of a Dean: Inge, W.R.

Diary of a desennuyée, The: Gore, Catherine

Diary of a country parson, The: Woodforde, James

Diary of a dryad: Brown, Alice

Diary of a goosegirl, The: Wiggin, K.D.

Diary of a hackney coachman, The: Ingraham, J.H.

Diary of a journey into North Wales, A: Johnson, Samuel

Diary of a man of fifty, The: James, Henry

Diary of a nobody: Grossmith, George and W.W. Grossmith

Diary of a pilgrimage: Jerome, Jerome K.

Diary of a provincial lady, The: †Delafield, E.M.

Diary of a public man, The: Adams, H.B.

Diary of a public schoolmaster: Mais, S.P.B.

Diary of a westward voyage, The: Tagore, *Sir* R.

Diary of an office seeker, The: (†Petroleum V. Nasby), Locke, D.R.

Diary of John Rous: Green, Mary Anne

Diary of Russell Beresford: Roberts, C.E.M.

Diary of Samuel Marchbanks, The: Davies, Robertson

Diary without dates, A: Bagnold, Enid

Dice of the goods, The: De Zilwa, Lucien

Dick and Tom in town: Van Doren, Mark

Dick and Tom, tales of two ponies: Van Doren, Mark

Dick of Downshire: Heywood, Thomas

Dick Rodney: Grant, James

Dick Turpin's ride: Noyes, Alfred

Dick Willoughby: Day Lewis, Cecil

Dickens: Gissing, George

Dickens: Pearson, Hesketh

Dickens: Sitwell, *Sir* Osbert

Dickens in his time: Brown, Ivor

Dickens of Grays Inn, The: Rubenstein, Harold F.

Dickon: †Bowen, Marjorie

Dick's desertion: Pickthall, M.L.C.

Dictator resigns, The: Joad, C.E.M.

Dictionary of abbreviations, A: Partridge, Eric

Dictionary of American history: Adams, J.T.

Dictionary of anonymous and pseudonymous literature: Halkett, Samuel, and John Laing

Dictionary of archaic and provincial words: Halliwell, J.O.

Dictionary of clichés, A: Partridge, Eric

Dictionary of national biography, The: Lee, *Sir* Sidney

Dictionary of obsolete and provincial English: Wright, Thomas

Dictionary of old English plays: Halliwell, J.O.

Dictionary of printers, 1558–1640: McKerrow, R.B.

Dictionary of R.A.F. slang, A: Partridge, Eric

Dictionary of slang and its analogues: Henley, W.E.

Dictionary of slang and unconventional English, A: Partridge, Eric

Dictionary of the English language, A: Johnson, Samuel

Dictionary of the Older Scottish tongue, A: Craigie, *Sir* W.A.

Dictionary of the underworld, British and American, A: Partridge, Eric

Dicts or sayings of the philosophers: Caxton, William

Did he deserve it?: Riddell, *Mrs.* J.H.

Did he steal it?: Trollope, Anthony

Did Polynesian voyagers know the Double Outrigger?: Best, Elsdon

Did she?: Glyn, Elinor

Did she fall?: Smith, Thorne

Did she love him?: Grant, James

Diderot and the encyclopaedists: Morley, John

Dido: Ritson, Joseph

Dido and Aeneas: Tate, Nahum

Dido, queen of hearts: Atherton, Gertrude

Dido Queene of Carthage: Nash, Thomas

Died in the wool: Marsh, Ngaio Edith

Dierdire: Bottomley, Gordon

Differences in judgment about water-baptism: Bunyan, John

Different days: Cornford, Francis

Different forms of flowers or plants of the same species, The: Darwin, Charles

Differing worships: Taylor, John

Difficult love: Strong, L.A.G.

Difficulties: Knox, R.A.

Dig: a drama of Central Australia: Clune, Frank

Digger Smith: Dennis, C.M.J.

Digging a grave: Hall, Anna Maria

Digging up the past: Woolley, *Sir* Leonard

Dilecta: Ruskin, John

Dilemma, The: Chesney, *Sir* G.T.

Dilemma: Phillpotts, Eden

Dilemma of the scientist, The: Bronowski, J.

Dilemmas: Dowson, E.C.

Dilemmas: Mason, A.E.W.

Diminutive dramas: Baring, Maurice

Dimple Hill: Richardson, D.M.

Ding and Co.: Munro, C.K.

Ding dong bell: De la Mare, Walter

Dining-room battle, The: Mackenzie, *Sir* Compton

Dinmont day by day: Lucas, E.V.

Dinner at eight: Ferber, Edna

Dinner at eight: Kaufman, G.S.

Dinner at the White House: Adamic, Louis

Dinner club, The: †Sapper

Dinner for eight: Benson, E.F.

Diogenes: Joad, C.E.M.

Diogines lanthorne: Rowlands, Samuel

Dione: Gay, John

Dionysia: Johnston, W.D.

Dionysus in doubt: Robinson, E.A.

Diospolis: Petrie, *Sir* William Flinders

Diplomacy: Nicolson, Hon. *Sir* Harold

Diplomacy of the American revolution, The: Bemis, S.F.

Diplomatic adventure, A: Mitchell, S.W.

Diplomatic history, 1713–1933: Petrie, *Sir* Charles

Diplomatic history of the United States, A: Bemis, S.F.

Diplomatic prelude, 1938–39: Namier, *Sir* Lewis

Diptych Rome–London: Pound, Ezra

Direadh: †McDiarmid, Hugh

Direct or indirect power of women: Higginson, T.W.

Directions for the gardiner at Says-Court: Evelyn, John

Directions to servants in general: Swift, Jonathan

Director, The: Dibdin, T.F.

Director, The: Strong, L.A.G.

Dirge and lyrics: Christesen, C.B.

Dirge for Lt. Col. McVicar: Hosmer, W.H.C.

"Dirge for the brave": Hosmer, W.H.C.

Dirty Eddie: Bemelmans, Ludwig

Dirty work: Pertwee, Roland

Disadvantages of being dead, The: Fairburn, A.R.D.

Disappearance of General Jason, The: Wren, P.C.

Disappearance of George Driffell, The: Payn, James

Disappearance of Martha Penny, The: Vachell, H.A.

Disappearance of Mr. Jeremiah Redworth, The: Riddell, *Mrs.* J.H.

Disappearing city, The: Wright, F.L.

Disappointment, The: Carey, Henry

Disappointment, The: Southern, Thomas

Disarmament: Madariaga, Salvador de

Disciple, The: Macdonald, George

Disciples of Emmaus, The: Neale, J.M.

Discipline and other sermons: Kingsley, Charles

Discipline of the Christian character: Church, Richard

Discommendatory verses: Blackmore, *Sir* R.D.

Discontented Colonell, The: Suckling, *Sir* John

Discordant encounters: Wilson, Edmund

Discource of horsemanshippe, A: Markham, Gervase

Discourse addressed to magistrates and men in authority, A: Berkeley, George

Discourse concerning earthquakes, A: Mather, Increase

Discourse concerning prayer ex tempore, A: Taylor, Jeremy

Discourse concerning the Stansfield tessellated pavement, A: Hearne, Thomas

Discourse, delivered at the opening of the Royal Academy: Reynolds, *Sir* Joshua

Discourse of baptisme, A: Taylor, Jeremy

Discourse of confirmation, A: Taylor, Jeremy

Discourse of education, A: Adams, J.Q.

Discourse of fish and fish-ponds, A: North, Roger

Discourse of matters pertaining to religion, A: Parker, Theodore

Discourse of monarchy, A: Wilson, John

Discourse of natural theology, A: Brougham, Henry

Discourse of the building, nature, excellency, and government of the House of God, A: Bunyan, John

Discourse of the liberty of prophesying, A: Taylor, Jeremy

Discourse of the nature, offices and mesures of friendship, A: Taylor, Jeremy

Discourse of the originall cause of naturall warre with the mysery of invasive warre, A: Ralegh, Sir Walter

Discourse of the Queens Majesties entertainment in Suffolk and Norffolk: Churchyard, Thomas

Discourse on ancient and modern learning, A: Addison, Joseph

Discourse on the aspects of war: Clarke, J.F.

Discourse on the evidences of the American Indians being the descendants of the lost tribes of Israel: Noah, M.M.

Discourse on the life and character of George Calvert, the first Lord Baltimore: Kennedy, J.P.

Discourse on the memory of Sir Robert Fletcher of Saltoun, A: Burnet, Gilbert

Discourse on the restoration of the Jews: Noah, M.M.

Discourse on the study of the laws, A: North, Roger

Discourse on 2 Corinthians i.q., A: Crabbe, George

Discourse upon the Pharisee and the Publicane, A: Bunyan, John

Discourse upon usurye, A: Wilson, Thomas

Discourses addressed to mixed congregations: Newman, J.H.

Discourses in America: Arnold, Matthew

Discourses on Christian nurture: Bushnell, Horace

Discourses on several important subjects: Seabury, Samuel

Discourses on several subjects: Seabury, Samuel

Discourses on the philosophy of religion: Ripley, George

Discourses on the scope and nature of University education: Newman, J.H.

Discourses on various important subjects: Edwards, Jonathan

Discovered isles: Holcroft, M.H.

Discoverie of Edmund Campion and his confederates, A: Munday, Anthony

Discoverie of Guiana, The: Ralegh, Sir Walter

Discoverie of the true causes why Ireland was never entirely subdued untill the beginning of his Majesties happie raigne, A: Davies, Sir John

Discoverie of witchcraft, The: Scot, Reginald

Discoveries: Sassoon, Siegfried

Discoveries: Yeats, W.B.

Discoveries and inventions: Mackaye, Percy

Discoveries: essays in literary criticism: Murry, John Middleton

Discoveries in England: Cammaerts, Emile

Discovering Australia: (†Donald Barr), Barrett, C.L.

Discovery: Bourinot, A.S.

Discovery: Drinkwater, John

Discovery, The: Huxley, Aldous

Discovery, The: Sheridan, Mrs. Frances

Discovery and settlement of Port Philip: Bonwick, James

Discovery of a most exquisite jewel, The: Urquhart, Sir Thomas

Discovery of America, The: Fiske, John

Discovery of America by John Cabot in 1497: Dawson, S.E.

Discovery of Britain, The: Lindsay, Jack

Discovery of Canada, The: Burpee, Lawrence, J.

Discovery of Eastern Australia, The: Halloran, Henry

Discovery of God, The: †King, Basil

Discovery of India, The: Nehru, J.

Discovery of New Zealand, The: Beaglehole, J.C.

Discovery of the consumer, The: Webb, Beatrice

Discovery of the future, The: Wells, H.G.

Discovery of the Great West, The: Parkman, Francis

Discovery of witches, The: Hopkins, Matthew

Discovery upon discovery: L'Estrange, Sir Roger

Discription of a maske, The: Campion, Thomas

Discursions on travel, art and life: Sitwell, Sir Osbert

Discussion of human affairs, The: Beard, C.A.

Discussions and argument on various subjects: Newman, J.H.

Disenchantment: Montague, C.E.

Disengaged: James, Henry

Disentanglers, The: Lang, Andrew

Disgrace to the college: Cole, G.D.H.

Dish of apples, A: Phillpotts, Eden

Dishonored lady: Barnes, Margaret

Disillusioned India: Mukherji, D.G.

Disinherited, The: Allen, Hervey

Disinherited, The: Gilmore, Mary

Disinherited and the ensnared, The: Bury, Lady C.S.M.

Disowned, The: Lytton, E.G.E.B., Ist Baron

Disputation betweene a hee conny-catcher and a shee conny-catcher, A: Greene, Robert

Disquisition concerning ecclesiastical councils, A: Mather, Increase

Disquisitions on several subjects: Jenyns, Soame

Disquisitions relating to matter and spirit: Priestley, Joseph

Dissertation on anecdotes, A: D'Israeli, Isaac

Dissertation on liberty and necessity, A: Franklin, Benjamin

Dissertation on the breed of Spanish sheep called merino: Humphreys, David

Dissertation on the theory and practice of benevolence, A: Dyer, George

Dissertation on the three parts of King Henry VI, A: Malone, Edmund

Dissertation upon pamphlets and the undertaking of Phœnix Britannicus to revive the most excellent among them, A: Oldys, William

Dissertation upon parties, A: Bolingbroke, Henry

Dissertations and discussions: Mill, John Stuart

Dissertations by Mr. Dooley: Dunne, Finley Peter

Dissertations moral and critical: Beattie, James

Dissertations on the English language: Webster, Noah

Dissolution of the religious houses, The: Neale, J.M.

Dissuasive from popery to the people of Ireland, A: Taylor, Jeremy

Distaff side, The: Van Druten, J.W.

Distant fields: Vachell, H.A.

Distant hours of summer, The: Bates, H.E.

Distant music, The: Davis, H.L.

Distant point: Griffith, Hubert

Distant relative, A: Jacobs, W.W.

Distant trumpet, A: Horgan, Paul

Distinguished villa: O'Brien, Kate

Distinguishing marks of a work of the spirit of God, The: Edwards, Jonathan

Distress in Lancashire, The: Myers, F.W.H.

Distress'd innocence: Settle, Elkanah

Distress'd wife, The: Gay, John

Distressing dialogues: (†Nancy Boyd), Millay, E.St. Vincent

Distrest mother, The: Philips, Ambrose

District of Columbia: Dos Passos, John

Disturbing affair of Noel Blake, The: †Bell, Neil

Disturbing element: Herbert, A.F.X.

Ditchampton Farm: Street, A.G.

Dithers and jitters: Skinner, C.O.

Ditty box, A: †Bartimeus

Diurnall of dangers, A: Jordan, Thomas

Diva's ruby, The: Crawford, Francis Marion

Divel conjured, The: Lodge, Thomas

Divers vanities: Morrison, Arthur

Divers views, opinions, and prophecies of yours truly: (†Petroleum V. Nasby), Locke, D.R.

Divers voyages, touching the discoverie of America, and the ilands adjacent unto the same: Hakluyt, Richard

Diversey: Kantor, MacKinlay

Diversion: Van Druten, J.W.

Diversions: Farjeon, Herbert

Diversions of Purley, The: Tooke, H.J.

Diversity of creatures: Kipling, Rudyard

Diverting history of John Bull and Brother Jonathan, The: Paulding, J.K.

Divided lady, The: Marshall, Bruce

Divided lines: Fawcett, Edgar

Divine adventure; The: †Macleod, Fiona

Divine and supernatural light, A: Edwards, Jonathan

Divine Comedy of Dante Alighieri, The: Longfellow, H.W.

Divine comedy of patriotism, The: (†Q. K. Philander Doesticks, P.B.) Thompson, Mortimer

Divine considerations of the soule: Breton, Nicholas

Divine fancies: Quarles, Francis

Divine fire, The: Sinclair, May

Divine folly, The: Orczy, Baroness

Divine gift, The: Jones, H.A.

Divine guidance: Dodge, May Abigail

Divine in man, The: Hubbard, Elbert

Divine King in England, The: Murray, Margaret

Divine lady, The: Beck, Mrs. Lily

Divine legation of Moses, The: Warburton, William

Divine passion, The: Fisher, V.A.

Divine pilgrim, The: Aiken, Conrad

Divine poem, A: Breton, Nicholas

Divine poems, The: Donne, John

Divine poems: Quarles, Francis

Divine psalm, A: Davies, John

Divine songs attempted in easy language for the use of children: Watts, Isaac

Divine tragedy, The: Longfellow, H.W.

Divine vagabond, The: Chattopadhyaya, Harindranath

Divine vision, The: Russell, G.W.

Division and reunion, 1829 to 1889: Wilson, Woodrow

Divorce: Williams, Charles

Divorce as I see it: Dreiser, Theodore

Divorce as I see it: Russell, Bertrand

Divorce of Catherine of Aragon, The: Froude, James Anthony

Divorced, The: Bury, Lady C.S.M.

Dix portraits: Stein, Gertrude

Dixon's return: Jacobs, W.W.

Dizzy: Pearson, Hesketh

Do not go down, O sun!: Vijayatunga, J.

Do tell me, Doctor Johnson: Marquand, J.P.

Do what you will: Huxley, Aldous

Do you know?: Mais, S.P.B.

Do you know your Bible?: Hannay, J.O.

Do you know your history?: Hannay, J.O.

Do you want to write?: Widdemer, Margaret
Doc Gordon: Freeman, M.W.
Doctor, The: Brown, T.E.
Doctor, The: †Connor, Ralph
Doctor, The: Hubbard, Elbert
Doctor, The: Rinehart, Mary Roberts
Doctor, The: Southey, Robert
Doctor and the devils, The: Thomas, Dylan
Dr. Angelus: †Bridie, James
Doctor Artz: Hichens, Robert Compton
Dr. Benes: Mackenzie, *Sir* Compton
Doctor Birch and his young friends: Thackeray, W.M.
Dr. Bluff in Russia: Gayarré, C.E.A.
Dr. Bradley remembers: Young, F.B.
Doctor Breen's practice: Howells, W.D.
Dr. Brent's household: Percy, Edward
Doctor Claudius: Crawford, Francis Marion
Doctor Cupid: Broughton, Rhoda
Doctor Darwin: Pearson, Hesketh
Doctor Dido: Lucas, F.L.
Dr. Dogbody's leg: Hall, J.N.
Dr. Dolittle and the secret lake: Lofting, Hugh
Dr. Dolittle in the moon: Lofting, Hugh
Dr. Dolittle's caravan: Lofting, Hugh
Dr. Dolittle's circus: Lofting, Hugh
Dr. Dolittle's garden: Lofting, Hugh
Dr. Dolittle's post office: Lofting, Hugh
Dr. Dolittle's return: Lofting, Hugh
Dr. Dolittle's zoo: Lofting, Hugh
Dr. Donne and Gargantua: Sitwell, Sacheverell
Dr. Fell omnibus, A: Carr, J.D.
Dr. Glennie's daughter: Farjeon, B.L.
Dr. Golightly: Campion, Sarah

Dr. Grenfell's parish: the deep sea fisherman: Duncan, Norman
Dr. Grimshawe's secret: Hawthorne, Nathaniel
Dr. Harmer's holidays: Pinero, *Sir* A.W.
Doctor Hathern's daughters: Holmes, M.J.
Dr. Heidenhoff's process: Bellamy, Edward
Doctor Huguet: Donnelly, I.L.
Dr. Jameson's raiders vs the Johannesburg reformers: Davis, R.H.
Dr. Johns: Mitchell, D.G.
Dr. Johnson (anth.): Hayward, John
Dr. Johnson: Hollis, Christopher
Dr. Johnson and company: Lynd, Robert
Dr. Johnson and his world: Brown, I.J.C.
Dr. Jonathan: Churchill, Winston
Dr. Kildare takes charge: †Brand, Max
Dr. Kildare's crisis: †Brand, Max
Dr. Krasinki's secret: Shiel, M.P.
Dr. Last in his chariot: Bickerstaffe, Isaac
Dr. Lavendar's people: Deland, Margaret
Doctor Livingstone: Hughes, Thomas
Doctor Luke of the Labrador: Duncan, Norman
Doctor Martino: Faulkner, William
Dr. Mesmer: Nichols, J.B.
Dr. North and his friends: Mitchell, S.W.
Dr. Oates's narrative of the Popish plot, vindicated: Phillips, John
Dr. Palliser's patient: Allen, Grant
Doctor Philligo: his journal and opinions: Vulliamy, C.E.
Dr. Quicksilver: Strong, L.A.G.
Doctor Rabelais: Lewis, D.B. Wyndham

Doctor Robert Child, the remonstrant: Kittredge, G.L.
Doctor Sally: Wodehouse, P.G.
Doctor Serocold: Ashton, Helen
Dr. Sevier: Cable, G.W.
Dr. Stiggins: †Machen, Arthur
Dr. Tancred begins: Cole, G.D.H.
Dr. Therne: Haggard, *Sir* H. Rider
Doctor Thorne: Trollope, Anthony
Dr. Thorne's idea: Mitchell, J.A.
Doctor Vandyke: Cooke, John
Dr. Wainwright's patient: Yates, E.H.
Dr. Warren's daughter: Davis, R.B.H.
Doctor Whitty: Hannay, J.O.
Dr. Wortle's school: Trollope, Anthony
Doctor Zay: Ward, E.S.
Doctors: Kipling, Rudyard
Doctors and masters in Bergendoff: Van Doren, Mark
Doctor's Christmas Eve, The: Allen, J.L.
Doctors' delusions: Shaw, G.B.
Doctor's dilemma, The: Shaw, G.B.
Doctor's son, The: O'Hara, J.H.
Doctor's wife, The: Braddon, M.E.
Doctor's wife comes to stay, The: Swinnerton, Frank
Doctrinal of princes, The: Elyot, *Sir* Thomas
Doctrinal of sapience (trn.): Caxton, William
Doctrine and discipline of divorce, The: Milton, John
Doctrine and discipline of human culture, The: Alcott, A.B.
Doctrine of Divine Providence, opened and applyed, The: Mather, Increase
Doctrine of evolution, The: Fiske, John
Doctrine of grace, The: Warburton, William
Doctrine of passive resistance, The: Ghose, Sri Aurobindo

Doctrine of philosophical necessity illustrated, The: Priestley, Joseph

Doctrine of the Church, The: Cotton, John

Doctrine of the law and grace unfolded, The: Bunyan, John

Doctrine of the Real Prescence, The: Pusey, E.B.

Doctrine to learn French and English (trn.): Caxton, William

Documents in the case, The: Sayers, Dorothy

Dodd family abroad, The: Lever, C.J.

Dodge Club, The: De Mille, James

Dodge Club abroad, The: De Mille, James

Dodo: Benson, E.F.

Dodo the second: Benson, E.F.

Dodo wonders: Benson, E.F.

Dodsworth: Lewis, H.S.

Dodu: Narayan, R.K.

Does slavery Christianize the Negro?: Higginson, T.W.

Does the Bible sanction American slavery?: Smith, Goldwin

Doesticks: what he says: (†Q.K. Philander Doesticks, P.B.), Thompson, Mortimer

Dog and Duck: †Machen, Arthur

Dog beneath the skin, The: Auden, W.H.

Dog beneath the skin, The: Isherwood, Christopher

Dog Crusoe, The: Ballantyne, R.M.

Dog days, other times, other dogs: White, S.E.

Dog of Flanders, A: †Ouida

Dog on the sun: Green, Paul

Dog Toby: Church, Richard

Dogberry bunch, The: Catherwood, Mary

Dogge of war, A: Taylor, John

Dogood papers, The: Franklin, Benjamin

Dogs, birds and others: Massingham, Harold

Dogs delight: Percy, Edward

Dog's mission, A: Stowe, Harriet Beecher

Dogs of war!: Yeats-Brown, F.C.C.

Dog's tale, A: (†Mark Twain), Clemens, S.L.

Dogtown Common: Mackaye, Percy

Doing his best: Trowbridge, J.T.

Doing their bit: Ewart, E.A.

Doings of Raffles Haw, The: Doyle, Sir Arthur Conan

Doll, The: Strong, L.A.G.

Doll and one other, The: Blackwood, Algernon

Doll doctor, The: Lucas, E.V.

Dollars and cents: Warner, A.B.

Dollars only: Bok, E.W.

Dolliver romance, The: Hawthorne, Nathaniel

Dolls'house, The: Godden, Rumer

Dolly: Burnett, Frances Hodgson

Dolly dialogues, The: (†Anthony Hope), Hawkins, Anthony Hope

Dolly reforming herself: Jones, H.A.

Dolores: Compton-Burnett, Ivy

Dolphin Cottage: Stern, G.B.

Dolphin in the wood, The: Bates, Ralph

Domain of physical science, The: Eddington, Sir A.S.

Dome of many-coloured glass, A: Lowell, Amy

Domesday Book: Masters, E.L.

Domestic affections, The: Hemans, Mrs. Felicia

Domestic anecdotes of the French nation: D'Israeli, Isaac

Domestic annals of Scotland from the Reformation to the Revolution: Chambers, Robert

Domestic annals of Scotland from the Revolution to the Rebellion of 1745: Chambers, Robert

Domestic experiment, A: †Grand, Sarah

Domestic manners of the Americans: Trollope, Frances

Domestic pictures and tales: Gatty, Margaret

Domestic relations: †O'Connor, Frank

Domestic stories: Craik, Mrs. Dinah M.

Domestic verses: Moir, D.M.

Domesticities: Lucas, E.V.

Domicilium: Hardy, Thomas

Dominant city, The: Fletcher, John Gould

Dominations and powers: Santayana, George

Dominie's legacy, The: Picken, Andrew

Dominion: Fairburn, A.R.D.

Dominion interests in Imperial administration: Miller, E.M.

Dominion of dreams, The: (†Macleod, Fiona), Sharp, William

Dominions of the boundary: O'Dowd, B.P.

Domitia: Baring-Gould, Sabine

Don: Besier, Rudolf

Don among the dead men: Vulliamy, C.E.

Don Careless: Beach, R.E.

Don Carlos, Prince of Spain: Otway, Thomas

Don Fernando: Maugham, Somerset

Don Gesualdo: †Ouida

Don J.Ewan: Wolfe, Humbert

Don John: Ingelow, Jean

Don John's mountain home: Raymond, Ernest

Don Juan: Byron, G.G.

Don Juan: Flecker, James Elroy

Don Juan: Lewisohn, Ludwig

Don Juan and the wheelbarrow: Strong, L.A.G.

Don Juan de Marana: Bennett, Arnold

Don Orsino: Crawford, Francis Marion

Don Quixote: Madariaga, Salvador de

Don Quixote drowned: Hanley, James

Don Quixote in England: Fielding, Henry

Don Quixote's profession: Van Doren, Mark

Don Sebastian: Porter, Anna Maria

Don Sebastian, King of Portugal: Dryden, John

Don Tarquinio: (†Baron Corvo), Rolfe, Frederick

Don, the story of a lion dog: Grey, Zane

Dona Ellen: Richter, Conrad

Don-a-Dreams: O'Higgins, H.J.

Donal Grant: Macdonald, George

Donalbane of Darien: Oxley, J.M.

Donald Grant's development: Oxley, J.M.

Donald Mackay and the clipper ships: Chase, M.E.

Donald Marcy: Ward, E.S.

Donald Ross of Heimra: Black, William

Donatello's ascension: Pope-Hennessy, J.W.

Done in the open: Wister, Owen

Done on both sides: Morton, J.M.

Donkey boy: Williamson, Henry

Donkey inside, The: Bemelmans, Ludwig

Donkey of God, The: Untermeyer, Louis

Donkey shoe, The: Stern, G.B.

Donna Florida: Simms, W.G.

Donne (anth.): Hayward, John

Donnellan lectures, The: Dunsany, E.J.M.D.P. *Lord*

Donovan: Lyall, Edna

Donovan Pasha, and some people of Egypt: Parker, *Sir* H.G.

Don't ask questions: Marquand, J.P.

Don't blame me: Hughes, R.A.W.

Don't expect any mercy: Treece, Henry

Don't get me wrong: †Cheyney, Peter

Don't go away mad: Saroyan, William

Don't open until Christmas: Morley, C.D.

Don't say that about Maine!: Roberts, Kenneth

Don't tell Alfred: Mitford, Nancy

Doom Castle: Munro, Neil

Doom of destiny, The: Ascher, I.G.

Doom of Devorgoil, The: Scott, *Sir* Walter

Doom of the Hapsburgs, The: Steed, H.W.

Doom of youth, The: Lewis, Wyndham

Doomed chief, The: Thompson, D.P.

Doomington wanderer, The: Golding, Louis

Doomsday: Alexander, William

Doomsday: Deeping, Warwick

Doomsday men, The: Priestley, J.B.

Doomsland: Leslie, *Sir* J.R. Shane

Doomswoman, The: Atherton, Gertrude

Door, The: Rinehart, Mary Roberts

Door between, The: †Queen, Ellery

Door in the wall, The: La Farge, Oliver

Door of dread, The: Stringer, A.J.A.

Door of humility, The: Austin, Alfred

Door with seven locks, The: Wallace, Edgar

Doormats: Davies, H.H.

Doors of perception, The: Huxley, Aldous

Doors of stone, The: Prince, F.T.

Doors of the night: Packard, F.L.

Doorway, The: Brighouse, Harold

Doorway in fairyland, A: Housman, Laurence

Doorways to poetry: Untermeyer, Louis

Dope Darling: Garnett, David

Dora: Kavanagh, Julia

Dora: Reade, Charles

Dora: Tennyson, Alfred *Lord*

Dora Deane: Holmes, M.J.

Dorando: Boswell, James

Doreen: Dennis, C.M.J.

Doreen: Lyall, Edna

Dorking thigh, The: Plomer, W.C.F.

Dormant: Nesbit, Edith

Dorothy: Woolson, C.F.

Dorothy, a country story: Munby, A.J.

Dorothy Chance: Moodie, Susanna

Dorothy Dovedale's tales: Miller, Thomas

Dorothy Forster: Besant, *Sir* Walter

Dorothy M. Richardson: Powys, J.C.

Dorothy South: Eggleston, G.C.

Dorothy Vernon of Haddon Hall: Major, Charles

Dorothy Wordsworth: De Selincourt, Ernest

Dorothy's wedding: Sidgwick, Ethel

Dorrien of Cranston: Mitford, Bertram

Dorrington deed-box, The: Morrison, Arthur

Dorset: De Selincourt, Aubrey

Dorset essays: Powys, Llewelyn

Dorset farm labourer, The: Hardy, Thomas

Dorsetshire labourer, The: Hardy, Thomas

Dosser in springtime, The: Stewart, D.A.

Dostoievsky: Powys, J.C.

Dostoievsky's Crime and Punishment: Ackland, Rodney

Doting: Green, Henry

Double, The: Wallace, Edgar

Double affair, A: Thirkell, Angela

Double agent, The: Blackmur, R.P.

Double alibi, The: Rinehart, M.R.

Double barrelled detective story, A: (†Mark Twain), Clemens, S.L.

Double bed dialogues: (†James, James), Adams, Arthur H.

Double blackmail: Cole, G.D.H.

Double cross purposes, Knox, R.A.

Double Dallilay: †Preedy, George

Double Dan: Wallace, Edgar

Double demon: Herbert, *Sir* A.P.

Double double: †Queen, Ellery

Double duel, The: Fay, T.S.

Double event, The: Gould, Nathaniel

Double falsehood: Theobald, Lewis

Double four: Oppenheim, E. Phillips

Double gallant, The: Cibber, Colley

Double harness: (†Anthony Hope), Hawkins, Anthony Hope

Double heart, The: Royde-Smith, Naomi

Double image, The: Heppenstall, Rayner

Double indemnity: Cain, J.M.

Double life: Richards, Grant

Double life, A: Wilcox, Ella Wheeler

Double life of Alfred Burton, The: Oppenheim, E.Phillips

Double lives: Plomer, William

Double lives: Sullivan, Alan

Double marriage, The: Reade, Charles

Double PP, The: Dekker, Thomas

Double prophecy, The: Carleton, William

Double scoop, A: Ewart, E.A.

Double traitor, A: Oppenheim, E.Phillips

Double-dealer, The: Congreve, William

Double-runner club, The: †Mrs. Partington

Doublets: †Carroll, Lewis

Doubtful heir, The: Shirley, James

Doubts of Dives, The: Besant, Sir Walter

Doughty deeds: Cunninghame Graham, Robert

Douglas: Home, John

Douglas Duane (together with Sinfire by Julian Hawthorne): Fawcett, Edgar

Douglas romance, The: Sladen, D.B.W.

Dove, The: Prior, Matthew

Dove Cottage: Brooke, S.A.

Dove in the eagle's nest, The: Yonge, C.M.

Dove in the mulberry tree, The: †Preedy, George

Dove of El-Djezaire, The: Salverson, L.G.

Dover Beach revisited: Finch, R.D.C.

Dover road, The: Milne, A.A.

Dover-Ostend: †Taffrail

Dove's nest, The: Mansfield, Katherine

Dowager, The: Gore, Catherine

Do-well and do-little: Sigerson, Dora

Down and out in Paris and London: †Orwell, George

Down by the sea: Greenwood, Walter

Down Dartmoor way: Phillpotts, Eden

Down north on the Labrador: Grenfell, Sir Wilfred

Down on the farm: Brown, Ivor

Down river: Church, Richard

Down river: Lehmann, John

Down the garden path: Nichols, Beverley

Down the long table: Birney, Earle

Down the ravine: †Craddock, C.E.

Down the river: Bates, H.E.

Down the river to the sea: Machar, A.M.

Down the sky: Lucas, E.V.

Down there on a visit: Isherwood, Christopher

Down to the sea: Grenfell, Sir Wilfred

Down under Donovan: Wallace, Edgar

Down wind: Peattie, D.C.

Down-adown-derry: De la Mare, Walter

Down-easters, The: Neal, John

Downfall and death of King Oedipus, The: Fitzgerald, Edward

Downfall of Robert, Earle of Huntington: Chettle, Henry

Downfall of Robert, Earle of Huntington, The: Munday, Anthony

Downfall of Temlaham, The: Barbeau, C.M.

Down-Hall: Prior, Matthew

Downing legends, The: De Forest, J.W.

Downland man: Massingham, Harold

Doyle's rock: Strong, L.A.G.

Dracula: Stoker, Bram

Draft of cantos XXXI–XLII, A: Pound, Ezra

Draft of XVI cantos, A: Pound, Ezra

Draft of the cantos 17–27, A: Pound, Ezra

Draft of XXX cantos, A: Pound, Ezra

Dragon, The: Gregory, Augusta Lady

Dragon, The: Shiel, M.P.

Dragon and the dove, The: †Bridie, James

Dragon harvest: Sinclair, Upton

Dragon in shallow waters, The: Sackville-West, V.

Dragon laughed, A: Linklater, Eric

Dragon of Tingalam, The: Palmer, H.E.

Dragon of Wantley, The: Carey, Henry

Dragon of Wantley, The: Wister, Owen

Dragon rampant: †Hyde, Robin

Dragon seed: Buck, Pearl

Dragon who was different, The: Trease, Geoffrey

Dragonfly: Cronin, B.C.

Dragon's blood: Wilson, Romer

Dragon's jaws, The: Packard, F.L.

Dragon's mouth: Priestley, J.B.

Dragon's teeth, The: †Queen, Ellery

Dragon's teeth: Sinclair, Upton

Drake: Noyes, Alfred

Drake's drum: Newbolt, Sir Henry

Drake-stone, The: †Onions, Oliver

Drama: Dukes, Ashley

Drama: MacCarthy, Sir Desmond

Drama and society in the age of Jonson: Knights, L.C.

Drama and the stage, The: Lewisohn, Ludwig

Drama and the weather: Green, Paul

Drama at Inish: Robinson, E.S.L.

Drama in muslin, A: Moore, George

Drama in sunshine, A: Vachell, H.A.

Drama of exile, A: Browning, Elizabeth Barrett

Drama of kings, The: Buchanan, R.W.

Drama of 365 days, The: Caine, *Sir* Thomas Hall

Dramas: Baillie, Joanna

Dramatic divertissements: Iyengar, V.V. Srinivasa

Dramatic documents from the Elizabethan playhouses: Greg, W.W.

Dramatic duologues: Masters, E.L.

Dramatic essays: Forster, John

Dramatic essays reprinted from the Examiner: Lewes, G.H.

Dramatic history of England: Peach, L. du Garde

Dramatic idyls: Browning, Robert

Dramatic legends: Colum, Padraic

Dramatic lyrics: Browning, Robert

Dramatic opinions and essays: Shaw, G.B.

Dramatic scene, A: Wells, C.J.

Dramatic scenes: Proctor, B.W.

Dramatic scenes from real life: Morgan, *Lady* Sydney

Dramatic scenes, sonnets and other poems: Mitford, Mary Russell

Dramatic tales: Hogg, James

Dramatic values: Montague, C.E.

Dramatis personae: Browning, Robert

Dramatis personae: Symons, Arthur

Dramatis personae: Yeats, W.B.

Dramatists of today: Hale, E.E.

Drapier's letters to the people of Ireland, The: Swift, Jonathan

Drapier's miscellany, The: Swift, Jonathan

Draw in your stool: †Onions, Oliver

Drawing room table book, The: Manning, Anne

Drawings by Hok'sai: Rothenstein, *Sir* William

Drawings from life: Gill, Eric

Drawings of Domenichino at Windsor Castle, The: Pope-Hennessy, J.W.

Drawings of the Florentine painters, The: Berenson, Bernhard

Dread voyage, The: Campbell, W.W.

Dreadful battle between a Taylor and a louse, A: Taylor, John

Dreadful dragon of Hay Hill, The: Beerbohm, *Sir* Max

Dreadful hollow, The: Day-Lewis, Cecil

Dreadnought of the Darling, The: Bean, C.E.

Dreads and drolls: †Machen, Arthur

Dream, The: Church, Richard

Dream, The: Masefield, John

Dream, The: Wells, H.G.

Dream and action: Bacon, Leonard

Dream and the business, The: †Hobbes, John Oliver

Dream come true: Binyon, R.L.

Dream days: Grahame, Kenneth

Dream department, The: Perelman, S.J.

Dream drops: Lowell, Amy

Dream girl: Rice, Elmer

Dream in the Luxembourg: Aldington, Richard

Dream keeper, The: Hughes, J.L.

Dream life: Mitchell, D.G.

Dream life and real life: Schreiner, Olive

Dream life of Balse Snell, The: †West, Nathaniel

Dream observed, A: Ridler, A.B.

Dream of a day, The: Percival, J.G.

Dream of Arcadia, The: Brooks, Van Wyck

Dream of destiny: Bennett, Arnold

Dream of Eugene Aram, The: Hood, Thomas

Dream of fair women, A: Tennyson, Alfred *Lord*

Dream of fair women, The: Williamson, Henry

Dream of Gerontius, The: Newman, J.H.

Dream of God, The: Watson, A.D.

Dream of John Ball, A: Morris, William

Dream of love, A: Williams, W.C.

Dream of Magi, The: Cunninghame Graham, Robert

Dream of the Lilybell, The: Morley, Henry

Dream of the red chamber, The: Waley, Arthur

Dream of two dimensions, A: White, W.H.

Dream physician, The: Martyn, Edward

Dream tea: Beck, *Mrs.* Lily

Dreamer, The: Carman, Bliss

Dreamer, The: Green, Julian

Dreamer and the worker, The: Horne, R.H.

Dreamer in Portugal, A: Dixon, Thomas

Dreamers, The: Bangs, J.K.

Dreamers, The: Robinson, E.S.L.

Dreamers of dreams: Jackson, Holbrook

Dreamers of the ghetto: Zangwill, Israel

Dreamer's tales, A: Dunsany, E.J.M.D.P. *Lord*

Dreaming: Bullett, Gerald

Dreaming dust, The: Johnston, W.D.

Dreamland: †Carroll, Lewis

Dreamland: Mair, Charles

Dreams: Brontë, Anne

Dreams: Schreiner, Olive

Dreams and days: Lathrop, G.P.

Dreams and delights: Beck, *Mrs.* Lily

Dreams and dust: Marquis, Don

Dreams and reveries of a quiet man: Fay, T.S.

Dreams come true: Mee, Arthur

Dream's end: Smith, Thorne

Dreams from China and Japan: Komai, Gonnosuké

Dreams o' mine: Bullett, Gerald

Dreams, waking thoughts, and incidents: Beckford, William

Dreamthorp: Smith, Alexander

Dreamy kid, The: O'Neill, Eugene

Dred: a tale of the great dismal swamp: Stowe, Harriet Beecher

Dress: Gill, Eric

Dress: Oliphant, Margaret

Dressing gown, The: Percy, Edward

D'ri and I: Bacheller, Irving

Drift: Hanley, James

Drift: Willson, H.B.

Drift: a sea-shore idyl: Arnold, George

Drift and mastery, an attempt to diagnose the current unrest: Lippmann, Walter

Drift fence, The: Grey, Zane

Drift from two shores: Harte, Bret

Drift of pinions, The: Pickthall, M.L.C.

Drift of romanticism, The: More, P.E.

Drifted in: Carleton, William (McKendree)

Drifting: Read, T.B.

Drift-weed: Thaxter, C.L.

Driftwood from Scandinavia: Wilde, *Lady* J.F.

Driftwood spars: Wren, P.C.

Drink for sale: Lindsay, N.V.

Drinking Academy, The: Randolph, Thomas

Drinking well, The: Gunn, Neil M.

Drive in June, A: Jones, H.A.

Droomme of Doomes day, The: Gascoigne, George

Drop to his death: †Carter Dickson

Dropping the hyphen: Kaye-Smith, Shiela

Drops of water: Wilcox, Ella Wheeler

Dross: Braddon, M.E.

Dross: †Seton, Merriman

Drovers, The: Esson, T.L.B.

Drowsie frighted steeds: Abercrombie, Lascelles

Drowsy: Mitchell, J.A.

Drug-shop, The: Benét, Stephen Vincent

Druid circle, The: Van Druten, John

Druid's rest, The: Williams, Emlyn

Drum, The: Mason, A.E.W.

Drummer, The: Addison, Joseph

Drummer boy, The: Trowbridge, J.T.

Drummer's coat, The: Fortescue, *Sir* John

Drummond of Hawthornden: Masson, David

Drums: Boyd, James

Drums afar: Gibbon, J.M.

Drums along the Mohawk: Edmonds, W.D.

Drums of Aulone, The: Chambers, R.W.

Drums of Dambala: Bedford-Jones, Henry

Drums of Dombali, The: Phillpotts, Eden

Drums of Father Ned, The: O'Casey, Sean

Drums under the windows: O'Casey, Sean

Drum-taps: Whitman, Walt

Drunk man looks at the thistle, A: †McDiarmid, Hugh

Drunkard's bible, The: Hall, A.M.

Drunkard's progress, The: Reynolds, G.

Drunken sailor, The: Cary, Joyce

Drury Lane boys' club, The: Burnett, F.H.

Drury Lane's last case: †Barnaby Ross

Dry Pickwick and other incongruities, The: Leacock, Stephen

Dry salvages, The: Eliot, T.S.

Dry season, The: Cowley, Malcolm

Dry sticks, fagoted: Landor, W.S.

Dryad: Mannin, Ethel

Dryad in Nanaimo, A: Brown, A.A.

Dryden: Hollis, Christopher

Dryden as an adapter of Shakespeare: Nicoll, Allardyce

Dryden library, A: Wise, T.J.

Du Barry: Belasco, David

Du Mauriers, The: Du Maurier, Daphne

Du Poissey anecdotes, The: McCrae, Hugh

Dual resurrection, A: Mitford, Bertram

Dublin days: Strong, L.A.G.

Dublin poems: †O'Sullivan, Seumas

Dublin Whiskey: Sala, G.A.H.

Dubliners: Joyce, James

Dubloons: Phillpotts, Eden

DuBose Heyward: Allen, Hervey

Ducdame: Powys, John Cowper

Duchenier: Neale, J.M.

Duchess de la Vallière, The: Lytton, E.G.E.B. *1st Baron*

Duchess Laura: Lowndes, M.A.

Duchess of Devonshire's cow, The: Combe, William

Duchess of Padua, The: Wilde, Oscar

Duchess of Popocatapetl, The: Turner, W.J.R.

Duchess of Portland's museum, The: Walpole, Horace

Duchess of Powysland, The: Allen, Grant

Duchess of Rosemary Lane, The: Farjeon, B.L.

Duchess of Trajetto, The: Manning, Anne

Duchess of Wrexe, The: Walpole, *Sir* Hugh

Duck Lake: Young, E.R.

Duck to water, A: Stern, G.B.

Ductor dubitantium: Taylor, Jeremy

Ductor historicus: Hearne, Thomas

Dude, The: †Brand, Max

Dude ranger: Grey, Zane

Due preparations for the plague: Defoe, Daniel

Dudley and Gilderoy, a nonsense: Blackwood, Algernon

Duel in the dark: Steen, Marguerite

Duel of queens, The: Beck, *Mrs.* Lily

Duellist, The: Churchill, Charles

Duello, The: Selden, John

Duenna, The: Sheridan, Richard Brinsley

Duet: Bates, H.E.

Duet for female voices: Campion, Sarah

Duet in floodlight: Priestley, J.B.

Duet with an occasional chorus, A: Doyle, *Sir* Arthur Conan

Duffels: Eggleston, Edward

Duke of Wellington, The: Guedalla, Philip

Duke and no duke, A: Tate, Nahum

Duke and the king, The: Carleton, William(McKendree)

Duke Christian of Luneburg: Porter, Jane

Duke Herring: Bodenheim, Maxwell

Duke in darkness, The: Hamilton, Patrick

Duke in the suburbs, The: Wallace, Edgar

Duke Jones: Sidgwick, Ethel

Duke of Albany's own Highlanders, The: Grant, James

Duke of Berwick, The: Douglas, *Lord* Alfred

Duke of Devonshire's bull to the Duchess of Devonshire's cow, The: Combe, William

Duke of Gandia, The: Swinburne, A.C.

Duke of Guise, The: Dryden, John

Duke of Guise, The: Lee, Nathaniel

Duke of Lipari, The: Percy, Edward

Duke of Marchmont, The: Reynolds, G.

Duke of Marlborough, The: Thomas, E.E.P.

Duke of Millaine, The: Massinger, Philip

Duke of Monmouth, The: Griffin, Gerald

Duke of Stockbridge, The: Bellamy, Edward

Duke's children, The: Trollope, Anthony

Duke's daughter, The: Thirkell, Angela

Duke's daughter and the fugitives, The: Oliphant, Margaret

Duke's funeral, The: Doyle, *Sir* F.H.C.

Dukes mistris, The: Shirley, James

Dukes of Buckingham, The: Coffin, Robert

Dukesborough tales: Johnston, R.M.

Dulce Cor: Crockett, S.R.

Dulcie Carlyon: Grant, James

Dulcie Everton: Linton, Eliza

Dulcy: Connelly, Marc

Dulcy: Kaufman, G.S.

Dull day in London, A: Sigerson, Dora

Dull Miss Archinard, The: Sedgwick, A.D.

Dumaresq's daughter: Allen, Grant

Dumb animal: Sitwell, *Sir* Osbert

Dumb belle, The: Bernard, W.B.

Dumb cake, The: Morrison, Arthur

Dumb gods speak, The: Oppenheim, E.Phillips

Dumb philosopher, The: Defoe, Daniel

Dumb wife of Cheapside, The: Dukes, Ashley

Dumb witness: Christie, Agatha

Dumbe knight, The: Markham, Gervase

Dummy, The: O'Higgins, H.J.

Dumphry: Pain, B.E.O.

Dun cow, The: Landor, W.S.

Duncan McClure: †Rudd, Steele

Dunciad, The: Pope, A.

Dunciad of today, The: Disraeli, Benjamin

Dundonald: Fortescue, *Sir* John

Dunkerley's: Spring, Howard

Dunkirk: Bryant, *Sir* Arthur

Dunkirk: Divine, A.D.

Dunkirk: Pratt, E.J.

Dunky Fitlow: Coppard, A.E.

Dunnigan's daughter: Behrman, S.N.

Dupe, The: Sheridan, *Mrs.* Frances

Duplicate death: Heyer, Georgette

Duplicate letters, the fisheries and the Mississippi, The: Adams, J.Q

Duplicity: Holcroft, Thomas

Durable riches: Mather, Cotton

Durham Company: Pope-Hennessy, *Dame* Una

During Her Majesty's pleasure: Braddon, M.E.

Dusantes, The: Stockton, F.R.

Dusk of dawn: Dubois, William

Dust and light: Wheelock, J.H.

Dust flower, The: †King, Basil

Dust in the eyes: Frost, Robert

Dust in the lion's paw: Stark, F.M.

Dust of New York: Bercovici, Konrad

Dust or polish?: Lindsay, Norman

Dust over the ruins: Ashton, Helen

Dust which is God: Benét, William Rose

Dustman, The: Carman, Bliss

Dusty: Davison, F.D.

Dusty answer: Lehmann, Rosamund

Dutch and Quaker Colonies in America, The: Fiske, John

Dutch are coming, The: Trease, Geoffrey

Dutch Barrier our's, The: Oldmixon, John

Dutch cheese, The: De la Mare, Walter

Dutch courage: London, Jack

Dutch courtezan, The: Marston, John

Dutch etchers of the seventeenth century: Binyon, Laurence

Dutch founding of New York, The: Janvier, T.A.

Dutch holiday: Mais, S.P.B.

Dutch interior: †O'Connor, Frank

Dutch lover, The: Behn, *Mrs.* Afra

Dutch pictures: Sala, G.A.H.

Dutch shoe mystery, The: †Queen, Ellery

Dutchman's fireside, The: Paulding, J.K.

Duties of clerks of Petty Sessions in Ireland, The: Stoker, Bram

Duties of educated young men in British America: Dawson, *Sir* J.W.

Duties of Massachusetts, The: Clarke, J.F.

Duties of women, The: Cobbe, F.P.

Duty: Smiles, Samuel

Duty of disobedience to the fugitive slave act, The: Child, Lydia Maria

Duty of the American scholar to politics and the times, The: Curtis, G.W.

Duveen: Behrman, S.N.

Dwarf's chamber, The: Hume, F.W.

Dweller on the threshold, The: Hichens, R.S.

Dwellers by the river: Praed, *Mrs.* C.

Dwelling-place of light, The: Churchill, Winston

Dwight Morrow: Nicolson, Hon. *Sir* Harold

Dyaloge of syr Thomas More of ymages, praying to sayntys, othere thynges touchyng the pestylent sect of Luther and Tyndale, A: More, *Sir* Thomas

Dye-hard, The: Brighouse, Harold

Dyer's hand, The: Auden, W.H.

Dyet of Poland, The: Defoe, Daniel

Dying fires: Monkhouse, A.N.

Dying gladiators, The: Gregory, Horace

Dying God, The: Frazer, *Sir* James

Dying Indian's dream, The: Rand, S.T.

Dying thoughts and last reflections, The: Brown, Thomas

Dylan Thomas. Dog among the fairies: Treece, Henry

Dymer: (†Clive Hamilton), C.S. Lewis

Dynamic defence: Liddell Hart, B.

Dynamite, the story of class violence in America: Adamic, Louis

Dynamiter, The: Stevenson, R.L.

Dynamo: O'Neill, Eugene

Dynasts, The: Hardy, Thomas

Dynasty of Stowe, The: Knight, G.W.

Dynever terrace: Yonge, C.M.

E

E. Grace Coombs: Pierce, Lorne

E.M. Forster: Trilling, Lionel

E.V. Lucas: Sherwood, R.E.

Each in his darkness: Green, Julian

Eagle and the dove, The: Sackville-West, V.

Eagle and the roots: Adamic, Louis

Eagle and the wren, The: Pertwee, Roland

Eagle in the egg, The: La Farge, Oliver

Eagles, The: Bayldon, Arthur

Eagles have flown, The: Treece, Henry

Eagle's heart, The: Garland, Hamlin

Eagle's nest, The: Ruskin, John

Eagles of the Andes: Beals, Carleton

Eagle's shadow, The: Cabell, James Branch

Ealasaid: Bottomley, Gordon

Ear of Vincent van Gogh, The: †Bridie, James

Ear trumpet, The: Dalton, A.C.

Earl of Beaconsfield, The: Davin, N.F.

Earl of Brecon, The: Landor, R.E.

Earl of Derby, The: Saintsbury, George

Earl of Elgin, The: Wrong, G.M.

Earl of Essex, The: Brooke, Henry

Earl of Mayo, The: Hunter, *Sir* William

Earl of Pawtuckete, The: Thomas, Augustus

Earlham: Lubbock, Percy

Earlier diplomatic history, 1492–1713: Petrie, *Sir* Charles

Earlier religion of Greece in the light of Cretan discoveries, The: Evans, *Sir* A.J.

Earlier Renaissance, The: Saintsbury, George

Earlier works of Sir Roderick Athelstane, The: Rubenstein, Harold F.

Earliest life of Milton, The: Phillips, John

Earl's promise, The: Riddell, *Mrs.* J.H.

Early American chroniclers, The: Bancroft, H.H.

Early Americana: Richter, Conrad

Early Aryans in Gujarati, The: Munshi, K.M.

Early attempts at Christian reunion: Hannay, J.O.

Early Autumn: Bromfield, Louis

Early birds: Pertwee, Roland

Early blossoms: Hemans, *Mrs.* Felicia

Early Chinese jades: Pope-Hennessy, *Dame* Una

Early days in Wellesley: Bradford, Gamaliel

Early days of Cornell, The: Smith, Goldwin

Early days of Melbourne: Bonwick, James

Early days of Van Diemen's land: Bonwick, James

Early diary of Frances Burney, The: Burney, Frances

Early drawings and etchings: Coulton, G.G.

Early eighteenth century, The: Dobrée, Bonamy

Early Greek elegists: Bowra, *Sir* Maurice

Early Hindu civilization: Dutt, R.C.

Early history of Charles James Fox, The: Trevelyan, *Sir* G.O.

Early history of Jacob Stahl, The: Beresford, J.D.

Early history of science, An: Lindsay, Jack

Early history of the university and its parent constitutions: Lodge, *Sir* Oliver

Early hours, The: Pickthall, M.W.

Early illustrated books: Pollard, A.W.

Early Italian poets from Ciullo d'Alcamo to Dante Alighieri, The: Rossetti, Dante Gabriel

Early kings of Norway, The: Carlyle, Thomas

Early lays: Simms, W.G.

Early lessons: Edgeworth, Maria

Early life and adventures of Sylvia Scarlett, The: Mackenzie, *Sir* Compton

Early life of Mark Rutherford, The: †Rutherford, Mark

Early life of Stephen Hind, The: Jameson, Storm

Early light: Wellesley, D.V.

Early London: Besant, *Sir* Walter

Early martyr, An: Williams, W.C.

Early mathematics, chiefly arithmetic: Lodge, *Sir* Oliver

Early memories for the children: Hughes, Thomas

Early moon: Sandburg, Carl

Early morning: Mottram, R.H.

Early notices of Toronto: Scadding, Henry

Early papers and some memories: Morley, Henry

Early Plantagenets, The: Stubbs, William

Early poems: Riley, J.W.

Early reminiscences: Baring-Gould, Sabine

Early spring: Tennyson, Alfred *Lord*

Early Spring in Massachusetts: Thoreau, H.D.

Early stories: Du Maurier, Daphne

Early Victorian novelists: Cecil, *Lord* David

Early whistler, The: Gibson, W.W.

Early Wordsworth, The: De Selincourt, Ernest

Early worm, The: Benchley, Robert

Early worm, The: †Lonsdale, Frederick

Early years of Alec Waugh, The: Waugh, Alec

Earth breadth, The: Russell, G.W.

Earth compels, The: Macneice, Louis

Earth deities: Carman, Bliss

Earth for sale, The: Monro, H.E.

Earth gives and takes all: Evans, Caradoc

Earth horizon: Austin, Mary

Earth kindred: Devaney, J.M.

Earth lover, The: †O'Sullivan, Seumas

Earth lover, The: Prichard, K.S.

Earth memories: Powys, Llewelyn

Earth moods: Allen, Hervey

Earth passion, The: Ficke, A.D.

Earth stopped: White, T.H.

Earth trembled, The: Roe, E.P.

Earth triumphant: Aiken, Conrad

Earthen vessels: Macartney, Frederick

Earthlings: King, G.E.

Earthly paradise, The: Forester, C.S.

Earthly paradise, The: Morris, William

Earthquake, The: Buchanan, R.W.

Earthquake, The: Galt, John

Earth-visitors: Slessor, Kenneth

Earth's voices: (†Macleod, Fiona), Sharp, William

Earthwork out of Tuscany: Hewlett, M.H.

East Africa: Huxley, Elspeth J.

East African Protectorate, The: Eliot, *Sir* Charles

East and west: Arnold, Edwin

East and West: Fenollosa, E.F.

East and west: Hale, E.E.

East and west: Thomas, F.W.

East and West in religion: Radhakrishan, Sarvepalli

East and West poems: Harte, Bret

East angels: Woolson, C.F.

East Anglia, England's eastern province: Mottram, R.H.

East Coker: Eliot, T.S.

East Indian, The: Lewis, M.G.

East is East: Stribling, T.S.

East is west: Stark, F.M.

East London: Besant, *Sir* Walter

East London Hospital for children: Dickens, Charles

East Lynne: Wood, Ellen

East of Eden: Morley, C.D.

East of Eden: Steinbeck, John

East of Malta, west of Suez: †Bartimeus

East of Suez: Maugham, Somerset

East of the city: Dudek, Louis

East of the setting sun: McCutcheon, G.B.

East side, west side: Davenport, Marcia

East Sussex: Lucas, E.V.

East to West: a journey round the world: Toynbee, Arnold

East wind: Lowell, Amy

East wind, The: Mackenzie, *Sir* C.

East wind: west wind: Buck, Pearl

Easter: Deamer, Dulcie

Easter: Masefield, John

Easter bells: Jackson, H.H.

Easter day: Coppard, A.E.

Easter garland, An: Scollard, Clinton

Easter gift, The: Landon, L.E.M.

Easter gleams: Larcom, Lucy

Easter greeting to every child who loves "Alice", An: †Carroll, Lewis

Easter poems: Machar, A.M.

Easter market, An: Carman, Bliss

Easter, 1916: Yeats, W.B.

Easter party, The: Sackville-West, V.

Easter song: Scollard, Clinton

Eastern epic: Mackenzie, *Sir* Compton

Eastern exploration: Petrie, *Sir* William Flinders

Eastern life, past and present: Martineau, Harriet

Eastern Mediterranean and early civilization in Europe, The: Breasted, J.H.

Eastern religions and western thought: Radhakrishan, Sarvepalli

Eastern schism, The: Runciman, *Sir* Steven

Eastward drift: Percy, Edward

Eastward hoe: Chapman, George

Easy chair: De Voto, Bernard

Easy distances: Ridge, W. Pett

Easy mathematics: Lodge, *Sir* Oliver

Easy readings in Anglo-Saxon: Craigie, *Sir* W.A.

Easy readings in Old Icelandic: Craigie, *Sir* W.A.

Easy virtue: Coward, Noel

Easy warriors: †Armstrong, Anthony

Eaten heart, The: Aldington, Richard

Eater of darkness, The: Coates, R.M.

Eavesdropper, The: Payn, James

Ebb and flood: Hanley, James

Ebb tide: Pickthall, M.L.C.

Ebbing of the tide, The: †Becke, Louis

Ebb-tide, The: Stevenson, R.L.

Eben Erskine: Galt, John

Eben Holden: Bacheller, Irving

Ebony and ivory: Powys, Llewelyn

Ebony flame: Starrett, Vincent

Ecarté: Richardson, John

Ecce Puella: †Macleod, Fiona

Eccentricities for Edinburgh: Colman, George, *the younger*

Ecchoes from the sixth trumpet: Wither, George

Ecclesia: Hawker, R.S.

Ecclesia restaurata: Heylyn, Peter

Ecclesia vindicata: Heylyn, Peter

Ecclesiastical history of Great Britain, An: Collier, Jeremy

Ecclesiastical sketches: Wordsworth, William

Echo, The: Alsop, Richard

Echo, The: Connecticut Wits

Echo, The: Hoffman, C.F.

Echo club and other literary diversions, The: Taylor, Bayard

Echo de Paris: Housman, Laurence

Echo of passion, An: Lathrop, G.P.

Echoes: Kipling, Rudyard

Echoes: Mackenzie, *Sir* Compton

Echoes from old Cornwall: Hawker, R.S.

Echoes from the Oxford Magazine: Godley, A.D.

Echoes from the Sabine farm: Field, Eugene

Echoes from Vagabondia: Carman, Bliss

Echoes of the Foot-Hills: Harte, Bret

Echoes of the war: †Barrie, *Sir* J.M.

Echoes of the year 1883: Sala, G.A.H.

Echoing grove, The: Lehmann, Rosamund

Echo's bones: Beckett, Samuel

Eclectic A.B.C., An: †George, Daniel

Eclectic Readers: McGuffey, W.H.

Eclipse: Mais, S.P.B.

Eclogues: Read, *Sir* Herbert

Eclogues and monodramas: Warren, J.B.L.

Economic basis of politics, The: Beard, C.A.

Economic chaos and the Peace Treaty, The: Angell, *Sir* Norman

Economic consequences of the Peace, The: Keynes, J.M.

Economic foundations of peace, The: Garvin, J.L.

Economic history of British India: Dutt, R.C.

Economic interpretation of the Constitution of the United States, The: Beard, C.A.

Economic notes on insular free trade: Balfour, A.J.

Economic origins of Jeffersonian democracy: Beard, C.A.

Economic studies: Bagehot, Walter

Economic system, The: Cole, G.D.H.

Economic tracts for the time: Cole, G.D.H.

Economic war after the war: Dickinson, G.L.

Economics of British India: Sarkar, Y.J.

Economics of Khadi: Gandhi, M.K.

Economics of the hour: Strachey, John St. Loe

Economy of abundance, The: Chase, Stuart

Economics for Helen: Belloc, Hilaire

Ecstasy of Angus, The: O'Flaherty, Liam

Eddy and the Archangel Mike: Benefield, Barry

Eden: Bridges, Robert

Eden: Saltus, E.E.

Eden end: Priestley, J.B.

Eden lost and won: Dawson, *Sir* J.W.

Eden river: Bullett, Gerald

Eden tree: Bynner, Witter

Eden versus Whistler: Whistler, James

Edgar: Rymer, Thomas

Edgar Allan Poe: Browning, Elizabeth Barrett

Edgar Allan Poe: Ransome, A.M.

Edgar Allan Poe: Reese, L.W.

Edgar Allan Poe: Woodberry, G.E.

Edgar Allan Poe: a critical biography: Pope-Hennessy, *Dame* Una

Edgar Allan Poe, a study in genius: Krutch, J.W.

Edgar and Emmeline: Hawkesworth, John

Edgar Huntly: Brown, C.B.

Edgar Montrose: Reynolds, G.

Edgar Poe and his critics: Whitman, S.H.

Edge of being, The: Spender, Stephen

Edge of darkness, The: Chase, M.E.

Edge of night, The: Derleth, A.W.

Edge of the abyss, The: Noyes, Alfred

Edgewater people: Freeman, M.W.

Edgeways and the Saint: Chattopadhyaya, Harindranath

Edict of the King of Prussia, An: Franklin, Benjamin

Edina: Wood, Ellen

Edinburgh: Sitwell, Sacheverell

Edinburgh: Stevenson, R.L.

Edinburgh eleven, An: Barrie, *Sir* J.M.

Edinburgh papers: Chambers, Robert

Edinburgh sketches and memories: Masson, David

Edinburgh tales, The: Mitford, Mary Russel

Edinburgh's address to the country: Ramsay, Allan

Edinburgh's salutation to the most honourable My Lord Marquess of Carnarvon: Ramsay, Allan

Edith: Baker, Elizabeth

Edith Lyle: Holmes, M.J.

Edith Sitwell: Bowra, *Sir* Maurice

Edith Sitwell: Lehmann, John

Edith Wharton: Brown, E.K.

Edith Wharton, a critical study: Gerould, Katharine

Editha's burglar: Burnett, F.H.

Editha's burglar: Thomas, Augustus

Editions of the life of Colonel Hutchinson: Firth, *Sir* Charles

Editor and his people, The: White, W.A.

Editorial jottings: Nitobe, Inazo

Editorial preface to the New England Courant: Franklin, Benjamin

Editorial problem in Shakespeare, The: Greg, W.W.

Editor's tales, An: Trollope, Anthony

Edmée, a tale of the French Revolution: Molesworth, *Mrs.*

Edmund Burke: a historical study: Morley, John

Edna Browning: Holmes, M.J.

Edna his wife: Barnes, Margaret

Edna St. Vincent Millay: Van Doren, Carl

Educated Evans: Wallace, Edgar

Educated man – good Evans! The: Wallace, Edgar

Educated women: Dawson, *Sir* J.W.

Educating the emotions: Stewart, J.I.M.

Education: Morton, Thomas

Education: Spencer, Herbert

Education and living: Bourne, Randolph

Education and significance of life: Krishnamurti, Jiddu

Education and the modern world: Russell, Bertrand

Education and the social order: Russell, Bertrand

Education and the spirit of the age: Livingstone, *Sir* Richard

Education and the University: Leavis, F.R.

Education as service: Krishnamurti, Jiddu

Education by violence: Canby, H.S.

Education for a world adrift: Livingstone, *Sir* Richard

Education for democracy: Cole, M.I.

Education for democracy: Russell, Bertrand

Education for girls: Moulton, E.L.

Education for life: Drake-Brockman, H.

Education for peace: Read, *Sir* Herbert

Education in a free society: Commager, H.S.

Education in India: Arnold, Edwin

Education of a philanderer, The: Mais, S.P.B.

Education of free men, The: Read, *Sir* Herbert

Education of Mr. Surrage, The: Monkhouse, A.N.

Education of Uncle Paul, The: Blackwood, Algernon

Education or Bringing up of children, The (trans. from Plutarch): Elyot, *Sir* Thomas

Education, politics and war: Radhakrishan, Sarvepalli

Education, the Socialist policy: Tawney, R.H.

Education through art: Read, *Sir* Herbert

Education today: Dewey, John

Education under the Nazis: Beard, C.A.

Educational essays: Dewey, John

Educational reconstruction in India: Panikkar, K.M.

Educational situation, The: Dewey, John

Edward: Moore, *Dr.* John

Edward and Eleonora: Thomson, James

Edward Austin: Ingraham, J.H.

Edward Barry: †Becke, Louis

Edward Blake: Sheldon, C.M.

Edward Burra: Rothenstein, *Sir* John

Edward Burton: Wood, Ellen

Edward Campion: Waugh, Evelyn

Edward Fitzgerald: Benson, A.C.

Edward Fitzgerald and Omar Khayyám: Jackson, Holbrook

Edward Gibbon and his age: Blunden, Edmund

Edward Gibbon Wakefield: Garnett, Richard

Edward Henry Harriman: Muir, John

Edward Livingston Youmans: Fiske, John

Edward Livingston Youmans interpreter of science for the people: Fiske, John

Edward Manning: Ingraham, J.H.

Edward Marsh, patron of the arts: Hassall, Christopher

Edward the Black Prince: Sladen, D.B.W.

Edwardians, The: Gow, Ronald

Edwardians, The: Sackville-West, V.

Edwards: Pain, B.E.O.

Edwin and Eleanor: Vulliamy, C.E.

Edwin and Eltruda: Williams, H.M.

Edwin and Emma: Mallet, David

Edwin Arlington Robinson: Van Doren, Mark

Edwin Arlington Robinson: Winters, Yvor

Edwin Austin Abbey: Lucas, E.V.

Edwin Brothertoft: Winthrop, Theodore

Edwin of Deira: Smith, Alexander

Edwin the fair: Taylor, *Sir* Henry

Eena Deena dynamo: Cresswell, W.D.

Effect of war on stock exchange transactions, The: Guedalla, Philip

Effects of cross- and self-fertilization in the vegetable kingdom, The: Darwin, Charles

Effects of slavery on morals and industry: Webster, Noah

Effendi, Frank Nelson Doubleday: Morley, C.D.

Effie Hetherington: Buchanan, R.W.

Effie Ogilvie: Oliphant, Margaret

Effigies Poeticae: Proctor, B.W.

Efforts. By an invalid: Galt, John

Effusions of love from Chatelar to Mary, Queen of Scotland: Ireland, W.H.

Egbert: Darlington, W.A.

Egeria: Simms, W.G.

Eggs and baker: Masefield, John

Eggs, beans and crumpets: Wodehouse, P.G.

Egil's saga: Eddison, Eric Rucker

Egloges of Alexander Barclay, The: Barclay, Alexander

Eglogs, epytaphes and sonettes: Googe, Barnabe

Eglogue. Gratulatorie, An: Peele, George

Eglogue upon the death of the Right Honourable Sir Francis Walsingham, An: Watson, Thomas

Egmont: Church, H.N.W.

Ego: Agate, J.E.

Egoist, The: Meredith, George

Egoists: Huneker, James

Egotism in German philosophy: Santayana, George

Egypt: Neale, J.M.

Egypt and Iceland in the year 1874: Taylor, Bayard

Egypt and Israel: Petrie, Sir William Flinders

Egypt and its monuments: Hichens, R.S.

Egypt and the English: Sladen, D.B.W.

Egypt through the stereoscope: Breasted, J. H.

Egyptian architecture: Petrie, Sir William Flinders

Egyptian belief and modern thought: Bonwick, James

Egyptian cross mystery, The: †Queen, Ellery

Egyptian elements in the Grail romance: Murray, Margaret

Egyptian hours: (†Donald Barr), Barrett, C.L.

Egyptian objects found in Malta: Murray, Margaret

Egyptian pillar, The: Gore-Booth, E.S.

Egyptian religious poetry: Murray, Margaret

Egyptian tales: Petrie, Sir William Flinders

Egyptian temples: Murray, Margaret

Egyptian wanderers, The: Neal, J.M.

Ehnasya: Petrie, Sir William Flinders

Eight American writers: Foerster, Norman

Eight Canadian poems: Klein, A.M.

Eight cousins: Alcott, Louisa May

Eight crooked trenches, The: †Beeding, Francis

Eight decades: Repplier, Agnes

Eight dramas of Calderón: Fitzgerald, Edward

Eight for eternity: Roberts, C.E.M.

Eight for immortality: Church, Richard

Eight Harvard poets: Cummings, E.E.

Eight Harvard poets: Dos Passos, John

Eight Harvard poets: Hillyer, Robert

Eight hours day, The: Webb, Sidney

Eight men: Wright, Richard

Eight modern writers: (†Michael Innes), Stewart J.I.M.

Eight more Harvard poems: Cowley, Malcolm

Eight o'clock: Ervine, St. John

Eight of swords, The: Carr, J.D.

Eight or nine wise words about letter-writing: †Carroll, Lewis

Eight Victorian poets: Lucas, F.L.

Eight ways of looking at Christianity: Hicks, Granville

Eight years in Canada: Richardson, John

Eighteen centuries of beginnings of Church history: Yonge, C.M.

1848: the revolution of the intellectuals: Namier, Sir Lewis

1844, or the power of the S.F.: English, T.D.

Eighteen hundred and eleven: Barbauld, Mrs. Anna Latitia

Eighteen hundred and thirteen: Grant, Anne

Eighteen months in India: Nehru, J.

Eighteen nineties, The: Jackson, Holbrook

1860–80. John Brown and Wm. Mahone: Bagby, G.W.

Eighteenth century English Romantic poetry: Partridge, Eric

Eighteenth century vignettes: Dobson, H.A.

Eighth commandment, The: Reade, Charles

Eighth sin, The: Morley, C.D.

Eighth wonder, The: Hutchinson, Arthur

Eighth wonder of the world, The: Taylor, John

Eighth year, a vital problem of married life, The: Gibbs, Sir Phillip

Eighty in the shade: †Dane, Clemence

LXXX sermons: Donne, John

Eighty years and after: Howells, W.D.

Eikonoklastes: Milton, John

Eileen: Masters, E.L.

Eimi: Cummings, E.E.

Einstein: MacLeish, Archibald

Eirenicon: Pusey, E.B.

Ekkoes from Kentucky: (†Petroleum V. Nasby), Locke, D.R.

El Fureidis: Cummins, M.S.

El goes south: Kantor, MacKinlay

El Ombú: Hudson, W.H.

El Rio de la Plata: Cunninghame, Graham Robert

Eleanor Sherwood: Ingraham, J.H.

Elder brother, The: Fletcher, John

Elder Conklin: Harris, J.T.

Elder sister, The: Swinnerton, Frank

Elder son, The: Lawson, Henry

Elder statesman, The: Eliot, T.S.

Elderbrook brothers, The: Bullett, Gerald

Elders and betters: Compton-Burnett, Ivy

Elder's people, The: Spofford, H.E.

Eldest, a drama of American life, The: Ferber, Edna

Eldest Miss Collingwood: Ridge, W.Pett

Eldest son, The: Galsworthy, John

Eldorado: Orczy, *Baroness*

Eldorado: Taylor, Bayard

Eldorado Jane: Bottome, Phyllis

Eleanor: Lippard, George

Eleanor: Ward, M.A.

Eleanor's enterprise: Hannay, J.O.

Eleanor's victory: Braddon, M.E.

Elect lady, The: Macdonald, George

Election, The: Sterling, John

Election, An: Swinburne, A.C.

Election Ball in poetical letters in the Zomerzetshire dialect, An: Anstey, Christopher

Election on Academy Hill, The: Canfield, Dorothy

Elections to the Hebdomadal Council, The: †Carroll, Lewis

Electorate and the legislature, The: Walpole, *Sir* Spencer

Electra: Treece, Henry

Electra of Euripides, The: Murray, Gilbert

Electrical precipitation: Lodge, *Sir* Oliver

Electricity: Bragg, *Sir* Laurence

Electricity: Gillette, William

Electrons: Lodge, *Sir* Oliver

Elegance of rebels, An: Langley, Noel

Elegant Edward: Jennings, Gertrude

Elegant Edward: Wallace, Edgar

Elegant wits and grand horizontals: Skinner, C.O.

Elegiac ballad, An: †Pindar, Peter

Elegiac poem on the death of the celebrated divine... George Whitefield, An: Wheatley, Phillis

Elegiac sonnets: Smith, Charlotte

Elegiac stanzas written during sickness at Bath: Bowles, W.L.

Elegie on the death of Prince Henrie, An: Alexander, William

Elegie on the never inough bewailed death (of Henry, Prince of Wales), An: Browne, William

Elegies on different occasions: Pye, H.J.

Elegies on Maggy Johnston, John Cowper, and Lucky Wood: Ramsay, Allan

Elegies. With an ode to the Tiber: Whitehead, William

Elegy for an airman: Stewart, D.A.

Elegy in autumn: Scollard, Clinton

Elegy in memory of Ralph Marshall, An: Tate, Nahum

Elegy on a pile of ruins: Cunningham, John

Elegy on an Australian schoolboy: Cross, Zora

Elegy on Captain Cook to which is added an ode to the sun: Seward, Anna

Elegy on dead fashion: Sitwell, Edith

Elegy on Dicky and Dolly, An: Swift, Jonathan

Elegy on Lucky Wood: Ramsay, Allan

Elegy on Mr. Pa(r)tri(d)ge, the Almanack-maker, An: Swift, Jonathan

Elegy on Patie Birnie, An: Ramsay, Allan

Elegy on the death of an amiable young lady, An: Boswell, James

Elegy on the death of Mr. Buckingham St. John, An: Trumbull, John

Elegy on the late Archbishop of Canterbury, An: Tate, Nahum

Elegy on the late Honorable Titus Hosmer, Esq.: Barlow, Joel

Elegy on the much lamented death of Mr. Demar, the famous rich man, An: Swift, Jonathan

Elegy on the much lamented death of William Beckford, Esq., An: Chatterton, Thomas

Elegy on Trottin' Nanny: Tennant, William

Elegy to the memory of the late Duke of Bedford, written on the evening of his interment, An: Opie, Amelia

Elegy to the memory of the Right Honourable William, late Earl of Bath, An: Kelly, Hugh

Elegy written at the Hot-Wells, Bristol: Bowles, William Lisle

Elegy written on Saint Mark's Eve, An: Cumberland, Richard

Elegy wrote in a country church yard, An: Gray, Thomas

Elementa philosophica: Johnson, Samuel

Elementary Coptic grammar: Murray, Margaret

Elementary Egyptian grammar: Murray, Margaret

Elementary geography, An: Stowe, Hariet Beecher

Elementary Jane: Pryce, Richard

Elementary mechanics: Lodge, *Sir* Oliver

Elementary primer, The: Webster, Noah

Elementary sketches of moral philosophy: Smith, Sydney

Elementary spelling book, The: Webster, Noah

Elementary world history: Beard, C.A.

Elements of architecture, The: Wotton, *Sir* Henry

Elements of Armories, The: Bolton, Edmund

Elements of Buddhist Iconography: Coomaraswamy, A.K.

Elements of drawing, The: Ruskin, John

Elements of English prosody for use in St. George's schools: Ruskin, John

Elements of logic: Whately, Richard

Elements of moral science: Beattie, James

Elements of perspective arranged for the use of schools, The: Ruskin, John

Elements of political economy: Mill, James

Elements of politics, The: Sidgwick, Henry

Elements of reconstruction, The: Wells, H.G.

Elements of rhetoric, The: De Mille, James

Elements of Rhetoric: Whately, Richard

Elements of the art of packing as applied to special juries: Bentham, Jeremy

Elements of the short story, The: Hale, E.E.

Elements of useful knowledge: Webster, Noah

Eleonora: Dryden, John

Eleonora Duse: Symons, Arthur

Elephant and the kangaroo, The: White, T.H.

Elephant's Head, The: †Bartimeus

Elephant's work: Bentley, E.C.

Eleusinia: †Machen, Arthur

Eleutheria: Mather, Cotton

Elevator, The: Howells, W.D.

Eleven essays in the European novel: Blackmur, R.P.

Eleven lectures on the French and Belgian Revolutions: Cobbett, William

Eleven new cantos, XXXI–XLI: Pound, Ezra

Eleven poems on the same theme: Warren, R.P.

Eleven weeks in Europe: Clarke, J.F.

Eleven were brave: †Beeding, Francis

Eleventh hour: †Armstrong, Anthony

Eleventh hour in the life of Julia Ward Howe, The: Elliott, M.H.

Elfin artist, The: Noyes, Alfred

Elfin Dell: Anderson, J.C.

Elfrid: Hill, Aaron

Elgar: Newman, Ernest

Eli Perkins at large: his sayings and doings: Landon, Melville

Elia: Lamb, Charles

Eliana: Lamb, Charles

Elijah: Brooker, Bertram

Elinor Barley: Warner, Sylvia Townsend

Elinor Colhouse: †Hudson, Stephen

Elinor Wyllys: Cooper, Susan Fenimore

Eliot: Channing, W.E.

Eliot, Hampden, and Pym: D'Israeli, Isaac

Elisa: Fletcher, Phineas

Elixir of life, The: Ransome, Arthur

Elixir of life, The: Satchell, William

Elixir of moonshine by the Mad Poet: Clarke, Macdonald

Eliza: Blackmore, Sir R.D.

Eliza: Pain, B.E.O.

Eliza books, The: Pain, B.E.O.

Eliza for common: Buchan, Anna

Eliza getting on: Pain, B.E.O.

Eliza's husband: Pain, B.E.O.

Eliza's son: Pain, B.E.O.

Elizabeth: Swinnerton, Frank

Elizabeth and Essex: Strachey, Lytton

Elizabeth and her German garden: Russell, E.M.

Elizabeth and Leicester: Jenkins, Elizabeth

Elizabeth and the Archdeacon: Hannay, J.O.

Elizabeth and the Prince of Spain: Irwin, Margaret

Elizabeth Appleton: O'Hara, J.H.

Elizabeth Barrett Browning in her letters: Lubbock, Percy

Elizabeth, captive Princess: Irwin, Margaret

Elizabeth Cooper: Moore, George

Elizabeth I and her parliaments, 1584–1601: Neale, J.E.

Elizabeth I and her parliaments, 1559–81: Neale, J.E.

Elizabeth Madox Roberts: Wescott, Glenway

Elizabeth of England: Dukes, Ashley

Elizabeth the Great: Jenkins, Elizabeth

Elizabeth the queen: Anderson, Maxwell

Elizabeth visits America: Glyn, Elinor

Elizabethan and other essays: Lee, Sir Sidney

Elizabethan commentary: Belloc, Hilaire

Elizabethan dramatists: Eliot, T.S.

Elizabethan essays: Eliot, T.S.

Elizabethan House of Commons, The: Neale, J.E.

Elizabethan lyric, The: Erskine, John

Elizabethan stage, The: Chambers, Sir E.K.

Elizabethan world picture, The: Tillyard, E.M.W.

Elizabethans, The: Nicoll, John Allardyce

Ellen: Calvert, G.H.

Ellen Adair: Niven, F.J.

Ellen Fitzarthur: Southey, C.A.

Ellen Glasgow: Sherman, S.P.

Ellen Gray: Bowles, W.L.

Ellen Hart: Ingraham, J.H.

Ellen Percy: Reynolds, G.

Ellen Prior: Brown, Alice

Ellen Rogers: Farrell, James

Ellen Story: Fawcett, Edgar

Ellen Terry and her secret self: Craig, Sir E.G.

Ellen Terry and Shaw: a correspondence: Shaw, G.B.

Ellesmere Lake: Montgomery, Robert

Ellie: Cooke, J.E.

Ellis: Colum, Padraic

Ellis: Hercules, Mangan, J.C.

Elm angel: Monro, H.E.

Elmer Gantry: Lewis, H.S.

Elmerick: Lillo, George

Elocutionist, The: Knowles, J.S.

Elopement: Jones, H.A.

Elopement into exile: Pritchett, V.S.

Eloping angels, The: Watson, Sir J.W.

Eloquence of the British senate, The: Hazlitt, William

Elsie and the child: Bennett, Arnold

Elsie Venner: Holmes, Oliver Wendell

Elsket: Page, T.N.

Elster's folly: Wood, Ellen

Eltham House: Ward, M.A.

Elton Hazelwood: Scott, F.G.

Elucidation, An: Stein, Gertrude

Elucidations of Dr. Hampden's theological statements: Newman, J.H.

Elusive Pimpernel, The: Orczy, Baroness

Elves and the shoemaker, The: Sidgwick, Ethel

Elvira: Mallet, David

Emancipated, The: Gissing, George

Embargo, The: Bryant, W.C.

Embarrassments: James, Henry

Embassy ball, The: Thomas, Augustus

Embassy to Provence, An: Janvier, T.A.

Ember lane: Kaye-Smith, S.

Embers: Beckett, Samuel

Embers: Parker, Sir H.G.

Embers; a lover's diary: Parker, Sir H.G.

Embezzler, The: Cain, J.M.

Emblemes: Quarles, Francis

Emblemland: Bangs, J. Kendrick

Emblems of fidelity, The: Allen, J.L.

Emblems of love: Ayres, Philip

Emerald of Catherine the Great, The: Belloc, Hilaire

Emergency exit: Coppard, A.E.

Emerson: Alcott, A.B.

Emerson: Arnold, Matthew

Emerson: Birrell, Augustine

Emerson: Garnett, Richard

Emerson and others: Brooks, Van Wyck

Emerson at home and abroad: Conway, M.D.

Emigrant, The: McLachlan, Alexander

Emigrant, The: O'Grady, Standish

Emigrant, The: Thomas, F.W.

Emigrants of Ahadarra, The: Carleton, William

Emigrant ship, The: Russell, W.C.

Emigrants, The: Bolitho, H.H.

Emigrants, The: Smith, Charlotte

Emigrant's guide, The: Cobbett, William

Emigrant's story, The: Trowbridge, J.T.

Emigration and settlement on wild land: Gourlay, R.F.

Emilia in England: Meredith, George

Emily climbs: Montgomey, L.M.

Emily of New Moon: Montgomery, L.M.

Emily Parker: Child, Lydia Maria

Emily's quest: Montgomery, L.M.

Emin, governor of Equatoria: Symons, A.J.A.

Eminent Victorians: Strachey, Lytton

Emma: Austen, Jane

Emma McChesney & Co.: Ferber, Edna

Emmanuel Burden: Belloc, Hilaire

Emmett Bonlore: Read, O.P.

Emotional discovery of America, The: Sherman, S.P.

Emotional moments: †Grand, Sarah

Empedocles on Etna: Arnold, Matthew

Emperor Constantine, The: Sayers, Dorothy

Emperor Jones, The: O'Neill, Eugene

Emperor of Haiti: Hughes, J.L.

Emperor of the moon, The: Behn, Mrs. Afra

Emperor of the West (Charles V): Lewis, D.B. Wyndham

Emperor Romanus Lecapenus, The: Runciman, Sir Steven

Emperor's candlesticks, The: Orczy, Baroness

Emperor's servant, The: †Pilgrim, David

Emperor's snuff box, The: Carr, J.D.

Emperour of the East, The: Massinger, Philip

Empire, The: Lecky, W.E.H.

Empire, The: Smith, Goldwin

Empire and commerce in Africa: Woolf, Leonard

Empire and communication: Innis, H.A.

Empire and the army, The: Fortescue, Sir John

Empire builders, The: Stead, R.J.C.

Empire City, The: Lippard, George

Empire of fur: Derleth, A.W.

Empire on stamps: Hamilton, Patrick

Empress Eugenie's boudoir, The: Reynolds, G.

Empress of Hearts, The: Beck, Mrs. Lily

Empress of Morocco, The: Settle, Elkanah

Empty clothes: Bolitho, H.H.

Empty hands: Stringer, A.J.A.

Empty house, The: Blackwood, Algernon

Empty house, The: Ward, E.S.

Empty purse, with odes to the comic, The: Meredith, George

Empty room, The: Morgan, Charles

Empty sack, The: †King, Basil

Emu parade: Moore, T.I.

Enbury Heath: Gibbons, Stella

Encaenia: Donne, John

Enchafèd flood, The: Auden, W.H.

Enchanted, The: Flavin, Martin

Enchanted April, The: Russell, E.M.

Enchanted blanket, The: Mackenzie, Sir Compton

Enchanted castle, The: Nesbit, E. Edith

Enchanted cottage, The: Pinero, Sir A.W.

Enchanted doll, The: Lemon, Mark

Enchanted fiddle, The: Brazil, Angela

Enchanted garden, The: Erskine, John

Enchanted garden, An: Molesworth, Mrs.

Enchanted garden, The: Vachell, H.A.

Enchanted island, The: Mackenzie, *Sir* Compton

Enchanted island, The: Noyes, Alfred

Enchanted island, The: Palmer, E.V.

Enchanted isles: Woollcott, A.H.

Enchanted land: Mee, Arthur

Enchanted sea, An: Martyn, Edward

Enchanted treasure, The: †Machen, Arthur

Enchanted typewriter, The: Bangs, J.K.

Enchanted wood, The: Philpotts, Eden

Enchanted woods, The: Lee, Vernon

Enchantment: Russell, G.W.

Enchyridion: Quarles, Francis

Encircling seas: Holcroft, M.H.

Encomion of Lady Pecunia, The: Barnfield, Richard

Encore: Maugham, W.S.

Encore, An: Deland, Margaret

Encounter, The: Sedgwick, A.D.

Encounters: Bowen, E.D.C.

Encounters and diversions: Lucas, E.V.

Encouragement to colonies, An: Alexander, William

Encyclopaedia Metropolitana: Talfourd, *Sir* T.N.

Encyclopaedia of Buddhism: Malalasekara, Gunapala

Encyclopaedia of pacifism, An: Huxley, Aldous

End and a beginning, An: Hanley, James

End and a beginning, An: Mitchison, Naomi

End and beginning: Masefield, John

Endgame: Beckett, Samuel

End of a chapter, The: Leslie, *Sir* J.R. Shane

End of a childhood, The: †Richardson, H.H.

End of a life, The: Phillpotts, Eden

End of a war, The: Read, *Sir* Herbert

End of an ancient mariner: Cole, G.D.H.

End of an era, The: Munshi, K.M.

End of Andrew Harrison, The: Crofts, F.W.

End of chapter: Day-Lewis, Cecil

End of day: Mason, R.A.K.

End of desire, The: Herrick, Robert

End of Elfintown, The: Barlow, Jane

End of empire, The: Strachey, John

End of her honeymoon, The: Lowndes, M.A.

End of Laissez-Faire, The: Keynes, J.M.

End of Mr. Garment, The: Starrett, Vincent

End of socialism in Russia, The: Eastman, Max

End of summer: Behrman, S.N.

End of the affair, The: Greene, Graham

End of the armament rings, The: Wells, H.G.

End of the Armistice: Chesterton, G.K.

End of the beginning, The: Churchill, *Sir* Winston

End of the chapter: Galsworthy, John

End of the coil, The: Warner, S.B.

End of the house of Alard, The: Kaye-Smith, S.

End of the Roman road, The: Chesterton, G.K.

End of the row, The: Green, Paul

End of the trail, The: Carman, Bliss

End of the world, The: Abercrombie, Lascelles

End of the world, The: Eggleston, Edward

End of this war, The: Jameson, Storm

Ende of Nero and beginning of Galba, The: Savile, *Sir* Henry

Endeavour of Jean Fernel, The: Sherrington, *Sir* Charles

Endimion and Phoebe: Drayton, Michael

Endimion, the man in the moone: Lyly, John

Ending in earnest: †West, Rebecca

Ending of hereditary American fortunes, The: Myers, Gustavus

Endless chain, The: †Bell, Neil

Endless furrow: Street, A.G.

Endless story: †Taffrail

Endowed schools of Ireland: Martineau, Harriet

Ends and means: Huxley, Aldous

Ends and means: Livingstone, *Sir* Richard

Endymion: Disraeli, Benjamin

Endymion: Keats, John

Enemies: Glaspell, Susan

Enemies, The: Lynd, Sylvia

Enemies of literature, The: (†Elzevir), Murdoch, *Sir* W.L.F.

Enemies of promise: Connolly, Cyril

Enemy camp, The: Weidman, Jerome

Enemy gods, The: La Farge, Oliver

Enemy had it too, The: Sinclair, Upton

Enemy of the stars: Lewis, Wyndham

Enemy unseen: Crofts, F.W.

Energy: Lodge, *Sir* Oliver

Eneydos (trn.): Caxton, William

Engaged: Gilbert, *Sir* W.S.

Engaged in writing: Spender, Stephen

Engagement ring, The: Hillyer, Robert

Engine fight-talk: Lewis, Wyndham

Engineers and the price system, The: Veblen, T.B.

Engineer's notebook, An: McFee, William

Engines: Andrade, E.N. da Costa

Engines of the human body: Keith, *Sir* Arthur

England: Binyon, Laurence

England: Inge, W.R.

England, a dying oligarchy: Bromfield, Louis

England and America in 1782: Tennyson, Alfred *Lord*

England and Europe: Fisher, H.A.L.

England and her soldiers: Martineau, Harriet

England and India: Dutt, R.C.

England and Ireland: Mill, John Stuart

England and Spain: Hemans, *Mrs.* Felicia

England and the disrupted States of America: Gratton, T.C.

England and the English: Kipling, Rudyard

England and the English: Lytton, E.G.E.B. *Ist Baron*

England and the Italian question: Arnold, Matthew

England and the War: Raleigh, *Sir* W.A.

England and yesterday: Guiney, L.I.

England at the close of the Middle Ages: Chambers, *Sir* Edmund

England day by day: Lucas, E.V.

England, Egypt and the Soudan: Traill, H.D.

England 1870–1914: Ensor, *Sir* R.C.K.

England have my bones: White, T.H.

England I remember, The: Mickle, A.D.

England in the age of the American revolution: Namier, *Sir* Lewis

England in the age of Wycliffe: Trevelyan, G.M.

England in time of war: Dobell, S.T.

England is my village: Rhys, John Llewellyn

England made me: Greene, Graham

England, my England: Lawrence, D.H.

England, my England! Lindsay, Jack

England of Charles II, The: Bryant, *Sir* Arthur

England of the windmills: Mais, S.P.B.

England our England: †Armstrong, Anthony and Treyer Evans

England reclaimed: Sitwell, *Sir* Osbert

England speaks: Gibbs, *Sir* Philip

England, their England: Macdonell, A.G.

England under Protector Somerset: Pollard, A.F.

England under Queen Anne: Trevelyan, G.M.

England under the House of Hanover: Wright, Thomas

England under the reigns of Edward VI and Mary: Tytler, P.F.

England under the Stuarts: Trevelyan, G.M.

Englandes mourning garment: Chettle, Henry

England's antiphon: Macdonald, George

England's character: Mais, S.P.B.

England's darling: Austin, Alfred

England's darling: †Dane, Clemence

England's effort: Ward, M.A.

Englands Elizabeth: her life and troubles, during her minoritie, from the cradle to the crowne: Heywood, Thomas

Englands heroicall epistles: Drayton, Michael

England's hour: Brittain, Vera

England's iron days: Bannister, N.H.

England's jubile: Chamberlayne, William

England's pleasance: Mais, S.P.B.

England's pleasant land: Forster, E.M.

England's work in India: Hunter, *Sir* William

English adventures: Boyle, Roger

English and Hebrew grammar, An: Johnson, Samuel

English and Scottish ballads: Child, F.J.

English and Scottish popular ballads: Child, F.J.

English anthology, The: Ritson, Joseph

English Arcadia, The: Markham, Gervase

English artists of the present day: Taylor, Tom

English as a colonizing nation, The: Hight, James

English ballad, The: Graves, Robert

English ballad: an answer to Mr. Despreaux's Pindarique Ode on the taking of Namur, An: Prior, Matthew

English bards and Scotch reviewers: Byron, George Gordon, *Lord*

English baronage, The: Collins, Arthur

English Bible, The: Grierson, *Sir* Herbert

English bookman's library: Pollard, A.W.

English Canadian literature, 1882–1932: Pierce, Lorne

English Captain, The: Strong, L.A.G.

English children: Lynd, Sylvia

English churches: Betjeman, John

English cities and small towns: Betjeman, John

English classics: a historical sketch of the literature of England from the earliest times to the accession of King George III, The: Johnston, R.M.

English comic characters, The: Priestley, J.B.

English comic drama, 1700–1750: Bateson, F.W.

English constitution, The: Bagehot, Walter

English country houses: Sackville-West, V.

English country life: Miller, Thomas

English countryman, The: Massingham, Harold

English course for army candidates, An: Mais, S.P.B.

English course for everybody, An: Mais, S.P.B.

English course for schools, An: Mais, S.P.B.

English dance of death, The: Combe, William

English diaries and journals: O'Brien, Kate

English downland: Massingham, Harold

English drama, The: Rubenstein, Harold F.

English dramatists of to-day: Archer, William

English drawings: Grigson, Geoffrey

English eccentrics, The: Sitwell, Edith

English economic history: Cole, G.D.H.

English economic history: Tawney, R.H.

English epic and its background, The: Tillyard, E.M.W.

English essayists: Dobrée, Bonamy

English essays from a French, pen: Jusserand, Jean

English excursions: Grigson, Geoffrey

English family Robinson: Reid, T.M.

English farming; why I turned it in: Bramah, E.

English festivals, The: Whistler, Laurence

English folk-play, The: Chambers, Sir E.K.

English for human beings: Partridge, Eric

English for pleasure: Strong, L.A.G.

English gardener, The: Cobbett, William

English girl, An: Ford, F.M.

English girl's account of a Moravian settlement, An: Manning, Anne

English gone wrong: Partridge, Eric

English grammar, The: Jonson, Ben

English history for American readers: Higginson, T.W.

English hours: James, Henry

English humour: Priestley, J.B.

English humourists of the eighteenth century, The: Thackeray, W.M.

English husbandman, The: Markham, Gervase

English in America, The: Haliburton, T.C.

English in India, The: Hockley, W.B.

English in Ireland in the eighteenth century, The: Froude, J.A.

English in love, The: †George, Daniel

English journey: Priestley, J.B.

English Kings in a nutshell: Dodge, M.A.

English lands, letters and kings: Mitchell, D.G.

English language, The: Smith, L.L.P.

English language, The: Weekley, Ernest

English language and literature: Chambers, Robert

English leaves: Lucas, E.V.

English letter writers: Vulliamy, C.E.

English literary autographs, 1550–1650: Greg, W.W.

English literature: Brooke, S.A.

English literature: Erskine, John

English literature: Johnston, R.M.

English literature: Gosse, Sir Edmund

English literature and society in the eighteenth century: Stephen, Sir Leslie

English literature at the close of the Middle Ages: Chambers, Sir E.K.

English literature from the beginning to the Norman Conquest: Brooke, S.A.

English literature in Japan: Saito, Takeshu

English literature in the earlier seventeenth century, 1600–1660: Bush, Douglas

English literature in the sixteenth century: Lewis, C.S.

English literature: mediaeval: Ker, W.P.

English local government: Webb, Sidney and Beatrice Webb

English love poems: Betjeman, John

English maiden: Swinnerton, Frank

English medley, An: Drinkwater, John

English men of science: Galton, Sir Francis

English merchant, The: Colman, George, the elder

English minstrelsie: Baring-Gould, Sabine

English miss, The: Mottram, R.H.

English muse, The: Elton, Oliver

English myrror, The: Whetstone, George

English mystics, The: Bullett, Gerald

English naturalists from Neckam to Ray: Raven, C.E.

English notebooks, The: Hawthorne, Nathaniel

English novel, The: Allen, Walter Ernest

English novel, The: Ford, F.M.

English novel, The: Priestley, J.B.

English novel, The: Raleigh, Sir Walter

English novel, The: Saintsbury, George

English novel, The: Walpole, Sir Hugh

English novel and the principle of its development, The: Lanier, Sidney

English novel in the time of Shakespeare, The: Jusserand, Jean

English novel of today, The: Gould, Gerald

English novelists: Bowen, E.D.C.

English ode, The: Binyon, Laurence

English of the line, The: Mulgan, A.E.

English orphans, The: Holmes, M.J.

English padlock, An: Prior, Matthew

English painters of the present day: Taylor, Tom

English paragon, The: †Bowen, Marjorie

English people, The: Brogan, Sir Denis

English people, The: †Orwell, George

English Physitian, The: Culpeper, Nicolas

English place-names: Bradley, *Dr.* Henry

English poems: Blunden, Edmund

English poems: Le Gallienne, Richard

English poetic mind, The: Williams, Charles

English poetry: a critical introduction: Bateson, F.W.

English poetry and the English language: Bateson, F.W.

English poetry in its relation to painting and the other arts: Binyon, Laurence

English poetry: the main currents: Bush, Douglas

English poets and the national ideal: De Selincourt, Ernest

English poets; Lessing, Rousseau, The: Lowell, J.R.

English political leaders: Trollope, Anthony

English political theory: Brown, Iver

English Poor Law history: Webb, Sidney and Beatrice Webb

English poor law policy: Webb, Sidney and Beatrice Webb

English Poor Law, will it endure?, The: Webb, Beatrice

English portraits: Rothenstein, *Sir* William

English portraits and essays: Freeman, John

English pottery: Read, *Sir* Herbert

English prayers: More, *Sir* Thomas

English prisons under Local Government: Webb, Sidney and Beatrice Webb

English prose: Brophy, John

English prose style: Read, *Sir* Herbert

English Public Schools: Warner, Rex

English rambles: Winter, William

English reading made easy: Craigie, *Sir* W.A.

English regional novel, The: Bentley, Phyllis

English Renaissance, fact or fiction, The: Tillyard, E.M.W.

English revolts: Dobrée, Bonamy

English revolution, 1688–1689, The: Trevelyan, G.M.

English rogue, The: Head, Richard

English rogue described in the life of Meriton Latroon, The: Kirkman, Francis

English Romayne lyfe, The: Munday, Anthony

English saga: Bryant, *Sir* Arthur

English scene today, The: Mais, S.P.B.

English sense of humour, The: Nicolson, Hon. *Sir* Harold

English social history: A survey of six centuries: Trevelyan, G.M.

English society at home: Du Maurier, George

English spelling: Craigie, *Sir* W.A.

English stage, The: Nicoll, John Allardyce

English stained glass: Read, *Sir* Herbert

English teacher, The: Narayan, R.K.

English theatre, The: Nicoll, John Allardyce

English title-borders, 1485–1640: McKerrow, R.B.

English towns in the last hundred years, The: Betjeman, John

English traits: Emerson, R.W.

English traveller, The: Heywood, Thomas

English utilitarians, The: Stephen, *Sir* Leslie

English villages: Blunden, Edmund

English vineyard vindicated by John Rose Gard'ner to his Majesty: Evelyn, John

English wayfaring life in the Middle Ages: Jusserand, Jean

English witchcraft and James the First: Kittredge, G.L.

English women: Sitwell, Edith

English women of letters: Kavanagh, Julia

English works, The: Roy, R.R.

English writers: Morley, Henry

Englishman, The: Steele, *Sir* Richard

Englishman and his history, The: Butterfield, Herbert

Englishman looks at the world, An: Wells, H.G.

Englishmans doctor, The: Harington, *Sir* John

Englishman's Flora, The: Grigson, Geoffrey

English-mans love to Bohemia, An: Taylor, John

Englishman's mentor, The: Hone, William

Englishman's thanks to the Duke of Marlborough, The: Steele, *Sir* Richard

Englishman's year, An: Massingham, Harold

Englishmen and Italians: Trevelyan, G.M.

Englishmen, Frenchmen, Spaniards: Madariaga, Salvador de

Englishness of English art, The: Pevsner, Nikolaus

English-South African's view of the situation, An: Schreiner, Olive

Englishwoman's love letters, An: Housman, Laurence

Engraved glass: Whistler, Laurence

Engravings by Eric Gill: Gill, Eric

Engravings 1928–1933: Gill, Eric

Enid: Pickthall, M.W.

Enid and Geraint: Rhys, Ernest

Enid and Nimuë: Tennyson, Alfred *Lord*

Enigmas of life: Greg, W.R.

Enjoying books: Trease, Geoffrey

Enjoying life: †Barbellion, W.N.P.

Enjoying pictures: Bell, Clive

Enjoying poetry: Day-Lewis, Cecil

Enjoyment of laughter: Eastman, Max

Enjoyment of poetry: Eastman, Max

Enoch Arden: Tennyson, Alfred *Lord*

Enoch Crane: Smith, F.H.

Enormous room, The: Cummings, E.E.

Enough rope: Parker, Dorothy

Enquirer, The: Godwin, William

Enquiries and observations respecting the university library: Montagu, Basil

Enquiries respecting the proposed alteration of the law of copyright as it affects authors and the universities: Montagu, Basil

Enquiry concerning the principles of morals, An: Hume, David

Enquiry concerning the principles of political justice, An: Godwin, William

Enquiry into industrial art in England, An: Pevsner, Nikolaus

Enquiry into the authenticity of the poems attributed to Thomas Rowley, An: Warton, Thomas

Enquiry into the causes of the late increase of robbers, An: Fielding, Henry

Enquiry into the effects of public punishments upon criminals, An: Rush, Benjamin

Enquiry into the measures of submission to the supream authority, An: Burnet, Gilbert

Enquiry into the merit of assassination, An: Hill, Aaron

Enquiry into the nature and origin of literary property, An: Warburton, William

Enquiry into the nature of peace and the terms of its perpetration, An: Veblen, T.B.

Enquiry into the present state of affairs, An: Burnet, Gilbert

Ensign Knightly: Mason, A.E.W.

Enslaved: Masefield, John

Entail, or the Lairds of Grippy, The: Galt, John

Enter a murderer: Marsh, Ngaio Edith

Enter Psmith: Wodehouse, P.G.

Enter Sir John: †Dane, Clemence and H. de G. Simpson

Enter Sir Robert: Thirkell, Angela

Enter without knocking: Glover, Denis

Entertainment, The: †Delafield, E.M.

Entertainment of His most excellent Majestie Charles II, The: Ogilby, John

Entertainment of the high and mighty Monarch Charles King of Great Britain, The: Drummond of Hawthornden, William

Entertainment of the Queen and King at Althorpe, The: Jonson, Ben

Enthralled: Saltus, E.E.

Enthusiasm: Byrom, John

Enthusiasm: Knox, R.A.

Enthusiasm: Moodie, Susanna

Enthusiast, The: Calder-Marshall, Arthur

Enthusiast, An: Somerville, E.

Enthusiast, The: Warton, Joseph

Entirely new and original drama, in four acts, entitled Brantinghame Hall, An: Gilbert, Sir W.S.

Envious Casca: Heyer, Georgette

Environment: Bentley, Phyllis

Envoi: Lewis, P. Wyndham

Envoy extraordinary: Brittain, Vera

Envoy extraordinary: Oppenheim, E. Phillips

Envy: Anstey, Christopher

Enzio's kingdom: Percy, W.A.

Enzymes: Haldane, J.B.S.

Eos: a prairie dream: Davin, N.F.

Eos: an epic of the dawn: Davin, N.F.

Eothen: Kinglake, A.W.

Ephemera, The: Franklin, Benjamin

Ephemera: Willis, N.P.

Ephemera: an Iliad of Albury: Farrell, John

Ephemera critica: Collins, J.C.

Ephemerides: Pringle, Thomas

Ephesian matron, The: Bickerstaffe, Isaac

Epic, The: Abercrombie, Lascelles

Epic and romance: Ker, W.P.

Epic of America, The: Adams, J.T

Epic of Arkansas, The: Fletcher, John Gould

Epic of golf, The: Scollard, Clinton

Epic of Hades, The: Morris, Sir Lewis

Epic of Jutland, The: Leslie, Sir J.R.Shane

Epic of women, An: O'Shaughnessy, A.W.E.

EPIC plan for California, The: Sinclair, Upton

Epic strain in the English novel, The: Tillyard, E.M.W.

Epicede or funerall song: on the death of Henry Prince of Wales, An: Chapman, George

Epicoene, or The silent woman: Jonson, Ben

Epics of the fancy: Farnol, J.J.

Epicurean, The: Moore, Thomas

Epigrammes: besides, two new made satyres: Taylor, John

Epigrams: Stringer, A.J.A.

Epigrams and humorous verses: Warburton, R.E.E.

Epigrams both pleasant and serious: Harington, Sir John

Epigrams: divine and moral: Urquhart, Sir Thomas

Epigrams in a cellar: Morley, C.D.

Epigrams of art, life and nature: Watson, Sir J.W.

Epilogue, An: †O'Sullivan, Seumas

Epilogue to Her Highness on her return from Scotland: Otway, Thomas

Epilogue to Tamerlane: Walpole, Horace

Epilogue to Venice Preserv'd spoken upon the Duke of York's coming to the theatre: Otway, Thomas

Epipsychidion: Shelley, Percy Bysshe

Episcopal elections ancient and modern: Dawson, Sir J.W.

Episode in Palmetta: Caldwell, Erskine Preston

Episode of sparrows, An: Godden, Rumer

Episodes before thirty: Blackwood, Algernon

Episodes in a life of adventure: Oliphant, Laurence

Episodes in an obscure life: Rowe, Richard

Epistle, The: Marprelate, Martin

Epistle dedicatory: Shaw, G.B.

Epistle from a lady in England, to a gentleman at Avignon, An: Tickell, Thomas

Epistle from a nobleman to a doctor of divinity, An: Hervey, John

Epistle humbly addressed to the Rt. Hon. John, Earl of Orrery, An: Theobald, Lewis

Epistle of comfort to the reverend preistes, An: Southwell, Robert

Epistle the second to Mrs. Clarke: †Pindar, Peter

Epistle to a friend, An: Rogers, Samuel

Epistle to a gentleman of the temple, An: Byrom, John

Epistle to a lady, who desired the author to make verses on her, An: Swift, Jonathan

Epistle to Cobham, An: Pope, Alexander

Epistle to Curio, An: Akenside, Mark

Epistle to David Garrick Esq., An: Lloyd, Evan

Epistle to Dr. Arbuthnot, An: Pope, Alexander

Epistle to Dr. Kenrick, An: Colman, George, *the elder*

Epistle to Dr. Oliver Wendell Holmes, An: Gosse, *Sir* Edmund

Epistle to Her Grace Henrietta, Dutchess of Marlborough, An: Gay, John

Epistle to his excellency John Lord Carteret Lord Lieutenant of Ireland, An: Swift, Jonathan

Epistle to James Lowther: †Pindar, Peter

Epistle to John Nichols: †Pindar, Peter

Epistle to Lord Lovelace, An: Jenyns, Soame

Epistle to Mr. Pope, An: Lyttelton, George *Baron*

Epistle to Prometheus: Deutch, Babette

Epistle to the Hebrews: Moffat, James

Epistle to the Honourable James Craggs, Esq. An: Philips, Ambrose

Epistle to the Quarterly and Monthly Meeting of Friends, An: Woolman, John

Epistle to the right honourable Charles Lord Halifax, An: Philips, Ambrose

Epistle to the Right Honourable the Lord Lansdown, An: Young, Edward

Epistle to Walter Scott, An: Brackenridge, H.H.

Epistle to W—H—, An: Ramsay, Allan

Epistle to William Hogarth, An: Churchill, Charles

Epistle to William Wilberforce Esq.: Barbauld, *Mrs.* A.L.

Epistle upon an epistle from a certain doctor to a great lord, An: Swift, Jonathan

Epistles, odes, and other poems: Moore, Thomas

Epistles to the King and Duke: Wycherley, William

Epistolary correspondence: Steele, *Sir* Richard

Epistolary letter, An: Hearne, Thomas

Epistolary poems: Hopkins, Charles

Epitaph: Dreiser, Theodore

Epitaph for a spy: Ambler, Eric

Epitaph for the race of man: Millay, E. St. Vincent

Epitaph on George Moore: Morgan, Charles

Epitaph on the admirable dramaticke poet, W. Shakespeare, An: Milton, John

Epitaphes, epigrams, songs and sonets, with a discourse of the friendly affections of Tymetes to Pyndara his ladie: Turberville, George

Epithalamia: Wither, George

Epithalamion: Spenser, Edmund

Epithalamium: Sitwell, Edith

Epithalamium in time of war: Gustafson, Ralph

Epitome, The: Marprelate, Martin

Epoch—the life of Steele Mackaye: Mackaye, Percy

Epochs of Chinese and Japanese art: Fenollosa, E.F.

Epping hunt, The: Hood, Thomas

Epsom-Wells: Shadwell, Thomas

Epullia: Blackmore, *Sir* R.D.

E.Q.s big book: †Queen, Ellery

Equal rights for women: Curtis, George

Equality: Bellamy, Edward

Equality: Tawney, R.H.

Equall ways of God, The: Hooker, Thomas

Equitable trust company of Atlantic City, The: Morley, C.D.

Era of Franklin D. Roosevelt, The: Brogan, *Sir* Denis

Era of reform, The: Commager, Henry Steele

Erasmus: Hollis, Christopher

Erato No. I: Gallagher, W.D.

Erato No. II: Gallagher, W.D.

Erato No. III: Gallagher, W.D.

Erb: Ridge, W. Pett

Erchie: my droll friend: Munro, Neil

Erechtheus: Swinburne, A.C.

Erema: Blackmore, *Sir* R.D.

Eremus: Phillips, Stephen

Erewhon: Butler, Samuel

Erewhon revisited: Butler, Samuel

Erez Israel: Mencken, H.L.

Eric Brighteyes: Haggard, *Sir* Henry Rider

Eric Gill: Rothenstein, *Sir* John

Eric, King of Norway: Ghose, Sri Aurobindo

Eric Lee-Johnson: McCormick, E.H.

Ericksons, The: Browne, Frances

Erie canal, The: Edmonds, W.D.

Erie Water: Edmonds, W.D.

Erik Dorn: Hecht, Ben

Erin: Bayly, T.H.

Erin-go-Bragh: Maxwell, W.H.

Eris: Chambers, R.W.

Erling the bold: Ballantyne, R.M.

Ermine, The: Pitter, Ruth

Ernest Clouet: Swinburne, A.C.

Ernest escaping: Ridge, W. Pett

Ernest Maltravers: Lytton, E.G.E.B. *Ist Baron*

Ernest Thompson Seton's trail and camp-fire stories: Seton-Thompson, E.

Ernestina: Lathom, Francis

Ernestine: Maltby, H.F.

Eros and Psyche: Bridges, Robert

Eros at breakfast: Davies, Robertson

Eros in dogma: Barker, George

Errata: Hopkinson, Francis

Erring woman's love, An: Wilcox, Ella Wheeler

Error of judgement, An: Johnson, Pamela H.

Errors of ecstasie, The: Darley, George

Errors of innocence, The: Lee, Harriet

Erskine Dale Pointer: Fox, John

Escapade: Scott, Evelyn

Escapade: Warner, Rex

Escapades of Anne, The: Dyson, E.G.

Escape: Benson, A.C.

Escape: Galsworthy, John

Escape from Spain: Divine, David

Escape me never! Kennedy, Margaret

Escape of Alice, The: Starrett, Vincent

Escape of Captain John Holliday from the Mexicans in 1837: Hall, B.R.

Escape of the notorious Sir William Heans, The: Hay, William

Escape to King Alfred: Trease, Geoffrey

Escape to yesterday: Frankau, Gilbert

Escape with me!: Sitwell, *Sir* Osbert

Escaped cock, The: Lawrence, D.H.

Escorial, The: Symonds, J.A.

Esmeralda: Burnett, Frances Hodgson

Espalier, The: Warner, Sylvia

Esperanza: Ervine, St.John

Esprit de Corps: Durrell, Lawrence

Essaies of Sir Francis Bacon Knight the kings solliciter generall, The: Bacon, Francis

Essay concerning humane understanding, An: Locke, John

Essay concerning preaching, An: Glanvill, Joseph

Essay concerning the effects of air on human bodies, An: Arbuthnot, John

Essay concerning the nature of ailments, An: Arbuthnot, John

Essay for a frame of government in Pennsylvania: Dickinson, John

Essay for promoting psalmody, An: Tate, Nahum

Essay for the recording of illustrious providences, An: Mather, Increase

Essay in aid of a grammar of assent, An: Newman, J.H.

Essay in physics: Samuel, Herbert *1st Viscount*

Essay in the God that failed: Spender, Stephen

Essay in Warburg Vorträge: Livingstone, *Sir* Richard

Essay of a character of Sir G.Treby, An: Tate, Nahum

Essay on a course of liberal education, An: Priestley, Joseph

Essay on abstinence from animal food as a moral duty, An: Ritson, Joseph

Essay on beauty: Jeffrey, *Lord* Francis

Essay on charity schools: Watts, Isaac

Essay on chivalry: Courthorpe, W.J.

Essay on Christian education, An: Trimmer, *Mrs*. Sarah

Essay on classification, An: Agassis, J.L.R.

Essay on colophons, An: Pollard, A.W.

Essay on criticism, An: Oldmixon, John

Essay on criticism, An: Pope, Alexander

Essay on Dante: Church, Richard

Essay on Flecker, An: Lawrence, T.E.

Essay on Greek Federal coinage, An: Warren, J.B.L.

Essay on human vanity: Franklin, Benjamin

Essay on India, An: Byron, Robert

Essay on intuitive morals, An: Cobbe, F.P.

Essay on man, An: Pope, Alexander

Essay on metaphysics, An: Collingwood, R.G.

Essay on Milton's use and imitation of the moderns in his Paradise Lost, An: Lauder, William

Essay on mind, An: Browning, Elizabeth Barrett

Essay on modern gardening: Walpole, Horace

Essay on philosophical method, An: Collingwood, R.C.

Essay on Pope's Odyssey, An: Spence, Joseph

Essay on ridicule, An: Whitehead, William

Essay on rime: Shapiro, Karl

Essay on sepulchres: Godwin, William

Essay on the character and practical writings of St.Paul, An: More, Hannah

Essay on the constitutional power of Great-Britain over the colonies in America, An: Dickinson, John

Essay on the development of Christian doctrine, An: Newman, J.H.

Essay on the different stiles of poetry, An: Parnell, Thomas

Essay on the external use of water, An: Smollett, Tobias

Essay on the first principles of government, An: Priestley, Joseph

Essay on the foundations of geometry, An: Russell, Bertrand

Essay on the genius and writings of Shakespeare, An: Dennis, John

Essay on the genius of George Cruikshank, An: Thackeray, W.M.

Essay on the human character of Jesus Christ, An: Austin, William

Essay on the influence of a low price of corn on the profits of stock: Ricardo, David

Essay on the life and genius of Henry Fielding, An: Murphy, Arthur

Essay on the life and genius of Samuel Johnson, An: Murphy, Arthur

Essay on the life of the Hon. Major General Israel Putnam: Humphreys, David

Essay on the manners and genius of the literary character, An: D'Israeli, Isaac

Essay on the memory of the late Queen, An: Burnet, Gilbert

Essay on the nature and immutability of truth, The: Beattie, James

Essay on the nature of contemporary England, An: Belloc, Hilaire

Essay on the nature of the lyric: Gould, Gerald

Essay on the navy, An: Dennis, John

Essay on the operas after the Italian manner, An: Dennis, John

Essay on the origin of the English stage particularly on the historical plays of Shakespeare, An: Percy, Thomas

Essay on the original authority of the King's Council, An: Palgrave, *Sir* Francis

Essay on the origins and prospects of man, An: Hope, Thomas

Essay on the philosophical writings of Cicero: Hallam, Arthur

Essay on the picturesque as compared with the sublime and the beautiful, An: Price, *Sir* Uvedale

Essay on the principles of human action, An: Hazlitt, William

Essay on the restoration of property, An: Belloc, Hilaire

Essay on the use and advantages of the Fine Arts, An: Trumbull, John

Essay on the usefulness of mathematical learning, An: Arbuthnot, John

Essay on the writings and genius of Pope: Warton, Joseph

Essay on the writings and genius of Shakespear, An: Montagu, *Mrs*. Elizabeth

Essay on translated verse, An: Roscommon, D.W. *Earl of*

Essay on Transylvania, An: Morley, C.D.

Essay on typography, An: Gill, Eric

Essay towards a new theory of vision, An: Berkeley, George

Essay towards a theory of art, An: Abercrombie, Lascelles

Essay towards an abridgement of the English history, An: Burke, Edmund

Essay towards preventing the ruin of Great-Britain, An: Berkeley, George

Essay upon gaming, An: Collier, Jeremy

Essay upon essays, An: Todhunter, John

Essay upon poetry, An: Sheffield, John

Essay upon prints, An: Gilpin, William

Essay upon publick spirit, An: Dennis, John

Essay upon taxes, An: Temple, *Sir* William

Essay upon the advancement of trade in Ireland, An: Temple, *Sir* William

Essay upon the King's friends to Dr. S—l J—n, An: Stevenson, J.H.

Essayes: Bacon, Francis

Essayes in divinity: Donne, John

Essayes of a prentise in the divine art of poesie, The: James VI of Scotland

Essayes of counsels, civill and morall, of Francis Lo. Verulam, Viscount St. Alban, The: Bacon, Francis

Essayes or morall, politike and militarie discourses of Lord Michaell de Montaigne, The: Florio, John

Essays about men, women, and books: Birrell, Augustine

Essays aesthetical: Calvert, G.H.

Essays and addresses: Balfour, A.J.

Essays and addresses: Grierson, *Sir* Herbert

Essays and addresses: Murray, Gilbert

Essays and criticisms: Stevenson, R.L.

Essays and historiettes: Besant, *Sir* Walter

Essays and literary studies: Leacock, S.B.

Essays and marginalia: Coleridge, Hartley

Essays and miscellanies: Bancroft, H.H.

Essays and phantasies: Thomson, James

Essays and recollections: †O'Sullivan, Seumas

Essays and selections: Montagu, Basil

Essays and sketches of life and character by a gentleman who has left his lodgings: Russell, *Lord* John

Essays and treatises on several subjects: Hume, David

Essays at large: (†Solomon Eagle), Squire, *Sir* J.C.

Essays, biographical and critical: Tuckerman, H.T.

Essays, biographical and critical: chiefly on English poets: Masson, David

Essays classical and modern: Myers, F.W.H.

Essays, critical and historical: Newman, J.H.

Essays critical and imaginative: Wilson, John

Essays familiar and humorous: Chambers, Robert

Essays from reviews: Stewart, George

Essays from the air: Grigson, Geoffrey

Essays from "the Guardian": Pater, Walter

Essays from the Quarterly Review: Hannay, James

Essays from the Times: Phillips, Samuel

Essays, historical and biographical, political and social, literary and scientific: Miller, Hugh

Essays historical and literary: Fiske, John

Essays in Anglo-Saxon law: Adams, H.B.

Essays in appreciation: Berenson, Bernhard

Essays in appreciation: Lowes, J.L.

Essays in Australian fiction: †Eldershaw, M.Barnard

Essays in biography: Dobrée, Bonamy

Essays in biography: Keynes, J.M.

Essays in Christian politics: Temple, William

Essays in common sense philosophy: Joad, C.E.M.

Essays in critical realism: Santayana, George

Essays in criticism: Arnold, Matthew

Essays in criticism and research: Tillotson, Geoffrey

Essays in Elizabethan history: Neale, J.E.

Essays in English literature 1780–1860: Saintsbury, George

Essays in experimental logic: Dewey, John

Essays in Fabian socialism: Shaw, G.B.

Essays in fallacy: Macphail, *Sir* Andrew

Essays in idleness: Repplier, Agnes

Essays in librarianship and bibliography: Garnett, Richard

Essays in little: Lang, Andrew

Essays in little: Phillpotts, Eden

Essays in London and elsewhere: James, Henry

Essays in mediaeval art: Berenson, Bernhard

Essays in miniature: Repplier, Agnes

Essays in modernity: Adams, Francis

Essays in national idealism: Coomaraswamy, A.K.

Essays in persuasion: Keynes, J.M.

Essays in politics: Macphail, *Sir* Andrew

Essays in popular science: Huxley, *Sir* Julian

Essays in Puritanism: Macphail, *Sir* Andrew

Essays in satire: Knox, R.A.

Essays in science and philosophy: Whitehead, A.N.

Essays in social and political theory: Cole, G.D.H.

Essays in the art of writing: Stevenson, R.L.

Essays in the public philosophy: Lippmann, Walter

Essays in verse: Sinclair, May

Essays in verse: Suhrawardy, Shahid

Essays in war-time: Ellis, Havelock

Essays, literary, critical and historical: O'Hagan, Thomas

Essays, literary, moral and philosophical: Rush, Benjamin

Essays modern and Elizabethan: Dowden, Edward

Essays moral and political: Hume, David

Essays never before published: Godwin, William

Essays of a biologist: Huxley, *Sir* Julian

Essays of a Catholic: Belloc, Hilaire

Essays of a humanist: Huxley, *Sir* Julian

Essays of an ex-librarian: Garnett, Richard

Essays of Joseph Addison: Frazer, *Sir* James

Essays of today and yesterday: Jackson, Holbrook

Essays of today and yesterday: Pain, B.E.O.

Essays of travel: Stevenson, R.L.

Essays on archaeological subjects: Wright, Thomas

Essays on art: Palgrave, F.T.

Essays on ballad poetry: Scott, *Sir* Walter

Essays on banking: Carey, Mathew

Essays on Catholic life: O'Hagan, Thomas

Essays on chivalry, romance and the drama: Scott, *Sir* Walter

Essays on educational reconstruction and the modern world: Panikkar, K.M.

Essays on Elizabethan drama: Eliot, T.S.

Essays on English: Matthews, J.B.

Essays on fiction: Senior, N.W.

Essays on free thinking and plain speaking: Stephen, *Sir* Leslie

Essays on German literature: Boyesen, H.H.

Essays on Gothic architecture: Warton, Thomas

Essays on government, jurisprudence: Mill, James

Essays on his own times: Coleridge, S.T.

Essays on human evolution: Keith, *Sir* Arthur

Essays on life, art and science: Butler, Samuel

Essays on literature and society: Muir, Edwin

Essays on mediaeval literature: Ker, W.P.

Essays on natural history: Waterton, Charles

Essays on our changing order: Veblen, T.B.

Essays on Parliamentary reform: Bagehot, Walter

Essays on philosophical subjects: Smith, Adam

Essays on poetry: Squire, *Sir* John

Essays on poetry and poets: Noel, R.B.W.

Essays on political economy: Carey, Mathew

Essays on questions of the day, political and social: Smith, Goldwin

Essays on Scandinavian literature: Boyesen, H.H.

Essays on several important subjects: Glanvill, Joseph

Essays on Sienese paintings: Berenson, Bernhard

Essays on social subjects: Higgins, M.J.

Essays on some of the modern guides of English thought in matters of faith: Hutton, R.H.

Essays on some of the peculiarities of the Christian religion: Whately, Richard

Essays on some unsettled questions of political economy: Mill, John Stuart

Essays on subjects connected with the literature, popular superstitions and history of England in the Middle Ages: Wright, Thomas

Essays on the early period of the French Revolution: Croker, J.W.

Essays on the French novelists: Saintsbury, George

Essays on the Gita: Ghose, Sri Aurobindo

Essays on the philosophy of Theism: Ward, W.G.

Essays on the rise of the Christian religion in the West of Europe from the reign of Tiberius to the end of the Council of Trent: Russell, *Lord* John

Essays on the superstitions of the Highlands: Grant, Anne

Essays on truth and reality: Bradley, F.H.

Essays on various subjects of taste, morals, and national policy: Tucker, George

Essays on various subjects, principally designed for young ladies: More, Hannah

Essays political and biographical: Walpole, *Sir* Spencer

Essays, scientific, political and speculative: Spencer, Herbert

Essays, speculative and political: Balfour, A.J.

Essays, speculative and suggestive: Symonds, J.A.

Essays, theological and literary: Hutton, R.H.

Essays upon several moral subjects: Collier, Jeremy

Essays upon some controverted questions: Huxley, T.H.

Essays with a purpose: Madariaga, Salvator de

Essays written in the intervals of business: Helps, *Sir* Arthur

Essence of nonsense upon sence, The: Taylor, John

Essence of tragedy, The: Anderson, Maxwell

Essential faith of the Universal Church deduced from the sacred records: Martineau, Harriet

Essential Shakespeare, The: Wilson, John Dover

Essentials and non-essentials in religion: Clarke, J.F.

Essentials of mysticism, The: Underhill, Evelyn

Essentials of psychology: Radhakrishan, Sarvepalli

Essentials of socialisation, The: Cole, G.D.H.

Essentials of spiritual unity, The: Knox, R.A.

Establishing relations: Jacobs, W.W.

Establishment of the Turks in Europe, The: Russell, *Lord* John

Estelle: Ingraham, J.H.

Esther: (†Frances Snow Compton), Adams, H.B.

Esther: Blunt, W.S.

Esther Vanhomrigh: Woods, M.L.

Esther Waters: Moore, George

Esthétique du Mal: Stevens, Wallace

Estimate of the religion of the fashionable world, An: More, Hannah

Estimations in criticism: Bagehot, Walter

Estimates of some Englishmen and Scotchmen: Bagehot, Walter

Esto perpetua: Belloc, Hilaire

Estrangement: Yeats, W.B.

Estrays: Starrett, Vincent

Et cetera: Birrell, Augustine

Etched in moonlight: Stephens, James

Etching and dry points: Whistler, J.A.M.

Eternal City, The: Caine, *Sir* Thomas

Eternal feminine, The: Cambridge, Ada

Eternal Greece: Warner, Rex

Eternal moment, The: Forster, E.M.

Eternal now, The: Jackson, Holbrook

Eternal quest, The: Kirkconnell, Watson

Ethan Frome: Wharton, Edith

Ethel Churchill: Landon, L.E.M.

Ethel Turner's birthday book: Turner, E.S.

Ethelinde: Smith, Charlotte

Ethelrinda's fairy: Housman, Laurence

Ethel's book: Faber, F.W.

Ethelstan: Darley, George

Ethelyn's mistake: Holmes, M.J.

Ether and reality: Lodge, *Sir* Oliver

Ether of space, The: Lodge, *Sir* Oliver

Ethical condition of the early Scandinavian peoples, The: Gosse, *Sir* Edmund

Ethical dilemma of science, The: Hill, A.V.

Ethical problems of the war: Murray, Gilbert

Ethical studies: Bradley, F.H.

Ethices elementa: Johnson, Samuel

Ethics: Dewey, John

Ethics in modern art: †Bowen, Marjorie

Ethics of boxing and manly sport: O'Reilly, J.B.

Ethics of literary art, The: Thompson, Maurice

Ethics of penal action, The: Temple, *Sir* William

Ethics of the dust, The: Ruskin, John

Eton: Hollis, Christopher

Eton Latin grammar: Inge, W.R.

Eton memorial ode: Bridges, Robert

Eton portrait: Fergusson, *Sir* Bernard

Eton reform: Cory, W.

Eton Shakespeariana: Greg, W.W.

Etruscan Bologna: Burton, *Sir* Richard

Etruscan places: Lawrence, D.H.

Ettricke garland, The: Hogg, James

Etymological dictionary of modern English, An: Weekley, Ernest

Etymological dictionary of the English Language, arranged on an historical basis, An: Skeat, W.W.

Eucharistic prayers from ancient liturgies: Underhill, Evelyn

Eudmon Blake: Walsh, Maurice

Eudocia: Phillpotts, Eden

Eugene Aram: Lytton, E.G.E.B. *1st Baron*

Eugene Onegin: Nabokov, Vladimir

Eugenia: Chapman, George

Eugenics: Galton, *Sir* Francis

Eugenics and other evils: Chesterton, G.K.

Eugenius: Graves, Richard

Eulogium of James Watt: Jeffrey, *Lord* Francis

Eulogium of the brave men who have fallen in the contest with Great Britain, An: Brackenridge, H.H.

Eulogy of Richard Jefferies, The: Besant, *Sir* Walter

Eulogy on the life and character of James Madison, An: Adams, J.Q.

Eulogy on the life and character of James Monroe, An: Adams, J.Q.

Eumenides (The furies) of Aeschylus, The: Murray, Gilbert

Euphemia: Lennox, Charlotte

Euphorion: Lee, Vernon

Euphranor: Fitzgerald, Edward

Euphrates: Vaughan, Thomas

Euphrenia: (†Fiona Macleod), Sharp, Whilliam

Euphrosyne: Graves, Richard

Euphrosyne: Strachey, Lytton

Euphues: Lyly, John

Euphues and his England: Lyly, John

Euphues his censure to Philautus: Greene, Robert

Euphues shadow: Lodge, Thomas

Eureka: Poe, Edgar Allan

Eureka: Turnbull, S.C.P.

Eureka stockade: Greenwood, Walter

Euripides and his age: Murray, Gilbert

Euripides and his influence: Lucas, F.L.

Europa's beast: Mottram, R.H.

Europe: Blake, William

Europe: Dudek, Louis

Europe after 8:15: Mencken, H.L. and G.J. Nathan

Europe and America since 1492: Commager, H.S.

Europe and elsewhere: (†Mark Twain), Clemens, S.L.

Europe and the faith: Belloc, Hilaire

Europe in arms: Liddell Hart, B.

Europe in decay, 1936–40: Namier, *Sir* Levis

Europe in the looking glass: Byron, Robert

Europe, Russia and the future: Cole, G.D.H.

Europe to let: Jameson, Storm

Europe unite: Churchill, *Sir* Winston

Europe—whither bound?: Graham, Stephen

Europe without Baedeker: Wilson, Edmund

European acquaintance: De Forest, J.W.

European anarchy, The: Dickinson, G.L.

European encounters: Griffith, Hubert

European heritage, The: Kirconnell, Watson

European journey: Gibbs, *Sir* Philip

European jungle: Yeats-Brown, F.C.C.

European painting and sculpture: Newton, Eric

European sobriety in the presence of the Balkan crisis: Beard, C.A.

European War, The: Belloc, Hilaire

European witness: Spender, Stephen

Europeans, The: James, Henry

Europe's apprenticeship: Coulton, G.G.

Europe's morning after: Roberts, Kenneth

Europe's optical illusion: Angell, *Sir* Norman

Europe's revels for the peace: Motteux, P.A.

Eurydice: Fielding, Henry

Eurydice: Mallet, David

Eurydice: †Taffrail

Eurydice hiss'd: Fielding, Henry

Eustace and Hilda: Hartley, L.P.

Eustace Conyers: Hannay, James

Eustace diamonds, The: Trollope, Anthony

Eustace Quentin: Reynolds, G.

Eutaw: Simms, W.G.

Euthanatos: Swinburne, A.C.

Euthymiae raptus: Chapman, George

Eutychus: Holtby, Winifred

Eva: Levin, Meyer

Eva: Lytton, E.G.E.B. *1st Baron*

Eva Gay: Scott, Evelyn

Eva Huntingdon: Leprohon, R.E.

Eva St. Clair: James, G.P.R.

Evadne: Rowcroft, Charles

Evan Harrington: Meredith, George

Evander: Phillpotts, Eden

Evanescent city, The: Sterling, George

Evangeline: Longfellow, H.W.

Evangelist, The: Jones, H.A.

Eve: Baring-Gould, Sabine

Eve: Hodgson, Ralph

Eve, an artist's model: Sladen, D.B.W.

Eve and the serpent: Douglas, *Lord* Alfred

Eve of St. John, The: Scott, *Sir* Walter

Eve of St. Mark, The: Anderson, Maxwell

Eve of the conquest, The: Taylor, *Sir* Henry

Eve of the revolution, The: Becker, C.L.

Eveleen O'Donnell: Leprohon, R.E.

Evelina: Burney, Frances

Evelyn Byrd: Eggleston, G.C.

Evelyn Innes: Moore, George

Even more for your garden: Sackville-West, V.

Even the parrot: Sayers, Dorothy

Evening: Macaulay, T.B. *Baron*

Evening clothes: Gale, Zona

Evening dress: Howells, W.D.

Evening in spring: Derleth, A.W.

Evening in Stepney: Bowes-Lyon, Lilian

Evening light: De Selincourt, Hugh

Evening walk, An: Wordsworth, William

Evenings at home: Barbauld, *Mrs*. A.L.

Evenings in Albany: Bax, Clifford

Evenings in Greece: Moore, Thomas

Evenings in New England: Child, Lydia Maria

Evenings in the library: Stewart, George

Evenings love, An: Dryden, John

Evenings with a reviewer: Spedding, James

Evenings with Australian authors: Stephens, A.G.

Evensong: Nichols, Beverley

Evensong: Tynan, Katherine

Events and embroideries: Lucas, E.V.

Events and signals: Scott, F.R.

Events of the year 1835, The: Morison, S.E.

Ever green: Levy, Benn W.

Ever since Paradise: Priestley, J.B.

Ever the twain: Robinson, E.S.L.

Evergreen: Webster, M.M.

Evergreen tree, The: Mackaye, Percy

Everlasting army, The: Mee, Arthur

Everlasting Gospel, The: Mather, Cotton

Everlasting man, The: Chesterton, G.K.

Everlasting mercy, The: Masefield, John

Every child: Garvin, J.L.

Every child's creed: Mee, Arthur

Every day is Saturday: White, E.B.

Every man a penny: Marshall, Bruce

Every man a stranger: Mannin, Ethel

Every man for himself: Duncan, Norman

Every man in his humour: Jonson, Ben

Every man is God: Postgate, Raymond

Every man out of his humour: Jonson, Ben

Every man's Bible: Inge, W.R.

Every mother's son: Lindsay, Norman

Every other gift: Jacob, Naomi

Every soul is a circus: Lindsay, N.V.

Every wife: Richards, Grant

Everybody's autobiography: Stein, Gertrude

Everybody's friend: †Billings, Josh

Everybody's friend: Brown, Ivor

Everybody's husband: Cannan, Gilbert

Everybody's letters: Riding, Laura

Everybody's political what's what: Shaw, G.B.

Everychild: Jackson, Holbrook

Everyday: Crothers, Rachel

Everyday Americans: Canby, H.S.

Everyday Bible, The: Sheldon, C.M.

Every-day book, The: Hone, William

Everyday life in prehistoric times: Quennell, Marjorie

Everyday life in the old stone age: Quennell, Marjorie

Everyday things in archaic Greece: Quennell, Marjorie

Everyday things in classical Greece: Quennell, Marjorie

Everyday things in Homeric Greece: Quennell, Marjorie

Every-day thoughts in prose and verse: Wilcox, Ella Wheeler

Every-day topics: Holland, J.G.

Everyman his own historian: Becker, C.L.

Everyman his own poet: Mallock, W.H.

Everyman remembers: Rhys, Ernest

Everyman's genius: Austin, Mary

Everyman's life of Jesus: Moffat, James

Everyone but thee and me: Nash, Ogden

Everyone has his fault: Inchbald, *Mrs*. Elizabeth

Everything has a history: Haldane, J.B.S.

Everywoman: Frankau, Gilbert

Eve's apples: Vachell, H.A.

Eve's diary: (†Mark Twain), Clemens, S.L.

Eve's orchard: Widdemer, Margaret

Eve's ransom: Gissing, George

Evidence as to man's place in nature: Huxley, T.H.

Evidence for the resurrection of Jesus Christ, as given by the Four evangelists, critically examined, The: Butler, Samuel

Evidences of the Christian religion briefly stated: Beattie, James

Evil eye, The: Carleton, William

Evil eye, The: Fitzgerald, F. Scott

Evil eye, The: Wilson, Edmund

Evil genius, The: Collins, Wilkie

Evil guest, The: Le Fanu, Sheidan

Evil kettle, The: Dunsany, E.J.M.D.P. *Lord*

Evil May-day: Allingham, William

Evil shepherd, The: Oppenheim, E.Phillips

Evil spirit, The: Pryce, Richard

Evil that men do, The: Fawcett, Edgar

Evil under the sun: Christie, Agatha

Evil was abroad: Lehmann, John

Evils of slavery, The: Child, Lydia Maria

Evolution: Ghose, Sri Aurobindo

Evolution and creation: Lodge, *Sir* Oliver

Evolution and ethics: Huxley, T.H.

Evolution and ethics: 1893–1943: Huxley, *Sir* Julian

Evolution and permanence of type: Agassis, J.L.R.

Evolution and religion: Fiske, John

Evolution in action: Huxley, *Sir* Julian

Evolution in Italian art: Allen, Grant

Evolution of an intellectual, The: Murry, John Middleton

Evolution of British policy towards Indian states, 1774–1858: Panikkar, K.M.

Evolution of diplomatic method: Nicolson, Hon. *Sir* Harold

Evolution of modesty, The: Ellis, Havelock

Evolution of Parliament, The: Pollard, A.F.

Evolution of physics, The: Einstein, Albert

Evolution of publishers' binding styles, 1770–1900: Sadleir, Michael

Evolution of Society, The: Besant, *Mrs*. Annie

Evolution of the idea of God, The: Allen, Grant

Evolution of the soul, The: Monro, H.E.

Evolution, old or new: Butler, Samuel

Evolution, the modern synthesis: Huxley, *Sir* Julian

Evolutionary ethics: Huxley, *Sir* Julian

Evolutionist at large, The: Allen, Grant

Ex Voto: Butler, Samuel

Exact catalogue of all the comedies etc. that were printed or published, till this present year 1680, An: Langbaine, Gerard

Exalt the Eglantine: Sitwell, Sacheverell

Examen: North, Roger

Examination and a criticism, An: Russell, Bertrand

Examination of certain abuses, An: Swift, Jonathan

Examination of Dr.Reid's inquiry, Dr. Beattie's essay and Dr. Oswald's appeal to common sense, An: Priestley, Joseph

Examination of Sir William Hamilton's philosophy: Mill, John Stuart

Examination of the charge of apostasy against Wordsworth, An: White, W.H.

Examination of the commercial principles of the late negotiations between Great Britain and France in 1761, An: Burke, Edmund

Examination of the conduct of the executive of the United States, towards the French republic, An: Gallatin, Albert

Examiner, The: Murphy, Arthur

Example, The: Shirley, James

Example of France a warning to England, The: Young, Arthur

Example of vertu, The: Hawes, Stephen

Examples of the interposition of Providence in the detection and the punishment of murder: Fielding, Henry

Excavations: Van Vechten, Carl

Excavations at Ur: Woolley, *Sir* Leonard

Excavations in Malta: Murray, Margaret

Excavations in Minorca: Murray, Margaret

Excavations in the citadel of Anuradhapura, The: Paranavitana, Senerat

Excellency of a publick spirit, The: Mather, Increase

Excellency of good women, The: Rich, Barnabe

Excellent becomes the permanent, The: Addams, Jane

Excellent comedy, The: Middleton, Thomas

Excellent comedy, called The Prince of Prigs revels, An: Shirley, James

Excellent conceited tragedie of Romeo and Juliet, An: Shakespeare, William

Excellent new ballad, An: Swift, Jonathan

Excellent new song, An: Swift, Jonathan

Excellent new song upon His Grace our good Lord Archbishop of Dublin, An: Swift, Jonathan

Excellent poem, An: Breton, Nicholas

Excelsior: Harwood, H.M.

Except the lord: Cary, Joyce

Exception, The: †Onions, Oliver

Excerpta Tudoriana: Brydges, *Sir* Samuel

Exchange no robbery: Hook, T.E.

Exchange of souls, An: Pain, B.E.O.

Exchange royal: †Bowen, Marjorie

Exciting term, An: Brazil, Angela

Excursion, The: Brooke, Frances

Excursion, The: Mallet, David

Excursion, The: Wordsworth, William

Excursions: Thoreau, H.D.

Excursions and enquiries: Brown, E.T.

Excursions in art and letters: Story, W.W.

Excursions in criticism: Watson, *Sir* J.W.

Excursions in Victorian bibliography: Sadleir, Michael

Excursions of an evolutionist: Fiske, John

Excuse it, please!: Skinner, C.O.

Ex-detective, The: Oppenheim, E.Phillips

Ex-duke, The: Oppenheim, E. Phillip

Execration against Vulcan: Jonson, Ben

Execution of Newcome Bowles, The: Mickle, A.D.

Execution of Sir Charles Bawdin, The: Chatterton, Thomas

Exemplary lives and memorable acts of nine of the most worthy women of the world, The: Heywood, Thomas

Exemplary theatre, The: Barker, Harley Granville

Exercise, An: Hopkinson, Francis

Exercises upon the first psalme: Wither, George

Exhibit C: Brighouse, Harold

Exhibition of paintings in fresco, poetical and historical inventions: Blake, William

Exhumations: Isherwood, Christopher

Exile: Aldington, Richard

Exile, The: Buck, Pearl

Exiled: Galsworthy, John

Exiled lover, The: Roberts, T. G.

Exiles, The: Davis, R. H.

Exiles: Deeping, Warwick

Exiles: Joyce, James

Exiles, The: Reeve, Clara

Exiles, The: Treece, Henry

Exiles of Faloo, The: Pain, B. E. O.

Exile's return: Cowley, Malcolm

Exile's trust, The: Browne, Frances

Exit: Wright, H. B.

Exit a dictator: Oppenheim, E. Phillip

Exit Eliza: Pain, B. E. O.

Exits and entrances: Starrett, Vincent

Exits and entrances: Stoddard, C. W.

Exits and farewells!: †Bowen, Marjorie

Exodiad, The: Cumberland, Richard

Exodus: Armstrong, M. D.

Exodus: Bercovici, Konrad

Exodus: Rubenstein, Harold, F.

Exotics and retrospections: Hearn, Lafcadio

Expanding universe, The: Eddington, Sir Arthur

Expansion of the universe, The: Jeans, Sir James

Expatriate, The: McCormick, Eric Hall

Expedition of Humphry Clinker, The: Smollett, Tobias

Expedition of Orsua, The: Southey, Robert

Expenditures of public funds in the administration of civil justice in New York City: Chase, Stuart

Expense of greatness, The: Blackmur, R. P.

Expenses of the war: Gallatin, Albert

Expensive halo, The: (†Josephine Tey), Mackintosh, Elizabeth

Experience: MacCarthy, Sir Desmond

Experience and art: Krutch, J. W.

Experience and education: Dewey, John

Experience and nature: Dewey, John

Experience of critics, An: Fry, Christopher

Experiences: Tynan, Katherine

Experiences and art: Krutch, J. W.

Experiences facing death: Austin, Mary

Experiences of a Bond street jeweller: Vachell, H. A.

Experiment in autobiography: Wells, H. G.

Experiment in criticism: Lewis, C. S.

Experiment of a free church, The: Clarke, J. F.

Experiment with St. George, An: Dunne, J. W.

Experiment with time, An: Dunne, J. W.

Experimenting with human lives: Wright, Frank Lloyd

Experiments: Douglas, Norman

Experiments and observations on different kinds of air: Priestley, Joseph

Experiments and observations on electricity: Franklin, Benjamin

Experiments and observations on the mineral waters of Philadelphia, Abington, and Bristol, in the province of Pennsylvania: Rush, Benjamin

Experiments and observations relating to various branches of natural philosophy: Priestley, Joseph

Experiments in crime: Frankau, Gilbert

Experiments in pangenesis: Galton, Sir Francis

Experiments of spiritual life and health: Williams, Roger

Expert evidence: Pertwee, Roland

Experts are puzzled: Riding, Laura

Expiation: Russell, E. M.

Expiation of Wynne Palliser, The: Mitford, Bertram

Explaining the editor: Bok, E. W.

Explanation of South Africa called The South Africans, An: Millin, Sarah Gertrude

Explanations: a sequel to "Vestiges": Chambers, Robert

Exploits of Brigadier Gerard: Doyle, Sir Arthur Conan

Exploits of Sherlock Holmes (with Adrian Conan Doyle): Carr, J. D.

Exploration: Palliser, John

Exploration of Jonathan Oldbuck, F.R.S.Q., The: Le-Moine, Sir J. M.

Exploration of the Pacific, The: Beaglehole, J. C.

Explorations: essays in literary criticism: Knights, L. C.

Explorations in civilization: Bedford, Randolph

Explorations in the interior of the Labrador Peninsula: Hind, H. Y.

Explorations of the highlands of Brazil: Burton, Sir Richard

Explorer, The: Maugham, Somerset

Explorers, The: Martin, C. E.

Explorers of Australia and their life-work, The: Favenc, Ernest

Explorers of the dawn: De la Roche, Mazo

Explosion: Wren, P. C.

Exposé of the vice of gaming as it lately existed in New England: Snelling, W. J.

Exposicion upon the v. vi. vii. chapters of Mathew, The: Tyndale, William

Exposition, The: Brooks, C. W. S.

Exposition of the epistles of St. John, The: Tyndale, William

Exposition of the false medium and barriers excluding men of genius from the public: Horne, R.H.

Exposition of the fyrste epistle of Seynt Jhon, The: Tyndale, William

Exposition upon the thirteenth chapter of the Revelation, An: Cotton, John

Expository lectures on St. Paul's epistles to the Corinthians: Robertson, F.W.

Expostulatory odes to a great Duke and a little Lord: †Pindar, Peter

Express and admirable: Agate, J.E.

Expressing Willie: Crothers, Rachel

Expression in America: Lewisohn, Ludwig

Expression of the emotions in man and animals, The: Darwin, Charles

Exquisite Perdita, The: Beck, *Mrs.* Lily

Extemporary essays: Hewlett, Mary

Exterior: Rice, Elmer

Extra day, The: Blackwood, Algernon

Extra pound, The: Canfield, Dorothy

Extract out of a book, entituled, an exact collection of the debates of the House of Commons held at Westminster, An: Swift, Jonathan

Extracts from a diary: Walpole, *Sir* Hugh

Extracts from Captain Stormfield's visit to heaven: (†Mark Twain), Clemens, S.L.

Extracts from some unpublished scenes of Manuel: Maturin, C.R.

Extracts from the strange interlude: O'Neill, Eugene

Extraneus vapulans: Heylyn, Peter

Extraordinary women: Mackenzie, *Sir* Compton

Extremes meet: Mackenzie, *Sir* Compton

Exultations: Pound, Ezra

Ex-wife, The: Lang, J.

Eye, The: Nabokov, Vladimir

Eye for a tooth, An: †Yates, Dornford

Eye for an eye, An: Darrow, C.S.

Eye for an eye, An: Trollope, Anthony

Eye of God, The: Bemelmans, Ludwig

Eye of love, The: Sharp, Margery

Eye of the lizard, The: Holcroft, M.H.

Eye of the needle: Scott, F.R.

Eye sore: Tagore, *Sir* R.

Eye witness, The: Belloc, Hilaire

Eyebright: Coolidge, Susan

Eyeless in Gaza: Huxley, Aldous

Eyes and no eyes: Gilbert, *Sir* W.S.

Eyes of a gypsy: Gibbon, J.M.

Eyes of Asia, The: Kipling, Rudyard

Eyes of Max Carrodos, The: Bramah, E.

Eyes of the panther, The: Bierce, Ambrose

Eyes of the sea: †Corelli, Marie

Eyes of the world, The: Wright, H.B.

Eyes of vigilance: †Maurice, Furnley

Eyes of youth: Colum, Padraic

Eyes of youth: Thompson, Francis

Eyewitness of eight months before the mast, An: Hart, James D.

Eynsham under the monks: Chambers, *Sir* E.K.

Ezekiel's chant, The: Lindsay, Norman

Ezra Pound his metric and poetry: Eliot, T.S.

F

Fabian: Devaney, J.M.

Fabian Dimitry: Fawcett, Edgar

Fabian election manifesto: Shaw, G.B.

Fabian socialism: Cole, G.D.H.

Fabian Society, The: Shaw, G.B.

Fabianism and Empire: Shaw, G.B.

Fable, A: Faulkner, William

Fable for critics, A: Lowell, J.R.

Fable for every day in the week, A: Stevenson, J.H.

Fable of Midas, The: Swift, Jonathan,

Fable of the goat, The: Pratt, E.J.

Fable of the widow and her cat, A: Swift, Jonathan

Fabled shores: Macaulay, *Dame* Rose

Fables: Gay, John

Fables: Powys, T.F.

Fables ancient and modern: Dryden, John

Fables, ancient and modern: Godwin, William

Fables and fairy tales: Morley, Henry

Fables and legends of many countries rendered in rhyme: Saxe, J.G.

Fables and other little tales: Patchen, Kenneth

Fables for grown gentlemen for the year 1770: Stevenson, J.H.

Fables for our time: Thurber, James

Fables for parents: Canfield, Dorothy

Fables for the female sex: Brooke, Henry

Fables for the Holy alliance: Moore, Thomas

Fables in song: (†Owen Meredith), Lytton, E. *1st Earl*

Fables in verse for the improvement of young and old: (†Abraham Aesop), Newbery, John

Fabulous histories: Trimmer, *Mrs.* S.

Fabulous invalid, The: Kaufman, G.S.

Fabulous Mogul: Karaka, D.F.

Fabulous money-maker, The: Ginsbury, Norman

Fabulous Mrs. V., The: Bates, H.E.

Façade: Sitwell, Edith

Face: Mais, Roger

Face beside the fire, The: Van der Post, L.J.

Face illuminated, A: Roe, E.P.

Face in candlelight, A: Squire, Sir J.

Face in the night, The: Wallace, Edgar

Face in the steam, The: Carman, Bliss

Face in Western art, The: Brophy, John

Face is familiar, The: Nash, Ogden

Face of clay, The: Vachell, H.A.

Face of England, The: Bates, H.E.

Face of England, The: Blunden, Edmund

Face of silence, The: Mukherji, D.G.

Face of the deep, The: Rossetti, Christina

Face of the earth, The: Tomlinson, H.M.

Face of the night, The: (Hueffer) Ford, Ford Madox

Face of time, The: Farrell, James

Face of violence, The: Bronowski, J.

Face to face: Grant, Robert

Faces for fortunes: Mayhew, Augustus Septimus

Facial justice: Hartley, L.P.

Facing death: Henty, G.A.

Facing east: Namier, Sir Levis

Facing the chair: Dos Passos, John

Facing the music: Turner, W.J.R.

Facsimiles of twelve manuscripts in T.C.C.: Greg, W.W.

Fact and faith: Haldane, J.B.S.

Fact and fiction: Child, Lydia Maria

Fact and fiction: Russell, Bertrand

Fact and fiction about Wagner: Newman, Ernest

Factories, The: Widdemer, Margaret

Factors in American history: Pollard, A.F.

Factors in modern history: Pollard, A.F.

Factors of organic evolution, The: Spencer, Herbert

Factory bell, The: Ricketson, D.

Factory controversy, The: Martineau, Harriet

Factory on the cliff, The: (†Neil Gordon), Macdonell, A.G.

Fact'ry 'ands: Dyson, E.G.

Facts and comments: Spencer, Herbert

Facts and conditions of progress in the North-west: Gallagher, W.D.

Facts and fancies in Baconian theory: Greg, W.W.

Facts and figures from Italy: Mahony, F.S.

Facts and ideas: Gibbs, Sir Philip

Facts and manners for day-school reading: Sedgwick, C.M.

Facts illustrative of the treatment of Napoleon Buonaparte in Saint Helena: Hook, T.E.

Facts of fiction, The: Collins, Norman

Facts you should know about California: Adamic, Louis

Fade out: Jacob, Naomi

Faded hope, The: Sigourney, L.H.

Faerie queene, The: Spenser, Edmund

Faery lands of the South Seas: Hall, J.N. and C.B. Nordhoff

Faerylands forlorn: Cripps, A.S.

Failure of Protestantism in New York and its causes, The: Dixon, Thomas

Failures: Nichols, Beverley

Faint perfume: Gale, Zona

Fair assembly, The: Ramsay, Allan

Fair barbarian, A: Burnett, Frances Hodgson

Fair bride, The: Marshall, Bruce

Fair captive, The: Haywood, Mrs. Eliza

Fair colonist, A: Glanville, Ernest

Fair day's work, A: Monsarrat, Nicholas

Fair dealing: Mather, Cotton

Fair device, A: Balestier, C.W.

Fair enough: Street, A.G.

Fair exchange: Richards, Grant

Fair France: Craik, Mrs. Dinah Maria

Fair girls and gray horses: Ogilvie, W.H.

Fair God, The: Wallace, Lew

Fair grit, The: Davin, N.F.

Fair haven, The: Butler, Samuel

Fair house, A: De Selincourt, Hugh

Fair Ines: Turner, E.S.

Fair Inez: Sladen, D.B.W.

Fair Lavinia, The: Freeman, Mary Wilkins

Fair maid of the west, The: Heywood, Thomas

Fair Margaret: Crawford, F. Marion

Fair Margaret: Haggard, Sir H. Rider

Fair Mississippian, The: †Craddock, C.E.

Fair of Emyvale and the master and scholar, The: Carleton, William

Fair of Mayfair, The: Gore, Catherine

Fair of St. James: Farjeon, Eleanor

Fair penitent, The: Rowe, Nicholas

Fair Rosamond: Miller, Thomas

Fair stood the wind for France: Bates, H.E.

Fair Syrian, The: Bage, Robert

Fair to middling, The: Calder-Marshall, Arthur

Fair Venetian: Farjeon, Eleanor

Fair weather: Mather, Cotton

Fair women in painting and poetry: †Macleod, Fiona

Fair world for all: Canfield, Dorothy

Fair young widow, The: †Preedy, George

Faire and fowle weather: Taylor, John

Faire quarrell, A: Middleton, Thomas

Fairer than a fairy: Grant, James

Faire-virtue, the mistresse of Phil'arete: Wither, George

Fairfax: Cooke, John Esten

Fairies, The: Allingham, William

Fairies afield: Molesworth, *Mrs.*

Fairies and fusiliers: Graves, Robert

Fairies—of sorts: Molesworth, *Mrs.*

Fairy book, The: Craik, *Mrs.* Dinah

Fairy caravan, The: Potter, Helen Beatrix

Fairy changeling, The: Sigerson, Dora

Fairy changeling, The: Spofford, H.E.

Fairy doll: Godden, Rumer

Fairy fables: †Bede, Cuthbert

Fairy feast, The: King, William

Fairy fingers: Ritchie, *Mrs.* A.C.M.

Fairy folk-tales of the Maoris: Cowan, James

Fairy gifts, The: Brazil, Angela

Fairy Godmother and other tales, The: Gatty, *Mrs.* Margaret

Fairy gold: Mackenzie, *Sir* Compton

Fairy gold: Rhys, Ernest

Fairy goose, The: O'Flaherty, Liam

Fairy in the window box, The: Mackenzie, *Sir* Compton

Fairy land: Hood, Thomas

Fairy legends and traditions of the south of Ireland: Croker, T.C.

Fairy stories and wonder tales: English, T.D.

Fairy tales: Lemon, Mark

Fairy tales: Morley, Henry

Fairy tales, far and near: (†Q), Quiller-Couch, *Sir* A.

Fairy tales from Grimm: Baring-Gould, S.

Fairy tales told by seven travellers at the Red Lion Inn: Belasco, David

Fairy water: Riddell, *Mrs.* J.H.

Fairy who couldn't tell a lie, The: Mitchison, Naomi

Fairy-queen, The: Settle, Elkanah

Fairy's dilemma, The: Gilbert, *Sir* W.S.

Faith: Cunninghame Graham, Robert

Faith: Inge, W.R.

Faith and duties of Christians, The: Dennis, John

Faith and freedom: Temple, *Sir* William

Faith and knowledge: Inge, W.R.

Faith and modern thought, The: Temple, *Sir* William

Faith and reason: Collingwood, R.G.

Faith and success: †King, Basil

Faith as unfolded by many prophets, The: Martineau, Harriet

Faith doctor, The: Eggleston, Edward

Faith healer, The: Moody, W.V.

Faith of a liberal, The: Cohen, M.R.

Faith of a rationalist, The: Russell, Bertrand

Faith of fieldsman: Massingham, Harold

Faith of Frances Craniford, The: Churchill, Winston

Faith of men, The: London, Jack

Faith of poetry, The: Mackaye, Percy

Faith, reason, civilisation: Laski, Harold

Faith to fight for, A: Strachey, John

Faith Tresilion: Phillpotts, Eden

Faith, war and policy: Murray, Gilbert

Faithful, The: Masefield, John

Faithful ally: Linklater, Eric

Faithful company: Swinnerton, Frank

Faithful for ever: Patmore, Coventry

Faithful heart, The: Hoffe, Monckton

Faithful Jenny Dove: Farjeon, Eleanor

Faithful lovers, The: Beresford, J.D.

Faithful man described and rewarded, A: Mather, Cotton

Faithful narrative, A: Edwards, Jonathan

Faithful narrative of the base and inhuman arts that were lately practised upon the brain of Habbakkuk Hilding, A: Smollett, Tobias

Faithful servants: Munby, A.J.

Faithful stranger: Kaye-Smith, S.

Faithful unto death: Machar, A.M.

Faithfull shepheardesse, The: Beaumont, Francis

Faithfull shepheardesse, The: Fletcher, John

Faithless world, A: Cobbe, Frances Power

Fake, The: †Lonsdale, Frederick

Fakeer of Jungheera, The: Derozio, H.L.V.

Falconberg: Boyesen, H.H.

Falconer of God, The: Benét, William Rose

Falconer's lassie, The: Bottomley, Gordon

Falconer's voice, The: Mannin, Ethel

Falconry in the valley of the Indus: Burton, *Sir* Richard

Falcons of France: Hall, J.N. and C.B. Nordhoff

Falkland: Lytton, E.G.E.B. *1st Baron*

Falkner: Shelley, Mary

Falkner Lyle: Lemon, Mark

Fall guy, The: Whitlock, Brand

Fall in, ghost: Blunden, Edmund

Fall in, Rookies: Jones, H.A.

Fall of a nation, The: Dixon, Thomas

Fall of a sparrow: Gielgud, Val

Fall of Constantinople, 1493, The: Runciman, *Sir* Steven

Fall of Egypt, The: Hawkesworth, John

Fall of Jerusalem, The: Milman, H.H.

Fall of Portugal, The: †Pindar, Peter

Fall of princis, The: Lydgate, John

Fall of Robespierre, The: Coleridge, S.T.

Fall of Robespierre, The: Southey, Robert

Fall of Somerset, The: Ainsworth, Harrison

Fall of the city, The: MacLeish, Archibald

Fall of the Dutch republic, The: Van Loon, Hendrik

Fall of the House of Heron: Phillpotts, Eden

Fall of the idols, The: Inge, W.R.

Fall of the Mughul empire: Sarkar, Y.J.

Fall of the Spanish American Empire, The: Madariaga, Salvador de

Fall of the sparrow, The: Balchin, Nigel

Fall of the year, The: Massingham, Harold

Fallacy of economics, The: Murry, John Middleton

Fallen angel: Fast, Howard M.

Fallen angels: Coward, Noel

Fallen fairies: Gilbert, *Sir* W.S.

Fallen fortunes: Payn, James

Fallen idol, A: †Anstey, F.

Fallen idol, The: Greene, Graham

Fallen leaves, The: Collins, Wilkie

Falling in love: Allen, Grant

Falling leaves: Vane, S.V.H.

Falling star, The: Oppenheim, E.Phillips

Falling upstairs: Pertwee, Roland

Fallodon papers: Grey of Fallodon, Edward

Fallow land, The: Bates, H.E.

Falmouth for orders: Villiers, A.J.

False alarm, The: Johnson, Samuel

False chevalier, The: Lighthall, W.D.

False colours, The: Heyer, Georgette

False Count, The: Behn, *Mrs.* Afra

False dawn (the 'forties): Wharton, Edith

False delicacy: Kelly, Hugh

False evidence: Oppenheim, E.Phillips

False friend, The: Vanbrugh, *Sir* John

False heir, The: James, G.P.R.

False hopes: Smith, Goldwin

False impressions: Cumberland, Richard

False premises: Housman, Laurence

False scent: Marsh, Ngaio Edith

False spring: Seymour, Beatrice Kean

Fame: Sinclair, May

Fame and confession of the fraternity, The: Vaughan, Thomas

Fame and fiction: Bennett, Arnold

Fame and the poet: Dunsany, E.J.M.D.P. *Lord*

Fame is the spur: Spring, Howard

Fames memoriall: Ford, John

Familiar and courtly letters: Farquhar, George

Familiar beliefs and transcendent reason: Balfour, A.J.

Familiar epistle in verse and prose [to Charles Baxter]: Stevenson, R.L.

Familiar epistles between W—H— and A— R—: Ramsay, Allan

Familiar epistles on the state of the Irish stage: Croker, J.W.

Familiar faces, The: Garnett, David

Familiar faces: Rinehart, Mary Roberts

Familiar fields: McArthur, Peter

Familiar friend, A: Lemon, Mark

Familiar letters: (Katherine Philips), †Orinda

Familiar letters: Thoreau, H.D.

Familiar Spanish travels: Howells, W.D.

Familiar studies of men and books: Stevenson, R.L.

Familie of love, The: Middleton, Thomas

Family, The: †Mordaunt, Elinor

Family affairs: Jennings, Gertrude

Family afloat: De Selincourt, Aubrey

Family and a fortune, A: Compton-Burnett, Ivy

Family at misrule, The: Turner, E.S.

Family circle: Skinner, C.O.

Family comedy, A: †Bowen, Marjorie

Family compact, The: Wallace, W.S.

Family credit, The: Marston, J.W.

Family cruise: Ashton, Helen

Family flight around home, A: Hale, E.E.

Family flight over Egypt and Syria, A: Hale, E.E.

Family flight through France and Switzerland, A: Hale, E.E.

Family flight through France, Germany, Norway, A: Hale, E.E.

Family flight through Mexico, A: Hale, E.E.

Family group: Seymour, Beatrice Kean

Family history: Canby, Henry Seidel

Family history: Sackville-West, V.

Family honour, The: Housman, Laurence

Family instructor, The: Defoe, Daniel

Family legend, The: Baillie, Joanna

Family magazine, The: Trimmer, *Mrs.* Sarah

Family man, A: Galsworthy, John

Family matters: Vulliamy, C.E.

Family names and their story: Baring-Gould, S.

Family nurse, The: Child, Lydia Maria

Family of islands, A: Waugh, Alec

Family on wheels, The: Oxley, J.M.

Family party, A: O'Hara, J.H.

Family picture, The: Holcroft, Thomas

Family pictures: Gunning, *Mrs.* Susannah

Family pictures: Manning, Anne

Family portrait, A: Wescott, Glenway

Family records: Bury, *Lady* C.S.M.

Family reunion, The: Eliot, T.S.

Family reunion: Nash, Ogden

Family Shakespeare, The: Bowdler, Thomas

Family that was, A: Raymond, Ernest

Family ties: Steen, Marguerite

Family tradition, A: Ford, Paul Leicester

Family tree, A: Matthews, J.B.

Family tree, The: Plomer, William

Family trouble: McFee, William

Family troubles: Molesworth, *Mrs.*

Family well-ordered, A: Mather, Cotton

Famine: O'Flaherty, Liam

Famine aspects of Bengal districts: Hunter, *Sir* W.W.

Famous American Negroes: Hughes, J.L.

Famous and memorable workes of Josephus, The: Lodge, Thomas

Famous and remarkable history of Sir Richard Whittington, The: Heywood, Thomas

Famous and renowned history of Amadis de Gaula, The: Kirkman, Francis

Famous animal stories: Seton-Thompson, E.

Famous boating party, The: Patchen, Kenneth

Famous British novelists: Cournos, John

Famous British poets: Cournos, John

Famous Chinese short stories: Lin Yu-T'ang

Famous chronicle of King Edwarde, The: Peele, George

Famous composers: Dole, N.H.

Famous cronycle of the warre agaynst Jugurth, The: Barclay, Alexander

Famous golf links: Lang, Andrew

Famous historie of Guy Earl of Warwick, The: Rowlands, Samuel

Famous history of Sir Thomas Wyat, The: Dekker, Thomas

Famous men of Britain: Peach, L. du Garde

Famous negro heroes of America: Hughes, J.L.

Famous Negro music makers: Hughes, J.L.

Famous old people: Hawthorne, Nathaniel

Famous persons and places: Willis, N.P.

Famous prediction of Merlin, the British Wizard, A: Swift, Jonathan

Famous Scottish regiments: Wallace, Edgar

Famous tragedy of the Queen of Cornwall, The: Hardy, Thomas

Famous tragedy of the rich Jew of Malta, The: Marlowe, Christopher

Famous, true and historicall life of Robert second Duke of Normandy, The: Lodge, Thomas

Famous whore, The: Markham, Gervase

Famous women of Britain: Peach, L. du Garde

Fan, The: Gay, John

Fan: Hudson, W.H.

Fanatic, The: Levin, Meyer

Fanatics, The: Malleson, Miles

Fanchette: Cooke, John Esten

Fanciad, The: Hill, Aaron

Fancies, The: Ford, John

Fancies and good nights: Collier, John

Fancies versus fads: Chesterton, G.K.

Fanciful tales: Stockton, F.T.

Fancy, The: Dickens, Monica

Fancy farm: Munro, Neil

Fancy free: Houghton, W.S.

Fancy free: Phillpotts, Eden

Fancy now: Knox, E.V.

Fancy tales: Isvaran, M.S.

Fancy's festivals: Jordan, Thomas

Fancy's following: Coleridge, Mary

Fancy's fool: Carman, Bliss

Fancy's Guerdon: Coleridge, Mary

Faneuil Hall address, The: Dana, R.H. *junior*

Fanfare: Brophy, John

Fanfare for Elizabeth: Sitwell, Edith

Fanfare for tin trumpets: Sharp, Margery

Fanfrolics and after: Lindsay, Jack

Fanny: Behrman, S.N.

Fanny: Halleck, Fitz-Greene

Fanny Burney: Dobson, Henry Austin

Fanny by gaslight: Sadleir, Michael

Fanny H—.: Ingraham, J.H.

Fanny herself: Ferber, Edna

Fanny the little milliner: Rowcroft, Charles

Fanny's fancies: Hall, Anna Maria

Fanny's first play: Shaw, G.B.

Fanshawe: Hawthorne, Nathaniel

Fantasia: Deeping, Warwick

Fantasia of the unconscious: Lawrence, D.H.

Fantasies: O'Dowd, B.P.

Fantasies and impromptus: Agate, J.E.

Fantastic fables: Bierce, Ambrose

Fantasticks serving for a perpetuall prognostication: Breton, Nicholas

Fantasy and passion: Fawcett, Edgar

Fantazius Mallare: Hecht, Ben

Far above rubies: Riddell, *Mrs.* J.H.

Far above rubies: Sutro, Alfred

Far and near: Blunden, Edmund

Far and near: Burroughs, John

Far away and long ago: Hudson, W.H.

Far away and long ago: Kemble, Frances

Far caravan: Timms, E.V.

Far country, A: Churchill, Winston

Far country, The: †Shute, Nevil

Far distant ships, The: Schull, J.J.

Far end: Sinclair, May

Far enough: Ashton, Helen

Far familiar, The: Mackaye, Percy

Far forest: Young, F.B.

Far from my home: Sitwell, Sacheverell

Far from the madding crowd: Hardy, Thomas

Far harbour, The: Mitchison, Naomi

Far horizons: Bedford-Jones, Henry

Far horizons: Carman, Bliss

Far in the forest: Mitchell, S.W.

Far lands, The: Hall, J.N.

Far off things: †Machen, Arthur

Faraway: Priestley, J.B.

Fardorougha the miser: Carleton, William

Fares please! Coppard, A.E.

Farewell: Aldrich, Thomas Bailey

Farewell, The: Churchill, Charles

Farewell and welcome: Bottrall, Ronald

Farewell. Entituled to the famous and fortunate generalls of our English forces Sir John Norris & Sir Frauncis Drake knights: Peele, George

Farewell for two years to England, A: Williams, H.M.

Farewell Manchester: Monkhouse, A.N.

Farewell, Miss Julie Logan: Barrie, Sir J.M.

Farewell, my friend: Tagore, Sir Rabindranath

Farewell my lovely: Chandler, Raymond

Farewell, my muse: Bax, Clifford

Farewell night, welcome day: Jameson, Storm

Farewell odes for the year 1786: †Pindar, Peter

Farewell romance: Frankau, Gilbert

Farewell sermon preached at the first precinct in Northampton, A: Edwards, Jonathan

Farewell Spain: O'Brien, Kate

Farewell to arms, A: Hemingway, Ernest

Farewell to poesy: Davies, W.H.

Farewell to Priorsford: Buchan, Anna

Farewell to sport: Gallico, Paul

Farewell to the children of the British Isles: (†Grey Owl), Belaney, G.S.

Farewell to youth: Jameson, Storm

Farewell, Victoria: White, T.H.

Farewell yesterday: Vachell, H.A.

Farina: Meredith, George

Faringdon Hill: Pye, H.J.

Farm: Bromfield, Louis

Farm and the fireside, The: †Arp, Bill

Farm ballads: Carleton, William (McKendree)

Farm festivals: Carleton, William (McKendree)

Farm in fairyland, A: Housman, Laurence

Farm legends: Carleton, William (McKendree)

Farm of Sertorius, The: Landor, Robert

Farm of the dagger, The: Phillpotts, Eden

Farm of three echoes: Langley, Noel

Farm on the hill, The: Uttley, Alison

Farmer, The: O'Keeffe, John

Farmer Giles of Ham: Tolkien, J.R.R.

Farmer refuted, The: Hamilton, Alexander

Farmer's boy, The: Bloomfield, Robert

Farmer's bride, The: Mew, Charlotte

Farmer's calendar, The: Young, Arthur

Farmer's daughter, The: Anstey, Christopher

Farmers' daughters, The: Williams, W.C.

Farmer's glory: Street, A.G.

Farmer's hotel, The: O'Hara, J.H.

Farmer's letter to the people of England, A: Young, Arthur

Farmer's return from London, The: Garrick, David

Farmer's six letters to the Protestants of Ireland, The: Brooke, Henry

Farmer's son, The: Graves, Richard

Farmer's story! The: Bernard, W.B.

Farmer's tour through the East of England, The: Young, Arthur

Farmer's wife, The: Phillpotts, Eden

Farmer's year, A: Haggard, Sir H. Rider

Farming England: Street, A.G.

Farming tour in the South and West of England, A: Young, Arthur

Farmington: Darrow, C.S.

Farnell's folly: Trowbridge, J.T.

Faro Nell and her friends: Lewis, A.H.

Far-off hills, The: Robinson, E.S.L.

Far-off things: Spittel, R.L.

Faro's daughter: Heyer, Georgette

Farther adventures of Robinson Crusoe, The: Defoe, Daniel

Farther defence of dramatick poetry, A: Settle, Elkanah

Farther shore, The: Coates, R.M.

Farthest from the truth: Lucas, E.V.

Farthing Hall: Priestley, J.B.

Farthing Hall: Walpole, Sir Hugh

Farthings: the story of a stray and a waif: Molesworth, Mrs.

Fascinating folly, The: McCormick, E.H.

Fascinating foundling, The: Shaw, G.B.

Fascinating Mr. Vanderveldt, The: Sutro, Alfred

Fascinating stranger, The: Tarkington, Booth

Fascism and social revolution: Dutt, R.P.

Fashion: Ritchie, Mrs. A.C.M.

Fashion in shrouds, The: Allingham, Margery

Fashionable adventures of Joshua Craig, The: Phillips, D.G.

Fashionable life: Trollope, Frances

Fashionable lover, The: Cumberland, Richard

Fashionable mysteries: Lathom, Francis

Fashionable philosophy and other sketches, Oliphant: Laurence

Fashionable tragedian, The: Archer, William

Fashions in literature: Warner, C.D.

Fast day, The: Combe, William

Fast friends: Trowbridge, J.T.

Fast of St. Magdalen, The: Porter, Anna Maria

Faster! Faster! †Delafield, E.M.

Fasti Etonenses: Benson, A.C.

Fasting cure, The: Sinclair, Upton

Fat contributor, The: Thackeray, W.M.

Fat King Melon and Princess Caraway: Herbert, *Sir* A.P.

Fat women, The: †Bridie, James

Fatal beauty: Cole, G.D.H.

Fatal boots, The: Thackeray, W.M.

Fatal contract, The: Heming, William

Fatal cord, The: Reid, T.N.

Fatal curiosity: Lillo, George

Fatal days, The: Drake-Brockman, H.

Fatal discovery, The: Home, John

Fatal extravagance, The: Hill, Aaron

Fatal falsehood, The: More, Hannah

Fatal interview: Millay, E. St. Vincent

Fatal jealousie, The: Payne, Henry Nevil

Fatal love: Settle, Elkanah

Fatal marriage, The: Southern, Thomas

Fatal message, The: Bangs, J.K.

Fatal revenge: Maturin, C.R.

Fatal second, The: †Sapper

Fatal secret, The: Theobald, Lewis

Fatal three, The: Braddon, Mary

Fatal venture: Crofts, F.W.

Fatal vision, The: Hill, Aaron

Fatal vow, The: Lathom, Francis

Fatality in Fleet Street: †Caudwell, Christopher

Fatall dowry, The: Massinger, Philip

Fate, The: James, G.P.R.

Fate cannot harm me: Masterman, *Sir* J.C.

Fate cries out: †Dane, Clemence

Fate of Adelaide, The: Landon, *Mrs.* Letitia

Fate of Admiral Kolchak, The: Fleming, Peter

Fate of Capua, The: Southern, Thomas

Fate of Franklin, The: Blackmore, *Sir* R.D.

Fate of Homo Sapiens, The: Wells, H.G.

Fate of Sparta, The: Cowley, *Mrs.* Hannah

Fate of the jury, The: Masters, E.L.

Fated to be free: Ingelow, Jean

Father: Russell, E.M.

Father Abbott: Simms, W.G.

Father Abraham: Bacheller, Irving

Father Abraham: Hardy, W.G.

Father and daughter: †Mordaunt, Elinor

Father and daughter, The: Opie, Amelia

Father and his fate, A: Compton-Burnett, Ivy

Father and I: Day, C.S.

Father and son: Farrell, James

Father and son: Gosse, *Sir* Edmund

Father Anthony: Buchanan, R.W.

Father Archangel of Scotland: Cunninghame Graham, Robert

Father Brighthopes: Trowbridge, J.T.

Father Butler: Carleton, William

Father confessor, The: Sigerson, Dora

Father Connell: Banim, John and Michael Banim

Father Damien: Stevenson, R.L.

Father Damien the martyr of Molokai: Stoddard, C.W.

Father, dear father: Bemelmans, Ludwig

Father Eustace: Trollope, Frances

Father Gregory: Wren, P.C.

Father Hilary's holiday: Marshall, Bruce

Father Hubbards tales: Middleton, Thomas

Father Junipero: Jackson, H.H.

Father Malachy's miracle: Marshall, Bruce

Father Marquette and the great rivers: Derleth, A.W.

Father of the forest, The: Watson, *Sir* J.W.

Father of the sea, The: Russell, W.C.

Father of women, A: Meynell, Alice

Father O'Flynn: Graves, Alfred Percival

Father Payne: Benson, A.C.

Father Rhine: Coulton, G.G.

Father Stafford: (†Anthony Hope), Hawkins, Anthony Hope

Father Varien: Hoffe, Monckton

Father William: Stewart, D.O.

Fathers, The: Fielding, Henry

Fathers and sons: Hook, T.E.

Father's legacy to his daughter, A: O'Keeffe, John

Fathers of men: Hornung, E.W.

Father's testament, A: Fletcher, Phineas

Father's tragedy, The: †Field, Michael

Faucit of Balliol: Merivale, H.C.

Faulkener: Godwin, William

Fault of angels, The: Horgan, Paul

Faultes faults, and nothing else but faultes: Rich, Barnabe

Faults of the Fabian Society: Wells, H.G.

Fauns and ladies: Lindsay, Jack

Faust: Bangs, John Kendrick

Faust: Phillips, Stephen

Faust: Reynolds, G.

Favourite studies in English literature: Blunden, Edmund

Fawn of Spring-Vale, The: Carleton, William (McKendree)

Fax: Carleton, William (McKendree)

Fayette: Stephens, J.B.

Fayre mayde of the Exchange: with the pleasaunt humours of the cripple of Fanchurch, The: Heywood, Thomas

Fazio: Milman, H.H.

Fear: Nesbit, E.

Fear and trembling: Wescott, Glenway

Fear comes to Chalfont: Crofts, F.W.

Fear is the same: Carr, J.D.

Fear lent us wings: Mais, S.P.B.

Fear of books, The: Jackson, Holbrook

Fear of the dead in primitive religion, The: Frazer, *Sir* James

Fear that walks by noonday, The: Canfield, Dorothy

Fearful joy, A: Cary, Joyce

Fearful pleasures: Coppard, A.E.

Fearful responsibility, A: Howells, W.D.

Fears in solitude: Coleridge, S.T.

Feast, The: Kennedy, Margaret

Feast of Bacchus, The: Bridges, Robert

Feast of Belshazzar, The: Arnold, Edwin

Feast of July, The: Bates, H.E.

Feast of ortolans, The: Anderson, Maxwell

Feast of St. Friend, The: Bennett, Arnold

Feast of the poets, The: Hunt, Leigh

Feast of youth, The: Chattopadhyaya, H.

Feather, The: (Hueffer), Ford, Ford Madox

Feather bed, The: Graves, Robert

Feather of the dawn, The: Naidu, Sarojini

Feather-bedding: Street, A.G.

Feathered nest, The: Leech, M.K.

Feathered serpent, The: Wallace, Edgar

Feathers: Van Vechten, Carl

Featherston's story: Wood, Ellen

February boys, The: Molesworth, *Mrs.*

Fed up: Hannay, J.O.

Fedele and Fortunio: Munday, Anthony

Federal India: Panikkar, K.M.

Federal story, The: Deakin, Alfred

Federalist, The: Hamilton, Alexander

Federalist Newburyport: Marquand, J.P.

Fee, fi, fo, fum: Massingham, Harold

Fee fi fo fum! Sitwell, *Sir* Osbert

Feed my swine: Powys, T.F.

Feet of clay: Barr, A.E.H.

Feet of the young men, The: Kipling, Rudyard

Feign'd curtizans, The: Behn, *Mrs.* Afra

Felice: Long, J.L.

Félicien Cossu: Swinburne, A.C.

Felicity Greene: Brophy, John

Felix: Hichens, Robert

Felix, an outcast: Molesworth, *Mrs.*

Felix Holt the radical: †Eliot, George

Felix O'Day: Smith, F.H.

Fell purpose: Derleth, A.W.

Fell sergeant, The: Mickle, A.D.

Fellow captains: Canfield, Dorothy

Fellow countrymen: Farrell, James

Fellowe and his wife, A: (†Macleod, Fiona), Sharp, William

Fellowship drinking song, The: Field, Eugene

Fellowship of the frog, The: Wallace, Edgar

Fellowship of the ring, The: Tolkien, J.R.R.

Fellowship with God: Temple, *Sir* William

Fellow-travellers: Vachell, H.A.

Female advocate, The: Radcliffe, *Mrs.* Ann

Female characters of Holy Scripture: Williams, Isaac

Female education: Cobbe, Frances Power

Female emigrant's guide, and hints on Canadian housekeeping, The: Traill, C.P.

Female felon, The: Simpson, H. de G.

Female grievances debated in six dialogues between two young ladies concerning love and marriage: Ward, Edward

Female of the species, The: Kipling, Rudyard

Female of the species: †Queen, Ellery

Female of the species, The: †Sapper

Female patriot, The: Rowson, S.H.

Female poets of America, The: Read, T.B.

Female prelate, The: Settle, Elkanah

Female Quixote, The: Lennox, Charlotte

Female spectator, The: Haywood, *Mrs.* Eliza

Feminine influence on the poets: Thomas, E.E.P.

Fenceless ranges, The: Bridges, Roy

Fenellosa and his circle: Brooks, Van Wyck

Fennel and rue: Howells, W.D.

Fenris the wolf: Mackaye, Percy

Fenton's quest: Braddon, Mary Elizabeth

Fenwick's career: Ward, M.A.

Ferdinand Magellan: Benson, E.F.

Fergus MacTavish: Oxley, J.M.

Ferishtah's Fancies: Browning, Robert

Fern on the rock, The: Dehn, Paul

Fernando de Lemos: Gayarré, C.E.A.

Festival: Basso, Hamilton

Festival at Faibridge: Priestley, J.B.

Festival guide: Yorkshire and Lancashire: Walmsley, Leo

Festival preludes: Bottomley, Gordon

Festivals, games and amusements, ancient and modern: Smith, Horatio

Festivals of fire: Bottrall, Ronald

Festive baked-potato cart, The: Allen, Walter Ernest

Festoon, The: Graves, Richard

Festus: Bailey, Philip James

Fetch: (†Joseph Shearing), †Bowen, Marjorie

Fetish of speed, The: Beerbohm, *Sir* Max

Feud, The: Garnett, Edward

Feud, The: Gordon, A.L.

Feud of Oakfield Creek, The: Royce, Josiah

Feudal times: Colman, George *the younger*

Few figs from thistles, A: Millay, E. St. Vincent

Few flowers for Shiner, A: Llewellyn, Richard

Few late chrysanthemums, A: Betjeman, John

Few love rhymes of a married life, A: Halloran, Henry

Few quick ones, A: Wodehouse, P.G.

Few sighs from Hell, A: Bunyan, John

Few verses for a few friends, A: Fields, J.T.

Fiametta: a summer idyl: Story, W.W.

Fiction as she is wrote: Knox, E.V.

Fiddle o' dreams: Morrison, Arthur

Fiddlededee: (Stephen Southwold), †Bell, Neill

Fiddler, The: Millin, Sarah

Fiddler of Carne, The: Rhys, Ernest

Fiddlers, The: Mee, Arthur

Fiddler's farewell: Speyer, *Mrs.* Leonora

Fiddler's house, The: Colum, Padraic

Fiddler's story, The: Hardy, Thomas

Fidelia: Wither, George

Fidelis: Cambridge, Ada

Fidelity: Glaspell, Susan

Fidgets: Hannay, J.O.

Field and hedgerow: Jefferies, Richard

Field fellowship: Massingham, Harold

Field god, The: Green, Paul

Field mouse, The: Traill, C.P.

Field of clover, The: Housman, Laurence

Field of honor: Byrne, Donn

Field of the forty footsteps, The: Porter, Jane

Field of Waterloo, The: Scott, *Sir* Walter

Field sports: Somerville, William

Field sports in the United States: Herbert, H.W.

Field theories, old and new: Einstein, Albert

Field-book, The: Maxwell, W.H.

Fields, The: Richter, Conrad

Fields at evening, The: Mannin, Ethel

Fields of paradise, The: Bates, Ralph

Fields of victory: Ward, M.A.

Fiend's delight, The: Bierce, Ambrose

Fiercest heart, The: Cloete, E.F.S.G.

Fiery dawn, The: Coleridge, Mary

Fiery dive, The: Armstrong, M.D.

Fiery ordeal, A: †Tasma

Fiery particles: Montague, C.E.

Fiesta: Hemingway, Ernest

Fife and drum at Louisbourg: Oxley, J.M.

Fifi: Bemelmans, Ludwig

Fifine at the fair: Browning, Robert

Fifteen and fair: Turner, E.S.

Fifteen drawings: Lewis, P. Wyndham

Fifteen dry points: Chattopadhyaya, H.

Fifteen oes, The: Caxton, William

Fifteen years of a drunkard's life: Jerrold, Douglas

Fifth arm, The: Steed, H.W.

Fifth child, The: Courage, J.F.

Fifth column and the first forty-nine stories, The: Hemingway, Ernest

Fifth commandant, The: Vachell, H.A.

Fifth decade of cantos, The: Pound, Ezra

Fifth gospel, The: Rubenstein, Harold F.

Fifth horseman, The: Chambers, R.W.

Fifth of November, The: Strong, L.A.G.

Fifth queen, The: (Hueffer), Ford, Ford Madox

Fifth queen crowned, The: (Hueffer), Ford, Ford Madox

Fifth series: Harris, James Thomas

Fifth victim, The: Collins, Dale

Fifty caricatures: Beerbohm, *Sir* Max

Fifty comedies and tragedies: Beaumont, Francis and John Fletcher

Fifty five: Frankau, Pamela

Fifty golden years: Craik, *Mrs.* Dinah

Fifty lyrical ballads: Bayly, Thomas Haynes

50 poems: Cummings, E.E.

Fifty poems: Godley, A.D.

Fifty sermons: Donne, John

Fifty three short stories: Garnett, Edward

Fifty years: Johnson, J.W.

Fifty years ago: Besant, *Sir* Walter

Fifty years of public service: a life of James L. Hughes: Pierce, Lorne

Fifty years of the L.L.C.: Mais, S.P.B.

Fifty years of work in Canada, scientific and educational: Dawson, *Sir* J.W.

Fifty-fifty: Maltby, H.F.

54–40 or fight: Hough, Emerson

51 stories by Sapper: †Sapper

Fig for Momus, A: Lodge, Thomas

Figaro at Hastings, St. Leonards: †Bede, Cuthbert

Figaro in London: Mayhew, Henry

Fight against war, The: Einstein, Albert

Fight of faith: Hall, Anna Maria

Fight to a finish, A: Phillpotts, Eden

Fighters for freedom: Van Loon, Hendrik

Fightin' fool: †Brand, Max

Fighting angel, portrait of a soul: Buck, Pearl

Fighting caravans: Grey, Zane

Fighting chance, The: Chambers, R.W.

Fighting France from Dunkerque to Belfort: Wharton, Edith

Fighting Littles, The: Tarkington, Booth

Fighting man: Treece, Henry

Fighting Scouts, The: Wallace, Edgar

Fighting Snub Reilly: Wallace, Edgar

Fighting Starkleys, The: Roberts, T.G.

Fighting stars: Cody, H.A.

Fighting the flames: Ballantyne, R.M.

Fighting tramp, The: Divine, A.D.

Fighting-slogan, The: Cody, H.A.

Figs and thistles: Tourgée, A.W.

Figure of Beatrice, The: Williams, Charles

Figure of eight: Mackenzie, *Sir* Compton

Figure of foure, The: Breton, Nicholas

Figures in a landscape: Horgan, Paul

Figures in modern literature: Priestley, J.B.

Figures in the foreground: Swinnerton, Frank

Figures of earth: Cabell, James Branch

Figures of several centuries: Symons, Arthur

Figures of speech or figures of thought: Coomaraswamy, A.K.

Figure-skating: Benson, E.F.

Fiji, Samoa, Tonga, the Islands of Wonder: Bolitho, H.H.

Files on parade: O'Hara, J.H.

Filibusters in Barbary: Lewis, P. Wyndham

Fill Gut and Pinch Belly: Taylor, John

Fille de chambre, The: Rowson, S.H.

Film and theatre: Nicoll, J.R.A.

Film commentary for The Queen is Crowned (Coronation Film 1953): Fry, Christopher

Film of memory, The: Leslie, *Sir* J.R. Shane

Film stories: Victory, Balaclava, etc.: Ewart, E.A.

Final appeal to the literary public relative to Pope, A: Bowles, William Lisle

Final count, The: †Sapper

Final curtain: Marsh, Ngaio Edith

Final edition: Benson, E.F.

Final memorials of Charles Lamb: Talfourd, *Sir* T.N.

Final reliques of Father Prout, The: Mahony, F.S.

Final test, The: Rattigan, Terence

Financial expert, The: Narayan, R.K.

Financier, The: Dreiser, Theodore

Finch's fortune: De la Roche, Mazo

Findernes' flowers: †Preedy, George

Finders-keepers: Kelly, G.E.

Finding a home: Wiggin, Kale

Finding his soul: Duncan, Norman

Fine and dandy: Stewart, D.O.

Fine art, chiefly contemporary: Rossetti, W.M.

Fine art of reading, The: Cecil, *Lord* David

Fine bird books 1700–1900: Sitwell, Sacheverell

Fine books: Pollard, A.W.

Fine clothes to the Jew: Hughes, J.L.

Fine companion, A: Marmion, Shackerley

Fine furniture: Dreiser, Theodore

Fine printing in California: Hart, James D.

Finer grain, The: James, Henry

Finest girl in Bloomsbury, The: Mayhew, Augustus Septimus

Finest walk in the world, The: Baughan, B.E.

Fingal: Macpherson, James

Finger in every pie, A: Davies, Rhys

Finger of fate, The: Reid, T.M.

Finger of fate, The: †Sapper

Finish to the adventures of Tom, Jerry and Logic in their pursuits through life in and out of London: Egan, Pierce

Finished: Haggard, *Sir* H. Rider

Finishing stroke: †Queen, Ellery

Finnegans wake: Joyce, James

Finnish grammar, A: Eliot, *Sir* Charles

Fiorello!: Weidman, Jerome

Firdausi in exile: Gosse, *Sir* Edmund

Fire!: Crane, Stephen

Fire and the robe, The: Bryant, *Sir* Arthur

Fire and wine: Fletcher, John Gould

Fire below: †Yates, Dornford

Fire brain: †Brand, Max

Fire, burn! Carr, J.D.

Fire divine, The: Gilder, R.W.

Fire down below: Irwin, Margaret

Fireflies: Tagore, *Sir* R.

Fire for the night: Deutsch, Babette

Fire in stubble: Orczy, *Baroness*

Fire in the ice: Divine, David

Fire in the woods: De Mille, James

Fire of driftwood, A: Broster, D.K.

Fire on the Andes: Beals, Carleton

Fire on the snow, The: Stewart, D.A.

Fire out of heaven: Millin, Sarah

Fire over England: Mason, A.E.W.

Fire tribe, The: Devaney, J.M.

Fire trumpet, The: Mitford, Bertram

Firebrand, The: Crockett, S.R.

Fire-bringer, The: Moody, W.V.

Firecrackers: Van Vechten, Carl

Firehead: Ridge, Lola

Fires: Gibson, Wilfred

Fires in the distance: Courage, J.F.

Fires in Smithfield: Lindsay, Jack

Fires of driftwood: MacKay, I.E.

Fires of hate, The: Bridges, Roy

Fires of spring, The: Michener, J.A.

Firefly's light, The: Hough, Emerson

Firelight stories: Moulton, E.L.

Firescreen, The: Sutro, Alfred

Fireside and sunshine: Lucas, E.V.

Fireside sphinx, The: Repplier, Agnes

Fireside studies: Kingsley, Henry

Fireside travels: Lowell, J.R.

Fire-weed: Royde-Smith, N.

Fireworks: Jennings, Gertrude

Fir-flower tablets: Lowell, Amy

Firing line, The: Chambers, R.W.

Firing squad, The: Wallace, Edgar

Firm of Girdlestone, The: Doyle, *Sir* Arthur Conan

Firmiliam: Aytoun, W.E.

First a lady: Kaufman, G.S.

First affair, The: Mitchell, J.A.

First and last: Belloc, Hilaire

First and last: Lardner, Ring

First and last loves: Betjeman, John

First and last things: Wells, H.G.

First and second love: Farjeon, Eleanor

First and second partes of King Edward the Fourth, The: Heywood, Thomas

First and the last, The: Galsworthy, John

First anniversary, The: Donne, John

First anniversary of the government under His Highness the Lord Protector, The: Marvell, Andrew

First assault on the Sorbonne, The: Kipling, Rudyard

First Athenian memories: Mackenzie, *Sir* Compton

First Bishop of Toronto, The: Scadding, Henry

First blood: Monkhouse, A.N.

First book in American history, A: Beard, C.A.

First book in American history, A: Eggleston, Edward

First book of Africa: Hughes, J.L.

First book of American history (for children): Commager, H.S.

First book of Canadian history, A: Wallace, W.S.

First book of English literature, A: Saintsbury, George

First book of jazz: Hughes, J.L.

First book of Negros: Hughes, J.L.

First book of rhymes: Hughes, J.L.

First book of rhythms, The: Hughes, J.L.

First book of the Caribbean, The: Hughes, J.L.

First book of the West Indies: Hughes, J.L.

First book of Urizen, The: Blake, William

First Bulgarian empire, The: Runciman, *Sir* Steven

First chapbook of rounds: Farjeon, Eleanor

First Childermas, The: Seymour, W.K.

First Christmas daily paper, The: Sheldon, C.M.

First Church of Christ Scientist, The: Eddy, M.B.

First college bowl question book: Weidman, Jerome

First Corinthians: Moffat, James

First Corinthians: Rubenstein, Harold F.

First croak: Carman, Bliss

First decade of the Australian Commonwealth, 1901–10, The: Turner, H.G.

First draft of Swinburne's "Anactoria", The: Gosse, *Sir* Edmund

First English book, A: Craigie, *Sir* W.A.

First English reader, A: Craigie, *Sir* W.A.

First episode: Rattigan, Terence

First family of Tasajara, A: Harte, Bret

First fam'lies in the Sierras (novel and play): †Miller, Joaquin

First five books of the Roman History, The: Bellenden, John

First five centuries of the Church, The: Moffat, James

First five chapters of a history of the United States for the use of schools: Fiske, John

First Fleet family, A: †Becke, Louis

First fowre bookes of the civile wars: Daniel, Samuel

First fruits of Australian poetry: Field, Baron

First gazetteer of Upper Canada: Scadding, Henry

First gentleman, The: Ginsbury, Norman

First gentleman of America, The: Cabell, James Branch

First half of the seventeenth century, The: Grierson, *Sir* Herbert

First hundred thousand, The: (†Ian Hay), Beith, *Sir* John Hay

First hundred years, 1848–1948, The: Edmonds, W.D.

First hymn to Lenin: †McDiarmid, Hugh

First impressions: Smith, Horatio

First impressions of England and its people: Miller, Hugh

First Lady Brendon, The: Hichens, Robert

First leaf, The: Riding, Laura

First lesson: White, T.H.

First lessons in story-writing: Pain, B.E.O.

First lessons in the principles of cooking: Barker, M.A.

First love: Cumberland, Richard

First love: Meynell, Viola

First love: Morgan, C.L.

First love: Pertwee, Roland

First love: Untermeyer, Louis

First love and last love: Grant, James

First love is best: Dodge, May Abigail

First lover, The: Boyle, Kay

First mate's log of a journey to Greece, The: Collingwood, R.G.

First men in the moon, The: Welles, H.G.

First Mrs. Fraser, The (novel and play): Ervine, St. John

First nights: Agate, J.E.

First notes on the general principles of employment for the destitute and criminal classes: Ruskin, John

First ode of the second book of Horace paraphras'd, The: Swift, Jonathan

First of April, The: Combe, William

First of April, The: Swift, Jonathan

First of the African diamonds, The: Browne, Frances

First of the Hoosiers, The: Eggleston, George Cary

First part of the elementarie which entreateth chefelie of the right writing of our English tung, The: Mulcaster, Richard

First part of the historie of England: Daniel, Samuel

First part of the life and raigne of King Henrie the IIII, The: Hayward, *Sir* John

First part of the true and honorable historie, of the life of Sir John Oldcastle, The: Drayton, Michael

First part of the true and honorable historie, of the life of Sir John Oldcastle, The: Munday, Anthony

First person singular, The: Benét, William Rose

First player: Brown, Ivor

First poor traveller, The: Dickens, Charles

First principles of the oracles of God, The: Shepard, Thomas

First principles of verse: Hillyer, Robert

First quarter: Mais, S.P.B.

First Russia, then Tibet: Byron, Robert

First satire of the second book of Horace, imitated, The: Pope, Alexander

First scene, The: †Bridie, James

First sermon preached to King Charles: Donne, John

First sett of Italian madrigalls Englished, The: Watson, Thomas

First Sir Percy, The: Orczy, *Baroness*

First sketch of English literature, A: Morley, Henry

First television murder, The: Gielgud, Val

First the blade: †Dane, Clemence

First three years, The: Partridge, Eric

"First time under fire, The": De Forest, John William

First to awaken, The: Hicks, Granville

First twenty years of Australia: Bonwick, James

First wife, The: Buck, Pearl

First will and testament: Patchen, Kenneth

First with the sun: Mulgan, A.E.

First words before spring: Untermeyer, Louis

First year in Canterbury settlement, A: Butler, Samuel

First years in Europe: Calvert, George Henry

Firstborn, The: Fry, Christopher

Firste (laste) volume of the Chronicles of England, Scotlande, and Irelande, etc., The: Holinshed, Raphael

Firste part of Churchyardes Chippes: Churchyard, Thomas

Fish and chips: Street, A.G.

Fish are such liars: Pertwee, Roland

Fish dinner in Memison, A: Eddison, Eric Rucker

Fish of Monsieur Quissard, The: Janvier, T.A.

Fish pool, The: Steele, *Sir* Richard

Fisher boy, The: Ireland, William Henry

Fisherman's creed, A: Blake, W.H.

Fisherman's song, The: Neale, J.M.

Fishermen at war: Walmsley, Leo

Fishermen's saint, The: Grenfell, *Sir* W.T.

Fisher's ghost: Stewart, Douglas

Fisher's juvenile scrap-book: Barton, Bernard

Fishers of men: Crockett, S.R.

Fishing fleets of New England, The: Chase, M.E.

Fishing methods and devices of the Maoris: Best, Elsdon

Fishing valley on the Clyde, A: Mitchison, Naomi

Fishing with hook and line: Herbert, H.W.

Fishmonger's fiddle: Coppard, A.E.

Fishpingle (novel and play): Vachell, H.A.

Fitness of the glories of Mary, The: Newman, J.H.

Fitz of Fitz-ford: Bray, Anna

Fitz-Boodle papers, The: Thackeray, W.M.

FitzGeorge: Sterling, John

Five arts: Frank, Waldo

Five bells: Slessor, Kenneth

Five birds in a cage: Jennings, Gertrude

Five books of song: Gilder, R.W.

Five books of youth, The: Hillyer, Robert

Five centuries of religion: Coulton, G.G.

Five children and it: Nesbit, E.

Five corners: O'Reilly, D.P.

Five days' entertainments at Wentworth Grange, The: Palgrave, F.T.

Five degrees south: Young, F.B.

Five flamboys, The: †Beeding, Francis

Five free trade essays: Reid, *Sir* G.H.

Five gifts, The: Masani, *Sir* R.P.

Five hundred points of good husbandry: Tusser, Thomas

Five hundred years of Chaucer criticism and allusion: Spurgeon, Caroline

Five jars, The: James, M.R.

Five jolly schoolgirls: Brazil, Angela

Five little pigs: Christie, Agatha

Five masters: Krutch, J.W.

Five men and pompey: Benét, Stephen Vincent

Five men and a swan: Mitchison, Naomi

Five minutes stories: Molesworth, *Mrs.*

Five nations: Kipling, Rudyard

Five people: †Bowen, Marjorie

Five pieces of Runic poetry translated from the Islandic language: Percy, Thomas

Five plays of other times: Dukes, Ashley

Five poems, 1470–1870: Tillyard, E.M.W.

Five red herrings, The: Sayers, Dorothy

Five Robin Hood plays: Gow, Ronald

Five Saints: Acton, Harold

Five silver daughters: Golding, Louis

Five sons of Le Faber, The: Raymond, Ernest

Five types: Chesterton, G.K.

Five variations on a theme: Sitwell, Edith

Five winds: †Bowen, Marjorie

Five years, The: Brophy, John

Five years of it: Austin, Alfred

Five years of youth: Martineau, Harriet

Five year's tryst, A: Besant, *Sir* Walter

Fivefold screen, The: Plomer, William

Fixed period, The: Trollope, Anthony

Fixin's: Green, Paul

Flag and good faith, The: Fitzpatrick, *Sir* J.P.

Flag of distress, The: Reid, T.M.

Flag of truce, The: Warner, S.B.

Flagon of beauty, A: MacDonald, W.P.

Flagons and apples: Jeffers, J.R.

Flag-raising, The: Wiggin, Kate

Flagships three: Bean, C.E.

Flame and adventure: Dalton, A.C.

Flame and dust, Starrett: Vincent

Flame and shadow: Dalton, A.C.

Flame and shadow: Teasdale, Sara

Flame and the light, The: Fausset, Hugh

Flame for doubting Thomas, A: Llewellyn, Richard

Flame in sunlight, A: Sackville-West, Edward

Flame of Ethirdova, The: Bolitho, H.H.

Flame of Hercules, The: Llewellyn, Richard

Flame of the forest, The: Ghose, S.N.

Flame trees of Thika, The: Huxley, Elspeth J.

Flamehair the Skald: Bedford-Jones, Henry

Flameless fire: Holcroft, M.H.

Flames: Hichens, Robert

Flames coming out of the top: Collins, Norman

Flaming jewel, The: Chambers, R.W.

Flaming sword, The: Dixon, Thomas

Flaming terrapin, The: Campbell, Roy

Flamingo feather: Van der Post, L.J.

Flamp, The: Lucas, E.V.

Flappers and philosophers: Fitzgerald, F. Scott

Flare path: Rattigan, Terence

Flashing stream, The: Morgan, Charles

Flashlights on nature: Allen, Grant

Flat iron for a farthing, A: Ewing, *Mrs.* Juliana Horatia

Flat 2: Wallace, Edgar

Flattering word, The: Kelly, G.E.

Flavor of Texas, The: Dobie, J.F.

Flaw in the crystal, The: Sinclair, May

Flawed blades: Wren, P.C.

Flax of dream, The: Williamson, Henry

Flecker of Dean Close: Williams, Charles

Fledgling, The: Nordhoff, C.B.

Fleece, The: Dyer, John

Fleet and convoy: McCrae, G.G.

Fleet in being, A: Kipling, Rudyard

Fleet Street: Davidson, John

Fleet Street eclogues: Davidson, John

Fleeting, The: De la Mare, Walter

Fleetwood: Godwin, William

Fleetwood: Sargent, Epes

Fleming Field: Ingraham, J.H.

Flemish painting: Cammaerts, Emile

Flesh and blood: Brophy, John

Flesh and the spirit, The: Stewart, D.A.

Flesh in armour: Mann, Leonard

Fleshly school of poetry, The: Buchanan, Robert Williams

Flies in the sun: †Novello, Ivor

Flight, The: Woodberry, G.E.

Flight from a lady: Macdonell, A.G.

Flight into darkness: Gustafson, Ralph

Flight of birds, A: Roberts, C.E.M.

Flight of fancies, A: Gale, Norman R.

Flight of Pony Baker, The: Howells, W.D.

Flight of swans, A: Tagore, *Sir* Rabindranath

Flight of the falcon, The: Du Maurier, Daphne

Flight of the heron, The: Broster, D.K.

Flight of the innocents, The: Lin Yu-T'ang

Flight of the shadow, The: Macdonald, George

Flight to the West: Rice, Elmer

Flim-flams!: D'Israeli, Isaac

Flint anchor, The: Warner, Sylvia Townsend

Flint and feather: Johnson, E.P.

Flint heart, The: Phillpotts, Eden

Flip and found at Blazing Star: Harte, Bret

Flirt, The: Tarkington, Booth

Flirt and the flapper, The: Glyn, Elinor

Flirtation: Bury, *Lady* C.S.M.

Flirtation: Maugham, Somerset

Flirtation at the Moultrie House: Simms, W.G.

Flitch of bacon, or the custom of Dunmow, The: Ainsworth, William H.

Flivver king, The: Sinclair, Upton

Floating admiral, The: Sayers, Dorothy

Floating island, The: Head, Richard

Floating prince, The: Stockton, F.R.

Floating republic, The: Dobrée, Bonamy

Floating world: Michener, J.A.

Flock, The: Austin, Mary

Flock at the fountain, The: Adams, Sarah

Flodden field: Austin, Alfred

Flood, A: Moore, George

Flood: Warren, Robert Penn

Flood of life: Church, Richard

Flood of Thessaly, The: Proctor, B.W.

Floodlight: Nichols, Beverley

Floor games: Wells, H.G.

Floorish upon fancie, A: Breton, Nicholas

Flora: De la Mare, Walter

Flora Lindsay: Moodie, Susanna

Flora of Cheshire, The: Warren, J.B.L.

Floral tribute: Vulliamy, C.E.

Flora's gems: Meredith, L.A.

Florence: Hare, A.J.C.

Florence Bardsley's story: Field, Eugene

Florence Fitz-Hardinge: Leprohon, R.E.

Florence Macarthy: Morgan, *Lady* Sydney

Florence miscellany: Thrale, *Mrs.* Hester Lynch

Florentine dagger, The: Hecht, Ben

Florentine journal: Bennett, Arnold

Florentine painters of the Renaissance: Berenson, Bernhard

Florentine portrait, A: Lewis, D.B. Wyndham

Florentine tragedy, A: Wilde, Oscar

Florida: Roberts, Kenneth

Florida days: Deland, Margaret

Florida: its scenery, climate, and history: Lanier, Sidney

Florida loafing: Roberts, Kenneth

Florien: Merivale, H.C.

Florio: More, Hannah

Florio his firste fruites: Florio, John

Florus Britannicus: Stevenson, Matthew

Flotsam: †Merriman, Seton

Flotsam and Jetsam: Domett, Alfred

Flourishing of romance and the rise of allegory, The: Saintsbury, George

Flower alphabet, The: Osgood, F.S.

Flower and the weed: Braddon, Mary

Flower and the wheel, The: Bell, Adrian

Flower and thorn: Aldrich, Thomas Bailey

Flower beneath the foot, The: Firbank, Ronald

Flower fables: Alcott, Louisa May

Flower for Catherine, A: Swinnerton, F.A.

Flower girls, The: †Dane, Clemence

Flower o' the lily: Orczy, *Baroness*

Flower o' the pine: Turner, E.S.

Flower of Gala Water, The: Barr, A.E.H.

Flower of grass, The: Cammaerts, Emile

Flower of May, The: O'Brien, Kate

Flower of old Japan, The: Noyes, Alfred

Flower of the Chapdelaines, The: Cable, George Washington

Flower of the rose: Carman, Bliss

Flower of youth: Tynan, Katherine

Flower o'-the-corn: Crockett, S.R.

Flower pieces: Allingham, William

Flower pieces: Colum, Padraic

Flower pot end: Mottram, R.H.

Flower show, The: Mackail, Denis

Flower-de-Luce: Longfellow, H.W.

Flowering earth: Peattie, D.C.

Flowering Judas: Porter, K.A.

Flowering of New England, The: Brooks, Van Wyck

Flowering of the gods: Phillpotts, Eden

Flowering of the rod: Doolittle, Hilda

Flowering peach, The: Odets, Clifford

Flowering reeds: Campbell, Roy

Flowering rifle: Campbell, Roy

Flowering stone, The: Dillon, George

Flowering thorn, The: Sharp, Margery

Flowering wilderness: Galsworthy, John

Flowers for a lady: Percy, Edward

Flowers for children: Child, Lydia Maria

Flowers for the judge: Allingham, Margery

Flowers from four gardens: Webster, M.M.

Flowers in the grass: Hewlett, M.H.

Flowers of Lodowicke of Granado, The: Lodge, Thomas

Flowers of loveliness: Bayly, Thomas Haynes

Flowers of loveliness: Landon, Letitia

Flowers of passion: Moore, George

Flowers of Sion: Drummond of Hawthornden, William

Flowers of speech: Squire, *Sir* J.C.

Flowers of the forest: †Bell, Neil

Flowers of the forest: Garnett, David

Flowers of the forest: Van Druten, J.W.

Flowers of virtue, The: Connelly, Marc

Flowers on the grass: Dickens, Monica

Flowery sword, The: Mannin, Ethel

Flowery walk: Temple, Joan

Flowing gold: Beach, R.E.

Flowing summer, The: Bruce, Charles

Flush: Woolf, Virginia

Flush times of Alabama and Mississippi, The: Baldwin, J.G.

Flute and violin: Allen, James Lane

Flute of Pan, The: †Hobbes, John Oliver

Flute player's story, The: Colum, Padraic

Fly fishing: Grey of Fallodon, Edward *Lord*

Fly leaves: Calverley, Charles Stuart

Fly with me: †Caudwell, Christopher

Flyaway highway, The: Lindsay, Norman

Flyer, The: McCutcheon, G.B.

Flying and sport in East Africa: Walmsley, Leo

Flying angel: Strong, L.A.G.

Flying bull, The: Kirkconnell, Watson

Flying colours: Forester, C.S.

Flying courier, The: Ewart, E.A.

Flying doctor calling: Hill, Ernestine

Flying Dutchman: Arlen, Michael

Fly-ing Dutchman, The: Saxe, J.G.

Flying emerald, The: Lewis, Ethelreda

Flying fifty-five, The: Wallace, Edgar

Flying goat, The: Bates, H.E.

Flying inn, The: Chesterton, G.K.

Flying islands of the night, The: Riley, J.W.

Flying king of Kurio, The: Benét, William Rose

Flying Plover: Roberts, T.G.

Flying scroll, A: Hodgson, Ralph

Flying shadow, The: Rhys, John Llewellyn

Flying swans: Colum, Padraic

Flying Teuton, The: Brown, Alice

Flying visit, The: Fleming, Peter

Flying wasp, The: O'Casey, Sean

Flying with Chaucer: Hall, J.N.

Flying years, The: Niven, F.J.

Flytting betwixt Montgomerie and [Sir Patrick Hume of] Polwart, The: Montgomerie, Alexander

Foch: the man of Orleans: Liddell Hart, B.

Fodor Dostoievsky: Murry, John Middleton

Foe-Farrell:(†Q),Quiller-Couch, Sir A.

Foes in law: Broughton, Rhoda

Foes of the fields, The: Carleton, William (McKendree)

Foggerty's fairy, Gilbert: Sir W.S.

Foggy night at Offord, The: Wood, Ellen

Foghorn stories, The: Atherton, Gertrude

Folded hills: White, S.E.

Foliage: Davies, W.H.

Foliage: Hunt, Leigh

Folk afield, The: Phillpotts, Eden

Folk idea in American life, The: Suckow, Ruth

Folk tales and fairy tales from India: Ghose, S.N.

Folk-lore in the Old Testament: Frazer, Sir James

Folklore of wells: Masani, Sir R.P.

Folks, The: Suckow, Ruth

Folle Farine: †Ouida

Follow my black plume: Trease, Geoffrey

Follow the call: Anthony, Frank S.

Follow thy fair sun: Meynell, Viola

Followers: Brighouse, Harold

Followers of St. Francis: Housman, Laurence

Following darkness: Reid, Forrest

Following of the star, The: Barclay, F.L.

Following the color line: Baker, R.S.

Following the drum: Fortescue, Sir John

Following the equator: (†Mark Twain), Clemens, S.L.

Following the sun-flag: Fox, John

Folly and fresh air: Phillpotts, Eden

Folly calling: Knox, E.V.

Folly Farm: Joad, C.E.M.

Folly field: Bell, Adrian

Folly of Eustace, The: Hichens, Robert

Fombombo: Stribling, T.S.

Fond adventures: Hewlett, Maurice

Fond fancy: †Bowen, Marjorie

Fontainebleau or Our Way in France: O'Keeffe, John

Food and drink: Untermeyer, Louis

Food for thought: Pertwee, Roland

Food of the gods and how it came to earth, The: Wells, H.G.

Fool and his money, A: McCutcheon, G.B.

Fool beloved, The: Farnol, J.J.

Fool divine: †Lancaster, G.B.

Fool errant, The: Hewlett, M.H.

Fool hath said, The: Nichols, Beverley

Fool i' the forest, A: Aldington, Richard

Fool of quality, The: Brooke, Henry

Fool in her folly, A: Broughton, Rhoda

Fool o' the moon: Lowell, Amy

Fool of joy, The: MacInnes, T.R.E.

Fool of love, The: Pearson, Hesketh

Fool of the family, The: Kennedy, Margaret

Fool of the world, The: Symons, Arthur

Fool of time, The: Seymour, Beatrice Kean

Fooles bolt is soon shott, A: Rowlands, Samuel

Foolish apprentices: Frankau, Pamela

Foolish gentlewoman, The: Sharp, Margery

Foolish immortals, The: Gallico, Paul

Foolish lovers, The: Ervine, St. John

Foolish matrons, The: Byrne, Donn

Foolish virgin, The: Dixon, Thomas

Foolish virgins, The: Sutro, Alfred

Foolishness of Solomon, The: Trevelyan, R.C.

Fool's errand, A: Tourgée, A.W.

Fool's gold: Fletcher, John Gould

Fools' harvest: (†The Chiel), Cox, Erle

Fools of nature: Brown, Alice

Fool's revenge, The: Taylor, Tom

Fools rush in: Green, Anne

Foolscap rose, The: Hergesheimer, Joseph

Foot of the cross, The: Faber, F.W.

Footfall of fate, The: Riddell, *Mrs.* J.H.

Footfarings: Scollard, Clinton

Foothills of Parnassus, The: Bangs, John Kendrick

Footman in powder: Ashton, Helen

Footnote on Capri: Douglas, Norman

Footnote to history, A: Stevenson, R.L.

Footnotes for a centennial: Morley, C.D.

Footpaths thro' the Veld: Slater, F.C.

Foot-prints: Stoddard, R.H.

Footprints in foreign lands: Rowcroft, Charles

Footprints of former men in far Cornwall: Hawker, Robert Stephen

Footsteps at the lock, The: Knox, R.A.

Footsteps in the dark: Heyer, Georgette

Footsteps of the master: Stowe, Harriet Beecher

For a song: Bercovici, Konrad

For adults only: Nichols, Beverley

For all we know: Stern, G.B.

For Australia: Lawson, Henry

For authors only: Roberts, Kenneth

For better, for worse: Cammaerts, Emile

For better, for worse: Yates, E.H.

For cash only: Payn, James

For Christ and Church: Sheldon, C.M.

For continuity: Leavis, F.R.

For daws to peck at: Gibbon, Monk

For Dick's sake: Riddell, *Mrs.* J.H.

For England: Watson, *Sir* J.W.

For England's sake: Henley, W.E.

For ever: Langley, Noel

For ever wilt thou love: Lewisohn, Ludwig

For faith and freedom: Besant, *Sir* Walter

For fifty years: Hale, E.E.

For free trade: Churchill, *Sir* Winston

For her to see: (†Joseph Shearing), †Bowen, Marjorie

For his people: Hayashi, Tadasu *Viscount*

For information received: Wallace, Edgar

For king and country: Machar, A.M.

For Lancelot Andrewes: Eliot, T.S.

For liberalism and free trade: Churchill, *Sir* Winston

For life: †Rudd, Steele

For love alone: Stead, C.E.

For love and life: Oliphant, Margaret

For love and money: Dehn, Paul

For love of the King: Wilde, Oscar

For Mamie's sake: Allen, Grant

For Maurice: Lee, Vernon

For my great folly: Costain, T.B.

For one sweet grape: O'Brien, Kate

For remembrance: Phillpotts, Eden

For revolution: Calverton, V.F.

For services rendered: Maugham, Somerset

For sale: Mackenzie, *Sir* C.

For some we loved: Mottram, R.H.

For summer afternoons: Coolidge, Susan

"For the country": Gilder, R.W.

For the crown: Davidson, John

For the crowning of the King, June 26th, 1902: MacInnes, T.R.E.

For the defence: Farjeon, B.L.

For the Iowa dead: Engle, Paul

For the love of Mike: Maltby, H.F.

For the luncheon interval: Milne, A.A.

For the major: Woolson, C.F.

For the pleasure of his company: Stoddard, C.W.

For the Queen: Oppenheim, E.Phillips

For the sacred memoriall of Charles Howard, Earle of Nottingham: Taylor, John

For the sake of the school: Brazil, Angela

For the school colours: Brazil, Angela

For the sexes: Blake, William

For the time being: Auden, W.H.

For the train: †Carroll, Lewis

For them that trespass: Raymond, Ernest

For this we fought: Chase, Stuart

For us in the dark: Royde-Smith, Naomi

For us the living: Woollcott, A.H.

For Virginians only: Bagby, G.W.

For what do we fight? Angell, *Sir* Norman

For whom the bell tolls: Hemingway, Ernest

For you, with love: Untermeyer, Louis

Foray of Queen Meave, The: De Vere, Aubrey

Forayers, The: Simms, W.G.

Forays and rebuttals: De Voto, Bernard

Forbes of Harvard: Hubbard, Elbert

Forbidden gold: Lawson, Will

Forc'd marriage, The: Behn, *Mrs.* Afra

Force and energy: Allen, Grant

Force of religion, The: Young, Edward

Force of women in Japanese history, The: Beard, Mary

Forces' slang (1939–45): Partridge, E.H.

Ford, The: Austin, Mary

Ford Madox Brown—life and work: Ford, Ford Madox

Fordham's feud: Mitford, Bertram

Forecasts of the coming century: Wallace, A.R.

Foregone conclusion, A: Howells, W.D.

Foreign exchange: Tarkington, Booth

Foreign faces: Pritchett, V.S.

Foreign policy for America, A: Beard, C.A.

Foreign policy of England, 1570–1870, The: Russell, *Lord* John

Foreign policy of Sir Edward Grey, The: Murray, Gilbert

Foreign relations: Walpole, *Sir* Spencer

Foreigner, The: †Connor, Ralph

Foreigners, The: †Lonsdale, Frederick

Foreigners: Walmsley, Leo

Foreigners aren't fools: Hollis, Christopher

Foreigners aren't knaves: Hollis, Christopher

Forerunners, The: Palmer, E.V.

Forest, The: Cresswell, W.D.

Forest, The: Galsworthy, John

Forest, The: White, S.E.

Forest and game-law tales: Martineau, Harriet

Forest and ice: Baughan, B.E.

Forest and stream: Robinson, R.E.

Forest days: James, G.P.R.

Forest exiles, The: Reid, T.M.

Forest fugitives: Roberts, T.G.

Forest hearth, A: Major, Charles

Forest lore of the Maoris: Best, Elsdon

Forest lovers, The: Hewlett, Maurice

Forest minstrel, The: Hogg, James

Forest of Bourg-Marie, The: †Seranus

Forest of happy dreams, The: Wallace, Edgar

Forest of terrible things, The: Hull, E.M.

Forest of wild thyme, The: Noyes, Alfred

Forest on the hill, The: Phillpotts, Eden

Forest orphans: Derleth, A.W.

Forest rose, The: Woodworth, Samuel

Forest sanctuary, The: Hemans, *Mrs.* Felicia

Forest songs: Todhunter, John

Forester, The: Alcott, A.B.

Foresters, The: Belknap, Jeremy

Foresters, The: Tennyson, Alfred *Lord*

Foresters, The: Wilson, John

Forester's daughter, The: Garland, Hamlin

Forester's manual, The: Seton-Thompson, E.

Forest-land: Chambers, R.W.

Forests of Pan: McCrae, Hugh

Forever growing: Green, Paul

Forever morning: Davison, F.D.

Forever to remain: Timms, E.V.

Forever wandering: Mannin, Ethel

Forever young: Akins, Zoë

Forfeit, The: Gratton, T.C.

Forge, The: Hall, M.R.

Forge, The: Stribling, T.S.

Forge in the forest, The: Colum, Padraic

Forger's wife, The: Lang, J.

Forgery, The: James, G.P.R.

Forges of freedom: McDowell, F.D.

Forget if you can: Erskine, John

Forget-me-not for 1823, The: Combe, William

Forget-me-nots: Kavanagh, Julia

Forging of the anchor, The: Fergusson, *Sir* Samuel

Forging the blades: Mitford, Bertram

Forgive us our trespasses: †Bell, Neil

Forgive us our virtues: Fisher, V.A.

Forgiveness and law: Bushnell, Horace

Forgiveness of sins, The: Williams, Charles

Forgotten island, The: Hall, M.R.

Forgotten journey, A: Fleming, Peter

Forgotten kingdom, A: Woolley, *Sir* Leonard

Forgotten one, The: Hall, J.N.

Forgotten peninsula, The: Krutch, J.W.

Forgotten smile, The: Kennedy, Margaret

Forgotten village, The: Steinbeck, John

Forks and hope: Huxley, Elspeth J.

Forlorn hope, The: Clune, Frank

Forlorn hope, The: Hall, Anna Maria

Forlorn river: Grey, Zane

Forlorn sunset: Sadleir, Michael

Form and content in English painting: Rothenstein, *Sir* William

Form and purpose of Home Rule, The: Childers, R.E.

Form and style in poetry: Ker, W.P.

Form and value in modern poetry: Blackmur, R.P.

Form in modern poetry: Read, *Sir* Herbert

Form of prayer, with thanksgiving to Almighty God, The: Hone, William

Formation of the alphabet, The: Petrie, *Sir* William Flinders

Formation of the Massachusetts constitution, The: Morison, S.E.

Formation of vegetable mould through the action of worms, The: Darwin, Charles

Former age, The: Chaucer, Geoffrey

Formidable to tyrants: Bottome, Phyllis

Forms of poetry, The: Untermeyer, Louis

Forms of things unknown, The: Read, *Sir* Herbert

Forrest House: Holmes, M.J.

Forrestal: Ingraham, J.H.

Forrigan reel, The: †Bridie, James

Fors clavigera: Ruskin, John

Forsyte saga, The: Galsworthy, John

Fort, The: Jameson, Storm

Fort Amity:(†Q), Quiller-Couch, *Sir* A.

Fort Braddock letters: Brainard, J.G.C.

Fort in the jungle, The: Wren, P.C.

Fort of the bear: Gibbons, Stella

Fort Sumter: Heyward, DuBose

Fortescue: Knowles, James Sheridan

Forth feasting: Drummond of Hawthornden, William

Fortitude: Walpole, *Sir* Hugh

Fortnight in September, The: Sherriff, R.C.

Fortnight of folly, A: Thompson, J.M.

Fortnight south of Skye: Strong, L.A.G.

Fortnightly review: Conway, Moncure Daniel

Fortress, The: Hook, T.E.

Fortress, The: Walpole, *Sir* Hugh

Fortress in the rice: Appel, Benjamin

Fortress of Quebec, 1608–1903, The: Doughty, *Sir* A.G.

Fortress of Sorrento, The: Noah, M.M.

Fortunate farewel to the most forward and noble Earle of Essex, The: Churchyard, Thomas

Fortunate foundlings, The: Haywood, *Mrs*. Eliza

Fortunate isles, The: Jonson, Ben

Fortunate lady, The: Swinnerton, Frank

Fortunate Mary, The: Porter, E.H.

Fortunate mistress, The: Defoe, Daniel

Fortunate simpleton, The: Connell, John

Fortunate term, A: Brazil, Angela

Fortunate wayfarer, The: Oppenheim, E. Phillips

Fortunatus the pessimist: Austin, Alfred

Fortune: Chaucer, Geoffrey

Fortune: Cunningham, John

Fortune and fortitude: Miller, Thomas

Fortune by land and sea: Heywood, Thomas

Fortune by land and sea: Rowley, William

Fortune heights: Dos Passos, John

Fortune hunter, The: Gilbert, *Sir* W.S.

Fortune hunter, The: Phillips, D.G.

Fortune hunter, The: Ritchie, *Mrs*. A.C.M.

Fortune my foe: Davies, Robertson

Fortune, my foe: Trease, Geoffrey

Fortune of the Republic: Emerson, R.W.

Fortunes and misfortunes of the famous Moll Flanders, The: Defoe, Daniel

Fortune's finger: Bottome, Phyllis

Fortune's fool: Sabatini, Rafael

Fortunes of Captain Blood, The: Sabatini, Rafael

Fortunes of Colonel Torlogh O'Brien, The: Le Fanu, Joseph Sheridan

Fortunes of Falstaff, The: Wilson, John Dover

Fortunes of Glencore, The: Lever, Charles

Fortunes of Harriet, The: Thirkell, Angela

Fortunes of Hector O'Halloran and his man Mark Anthony O'Toole, The: Maxwell, W.H.

Fortunes of Hugo, The: Mackail, Denis

Fortunes of Nigel, The: Scott, *Sir* Walter

Fortunes of Oliver Horn, The: Smith, F.H.

Fortunes of Perkin Warbeck, The: Shelley, Mary

Fortunes of Philippa, The: Brazil, Angela

Fortunes of Philippa Fairfax, The: Burnett, Frances Hodgson

Fortunes of Rachel, The: Hale, E.E.

Fortunes of the Colville family, The: Smedley, F.E.

Fortunes of Toby Trafford, The: Trowbridge, J.T.

Fortvnatvs: Robinson, E.A.

Forty Dartmouth poems: Eberhart, Richard

Forty favourite flowers: Nichols, Beverley

Forty four months in Germany and Turkey: Hardayal, Lala

Forty liars and other lies: (†Bill Nye), Nye, E.W.

Forty minutes later: Smith, F.H.

Forty singing seamen: Noyes, Alfred

Forty thieves, The: Colman, George, *the younger*

Forty thieves, The: Sheridan, R.B.

Forty thieves pantomime, The: Adams, Arthur H.

Forty years at Hull House: Addams, Jane

Forty years for Labrador: Grenfell, *Sir* Wilfred

Forty years of it: Whitlock, Brand

Forty years of psychic research: Garland, Hamlin

Forty years on Main Street: White, W.A.

Forty-eight short stories: Wallace, Edgar

Forty-nine: †Miller, Joaquin

Forty-nine stories: O'Hara, J.H.

'49: the gold-seeker of the Sierras: †Miller, Joaquin

Forty-niners, The: White, S.E.

XLI poems: Cummings, E.E.

42nd parallel, The: Dos Passos, John

'42 to '44: Wells, H.G.

Forward child, A: De la Mare, Walter

Forward from Babylon: Golding, Louis

Forward from Liberalism: Spender, Stephen

Forward the nation: Peattie, D.C.

Foscari: Mitford, Mary Russell

Fossett's memory: Hollis, Christopher

Fossicher, The: Glanville, Ernest

Fossie for short: Brighouse, Harold

Fossils of a future time? Turner, W.J.R.

Foster brothers, The: Payn, James

Foster-mother and fifty-four conceits, The: Armstrong, M.D.

Fotheringay and Mary Queen of Scots: †Bede, Cuthbert

Foul play: Reade, Charles

Found drowned: Phillpotts, Eden

Found floating: Crofts, F.W.

Found money: Hannay, J.O.

Found, yet lost: Roe, E.P.

Foundation Day address (Bembridge School), A: Masefield, John

Foundation of the American colonies: Smith, Goldwin

Foundation of the origin of species, The: Darwin, Charles

Foundations, The: Galsworthy, John

Foundations of a league of peace, The: Dickinson, Goldsworthy Lowes

Foundations of a national drama, The: Jones, H.A.

Foundations of aesthetics, The: Richards, I.A.

Foundations of belief, The: Balfour, A.J.

Foundations of empirical knowledge, The: Ayer, A.J.

Foundations of Indian culture: Ghose, Sri Aurobindo

Foundations of international polity, The: Angell, *Sir* Norman

Foundations of new India, The: Panikkar, K.M.

Foundations of Shakespeare's text, The: Pollard, A.W.

Foundations of sovereignty: Laski, Harold

Founder of Christendom, The: Smith, Goldwin

Founder of the house, The: Jacob, Naomi

Founders, The: Green, Paul

Founder's day: Bridges, Robert

Founders of the empire: Gibbs, *Sir* Philip

Founding of fortunes, The: Barlow, Jane

Founding of Harvard college, The: Morison, S.E.

Founding of New England, The: Adams, J.T.

Foundling, The: Heyer, Georgette

Foundling of the fens, The: Browne, Frances

Foundry, The: Halper, Albert

Foundry, The: Morley, C.D.

Fountain, The: Bryant, William Cullen

Fountain, The: Morgan, Charles

Fountain, The: O'Neill, Eugene

Fountain of Arethusa, The: Landor, Robert Eyres

Fountain of magic: †O'Connor, Frank

Fountain of youth, The: Colum, Padraic

Fountain overflows, The: †West, Rebecca

Fountain sealed, A: Besant, *Sir* Walter

Fountain sealed, A: Sedgwick, A.D.

Fountain-head, The: Dukes, Ashley

Fountaine of selfe-love, The: Jonson, Ben

Fountains in the sand: Douglas, Norman

Fountains in Trafalgar Square, The: Munro, C.K.

Fountains of Rome: Morton, H.V.

Four absentees: Heppenstall, Rayner

Four ages of poetry, The: Peacock, Thomas Love

Four and five: Hale, E.E.

Four and twenty blackbirds: Thomas, E.E.P.

Four and twenty toilers: Lucas, E.V.

Four armourers, The: †Beeding, Francis

Four ballads and a play: (†Seranus), Harrison, S.F.

Four boasting disputers of this world briefly rebuked: Pastorius, F.D.

Four chapters: Tagore, *Sir* R.

Four contemporary novelists: Cross, W.L.

Four continents, The: Sitwell, *Sir* Osbert

Four corners of the world, The: Mason, A.E.W.

Four countries: Plomer, William

Four days: Hoffe, Monckton

Four days of God: Spofford, H.E.

Four days' wonder: Milne, A.A.

Four dissertations: Hume, David

Four epistles of A.G.Bushbequius, The: Tate, Nahum

Four false weapons, The: Carr, J.D.

Four fantasies: Brighouse, Harold

Four faultless felons: Chesterton, G.K.

Four favourites: Lewis, D.B. Wyndham

Four feathers, The: Mason, A.E.W.

Four feathers, The: Sherriff, R.C.

4.50 from Paddington: Christie, Agatha

Four Forsyte stories: Galsworthy, John

Four foundlings, The: Allen, C.R.

Four French women: Dobson, Henry Austin

Four gardens: Sharp, Margery

Four generations: Jacob, Naomi

Four generations of a literary family: Hazlitt, William Carew

Four Georges, The: Thackeray, W.M.

Four Georges: a revaluation, The: Petrie, *Sir* Charles

Four ghost stories: Molesworth, *Mrs.*

Four Gospels in one story, The: Crofts, F.W.

Four great religions: Besant, *Mrs.* Annie

Four guineas: a journey through West Africa: Huxley, Elspeth J.

Four in America: Stein, Gertrude

Four in hand: Priestley, J.B.

Four Jameses, The: Deacon, W.A.

Four just men, The: Wallace, Edgar

Four last things, The: More, *Sir* Thomas

Four letters containing some arguments in proof of a Diety. To Doctor [Richard] Bentley: Newton, *Sir* Isaac

Four loves, The: Lewis, C.S.

Four Macnicols, The: Black, William

Four million, The: †Henry, O.

Four Molière comedies: †Anstey, F.

Four men, The: Belloc, Hilaire

Four necessary cases of conscience: Shepard, Thomas

Four new dialogues of the dead: Lyttelton, George *Baron*

Four of a kind: Marquand, J.P.

Four of hearts, The: †Queen, Ellery

Four of them: Moulton, E.L.

Four people: Malleson, Miles

Four plays for dancers: Yeats, W.B.

Four plays of St. Clare: Housman, Laurence

Four portraits: Quennell, P.C.

Four quartets: Eliot, T.S.

Four roads to death: Appel, Benjamin

Four saints in three acts: Stein, Gertrude

Four seasons, The: Motteux, P.A.

Four short plays: Abercrombie, Lascelles

Four songs of the Italian earth: Sitwell, *Sir* Osbert

Four sonnets to Sir P. Sidney's soul: Constable, Henry

Four sons of Aymon: Caxton, William

Four square Jane: Wallace, Edgar

Four stages of Greek religion: Murray, Gilbert

Four stories high: Clarke, Marcus

Four stragglers, The: Packard, F.L.

Four trials at Kingston: Hone, William

Four unposted letters to Catherine: Riding, Laura

Four winds: Pertwee, Roland

Four wind's farm: Molesworth, *Mrs.*

Four winds of love, The: Mackenzie, *Sir* Compton

Four wishes, The: Brontë, Charlotte

Four years, The: Binyon, Laurence

Four years: Yeats, W.B.

Foure ages of England, The: Cowley, Abraham

Foure birds of Noahs Arke: Dekker, Thomas

Foure bookes of husbandrie, collected by Conradus Heresbachius: Googe, Barnabe

Foure godly and learned treatises: Hooker, Thomas

Foure letters and certaine sonnets: especially touching Robert Greene: Harvey, Gabriel

Foure prentises of London, The: Heywood, Thomas

Foure-fould meditation of the foure last things, A: Southwell, Robert

Fourfold tradition, The: Heppenstall, Rayner

Fourscore: Grant, Robert

Fourscore years: Coulton, G.G.

14A: †Riding, Laura

Fourteen minutes: Green, H.M.

Fourteen notes: Craig, Gordon

Fourteen sonnets: Bowles, W.L.

Fourteen to one: Ward, E.S.

Fourteen years: Palmer, Nettie

Fourth Avatar, The: Isvaran, M.S.

Fourth book of Jorkens, The: Dunsany, Edward Plunkett, *Baron*

Fourth canto, The: Pound, Ezra

Fourth chamber, The: †Preedy, George

Fourth dimension, The: Vachell, H.A.

Fourth form friendship, A: Brazil, Angela

Fourth generation, The: Besant, *Sir* Walter

Fourth hundred of epygrams, newly invented, A: Heywood, John

Fourth of August, The: Wolfe, Humbert

Fourth of July breakfast and floral exhibition: Emerson, R.W.

Fourth paper presented by Major Butler, The: Williams, Roger

Fourth pig: Mitchison, Naomi

Fourth plague, The: Wallace, Edgar

Fourth queen, The: Paterson, Isabel M.

Fourth series: Harris, J.T.

Fourth wall, The: Milne, A.A.

Fourth watch, The: Cody, H.A.

Fourth watch, The: Warner, A.B.

Foveaux: Tennant, Kylie

Fowler and King's English: Coulton, G.G.

Fox Farm: Deeping, Warwick

Fox in the attic, The: Hughes, R.A.W.

Fox meditates, The: Kipling, Rudyard

Fox of Peapack, The: White, E.B.

Fox under my cloak, A: Williamson, Henry

Foxglove Manor: Buchanan, R.W.

Fox-woman, The: Long, J.L.

Fra Angelico: Pope-Hennessy, J.W.

Fra Rupert: Landor, W.S.

Fragilia Labilia: Symonds, J.A.

Fragment, A: †Bridie, James

Fragment of life, A: †Machen, Arthur

Fragment on government, A: Bentham, Jeremy

Fragment on Mackintosh, A: Mill, James

Fragment on the Irish Roman Catholic Church, A: Smith, Sydney

Fragmenta Aurea: Suckling, *Sir* John

Fragmentary thoughts: Parkes, *Sir* Henry

Fragments from an unwritten autobiography: Van Vechten, Carl

Fragments of a play: Wiggin, Kate

Fragments of ancient poetry collected in the Highlands of Scotland: Macpherson, James

Fragments of autobiography: Hughes, Thomas

Fragments of prose and poetry: Myers, F.W.H.

Fragments on ethical subjects: Grote, George

Framework of Home Rule, The: Childers, Erskine

Framley Parsonage: Trollope, Anthony

France: Kipling, Rudyard

France: Morgan, *Lady* Sydney

France and the European settlement: Lippmann, Walter

France at war: Kipling, Rudyard

France at war: Maugham, Somerset

France in 1829–30: Morgan, *Lady* Sydney

France, in the lives of her great men: James, G.P.R.

France painted to the life: Heylyn, Peter

Francesca da Rimini: Boker, G.H.

Francesca Da Rimini: Crawford, F. Marion

Francesca of Rimini: Hardy, A.S.

Francesco Carrara: Landon, L.E.M.

Franchise affair, The: (†Josephine Tey), Mackintosh, Elizabeth

Francis and Riversdale Grenfell: Buchan, John

Francis Bacon: Rothenstein, *Sir* John

Francis Berrian: Flint, Timothy

Francis Dana: Dana, R.H. *junior*

Francis Drake, a tragedy of the sea: Mitchell, S.W.

Francis of Assisi: Oliphant, Margaret

Francis Place: Ervine, St. John

Francis the first: Kemble, F.A.

Francis Thompson and Wilfred Meynell: Meynell, Viola

Francis Waldeaux: Davis, Rebecca

François Mauriac, novelist and moralist: Iyengar, K.R. Srinivasa

François Villon: Lewis, D.B. Wyndham

Franconian fancy, A: Bangs, J.K.

Franco-Prussian war in a nutshell, The: (†Eli Perkins), Landon, Melville

Frank: Edgeworth, Maria

Frank Fairleigh: Smedley, F.E.

Frank Forester and his friends: Herbert, H.W.

Frank Forester's fish and fishing: Herbert, H.W.

Frank Forester's fugitive sporting sketches: Herbert, H.W.

Frank Forester's horse and horsemanship of the United States: Herbert, H.W.

Frank Freeman's barber shop: Hall, B.R.

Frank Hilton: Grant, James

Frank Miller of Mission Inn: Gale, Zona

Frank Rivers: Ingraham, J.H.

Frank Sinclair's wife: Riddell, *Mrs.* J.H.

Frank Swinnerton: Bennett, Arnold

Frank Wilmot (Furnley Maurice), Palmer, E.V.

Frankenstein: Shelley, Mary

Frankie and Johnnie: Levin, Meyer

Franklin Evans: Whitman, Walt

Franklin in France: Hale, E.E.

Franklin Winslow Kane: Sedgwick, A.D.

Frank's debt: Yonge, Charlotte M.

Frans Hals: Lucas, E.V.

Franz Liszt: Huneker, J.G.

Fraternity: Galsworthy, John

Fraud detected: Swift, Jonathan

Frauds: Aldington, Richard

Fräulein Schmidt and Mr. Anstruther: Russell, E.M.

Freaks, The: Pinero, *Sir* A.W.

Freaks of fortune: Jones, J.B.

Freaks of Mayfair, The: Benson, E.F.

Freckles: Stratton-Porter, Gene

Fred and the gorillas: Miller, Thomas

Fred Leicester: Rowe, Richard

Fred Travis, A.B.: †Taffrail

Frederica: Heyer, Georgette

Frederick Baron Corvo: Symons, A.J.A.

Frederick Douglass: Chestnutt, C.W.

Frederick Douglass: Washington, B.T.

Frederick, Duke of Brunswick-Lunenburgh: Haywood, *Mrs.* Eliza

Frederick Locker-Lampson: Birrell, Augustine

Frederick York Powell: Elton, Oliver

Fredolfo: Maturin, C.R.

Free: Dreiser, Theodore

Free address to Protestant Dissenters as such, A: Priestley, Joseph

Free air: Lewis, H.S.

Free and easy land: Clune, Frank

Free and offenceles justification of Andromeda liberata, A: Chapman, George

Free company presents, The: Boyd, James

Free discussion on the doctrines of materialism, &c., A: Priestley, Joseph

Free enquiry into the nature and origin of evil, A: Jenyns, Soame

Free fishers, The: Buchan, John

Free house!, A: Sitwell, *Sir* Osbert

Free Joe: Harris, J.C.

Free Lances, The: Reid, T.M.

Free man, The: Richter, Conrad

Free opinions freely expressed: †Corelli, Marie

Free press, The: Belloc, Hilaire

Free society, The: Murry, John Middleton

Free State, The: Brogan, *Sir* Denis

Free thought and official propaganda: Russell, Bertrand

Free thoughts on faith: Hill, Aaron

Free thoughts on public affairs: or advice to a patriot: Hazlitt, William

Free thoughts on the proceedings of the Continental Congress, held at Philadelphia: Seabury, Samuel

Free wheeling: Nash, Ogden

Freedman's book, The: Child, L.M.

Freedom: Cannan, Gilbert

Freedom: Glaspell, Susan

Freedom: Sutro, Alfred

Freedom and culture: Dewey, John

Freedom and culture: Radhakrishan, Sarvepalli

Freedom and fellowship in religion: Alcott, A.B.

Freedom and organization, 1814–1914: Russell, Bertrand

Freedom and responsibility in the American way of life: Becker, C.L.

Freedom, farewell! Bentley, Phyllis

Freedom first and last: Krishnamurti, Jiddu

Freedom in contemporary society: Morison, S.E.

Freedom is the right to choose: MacLeish, Archibald

Freedom, love and truth: Inge, W.R.

Freedom, loyalty, dissent: Commager, H.S.

Freedom of nations and of men, The: Temple, William

Freedom of the parish: Grigson, Geoffrey

Freedom Road: Fast, Howard M.

Freedom's plow: Hughes, J.L.

Freeholder's political catechism, The: Bolingbroke, Henry St. John

Freelands, The: Galsworthy, John

Freeman, The: Glasgow, Ellen

Freemantle: Ingraham, J.H.

Freethinker, The: Philips, Ambrose

Free-thinkers:Winchilsea, Anne, *Countess of*

Free-trader, The: Ingraham, J.H.

French ambassador at the court of Charles II, A: Jusserand, Jean

French art: Brownell, W.C.

French dramatists of the nineteenth century: Matthews, J.B.

French Eton, A: Arnold, Matthew

French faith represented in the present state of Dunkirk, The: Steele, *Sir* Richard

French for love: Steen, Marguerite

French girls are vicious: Farrell, James

French humorists, The: Besant, *Sir* Walter

French in the West Indies, The: Roberts, W. Adolphe

French leave: Somerville, Edith

French leave: Wodehouse, P.G.

French leaves: Lucas, E.V.

French Liberal thought in the eighteenth century: Martin, B.K.

French life in letters: Molesworth, *Mrs.*

French literature: Babbitt, Irving

French lyrics: Saintsbury, G.E.B.

French nation, The: Brogan, *Sir* Denis

French of Paris, The: Huxley, Aldous

French personalities and problems: Brogan, *Sir* Denis

French poets and novelists: James, Henry

French powder mystery, The: †Queen, Ellery

French profiles: Gosse, *Sir* Edmund

French Renaissance in England, The: Lee, *Sir* Sidney

French retreat from Moscow, The: Stanhope, Philip, *Earl*

French Revolution, The: Belloc, Hilaire

French Revolution, The: Blake, William

French Revolution, The: Carlyle, Thomas

French Revolution and English literature, The: Dowden, Edward

French Revolution of 1848, The: English, T.D.

French Romantics' knowledge of English literature, The: Partridge, Eric

French school at Middlebury, The: Canfield, Dorothy

French self instructor, The: Reynolds, G.

French set, The: Rothenstein, *Sir* William

French strikes oil: Crofts, F.W.

French studies and reviews: Aldington, Richard

French traits: Brownell, W.C.

French ways and their meaning: Wharton, Edith

French without tears: Rattigan, Terence

French women of letters: Kavanagh, Julia

Frenchman must die, A: Boyle, Kay

Frenchman's Creek: Du Maurier, Daphne

Frenzied fiction: Leacock, Stephen

Frescoes: dramatic sketches: †Ouida

Frescoes for Mr. Rockefeller's city: MacLeish, Archibald

Frescoes from buried temples: Bottomley, Gordon

Fresh air: Warner, A.B.

Fresh fields: Burroughs, John

Fresh fields: †Novello, Ivor

Fresh gleanings: Mitchell, D.G.

Fresh hearts that failed three thousand years ago: Lowell, Robert

Freston Tower: Cobbold, Richard

Freud and the crisis of our culture: Trilling, Lionel

Frey and his wife: Hewlett, Maurice

Friar's lantern: Coulton, G.G.

Friday mornings: Nicolson, Hon. *Sir* Harold

Friday nights: Garnett, Edward

Friday's business: Baring, Maurice

Friday's child: Heyer, Georgette

Friend of man, The: Cobbe, F.P.

Friend of Shelley, The: Massingham, Harold

Friend Olivia: Barr, A.E.H.

Friendly acres: McArthur, Peter

Friendly Arctic, The: Stefansson, V.

Friendly check from a kind relation, A: Wise, John

Friendly four, The: †Connor, Ralph

Friendly Joey: Molesworth, *Mrs.*

Friendly relations, Langley, Noel

Friendly road, The: Baker, R.S.

Friendly tree, The: Day-Lewis, C.

Friends: Farjeon, Herbert

Friends: Gibson, Wilfred

Friends, The: Hall, J.N.

Friends: a duet: Ward, E.S.

Friends and acquaintances: Rowe, Richard

Friends and enemies: Mitchison, Naomi

Friends and relations: Bowen, E.D.C.

Friends and relations: Ervine, St. John

Friends apart: Toynbee, Philip

Friends, foes and foreigners: Lockhart, *Sir* Robert Bruce

Friends in council: Helps, *Sir* Arthur

Friends in feathers: Stratton-Porter, Gene

Friends of the swallow: Seymour, W.K.

Friendship: Lecky, W.E.

Friendship: †Ouida

Friendship improv'd: Hopkins, Charles

Friendship in fashion: Otway, Thomas

Friendship of art, The: Carman, Bliss

Friendship village: Gale, Zona

Friendship village love stories: Gale, Zona

Friendship's garland: Arnold, Matthew

Frightened lady, The: Wallace, Edgar

Fringes of the fleet: Kipling, Rudyard

Fringilla: Blackmore, *Sir* R.D.

Frisky Mrs. Johnson, The: Fitch, C.W.

Frithjof and Ingebjorg: Sladen, D.B.W.

Frobishers, The: Baring-Gould, Sabine

Frog, The: (†Ian Hay), Beith, *Sir* John Hay

Frolic lady: Mais, S.P.B.

Frolic wind: Pryce, Richard

Frolick to Horn-Fair, A: Ward, Edward

From a college window: Benson, A.C.

From a Cornish window: Quiller-Couch, *Sir* Arthur

From a garden in the Antipodes: †Bethell, M.U.

From a Paris garret: Le Gallienne, Richard

From a Paris scrapbook: Le Gallienne, Richard

From a view to a death: Powell, Anthony

From a writer's notebook: Brooks, Van Wyck

From an antique land: Huxley, *Sir* Julian

From an old house: Hergesheimer, Joseph

From an unknown isle: Drinkwater, John

From another world: Untermeyer, Louis

From Bapaume to Passchendaele: Gibbs, *Sir* Philip

From bed to worse: Benchley, Robert

From boundary-rider to Prime Minister: Sladen, D.B.W.

From cabin boy to archbishop: Leslie, *Sir* J.R. Shane

From Cairo to Soudan: Traill, H.D.

From chaos to control: Angell, *Sir* Norman

From city unto sea: Hardy, W.G.

From Connaught to Chicago: Hannay, J.O.

From death to life: Kingsley, Charles

From death to morning: Wolfe, T.C.

From dusk till dawn: Street, A.G.

From dusk to dawn: Maltby, H.F.

From exile: Payn, James

From feathers to iron: Day-Lewis, C.

From friend to friend: Buck, Pearl

From Grave to Gay: Strachey, John St. Loe

From Henry V to Hamlet: Barker, Harley Granville

From inland: Ford, Ford Madox

From jest to earnest: Roe, E.P.

From Jordan's delight: Blackmur, R.P.

From king to king: Dickinson, G.L.

From Land to Lindbergh: Kingston, G.A.

From London far: (†Michael Innes), Stewart, J.I.M.

From man to man, or perhaps only: Schreiner, Olive

From many times and lands: Lucas, F.L.

From Mimosa land: Slater, F.C.

From Minas to the Wotan line: MacMechan, A.M.

From my arm-chair: Longfellow, H.W.

From my experience: Bromfield, Louis

From now on: Packard, F.L.

From Olympus to the Styx: Lucas, F.L.

From one generation to another: †Merriman, Seton

From pillar to post: Bangs, J.K.

From Ponkapog to Pesth: Aldrich, T.B.

From Quebec to Piccadilly: Willson, H.B.

From range to sea: (†Donald Barr), Barrett, C.L.

From Rousseau to Proust: Ellis, Havelock

From rung to rung: Oxley, J.M.

From St. Francis to Dante: Coulton, G.G.

From sand hill to pine: Harte, Bret

From Sanskrit to Brazil: Partridge, Eric

From sea to sea: Kipling, Rudyard

From selection to city: †Rudd, Steele

From Shakespeare to O. Henry: Mais, S.P.B.

From Shakespeare to Pope: Gosse, *Sir* Edmund

From small beginnings: Andrade, E.N. da Costa

From snow to snow: Frost, Robert

From stores of memory: Bacheller, Irving

From Sunset Ridge: Howe, Julia Ward

From sunset to dawn: Ogilvie, W.H.

From the angle of 88: Phillpotts, Eden

From the angle of seventeen: Phillpotts, Eden

From the book of myths: Carman, Bliss

From the book of valentines: Carman, Bliss

From the eastern sea: Noguchi, Yone

From the easy chair: Curtis, G.W.

From the green book of the bards: Carman, Bliss

From the ground up: Mumford, Lewis

From the heart of the hills: Scollard, Clinton

From the hidden way: Cabell, James Branch

From the hills of dream: †Macleod, Fiona

From the isles: Ficke, Arthur

From the land of dreams: Todhunter, John

From the League to U.N.: Murray, Gilbert

From the life: Bottome, Phyllis

From the life: O'Higgins, H.J.

From the lips of the sea: Scollard, Clinton

From the log of the Velsa: Bennett, Arnold

From the Maori Sea: Mackay, Jessie

From the oak to the olive: Howe, Julia Ward

From the other side: Fuller, H.B.

From the outposts: Gouldsbury, H.C.

From the shadow of the mountain: my post-meridian years: Brooks, Van Wyck

From the Shiffolds: Trevelyan, R.C.

From the soul's observatory: Logan, J.D.

From the South of France: Janvier, T.A.

From the South Seas: Mead, Margaret

From the terrace: O'Hara, J.H.

From the vasty deep: Lowndes, M.A.

From Toulouse-Lautrec to Ropin: Symons, Arthur

From Virgil to Milton: Bowra, Sir Maurice

From war to war: Graham, Stephen

From Waterloo to the Peninsula: Sala, G.A.H.

Fronded isle, A: Lucas, E.V.

Front door key, The: Brophy, John

Front line, The: Montague, C.E.

Front lines: Ewart, E.A.

Front page, The: Hecht, Ben

Front yard, The: Woolson, C.F.

Frontier: Kantor, Mackinlay

Frontier: Turnbull, S.C.P.

Frontier forsaken: Mason, R.A.K.

Frontier mystery, A: Mitford, Bertram

Frontiers, The: Strachey, John

Frontiers and wars: Churchill, Sir Winston

Frontiers of American culture: Adams, J.T.

Frontiers of criticism, The: Eliot, T.S.

Frontiersman, The: Cody, H.A.

Frontiersman, The: †Craddock, C.E.

Frost at morning: Seymour, Beatrice Kean

Frozen assets: Wodehouse, P.G.

Frozen deep, The: Collins, Wilkie

Frozen earth, The: Holtby, Winifred

Frozen ocean, The: Meynell, Viola

Frozen pirate, The: Russell, W.C.

Frugal housewife, The: Child, L.M.

Fruit of tree, The: Wharton, Edith

Fruit stoners, being the adventures of Maria among the fruit stoners, The: Blackwood, Algernon

Fruitefull and godly treatise expressing the right institution of the Sacraments, A: Tyndale, William

Fruitful vine, The: Hichens, Robert

Fruitfull and comfortable exhortation anent death: Melville, James

Fruit-gathering: Tagore, Sir R.

Fruitless enquiry, The: Haywood, Mrs. Eliza

Fruits of silence: Fausset, Hugh

Fruits of the earth: Grove, F.P.

Fruits of the spirit, The: Underhill, Evelyn

Fruits of victory, The: Angell, Sir Norman

Fruteful and pleasaunt work of the newe yle called Utopia translated into Englyshe by Raphe Robynson, A: More, Sir Thomas

Fudge doings: Mitchell, D.G.

Fudge family in Paris, The: Moore, Thomas

Fudges in England, The: Moore, Thomas

Fuel: Gibson, W.W.

Fuel for the flame: Waugh, Alec

Fugitive, The: Bridges, Roy

Fugitive, The: Galsworthy, John

Fugitive, The: Tagore, Sir R.

Fugitive Anne: Praed, Mrs. C.

Fugitive essays: Royce, Josiah

Fugitive pieces: Byron, Lord G.G.

Fugitive pieces: Knowles, J.S.

Fugitive pieces: Riley, J.W.

Fugitive pieces in verse and prose: Walpole, Horace

Fugitive poetry: Willis, N.P.

Fugitive verses: Baillie, Joanna

Fugitives: Sabatini, Rafael

Fugitives from fortune: Turner, E.S.

Fugitive's return, The: Glaspell, Susan

Fugue in time: Godden, Rumer

Fuji from Hampstead Heath: Komai, Gonnosuké

Full account of the present state of the Ottoman Empire, A: Hill, Aaron

Full and authentick account of Stephen Duck, the Wiltshire poet, A: Spence, Joseph

Full and true account of the wonderful mission of Earl Lavender, A: Davidson, John

Full annals of the Revolution in France: Hone, William

Full circle: Blackwood, Algernon

Full circle: Jameson, Storm

Full circle: †Mordaunt, Elinor

Full enjoyment: Herbert, *Sir* A.P.

Full house: †Novello, Ivor

Full meridian: Jacob, Naomi

Full moon: Williams, Emlyn

Full moon: Wodehouse, P.G.

Full moon in March, A: Yeats, W.B.

Full relation of two journeys: the one into the main-land of France. The other into some of the adjacent Ilands, A: Heylyn, Peter

Full vindication of the measures of the Congress, A: Hamilton, Alexander

Fumifugium: Evelyn, John

Fun and games: Greenwood, Walter

Fun and games; how to win at almost anything: †Spade, Mark

Fun jottings: Willis, N.P.

Fun of the fair, The: Phillpotts, Eden

Fun to be free: Hecht, Ben

Function of criticism, The: Winters, Yvor

Function of reason, The: Whitehead, A.N.

Fundamental theory: Eddington, *Sir* Arthur

Fundamentals of good writing: Brooks, Cleanth

Fundamentals of good writing: Warren, Robert Penn

Funeral, The: Steele, *Sir* Richard

Funeral elegie, upon King James, An: Heywood, Thomas

Funeral furniture and stone and metal vases: Petrie, *Sir* William Flindes

Funeral of Adam Willis Wagnalls: Markham, Edwin

Funeral poems: Tate, Nahum

Funerall elegie in memory of Lancelot, Bishop of Winchester, A: Taylor, John

Funerall elegie upon the death of B. Jonson, poet, A: Taylor, John

Funerall elegie, upon the death of Henry, Prince of Wales, A: Heywood, Thomas

Funerall idyll, A: Oldmixon, John

Funerall poeme, A. Upon the death of Sir Francis Vere, Knight: Tourneur, Cyril

Funerall poeme uppon the death of the Earle of Devonshyre: Daniel, Samuel

Funerall sermon, preached at the obsequies of the Right Honourable and most vertuous lady, the Lady Frances, Countesse of Carbery, A: Taylor, Jeremy

Funerals of the Quakers, The: Montagu, Basil

Funk-hole, The: Brighouse, Harold

Funny: Turner, E.S.

Funny face: Gershwin, Ira

Funny farmyard: Slessor, Kenneth

Funny figures: †Bede, Cuthbert

Funny pieces: Leacock, Stephen

Fur masters, The: Sullivan, Alan

Furioso, The: Bacon, Leonard

Furmetary, The: King, William

Furnace, The: Macaulay, *Dame* Rose

Furnace, The: Young, Francis Brett

Furness Abbey and its neighbourhood: Payn, James

Furniture of a woman's mind, The: Swift, Jonathan

Further adventures of Jimmy Dale, The: Packard, F.L.

Further adventures of Mr. Verdant Green, The: †Bede, Cuthbert

Further chronicles of Avonlea: Montgomery, L.M.

Further confessions of a story writer: Gallico, Paul

Further considerations concerning raising the value of money: Locke, John

Further experiences of an Irish R.M.: Somerville, E.

Further explication of the doctrine of original sin, A: Taylor, Jeremy

Further explorations: Knights, L.C.

Further fables for our time: Thurber, James

Further foolishness: Leacock, Stephen

Further nonsense verse: †Carroll, Lewis

Further papers on Dante: Sayers, Dorothy

Further particulars regarding the works of Shakespeare: Collier, John Payne

Further range, A: Frost, Robert

Further records: Kemble, Fanny

Further reminiscences: Baring-Gould, Sabine

Further reminiscences of a South African pioneer: Scully, W.C.

Further stories of Ireland: Lover, Samuel

Further studies in a dying culture: †Caudwell, Christopher

Furthermore: Runyon, Damon

Fury, The: Timms, E.V.

Furys, The: Hanley, James

Furze bloom: Baring-Gould, Sabine

Fusilier Bluff: Vulliamy, C.E.

Future Australian race, The: Clarke, Marcus

Future comes, The: Beard, C.A.

Future in America, The: Wells, H.G.

Future in education, The: Livingstone, *Sir* Richard

Future indefinite: Coward, Noel

Future of architecture, The: Wright, Frank Lloyd

Future of Constantinople, The: Woolf, Leonard

Future of English poetry, The: Gosse, *Sir* Edmund

Future of industrial design, The: Read, *Sir* Herbert

Future of infantry, The: Liddell Hart, B.

Future of Islam, The: Blunt, Wilfred

Future of life, The: Joad, C.E.M.

Future of local government, The: Cole, G.D.H.

Future of our poetry, The: Dalton, A.C.

Future of political science in America, The: Shaw, G.B.

Future of sculpture, The: Gill, Eric

Future of South East Asia: Panikkar, K.M.

Future of the American negro, The: Washington, B.T.

Future of the covenant, The: Dickinson, G.L.

Future of the English-speaking world: Nicolson, *Hon. Sir* Harold

Future of the Liberal College, The: Foerster, Norman

Future of the press, The: Ervine, St.John

Future of the social studies, The: Michener, J.A.

Future of the theatre, The: Palmer, J.L.

Future perfect: Bryant, *Sir* Arthur

Future poetry, The: Ghose, Sri Aurobindo

Futurist fifteen: Pain, B.E.O.

Fuzzypeg goes to school: Uttley, Alison

Fyfte eglog of Alexandre Barclay of the cytezen and uplondyshman, The: Barclay, Alexander

G

G.B.S. a postscript: Pearson, Hesketh

G.F.Watts: Chesterton, G.K.

G.T.T.: Hale, E.E.

Gabriel Conroy: Harte, Bret

Gabriel Samara: Oppenheim, E.Phillips

Gabriel Tolliver: Harris, Joel Chandler

Gabrielle de Bergerac: James, H.

Gad's hill Gazette, The: Dickens, Charles

Gai saber: Hewlett, Maurice

Gaieties and gravities: Smith, Horatio

Gaily, gaily: Hecht, Ben

Gaily the troubadour: Macartney, Frederick

Gala-days: Dodge, M.A.

Galahad at Blandings: Wodehouse, P.G.

Galahad, enough of his life to explain his reputation: Erskine, John

Galahad Jones: Adams, Arthur H.

Galatea: Cain, James

Galaxy: Waugh, Alec

Galaxy of fathers, A: Swinnerton, F.A.

Gale Middleton: Smith, Horatio

Gale warning: †Yates, Dornford

Gallant lady: Widdemer, Margaret

Gallantry: Cabell, James Branch

Gallants, The: Beck, *Mrs.* Lily

Gallathea: Lyly, John

Gallegher: Davis, R.H.

Gallery, A: Guedalla, Philip

Gallery of children, A: Milne, A.A.

Gallery of illustrious literary characters, A: Maginn, William

Gallery of women, A: Dreiser, Theodore

Gallions Reach: Tomlinson, H.M.

Gallipoli: Masefield, John

Gallipoli memories: Mackenzie, *Sir* Compton

Galloping shoes: Ogilvie, W.H.

Galloping wheels: Lawson, Will

Gallow's Foot: Gielgud, Val

Gallows glorious: Gow, Ronald

Gallows of chance, The: Oppenheim, E.Phillips

Gallows-cross, The: Palmer, H.E.

Gallybird: Kaye-Smith, Shiela

Gamaliel Bradford: Mencken, H.L.

Game, The: Brighouse, Harold

Game, The: London, Jack

Game and play of the chess, The (trn.): Caxton, William

Game and the candle, The: Broughton, Rhoda

Game and the candle, The: Kennedy, Margaret

Game at chesse, A: Middleton, Thomas

Game of euchre campared to a game of life: Saxe, J.G.

Game of liberty, The: Oppenheim, E.Phillips

Game of logic, The: †Carroll, Lewis

Game of the season, The: De Selincourt, Hugh

Gamekeeper at home, The: Jefferies, Richard

Games and pastimes of the Maoris: Best, Elsdon

Gamesmanship: Potter, Stephen

Gamester, The: Sabatini, Rafael

Gamester, The: Shirley, James

Gammer Gurton's famous histories of Sir Guy of Warwick, Sir Bevis of Hampton: Thoms, W.J.

Gammer Gurton's garland: Ritson, Joseph

Gammer Gurton's pleasant stories of patient Grissel, the Princess Rosetta: Thoms, W.J.

Ganconagh, John Sherman, and Dhoya: Yeats, W.B.

Gander and his geese, A: Housman, Laurence

Gandhi and Gandhism: Gupta, Nagendranath

Gandhi: the master: Munshi, K.M.

Gandhi-Jinnah talks: Gandhi, M.K.

Gandle follows his nose: Broun, Heywood

Ganga Singh of Bikaner: Panikkar, K.M.

Gap in the curtain, The: Buchan, John

Gap of brightness, The: Higgins, F.R.

Garbage man, a parade with shouting, The: Dos Passos, John

Garden, The: Sackville-West, Victoria

Garden, The: Strong, L.A.G.

Garden, The: Tagore, *Sir* R.

Garden behind the moon, The: Pyle, Howard

Garden by the sea, A: Reid, Forrest

Garden of Allah, The: Hichens, Robert

Garden of contentment, The: †Mordaunt, Elinor

Garden of dreams, The: Cawein, Madison

Garden of folly, The: Leacock, Stephen

Garden of survival, The: Blackwood, Algernon

Garden of vision, The: Beck, *Mrs.* Lily

Garden open today: Nichols, Beverley

Garden party, A: Jones, H.A.

Garden party, The: Mansfield, Katherine

Garden poems: Nesbit, E.

Garden revisited, A: Lehmann, John

Garden secrets: Marston, P.B.

Garden that I love, The: Austin, Alfred

Garden to the sea, The: Toynbee, Philip

Gardenage: Grigson, Geoffrey

Gardener, The: Tagore, *Sir* R.

Gardener, The: Wheelock, J.H.

Gardeners and astronomers: Sitwell, Edith

Gardener's daughter, The: Tennyson, Alfred *Lord*

Gardener's world, The: Krutch, J.W.

Gardener's year, A: Haggard, *Sir* Henry Rider

Gardenia, The: Hichens, Robert

Gardening by myself: Warner, A.B.

Garden-land: Chambers, R.W.

Gardens of Aphrodite, The: Saltus, E.E.

Gardens of South Africa: Fairbridge, Dorothea

Gardens of this world: Fuller, H.B.

Gareth and Linette: Tennyson, Alfred *Lord*

Gargoyles: Hecht, Ben

Garibaldi: Braddon, M.E.

Garibaldi: Davenport, Marcia

Garibaldi: Drinkwater, John

Garibaldi and the making of Italy: Trevelyan, G.M.

Garibaldi and the thousand: Trevelyan, G.M.

Garibaldi rebuked by one of his best friends: Reid, T.M.

Garibaldi's defence of the Roman Republic: Trevelyan, G.M.

Garland for girls, A: Alcott, Louisa M.

Garland from the vernacular, A: Skinner, John

Garland in the wind: Webster, M.M.

Garland of country song, A: Baring-Gould, Sabine

Garland of good will, The: Deloney, Thomas

Garland of Rachel, The: Bridges, Robert

Garland of straw, A: Warner, Sylvia Townsend

Garland to Sylvia, A: Mackaye, Percy

Garnered sheaves: Frazer, *Sir* James

Garnered sheaves: Holland, J.G.

Garnet's ghost: Oldham, John

Garrotters, The: Howells, W.D.

Garry Owen: Edgeworth, Maria

Garryowen sketches, The: Finn, Edmund

Garside's career: Brighouse, Harold

Gary schools, The: Bourne, Randolph

Gas light: Hamilton, Patrick

Gas-house McGinty: Farrell, James

Gaslight and daylight: Sala, G.A.H.

Gasology: English, T.D.

Gaspar the Gaucho: Reid, T.M.

Gaspard de Coligny: Besant, *Sir* Walter

Gaspards of Pine Croft, The: †Connor, Ralph

Gaston de Blondeville: Radcliffe, *Mrs.* Ann

Gaston de Foix: Baring, Maurice

Gaston de Latour: Pater, Walter

Gate, The: Day-Lewis, C.

Gate of death, The: Benson, A.C.

Gate of flowers, A: O'Hagan, Thomas

Gate of life, The: Inge, W.R.

Gate of peace, The: Carman, Bliss

Gate of Smaragdus, The: Bottomley, Gordon

Gates between, The: Ward, E.S.

Gates ajar, The: Ward, E.S.

Gates of Bannerdale, The: Trease, Geoffrey

Gates of birth: Bridges, Roy

Gates of doom, The: Sabatini, Rafael

Gates of horn: Levin, Harry

Gates of paradise, The: Hichens, Robert

Gates of Paradise: Markham, Edwin

Gates of the Caribbean, The: McFee, William

Gates of the compass, The: Hillyer, Robert

Gates of wrath, The: Bennett, Arnold

Gateways to literature: Matthews, J.B.

Gathered leaves: Coleridge, Mary

Gathered leaves: Smedley, F.E.

Gathered songs: Swinburne, A.C.

Gathering of Brother Hilarius, The: †Fairless, Michael

Gathering of eagles: Gielgud, Val

Gathering of fugitives, A: Trilling, Lionel

Gathering of the West, The: Galt, John

Gathering storm, The: Empson, William

Gatherings from Spain: Ford, Richard

Gaudier-Bzreska: Pound, Ezra

Gaudy night: Sayers, Dorothy

Gauguin, 1848–1903: Read, *Sir* Herbert

Gaulantus: Bannister, N.H.

Gaunt stranger, The: Wallace, Edgar

Gaut Gurley: Thompson, D.P.

Gautama the Buddha: Radhakrishan, Sarvepalli

Gautama the enlightened: Masefield, John

Gauvinier takes to bowls: De Selincourt, Hugh

Gaverocks, The: Baring-Gould, Sabine

Gay and melancholy flux, The: Saroyan, William

Gay crusader, The: †Connor, Ralph

Gay deceivers, The: Colman, George, *the younger*

Gay galliard, The: Irwin, Margaret

Gay genius, The: Lin Yu-T'ang

Gay hunter: Mitchell, J.L.

Gay life: †Delafield, E.M.

Gay Lord Quex, The: Pinero, *Sir* A.W.

Gay rebellion, The: Chambers, R.W.

Gay-neck: the story of a pigeon: Mukherji, D.G.

Gay's the word: †Novello, Ivor

Gazella: Cloete, E.F.S.G.

Gazelles, The: Moore, T.S.

Gebir: Landor, W.S.

Gehenna: Aiken, Conrad

Gemel in London: Agate, J.E.

Gemini: Collier, John

Gems: Croly, George

Gems: Wilcox, E.W.

Gems of English art of this century: Palgrave, F.T.

Genealogy: Webster, Noah

Genealogy of the family of Benson: Benson, A.C.

General, The: Boyle, Roger

General, The: Forester, C.S.

General Besserley's puzzle box: Oppenheim, E.Phillips

General Bounce: Whyte-Melville, G.J.

General Buntop's miracle: Armstrong, M.D.

General cargo: Herbert, *Sir* A.P.

General Crack: †Preedy, George

General description of Nova Scotia, A: Haliburton, T.C.

General Election, and after, The: Cole, M.I.

General epistles, The: Moffatt, James

General Gage's confession: Freneau, Philip

General Gage's soliloquy: Freneau, Philip

General Grant: an estimate: Arnold, Matthew

General history of Europe from November 1688 to July 1690, The: Phillips, John

General history of Ireland from the earliest accounts to those of the 12th century: O'Halloran, Sylvester

General history of quadrupeds, A: Bewick, Thomas

General history of the science and practice of music: Burney, *Dr*. Charles

General impressions: †Delafield, E.M.

General John Regan: Hannay, J.O.

General report on inclosures: Young, Arthur

General Smuts: Millin, Sarah Gertrude

General theory of employment, interest and money, The: Keynes, John Maynard

General theory of relativity: Einstein, Albert

General view of the African slave-trade, A: Roscoe, William

General Washington and the water witch: Fast, Howard M.

General William Booth enters into Heaven: Lindsay, N.V.

Generall historie of Virginia, New-England, and the Summer Isles, The: Smith, John

Generall rehearsall of warres, A: Churchyard, Thomas

Generally speaking: Chesterton, G.K.

Generals and generalship: Wavell, A.P. *1st Earl*

General's lady, The: Forbes, Esther

Generation without farewell: Boyle, Kay

Generic images: Galton, *Sir* Francis

Generous heart, The: Fearing Kenneth

Genesis: Wellesley, D.V.

Genesis of Christian art, The: O'Hagan, Thomas

Genesis of Religion, The: Murray, Margaret

Geneva: Shaw, G.B.

Genevra's money: Lucas, E.V.

Genial idiot, The: Bangs, J.K.

Genius, The: Colman, George, *the elder*

Genius, The: Dreiser, Theodore

Genius: Stedman, E.C.

Genius and character of Emerson, The: Alcott, A.B.

Genius and morality: a curious but sincere appreciation of Poe: Thompson, J.M.

Genius and the goddess, The: Huxley, Aldous

Genius and the mobocracy: Wright, Frank Lloyd

Genius Loci: †Lee, Vernon

Genius of America, The: Sherman, S.P.

Genius of England: Massingham, Harold

Genius of English poetry, The: Temple, William

Genius of Judaism: D'Israeli, Isaac

Genius of nonsense, The: Colman, George, *the elder*

Genius of oblivion, The: Hale, S.J.B.

Genius of Spain, The: Madariaga, Salvador de

Genius of Spenser, The: Courthorpe, W.J.

Genius of style, The: Brownell, William C.

Genius of the Church of England, The: Temple, William

Genius of the Thames, The: Peacock, Thomas Love

Genoveva: Trench, R.C.

Genteel tradition at bay, The: Santayana, George

Gentilesse: Chaucer, Geoffrey

Gentle Annie: Kantor, Mackinlay

Gentle art of lexicography, The: Partridge, Eric

Gentle art of making enemies, The: Whistler, James McNeill

Gentle art of theatre-going, The: Drinkwater, John

Gentle art of tramping: Graham, Stephen

Gentle assassin, The: Spring, Howard

Gentle Caesar: Sitwell, *Sir* Osbert

Gentle craft, The: Deloney, Thomas

Gentle grafter, The: †Henry, O.

Gentle Greaves: Raymond, Ernest

Gentle Julia: Tarkington, Booth

Gentle knight of old Brandenburg, A: Major, Charles

Gentle lover, The: Reid, Forrest

Gentle people, The: Shaw, Irwin

Gentle powers, The: Gibbons, S.D.

Gentle shepherd, The: Ramsay, Allan

Gentleman, The: Calvert, G.H.

Gentleman, The: Colman, George, *the elder*

Gentleman dancing-master, The: Wycherley, William

Gentleman from Indiana, The: Tarkington, Booth

Gentleman in black, The: Gilbert, *Sir* W.S.

Gentleman in black, The: Lemon, Mark

Gentleman in grey, The: Mackenzie, *Sir* Compton

Gentleman of France, A: Weyman, Stanley

Gentleman of Japan and a lady, A: Long, J.L.

Gentleman of leisure, A: Fawcett, Edgar

Gentleman of leisure, The: Mottram, R.H.

Gentleman of leisure, A: Wodehouse, P.G.

Gentleman of Lyons, The: Bannister, N.H.

Gentleman of Stratford: Brophy, John

Gentleman of the old school, The: James, G.P.R.

Gentleman of the party, The: Street, A.G.

Gentleman of Venice, The: Shirley, James

Gentleman usher, The: Chapman, George

Gentleman vagabond, A: Smith, F.H.

Gentleman's academy, The: Markham, Gervase

Gentlemans accomplish'd jockey, The: Markham, Gervase

Gentleman's exercise for drawing all manner of beasts, The: Peacham, Henry

Gentleman's tour through Monmouthshire, A: Lyttelton, George *Baron*

Gentlemen, I address you privately: Boyle, Kay

Gentlemen in the parlour, The: Maugham, Somerset

Gentlemen of the Press: Wolfe, T.C.

Gentlemen prefer blondes: Loos, Anita

Gentles, attend!: Morley, C.D.

Genuine arguments of the Council why an information should not be exhibited against Thomas Leigh for a conspiracy to deprive Charles Macklin of his livelihood, The: Macklin, Charles

Genuine remains, The: Butler, Samuel

Geoffrey Chaucer: Lowes, J.L.

Geoffrey Chaucer, and the development of his genius: Lowes, J.L.

Geoffrey Gambado: Cobbold, Richard

Geoffrey Moncton: Moodie, Susanna

Geographical factors in Indian history: Panikkar, K.M.

Geographical history of America, The: Stein, Gertrude

Geographical memoirs of New South Wales: Field, *Baron*

Geography and plays: Stein, Gertrude

Geography for my children: Stowe, Harriet Beecher

Geography of South Carolina, The: Simms, W.G.

Geological sketches: Agassis, J.L.R.

George: Williams, Emlyn

George and the Crown, The: Kaye-Smith, Sheila

George and the General: Ridge, W. Pett

George Balcombe: Tucker, N.B.

George Bernard Shaw: Chesterton, G.K.

George Bernard Shaw: Palmer, J.L.

George Bernard Shaw, his plays: Mencken, H.L.

George Borrow: Armstrong, M.D.

George Borrow: Shorter, C.K.

George Borrow: Thomas, E.E.P.

George Brown's schooldays: Marshall, Bruce

George Calderon: Lubbock, Percy

George Canning: Petrie, *Sir* Charles

George Canterbury's will: Wood, Ellen,

George Castriot: Moore, C.C.

George Chapman: Swinburne, A.C.

George Edward Woodbury, 1855–1930: Erskine, John

George Eliot: Allen, Walter Ernest

George Eliot: Meynell, Viola

George Eliot: Stephen, *Sir* Leslie

George Eliot, her life and books: Bullett, Gerald

George Eliot's Middlemarch: Daiches, David

George Fox digged out of his burrowes: Williams, Roger

George Geith of Fen Court: †Trafford, F.G.

George Gissing, a critical study: Swinnerton, Frank

George Helm: Phillips, D.G.

George Leatrim: Moodie, Susanna

George Lovell: Knowles, J.S.

George MacDonald: an anthology: Lewis, C.S.

George Mason, the young backwoodsman: Flint, Timothy

George Mayford: Rowcroft, Charles

George Meredith: Barrie, *Sir* J.M.

George Meredith: Le Gallienne, Richard

George Meredith: Priestley, J.B.

George Moore: Wolfe, Humbert

George Moore, merchant and philanthropist: Smiles, Samuel

George Sylvester Viereck: Lewisohn, Ludwig

George V: Bryant, *Sir* Arthur

George IV: Fulford, Roger

George the Fourth: Leslie, *Sir* J.R. Shane

George VI: Bolitho, H.H.

George the third and Charles Fox: Trevelyan, *Sir* G.O.

George III and the historians: Butterfield, Herbert

George the third, his court and family: Galt, John

George III, Lord North and the people: Butterfield, Herbert

George Washington: Hubbard, Elbert

George Washington: Mackaye, Percy

George Washington: Wilson, Woodrow

George Washington and other American addresses: Harrison, Frederic

George Westover: Phillpotts, Eden

George's mother: Crane, Stephen

Georgia boy: Caldwell, Erskine Preston

Georgia scenes, characters, incidents, etc.: Longstreet, A.B.

Georgiad, The: Campbell, Roy

Georgian house, The: Swinnerton, Frank

Georgian literary scene, The: Swinnerton, Frank

Georgian novel and Mr. Robinson, The: Jameson, Storm

Georgie May: Bodenheim, Maxwell

Gerald, a dramatic poem: Marston, J.W.

Gerald, a portrait: Du Maurier, Daphne

Gerald Cranston's lady: Frankau, Gilbert

Gerald Fitzgerald the chevalier: Lever, C.J.

Gerar: Petrie, *Sir* William Flindes

Gerard: Braddon, M.E.

Gerard Manley Hopkins: Grigson, Geoffrey

Gerard Manley Hopkins, the man and the poet: Iyengar, K.R. Srinivasa

Germ, The: Rossetti, C. G., Rossetti, D.G. and Rossetti, W.M.

German Baroque art: Sitwell, Sacheverell

German Baroque sculpture: Pevsner, Nikolaus

German Baroque sculpture: Sitwell, Sacheverell

German hotel, The: Holcroft, Thomas

German idyll, A: Bates, H.E.

German influence on British Cavalry: Childers, Erskine

German life and manners in Saxony: Mayhew, Henry

German myth, The: Myers, Gustavus

German philosophy and politics: Dewey, John

German prisoner, The: Hanley, James

German romance: Carlyle, Thomas

German social democracy: Russell, Bertrand

German war, The: Doyle, *Sir* Arthur Conan

Germans on the Somme, The: Gibbs, *Sir* Philip

Germany: Baring-Gould, Sabine

Germany: Bullett, Gerald

Germany and Eastern Europe: Namier, *Sir* Lewis

Germany in the early Middle Ages: Stubbs, William

Germany in the later Middle Ages: Stubbs, William

Germany past and present: Baring-Gould, Sabine

Germany's great lie: Sladen, D.B.

Gertie: Bagnold, Enid

Gertie Maude: Van Druten, J.W.

Gertrude: Trollope, Frances

Gertrude of Wyoming: Campbell, Thomas

Geste of Duke Jocelyn, The: Farnol, J.J.

Get away, old man: Saroyan, William

Get out or get in line: Hubbard, Elbert

Getting a wrong start: Hough, Emerson

Getting married: Shaw, G.B.

Getting of wisdom, The: †Richardson, H.H.

Gettysburg: Kantor, Mackinlay

Gettysburg: Lathrop, G.P.

Gettysburg: Masters, E.L.

Ghastly good taste: Betjeman, John

Ghetto, The: Ridge, Lola

Ghetto comedies: Zangwill, Israel

Ghetto di Roma: Parsons, T.W.

Ghetto tragedies: Zangwill, Israel

Ghitza: Bercovici, Konrad

Ghond, the hunter: Mukherji, D.G.

Ghost, The: Bennett, Arnold

Ghost, The: Churchill, Charles

Ghost, The: Praed, *Mrs.* C.

Ghost and the burglar, The: McArthur, Peter

Ghost and the maiden, The: Mottram, R.H.

Ghost camp, The: †Boldrewood, Rolf

Ghost girl, The: Saltus, E.E.

Ghost in the Isle of Wight, A: Leslie, *Sir* J.R. Shane

Ghost kings, The: Haggard, *Sir* Henry Rider

Ghost of Abel, The: Blake, William

Ghost of Black Hawk Island, The: Derleth, A.W.

Ghost of Captain Brand, The: Pyle, Howard

Ghost of Doctor Harris, The: Hawthorne, Nathaniel

Ghost of Down Hill, The: Wallace, Edgar

Ghost of Guy Thryle, The: Fawcett, Edgar

Ghost of Jerry Bundler, The: Jacobs, W.W.

Ghost of Napoleon, The: Liddell Hart, B.

Ghost of Richard III, The: Brooke, Christopher

Ghost of Yankee Doodle, The: Howard, S.C.

Ghost plane, The: Stringer, A.J.A.

Ghost stories: Arlen, Michael

Ghost stories and tales of mystery: Le Fanu, Joseph

Ghost stories of an antiquary: James, M.R.

Ghost story, The: Tarkington, Booth

Ghost-bereft: Barlow, Jane

Ghost-hunter and his family, The: Banim, Michael

Ghostly Japan: Hearn, Lafcadio

Ghosts: Wharton, Edith

Ghosts I have met: Bangs, J.K.

Ghosts in daylight: †Onions, Oliver

Ghosts of London: Morton, H.V.

Giacomo Casanova, Chevalier de Seingalt: Dobrée, Bonamy

Giant: Ferber, Edna

Giant and the star, The: Cawein, Madison

Giant in chains: †Bowen, Marjorie

Giant swing, The: Burnett, W.R.

Giant weapon, The: Winters, Yvor

Giant's bread: Christie, Agatha

Giants cast long shadows: Lockhart, Sir Robert Bruce

Giants gone: men who made Chicago: Poole, Ernest

Giants in the earth: Rölvaag, O.E.

Giants' robe, The: †Anstey, F.

Giant's strength, The: †King, Basil

Giaour, The: Byron, George Gordon Lord

Gibbon: Young, G.M.

Gibraltar: Dennis, John

Gibson upright, The: Tarkington, Booth

Giddy minds and foreign quarrels: Beard, C.A.

Gideon: Hill, Aaron

Gideon Giles, the roper: Miller, Thomas

Gideon Planish: Lewis, H.S.

Gideon's band: Cable, G.W.

Gift, The: Nabokov, Vladimir

Gift, The: Steinbeck, John

Gift, The: Williams, W.C.

Gift from fairy-land, A: Paulding, J.K.

Gift from God: Vachell, H.A.

Gift from the grave, A: Wharton, Edith

Gift from the sea, A: Brazil, Angela

Gift of the black folk, The: Dubois, William

Gifted family, The: Pain, B.E.O.

Gifts of fortune: Tomlinson, H.M.

Gifts of the Christ child, The: Macdonald, George

Giglet Market: Phillpotts, Eden

Gigolo: Ferber, Edna

Gilbert: Pearson, Hesketh

Gilbert and Sullivan: Pearson, Hesketh

Gilbert Gurney: Hook, T.E.

Gilded age, The: (†Mark Twain), Clemens, S.L.

Gilded age, The: Warner, C.D.

Gilded India: Fyzee Rahamin, S.

Gilded man, The: †Carter Dickson

Giles Corey: Yeoman, Freeman M.W.

Gilgamesh: Lucas, F.L.

Gilian the dreamer: Munro, Neil

Gilt cage: Steen, Marguerite

Gin Mill Primer, The: Bengough, J.W.

Ginger and Pickles: Potter, Helen Beatrix

Gingerbread boy, The: Tietjens, E.S.

Gingertown: McKay, Claude

Ginn and Bitters: †Mordaunt, Elinor

Gioconda smile, The: Huxley, Aldous

Giorgione: Lucas, E.V.

Giotto and his works in Padua: Ruskin, John

Giovanni: Burnett, Frances Hodgson

Giovanni Boccaccio, man and author: Symonds, J.A.

Giovanni di Paolo: Pope-Hennessy, J.W.

Giovio and Julia: Scollard, Clinton

Gipsy chief: Reynolds, G.

Gipsy in the parlour, The: Sharp, Margery

Gipsy King: Howitt, Richard

Gipsy night: Hughes, R.A.W.

Gipsy of the Highlands, The: Ingraham, J.H.

Gipsy trail, The: Kipling, Rudyard

Gipsy wagon: Kaye-Smith, S.

Giraffe hunters, The: Reid, T.M.

Girl adoring, A: Meynell, Viola

Girl and the faun, The: Phillpotts, Eden

Girl and the kingdom, The: Wiggin, Kate

Girl at Bullet Lake, The: Cody, H.A.

Girl at the halfway house, The: Hough, Emerson

Girl behind the bar, The: Jennings, Gertrude

Girl behind the gun, The: Macdonald, W.P.

Girl behind the gun, The: Wodehouse, P.G.

Girl crazy: Gershwin, Ira

Girl from Glengarry, The: Connor, Ralph

Girl from Lübeck, A: Marshall, Bruce

Girl from the Big Horn country, The: Chase, M.E.

Girl he married, The: Grant, James

Girl I left behind me, The: Belasco, David

Girl in black and bronze, The: Molesworth, Mrs.

Girl in golden rags, The: Chambers, R.W.

Girl in May: Marshall, Bruce

Girl in the Tube, The: Brighouse, Harold

Girl like I, A: Loos, Anita

Girl of the golden west, The: Belasco, David

Girl of the Limberlost, A: Stratton-Porter, Gene

Girl of the period, The: Linton, Eliza

Girl on the boat, The: Wodehouse, P.G.

Girl Oone, The: Devaney, J.M.

Girl Philippa, The: Chambers, R.W.

Girl waiting in the shade: Davies, Rhys

Girl who did not want to go to Kuala Lumpur, The: †Bridie, James

Girl who kills to save, The: Dhlomo, H.I.E.

Girl who sat by the ashes, The: Colum, Padraic

Girl with green eyes, The: Fitch, C.W.

Girl with red hair, A: Stewart, D.A.

Girls, The: Ferber, Edna

Girls and I, The: Molesworth, Mrs.

Girls are silly: Nash, Ogden

Girls at Cobhurst, The: Stockton, F.R.

Girl's best friend, A: Harwood, H.M.

Girls' education: Mackenzie, Henry

Girl's journey, The: Bagnold, Enid

Girls of a feather: Barr, A.E.H.

Girls of St. Cyprians, The: Brazil, Angela

Girondin, The: Belloc, Hilaire

Gisippus: Griffin, Gerald

Gitana: Chambers, R.W.

Gitanjali: Tagore, Sir R.

Give me back my heart: Jones, Jack

Give me liberty: the story of an innocent bystander: Erskine, John

Give me my sin again: Royde-Smith, N.

Give me possession: Horgan, Paul

Give me yesterday: Percy, Edward

Give me your love: Weidman, Jerome

Give up your lovers: Golding, Louis

Give us this day: Greenwood, Walter

Give your heart to the hawks: Jeffers, J.R.

Givers, The: Freeman, Mary

Giving and receiving: Lucas, E.V.

Gizeh and Rifeh: Petrie, Sir William Flindes

Gl'Ingannati: the deceived: Peacock, Thomas Love

Glad day, A: Boyle, Kay

Glad ghosts: Lawrence, D.H.

Glad returning, The: †Bethell, M.U.

Glad summer, The: Farnol, J.J.

Gladiator, The: Bird, R.M.

Gladiators, The: Whyte-Melville, G.J.

Gladys Fane: Reid, Sir Thomas

Glamming: MacMechan, A.M.

Glamorous night: Hassall, Christopher

Glamorous night: †Novello, Ivor

Glamour: Williams, Emlyn

Glance at New York, A: Green, Asa

Glance backward, The: Church, Richard

Glass blowers, The: Du Maurier, Daphne

Glass cage, The: Priestley, J.B.

Glass houses: ten years of freelancing: Beals, Carleton

Glass key, The: Hammett, S.D.

Glass of bitter, A: Priestley, J.B.

Glass of water, A: Dukes, Ashley

Glass princess, The: Vijayatunga, J.

Glass slipper, The: Farjeon, Eleanor and Herbert Farjeon

Glass stamps, and weight: Petrie, Sir William Flindes

Glas village: †Queen, Ellery

Glass wall, The: †Delafield, E.M.

Glasse of government, The: Gascoigne, George

Glasse of time in the first age, The: Peyton, Thomas

Glasse of time in the second age, The: Peyton, Thomas

Glasshouse, The: †Eldershaw, M. Barnard

Glassmender, The: Baring, Maurice

Glastonbury romance, A: Powys, John Cowper

Glaucus: Boker, G.H.

Glaucus: Kingsley, Charles

Glaucus: Traill, H.D.

Gleam in the North, The: Broster, D.K.

Gleaming archway, The: Stephen, A.M.

Gleams of memory with some reflections: Payn, James

Gleanings by an undergraduate: Soutar, William

Gleanings from a gathered harvest: Noah, M.M.

Gleanings from the menagerie and aviary at Knowsley Hall: Lear, Edward

Gleanings in Buddha-fields: Hearn, Lafcadio

Gleanings in Europe: Cooper, James Fenimore

Glen o' weeping, The: †Bowen, Marjorie

Glen of the high north: Cody, H.A.

Glen of the white man's grave, The: Kendall, Henry

Glenarvon: Lamb, Lady Caroline

Glenaveril: (†Owen Meredith), Lytton, E.R.B. Earl

Glencoe: Stewart, D.A.

Glencoe: Talfourd, Sir T.N.

Glencreggan: †Bede, Cuthbert

Glengarry school days: †Connor, Ralph

Glenlitten murder, The: Oppenheim, E.Phillips

Glimpse, The: Bennett, Arnold

Glimpse of reality, The: Shaw, G.B.

Glimpses and reflections: Galsworthy, John

Glimpses of antiquity: Warren, J.B.L.

Glimpses of Bengal life: Tagore, Sir R.

Glimpses of California and the missions: Jackson, H.H.

Glimpses of New Zealand scenery: Baughan, B.E.

Glimpses of Quebec during the last ten years of French domination in Canada, 1749–1759: LeMoine, Sir J.M.

Glimpses of the moon, The: Wharton, Edith

Glimpses of three coasts: Jackson, H.H.

Glimpses of unfamiliar Japan: Hearn, Lafcadio

Glimpses of world history: Nehru, J.

Glittering gate, The: Dunsany, Edward Plunkett, *Baron*

"Globe" Chaucer: Pollard, A.W.

Gloria in profundis: Chesterton, G.K.

Gloria Mundi: Frederic, Harold

Gloriana: Lee, Nathaniel

Gloriana: Plomer, William

Glories of Mary for the sake of her son, The: Newman, J.H.

Glorious Apollo: Beck, *Mrs.* Lily

Glorious Devon: Mais, S.P.B.

Glorious first of June, The: Sheridan, R.B.

Glorious fourth, A: Alcott, Louisa, M.

Glorious mystery, The: †Machen, Arthur

Glorious oyster, The: Bolitho, H.H.

Glorious pool, The: Smith, Thorne

Glory dead: Calder-Marshall, Arthur

Glory hole, The: White, S.E.

Glory never guesses: Patchen, Kenneth

Glory of Egypt, The: Beck, *Mrs.* Lily

Glory of Elsie Silver, The: Golding, Louis

Glory of life: Powys, L.C.

Glory of the conquered, The: Glaspell, Susan

Glory of the Nightingales, The: Robinson, E.A.

Glory that was Guvjaradesa, The: Munshi, K.M.

Glossary, or collection of words, phrases, names and allusions to customs, proverbs,...in the works of English authors, particularly Shakespeare and his contemporaries, A: Halliwell, J.O.

"Glourie ghost", The: Sherwood, R.E.

Glow-worm tales: Payn, James

Gluck and the opera: Newman, Ernest

Glue and lacquer: Acton, Harold

Glugs of Gosh, The: Dennis, C.M.J.

Gnomica: Brydges, *Sir* S.E.

Gnomobile, The: Sinclair, Upton

Go back for murder: Christie, Agatha

Go down, Moses: Faulkner, William

Go north, where the world is young: Niven, F.J.

Go she must!: Garnett, David

Go up higher: Clarke, J.F.

Goa, and the Blue Mountains: Burton, *Sir* Richard

Goal, The: Bottome, Phyllis

Goal, The: Jones, H.A.

Goals for America: Chase, Stuart

Goat and compasses, The: Armstrong, M.D.

Goat for Azazel, A: Fisher, V.A.

Goat green: Powys, T.F.

Goat's beard, The: Whitehead, William

Gobbler of God, The: Mackaye, Percy

Go-between, The: Hartley, L.P.

Gobi or Shamo: Murray, Gilbert

Goblin gold: MacKay, I.E.

Goblin Market: Rossetti, Christina

Goblins and pagodas: Fletcher, John Gould

God: an introduction to the science of metabiology: Murry, John Middleton

God and evil: Joad, C.E.M.

God and his gifts, A: Compton-Burnett, Ivy

God and King: †Bowen, Marjorie

God and Mammon: Davidson, John

God and my country: Kantor, Mackinlay

God and my father: Day, C.S.

God and the astronomers: Inge, W.R.

God and the atom: Knox, R.A.

God and the Bible: Arnold, Matthew

God and the groceryman: Wright, H.B.

God and the man: Buchanan, R.W.

God and the story of Judaism: Levin, Meyer

God and the wedding dress: †Bowen, Marjorie

God glorified in the work of redemption: Edwards, Jonathan

God help us to be brave: Lindsay, N.V.

God in Christ: Bushnell, Horace

God in the car, The: †(Anthony Hope), Hawkins, Anthony Hope

God knows: Mee, Arthur

God likes them plain: Linklater, Eric

God of his fathers, The: London, Jack

God of quiet, The: Drinkwater, John

God of the machine, The: Paterson, Isabel

God of the witches, The: Murray, Margaret

God or Caesar: Fisher, V.A.

God rest you merry gentlemen: Hemingway, Ernest

God the invisible king: Wells, H.G.

God the known and the unknown: Butler, Samuel

God within Him, The: Hichens, Robert

God without thunder: Ransom, J.C.

Godbey: Masters, E.L.

Goddess named gold, A: Bhattacharya, B.

Godfrey Malvern: Miller, Thomas

Godfrey of Bologne: Caxton, William

Godfrida: Davidson, John

Godhead of Jesus, The: Temple, William

Godolphin: Lytton, E.G.E.B. *1st Baron*

Godolphin Arabian, The: Stephens, J.B.

God's acre: Hough, Emerson

Gods and their makers: Housman, Laurence

Gods arrive, The: Wharton, Edith

God's counterpoint: Beresford, J.D.

Gods, demons and others: Narayan, R.K.

God's eye's a twinkle: Powys, T.F.

God's good man: †Corelli, Marie

Gods in twilight, The: Sandwell, B.K.

God's Iron: Hannay, J.O.

God's little acre: Caldwell, Erskine Preston

God's men: Buck, Pearl

Gods mercie mixed with his justice: Cotton, John

Gods of Mount Olympus, The: Warren, Robert Penn

Gods of Pegana, The: Dunsany, Edward Plunkett, *Baron*

Gods of the lightning: Anderson, Maxwell

Gods of the mountain, The: Dunsany, Edward Plunkett, *Baron*

Gods of war: Russell, G.W.

God's outpost: Gouldsbury, H.C.

God's playthings: †Bowen, Marjorie

Gods promise to his plantation: Cotton, John

God's promises: Bale, John

God's puppets: White, W.A.

God's soldier, General William Booth: Ervine, St.John

Gods, some mortals and Lord Wickenham, The: †Hobbes, John Oliver

God's sparrows: Child, P.A.

God's stepchildren: Millin, Sarah Gertrude

God's trombones: Johnson, J.W.

God-seeker, The: Lewis, H.S.

Godstone and the blackymor, The: White, T.H.

Godstow Nunnery: Binyon, Robert Laurence

Godwits fly, The: †Hyde, Robin

Goethals and the Panama Canal: Fast, Howard M.

Goethe: Calvert, G.H.

Goethe: Hayward, Abraham

Goethe and Faust: Dickinson, G.L.

Goethe and Schiller: Boyesen, H.H.

Goethe: the story of a man: Lewisohn, Ludwig

Goethe's Iphigenie in Taurus: Boyd, James

Go-getter, The: Mann, Leonard

Goggle-box affair, The: Gielgud, Val

Going abroad: Macaulay, *Dame* Rose

Going down from Jerusalem: Duncan, Norman

Going home: Pain, B.E.O.

Going into society: Dickens, Charles

Going native: Gogarty, O.St.John

Going of the white swan, The: Parker, *Sir* H.G.

Going some: Beach, R.E.

Going their own ways: Waugh, Alec

Going to pieces: Woollcott, A.H.

Going to the bad: Taylor, Tom

Going up: Priestley, J.B.

Going west: †King, Basil

Going-to-the-stars: Lindsay, N.V.

Going-to-the-sun: Lindsay, N.V.

Gokhale: My political Guru: Gandhi, M.K.

Golconda: Palmer, E.V.

Gold: O'Neill, Eugene

Gold: Reade, Charles

Gold: White, S.E.

Gold and iron: Hergesheimer, Joseph

Gold bat, The: Wodehouse, P.G.

Gold brick, The: Whitlock, Brand

Gold chase, The: Chambers, R.W.

Gold Coast customs: Sitwell, Edith

Gold, credit and unemployment: Cole, G.D.H.

Gold cure, The: Duncan, S.J.

Gold gauze veil: Read, O.P.

Gold Hesperidee, The: Frost, Robert

Gold mine, A: Matthews, J.B.

Gold mines of Midian: Burton, *Sir* Richard

Gold mines of the Gila, The: Webber, C.W.

Gold of Chickaree, The: Warner, S.B.

Gold of Fairmilee, The: Lang, Andrew

Gold seekers, The: Burnett, W.R.

Gold, silver and precious stones: Thompson, Maurice

Gold skull murders, The: Packard, F.L.

Gold stealers, The: Dyson, E.G.

Gold: the romance of its discovery in Australia: (†Donald Barr), Barrett, C.L.

Gold tree, The: Squire, *Sir* J.C.

Goldcross: Phillpotts, Eden

Golden age, The: Austin, Alfred

Golden age, The: Darwin, Erasmus

Golden age, The: Grahame, Kenneth

Golden age, The: Heywood, Thomas

Golden age, The: Massingham, Harold

Golden age restored, The: Jonson, Ben

Golden ages of the Greek cities: Bowra, *Sir* Maurice

Golden apple, The: Gregory, *Lady* Augusta

Golden apple: Hannay, J.O.

Golden apples: Rawlings, Marjorie

Golden arrow, The: Webb, Mary

Golden ashes: Crofts, F.W.

Golden asse, The: Chase, M.E.

Golden ball, The: Brown, Alice

Golden basket: Bemelmans, Ludwig

Golden beast, The: Oppenheim, E.Phillips

Golden bird, The: Ridler, A.B.

Golden boat, The: Tagore, *Sir* R.

Golden book of Springfield, The: Lindsay, N.V.

Golden book of the Dutch navigators, The: Van Loon, Hendrik

Golden bottle, The: Donnelly, Ignatius Loyola

Golden bough, The: Frazer, *Sir* James

Golden bowl, The: James, Henry

Golden boy: Odets, Clifford

Golden breath, The: Anand, M.R.

Golden butterfly, The: Besant, *Sir* Walter and James Rice

Golden calf, The: Boyesen, H.H.

Golden calf, The: Braddon, Mary Elizabeth

Golden calf, The: Harwood, H.M.

Golden casket, The: Hall, Anna Maria

Golden casket, The: Wood, Ellen

Golden chalice, The: Gustafson, Ralph

Golden child: Engle, Paul

Golden Christmas, The: Simms, W.G.

Golden coney: Farjeon, Eleanor

Golden crowns: Reade, Charles

Golden cuckoo, The: Johnston, W.D.

Golden day, The: Mumford, Lewis

Golden dog, The: Kirby, William

Golden doom, The: Dunsany, Edward Plunkett, *Baron*

Golden door, The: Scott, Evelyn

Golden Dragon City: Dunsany, Edward Plunkett, *Baron*

Golden eagle: Bax, Clifford

Golden Echo, The: Garnett, David

Golden face: Mitford, Bertram

Golden falcon: Coffin, Robert

Golden fetich, The: Phillpotts, Eden

Golden fetters: Lemon, Mark

Golden fleece: Benét, W.R.

Golden Fleece, The: Graves, Robert

Golden fleece: Phillips, D.G.

Golden fleece, The: Priestley, J.B.

Golden fleece and the heroes who lived before Achilles, The: Colum, Padraic

Golden fleece of California, The: Masters, E.L.

Golden fool, The: †Divine, David

Golden foundling: †Sinclair Murray

Golden friends I had: Widdemer, Margaret

Golden gate, The: Atherton, Gertrude

Golden goat, The: Byrne, Donn

Golden Goliath: Clune, Frank

Golden grain: Farjeon, B.L.

Golden Grove, The: Taylor, Jeremy

Golden Hades, The: Wallace, Edgar

Golden helm, The: Gibson, Wilfred

Golden helmet, The: Yeats, W.B.

Golden highlanders, The: Roberts, T.G.

Golden Hope, The: Russell, W.C.

Golden Horn: Yeats-Brown, Francis

Golden Hour, The: Conway, Moncure Daniel

Golden house, The: Vachell, H.A.

Golden house, The: Warner, C.D.

Golden Hynde, The: Noyes, Alfred

Golden Island: Phillpotts, Eden

Golden journey to Samarkand: Flecker, J.E.

Golden Jubilee of Wesley College, Winnipeg, The: Kirkconnell, Watson

Golden keys, The: †Lee, Vernon

Golden labyrinth, The: Knight, G.W.

Golden land, The: Farjeon, B.L.

Golden legend, The: Caxton, William

Golden legend, The: Longfellow, H.W.

Golden legend of Shults, The: †Bridie, James

Golden Lion of Granpere, The: Trollope, Anthony

Golden lover, The: Stewart, D.A.

Golden miles: Prichard, K.S.

Golden moth: †Novello, Ivor

Golden moth, The: Wodehouse, P.G.

Golden mountain, The: Levin, Meyer

Golden one, The: Treece, Henry

Golden oriole, The: Bates, H.E.

Golden peacock: Atherton, Gertrude

Golden phoenix: Barbeau, C.M.

Golden pound, The: Hutchinson, Arthur

Golden rain: Widdemer, Margaret

Golden reign of Queen Elizabeth: †Dane, Clemence

Golden road, The: Montgomery, L.M.

Golden rock, The: Glanville, Ernest

Golden roof, The: †Bowen, Marjorie

Golden room, The: Gibson, Wilfred

Golden rooms, The: Fisher, V.A.

Golden rowan: Carman, Bliss

Golden sayings: Hannay, J.O.

Golden scarecrow, The: Walpole, *Sir* Hugh

Golden secret, The: O'Reilly, J.B.

Golden sequence, The: Underhill, Evelyn

Golden Shakespeare, The: Smith, L.L.P.

Golden shanty, The: Dyson, E.G.

Golden six, The: Anderson, Maxwell

Golden sovereign, The: Church, Richard

Golden sovereign, The: Housman, Laurence

Golden spike, The: Dell, Floyd

Golden string, A: Morley, C.D.

Golden strangers, The: Treece, Henry

Golden summer, The: †Queen, Ellery

Golden threshold, The: Naidu, Sarojini

Golden treasury, The: Palgrave, F.T.

Golden treasury of Scottish poetry: †McDiarmid, Hugh

Golden vanity, The: Paterson, Isabel

Golden vase, The: Lewisohn, Ludwig

Golden violet: (†Joseph Shearing), †Bowen, Marjorie

Golden violet, The: Landon, L.E.M.

Golden virgin, The: Williamson, Henry

Golden wall and mirador from England to Peru: Sitwell, Sacheverell

Golden Wang-ho, The: Hume, F.W.

Golden waterwheel, The: Walmsley, Leo

Golden wedding: Mulgan, A.E.

Golden wedding, A: Phillpotts, Eden

Golden wedding, The: Taylor, Bayard

Golden West, The: Gow, Ronald

Golden whales of California, The: Lindsay, N.V.

Golden wildcat, The: Widdemer, Margaret

Golden years, The: Finlayson, Roderick

Golden years, The: Gibbs Sir Philip

Golden yesterdays: Deland, Margaret

Goldfinches, The: Lynd, Sylvia

Goldfish, The: Lynd, Robert

Goldfish under the ice, The: Morley, C.D.

Gold-foil, hammered from popular proverbs: Holland, J.G.

Goldsmith's wife, The: Ainsworth, Harrison

Goldsworthy Lowes Dickinson: Forster, E.M.

Golf is a friendly game: Gallico, Paul

Gollan, The: Coppard, A.E.

Gollantz: Jacob, Naomi

Gollantz and partners: Jacob, Naomi

Gombo Zhèbes: Hearn, Lafcadio

Gondal poems: Brontë, Emily

Gondola days: Smith, F.H.

Gondoliers, The: Gilbert, Sir W.S.

Gone afield: Roberts, C.E.M.

Gone astray: Dickens, Charles

Gone rustic: Roberts, C.E.M.

Gone sunwards: Roberts, C.E.M.

Gone to earth: Webb, Mary

Gone to ground: White, T.H.

Gone with the wind: Mitchell, Margaret

Good and the badde, The: Breton, Nicholas

Good bargain, A: Dunsany, Edward Plunkett, Baron

Good behaviour: Nicolson, Hon. Sir Harold

Good boy Seldom: †Onions, Oliver

Good companions, The: Priestley, J.B.

Good companions, The: Woollcott, A.H.

Good company, a rally of men: Lucas, E.V.

Good conduct: Hannay, J.O.

Good days: Cardus, Neville

Good earth, The: Buck, Pearl

Good egg: †Armstrong, Anthony and Fred Robinson

Good European, The: Blackmur, R.P.

Good family, The: Kantor, Mackinlay

Good fellow, The: Kaufman. G.S.

Good fight, A: Reade, Charles

Good fight, A: Sheldon, C.M.

Good food guide: Postgate, Raymond

Good for nothing: Whyte-Melville, G.J.

Good for the soul: Deland, M.W.C.

Good Friday: Masefield, John

Good genius that turned everything into gold, The: Mayhew, Augustus Septimus

Good Gestes, The: Wren, P.C.

Good health and how we won it: Sinclair, Upton

Good intentions: Hannay, J.O.

Good intentions: Nash, Ogden

Good King Charles: Shaw, G.B.

Good losers: Arlen, Michael

Good luck: (†Ian Hay), Beith, Sir John Hay

Good man of Paris, The: Power, Eileen

Good man's love, A: †Delafield, E.M.

Good men and true: Rhodes, E.M.

Good morning, America: Sandburg, Carl

Good morning, Bill: Wodehouse, P.G.

Good morning, Rosamond!: Skinner, C.L.

Good natur'd man, The: Goldsmith, Oliver

Good neighbours: Burpee, Lawrence J.

Good neighbours: Jennings, Gertrude

Good new days, The: Quennell, Marjorie

Good newes and bad newes: Rowlands, Samuel

Good news for the vilest of men: Bunyan, John

Good news of God, The: Kingsley, Charles

Good news of God: Raven, C.E.

Good night: Aldrich, T.B.

Good night and good morning: Milnes, R.M.

Good old Anna: Lowndes, M.A.

Good old days, The: Phillpotts, Eden

Good old times, The: Ainsworth, William H.

Good old times, The: Manning, Anne

Good old-fashioned Christmas, A: Mottram, R.H.

Good Queen Anne vindicated: Bolingbroke, Henry St. John

Good red earth, The: Phillpotts, Eden

Good St. Louis and his times, The: Bray, Anna Eliza

Good samaritans: Read, T.B.

Good shepherd, The: Forester, C.S.

Good ship Gryphon, The: Oxley, J.M.

Good ship Mohock, The: Russell, W.C.

Good soldier, The: (Hueffer) Ford, Ford Madox

Good soldier, The: Wavell, A.P. *1st Earl*

Good stories of man and other animals: Reade, Charles

Good theatre: Morley, C.D.

Good thoughts in bad times: Fuller, Thomas

Good thoughts in worse times: Fuller, Thomas

Good tidings: Bloomfield, Robert

Good tidings: Van Loon, Hendrik

Good time coming, The: Hale, E.E.

Good time was had by all, A: Smith, Stevie

Good wives: Child, Lydia Maria

Good wolf, The: Burnett, Frances Hodgson

Good woman, A: Bromfield, Louis

Goodbye, The: Green, Paul

Goodbye, dear England: Millin, Sarah

Goodbye earth: Richards, I.A.

Goodbye, Mr. Chips: Hilton, James

Goodbye Mr. Chips: Sherriff, R.C.

Good-bye my fancy: Whitman, Walt

Goodbye nice types: †Armstrong, Anthony and Raff

Goodbye stranger: Benson, Stella

"Goodbye, sweetheart":Broughton, Rhoda

Goodbye to all that: Graves, Robert

Goodbye to Berlin: Isherwood, Christopher

Goodbye to Ithaca: Golding, Louis

Goodbye to the past: Burnett, W.R.

Good-bye to the West Country: Williamson, Henry

Goodbye to Western culture: Douglas, Norman

Good-bye, Wisconsin: Wescott, Glenway

Goodhues of Sinking Creek, The: Burnett, W.R.

Goodly fellowship: Chase, M.E.

Goodly heritage, A: Chase, M.E.

Goodly pearls: Hannay, J.O.

Goodnight, children: Priestley, J.B.

Goodwill: Phillpotts, Eden

Goody Platts: Miller, Thomas

Goody two shoes: Clarke, Marcus

Goody two-shoes: Freeman, Mary

Goody-witch, The: Sidgewick, Ethel

Goose on the Capitol, The: Bacon, Leonard

Goose woman, The: Beach, R.E.

Goosegirl, The: Sidgwick, Ethel

Goose-quill papers: Guiney, L.I.

Goose-step, The: Sinclair, Upton

Goostly psalmes: Coverdale, Miles

Gora: Tagore, *Sir* R.

Gordian knot, The: Brooks, C.W.S.

Gordon at Khartoum: Blunt, Wilfred

Gordon at Khartoum: Buchan, John

Gordon Bailey: Leslie, *Sir* J.R. Shane

Gordon Craip's book of penny toys, Craig, Gordon

Gordon Keith: Page, T.N.

Gordon riots, The: Johnson, L.P.

Gorgeous George: Gielgud, Val

Gorgeous isle, The: Atherton, Gertrude

Gorgeous lovers, The: †Bowen, Marjorie

Gorgeous times: Knox, E.V.

Gorgon's head, The: Frazer, *Sir* James

Gorilla hunters, The: Ballantyne, R.M.

Gorilla land, and the cataracts of Congo: Burton, *Sir* Richard

Goshawk, The: White, T.H.

Goslings: Beresford, J.D.

Goslings, The: Sinclair, Upton

Gospel and the Church, The: Raven, C.E.

Gospel attributed to Matthew is the record of the whole original apostlehood, The: Knowles, James Sheridan

Gospel in slow motion, The: Knox, R.A.

Gospel of beauty, The: Lindsay, N.V.

Gospel of freedom, The: Herrick, Robert

Gospel of selfless action, The: Gandhi, M.K.

Gospel of the dirty hand, The: Munshi, K.M.

Gospel of the Pentateuch, The: Kingsley, Charles

Gospel truth demonstrated:Fox, George

Gospels of anarchy: †Lee,Vernon

Gossamer: Hannay, J.O.

Gossip, The: Clarke, Macdonald

Gossip: Morley, Henry

Gossip in a library: Gosse, *Sir* Edmund

Gotham: Churchill, Charles

Gothic architecture: Morris, William

Gothick North, The: Sitwell, Sacheverell

Goths, The: Bradley, *Dr.* Henry

Governance of empire: Lighthall, W.D.

Governaunce of kynges and prynces, The: Lydgate, John

Governess, The: Blessington, Marguerite

Governess, The: Fielding, Sarah

Governess, The: Hall, Anna Marie

Governess, The: Hamilton, Patrick

Governess of Ashburton Hall, The: †Bell, Neil

Government in business: Chase, Stuart

Government research, past, present and future: Beard, C.A.

Governor of Chi-Foo, The: Wallace, Edgar

Governor of Cyprus, The: Oldmixon, John

Governor of England, The: †Bowen, Marjorie

Governors, The: Oppenheim, E. Phillips

Governor's lady, The: Collins, Norman

Governor's lady, The: Raddall, T.H.

Gower Street poltergeist, The: Fleming, Peter

Grab and Grace: Williams, Charles

Grace abounding to the chief of sinners: Bunyan, John

Grace after meat: Ransom, J.C.

Grace Darling: Reynolds, G.

Grace Darling: Swinburne, A.C.

Grace Darling: Wordsworth, William

Grace divorce, The: Swinnerton, Frank

Grace in the New Testament: Moffat, James

Grace Latouche: †Bowen, Marjorie

Grace Lee: Kavanagh, Julia

Grace Lorraine: Sladen, D.B.W.

Grace Mary: Jones, H.A.

Grace Weldon: Ingraham, J.H.

Graces, The: Beck, Mrs. Lily

Graduate fictioneer, The: Bedford-Jones, Henry

Graeme and Cyril: Pain, B.E.O.

Graeme and the dragon: Mitchison, Naomi

Graffiti d'Italia: Story, W.W.

Graft: Brighouse, Harold

Graham Hamilton: Lamb, Lady Caroline

Grain: Stead, R.J.C.

Grain of dust, The: Phillips, D.G.

Grain of mustard seed, The: Harwood, H.M.

Grammar of motives: Burke, Kenneth

Grammar of politics, A: Laski, Harold

Grammar of the English language, A: Cobbett, William

Grammatical institute of the English language, A: Webster, Noah

Gramophone nights: Mackenzie, Sir Compton

Granada window: Steen, Marguerite

Granadas devotion: Meres, Francis

Granadas spirituall and heavenlie exercises: Meres, Francis

Grand Army man, A: Belasco, David

Grand Army man, A: O'Higgins, H.J.

Grand Babylon hotel, The: Bennett, Arnold

Grand Canary: Cronin, A.J.

Grand Canyon: Krutch, J.W.

Grand Canyon: Sackville-West, V.

Grand Canyon: today and all its yesterdays: Krutch, J.W.

Grand chain: Stern, G.B.

Grand Cham's diamond, The: Monkhouse, A.N.

Grand cruise, The: Roberts, C.E.M.

Grand design, The: Dos Passos, John

Grand design, The: †Pilgrim, David

Grand Duchess, The: Hannay, J.O.

Grand Duke, The: Gilbert, Sir W.S.

Grand manner, The: Day-Lewis, C.

Grand national, historical and chivalric pantomime: Sala, G.A.H.

Grand parade, etc.: †Lancaster, G.B.

Grand Sophy, The: Heyer, Georgette

Grand tour, The: Wilson, Romer

Grande trouvaille, The: †Machen, Arthur

Grandfather Whitehead: Lemon, Mark

Grandfather's chair: Hawthorne, Nathaniel

Grandissimes, The: Cable, G.W.

Grandmama's pockets: Hall, Anna Maria

Grandmamma's verse book for young Australia: Meredith, L.A.

Grandmother dear: Molesworth, Mrs.

Grandmothers, The: Wescott, Glenway

Grandpa's selection: †Fudd, Steele

Grand-Pré: Herbin, J.F.

Grandsons: Adamic, Louis

Grange garden, The: Kingsley, Henry

Grangecolman: Martyn, Edward

Granite: †Dane, Clemence

Grannie's a hundred: Gow, Ronald

Granny Gray: Farjeon, Eleanor

Granny's wonderful chair and its tales of fairy times: Browne, Frances

Grant: Guiney, L.I.

Grants in aid: Webb, Sidney

Grape from a thorn, A: Payn, James

Grapes of wrath: Ewart, E.A.

Grapes of wrath, The: Steinbeck, John

Grasp your nettle: Linton, Eliza

Grass for my feet: Vijayatunga, J.

Grass grown trails: Clark, C.B.

Grass of Parnassus: Lang, Andrew

Grass roots of art, The: Read, Sir Herbert

Grasshoppers come, The: Garnett, David

Grassleyes mystery, The: Oppenheim, E. Phillips

Grateful sparrow, The: Thirkell, Angela

Gratefull servant, The: Shirley, James

Graustark: McCutcheon, G.B.

Grave, The: Blair, Robert

Grave, gay and grim: Lizars, Robina and K.M. Lizars

Grave of Arthur, The: Chesterton, G.K.

Grave of Howard, The: Bowles, William Lisle

Grave of the last Saxon, The: Bowles, William Lisle

Gravelhanger: Gielgud, Val

Graven image: Widdemer, Margaret

Graves of the fallen: Kipling, Rudyard

Grave-tree, The: Carman, Bliss

Graveyard to let, A: †Carter Dickson

Graveyard watch: Divine, A.D.

Gray: Gosse, Sir Edmund

Gray dawn, The: White, S.E.

Gray days and gold: Winter, William

Gray youth: †Onions, Oliver

Graysons, The: Eggleston, Edward

Great acting in English: Symons, Arthur

Great adventure, The: Bennett, Arnold

Great adventure, The: Lodge, G.C.

Great all-star animal league ball game: Starrett, Vincent

Great American novel, The: Williams, W.C.

Great American short stories: Graham, Stephen

Great American writers: Erskine, John

Great analysis, The: Archer, William

Great and the goods, The: Brown, Ivor

Great argument: Gibbs, Sir Philip

Great auction sale of slaves, at Savannah, Georgia: (†Q.K. Philander Doesticks) Thompson, Mortimer

Great Australian loneliness, The: Hill, Ernestine

Great Australian plain, The: Favenc, Ernest

Great authors of all ages: Allibone, S.A.

Great awakening, The: Oppenheim, E. Phillips

Great barrier reef, The: Bedford, Randolph

Great battles of the world: Crane, Stephen

Great bear, The: Oppenheim, E. Phillips

Great black oxen: Jacob, Naomi

Great blessing of primitive counsellours, The: Mather, Increase

Great Boer War, The: Doyle, Sir Arthur Conan

Great Britain and her colonies: Vogel, Sir Julius

Great Britain and Prussia in the eighteenth century: Lodge, Sir Richard

Great Britain at war: Farnol, J.J.

Great Britain in the post-war world: Cole, G.D.H.

Great Britaine all in blacke: Taylor, John

Great Broxopp, The: Milne, A.A.

Great captains: Treece, Henry

Great captains unveiled: Liddell Hart, B.

Great Catherine: Shaw, G.B.

Great chain of life, The: Krutch, J.W.

Great chameleon: Vachell, H.A.

Great Christian doctrine of original sin defended, The: Edwards, Jonathan

Great circle: Aiken, Conrad

Great circle: further adventures in free-lancing, The: Beals, Carleton

Great city, The: Mickle, A.D.

Great companions; critical memoirs of some famous friends: Eastman, Max

Great company, The: Willson, H.B.

Great constitution, The: Commager, H.S.

Great contemporaries: Churchill, Sir Winston

Great cry and little wool: †Pindar, Peter

Great cryptogram, The: Donnelly, Ignatius Loyola

Great dark, The: Brighouse, Harold

Great days, The: Dos Passos, John

Great days in New Zealand writing: Mulgan, A.E.

Great declaration, The: Commager, H.S.

Great divide, The: Moody, W.V.

Great divide, The: Sullivan, Alan

Great divorce, The: Lewis, C.S.

Great drama; an appeal to Maryland, The: Kennedy, J.P.

Great Duke of Florence, The: Massinger, Philip

Great emergency, A: Ewing, Mrs. Juliana Horatia

Great English novelists: Jackson, Holbrook

Great Englishmen of the sixteenth century: Lee, Sir Sidney

Great epics of ancient India condensed into English verse, The: Dutt, R.C.

Great exemplar of sanctity and holy life according to Christian institution, The: Taylor, Jeremy

Great Exhibition, The: Sala, G.A.H.

Great expectations: Dickens, Charles

Great fight, The: Drummond, W.H.

Great flights: †Caudwell, Christopher

Great flower books: Sitwell, Sacheverell

Great French romances: Aldington, Richard

Great Gatsby, The: Fitzgerald, F. Scott

Great god Brown, The: O'Neill, Eugene

Great God Pan, The: †Machen, Arthur

Great God success, The: Phillips, D.G.

Great healer, The: Levy, Benn W.

Great heresies, The: Belloc, Hilaire

Great historic animals: Seton-Thompson, E.

Great historical, geographical, genealogical and poetical dictionary, The: Collier, Jeremy

Great Hotel murder, The: Starrett, Vincent

Great house, The: Weyman, Stanley

Great houses of Europe: Gibbon, Monk

Great illusion, The: Angell, Sir Norman

Great illusion, 1933, The: Angell, Sir Norman

Great impersonation, The: Oppenheim, E. Phillips

Great Italian artists and the world: Lucas, E.V.

Great K & A robbery, The: Ford, Paul Leicester

Great longing, The: Mickle, A.D.

Great magoo, The: Hecht, Ben

Great man, A: Bennett, Arnold

Great man's wife, A: Tarkington, Booth

Great meadow, The: Roberts, E.M.

Great men, The: Davidson, John

Great Miss Driver, The: (†Anthony Hope), Hawkins, Anthony Hope

Great mistake, The: Rinehart, Mary Roberts

Great mistery of the great whore unfolded, The: Fox, George

Great moment, The: Glyn, Elinor

Great moments in the life of Washington: Bacheller, Irving

Great moments of life: Bacheller, Irving

Great morning: Sitwell, *Sir* Osbert

Great mountains, The: Steinbeck, John

Great musicians: Hubbard, Elbert

Great mysteries and little plagues: Neal, John

Great Northern?: Ransome, Arthur

Great novelists and their novels (essays): Maugham, Somerset

Great oak, The: Lindsay, Jack

Great O'Neill, The: O'Faolain, Sean

Great O'Toole, The: Taylor, John

Great palaces of Europe: Gibbon, Monk

Great peace-maker, The: Horne, R.H.

Great philosophies: Joad, C.E.M.

Great Pine's story, The: Widdemer, Margaret

Great plateau of Northern Rhodesia, The: Gouldsbury, H.C.

Great Porter Square: Farjeon, B.L.

Great possessions: Baker, Ray Stannard

Great possessions: Housman, Laurence

Great powers and the Eastern Christians, The: Reeves, W.P.

Great praises: Eberhart, Richard

Great Prince Shan, The: Oppenheim, E.Phillips

Great procession, The: Spofford, H.E.

Great proclamation, The: Commager, H.S.

Great Quillow, The: Thurber, James

Great Ralegh: De Selincourt, Hugh

Great refusal, The: More, P.E.

Great rehearsal, The:Van Doren, Carl

Great remembrance, The: Gilder, R.W.

Great return, The: †Machen, Arthur

Great river: the Rio Grande in North American history, The: Horgan, Paul

Great romantic, The: Beck, *Mrs.* Lily

Great Roxhythe, The: Heyer, Georgette

Great security: †Bartimeus

Great ship: Linklater, Eric

Great Southern mystery, The: Cole, G.D.H.

Great shadow, The: Doyle, *Sir* Arthur Conan

Great short stories, The:O'Hara, J.H.

Great son: Ferber, Edna

Great state, The: Wells, H.G.

Great stone of Sardis, The: Stockton, F.R.

Great success, A: Ward, *Mrs.* Humphrey

Great taboo, The: Allen, Grant

Great trade route: Ford, Ford Madox

Great tradition, The: Gerould, Katharine

Great tradition, The: Hicks, Granville

Great tradition: George Eliot, James and Conrad, The: Leavis, F.R.

Great Uncle Hoot-Toot: Molesworth, *Mrs.*

Great valley, The: Masters, E.L.

Great wall of India, The: (†Ian Hay), Beith, *Sir* John Hay

Great War as I saw it, The: Scott, F.G.

Great war syndicate, The: Stockton, F.R.

Great well, The: Sutro, Alfred

Great white hills of New Hampshire, The: Poole, Ernest

Great white wall, The: Benét, W.R.

Great winds: Poole, Ernest

Great writers: Cervantes, Scott, Milton, Virgil, Montaigne, Shakespeare: Woodberry, G.E.

Greater Apollo, The: Fitzgerald, R.D.

Greater inclination, The: Wharton, Edith

Greater India: Tagore, *Sir* R.

Greater infortune, The: Heppenstall, Rayner

Greater love hath no man: Packard, F.L.

Greater poems of the Bible: MacDonald, W.P.

Greater than Napoleon, A: Liddell Hart, B.

Greater trumps, The: Williams, Charles

Greatest heiress in England, The: Oliphant, Margaret

Greatest liar on earth, The: Clune, Frank

Greatest people in the world, The: Bates, H.E.

Greatest plague of life, The: Mayhew, Augustus Septimus

Greatest problem, The: Lucas, F.L.

Great-grandmother, The: Hannay, J.O.

Greatness of the soul, The: Bunyan, John

Grecian captive, The: Noah, M.M.

Grecian daughter, The: Murphy, Arthur

Grecian history, from the earliest state to the death of Alexander the Great, The: Goldsmith, Oliver

Greece: Miller, Henry

Greece: Thomson, James

Greece in my life: Mackenzie, *Sir* Compton

Greek anthology, The: Leslie *Sir* J.R. Shane

Greek boy, The: Lover, Samuel

Greek civilisation and character: Toynbee, Arnold

Greek coffin mystery, The: †Queen, Ellery

Greek coins: Glaspell, Susan

Greek experience, The: Bowra, *Sir* Maurice

Greek garland, A: Lucas, F.L.

Greek genius and its meaning to us, The: Livingstone, *Sir* Richard

Greek historical thought: Toynbee, Arthur

Greek holiday: Mais, S.P.B.

Greek ideals and modern life: Livingstone, *Sir* Richard

Greek influence on English poetry: Collins, John Churton

Greek lyric poetry: Bowra, *Sir* Maurice

Greek memories: Mackenzie, *Sir* Compton

Greek philosophers, The: Warner, Rex

Greek poets, The: Dole, N.H.

Greek slave, The: Sladen, D.B.W.

Greek studies: Murray, Gilbert

Greek studies: a series of essays: Pater, W.H.

Greek tradition, The: More, P.E.

Greek tragedy: Cole, G.D.H.

Greek view of life, The: Dickinson, G.L.

Greeks and Trojans: Warner, Rex

Green alleys, The: Phillpotts, Eden

Green and the grey and the red, The: Stephens, A.G.

Green apple harvest: Kaye-Smith, Sheila

Green archer, The: Wallace, Edgar

Green Arras: Housman, Laurence

Green bay tree, The: Bromfield, Louis

Green bay tree, The: Churchill, Winston

Green bay tree, The: White, T.H.

Green Bays: †Quiller-Couch, *Sir* Arthur

Green beret, The: Saunders, H.A. St. George

Green book of the bards, The: Carman, Bliss

Green bough, The: Austin, Mary

Green bough, A: Faulkner, William

Green branches: Stephens, James

Green butterflies: Bridges, Roy

Green carnation, The: Hichens, Robert

Green casket, The: Molesworth, *Mrs.*

Green child, The: Read, *Sir* Herbert

Green cloister, The: Scott, D.C.

Green crow, The: O'Casey, Sean

Green curtain, The: Braddon, Mary Elizabeth

Green door, The: Freeman, Mary Wilkins

Green eye of Goona, The: Morrison, Arthur

Green fairy book, The: Lang, Andrew

Green fancy: McCutcheon, G.B.

Green Ferne Farm: Jefferies, Richard

Green fields and running brooks: Riley, J.W.

Green figs: Mannin, Ethel

Green fire: (†Macleod, Fiona), Sharp, William

Green flag, The: Doyle, *Sir* Arthur Conan

Green fruit: Bishop, John Peale

Green Ginger: Morrison, Arthur

Green glory: Brophy, John

Green goddess, The: Archer, William

Green grey homestead: †Rudd, Steele

Green grows the city: Nichols, Beverley

Green hat, The: Arlen, Michael

Green helmet, The: Yates, W.B.

Green hills of Africa: Hemingway, Ernest

Green isle of the great deep, The: Gunn, Neil M.

Green ladies: Brophy, John

Green laurels: Peattie, D.C.

Green lions: Stewart, D.A.

Green man, The: Jameson, Storm

Green man, The: Lynd, Robert

Green man, The: Treece, Henry

Green man, The: Young, A.J.

Green mansions: Hudson, W.H.

Green memories: Mumford, Lewis

Green memory: †Eldershaw, M. Barnard

Green memory: Strong, L.A.G.

Green mirror, The: Walpole, *Sir* Hugh

Green mountain boys, The: Thompson, D.P.

Green mouse, The: Chambers, R.W.

Green overcoat, The: Belloc, Hilaire

Green pack, The: Wallace, Edgar

Green pastures, The: Connelly, Marc

Green pastures and Piccadilly: Black, William

Green pitcher: Livesay, Dorothy

Green popinjays, The: Fairburn, A.R.D.

Green ribbon, The: Wallace, Edgar

Green rocket, The: Walmsley, Leo

Green room: Basso, Hamilton

Green round, The: †Machen, Arthur

Green rushes: Walsh, Maurice

Green rust, The: Wallace, Edgar

Green song: Sitwell, Edith

Green thoughts, etc.: Collier, John

Green tide: Church, Richard

Green Timber Thoroughbreds: Roberts, T.G.

Green wave, The: Rukeyser, Muriel

Green willow: Mannin, Ethel

Green years, The: Cronin, A.J.
Greenery Street: Mackail, Denis
Greenes funeralls: Barnfield, Richard
Greenes ghost haunting conie-catchers: Rowlands, Samuel
Greenes newes both from Heaven and Hell: Rich, Barnabe
Greengage summer, The: Godden, Rumer
Greengates: Sherriff, R.C.
Greenland: Montgomery, James
Greenland: Stefansson, V.
Greenlow: Wilson, Romer
Greenmantle: Buchan, John
Greenstone Door, The: Satchell, William
Greenwood hat, The: Barrie, Sir J.M.
Gregory VII: Horne, R.H.
Greifenstein: Crawford, Francis Marion
Grenstone poems: Bynner, Witter
Gretchen: Gilbert, Sir W.S.
Gretchen: Holmes, M.J.
Gretna Green: O'Keeffe, John
Gretta: Caldwell, Erskine Preston
Grettir the outlaw: Baring-Gould, Sabine
Grettis saga: Morris, William
Greville: Gore, Catherine
Grey adventurer, The: Trease, Geoffrey
Grey brethren, The: †Fairless, Michael
Grey children: Hanley, James
Grey clouds and white showers: Chattopadhyaya, H.
Grey coast: Gunn, Neil M.
Grey eminence: Huxley, A.L.
Grey fairy book, The: Lang, Andrew
Grey goose comedy company, The: Dyson, E.G.
Grey granite: †Gibbon, L.G.
Grey lady, The: †Merriman, Seton
Grey man, The: Crockett, S.R.
Grey of Fallodon: Trevelyan, G.M.
Grey parrot, The: Jacobs, W.W.
Grey Rabbit and the wandering hedgehog: Uttley, Alison
Grey river, The: Praed, Mrs. C.

Grey room, The: Phillpotts, Eden
Grey ship moving: Bruce, Charles
Grey stocking, The: Baring, Maurice
Grey Timothy: Wallace, Edgar
Grey wethers: Buchan, John
Grey Wethers: Sackville-West, V.
Grey wig, The: Zangwill, Israel
Grey woman, The: Gaskell, Mrs. Elizabeth
Grey world, The: Underhill, Evelyn
Greybeards at play: Chesterton, G.K.
Greyling Towers: Molesworth, Mrs.
Greyslaer: a romance of the Mohawk: Hoffman, C.F.
Grief goes over: Hodge, H.E.
Griefe on the death of Prince Henrie, A: Tourneur, Cyril
Grif: a story of Australian life: Farjeon, B.L.
Grif: a story of Colonial life: Farjeon, B.L.
Griffilwraith, The: Stephens, A.G.
Griffith Gaunt: Reade, Charles
Grim house, The: Molesworth, Mrs.
Grim smile of the five towns, The: Bennett, Arnold
Grim tales: Nesbit, E.
Grimellos fortunes: Breton, Nicholas
Grip cartoons, The: Bengough, J.W.
Grip-sack, The: Bengough, J.W.
Griselda: Blunt, Wilfred
Griselda: †King, Basil
Griselda, a tragedy, and other poems: Arnold, Sir Edwin
Grocer Greatheart: Adams, Arthur H.
Groote Park murder, The: Crofts, F.W.
Groping: Jacob, Naomi
Grotto, The: Green, Matthew
Grounds of criticism in poetry, The: Dennis, John
Group of Londoners, A: Lucas, E.V.
Group of noble dames, A: Hardy, Thomas

Grouped thoughts and scattered fancies: Simms, W.G.
Grove, The: Freeman, John
Grove, The: Oldmixon, John
Grove, The: Theobald, Lewis
Grover Cleveland: a record of friendship: Gilder, R.W.
Growing: Woolf, Leonard
Growing up: Thirkell, Angela
Growing up in New Guinea: Mead, Margaret
Growing up into revolution: Cole, M.I.
Growth and culture: Mead, Margaret
Growth in Holiness: Faber, F.W.
Growth of a man: De la Roche, Mazo
Growth of Canadian national feeling, The: Wallace, W.S.
Growth of love, The: Bridges, Robert
Growth of physical science, The: Jeans, Sir James
Growth of Plato's ideal theory, The: Frazer, Sir James
Growth of the American republic, The: Commager, H.S.
Growth of the American republic: Morison, S.E.
Growth of the Empire, The: (†Ishmael Dare), Jose, A.W.
Growth of the English novel, The: Church, Richard
Growth of the Gospels, The: Petrie, Sir William Flinders
Growth of the law, The: Cardozo, B.N.
Gruach and Britain's daughter: Bottomley, Gordon
Grub Street nights entertainments, The: Squire, Sir J.C.
Grubstreet nae Satyre: Ramsay, Allan
Grumbler, The: Grose, Francis
Gryll Grange: Peacock, Thomas Love
Guard of honour: Cozzens, James Gould
Guardian, The: Cowley, Abraham
Guardian, The: Garrick, David
Guardian, The: Massinger, Philip

Guardian angel, The: Brooks, C.W.S.

Guardian angel, The: Holmes, Oliver Wendell

Guardian of education, The: Trimmer, *Mrs.* Sarah

Guardians, The: (†Michael Innes), Stewart, J.I.M.

Guards came through, The: Doyle, *Sir* Arthur Conan

Guards in Canada, The: Richardson, John

Guarica, the Charib bride: Herbert, H.W.

Guasvas the tinner: Baring-Gould, S.

Gub Gub's book: Lofting, Hugh

Gudrid the fair: Hewlett, Maurice

Guendolen: Carman, Bliss

Guerdon, The: Beerbohm, *Sir* Max

Guerilla: Dunsany, Edward Plunkett, *Baron*

Guerilla chief, The: Reid, T.M.

Guernsey lily, A: Coolidge, Susan

Guesses at the riddle of existence: Smith, Goldwin

Guest at the Ludlow, A: (†Bill Nye), Nye, E.W.

Guest book: Bynner, Witter

Guest of Thomas Hardy: Blunden, Edmund

Guests arrive, The: Roberts, C.E.M.

Guests of the Nation: †O'Connor, Frank

Guide, The: Narayan, R.K.

Guide book to women, A: (†James James), Adams, Arthur H.

Guide for the bedevilled, A: Hecht, Ben

Guide through the district of the lakes in the North of England, A: Wordsworth, William

Guide to English literature, A: Bateson, F.W.

Guide to good English, A: Partridge, Eric

Guide to health, A: Gandhi, M.K.

Guide to Keswick and its environs: Martineau, Harriet

Guide to life and literature of the Southwest: Dobie, J.B.

Guide to modern English history, 1815–1835, A: Cory, W.J.

Guide to modern politics, A: Cole, G.D.H. and M.I. Cole

Guide to modern thought: Joad, C.E.M.

Guide to modern wickedness: Joad, C.E.M.

Guide to philosophy: Joad, C.E.M.

Guide to the Caterham railway, and to the country around it: Wright, Thomas

Guide to the collection of Egyptian antiquities in the Edinburgh Museum of science and art: Murray, Margaret

Guide to the Crystal Palace and Park: Phillips, Samuel

Guide to the diplomatic history of the United States, 1775–1921: Bemis, S.F.

Guide to the new world: Wells, H.G.

Guide to the philosophy of morals and politics: Joad, C.E.M.

Guide to the principal pictures in the academy of Fine Arts at Venice: Ruskin, John

Guide to the Roman wall, A: Collingwood, R.G.

Guide to the study of book plates, A: Warren, J.B.L.

Guide to the varieties and rarity of English regal copper coins: Bramah, E.

Guide to Windermere: Martineau, Harriet

Guides to service: Martineau, Harriet

Guides to straight thinking: Chase, Stuart

Guild Court: Macdonald, George

Guild socialism: Cole, G.D.H.

Guild socialism, a plan for economic democracy: Cole, G.D.H.

Guild socialism restated: Cole, G.D.H.

Guilderoy: †Ouida

Guillotine, The: Hopkins, Lemuel

Guillotine club, The: Mitchell, S.W.

Guillotine party: Farrell, James

Guilty river, The: Collins, Wilkie

Guinea Fowl and other poultry: Bacon, Leonard

Gujarat and its literature: Munshi, K.M.

Gulab Singh, founder of Kashmir: Panikkar, K.M.

Gulf Coast stories: Caldwell, Erskine Preston

Gullible's travels: Lardner, Ring

Gulliver's travels: Swift, Jonathan

Gully, The: †Maurice, Furnley

Guls horne-booke, The: Dekker, Thomas

Gum leaves: Turner, E.S.

Gum trees, The: Campbell, Roy

Gun, The: Forester, C.S.

Gun for sale, A: Greene, Graham

Gun runner, The: Mitford, Bertram

Gun tamer: †Brand, Max

Gunhild: Canfield, Dorothy

Gunman's gold: †Brand, Max

Gunnar: Boyesen, H.H.

Gunner, The: Wallace, Edgar

Gunroom, The: Morgan, Charles

Gun-runner, The: Stringer, A.J.A.

Gun-runners, The: Hannay, J.O.

Guns, The: Frankau, Gilbert

Guns or butter?: Lockhart, *Sir* Robert Bruce

Gurney married: Hook, T.E.

Gurneys of Earlham, The: Hare, A.J.C.

Gusher, The: (†Ian Hay), Beith, *Sir* John Hay

Gustav Mahler: his mind and his music: Cardus, Neville

Gustavus Adolphus: a history of Sweden, 1611–1632: Roberts, Michael

Gustavus Vasa: Brooke, Henry

Gutta Percha Willie, the working genius: Macdonald, George

Guv'nor, The: Wallace, Edgar
Guy and Pauline: Mackenzie, *Sir* Compton
Guy Deverell: Le Fanu, Sheridan
Guy Faux: Mayhew, Horace
Guy Fawkes, or the Gunpowder Treason: Ainsworth, Harrison
Guy Livingstone: Lawrence, George Alfred
Guy Mannering: Scott, *Sir* Walter

Guy of Warwick: Lydgate, John
Guy Renton: Waugh, Alec
Guy Rivers: Simms, W.G.
Guys and Dolls: Runyon, Damon
Guzman: Boyle, Roger
Gwen: †Connor, Ralph
Gwen: Morris, *Sir* Lewis
Gwen Wynn: Reid, T.M.
Gwendoline's harvest: Payn, James
Gwydonius: Greene, Robert

Gycia: Morris, *Sir* Lewis
Gyfford of Weare: Farnol, J.J.
Gypsy Breynton: Ward, E.S.
Gypsy gypsy: Godden, Rumer
Gypsy's baby, The: Lehmann, Rosamund
Gypsy's cousin Joy: Ward, E.S.
Gypsy's sowing and reaping: Ward, E.S.
Gypsy's year at the Golden Crescent: Ward, E.S.

H

H.G.Wells: Beresford, J.D.
H.G.Wells: Brown, Ivor
H.L.Mencken: Lippmann, Walter
H.M.Pulham, Esquire: Marquand, J.P.
H.M.Stanley: Symons, A.J.A.
H. M. S. Pinafore: Gilbert, *Sir* W. S.
H.M.S.Marlborough will enter harbour: Monsarrat, Nicholas
H.P.L., a memoir: Derleth, A.W.
Habit of Empire, The: Horgan, Paul
Habitant of dusk: Derleth, A.W.
Hacienda: Porter, K.A.
Hades: Scott, W.B.
Hadrian the seventh: (†Baron Corvo), Rolfe, Frederick
Hagarene: Lawrence, G.A.
Hag's nook: Carr, J.D.
Haifa: Oliphant, Laurence
Haig: Cooper, Alfred Duff
Hail and farewell!: Moore, George
Hail tomorrow: Palmer, E.V.
Hair powder: †Pindar, Peter
Hairy ape, The: O'Neill, Eugene
Hakluytus Posthumus: Purchas, Samuel
Hal o' the Ironsides: Crockett, S.R.
Halcyon: Brittain, Vera
Halcyone: Glyn, Elinor
Halelujah: Wither, George
Hale's Indians of North-west America: Gallatin, Albert

Half a century of the British Empire: Martineau, Harriet
Half a hero: (†Anthony Hope), Hawkins, Anthony Hope
Half a minute's silence: Baring, Maurice
Half blood, The: Reid, T.M.
Half caste,The: Robertson,T.W.
Half century of conflict, A: Parkman, Francis
Half crown house, The: Ashton, Helen
Half gods: Howard, S.C.
Half hours: Barrie, *Sir* J.M.
Half hours with Jimmieboy: Bangs, J.K.
Half hours with the idiot: Bangs, J.K.
Half mile down: Beebe, William
"Half Moon", The: (Hueffer), Ford, Ford Madox
Half pint flask, The: Heyward, DuBose
Half portions: Ferber, Edna
Half way: Roberts, C.E.M.
Half-a-dozen housekeepers: Wiggin, Kate
Half-a-sovereign: (†Ian Hay), Beith, *Sir* John Hay
Half-an-eye: Hanley, James
Half-crown Bob: †Warung, Price
Half-day's ride, A: Colum, Padraic
Half-hearted, The: Buchan, John
Half-hours at Helles: Herbert, *Sir* A.P.

Half-sisters, The: Jewsbury, G.E.
Halfway house: Blunden, Edmund
Halfway house: Hewlett, Maurice
Halfway house: †Queen, Ellery
Half-way sun, The: Moore, T.I.
Halfway to anywhere: Lindsay, Norman
Halidon Hill: Scott, *Sir* Walter
Halifax, warden of the north: Raddall, T.H.
Hall of Hellingsley, The: Brydges, *Sir* S.E.
Hall porter, The: Lover, Samuel
Hallam succession, The: Barr, A.E.H.
Hallmarked: Galsworthy, John
Hallowed ground: Brighouse, Harold
Halo, The: Temple, John
Halt and parley: Clarke, G.H.
Halt in the garden, The: Hillyer, Robert
Halt! Who goes there?: Meynell, Wilfred
Halves: Payn, James
Ham funeral, The: White, Patrick
Hamilton wedding, The: Maxwell, W.H.
Hamiltons, The: Gore, Catherine
Hamlet, The: Faulkner, William
Hamlet: Shakespeare, William
Hamlet: a philosophic correspondence: Miller, Henry

Hamlet and Orestes: Murray, Gilbert

Hamlet had an uncle: Cabell, James Branch

Hamlet in Springfield: Lindsay, N.V.

Hamlet, revenge!: (†Michael Innes), Stewart, J.I.M.

Hamlet travestie: Poole, John

Hammer and rapier: Cooke, J.E.

Hampdens, The: Martineau, Harriet

Hampdenshire wonder, The: Beresford, J.D.

Hampshire days: Hudson, W.H.

Hand and heart and Bessy's troubles at home: Gaskell, *Mrs.* Elizabeth

Hand in glove: Marsh, Ngaio Edith

Hand in the dark, The: Cambridge, Ada

Hand of Ethelberta, The: Hardy, Thomas

Hand of God, The: Allen, Grant

Hand of Kornelius Voyt, The: †Onions, Oliver

Hand of Mary Constable, The: Gallico, Paul

Hand of peril, The: Stringer, A.J.A.

Hand of Siva, The: Hecht, Ben

Hand of the hunter, The: Weidman, Jerome

Hand of the potter, The: Dreiser, Theodore

Hand on her shoulder: Widdemer, Margaret

Handbook for Berkshire: Falkner, John Meade

Handbook for the Dominion of Canada: Dawson, S.E.

Handbook for travellers in Berks, Bucks and Oxfordshire, A: Hare, A.J.C.

Handbook for travellers in Northern Italy: Palgrave, *Sir* Francis

Handbook for travellers in Spain: Ford, Richard

Handbook for travellers to Durham and Northumberland, A: Hare, A.J.C.

Handbook of Egyptian sculpture: Murray, Margaret

Handbook of freedom: Lindsay, Jack

Handbook of literature and the fine arts: Ripley, George

Handbook of the pictures in the International Exhibition of 1862: Taylor, Tom

Handbook to the centenary present: Peach, L. du Garde

Handbook to the English Lakes, A: Payn, James

Handbook to the fine art collection in the International Exhibition of 1862: Palgrave, F.T.

Handbook to the popular, poetical and dramatic literature of Great Britain, from the invention of printing to the Restoration: Hazlitt, William Carew

Handefull of gladsome verses, A: Churchyard, Thomas

Handel: Bray, A.E.

Handful of dust, A: Waugh, Evelyn

Handful of earth, A: Soutar, William

Handful of lavendar, A: Reese, L.W.

Handful of leather, A: Ogilvie, W.H.

Handley Cross: Surtees, R.S.

Handling of words, The: †Lee, Vernon

Handlist of upwards of a thousand volumes of Shakespeariana, A: Halliwell, J.O.

Hand-made gentleman, The: Bacheller, Irving

Handmaid of the Lord, The: †McDiarmid, Hugh

Hands all round: Tennyson, Alfred *Lord*

Hands and other stories: Anderson, Sherwood

Hands of compulsion, The: Barr, A.E.H.

Hands of Dr. Locke, The: Beach, R.E.

Hands of Esau, The: Deland, Margaret

Hands off: Hale, E.E.

Hands off China!: Dickinson G.L.

Hands off Rusia: Zangwill, Israel

Hands up!: Niven, F.J.

Handsome and the deformed leg, The: Franklin, Benjamin

Handsome Brandons, The: Tynan, Katherine

Handsome Humes, The: Black, William

Handsome Langleys, The: †Bell, Neil

Handsome Phil: Riddell, *Mrs.* J.H.

Handy Andy: Lover, Samuel

Handy Dickens, A: †Machen, Arthur

Handy guide for beggars, A: Lindsay, N.V.

Hanging and marriage: Carey, Henry

Hanging judge, The: Stevenson, R.L.

Hanging of the crane, The: Longfellow, H.W.

Hangman's holiday: Sayers, Dorothy

Hangman's house: Byrne, Donn

Hangover Square: Hamilton, Patrick

Hannah: Craik, *Mrs.* D.M.

Hannah: Smart, Christopher

Hannah Jane: †Nasby, Petroleum V.

Hannah Lightfoot: Thoms, W.J.

Hannah Thursten: a story of American life: Taylor, Bayard

Hannap Hewit: Dibdin, Charles

Hannibal takes a hand: Lindsay, Jack

Hannibal Brown: Robinson, E.A.

Hannibal's legacy: Toynbee, A.J.

Hanno: Mitchell, J.L.

Hanover by gaslight: Hovey, Richard

Hanover to Windsor: Fulford, Roger

Hans Christian Andersen: Godden, Rumer

Hans Frost: Walpole, *Sir* Hugh

Hans Holbein the Younger: Ford, Ford Madox

Hansi: Bemelmans, Ludwig

Hansom cab and the pigeons, The: Strong, L.A.G.

Happenings to Forester: Oppenheim, E.Phillips

Happier Eden, The: Seymour, Beatrice Kean

Happiest day of my life, The: Sheldon, C.M.

Happiest days of my life, The: Mais, S.P.B.

Happiness: Lampman, Archibald

Happy Arcadia: Gilbert, *Sir* W.S.

Happy as a King: Jennings, Gertrude

Happy average, The: Whitlock, Brand

Happy birds: Mottram, R.H.

Happy birthday: Greenwood, Walter

Happy birthday: Loos, Anita

Happy captives, The: Theobald, Lewis

Happy critic, The: Van Doren, Mark

Happy days: Beckett, Samuel

Happy days: Greenwood, Walter

Happy days: Milne, A.A.

Happy days: Nash, Ogden

Happy days!: Somerville, Edith

Happy days, 1880–1892: Mencken, H.L.

Happy Dodd: Cooke, R.T.

Happy end, The: Hergesheimer, Joseph

Happy ending, The: (†Ian Hay), Beith, *Sir* John Hay

Happy ending, The: Walmsley, Leo

Happy episode, The: Hillyer, Robert

Happy ever after: †Armstrong, Anthony

Happy ever after: Seymour, Beatrice Kean

Happy families: (Southwold, Stephen), †Bell, Neil

Happy family, The: Swinnerton, Frank

Happy fool, The: Palmer, J.L.

Happy foreigner, The: Bagnold, Enid

Happy go-lucky: (†Ian Hay), Beith, *Sir* John Hay

Happy grandmother, The: Child, L.M.

Happy half-century, A: Repplier, Agnes

Happy hangman, The: Brighouse, Harold

Happy harvest, The: Farnol, J.J.

Happy hearts: Turner, E.S.

Happy highways, The: Jameson, Storm

Happy hours at Wynford Grange: †Bede, Cuthbert

Happy housewife, The: Simpson, H. de G.

Happy hypocrite, The: Beerbohm, *Sir* Max

Happy hypocrite, The: †Dane, Clemence

Happy isles, The: †King, Basil

Happy Jack: †Brand, Max

Happy journey, The: Wilder, Thornton

Happy kingdom, The: Peattie, D.C.

Happy land: Kantor, Mackinlay

Happy land, The: Gilbert, *Sir* W.S.

Happy little Harper's weekly: Bangs, J.K.

Happy man, The: Lover, Samuel

Happy mariners, The: Bullett, Gerald

Happy marriage, A: Cambridge, Ada

Happy marriage, The: MacLeish, Archibald

Happy meddler, The: Stern, G.B.

Happy memories: Jennings, Gertrude

Happy pair, The: Sedley, *Sir* Charles

Happy Parrot, The: Chambers, R.W.

Happy place, The: Bemelmans, Ludwig

Happy Prince, The: Wilde, Oscar

Happy princess, The: Ficke, Arthur

Happy prisoner, The: Dickens, Monica

Happy recruit, The: Ridge, W.Pett

Happy return, The: Forester, C.S.

Happy returns: Thirkell, Angela

Happy stories, just to laugh at: Leacock, Stephen

Happy the bride: Pertwee, Roland

Happy tree, The: Gould, Gerald

Happy tree, The: Kaye-Smith, S.

Happy turning, The: Wells, H.G.

Happy valley, The: †Brand, Max

Happy valley, The: Green, H.M.

Happy valley: White, Patrick

Happy warrior, The: Hutchinson, Arthur

Happy-go-lucky Morgans, The: Thomas, E.E.P.

Hapsburg monarchy, The: Steed, H.W.

Harbinger, The: Holmes, Oliver Wendell

Harbor, The: Poole, Ernest

Harbor master, The: Roberts, T.G.

Harbour tales down north: Duncan, Norman

Harbourmaster, The: McFee, William

Harbours of England, The: Ruskin, John

Harbours of memory: McFee, William

Hard cash: Reade, Charles

Hard facts: Spring, Howard

Hard light: Macartney, Frederick

Hard lines: Nash, Ogden

Hard maple: Warner, A.B.

Hard measure: Hall, Joseph

Hard struggle, A: Marston, J.W.

Hard times: Dickens, Charles

Harding's luck: Nesbit, E.

Hardscrabble: Richardson, John

Hardy Norseman, A: Lyall, Edna

Hardy, the novelist: Cecil, *Lord* David

Hardyknute: Ramsay, Allan

Hare and the Easter eggs: Uttley, Alison

Hare joins the Home Guard: Uttley, Alison

Hare sitting up: (†Michael Innes), Stewart, J. I. M.

Hargrave: Trollope, Frances

Hari, the jungle lad: Mukherji, D. G.

Hark the herald: Aldington, Richard

Hark to these three; talk about style: Moore, T. S.

Harkriders, The: Read, O. P.

Harlan miners speak: Dos Passos, John

Harlan miners speak: Dreiser, Theodore

Harleian Miscellany, The: Oldys, William

Harlem: Benét, W. R.

Harlem shadows: McKay, Claude

Harlequin a sorcerer: Theobald, Lewis

Harlequin and Columbine: Tarkington, Booth

Harlequin, Cock-Robin and Jenny Wren: Gilbert, *Sir* W. S.

Harlequin house: Sharp, Margery

Harlequin opal: Hume, F. W.

Harlequin teague: Colman, George, *the elder*

Harlequinade, The: Barker, Harley Granville

Harlequinade: Rattigan, Terence

Harley Greenoak's charge: Mitford, Bertram

Harmer John: Walpole, *Sir* Hugh

Harmonics: Hovey, Richard

Harmonie of the Church, The: Drayton, Michael

Harmonium: Stevens, Wallace

Harmony: Jones, H. A.

Harold: Phillips, Stephen

Harold: Tennyson, Alfred *Lord*

Harold: Willson, H. B.

Harold Adams Junior: Creighton, D. G.

Harold Gilman: Lewis, P. Wyndham

Harold Laski: Martin, B. K.

Harold the dauntless: Scott, *Sir* Walter

Harold, the last of the Saxons: Lytton, E. G. E. B. *1st Baron*

Harold's leap: Smith, Stevie

Harp, The: Lewis, Ethelreda

Harp of a thousand strings: Davis, H. L.

Harp of Aeolus, The: Grigson, Geoffrey

Harper of Heaven: Service, Robert

Harpe's Head: a legend of Kentucky, The: Hall, James

Harps in the wind: Hichens, Robert

Harp-weaver, The: Millay, E. St. Vincent

Harriet: Jenkins, Elizabeth

Harriet Hume: †West, Rebecca

Harrigan, †Brand, Max

Harrington: Edgeworth, Maria

Harrington's interpretation of his age: Tawney, R. H.

Harrow, The: Scully, W. C.

Harry and Lucy: Edgeworth, Maria

Harry Coverdale's courtship and all that came of it: Smedley, F. E.

Harry Dale's jockey Wild Rose: Gould, Nathaniel

Harry Guy, the widow's son: Hale, S. J. B.

Harry Harefoot: Ingraham, J. H.

Harry Heathcote of Gangoil: Trollope, Anthony

Harry Joscelyn: Oliphant, Margaret

Harry Muir: Oliphant, Margaret

Harry Ogilvie: Grant, James

Harry Treverton, his tramps and troubles: Barker, M. A.

Harsh voice, The: †West, Rebecca

Hartland Forest: Bray, Anna Eliza

Hartley's theory of the human mind: Priestley, Joseph

Hartopp Jubilee, The: Hall, Anna Maria

Harum, The: Percy, Edward

Harum-scarum schoolgirl, A: Brazil, Angela

Harunobu: Noguchi, Yone

Harvard college in the seventeenth century: Morison, S. E.

Harvest: Ward, *Mrs.* Humphrey

Harvest comedy: Swinnerton, Frank

Harvest moon, The: Kirby, William

Harvest moon, The: Thomas, Augustus

Harvest of stories from half a century of writing: Canfield, Dorothy

Harvest of the sea, The: Grenfell, *Sir* Wilfred

Harvest poems, 1910–1960: Sandburg, Carl

Harvest triumphant: Denison, Merrill

Harvester, The: Stratton, Porter Gene

Harvesters, The: Symons, Arthur

Harvest-home, The: Dibdin, Charles

Harvesting: Bacheller, Irving

Harvesting, A: Phillpotts, Eden

Harvest-tide: Morris, *Sir* Lewis

Harvey: Chase, M. C.

Harvey Garrard's crime: Oppenheim, E. Phillips

Harveys, The: Kingsley, Henry

Has Man a future?: Russell, Bertrand

Has religion made useful contribution to civilization?: Russell, Bertrand

Hash Knife outfit, The: Grey, Zane

Hassan: Flecker, James Elroy

Hasta la vista: Morley, C. D.

Hasting day, The: Clarke, G. H.

Hastings, Lewes, Rye, and the Sussex Marshes: Patmore, Coventry

Hasty marriage: Richards, Grant

Hasty-pudding, The: Barlow, Joel

Hat on the bed, The: O'Hara, J. H.

Hatch not a Jew: Klein, A. M.

Hatchment, A: Cunninghame Graham, Robert

Hatchways: Sidgewick, Ethel

Hate of treason, The: Breton, Nicholas

Hated servants: Rubenstein, Harold F.

Hathercourt Rectory: Molesworth, *Mrs.*

Hats of humanity historically, humorously and aesthetically considered, The: Sala, G. A. H.

Hatter's castle: Cronin, A.J.

Hau Kiou Choaan: Percy, Thomas

Haunch of venison, The: Goldsmith, Oliver

Haunted: De la Mare, Walter

Haunted: Maltby, H.F.

Haunted and the haunters, The: Lytton, E.G.E.B. *1st Baron*

Haunted biographer, The: Bradford, Gamaliel

Haunted bookshop, The: Morley, C.D.

Haunted forest, The: Tomlinson, H.M.

Haunted gallery, The: †Bethell, M.U.

Haunted garden, The: Treece, Henry

Haunted hearts: Cummins, M.S.

Haunted hotel, The: Collins, Wilkie

Haunted house, The: Belloc, Hilaire

Haunted house, The: Woolf, Virginia

Haunted lady: Rinehart, Mary Roberts

Haunted lives: Le Fanu, Shendan

Haunted man, The: Dickens, Charles

Haunted mirror, The: Roberts, E.M.

Haunted river, The: Riddell, *Mrs.* J.H.

Haunted vintage, The: †Bowen, Marjorie

Hauntings: †Lee, Vernon

Haunts of men, The: Chambers, R.W.

Havana bound: Roberts, C.E.M.

Have a heart: Maltby, H.F.

Have a heart: Wodehouse, P.G.

Have his carcase: Sayers, Dorothy

Have they attacked Mary. He giggled: Stein, Gertrude

Have with you to Saffron-Walden: Nash, Thomas

Have you anything to declare?: Baring, Maurice

Have you anything to declare?: Jennings, Gertrude

Have you read "casuals of the sea"?: Morley, C.D.

Havelock Ellis: Calder-Marshall, Arthur

Havelock's march: Massey, Gerald

Haven, The: Collins, Dale

Haven: Lewisohn, Ludwig

Haven, The: Phillpotts, Eden

Haven of rest and Dr. Pertwee's poor patients, The: Rowe, Richard

Haven of the spirit: Denison, Merrill

Haven's End: Marquand, J.P.

Haveth childers everywhere: Joyce, James

Haviland's chum: Mitford, Bertram

Having fun: Mackail, Denis

Having the last word: Brown, Ivor

Havoc: Oppenheim, E. Phillips

Hawaii: Michener, J.A.

Hawaii, scenes and impressions: Gerould, Katharine

Hawaiian life: Stoddard, C.W.

Hawaiian tales: Colum, Padraic

Hawara: Petrie, *Sir* William Flinders

Hawara portfolio, The: Petrie, *Sir* William Flinders

Hawbuck Grange: Surtees, R.S.

Hawbucks, The: Masefield, John

Hawk and the handsaw, The: (†Michael Innes), Stewart, J.I.M.

Hawk on the wind: Derleth, A.W.

Hawks of Hawk-hollow, The: Bird, R.M.

Hawkstone bow-meeting, The: Warburton, R.E.E.

Haworth's: Burnett, Frances Hodgson

Hawthorn and lavender: Henley, W.E.

Hawthorn tree, The: Dole, N.H.

Hawthorn tree, The: Green, Paul

Hawthorne: James, Henry

Hawthorne: Stedman, E.C.

Haxby's circus: Prichard, K.S.

Haxtons, The: Walpole, *Sir* Hugh

Hay any worke for cooper: †Marprelate, Martin

Hay fever: Coward, Noel

Hayling family, The: Monkhouse, A.N.

Haym Salomon: Fast, Howard M.

Hayward's fight: Ridge, W. Pett

Haywire: Bolitho, H.H.

Hazard of new fortunes, A: Howells, W.D.

Hazards: Gibson, Wilfrid

Hazards of Smith, The: Bedford-Jones, Henry

Hazel-blossoms: Whittier, J.G.

Hazelwood-Hall: Bloomfield, Robert

He: Lang, Andrew

He and she: Crothers, Rachel

He and she: Story, W.W.

He brings great news: †Dane, Clemence

He came down from Heaven: Williams, Charles

He could not have slipped: †Beeding, Francis

He dwelt among us: †Connor, Ralph

He fell in love with his wife: Roe, E.P.

He is here: Sheldon, C.M.

He knew he was right: Trollope, Anthony

He knew Lincoln: Tarbell, Ida

He looked for a city: Hutchinson, Arthur

He sent forth a raven: Roberts, E.M.

He shall not rise: Fairburn, A.R.D.

He that will not when he may: Oliphant, Margaret

He was born gay: Williams, Emlyn

He was found in the road: †Armstrong, Anthony

He who rides a tiger: Bhattacharya, B.

He who whispers: Carr, J.D.

He wou'd if he cou'd: Bickerstaffe, Isaac

He wouldn't kill Patience: †Carter Dickson

Head and heart of Thomas Jefferson, The: Dos Passos, John

Head girl at the Gables, The: Brazil, Angela

Head in green bronze: Walpole, *Sir* Hugh

Head of a traveller: Day-Lewis, C.

Head of Kay's, The: Wodehouse, P.G.

Head of the family, The: Craik, *Mrs.* Dinah

Head of the firm, The: Riddell, *Mrs.* J.H.

Head of the house of Coombe, The: Burnett, Frances Hodgson

Head station, The: Praed, *Mrs.* C.

Headless horseman, The: Benét, S.V.

Headless horseman, The: Reid, T.M.

Headless hound, The: Mottram, R.H.

Headlong Hall: Peacock, Thomas Love

Headmistress, The: Thirkell, Angela

Heads of all fashion: Taylor, John

Heads of the people: Hunt, Leigh

Heads of the people: Jerrold, Douglas

Headsman, The: Cooper, James Fenimore

Head-waters of Canadian Literature: MacMechan, A.M.

Healer, The: Herrick, Robert

Healing of heaven, The: Fausset, Hugh

Healing touch, The: Gibbs, *Sir* Philip

Health: Brown, *Dr.* John

Health: Ramsay, Allan

Health and education: Kingsley, Charles

Health and holiness: Thompson, Francis

Health and wealth: Hubbard, Elbert

Health, husbandry and handicraft: Martineau, Harriet

Health to the gentlemanly profession of servingmen, A: Markham, Gervase

Health trip to the tropics: Willis, N.P.

Hear both sides: Holcroft, Thomas

Hear us O Lord from Thy dwelling place: Lowry, M.B.

Heart and Cross: Oliphant, Margaret

Heart and science: Collins, Wilkie

Heart and the world, The: Marston, John W.

Heart for the gods of Mexico, A: Aiken, Conrad

Heart of a child, The: Bottome, Phyllis

Heart of a child, The: Frankau, Gilbert

Heart of a goof, The: Wodehouse, P.G.

Heart of England, The: Brown, Ivor

Heart of England, The: Thomas, E.E.P.

Heart of Hindustan, The: Radhakrishan, Sarvepalli

Heart of jade, The: Madariaga, Salvador de

Heart of Jessy Laurie, The: Barr, A.E.H.

Heart of life, The: Mallock, W.H.

Heart of London, The: Dickens, Monica

Heart of London, The: Morton, H.V.

Heart of man: Woodberry, G.E.

Heart of Maryland, The: Belasco, David

Heart of Oak: Russell, W.C.

Heart of Paddy Whack, The: Crothers, Rachel

Heart of peace, The: Housman, Laurence

Heart of Penelope, The: Lowndes, M.A.

Heart of Princess Osra, The: (†Anthony Hope), Hawkins, Anthony Hope

Heart of Rome, The: Crawford, F. Marion

Heart of spring: Neilson, J.S.

Heart of the bush, The: Grossmann, Edith

Heart of the country, The: Bates, H.E.

Heart of the country, The: Ford, Ford Madox

Heart of the hills, The: Fox, John

Heart of the hills: Watson, A.D.

Heart of the house, The: Jacob, Naomi

Heart of the hunter, The: Van der Post, Laurens

Heart of the matter, The: Greene, Graham

Heart of the new thought, The: Wilcox, Ella Wheeler

Heart of the sunset: Beach, R.E.

Heart of the West: †Henry, O.

Heart of the world: Haggard, *Sir* H. Rider

Heart of the world, The: Sheldon, C.M.

Heart songs: Blewett, Jean

Heart stories: Blewett, Jean

Heart stories: Sheldon, C.M.

Heartache in Canaan: Willson, H.B.

Heartbreak House: Shaw, G.B.

Hearts and diamonds: Wodehouse, P.G.

Hearts and faces: Gibbon, J.M.

Hearts are trumps: Hannay, James

Hearts are trumps: Lemon, Mark

Heart's desire: Hough, Emerson

Hearts enduring: Erskine, John

Heart's highway, The: Freeman, Mary

Heart's journey, The: Sassoon, Siegfried

Heart's kindred: Gale, Zona

Hearts of controversy: Meynell, Alice

Hearts of gold: Ogilvie, W.H.

Hearts of oak: Jones, H.A.

Hearts of steel, The: McHenry, James

Hearts of three: London, Jack

Hearts to sell: Jennings, Gertrude

Heartsease: Yonge, Charlotte M.

Heartsease and rue: Lowell, J.R.

Heat of the day, The: Bowen, E.D.C.

Heat of the sun, The: O'Faolain, Sean

Heat wave: Pertwee, Roland

Heath Hover mystery, The: Mitford, Bertram

Heathen days, 1890–1936: Mencken, H.L.

Heather and snow: Macdonald, George

Heather field and Maeve, The: Martyn, Edward

Heather of the high land: Stringer, A.J.A.

Heatwave in Berlin: Cusack, E.D.

Heaven and Charing Cross: Knox, R.A.

Heaven and earth: Murry, John Middleton

Heaven and Hell: Huxley, Aldous

Heaven lies about us: Spring, Howard

Heavenly city of the eighteenth century philosophers, The: Becker, C.L.

Heavenly footman, The: Bunyan, John

Heavenly guest, The: Thaxter, C.L.

Heavenly ladder, The: Mackenzie, *Sir* Compton

Heavenly promises: Faber, F.W.

Heavenly twins, The: †Grand, Sarah

Heavens: Untermeyer, Louis

Heaven's alarm to the world: Mather, Increase

Heavens and earth: Benét, S.V.

Heavens glory, seeke it: Rowlands, Samuel

Heaven's my destination: Wilder, Thornton

Heaven's treasury opened: Hooker, Thomas

Heavy weather: Wodehouse, P.G.

Hebrew melodies: Byron, George Gordon *Lord*

Hebrew myths. Genesis: Graves, Robert

Hebridean journey: Sutherland, H.G.

Heckington: Gore, Catherine

Hedge and the horse, The: Belloc, Hilaire

Hedge leaves: Ensor, *Sir* R.C.K.

Hedge trimmings: Street, A.G.

Hedged in: Ward, E.S.

Hedgehog, The: Doolittle, Hilda

Hedonistic theories from Aristippus to Spencer: Watson, John

Heel of Achilles, The: †Delafield, E.M.

Heemskerck shoals: Fitzgerald, R.D.

Heidelberg: James, G.P.R.

Heidenmauer, The: Cooper, James Fenimore

Heimweh: Long, J.L.

Heinemann's international library (Introductions to all volumes): Gosse, *Sir* Edmund

Heinrich Heine: Arnold, Matthew

Heinrich Heine: paradox and poet: Untermeyer, Louis

Heir, The: Sackville-West, Victoria

Heir at law, The: Colman, George, *the younger*

Heir of Fairmount Grange, The: Machar, A.M.

Heir of Gaymount, The: Cooke, John

Heir of Linne, The: Buchanan, R.W.

Heir of Morocco, The: Settle, Elkanah

Heir of Redclyffe, The: Yonge, Charlotte M.

Heir of Selwood, The: Gore, Catherine

Heir of the ages, The: Payn, James

Heir of the world, The: Fairfield, S.L.

Heir presumptive and the heir apparent, The: Oliphant, Margaret

Heir to Grand-Pré, The: Herbin, J.F.

Heir to millions, An: Fawcett, Edgar

Heire, The: May, Thomas

Heirefter followis the quair maid be King James of Scotland: James I

Heiress, The: Burgoyne, *Sir* John

Heiress of Bruges, The: Gratton, T.C.

Heirs apparent: Gibbs, *Sir* Philip

Helbeck of Bannisdale: Ward, *Mrs.* Humphrey

Held by the enemy: Gillette, William

Held in bondage: †Ouida

Helen: Edgeworth, Maria

Helen: (†E.V. Cunningham), Fast, Howard M.

Helen: Hardy, A.S.

Helen: Herbert, *Sir* A.P.

Helen: Heyer, Georgette

Helen: Lamb, Mary

Helen Adair: †Becke, Louis

Helen and Aphrodite: Doughty, *Sir* A.G.

Helen and Olga: Manning, Anne

Helen comes of age: Lindsay, Jack

Helen Halsey: Simms, W.G.

Helen in Egypt: Doolittle, Hilda

Helen Keller: Brooks, Van Wyck

Helen of Lancaster Gate: Gibbs, *Sir* Philip

Helen of the old house: Wright, H.B.

Helen of Troy: Lang, Andrew

Helen of Troy: Teasdale, Sara

Helen redeemed: Hewlett, Maurice

Helen retires: Erskine, John

Helen with the high hand: Bennett, Arnold

Helena: More, P.E.

Helena: Waugh, Evelyn

Helena in Troas: Todhunter, John

Helena's household: De Mille, James

Helenore: Ross, Alexander

Helen's lovers: Bullett, Gerald

Helen's tower: Nicolson, Hon. *Sir* Harold

Helen's tower: Tennyson, Alfred *Lord*

Helianthus: †Ouida

Helicon home colony, The: Sinclair, Upton

Heliodora: Doolittle, Hilda

Heliogabalus: Mencken, H.L.

Heliopolis: Petrie, *Sir* William Flinders

Hell: Sinclair, Upton

Hell: Tarkington, Booth

"Hell fer sartain": Fox, John

Hell! said the Duchess: Arlen, Michael

Hellas: Shelley, P.B.

Hell-bent for heaven: Hughes, Hatcher

Hellbox: O'Hara, J.H.

Hellenism: Toynbee, Arnold

Hellenism and the modern world: Murray, Gilbert

Hellenistic philosophies: More, P.E.

"Hello Soldier!": Dyson, E.G.

Hello towns!: Anderson, Sherwood

Hell's broke loose: Rowlands, Samuel

Hell's loose: Pertwee, Roland

Helogabalus: Nathan, G.J.

Héloïse and Abélard: Moore, George

Help to English history, A: Heylyn, Peter

Help yourself!: Maltby, H.F.

Helpful hints for business helpers: Hubbard, Elbert

Helping hand, The: Gould, Gerald

Helping hands, The: Jennings, Gertrude

Helpmate, The: Sinclair, May

Helter Skelter: Swift, Jonathan

Hemlock for eight: Bax, Clifford

Hemming, the adventurer: Roberts, T.G.

Hempfield: Baker, Ray Stannard

Hen upon a steeple, A: Temple, Joan

Henri Julien: Barbeau, C.M.

Henri quatre: Morton, Thomas

Henrietta, The: Howard, B.C.

Henrietta: Lennox, Charlotte

Henrietta Temple: Disraeli, Benjamin

Henry: Adams, Francis

Henry: Cumberland, Richard

Henry: Gow, Ronald

Henry Adams: Adams, J.T.

Henry Airbubble: Turner, W.J.R.

Henry Bly: Ridler, A.B.

Henry Bournes Higgins: †Palmer, Nettie

Henry Bradley: Bridges, Robert

Henry Brocken: De la Mare, Walter

Henry David Thoreau: Van Doren, Mark

Henry de Pomeroy: Bray, Anna Eliza

Henry Dunbar: Braddon, Mary Elizabeth

Henry Fielding: Dobson, Henry Austin

Henry Fielding: Jenkins, Elizabeth

Henry for Hugh: Ford, Ford Madox

Henry Handel Richardson: Palmer, Nettie

Henry Howard: Ingraham, J.H.

Henry Hudson: Denison, Merrill

Henry Hudson: Janvier, T.A.

Henry Hudson: Powys, L.C.

Henry Irving: Craig, Gordon

Henry Irving: Winter, William

Henry Irving: actor and manager: Archer, William

Henry James: Ford, Ford Madox

Henry James: †West, Rebecca

Henry James, man and author: Edgar, O.P.

Henry Kendall: Stephens, A.G.

Henry Masterton: James, G.P.R.

Henry Moore: Grigson, Geoffrey

Henry Moore: life and works: Read, Sir Herbert

Henry Moore, sculptor: Read, Sir Herbert

Henry Moore: sculpture and drawings: Read, Sir Herbert

Henry of Agincourt: Strong, L.A.G.

Henry of Guise: James, G.P.R.

Henry of Navarre: Pearson, Hesketh

Henry Plumdew: Vulliamy, C.E.

Henry St. John, Gentleman of "Flower of hundreds": Cooke, John Esten

Henry Smeaton: James, G.P.R.

Henry the Seventh: Macklin, Charles

Henry Wadsworth Longfellow: Higginson, T.W.

Henry Williamson animal saga, The: Williamson, Henry

Henry IV (Pts. I and II): Shakespeare, William

Henry V: Shakespeare, William

Henry VI (Pts. I, II and III): Shakespeare, William

Henry VII: Williams, Charles

Henry VIII: Beaumont, Francis

Henry VIII: Pollard, A.F.

Henry VIII: Shakespeare, William

Henry VIII: Simpson, H. de G.

Hephaestus: Stringer, A.J.A.

Hephzibah Guiness: thee and me: Mitchell, S.W.

Hepplestalls: Brighouse, Harold

Heptalogia, The: Swinburne, A.C.

Heptameron of civill discourses, An: Whetstone, George

Her baby brother: Moulton, E.L.

Her cardboard lover: Wodehouse, P.G.

Her convict: Braddon, Mary Elizabeth

Her fair fame: Fawcett, Edgar

Her foot is on the brass rail: Marquis, Don

Her great match: Fitch, Clyde William

Her infinite variety: Whitlock, Brand

Her Ladyship: Mackail, Denis

Her majesty the Queen: Cooke, John Esten

Her Majesty's: Fry, Christopher

Her mother's darling: Riddell, Mrs. J.H.

Her mountain lover: Garland, Hamlin

Her own way: Fitch, Clyde William

Her pilgrim: Mackaye, Percy

Her serene Highness: Phillips, D.G.

Her son: Vachell, H.A.

Her son's wife: Canfield, Dorothy

Her tongue: Jones, H.A.

Her weight in gold: McCutcheon, G.B.

Her wild oats: Rubenstein, Harold F.

Heraclitus: Ghose, Sri Aurobindo

Herakles: Lodge, G.C.

Herald of literature, The: Godwin, William

Herald of spring, The: Tagore, Sir R.

Heralds of Australian literature: †Boldrewood, Rolf

Heralds of the dawn, The: Watson, Sir J.W.

Herb basket, An: Eberhart, Richard

Herb moon, The: †Hobbes, John Oliver

Herb of the field, The: Yonge, Charlotte M.

Herb o'grace: Tynan, Katherine

Herbal of all sorts, A: Grigson, G.E.H.

Herball, The: Gerard, John

Herbert Beerbohm Tree: Beerbohm, *Sir* Max

Herbert Read: Treece, Henry

Herbert Spencer: an estimate and a view: Royce, Josiah

Herbert Tracy: Lippard, George

Hercule Poirot's Christmas: Christie, Agatha

Hercules my shipmate: Graves, Robert

Here after foloweth a lytell boke called Collyn Clout: Skelton, John

Here after foloweth a lytell boke, which hath to name, why come ye nat to courte: Skelton, John

Here after foloweth certayne bokes whose names here after shall appere Speke Parrot The deth of the noble prince Kyng Edwarde the fourth: Skelton, John

Here after foloweth the boke of Phyllyp Sparowe: Skelton, John

Here and beyond: Wharton, Edith

Here and hereafter: Pain, B.E.O.

Here and now: Layton, Irving

Here and there: Maugham, Somerset

Here are ladies: Stephens, James

Here are my lectures and stories: Leacock, Stephen

Here be blue and white violets from the garden: Gale, Norman

Here be dragons: Gibbons, Stella

Here begynneth a lytel treatyse named the bowge of courte: Skelton, John

Here come the clowns: Barry, Philip

Here comes the lady: Shiel, M.P.

Here comes, there goes, you know who: Saroyan, William

Here followes ye melancholie tale...of Amelia: Strong, L.A.G.

Here followythe dyvers balettys and dyties solacyous: Skelton, John

Here is America: Bentley, Phyllis

Here is Faery: †Maurice, Furnley

Here is New York: White, E.B.

Here lies: Parker, Dorothy

Here, my son: Bean, C.E.

Here on a darkling plain: Derleth, A.W.

Here stays good Yorkshire: Bird, W.R.

Here, there and everywhere: Partridge, Eric

Here today and gone tomorrow: Bromfield, Louis

Here we come gathering: †Armstrong, Anthony and Philip King

Heredity and politics: Haldane, J.B.S.

Hereditary genius: Galton, *Sir* Francis

Here's a new day: Uttley, Alison

Here's misery: Knox, E.V.

Here's O'Hara: O'Hara, J.H.

Heresy of Appollinaris, The: Newman, J.H.

Heretics: Chesterton, G.K.

Hereward: Lindsay, Jack

Hereward the Wake: Kingsley, Charles

Heritage: Sackville-West, Victoria

Heritage and its history, A: Compton-Burnett, Ivy

Heritage of America, The: Commager, H.S.

Heritage of Dedlow Marsh, The: Harte, Bret

Heritage of Hatcher Ide, The: Tarkington, Booth

Heritage of man, The: Massingham, Harold

Heritage of stone, old Tasmanian buildings: (†Donald Barr), Barrett, C.L.

Heritage of symbolism, The: Bowra, *Sir* Maurice

Heritage of the desert, The: Grey, Zane

Herman de Ruyter: Ingraham, J.H.

Herman Melville: Freeman, John

Herman Melville: Mumford, Lewis

Hermia Suydam: Atherton, Gertrude

Hermione: Sill, E.R.

Hermione, a knight of the HolyGhost:Grossmann,Edith

Hermione and her little group of serious thinkers: Marquis, Don

Hermit and the wild woman, The: Wharton, Edith

Hermit in Van Diemen's land, The: Savery, Henry

Hermit of Carmel, A: Santayana, George

Hermit of Warkworth, The: Percy, Thomas

Hermitage, The: Sill, E.R.

Hermits, The: Kingsley, Charles

Hermit's tale, A: Lee, Sophia

Hermsprong: Bage, Robert

Hermy: Molesworth, *Mrs.*

Hernán Cortés: Madariaga, Salvador de

Hernando de Soto: Cunninghame Graham, R.B.

Herne's egg, The: Yeats, W.B.

Hero, A: Craik, *Mrs.* Dinah

Hero, The: Maugham, Somerset

Hero and a martyr, A: Reade, Charles

Hero and Leander: Marlowe, Christopher

Hero and Leander: Wycherley, William

Hero and Leander, and, Bacchus and Ariadne: Hunt, Leigh

Hero in man, The: Russell, G.W.

Hero of Delhi, The: Pearson, Hesketh

Hero of Santa Maria: Hecht, Ben

Hero of Start Point, The: Oxley, J.M.

Hero of Ticonderoga, A: Robinson, R.E.

Hero stories of New Zealand: Cowan, James

Herod: Phillips, Stephen

Herod and Antipater: Markham, Gervase

Herod and Marianne, †Dane, Clemence

Herod and Marianne: Pordage, Samuel

Herod the Great: Boyle, Roger

Heroes, The: Kingsley, Charles

Heroes all: Wallace, Edgar

Heroes and heroines: Farjeon, Eleanor and Herbert Farjeon

Heroes and heroines of Bitter, Sweet: Beerbohm, Sir Max

Heroes and kings: Williams, Charles

Heroes I have known, twelve who lived great lives: Eastman, Max

Heroes of Canada: Machar, A.M.

Heroes of Clone, The: Kennedy, Margaret

Heroes of freedom: Mee, Arthur

Heroes of the desert: Manning, Anne

Heroes of the Bible: Mee, Arthur

Heroes of the Kalevala: Deutsch, Babette

Heroes of the middle West: Catherwood, Mary

Heroes of time, The: Lindsay, N.V.

Heroic epistle answered by the R..... H.... Lord C..., The: Combe, William

Heroic epistle to a noble D....: Combe, William

Heroic epistle to an unfortunate monarch, An: Combe, William

Heroic epistle to Sir James Wright, An: Combe, William

Heroic epistle to the noble author of the Duchess of Devonshire's Cow, An: Combe, William

Heroic epistle to the Right Honourable the Lord Craven: Combe, William

Heroic idylls: Landor, W. S.

Heroic lives: Sabatini, Rafael

Heroic poem in praise of wine, An: Belloc, Hilaire

Heroic poetry: Bowra, Sir Maurice

Heroic Stubbs, The: Jones, H.A.

Heroick friendship: Otway, Thomas

Heroine in bronze, The: Allen, James Lane

Heroine of Acadia, The: Hannay, James

Heroines of fiction: Howells, W.D.

Hero's funeral, The: Montgomery, Robert

Heroycall epistles of the learned poet Publius Ovidius Naso, The: Turberville, George

Herr Baby: Molesworth, Mrs.

Herr Paulus: Besant, Sir Walter

Herr witch doctor, The: Millin, Sarah Gertrude

Herrick: Pollard, A.W.

Herridge of reality swamp: Hay, William

Herries chronicle, The: Walpole, Sir Hugh

Herself: Sidgewick, Ethel

Herself surprised: Cary, Joyce

He's much to blame: Holcroft, Thomas

Hesper: Garland, Hamlin

Hesperides: Herrick, Robert

Hesperides, The: Palmer, J.L.

Hesperus: Sangster, Charles

Hessian prisoner, The: Bates, H.E.

Hester: Oliphant, Margaret

Hester Stanley at St. Marks: Spofford, H.E.

Hester Stanley's friends: Spofford, H.E.

Hester's mystery: Pinero, Sir A.W.

Hetty: Kingsley, Henry

Hetty Wesley: †Quiller-Couch, Sir Arthur

Hetty's strange history: Jackson, H.H.

Heu-Heu: Haggard, Sir H. Rider

He-who-came?: Holme, Constance

Hey, diddle diddle: (Stephen Southwold), †Bell, Neil

Hey for honesty, down with knavery: Randolph, Thomas

Hey rub-a-dub-dub: Dreiser, Theodore

Hiatus: Phillpotts, Eden

Hiawatha the Hochelagan: Lighthall, W.D.

Hibernian nights' entertainments: Fergusson, Sir Samuel

Hibernian patriot, The: Swift, Jonathan

Hickory Dickory Dock: Christie, Agatha

Hidden children, The: Chambers, R.W.

Hidden city, The: Gibbs, Philip

Hidden door, The: Packard, F.L.

Hidden doors: Gunn, Neil

Hidden flower: Buck, Pearl

Hidden God, The: Brooks, Cleanth

Hidden hand, The: Phillpotts, Eden

Hidden kingdom, The: †Beeding, Francis

Hidden player, The: Noyes, Alfred

Hidden river, The: Jameson, Storm

Hidden sin, The: Browne, Frances

Hidden son, The: Kaye-Smith, Sheila

Hidden stream, The: Knox, R.A.

Hidden tide, The: Quinn, R.J.

Hidden witness, The: †Sapper

Hide and seek: Collins, Wilkie

Hide and seek: Malleson, Miles

Hide and seek: Morley, C.D.

Hide and seek in forest-land: Chambers, R.W.

Hide my eyes: Allingham, Margery

Hide Park: Shirley, James

Hierakonpolis I: Petrie, Sir William Flinders

Hierarchie of the blessed Angells, The: Heywood, Thomas

Hieroglyphic tales: Walpole, Horace

Hieroglyphics: †Machen, Arthur

Hieroglyphikes of the life of man: Quarles, Francis

Higden's Polychronicon: Trevisa, John of

Higgins, a man's Christian: Duncan, Norman

Higgler, The: Coppard, A.E.

High adventure, The: De Selincourt, Hugh

High adventure: Farnol, J.J.

High adventure: Hall, J.N.

High altitude: Webster, E.C.

High altitude: Webster, M.M.

High are the mountains: Cloete, E.F.S.G.

High August: Van Doren, Mark

High Barbaree, The: Hall, J.N. and C.B. Nordhoff

High brows: Marshall, Bruce

High calling, The: Sheldon, C.M.

High country: Burdon, R.M.

High falcon: Adams, Leonie

High forfeit, The: †King, Basil

High Germany: Ford, Ford Madox

High heart, The: †King, Basil

High jump, The: Gielgud, Val

High Jungle: Beebe, William

High life below stairs: Garrick, David

High low along: MacInnes, T.R.E.

High meadows: Uttley, Alison

High noon: Brown, Alice

High place, The: Cabell, James Branch

High price of bullion, The: Ricardo, David

High priestess, The: Grant, Robert

High rising: Thirkell, Angela

High road, The: †Lonsdale, Frederick

High Sierra: Burnett, W.R.

High society: Parker, Dorothy

High spirits: Coward, Noel

High spirits: Payn, James

High summer: Church, Richard

High Toby, The: Priestley, J.B.

High Tor: Anderson, Maxwell

High towers: Costain, T.B.

High Victorian design: Pevsner, Nikolaus

High wind in Jamaica, A: Hughes, R.A.W.

High window, The: Chandler, Raymond

High world, The: Bemelmans, Ludwig

Highbrows, The: Joad, C.E.M.

Higher education of women: Trollope, Anthony

Higher learning in America, The: Veblen, T.B.

High-ho to London: Clune, Frank

Highland cousins: Black, William

Highland dawn: Gibson, Wilfred

Highland fling: Mitford, Nancy

Highland night: Gunn, Neil

Highland pack: Gunn, Neil

Highland rambles and legends to shorten the way: Lauder, Sir T.D.

Highland reel, The: O'Keeffe, John

Highland river: Gunn, Neil

Highlander, The: Macpherson, James

Highlanders, The: Grant, Anne

Highlanders of Glen Ora, The: Grant, James

Highlands of Britain, The: Mais, S.P.B.

Highway and the city, The: Mumford, Lewis

Highway to happiness: Le Gallienne, Richard

Highways and byways: Gratton, T.C.

Highways and byways in Essex: Bax, Clifford

Highways and byways in Sussex: Lucas, E.V.

Highways and byways in the Border: Lang, Andrew

Highways and byways in the Welsh Marches: Mais, S.P.B.

Highways and byways of Buckinghamshire: Shorter, C.K.

Highways of Canadian literature: Logan, J.D.

Hike and the aeroplane: Lewis, H.S.

Hilary St.Ives: Ainsworth, Harrison

Hilary Trent: Vachell, H.A.

Hilda: Duncan, S.J.

Hilda Lessways: Bennett, Arnold

Hilda Wade: Allen, Grant

Hildebrand: Campbell, W.W.

Hill, The: Fast, Howard M.

Hill, The: Vachell, H.A.

Hill figures of England: Petrie, Sir William Flinders

Hill garden: Widdemer, Margaret

Hill is mine, The: Walsh, Maurice

Hill of cloves, The: Wilson, Romer

Hill of Devi, The: Forster, E.M.

Hill of doves, The: Cloete, E.F.S.G.

Hill of dreams, The: †Machen, Arthur

Hill of Howth, The: Strong, L.A.G.

Hill of pains, The: Parker, Sir H.G.

Hill of stones, The: Mitchell, S.W.

Hill of trouble, The: Benson, A.C.

Hill of vision, The: Stephens, James

Hill side, The: Manning, Anne

Hillarys, The: Brighouse, Harold

Hilliad, The: Smart, Christopher

Hillingdon Hall: Surtees, R.S.

Hillman, The: Oppenheim, E. Phillips

Hills and the sea, The: Belloc, Hilaire

Hills and the vale, The: Jefferies, Richard

Hills beyond, The: Wolfe, T.C.

Hills give promise, The: Hillyer, Robert

Hills grow smaller, The: Akins, Zoë

Hills of hate, The: Timms, E.V.

Hills of song, The: Scollard, Clinton

Hills of the Shatemuc, The: Warner, S.B.

Hills of the South: Mais, S.P.B.

Hills of Varna, The: Trease, Geoffrey

Hills stand watch, The: Derleth, A.W.

Hills were joyful together, The: Mais, Roger

Hillsboro people: Canfield, Dorothy

Hillside and Border sketches: Maxwell, W.H.

Hillside and seaside in poetry: Larcom, Lucy

Hillside thaw, A: Frost, Robert

Hillyars and the Burtons, The: Kingsley, Henry

Hilt to hilt: Cooke, J.E.

Hilton's scale of perfection: Underhill, Evelyn

Him (play): Cummings, E.E.

Himatia-Poleos: Munday, Anthony

Hind and the panther, The: Dryden, John

Hind and the panther transvers'd to the story of the country mouse and the City mouse, The: Prior, Matthew

Hind in Richmond Park, A: Hudson, W.H.

Hind let loose, A: Montague, C.E.

Hind Swaraf: Gandhi, M.K.

Hinderers, The: Lyall, Edna

Hindle wakes: Brighouse, Harold

Hindle wakes: Houghton, W.S.

Hindu Dharma: Gandhi, M.K.

Hindu society at cross roads: Panikkar, K.M.

Hindu view of art, The: Anand, M.R.

Hindu view of life, The: Radhakrishan, Sarvepalli

Hinduism and Buddhism: Coomaraswamy, A.K.

Hinduism and Buddhism: Eliot, Sir Charles

Hinduism and the modern world: Panikkar, K.M.

Hint to husbands, A: Cumberland, Richard

Hints addressed to the inhabitants of Edinburgh: Scott, Sir Walter

Hints for Eton masters: Cory, W.J.

Hints on manning the navy: Cooper, James Fenimore

Hints on writing and speech-making: Higginson, T.W.

Hints to a soldier in service: Maxwell, W.H.

Hints to horsekeepers: Herbert, H.W.

Hints to stammerers: Kingsley, Charles

Hints towards forming the character of a young princess: More, Hannah

Hints towards the formation of a more comprehensive theory of life: Coleridge, S.T.

Hippolytus and Bacchae of Euripides, The: Murray, Gilbert

Hippolytus temporizes: Doolittle, Hilda

Hips and haws: Coppard, A.E.

Hireling, The: Hartley, L.P.

Hireling ministry none of Christs, The: Williams, Roger

Hiroshige and Japanese landscapes: Noguchi, Yone

Hiroshima: Knight, G.W.

His apologies: Kipling, Rudyard

His birthday: Chase, M.E.

His brother's keeper: Phillpotts, Eden

His brother's keeper: Sheldon, C.M.

His darling sin: Braddon, M.E.

His daughter first: Hardy, A.S.

His Excellency: Gilbert, Sir W.S.

His family: Poole, Ernest

His fatal beauty: Lucas, E.V.

His father's son: Matthews, J.B.

His fellow men: Dunsany, Edward Plunkett Baron

His fortunate grace: Atherton, Gertrude

His German wife: Sladen, D.B.W.

His gifts and promises: Moffat, James

His grace of Osmonde: Burnett, Frances, Hodgson

His Grace's answer to Jonathan: Swift, Jonathan

His great adventure: Herrick, Robert

His Honour and a lady: Duncan, S.J.

His hour: Glyn, Elinor

His house in order: Pinero, Sir A.W.

His human majesty: Boyle, Kay

His island princess: Russell, W.C.

His last bow: Doyle, Sir Arthur Conan

His last legs: Bernard, W.B.

His level best: Hale, E.E.

His little mother: Craik, Mrs. D.M.

His Lordship: Gibbs, Sir Philip

His Majesties poeticall exercises at vacant houres: James VI of Scotland

His Majesty: Barker, Harley Granville

His majesty, myself: †Harrington, George F.

His Majesty's embassy: Baring, Maurice

His Majesty's well-beloved: Orczy, Baroness

His Majesty's Yankees: Raddall, T.H.

His monkey wife: Collier, John

His mother: O'Higgins, H.J.

His native wife: †Becke, Louis

His natural life: Clarke, Marcus

His observations in his travailes upon the state of the XVII Provinces as they stood in 1609: Overbury, Sir Thomas

His one fault: Trowbridge, J.T.

His own master: Trowbridge, J.T.

His own people: Tarkington, Booth

His Pa's romance: Riley, J.W.

His people: Cunninghame Graham, Robert

His Royal Happiness: Duncan, S.J.

His second campaign: Thompson, Maurice

His second war: Waugh, Alec

His second wife: Poole, Ernest

His sombre rivals: Roe, E.P.

His vanished star: †Craddock, C.E.

His Worship the Mayor: Greenwood, Walter

Historia amoris: Saltus, E.E.

Historians and historical societies: Adams, C.F.

Historian's holiday: Bryant, Sir Arthur

Historic Boston and its neighbourhood: Hale, E.E.

Historic certainties respecting the early history of America: Whately, Richard

Historic doubt on the life and reign of King Richard the Third: Walpole, Horace

Historic doubts relative to Napoleon Bonaparte: Whately, Richard

Historic farms of South Africa: Fairbridge, Dorothea

Historic houses of South Africa: Fairbridge, Dorothea

Historic Nova Scotia: Bird, W.R.

Historic oddities and strange events: Baring-Gould, Sabine

Historic Thames, The: Belloc, Hilaire

Historical account of the heathen gods and heroes, An: King, William

Historical and biographical essays: Forster, John

Historical and descriptive account of the caricatures of James Gillray: Wright, Thomas

Historical and descriptive sketch of Ludlow Castle: Wright, Thomas

Historical and military essays: Fortescue, *Sir* John

Historical and miscellaneous tracts: Heylyn, Peter

Historical and moral view of the origin and progress of the French Revolution, An: Wollstonecraft, Mary

Historical and philosophical essays: Senior, Nassan

Historical and political essays: Lecky, W.E.H.

Historical and posthumous memoirs, 1772–84: Wraxall, *Sir* William

Historical and revolutionary incidents of the early settlers of the United States: Webber, C.W.

Historical and sporting notes on Quebec and its environs: LeMoine, *Sir* J.M.

Historical appendices I–V to the report of the Commissioners appointed to inquire into the constitution and working of the ecclesiastical courts: Stubbs, William

Historical background for the Massachusetts Bay tercentenary in 1930: Morison, S.E.

Historical causes of the present state of affairs in Italy, The: Trevelyan, G.M.

Historical collections of the noble families of Cavendishe, Holles, Vere, Harley and Ogle: Collins, Arthur

Historical collections of the noble family of Windsor: Collins, Arthur

Historical deluge: Dawson, *Sir* J.W.

Historical dictionary of American English, A: Craigie, *Sir* William Alexander

Historical discourse, delivered before the citizens of Concord, A: Emerson, R.W.

Historical disquisition concerning the knowledge which the ancients had of India, An: Robertson, William

Historical dramas: Taylor, Tom

Historical dramas: Yonge, C.M.

Historical essay on architecture, An: Hope, Thomas

Historical essay on the dress of the ancient and modern Irish: Walker, J.C.

Historical essay on the life and writings of Michael Drayton, An: Oldys, William

Historical essays and studies: Acton, John

Historical gleanings: Hind, H.Y.

Historical imagination, The: Collingwood, R.G.

Historical introductions to the Rolls Series: Stubbs, William

Historical lectures and essays: Kingsley, Charles

Historical manual of English prosody, A: Saintsbury, George

Historical memoir on Italian tragedy: Walker, J.C.

Historical memoires on the reigns of Queen Elizabeth and King James: Osborne, Francis

Historical memoirs of the Irish bards: Walker, J.C.

Historical mysteries: Lang, Andrew

Historical narration concerning heresie and the punishment thereof, An: Hobbes, Thomas

Historical New Testament, The: Moffat, James

Historical nights' entertainment, The: Sabatini, Rafael

Historical notes on Quebec and its environs: LeMoine, *Sir* J.M.

Historical novel, The: Butterfield, Herbert

Historical novel, The: Matthews, J.B.

Historical odes: Dixon, R.W.

Historical preface to Tract No. 90: Pusey, E.B.

Historical register, for the year, 1736, The: Fielding, Henry

Historical remains of my own time (1772–84): Wraxall, *Sir* William

Historical scarabs: Petrie, *Sir* William Flinders

Historical sketch of Christian science mind-healing: Eddy, M.D.

Historical sketch of Stokesay Castle, Salop.: Wright, Thomas

Historical sketch of the Nova Scotia Baptist Association, A: Rand, S.T.

Historical sketches: Newman, J.H.

Historical sketches of Ceylon Church history: Perera, Simon

Historical sketches of statesmen in the time of George III: Brougham, H.P.

Historical sketches of the reign of George II: Oliphant, Margaret

Historical sketches of the reign of Queen Anne: Oliphant, Margaret

Historical studies: Petrie, *Sir* William Flinders

Historical survey of English literature, with special reference to the spirit of the times: Saito, Takeshi

Historical tradition and oriental research: Breasted, J.H.

Historical traveller, The: Gore, Catherine

Historical view of the progress of discovery on the more northern coasts of America: Tytler, P.F.

Historie of ane nobil and wailzeand squyer William Meldrum, The: Lindsay, *Sir* David

Historie of Calanthrop and Lucilla, The: Kennedy, John

Historie of Edward the Fourth, The: Habington, William

Historie of Orlando Furioso, The: Greene, Robert

Historie of Samson, The: Quarles, Francis

Historie of the Holy Warre, The: Fuller, Thomas

Historie of the raigne of King Henry the Seventh, The: Bacon, Francis

Historie of tithes, The: Selden, John

Historie of Troylus and Cresseida, The: Shakespeare, William

History and adventures of an atom, The: Smollett, Tobias

History and antiquities of Cumberland and Westmoreland: Wright, Thomas

History and antiquities of Hinckley, in the County of Leicester, The: Nichols, John

History and antiquities of London, Westminster, Southwark and parts adjacent, The: Wright, Thomas

History and antiquities of the colleges and halls in the University of Oxford, The: Wood, Anthony à

History and antiquities of the County Palatine of Durham, The: Surtees, Robert

History and fall of Caius Marius, The: Otway, Thomas

History and fate of sacrilege, The: Spelman, *Sir* Henry

History and human relations: Butterfield, Herbert

History and life of Robert Blake, The: Oldmixon, John

History and motives of literary forgeries, The: Chambers, *Sir* E.K.

History and present state of discoveries relating to vision, light and colours, The: Priestley, Joseph

History and present state of electricity, The: Priestley, Joseph

History and present state of Virginia, The: Beverley, Robert

History and records of the Elephant Club, The: (†Q.K. Philander Doesticks) Thompson, Mortimer

History and remarkable life of Jack, The: Defoe, Daniel

History and the reader: Trevelyan, G.M.

History and topography of the county of Essex, The: Wright, Thomas

History as a literary art: Morison, S.E.

History in English words: Barfield, A. Owen

History is one: Wells, H.G.

History of a flirt, related by herself, The: Bury, *Lady* C.S.M.

History of a lifeboat: Rowe, Richard

History of a literary Radical: Bourne, Randolph

History of a six weeks' tour through a part of France: Shelley, Mary, and P.B. Shelley

History of Acadia, The: Hannay, James

History of addresses, The: Oldmixon, John

History of Alaska: Bancroft, H.H.

History of America, The: Robertson, William

History of American idealism, The: Myers, Gustavus

History of American life, A: Adams, J.T.

History of American poetry, 1900–1940, A: Gregory, Horace

History of an adopted child, The: Jewsbury, G.E.

History of an autumn: Morley, C.D.

History of ancient Greek literature, A: Murray, Gilbert

History of animals: Webster, Noah

History of Anthony Waring, The: Sinclair, May

History of Antonio and Mellida, The: Marston, John

History of Arizona and New Mexico: Bancroft, H.H.

History of Arsaces, Prince of Betlis, The: Johnstone, Charles

History of Aurangzib: Sarkar, Y.J.

History of Australia: Rusden, G.W.

History of Australian exploration, 1788–1888: Favenc, Ernest

History of Australian literature, 1778–1950: Green, H.M.

History of banks, The: Hildreth, Richard

History of Braintree: Adams, C.F.

History of Brasenose College, A: Buchan, John

History of Brazil: Southey, Robert

History of Britain, that part especially now call'd England, The: Milton, John

History of British Columbia: Bancroft, H.H.

History of British India, A: Hunter, *Sir* William

History of British India, The: Mill, James

History of California: Bancroft, H.H.

History of Canadian wealth: Myers, Gustavus

History of caricature and grotesque in literature and art, A: Wright, Thomas

History of Central America: Bancroft, H.H.

History of Ceylon for schools, 1505–1911, A: Perera, Simon

History of chivalry, The: James, G.P.R.

History of Christian names: Yonge, Charlotte

History of Christianity to the abolition of Paganism in the Roman Empire, The: Milman, H.H.

History of civilization in ancient India, A: Dutt, R.C.

History of criticism and literary taste in Europe, The: Saintsbury, George

History of David Grieve, The: Ward, *Mrs.* Humphrey

Historie of domestic manners and sentiments in England during the Middle Ages, A: Wright, Thomas

History of early eighteenth century drama, A: Nicoll, Allardyce

History of early English Literature, The: Brooke, Stopford

History of early nineteenth century drama, A: Nicoll, J.R.A.

History of Edward the Black Prince, A: James, G.P.R.

History of Egg Pandervil, The: Bullett, Gerald

History of Egypt, A: Breasted, J.H.

History of Egypt: Petrie, *Sir* William Flinders

History of eighteenth-century literature, 1660–1780, A: Gosse, *Sir* Edmund

History of Elizabethan literature A: Saintsbury, George

History of Emily Montague, The: Brooke, Frances

History of England: Belloc, Hilaire

History of England, The: Godwin, William

History of England, The: Kipling, Rudyard

History of England: Palgrave, *Sir* Francis

History of England, A: Pollard, A.F.

History of England: Trevelyan, G.M.

History of England and France under the House of Lancaster: Brougham, Henry

History of England comprising the reign of Anne until the Peace of Utrecht: Stanhope, Philip Henry *Earl of Chesterfield*

History of England, during the reigns of Henry VIII, Edward VI, Queen Mary, Queen Elizabeth, The: Oldmixon, John

History of England, during the reigns of King William and Queen Mary, Queen Anne, King George I, The: Oldmixon, John

History of England, during the reigns of the royal house of Stuart, The: Oldmixon, John

History of England during the thirty years peace, 1816–46: Martineau, Harriet

History of England from the accession of James II, The: Macaulay, Thomas *Baron*

History of England from the conclusion of the Great War in 1815, A: Walpole, *Sir* Spencer

History of England, from the earliest times to the death of George II, The: Goldsmith, Oliver

History of England from the fall of Wolsey to the death of Elizabeth: Froude, J.A.

History of England from the invasion of Julius Caesar to the Revolution of 1688: Hume, David

History of England from the Peace of Utrecht to the Peace of Aix-la-Chapelle: Stanhope, Philip Stanhope *Earl*

History of England in a series of letters from a nobleman to his son, An: Goldsmith, Oliver

History of England in the eighteenth century, A: Lecky, W.E.

History of English criticism, A: Saintsbury, George

History of English drama, 1600–1900, A: Nicoll, Allardyce

History of English dramatic poetry to the time of Shakespeare, The: Collier John Payne

History of English in the twentieth century, A: Partridge, Eric

History of English literature, A: Moody, W.V.

History of English literature from *Beowulf* to Swinburne: Lang, Andrew

History of English poetry, The: Courthorpe, W.J.

History of English poetry from the close of the 11th to the commencement of the 18th century, The: Warton, Thomas

History of English prose rhythm, A: Saintsbury, George

History of English prosody from the twelfth century to the present day, A: Saintsbury, George

History of English thought in the eighteenth century: Stephen, *Sir* Leslie

History of Episcopacie, The: Heylyn, Peter

History of Europe, A: Fisher, H.A.L.

History of Europe: ancient and medieval: Breasted, J.H.

History of European morals from Augustus to Charlemagne: Lecky, W.E.H.

History of everyday things in England, A: Quennell, Marjorie

History of France, The: Wright, Thomas

History of freedom, and other essays, The: Acton, John

History of freedom in antiquity, The: Acton, John

History of freedom in Christianity, The: Acton, John

History of French literature, A: Dowden, Edward

History of Friedrich II of Prussia, called Frederick the Great, The: Carlyle, Thomas

History of Glyn's: Fulford, Roger

History of government, The: Petrie, *Sir* Charles

History of Grand Pré, The: Herbin, J.F.

History of Great Britaine, The: Speed, John

History of Great Britain from the Restoration to the accession of the House of Hanover, The: Macpherson, James

History of Greece, A: Grote, George

History of Harvard University, The: Quincy, Josiah

History of Henrie the fourth, The: Shakespeare, William

History of Henry Esmond, Esq., The: Thackeray, W.M.

History of Henry Fielding: Cross, W.L.

History of Henry the Fifth, The: Boyle, Roger

History of Hungary and the Magyars, The: Godkin, E.L.

History of imbanking and drayning of divers fenns and marshes: Dugdale, Sir William

History of "In his steps", The: Sheldon, C.M.

History of Indian and Indonesian art: Coomaraswamy, A.K.

History of Ireland, The: Wright, Thomas

History of Ireland and the Irish people, under the government of England: Smiles, Samuel

History of Ireland from the earliest times proposed, A: Brooke, Henry

History of Jason, The: Caxton, William

History of Jemmy and Jenny Jessamy, The: Haywood, Mrs. Eliza

History of John Bull, The: Arbuthnot, John

History of Johnny Quae Genus, The: Combe, William

History of King Lear, The: Tate, Nahum

History of King Richard the Second, The: Tate, Nahum

History of King Richard III (Ed. S. W. Singer): More, Sir Thomas

History of Lady Julia Mandeville, The: Brooke, Frances

History of late eighteenth century drama, A: Nicoll, Allardyce

History of late nineteenth century drama, A: Nicoll, Allardyce

History of Latin Christianity: Milman, H.H.

History of liquor-licensing: Webb, Sidney and Beatrice Webb

History of literary criticism in the Renaissance, A: Spingarn, J.E.

History of Little Davy's new hat: Bloomfield, Robert

History of little Goody Two-shoes, The: Newbery, John

History of London, The: Besant, Sir Walter

History of London, A: Brown, I.J.C.

History of Louisiana: Gayarré, C.E.A.

History of Louisiana: King, G.E.

History of love, The: Hopkins, Charles

History of Ludlow and its neighbourhood, The: Wright, Thomas

History of Marcus Aurelius, emperor of Rome: Sigourney, L.H.

History of Margaret Catchpole, a Suffolk girl, The: Cobbold, Richard

History of Matthew Wald, The: Lockhart, J.G.

History of Mexico: Bancroft, H.H.

History of Miss Betsy Thoughtless, The: Haywood, Mrs. Eliza

History of modern Greece, The: Tennent, Sir J.E.

History of Mr. Polly, The: Wells, H.G.

History of my times, Xenophon: Warner, Rex

History of myself, Dawn, A: Dreiser, Theodore

History of Napoleon, The: Horne, R.H.

History of Napoleon Buonaparte, The: Lockhart, J.G.

History of Nevada, Colorado and Wyoming: Bancroft, H.H.

History of New Bedford, The: Ricketson, Daniel

History of New Brunswick: Hannay, James

History of New York, A: (†Geoffrey Crayon), Irving, Washington

History of New Zealand, A: Mulgan, A.E.

History of New Zealand: Rusden, G.W.

History of New-Hampshire, The: Belknap, Jeremy

History of Newton, Massachusetts: Smith, S.F.

History of Niagara: Carnochan, Janet

History of nineteenth century literature, A: Saintsbury, George

History of Normandy and of England, The: Palgrave, Sir Francis

History of Nourjahad, The: Sheridan, Mrs. Frances

History of Ophelia, The: Fielding, Sarah

History of Oxfordshire, A: Falkner, John Meade

History of Pendennis, The: Thackeray, W.M.

History of Perourou, The: Williams, H.M.

History of philosophy, The Stanley, Thomas

History of philosophy, Eastern and Western: Radhakrishan, Sarvepalli

History of political economy, A: Ingram, J.K.

History of political parties in the province of New York, 1760–1776, The: Becker, C.L.

History of printing in New Zealand: Anderson, J.C.

History of religion, The: Evelyn, John

History of Restoration drama, A: Nicoll, Allardyce

History of Reynard the fox, The: Thoms, W.J.

History of Rome: Arnold, Thomas

History of St. Pauls Cathedral in London, The: Dugdale, *Sir* William

History of Samuel Titmarsh, The: Thackeray, W.M.

History of Sarawak under its two white rajahs, A: Baring-Gould, Sabine

History of Scotland: Burton, J.H.

History of Scotland, The: Chambers, Robert

History of Scotland: Scott, *Sir* Walter

History of Scotland: Tytler, P.F.

History of Scotland, The: Wright, Thomas

History of Scotland during the reigns of Queen Mary and of King James VI, The: Robertson, William

History of Scotland from the Roman occupation, A: Lang, Andrew

History of Scotland, from the year 1423, until the year 1542, The: Drummond of Hawthornden, William

History of Sir Charles Grandison, The: Richardson, Samuel

History of Sir Charles Napier's administration of Scinde: Napier, *Sir* W.F.P.

History of Sir George Warrington, The: Lennox, Charlotte

History of Sir Thomas Thumb, The: Yonge, Charlotte

History of slavery and serfdom, A: Ingram, J.K.

History of South Africa, A: Fairbridge, Dorothea

History of South Africa from the earliest days to the Union, A: Scully, W.C.

History of South Carolina, The: Simms, W.G.

History of Spain: Petrie, *Sir* Charles

History of spiritualism, The: Doyle, *Sir* Arthur Conan

History of story-telling, A: Ransome, Arthur

History of Susan Spray, The: Kaye-Smith, Shiela

History of Tammany Hall, The: Myers, Gustavus

History of that most famous saynt and souldier St. George of Cappadocia, The: Heylyn, Peter

History of the admirable Crichton, The: Urquhart, *Sir* Thomas

History of the adventures of Joseph Andrews and his friend Mr. Abraham Adams, The: Fielding, Henry

History of the American compromises, A: Martineau, Harriet

History of the American people, A: Beard, C.A.

History of the American people, A: Wilson, Woodrow

History of the ancient Egyptians, A: Breasted, J.H.

History of the Anglo-Saxons: Miller, Thomas

History of the Baptists of the Maritime Provinces: Saunders, E.M.

History of the Battle of Lake Erie: Bancroft, George

History of the Bene-Israelites of India: Fyzee Rahamin, S.

History of the Boston Athenaeum, The: Quincy, Josiah

History of the British Army. 1899–1929: Fortescue, *Sir* John

History of the British workers: Postgate, Raymond

History of the Canadian Pacific railway, A: Innis, H.A.

History of the Civil Wars of England, The: Hobbes, Thomas

History of the colonization of the United States: Bancroft, George

History of the Colony of Victoria, 1797–1900: Turner, H.G.

History of the Commonwealth of England, from its commencement to the restoration of Charles II: Godwin, William

History of the condition of women, The: Child, Lydia Maria

History of the conquest of Mexico: Prescott, W.H.

History of the conquest of Peru: Prescott, W.H.

History of the conspiracy of Pontiac and the War of the North American tribes: Parkman, Francis

History of the constitution of Massachusetts, A: Morison, S.E.

History of the corruptions of Christianity, An: Priestley, Joseph

History of the Crusades, A: Runciman, *Sir* Steven

History of the Dean Case: Stephens, A.G.

History of the earth, and animated nature, An: Goldsmith, Oliver

History of the English government from the reign of Henry VII: Russell, *Lord* John

History of the English turf: Rice, James

History of the English-speaking peoples, A: Churchill, *Sir* Winston

History of the family of the Percys, An: Collins, Arthur

History of the formation of the Constitution of the United States of America: Bancroft, George

History of the four last years of the Queen, The: Swift, Jonathan

History of the French novel to the close of the nineteenth century, A: Saintsbury, George

History of the great American fortunes, The: Myers, Gustavus

History of the Great War, A: Buchan, John

History of the guillotine: Croker, J.W.

History of the Holy Eastern Church, A: Neale, J.M.

History of the Indian tribes of North America: Hall, James

History of the Indians of Connecticut from the earliest known period to 1850: De Forest, John William

History of the Irish Rebellion in 1798: Maxwell, W.H.

History of the island of Minorca, The: Armstrong, John

History of the Jews, The: Milman, H.H.

History of the Jews, A: Neale, J.M.

History of the King's Bodyguard for Scotland, The: (†Ian Hay), Beith, *Sir* John Hay

History of the Labour party from 1914, A: Cole, G.D.H.

History of the late revolution in the Dutch Republic: Ellis, George

History of the late war, The: Lockhart, J.G.

History of the life and adventures of Mr. Duncan Campbell, The: Defoe, Daniel

History of the life and reign of the Empress Catharine of Russia, The: Mottley, John

History of the life and voyages of Christopher Columbus, A: (†Geoffrey Crayon), Irving, Washington

History of the life of King Henry the Second and of the age in which he lived, The: Lyttelton, George *Baron*

History of the life of Peter I, Emperor of Russia, The: Mottley, John

History of the life of William Gilpin: Bancroft, H.H.

History of the lives, actions, travels, sufferings, and deaths of the most eminent martyrs, and primitive fathers of the Church, An: Goldsmith, Oliver

History of the London Clubs, The: Ward, Edward

History of the Marquis of Lussan and Isabella, The: Lennox, Charlotte

History of the Navy of the United States of America, The: Cooper, James Fenimore

History of the Netherlands: Gratton, T.C.

History of the next French Revolution, The: Thackeray, W.M.

History of the noble family of Carteret, A: Collins, Arthur

History of the Northern Mexican States and Texas: Bancroft, H.H.

History of the North-West Coast: Bancroft, H.H.

History of the nun, The: Behn, *Mrs.* Afra

History of the old French port at Toronto: Scadding, Henry

History of the origin and rise of the Republic of Venice, The: Hazlitt, W.C.

History of the Passion: More, *Sir* Thomas

History of the Peninsular War: Southey, Robert

History of the present rebellion in Scotland, The: Fielding, Henry

History of the press and public opinion in China, A: Lin Yu-T'ang

History of the Protestant Reformation in England and Ireland, A: Cobbett, William

History of the rebellion and Civil Wars in England, The: Clarendon, Edward Hyde

History of the rebellion and civil wars in Ireland, The: Clarendon, Edward Hyde

History of the Rebellion in 1745, The: Home, John

History of the rebellion in Scotland, 1745–1746: Chambers, Robert

History of the rebellions in Scotland under the Marquis of Montrose and others, from 1638 till 1660: Chambers, Robert

History of the rebellions in Scotland under the Viscount of Dundee and The Earl of Mar, in 1689 and 1715: Chambers, Robert

History of the reformation of the church of England, The: Burnet, Gilbert

History of the regency and reign of King George the Fourth: Cobbett, William

History of the reign of Ferdi-

nand and Isabella, the Catholic: Prescott, W.H.

History of the reign of Philip the Second: Prescott, W.H.

History of the reign of Queen Anne: Burton, J.H.

History of the reign of the Emperor Charles V, The: Robertson, William

History of the rights of princes in the disposing of ecclesiastical benefices and churchlands, The: Burnet, Gilbert

History of the rise and influence of the spirit of rationalism in Europe: Lecky, W.E.

History of the Royal Bank of Scotland, The: Munro, Neil

History of the Royal-Society of London for the improving of natural knowledge, The: Sprat, Thomas

History of the Sabbath, The: Heylyn, Peter

History of the Second World War, A: Liddell Hart, B.

History of the 17th Lancers: Fortescue, *Sir* John

History of the Standard Oil Company, The: Tarbell, Ida

History of the sufferings of the Church of Scotland, The: Wodrow, Robert

History of the Supreme Court of the United States: Myers, Gustavus

History of the three late famous impostors, The: Evelyn, John

History of the town of Montpelier: Thompson, D.P.

History of the Triumvirates, The: Otway, Thomas

History of the troubles and memorable transactions in Scotland from the year 1625 to 1645: Spalding, John

History of the Union of Great Britain, The: Defoe, Daniel

History of the United Netherlands, from the death of William the Silent, to the Twelve Years' Truce––1609: Motley, J.L.

History of the United States: Adams, J.T.

History of the United States, A: Bancroft, George

History of the United States: Beard, C. and M. Beard

History of the United States, A: Eggleston, Edward

History of the United States: Hale, E.E.

History of the United States, The: Tucker, George

History of the United States: Webster, Noah

History of the United States for schools, A: Fiske, John

History of the United States of America 1856–1860, The: Hildreth, Richard

History of the United States of America during the first administration of James Madison: Adams, H.B.

History of the United States of America during the first administration of Thomas Jefferson: Adams, H.B.

History of the United States of America during the second administration of James Madison: Adams, H.B.

History of the United States of America during the second administration of Thomas Jefferson, 1805–09: Adams, H.B.

History of the United States of America, from the adoption of the federal constitution to the end of the Sixteenth Congress, The: Hildreth, Richard

History of the United States of America, from the discovery of the continent to the organization of government under the federal constitution, The: Hildreth, Richard

History of the University of Toronto, 1827–1927, A: Wallace, W.S.

History of the unreformed Parliament and its lessons, The: Bagehot, Walter

History of the war in the Peninsula and in the south of France: Napier, *Sir* W.F.P.

History of the war of 1812: Hannay, James

History of the war of the Succession of Spain: Stanhope, Philip Stanhope, *Earl*

History of the Working Tailor's Association: Hughes, Thomas

History of the world, The: Ralegh, *Sir* Walter

History of the worthies of England, The: Fuller, Thomas

History of Timon of Athens, the man hater, The: Shadwell, Thomas

History of Tom Jones, a foundling, The: Fielding, Henry

History of Trade Unionism: Webb, Beatrice and Sidney Webb

History of twenty-five years (1856–1880), The: Walpole, *Sir* Spencer

History of United States naval operations in World War II: Morison, S.E.

History of universities, The: Morison, S.E.

History of Western Massachusetts: Holland, J.G.

History of western philosophy, A: Russell, Bertrand

History of wood-engraving, A: Woodberry, G.E.

History unearthed: Woolley, *Sir* Leonard

History with a match: Van Loon, Hendrik

Histriophone, a dialogue on dramatic diction: Dobrée, Bonamy

Hitler: Lewis, P. Wyndham

Hitler cult, The: Lewis, P. Wyndham

Hitler, from power to ruin: Appel, Benjamin

Hitler through the ages: Golding, Louis

Hitler: whence and whither?: Steed, H.W.

Hitleriad, The: Klein, A.M.

Hitler's whistle: Street, A.G.

Hittite seals: Hogarth, D.G.

Hive of the bee hunter, The: Thorpe, T.B.

Ho!: Mackail, Denis

Hobbes: Stephen, *Sir* Leslie

Hobbinol: Somerville, William

Hobbit, The: Tolkien, J.R.R.

Hobby horse: †Mordaunt, Elinor

Hobby-horse, The: Pinero, *Sir* A.W.

Hobomok: Child, Lydia Maria

Hobson's: Brighouse, Harold

Hobson's choice: Brighouse, Harold

Hobsons horse-load of letters: Markham, Gervase

Hocken and Hunken: †Quiller-Couch, *Sir* Arthur

Hocus Pocus: Langley, Noel

Hodge and his masters: Jefferies, Richard

Hogarth: Garnett, Edward

Hogarth as a satirist: Hannay, James

Hogarth's Arabia: Doughty, C.M.

Hogarth's progress: Quennell, P.C.

Hog's Back mystery, The: Crofts, F.W.

Hohenzollerns in America, The: Leacock, Stephen

Hokusai: Noguchi, Yone

Hokusai sketchbook, The: Michener, J.A.

Holbein's dance: Butler, Samuel

Holdfast: Street, A.G.

Hold-up, The: White, S.E.

Hole in the wall, The: Morrison, Arthur

Hole in the wall, The: Poole, John

Holes in the sky: Macneice, Louis

Holi prophete Dauid seith, The: Wycliffe, John

Holiday: Barry, Philip

Holiday: Davidson, John

Holiday: Deamer, Dulcie

Holiday: Frank, Waldo

Holiday: †George, Daniel

Holiday, The: Smith, Stevie

Holiday book: Rowe, Richard

Holiday in bed: Barrie, *Sir* J.M.

Holiday peak: Clarke, Marcus

Holiday round, The: Milne, A.A.

Holiday stories for boys and girls: Barker, M.A.

Holiday tasks: Payn, James

Holiday time: Lathom, Francis

Holidays among the Russians: Cusack, E.D.

Hollander, The: Glapthorne Henry

Hollands leaguer: Marmion Shackerley

Holland-tide: Griffin, Gerald

Hollow, The: Christie, Agatha

Hollow and sallow: Bates, H. E.

Hollow man, The: Carr, J.D.

Hollow of her hand, The: McCutcheon, G.B.

Hollow sea: Hanley, James

Hollow tree house: Molesworth, Mrs.

Hollyhocks and golden glow: Hubbard, Elbert

Hollywood cemetery: O'Flaherty, Liam

Hollywood Hall: Grant, James

Hollywood holiday: Levy, Benn W.

Hollywood holiday: Van Druten, J.W.

Hollywood mystery!: Hecht, Ben

Holman hunt: Coleridge, Mary

Holmby House: Whyte-Melville, G.J.

Holy Bible, The: Knox, R.A.

Holy City, The: Bunyan, John

Holy deadlock: Herbert, Sir A.P.

Holy face: Huxley, Aldous

Holy flower, The: Haggard, Sir H. Rider

Holy Graal and other fragments, The: Hovey, Richard

Holy Grail, The: Tennyson, Alfred Lord

Holy isle: †Bridie, James

Holy Land, The: Hichens, Robert

Holy life, A: Bunyan, John

Holy Orders: †Corelli, Marie

Holy places, The: Waugh, Evelyn

Holy Roode, The: Davies, John

Holy Rose, The: Besant, Sir Walter

Holy State, The Profane State, The: Fuller, Thomas

Holy terror, The: Wells, H.G.

Holy terrors: †Machen, Arthur

Holy War, The: Bunyan, John

Holy war, The: Kipling, Rudyard

Holy War, The: Tynan, Katherine

Holy-cross, The: Field, Eugene

Homage to Baudelaire: Engle, Paul

Homage to Catalonia: †Orwell, George

Homage to Clio: Auden, W.H.

Homage to John Dryden: Eliot, T.S.

Homage to Sappho, Theocritos, Herondas, Catallus, Ausonius, A: Lindsay, Jack

Homage to Sextus Propertius: Pound, Ezra

Home: Gibson, Wilfred

Home: Sedgwick, C.M.

Home, a colonial's adventure: Mulgan, A.E.

Home acre, The: Roe, E.P.

Home again: Macdonald, George

Home and a changing civilization, The: Mitchison, Naomi

Home and beauty: Herbert, Sir A.P.

Home and beauty: Maugham, Somerset

Home and the world, The: Tagore, Sir R.

Home as found: Cooper, James Fenimore

Home at seven: Sheriff, R.C.

Home ballads: Whittier, J.G.

Home chat: Coward, Noel

Home colony, A: Sinclair, Upton

Home fires in France: Canfield, Dorothy

Home for the holidays: Mottram, R.H.

Home guard: Pertwee, Roland

Home idyl, A: Trowbridge, J. T.

Home in Tasmania: Meredith, L.A.

Home influence: Aguilar, Grace

Home is the sailor: Godden, Rumer

Home is tomorrow: Priestley, J.B.

Home letters, 1830–1: Disraeli, Benjamin

Home life in colonial days: Earle, A.M.

Home life in Ireland: Lynd, Robert

Home of mankind, The: Van Loon, Hendrik

Home pastorals, ballads, and lyrics: Taylor, Bayard

Home of the free, The: Rice, Elmer

Home scenes and heart studies: Aguilar, Grace

"Home, sweet home": Payne, J.H.

Home, sweet home: Riddell, Mrs. J.H.

Home thoughts and home scenes: Craik, Mrs. Dinah

Home thoughts and home scenes: Ingelow, Jean

Home to Harlem: McKay, Claude

Home town: Anderson, Sherwood

Home wine cellar: Postgate, Raymond

Homecoming: Dell, Floyd

Homecoming of Beorhtnoth, The: Tolkien, J.R.R.

Homecomings: Snow, C.P.

Home-folks: Riley, J.W.

Homely heroine, The: Ferber, Edna

Homely Lilla: Herrick, Robert

Home-maker, The: Camfield, Dorothy

Homer and Aether: Powys, John Cowper

Homer and David: Hale, E.E.

Homer and his age: Lang, Andrew

Homer and history: Leaf, Walter

Homer and the epic: Lang, Andrew

Homer's daughter: Graves, Robert

Homes for the millions: Davin, N.F.

Homespun and gold: Brown, Alice

Homespun tales: Wiggin, Kate

Homestead on the hillside, The: Holmes, M.J.

Homesteaders, The: Stead, R.J.C.

Homeward: Russell, G.W.

Homeward bound: Cooper, James Fenimore

Homicide act, The: Hollis, Christopher

Homilies and recreations: Buchan, John

Homing of the winds, The: Sitwell, Sacheverell

Homoeopathy, and its kindred delusions: Holmes, Oliver Wendell

Hon. Henry Caldwell, The: LeMoine, *Sir* J.M.

Hone Tiki Dialogues: Grace, A.A.

Hone's political showman—at home! Hone, William

Honest counsaile: Breton, Nicholas

Honest fisherman, The: Walsh, Maurice

Honest fool: Roberts, T.G.

Honest John Vane: De Forest, J.W.

Honest whore, The: Dekker, Thomas

Honest whore, The: Middleton, Thomas

Honest Yorkshire-man, The: Carey, Henry

Honestie of this age, The: Rich, Barnabe

Honey and bread: Davies, Rhys

Honey and salt: Sandburg, Carl

Honey bird: Cloete, E.F.S.G.

Honey flow, The: Tennant, Kylie

Honey for the ghost: Golding, Louis

Honey in the horn: Davies, H.L.

Honey out of the rock: Deutsch, Babette

Honeybubble and Co.: Herbert, *Sir* A.P.

Honeycomb: Richardson, D.M.

Honeymoon, The: Bennett, Arnold

Honeymoon experiment, A: Chase, Stuart and Margaret Chase

Honeysuckle and the bee, The: Squire, *Sir* J.

Hong Kong house: Blunden, Edmund

Honor: Elliott, M.H.

Honor bright: Nicholson, Meredith

Honor More: Cary, Joyce

Honor Neale: Trench, R.C.

Honor O'Hara: Porter, Anna Maria

Honor triumphant: Ford, John

Honorable entertainments: Middleton, Thomas

Honorable historie of frier Bacon, and frier Bongay, The: Greene, Robert

Honoratissimo Viro, Henrico Saint John Armigero, Ode: Philips, John

Honoria and Mammon: Shirley, James

Honour come back: Jacob, Naomi

Honour conceal'd strangely reveal'd: Taylor, John

Honour in his perfection: Markham, Gervase

Honour of the flag, The: Russell, W.C.

Honour of the Garter, The: Peele, George

Honour of the station, The: Ogilvie, W.H.

Honour of valour, The: Breton, Nicholas

Honour thy father: Harwood, H.M.

Honourable Algernon Knox, detective, The: Oppenheim, E. Phillips

Honourable estate: Brittain, Vera

Honourable Jim, The: Orczy, *Baroness*

Honourable Lorde and Lady of Huntingdons entertainement of theire right noble mother Alice, The: Marston, John

Honourable men—Livingstone, Lincoln, Gordon: Quiller-Couch, *Sir* Arthur

Honourable Mr. Tawnish, The: Farnol, J.J.

Honourable Peggy, The: †Lancaster, G.B.

Honourable Peter Stirling and what the people thought of him, The: Ford, P.L.

Honourable reputation of a souldier, The: Whetstone, George

Honour's a mistress: Jacob, Naomi

Honours easy: Pertwee, Roland

Honours physiography: Wells, H.G.

Hooded hawk, The: Lewis, D.B. Wyndham

Hoodie: Molesworth, *Mrs.*

Hood's own: Hood, Thomas

Hoofmarks of the faun, The: Ransome, Arthur

Hoosier Chronicle, A: Nicholson, Meredith

Hoosier holiday, A: Dreiser, Theodore

Hoosier lyrics: Field, Eugene

Hoosier mosaics: Thompson, Maurice

Hoosier romance, A: Riley, J.W.

Hoosier school-boy, The: Eggleston, Edward

Hoosier school-master, The: Eggleston, Edward

Hoosiers, The: Nicholson, Meredith

Hope: Bowles, W.L.

Hope: Cunninghame Graham, L.B.

Hope against hope: Benson, Stella

Hope for America: Strachey, John

Hope for poetry, A: Day-Lewis, C.

Hope in vain: Gissing, George

Hope is not for the wise: Jeffers, J.R.

Hope Leslie: Sedgwick, C.M.

Hope of a new world, The: Temple, William

Hope of Europe, The: Gibbs, *Sir* Philip

Hope of happiness, The: Nicholson, Meredith

Hope of Heaven: O'Hara, J.H.

Hope of the Gospel, The: Macdonald, George

Hope of the great community, The: Royce, Josiah

Hope of the world, The: Dixon, Thomas

Hope of the world, The: Watson, *Sir* J.W.

Hope the hermit: †Lyall, Edna

Hope vases, The: Tillyard, E.M.W.

Hopeful heart, The: Gibbs, *Sir* Philip

Hopeful journey, The: Seymour, Beatrice Kean

Hopeless case, A: Fawcett, Edgar

Hopes and fears: Yonge, Charlotte

Hopes and fears for art: Morris, William

Hopes of the human race, The: Cobbe, Frances Power

Hopkins manuscript, The: Sherriff, R.C.

Horae subsecivae: Brown, Dr. John

Horace at the University of Athens: Trevelyan, Sir G.O.

Horace Chase: Woolson, C.F.

Horace Elisha Scudder: Higginson, T.W.

Horace Howard Furness: Repplier, Agnes

Horace in London: Smith, Horatio and James Smith

Horace, Lib. 1, Epist. ix Imitated, To the Right Honourable Mr. Harley: Prior, Matthew

Horace Lyricae: Watts, Isaac

Horace Walpole: Dobson, Henry Austin

Horae Sabbaticae: Stephen, Sir J.F.

Horae solitariae: Thomas, E.E.P.

Horatio: Smith, Horatio

Horation canons of friendship, The: Smart, Christopher

Horatius: †Armstrong, Anthony

Horn of plenty, The: Alcott, Louisa M.

Hornblower and the Atropos: Forester, C.S.

Hornblower and the Hotspur: Forester, C.S.

Hornblower companion, The: Forester, C.S.

Hornblower in the West Indies: Forester, C.S.

Hornby Mills: Kingsley, Henry

Horned helmet, The: Treece, Henry

Hornet's nest: Ashton, Helen

Hornet's nest, The: Roe, E.P.

Horns of a goat: Basso, Hamilton

Horrors of bribery, The: †Pindar, Peter

Horrors of the countryside, The: Joad, C.E.M.

Horse! A horse!, A: Peach, L. du Garde

Horse and his boy, The: Lewis, C.S.

Horse knows the way, The: O'Hara, J.H.

Horse that could whistle "Dixie", The: Weidman, Jerome

Horse, the ghoos and the sheep, The: Lydgate, John

Horse-flesh for the observator: Phillips, John

Horseman in the sky, A: Bierce, Ambrose

Horseman's manual, The: Surtees, R.S.

Horsemen of Tarentum: Evans, Sir A.J.

Horses and men: Anderson, Sherwood

Horse's mouth, The: Cary, Joyce

Horses of the conquest, The: Cunninghame Graham, R.B.

Horse's tale, A: (†Mark Twain), Clemens, S.L.

Horseshoe Robinson: Kennedy, J.P.

Hortus inclusus: Ruskin, John

Hortus vitae: †Lee, Vernon

Hospital, The: Fearing, Kenneth

Hospital sketches: Alcott, Louisa M.

Hostages, The: Mitchison, Naomi

Hostages to fortune: Braddon, Mary Elizabeth

Hostages to fortune: Morley, C.D.

Hot iron, The: Green, Paul

Hot plowshares: Tourgée, A.W.

Hot water: Wodehouse, P.G.

Hot water sailor: Glover, Denis

Hotel, The: Bowen, E.D.C.

Hotel, The: Woolf, Leonard

Hotel Bemelmans: Bemelmans, Ludwig

Hotel mouse, The: Harwood, H.M.

Hotel Splendide: Bemelmans, Ludwig

Hotel universe: Barry, Philip

Hound dog Moses and the promised land: Edmonds, W.D.

Hound of death, The: Christie, Agatha

Hound of Ireland, The: Byrne, Donn

Hound of the Baskervilles, The: Doyle, Sir Arthur Conan

Hound of the road: Gilmore, Mary

Hounds of God, The: Sabatini, Rafael

Hounds of the king: Treece, Henry

Hour: De Voto, Bernard

Hour after Westerly, The: Coates, R.M.

Hour and the man, The: Martineau, Harriet

Hour before dawn, The: Maugham, W. Somerset

Hour from Victoria, An: Knox, E.R.V.

Hour on American history, An: Morison, S.E.

Hour of fame: Chaucer, Geoffrey

Hour of God, The: Ghose, Sri Aurobindo

Hour of magic, The: Davies, W.H.

Hour on Christianity, An: Powys, Llewelyn

Hour with the fairies, An: Wiggin, K.D.

Hour-glass, The: Yeats, W.B.

Hours in a library: Stephen, Sir Leslie

Hours of idleness: Byron, George Gordon Lord

Hours of life: Whitman, S.H.

House, The: Field, Eugene

House, The: Rubenstein, Harold F.

House and hearth: Spofford, H.E.

House and home papers: Stowe, Harriet Beecher

House and its head, A: Compton-Burnett, Ivy

House at High Bridge, The: Fawcett, Edgar

House at Pooh Corner, The: Milne, A.A.

House at Satan's Elbow, The: Carr, J.D.

House behind the cedars, The: Chestnutt, C.W.

House by Herod's gate, The: Connell, John

House by Stable, The: Williams, Charles

House by the church-yard, The: Le Fanu, Sheridan

House by the river, The: Derleth, A.W.

House by the river, The: Herbert, *Sir* A.P.

House by the sea, The: Lowndes, M.A.

House by the sea, The: Read, T.B.

House divided, A: Buck, Pearl

House divided against itself, A: Oliphant, Margaret

House in Antigua, The: Adamic, Louis

House in Blind Alley, The: Rice, Elmer

House in Bloomsbury, The: Oliphant, Margaret

House in Demetrius road, The: Beresford, J.D.

House in disorder: Strong, L.A.G.

House in Dormer Forest, The: Webb, Mary

House in Half Moon Street, The: Bolitho, H.H.

House in Lordship Lane, The: Mason, A.E.W.

House in Mexico: Beals, Carleton

House in Paris, The: Bowen, E.D.C.

House in the uplands: Caldwell, Erskine Preston

House in town, The: Warner, S.B.

House is built, A: †Eldershaw, M. Barnard

House of a thousand candles, The: Nicholson, Meredith

House of adventure, The: Deeping, Warwick

House of all nations: Stead, C.E.

House of Arden, The: Nesbit, E.

House of Assignation: Dukes, Ashley

House of children, A: Cary, Joyce

House of Coalport, The: Mackenzie, *Sir* Compton

House of Cobwebs, The: Gissing, George

House of Commons and the monarchy, The: Belloc, Hilaire

House of Connelly, The: Green, Paul

House of defence, The: Benson, E.F.

House of Dr. Edwardes, The: †Beeding, Francis

House of Dooner, The: Morley, C.D.

House of dreams, The: Campbell, W.W.

House of dust, The: Aiken, Conrad

House of earth: Buck, Pearl

House of Fame: Chaucer, Geoffrey

House of fear, The: Service, Robert

House of Fendon, The: Bridges, Roy

House of fulfilment, The: Beck, *Mrs.* Lily

House of Gair: Linklater, Eric

House of gold, The: O'Flaherty, Liam

House of Halliwell, The: Wood, Ellen

House of intrigue, The: Stringer, A.J.A.

House of Islâm, The: Pickthall, M.W.

House of Israel, The: Warner, S.B.

House of Isstens, The: Roberts, T.G.

House of joy, The: Housman, Laurence

House of Lee: Atherton, Gertrude

House of life, The: Rossetti, Dante Gabriel

House of Lords during the Civil War, The: Firth, *Sir* Charles

House of Lynch, The: Merrick, Leonard

House of Macmillan, The: Morgan, Charles

House of Martha, The: Stockton, F.R.

House of Menerdue, The: Benson, A.C.

House of mirth, The: Wharton, Edith

House of moonlight, The: Derleth, A.W.

House of Moreys, The: Bentley, Phyllis

House of orchids, The: Sterling, George

House of peril, The: Vachell, H.A.

House of Pomegranates, A: Wilde, Oscar

House of pride, The: London, Jack

House of prophecy, The: Cannan, Gilbert

House of quiet, The: Benson, A.C.

House of Ravensburg, The: Noel, R.B.W.

House of Ryerson, The: Pierce, Lorne

House of Satan, The: Nathan, G.J.

House of Shivaji: Sarkar, Y.J.

House of silk, The: Wurdemann, Audrey

House of souls, The: †Machen, Arthur

House of spies, The: Deeping, Warwick

House of strangers, The: Bullett, Gerald W.

House of sun-goes-down, The: De Voto, Bernard

House of Templemore, The: Lawlor, P.A.

House of the arrow, The: Mason, A.E.W.

House of the four winds, The: Buchan, John

House of the octopus, The: Williams, Charles

House of the Seven Gables, The: Hawthorne, Nathaniel

House of the soul, The: Underhill, Evelyn

House of the Titans, The: Russell, G.W.

House of the wolf, The: Weyman, Stanley

House of three ganders, The: Bacheller, Irving

House of three windows, The: Gore-Booth, E.S.

House of Usna, The: †Macleod, Fiona

House of war, The: Pickthall, M.W.

House of white shadows, The: Farjeon, B.L.

House of windows, The: Mac-Kay, I.E.

House of woman, A: Bates, H.E.

House on Cherry Street, The: Barr, A.E.H.

House on the beach, The: Meredith, George

House on the bridge, The: Percy, Edward

House on the moor, The: Oliphant, Margaret

House on the mound, The: Derleth, A.W.

House party, A: †Ouida

House that Berry built, The: †Yates, Dornford

House that grew, The: Molesworth, *Mrs.*

House that is our own, The: Buchan, Anna

House that Jack built, The: †Novello, Ivor

House to let, A: Molesworth, *Mrs.*

House under the water, The: Young, Francis Brett

House with the apricot and twenty tales, The: Bates, H.E.

House with the echo, The: Powys, T.F.

House with the green shutters, The: Brown, G.D.

House-boat on the Styx, A: Bangs, J.K.

Household book of English poetry, A: Trench, R.C.

Household education: Martineau, Harriet

Household furniture and interior decorating: Hope, Thomas

Household of McNeil, The: Barr, A.E.H.

Household of Sir Thomas More, The: Manning, Anne

Household poems: Longfellow, H.W.

Household verses: Barton, Bernard

Housemaid, The: Royde-Smith, Naomi

Housemaster: (†Ian Hay), Beith, *Sir* John Hay

House-mates: Beresford, J.D.

Houses and housekeeping: Barker, M.A.

Houses by the sea: †Hyde, Robin

Houses in between, The: Spring, Howard

Housewarming at the fireside of the Hampshire bookshop: Frost, Robert

Housing America: MacLeish, Archibald

Housman: 1897–1936: Richards, Grant

How a husband forgave: Fawcett, Edgar

How about Europe?: Douglas, Norman

How amusing!: Mackail, Denis

How are they at home?: Priestley, J.B.

How best to do away with the sweating system: Webb, Beatrice

How Bigger was born: Wright, Richard

How blind is he?: Bierce, Ambrose

How can war ever be right?: Murray, Gilbert

How dear is life?: Williamson, Henry

How do you do?: Dibdin, Charles

How doth the simple spelling bee: Wister, Owen

How Edith McGillcuddy met R.L.S.: Steinbeck, John

How green was my valley: Llewellyn, Richard

How he died: Farrell, John

How he lied to her husband: Shaw, G.B.

How I became Attorney-General of New Barataria: Deniehy, D.H.

How I built myself a house: Hardy, Thomas

How I found my brother: Hubbard, Elbert

How I managed and improved my estate: Patmore, Coventry

How I see Apocalypse: Treece, Henry

How I tamed Mrs. Cruiser: Sala, G.A.H.

How it happens: Buck, Pearl

How like an angel: Macdonell, A.G.

How Lisa loved the King: †Eliot, George

How Little Grey Rabbit got back her tale: Uttley, Alison

How new will the better world be?: Becker, C.L.

How now, brown cow!: Jennings, Gertrude

How now England?: Gibbs, *Sir* Philip

How one friar met the devil and two pursued him: Field, Eugene

How one may take profite of his enmyes (trans. from Plutarch): Elyot, *Sir* Thomas

How our working people live: Rowe, Richard

How runs the road: Cronin, B.C.

How Salvator won: Wilcox, Ella Wheeler

How Shakespeare spent the day: Brown, Ivor

How sleep the brave: Bates, H.E.

How Texas won her freedom: Warren, Robert Penn

How the bishop built his college in the woods: Piatt, J.J.

How the children raised the wind: †Lyall, Edna

How the "Mastiffs" went to Iceland: Trollope, Anthony

How the old woman got home: Shiel, M.P.

How the other man lives: Greenwood, Walter

How the Reformation happened: Belloc, Hilaire

How they lived in Hampton: Hale, E.E.

How to be free and happy: Russell, Bertrand

How to be healthy though married: Harwood, H.M.

How to become an author: Bennett, Arnold

How to do it: †Armstrong, Anthony

How to do it: Hale, E.E.

How to do it: Van Loon, Hendrik

How to educate yourself: Eggleston, G.C.

How to fail in literature: Lang, Andrew

How to find the stars: Clarke, J.F.

How to get the best out of books: Le Gallienne, Richard

How to have Europe all to yourself: Bemelmans, Ludwig

How to live: Hale, E.E.

How to look at pictures: Van Loon, Hendrik

How to make a living: Eggleston, G.C.

How to make home unhealthy: Morley, Henry

How to make a revolution: Postgate, Raymond

How to make the best of life: Bennett, Arnold

How to observe: Martineau, Harriet

How to pay for the War: Keynes, John Maynard

How to read: Pound, Ezra

How to read a page: Richards, I.A.

How to read an annual report: Chase, Stuart

How to run a Bassoon factory: Balchin, Nigel

How to see Italy by rail: Sladen, D.B.W.

How to see the Vatican: Sladen, D.B.W.

How to settle the Irish question: Shaw, G.B.

How to tell a story: (†Mark Twain), Clemens, S.L.

How to train in archery: Thompson, J.M.

How to travel incognito: Bemelmans, Ludwig

How to try a lover: Barker, J.N.

How to win love: Craik, *Mrs.* D.M.

How to write: Leacock, Stephen

How to write: Stein, Gertrude

How to write a play: Ervine, St. John

How to write broadcast plays: Gielgud, Val

How to write short stories: Lardner, Ring

How to write, think and speak correctly: Joad, C.E.M.

How to write and sell film stories: Sherwood, R.E.

How we celebrate the Coronation: Byron, Robert

How we think: Dewey, John

How well George does it: Gillette, William

How white is my sepulchre: Royde-Smith, Naomi

Howadji in Syria, The: Curtis, G.W.

Howard: Ingraham, J.H.

Howard Chase: Sheldon, C.M.

Howard Pinckney: Thomas, F.W.

Howard's end: Forster, E.M.

Howdie and other tales, The: Galt, John

How's your health?: Tarkington, Booth

Hubert's Arthur: (†Baron Corvo), Rolfe, Frederick

Huckleberries gathered from New England hills: Cooke, R.T.

Huddleston House: Mackail, Denis

Hudibras: Butler, Samuel

Hudson anthology: Garnett, Edward

Hudson River bracketed: Wharton, Edith

Hue and cry after Dismal, A: Swift, Jonathan

Hue and cry after M... K, A: Carey, Henry

Hugh Lane's life and achievement: Gregory, *Lady* Augusta

Hugh: memoirs of a brother: Benson, A.C.

Hugh Selwyn Mauberley: Pound, Ezra

Hugh Walpole: Steen, Marguerite

Hugh Walpole, an appreciation: Hergesheimer, Joseph

Hugh Worthington: Holmes, M.J.

Hugh Wynne: Mitchell, S.W.

Hugo: Bennett, Arnold

Hugo Wolf: Newman, Ernest

Huguenot, The: James, G.P.R.

Huguenots in France after the revocation of the Edict of Nantes, The: Smiles, Samuel

Huguenots, their settlements, churches and industries in England and Ireland, The: Smiles, Samuel

Hullo stranger: Lindsay, Jack

Human age, The: Lewis, P. Wyndham

Human being: Morley, C.D.

Human beings: Lathom, Francis

Human body, The: Keith, *Sir* Arthur

Human boy, The: Phillpotts, Eden

Human boy again, The: Phillpotts, Eden

Human boy and the war, The: Phillpotts, Eden

Human boy's diary, A: Phillpotts, Eden

Human chase, The: Oppenheim, E. Phillips

Human chord, The: Blackwood, Algernon

Human clay: †Sinclair Murray

Human comedy, The: Saroyan, William

Human crisis, The: Huxley, *Sir* Julian

Human cycle, The: Ghose, Sri Aurobindo

Human document, A: Mallock, W.H.

Human drift, The: London, Jack

Human drift: Mann, Leonard

Human face, The: Brophy, John

Human face divine, The: Gatty, Margaret

Human face reconsidered, The: Brophy, John

Human fantasy, The: Wheelock, J.H.

Human fate: Brydges, *Sir* Samuel Egerton

Human happiness: Holcroft, Thomas

Human immortality: James, William

Human inheritance, The: †Macleod, Fiona

Human knowledge, its scope and its limits: Russell, Bertrand

Human ladder, The: Oppenheim, E. Phillips

Human life: Rogers, Samuel

Human life and its conditions: Church, Richard

Human life of Jesus: Erskine, John

Human longevity: Thomas, W.J.

Human machine, The: Bennett, Arnold

Human nature: Wharton, Edith

Human nature and conduct: Dewey, John

Human nature and human history: Collingwood, R.G.

Human nature and the human condition: Krutch, J.W.

Human odds and ends: Gissing, George

Human personality and its survival of bodily death: Myers, F.W.H.

Human prospects, The: Mumford, Lewis

Human quest, The: †Grand, Sarah

Human sacrifice among the Eastern Jews: Burton, *Sir* Richard

Human shows: Hardy, Thomas

Human society in ethics and politics: Russell, Bertrand

Human touch, The: †Sapper

Human tragedy, The: Austin, Alfred

Human vibration: Richter, Conrad

Human way out, The: Mumford, Lewis

Humanism in the continuation school: Wilson, John Dover

Humanist and specialist: Babbitt, Irving

Humanities: MacCarthy, *Sir* Desmond

Humanities and the common man, The: Foerster, Norman

Humanities in Canada, The: Kirkconnell, Watson

Humanity: Vane, S.V.H.

Humanity in politics: Bryant, *Sir* Arthur

Humanity unlimited: Van Doren, Mark

Humble attempt to promote explicit agreement, An: Edwards, Jonathan

Humble enterprise, A: Cambridge, Ada

Humble inquiry into the rules of the word of God concerning ... Communion: Edwards, Jonathan

Humble offering to the sacred memory of Charles II, An: Phillips, John

Humble powers: Horgan, Paul

Humble remonstrance to the High Court of Parliament by a dutiful sonne of the Church, An: Hall, Joseph

Humble romance, A: Freeman, Mary

Humble supplication to Her Majestie, An: Southwell, Robert

Humbler creation, The: Johnson, Pamela Hansford

Humbug: †Delafield, E.M.

Humbug: Jones, Henry Arthur

Humdrum: Acton, Harold

Hume: Huxley, T.H.

Humerous dayes myrth, An: Chapman, George

Humfrey, Duke of Gloucester: Philips, Ambrose

Humiliation with honour: Brittain, Vera

Humiliations follow'd with deliverances: Mather, Cotton

Humming bird: Farjeon, Eleanor

Humor, its theory and technique: Leacock, Stephen

Humoresque: Wolfe, Humbert

Humorists, The: Shadwell, Thomas

Humorous and satirical poems: Saxe, J.G.

Humorous Lieutenant, The: Beaumont, Francis

Humorous poems: Holmes, O.W.

Humorous stories: Pain, B.E.O.

Humorous tales: Kipling, Rudyard

Humorous verses: Lawson, Henry

Humour and humanity: Leacock, Stephen

Humour anthology: Potter, Stephen

Humour of Homer, The: Butler, Samuel

Humour out of breath: Day, John

Humour, wit and satire: †Bede, Cuthbert

Humourous courtier, The: Shirley, James

Humours heav'n on earth: Davies, John

Humours looking glasse: Rowlands, Samuel

Humours of a coffee-house, The: Ward, Edward

Humours of the court, The: Bridges, Robert

Humours of '37: Lizars, Robina, and K.M. Lizars

Humpty Dumpty: Hecht, Ben

Humpty Dumpty: Vachell, H.A.

Hunchback, The: Knowles, J.S.

Hunchback's charge, The: Russell, W.C.

Hundred and one dalmations, The: Smith, Dodie

Hundred and one harlequins, The: Sitwell, Sacheverell

170 Chinese poems: Waley, Arthur

Hundred days, The: Guedalla, Philip

Hundred epigrammes, An: Heywood, John

Hundred good pointes of husbandrie, A: Tusser, Thomas

Hundred lyrics, A: Phillpotts, Eden

100%, the story of a patriot: Sinclair, Upton

Hundred poems of Kabir, A: Tagore, *Sir* R.

Hundred pounds, A: Stephen, J.B.

Hundred sonnets, A: Phillpotts, Eden

Hundred year history of the P. & O. Steam Navigation Company, A: Ewart, E.A.

Hundred years, The: Guedalla, Philip

100 years of Army nursing: (†Ian Hay), Beith, *Sir* John Hay

100 years of postage stamps: Hamilton, Patrick

Hundredth man, The: Stockton, F.R.

Hundredth story, The: Coppard, A.E.

Hundredth sundrie flowers, A: Gascoigne, George

Hundredth year, The: Guedalla, Philip

Hungarian brothers, The: Porter, Anna Maria

Hungarian tales: Gore, Catherine

Hunger, a Dublin story: Stephens, James

Hunger of the sea: Mannin, Ethel

Hungerers, The: Saroyan, William

Hungers prevention: Markham, Gervase

Hungry heart, The: Phillips, D.G.

Hungry Hill: Du Maurier, Daphne

Hungry Ireland: Munro, Neil

Hungry year, The: Kirby, William

Hunted, The: Lee, J.A.

Hunted down: Dickens, Charles

Hunted one, The: (Stephen Southwold), †Bell, Neil

Hunted riders, The: †Brand, Max

Hunter, The: Glanville, Ernest

Hunter, The: Langbaine, Gerard

Hunter, The: Turner, W.J.R.

Hunter and the trap, The: Fast, Howard M.

Hunter cats of Conorloa, The: Jackson, H.H.

Hunter hunted: Treece, Henry

Hunter-naturalist, The: Webber, C.W.

Hunters and the hunted, The: Sitwell, Sacheverell

Hunter's feast, The: Reid, T.M.

Hunter's moon, The: Poole, Ernest

Hunters of the great north: Stefansson, V.

Hunting hand, The: Roberts, W. Adolphe

Hunting of Badlewe, The: Hogg, James

Hunting of Cupid, The: Peele, George

Hunting of Hilary, The: †Winch, John

Hunting of the snark, The: †Carroll, Lewis

Hunting poems: Whyte-Melville, G.J.

Hunting rhymes: Ogilvie, W.H.

Hunting sketches: Trollope, Anthony

Hunting songs, ballads, etc.: Warburton, R.E.E.

Hunting start, A: Davies, Robertson

Hunting the Bismarck: Forester, C.S.

Hunting the fairies: Mackenzie, Sir Compton

Hunting the highbrow: Woolf, Leonard

Hunting without a gun: Robinson, R.E.

Hunting-tower: Buchan, John

Huntsman, what quarry?: Millay, E. St. Vincent

Hurrah for anything: Patchen, Kenneth

Hurrah for you, old glory: English, T.D.

Hurricane: Church, Richard

Hurricane, The: Hall, J.N. and C.B. Nordhoff

Hurricane story, The: Gallico, Paul

Hurrygraphs: Willis, N.P.

Hurt of sedition, The: Cheke, Sir John

Husband, The: Brooke, Christopher

Husband in clover, A: Merivale, H.C.

Husband of Delilah: Linklater, Eric

Husbandmans jewel, The: Markham, Gervase

Husbands of Edith, The: McCutcheon, G.B.

Husband's story, The: Phillips, D.G.

Hussey-Cumberland mission and American independence, The: Bemis, S.F.

Hustled history: Lucas, E.V.

Hustler Joe: Porter, E.H.

Hwomely rhymes: Barnes, William

Hyacinth: Hannay, J.O.

Hyacinth: Sassoon, Siegfried

Hydriotaphia: Browne, Sir Thomas

Hygiasticon in three treatises: Herbert, George

Hyksos and Israelite cities: Petrie, Sir William Flindes

Hymen: Doolittle, Hilda

Hymenaei: Jonson, Ben

Hymens triumph: Daniel, Samuel

Hymn (An effort of his early childhood): Macaulay, Baron T.B.

Hymn before action: Kipling, Rudyard

Hymn for the eighty-seventh anniversary of American Independence: Boker, G.H.

Hymn for use during the cattle plague: Neale, J.M.

Hymn of empire, A: Scott, F.G.

Hymn of the breaking strain: Kipling, Rudyard

Hymn to harmony, A: Congreve, William

Hymn to Miss Laurence in the pump-room at Bath: Stevenson, J.H.

Hymn to Moloch: Hodgson, Ralph

Hymn to the light of the world, A: Blackmore, Sir R.D.

Hymn to the nymph of Bristol Spring, An: Whitehead, William

Hymn to the pillory, A: Defoe, Daniel

Hymn to the rising sun: Green, Paul

Hymn to the Spirit Eternal: Clarke, G.H.

Hymn to the Supreme Being on recovery from a dangerous fit of illness: Smart, Christopher

Hymn tunes of the Oratory, Birmingham: Newman, J.H.

Hymnes and songs of the Church, The: Wither, George

Hymns: Bryant, W.C.

Hymns (complete edition 1861): Faber, F.W.

Hymns and anthems: Adams, Sarah Fuller

Hymns and spiritual songs: Watts, Isaac

Hymns for amusement of children: Smart, Christopher

Hymns for childhood: Hemans, *Mrs.* Felicia

Hymns for children, in accordance with the catechism: Neale, J.M.

Hymns for the free Religion Association, June 2nd 1882: Emerson, R.W.

Hymns for the sick: Neale, J.M.

Hymns for the use of the Birmingham Oratory: Newman, J.H.

Hymns in prose for children: Barbauld, A.L.

Hymnes of Astraea in acrosticke verse: Davies, *Sir* John

Hymns of the church militant: Warner, A.B.

Hymns of the Eastern church: Neale, J.M.

Hymns on the Catechism: Williams, Isaac

Hymns on the Holy Communion: Cambridge, Ada

Hymns on the Litany: Cambridge, Ada

Hymns on the works of nature for the use of children: Hemans, *Mrs.* Felicia

Hymns suitable for invalids: Neale, J.M.

Hymns to the gods: Pike, Albert

Hymns to the mystic fire: Ghose, Sri Aurobindo

Hymn-tune mystery, The: Hannay, J.O.

Hypatia: Kingsley, Charles

Hyperborea: Lindsay, Norman

Hypercritica: Bolton, Edmund

Hyperion: Keats, John

Hyperion: Longfellow, H.W.

Hyperthuliana: Gogarty, O. St. John

Hypocrite taken from Molière and Cibber, The: Bickerstaffe, Isaac

Hypocrites, The: Jones, H.A.

Hypolympia: Gosse, *Sir* Edmund

Hystorye Sege and Dystruccyon of Troy, The: Lydgate, John

I

I.M.H.: Baring, Maurice

I am a Roman: Lindsay, Jack

I am my brother: Lehmann, John

I, Americans: Madariaga, Salvador de

I believe: Knox, R.A.

I believe that —: Sullivan, Alan

I break my word: Brown, Ivor

I came and saw: Blackburn, Douglas

I can get it for you wholesale: Weidman, Jerome

I, candidate for governor, and how I got licked: Sinclair, Upton

I cannot go hunting tomorrow: Treece, Henry

I capture the castle: Smith, Dodie

I, Claudius: Graves, Robert

I commit to the flames: Brown, Ivor

I. Compton-Burnett: Johnson, Pamela Hansford

I crossed the Minch: Macneice, Louis

I dips me lid to the Sydney Harbour Bridge: Dennis, C.M.J.

I do what I like: Darlington, W.A.

I don't mind if I do: Huxley, Elspeth J.

I dwelt in high places: †Bowen, Marjorie

I cannot go hunting tomorrow: Treece, Henry

I find four people: Frankau, Pamela

I follow St. Patrick: Gogarty, O. St. John

I follow the Mahatma: Munshi, K.M.

I for one: Priestley, J.B.

I give you my word: Brown, Ivor

I go out: Rukeyser, Muriel

I go west: Karaka, D.F.

I, governor of California and how I ended poverty: Sinclair, Upton

I had a sister: Ashton, Helen

I hate actors! Hecht, Ben

I have been here before: Priestley, J.B.

I have seen Quebec: Barbeau, C.M.

I heard a sailor: Gibson, Wilfred

I heard Immanuel singing: Lindsay, N.V.

I, James Blunt: Morton, H.V.

I, Jones, soldier: Schull, J.J.

I knock at the door: O'Casey, Sean

I know a secret: Morley, C.D.

I know all this when gipsy fi d dles cry: Lindsay, N.V.

I let him go: Brophy, John

I like America: Hicks, Granville

I like to remember: Ridge, W.Pett

I live again: Deeping, Warwick

I live under a black sun: Sitwell, Edith

I lived with you: †Novello, Ivor

I love you, I love you, I love you: Bemelmans, Ludwig

I loved you once: Mais, S.P.B.

I made you possible: Brown, Ivor

I met a lady: Spring, Howard

I paint your world: †Bell, Neil

I pose: Benson, Stella

I pray you be not angrie: Breton, Nicholas

I remember: Read, O.P.

I remember! I remember!: O'Faolain, Sean

I return to Ireland: Mais, S.P.B.

I return to Scotland: Mais, S.P.B.

I return to Switzerland: Mais, S.P.B.

I return to Wales: Mais, S.P.B.

I saw three ships: †Quiller-Couch, *Sir* A.

I saw two Englands: Morton, H.V.

I say no: Collins, Wilkie

I serve: Pertwee, Roland

I shall not want: Collins, Norman

I sing of man: Chattopadhyaya, Harindranath

I sometimes think: Robinson, E.S.L.

I speak of Africa: Plomer, W.C.F.

I thought of Daisy: Wilson, Edmund

I, too, have lived in Arcadia: Lowndes, M.A.

I took a journey: Mackenzie, *Sir* Compton

I tremble to think: Lynd, Robert

I visit the Soviet: †Delafield, E.M.

I walked along a stream: Marlowe, Christopher

I want: Holme, Constance

I want! I want!: Masefield, John

I wanted to write: Roberts, Kenneth

I wanted to write a poem: Williams, W.C.

I went to Russia: O'Flaherty, Liam

I will maintain: †Bowen, Marjorie

I will pray with the spirit, and I will pray with the understanding also: Bunyan, John

I will repay: Orczy, *Baroness*

I wonder as I wonder: Hughes, J.L.

I would and would not: Breton, Nicholas

I would be private: Macaulay, *Dame* Rose

Ian and Felicity: Mackail, Denis

Ian Hamilton's march: Churchill, *Sir* Winston

Ian of the Orcades: Campbell, W.W.

Ibant obscuri: Bridges, Robert

Iberia liberata: Oldmixon, John

Ibrahim the illustrious Bassa: Settle, Elkanah

Ibsen: Gosse, *Sir* Edmund

Ibsen: Knight, G.Wilson

Ibsen and Strindberg: Lucas, F.L.

Icarus: Russell, Bertrand

Ice in the bedroom: Wodehouse, P.G.

Ice palace: Ferber, Edna

Iceland: Baring-Gould, Sabine

Iceland: Trollope, Anthony

Iceland: first American republic: Stefansson, V.

Icelander's sword, The: Baring-Gould, Sabine

Icelandic sagas: Craigie, *Sir* W.A.

Iceman cometh, The: O'Neill, Eugene

Ichabod!: Barton, Bernard

Ichabod: Mather, Increase

Icknield way, The: Thomas, E.E.P.

Icon and idea: Read, *Sir* Herbert

Iconoclastes: Griffith, Hubert

Iconoclasts: Huneker, J.G.

I'd rather be right: Kaufman, G.S.

Ida: Stein, Gertrude

Ida Beresford: Leprohon, R.E.

Idalia: Haywood, *Mrs.* Eliza

Idalia: †Ouida

Idea: Drayton, Michael

Idea of a Christian society, The: Eliot, T.S.

Idea of a league of nations, The: Wells, H.G.

Idea of a world encyclopaedia, The: Wells, H.G.

Idea of an English Association, The: Newbolt, *Sir* Henry

Idea of Christ in the Gospels, The: Santayana, George

Idea of God as affected by modern knowledge, The: Fiske, John

Idea of great poetry, The: Abercrombie, Lascelles

Idea of history, The: Collingwood, R.G.

Idea of national interest, The: Beard, C.A.

Idea of nature, The: Collingwood, R.G.

Idea of progress, The: Inge, W.R.

Idea of the English school: Franklin, Benjamin

Ideal giant, The: Lewis, P. Wyndham

Ideal husband, An: Wilde, Oscar

Ideal of a Christian Church considered in comparison with existing practice, The: Ward, W.G.

Ideal of human unity, The: Ghose, Sri Aurobindo

Ideal of the Karmayogin, The: Ghose, Sri Aurobindo

Ideal university, The: Birrell, Augustine

Ideala: †Grand, Sarah

Idealist view of life, An: Radhakrishan, Sarvepalli

Ideals: Scott, Evelyn

Ideals and progress: Ghose, Sri Aurobindo

Ideals of religion: Bradley, A.C.

Ideals of the East, The: †Okakura, Tenshin

Ideas about India: Blunt, Wilfred

Ideas and people: Bax, Clifford

Ideas and places: Connolly, Cyril

Ideas mirrour: Drayton, Michael

Ideas of good and evil: Yeats, W.B.

Ideas of order: Stevens, Wallace

Ideas of the apostle Paul translated into their modern equivalents: Clarke, J.F.

Identity of man, The: Bronowski, J.

Ides of March, The: Wilder, Thornton

Idiot, The: Bangs, J.K.

Idiot at home, The: Bangs, J.K.

Idiot's delight: Sherwood, R.E.

Idle days in Patagonia: Hudson, W.H.

Idle ideas in 1905: Jerome, Jerome K.

Idle man, The: Dana, Richard Henry, *senior*

Idle money idle men: Chase, Stuart

Idle tales: Riddell, *Mrs.* J.H.

Idle thoughts of an idle fellow: Jerome, Jerome K.

Idleness of business, The: Wycherley, William

Idler, The: Johnson, Samuel

Idler in France, The: Blessington, Marguerite

Idler in Italy, The: Blessington, Marguerite

Idlers' gate: †Winch, John

Idol and the shrine, The: Royde-Smith, Naomi

Idol demolished by its own priest, The: Knowles, J.S.

Idolaters: Collins, Dale

Idols, The: Binyon, Laurence

Idols and ideals: Conway, M.D.

Idols of the cave, The: Prokosch, Frederic

Idyll in the desert: Faulkner, William

Idyll of the Alps, An: Manning, Anne

Idyll of the shops, An: Hecht, Ben

Idyll of work, An: Larcom, Lucy

Idyll on the peace, An: Oldmixon, John

Idyllia: McCrae, Hugh

Idyllic monologues: Cawein, Madison

Idylls and epigrams: Garnett, Richard

Idylls and legends of Inverburn: Buchanan, R.W.

Idylls and lyrics: Morris, *Sir* Lewis

Idylls of the hearth: Tennyson, Alfred *Lord*

Idylls of the King: Tennyson, Alfred *Lord*

Idyls and lyrics of the Ohio valley: Piatt, J.J.

Idyls and pastorals: Thaxter, C.L.

Idyls and songs: Palgrave, F.T.

Idyls of Norway: Boyesen, H.H.

Ierne defended: O'Halloran, Sylvester

If: Kipling, Rudyard

If, a nightmare in the conditional mood: Lucas, E.V.

If, a play in four acts: Dunsany, E.J.M.D.P.

If all these young men: Wilson, Romer

If any man sin: Cody, H.A.

If Britain is to live: Angell, *Sir* Norman

If dogs could write: Lucas, E.V.

If four walls told: Percy, Edward

If I forget thee: Levin, Meyer

If I had money: Tarkington, Booth

If I may: Milne, A.A.

If I were dictator: Dunsany, E.J.M.D.P.

If I were dictator: Ervine, St. John

If I were dictator: Huxley, *Sir* Julian

If I were God: Le Gallienne, Richard

If I were you: Green, Julian

If I were you: Levy, Benn W.

If I were you: Wodehouse, P.G.

If it be not good, the Divel is in it: Dekker, Thomas

If it prove fair weather: Paterson, Isabel

If Jesus came to Boston: Hale, E.E.

If men played cards as women do: Kaufman, G.S.

If Shakespear lived today: Dunsany, E.J.M.D.P.

If she is wise: Campion, Sarah

If so the man you are: Lewis, P. Wyndham

If stones could speak: Mottram, R.H.

If summer don't: Pain, B.E.O.

If the general strike had succeeded: Knox, R.A.

If the Germans conquered England: Lynd, Robert

If the South had won the Civil War: Kantor, Mackinlay

If this be I as I suppose it be: Deland, Margaret

"If this be treason...": Pound, Ezra

If this were true: Beresford, J.D.

If winter comes: Hutchinson, Arthur

If winter don't: Pain, B.E.O.

If wishes were horses: Fowler, H.W.

If, yes, and perhaps: Hale, E.E.

If you don't mind my saying so: Krutch, J.W.

If you know not me, you know no bodie: Heywood, Thomas

Ignatius his conclave: Donne, John

Ignes fatui: Guedalla, Philip

Ike Partington: †Mrs. Partington

Il Paddy Whack in Italia: Lover, Samuel

Il quod: Gill, Eric

Ile: O'Neill, Eugene

Ile of guls, The: Day, John

Iliad of Homer, The (trn.): Pope, A.

Iliana: Bercovici, Konrad

Ilicit: Carman, Bliss

Ill wind: Hilton, James

Ilion: Ghose, Sri Aurobindo

Ilka on the hill-top: Boyesen, H.H.

I'll leave it to you: Coward, Noel

I'll never be young again: Du Maurier, Daphne

I'll never go there any more: Weidman, Jerome

I'll pay your fare: Jennings, Gertrude

I'll say she does: †Cheyney, Peter

I'll take my stand: Fletcher, John Gould

I'll take my stand: Ransom, J.C.

I'll tell the world: Knox, E.V.

I'll tell you a tale: Dobie, J.F.

I'll tell you everything: Bullett, Gerald

I'll tell you everything: Priestley, J.B.

I'll tell you what: Inchbald, *Mrs.* Elizabeth

Illahun: Petrie, *Sir* William Flinders

Illinois boyhood, An: Van Doren, Carl

Illinois poems: Masters, E.L.

Ill-made knight, The: White, T.H.

Ill-tempered clavichord, The: Perelman, S.J.

Illumination: Frederic, Harold

Illusion: Tomlinson, H.M.

Illusion and reality: †Caudwell, Christopher

Illusion of the first time in acting, The: Gillette, William

Illustrated book about South America, including Mexico and Central America, The: Appel, Benjamin

Illustrated catalogue of rare books on the East Indies and a letter to a friend, An: Tomlinson, H.M.

Illustrated excursions in Italy: Lear, Edward

Illustrated history of the State of Montana, An: †Miller, Joaquin

Illustrated poems: Holmes, O.W.

Illustrated poems: Sigourney, L.H.

Illustrated Quebec ... under French and English occupancy: Adam, G.M.

Illustrated record of English literature: Garnett, Richard

Illustrations, historical and critical, of the life of Lorenzo de' Medici: Roscoe, William

Illustrations of early English popular literature: Collier, J.P.

Illustrations of human life: Ward, R.P.

Illustrations of lying, in all its branches: Opie, Amelia

Illustrations of Old English literature: Collier, J.P.

Illustrations of political economy: Martineau, Harriet

Illustrations of taxation: Martineau, Harriet

Illustrations of Tennyson: Collins, J.C.

Illustrations of the author of Waverley: Chambers, Robert

Illustrations of the life of Shakespeare in a discursive series of essays: Halliwell, J.O.

Illustrations of the literary history of the eighteenth century: Nichols, John

Illustrations of the manners and expences of antient times in England: Nichols, John

Illustrators of the sixties: Reid, Forrest

Illustrious prince, The: Oppenheim, E.Phillips

Illyria reborn: Cusack, E.D.

Illyrian letters: Evans, Sir A.J.

Ilonka speaks of Hungary: Brophy, John

I'm a stranger here myself: Nash, Ogden

I'm sorry—it's out!: Jennings, Gertrude

Image, The: Gregory, Lady Augusta

Image and superscription: Mitchell, J.L.

Image in the sand, The: Benson, E.F.

Image of America: our literature from Puritanism to the space age: Foerster, Norman

Image of governance compiled of actes of Alexander Severus, The: Elyot, Sir Thomas

Image of his father, The: Mayhew, Augustus Septimus

Image of Josephine: Tarkington, Booth

Images: Aldington, Richard

Images of desire: Aldington, Richard

Images of good and evil: Symons, Arthur

Images of truth: Wescott, Glenway

Images of war: Aldington, Richard

Imaginary conversation of King Carlo Alberto and the Duchess Belgioioso: Landor, W.S.

Imaginary conversations: Heppenstall, Rayner

Imaginary conversations of Greeks and Romans: Landor, W.S.

Imaginary conversations of literary men and statesmen: Landor, W.S.

Imaginary interview between W. Hone and a lady, An: Hone, William

Imaginary interviews: Howells, W.D.

Imaginary invalid, The: Malleson, Miles

Imaginary letters: Pound, Ezra

Imaginary obligations: Colby, F.M.

Imaginary portrait, An: Pater, W.H.

Imaginary portraits: Pater, Walter

Imaginary speeches and other parodies in prose and verse: Squire, Sir John

Imagination and fancy: Hunt, Leigh

Imagination and the university: Bronowski, J.

Imagination and thinking: Day-Lewis, C.

Imagination of Vanbrugh and his fellow artists, The: Whistler, Laurence

Imaginations and reveries: Russell, G.W.

Imaginative biography: Brydges, Sir Samuel

Imaginative literature of England, The: Swinburne, A.C.

Imaginative man, An: Hichens, R.S.

Imagined corners: Muir, Willa

Imitation of the sixth satire of the second book of Horace, An: Swift, Jonathan

Immanence: Underhill, Evelyn

Immediate EPIC: Sinclair, Upton

Immersion: Isvaran, M.S.

Immobile wind, The: Winters, Yvor

Immoment toys: Agate, J.E.

Immoral effects of ignorance in sex relations, The: Housman, Laurence

Immortal dawn, The: Bridges, Roy

Immortal dawn: Mee, Arthur

Immortal Dyer: (Stephen Southwold), †Bell, Neil

Immortal friend, The: Krishnamurti, Jiddu

Immortal hour, The: †Macleod, Fiona

Immortal legions: Noyes, Alfred

Immortal man: Vulliamy, C.E.

Immortal marriage, The: Atherton, Gertrude

Immortal memories, essays and addresses: Shorter, C.K.

Immortal rock: Salverson, L.G.

Immortal sergeant: Brophy, John

Immortal soul, An: Mallock, W.H.

Immortal village: Peattie, D.C.

Imogen: Molesworth, Mrs.

Impact of science upon society, The: Russell, Bertrand

Impartial, The: Hill, Aaron

Impartial critick, The: Dennis, John

Impartial portrait of Lord Byron, as a poet and a man, An: Brydges, Sir Samuel

Impartiallest satyre that ever was seen, The: Taylor, John

Impassioned clay: Powys, L. C.

Impatient poverty: McKerrow, R.B.

Impendin crisis uv the Dimocracy, The: †Nasby, Petroleum V.

Impending fast of Mahatma Gandhi, The: Rahagopalachari, Chakravati

Impending sword, An: Vachell, H.A.

Impending sword, The: Yates, E.H.

Impenetrability: Graves, Robert

Impenetrable secret: find it out!, The: Lathom, Francis

Imperaitve duty, An: Howells, W.D.

Imperfect gift, The: Bottome, Phyllis

Imperfect mother, An: Beresford, J.D.

Imperial Caesar: Warner, Rex

Imperial captives, The: Mottley, John

Imperial city: Rice, Elmer

Imperial Germany and the industrial revolution: Veblen, T.B.

Imperial India: †Hobbes, John Oliver

Imperial orgy, The: Saltus, E.E.

Imperial palace: Bennett, Arnold

Imperial Peking: Lin Yu-T'ang

Imperial pilgrimage: Byron, Robert

Imperial purple: Saltus, E.E.

Imperial theme, The: Knight, G.W.

Imperial tragedy, The: Killigrew, *Sir* William

Imperial treasure: Gielgud, Val

Imperial woman: Buck, Pearl

Imperialism and civilization: Woolf, Leonard

Imperialism and the open conspiracy: Wells, H.G.

Imperialist, The: Duncan, S.J.

Imperium Pelagi: Young, Edward

Impertinent, The: Pope, Alexander

Imperturbable duchess, The: Beresford, J.D.

Impious feast, The: Landor, R.E.

Importance of being Ernest, The: Wilde, Oscar

Importance of Dunkirk considered, The: Steele, *Sir* Richard

Importance of literature to men of business, The: Talfourd, *Sir* T.N.

Importance of living, The: Lin Yu-T'ang

Importance of understanding, The: Lin Yu-T'ang

Importance of the Guardian considered in a second letter to the Bailiff of Stockbridge, The: Swift, Jonathan

Important man, An: Ridge, W.Pett

Important speeches: Nehru, J.

Impossibilities of anarchism, The: Shaw, G.B.

Impossible marriage, An: Johnson, Pamela H.

Impossible thing, An: Congreve, William

Impostors, The: Cumberland, Richard

Imposture, The: Shirley, James

Impregnable women: Linklater, Eric

Impressions and comments: Ellis, Havelock

Impressions and experiences: Howells, W.D.

Impressions and opinions: Moore, George

Impressions from Italy: Jacob, Naomi

Impressions of Australia Felix: Howitt, Richard

Impressions of Scandinavia in war time: Murray, Gilbert

Impressions of Soviet Russia and the revolutionary world: Dewey, John

Impressions of Theophrastus Such: †Eliot, George

Impromptu in Moribundia: Hamilton, Patrick

Impromptu verses read at the bookseller's dinner: Fields, J.T.

Improper people: Ackland, Rodney

Improper Peter: Hoffe, Monckton

Improved binoculars, The: Layton, Irving

Improvisatore: Beddoes, T.L.

Improvisatrice, The: Landon, L.E.M.

Impudence of youth, The: Deeping, Warwick

Impunity Jane: Godden, Rumer

In a Belgian garden: Call, F.O.

In a Canadian canoe: Pain, B.E.O.

In a fishing country: Blake, W.H.

In a garden: Barry, Philip

In a German Pension: Mansfield, Katherine

In a glass darkly: Le Fanu, Sheridan

In a green shade: Hewlett, Maurice

In a hollow of the hills: Harte, Bret

In a library: De la Mare, Walter

In a music hall: Davidson, John

In a province: Van der Post, Laldrens

In a quiet village: Baring-Gould, Sabine

In a silver sea: Farjeon, B.L.

In a strange land: Gill, Eric

In a winter city: †Ouida

In Abraham's bosom: Green, Paul

In accordance with the evidence: †Onions, Oliver

In all countries: Dos Passos, John

In all shades: Allen, Grant

In amber lands: MacInnes, T.R.E.

In an auction room: Morley, C.D.

In an enchanted island: Mallock, W.H.

In another land: Mackaye, Percy

In apple time: Carman, Bliss

In April once: Percy, W.A.

In Aunt Mahaly's cabin: Green, Paul

In Australia: †Rudd, Steele

In Australian Wilds: (†Donald Barr), Barrett, C.L.

In bad company: †Boldrewood, Rolf

In bad with Sinbad: Stringer, A.J.A.

In Barton Woods: Child, L.M.

In battle for peace: Dubois, William

In Ben Boyd's day: Lawson, Will

In between stories: (Stephen Southwold), †Bell, Neil

In black and white: Kipling, Rudyard

In Bohemia: O'Reilly, J.B.

In brief authority: Anstey, F.

In camp with a tin soldier: Bangs, J.K.

In chancery: Galsworthy, John

In Chancery: Pinero, *Sir* A.W.

In childhood's country: Moulton, E.L.

In classic shades: †Miller, Joaquin

In conference with the best minds: Pierce, Lorne

In connection with the De Quilloughby claim: Burnett, Frances Hodgson

In Cornwall and across the sea: Sladen, D.B.W.

In country sleep: Thomas, Dylan

In Deacon's Orders: Besant, *Sir* Walter

In defence of liberalism: Panikkar, K.M.

In defence of pink: Lynd, Robert

In defence of sensuality: Powys, John Cowper

In defence of Shelley: Read, *Sir* Herbert

In defense of ignorance: Shapiro, Karl

In defense of reason: Winters, Yvor

In defense of women: Mencken, H.L.

In Dewisland: Baring-Gould, Sabine

In Dickens's London: Smith, F.H.

In double harness: Williams, G.P. and W.P. Reeves

In dreamland: O'Hagan, Thomas

In dubious battle: Steinbeck, John

In excelsis: Carman, Bliss

In excelsis: Douglas, *Lord* Alfred

In exile: Cournos, John

In exitu Israel: Baring-Gould, Sabine

In far Lochaber: Black, William

In Flanders fields: McCrae, John

In general and particular: Bowra, *Sir* Cecil

In good King Charles's golden days: Shaw, G.B.

In great waters: Janvier, T.A.

In happy valley: Fox, John

In haste and at leisure: Linton, Eliza

In hazard: Hughes, R.A.W.

In her earliest youth: †Tasma

In high places: Braddon, M.E.

In his name: Hale, E.E.

In his own country: Street, A.G.

In his own image: (†Baron Corvo), Rolfe, Frederick

In his steps: Sheldon, C.M.

In his steps today: Sheldon, C.M.

In Hoc Vince: Barclay, F.L.

In homespun: Nesbit, E.

In Kedar's tents: †Merriman, Seton

In Kings' byways: Weyman, Stanley

In Lincoln's chair: Tarbell, Ida

In many keys: Bengough, J.W.

In Maremma: †Ouida

In marked overt: Payn, James

In memorabilis mortis: Sherman, F.J.

In memoriam: Alcott, A.B.

In Memoriam: Tennyson, Alfred *Lord*

In memoriam: Auberon Herbert: Baring, Maurice

In memoriam: C.G. Gordon: Rusden, G.W.

In memoriam: Charles W. Jeffrys, 1869–1951: Pierce, Lorne

In memoriam—free competition: Chase, Stuart

In memoriam George Paul MacDonell: Allen, Grant

In memoriam James Joyce: †McDiarmid, Hugh

In memoriam Mrs. Katherine Donnelly: Donnelly, I.L.

In memoriam: Nicol Drysdale Stenhouse: Kendall, Henry

In memoriam, Peter Redpath: Dawson, *Sir* J.W.

In memoriam: recollections of Father Dawson: Morgan, H.J.

In memoriam 2567: Bynner, Witter

In memory of John William Spencer, Earl Brownlow: Massey, Gerald

In memory of Joseph Washington Esq.: Tate, Nahum

In memory of our Late Most Gracious Lady Mary, Queen of Great Britain, France and Ireland: Phillips, John

In memory of R.D. Fitzgerald: Woolls, William

In Mizoura: Thomas, Augustus

In modern dress: Morley, C.D.

In Morocco: Wharton, Edith

In Mr. Knox's country: Somerville, Edith

In my good books: Pritchett, V.S.

In my lady's praise: Arnold, Edwin

In my path: Sutherland, H.G.

In my view: Newton, Eric

In narrow edge: †Bell, Neil

In nature's workshop: Allen, Grant

In New England fields and woods: Robinson, R.E.

In Noah's ark: Godden, Rumer

In northern skies: †Seranus

In old Narragansett: Earle, A.M.

In old New York: Janvier, T.A.

In old school days: Carleton, William (McKendree)

In ole Virginia: Page, T.N.

In our convent days: Repplier, Agnes

In our time: Hemingway, Ernest

In our town: Runyon, Damon

In our town: White, W.A.

In Palestine: Gilder, R.W.

In partnership: Bunner, H.C.

In partnership: Matthews, J.B.

In pastures green: McArthur, Peter

In paths of peril: Oxley, J.M.

In Pentland wine: Ogilvie, W.H.

In peril and privation: Payn, James

In peril of his life: Cole, G.D.H.

In powder and crinoline: Quiller-Couch, *Sir* A.

In praise of Aussie girls: Stephens, A.G.

In praise of birds: Raven, C.E.

In praise of England: Massingham, Harold

In praise of idleness: Russell, Bertrand

In praise of peace: Gower, John

In praise of wine: Waugh, Alec

In pursuit of laughter: Repplier, Agnes

In pursuit of poetry: Hillyer, Robert

In pursuit of Spring: Thomas, E.E.P.

In quest of El Dorado: Graham, Stephen

In quest of light: Smith, Goldwin

In quest of the Holy Graal: Evans, Sebastian

In re Logan Pearsall Smith: Morley, C.D.

In re: Sherlock Holmes: Derleth, A.W.

In retreat: Read, *Sir* Herbert

In retrospect; the history of a historian: Schlesinger, Arthur

In revolt: Grossman, E.H.

In russet and silver: Gosse, *Sir* Edmund

In scarlet and grey: Hardy, Thomas

In Scotland again: Morton, H.V.

In search: Levin, Meyer

In search of a character: Greene, Graham

In search of Bisco: Caldwell, Erskine Preston

In search of Canadian Liberalism: Underhill, F.H.

In search of Egeria: Mais,S.P.B.

In search of England: Morton, H.V.

In search of Ireland: Morton, H.V.

In search of London: Morton, H.V.

In search of myself: Grove, F.P.

In search of reality: Samuel, Herbert *1st Viscount*

In search of Scotland: Morton, H.V.

In search of South Africa: Morton, H.V.

In search of Swift: Johnston, W.D.

In search of the okapi: Glanville, Ernest

In search of the unknown: Chambers, R.W.

In search of Wales: Morton, H.V.

In search of winter sport: Gibbon, Monk

In secret: Chambers, R.W.

In Sicily: Sassoon, Siegfried

In Sicily: Sladen, D.B.W.

In silk attire: Black, William

In single strictness: Moore, George

In small proportions we just beauties see: Morley, C.D.

In sober livery: Vachell, H.A.

In soft garments: Knox, R.A.

In South Africa: Young, Francis Brett

In spite of: Powys, John Cowper

In spite of all: †Lyall, Edna

In spite of thunder: Carr, J.D.

In spring: Sitwell, Edith

In such a night: Deutsch, Babette

In sugar-cane land: Phillpotts, Eden

In summer: Blunden, Edmund

In sun and shade: Scott, F.G.

In tenebris lux: Evans, G.E.

In Thackeray's London: Smith, F.H.

In that far land: Van Doren, Mark

In the Alamo: Read, O.P.

In the American grain: Williams, W.C.

In the American jungle: Frank, Waldo

In the arena: Tarkington, Booth

In the balance: Churchill, Winston

In the battle silences: Scott, F.G.

In the beginning: Deamer, Dulcie

In the beginning: Douglas, Norman

In the beginning: Sullivan, Alan

In the blackout: Jennings, Gertrude

In the blood: Trease, Geoffrey

In the cage: James, Henry

In the Carquinez Woods: Harte, Bret

In the cellar: Jennings, Gertrude

In the closed room: Burnett, Frances Hodgson

In the clouds: †Craddock, C.E.

In the company of dolphins: Shaw, Irwin

In the Darwinian hypothesis of sexual selection: Douglas, Norman

In the days of McKinley: Leech, M.K.

In the days of poor Richard: Bacheller, Irving

In the days of the Canada Company: Lizars, Robina, and K.M. Lizars

In the days of the comet: Wells, H.G.

In the days when the world was wide: Lawson, Henry

In the distance: Lathrop, G.P.

In the dozy hours: Repplier, Agnes

In the end is my beginning: Baring, Maurice

In the endless sands: Scott, Evelyn

In the fog: Davis, R.H.

In the fog: Jennings, Gertrude

In the footprints of the Padres: Stoddard, C.W.

In the footsteps of the Lincolns: Tarbell, Ida

In the forest: Traill, C.P.

In the fourth year: anticipation of a world peace: Wells, H.G.

In the garden: Burnett, Frances Hodgson

In the garden of Arden: Dennis, C.M.J.

In the garden of charity: †King, Basil

In the garden of dreams: Moulton, E.L.

In the garret: Van Vechten, Carl

In the golden days: †Lyall, Edna

In the great steep's garden: Roberts, E.M.

In the green mountain country: Day, Clarence

In the green wood: Robinson, R.E.

In the hands of the Senecas: Edmonds, W.D.

In the harbor: Ultima Thule: Longfellow, H.W.

In the heart of a fool: White, W.A.

In the heart of the hills: Carman, Bliss

In the heart of the meadow: O'Hagan, Thomas

In the heights: Gilder, R.W.

In the High Valley: Coolidge, Susan

In the High Woods: Roberts, T.G.

In the hush of the autumn night: Aldrich, T.B.

In the hushes of the midnight: Aldrich, T.B.

In the key of blue: Symonds, J.A.

In the land of the Mogul: Trease, Geoffrey

In the land of youth: Stephens, James

In the Levant: Warner, C.D.

In the library: Jacobs, W.W.

In the manner of men: Mason, R.A.K.

In the margin of history: Namier, *Sir* Lewis

In the meantime: Spring, Howard

In the middle watch: Russell, W.C.

In the midst of life: Bierce, Ambrose

In the midst of my fever: Layton, Irving

In the mist of the mountains: Turner, E.S.

In the mill: Masefield, John

In the money: Williams, W.C.

In the mountains: Russell, E.M.

In the name of sanity: Mumford, Lewis

In the name of the Bodleian: Birrell, Augustine

In the name of time: †Field, Michael

In the Nazi era: Namier, *Sir* Lewis

In the net of the stars: Flint, F.S.

In the night: Swinnerton, Frank

In the old church tower: Aldrich, T.B.

In the old of my age: MacInnes, T.R.E.

In the palace of the king: Crawford, F.M.

In the quarter: Chambers, R.W.

In the Queen's parlor: †Queen, Ellery

In the ranks of the C.I.V.: Childers, R.E.

In the roar of the sea: Baring-Gould, Sabine

In the roaring 'Fifties: Dyson, E.G.

In the St. Peter's set: Janvier, T.A.

In the Sargasso Sea: Janvier, T.A.

In the second year: Jameson, Storm

In the seven woods: Yeats, W.B.

In the shadows: Johnson, E.P.

In the snare: Sabatini, Rafael

In the South Seas: Stevenson, R.L.

In the spotlight: Hubbard, Elbert

In the steps of Jesus: Morton, H.V.

In the steps of John Bunyan: Brittain, Vera

In the steps of Mary, Queen of Scots: †Bowen, Marjorie

In the steps of Moses the conqueror: Golding, Louis

In the steps of Moses the lawgiver: Golding, Louis

In the steps of St. Francis: Raymond, Ernest

In the steps of St. Paul: Morton, H.V.

In the steps of the Brontës: Raymond, Ernest

In the steps of the Master: Morton, H.V.

In the stranger people's country: †Craddock, C.E.

In the studio: Evans, Sebastian

In the sweet dry and dry: Morley, C.D.

In the swing of the sea: Oxley, J.M.

In the teeth of the evidence: Sayers, Dorothy

In the Tennessee mountains: †Craddock, C.E.

In the tent door: Carman, Bliss

In the time of the tyrants: Soutar, William

In the train: †O'Connor, Frank

In the twilight: Swinburne, A.C.

In the valley: Frederic, Harold

In the valley: Green, Paul

In the vestibule limited: Matthews, J.B.

In the village of Viger: Scott, D.C.

In the vine country: Somerville, Edith

In the wake of the wind ships: Wallace, F.W.

In the wet: †Shute, Nevil

In the whirl of the rising: Mitford, Bertram

In the wilderness: Hichens, R.S.

In the wilderness: Warner, C.D.

In the wilds of the west coast: Oxley, J.M.

In the wood: Royde-Smith, N.

In the wood: Williamson, Henry

In the wrong Paradise: Lang, Andrew

In the year of Jubilee: Gissing, George

In the Ypres Salient: Willson, H.B.

In the zone: O'Neill, Eugene

In their own image: Basso, Hamilton

In these days: Bancroft, H.H.

In this our life: Glasgow, Ellen

In three tongues: Knox, R.A.

In time like glass: Turner, W.J.R.

In time of mistrust: Hillyer, Robert

In time of peace: Boyd, Thomas

In time of "the breaking of nations": Hardy, Thomas

In time of war: Trench, R.C.

In Titian's garden: Spofford, H.E.

In tragic life: Fisher, V.A.

In troubadour land: Baring-Gould, Sabine

In trust: Oliphant, Margaret

In two Chinas: memoirs of a diplomat: Panikkar, K.M.

In two years time: Cambridge, Ada

In Tyrrell's book shop: Slessor, Kenneth

In Veronica's garden: Austin, Alfred

In vinculis: Blunt, Wilfred

In war time: Macartney, Frederick

In war time: Mitchell, S.W.

In war time: Whittier, J.G.

In Wicklow, West Kerry, and Connemara: Synge, J.M.

In winter: Davies, W.H.

In your garden: Sackville-West, Victoria

In your garden again: Sackville-West, Victoria

In your hands, Australians!: Bean, C.E.

Inadequacy of natural selection, The: Spencer, Herbert

Inalienable heritage, The: Lawless, Emily

Inaugural address at the University of St. Andrews: Mill, John Stuart

Inaugural address to the Shelley Society, The: Brooke, S.A.

Inaugural discourse on being installed Lord Rector of the University of Glasgow: Brougham, H.P.

Inaugural lecture on the present state of historical scholarship: Butterfield, Herbert

Inaugural lecture on the study of modern history: Butterfield, Herbert

Inaugural oration, An: Adams, J.Q.

Inca's treasure, The: Glanville, Ernest

Inca of Perusalem, The: Shaw, G.B.

Incarnation and principles of evidence: Hutton, R.H.

Incident at the Merry Hippo, The: Huxley, Elspeth J.

Incidental Bishop, The: Allen, Grant

Incidental numbers: Wylie, Elinor

Incidents of the insurrection in the western parts of Pennsylvania: Brackenridge, H.H.

Inclinations: Firbank, Ronald

Inclinations: Sackville-West, Edward

Including Horace: Untermeyer, Louis

Incognita: Congreve, William

Incognito: Hichens, R.S.

Income and outcome: Balchin, Nigel

Income-tax, The: Gilbert, Sir W.S.

Incoming summer, The: Williamson, Henry

Incomplete amorist, The: Nesbit, E.

Inconstant, The: Farquhar, George

Inconstant moon, The: Langley, Noel

Inconstant wife, The: (Stephen Southwold), Bell, Neil

Incorruptible Irishman, An: Somerville, E.

Incredible adventures: Blackwood, Algernon

Incredible Balkans: Bercovici, Konrad

Incredible honeymoon, The: Nesbit, E.

Incredible journey, The: Martin, C.E.

Incredible tale: Royde-Smith, Naomi

Incredible Tito: Fast, Howard M.

Incredible year: An Australian sees Europe, The: Chisholm, A.H.

Incredulity of Father Brown, The: Chesterton, G.K.

Indefinite American attitude toward the war and when shall it change?, The: Hough, Emerson

Independence: Churchill, Charles

Independence: Kipling, Rudyard

Independence: Sen, Keshub Chunder

Independence and after: Nehru, Jawarhalal

Independence day, a sketchbook: Guedalla, Philip

Independence of the New World: Fiske, John

Independent means: Houghton, W.S.

Independent member: Herbert, Sir A.P.

Index of names and titles in the Old Kingdom: Murray, Margaret

Index to mankind, An: Smart, Christopher

Index to the achievements of near kinsfolk, An: Galton, Sir Francis

Index to the story of my days: Craig, Sir E.G.

India: Churchill, Sir Winston

India and China: Panikkar, K.M.

India and China: Radhakrishan, Sarvepalli

India and the Indian Ocean: Panikkar, K.M.

India and the Prince of Wales: Sala, G.A.H.

India and the world: Nehru, Jawaharlal

India Christiana: Mather, Cotton

India in the Victorian age: Dutt, R.C.

India of Aurangzib, The: Sarkar, Y.J.

India of the Queen, The: Hunter, Sir William

India on the march: Nehru, Jawaharlal

India, our eastern empire: Gibbs, P.H.

India revisited: Arnold, Edwin

India through the ages: Sarkar, Y.J.

India today: Dutt, R.P.

India today and tomorrow: Dutt, R.P.

India under Ripon: Blunt, W.S.

India ventures of Fisher Ames, 1794–1804, The: Morison, S.E.

India—what next?, Nehru, Jawaharlal

Indian ass, An: Acton, Harold

Indian bangle, The: Hume, F.W.

Indian cavalcade: Bhattacharya, Bhabani

Indian Civil Service, The: Macaulay, T.B. Baron

Indian contribution to English literature, The: Iyengar, K.R. Srinivasa

Indian craftsman, The: Coomaraswamy, A.K.

Indian currency and finance: Keynes, J.M.

Indian days in the Canadian Rockies: Barbeau, C.M.

Indian drawings: Coomaraswamy, A.K.

Indian earth: Bynner, Witter

Indian education minutes, The: Macaulay, T.B. *Baron*

Indian Emperour, The: Dryden, John

Indian Empire, The: Hunter, *Sir* William

Indian fairy tales retold: Anand, M.R.

Indian famines, their causes and prevention: Dutt, R.C.

Indian farewell, The: Hubbard, Elbert

Indian giver, An: Howells, W.D.

Indian Musalmans, The: Hunter, *Sir* William

Indian nights: MacKay, I.E.

Indian Ocean, The: Villiers, A.J.

Indian pageant: Yeats-Brown, Francis

Indian passion: Woodberry, G.E.

Indian philosophy: Radhakrishan, Sarvepalli

Indian poetry: Arnold, Edwin

Indian poetry: Austin, Mary

Indian poetry selections: Dutt, R.C.

Indian polity: Chesney, *Sir* George

Indian pottery of the Rio Grande: Austin, Mary

Indian princes in council, The: Panikkar, K.M.

Indian princess, The: Barker, J.N.

Indian prophecy, The: Custis, G.W.P.

Indian Queen, The: Dryden, John

Indian revolution: Panikkar, K.M.

Indian speaks, The: Barbeau, C.M.

Indian speeches: Morley, John

Indian states and the government of India: Paikkar, K.M.

Indian summer: Howells, W.D.

Indian summer: Thomas, Augustus

Indian summer of a Forsyte, The: Galsworthy, John

Indian tragedy, An: Anand, M.R.

Indian wars of the West: Flint, Timothy

Indian writing in English: Iyengar, K.R. Srinivasa

Indiana Jane: Roberts, C.E.M.

India-rubber men, The: Wallace, Edgar

Indicator and the companion, The: Hunt, Leigh

Indictment of the Government: Kipling, Rudyard

Indiscreet itinerary, An: Van Loon, Hendrik

Indiscretion in the life of an heiress, An: Hardy, Thomas

Indiscretion of the duchess, The: Hawkins, A.H.

Indiscretions: Pound, Ezra

Indiscretions of Archie, The: Wodehouse, P.G.

Indispensible information for infants: Wister, Owen

Individual in the animal kingdom, The: Huxley, *Sir* Julian

Individualism, old and new: Dewey, John

Individualist, The: Gibbs, *Sir* Philip

Individualist, The: Mallock, W.H.

Indo-Anglian literature: Iyengar, K.R. Srinivasa

Indo-Aryan faith and doctrine, The: Pike, Albert

Indoor studies: Burroughs, John

Inductive metrology: Petrie, *Sir* Williams Flinders

Induna's wife, The: Mitford, Bertram

Industrial biography: iron workers and tool makers: Smiles, Samuel

Industrial democracy: Webb, Beatrice and Sidney Webb

Industrial future, The: Guedalla, Philip

Industrial republic, The: Sinclair, Upton

Industrial revolution, The: Beard, C.A.

Industrial revolution, 1750–1850, The: Power, Eileen

Inebriety: Crabbe, George

Inequality of Man, The: Haldane, J.B.S.

Inevitable millionaires, The: Oppenheim, E.Phillips

Inez: a tale of the Alamo: Evans, A.J.

Infallible astrologer, The: Brown, Thomas

Infamous army, An: Heyer, Georgette

Infant bridal, The: De Vere, Aubrey

Infatuation: Hecht, Ben

Infelice: Evans, A.J.

Infernal world of Branwell Brontë, The: Du Maurier, Daphne

Infidel, The: Bird, R.M.

Infidel, The: Braddon, M.E.

Infidelity: Bannister, N.H.

Inflation at the cross roads: †Nasby, Petroleum V.

Inflexible captive, The: More, Hannah

Influence of Darwin on philosophy, The: Dewey, John

Influence of Greek and Hebraic traditions on Western ideals, The: Livingstone, *Sir* Richard

Influence of Homer, The: Milnes, R.M.

Influence of the audience, The: Bridges, Robert

Influence of the mechanic arts on the human race: Gayarré, C.E.A.

Influence of the neighbourhood of a rich Asiatic: Mackenzie, Henry

Influence of women and its cure, The: Erskine, John

Influential books: Blunden, Edmund

Informal grammar, An: Strong, L.A.G.

Information to those who would remove to America: Franklin, Benjamin

Informer, The: O'Flaherty, Liam

Ingenious contention by way of letter between Mr. Wanley, a son of the Church and Dr. Wild a Nonconformist, An: Wanley, Nathaniel

Ingham papers, The: Hale, E.E.

Ingleborough Hall: Herbert, H.W.

Ingoldsby legends, The: Barham, R.H.

Ingoldsby lyrics: Barham, R.H.

Ingratitude of a Common-Wealth, The: Tate, Nahum

Inhale and exhale: Saroyan,William

Inheritance: Bentley, Phyllis

Inheritance: Drinkwater, John

Inheritance, The: Ferrier, Susan

Inheritance, An: Spofford, H.E.

Inheritor, The: Benson, E.F.

Inheritor, The: Beresford, J.D.

Inheritors, The: Church, Richard

Inheritors, The: Conrad, Joseph

Inheritors, The: Ford, F.M.

Inheritors: Glaspell, Susan

Inheritors: Penton, B.C.

Inimitable Jeeves, The: Wodehouse, P.G.

Iniquity of us all, The: Royde-Smith, Naomi

Inisfail: De Vere, Aubrey

Inishfallen, fare thee well: O'Casey, Sean

Initials, The: Tautphoeus, *Baroness* Jemima

Initials in the heart, The: Whistler, Laurence

Injur'd love: Tate, Nahum

Inkle and Yarico: Colman, George, *the younger*

Inklings of adventure: Willis, N.P.

Inland eye, The: McCormick, E.H.

Inland far: Bax, Clifford

Inland voyage, An: Stevenson, R.L.

Inmates, The: Powys, John Cowper

Inmost light, The: †Machen, Arthur

Inn album, The: Browning, Robert

Inn at the end of the world, The: Logan, J.D.

Inn of the hawk and the raven, The: McCutcheon, G.B.

Inn of tranquillity, The: Galsworthy, John

Inner door, The: Sullivan, Alan

Inner house, The: Besant, *Sir* Walter

Inner kingdom, The: Gore-Booth, E.S.

Inner life of the House of Commons, The: White, W.H.

Inner shrine, The: †King, Basil

Inner Temple masque: Browne, William

Inner-Temple Masque, The: Middleton, Thomas

Innocence and experience: Bottome, Phyllis

Innocence is drowned: Allen, Walter Ernest

Innocence of Father Brown, The: Chesterton, G.K.

Innocence of G.K.Chesterton, The: Bullett, Gerald

Innocencies: Tynan, Katherine

Innocency with her open face: Penn, William

Innocent: †Corelli, Marie

Innocent: Oliphant, Margaret

Innocent amusements: Pain, B.E.O.

Innocent birds: Powys, T.F.

Innocent criminal, An: Beresford, J.D.

Innocent eye, The: Calder-Marshall, Arthur

Innocent eye, The: Read, *Sir* Herbert

Innocent moon, The: Williamson, Henry

Innocent party, The: Harwood, H.M.

Innocent witch, The: Herbert, H.W.

Innocents, The: Lewis, H.S.

Innocents abroad, The: (†Mark Twain), Clemens, S.L.

Inquilab: Abbas, K.A.

Inquiries and opinions: Matthews, J.B.

Inquiries into the human faculty: Galton, *Sir* Francis

Inquiry concerning virtue in two discourses, An: Shaftesbury, Anthony, *Earl of*

Inquiry into meaning and truth, An: Russell, Bertrand

Inquiry into some of the conditions at present affecting the study of architecture in our schools, An: Ruskin, John

Inquiry into the authenticity of certain papers attributed to Shakespeare, Queen Elizabeth and Henry, Earl of Southampton, An: Malone, Edmund

Inquiry into the colonial policy of the European powers, An: Brougham, H.P.

Inquiry into the cultural stability in Polynesia, An: Mead, Margaret

Inquiry into the effects of our foreign carrying trade, An: Moore, C.C.

Inquiry into the effects of spirituous liquors upon the human body, An: Rush, Benjamin

Inquiry into the literary and political character of James I: D'Israeli, Isaac

Inquiry into the nature and causes of the wealth of nations, An: Smith, Adam

Inquiry into the principles of the good society, An: Lippmann, Walter

Inquiry into the propriety of applying wastes to the maintenance of the poor, An: Young, Arthur

Inquisition, The: Coulton, G.G.

Inquisitor, The: Holcroft, Thomas

Inquisitor, The: Rowson, S.H.

Inquisitor, The: Walpole, *Sir* Hugh

Inrichment of the weald of Kent, The: Markham, Gervase

Insane root, The: Praed, *Mrs.* C.

Insatiate countesse, The: Marston, John

Inscription for the rose-tree brought from Omar's tomb, and planted on the grave of Edward Fitzgerald: Gosse, *Sir* Edmund

Inscription of a fountain head: Quennell, P.C.

Inscriptions and graves in the Niagara peninsula: Carnochan, Janet

Insheeny: Hannay, J.O.

Inside: a chronicle of secession: Baker, W.M.

Inside America: Nehru, Jawaharlal

Inside Benchley: Benchley, Robert

Inside of life, The: Underhill, Evelyn

Inside of the cup, The: Churchill, Winston

Inside stand, The: Wodehouse, P.G.

Inside story of the Harding tragedy, The: Dixon, Thomas

Inside the whale: †Orwell, George

Inside Yugoslavia: Adamic, Louis

Insight: Bronowski, J.

Insolvent, The: Hill, Aaron

Inspector calls, An: Priestley, J.B.

Inspector Dickens retires: Oppenheim, E.Phillips

Inspector French and the Cheyne mystery: Crofts, F.W.

Inspector French's case book: Crofts, F.W.

Inspector French's greatest case: Crofts, F.W.

Inspector Queen's own case: †Queen, Ellery

Inspiration and poetry: Bowra, *Sir* Maurice

Inspiration of poetry, The: Woodberry, G.E.

Inspiring vision, An: Malalasekara, Gunapala

Instead of the thorn: Heyer, Georgette

Instigations: Pound, Ezra

Instinct of workmanship, The: Veblen, T.B.

Institutes of natural and revealed theology: Priestley, Joseph

Institution of the Garter, The: Garrick, David

Instruction for the ignorant: Bunyan, John

Instructions to a celebrated Laureat: †Pindar, Peter

Instructions to a painter for the drawing of the posture and progress of his Majesties forces at sea: Waller, Edmund

Instructions to his sonne: Ralegh, *Sir* Walter

Instructions to Vander Bank: Blackmore, *Sir* R.D.

Instructive epistle to the Lord Mayor, An: †Pindar, Peter

Instrument of destiny, The: Beresford, J.D.

Insula sacra: O'Halloran, Sylvester

Insulters of death: Logan, J.D.

Insurrection: O'Flaherty, Liam

Insurrection in Dublin, The: Stephens, James

Insurrections: Stephens, James

Intellectual and moral development of the present age, The: Warren, Samuel

Intellectual life of Colonial New England, The: Morison, S.E.

Intellectual mansions: Gibbs, *Sir* Philip

Intellectual part, The: Heppenstall, Rayner

Intellectual vagabondage: Dell, Floyd

Intelligencer, The: L'Estrange, *Sir* Roger

Intelligencer, The: Swift, Jonathan

Intelligent man's guide through world chaos, The: Cole, G.D.H.

Intelligent man's guide to the post-war world, The: Cole, G.D.H.

Intelligent man's review of Europe today, The: Cole, G.D.H. and M.I. Cole

Intelligent woman's guide to Socialism and Capitalism, The: Shaw, G.B.

Intentions: Wilde, Oscar

Inter arma: Gosse, *Sir* Edmund

Intercepted letter from Canton, An: Croker, J.W.

Intercepted letters: Moore, Thomas

Intercepted letters about the Infirmary Bazaar: Praed, W.M.

Intercessor, The: Sinclair, May

Intercourse between the United States and Japan, The: Nitobe, Inazo

Interest and effort in education: Dewey, John

Interest of England with regard to foreign alliances explained in two discourses, The: Ralegh, *Sir* Walter

Interest of Great Britain considered, The: Franklin, Benjamin

Interesting biographical sketch: Harris, G.W.

Interesting letter to the Duchess of Devonshire, An: Combe, William

Interests of Ireland considered, The: Brooke, Henry

Interference: (Ercole, Velia) †Gregory, Margaret

Interference: Pertwee, Roland

Interim: Richardson, D.M.

Interlopers: Harwood, H.M.

Interlude: Mais, S.P.B.

Interlude first: Kirby, William

Interlude for Sally: Seymour, B.K.

Interlude of youth: McKerrow, R.B.

Interludes: Austin, Alfred

Interludes and poems: Abercrombie, Lascelles

Interludes in verse and prose: Trevelyan, *Sir* G.O.

Internal constitution of the stars, The: Eddington, *Sir* A.S.

Internal revenue: Morley, C.D.

International anarchy 1904–1914, The: Dickinson, G.L.

International conflict in the twentieth century: Butterfield, Herbert

International during the war, The: Postgate, Raymond

International episode, An: James, Henry

International experiment, An: Fisher, H.A.L.

International government: Woolf, Leonard

International law and international relations: Stephen, J.K.

International policy of the Great Powers, The: Bailey, P.J.

Internationale, The: Dutt, R.P.

Interpretation in teaching: Richards, I.A.

Interpretation of Genesis, An: Powys, T.F.

Interpretation of religious experience, The: Watson, John

Interpretations: Akins, Zoë

Interpretations of poetry and religion: Santayana, George

Interpreter, The: Beresford, J.D.

Interpreter, The: Gibbs, *Sir* Philip

Interpreter, The: Whyte-Melville, G.J.

Interpreters, The: Russell, G.W.

Interpreters and interpretations: Van Vechten, Carl

Interrupted wedding, An: Manning, Anne

Interviews: Stephens, A.G.

Intimacies in Canadian life and letters: O'Hagan, Thomas

Intimate strangers: Prichard, K.S.

Intimate strangers, The: Tarkington, Booth

Intimations: Gogarty, O. St. John

Intimations of Eve: Fisher, V.A.

Intimations of the beautiful: Cawein, Madison

Into action (Dieppe): Lindsay, Jack

Into battle: Churchill, *Sir* Winston

Into Hades: Young, A.J.

Into the land of Nod: Vachell, H.A.

Introducing irony: Bodenheim, Maxwell

Introducing London: Lucas, E.V.

Introducing Paris: Lucas, E.V.

Introduction to American politics: Brogan, *Sir* Denis

Introduction to bibliography for literary students: McKerrow, R.B.

Introduction to contemporary knowledge: Joad, C.E.M.

Introduction to crystal analysis, An: Bragg, *Sir* William

Introduction to dramatic theory, An: Nicoll, J.R.A.

Introduction to economic history, 1750–1951: Cole, G.D.H.

Introduction to English historians, An: Beard, C.A.

Introduction to English literature, An: Mulgan, J.A.E.

Introduction to English painting, An: Rothenstein, *Sir* John

Introduction to Indian art, An: Coomaraswamy, A.K.

Introduction to Kiki of Montparnasse: Hemingway, Ernest

Introduction to Logan's Cato's Moral Distiches: Franklin, Benjamin

Introduction to logic and scientific method, An: Cohen, M.R.

Introduction to mathematical philosophy, An: Russell, Bertrand

Introduction to mathematics: Whitehead, A.N.

Introduction to Mistral: Aldington, Richard

Introduction to modern philosophy: Joad, C.E.M.

Introduction to poetry: Van Doren, Mark

Introduction to politics, An: Laski, Harold

Introduction to Sally: Russell, E.M.

Introduction to social science: Calvert, G.H.

Introduction to study of anthropoid apes: Keith, *Sir* Arthur

Introduction to the history of England, An: Temple, *Sir* William

Introduction to the history of Great Britain and Ireland, An: Macpherson, James

Introduction to the history of the peace from 1800 to 1815: Martineau, Harriet

Introduction to the knowledge of rare and valuable editions of the Greek and Roman classics, An: Dibdin, Thomas

Introduction to the literature of Europe in the 15th, 16th, and 17th centuries: Hallam, Henry

Introduction to the literature of the New Testament, An: Moffat, James

Introduction to the principles of morals and legislation, An: Bentham, Jeremy

Introduction to the study of Australian literature: Cross, Zora

Introduction to the study of Browning, An: Symons, Arthur

Introduction to the study of Chinese painting: Waley, Arthur

Introduction to the study of Dante: Symonds, J.A.

Introduction to the study of natural history, An: Agassis, J.L.R.

Introduction to the history and antiquities of Ireland, An: O'Halloran, Sylvester

Introduction to trade unionism, An: Cole, G.D.H.

Introductory essay to the Speculum Humanae salvations: Berenson, Bernhard

Introductory lecture, University College, London: Housmann, A.E.

Introductory lectures on modern history: Arnold, Thomas

Introductory lectures on political economy: Whately, Richard

Introductory papers on Dante: Sayers, Dorothy

Introductory to wryte and to pronounce Frenche, The: Barclay, Alexander

Intruder, The: Jameson, Storm

Intruder at the ballet, An: Gibbon, Monk

Intruder in the dust: Faulkner, William

Intruders in Eden: Stringer, A.J.A.

Intrusion: Seymour, B.K.

Intrusions of Peggy, The: (†Anthony Hope), Hawkins, Anthony Hope

Inundation, or Pardon and peace, The: Gore, Catherine

Invader, The: Woods, M.L.

Invader of his country, The: Dennis, John

Invaders: Frank, Waldo

Invaders, The: Plomer, W.C.F.

Invalid, The: Graves, Richard

Invariable principles of poetry, The: Bowles, W.L.

Invasion, The: Griffin, Gerald

Invasion, The: Hill, Aaron

Invasion: Van Loon, H.W.

Invasion 1940: Fleming, Peter

Invasion of France and Germany, 1944–45, The: Morison, S.E.

Invasion of the Crimea, The: Kinglake, A.W.

Inveni portam, Joseph Conrad: Cunninghame Graham, Robert

Invented gods: Fyzee Rahamin, S.

Invention performed for the service of ye Right Honorable Edward Barbham, L. Mayor of the Cittie of London, An: Middleton, Thomas

Inventions of the idiot, The: Bangs, J.K.

Investigations on the theory of the Brownian movement: Einstein, Albert

Invincibles, The: Morton, Thomas

Invincibles, The: †O'Connor, Frank

Inviolable sanctuary, The: Hannay, J.O.

Invisible cargo: Walmsley, Leo

Invisible event, The: Beresford, J.D.

Invisible girl, The: Hook, T.E.

Invisible landscapes: Masters, E.L.

Invisible man: Sherriff, R.C.

Invisible man, The: Wells, H.G.

Invisible tides: Seymour, B.K.

Invisible voices, The: Shiel, M.P.

Invitation and warning: Treece, Henry

Invitation to a beheading: Nabokov, Vladimir

Invitation to cast out care: Sackville-West, Victoria

Invitation to immortality (novel and play): Abbas, K.A.

Invitation to the waltz: Lehmann, Rosamund

Invocation to music: Bridges, Robert

Involuntary prophet, The: Smith, Horatio

Inward companion: De la Mare, Walter

Inward ho!: Morley, C.D.

Iolanthe: Gilbert, Sir W.S.

Iole: Chambers, R.W.

Ion: Talfourd, Sir T.N.

Iona: †Macleod, Fiona

Ione March: Crockett, S.R.

Ionia: a quest: Stark, Freya

Ionia and the East: Hogarth, D.G.

Ionica: Cory, W.J.

Iophon: Cory, W.J.

Iorana! Gibbings, Robert

Iowa interiors: Suckow, Ruth

Iowa, O Iowa!: Garland, Hamlin

Ipané, The: Cunninghame Graham, Robert

Iphigeneia in Delphi: Garnett, Richard

Iphigenia: Dennis, John

Iphigenia in Tauris: Bynner, Witter

Iphigenia in Tauris of Euripides, The: Murray, Gilbert

Ira and Isabella: Brown, W.H.

Ireland: Johnson, L.P.

Ireland: Lawless, Emily

Ireland, a nation: Lynd, Robert

Ireland and her books: Mencken, H.L.

Ireland arisen: Watson, Sir J.W.

Ireland the rock whence I was hewn: Byrne, Donn

Ireland unfreed: Watson, Sir J.W.

Ireland's Abbey Theatre: Robinson, E.S.L.

Irene: Johnson, Samuel

Irene of the mountains: Eggleston, G.C.

Irene the missionary: De Forest, J.W.

I-Rinka the messenger: Devaney, J.M.

Iris: Pinero, Sir A.W.

Irish, The: O'Faolain, Sean

Irish and English, portraits and impressions: Lynd, Robert

Irish attorney, The: Bernard, W.B.

Irish beauties, The: Beck, Mrs. Lily

Irish boy, The: Jacob, Naomi

Irish cousin, An: Somerville, E.A.O.

Irish druids and old Irish religions: Bonwick, James

Irish essays and others: Arnold, Matthew

Irish fairy tales: Stephens, James

Irish Faustus, An: Durrell, Lawrence

Irish folk-history: Gregory, Augusta Lady

Irish footman's poetry, The: Taylor, John

Irish Guards, The: Kipling, Rudyard

Irish heart, An: Wright, D.M.

Irish hubbub, The: Rich, Barnabe

Irish idylls: Barlow, Jane

Irish impressions: Chesterton, G.K.

Irish journey, An: O'Faolain, Sean

Irish journey: Sutherland, H.G.

Irish land question, The: George, Henry

Irish lyrics and ballads: Dollard, J.B.

Irish melodies. With an appendix, containing the ... prefatory letter on music: Moore, Thomas

Irish melodies and a melologue upon national music: Moore, Thomas

Irish memoirs: Somerville, E.

Irish miles: †O'Connor, Frank

Irish mimic, The: O'Keeffe, John

Irish mist and sunshine: Dollard, J.B.

Irish movements, their rise, progress and certain termination, The: Maxwell, W.H.

Irish neighbours: Barlow, Jane

Irish poems: Stringer, A.J.A.

Irish poems: Tynan, Katherine

Irish poetic gems: Mangan, J.C.

Irish short stories and plays: Carroll, P.V.

Irish sketch-book, The: Thackeray, W.M.

Irish songs and ballads: Graves, A.P.

Irish songs and poems: Allingham, William

Irish tangle for English readers, The: Leslie, *Sir* J.R. Shane

Irish widow, The: Garrick, David

Irishman in Canada, The: Davin, N.F.

Irishman looks at his world, An: Hannay, J.O.

Irishmen all: Hannay, J.O.

Iron age, The: Heywood, Thomas

Iron age, The: Young, F.B.

Iron and smoke: Kaye-Smith, Shiela

Iron chest, The: Colman, George, *the younger*

Iron Curtain: Gielgud, Val

Iron door, The: Pratt, E.J.

Iron gate, The: Holmes, O.W.

Iron grip, The: Wallace, Edgar

Iron heel, The: London, Jack

Iron horse, The: Ballantyne, R.M.

Iron ladies, The: †Divine, David

Iron Laurel, The: Keyes, S.A.K.

Iron man: Burnett, W.R.

Iron man and the tin woman, The: Leacock, Stephen

Iron rations: Pearson, Hesketh

Iron trail, The: Beach, R.E.

Iron trail, The: †Brand, Max

Iron woman, The: Deland, Margaret

Ironical tales: Housman, Laurence

Ironicall expostulation for the horse of the Lord Mayor of London, An: Taylor, John

Ironing board, The: Morley, C.D.

Ironmaster, The: Sullivan, Alan

Irradiations, sand and spray: Fletcher, John Gould

Irralie's bushranger: Hornung, E.W.

Irrational knot, The: Shaw, G.B.

Irregulars strike again, The: Derleth, A.W.

Irresponsibles, The: MacLeish, Archibald

Irving: Tuckerman, H.T.

Irving Babbitt and the teaching of literature: Levin, Harry

Is advertising today a burden or—a boon?: Cole, G.D.H.

Is cheap sugar the triumph of free trade?: Higgins, M.J.

Is Christianity true?: Joad, C.E.M.

Is 5: Cummings, E.E.

Is free trade alive or dead?: Shaw, G.B.

Is he Popenjoy?: Trollope, Anthony

Is he the man?: Russell, W.C.

Is immortality desirable?: Dickinson, G.L.

Is innocence enough?: Brogan, *Sir* Denis

Is it true?: Craik, *Mrs.* D.M.

Is life worth living?: Mallock, W.H.

Is life worth living?: Robinson, E.S.L.

Is polite society polite?: Howe, Julia

Is sex necessary?: Thurber, James

Is sex necessary?: White, E.B.

Is Shakespeare dead?: (†Mark Twain), Clemens, S.L.

Is she a wife?: Russell, W.C.

Is she his wife?: Dickens, Charles

Is the Gaelic League political?: Hannay, J.O.

Is the Roman Church anti-social: Coulton, G.G.

Is the truth obscene?: Eastman, Max

Is this called civilization?: Dutt, M.M.

Is this peace?: Radhakrishnan, Sarvepalli

Is war obsolete?: Raven, C.E.

Is woman suffrage important?: Eastman, Max

Isaac Casaubon, 1559–1614: Pattison, Mark

Isaac Comnenus: Taylor, *Sir* Henry

Isaac Newton: Andrade, E.N. da Costa

Isaac Newton: Einstein, Albert

Isaac T. Hopper: Child, L.M.

Isabel: Gould, Gerald

Isabel: Tuckerman, H.T.

Isabel Clarendon: Gissing, George

Isabel, Edward, and Anne: Jennings, Gertrude

Isabel Graham: Herbert, H.W.

Isabella Vincent: Reynolds, G.

Isaiah: Hannay, J.O.

Iscariot, The: Phillpotts, Eden

Iseult of Brittany: Symons, Arthur

Isha Upanishad: Ghose, Sri Aurobindo

Ishmael: Braddon, M.E.

Isidro: Austin, Mary

Island, The: Byron, George Gordon, *Lord*

Island, The: Hodge, H.E.

Island, The: †Mordaunt, Elinor

Island, The: Royde-Smith, Naomi

Island, The: Young, Francis Brett

Island blood: Higgins, F.R.

Island garden, An: Thaxter, C.L.

Island in the Atlantic: Frank, Waldo

Island in the sun: Waugh, Alec

Island mystery, The: Hannay, J.O.

Island night's entertainments: Stevenson, R.L.

Island of Cipango, The: Levy, Benn W.

Island of Doctor Moreau, The: Wells, H.G.

Island of Eden, An: Mitford, Bertram

Island of fantasy: Hume, F.W.

Island of Galloping gold, The: Wallace, Edgar

Island of innocence, The: †Pindar, Peter

Island of Kawau, The: Bolitho, H.H.

Island of sheep, The: Buchan, John

Island of terror, The: †Sapper

Island of the innocent, The: Fisher, V.A.

Island of the mighty, The: Colum, Padraic

Island of the red god: Akins, Zoë

Island of tranquil delights, The: Stoddard, C.W.

Island of youth, The: Byrne, Donn

Island pearl, An: Farjeon, B.L.

Island Pharisees, The: Galsworthy, John

Island princess, The: Beaumont, Francis

Island princess, The: Motteux, P.A.

Island Providence, The: Niven, F.J.

Island race, The: Newbolt, *Sir* Henry

Island world, The: (†Donald Barr), Barrett, C.L.

Islanders, The: Wurdemann, Audrey

Island-princess, The: Tate, Nahum

Islands: Gibson, Wilfred

Islands of adventure, The: Roberts, T.G.

Islands of innocence: Holcroft, M.H.

Isle in the water, An: Tynan, Katherine

Isle of Columcille, The: Leslie, *Sir* J.R.Shane

Isle of devils, The: Lewis, M.G.

Isle of lies: Shiel, M.P.

Isle of Man, The: Mais, S.P.B.

Isle of mountains, Tasmania: (†Donald Barr), Barrett, C.L.

Isle of palms, The: (†Donald Barr), Barrett, C.L.

Isle of palms, The: Wilson, John

Isle of Pines, The: Nevile, Henry

Isle of thorns: Kaye-Smith, Shiela

Isle of unrest, The: †Merriman, Seton

Isle of Wight: De Selincourt, Aubrey

Isle of Wight, The: Thomas, E.E.P.

Isles of Greece, Sappho and Alcaeus, The: Tennyson, Frederick

Isles of Scilly, The: Grigson, Geoffrey

Isles of sunset, The: Benson, A.C.

Isles of the island: Mais, S.P.B.

Isles of unwisdom, The: Graves, Robert

Islington: Nichols, John

Ismael: Lytton, E.

Isn't that just like a man!: Rinehart, M.R.

Isolation and alliances: Lippmann, Walter

Isolt of Ireland:Todhunter, John

Israel: Lewisohn, Ludwig

Israel and problems of identity: Mead, Margaret

Israel Potter: Melville, Herman

Israel set free: Rubenstein, Harold F.

Israelitish question, The: Traill, H.D.

Israfel: Allen, Hervey

Issues of faith: Temple, William

Isthmus of Suez, The: Mallock, W.H.

It: Glyn, Elinor

It all goes together: Gill, Eric

It can't happen here (novel and play): Lewis, H.S.

It couldn't matter less: †Cheyney, Peter

It depends what you mean: †Bridie, James

It had to happen: Bromfield, Louis

It happened like that: Phillpotts, Eden

It happened like this: Hutchinson, Arthur

It happened to Didymus: Sinclair, Upton

It happened to them: Davidson, Donald

It has come to pass: Farrell, James

It is a secret: Deutsch, Babette

It isn't far from London: Mais, S.P.B.

It isn't this time of year at all!: Gogarty, O.St.John

It makes the world go round: Mackail, Denis

It may never happen: Pritchett, V.S.

It means mischief: Pertwee, Roland

It must be your tonsils: Roberts, Kenneth

It needs to be said: Grove, F.P.

It never can happen again: De Morgan, W.F.

It occurs to me: Knox, E.V.

It seems to me, 1925–1935: Broun, Heywood

It takes all kinds: Bromfield, Louis

It walks by night: Carr, J.D.

It was a knight of Aragon: Aldrich, T.B.

It was a lover and his lass: Oliphant, Margaret

It was like this: Allen, Hervey

It was the nightingale: Ford, Ford Madox

It was the nightingale: Williamson, Henry

It was with doubt and trembling: Aldrich, T.B.

Italian, The: Radcliffe, *Mrs.* Ann

Italian backgrounds: Wharton, Edith

Italian book illustrations: Pollard, A.W.

Italian book illustrations and early printing: Pollard, A.W.

Italian bride, The: Payne, J.H.

Italian by-ways: Symonds, J.A.

Italian chest, The: †Onions, Oliver

Italian conjurer,The:Blackwood, Algernon

Italian element in Milton's verse, The: Prince, F.T.

Italian fantasies: Zangwill, Israel

Italian Gothic sculpture: Pope-Hennessy, J.W.

Italian Gothic sculpture in the Victoria and Albert Museum: Pope-Hennessy, J.W.

Italian High Renaissance and Baroque sculpture: Pope-Hennessy, J.W.

Italian holiday: Bemelmans, Ludwig

Italian holiday: Mais, S.P.B.

Italian hours: James, Henry

Italian journeys: Howells, W.D.

Italian life and legends: Ritchie, *Mrs.* A.C.M.

Italian mother, The: Swinburne, A.C.

Italian mysteries: Lathom, Francis

Italian painters of the Renaissance, The: Berenson, Bernhard

Italian peep-show and other tales: Farjeon, Eleanor

Italian pictures of the Renaissance: Berenson, Bernhard

Italian Renaissance sculpture: Pope-Hennessy, J.W.

Italian sketch book, The: Tuckerman, H.T.

Italian stories of today: Lehmann, J.F.

Italian story, The: Trease, Geoffrey

Italian villas and their gardens: Wharton, Edith

Italian visit, An: Day-Lewis, Cecil

Italy: Morgan, *Lady* Sydney

Italy: Rogers, Samuel

Italy and the World War: Page, T.N.

Italy in Africa: Hollis, Christopher

Italy in arms: Scollard, Clinton

Italy; with sketches of Spain and Portugal: Beckford, William

Italy under Mussolini: Bolitho, William

Itinerary of John Leland the antiquary, The: Leland, John

It's a battlefield: Greene, Graham

It's a boy's world: Derleth, A.W.

It's a fine world: Lynd, Robert

It's about crime: Kantor, Mackinlay

It's loaded, Mr. Bauer: Marquand, J.P.

It's me, O Lord!: Coppard, A.E.

It's never over: Callaghan, M.E.

It's never too late to mend: Reade, Charles

It's not very nice: Strong, L.A.G.

It's the gypsy in me: Bercovici, Konrad

It's too late now: Milne, A.A.

Ivan de Biron: Helps, *Sir* Arthur

Ivan Greet's masterpiece: Allen, Grant

Ivanhoe: Scott, *Sir* Walter

I've got sixpence: Van Druten, John

I've married Marjorie: Widdemer, Margaret

I've shed my tears: Karaka, D.F.

Ivory, apes, and peacocks: Huneker, J.G.

Ivory child, The: Haggard, *Sir* Rider

Ivory door, The: Milne, A.A.

Ivory gate, The: Barnard, M.

Ivory gate, The: Besant, *Sir* Walter

Ivory tower, The: James, Henry

Ixion in heaven: Disraeli, Benjamin

J

J.B.: MacLeish, Archibald

J.C. Williamson's life story: Stephens, A.G.

J. Hardin & Son: Whitlock, Brand

J.L. Strachan-Davidson, a memoir: Mackail, J.W.

J.M. Barrie: Darlington, W.A.

J.McT.E. McTaggart: Dickinson, G.L.

J. William White, M.D.: Repplier, Agnes

Jabberwocky: †Carroll, Lewis

Jacaranda tree, The: Bates, H.E.

Jacinth: Mackail, Denis

Jack Adams: Chamier, Frederick

Jack afloat and ashore: Rowe, Richard

Jack a'Manory: Stern, G.B.

Jack and Jill: Alcott, Louisa May

Jack and Jill: Turner, W.J.R.

Jack and Jill: a study of our Christian names: Weekley, Ernest

Jack and the beanstalk: Erskine, John

Jack and the check book: Bangs, J.K.

Jack and the Tanner of Wymondham: Manning, Anne

Jack Bass, Emperor of England: Jefferies, Richard

Jack Brag: Hook, T.E.

Jack Chaloner: Grant, James

Jack Frost's little prisoners: Baring-Gould, Sabine

Jack Hall: Grant, Robert

Jack Hazard and his fortunes: Trowbridge, J.T.

Jack in the Bush: Grant, Robert

Jack Junk: Ireland, W.H.

Jack Kelso: Masters, E.L.

Jack Malcolm's log: Chamier, Frederick

Jack Manly: Grant, James

Jack o' Judgement: Wallace, Edgar

Jack O'Diamonds: Maltby, H.F.

Jack O'Dreams: Herrick, Robert

Jack of Newberry: Deloney, Thomas

Jack Shelby: Eggleston, G.C.

Jack Sheppard: Ainsworth, Harrison

Jack Straw: Maugham, Somerset

Jack the fisherman: Ward, E.S.

Jack Tier: Cooper, J. Fenimore

Jackanapes: Ewing, *Mrs.* J.H.

Jackdaw in Georgia, A: Seymour, W.K.

Jackdaw's nest, The: Bullett, Gerald

Jack-of-all-trades: Miller, Thomas

Jackpot: Caldwell, Erskine Preston

Jack's courtship: Russell, W.C.

Jackson trail, The: †Brand, Max

Jacob Faithful: Marryatt, Frederick

Jacob Schuyler's millions: English, T.D.

Jacob Ussher: Jacob, Naomi

Jacobean poets, The: Gosse, *Sir* Edmund

Jacobite movement, The: Petrie, *Sir* Charles

Jacobite's journal, The: Fielding, Henry

Jacob's ladder: Dickinson, G.L.

Jacob's ladder: Rawlings, Marjorie

Jacob's room: Woolf, Virginia

Jacopone de Todi: Underhill, Evelyn

Jacqueline: Rogers, Samuel

Jacquerie, The: James, G.P.R.

Jacques Bonneval: Manning, Anne

Jacquetta: Baring-Gould, Sabine

Jade god, The: Sullivan, Alan

Jade lizard, The: †Taffrail

Jade of destiny, The: Farnol, J.J.

Jake: Royde-Smith, Naomi

Jake: Tietjens, E.S.

Jalasco brig, The: †Becke, Louis

Jalna: De la Roche, Mazo

Jamaica and Cuba: DeLisser, Herbert G.

Jamaica and the Great War: DeLisser, Herbert G.

Jamaica Inn: Du Maurier, Daphne

James and John: Cannan, Gilbert

James Boswell: Vulliamy, C.E.

James Bowie, big dealer: Dobie, J.F.

James Branch Cabell: Mencken, H.L.

James Branch Cabell: Van Doren, Carl

James Burnham and the managerial revolution: †Orwell, George

James! Don't be a fool: Timms, E.V.

James Fraser, second Bishop of Manchester: Hughes, Thomas

James G.Blanc: a sketch of his life: Balestier, C.W.

James! How dare you: Timms, E.V.

James Joyce: Golding, Louis

James Joyce: a critical introduction: Levin, Harry

James Joyce, 1882–1941: Wilder, Thornton

James Lyle Mackay: Bolitho, H.H.

James Melvin, Rector of the Grammar School of Aberdeen: Masson, David

James Nasmyth: Smiles, Samuel

James Russell Lowell: Curtis, G.W.

James Russell Lowell and his friends: Hale, E.E.

James Russell Lowell centenary poem: Mackaye, Percy

James Shaver Woodsworth: Underhill, F.H.

James Shore's daughter: Benét, S.V.

James Tarrant, adventurer: Crofts, F.W.

James I: Williams, Charles

James the fogey: Jones, H.A.

James the second, or the revolution of 1688: Ainsworth, William H.

James VI and the Gowrie mystery: Lang, Andrew

James Wallace: Bage, Robert

James Whitcombe Riley: Carman, Bliss

Jamesie: Sidgwick, Ethel

Jan Masaryk: Lockhart, Sir Robert

Jan of the windmill: Ewing, Mrs. J.H.

Jan Vedder's wife: Barr, A.E.H.

Jane: †Corelli, Marie

Jane: Linton, Eliza

Jane: a story of Jamaica: DeLisser, Herbert G.

Jane Annie: Barrie, Sir J.M.

Jane Austen: Cecil, Lord David

Jane Austen: Jenkins, Elizabeth

Jane Austen: Kennedy, Margaret

Jane Austen: Seymour, B.K.

Jane Austen, a critical bibliography: Chapman, R.W.

Jane Austen: facts and problems: Chapman, R.W.

Jane Austen's novels and letters: Chapman, R.W. (Ed.)

Jane Barston: Sitwell, Edith

Jane Cable: McCutcheon, G.B.

Jane Clegg: Ervine, St. John

Jane Eyre: Brontë, Charlotte

Jane Fairfax: Royde-Smith, Naomi

Jane Field: Freeman, Mary

Jane Lomax: Smith, Horatio

Jane Mecom, the favorite sister of Benjamin Franklin: Van Doren, Carl

Jane of Lantern Hill: Montgomery, L.M.

Jane Oglander: Lowndes, M.A.

Jane Seton, or The King's advocate: Grant, James

Jane Talbot: Brown, C.B.

Janeites, The: Kipling, Rudyard

Jane's career: DeLisser, Herbert G.

Jane's legacy: Phillpotts, Eden

Jane's parlour: Buchan, Anna

Janet: Oliphant, Margaret

Janet March: Dell, Floyd

Janice Meredith: Ford, P.L.

Janitor's boy, The: Crane, Nathalia

Janus: Barker, George

Janus: Lockhart, J.G.

Janus: Wilson, John

Janus in modern life: Petrie, Sir William Flinders

Japan: Tietjens, E.S.

Japan: an attempt at interpretation: Hearn, Lafcadio

Japan and America: Noguchi, Yone

Japan as it was and is: Hildreth, Richard

Japanese artist in London, A: Markino, Yoshio

Japanese Buddhism: Eliot, Sir Charles

Japanese Dumpy Book, The: Markino, Yoshio

Japanese garland, A: Blunden, Edmund

Japanese marriage, A: Sladen, D.B.W.

Japanese miscellany, A: Hearn, Lafcadio

Japanese nation, its land, its people and its life, The: Nitobe, Inazo

Japanese poetry: Waley, Arthur

Japanese prints: Fletcher, John Gould

Japanese prints: Michener, J.A.

Japanese traits and foreign influences: Nitobe, Inazo

Japanese view of Quakerism, A: Nitobe, Inazo

Japhet in search of a father: Marryatt, Frederick

Japonette: Chambers, R.W.

Japonica: Arnold, Edwin

Japs at home, The: Sladen, D.B.W.

Jaqueline of Holland: Gratton, T.C.

Jar of honey from Mount Hybla, A: Hunt, Leigh

Jarl's daughter: Burnett, Frances Hodgson

Jarn Mound: Evans, *Sir* A.J.

Jasbo Brown: Heyward, DuBose

Jasmin: barber, poet, philanthropist: Smiles, Samuel

Jasmine farm, The: Russell, E.M.

Jason: Glover, Richard

Jason: Treece, Henry

Jason Edwards, an average man: Garland, Hamlin

Jasper: Molesworth, *Mrs.*

Jaunty Jock: Munro, Neil

Java Head: Hergesheimer, Joseph

Javni: Rao, Raja

Jaw breakers alphabet, The: Tietjens, E.S.

Jaws of death, The: Allen, Grant

Jayadeva: Chattopadhyaya, Harindranath

Jaybird, The: Kantor, MacKinlay

Jayhawker: Lewis, H.S.

Jay's treaty: a study in commerce and diplomacy: Bemis, S.F.

Jazz: Hecht, Ben

Je ne parle pas français: Mansfield, Katherine

Jealous ghost, The: Strong, L.A.G.

Jealous god, The: Levy, Benn W.

Jealous gods, The: Atherton, Gertrude

Jealous lovers, The: Randolph, Thomas

Jealous wife, The: Colman, George, *the elder*

Jealous woman: Cain, J.M.

Jeames's diary:Thackeray,W.M.

Jean Baptiste La Moyne, sieur de Bienville: King, G.E.

Jean Huguenot: Benét, S.V.

Jeanne d'Arc: Mackaye, Percy

Jeanne d'Arc: her life and death: Oliphant, Margaret

Jeanne of the marshes: Oppenheim, E.Phillips

Jean's golden term: Brazil, Angela

Jeeves and the feudal spirit: Wodehouse, P.G.

Jeeves in the offing: Wodehouse, P.G.

Jeeves omnibus: Wodehouse, P.G.

Jefferson and/or Mussolini: Pound, Ezra

Jefferson, corporations and the Constitution: Beard, C.A.

Jeffersons, The: Winter, William

Jelf's: Vachell, H.A.

Jemmy Daily: Ingraham, J.H.

Jen of the marshes: Herbin, J.F.

Jennerton and Co.: Oppenheim, E.Phillips

Jennette Alison: Ingraham, J.H.

Jennie Gerhardt: Dreiser, Theodore

Jennifer: Palmer, J.L.

Jennifer J.: Turner, E.S.

Jennifer Lorn: a sedate extravaganza: Wylie, Elinor

Jenny: Barnes, Margaret

Jenny and Meggy: Ramsay, Allan

Jenny by nature: Caldwell, Erskine Preston

Jenny Jones: Gow, Ronald

Jenny Newstead:Lowndes, M.A.

Jenny Villiers: Priestley, J.B.

Jephthah's daughter:Heavysege, Charles

Jeremiah and the princess: Oppenheim, E.Phillips

Jeremy: Walpole, *Sir* Hugh

Jeremy and Hamlet:Walpole, *Sir* Hugh

Jeremy at Crale: Walpole, *Sir* Hugh

Jeremy Hamlin: Brown, Alice

Jeremy Taylor: Gosse, *Sir* Edmund

Jerome: Freeman, Mary

Jerry of the islands: London, Jack

Jersey Street and Jersey Lane: Bunner, H.C.

Jerusalem: Besant, *Sir* Walter

Jerusalem: Blake, William

Jerusalem diary: Gill, Eric

Jerusalem: its history and hope: Oliphant, Margaret

Jervaise comedy, The:Beresford, J.D.

Jess: Barrie, *Sir* J.M.

Jess: Haggard, *Sir* Rider

Jess of the rebel trail: Cody, H.A.

Jess of the river: Roberts, T.G.

Jessica letters, The: More, P.E.

Jessica's first prayer: †Stretton, Hesba

Jessie Phillips: Trollope, Frances

Jessie Trim: Farjeon, B.L.

Jessie's neighbor: Moulton, E.L.

Jest, The: †Bowen, Marjorie

Jesting army, The: Raymond, Ernest

Jesting Pilate: Huxley, Aldous

Jests to make you merie:Dekker, Thomas

Jesuits in Ceylon in the XVI and XVII centuries, The: Perera, Simon

Jesuits in North America in the 17th C., The: Parkman, Francis

Jesuits in Poland, The: Pollard, A.F.

Jesus and the Gospel of love: Raven, C.E.

Jesus came again: Fisher, V.A.

Jesus Christ, the only foundation: Belknap, Jeremy

Jesus Christ the same: Moffat, James

Jesus in London: Nesbit, Edith

Jesus in Rome: Graves, Robert

Jesus said: Mee, Arthur

Jet beads, The: Treece, Henry

Jew, The: Cumberland, Richard

Jew in love, A: Hecht, Ben

Jew in our day: Frank, Waldo

Jew of Mogodore, The: Cumberland, Richard

Jew Süss: Dukes, Ashley

Jew, the gypsy, and El Islam, The: Burton, *Sir* Richard

Jewel merchants, The: Cabell, James Branch

Jewel of seven stars, The: Stoker, Bram

Jewes tragedy, The: Heming, William

Jewish problem, The: Golding, Louis

Jewish studies of peace and postwar problems: Cohen, M.R.

Jews, The: Belloc, Hilaire

Jews—are they human, The: Lewis, P.Wyndham

Jews in America: MacLeish, Archibald

Jezebal: Frankau, Pamela

Jezebel: Pryce, Richard

Jezebel Mort: Symons, Arthur

Jezebel's daughter: Collins, Wilkie

Jig for the gypsy, A: Davies, Robertson

Jig of Forslin, The: Aiken, Conrad

Jig-saw: Phillpotts, Eden

Jill: †Delafield, E.M.

Jill Somerset: Waugh, Alec

Jill the reckless: Wodehouse, P.G.

Jill's jolliest school: Brazil, Angela

Jilt, The: Reade, Charles

Jim and the pirates: Farjeon, Eleanor

Jim at the corner: Farjeon, Eleanor

Jim Brent: †Sapper

Jim Dandy: Saroyan, William

Jim Davis: Masefield, John

Jim Maitland: †Sapper

Jim of the hills: Dennis, C.M.J.

Jim of the Ranges: †Lancaster, G.B.

Jim Redlake: Young, Francis Brett

Jimbo, a fantasy: Blackwood, Algernon

Jimmie Higgins: Sinclair, Upton

Jimmy Dale and the blue envelope murder: Packard, F.L

Jimmy Dale and the missing hour: Packard, F.L.

Jimmy Dale and the phantom clue: Packard, F.L.

Jimmy, the dog in my life: Bryant, *Sir* Arthur

Jimmyjohn boss, The: Wister, Owen

Jingalo in revolution: Housman, Laurence

Jingling in the wind: Roberts, E.M.

Jinnah, creator of Pakistan: Bolitho, H.H.

Jinny Morgan: Spring, Howard

Jinny the carrier: Zangwill, Israel

Jitta's atonement: Shaw, G.B.

Joan: Broughton, Rhoda

Joan, a romance of an English mining village: Barr, A.E.H.

Joan and Peter: Wells, H.G.

Joan Haste: Haggard, *Sir* H. Rider

Joan of Arc: Belloc, Hilaire

Joan of Arc: Calvert, G.H.

Joan of Arc: Farjeon, Eleanor

Joan of Arc: Southey, Robert

Joan of Arc, and the times of Charles VII, King of France: Bray, Anna Eliza

Joan of Lorraine: Anderson, Maxwell

Joan of the sword hand: Crockett, S.R.

Joan of the Tower: Deeping, G.W.

Joanna at Littlefold: Ashton, Helen

Joanna Godden: Kaye-Smith, Sheila

Joanna Godden married: Kaye-Smith, Sheila

Joan's best chum: Brazil, Angela

Joan's door: Farjeon, Eleanor

Joaquin et al.: †Miller, Joaquin

Job, The: Lewis, H.S.

Job of living, The: White, S.E.

Jobber Skald: Powys, John Cowper

Jocelyn: (†John Sinjohn) Galsworthy, John

Jock O'Dreams: Herrick, Robert

Jock of the Bushveld: Fitzpatrick, *Sir* J.P.

Jockey's downfall: Phillips, John

Jocoseria: Browning, Robert

Joe Lambert's ferry: Eggleston, G.C.

Joe Miller's jests: Mottley, John

Joe Quinney's Jodie: Vachell, H.A.

Joe Wilson: Lawson, Henry

Joe Wilson and his mates: Lawson, Henry

Joe Wilson's mates: Lawson, Henry

Joey goes to sea: Villiers, A.J.

Johannes in Eremo: Mather, Cotton

John: Barry, Philip

John: Oliphant, Margaret

John a Kent and John a Cumber: Munday, Anthony

John A. Macdonald: Creighton, D.G.

John Adams: independence forever: Cournos, John

John Addington Symonds: Brooks, Van Wyck

John Ames Mitchell: Lewis, H.S.

John Ames, native commissioner: Mitford, Bertram

John Andross: Davis, Rebecca

John at the old farm: Uttley, Alison

John Aubrey and his friends: Powell, Anthony

John Austen and the inseparables: Richardson, D.M.

John Baliol: Tennant, William

John Baptist: Bale, John

John Barleycorn: London, Jack

John Barleycorn: Uttley, Alison

John Batman, founder of Victoria: Bonwick, James

John Benn and the Progressive movement: Gardiner, A.G.

John Brent: Winthrop, Theodore

John Brougham: Winter, William

John Brown: Dubois, William

John Brown, and the heroes of Harper's ferry: Channing, W.E.

John Brown: the making of a martyr: Warren, Robert Penn

John Brown's body: Benét, S.V.

John Bull: Colman, George, *the younger*

John Bull calling: Drinkwater, John

John Bull in America: Paulding, J.K.

John Bull's other island: Shaw, G.B.

John Bunyan: Lindsay, Jack

John Bunyan: White, W.H.

John Burnet of Barns: Buchan, John

John C. Duval: first Texas man of letters: Dobie, J.F.

John Caldigate: Trollope, Anthony

John Charity: Vachell, H.A.

John Clare: Grigson, Geoffrey

John Clare and other studies: Murry, John Middleton

John Constable the painter: Lucas, E.V.

John Cornelius: Walpole, *Sir* Hugh

John Crome and John Sell Cotman: Binyon, Laurence

John Crome of Norwich: Mottram, R.H.

John Cumberland: Michael, J.L.
John Dawn: Coffin, Robert
John de Lancaster: Cumberland, Richard
John Deth: Aiken, Conrad
John Dobbs: Morton, J.M.
John Doe: Banim, Michael
John Donne, a study in discord: Fausset, Hugh
John Dorrien: Kavanagh, Julia
John Dos Passos: Hicks, Granville
John Dos Passos' Manhattan transfer: Lewis, H.S.
John Dryden: Eliot, T.S.
John Dryden: Nicoll, J.R.A.
John Dryden: Saintsbury, George
John Dryden: a study of his poetry: Van Doren, Mark
John Eax and Mamelon: Tourgée, A.W.
John Eliot: the man who loved the Indians: Beals, Carleton
John Elliott, the story of an artist: Elliott, M.H.
John Ermine of the Yellowstone: Remington, Frederic
John Fanning's legacy: Royde-Smith, Naomi
John Ferguson: Ervine, St. John
John Frensham, K.C.: †Sinclair, Murray
John Galsworthy: Kaye-Smith, Sheila
John Gayther's garden: Stockton, F.R.
John Glayde's honour: Sutro, Alfred
John Godfrey's fortunes, related by himself: Taylor, Bayard
John Graham (convict): Gibbings, Robert
John Graves Simcoe: Scott, D.C.
John Gray: Allen, James Lane
John Greenleaf Whittier: Higginson, T.W.
John H. Steggall: Cobbold, Richard
John Halifax, gentleman: Craik, *Mrs.* Dinah
John Hampden's England: Drinkwater, John
John Henry Newman: Meynell, Wilfred

John Holdsworth, chief mate: Russell, W.C.
John Ingerfield: Jerome, Jerome K.
John Inglesant: Shorthouse, J.H.
John Jackson's Arcady: Fitzgerald, F.Scott
John James Audubon: Burroughs, John
John Jerome: Ingelow, Jean
John Jone's tales for little John Joneses: James, G.P.R.
John Keats: Blunden, Edmund
John Keats: Bridges, Robert
John Keats: Lowell, Amy
John Keats: his life and poetry: Colvin, *Sir* Sidney
John Keats, the apothecary poet: Osler, *Sir* William
John Keble's parishes: Yonge, C.M.
John Kemp's wager: Graves, Robert
John King's question class: Sheldon, C.M.
John Knox: †Bridie, James
John Knox: Muir, Edwin
John Knox and the Reformation: Lang, Andrew
John Law, the Projector: Ainsworth, Harrison
John Lothrop Motley: Holmes, Oliver Wendell
John M. Daniel's latch-key: Bagby, G.W.
John M. Synge: Masefield, John
John Macnab: Buchan, John
John Manesty, the Liverpool merchant: Maginn, William
John March Southerner: Cable, G.W.
John Marchmont's legacy: Braddon, Mary Elizabeth
John Marr and other sailors: Melville, Herman
John Marvel: assistant: Page, T.N.
John Masefield: Strong, L.A.G.
John McCormack: the story of a singer: Strong, L.A.G.
John Middleton Murry: Heppenstall, J.R.
John Millington Synge: Strong, L.A.G.
John Milton: Bush, Douglas

John Milton: Daiches, David
John Milton: Warner, Rex
John Mistletoe: Morley, C.D.
John o' the forest: Tennant, Kylie
John of Daunt: Turner, E.S.
John of Ruysbroeck: Underhill, Evelyn
John of Salisbury in essays and studies: Waddell, Helen
John of the mountains: Muir, John
John Oldcastle's guide for literary beginners: †Oldcastle, John
John Palmer: 1885–1944: Saunders, H.A.St.George
John Paul Jones: Morison, S.E.
John Phillip: Greg, W.W.
John Piper: Betjeman, John
John Quincy Adams and the foundations of American foreign policy: Bemis, S.F.
John Quincy Adams and the Union: Bemis, S.F.
John Randolph: Adams, H.B.
John Randolph of Roanoke: Thomas, F.W.
John Rawn, prominent citizens: Hough, Emerson
John Ray, naturalist: Raven, C.E.
John Reed: Hicks, Granville
John Richardson: Riddell, W.R.
John Rous: a Queen Anne story: McCrae, G.G.
John Ruskin: Harrison, Frederic
John Ruskin: Masefield, John
John Ruskin: Meynell, Alice
John Ruskin: the portrait of a prophet: Quennell, P.C.
John Silence, physician extraordinary: Blackwood, Algernon
John Sloan: Brooks, Van Wyck
John Smedley of Matlock and his Hydro: Peach, L. du Garde
John Smith—also Pocahontas: Fletcher, John Gould
John Smith's letters, with "picters" to match: Smith, Seba
John Splendid: Munro, Neil
John Stuart Mill: Hayward, Abraham
John Verney: Vachell, H.A.

John Ward, preacher: Deland, Margaret

John Webb's end: Adams, Francis

John Webster and the Elizabethan drama: Brooke, Rupert

John Wesley: Dobrée, Bonamy

John Wesley: Vulliamy, C.E.

John Wheeler's two uncles: De Mille, James

John Winterbourne's family: Brown, Alice

John Wood case, The: Suckow, Ruth

John Woodvil: Lamb, Charles

John-Barbara: O'Brien, Kate

Johnnie Courteau: Drummond, W.H.

Johnny Appleseed: Lindsay, N.V.

Johnny Bear, Lobo and other stories: Seton-Thompson, E.

Johnny Cowslip: Street, A.G.

Johnny Crimson: Mackaye, Percy

Johnny forsaken: Stern, G.B.

Johnny Hack and his beginnings: Buck, Pearl

Johnny Johnson: Green, Paul

Johnny Ludlow: Wood, Ellen

Johnny Pye and the fool-killer: Benét, S.V.

Johnny Tremain: Forbes, Esther

John's alive: Thompson, W.T.

Johnson and Boswell: Pearson, Hesketh

Johnson and Garrick: Reynolds, Sir Joshua

Johnson over Jordan: Priestley, J.B.

Johnson was no gentleman: Rubenstein, H.F.

Johnsonian and other essays: Chapman, R.W.

Johnson's and Boswell's tour to the Hebrides: Chapman, R.W.

Joining Charles: Bowen, E.D.C.

Joint and humble address of the Tories and Whigs concerning the bill of Peerage, The: Steele, Sir Richard

Joint owners in Spain: Brown, Alice

Joker, The: Wallace, Edgar

Jolliest term on record, The: Brazil, Angela

Jolly fellowship, A: Stockton, F.R.

Jolly rover, The: Trowbridge, J.T.

Jonah: Stone, Louis

Jonah and Co.: †Yates, Dornford

Jonah and the whale: †Bridie, James

Jonah comes to Nineveh: Palmer, H.E.

Jonah 3: †Bridie, James

Jonah's luck: Hume, F.W.

Jonathan: Cripps, A.S.

Jonathan and David: Ward, E.S.

Jonathan Fisher, Maine parson, 1768–1847: Chase, M.E.

Jonathan Gentry: Van Doren, Mark

Jonathan Swift: Collins, John Churton

Jonathan Swift: Jeffrey, Lord Francis

Jonathan Swift: a critical biography: Murry, John Middleton

Jones: a gentleman of Wales: Vulliamy, C.E.

Jonson's Masque of Gipsies: Greg, W.W.

Jordans, The: Millin, S.G.

Jordanstown: Johnson, J.W.

Jorkens borrows another whiskey: Dunsany, E.J.M.D.P.

Jorkens has a large whiskey: Dunsany, E.J.M.D.P.

Jorrocks' jaunts and jollities: Surtees, R.S.

Jo's boys: Alcott, Louisa M.

José Antonio Páez: Cunninghame Graham, R.B.

Joseph Addison: Courthorpe, W.J.

Joseph and his brethren: Wells, C.J.

Joseph and his brothers: Van Doren, Mark

Joseph and his friend: Taylor, Bayard

Joseph Chamberlain: Mee, Arthur

Joseph Conrad: Ford, F.M.

Joseph Conrad; a study: Walpole, Sir Hugh

Joseph Conrad, an appreciation: O'Flaherty, Liam

Joseph entangled: Jones, H.A.

Joseph Furphy: Franklin, Miles

Joseph Hergesheimer: Cabell, James Branch

Joseph Howe: Grant, G.M.

Joseph Jefferson at home: Dole, N.H.

Joseph of Arimathaea: Percy, Edward

Joseph Rushbrook: Marryatt, Frederick

Joseph Story: Commager, H.S.

Joseph the dreamer: Zangwill, Israel

Joseph Vance: De Morgan, W.F.

Joseph Wilmot: Reynolds, G.

Joseph's dreams: Lawson, Henry

Josh Billings' farmers' allmibax for the year 1870: †Billings, Josh

Josh Billings, hiz sayings: †Billings, Josh

Josh Billings, his works complete: †Billings, Josh

Josh Billings' farmers' allminax, 1870–80: †Billings, Josh

Josh Billings on ice, and other things: †Billings, Josh

Josh Billings' spice box: †Billings, Josh

Josh Billings struggling with things: †Billings, Josh

Josh Billings' trump kards: †Billings, Josh

Joshua Haggard's daughter: Braddon, Mary Elizabeth

Joshua Marvel: Farjeon, B.L.

Josiah Shirley: Moodie, Susanna

Josiah Tucker and his writings: Ford, Paul Leicester

Josiah Wedgwood: his personal history: Smiles, Samuel

Jottings from my journal: Cook, Eliza

Joungleur strayed, A: Le Gallienne, Richard

Journal: Bennett, Arnold

Journal: Kemble, F.A.

Journal: Thoreau, H.D.

Journal, 1928–58: Green, Julian

Journal, The: Swift, Jonathan

Journal during a residence in France, A: Moore, Dr. John

Journal kept in Turkey and Greece. 1857–8, A: Senior, N.W.

Journal of a disappointed man, The: †Barbellion, W.N.P.

Journal of a Dublin lady, The: Swift, Jonathan

Journal of a landscape painter in Albania, Illyria etc.: Lear, Edward

Journal of a landscape painter in Corsica: Lear, Edward

Journal of a London playgoer from 1851–1866, The: Morley, Henry

Journal of a residence on a Georgian plantation in 1838–39: Kemble, Frances Anne

Journal of a second voyage, 1821–1823: Parry, *Sir* W.E.

Journal of a third voyage, 1824–1825: Parry, *Sir* W.E.

Journal of a tour in Scotland in 1819: Southey, Robert

Journal of a tour in the Netherlands in the autumn of 1815: Southey, Robert

Journal of a tour to the Hebrides, with Samuel Johnson, The: Boswell, James

Journal of a tour to the White Mountains: Belknap, Jeremy

Journal of a visit to Europe and the Levant: Melville, Herman

Journal of a visit to London and the Continent: Melville, Herman

Journal of a voyage for the discovery of a North-West passage, 1819–1820: Parry, *Sir* W.E.

Journal of a voyage from London to Philadelphia: Franklin, Benjamin

Journal of a voyage into the Mediterranean: Digby, *Sir* Kenelm

Journal of a voyage round the world, A: Banks, *Sir* Joseph

Journal of a voyage to Lisbon, The: Fielding, Henry

Journal of a West India proprietor, kept during a residence in the island of Jamaica: Lewis, M.G.

Journal of Albion Moonlight: Patchen, Kenneth

Journal of Arthur Stirling, The: Sinclair, Upton

Journal of Captain Cook's last voyage to the Pacific Ocean, A: Ledyard, John

Journal of discovery of the source of the Nile: Speke, J.H.

Journal of impressions in Belgium, A: Sinclair, May

Journal of Joachim Hane: Firth, *Sir* Charles Harding

Journal of Katherine Mansfield, The: Murry, John Middleton

Journal of Mary Hervey Russell, The: Jameson, Storm

Journal of mission to interior of Africa: Park, Mungo

Journal of researches into the geology and natural history of the various countries visited by H.M.S. Beagle: Darwin, Charles

Journal of the heart: Bury, *Lady* C.S.M.

Journal of the movements of the British Legion: Richardson, John

Journal of the negotiations for peace: Franklin, Benjamin

Journal of the plague year, A: Defoe, Daniel

Journal of the printing office at Strawberry Hill: Walpole, Horace

Journal of the reign of King George the third, 1771–1783: Walpole, Horace

Journal of the Rev. Timothy Flint: Flint, Timothy

Journal or historical account of the life, travels, sufferings, Christian experiences etc., A: Fox, George

Journal to Stella, The: Swift, Jonathan

Journal under the terror, A: Lucas, F.L.

Journal up the Straits: Melville, Herman

Journalism: Steed, H.W.

Journalism for women: Bennett, Arnold

Journalism versus art: Eastman, Max

Journalist and two bears, A: Edmond, James

Journalist's London, The: Gibbs, *Sir* Philip

Journals and journalism: (†John Oldcastle), Wilfred, Meynell

Journals, conversations and essays relating to Ireland: Senior, N.W.

Journals kept in France and Italy from 1848 to 1852: Senior, N.W.

Journals of Arnold Bennett: Bennett, Arnold

Journals of the ocean: Leggett, William

Journals of visits to the country seats: Walpole, Horace

Journals relating to Montana and adjacent regions: Thompson, David

Journey, The: Churchill, Charles

Journey, A: Dunsany, E.J.M.D.P.

Journey, The: Gould, Gerald

Journey, The: Winters, Yvor

Journey down a rainbow: Priestley, J.B.

Journey due north, A: Sala, G.A.H.

Journey due south, A: Sala, G.A.H.

Journey from Philadelphia to New York: Freneau, Philip

Journey from Prince of Wales's Fort in Hudson's Bay, to the Northern Ocean, A: Hearne, Samuel

Journey in Brazil, A: Agassis, Jean L.R.

Journey in search of Christmas, A: Wister, Owen

Journey in the dark: Flavin, Martin

Journey into America: Peattie, D.C.

Journey into fear: Ambler, Eric

Journey into Russia: Van der Post, L.J.

Journey made in the summer of 1794 through Holland and the Western Frontier of Germany, A: Radcliffe, *Mrs.* Ann

Journey of John Gilpin, The: Cowper, William

Journey of the Magi: Eliot, T.S.

Journey through Albania: Broughton, J.C.H.

Journey through Persia, Armenia and Asia Minor to Constantinople: Morier, J.J.

Journey through the war mind: Joad, C.E.M.

Journey to a war: Auden, W.H. and Christopher Isherwood

Journey to Boston, A: Chase, M.E.

Journey to Central Africa, A: Taylor, Bayard

Journey to China, A: Toynbee, Arnold

Journey to Java: Nicolson, Hon. *Sir* Harold

Journey to Jerusalem: Anderson, Maxwell

Journey to Jerusalem, A: Ervine, St. John

Journey to Katmandu, A: Oliphant, Laurence

Journey to London, A: Vanbrugh, *Sir* John

Journey to love: Williams, W.C.

Journey to the edge of morning: Partridge, Eric

Journey to the sandalwood forest, The: Bates, Ralph

Journey to the Western front: Mottram, R.H.

Journey to the Western Islands of Scotland, A: Johnson, Samuel

Journey to the world on the moon, A: Defoe, Daniel

Journey together: Rattigan, Terence

Journey up, The: Hichens, R.S.

Journey with genius: Bynner, Witter

Journey without maps: Greene, Graham

Journeyman: Caldwell, Erskine Preston

Journeys across the Pampas: Head, *Sir* F.B.

Journeys and places: Muir, Edwin

Journeys between wars: Dos Passos, John

Journey's echo, The: Stark, Frey

Journey's end: Sherriff, R.C. and Vernon Bartlett

Joy: Galsworthy, John

Joy and Josephine: Dickens, Monica

Joy as it flies: Seymour, B.K.

Joy in the morning: Wodehouse, P.G.

Joy in tribulation: Fletcher, Phineas

Joy of life, The: Lucas, E.V.

Joy of the theatre, The: Cannan, Gilbert

Joy of youth, A: Phillpotts, Eden

Joy to my soul: Hughes, J.L.

Joyce: Oliphant, Margaret

Joyce Cary: Allen, Walter Ernest

Joyce, the artificer: Huxley, Aldous

Joyful condemned, The: Tennant, Kylie

Joyful Delaneys, The: Walpole, *Sir* Hugh

Joyfull medytacyon to all Englande of the coronacyon of Kynge Henry the eyght, A: Hawes, Stephen

Joyfull new ballad, declaring the happie obtaining of the great Galleazzo, A: Deloney, Thomas

Joyous adventure, A: Orczy, *Baroness*

Joyous Gard: Benson, A.C.

Joyous miracle, The: †Norris, Frank

Joyous season, The: Barry, Philip

Joyous story of Astrid, The: Beck, *Mrs*. Lily

Juan in America: Linklater, Eric

Jubilee, The: Garrick, David

Jubilee blues: Davies, Rhys

Jubilee days: Aldrich, Thomas

Jubilee greeting at Spithead to the men of Greater Britain: Watts-Dunton, W.T.

Jubilee history of South Canterbury: Anderson, J.C.

Jubilee Ode, in commemoration of the fiftieth year of her majesty's reign: Halloran, Henry

Jubilee of the Constitution, The: Adams, J.Q.

Jucklins, The: Read, O.P.

Judah: Jones, H.A.

Judas: Linklater, Eric

Judas: Monro, H.E.

Judas: Moore, T.S.

Judas Iscariot: Horne, R.H

Judas Maccabeus: Vulliamy, C.E.

Judas tree, The: Cronin, A.J.

Judas window, The: †Carter Dickson

Judd Rankin's daughter: Glaspell, Susan

Jude the obscure: Hardy, Thomas

Judge, The: †West, Rebecca

Judge Elbridge: Read, O.P.

Judge not: †Mordaunt, Elinor

Judgement and mercy for afflicted soules: Quarles, Francis

Judgement day: Farrell, James

Judgement Day: Rice, Elmer

Judgement house, The: Parker, *Sir* H.G.

Judgement in suspense: Bullett, Gerald

Judgement of Borso, The: Hewlett, Maurice

Judgement of connoisseurs upon works of art compared with that of professional men; in reference more particularly to the Elgin Marbles, The: Haydon, Benjamin

Judgement of Eve, The: Sinclair, May

Judgement of François Villon, The: Palmer, H.E.

Judgement of Martin Bucer, The: Milton, John

Judgement of Valhalla, The: Frankau, Gilbert

Judgement on Deltchev: Ambler, Eric

Judgement seat, The: Maugham, W. Somerset

Judgements in the Admiralty of Pennsylvania: Hopkinson, Francis

Judge's chair, The: Phillpotts, Eden

Judge's story, The: Morgan, Charles

Judging of Jurgen, The: Cabell, James Branch

Judgment: Brown, Alice

Judgment at Chelmsford: Williams, Charles

Judgment books: Benson, E.F.

Judgment glen: Bird, W.R.

Judgment of Dr. Johnson, The: Chesterton, G.K.

Judgment of Hercules, The: Shenstone, William

Judgment of Paris, The: Beattie, James

Judgment of Paris, The: Congreve, William

Judgment-Day, The: Hill, Aaron

Judith: Bennett, Arnold

Judith: Bickerstaffe, Isaac

Judith: Neale, J.M.

Judith and Holofernes: Aldrich, Thomas Bailey

Judith of Bethulia: Aldrich, Thomas Bailey

Judith Paris: Walpole, *Sir* Hugh

Judith Shakespeare: Black, William

Judith Silver: Bolitho, H.H.

Judy and Lakshmi: Mitchison, Naomi

Judy and Punch: Turner, E.S.

Judy of Bunter's buildings: Oppenheim, E.Phillips

Juggernaut: Eggleston, G.C.

Juggler, The: †Craddock, C.E.

Julia: Payne, J.H.

Julia: Williams, H.M.

JuliaBallantyne:†Preedy,George

Julia Bride: James, Henry

Julia de Roubigne: Mackenzie, Henry

Julia Domna: †Field, Michael

Julia Elizabeth: Stephens, James

Julia France and her times: Atherton, Gertrude

Julia Roseingrave:†Paye, Robert

Julia Ward Howe: Elliott, M.H.

Julian: Mitford, Mary Ruttell

Julian: Ware, William

Julian Fane: (†Owen Meredith), Lytton, *Earl* E.R.B.

Julian Grenfell: Meynell, Viola

Julian's way: Brophy, John

Julie: Mannin, Ethel

Julie Cane: O'Higgins, H.J.

Julien Benda and the new Humanism: Read, *Sir* Herbert

Juliet Grenville: Brooke, Henry

Julius Caesar: Buchan, John

Julius Caesar: Shakespeare, William

Julius Ceasar acquitted: Dennis, John

Julius De Vallon, an episode: Blackwood, Algernon

Jumble warfare: †Armstrong, Anthony

Jumpers, The: (Stephen Southwold), †Bell, Neil

Jumping lions of Borneo, The: Dunne, J.W.

Jump-to-Glory Jane: Meredith, George

June dance: Drinkwater, John

June moon: Kaufman, G.S.

June moon: Lardner, Ring

June romance, A: Gale, Norman

Jungfrau: Cusack, E.D.

Jungle, The: Sinclair, Upton

Jungle book, The: Kipling, Rudyard

Jungle captive: Hull, E.M.

Jungle gold: Beach, R.E.

Jungle journey: Mannin, Ethel

Jungle maid: Collins, Dale

Jungle peace: Beebe, William

Jungle tide, The: Still, John

Jungling in Jasper: Burpee, Lawrence

Juniper Loa: Lin Yu-T'ang

Junipero Serra: Repplier, Agnes

Junk-man, The: Le Gallienne, Richard

Juno and the paycock: O'Casey, Sean

Juno Clifford: Moulton, E.L.

Jupiter and the nun: Wellesley, D.V.

Jupiter laughs: a play: Cronin, A.J.

Jupiter lights: Woolson, C.F.

Jure divino: Defoe, Daniel

Jurgen: Cabell, James Branch

Jury, The: Bullett, Gerald

Jury, The: Phillpotts, Eden

Jury of her peers, A: Glaspell, Susan

Just about us: Jacob, Naomi

Just and the unjust, The:Cozzens, James Gould

Just another word: Brown, Ivor

Just as I am: Braddon, Mary Elizabeth

Just David: Porter, E.H.

Just dogs: Young, E.R.

Just flesh: Karaka, D.F.

Just impediment: Pryce, Richard

Just like Aunt Bertha: Ridge, W.Pett

Just men of Cordova, The: Wallace, Edgar

Just Mother: Porter, E.H.

Just open: Ridge, W.Pett

Just sixteen: Coolidge, Susan

Just so stories: Kipling, Rudyard

Just the other day: Collier, John

Just vengeance, The: Sayers, Dorothy

Just wild about Harry: Miller, Henry

Justice: Galsworthy, John

Justice: Kipling, Rudyard

Justice and expediency: Whittier, J.G.

Justice and liberty: Dickinson, Goldsworthy Lowes

Justice for Judy: Vulliamy, C.E.

Justice in war-time: Russell, Bertrand

Justice of the Duke, The: Sabatini, Rafael

Justice of the peace: Niven, F.J.

Justification, The: Combe, William

JustinHarley: Cooke,John Esten

Justine's lovers: De Forest, John William

JutlandCottage:Thirkell,Angela

Juvenile employment and education: Tawney, R.H.

Juvenile poems on various subjects: Godfrey, Thomas

Juvenilia: Donne, John

Juvenilia: Hunt, J.H.L.

Juvenilia: Lee, Vernon

Juxta salices: Knox, R.A.

K

K: Rinehart, Mary Roberts
K.Henry IV: Betterton, Thomas
Kafir stories: Scully, W.C.
Kahun: Petrie, *Sir* William Flinders
Kai-Lung under the mulberry tree: Bramah, E.
Kai-Lung unrolls his mat: Bramah, E.
Kai-Lung's golden hours: Bramah, E.
Kaiser and English relations, The: Benson, E.F.
Kaiser dead, a poem: Arnold, Matthew
Kak, the copper eskimo: Stefansson, V.
Kalee's Shrine: Allen, Grant
Kaleidoscope: Farjeon, Eleanor
Kalidasa: Ghose, Sri Aurobindo
Kalendrium hortense: Evelyn, John
Kamakura: Noguchi, Yone
Kamla: Singh, Jogendra
Kamni: Singh, Jogendra
Kanga Creek: Ellis, Havelock
Kangaroo: Lawrence, D.H.
Kangaroo and his kin: (†Donald Barr), Barrett, C.L.
Kangaroo rhymes: Cronin, B.C.
Kansas and Nebraska: Hale, E.E.
Kant and his English critics: Watson, John
Kanthapura: Rao, Raja
Kant's doctrine of freedom: Miller, E.M.
Kapuskasing: Kirkconnell, Watson
Karaman: Reynolds, G.
Karensgaard: Mitchison, Naomi
Kari, the elephant: Mukherji, D.G.
Karina with love: Linklater, Eric
Karl Marx: Postgate, R.W.
Karma: Besant, *Mrs.* Annie
Karma, a re-incarnation play: Blackwood, Algernon
Karroo, The: Slater, F.C.
Kasidah of Haji Abdu-el-Yezdi, The: Burton, *Sir* Richard

Kate: Howard, B.C.
Kate and Emma: Dickens, Monica
Kate Beaumont: DeForest,John William
Kate Bonnet: Stockton, F.R.
Kate Coventry: Whyte-Melville, G.J.
Kate Fennigate: Tarkington, Booth
Kate Kennedy: Bottomley, Gordon
Kate Peyton: Reade, Charles
Kate plus ten: Wallace, Edgar
Katerfelto: Whyte-Melville, G.J.
Katharine Walton: Simms, W.G.
Katharine Lauderdale: Crawford, F.Marion
Katherine: Bangs, J.K.
Katherine Christian: Walpole, *Sir* Hugh
Katherine Mansfield and other literary portraits: Murry,John Middleton
Katherine Regina: Besant, *Sir* Walter
Kathie Morris: Aldrich, Thomas Bailey
Kathleen: Burnett, Frances Hodgson
Kathleen: Morley, C.D.
Kathrina: her life and mine: Holland, J.G.
Kathy the Snow child: Seton-Thompson, E.
Katie Johnstone's Cross: Machar, A.M.
Katie Stewart: Oliphant, Margaret
Katy Kruse at the seaside: Farjeon, Eleanor
Kavanagh: Longfellow, H.W.
Kays, The: Deland, Margaret
Keats: Colvin, *Sir* Sidney
Keats: Murry, John Middleton
Keats: Thomas, E.E.P.
Keats, a study in development: Fausset, Hugh
Keats and Shakespeare: Murry, John Middleton

Keats's publisher: a memoir of John Taylor: Blunden, Edmund
Keats's Shakespeare: Spurgeon, Caroline
Keats's view of poetry: Saito, Takeshi
Keep cool: Neal, John
Keep it crisp: Perelman, S.J.
Keep the aspidistra flying: †Orwell, George
Keep the home fires burning: †Novello, Ivor
Keep the Home Guard turning: Mackenzie, *Sir* Compton
Keeper of the bees, The: Stratton-Porter, Gene
Keepers of the King's peace: Wallace, Edgar
Keeping Christmas: Smith,Goldwin
Keeping cool: Haldane, J.B.S.
Keeping house and house keeping: Hale, S.J.B.
Keeping up appearances: Jacobs, W.W.
Keeping up appearances: Macaulay, *Dame* Rose
Keeping up with Lizzie: Bacheller, Irving
Keeping up with William: Bacheller, Irving
Keepsake for 1828, The: Hunt, Leigh
Kellyana: Turnbull, S.C.P.
Kellys and the O'Kellys, The: Trollope, Anthony
Kelp-gatherer, The: Griffin, Gerald
Kelp-gatherers, The: Trowbridge, J.T.
Kelpic riders, The: Carman, Bliss
Kempton-Wace letters, The: London, Jack
Ken Ward in the jungle: Grey, Zane
Kena Upanishad: Ghose, Sri Aurobindo
Kenelm Chillingly: Lytton, E.G.E.B. *1st Baron*
Kenilworth: Scott, *Sir* Walter

Kennebec, cradle of Americans: Coffin, Robert

Kennedy people, The: Ridge, W. Pett

Kennedy Square: Smith, F.H.

Kenneth: Yonge, C.M.

Kenneth, a romance of the Highlands: Reynolds, G.

Kenny: Bromfield, Louis

Kensington Garden: Tickell, Thomas

Kensington Garden in wartime: Wolfe, Humbert

Kensington gardens: Wolfe, Humbert

Kensington rhymes: Mackenzie, *Sir* Compton

Kent: Church, Richard

Kent Hampden: Davis, Rebecca

Kentish worthies, The: Tate, Nahum

Kentons, The: Howells, W.D.

Kentuckian in New York, The: Caruthers, W.A.

Kentuckians, The: Fox, John

Kentucky: Hall, James

Kentucky Cardinal, A: Allen, James Lane

Kentucky colonel, A: Read, O.P.

Kentucky Mountain fantasies: Mackaye, Percy

Kentucky warbler, The: Allen, James Lane

Kept: Waugh, Alec

Kept in the dark: Trollope, Anthony

Kéramos: Longfellow, H.W.

Kerrell: †Taffrail

Kestrel: De Selincourt, Aubrey

Kestrel edge: Gibson, Wilfred

Kettle of fire: Davis, H.L.

Kew Gardens: Woolf, Virginia

Key above the door, The: Walsh, Maurice

Key into the language of America, A: Williams, Roger

Key largo: Anderson, Maxwell

Key of dreams, The: Beck, *Mrs.* Lily

Key of life, The: Scott, F.G.

Key of life, The: Young, Francis Brett

Key of the chest, The: Gunn, Neil M.

Key of the field, The: Powys, T.F.

Key of the house, The: Darlington, W.A.

Key of the strong room, The: Gilbert, *Sir* W.S.

Key to modern poetry: Durrell, Lawrence

Key to my heart, The: Pritchett, V.S.

Key to the disunion conspiracy, A: Tucker, N.B.

Key to the New Testament, A: Percy, Thomas

Key to Uncle Tom's cabin, A: Stowe, Harriet Beecher

Keyes of the Kingdom of Heaven, The: Cotton, John

Keys of the kingdom, The: Cronin, A.J.

Keystone of Europe, The: Cammaerts, Emile

Khaki boys, The: Brazil, Angela

Khaled: Crawford, F.Marion

Kick for a bite, A: Rowson, S.H.

Kickleburys on the Rhine, The: Thackeray, W.M.

Kicksy winsey, A: Taylor, John

Kid, The: Aiken, Conrad

Kid McGhie: Crockett, S.R.

Kidders, The: Stewart, D.O.

Kidnapped: Stevenson, R.L.

Kif: (†Josephine Tey), Mackintosh, Elizabeth

Kilburn tale, The: Raymond, Ernest

Killer, The: White, S.E.

Killer and the slain, The: Walpole, *Sir* Hugh

Killer Dolphin: Marsh, Ngaio Edith

Killer in dark glasses: Treece, Henry

Killer in the rain: Chandler, Raymond

Killing bottle, The: Hartley, L.P.

Killing no murder: Hock, T.E.

Killycreggs in twilight: Robinson, E.S.L.

Kilmeny: Black, William

Kilmeny of the orchard: Montgomery, L.M.

Kiltartan history book, The: Gregory, *Lady* Augusta

Kiltartan wonder book, The: Gregory, *Lady* Augusta

Kim: Kipling, Rudyard

Kincaid's battery: Cable, George Washington

Kincora: Gregory, *Lady* Augusta

Kind harts dreame: Chettle, Henry

Kind keeper, The: Dryden, John

Kind of anger, A: Ambler, Eric

Kind of poetry I want, The: †McDiarmid, Hugh

Kind of visit I like to make, The: Lindsay, N.V.

Kindling: †Shute, Nevil

Kindling and ashes: McCutcheon, G.B.

Kindly ones, The: Powell, Anthony

Kindness in a corner: Powys, T.F.

Kindness in women: Bayly, Thomas Haynes

Kindness of the celestial: Pain, B.E.O.

Kinds of love: Eastman, Max

Kinds of poetry, The: Erskine, John

Kinfolk of Robin Hood: Mackaye, Percy

King, The: Phillips, Stephen

King Alfonso XIII: Petrie, *Sir* Charles

King Alfred, as educator of his people and man of letters: Brooke, Stopford

King and a few dukes, A: Chambers, R.W.

King and Emperor: Mee, Arthur

King and no king, A: Beaumont, Francis and John Fletcher

King and Queen of Hearts, The: Lamb, Charles

King and the sea, The: Kipling, Rudyard

King Anne: Turner, E.S.

King Argimenes and the unknown warrior: Dunsany, E.J.M.D.P.

King Arthur: Blackmore, *Sir* R.D.

King Arthur: Craik, *Mrs.* Dinah

King Arthur: Dryden, John

King Arthur: Lytton, E.G.E.B. *1st Baron*

King Arthur's socks: Dell, Floyd

King behind the King, The: Deeping, Warwick

King bird rides, The: †Brand, Max

King by night, A: Wallace, Edgar

King Charles II: Bryant, *Sir* Arthur

King Coal: Sinclair, Upton

King Coffin: Aiken, Conrad

King Cole: Burnett, W.R.

King Cole: Masefield, John

King David: Benét, S.V.

King Dick: Burdon, R.M.

King Dobbs: Hannay, James

King Edward: Caine, *Sir* Thomas Henry Hall

King Edward VII: Benson, E.F.

King Edward VII: Lee, *Sir* Sidney

King Edward VIII: Bolitho, H.H.

King Erik: Gosse, *Sir* Edmund

King George V: his life and reign: Nicolson, Hon. *Sir* Harold

King Hart: Douglas, Gavin

King Henry the fifth: Hill, Aaron

King Henry the Second: Helps, *Sir* Arthur

King in Prussia: Sabatini, Rafael

King in yellow, The: Chambers, R.W.

King is dead: †Queen, Ellery

King James Bible: A study of its sources and development, The: Daiches, David

King Jasper: Robinson, E.A.

King Jesus: Graves, Robert

King John: Shakespeare, William

King John of Jingalo: Housman, Laurence

King John's treasure: Sherriff, R.C.

King Josiah: Neale, J.M.

King Lear: Shakespeare, William

King Lear's wife: Bottomley, Gordon

King liveth, The: Farnol, J.J.

King Midas: Sinclair, Upton

King Nihil's round table: Horne, Richard Henry

King of Alsander, The: Flecker, James Elwy

King of Barvender, The: Monkhouse, A.N.

King of Cadonia, The: †Lonsdale, Frederick

King of China's daughter, The: Sitwell, Edith

King of Elfland's daughter, The: Dunsany, E.J.M.D.P.

King of Fassarai, The: †Divine, David

King of Folly Island, The: Jewett, S.O.

King of Gee-Whiz, The: Hough, Emerson

King of Honey Island, The: Thompson, Maurice

King of Irelands son, The: Colum, Padraic

King of Noland, The: Farjeon, B.L.

King of Nowhere, The: †Bridie, James

King of pirates, The: Defoe, Daniel

King of Schnorrers, The: Zangwill, Israel

King of Spain: Bodenheim, Maxwell

King of the bastards: Millin, Sarah Gertrude

King of the beggars: a biography: O'Faolain, Sean

King of the Castle: Herbert, *Sir* A.P.

King of the Dark Chamber, The: Tagore, *Sir* R.

King of the Golden River, The: Ruskin, John

King of the great clock tower, The: Yeats, W.B.

King Poppy: (†Owen Meredith), Lytton, E.R.B. *Earl*

King, Queen, Knave: Harwood, H.M.

King Richard's land: Strong, L.A.G.

King Solomon and Queen Balkis: Virtue, Vivian L.

King Solomon's Mines: Haggard, *Sir* Henry Rider

King spider: Louis XI of France: Lewis, D.B. Wyndham

King Tommy: Hannay, J.O.

King Victor and King Charles: Browning, Robert

King waits, The: †Dane, Clemence

King was in his counting house, The: Cabell, James Branch

King who loved old clothes, The: Stringer, A.J.A.

King who was a king, The: Wells, H.G.

King with two faces, The: Coleridge, Mary

Kingdom in the sky, The: Brown, Alice

Kingdom of All-Souls, The: Woodberry, G.E.

Kingdom of evil, The: Hecht, Ben

Kingdom of God, The: Temple, William

Kingdom of happiness, The: Krishnamurti, Jiddu

Kingdom of Heaven: Mitchison, Naomi

Kingdom of Judah, The: Warner, S.B.

Kingdom of love: Wilcox, Ella Wheeler

Kingdom of Saguenay, The: Barbeau, C.M.

Kingdom of the beasts: Huxley, *Sir* Julian

Kingdom of the blind, The: Oppenheim, E. Phillips

Kingdom of the sun, The: Stephen, A.M.

Kingfisher, The: Bottome, Phyllis

Kingfishers catch fire: Godden, Rumer

Kingis quair, The: James I

Kings and Queens: Besier, Rudolf

Kings and queens: Farjeon, Eleanor and Herbert Farjeon

Kings and the moon: Stephens, James

King's arrow, The: Cody, H.A.

King's Assegai, The: Mitford, Bertram

Kings at arms: †Bowen, Marjorie

King's bell, The: Stoddard, R.H.

Kings blood Royal: Lewis, H.S.

King's book of Quebec, The: Doughty, *Sir* A.G.

King's Corsair: Trease, Geoffrey

Kings, courts and monarchy: Nicolson, *Hon. Sir* Harold

King's daughter, A: Masefield, John

King's daughter: Sackville-West, Victoria

King's end: Brown, Alice

King's England, The: Mee, Arthur

King's English, The: Fowler, H.W.

King's favourite: Gibbs, *Sir* Philip

King's general, The: Du Maurier, Daphne

King's grace, The: Buchan, John

King's henchman, The: Millay, E. St. Vincent

King's highway, The: Barr, A.E.H.

King's highway, The: James, P.R.

King's jackal, The: Davis, R.H.

Kings, Lords and Commons: †O'Connor, Frank

King's men, The: Grant, Robert

King's men, The: O'Reilly, J.B.

King's men, The: Palmer, J.L.

King's mirror, The: (†Anthony Hope), Hawkins, Anthony Hope

King's missive, The: Whittier, J.G.

Kings most excellent majesties wellcome to his owne house, The: Taylor, John

Kings of the Hittites: Hogarth, David George

King's own, The: Marryatt, Frederick

King's Own Borderers, The: Grant, James

King's pardon, The: Bedford-Jones, Henry

King's passport, The: Bedford-Jones, Henry

King's peace, The: Wedgwood, C.V.

King's pilgrimage, The: Kipling, Rudyard

Kings, queens and pawns: Rinehart, Mary Roberts

King's revoke, The: Woods, M.L.

King's Rhapsody: Hassall, Christopher

King's rhapsody: †Novello, Ivor

King's rival, The: Reade, Charles

King's servants, The: †Stretton, Hesba

King's service, The: (†Ian Hay), Beith, *Sir* John Hay

King's stratagem, The: Lewis, S.A.

King's threshold, The: Yeats, W.B.

King's war, The: Wedgwood, C.V.

Kinsfolk: Buck, Pearl

Kinship in the Admiralty Islands: Mead, Margaret

Kinship of nature, The: Carman, Bliss

Kinsmen, The: Simms, W.G.

Kinsmen at war: McIlwraith, J.N.

Kipling Calendar: Kipling, Rudyard

Kipling pageant, A: Kipling, Rudyard

Kipling reader for elementary grades: Kipling, Rudyard

Kipling's message: Kipling, Rudyard

Kipling's regrets: Kipling, Rudyard

Kipps: Besier, Rudolf

Kipps: Wells, H.G.

Kirk in Scotland, The: Buchan, John

Kirsteen: Oliphant, Margaret

Kiss me again, stranger: Du Maurier, Daphne

Kiss on the lips: Prichard, K.S.

Kisses can: Stein, Gertrude

Kisses of Marjorie, The: Tarkington, Booth

Kissing the rod: Meynell, Viola

Kissing the rod: Yates, E.H.

Kist of whistles, A: †McDiarmid, Hugh

Kit: Payn, James

Kit and Kitty: Blackmore, R.D.

Kit Brandon: Anderson, Sherwood

Kit Kennedy: Crockett, S.R.

Kit O'Brien: Masters, E.L.

Kit-Cats, The: Blackmore, R.D.

Kitchen comedy, The: †Bridie, James

Kitchen fugue: Kaye-Smith, Shiela

Kitchener: Stead, R.J.C.

Kitchener's army and the territorial forces: Wallace, Edgar

Kitchener's mob: Hall, J.N.

Kite's dinner, A: Wingfield, Shiela

Kith and kin: Bentley, Phyllis

Kitten who barked, The: Untermeyer, Louis

Kittle cattle: Street, A.G.

Kitty: Deeping, G.W.

Kitty alone: Baring-Gould, Sabine

Kitty Foyle: Morley, C.D.

Kitty Lamere: Mayhew, Augustus Septimus

Kitty Tailleur: Sinclair, May

Kitty's class day: Alcott, Louisa M.

Kitty's rival: Russell, W.C.

Klee: Read, *Sir* Herbert

Klondike Mike: Denison, Merrill

Kloof bride, The: Glanville, Ernest

Kloof yarns: Glanville, Ernest

Klosterheim: De Quincey, Thomas

Knave of clubbes, The: Rowlands, Samuel

Knave of harts, The: Rowlands, Samuel

Knave of hearts, The: Grant, Robert

Knave of hearts, 1894–1908: Symons, Arthur

Knave or not?: Holcroft, Thomas

Knave takes queen: †Cheyney, Peter

Kneel to the rising sun: Caldwell, Erskine Preston

Knickerbocker holiday: Anderson, Maxwell

Knife, The: Jones, H.A.

Knife in the dark: Cole, G.D.H.

Knife of the times, The: Williams, W.C.

Knight of a night: †Armstrong, Anthony

Knight of Gwynne, The: Lever, Charles James

Knight of St. John, The: Porter, A.M.

Knight of Scotland, The: †Gibbon, L.G.

Knight of Snowdoun, The: Morton, Thomas

Knight of Spain, A: †Bowen, Marjorie

Knight of the burning pestle, The: Beaumont, Francis and John Fletcher

Knight of the Cumberland, A: Fox, John

Knight of the highway, A: Scollard, Clinton

Knight of the maypole, The: Davidson, John

Knight of the motor launch, The: Adams, Arthur H.

Knight of the nineteenth century, A: Roe, E.P.

Knight of the tower, The (trn.): Caxton, William

Knight of the White Feather, A: †Tasma

Knight on wheels, A: (†Ian Hay), Beith, Sir John Hay

Knight without armour: Hilton, James

Knight-errant: Lyall, Edna

Knighting of the twins, The: Fitch, Clyde William

Knight's gambit: Faulkner, William

Knights of Araby: Pickthall, M.W.

Knights of St. John, The: Faber, F.W.

Knights of seven lands, The: Ingraham, J.H.

Knights of the Horseshoe, The: Caruthers, W.A.

Knights of the range: Grey, Zane

Knit one, purl one: Jennings, Gertrude

Knitting work: †Mrs. Partington

Knock at a venture: Phillpotts, Eden

Knock four times: Irwin, Margaret

Knocking round: Brereton, John Le G.

Knock-out: †Sapper

Knole and the Sackvilles: Sackville-West, Victoria

Knot garden, The: †Preedy, George

Knot of life, The: Shiel, M.P.

Knot squirrel tied, The: Uttley, Alison

Know nothingism unveiled: Longstreet, A.B.

Know your own mind: Murphy, Arthur

Knowledge and experience in the philosophy of F.H. Bradley: Eliot, T.S.

Knowledge, error, prejudice and reform: Montagu, Basil

Knowledge for what?: Lynd, R.S.

Knowledge is power: Gibbs, Sir Philip

Koala: (†Donald Barr), Barrett, C.L.

Kokoro: Hearn, Lafcadio

Kometographia: Mather, Increase

Königsmark: Mason, A.E.W.

Königsmark the legend of the hounds: Boker, G.H.

Koningsmarke: the long Finne: Paulding, J.K.

Kooborr the Koala: (†Donald Barr), Barrett, C.L.

Koonwarra: (†Donald Barr), Barrett, C.L.

Koptos: Petrie, Sir William Flinders

Kora in hell: Williams, W.C.

Korin: Noguchi, Yone

Kotto: Hearn, Lafcadio

Krag and Johnny Bear: Seton-Thompson, E.

Krag, the Kootenay ram: Seton-Thompson, E.

Kramer girls, The: Suckow, Ruth

Krapp's last tape: Beckett, Samuel

Krindlesyke: Gibson, Wilfred

Kwaidan: Hearn, Lafcadio

Kwan-Yin: Benson, Stella

Kynge Johan: Bale, John

L

La bonita cigarera: Ingraham, J.H.

La Corne St. Luc: Lighthall, W.D.

La Cuisine Creole: Hearn, Lafcadio

La Dame de Sainte Hermine: King, G.E.

La Fayette: Whitlock, Brand

La Fayette: Woodworth, Samuel

La Jeanne d'Arc de M. Anatole France: Lang, Andrew

La Saisiaz: Browning, Robert

La salle: Bourinot, A.S.

La Strega: †Ouida

La Vendée: Trollope, Anthony

La vie parisienne: Herbert, Sir A.P.

La vie Parisienne: Sitwell, Sacheverell

La vivandière: Gilbert, Sir W.S.

Labby: Pearson, Hesketh

Labels: Waugh, Evelyn

Labor and the angel: Scott, D.C.

Labor, cheer and love: Bangs, J.K.

Labor injunction, The: Frankfurter, Felix

Labor spy, The: Howard, S.C.

Laboryouse journey and serche of Johan Leylande, The: Leland, John

Labour and profits: Ewart, E.A.

Labour in the coal-mining industry (1914–21): Cole, G.D.H.

Labour in the Commonwealth: Cole, G.D.H.

Labour in the longest reign: Webb, S.J.

Labour in war time, Cole: G.D.H.

Labour: its rights, difficulties, dignity and consolations: Warren, Samuel

Labour supply and regulation: Wolfe, Humbert

Labour unrest, The: Wells, H. G.

Labouring life, The: Williamson, Henry

Labours of Hercules, The: Christie, Agatha

Labours of idleness, The: Darley, George

Labour's task: Strachey, John

Labrador days: Grenfell, *Sir* Wilfred

Labrador doctor, A: Grenfell, *Sir* Wilfred

Labrador logbook, A: Grenfell, *Sir* Wilfred

Labrador looks at the Orient: Grenfell, *Sir* Wilfred

Labrador, the country and the people: Grenfell, *Sir* Wilfred

Labrador's fight for economic freedom: Grenfell, *Sir* Wilfred

Laburnum branch, The: Mitchison, Naomi

Laburnum Grove: Priestley, J. B.

Labyrinth, The: Muir, Edwin

Labyrinth, The: Petrie, *Sir* William Flinders

Labyrinthine ways, The: Greene, Graham

Lachish: Petrie, *Sir* William Flinders

Lachrymae Lachrymarum: Donne, John

Lachrymae Musarum: Watson, *Sir* J.W.

Lack of the Leura, The: Praed, *Mrs*. C.

Lackey's carnival, The: Jones, H.A.

Laconics: Brown, Thomas

Ladder of learning, The: Trimmer, *Mrs*. Sarah

Ladder of swords, A: Parker, *Sir* H.G.

Laddie: Stratton-Porter, Gene

Ladies!, The: Beck, *Mrs*. Lily

Ladies, The: Nevile, Henry

Ladies and gentlemen: Cabell, James Branch

Ladies and gentlemen in Victorian fiction: †Delafield, E.M.

Ladies' battle, The: Reade, Charles

Ladies' gallery, The: Praed, *Msr*. C.

Ladies go masked: Widdemer, Margaret

Ladies in Parliament, The: Trevelyan, *Sir* G.O.

Ladies in retirement: Percy, Edward

Ladies in waiting: Wiggin, K.D.

Ladies Lindores, The: Oliphant, Margaret

Ladies of Bever Hollow, The: Manning, Anne

Ladies of Lyndon, The: Kennedy, Margaret

Ladies of the corridor, The: Parker, Dorothy

Ladies priviledge, The: Glapthorne, Henry

Ladies triall, The: Ford, John

Ladies whose bright eyes...: (Hueffer) Ford, Ford Madox

Ladies won't wait: †Cheyney, Peter

Lads of the village: Aldington, Richard

Lad's love: Crockett, S.R.

Lady, The: Richter, Conrad

Lady Adela: Gould, Gerald

Lady Adelaide's oath: Wood, *Mrs*. Ellen

Lady Alcuin, The: Fausset, Hugh

Lady and the arsenic: (†Joseph Shearing), †Bowen, Marjorie

Lady and the pirate, The: Hough, Emerson

Lady and unicorn: Godden, Rumer

Lady Anna: Trollope, Anthony

Lady Anne Barnard at the Cape of Good Hope: Fairbridge, Dorothea

Lady Anne Granard: Landon, L.E.M.

Lady A-S-N weary of the Dean: Swift, Jonathan

Lady Athlyne: Stoker, Bram

Lady Audley's secret: Braddon, M.E.

Lady Baltimore: Wister, Owen

Lady, be good: Gershwin, Ira

Lady behave: †Cheyney, Peter

Lady Bountiful: Hannay, J.O.

Lady Bountiful: Pinero, *Sir* A.W.

Lady Bridget in the Never Never Land: Praed, *Mrs*. C.

Lady Byron vindicated: Stowe, Harriet Beecher

Lady Calphurnia Royal, The: Stephens, A.G.

Lady Caprice: Jones, H.A.

Lady Car: Oliphant, Margaret

Lady Caroline Lamb: Jenkins, Elizabeth

Lady Chatterley's lover: Lawrence, D.H.

Lady Chesterfield's letters to her daughter: Sala, G.A.H.

Lady Connie, Ward, M.A.

Lady Cristilinda, The: Hoffe, Monckton

Lady Dorothy Nevill: Gosse, *Sir* Edmund

Lady Epping's lawsuit: Davies, H.H.

Lady Frederick: Maugham, Somerset

Lady Glendonwyn: Grant, James

Lady good for nothing: †Quiller-Couch, *Sir* A.

Lady Grace: Wood, *Mrs*. Ellen

Lady Gresham's fête: Aguilar, Grace

Lady Hamilton: Sherriff, R.C.

Lady Hamilton and her Nelson: Tarkington, Booth

Lady Hester Stanhope: Armstrong, M.D.

Lady in a veil: †Preedy, George

Lady in her own right, A: Marston, J.W.

Lady in red, The: Jennings, Gertrude

Lady in the dark: Gershwin, Ira

Lady in the lake, The: Chandler, Raymond

Lady into fox: Garnett, David

Lady into woman: Brittain, Vera

Lady is cold, The: White, E.B.

Lady Jane, The: Willis, N.P.

Lady Jane Grey: Miller, Thomas

Lady John Russell: MacCarthy, *Sir* Desmond

Lady Kilpatrick: Buchanan, R.W.

Lady Larkspur: Nicholson, Meredith

Lady Lisle: Braddon, M.E.

Lady Lovan: (†Agnes Farrell), Adams, Francis

Lady Maisie's bairn: Swinburne, A.C.

Lady Mary: †Lonsdale, Frederick

Lady Mary and her nurse: Traill, C.P.

Lady Maud, The: Russell, W.C.

Lady mother, The: Glapthorne, Henry

Lady of Aroostook, The: Howells, W.D.

Lady of Ascot, The: Wallace, Edgar

Lady of Belmont, The: Ervine, St. John

Lady of Blossholme, The: Haggard, *Sir* Henry Rider

Lady of fashion, The: Bury, *Lady* C.S.M.

Lady of Fort St. John, The: Catherwood, Mary

Lady of Launay, The: Trollope, Anthony

Lady of leisure, A: Sidgwick, Ethel

Lady of limited income, The: Manning, Anne

Lady of little hell, The: Wallace, Edgar

Lady of Lynn, The: Besant, *Sir* Walter

Lady of Lyons, The: Lytton, E.G.E.B., *1st Baron*

Lady of Lyons married and settled, The: Merivale, H.C.

Lady of pleasure, The: Shirley, James

Lady of quality, A: Burnett, Frances Hodgson

Lady of Rome, A: Crawford, Francis Marion

Lady of Shalott, The: Tennyson, Alfred *Lord*

Lady of the Abbey, The: Hannay, J.O.

Lady of the barge, The: Jacobs, W.W.

Lady of the crossing, The: Niven, F.J.

Lady of the gulf, The: Ingraham, J.H.

Lady of the heather, The: Lawson, Will

Lady of the hundred dresses, The: Crockett, S.R.

Lady of the ice, The: De Mille, James

Lady of the lake, The: (†Q.K. Philander Doesticks, P.B.), Thompson, Mortimer Neal

Lady of the lake, The: Scott, *Sir* Walter

Lady of the Mohawks: Widdemer, Margaret

Lady of the rock, The: Holcroft, Thomas

Lady of the rose: Flavin, Martin

Lady of the Rose, The: †Lonsdale, Frederick

Lady of the shroud, The: Stoker, Bram

Lady Olivia: Falkner, W.C.

Lady on the drawingroom floor, The: Coleridge, Mary

Lady or the tiger?, The: Stockton, F.R.

Lady Patricia: Besier, Rudolf

Lady quite lost, A: Stringer, A.J.A.

Lady Rose's daughter: Ward, M.A.

Lady Silverdale's sweetheart: Black, William

Lady Susan: Austen, Jane

Lady Susan and life: Jameson, Storm

Lady Wedderburn's wish: Grant, James

Lady who dwelt in the dark, The: Hoffe, Monckton

Lady who loved insects, The: Waley, Arthur

Lady William: Oliphant, Margaret

Lady Windermere's fan: Wilde, Oscar

Lady Wu: Lin Yu-T'ang

Ladybird, The: Lawrence, D.H.

Ladybrook: Farjeon, Eleanor

Ladye Annabel, The: Lippard, George

Lady's dressing room, The: Swift, Jonathan

Lady's guide: Nichols, Beverley

Lady's last stake, The: Cibber, Colley

Lady's lecture, The: Cibber, Colley

Lady's mile, The: Braddon, M.E.

Lady's Museum, The: Lennox, Charlotte

Lady's New-Years gift, The: Savile, George

Lady's not for burning, The: Fry, Christopher

Lady's prisoner, The: †Bowen, Marjorie

Lady's shoe, A: Barrie, *Sir* J.M.

Lady's triumph, The: Settle, Elkanah

Lady's walk, The: Oliphant, Margaret

Lafayette Flying Corps, The: Hall, J.N. and C.B. Nordhoff

Lafayette in Brooklyn: Whitman, Walt

Lafcadio Hearn: Thomas, E.E.P.

Lafcadio Hearn in Japan: Noguchi, Yone

Lafitte: Ingraham, J.H.

Lahun I: Petrie, *Sir* William Flinders

Lahun II: Petrie, *Sir* William Flinders

Laid up in lavender: Weyman, Stanley

Lair of the white worm, The: Stoker, Bram

Laird of Abbotsford, The: Pope-Hennessy, *Dame* Una

Laird of Nordlaw, The: Oliphant, Margaret

Laird's luck, The: †Quiller-Couch, *Sir* A.

Lak of stedfastnesse: Chaucer, Geoffrey

Lake, The: Moore, George

Lake and war: Cripps, A.S.

Lake Country, The: Linton, Eliza

Lake lyrics: Campbell, W.W.

Lake of darkness, The: Percy, Edward

Lake of Geneva, The: Brydges, *Sir* S.E.

Lake of Killarney, The: Porter, Anna Maria

Lake of Palms: a story of Indian domestic life, The: Dutt, R.C.

Lake Pontchartrain: Roberts, W. Adolphe

Lake region of Central Africa: Burton, *Sir* Richard

Lake Superior and the Red River settlement: Hind, H.Y.

Lake Superior, its physical character, vegetation and animals: Agassis, Jean L.R.

Lakeland mystery: Treate, Geoffrey

Lakes in sunshine, The: Payn, James

Lalage's lovers: Hannay, J.O.

Lalla Rookh: Moore, Thomas

Lamb as a letter writer: Palgrave, F.T.

Lamb in his bosom: Miller, Caroline

Lamb on Coleridge: Forster, John

Lambkins remains: Belloc, Hilaire

Lambs, The: Grant, Robert

Lamb's criticism: Tillyard, E.M.W.

Lambs: their lives, their friends and their correspondence, The: Hazlitt, William

Lame dog, The: Mottram, R.H.

Lame Englishman, The: Deeping, George Warwick

Lament and triumph: Barker, George

Lament befitting these "Times of Night": Brontë, Charlotte

Lament for a maker: (†Michael Innes), Stewart, J.I.M.

Lament for dark peoples: Hughes, J.L.

Lament of Tasso, The: Byron, George Gordon, *Lord*

Lament on the death of a Master of Arts: Anand, M.R.

Lamentable, and pitifull description, of the wofull warres in Flaunders, A: Churchyard, Thomas

Lamentable tragedie, mixed full of plesant mirth, containing the life of Cambises king of Percia, A: Preston, Thomas

Lamentation of our Lady, The: Lydgate, John

Laments for the living: Parker, Dorothy

Lamia, Isabella, The Eve of St. Agnes, and other poems: Keats, John

Lamia's winter quarters: Austin, Alfred

L'amour à-la-mode: Kelly, Hugh

Lamp, The: Church, Richard

Lamp and the bell, The: Millay, E.St.Vincent

Lamp and the lute, The: Dobrée, Bonamy

Lamp for nightfall: Caldwell, Erskine Preston

Lamp in the valley, The: Stringer, A.J.A.

Lamp of poor souls, The: Pickthall, M.L.C.

Lamp of Psyche: Anderson, J.C.

Lamp on the plains, A: Horgan, Paul

Lamplighter, The: Cummins, M.S.

Lamplighter, The: Dickens, Charles

Lamplighter, The: †O'Sullivan, Seumas

Lampoons: Wolfe, Humbert

Lancashire: Greenwood, Walter

Lancashire witches, The: Ainsworth, Harrison

Lancashire witches, The: Shadwell, Thomas

Lance for the Arabs, A: Mannin, Ethel

Lancelot: †Bridie, James

Lancelot: Robinson, E.A.

Lancelot: Swinburne, A.C.

Lancelot and Guenevre: Rhys, Ernest

Lancer at large: Yeats-Brown, Francis

Lances of Lynwood, The: Yonge, C.M.

Land, The: Colum, Padraic

Land, The: Macphail, *Sir* Andrew

Land: O'Flaherty, Liam

Land, The: Sackville-West, Victoria

Land and labour in China: Tawney, R.H.

Land and sea tales: Kipling, Rudyard

Land at last: Yates, E.H.

Land everlasting: Street, A.G.

Land is bright: Ferber, Edna

Land monopoly, The: Jones, Ebenezer

Land of Burns, The: Wilson, John

Land of darkness, The: Oliphant, Margaret

Land of Evangeline, The: Herbin, J.F.

Land of fire, The: Reid, T.M.

Land of footprints, The: White, S.E.

Land of Gilead, The: Oliphant, Laurence

Land of gray gold: Derleth, A.W.

Land of green ginger, The: Holtby, Winifred

Land of heart's desire, The: Yeats, W.B.

Land of hope and glory: Clune, Frank

Land of home rule, The: Walpole, *Sir* Spencer

Land of journeys ending, The: Austin, Mary

Land of Khemi, The: Oliphant, Laurence

Land of little rain, The: Austin, Mary

Land of Lorne, The: Buchanan, R.W.

Land of Manitou, The: Lighthall, W.D.

Land of Midian, revisited: Burton, *Sir* Richard

Land of mist, The: Doyle, *Sir* Arthur Conan

Land of mist and mountain: Tynan, Katherine

Land of my birth: Clune, Frank

Land of my fathers: Jones, Jack

Land of promise, The: Maugham, Somerset

Land of shorter shadow, The: (†A.A. Fair), Gardner, Erle Stanley

Land of singing waters, The: Stephen, A.M.

Land of sky-blue waters: Derleth, A.W.

Land of spices, The: O'Brien, Kate

Land of Teck and its neighbourhood, The: Baring-Gould, Sabine

Land of the Bey, The: Reid, *Sir* Thomas Wemyss

Land of the Blessed Virgin, The: Maugham, Somerset

Land of the blue flower, The: Burnett, Frances Hodgson

Land of the Cinque ports, The: Mais, S.P.B.

Land of the crested lion: Mannin, Ethel

Land of the free: MacLeish, Archibald

Land of the lost, The: Satchell, William

Land of the morning: Mackay, Jessie

Land of the pilgrims' pride: Nathan, G.J.

Land of the Spirit, The: Page, T.N.

Land sharks and sea gulls: Glascock, W.N.

Land the ravens found, The: Mitchison, Naomi

Land war in Ireland, The: Blunt, Wilfred

Land we live in, The: Martineau, Harriet

Land we love, The: Ogilvie, W.H.

Land workers: Masefield, John

Landed gentry: Maugham, Somerset

Landfall: †Shute, Nevil

Landleaguers, The: Trollope, Anthony

Landlopers: Brereton, John Le G.

Landlord at Lion's Head, The: Howells, W.D.

Landor: Colvin, *Sir* Sydney

Landmark, The: Allen, J.L.

Landmarks: Lucas, E.V.

Landmarks: Piatt, J.J.

Landmarks: Street, A.G.

Landmarks in French literature: Strachey, Lytton

Landmarks in nineteenth century painting: Bell, Clive

Land's end, The: Hudson, W.H.

Land's End: Lucas, F.L.

Lands of the dawning morrow: Beals, Carleton

Lands of the inner sea: Roberts, W. Adolphe

Lands of the Saracen, The: Taylor, Bayard

Landscape in American poetry: Larcom, Lucy

Landscape in English art and poetry: Binyon, Laurence

Landscape in poetry, from Homer to Tennyson: Palgrave, F.T.

Landscape of Cytherea: Turner, W.J.R.

Landscape west of Eden: Aiken, Conrad

Landscape with figures: Rice, Elmer

Landtakers: Penton, B.C.

Lane that had no turning, The: Parker, *Sir* H.G.

Langemarck: Campbell, W.W.

Langley-on-Lea: Miller, Thomas

Language as gesture: Blackmur, R.P.

Language of love, The: Percy, Edward

Language, truth and logic: Ayer, A.J.

Lanky for luck: †Brand, Max

Lantana Lane: Dark, Eleanor

Lantern Lane: Deeping, George

Lanterns and lances: Thurber, James

Lanterns on the levee: Percy, W.A.

Lanthorne and candle-light: Dekker, Thomas

Laocoon, The: Blake, William

Laodice and Danaë: Bottomley, Gordon

Laodicean, A: Hardy, Thomas

Laon and Cythna: Shelley, P.B.

Lao-Tzŭ. The wisdom of Laotse: Lin Yu-T'ang

Lapland journey: Sutherland, H.G.

Lapsus calami: Stephen, J.K.

Lara: Byron, G.G. *Lord*

Lardners and the Laurelwoods, The: Kaye-Smith, S.

Lardner's cabinet cyclopaedia: Scott, *Sir* Walter

Larger history of the United States of America, A: Higginson, T.W.

Larger success, The: Johnson, J.W.

Larger than life: Herbert, A.F.X.

Lark, The: Nesbit, Edith

Lark ascending: De la Roche, Mazo

Lark rise: Thompson, Flora

Lark rise to Candleford: Thompson, Flora

Larkmeadow: Pickthall, M.W.

Larry Munro: Stern, G.B.

Lars: a pastoral of Norway: Taylor, Bayard

Lars Porsena: Graves, Robert

Lasselia: Haywood, *Mrs*. Eliza

Last actor-managers, The: Pearson, Hesketh

Last Adam, The: Cozzens, J.G.

Last adventure, The: Wallace, Edgar

Last age of the Church: Wycliffe, John

Last American, The: Mitchell, J.A.

Last and first: Symonds, J.A.

Last appearance: Malleson, Miles

Last ballad, The: Davidson, John

Last battle, The: Lewis, C.S.

Last birthright: Lindsay, Jack

Last blackbird, The: Hodgson, Ralph

Last Boer War, The: Haggard, *Sir* Henry Rider

Last bouquet, The: †Bowen, Marjorie

Last Bourbons of Naples, The: Acton, Harold

Last bread, The: Bates, H.E.

Last bus, The: (Stephen Southwold), †Bell, Neil

Last cache, The: MacKay, I.E.

Last chance, The: †Boldrewood, Rolf

Last Christmas tree, The: Allen, J.L.

Last chronicle of Barset, The: Trollope, Anthony

Last chukka, The: Waugh, Alec

Last circle, The: Benét, S.V.

Last day, The: Seymour, B.K.

Last days, The: Fausset, Hugh

Last days of Lincoln, The: Van Doren, Mark

Last days of Pompeii, The: Lytton, E.G.E.B., *1st Baron*

Last days of Shylock, The: Lewisohn, Ludwig

Last days of the French monarchy, The: Belloc, Hilaire

Last days with Cleopatra: Lindsay, Jack

Last diary, A: †Barbellion

Last dream of Attila, The: Scollard, Clinton

Last duel in Spain, The: Payne, J.H.

Last enemy, The: Strong, L.A.G.

Last entry, The: Russell, W.C.

Last essays: Conrad, Joseph

Last essays: Gill, Eric

Last essays of Elia, The: Lamb, Charles

Last essays on church and religion: Arnold, Matthew

Last flower, The: Thurber, James

Last frontier, The: Fast, Howard M.

Last fruit off an old tree, The: Landor, W.S.

Last galley, The: Doyle, *Sir* Arthur Conan

Last harvest, The: Burroughs, John

Last harvest, A: Marston, P.B.

Last holiday: Priestley, J.B.

Last hope, The: †Merriman, Seton

Last hundred years, The: Webb, Sidney and Beatrice Webb

Last joke, The: Bagnold, Enid

Last laugh, Mr. Moto: Marquand, J.P.

Last leaves: Leacock, Stephen

Last leaves: Smith, Alexander

Last leaves from Beechwood: Smedley, F.E.

Last leaves from Dunk Island: Banfield, E.J.

Last letters: Beardsley, Aubrey

Last letters of Edgar Allen Poe to Sarah Helen Whitman, The: Whitman, S.H.

Last letters to a friend, 1952–58: Macaulay, *Dame* R.

Last load, The: †Anstey, F.

Last look, The: Van Doren, Mark

Last man, The: Noyes, Alfred

Last man, The: Shelley, Mary

Last Medici, The: Acton, Harold

Last meeting, The: Matthews, J.B.

Last million, The: (†Ian Hay), Beith, *Sir* John Hay

Last miracle, The: Shiel, M.P.

Last night of Pompeii, The: Fairfield, S.L.

Last nine days of the Bismarck, The: Forester, C.S.

Last of Mr. Moto: Marquand, J.P.

Last of Mr. Norris, The: Isherwood, C.

Last of Mrs. Cheyney, The: †Lonsdale, Frederick

Last of six, The: Favenc, Ernest

Last of summer, The: O'Brien, Kate

Last of the Australian explorers: Clune, Frank

Last of the barons, The: Lytton, E.G.E.B., *1st Baron*

Last of the fairies, The: James, G.P.R.

Last of the flatboats, The: Eggleston, G.C.

Last of the foresters, The: Cooke, J.E.

Last of the Incas, The: Knight, G.W.

Last of the Lairds, The: Galt, John

Last of the Lowries, The: Green, Paul

Last of the Macallisters, The: Barr, A.E.H.

Last of the Mohicans, The: Cooper, James Fenimore

Last of the Mortimers, The: Oliphant, Margaret

Last of the plainsmen, The: Grey, Zane

Last of the radicals, The: Wedgwood, C.V.

Last of the Tasmanians, The: Bonwick, James

Last of the troubadours, The: Van Loon, Hendrik

Last of the Vikings, The: Treece, Henry

Last of the wind ships: Villiers, A.J.

Last operas and plays: Stein, Gertrude

Last pirate, The: Untermeyer, Louis

Last poems: Housman, A.E.

Last poet, The: Fortescue, *Sir* John

Last post: Ford, Ford Madox

Last Puritan, The: Santayana, George

Last rally, The: Belloc, Hilaire

Last rambles amongst the Indians of the Rocky Mountains and the Andes: Catlin, George

Last recollections of my Uncle Charles: †Balchin, Nigel

Last refuge, The: Fuller, H.B.

Last resort, The: Johnson, Pamela H.

Last revolution, The: Dunsany, E.J.M.D.P. *Lord*

Last score: Jameson, Storm

Last scrap book, A: Saintsbury, George

Last September, The: Bowen, E.D.C.

Last sheaf, The: Thomas, E.E.P.

Last song of Lucifer, The: Lindsay, N.V.

Last songs: Ledwidge, Francis

Last songs from Vagabondia: Carman, Bliss

Last songs from Vagabondia: Hovey, Richard

Last speech of John the Good, vulgarly called Jack the giant queller, The: Brooke, Henry

Last stand of dialectic materialism, The: Eastman, Max

Last straw, The: Percy, Edward

Last straw—brotherhood, The: McArthur, Peter

Last straws: Aldington, Richard

Last supper, The: Fast, Howard M.

Last tenant, The: Farjeon, B.L.

Last time, The: Hichens, R.S.

Last to rest, The: Raymond, Ernest

Last trail, The: Grey, Zane

Last train out, The: Oppenheim, E. Phillips

Last Tresilians, The: (†Michael Innes), Stewart, J.I.M.

Last trump, The: †Bridie, James

Last Trump, The: Wells, H.G.

Last tycoon, The: Fitzgerald, F. Scott

Last verses: Coolidge, Susan

Last voyage, The: Hanley, James

Last voyage, The: Noyes, Alfred

Last watch, The: Carman, Bliss

Last will and testament: Cole, G.D.H.

Last words: Crane, Stephen

Last words of Cleanthes, The: Horne, R.H.

Last years of the Protectorate, The: Firth, *Sir* Charles

Late and soon: †Delafield, E.M.

Late Christopher Bean, The: Howard, S.C.

Late converts exposed, The: Brown, Thomas

Late George Apley, The (novel and play): Marquand, J.P.

Late harvest: Douglas, Norman

Late harvest: MacMechan, A.M.

Late have I loved thee: Mannin, Ethel

Late in the day: Raymond, Ernest

Late John Wilkes's catechism, The: Hone, William

Late Lancashire witches, The: Heywood, Thomas

Late lark singing, A: Jacob, Naomi

Late M.D., The: Sala, G.A.H.

Late Mr. Justice Talfourd, The: Dickens, Charles

Late Mrs. Null, The: Stockton, F.R.

Late regulations respecting the British Colonies ... considered, The: Dickinson, John

Late songs: Tynan, Katherine

Later days: Davies, W.H.

Later Hazlitts, The: Hazlitt, W.C.

Later Hindu civilization: Dutt, R.C.

Later lays and lyrics: Hosmer, W.H.C.

Later nineteenth century, The: Saintsbury, G.E.B.

Later years, The: Pain, B.E.O.

Latest gleanings: Brontë, Charlotte

Latin literature: Mackail, J.W.

Latin-America between the Eagle and the Bear: Madariaga, Salvador de

Latin-America; world in revolution: Beals, Carleton

Latin-American policy of the United States, The: Bemis, S.F.

Latitudes: Muir, Edwin

Latter-day pamphlets: Carlyle, Thomas

Latterday symphony: Wilson, Romer

Laud, storm center of Stuart England: Coffin, Robert

Laugh parade: Leacock, S.B.

Laughable lyrics: Lear, Edward

Laughing Ann: Herbert, *Sir* A.P.

Laughing Anne: Conrad, Joseph

Laughing Bill Hyde: Beach, R.E.

Laughing boy: La Farge, Oliver

Laughing buccaneer, The: Lawson, Will

Laughing Buddha, The: Starrett, Vincent

Laughing cavalier, The: Orczy, *Baroness*

Laughing gas: Wodehouse, P.G.

Laughing girl, The: Chambers, R.W.

Laughing house: Deeping, G.W.

Laughing in the jungle: Adamic, Louis

Laughing lady, The: Sutro, Alfred

Laughing matter, The: Saroyan, William

Laughing pioneer, The: Green, Paul

Laughing prophet, The: Cammaerts, Emile

Laughing queen, The: Beck, *Mrs.* Lily

Laughing to keep from crying: Hughes, J.L.

Laughing water: Turner, E.S.

Laughing woman, The: (†Gordon Daviot), Mackintosh, Elizabeth

Laughter from a cloud: Raleigh, *Sir* W.A.

Laughter in the dark: Nabokov, Vladimir

Laughter in the next room: Sitwell, *Sir* Osbert

Laughter of fools, The: Maltby, H.F.

Laughter of Peterkin, The: †Macleod, Fiona

Laughter of the gods, The: Dunsany, E.J.M.

Laughter omnibus: †Armstrong, Anthony

Laughter parade: †Armstrong, Anthony

Laughter on the stairs: Nichols, Beverley

Launcelot and Guenevere: Hovey, Richard

Laura: Sidgwick, Ethel

Laura and Francisca: Riding, Laura

Laura Arden: Crawford, F. Marion

Laura Bridgman: Elliott, M.H.

Laura Creichton: †Mordaunt, Elinor

Laura Dibalzo: Horne, R.H.

Laura Ruthven's widowhood: Davidson, John

Laura's Bishop: Hannay, J.O.

Laureate of peace: Knight, G.W.

Laureate of the Centaurs, The: Gordon, A.L.

Laureateship, The: Broadus, E.K.

Laurel, The: Hovey, Richard

Laurel bush, The: Craik, *Mrs.* Dinah

Laurel walk, The: Molesworth, *Mrs.*

Laurelia: Todhunter, John

Laurell'd captains: †Preedy, George

Laurence Bloomfield in Ireland: Allingham, William

Laurence of Arabia: Aldington, Richard

Laurentian lyrics: Bourinot, A.S.

Laurier: Dafoe, J.W.

Lauringtons, The: Trollope, Frances

Laurus nobilis: Lee, Vernon

Lava lane: Crane, Nathalia

Lavender dragon, The: Phillpotts, Eden

Lavengro: Borrow, George

Lavinia: Broughton, Rhoda

Law and literature: Cardozo, B.N.

Law and politics: occasional papers: Frankfurter, Felix

Law and practice of election committees, The: Warren, Samuel

Law and the family: Grant, Robert

Law and the lady, The: Collins, Wilkie

Law and the social order: Cohen, M.R.

Law and the testimony, The: Warner, S.B.

Law, association and the trade union movement: Barfield, A.O.

Law is justice: notable opinions: Cardozo, B.N.

Law, literature and other essays: Cardozo, B.N.

Law of copyright, The: Wordsworth, William

Law of Java, The: Colman, George, *the younger*

Law of population, The: Besant, *Mrs.* Annie

Law of the four just men, The: Wallace, Edgar

Law of the land of Miss Lady, The: Hough, Emerson

Law of the sea, The: McFee, William

Law unto herself, A: Davis, R.B.H.

Law-abiding, The: Housman, Laurence

Law-breaker, The: Grant, Robert

Law-bringers, The: †Lancaster, G.B.

Lawd today: Wright, Richard

Lawless roads, The: Greene, Graham

Lawless voyage: Divine, A.D.

Lawley Road: Narayan, R.K.

Lawn tennis masters unveiled: Liddell Hart, B.

Lawn tennis tournament: Bangs, John Kendrick

Lawrence and the Arabs: Graves, Robert

Lawrence Clavering: Mason, A.E.W.

Lawrence's adventures among the ice-cutters: Trowbridge, J.T.

Lawrie Todd: Galt, John

Laws of Fiesole, The: Ruskin, John

Laws of life: Sutherland, H.G.

Laws of verse: Anderson, J.C.

Laws of wages, profits, and rent, investigated, The: Tucker, George

Laws we live under, The: Spence, C.H.

Lawton: Scollard, Clinton

Lawton girl, The: Frederic, Harold

Law-trickes: Day, John

Lawyer of Springfield, The: Gow, Ronald

Lawyer that tempted Christ, The: Smith, Sydney

Laxdale Hall: Linklater, Eric

Lay Anthony, The: Hergesheimer, Joseph

Lay confessor, The: Graham, Stephen

Lay morals: Stevenson, R.L.

Lay of an Irish harp, The: Morgan, *Lady* Sydney

Lay of lilies, A: Swinburne, A.C.

Lay of Norman's codpiece, The: Lindsay, Jack

Lay of the last minstrel, The: Scott, *Sir* Walter

Lay of the Laureate, The: Southey, Robert

Lay of the Scottish fiddle, The: Paulding, J.K.

Lay preacher, A: Cooke, Rose Terry

Lay preacher, The: Dennie, Joseph

Lay sermons, addresses and reviews: Huxley, T.H.

Lay thoughts of a Dean: Inge, W.R.

Laying the devil: Drinkwater, John

Layman and his conscience, The: Knox, R.A.

Layman's faith, A: Hughes, Thomas

Laymen's mission report, The: Buck, Pearl

Lay-monastery, The: Blackmore, *Sir* R.D.

Lays and ballads: Read, T.B.

Lays and legends: Nesbit, E.

Lays and legends of various nations: Thoms, W.J.

Lays and lyrics: Bayldon, Arthur

Lays for the dead: Opie, Amelia

Lays from Strathearn: Nairne, Caroline, *Baroness*

Lays of a wild harp: Cook, Eliza

Lays of ancient India: Dutt, R.C.

Lays of Ancient Rome: Macaulay, T.B. *Baron*

Lays of France: O'Shaughnessy, A.W.E.

Lays of many lands: Hemans, *Mrs.* Felicia

Lays of Melpomene: Fairfield, S.L.

Lays of my home: Whittier, J.G.

Lays of the Palmetto: Simms, W.G.

Lays of the red branch: Fergusson, *Sir* Samuel

Lays of the Scottish Cavaliers and other poems: Aytoun, William Edmondstone

Lays of the true North: Machar, A.M.

Lays of the Western Gael: Fergusson, *Sir* Samuel

Lazarre: Catherwood, Mary

Lazarus: Gilbert, G.R.

Lazarus laughed: O'Neill, Eugene

Lazy Bear Lane: Smith, Thorne

Lazy tour of two idle apprentices, The: Collins, Wilkie

Lazy tour of two idle apprentices, The: Dickens, Charles and Wilkie Collins

Lazy tours in Spain and elsewhere: Moulton, E.L.

Le bon oncle d'Amérique: Janvier, T.A.

Le cahier jaune: Benson, A.C.

Le Fauborg Saint-Germain: Reade, Charles

Le Forester: Brydges, *Sir* Samuel Egerton

Le gentleman: Sidgwick, Ethel

Le Manoir de Villerai: Leprohon, R.E.

Le morte Darthur reduced in to englysshe: Malory, *Sir* Thomas

Le mouchoir: Cooper, James Fenimore

Le Selve: †Ouida

Leader of the lower school, The: Brazil, Angela

Leaders of public opinion in Ireland, The: Lecky, W.E.

Leadership in education: Livingstone, *Sir* Richard

Leading American novelists: Erskine, John

Leading articles on various subjects: Miller, Hugh

Leaf and tendril: Burroughs, John

Leaf burners, The: Rhys, Ernest

Leaf by niggle: Tolkien, J.R.R.

Leaf from the 1611 King James Bible with "The noblest monument of English prose", A: Lowes, J.L.

Leaf in the storm, A: Lin Yu-T'ang

League and its guarantees, The: Murray, Gilbert

League of discontent, The: †Beeding, Francis

League of frightened Philistines, The: Farrell, James

League of nations, A: Gibbs, Sir Philip

League of Nations, The: Pollard, A.F.

League of Nations, The: Shaw, G.B.

League of Nations and the democratic idea, The: Murray, Gilbert

League of the Lord, The: Bridges, Roy

League of the Scarlet Pimpernel, The: Orczy, Baroness

Leaguer of Lathom, The: Ainsworth, Harrison

Lean forward, Spring!: Hesketh, Phoebe

Lean men: Bates, Ralph

Leaning tower, The: Porter, Katharine Anne

Leap before you look: Waugh, Alec

Leaps and bounds: Ridge, W. Pett

Learn one thing every day: Garland, Hamlin

Learn or perish: Canfield, Dorothy

Learned and comfortable sermon of the certaintie of faith, A: Hooker, Richard

Learned city, A: Toynbee, Philip

Learned comment upon Dr. Hare's excellent sermon preach'd before the D. of Marlborough, A: Swift, Jonathan

Learned dissertation on dumpling, A: Carey, Henry

Learned dissertation on old women, A: Carey, Henry

Learned sermon of the nature of pride, A: Hooker, Richard

Learning how to behave: Schlesinger, A.M.

Learning laughter: Spender, Stephen

Learning to love: Maltby, H. F.

Least of these, The: Steffens, Lincoln

Leather bottle, The: Roberts, T.G.

Leather face: Orczy, Baroness

Leather stocking and silk: Cooke, John Esten

Leatherwood, God, The: Howells, W.D.

Leave her to Heaven: Van Druten, J.W.

Leave it to Jane: Wodehouse, P.G.

Leave it to Psmith: Wodehouse, P.G.

Leaven: a black and white story: Blackburn, Douglas

Leaven of malice: Davies, Robertson

Leaves and fruit: Gosse, Sir Edmund

Leaves darken, The: Wingfield, Shiela

Leaves from a journal of our life in the Highlands: Victoria, Queen of England

Leaves from Arcady: Vachell, H.A.

Leaves from Australian forests: Kendall, Henry

Leaves from Lakeland: Payn, James

Leaves from Margaret Smith's journal: Whittier, J.G.

Leaves from the diary of a dreamer: Tuckerman, H.T.

Leaves from the garland woven by Max Beerbohm: Beerbohm, Sir Max

Leaves in the wind: Gardiner, A.G.

Leaves in windy weather: Tietjens, E.S.

Leaves of grass: Whitman, Walt

Leaves of life: Nesbit, E.

Leaves of the tree, The: Benson, A.C.

Leaves of the tree, The: Masters, E.L.

Lebanon: Miller, Caroline

Lebanon; impressions of a Unesco conference: Holcroft, M.H.

Lecture on Condorcet: Frazer, Sir James

Lecture on lectures, A: †Quiller-Couch, Sir A.

Lecture on Nicholas Hilliard, A: Pope-Hennessy, J.W.

Lecture on the history and objects of co-operation: Hughes, Thomas

Lecture on the shop system, A: Hughes, Thomas

Lecture on the study of history, A: Acton, John E.E.D.

Lecture on the study of the law, A: Tucker, N.B.

Lectures and addresses: Tagore, Sir R.

Lectures and addresses on literary and social topics: Robertson, F.W.

Lectures and biographical sketches: Emerson, Ralph Waldo

Lectures and essays on university subjects: Newman, J.H.

Lectures chiefly on the dramatic literature of the age of Elizabeth: Hazlitt, William

Lectures delivered in America in 1874: Kingsley, Charles

Lectures in America: Stein, Gertrude

Lectures in India: Sen, Keshub Chunder

Lectures on art delivered before the University of Oxford in Hilary Term, 1870: Ruskin, John

Lectures on an entire new state of society: Owen, Robert

Lectures on architecture and painting: Ruskin, John

Lectures on certain difficulties felt by Anglicans in submitting to the Catholic Church: Newman, J.H.

Lectures on dramatic literature: Knowles, James Sheridan

Lectures on early English history: Stubbs, William

Lectures on European history: Stubbs, William

Lectures on fashion: Willis, N.P.

Lectures on Greek poetry: Mackail, J.W.

Lectures on Japan: Nitobe, Inazo

Lectures on justification: Newman, J.H.

Lectures on Landscape: Ruskin, John

Lectures on modern history: Smith, Goldwin

Lectures on modern idealism: Royce, Josiah

Lectures on painting and design: Haydon, Benjamin

Lectures on poetry: Mackail, J.W.

Lectures on poetry: Montgomery, James

Lectures on poetry, delivered at Oxford: Doyle, *Sir* F.H.C.

Lectures on poetry, 1832–1841: Keble, John

Lectures on rhetoric and oratory: Adams, John Quincy

Lectures on the early history of the kingship: Frazre, *Sir* James

Lectures on the English comic writers: Hazlitt, William

Lectures on the English poets: Hazlitt, William

Lectures on the ethics of Green, Spencer and Martineau: Sidgwick, Henry

Lectures on the French Revolution: Acton, John E.E.D.

Lectures on the history of literature: Carlyle, Thomas

Lectures on the history of the Turks in its relation to Christianity: Newman, J.H.

Lectures on the present position of Catholics in England: Newman, J.H.

Lectures on the prophetical office of the Church, viewed relatively to Romanism and popular Protestantism: Newman, J.H.

Lectures on the "Ramayana": Sastri, Srinivasa

Lectures on the works and genius of Washington Allston: Ware, William

Lectures printed at the Chiswick Press: Morris, William

Lectures upon natural history, geology, chemistry, the application of steam and interesting discoveries in the arts: Flint, Timothy

Led by a dream: Tynan, Katherine

Led by Westmacott: Ridge, W. Pett

Leda: Huxley, Aldous

Ledger is kept, The: Postgate, Raymond

Lee: Masters, E.L.

Lee and Grant at Appomattox: Kantor, Mackinlay

Lee at Appomattox: Adams, C.F.

Lee in the mountains: Davidson, D.G.

Lee Shore, The: Macaulay, *Dame* Rose

Lee the American: Bradford, Gamaliel

Left bank, The: Rice, Elmer

Left hand! Right hand!: Sitwell, *Sir* Osbert

Left hand shake, The: Saunders, H.A.St.George

Left leg, The: Powys, T.F.

Left wings over Europe: Lewis, P. Wyndham

Legacy: †Shute, Nevil

Legacy of Cain, The: Collins, Wilkie

Legacy of the Civil War, The: Warren, Robert Penn

Legacy of the granite hills, A: Mitford, Bertram

Legal profession in Upper Canada in its early periods, The: Riddell, W.R.

Legal vocabulary, The: Reade, Charles

Legal wreck, A: Gillette, William

Legend: †Dane, Clemence

Legend for Sanderson: Palmer, E.V.

Legend of Camelot, A: Du Maurier, George

Legend of Florence, A: Hunt, Leigh

Legend of Geneviève, The: Moir, D.M.

Legend of Ghost Lagoon, The: Schull, J.J.

Legend of Glandalough, A: Sigerson, Dora

Legend of good women: Chaucer, Geoffrey

Legend of great Cromwel, The: Drayton, Michael

Legend of Jubal, The: †Eliot, George

Legend of Monte della Sibilla, or le paradis de la reine Sibille, The: Bell, Clive

Legend of Quincibald, The: Bacon, Leonard

Legend of Saint Columbia, The: Colum, Padraic

Legend of Siwash Rock: Johnson, E.P.

Legend of Stauffenberg, The: Todhunter, John

Legend of the lake, A: Whittier, J.G.

Legend of the nineties, The: Palmer, Edward Vance

Legend of the Rhine, A: Thackeray, W.M.

Legenda Suecana: Grigson, Geoffrey

Legendary, The: Willis, N.P.

Legendary ballads: Moore, Thomas

Legendary lore of the Lower St. Lawrence, The: LeMoine, *Sir* J.M.

Legendary lyrics: Kingston, G.A.

Legendary tales: Gatty, *Mrs.* Margaret

Legendary tales of the Highlands: Lauder, *Sir* Thomas Dick

Legends: Crane, Stephen

Legends and lyrics: Hayne, P.H.

Legends and records of the Church and the Empire: De Vere, Aubrey

Legends and stories of Ireland: Lover, Samuel

Legends of Angria: Brontë, Charlotte

Legends of Mexico: Lippard, George

Legends of New England: Whittier, J.G.

Legends of Saint Patrick, The: De Vere, Aubrey Thomas

Legends of the American revolution "1776", The: Lippard, George

Legends of the Black Watch: Grant, James

Legends of the City of Mexico: Janvier, T.A.

Legends of the Lakes: Croker, T.C.

Legends of the Micmacs: Rand, S.T.

Legends of the Rhine and of the Low Countries: Gratton, T.C.

Legends of the St. Lawrence, The: LeMoine, *Sir* J.M.

Legends of the Saxon saints: De Vere, Aubrey

Legends of the West: Hall, James

Legends of Thomas Didymus, the Jewish sceptic, The: Clarke, J.F.

Legends of Vancouver: Johnson, E.P.

Legion: for we are many: Bridges, Roy

Legion of Honour, The: Orczy, *Baroness*

Legions of the eagle: Treece, Henry

Legislative Black List of Upper Canada, The: Mackenzie, W.L.

Leicester Square: its associations and its worthies: Taylor, Tom

Leigh Hunt: a biography: Blunden, Edmund

Leigh Hunt's "Examiner" examined: Blunden, Edmund

Leighton Court: Kingsley, Henry

Leila: Lytton, E.G.E.B., *1st Baron*

Leila: Reynolds, G.

Leinster, Munster and Connacht: †O'Connor, Frank

Leisler: Ingraham, J.H.

Leisure hours at sea: Leggett, William

Leisure-day rhymes: Saxe, J.G.

Leith Sands: (†Gordon Daviot), Mackintosh, Elizabeth

Lemon farm, The: Boyd, Martin

Lemon verbena: Lucas, E.V.

Len Gansett: Read, O.P.

Lena Rivers: Holmes, M.J.

Lend a hand: Sheldon, C.M.

Lenient God, The: Jacob, Naomi

Lenin: Dutt, R.P.

Lenin: Hollis, Christopher

Lenten prologue, A: Shadwell, Thomas

Lenten sermons: Pusey, E.B.

Lenvoy à Bukton: Chaucer, Geoffrey

Lenvoy à Scogan: Chaucer, Geoffrey

Leo, the Royal cadet: Cameron, G.F.

Leoline and Sydonis: Kynaston, *Sir* Francis

Léon Bloy: Heppenstall, Rayner

Leon Trotsky: the portrait of a youth: Eastman, Max

Leona: Molesworth, *Mrs.*

Leonardo da Vinci: Bax, Clifford

Leonardo da Vinci: Lucas, E.V.

Leonor de Guzman: Boker, G.H.

Leonora: Bennett, Arnold

Leonora D'Orco: James, G.P.R.

Leonora: Edgeworth, Maria

Leopard and the lily, The: †Bowen, Marjorie

Leopard woman, The: White, S.E.

Leopards and spots: Jacob, Naomi

Leopard's spots, The: Dixon, Thomas

Lepers of Molokai, The: Stoddard, C.W.

Les Bellini—an essay in art criticism: Cammaerts, Emile

Les Fleurs du Mal: Swinburne, A.C.

Lesbia: Symons, Arthur

Lesbia Brandon: Swinburne, A.C.

Leslie Stephen: MacCarthy, *Sir* Desmond

Less black than we're painted: Payn, James

Less familiar nursery rhymes, The: Graves, Robert

Less nonsense: Herbert, *Sir* A.P.

Less in fortune, The: Heppenstall, Rayner

Lesson, The: Temple, Joan

Lesson in crime, A: Cole, G.D.H.

Lesson of Balzac, The: James, Henry

Lesson of Black Friday, The: Gould, Gerald

Lesson of life, The: Boker, G.H.

Lesson of the master, The: James, Henry

Lessons for children from two to three years old: Barbauld, Anna Letitia

Lessons in life: Holland, J.G.

Lest we forget: Wilcox, Ella Wheeler

Lester the loyalist: Sladen, D.B.W.

Lesters, The: Chesney, *Sir* George Tomkyns

L'Estrange's case in a civil dialogue between "Zekiel and Ephraim": L'Estrange, *Sir* Roger

Let dons delight: Knox, R.A.

Let 'em eat cake: Gershwin, Ira

Let 'em eat cake: Kaufman, G.S.

Let me feel your pulse: †Henry, O.

Let me have wings: Widdemer, Margaret

Let me lie: Cabell, James Branch

Let not man put asunder: †King, Basil

Let the birds fly: Palmer, Edward Vance

Let the flag wave: Scollard, Clinton

Let the people know: Angell, *Sir* Norman

Let the people sing: Priestley, J.B.

Let the people think: Russell, Bertrand

Let understanding be the law: Krishnamurti, Jiddu

Let us be gay: Crothers, Rachel

Let us be glum: Herbert, *Sir* A.P.

Let us do the best that we can: Cawein, Madison

Let us go afield: Hough, Emerson

Let us have faith: Keller, Helen

Let your mind alone!: Thurber, James

Lethe: Garrick, David

Let's get out here: Mais, S.P.B.

Let's laugh: †Nasby, Petroleum V.

Let's learn to fly!: †Caudwell, Christopher

Let's talk it over: Sheldon, C.M.

Letter, The: Maugham, Somerset

Letter about my four programmes, A: Lindsay, N.V.

Letter about the lions, A: Osgood, F.S.

Letter addressed to his Grace the Duke of Norfolk on occasion of Mr. Gladstone's recent expostulation, A: Newman, J.H.

Letter addressed to the people of Piedmont, A: Barlow, Joel

Letter addressed to the Rev. R.W. Jelf in explanation of No. 90 in the series called The Tracts for the Times, A: Newman, J.H.

Letter and spirit: Rossetti, Christina

Letter bag of the Great Western, The: Haliburton, T.C.

Letter box rattles, The: †Bridie, James

Letter concerning enthusiasm, A: Shaftesbury, Anthony, Earl of

Letter, containing some reflections on his Majesties declaration for liberty of conscience, A: Burnet, Gilbert

Letter describing the ride to Hulme Abbey, A: Percy, Thomas

Letter for your wicked private ear only, A: Lindsay, N.V.

Letter from a father to his son at the University, A: Graves, Richard

Letter from a lay-patron, to a gentleman designing for holy orders, A: Swift, Jonathan

Letter from a member of the House of Commons in Ireland, to a member of the House in England, concerning the sacramental test, A: Swift, Jonathan

Letter from Alabama on various subjects: Royall, A.N.

Letter from an author to a member of Parliament, concerning literary property, A: Warburton, William

Letter from Li Po, A: Aiken, Conrad

Letter from one of the special constables in London on the occasion of their being called out to keep the peace, A: Helps, Sir Arthur

Letter from Paris: Smith, Dodie

Letter from Pontus, A: Masefield, John

Letter from the earl of Mulgrave to Dr. Tillotson, A: Sheffield, John

Letter from the man on the moon, A: Defoe, Daniel

Letter from the Pretender, to a Whig-Lord, A: Swift, Jonathan

Letter from the Rev. R.W. Emerson, to the second church and society: Emerson, R.W.

Letter of abuse to D...d G...k, Esq., A: Colman, George, the elder

Letter of advice to a young poet, A: Swift, Jonathan

Letter of credit, The: Warner, S.B.

Letter of credit: Weidman, Jerome

Letter of Cupid, The: Hoccleve, Thomas

Letter of introduction, A: Howells, W.D.

Letter of †Mr. Paul Ambrose on the great rebellion in the United States: Kennedy, J.P.

Letter of thanks from my Lord W*****n to the Lord Bp of S. Asaph, A: Swift, Jonathan

Letter of the contract, The: †King, Basil

Letter on a legal provision for the Irish poor: Senior, N.W.

Letter on a possible source of the Tempest: Kipling, Rudyard

Letter on administrative reform, A: Higgins, M.J.

Letter on "Uncle Tom's Cabin", A: Helps, Sir Arthur

Letter to a friend of Robert Burns [James Gray], A: Wordsworth, William

Letter to a lady, A: Gay, John

Letter to a member concerning the condemn'd Lords, A: Steele, Sir Richard

Letter to a member of Parliament concerning the Bill for Preventing the growth of Schism, A: Steele, Sir Richard

Letter to a member of the National Assembly: Burke, Edmund

Letter to a modern novelist, A: Walpole, Sir Hugh

Letter to a new-married-lady, A: Chapone, Hester

Letter to a peer of Ireland [Viscount Kenmare] on the Penal Laws: Burke, Edmund

Letter to a returning serviceman: Priestley, J.B.

Letter to a sister, A: Lehmann, Rosamund

Letter to a young painter, A: Read, Sir Herbert

Letter to a young poet, A: Woolf, Virginia

Letter to Adolf Hitler, A: Golding, Louis

Letter to American teachers of history, A: Adams, H.B.

Letter to Archdeacon Singleton, on the Ecclesiastical Commission, A: Smith, Sydney

Letter to Conrad: Kipling, Rudyard

Letter to critics, A: Lewis, H.S.

Letter to Dr. Harwood, A: Mickle, William Julius

Letter to Earl Camden connected with the late duel, A: Canning, George

Letter to General Hamilton, A: Webster, Noah

Letter to General Lord Viscount Beresford, A: Napier, Sir W.F.P.

Letter to grandfather, A: †West, Rebecca

Letter to H. Repton on the application of the principles of landscape painting to landscape architecture: Price, Sir Uvedale

Letter to her Grace the Duchess of Devonshire, A: Combe, William

Letter to His Excellency Marcus Morton, on banking and the currency, A: Hildreth, Richard

Letter ... to Joel Lewis Griffing, A: Halleck, Fitz-Greene

Letter to John Farr and John Harris, the sherriffs of Bristol on the affairs of America: Burke, Edmund

Letter to John Murray, Esq., "touching" Lord Nugent: Southey, Robert

Letter to Leonora, A: Morley, C.D.

Letter to Lord Ellenborough, A: Shelley, P.B.

Letter to Lord John Russell on the Church Bills, A: Smith, Sydney

Letter to Lucian, A: Noyes, Alfred

Letter to M. de Voltaire or The desert island, A: Murphy, Arthur

Letter to Madam Blanchard: Forster, E.M.

Letter to Monsieur Boileau Despreaux occasion'd by the Victory at Blenheim, A: Prior, Matthew

Letter to Mr. Harding the printer, A: Swift, Jonathan

Letter to Mr. Tickell, A: Young, Edward

Letter to Mr. Williams, A: Cotton, John

Letter to Mrs. Virginia Woolf, A: Quennell, P.C.

Letter to my son, A: Sitwell, Sir Osbert

Letter to parishioners on laying the first stone of the church at Littlemore: Newman, J.H.

Letter to Richard (Bagot), Bishop of Oxford, A: Newman, J.H.

Letter to Richard, Lord Bishop of Llandaff, A: Cumberland, Richard

Letter to Robert Frost and others, A: Hillyer, Robert

Letter to Sir Hercules Langrishe, A: Burke, Edmund

Letter to Sir M.W[harton] concerning occasional Peers, A: Steele, Sir Richard

Letter to Sir Samuel Romilly upon the abuse of charities, A: Brougham, Henry Peter

Letter to Sir Thomas Osborn, A: Buckingham, G.V.

Letter to Sir William Windham: Bolingbroke, Henry St. John

Letter to the Archbishop of Canterbury: Pusey, E.B.

Letter to the Bishop of London, A: Pusey, E.B.

Letter to the Earl of O—d concerning the Bill of Peerage, A: Steele, Sir Richard

Letter to the editor of the letters on the spirit of patriotism, A: Warburton, William

Letter to the editor of the miscellanies of Thomas Chatterton, A: Walpole, Horace

Letter to the electors, upon the Catholic question, A: Smith, Sydney

Letter to the Examiner, A: Bolingbroke, Henry St.John

Letter to the late Cabinet Minister on the crisis, A: Lytton, E.G.E.B. 1st Baron

Letter to the K[ing] at Arms from a reputed esquire one of the subscribers to the bank, A: Swift, Jonathan

Letter to the Margaret Professor of Divinity on Mr. R.H. Froude's statements on the Holy Eucharist: Newman, J.H.

Letter to the most insolent man alive, A: †Pindar, Peter

Letter to the National Convention of France, A: Barlow, Joel

Letter to the people of the United States touching the matter of slavery, A: Parker, Theodore

Letter to the Queen on a late court martial: Warren, Samuel

Letter to the Rev. E.B.Pusey, D.D., A: Newman, J.H.

Letter to the Rev. Godfrey Faussett, on certain points of faith and practice, A: Newman, J.H.

Letter to the Rev. Mr. Douglas, occasioned by his vindication of Milton, A: Lauder, William

Letter to the Reverend Mr. Noah Hobart, A: Wolcott, Roger

Letter to the Right Honourable H. Flood concerning Irish Affairs, 18 May, 1765: Burke, Edmund

Letter to the Right Honourable the Lord Viscount Molesworth, A: Swift, Jonathan

Letter to the Right Honourable William Windham, A: Holcroft, Thomas

Letter to the Right Reverend Lord Bishop of Worcester concerning some passages relating to Mr. Locke's essay on human understanding, A: Locke, John

Letter to the Roman Catholics of Dublin, A: Moore, Thomas

Letter to the shop-keepers, A: Swift, Jonathan

Letter to the whole people of Ireland, A: Swift, Jonathan

Letter to the young men of Maine, A: Curtis, G.W.

Letter to T[homas] B[urgh] Esq. on Irish affairs: Burke, Edmund

Letter to W.B.Yeats, A: Strong, L.A.G.

Letter to William Gifford, Esq., A: Hazlitt, William

Letter to William Smith, Esq., M.P., A: Southey, Robert

Letter: whearin part of the entertainment untoo the Queenz Majesty at Killingwoorth Castl, in Warwik Sheer in this soomerz progress 1575 iz signified: Laneham, Robert

Letter: wherein, part of the entertainment untoo the Queenz Majesty at Killingwoorth Castl, A: Laneham, Robert

Letter written to a gentleman in the country, A: Milton, John

Letters: Arnold, Matthew

Letters about Shelley: Garnett, Richard

Letters about Shelley interchanged by Edward Dowden, Robert Garnett, and Wm. Michael Rossetti: Dowden, Edward

Letters addressed to a college friend: Ruskin, John

Letters and addresses on freemasonry: Adams, John Quincy

Letters and art in New Zealand: McCormick, E.H.

Letters and correspondence, public and private, during the time he was Secretary of State to Queen Anne: Bolingbroke, Henry St. John

Letters and dispatches, 1617–1620: Wotton, *Sir* Henry

Letters and journals of Lord Byron: Moore, Thomas

Letters and leadership: Brooks, Van Wyck

Letters and memoranda to H. Buxton Forman: Wise, T.J.

Letters and memorials of State in the reigns of Queen Mary, Queen Elizabeth, King James, King Charles the first, part of the reign of King Charles the second, and Oliver's usurpation: Collins, Arthur

Letters and notes on the manners and customs of the North American Indians: Catlin, George

Letters and social aims: Emerson, Ralph Waldo

Letters and speeches of Charles II, The: Bryant, *Sir* Arthur

Letters at the pastry-cook's: Mayhew, Horace

Letters by an American: Hamilton, Alexander

Letters containing a sketch of the politics of France: Williams, H.M.

Letters for literary ladies: Edgeworth, Maria

Letters from a cat: Jackson, H.H.

Letters from a Chinese official: Dickinson, Goldsworthy Lowes

Letters from a distance: Cannan, Gilbert

Letters from a farmer in Pennsylvania to the inhabitants of the British Colonies: Dickinson, John

Letters from a father to his daughter: Nehru, Jawaharlal

Letters from a late eminent prelate to one of his friends [Richard Hurd]: Warburton, William

Letters from a Persian in England to his friend at Ispahan: Lyttelton, George *Baron*

Letters from a silent study: †Hobbes, John Oliver

Letters from abroad: Tagore, *Sir* R.

Letters from abroad to kindred at home: Sedgwick, C.M.

Letters from America: Brooke, Rupert

Letters from America: Rölvaag, O.E.

Letters from an American Farmer: Crèvecœur, Jean de

Letters from Bohemia: Hecht, Ben

Letters from China and Japan: Dewey, John

Letters from Cockney lands: Ainsworth, Harrison

Letters from France: Bean, C.E.

Letters from Honolulu: Clemens, S.L.

Letters from Iceland: Auden, W.H.

Letters from Iceland: Macneice, Louis

Letters from India: Eden, Emily

Letters from Ireland: Martineau, Harriet

Letters from John Chinaman: Dickinson, Goldsworthy Lowes

Letters from limbo: Rhys, Ernest

Letters from London: Austin, William

Letters from New York: Child, L.M.

Letters from Orinda to Poliarchus: (Katherine Philips), †Orinda

Letters from Palmyra: Ware, William

Letters from Paris to the citizens of the United States of America: Barlow, Joel

Letters from "Phocion": Hamilton, Alexander

Letters from President Longstreet: Longstreet, A.B.

Letters from Russia: Tagore, *Sir* R.

Letters from Spain: Glyn, Elinor

Letters from Syria: Stark, Freya

Letters from the Aegean: Tennent, *Sir* J.E.

Letters from the battlefields of Paraguay: Burton, *Sir* Richard

Letters from the East: Bryant, W.C.

Letters from the Far East: Eliot, *Sir* Charles

Letters from the Levant: Galt, John

Letters from the Levant: Montagu, *Lady* M.W.

Letters from the mountains: Grant, Anne

Letters from the Orient: Phillips, Samuel

Letters from the South: Campbell, Thomas

Letters from the South: Paulding, J.K.

Letters from the West: Hall, James

Letters from under a bridge: Willis, N.P.

Letters from Yorick to Eliza: Sterne, Laurence

Letters home: Howells, W.D.

Letters in criticism to William Roscoe: Bowles, William Lisle

Letters of a Chinese Amazon: Lin Yu-T'ang

Letters of a Conservative, The: Landor, W.S.

Letters of a man of the times, to the citizens of Baltimore: Kennedy, J.P.

Letters of a traveller: Bryant, W.C.

Letters of a Westchester farmer: Seabury, Samuel

Letters of advice: touching the choice of Knights and Burgesses for the Parliament: Wither, George

Letters of an American, mainly on Russia and Revolution: Landor, W.S.

Letters of an Italian nun and an English gentleman: Combe, William

Letters of askance: Morley, C.D.

Letters of Cardinal Vaughan to Lady Herbert of Lea: Leslie, *Sir* J.R. Shane

Letters of Charles Lamb, with a sketch of his life, The: Talfourd, *Sir* T.N.

Letters of Elizabeth Barrett Browning: Horne, R.H.

Letters of Eric Gill: Gill, Eric

Letters of Fabius, The: Dickinson, John

Letters of Jonathan Oldstyle, Gent.: (†Geoffrey Crayon), Irving, Washington

Letters of life: Sigourney, L.H.

Letters of Lucius M. Piso from Palmyra: Ware, William

Letters of Marque: Kipling, Rudyard

Letters of Mozis Addums to Billy Ivvins, The: Bagby, G.W.

Letters of Mr. Addison and Mr. Pope: Addison, Joseph

Letters of Mrs. Fitzherbert: Leslie, *Sir* J.R. Shane

Letters of Peter Plymley to my brother Abraham who lives in the country, The: Smith, Sydney

Letters of Queen Henrietta Maria: Green, Mary Anne

Letters of Quintus Curtius Snodgrass, The: (†Mark Twain), Clemens, S.L.

Letters of Robert Burns, The. Ed. from the original manuscripts by J. De L. Ferguson: Burns, Robert

Letters of royal and illustrious ladies of Great Britain: Green, Mary Anne

Letters of St. Evremond: Hayward, J.D.

Letters of state: Milton, John

Letters of the British spy, The: Wirt, William

Letters of travel: Kipling, Rudyard

Letters of Tsar Nicholas II: Vulliamy, C.E.

Letters of Virginia Woolf and Lytton Strachey: Woolf, L.S.

Letters of William Cowper: Frazer, *Sir* James

Letters of wit, politicks and morality: Farquhar, George

Letters on American debts: Smith, Sydney

Letters on army reform: Higgins, Matthew James

Letters on art and literature: Ruskin, John

Letters on Charlotte Brontë: Caskell, Elizabeth

Letters on demonology and witchcraft: Scott, *Sir* Walter

Letters on India: Anand, M.R.

Letters on literature: Lang, Andrew

Letters on mesmerism: Martineau, Harriet

Letters on military education: Higgins, Matthew James

Letters on religious persecution: Carey, Mathew

Letters on "Savitri": Ghose, Sri Aurobindo

Letters on several subjects: More, Henry

Letters on Silesia: Adams, J.Q.

Letters on the character and poetical genius of Lord Byron: Brydges, *Sir* Samuel Egerton

Letters on the events which have passed in France since the Restoration in 1815: Williams, H.M.

Letters on the Factory Act: Senior, N.W.

Letters on the French Revolution: Williams, H.M.

Letters on the improvement of the mind, addressed to a young lady: Chapone, Hester

Letters on the latest forms of infidelity: Ripley, George

Letters on the laws of man's nature and development: Martineau, Harriet

Letters on the Masonic Institution: Adams, J.Q.

Letters on the spirit of patriotism: Bolingbroke, Henry St. John

Letters on the study and use of history: Bolingbroke, Henry St. John

Letters on the war: Hardy, Thomas

Letters to a friend: Holtby, Winifred

Letters to a friend: Macaulay, *Dame* R.

Letters to a friend: Muir, John

Letters to a friend: Sterling, John

Letters to a friend: Tagore, *Sir* R.

Letters to a king: Tourgée, A.W.

Letters to a niece: Adams, H.B.

Letters to a sister: Hollis, Christopher

Letters to a sister: Macaulay, *Dame* R.

Letters to a young gentleman commencing his education: Webster, Noah

Letters to an editor: Stevenson, R.L.

Letters to an old Garibaldian: Chesterton, G.K.

Letters to an unphilosophical believer: Priestley, Joseph

Letters to and from the late Samuel Johnson, LL.D. to which are added some poems never before printed: Thrale, H.L.

Letters to Anaïs Nin: Miller, Henry

Letters to Burke occasioned by his reflections on the French Revolution: Priestley, Joseph

Letters to Caroline: Glyn, Elinor

Letters to Charles Baxter: Stevenson, R.L.

Letters to dead authors: Lang, Andrew

Letters to Ernest Chesneau: Ruskin, John

Letters to Frances Anne: Disraeli, Benjamin

Letters to his mother, Ann Borrow: Borrow, George

Letters to his wife, Mary Borrow: Borrow, George

Letters to J.J. Furnivall: Ruskin, John

Letters to Guy: Barker, M.A.

Letters to John Bull Esquire: Lytton, E.G.E.B., *1st Baron*

Letters to Judd: Sinclair, Upton

Letters to Julia, in rhyme: Luttrell, Henry

Letters to L.U. Wilkinson: Powys, John Cowper

Letters to M.G. & H.G. (Mary and Helen Gladstone): Ruskin, John

Letters to Miss Alma Murray: Shaw, G.B.

Letters to R. Molesworth Esq.: Shaftesbury, Anthony, *3rd Earl of*

Letters to mothers: Sigourney, L.H.

Letters to my neighbours on the present election: Ward, M.A.

Letters to my pupils: Sigourney, L.H.

Letters to New Island: Yeats, W.B.

Letters to Rev. F.J.Faunthorpe: Ruskin, John

Letters to Sanchia: Hewlett, Maurice

Letters to Sir Edmund Bacon: Wotton, *Sir* Henry

Letters to the Bishop of Carlisle: Rymer, Thomas

Letters to the British and Foreign Bible Society: Borrow, George

Letters to the family: Kipling, Rudyard

Letters to the Joneses: Holland, J.G.

Letters to the Sphinx: Wilde, Oscar

Letters to the "Times" on the principal Pre-Raphaelite pictures: Ruskin, John

Letters to three friends: White, W.H.

Letters to various persons: Thoreau, H.D.

Letters to X: Massingham, Harold

Letters to young ladies: Sigourney, L.H.

Letters to young men on betting and gambling: Kingsley, Charles

Letters upon several occasions: Congreve, William

Letters written by Sir W* Temple, Bar, and other Ministers of State: Swift, Jonathan

Letters written during a short residence in Spain and Portugal: Southey, Robert

Letters written during a short residence in Sweden, Norway, and Denmark: Wollstonecraft, Mary

Letters written during the President's tour down East: Smith, Seba

Letters written in France to a friend in England: Williams, H.M.

Letters written in Holland: Bowdler, Thomas

Letters written to and for particular friends, directing the requisite style and forms to be observed in writing familiar letters: Richardson, Samuel

Letter-writers, The: Fielding, Henry

Lettice: Molesworth, *Mrs.*

Letting of humours blood in the head-vaine, The: Rowland, Samuel

Lettre de cachet, The: Gore, Catherine

Letty: Pinero, *Sir* A.W.

Letty Fox, her luck: Stead, C.E.

Letty Hyde's lovers: Grant, James

Letty Landon: Ashton, Helen

Letty Lynton: Lowndes, M.A.

Leucothoe: Bickerstaffe, Isaac

Level crossing: Bottome, Phyllis

'Leven more poems: Riley, J.W.

Leviathan: Bolitho, William

Leviathan: Hobbes, Thomas

Levine: Hanley, James

Levy Mayer and the new industrial era: Masters, E.L.

Lewis Arundel: Smedley, F.E.

Lewis Carroll: De la Mare, Walter

Lewis Seymour, and some women: Moore, George

Lexington: Howard, S.C.

Leyton Hall: Lemon, Mark

L'Hasa at last: Oxley, J.M.

Liar, The: James, Henry

Liar, The: Parker, *Sir* H.G.

Liars, The: Jones, H.A.

Libel on D— D— and a certain great lord, A: Swift, Jonathan

Liber amoris: or, the new Pygmalion: Hazlitt, William

Liber juniorum: Rothenstein, *Sir* William

Liberal case, The: Fulford, R.T.B.

Liberal education: Van Doren, Mark

Liberal imagination, The: Trilling, Lionel

Liberal movement in English literature, The: Courthorpe, W.J.

Liberal tradition, The: Belloc, Hilaire

Liberalism and the social problem: Churchill, *Sir* Winston

Liberalism in America: Stearns, H.E.

Liberalism: its principles and proposals: Samuel, Herbert *1st Viscount*

Liberality and civilisation: Murray, Gilbert

Liberality or the decayed Macaroni: Anstey, Christopher

Liberation: Adamic, Louis

Liberation of American literature, The: Calverton, V.F.

Liberation of mankind, The: Van Loon, H.W.

Liberation of the Philippines: Luzon, Mindanao, the Visayas, The: Morison, S.E.

Liberators, The: Guedalla, Philip

Liberators, The: Hubbard, Elbert

Liberia: Hale, S.J.B.

Liberties of the mind: Morgan, Charles

Libertine, The: Shadwell, Thomas

Liberty!: Bennett, Arnold

Liberty: Thomson, James

Liberty and authority in matters of taste: Courthorpe, W.J.

Liberty and learning: Hight, James

Liberty and morality: Conway, M.D.

Liberty and the news: Lippmann, Walter

Liberty asserted: Dennis, John

Liberty, equality, fraternity: Stephen, *Sir* J.F.

Liberty in the modern state: Laski, Harold

Liberty Jones: Barry, Philip

Liberty to-day: Joad, C.E.M.

Liberty tree: Hawthorne, Nathaniel

Liberty's last squeak: †Pindar, Peter

Libraries and education: Miller, E.M.

Library, The: Crabbe, George

Library, The: Lang, Andrew

Library companion, The: Dibdin, T.F.

Library of Parliament, N.S.W.: Stephens, A.G.

Libretto of Menna: Griffith, Llewelyn

Licensers for the Press, etc. to 1640: Greg, W.W.

Lichee nuts: Masters, E.L.

Licia: Fletcher, Giles, *the elder*

Lie, The: Jones, H.A.

Lie factory starts, The: Sinclair, Upton

Lie of the day, The: O'Keeffe, John

Lieutenant Bones: Wallace, Edgar

Lieutenant and others, The: †Sapper

Lieutenant Commander: Hannay, J.O.

Life: Cobbe, Frances Power

Life, character and writings of W.C. Bryant, The: Curtis, G.W.

Life adventurous, The: Farrell, James

Life along the Passaic river: Williams, W.C.

Life among the English: Macaulay, *Dame* R.

Life among the Indians: Catlin, George

Life amongst the Modocs: †Miller, Joaquin

Life and achievements of E.H. Palmer, The: Besant, *Sir* Walter

Life and administration of Cardinal Wolsey, The: Galt, John

Life and adventures: Harris, J.T.

Life and adventures, and pyracies of the famous Captain Singleton, The: Defoe, Daniel

Life and adventures of a clever woman, The: Trollope, Frances

Life and adventures of a country merchant, The: Jones, J.B.

Life and adventures of a dog, The: Miller, Thomas

Life and adventures of Ambrose Gwinnett, The: Bickerstaffe, Isaac

Life and adventures of Arthur Clenning, The: Flint, Timothy

Life and adventures of Carl Laemmle: Drinkwater, John

Life and adventures of Dr. Dodimus Duckworth, A.N.Q., The: Green, Asa

Life and adventures of Jeff Davis: Arnold, George

Life and adventures of John Marston Hall, The: James, G.P.R.

Life and adventures of Jonathan Jefferson Whitlaw, The: Trollope, Frances

Life and adventures of Martin Chuzzlewit, The: Dickens, Charles

Life and adventures of Mervyn Clitheroe: Ainsworth, Harrison

Life and adventures of Michael Armstrong, the factory boy, The: Trollope, Frances

Life and adventures of Nicholas Nickleby, The: Dickens, Charles

Life and adventures of Oliver Goldsmith, The: Forster, John

Life and adventures of Peter Porcupine, The: Cobbett, William

Life and adventures of Peter Wilkins, a Cornish man, The: Paltock, Robert

Life and adventures of Sylvia Scarlett, The: Mackenzie, *Sir* Compton

Life and adventures, songs, services and speeches of Private Miles O'Reilly, The: Halpine, C.G.

Life and Andrew Otway: †Bell, Neil

Life and art of Edwin Booth, The: Matthews, J.B.

Life and art of Edwin Booth: Winter, William

Life and art of Richard Mansfield, The: Winter, William

Life and correspondence of David Hume: Burton, J.H.

Life and death of Conder, The: Rothenstein, *Sir* John

Life and death of Dr. Donne, The: Walton, Izaak

Life and death of Garfield, The: Conway, M.D.

Life and death of Harriet Frean, The: Sinclair, May

Life and death of Jason, The: Morris, William

Life and death of John of Barneveld, The: Motley, J.L.

Life and death of Julius Caesar, The: Shakespeare, William

Life and death of King John, The: Shakespeare, William

Life and death of Leo the Armenian, The: Morris, *Sir* Lewis

Life and death of Lord Edward Fitzgerald, The: Moore, Thomas

Life and death of Mother Shipton, The: Head, Richard

Life and death of Mr. Badman, The: Bunyan, John

Life and death of Queene Elizabeth, The: Heywood, Thomas

Life and death of Richard Mather, The: Mather, Increase

Life and death of Richard Yea-and-Nay, The: Hewlett, Maurice

Life and death of Sir Matthew Hale sometime Lord Chief Justice of His Majesties Court of Kings Bench, The: Burnet, Gilbert

Life and death of William Long Beard, The: Lodge, Thomas

Life—and Erica: Frankau, Gilbert

Life and extraordinary adventures of Captain John Smith, The: Belknap, Jeremy

Life and Gabriella: Glasgow, Ellen

Life and genuine character of Doctor Swift, The: Swift, Jonathan

Life and glorious actions of Edward Prince of Wales, The: Collins, Arthur

Life and habit: Butler, Samuel

Life and heroic exploits of Israel Putnam, The: Humphreys, David

Life and history of Belisarius, The: Oldmixon, John

Life and I: Bradford, Gamaliel

Life and labour: Smiles, Samuel

Life and labour of the people in London: Booth, Charles

Life and labours of Blessed John Baptist de la Salle, The: Thompson, Francis

Life and labours of Mr. Thomas Brassey, The: Helps, *Sir* Arthur

Life and labours of the Rev. Daniel Baker, The: Baker, W.M.

Life and language in the Old Testament: Chase, M.E.

Life and last words of Wilfrid Ewart: Graham, Stephen

Life and letters: Godkin, E.L.

Life and letters: Squire, *Sir* J.C.

Life and letters of Dr. Samuel Butler, The: Butler, Samuel

Life and letters of Frances, Baroness Bunsen: Hare, A.J.C.

Life and letters of J.G. Lockhart, The: Lang, Andrew

Life and letters of James Wolfe, The: Willson, H.B.

Life and letters of John Donne, The: Gosse, *Sir* Edmund

Life and letters of Joseph Hardy Neesima: Hardy, A.S.

Life and letters of Joseph Severn, The: †Macleod, Fiona

Life and letters of Lord Macaulay, The: Trevelyan, *Sir* G.O.

Life and letters of Maggie Benson: Benson, A.C.

Life and letters of Maria Edgeworth, The: Hare, A.J.C.

Life and letters of Sir Austen Chamberlain: Petrie, *Sir* Charles

Life and letters of Sir Henry Wotton: Smith, L.L.P.

Life and letters of the Rev. F.W. Robertson, The: Brooke, Stopford

Life and letters of Woodrow Wilson: Baker, Ray Stannard

Life and liberty: Temple, William

Life and literary remains of Ralph Bathurst, M.D., The: Warton, Thomas

Life and Lord Strathcona and Mount Royal, The: Willson, H.B.

Life and matter: Lodge, Oliver

Life and myself: Chattopadhyaya, H.

Life and opinions of General Sir C.J. Napier, The: Napier, *Sir* W.F.P.

Life and opinions of John Buncle, Esq., The: Amory, Thomas

Life and opinions of Tristram Shandy, gentleman, The: Sterne, Laurence

Life and phantasy: Allingham, William

Life and pontificate of Leo the tenth, The: Roscoe, William

Life and posthumous works of Arthur Maynwaring, Esq., The: Oldmixon, John

Life and public services of Henry Clay, The: Sargent, Epes

Life and raigne of King Edward the sixt, The: Hayward, *Sir* John

Life and raigne of King Henry the eighth, The: Herbert, Edward

Life and remains of Theodore Edward Hook, The: Barham, R.H.

Life and sport on the Pacific slope: Vachell, H.A.

Life and strange surprizing adventures of Robinson Crusoe, of York, mariner, The: Defoe, Daniel

Life and studies of Benjamin West, The: Galt, John

Life and teaching of Jesus Christ, The: Raven, C.E.

Life and the poet: Spender, Stephen

Life and times of Captain John Piper, The: †Eldershaw, M. Barnard

Life and times of Charles James Fox, The: Russell, *Lord* John

Life and times of Jesus as related by Thomas Didymus: Clarke, J.F.

Life and times of Johann Sebastian Bach, The: Van Loon, Hendrik

Life and times of Laurence Sterne: Cross, W.L.

Life and times of Louis the Fourteenth, The: James, G.P.R.

Life and times of Peter Cooper: Hughes, Thomas

Life and times of Phirozeshah Mehta: Sastri, Srinivasa

Life and times of Pieter Stuyvesant: Van Loon, Hendrik

Life and times of Po Chu-i, The: Waley, Arthur

Life and times of Rembrandt, The: Van Loon, Hendrik

Life and times of Rev. John Wiswall, M.A., The: Saunders, E.M.

Life and times of Salvator Rosa, The: Morgan, *Lady* Sydney

Life and times of Simon Bolivar, The: Van Loon, Hendrik

Life and times of Sir Joshua Reynolds: Taylor, Tom

Life and times of Sir Julius Vogel: Burdon, R.M.

Life and times of Sir Leonard Tilley, The: Hannay, James

Life and times of Stephen Higginson: Higginson, T.W.

Life and work of Lady Butler, The: Meynell, Wilfred

Life and works of Goethe, The: Lewes, G.H.

Life and writings of Major Jack Downing of Downingville, The: Smith, Seba

Life and writings of Mrs. Piozzi, The: Hayward, Abraham

Life, art and America: Dreiser, Theodore

Life as prayer: Underhill, Evelyn

Life at Happy Knoll: Marquand, J.P.

Life at the Mermaid: Squire, *Sir* J.C.

Life class: Bemelmans, Ludwig

Life comes to Seathorpe: †Bell, Neil

Life, death: Calvert, G.H.

Life divine, The: Ghose, Sri Aurobindo

Life everlasting, The: †Corelli, Marie

Life everlasting: Fiske, John

Life for a life, A: Craik, *Mrs.*

Life for a life, A: Herrick, Robert

Life here and there: Willis, N.P.

Life histories of Northern animals: Seton-Thompson, E.

Life history album: Galton, *Sir* Francis

Life in a country manse: Barrie, *Sir* J.M.

Life in a Devon village: Williamson, Henry

Life in a New England town: Adams, J.Q.

Life in an hospital: Besant, *Sir* Walter

Life in English Literature: Strong, L.A.G.

Life in freedom: Krishnamurti, Jiddu

Life in London: Egan, Pierce

Life in Manchester: Gaskell, Elizabeth

Life in Paris: Reynolds, G.

Life in poetry: Courthorpe, W.J.

Life in Shakespeare's England: Wilson, J.D.

Life in the backwoods: Moodie, Susanna

Life in the clearings versus the bush: Moodie, Susanna

Life in the eighteenth century: Eggleston, G.C.

Life in the Middle Ages: Coulton, G.G.

Life in the open air: Winthrop, Theodore

Life in the sick-room: Martineau, Harriet

Life in the war zone: Atherton, Gertrude

Life is a four letter word: Monsarrat, N.J.T.

Life is my song: Fletcher, John Gould

Life, letters and diaries of Sir Stafford Northcote: Lang, Andrew

Life, letters, and friendships of Richard Monckton Milnes, The: Reid, *Sir* Thomas Wemyss

Life, letters and literary remains, The: Lytton, E.

Life, letters, and literary remains of John Keats, The: Milnes, R.M.

Life, love and light: Pollard, A.W.

Life of a little college, The: MacMechan, A.M.

Life of a lover, The: Lee, Sophia

Life of a sailor, The: Chamier, Frederick

Life of a Scotch naturalist: Thomas Edward: Smiles, Samuel

Life of Abraham Lincoln, The: Holland, J.G.

Life of Abraham Lincoln, The: Tarbell, Ida

Life of Albert Gallatin, The: Adams, H.B.

Life of Alcibiades, The: Benson, E.F.

Life of Alexander H. Stephens: Johnston, R.M.

Life of Alexander II, Tsar of Russia: Graham, Stephen

Life of Algernon Charles Swinburne, The: Gosse, *Sir* Edmund

Life of Ali Baba: Hubbard, Elbert

Life of an actor, The: Egan, Pierce

Life of Andrew Jackson: Cobbett, William

Life of Andrew Marvell: Coleridge, Hartley

Life of Belisarius, The: Stanhope, P.H., *Earl*

Life of Ben Jonson: Symonds, J.A.

Life of Bernard Shaw: Harris, James Thomas

Life of Bishop Percival: Temple, William

Life of Blake, The: Gilchrist, Alexander

Life of Brian Houghton Hodgson: Hunter, *Sir* William Wilson

Life of Captain John Smith, The: Simms, W.G.

Life of Captain [Meriwether] Lewis: Jefferson, Thomas

Life of Cardinal Manning: Leslie, *Sir* J.R.

Life of Cardinal Wolsey: Cavendish, George

Life of Cesare Borgia, The: Sabatini, Rafael

Life of Charles Dickens, The: Forster, John

Life of Charles Lamb, The: Lucas, E.V.

Life of Charles the Fifth after his abdication, The: Prescott, W.H.

Life of Charlotte Brontë, The: Birrell, Augustine

Life of Charlotte Brontë, The: Gaskell, *Mrs.* Elizabeth

Life of Chatham, The: Godwin, William

Life of Christ: Caine, *Sir* T.H. Hall

Life of Christopher Columbus, The: Hale, E.E.

Life of Cicero, The: Trollope, Anthony

Life of Coleridge: Caine, *Sir* T.H. Hall

Life of Columbus, The: Helps, *Sir* Arthur

Life of Count Tolstoi: Dole, N.H.

Life of Cowper: Smith, Goldwin

Life of David Belasco, The: Winter, William

Life of David Garrick, The: Murphy, Arthur

Life of Dickens: Lindsay, Jack

Life of Dr. George Abbot, Lord Archbishop of Canterbury, The: Oldys, William

Life of Dr. Sanderson, The: Walton, Izaak

Life of Edgar Allan Poe, The: Woodberry, G.E.

Life of Edmund Kean, The: Proctor, B.W.

Life of Edward Gibbon, The: Milman, H.H.

Life of Edward Irving, The: Oliphant, Margaret

Life of Edward White, sometime Archbishop of Canterbury: Benson, A.C.

Life of Emerson, The: Brooks, Van Wyck

Life of Etty: Gilchrist, Alexander

Life of F.W. Maitland: Fisher, H.A.L.

Life of Father Jacome Goncawez: Perera, Simon

Life of Field-Marshal the Duke of Wellington: Maxwell, W.H.

Life of Francis Bacon, The: Mallet, David

Life of Francis Drake, The: Mason, A.E.W.

Life of Francis Marion, The: Simms, W.G.

Life of Francis Worth, Baron of Guilford, The: †North, Roger

Life of Franklin Pierce, The: Hawthorne, Nathaniel

Life of Gen. Robert E. Lee, A: Cooke, John Esten

Life of General Sir David Baird: Hook, T.E.

Life of General Smuts, The: Millin, Sarah Gertrude

Life of Geoffrey Chaucer, The: Godwin, William

Life of George Cabot Lodge, The: Adams, H.B.

Life of George Cadbury, The: Gardiner, A.G.

Life of George Lansbury: Postgate, Raymond

Life of George Stephenson, The: Smiles, Samuel

Life of George Washington, The: (†Geoffrey Crayon), Irving, Washington

Life of George Washington, The: Hale, E.E.

Life of George Wyndham: Mackail, J.W.

Life of Geronimo Cardano, of Milan, physician, The: Morley, Henry

Life of Goethe: Ritchie, *Mrs.* A.C.M.

Life of Goya, A: Rothenstein, *Sir* William

Life of H.R.H. the Prince Consort: Yonge, C.M.

Life of Harriot Stuart, The: Lennox, Charlotte

Life of Harrison Gray Otis, The: Morison, S.E.

Life of Heinrich Heine: †Macleod, Fiona

Life of Henry Fawcett: Stephen, *Sir* Leslie

Life of Henry St. John, Lord Viscount Bolingbroke, The: Goldsmith, Oliver

Life of Ivan the Terrible: Graham, Stephen

Life of J.C. Patteson: Yonge, C.M.

Life of James Crichton, of Cluny: Tytler, P.F.

Life of Jane Austen: Smith, Goldwin

Life of Jefferson S. Batkins, member from Cranberry Centre: Jones, J.S.

Life of Jesus, The: Murry, John Middleton

Life of Jesus Christ illustrated from the Italian painters of the 14th, 15th and 16th centuries, The: Palgrave, F.T.

Life of John Bright, The: Trevelyan, G.M.

Life of John Graves Simcoe, The: Riddell, W.R.

Life of John Home: Mackenzie, Henry

Life of John Keats: Rossetti, W.M.

Life of John Knox, The: †Preedy, George

Life of John Milton, The: Masson, David

Life of John Owen, The: Moffatt, James

Life of John Pendleton Kennedy, The: Tuckerman, H.T.

Life of John Sterling: Carlyle, Thomas

Life of John Williams: Philips, Ambrose

Life of John Wyckliff, The: Tytler, P.F.

Life of Jonathan Swift, The: Forster, John

Life of Joseph Chamberlain, The: Garvin, J.L.

Life of Katharine Mansfield, The: Murry, John Middleton

Life of King Arthur, The: Ritson, Joseph

Life of King James the First, The: Chambers, Robert

Life of Lady Jane Grey, and of Guildford Dudley, her husband, The: Godwin, William

Life of Lord Bryce: Fisher, H.A.L.

Life of Lord Byron, The: Galt, John

Life of Lord Byron: Noel, R.B.W.

Life of Lord John Russell, The: Walpole, *Sir* Spencer

Life of Lorenzo de' Medici, The: Roscoe, William

Life of Mansie Waugh, The: Moir, D.M.

Life of Maximilien Robespierre, The: Lewes, G.H.

Life of Merlin, surnamed Ambrosius, The: Heywood, Thomas

Life of Michelangelo Buonarotti, The: Symonds, J.A.

Life of Mr. George Herbert, The: Walton, Izaak

Life of Mr. Jonathan Wild the Great, The: Fielding, Henry

Life of Mr. Richard Hooker, The: Walton, Izaak

Life of Mrs. Fitzherbert, The: Leslie, *Sir* J.R. Shane

Life of Mrs. Godolphin, The: Evelyn, John

Life of Mrs. Siddons, The: Campbell, Thomas

Life of Nancy, The: Jewett, S.O.

Life of Napoleon: Baring-Gould, Sabine

Life of Napoleon Buonaparte, The: Hazlitt, William

Life of Napoleon Buonoparte, Emperor of the French, The: Scott, *Sir* Walter

Life of Nathanael Greene, The: Simms, W.G.

Life of Nathaniel Hawthorne: Conway, M.D.

Life of Nelson, The: Southey, Robert

Life of Nelson in a series of episodes, The: Russell, W.C.

Life of Oliver Goldsmith, The: (†Geoffrey Crayon), Irving, Washington

Life of Oscar Wilde, The: Pearson, Hesketh

Life of our Lord, The: Dickens, Charles

Life of P.B. Shelley: †Macleod, Fiona

Life of Patrick Sarsfield, Earl of Lucan: Todhunter, John

Life of Percy Bysshe Shelley, The: Dowden, Edward

Life of Peter the Great: Graham, Stephen

Life of Petrarch, The: Campbell, Thomas

Life of Philip Henry Gosse, The: Gosse, *Sir* Edmund

Life of poetry, The: Rukeyser, Muriel

Life of Pope, The: Courthorpe, W.J.

Life of Rear-Admiral John Paul Jones, The: †Preedy, George

Life of reason, The: Santayana, George

Life of Richard Cobden, The: Morley, John

Life of Richard Jefferies: Thomas, E.E.P.

Life of Richard Nash, of Bath, Esq.: Goldsmith, Oliver

Life of Richard Wagner, The: Newman, Ernest

Life of Robert Browning: †Macleod, Fiona

Life of Robert Burns, The: Chambers, Robert

Life of Robert Burns: Lockhart, J.G.

Life of Ronald Knox, The: Waugh, Evelyn

Life of Rubens, The: Calvert, G.H.

Life of Rudyard Kipling: Dole, N.H.

Life of St. Anselm: Church, Richard

Life of St. David, The: Rhys, Ernest

Life of St. Winifred (trn.): Caxton, William

Life of Samuel Johnson, LL.D.: Boswell, James

Life of Samuel Lover, R.H.A., The: Bernard, W.B.

Life of Schiller, The: Carlyle, Thomas

Life of Shakespeare, The: Pearson, Hesketh

Life of Silas Talbot, The: Tuckerman, H.T.

Life of Sir Alfred Fripp: Roberts, C.E.M.

Life of Sir Arthur Conan Doyle, The: Carr, J.D.

Life of Sir Dudley North, and of Dr. John North, The: North, Roger

Life of Sir Henry Wotton, The: Walton, Izaak

Life of Sir James Fitzjames Stephen, The: Stephen, *Sir* Leslie

Life of Sir John Franklin: Traill, H.D.

Life of Sir Mark Sykes: Leslie, *Sir* J.R. Shane

Life of Sir Martin Frobisher: McFee, William

Life of Sir Paul Vinogradoff: Fisher, H.A.L.

Life of Sir Ralph Lane, The: Hale, E.E.

Life of Sir T. Pope, founder of Trinity College, Oxford, The: Warton, Thomas

Life of Sir Walter Raleigh: Oldys, William

Life of Sir Walter Raleigh: Shirley, John

Life of Sir Walter Raleigh: Tytler, P.F.

Life of Sir Walter Scott: Chambers, Robert

Life of Sir William Harcourt, The: Gardiner, A.G.

Life of Spencer Perceval, The: Walpole, *Sir* Spencer

Life of Stonewall Jackson, The: Cooke, John Esten

Life of the bee, The (trn.): Sutro, Alfred

Life of the Buddha, The: Beck, *Mrs.* Lily

Life of the Chevalier Bayard, The: Simms, W.G.

Life of the dead, The: Riding, Laura

Life of the Duke of Newcastle, The: Firth, *Sir* Charles Harding

Life of the Earl of Mayo, A: Hunter, *Sir* William Wilson

Life of the fields, The: Jefferies, Richard

Life of King Henry the eighth, The: Shakespeare, William

Life of King Henry the eighth: Tytler, P.F.

Life of the Marquis of Dufferin and Ava, The: Lyall, *Sir* Alfred C.

Life of the renowned Sir Philip Sidney, The: Grenville, *Sir* Fulke

Life of the Rev. Andrew Bell, The: Southey, Robert

Life of the spirit and the life of today, The: Underhill, Evelyn

Life of the white devil, The: Bax, Clifford

Life of Thomas Cranmer, A: Pollard, A.F.

Life of Thomas Jefferson, third president of the United States, The: Tucker, George

Life of Thomas Ken D.D., The: Bowles, William Lisle

Life of Thomas Love Peacock, The: Van Doren, Carl

Life of Thomas Paine, The: Conway, Moncure Daniel

Life of Thomas Stothard, The: Bray, Anna Eliza

Life of Tim Healy, The: O'Flaherty, Liam

Life of Vice-Admiral William Bligh, The: Mackaness, George

Life of W.E. Forster: Reid, *Sir* Thomas Wemyss

Life of W.E. Gladstone, The: Reid, *Sir* Thomas Wemyss

Life of W.M. Thackeray: Merivale, H.C.

Life of Washington, A: Paulding, J.K.

Life of Washington Irving, The: Stoddard, R.H.

Life of Wesley, The: Southey, Robert

Life of William Bedell, The: Burnet, Gilbert

Life of William Cecil: Collins, Arthur

Life of William Cobbett, The: Hone, William

Life of William Congreve, The: Gosse, *Sir* Edmund

Life of William Dummer Powell, The: Riddell, W.R.

Life of William Ewart Gladstone, The: Morley, John

Life of William Lord Russell, The: Russell, *Lord* John

Life of William Morris: Mackail, J.W.

Life of William Pitt: Stanhope, P.H., *Earl*

Life of William Shakespeare, The: Halliwell, J.O.

Life of William Shakespeare, The: Lee, *Sir* Sidney

Life on the Mississippi: (†Mark Twain), Clemens, S.L.

Life rarely tells: Lindsay, Jack

Life romantic, The: Le Gallienne, Richard

Life story: Bentley, Phyllis

Life the goal: Krishnamurti, J.

Life, travels and books of Alexander von Humboldt, The: Stoddard, R.H.

Life with father: Day, C.S.

Life with mother: Day, C.S.

Life with Topsy: Mackail, Denis

Life within reason: Brown, Ivor

Life without and life within: Fuller, Margaret

Life worth living, The: Dixon, Thomas

Life-line, The: Bottome, Phyllis

Lifemanship: Potter, Stephen

Life's assize, A: Riddell, *Mrs*. J.H.

Life's fairy tales: Mitchell, J.A.

Life's handicap: Kipling, Rudyard

Life's lessons, A: Gore, Catherine

Life's little ironies: Hardy, Thomas

Life's little oddities: Lynd, Robert

Life's morning, A: Gissing, George

Life's picture history of World War II: Dos Passos, John

Life's progress through the passions: Haywood, *Mrs*. Eliza

Life's ransom, A: Marston, J.W.

Life's secret, A: Wood, Ellen

Life's sunny side: Nesbit, Edith

Life's testament: Blocksidge, C.W.

Life's treasure book: Sheldon, C.M.

Life's vagaries: O'Keeffe, John

Lift up your hearts: Scott, F.G.

Lifted and subsided rocks of America: Catlin, George

Lifted masks: Glaspell, Susan

Lifted spear, The: Moll, E.G.

Lifted veil, The: †Eliot, George

Lifted veil, The: †King, Basil

Light: a narrative poem: †Miller, Joaquin

Light above the lake: Strong, L.A.G.

Light and the dark, The: Snow, C.P.

Light and twilight: Thomas, E.E.P.

Light articles only: Herbert, *Sir* A.P.

Light beyond, The: Oppenheim, E. Phillips

Light bondell of livly discourses, A: Churchyard, Thomas

Light for them that sit in darkness: Bunyan, John

Light freights: Jacobs, W.W.

Light heart, The: Hewlett, Maurice

Light horse: Higgins, Matthew James

Light horse Harry Lee: Boyd, Thomas

Light in August: Faulkner, William

Light in Italy: Lindsay, Jack

Light in the clearing, The: Bacheller, Irving

Light in the forest, The: Richter, Conrad

Light infantry ball, The: Basso, Hamilton

Light of Asia, or the great renunciation, The: Arnold, Edwin

Light of Christ: Underhill, Evelyn

Light of day, The: Ambler, Eric

Light of day, The: Burroughs, John

Light of heart, The: Williams, Emlyn

Light of her countenance, The: Boyesen, H.H.

Light of the star, The: Garland, Hamlin

Light of the world, or the great consummation, The: Arnold, Edwin

Light of western stars, The: Grey, Zane

Light on a dark horse: Campbell, Roy

Light over Lundy: Mais, S.P.B.

Light princess, The: Macdonald, George

Light refreshment: Ridge, W. Pett

Light that failed, The: Kipling, Rudyard

Light that lies, The: McCutcheon, G.B.

Light that never was, The: Gerould, Katharine

Light the lights: Herbert, *Sir* A.P.

Light through the cloud: Strong, L.A.G.

Light woman: Gale, Zona

Lightbody on liberty: Balchin, Nigel

Lighted way, The: Oppenheim, E. Phillips

Lighter side of Irish life, The: Hannay, J.O.

Lighter side of school life, The: (†Ian Hay), Beith, *Sir* John Hay

Light-fingered gentry: Phillips, D.G.

Lighting-up time: Brown, Ivor

Lightning conductors and lightning guards: Lodge, *Sir* Oliver

Lightning meditations: Knox, R.A.

Lightning-rod dispenser, The: Carleton, William (McKendree)

Lights and shadows of American life: Mitford, Mary Russell

Lights and shadows of Irish life: Hall, Anna Maria

Lights and shadows of London life: Payn, James

Lights around the shore, The: Weidman, Jerome

Lights in the alley: Bodenheim, Maxwell

Lights on Yoga: Ghose, Sri Aurobindo

Lik: Nabokov, Vladimir

Like a bulwark: Moore, M.C.

Like a lover: Wescott, Glenway

Like and Unlike: Braddon, M.E.

Like father, like son: Payn, James

Likely story, A: De Morgan, W.F.

Likely story, A: Housman, Laurence

Likely story, A: Howells, W.D.

Lilac domino, The: Maltby, H.F.

Lilac fairy book, The: Lang, Andrew

Lilac sunbonnet, The: Crockett, S.R.

Lilian: Bennett, Arnold

Lilies and leopards: Dalton, A.C.

Lilith: Macdonald, George

Lilith: Sterling, George

Lilla, a part of her life: Lowndes, M.A.

Lillian: Praed, W.M.

Lilliesleaf: Oliphant, Margaret

Lilliput: Garrick, David

Lilliput lectures: Rands, W.B.

Lilliput legends: Rands, W.B.

Lilliput levee: Rands, W.B.

Lilliput revels: Rands, W.B.

Lilt of life, The: Cross, Zora

Lily and the bee, The: Warren, Samuel

Lily and the cross, The: De Mille, James

Lily and the cross, The: Nesbit, Edith

Lily and the totem, The: Simms, W.G.

Lily Christine: Arlen, Michael

Lily of Malud, The: Squire, Sir J.C.

Lily of the valley: Jones, Jack

Limbo: Huxley, Aldous

Limbo: Lee, Vernon

Limestone tree, The: Hergesheimer, Joseph

Limitations: Benson, E.F.

Limits and renewals: Kipling, Rudyard

Limits of exact science as applied to history, The: Kingsley, Charles

Lin McLean: Wister, Owen

Lincoln: Markham, Edwin

Lincoln: Mee, Arthur

Lincoln and Whitman miscellany, A: Sandburg, Carl

Lincoln centenary ode: Mackaye, Percy

Lincoln frees the slaves: Leacock, Stephen

Lincoln the leader, and Lincoln's genius for expression: Gilder, R.W.

Lincoln, the man: Masters, E.L.

Lincoln, the world emancipator: Drinkwater, John

Lincoln's grave: Thompson, J.M.

Lincolnshire tragedy, The: Manning, Anne

Linda Condon: Hergesheimer, Joseph

Linda Shawn: Mannin, Ethel

Linda Tressel: Trollope, Anthony

Linden tree, The: Priestley, J.B.

Lindleys Kays: Pain, B.E.O.

Lindsay's luck: Burnett, Frances Hodgson

Line o' cheer for each day o' the year, A: Bangs, J.K.

Line of life, A: Ford, John

Line of love, The: Cabell, James Branch

Lineage of Lichfield, The: Cabell, James Branch

Lines: McArthur, Peter

Lines from Deepwood: Bourinot, A.S.

Lines in memory of Edmund Morris: Scott, D.C.

Lines in pleasant places: †Mrs. Partington

Lines long and short: Fuller, Henry Blake

Lines of religious enquiry: Smith, Goldwin

Lines on leaving the Bedford Street schoolhouse: Santayana, George

Lines on the death of ... [i.e. R.B. Sheridan]: Moore, Thomas

Lines on the death of Princess Charlotte: Croly, George

Lines on the inaugural meeting of the Shelley Society: Lang, Andrew

Lines sacred to the memory of the Rev. James Grahame: Wilson, John

Lines to the recorder: Halleck, Fitz-Greene

Lines written at Ampthill Park in the autumn of 1818: Luttrell, Henry

Lines written in the 'Prometheus unbound': Beddoes, T.L.

Lines written to an Indian air: Anand, M.R.

Lingua: Tomkis, Thomas

Lingual exercises for advanced vocabularies: Sassoon, Siegfried

Linhay on the downs: Williamson, Henry

Links in the chain of life: Orczy, Baroness

Linnet: Allen, Grant

Linnet's nest, The: Newbolt, Sir Henry

Linwoods, The: Sedgwick, C.M.

Lion and jackal: Brownlee, Frank

Lion and the fox, The: Lewis, P. Wyndham

Lion and the honeycomb, The: Blackmur, R.P.

Lion and the lamb, The: Oppenheim, E. Phillips

Lion and the unicorn, The: †Dane, Clemence

Lion and the unicorn, The: Davies, R.H.

Lion and the unicorn: Linklater, Eric

Lion and the unicorn, The: †Orwell, George

Lion in the garden, A: Stern, G.B.

Lion of St. Mark, The: Henty, G.A.

Lion of the north, The: Henty, G.A.

Lion tamer, The: Hull, E.M.

Lion, the witch and the wardrobe, The: Lewis, C.S.

Lionel and Clarissa: Bickerstaffe, Isaac

Lionel Deerhurst: Blessington, Marguerite

Lionel Lincoln: Cooper, J. Fenimore

Lion-man: Cripps, A.S.

Lions and lambs: †West, Rebecca

Lions and shadows: Isherwood, Christopher

Lion's cub, The: Stoddard, R.H.

Lions in the path: White, S.E.

Lion's share, The: Bennett, Arnold

Lion's skin, The: Sabatini, Rafael

Lion's whelp, The: Barr, A.E.H.

Lion-tamer, The: Drake, Brockman, H.

Lipton story, The: Waugh, Alec

Lise Lillywhite: Sharp, Margery

List of English plays, A: Greg, W.W.

List of masques, A: Greg, W.W.

List of the members of the Society of Antiquaries, from 1717–96, A: Nichols, John

List, ye landsmen!: Russell, W.C.

Listen again, children!: (Stephen Southwold), †Bell, Neil

Listen children!: (Stephen Southwold), †Bell, Neil

Listen to the country: Mais, S.P.B.

Listen to the mocking-bird: Perelman, S.J.

Listen to the people: Benét, S.V.

Listener, The: Blackwood, Algernon

Listeners, The: De la Mare, Walter

Listener's guide to invitation to learning, A: Van Doren, Mark

Listener's lure: Lucas, E.V.

Listerdale mystery, The: Christie, Agatha

Liszt: Sitwell, Sacheverell

Litany for those in the train, A: Baring, Maurice

Litany of Washington street, The: Lindsay, N.V.

Literally true: Stein, Gertrude

Literary and general lectures and essays: Kingsley, Charles

Literary and social essays: Curtis, G.W.

Literary and social judgments: Greg, W.R.

Literary and social silhouettes: Boyesen, H.H.

Literary anecdotes of the eighteenth century: Nichols, John

Literary capital of the United States, The: Mencken, H.L.

Literary chameleon, A: Logan, J.D.

Literary chronicle, 1920–1950: Wilson, Edmund

Literary criticism: a short history: Brooks, Cleanth

Literary discipline, The: Erskine, John

Literary distractions: Knox, R.A.

Literary essays: Daiches, David

Literary essays: Morley, John

Literary fallacy: De Voto, Bernard

Literary friends and acquaintances: Howells, W.D.

Literary geography: †Macleod, Fiona

Literary heritage of New Jersey, The: Williams, W.C.

Literary history of England in the end of the eighteenth and beginning of the nineteenth century: Oliphant, Margaret

Literary history of the English people, A: Jusserand, Jean

Literary history of the United States: Canby, Henry Seidel

Literary ideals in Ireland: Yeats, W.B.

Literary illustrations of the Bible: Moffat, James

Literary industries: Bancroft, H.H.

Literary lapses: Leacock, Stephen

Literary life and miscellanies, The: Galt, John

Literary love-letters: Herrick, Robert

Literary memoirs of the nineteenth century: Woodberry, G.E.

Literary mind, its place in an age of science, The: Eastman, Max

Literary pilgrim in England, A: Thomas, E.E.P.

Literary recreations and miscellanies: Whittier, J.G.

Literary relics: Addison, Joseph

Literary remains, The: Coleridge, S.T.

Literary remains of William Hazlitt: Lytton, E.G.E.B., *1st Baron*

Literary sense, The: Nesbit, Edith

Literary sessions: Partridge, Eric

Literary situation, The: Cowley, Malcolm

Literary studies: Bagehot, Walter

Literary studies and reviews: Aldington, Richard

Literary taste: Bennett, Arnold

Literary values: Burroughs, John

Literati, The: Poe, Edgar Allen

Literature and authorship in India: Iyengar, K.R. Srinivasa

Literature and authorship in New Zealand: Mulgan, A.E.

Literature and dogma: Arnold, Matthew

Literature and life: Howells, W.D.

Literature and morality: Farrell, James

Literature and politics: Cole, G.D.H.

Literature and psychology: Lucas, F.L.

Literature and reality: Fast, Howard M.

Literature and revolution: Hicks, Granville

Literature and society: Daiches, David

Literature and the American college: Babbitt, Irving

Literature and the press: Dudek, Louis

Literature and western man: Priestley, J.B.

Literature at nurse: Moore, George

Literature in my time: Mackenzie, *Sir* Compton

Literature in New South Wales: Barton, George

Literature in the making: Kilmer, Joyce

Literature in the making, A: McFarlane, J.E.C.

Literature in the theatre: Darlington, W.A.

Literature of Bengal, The: Dutt, R.C.

Literature of crime: †Queen, Ellery

Literature of Nova Scotia, The: MacMechan, A.M.

Literature of the Rail, The: Phillips, Samuel

Lithuania: Brooke, Rupert

Litter of the rose leaves, The: Benét, S.V.

Little accident: Dell, Floyd

Little Admiral, The: McIlwraith, J.N.

Little and good: Housman, Laurence

Little angel, The: Lynd, Robert

Little Anna Mark: Crockett, S.R.

Little ark, A: Shirley, James

LittleArthur's guide to Humbug: Vulliamy, C.E.

Little black dog: Herrick, Robert

Little black pony, The: Moodie, Susanna

Little blue ghost, The: Logan, J.D.

Little Blue Hood: Miller, Thomas

Little blue light, The: Wilson, Edmund

Little book for every day, A: Sheldon, C.M.

Little book of Canadian essays, A: Burpee, Lawrence J.

Little book of friends, A: Spofford, H.E.

Little book of profitable tales, A: Field, Eugene

Little book of Tribune verse, A: Field, Eugene

Little book of Western verse, A: Field, Eugene

Little book, thy pages stir: Lampman, Archibald

Little bookroom, The: Farjeon, Eleanor

Little boy lost, A: Hudson, W.H.

Little brother: Cannan, Gilbert

Little brown jug at Kildare, The: Nicholson, Meredith

Little boxes: Mitchison, Naomi

Little brick church, The: Falkner, W.C.

Little Brown Mouse books: Uttley, Alison

Little Caesar: Burnett, W.R.

Little cages, The: Seymour, W.K.

Little camp on Eagle Hill, The: Warner, S.B.

Little Charlie: Aldrich, Thomas Bailey

Little chatterbox: Hall, Anna Maria

Little children: Saroyan, William

Little child's monument, A: Noel, R.B.W.

Little child's prayer, A: Carman, Bliss

Little church of the leaves, The: Carman, Bliss

Little city of hope, The: Crawford, F.Marion

Little clown lost, A: Benefield, Barry

Little company, The: Dark, Eleanor

Little country girl, A: Coolidge, Susan

Little critic, The: Lin Yu-T'ang

Little damozel, The: Hoffe, Monckton

Little dark man, The: Poole, Ernest

Little David: Connelly, Marc

Little Devil Doubt: †Onions, Oliver

Little dinner at Timmins's and the Bedford-Row conspiracy, A: Thackeray, W.M.

Little dinners with the Sphinx: Le Gallienne, Richard

Little dog laughed, The: Merrick, Leonard

Little Dorrit: Dickens, Charles

Little dream, The: Galsworthy, John

Little drummer, The: Harte, Bret

Little dry thorn, The: (†Gordon Daviot), Mackintosh, Elizabeth

Little Duke, The: Yonge, C.M.

Little England: Kaye-Smith, Shiela

Little England beyond Wales: Mais, S.P.B.

Little English gallery, A: Guiney, L.I.

Little entertainments: Pain, B.E.O.

Little essays: Santayana, George

Little essays of love and virtue: Ellis, Havelock

Little Esson: Crockett, S.R.

Little field by the sea, The: Carman, Bliss

Little fire engine, The: Greene, Graham

Little flocks guarded against grievous wolves: Mather, Cotton

Little flutter: Bramah, E.

Little folk life: Dodge, May Abigail

Little foxes: Cooke, Rose Terry

Little foxes: Stowe, Harriet Beecher

Little French girl, The: Sedgwick, A.D.

Little Frenchman and his water lots, The: Morris, G.P.

Little friend, The: Marshall, Bruce

Little gentleman from Okehampstead, The: Oppenheim, E. Phillips

Little giant, The: English, T.D.

Little Gidding: Eliot, T.S.

Little girl among the Old Masters, A: Howells, W.D.

Little girl and boy land: Widdemer, Margaret

Little girls, The: Bowen, E.D.C.

Little green man, The: Wallace, Edgar

Little green school, The: Brazil, Angela

Little green shutter, The: Whitlock, Brand

Little Grey Rabbit and the weasels: Uttley, Alison

Little Grey Rabbit goes to sea: Uttley, Alison

Little Grey Rabbit makes lace: Uttley, Alison

Little Grey Rabbit to the rescue: Uttley, Alison

Little Grey Rabbit's birthday: Uttley, Alison

Little Grey Rabbit's Christmas: Uttley, Alison

Little Grey Rabbit's party: Uttley, Alison

Little Grey Rabbit's washing day: Uttley, Alison

Little guest, The: Molesworth, Mrs.

Little Ham: Hughes, J.L.

Little Hannah Lee: Wilson, John

Little hearts: Pickthall, M.L.C.

Little Henrietta: Reese, L.W.

Little horse bus, The: Greene Graham

Little hunch-back, The: O'Keeffe, John

Little hunchback Zia, The: Burnett, Frances Hodgson

Little Ike Templin: Johnston, R.M.

Little Iliad, The: Hewlett, Maurice

Little Joe: Bonwick, James

Little journey, A: Crothers, Rachel

Little journey in the world, A: Warner, C.D.

Little journeys: Hubbard, Elbert

Little Karoo, The: Smith, Pauline

Little king, The: Bynner, Witter

Little king, A: Major, Charles

Little knife that did all the work, The: Uttley, Alison

Little knight of labor, A: Coolidge, Susan

Little lady of the big house, The: London, Jack

Little ladyship: (†Ian Hay), Beith, *Sir* John Hay

Little lambs eat ivy: Langley, Noel

Little lame prince, The: Craik, *Mrs.* Dinah

Little land, The: Housman, Laurence

Little Larrikin, The: Turner, E.S.

Little learning, A: Waugh, Evelyn

Little less than gods, A: Ford, Ford Madox

Little liberty, The: Brighouse, Harold

Little Lion: Mieke: Whitlock, Brand

Little Loo, The: Russell, W.C.

Little loot, A: Knox, E.V.

Little Lord Fauntleroy: Burnett, Frances Hodgson

Little maid and the gentleman, The: Wordsworth, William

Little man and other satires, The: Galsworthy, John

Little Manx nation, The: Caine, *Sir* T.H. Hall

Little master, The: Trowbridge, J.T.

Little masters, The: Scott, W.B.

Little Maud: Aldrich, Thomas Bailey

Little men: Alcott, Louisa M.

Little men: Burnett, W.R.

Little Mexican: Huxley, Aldous

Little Minister, The: Barrie, *Sir* J.M.

Little Minx, A: Cambridge, Ada

Little miracle, The: Akins, Zoë

Little Miss Joy-Sing: Long, J. L.

Little Miss Mischief: Coolidge, Susan

Little Miss Peggy: Molesworth, *Mrs.*

Little monasteries, The: †O'Connor, Frank

Little Mother Bunch: Molesworth, *Mrs.*

Little Mother Meg: Turner, E.S.

Little Mr. Bouncer and his friend, Verdant Green: †Bede, Cuthbert

Little Mr. Thimblefinger and his queer country: Harris, Joel Chandler

Little Mrs. Manington: Roberts, C.E.M.

Little New World idyls: Piatt, J.J.

Little Norsk, A: Garland, Hamlin

Little novels: Collins, Wilkie

Little novels of Italy: Hewlett, Maurice

Little novels of nowadays: Gibbs, *Sir* Philip

Little nugget, The: Wodehouse, P.G.

Little nurse of Cape Cod, The: Warner, S.B.

Little old Admiral, The: Golding, Louis

Little old portrait: Molesworth, *Mrs.*

Little Orvie: Tarkington, Booth

Little pardner: Porter, E.H.

Little Pedlington and the Pedlingtonians: Poole, John

Little people, The: Halper, Albert

Little pilgrim in the unseen, A: Oliphant, Margaret

Little plays for children: Edgeworth, Maria

"Little plays" handbook, The: Housman, Laurence

Little plays of St. Francis: Housman, Laurence

Little plum: Godden, Rumer

Little poems from the Greek: Leaf, Walter

Little pretty pocket book intended for the instruction and amusement of little Master Tommy and pretty Miss Polly, A: Newbery, John

Little princess, The: Traill, C.P.

Little prisoner, The: Moodie, Susanna

Little Pussy Willow: Stowe, Harriet Beecher

Little red foot, The: Chambers, R.W.

Little red fox and the wicked uncle: Uttley, Alison

Little red horses: Stern, G.B.

Little red shoes: Brighouse, Harold

Little regiment, The: Crane, Stephen

Little Saint Elizabeth: Burnett, Frances Hodgson

Little savage, The: Marryatt, Frederick

Little school, The: Moore, T.S.

Little schoolmaster Mark, The: Shorthouse, J.H.

Little shepherd of kingdom come, The: Fox, John

Little sister, The: Chandler, Raymond

Little songs: Pickthall, M.L.C.

Little soul, The: †Mordaunt, Elinor

Little steamroller, The: Greene, Graham

Little steel: Sinclair, Upton

Little stories: Mitchell, S.W.

Little Sunshine's holiday: Craik, *Mrs.* Dinah

Little Swiss sojourn, A: Howells, W.D.

Little tales of Smethers, The: Dunsany, E.J.M.D.P.

Little tea, a little chat, A: Stead, C.E.

Little things: Stephens, James

Little Tiger: (†Anthony Hope), Hawkins, Anthony Hope

Little tin gods-on-wheels, The: Grant, Robert

Little Tommy Ticker: Coolidge, Susan

Little tour in France, A: James, Henry

Little tour in Ireland, A: Hole, Samuel Reynolds

Little Treasure Island: Mee, Arthur

Little Tu'penny: Baring-Gould, Sabine

Little tyrannies: Vachell, H.A.

Little Union Scout, A: Harris, Joel Chandler

Little verses and big names: Allen, James Lane

Little wars: Wells, H.G.

Little way ahead, A: Sullivan, Alan

Little white bird, The: Barrie, *Sir* J.M.

Little white hag, The: †Beeding, Francis

Little white king: Steen, Marguerite

Little white thought, The: Malleson, Miles

Little women: Alcott, Louisa M.

Little wonder-horn, The: Ingelow, Jean

Little world, The: Benson, Stella

Littleholme: Bottomley, Gordon

Live and kicking Ned: Masefield, John

Live and learn: Lathom, Francis

Live and let live: Chase, Stuart

Live and let live: Sedgwick, C.M.

Livelihood: Gibson, Wilfred

"Lively boys! Lively boys!": (†Mrs. Partington), Shillaber, B.P.

Lively lady, The: Roberts, Kenneth

Lively Peggy, The: Weyman, Stanley

Livery companies of the City of London, The: Hazlitt, W.C.

Lives and characters of the English dramatick poets, The: Langbaine, Gerard

Lives and exploits of English Highwaymen, The: Whitehead, Charles

Lives and speeches of Abraham Lincoln and Hannibal Hamlin: Howells, W.D.

Lives of a Bengal Lancer: Yeats-Brown, F.C.C.

Lives of Boulton and Watt: Smiles, Samuel

Lives of celebrated statesmen: Adams, John Quincy

Lives of Cleopatra and Octavia: Fielding, Sarah

Lives of destiny, as told for the Reader's Digest: Peattie, D.C.

Lives of distinguished American Naval Officers: Cooper, James Fenimore

Lives of Edward and John Philips, nephews and pupils of Milton, The: Godwin, William

Lives of eminent men: Aubrey, John

Lives of famous poets: Rossetti, W.M.

Lives of game animals: Seton-Thompson, E.

Lives of good servants: Manning, Anne

Lives of James Madison and James Monroe, The: Adams, J.Q.

Lives of men of letters and science, in the time of George III: Brougham, Henry

Lives of Robert Young Hayne and Hugh Swinton Legaré: Hayne, P.H.

Lives of Scottish worthies: Tytler, P.F.

Lives of Simon Lord Lovat, and Duncan Forbes of Culloden: Burton, John Hill

Lives of the British admirals: Southey, Robert

Lives of the British Saints: Baring-Gould, Sabine

Lives of the engineers: Smiles, Samuel

Lives of the English Saints: Church, Richard

Lives of the English saints, The: Pattison, Mark

Lives of the hunted: Seton-Thompson, E.

Lives of the literary and scientific men of Italy, Spain, etc.: Montgomery, James

Lives of the Necromancers: Godwin, William

Lives of the noble Grecians and Romanes, The: North, *Sir* Thomas

Lives of the novelists: Scott, *Sir* Walter

Lives of the players, The: Galt, John

Lives of the poets: Untermeyer, Louis

Lives of the princesses of England, from the Conquest: Green, Mary Anne

Lives of the saints, The: Baring-Gould, Sabine

Lives of the saints for children: Molesworth, *Mrs.*

Lives of the III Normans, Kings of England, The: Hayward, *Sir* John

Lives of the wits: Pearson, Hesketh

Lives of wives: Riding, Laura

Livestock in barracks: †Armstrong, Anthony

Living: Green, Henry

Living alone: Benson, Stella

Living and the dead, The: White, Patrick

Living city: Wright, Frank Lloyd

Living for appearances: Mayhew, Augustus Septimus

Living ideas in America: Commager, H.S.

Living Jefferson, The: Adams, J.T.

Living languages, The: Stephen, J.K.

Living link, The: De Mille, James

Living London: Sala, G.A.H.

Living lotus, The: Mannin, Ethel

Living machinery: Hill, A.V.

Living novel, The: Hicks, Granville

Living novel, The: Pritchett, V.S.

Living present, The: Atherton, Gertrude

Living room, The: Greene, Graham

Living sadness, A: Taylor, John

Living space: Allen, Walter Ernest

Living theatre: Rice, Elmer

Living theatre: the Gordon Craig School, A: Craig, *Sir* Edward Gordon

Living thoughts of Darwin, The: Huxley, *Sir* Julian

Living thoughts of Tom Paine, The: Dos Passos, John

Living together: Sutro, Alfred

Living torch, The: Gibbon, Monk

Living torch, The: Russell, W.G.

Livingstone in Africa: Noel, R.B.W.

Liza of Lambeth: Maugham, Somerset

Lizzie Borden: Lowndes, M.A.

Lizzie Leigh: Gaskell, *Mrs.* Elizabeth

Lizzie Norton of Greygrigg: Linton, Eliza

Llangollen Vale: Seward, Anna

Loaded dice: Fawcett, Edgar

Loaded stick, The: Jacob, Naomi

Loaves and fishes: Maugham, Somerset

Lobelia Grove: Vulliamy, C.E.

Lob-lie-by-the-fire: Ewing, *Mrs.* Juliana Horatia

Lobo: Kantor, Mackinlay

Lobo, Rag and Vixen: Seton-Thompson, E.

Lobsters on the agenda: Mitchison, Naomi

Local and regional government: Cole, G.D.H.

Local government for beginners: Cole, M.I.

Local habitation, A: Lindsay, Jack

Local self-government in Bombay: Masani, *Sir* R.P.

Lochandu: Lauder, *Sir* Thomas Dick

Lochinvar: Crockett, S.R.

Loci critici: Saintsbury, G.E.B.

Locke Amsden: Thompson, D.P.

Locked book, The: Packard, F.L.

Locked chest, The: Masefield, John

Locke's travels in France, 1675–9: Locke, John

Locket, The: Masters, E.L.

Locksley Hall: Tennyson, Alfred *Lord*

Locksley Hall sixty years after: Tennyson, Alfred *Lord*

Lockwood concern, The: O'Hara, J.H.

Locrine: Swinburne, A.C.

Locusts and wild honey: Burroughs, John

Lodge in the wilderness, A: Buchan, John

Lodger, The: Lowndes, M.A.

Lodges in the wilderness: Scully, W.C.

Lodgings for single gentlemen: Poole, John

Lodore: Shelley, Mary

Log from the Sea of Cortez, The: Steinbeck, John

Log of a cowboy, The: Adams, Andy

Log of a Halifax privateer, The: MacMechan, A.M.

Log of a lame duck, The: Brown, A.A.

Log of the sun, The: Beebe, William

Logan: Neal, John

Logic of political economy, The: De Quincey, Thomas

Logic, the theory of inquiry: Dewey, John

Logopandecteision: Urquhart, *Sir* Thomas

Lohengrin: Bangs, John Kendrick

Lois the witch: Gaskell, *Mrs.* Elizabeth

Loiterer's harvest: Lucas, E.V.

Loiterings of travel: Willis, N. P.

Lola of the chocolates: (†James James), Adams, Arthur H.

Lolita: Nabokov, Vladimir

Lollington Downs: Masefield, John

Lolly Dink's doings: Stoddard, E.D.

Lolly Willowes: Warner, Sylvia Townsend

Lombard Street: Bagehot, Walter

Londini Artium & Scientiarum Scaturigo: Heywood, Thomas

Londini Emporia: Heywood, Thomas

Londini sinus salutis: Heywood, Thomas

Londini speculum: Heywood, Thomas

Londini status pacatus: Heywood, Thomas

Londinium defensum: Knox, R.A.

Londinium Redivivum: Evelyn, John

London: Besant, *Sir* Walter

London: Brown, Ivor

London: Knight, Charles

London: Lathom, Francis

London: Lucas, E.V.

London: Morton, H.V.

London, a book of aspects: Symons, Arthur

London: a poem: Johnson, Samuel

London adventure, The: †Machen, Arthur

London afresh: Lucas, E.V.

London belongs to me: Collins, Norman

London book of English verse, The: Dobrée, Bonamy

London bookman, A: Swinnerton, Frank

London characters: Mayhew, Henry

London craftsmen: Quennell, Marjorie

London diary (1717–21), The: Byrd, William

London drollery: or, the wits academy: Hicks, William "Captain"

London education: Webb, Sidney

London farrago, A: Lewis, D.B. Wyndham

London films: Howells, W.D.

London front: Brighouse, Harold

London has a garden: †Dane, Clemence

London hermit, The: O'Keeffe, John

London impressions: Meynell, Alice

London in the eighteenth century: Besant, *Sir* Walter

London in the nineteenth century: Besant, *Sir* Walter

London in the time of the Stuarts: Besant, *Sir* Walter

London in the time of the Tudors: Besant, *Sir* Walter

London labour and the London poor: Mayhew, Henry

London lavender: Lucas, E.V.

London life: Bennett, Arnold

London life, A: James, Henry

London looke backe: Dekker, Thomas

London lovers: Mackail, Denis

London Magazine, The: Hood, Thomas

London merchant, The: Lillo, George

London morning: Coward, Noel

London music in 1888-1889: Shaw, G.B.

London nights: Graham, Stephen

London nights: Symons, Arthur

London only: Ridge, W.Pett

London perceived: Pritchett, V.S.

London please: Ridge, W.Pett

London poems: Buchanan, R.W.

London pride: Bottome, Phyllis

London pride: Braddon, M.E.

London Programme, The: Webb, S.J.

London reverie, A: Squire, *Sir* J.C.

London Review, The: Cumberland, Richard

London revisited: Lucas, E.V.

London river: Tomlinson, H.M.

London rose, A: Rhys, Ernest

London scene: Massingham, Harold

London sonnets: Wolfe, Humbert

London south of the Thames: Besant, *Sir* Walter

London spy, The: Ward, Edward

London stone: Rubenstein, H.F.

London street games: Douglas, Norman

London Terraefilius, The: Ward, Edward

London to Ladysmith via Pretoria: Churchill, *Sir* Winston

London tradesmen: Trollope, Anthony

London types: Henley, W.E.

London types taken from life: Ridge, W.Pett

London up to date: Sala, G.A.H.

London venture, The: Arlen, Michael

London visions: Binyon, Laurence

London voluntaries: Henley, W.E.

London Wall: Van Druten, J.W.

London year, The: Morton, H.V.

Londoners, The: Hichens, R.S.

Londoner's Post: Swinnerton, Frank

London's heart: Farjeon, B.L.

Londons jus honorarium: Heywood, Thomas

Londons lamentable estate, in any great visitation: Massinger, Philip

Londons love: Munday, Anthony

London's river: Rothenstein, *Sir* John

Londons tempe: Dekker, Thomas

Lone house, The: Barr, A.E.H.

Lone House Mystery, The: Wallace, Edgar

Lone inn, The: Hume, F.W.

Lone ranche, The: Reid, T.M.

Lone Star Ranger, The: Grey, Zane

Lone striker, The: Frost, Robert

Lone swallows, The: Williamson, Henry

Lone wolf. The story of Jack London: Calder-Marshall, Arthur

Loneliest girl in the world: Fearing, Kenneth

Loneliest mountain: Davies, W.H.

Lonely, The: Gallico, Paul

Lonely bungalow, The: †Taffrail

Lonely dancer, The: Le Gallienne, Richard

Lonely God,: The Stephens, James

Lonely house, The: Lowndes, M.A.

Lonely lady of Dulwich, The: Baring, Maurice

Lonely man, The: Frankau, Gilbert

Lonely O'Malley: Stringer, A.J.A.

Lonely pleasures: †George, Daniel

Lonely plough, The: Holme, Constance

Lonely road, The: Farnol, J.J.

Lonely road, The: †Shute, Nevil

Lonely unicorn, The: Waugh, Alec

Lonely voice, The: †O'Connor, Frank

Lonesome bar: MacInnes, T.R.E.

Lonesome places: Derleth, A.W.

Lonesome road: Green, Paul

Lonesome-like: Brighouse, Harold

Long ago: †Field, Michael

Long ago told: Wright, H.B.

Long alert, The: Gibbs, *Sir* Philip

Long arm, The: Oppenheim, E.Phillips

Long arm of Mannister, The: Oppenheim, E.Phillips

Long chance: †Brand, Max

Long Christmas dinner, The: Wilder, Thornton

Long day's journey into night: O'Neill, Eugene

Long dream, The: Wright, Richard

Long farewell: (†Michael Innes), Stewart, J.I.M.

Long feud, The: Untermeyer, Louis

Long goodbye, The: Chandler, Raymond

Long horns, The: Dobie, J.F.

Long hunt: Boyd, James

Long journey, The: Housman, Laurence

Long knives: Eggleston, G.C.

Long land Chile, The: Beals, Carleton

Long live the King!: Rinehart, Mary Roberts

Long love, The: Buck, Pearl

Long mirror, The: Priestley, J.B.

Long night, The: Weyman, Stanley

Long odds: Clarke, Marcus

Long patrol, The: Cody, H.A.

Long pea-shooter, The: Layton, Irving

Long pennant: La Farge, Oliver

Long remember: Kantor, MacKinlay

Long retrospect, A: †Anstey, F.

Long rifle, The: White, S.E.

Long road of woman's memory, The: Addams, Jane

Long story, A: Pye, H.J.

Long street, The: Davidson, Donald

Long sunset, The: Sherriff, R.C.

Long time ago, A: Kennedy, Margaret

Long trail, The: Garland, Hamlin

Long trick, The: †Bartimeus

Long valley, The: Steinbeck, John

Long view, The: Beresford, J.D.

Long way from home, A: McKay, Claude

Long week-end, The: Graves, Robert

Long week-end, A: Kennedy, Margaret

Long white cloud, The: Reeves, W.P.

Longest day, The: Clough, Arthur Hugh

Longest journey, The: Forster, E.M.

Longest lane, The: (Stephen Southwold), †Bell, Neil

Longest reign, The: Courthorpe, W.J.

Longhorn feud: †Brand, Max

Longleat of Kooralbyn: Praed, *Mrs*. C.

Long-lost father: Stern, G.B.

Longus: Moore, George

Look after Lulu: Coward, Noel

Look at all those roses: Bowen, E.D.C.

Look back and laugh: Herbert, *Sir* A.P.

Look homeward, angel: Wolfe, T.C.

Look out upon the stars, my love: Pinkney, E.C.

Look round literature, A: Buchanan, R.W.

Look, stranger!: Auden, W.H.

Look: the sun: Sitwell, Edith

Look to the lady: Allingham, Margery

Look! we have come through: Lawrence, D.H.

Look who's talking!: Perelman, S.J.

Looke to it: Rowlands, Samuel

Looke up and see wonders: Dekker, Thomas

Looker-on, The: Munro, Neil

Looking after Joan: Palmer, J.L.

Looking at life: Dell, Floyd

Looking at life: Sala, G.A.H.

Looking back: Douglas, Norman

Looking backward 2000–1887: Bellamy, Edward

Looking before and after: Murry, John Middleton

Looking beyond: Lin Yu-T'ang

Looking forward and others: Tarkington, Booth

Looking glass, The: Cloete, E.F.S.G.

Looking glass, The: Godwin, William

Looking glass conference, The: Blunden, Edmund

Looking glass 9: Steen, Marguerite

Looking glasse for London and England, A: Lodge, Thomas and Robert Greene

Looking toward sunset: Child, Lydia Maria

Looking-glass for landlords, A: Warburton, R.E.E.

Looking-glass house and what Alice saw there: †Carroll, Lewis

Loom of destiny, The: Stringer, A.J.A.

Loom of dreams, The: Symons, Arthur

Loom of years, The: Noyes, Alfred

Loom of youth, The: Waugh, Alec

Loony Cove, The: Mickle, A.D.

Loose leaves: (†Elzevir), Murdoch, *Sir* W.L.F.

Loose sketches: Thackeray, W.M.

Loosening, The: Bottrall, Ronald

Loot from the Temple of Fortune: Vachell, H.A.

Loot of cities, The: Bennett, Arnold

Loraine: Evans, G.E.

Lorca: Campbell, Roy

Lord Adrian: Dunsany, E.J.M.D.P.

Lord and the Vassal, The: Palgrave, *Sir* Francis

Lord Arthur Savile's crime: Wilde, Oscar

Lord Auckland's triumpho: †Pindar, Peter

Lord Baden-Powell: Fast, Howard M.

Lord Brokenhurst: Brydges, *Sir* Samuel Egerton

Lord Byron and some of his contemporaries: Hunt, Leigh

Lord Byron, Christian virtues: Knight, G.W.

Lord Byron's helmet: Elliott, M.H.

Lord Byron's marriage: Knight, G.W.

Lord Chancellor's speech on parliamentary reform, in the House of Lords, The: Brougham, Henry

Lord Chatham at Chevening: Stanhope, P.H., *Earl*

Lord Chesterfield, his life, character and opinions: and George Selwyn, his life and times: Hayward, Abraham

Lord Chumley: Belasco, David

Lord Cromer: Traill, H.D.

Lord Cromer as a man of letters: Gosse, *Sir* Edmund

Lord Edgeware dies: Christie, Agatha

Lord Emsworth and others: Wodehouse, P.G.

Lord fish, The: De la Mare, Walter

Lord Grey of the Reform Bill: Trevelyan, G.M.

Lord Harry Bellair: Manning, Anne

Lord Hermitage, The: Grant, James

Lord Hornblower: Forester, C.S.

Lord, I was afraid: Balchin, Nigel

Lord Jim: Conrad, Joseph

Lord John Russell and Mr. Macaulay on the French Revolution: Stanhope, P.H., *Earl*

Lord Kilgobbin: Lever, Charles James

Lord Kitchener: Bridges, Robert

Lord M.: Cecil, *Lord* David

Lord Macaulay: Milman, H.H.

Lord Mayor of London: Ainsworth, Harrison

Lord Milner and his work: Fitzpatrick, *Sir* J.P.

Lord Minto: Buchan, John

Lord Montagu's page: James, G.P.R.

Lord Oakburn's daughters: Wood, Ellen

Lord of life, The: †Bell, Neil

Lord of misrule, The: Noyes, Alfred

Lord of the Bedchamber, The: Howe, Joseph

Lord of the harvest: Housman, Laurence

Lord of the isles, The: Scott, *Sir* Walter

Lord of the manor, The: Burgoyne, *Sir* John

Lord of the manor, The:Herbert, H.W.

Lord of the rings, The: Tolkien, J.R.R.

Lord of the sea, The: Shiel, M.P.

Lord of the silver dragon: Salverson, L.G.

Lord of the sorcerers: †Carter Dickson

Lord of Wensley, The: Raymond, Ernest

Lord Ormont and his Aminta: Meredith, George

Lord Pengo: Behrman, S.N.

Lord Peter views the body: Sayers, Dorothy

Lord Raingo: Bennett, Arnold

Lord Randolph Churchill: Churchill, *Sir* Winston

Lord Salisbury: Mee, Arthur

Lord Samarkand: Vachell, H.A.

Lord Saxondale: Reynolds, G.

Lord Scales: Swinburne, A.C.

Lord Soulis: Swinburne, A.C.

Lord Strathcona, the story of his life: Willson, H.B.

Lord Timothy Dexter of Newburyport, Mass.: Marquand, J.P.

Lord Tony's wife: Orczy, *Baroness*

Lord Vyet: Benson, A.C.

Lords and Commons: †O'Connor, Frank

Lords and masters: Garnett, Edward

Lords and masters: Macdonell, A.G.

Lords of high decision, The: Nicholson, Meredith

Lords of the air: Stephen, A.M.

Lords of the ghostland, The: Saltus, E.E.

Lord's song: a sermon, The: Gill, Eric

Lord's supper in the wilderness, The: Kirby, William

Lord's will, The: Green, Paul

Lorenzo bunch, The: Tarkington, Booth

Lorenzo Lotto: Berenson, Bernhard

Loretta Mason Potts: Chase, M.C.

Lorgnette, The: Bangs, John Kendrick

Lorgnette, The: Mitchell, D.G.

Loring mystery, The: Farnol, J.J.

Lorna Doone: Blackmore, *Sir* R.D.

Lorraine: Chambers, R.W.

Los cerritos: Atherton, Gertrude

Lose with a smile: Lardner, Ring

Loser takes all: Greene, Graham

Losing game, The: Crofts, F.W.

Losing of Virel, The: Willson, H.B.

Loss and gain: Newman, J.H.

Loss of Atalante, The: MacMechan, A.M.

Loss of the Jane Vosper, The: Crofts, F.W.

Lost: Collins, Dale

Lost and won: Machar, A.M.

Lost battle: Graham, Stephen

Lost borders: Austin, Mary

Lost Buffalo: Bacon, Leonard

Lost cabin mine, The: Niven, F.J.

Lost cause, The: Mackenzie, *Sir* Compton

Lost chart, The: Gunn, Neil M.

Lost child, The: Anand, M.R.

Lost child, The: Flint, Timothy

Lost child, The: Kingsley, Henry

Lost childhood, The: Greene, Graham

Lost Christmas presents, The: Mottram, R.H.

Lost colony, The: Green, Paul

Lost crusade, The: Muir, D.C.A.

Lost earl, The: Trowbridge, J.T.

Lost Earl of Ellan, The: Praed, *Mrs.* C.

Lost ecstasy: Rinehart, Mary Roberts

Lost Eden, A: Braddon, M.E.

Lost Eden, The: Watson, *Sir* J.W.

Lost empires: Priestley, J.B.

Lost Endeavour: Masefield, John

Lost face: London, Jack

Lost for love: Braddon, M.E.

Lost Galleon, The: Harte, Bret

Lost gallows, The: Carr, J.D.

Lost Gip, †Stretton, Hesba

Lost girl, The: Lawrence, D.H.

Lost glen, The: Gunn, Neil M.

Lost hat, The: Percy, Edward

Lost haven: Tennant, Kylie

Lost heiress, The: Glanville, Ernest

Lost hero, A: Ward, E.S.

Lost horizon: Hilton, James

Lost in the backwoods: Traill, C.P.

Lost in the fog: De Mille, James

Lost in the stars: Anderson, Maxwell

Lost island: Hall, J.N.

Lost jewel, A: Spofford, H.E.

Lost king, The: Sabatini, Rafael

Lost lady, A: Cather, Willa

Lost lady of old years, A: Buchan, John

Lost lawyer, The: Hannay, J.O.

Lost leader: Cournos, John

Lost leader, The: Fausset, Hugh

Lost leader, The: Oppenheim, E. Phillips

Lost leader, The: Robinson, E.S.L.

Lost leaders: Lang, Andrew

Lost lectures: Baring, Maurice

Lost Lenore: Reid, T.M.

Lost lover, The: Manley, *Mrs.*

Lost morning: Heyward, DuBose

Lost mountain, The: Reid, T.M.

Lost name, A: Le Fanu, Sheridan

Lost one, The: Steen, Marguerite

Lost paradise: Coffin, Robert

Lost Pibroch, The: Munro, Neil

Lost planet: Wellesley, D.V.

Lost poem, A: Crane, Stephen

Lost prince, The: Burnett, Frances Hodgson

Lost property: Ridge, W.Pett

Lost pueblo: Grey, Zane

Lost regiment, The: Glanville, Ernest

Lost road, The: Davis, R.H.

Lost shipmate, The: Roberts, T.G.

Lost silk hat, The: Dunsany, E.J.

Lost silver of Briffault, The: Barr, A.E.H.

Lost Sir Massingbird: Payn, James

Lost son, The: Gore, Catherine

Lost, stolen, or strayed: Molesworth, *Mrs.*

Lost Stradivarius, The: Falkner, John Meade

Lost tales of Miletus: Lytton, E.

Lost Tasmanian race, The: Bonwick, James

Lost 300, The: Cullen, Countée

Lost Titian, The: Stringer, A.J.A.

Lost tools of learning, The: Sayers, Dorothy

Lost tribes, The: Hannay, J.O.

Lost trumpet, The: Mitchell, J.L.

Lost valley, The: Blackwood, Algernon

Lost valley: Gerould, Katharine

Lost viol, The: Shiel, M.P.

Lost wagon train, The: Grey, Zane

Lost word, The: Underhill, Evelyn

Lost world, The: Doyle, *Sir* Arthur Conan

Lost world of the Kalahari, The: Van der Post, Laurens

Lot Barrow: Meynell, Viola

Lot of gems, A: Cole, E.W.

Lot of talk, A: Ashton, Helen

Lothair: Disraeli, Benjamin

Lotos-eating: Curtis, G.W.

Lots lane: Wellesley, D.V.

Lot's wife: Eastman, Max

Lotta Schmidt: Trollope, Anthony

Lottery, The: Fielding, Henry

Lottery of life, The: Blessington, Marguerite

Lottery of marriage, The: Trollope, Frances

Lottery ticket, The: Trowbridge, J.T.

Lottie Dundass: Bagnold, Enid

Lotus and Jewel: Arnold, Edwin

Lotus eaters, The: Tennyson, Alfred *Lord*

Lotus flower: Quinn, R.J.

Lou Gehrig: Gallico, Paul

Louder and funnier: Wodehouse, P.G.

Lough Corrib and Lough Mask: Wilde, *Sir* William Robert Wills

Louis Norbert: Lee, Vernon

Louisa: Seward, Anna

Louisa Pallant: James, Henry

Louisana: Burnett, Frances Hodgson

Louise: Meynell, Viola

Louise de la Vallière: Tynan, Katharine

Louise Imogen Guiney: Brown, Alice

Lounger, The: Mackenzie, Henry

Loup-Garou!: Phillpotts, Eden

Lousiad, The: †Pindar, Peter

Love: Bury, *Lady* C.S.M.

Love: Cannan, Gilbert

Love: De la Mare, Walter

Love: Dobell, Sydney Thompson

Love: Hale, S.J.B.

Love: Russell, E.M.

Love à la mode: Macklin, Charles

Love, a poem: Elliott, Ebenezer

Love affair: Farjeon, Eleanor

Love affairs of a bibliomaniac, The: Field, Eugene

Love all: Sayers, Dorothy

Love among the artists: Shaw, G.B.

Love among the chickens: Wodehouse, P.G.

Love among the haystacks: Lawrence, D.H.

Love among the lions: †Anstey, F.

Love among the paint pots: Jennings, Gertrude

Love among the ruins: Deeping, Warwick

Love among the ruins: Thirkell, Angela

Love among the ruins: Waugh, Evelyn

Love and a birdcage: Royde-Smith, Naomi

Love and a bottle: Farquhar, George

Love and a sword: Brown, G.D.

Love and business: Farquhar, George

Love and death: Fisher, V.A.

Love and death: Ghose, Sri Aurobindo

Love and death: Powys, L.C.

Love and desire and hate: †Bell, Neil

Love and friendship: Austen, Jane

Love and hatred: Lowndes, M.A.

Love, and how to cure it: Wilder, Thornton

Love and Julian Farne: †Bell, Neil

Love and liberation: Wheelock, J.H.

Love and lore: Saltus, E.E.

Love and Lucy: Hewlett, Maurice

Love and marriage: Ashford, Daisy

Love and mesmerism: Smith, Horatio

Love and money: Bentley, Phyllis

Love and money: Caldwell, Erskine Preston

Love and money: Reade, Charles

Love and Mr. Lewisham: Wells, H.G.

Love and pride: Hook, T.E.

Love and revenge: Settle, Elkanah

Love and sleep: Morris, *Sir* Lewis

Love and the Lieutenant: Chambers, R.W.

Love and the loveless: Williamson, Henry

Love and the philosopher: †Corelli, Marie

Love and the soul hunters: †Hobbes, John Oliver

Love and the soul maker: Austin, Mary

Love and the universe: Watson, A.D.

Love and truth: Walton, Izaak

Love at all ages: Thirkell, Angela

Love at first sight: Royde-Smith, Naomi

Love at Paddington: Ridge, W.Pett

Love at second sight: Malleson, Miles

Love by express: Wiggin, K.D.

Love complex, The: Dixon, Thomas

Love concealed, The: Housman, Laurence

Love conquers all: Benchley, Robert

Love eternal: Haggard, *Sir* H. Rider

Love finds the way: Ford, Paul Leicester

Love for an hour is love forever: Barr, A.E.H.

Love for love: Congreve, William

Love for Lydia: Bates, H.E.

Love, freedom and society: Murry, John Middleton.

Love from a stranger: Christie, Agatha

Love has no resurrection: †Delafield, E.M.

Love, here is my hat: Saroyan, William

Love hunger: Maltby, H.F.

Love idylls: Crockett, S.R.

Love in a City: Bickerstaffe, Isaac

Love in a cold climate: Mitford, Nancy

Love in a cottage: Deniehy, D.H.

Love in a Greenwich village: Dell, Floyd

Love in a life: Monkhouse, A.N.

Love in a mist: Cunningham, John

Love in a riddle: Cibber, Colley

Love in a village: Bickerstaffe, Isaac

Love in a wood: Wycherley, William

Love in Albania: Linklater, Eric

Love in excess: Haywood, *Mrs.* Eliza

Love in idleness: Crawford, Francis Marion

Love in idleness: Rattigan, Terence

Love in Mildensee: Royde-Smith, Naomi

Love in old cloathes: Bunner, Henry Cuyler

Love in our time: Collins, Norman

Love in Pernicketty Town: Crockett, S.R.

Love in several masques: Fielding, Henry

Love in the desert: Binyon, Laurence

Love in the machine age: Dell, Floyd

Love in the New Testament: Moffat, James

Love in the sun: Walmsley, Leo

Love in the United States: Hergesheimer, Joseph

Love in these days: Waugh, Alec

Love in winter: Jameson, Storm

Love is enough: Morris, William

Love is less than God: Cannan, Gilbert

Love is like that: Roberts, C.E.M.

Love is the sum of it all: Eggleston, G.C.

Love laughs at locksmiths: Colman, George, *the younger*

Love letters between a nobleman and his sister: Behn, *Mrs.* Afra

Love letters of Mrs. Piozzi, written when she was eighty, to W.A. Conway: Thrale, H.L.

Love letters of the king: Le Gallienne, Richard

Love lyrics and songs of Proteus, The: Blunt, W.S.

Love makes a man: Cibber, Colley

Love match, The: Bennett, Arnold

Love me for ever: Buchanan, R.B.

"Love me little love me long": Reade, Charles

Love Muti: Blackburn, Douglas

Love nest, The: Lardner, Ring

Love of books, The: Hunt, Leigh

Love of fame: Young, Edward

Love of gain, The: Lewis, M.G.

Love of Ireland: poems and ballads: Sigerson, Dora

Love of King David and fair Bethsabe, and the tragedie of Absalon, The: Peele, George

Love of life: London, Jack

Love of long ago, The: †Corelli, Marie

Love of order, The: Graves, Richard

Love of Parson Lord, The: Freeman, Mary

Love of Proserpine: Hewlett, Maurice

Love of seven dolls: Gallico, Paul

Love on Smoky River: Roberts, T.G.

Love on the dole: Greenwood, Walter

Love or marriage: Black, William

Love or money: Hannay, J.O.

Love passage, A: Jacobs, W.W.

Love poems: Davies, W.H.

Love poems: Patchen, Kenneth

Love poems and others: Lawrence, D.H.

Love poems of Myrrhine and Konallis, The: Aldington, Richard

Love provoked: Davies, Rhys

Love rack, The: Roberts, C.E.M.

Love redeemed: †Baylebridge, W.

Love respelt: Graves, Robert

Love songs: Teasdale, Sara

Love songs and elegies: Ghose, Manmohan

Love sonnets of a cave man: Marquis, Don

Love sonnets of Proteus, The: Blunt, Wilfred

Love stories: Rinehart, M.R.

Love the conqueror worm: Layton, Irving

Love thief, The: †Bowen, Marjorie

Love triumphant: Dryden, John

Love without money: Dell, Floyd

Love-at-arms: Sabatini, Rafael

Love-chase, The: Knowles, James Sheridan

Loved and envied, The: Bagnold, Enid

Loved and lost!: Meredith, L.A.

Loved and the lost, The: Callaghan, M.E.

Loved at last: Lemon, Mark

Loved Helen: White, T.H.

Loved one, The: Waugh, Evelyn

Love-in-a-Mist: Gale, Norman

Lovel the widower: Thackeray, W.M.

Love-letters of Walter Bagehot and Eliza Wilson, The: Bagehot, Walter

Loveliest stories in the world, The: Mee, Arthur

Loveliest thing, The: Pertwee, Roland

Lovelight: †Maurice, Furnley

Loveliness: Ward, E.S.

Lovels of Arden, The: Braddon, M.E.

Lovely ambition, The: Chase, M.E.

Lovely is the Lee: Gibbings, Robert

Lovely lady, The: Austin, Mary

Lovely lady, The: Lawrence, D.H.

Lovely land, The: Mannin, Ethel

Lovely shall be choosers, The: Frost, Robert

Lovely ship, The: Jameson, Storm

Lover, The: †Dane, Clemence

Lover, The: Royde-Smith, Naomi

Lover, The: Steele, *Sir* Richard

Lover and husband: (†Ennis Graham), Molesworth, *Mrs.*

Lover and the reader, The: Steele, *Sir* Richard

Lover of the land, A: Niven, F.J.

Lover under another name: Mannin, Ethel

Lovers, The: Phillpotts, Eden

Lovers and friends: Smith, Dodie

Lovers and heroines of the poets, The: Stoddard, R.H.

Lovers are losers: Pertwee, Roland

Lover's breast-knot, A: Tynan, Katherine

Lovers courageous (film):†Lonsdale, Frederick

Lover's ephemeris, A: Lavater, Louis

Lover's diary, A: Parker, *Sir* H.G.

Lover's gift: Tagore, *Sir* R.

Lovers in London: Milne, A.A.

Lover's knots: †Bowen, Marjorie

Lover's Lane: Fitch, Clyde William

Lover's leap: Armstrong, M.D.

Lovers made men: Jonson, Ben

Lovers melancholy, The: Ford, John

Lovers of Louisiana: Cable, George Washington

Lovers of silver: Mais, S.P.B.

Lover's revolt, A: De Forest, John William

Lovers' Saint Ruth's: Guiney, L.I.

Lovers' song book, The: Davies, W.H.

Lover's tale, A: Hewlett, Maurice

Lover's tale, The: Tennyson, Alfred *Lord*

Love's a jest: Motteux, P.A.

Love's alibi: Widdemer, Margaret

Love's blindness: Glyn, Elinor

Love's calendar: Hoffman, C.F.

Love's cross currents: Swinburne, A.C.

Loves crueltie: Shirley, James

Love's cruelty: Symons, Arthur

Love's cure: Beaumont, Francis

Love's dilemmas: Herrick, Robert

Love's frailties: Holcroft, Thomas

Love's hour: Glyn, Elinor

Love's illusion: Beresford, J.D.

Love's labour lost: Grant, James

Love's labours lost: Shakespeare, William

Love's last shift: Cibber, Colley

Love's lovely counterfeit: Cain, J.M.

Loves maistresse: Heywood, Thomas

Love's martyr: Reid, T.M.

Love's meinie: Ruskin, John

Loves metamorphosis: Lyly, John

Love's morrow: Alcott, A.B.

Loves of Lancelot, The: Dyson, E.G.

Loves of Mars and Venus, The: Motteux, P.A.

Loves of Miss Anne, The: Crockett, S.R.

Loves of Pelleas and Etarre, The: Gale, Zona

Loves of Sally Brown and Ben the Carpenter, The: Hood, Thomas

Loves of the angels, The: Moore, Thomas

Loves of the Harem: Reynolds, G.

Loves of the plants, The: Darwin, Erasmus

Loves of the poets: Le Gallienne, Richard

Love's old sweet song: Saroyan, William

Love's pilgrim: Beresford, J.D.

Love's pilgrim: Logan, J.D.

Love's pilgrimage: Sinclair, Upton

Love's provocations: †Bede, Cuthbert

Love's revenge: Moore, T.I.

Loves riddle: Cowley, Abraham

Loves sacrifice: Ford, John

Love's triumph: Motteux, P.A.

Loves triumph through Callipos: Jonson, Ben

Love's victory: Chamberlayne, William

Love's victory: Farjeon, B.L.

Love's widowhood, and other poems: Austin, Alfred

Love's winnowing: Mannin, Ethel

Love-songs of childhood: Field, Eugene

Love-story of Aliette Brunton, The: Frankau, Gilbert

Loving: Green, Henry

Loving ballad of Lord Bateman, The: Thackeray, W.M.

Loving brothers, The: Golding, Louis

Loving history of Peridore and Paravail, The: Hewlett, Maurice

Loving mad Tom: Lindsay, Jack

Loving spirit, The: du Maurier, Daphne

Low life: De la Roche, Mazo

Low notes on a high level:Priestley, J.B.

Low tide on the Grand-Pré: Carman, Bliss

Lower slopes, The: Allen, Grant

Lower than vermin: †Yates, Dornford

Lower thirteen: Carleton, William (McKendree)

Lowery road, The: Strong, L.A.G.

Lowest rung, The: Cholmondeley, Mary

Lowland soldier: Fergusson, *Sir* Bernard

Lowland Venus, The: Gibbons, Stella

Low's Russian sketch book: Martin, B.K.

Loyal brother, The: Southern, Thomas

Loyal general, The: Tate, Nahum

Loyal incendiary, The: Pordage, Samuel

Loyal lover: Widdemer, Margaret

Loyal subject, The: Beaumont, Francis

Loyal to the school: Brazil, Angela

Loyalists: Roberts, T.G.

Loyall convert, The: Quarles, Francis

Loyalties: Drinkwater, John

Loyalties: Galsworthy, John

Loyalty and devotion of colored Americans in the revolution and war of 1812, The: Garrison, W.L.

Loyalty, aristocracy and jingoism: Smith, Goldwin

Lu of the Ranges: †Mordaunt, Elinor

Lucan's Pharsalia: May, Thomas

Lucas, king of the Balucas: Adamic, Louis

Lucasta: Lovelace, Richard

Lucia in London: Benson, E.F.

Lucia's progress: Benson, E.F.

Lucid intervals: (†Elzevir), Murdoch, *Sir* W.L.F.

Lucifer: Powys, John Cowper

Lucifer: Santayana, George

Lucifer and the child: Mannin, Ethel

Lucile: (†Owen Meredith), Lytton, E.B. *Earl*

Lucinda: (†Anthony Hope), Hawkins, Anthony Hope

Lucinda Brayford: Boyd, Martin

Lucius: Manley, *Mrs.*

Lucius Davoren, of publicans and sinners: Braddon, M.E.

Lucius Junius Brutus: Lee, Nathaniel

Luck of Barry Lyndon, The: Thackeray, W.M.

Luck of Gerard Ridgeley, The: Mitford, Bertram

Luck of Norman Dale, The: Pain, B.E.O.

Luck of Roaring Camp, The: Harte, Bret

Luck of the Bodkins, The: Wodehouse, P.G.

Luck of the Darrells, The: Payn, James

Luck of the Grilse, The: MacMechan, A.M.

Luck of the vails, The: Benson, E.F.

Luck of the year: Lucas, E.V.

Luck or cunning: Butler, Samuel

Luckiest girl in the school, The: Brazil, Angela

Lucky bag: Rowe, Richard

Lucky chance, The: Behn, *Mrs.* Afra

Lucky dog: (†Ian Hay), Beith, *Sir* John Hay

Lucky ducks: Molesworth, *Mrs.*

Lucky finger, The: Robinson, E.S.L.

Lucky Lear: Jones, Jack

Lucky mistake, The: Behn, *Mrs.* Afra

Lucky number, The: (†Ian Hay), Beith, *Sir* John Hay

Lucky one, The: Milne, A.A.

Lucky penny, The: Hall, Anna Maria

Lucky poet: †McDiarmid, Hugh

Lucky Sam McCarver: Howard, S.C.

Lucky Spence's last advice: Ramsay, Allan

Luckypenny: Marshall, Bruce

Lucrece: Shakespeare, William

Lucretia: Lytton, E.G.E.B., *1st Baron*

Lucretia Borgia: Swinburne, A.C.

Lucretilius: Cory, W.

Lucretius: Mallock, W.H.

Lucretius on life and death: Mallock, W.H.

Luctor and Emergo: †Bowen, Marjorie

Lucubrations: Graves, Richard

Lucy: De la Mare, Walter

Lucy and Colin: Tickell, Thomas

Lucy Arlyn: Trowbridge, J.T.

Lucy Carmichael: Kennedy, Margaret

Lucy Crofton: Oliphant, Margaret

Lucy Crown: Shaw, Irwin

Lucy Gayheart: Cather, Willa

Lucy Harding: Holmes, M.J.

Lucy Hosmer: Thompson, D.P.

Lucy Howard's journal: Sigourney, L.H.

Lucy in her pink jacket: Coppard, A.E.

Lucy Raymond: Machar, A.M.

Lucy Temple: Rowson, S.H.

Ludibria Lunae: Courthorpe, W.J.

Ludlow's memoirs: Firth, *Sir* Charles Harding

Ludmila: Gallico, Paul

Luigi of Cantazaro: Golding, Louis

Luke Baldwin's vow: Callaghan, M.E.

Luke Branwhite: †Bell, Neil

Lume spento, A: Pound, Ezra

Lunatic republic, The: Mackenzie, *Sir* Compton

Lunch: †George, Daniel

Lunch basket, The: Ridge, W. Pett

Luncheon, A: Beerbohm, *Sir* Max

Lundy's Lane: Scott, D.C.

Lure of New Zealand book collecting: Anderson, J.C.

Lure of Piper's Glen, The: Roberts, T.G.

Lure of Thunder Island, The: Walmsley, Leo

Luria: Browning, Robert

Lusiad, The (trans. from Camoens): Mickle, W.J.

Lusoria: Feltham, Owen

Lustra: Pound, Ezra

Lute-girl of Rainyvale, The: Cross, Zora

Luther: Montgomery, Robert

Luttrell of Arran: Lever, C.J.

Lux orientalis: Glanvill, Joseph

Lycanthrope: Phillpotts, Eden

Lycian shore, The: Stark, Freya

Lycidas: Milton, John

Lydia: (†E.V. Cunningham) Fast, Howard M.

Lydia Bailey: Roberts, Kenneth

Lydia Gilmore: Jones, H.A.

Lyf of our Lady, The: Lydgate, John

Lyfe of Johan Picus Erle of Myrandula, The: More, *Sir* Thomas

Lyfe of Seint Albon and the Lyfe of Saint Amphabel, The: Lydgate, John

Lyfe of the blessed martyr Saynte Thomas, The: Barclay, Alexander

Lying lover, The: Steele, *Sir* Richard

Lying prophets: Phillpotts, Eden

Lying valet, The: Garrick, David

Lyme garland, A: Palgrave, F.T.

Lynde Weiss: an autobiography: Thorpe, T.B.

Lyndesay: Connell, John

Lyndley waters: †Preedy, George

Lyra Apostolica: Keble, John

Lyra Apostolica: Newman, J.H.

Lyra apostolica: Williams, Isaac

Lyra Australia: Leakey, C.W.

Lyra Evangelistica: Cripps, A.S.

Lyra frivola: Godley, A.D.

Lyra innocentium: Keble, John

Lyra sacra: Kirkconnell, Watson

Lyre and lancet: †Anstey, F.

Lyric, The: Drinkwater, John

Lyric bough, The: Scollard, Clinton

Lyric consolations: Stevenson, J.H.

Lyric gems: Smith, S.F.

Lyric odes for the year 1785: †Pindar, Peter

Lyric odes to the Royal Academicians: †Pindar, Peter

Lyric plays: Bottomley, Gordon

Lyric year, The: MacDonald, W.P.

Lyrical poems: Dixon, R.W.

Lyrical poetry of Thomas Hardy, The: Day-Lewis, C.

Lyrics and legends of Christmastide: Scollard, Clinton

Lyrics and love songs: Pike, Albert

Lyrics by † The Letter H: Halpine, C.G.

Lyrics from a library: Scollard, Clinton

Lyrics from the Chinese: Waddell, Helen

Lyrics from the hills: Bourinot, A.S.

Lyrics of a low brow: Service, Robert

Lyrics of earth: Lampman, Archibald

Lyrics of Florida: Scollard, Clinton

Lyrics of iron and mist: Campbell, W.W.

Lyrics of nature: O'Hara, J.B.

Lyrics of the dawn: Scollard, Clinton

Lyrics of the dread Redoubt: Campbell, W.W.

Lyrics on freedom, love and death: Cameron, G.F.

Lyrics unromantic: Gustafson, Ralph

Lysbeth: Haggard, *Sir* H.Rider

Lysistrata: Housman, Laurence

Lytton Strachey: Beerbohm, *Sir* Max

Lytton Strachey, a critical study: Iyengar, K.R.Srinivasa

M

M. or N.: Whyte-Melville, G.J.

M.P.: Moore, Thomas

M.P.: Robertson, T.W.

M.P. for the Rotten Borough, The: Lemon, Mark

MW-XX3: Pertwee, Roland

Ma Cinderella: Wright, H.B.

Ma Jones: Tennant, Kylie

Mabel in Queer Street: Mackenzie, *Sir* Compton

Mabel Martin: Whittier, J.G.

Mabel Vaughan: Cummins, Maria Susanna

Macaire: Henley, W.E.

Macaire: Stevenson, R.L.

Macaque: Cloete, E.F.S.G.

Macaria: Evans, A.J.

Macaulay: Bryant, *Sir* Arthur

Macbeth: Shakespeare, William

Macbeth production, A: Masefield, John

MacCarthy More: Lover, Samuel

Macdermots of Ballycloran, The: Trollope, Anthony

Macduff: Uttley, Alison

MacFlecknoe: Dryden, John

Machiavelli: Morley, John

Machiavells dogge: Breton, Nicholas

Machiavels ghost: Heywood, Thomas

Machine, The: Sinclair, Upton

Machine politics and the remedy: Curtis, G.W.

Machiners of socialist planning, The: Cole, G.D.H.

Mackenzie, Baldwin, LaFontaine, Hincks: Leacock, Stephen

Mackerel sky: Ashton, Helen

Mackinac and Lake stories: Catherwood, Mary

Macleod of Dare: Black, William

Macquarie's world: Barnard, M.

Mad Anthony Wayne: Boyd, Thomas

Mad Barbara: Deeping, Warwick

Mad fashions, od fashions, all out of fashion: Taylor, John

Mad grandeur: Gogarty, O. St. John

Mad hatter mystery, The: Carr, J.D.

Mad lady's garland, A: Pitter, Ruth

Mad lover, The: Motteux, P.A.

Mad Sir Uchtred of the hills: Crockett, S.R.

Mad verse, sad verse, glad verse and bad verse: Taylor, John

Mad Willoughby's, The: Linton, Eliza

Mad world, my masters, A: Middleton, Thomas
Madagascar: Defoe, Daniel
Madam: Oliphant, Margaret
Madam: Sidgwick, Ethel
Madam Crowl's ghost: Le Fanu, Sheridan
Madam How and Lady Why: Kingsley, Charles
Madam Izán: Praed, *Mrs.* C.
Madam Jolicoeur's cat: Janvier, T.A.
Madam Julia's tale: Royde-Smith, Naomi
Madam Life's lovers: Lindsay, Norman
Madame: Oppenheim, E. Phillips
Madame Bovary: Levy, Benn W.
Madame Butterfly: Belasco, David
Madame Butterfly: Long, J.L.
Madame de Pompadour: Mitford, Nancy
Madame de Treymes: Wharton, Edith
Madame Delphine Carancro: Cable, G.W.
Madame fears the dark: Irwin, Margaret
Madame Midas: Hume, F.W.
Madame Pompadour: †Lonsdale, Frederick
Madame Prince: Ridge, W. Pett
Madame Roland: Tarbell, Ida
Madcap of the school, The: Brazil, Angela
Madcap violet: Black, William
Made for man: Herbert, *Sir* A.P.
"Made in France": Bunner, H.C.
Madeira holiday: Mais, S.P.B.
Madeira party, A: Mitchell, S.W.
Madeleine: Holmes, M.J.
Madeleine: Kavanagh, Julia
Madeleine heritage, The: (†Martin Mills), Boyd, Martin
Madeline: Bemelmans, Ludwig
Madeline: Opie, Amelia
Madeline and the bad hat: Bemelmans, Ludwig
Madeline and the gypsies: Bemelmans, Ludwig
Madeline Brown's murderer: Adams, Francis

Madeline in London: Bemelmans, Ludwig
Madeline's rescue: Bemelmans, Ludwig
Madelon: Freeman, Mary
Mademoiselle Maria Gloria: †Bowen, Marjorie
Mademoiselle Mathilde: Kingsley, Henry
Made-to-order stories: Canfield, Dorothy
Madge Linsey: Sigerson, Dora
Madir Shah in India: Sarkar, Y.J.
Madness of May, The: Nicholson, Meredith
Madoc: Southey, Robert
Madonna: Carman, Bliss
Madonna Mary: Oliphant, Margaret
Madonna of Carthagena, The: Lowell, Amy
Madonna of the barricades, The: Strachey, J. St. Loe
Madonna of the future, The: James, Henry
Madonna of the peach tree: Hewlett, Maurice
Madonna of the tubs, The: Ward, E.S.
Madonna's Child: Austin, Alfred
Mador of the Moor: Hogg, James
Madras house, The: Granville-Barker, Harley
Madrigals, songs and sonnets: Gosse, *Sir* Edmund
Maelcho: Lawless, Emily
Maelstrom, The: Hanley, James
Maelstrom: Timms, E.V.
Maeoniae: Southwell, Robert
Maga papers about Paris: Tuckerman, H.T.
Magazine miscellanies: Maginn, William
Magdalen, The: McFarlane, John E. Clare
Magdalen Hepburn: Oliphant, Margaret
Magdalene College, Cambridge: Benson, A.C.
Magdalen's husband, A: Percy, Edward
Magde o' the pool: †Macleod, Fiona
Maggie: Crane, Stephen

Maggie: Maltby, H.F.
Maggie Mackenzie: Mottram, R.H.
Maggie Miller: Holmes, M.J.
Magia Adamica: Vaughan, Thomas
Magic: Chesterton, G.K.
Magic and religion: Lang, Andrew
Magic art and the evolution of kings, The: Frazer, *Sir* James
Magic casements: Cripps, A.S.
Magic casements: Farjeon, Eleanor
Magic city, The: Nesbit, E.
Magic egg, The: Stockton, F.R.
Magic flute, The: Dickinson, Goldsworthy Lowes
Magic for Marigold: Montgomery, L.M.
Magic forest, The: White, S.E.
Magic house, The: Scott, D.C.
Magic in my pocket: Uttley, Alison
Magic inkstand, The: Black, William
Magic jacket, The: De la Mare, Walter
Magic lantern, The: Blessington, Marguerite
Magic makers, The: Sullivan, Alan
Magic mirror, The: Wilson, John
Magic number, The: Potter, Stephen
Magic nuts, The: Molesworth, *Mrs.*
Magic of kindness, The: Mayhew, Augustus Septimus
Magic of melody, The: Gibbon, J.M.
Magic of monarchy, The: Martin, B.K.
Magic of my youth, The: Calder-Marshall, Arthur
Magic of sport, mainly autobiographical, The: Gould, Nathaniel
Magic pudding, The: Lindsay, Norman
Magic seas, The: Le Gallienne, Richard
Magic tree, The: Chattopadhyaya, H.
Magic walking-stick, The: Buchan, John

Magic world, The: Nesbit, E.

Magician, The: Maugham, Somerset

Magicians, The: Priestley, J.B.

Magician's nephew, The: Lewis, C.S.

Magician's own book, The: Arnold, George

Magic-lantern murders, The: †Carter Dickson

Magilligan Strand: Hannay, J.O.

Magistrate, The: Pinero, *Sir* A.W.

Magna: Gale, Zona

Magnalia Christi Americana: Mather, Cotton

Magnanimous lover, The: Ervine, St. John

Magnetic lady, The: Jonson, Ben

Magnetic mountain, The: Day-Lewis, C.

Magnificent adventure, The: Hough, Emerson

Magnificent Ambersons, The: Tarkington, Booth

Magnificent entertainment, The: Dekker, Thomas

Magnificent entertainment, The: Middleton, Thomas

Magnolia, The: Parsons, T.W.

Magnolia: Tarkington, Booth

Magnolia Street: Golding, Louis

Magnus Merriman: Linklater, Eric

Magnyfycence: Skelton, John

Magpie and her brood, The: Walpole, Horace

Magpie's nest, The: Paterson, Isabel M.

Mahabharata: Rajagopala-chari, C.

Maharanee: Vijayatunga, Jawaharlal

Mahasen, A: Baring, Maurice

Mahatma and the hare, The: Haggard, *Sir* H.Rider

Mahatma Gandhi: Nehru, Jawa-harlal

Mahatma Gandhi: essays and reflections on his life and work: Radhakrishan, S.

Mahatmaji and the depressed humanity: Tagore, *Sir* R.

Mahomet and his successors: (†Geoffrey Crayon), Irving, Washington

Maid he married, The: Spofford, H.E.

Maid in waiting: Galsworthy, John

Maid Margaret of Galloway: Crockett, S.R.

Maid Marian: Peacock, Thomas Love •

Maid no more: Simpson, H. de G.

Maid of Arragon, The: Cowley, *Mrs.* Hannah

Maid of Brattleboro, The: Carle-ton, William (McKendree)

Maid of France: Brighouse, Harold

Maid of France, The: Lang, Andrew

Maid of honour, The: Massinger, Philip

Maid of Killeena, The: Black, William

Maid of Maiden Lane, The: Barr, A.E.H.

Maid of Old New York, A: Barr, A.E.H.

Maid of Orleans, The: Calvert, G.H.

Maid of Orleans, The: Ireland, W.H.

Maid of Sker, The: Blackmore, *Sir* R.D.

Maid of the marshes: Bird, W.R.

Maid of the mill, The: Bicker-staffe, Isaac

Maid of the mountains, The: †Lonsdale, Frederick

Maid of the Oaks, The: Bur-goyne, *Sir* John

Maid of the river, The: Praed, *Mrs.* C.

Maid-at-arms, The: Chambers, R.W.

Maiden, The: Calvert, G.H.

Maiden and married life of Mary Powell, The: Manning, Anne

Maiden Castle: Powys, John Cowper

Maiden stakes: †Yates, Dorn-ford

Maidens beware: Mitchell, Mary

Maides revenge, The: Shirley, James

Maids and mistresses: Seymour, B.K.

Maids last prayer, The: Southern, Thomas

Maids of Athens: Bottomley, Gordon

Maids of Paradise, The: Cham-bers, R.W.

Maid's tragedy, altered, The: Waller, Edmund

Maids, wives and bachelors: Barr, A.E.H.

Main chance, The: Nicholson, Meredith

Main currents in American thought: Parrington, V.L.

Main entrance: Bercovici, Kon-rad

Main illusions of pacificism, The: Coulton, G.G.

Main line west: Horgan, Paul

Main stream, The: Sherman, S.P.

Main Street: Kilmer, Joyce

Main street: Lewis, H.S.

Maine, a state of grace: Coffin, Robert

Maine ballads: Coffin, Robert

Maine doings: Coffin, Robert

Maine of the sea and pines: Dole, N.H.

Maine woods, The: Thoreau, H.D.

Mainly about fishing: Ransome, A.M.

Mainly on the air: Beerbohm, *Sir* Max

Mainsail haul, A: Masefield, John

Mainstays of Maine: Coffin, Robert

Mainstream: Basso, Hamilton

Main-travelled roads: Garland, Hamlin

Mainwaring: Hewlett, Maurice

Maitland Folio Manuscript, The: Craigie, *Sir* W.A.

Maitland Quarto Manuscript, The: Craigie, *Sir* W.A.

Maiwa's revenge: Haggard, *Sir* H.Rider

Majestic mystery, The: Mackail, Denis

Majesty's rancho: Grey, Zane

Majolo, The: Galt, John

Major, The: †Connor, Ralph

Major Barbara: Shaw, G.B.

Major critical essays: Shaw, G.B.

Major Gahagan: Thackeray, W.M.

Major Jones's courtship: Thompson, W.T.

Major Jones's scenes in Georgia: Thompson, W.T.

Major Jones's sketches of travel: Thompson, W.T.

Major Vigoureux: (†Q) Quiller-Couch, Sir A.

Major Wither's disclaimer: Wither, George

Majorca observed: Graves, Robert

Majorcan holiday: Mais, S.P.B.

Majority rule and minority rights: Commager, H.S.

Majors and their marriages, The: Cabell, James Branch

Major's candlesticks, The: Hannay, J.O.

Major's niece, The: Hannay, J.O.

Makarony fables: Stevenson, J.H.

Make and mend, A: †Bartimeus

Make bright the arrows: Millay, E.St. Vincent

Make it new: Pound, Ezra

Make light of it: Williams, W.C.

Make this your Canada: Scott, F.R.

Make thyself many: Powys, T.F.

Make ventures for Christ's Sake: Newman, J.H.

Make way for Lucia: Van Druten, John

Make your game: Sala, G.A.H.

Make-believe: Milne, A.A.

Maker of history, A: Oppenheim, E.Phillips

Maker of moons, The: Chambers, R.W.

Maker of rainbows: Le Gallienne, Richard

Makers of Australasia, The: Hight, James

Makers of Florence, The: Oliphant, Margaret

Makers of literature: Woodberry, G.E.

Makers of modern Rome, The: Oliphant, Margaret

Makers of the Labour Movement: Cole, M.I.

Makers of the modern world: Untermeyer, Louis

Makers of Venice, The: Oliphant, Margaret

Makeshift: Campion, Sarah

Making a better world: Becker, C.L.

Making crime pay: †Cheyney, Peter

Making his way: Oxley, J.M.

Making, knowing and judging: Auden, W.H.

Making of a bigot, The: Macaulay, Dame Rose

Making of a fortune, The: Spofford, H.E.

Making of a man, The: (†George F.Harrington), Baker, W.M.

Making of a marchioness, The: Burnett, Frances Hodgson

Making of a New Zealander, The: Mulgan, A.E.

Making of a poem, The: Spender, Stephen

Making of a saint, The: Maugham, Somerset

Making of a sentimental bloke, The: Chisholm, A.H.

Making a president: Mencken, H.L.

Making a sister, a mock initiation for ladies: Sargent, Epes

Making of a statesman, The: Harris, Joel Chandler

Making of American civilization, The: Beard, C. and M. Beard

Making of Americans, The: Stein, Gertrude

Making of an immortal, The: Moore, George

Making of Australia, The: (†Elzevir), Murdoch, Sir W.L.F.

Making of Bristol, The: Beals, Carleton

Making of Egypt: Petrie, Sir William Flinders

Making of English, The: Bradley, Dr. Henry

Making of Greater New Haven, The: Beals, Carleton

Making of Man: Lodge, Sir Oliver

Making of Mary, The: McIlwraith, J.N.

Making of personality, The: Carman, Bliss

Making of Rachel Rowe, The: Cambridge, Ada

Making of religion, The: Lang, Andrew

Mal moulée: Wilcox, Ella Wheeler

Malabar and the Dutch: Panikkar, K.M.

Malabar and the Portuguese: Panikkar, K.M.

Malabar farm: Bromfield, Louis

Malady of the ideal, The: Brooks, Van Wyck

Malay archipelago, The: Wallace, A.R.

Malay waters: Tomlinson, H.M.

Malbone: Higginson, T.W.

Malcolm: Macdonald, George

Malcolm Kirk: Sheldon, C.M.

Malcontent, The: Marston, John

Male and female: Mead, Margaret

Male animal, The: Thurber, James

Male coquette, The: Garrick, David

Malgudi days: Narayan, R.K.

Malherbe and the classical reaction in the seventeenth century: Gosse, Sir Edmund

Malice domestic: Percy, Edward

Malice in wonderland: Day-Lewis, C.

Malice of men, The: Deeping, Warwick

Malign fiesta: Lewis, P.Wyndham

Mall, The: Dryden, John

Mallow and Asphodel: Trevelyan, R.C.

Malone dies: Beckett, Samuel

Malt: Buchanan, R.B.

Malta: Sitwell, Sacheverell

Malta invicta: †Bartimeus

Maltese falcon, The: Hammett, S.D.

Maltese folk-tales: Murray, Margaret

Malvina of Brittany: Jerome, K. Jerome

Malyn's daisy: Carman, Bliss

Mama, I love you: Saroyan, William

Mamba: Cloete, E.F.S.G.

Mamba, the bright-eyed: McCrae, G.G.

Mamba's daughters (novel and play): Heyward, DuBose

Mamillia: Greene, Robert

Mamma: Broughton, Rhoda

Mamma Milly: Hall, Anna Maria

Mammals of Manitoba: Seton-Thompson, E.

Mammon: Elliott, M.H.

Mammon: Gore, Catherine

Mammon and Co.: Benson, E.F.

Mammon of righteousness, The: Wren, P.C.

Mammon of unrighteousness, The: Boyesen, H.H.

Mammonart: Sinclair, Upton

Mammy Tittleback and her family: Jackson, H.H.

Mamon and the black goddess: Graves, Robert

Mam'zelle Guillotine: Orczy, *Baroness*

Man: Fyzee Rahamin, S.

Man, The: Stoker, Bram

Man: Tagore, *Sir* R.

Man about the house, A: Young, Francis Brett

Man about town, The: Herbert, *Sir* A.P.

Man against the sky, The: Robinson, E.A.

Man alone: Mulgan, J.A.E.

Man and beast: Bottome, Phyllis

Man and boy: Rattigan, Terence

Man and his kingdom, The: Oppenheim, E.Phillips

Man and maid: Glyn, Elinor

Man and maid: Nesbit, E.

Man and superman: Shaw, G.B.

Man and the atom: Vulliamy, C.E.

Man and the supernatural: Underhill, Evelyn

Man and the universe: Jeans, *Sir* James

Man and the universe: Lodge, *Sir* Oliver

Man and time: Priestley, J.B.

Man and wife: Collins, Wilkie

Man and wife: Colman, George, *the elder*

Man and woman: Ellis, Henry Havelock

Man arose, A: Roberts, C.E.M.

Man as he is: Bage, Robert

Man as interpreter: Mumford, Lewis

Man at arms, The: James, G.P.R.

Man at Lone Tree: Sullivan, Alan

Man at the Carlton, The: Wallace, Edgar

Man between, The: Barr, A.E.H.

Man born to be hanged, The: Hughes, R.A.W.

Man born to be king, The: Sayers, Dorothy

Man called Spade, A: Hammett, S.D.

Man child's prayer, A: Carman, Bliss

Man comes down from the moon, The: Gibbon, J.M.

Man could stand up, A: Ford, Ford Madox

Man David, The: Jones, Jack

Man does, woman is: Graves, Robert

Man for Castle Gillian, A: Walsh, Maurice

Man for the ages, A: Bacheller, Irving

Man from Brodney's, The: McCutcheon, G.B.

Man from Devil's Island, The: Calder-Marshall, Arthur

Man from Glengarry, The: †Connor, Ralph

Man from home, The: Tarkington, Booth

Man from Kilsheelan, The: Coppard, A.E.

Man from Maine, A: Bok, E.W.

Man from nowhere, A: Huxley, Elspeth J.

Man from Scapa Flow, The: †Taffrail

Man from Snowy River, The: (†The Banjo), Paterson, A.B.

Man from the North, A: Bennett, Arnold

Man from the river, The: Cole, G.D.H.

Man from the sea: (†Michael Innes), Stewart, J.I.M.

Man, God and immortality: Frazer, *Sir* James

Man goes alone: Gunn, Neil M.

Man Hamilton, The: Palmer, E.V.

Man in black, The: Weyman, Stanley

Man in brown: Walsh, Maurice

Man in chains: Deeping, Warwick

Man in gray, The: Dixon, Thomas

Man in grey, The: Orczy, *Baroness*

Man in lower ten, The: Rinehart, Mary Roberts

Man in possession, The: Harwood, H.M.

Man in Ratcatcher, The: †Sapper

Man in the bowler hat, The: Milne, A.A.

Man in the brown suit, The: Christie, Agatha

Man in the case, The: Ward, E.S.

Man in the iron mask, The: McCrae, G.G.

Man in the modern world: Huxley, *Sir* Julian

Man in the moon, The: Hone, William

Man in the purple gown, The: Palmer, J.L.

Man in the queue, The: (†Josephine Tey), Mackintosh, Elizabeth

Man in the stalls, The: Sutro, Alfred

Man in the street, The: Nicholson, Meredith

Man in the zoo, A: Garnett, David

Man inside, The: Calverton, V.F.

Man Jesus, The: Austin, Mary

Man just ahead of you: Coates, R.M.

Man lay dead, A: Marsh, Ngaio Edith

Man Liszt, The: Newman, Ernest

Man lost: Stringer, A.J.A.

Man made of money, A: Jerrold, Douglas William

Man next door, The: Hough, Emerson

Man of a ghost, The: Wren, P.C.

Man of business, The: Colman, George, *the elder*

Man of destiny, The: Shaw, G.B.

Man of Devon, A: (†John Sinjohn) Galsworthy, John

Man of feeling, The: Mackenzie, Henry

Man of fortune, The: Gore, Catherine

Man of forty, A: Bullett, Gerald W.

Man of his time, A: Simpson, H. de G.

Man of honor, A: Eggleston, G.C.

Man of honour, A: Maugham, Somerset

Man of ideas, A: Malleson, Miles

Man of mark, A: (†Anthony Hope), Hawkins, Anthony Hope

Man of mode, The: Etherege, *Sir* George

Man of property, The: Galsworthy, John

Man of sorrow, by †Alfred Allendale, The: Hook, T.E.

Man of sorrows, The: Hubbard, Elbert

Man of taste, The: Bramston, James

Man of the forest, The: Grey, Zane

Man of the Marne, The: Carman, Bliss

Man of the people, A: Dixon, Thomas

Man of ten thousand, The: Holcroft, Thomas

Man of the world, The: Mackenzie, Henry

Man of the world, The: Macklin, Charles

Man on all fours, The: Derleth, A.W.

Man on his nature: Sherrington, *Sir* Charles Scott

Man on his past: Butterfield, Herbert

Man on horseback, The: Tarkington, Booth

Man on my back, The: Linklater, Eric

Man on the hilltop, The: Ficke, A.D.

Man on the house, The: Green, Paul

Man on the kerb, The: Sutro, Alfred

Man on the white horse: Deeping, G.W.

Man over forty, A: Linklater, Eric

Man overboard: Crawford, F. Marion

Man overboard!: Crofts, F.W.

Man overboard: Dickens, Monica

Man possessed: Benét, William Rose

Man reprieved, A: Calder-Marshall, Arthur

Man Shakespeare, The: Harris, J.T.

Man stealers: Shiel, M.P.

Man that corrupted Hadleyburg, The: (†Mark Twain), Clemens, S.L.

Man that was used up, The: Poe, Edgar Allan

Man, the miracle maker: Van Loon, Hendrik

Man the reformer: Emerson, Ralph Waldo

Man they hanged, The: Chambers, R.W.

Man track here: Derleth, A.W.

Man upstairs, The: Hamilton, Patrick

Man upstairs, The: Thomas, Augustus

Man upstairs, The: Wodehouse, P.G.

Man versus the state, The: Spencer, Herbert

Man Whistler, The: Pearson, Hesketh

Man who asked questions, The: Strong, L.A.G.

Man who ate the Phoenix, The: Dunsany, E.J.

Man who bought London, The: Wallace, Edgar

Man who came back, The: Ferber, Edna

Man who came to dinner, The: Kaufman, G.S.

Man who changed China: Buck, Pearl

Man who changed his name, The: Wallace, Edgar

Man who changed his plea, The: Oppenheim, E. Phillips

Man who could not lose, The: Davis, R.H.

Man who could not shudder, The: Carr, J.D.

Man who couldn't sleep, The: Stringer, A.J.A.

Man who died, The: Lawrence, D.H.

Man who died at twelve o'clock, The: Green, Paul

Man who died twice, The: Robinson, E.A.

Man who found himself, The: Jacob, Naomi

Man who had everything, The: Bromfield, Louis

Man who ignored the war, The: Brighouse, Harold

Man who knew, The: Wallace, Edgar

Man who knew Coolidge, The: Lewis, H.S.

Man who knew too much, The: Chesterton, G.K.

Man who lost himself, The: Sitwell, *Sir* Osbert

Man who loved children, The: Stead, C.E.

Man who made friends with himself, The: Morley, C.D.

Man who made gold, The: Belloc, Hilaire

Man who missed the 'bus, The: Benson, Stella

Man who outlived himself, The: Tourgée, A.W.

Man who pays the piper, The: Stern, G.B.

Man who saw, The: Watson, *Sir* J.W.

Man who thought he was a pauper, The: Oppenheim, E. Phillips

Man who understood women, The: Merrick, Leonard

Man who was good, The: Merrick, Leonard

Man who was nobody, The: Wallace, Edgar

Man who was Thursday, The: Chesterton, G.K.

Man who went away, The: Wright, H.V.

Man who went back, The: Deeping, Warwick

Man who wins, The: Herrick, R.

Man who won the Pools, The: (†Michael Innes), Stewart, J.I.M.

Man who wrote detective stories, The: (†Michael Innes), Stewart, J.I.M.

Man with a heart, A: Sutro, A.

Man with a load of mischief, The: Dukes, Ashley

Man with a sword: Treece, Henry

Man with expensive tastes, The: Percy, Edward

Man with red hair, A: Levy, Benn W.

Man with the blue guitar, The: Stevens, Wallace

Man with the golden arm, The: Algren, Nelson

Man with the hoe, The: Markham, Edwin

Man with the oblong box, The: Clarke, Marcus

Man with the pan-pipes, The: Molesworth, Mrs.

Man with the scales, The: †Bowen, Marjorie

Man with the spats, The: Cournos, John

Man with two left feet, The: Wodehouse, P.G.

Man with two names, The: Palmer, J.L.

Man within, The: Greene, Graham

Man without a country, The: Hale, E.E.

Man without a mask, A: Bronowski, J.

Man without a profession, A: Rowcroft, Charles

Man, woman and child: Brophy, John

Manager in distress, The: Colman, George, *the elder*

Manalive: Chesterton, G.K.

Manassas: Sinclair, Upton

Man-at-arms, A: Scollard, Clinton

Manchester: Mee, Arthur

Manchester: a history of the town: Saintsbury, George

Manchester portraits: Rothenstein, *Sir* William

Manchester stage, The: Elton, Oliver

Mandarin in Manhattan: Morley, C.D.

Mandeville: Godwin, William

Mandoa, Mandoa: Holtby, Winifred

Mandragola: Dukes, Ashley

Mandragora: Palmer, J.L.

Mandragora: Powys, John Cowper

Mandrake over the water-carrier: Sackville-West, E.C.

Man-eater of Malgudi, The: Narayan, R.K.

Manet: Rothenstein, *Sir* John

Manfred: Byron, George Gordon *Lord*

Manfroy: Baring, Maurice

Manhandled: Stringer, A.J.A.

Manhattan side-show: Bercovici, Konrad

Manhattan transfer: Dos Passos, John

Manhold: Bentley, Phyllis

Manifesto, A: Fabian tract No. 2.: Shaw, G.B.

Manifests of love, The: Mais, S.P.B.

Manin and the Venetian revolution of 1848: Trevelyan, G.M.

Manitoba and the north-west frauds: Hind, H.Y.

Manitoba symphony: Kirkconnell, Watson

Mankind in the making: Wells, H.G.

Manliness of Christ, The: Hughes, Thomas

Man-mouse taken in a trap, The: Vaughan, Thomas

Manner of the encounter between the French and Spanish Embassadours, at the landing of the Swedish Embassadour: Evelyn, John

Mannerhouse: Wolfe, T.C.

Mannerings, The: Brown, Alice

Manners: Hale, S.J.B.

Mano: Dixon, Richard Watson

Manoeuvres of Jane, The: Jones, H.A.

Manoeuvring mother, The: Bury, *Lady* C.S.M.

Manor and the borough, The: Webb, Sidney and Beatrice Webb

Manor House, The: Cambridge, Ada

Manor House School, The: Brazil, Angela

Man-power story, The: Priestley, J.B.

Man's faith, A: Grenfell, *Sir* Wilfred

Man's great adventure: (Stephen Southwold), †Bell, Neil

Man's helpers, A: Grenfell, *Sir* Wilfred

Man's house, A: Drinkwater, John

Man's life, A: Adams, Arthur H.

Man's man, A: (Ian Hay), Beith, *Sir* John Hay

Man's mortality: Arlen, Michael

Man's place in the universe: Wallace, A.R.

Man's redemption of man: Osler, *Sir* William

Man's right to knowledge: Van Doren, Mark

Man's will, A: Fawcett, Edgar

Man's woman, A: †Norris, Frank

Man's world, A: Crothers, Rachel

Mansart builds a school: Dubois, William

Manservant and maidservant: Compton-Burnett, Ivy

Mansfield Park: Austen, Jane

Man-shy: Davison, F.D.

Mansion, The: Faulkner, William

Mansions of philosophy, The: Durant, W.J.

Mansoul: Doughty, C.M.

Mantel-piece minstrels, The: Bangs, J.K.

Mantis: Lewis, Ethelreda

Mantle of Elijah, The: Zangwill, Israel

Mantrap: Lewis, H.S.

Manual, The: Eggleston, Edward

Manual for the collector and amateur of Old English plays, A: Hazlitt, W.C.

Manual of Parliamentary practice, A: Jefferson, Thomas

Manual of prayers for wartime, A: Temple, William

Manual of scouting: Seton-Thompson, E.

Manual of the Parliamentary Election Law, A: Warren, Samuel

Manual of Unitarian belief: Clarke, J.F.

Manual on the culture of small fruits, A: Roe, E.P.

Manual to accompany the history of the American people, A: Beard, C.A.

Manuel: Maturin, C.R.

Manufacture of paupers, The: Strachey, J.St. Loe

Manuscript commonplace book, 1780–1783: Walpole, Horace

Manuscript of Shakespeare's Hamlet, The: Wilson, John Dover

Manuscript of the Queen's Court: Bowring, *Sir* John

Manx witch, The: Brown, T.E.

Manxman, The: Caine, *Sir* T.H. Hall

Many a green isle: Bax, Clifford

Many a slip: Crofts, F.W.

Many cargoes Jacobs, W.W.

Many cities: Belloc, Hilaire

Many dimensions: Williams, Charles

Many furrows: Gardiner, A.G.

Many happy returns: Pertwee, Roland

Many inventions: Kipling, Rudyard

Many long years ago: Nash, Ogden

Many loves: Williams, W.C.

Many marriages: Anderson, Sherwood

Many minds: Van Doren, Carl

Many moods: Pratt, E.J.

Many moods: Symonds, J.A.

Many moons: Thurber, James

Many thousands gone: Bishop, John Peale

Many waters: †Bell, Neil

Many waters: Hoffe, Monckton

Many-coloured coat, The: Callaghan, M.E.

Many-mansioned house, The: Thomson, E.W.

Many-sided Franklin, The: Ford, Paul Leicester

Mao Tse-tung's "democracy": Lin Yu-T'ang

Maori agriculture: Best, Elsdon

Maori and Pakeha: Mulgan, A.E.

Maori as he was, The: Best, Elsdon

Maori canoe, The: Best, Elsdon

Maori division of time, The: Best, Elsdon

Maori folk-tales of the Port Hills: Cowan, James

Maori life in Aotea: Anderson, J.C.

Maori music with its Polynesian background: Anderson, J.C.

Maori place names: Anderson, J.C.

Maori school of learning, The: Best, Elsdon

Maori store houses and kindred structures: Best, Elsdon

Maori string figures: Anderson, J.C.

Maori tales: Anderson, J.C.

Maori tales: Lawlor, P.A.

Maori wars, 1843–1872, The: Hight, James

Maori yesterday and today, The: Cowan, James

Maoriland: Adams, Arthur H.

Maoriland stories: Grace, A.A.

Maoris, The: Best, Elsdon

Maoris and their arts, The: Mead, Margaret

Maoris in the Great War, The: Cowan, James

Maoris of New Zealand, The: Cowan, James

Maoris of New Zealand, The: Finlayson, Roderick

Map of life, The: Lecky, W.E.

Map of love, The: Thomas, Dylan

Map of Virginia, with a description of the countrey, A: Smith, John

Maple leaf as an emblem of Canada, The: Scadding, Henry

Maple leaf songs: Niven, F.J.

Maple leaves: LeMoine, *Sir* J.M.

Mapp and Lucia: Benson, E.F.

Mapp shewing the order and causes of salvation and damnation, A: Bunyan, John

Maracot deep, The: Doyle, *Sir* Arthur Conan

Maradick at forty: Walpole, *Sir* Hugh

Marah: (†Owen Meredith), Lytton, E.R.B. *Earl*

Marathon and Salamis: Mackenzie, *Sir* C. Compton

Marazan: †Shute, Nevil

Marbeck Inn, The: Brighouse, Harold

Marble faun, The: Faulkner, William

Marble faun, The: Hawthorne, Nathaniel

Marble prophecy, The: Holland, J.G.

Marbleface: †Brand, Max

Marcella: Ward, M.A.

March hares by George Forth: Frederic, Harold

March of democracy, The: Adams, James Truslow

March of fate, The: Farjeon, B.L.

March of literature from Confucius to modern times, The: Ford, Ford Madox

March of the white guard, The: Parker, *Sir* H.G.

March to Quebec: Roberts, Kenneth

Marching men: Anderson, Sherwood

Marching men: Coleman, H.J.

Marching on: Boyd, James

Marching on Tanga: Young, Francis Brett

Marching soldier: Cary, Joyce

Marching Spain: Pritchett, V.S.

Marchmont: Smith, Charlotte

Marcia gets her own back: Darlington, W.A.

Marcian Colonna, an Italian tale: Proctor, B.W.

Marcia's farmhouse: Widdemer, Margaret

Marco Bozzaris: Halleck, Fitz-Greene

Marco Millions: O'Neill, Eugene

Marden Fee: Bullett, Gerald

Marden Mystery, The: Nesbit, Edith

Mardi: Melville, Herman

Mardi Gras mystery, The: Bedford-Jones, Henry

Mare Clausam: Settle, Elkanah

Margaret: Adams, Francis

Margaret: Reynolds, G.

Margaret: a tale of the real and the ideal: Judd, Sylvester

Margaret Foster: Sala, G.A.H.

Margaret Fuller (Margaret Ossoli): Howe, Julia

Margaret Fuller Ossoli: Higginson, T.W.

Margaret Fuller to Sarah Helen Whitman, an unpublished letter: Hicks, Granville

Margaret Graham: James, G.P.R.

Margareth Howth: Davis, Rebecca

Margaret McMillan, a memoir: Cresswell, W.D.

Margaret More's Tagebuch: Manning, Anne

Margaret Ogilvy: Barrie, Sir J.M.

Margaret Warrener: Brown, Alice

Margaret Winthrop: Earle, A.M.

Margarite of America, A: Lodge, Thomas

Marge Askinforit: Pain, B.E.O.

Margery: Carey, Henry

Margery of Quether: Baring-Gould, Sabine

Margie: (†E.V.Cunningham) Fast, Howard M.

Margin of hesitation, The: Colby, F.M.

Margin released: Priestley, J.B.

Marginal comment: Nicolson, Hon. Sir Harold

Marginal notes by Lord Macaulay: Trevelyan, Sir G.O.

Marginalia: Harvey, Gabriel

Marguerite: Holmes, M.J.

Maria: Motteux, P.A.

Maria and some other dogs: Somerville, Edith

Maria Edgeworth: Lawless, Emily

Maria (of England) in the rain: Blackwood, Algernon

Mariamne: Moore, T.S.

Marian: Brooke, Frances

Marian: Hall, Anna Maria

Marian Fay: Trollope, Anthony

Marian Grey: Holmes, M.J.

Marian Withers: Jewsbury, G.E.

Mariana: Dickens, Monica

Mariana: Tennyson, Alfred Lord

Marianne: Davies, Rhys

Marianne Moore reader, A: Moore, M.C.

Marianne Thornton: Forster, E.M.

Marie: Haggard, Sir H.Rider

Marie: Ingraham, J.H.

Marie Antoinette: Belloc, Hilaire

Marie Antoinette: Sinclair, Upton

Marie De Berniere: Simms, W.G.

Marie Halkett: Chambers, R.W.

Marie Magdalens funerall teares: Southwell, Robert

Marie Magdalens lamentations: Markham, Gervase

Marie Tempest: Bolitho, H.H.

Marietta: Crawford, F.Marion

Marietta: Green, Anne

Marigold, an idyll of the sea: Turner, W.J.R.

Marina: Bemelmans Ludwig,

Marina: Eliot, T.S.

Marina: Lillo, George

Marine Parade: Brown, Ivor

Mariner of St. Malo, The: Leacock, Stephen

Mariners: †Dane, Clemence

Marines were there, The: Lockhart, Sir R.B.

Marino Faliero: Doge of Venice: Byron, George Gordon Lord

Marino Faliero: Lindsay, Jack

Marino Faliero: Swinburne, A.C.

Mario on the beach: Golding, Louis

Marion: Noah, M.M.

Marion Darche: Crawford, F.Marion

Marion-Ella: Ackland, Rodney

Marionette, The: Muir, Edwin

Marionettes: Lucas, F.L.

Marionette, The: Craig, Sir Gordon

Maritime history of Massachusetts: Morison, S.E.

Maritime observations: Franklin, Benjamin

Marius the Epicurean: his sensations and ideas: Pater, Walter

Marivosa: Orczy, Baroness

Marjorie Daw: Aldrich, Thomas Bailey

Marjorie Daw: Braddon, M.E.

Marjorie Fleming: Brown, Dr. John

Marjorie Pickthall: Logan, J.D.

Marjorie Pickthall: Pierce, Lorne

Marjorie's Almanac: Aldrich, Thomas Bailey

Marjorie's Canadian winter: Machar, A.M.

Marjory Darrow: Carman, Bliss

Mark Antony: Lindsay, Jack

Mark Hurdlestone: Moodie, Susanna

Mark Lambert's supper: (†Michael Innes), Stewart, J.I.M.

Mark of Cain, The: Lang, Andrew

Mark on the wall, The: Woolf, Virginia

Mark only: Powys, T.F.

Mark Rutherford's deliverance: †Rutherford, Mark

Mark Twain: Leacock, Stephen

Mark Twain: Masters, E.L.

Mark Twain and I: Read, O.P.

Mark Twain at work: De Voto, Bernard

Mark Twain's America: De Voto, Bernard

Marked man: some episodes in his life, A: Cambridge, Ada

Market Harborough: Whyte-Melville, G.J.

Market-money, The: Phillpotts, Eden

Market-place, The: Frederic, Harold

Marlborough: Fortescue, Sir John

Marlborough: Saintsbury, George

Marlborough: Sorley, C.H.

Marlborough; his life and times: Churchill, Sir Winston

Marling Hall: Thirkell, Angela

Marlowe's Doctor Faustus: Greg, W.W.

Marm Lisa: Wiggin, K.D.

Marmaduke: Monkhouse, A.N.

Marmaduke Wyvil: Herbert, H.W.

Marmion: Barker, James Nelson

Marmion: a tale of Flodden field: Scott, *Sir* Walter

Marne, The: Wharton, Edith

Maroon, The: Reid, T.M.

Marooned: Russell, W.C.

Marooned on Australia: Favenc, Ernest

Marpessa: Phillips, Stephen

Marquess of Dalhousie, The: Hunter, *Sir* William

Marquis of Carabas, The: Sabatini, R.

Marquis of Carabas, The: Spofford, H.E.

Marquis of Dalhousie's administration of British India, The: Arnold, Edwin

Marquis of Lossie, The: Macdonald, George

Marquis of Salisbury, The: Traill, H.D.

Marriage: Ferrier, Susan

Marriage: Tarkington, Booth

Marriage: Wells, H.G.

Marriage à-la-mode: Dryden, John

Marriage and morals: Russell, Bertrand

Marriage at sea, A: Russell, W.C.

Marriage by capture, A: Buchanan, R.W.

Marriage by capture: Stringer, A.J.A.

Marriage by conquest: Deeping, Warwick

Marriage by ordeal: †Gregory, Margaret, (Ercole, Velia)

Marriage ceremony, A: Cambridge, Ada

Marriage feast, The: Brown, Alice

Marriage guest, The: Bercovici, Konrad

Marriage has been arranged, A: Sutro, Alfred

Marriage in high life, A: Bury, *Lady* C.S.M.

Marriage is no joke: †Bridie, James

Marriage is possible: Widdemer, Margaret

Marriage lines: Nash, Ogden

Marriage made on earth: †Gregory, Margaret, (Ercole, Velia)

Marriage memorial, A: Taylor, Tom

Marriage of convenience, A: Green, Anne

Marriage of Elinor, The: Oliphant, Margaret

Marriage of Figaro, The: Harwood, H.M.

Marriage of Harlequin: Frankau, Pamela

Marriage of Heaven and Hell, The: Blake, William

Marriage of Marie Antoinette with the Dauphin, The: Lawrence, G.A.

Marriage of Mona Lisa, The: Swinburne, A.C.

Marriage of music, The: Dalton, A.C.

Marriage of Simon Harper, The: †Bell, Neil

Marriage of the Old and New Testament, The: Middleton, Thomas

Marriage of Venus, The: Santayana, George

Marriage of William Ashe, The: Ward, M.A.

Marriage past and present: Cole, M.I.

Marriage triumphe, A: Heywood, Thomas

Marriage will not take place, The: Steen, Marguerite

Marriage ... will not take place, The: Sutro, Alfred

Marriage-broker, The: Lowndes, M.A.

Marriages, The: James, Henry

Marri'd: Gilmore, Mary

Married beneath him: Braddon, M.E.

Married beneath him: Payn, James

Married in haste: Braddon, Mary Elizabeth

Married man, The: Grant, Robert

Married or single?: Sedgwick, C.M.

Married or unmarried: Hichens, R.S.

Married people: Rinehart, Mary Roberts

Marrow of tradition, The: Chestnutt, C.W.

Marryers: Bacheller, Irving

Marrying and giving in marriage: Molesworth, *Mrs.*

Marrying man, A: Brighouse, Harold

Marrying man, A: Stern, G.B.

Marrying sort, The: Gow, Ronald

Mars his idiot: Tomlinson, H.M.

Mars stript of his armour: Ward, Edward

Marsden case, The: Ford, Ford Madox

Marsena: Frederic, Harold

Marsh, The: Raymond, Ernest

Marsh island, A: Jewett, S.O.

Marshal Duke of Berwick, The: Petrie, *Sir* Charles

Marshal Ney: Masterman, *Sir* J.C.

Marshal Tito and his gallant bands: Adamic, Louis

Marshdikes: Ashton, Helen

Marshlands, The: Herbin, J.F.

Marston: Croly, George

Marsupial Bill: Stephens, J.B.

Martha: Mannin, Ethel

Martha, Eric and George: Sharp, Margery

Martha in Paris: Sharp, Margery

Martha Vine: Meynell, Viola

Martial adventures of Henry and me, The: White, W.A.

Martial India: Yeats-Brown, Francis

Martiall conference, pleasantly discoursed between two souldiers only practised in Finsbury Fields, A: Rich, Barnabe

Martian, The: Du Maurier, George

Martin Arrowsmith: Lewis, H.S.

Martin Conisby's vengeance: Farnol, J.J.

Martin Eden: London, Jack

Martin Faber: Simms, W.G.

Martin Hewitt, investigator: Morrison, Arthur

Martin Hyde: Masefield, John

Martin Junior: Marprelate, Martin

Martin Luther: Moore, George

Martin make believe: Frankau, Gilbert

Martin Pippin in the apple orchard: Farjeon, Eleanor

Martin Pippin in the daisy field: Farjeon, Eleanor

Martin Rattler: Ballantyne, R.M.

Martin Schüler: Wilson, Romer

Martin Senior: Marprelate, Martin

Martin Toutrond: Morier, J.J.

Martin Valliant: Deeping, Warwick

Martin Van Buren to the end of his public career: Bancroft, George

Martins of Cro' Martin, The: Lever, C.J.

Martyr, The: Baillie, Joanna

Martyr, The: O'Flaherty, Liam

Martyr age of the United States of America, The: Martineau, Harriet

Martyr nurse, The: Blackburn, Douglas

Martyr of Antioch, The: Milman, H.H.

Martyr of destiny, A: Fawcett, Edgar

Martyr of the catacombs, The: De Mille, James

Martyr President, The: (†Orpheus C. Kerr), Newell, R.H.

Martyrdom of Madeleine, The: Buchanan, R.W.

Martyr's heir, A: Cripps, A.S.

Martyr's idyl, The: Guiney, L.I.

Martyr's servant, A: Cripps, A.S.

Maruja: Harte, Bret

Marx, Lenin and the science of revolution: Eastman, Max

Marx, the man and his work: Prichard, K.S.

Marxism and contemporary science: Lindsay, Jack

Marxism, is it science? Eastman, Max

Marxist philosophy and the sciences, The: Haldane, J.B.S.

Mary: Braddon, M.E.

Mary: Molesworth, *Mrs.*

Mary: Rowson, S.H.

Mary: Wollstonecraft, Mary

Mary Adams: Ward, E.S.

Mary and the bramble: Abercrombie, Lascelles

Mary Anerley: Blackmore, *Sir* R.D.

Mary Ann Wellington: Cobbold, Richard

Mary Anne: Du Maurier, Daphne

Mary Arnold: Guedalla, Philip

Mary Barton: Gaskell, *Mrs.* Elizabeth

Mary Broome: Monkhouse, A.N.

Mary Cholmondeley: Lubbock, Percy

Mary Christmas: Chase, M.E.

Mary darling: Percy, Edward

Mary de Clifford: Brydges, *Sir* Samuel Egerton

Mary Glenn: Millin, Sarah Gertrude

Mary goes first: Jones, H.A.

Mary Lavelle: O'Brien, Kate

Mary Leith: Raymond, Ernest

Mary Lincoln, wife and widow: Sandburg, Carl

Mary Magdalen: Saltus, E.E.

Mary Marie: Porter, E.H.

Mary Marston: Macdonald, George

Mary, Mary, quite contrary: Ervine, St. John

Mary Middleton: Reynolds, G.

Mary Midthorne: McCutcheon, G.B.

Mary of Burgundy: James, G.P.R.

Mary of delight: Jacob, Naomi

Mary of Lorraine: Grant, James

Mary of Marion Isle: Haggard, *Sir* H. Rider

Mary of Scotland: Anderson, Maxwell

Mary Olivier: a life: Sinclair, May

Mary Pechell: Lowndes, M.A.

Mary Peters: Chase, M.E.

Mary Price: Reynolds, G.

Mary, Queen of Scots: Linklater, Eric

Mary, Queen of Scots: Mitford, Mary Russell

Mary Queen of Scots; daughter of debate: †Bowen, Marjorie

Mary Raymond: Gore, Catherine

Mary Read: †Bridie, James

Mary Shelley: Church, Richard

Mary Stewart: Grahame, James

Mary Stuart: Drinkwater, John

Mary Stuart: Swinburne, A.C.

Mary Stuart, Queen of Scots: Reynolds, G.

Mary, the mother of Jesus: Meynell, Alice

Mary the third: Crothers, Rachel

Mary tired: Pickthall, M.L.C.

Mary Wakefield: De la Roche, Mazo

Mary Wilbur: Ingraham, J.H.

Marylebone miser, The: Phillpotts, Eden

Mary's John: Brighouse, Harold

Mary's meadow: Ewing, *Mrs.* Juliana Horatia

Mary's neck: Tarkington, Booth

Mary's wedding: Cannan, Gilbert

Marzio's crucifix: Crawford, F. Marion

Ma's bit o' brass: Gow, Ronald

Mashallah! A flight into Egypt: Stoddard, C.W.

Mashi: Tagore, *Sir* R.

Mask, A: Brennan, C.J.

Mask, A: Brereton, John Le G.

Mask, The: Cloete, E.F.S.G.

Mask, The: Cournos, John

Mask, The: Harwood, H.M.

Mask of Apollo, The: Russell, G.W.

Mask of Cthulhu, The: Derleth, A.W.

Mask of Dimitrios, The: Ambler, Eric

Mask of Silenus: Deutsch, Babette

Mask of virtue, The: Dukes, Ashley

Maske presented at Ludlow Castle, 1634, A: Milton, John

Masked women: Beach, R.E.

Masks and faces: Bottome, Phyllis

Masks and faces: Lindsay, Jack

Masks and faces: Reade, Charles

Masks and farewells: Chattopadhyaya, H.

Masks, mimes and miracles: Nicoll, J.R.A.

Masks of times, The: Blunden, Edmund

Masks or faces? Archer, William

Masollam: Oliphant, Laurence

Masque, A: Mitchell, S.W.

Masque at Ludlow, The: Manning, Anne

Masque of Acis and Galatea, The: Motteux, P.A.

Masque of Aesop, A: Davies, Robertson

Masque of anarchy, The: Shelley, P.B.

Masque of augures, The: Jonson, Ben

Masque of blacknesse: Jonson, Ben

Masque of dead Florentines, A: Hewlett, Maurice

Masque of gypsies, The: Jonson, Ben

Masque of judgement, The: Moody, W.V.

Masque of kings, The: Anderson, Maxwell

Masque of mercy, A: Frost, Robert

Masque of Mr. Punch, A: Davies, Robertson

Masque of painters, The: Gosse, Sir Edmund

Masque of Pandora, The: Longfellow, H.W.

Masque of perusal, The: Williams, Charles

Masque of poets, A: Aldrich, Thomas Bailey

Masque of queenes: Jonson, Ben

Masque of reason, A: Frost, Robert

Masque of the gods, The: Taylor, Bayard

Masque of the Inner Temple and Grayes Inne, The: Beaumont, Francis

Masque of the manuscript, The: Williams, Charles

Masquerade, The: Fielding, Henry

Masquerade, The: Hillyer, Robert

Masquerade, The: Saxe, J.G.

Masqueraders, The: Heyer, Georgette

Masqueraders, The: Jones, H.A.

Masquerades: Leslie, Sir J.R. Shane

Masques and phases: Brown, Ivor

Masques and poems: Quennell, P.C.

Masques in a pageant: White, W.A.

Mass civilization and minority culture: Leavis, F.R.

Mass in slow motion, The: Knox, R.A.

Massachusetts: its historians and its history: Adams, C.F.

Massacre at Paris, The: Marlowe, Christopher

Massacre of Glencoe: The: Buchan, John

Massacre of Glencoe: Reynolds, G.

Massacre of Paris, The: Lee, Nathaniel

Massacre of the innocents, The: Kingsley, Charles

Massaniello: Smith, Horatio

Massarenes, The: †Ouida

Massa's in the cold ground: Foster, S.C.

Master, The: Bacheller, Irving

Master, The: White, T.H.

Master, The: Zangwill, Israel

Master builders: Pierce, Lorne

Master Christian, The: †Corelli, Marie

Master craftsman, The: Besant, Sir Walter

Master Fink's apprenticeship: Farjeon, B.L.

Master hope, The: Bottome, Phyllis

Master Humphrey's clock: Dickens, Charles

Master Jim Probity: Swinnerton, Frank

Master Mariner: Walmsley, Leo

Master mariners: Jacobs, W.W.

Master mummer, The: Oppenheim, E. Phillips

Master of a microbe, The: Service, Robert

Master of Aberfeldie, The: Grant, James

Master of Badgers Hall: Treece, Henry

Master of Ballantrae, The: Stevenson, R.L.

Master of chaos: Bacheller, Irving

Master of craft, A: Jacobs, W.W.

Master of Greylands, The: Wood, Ellen

Master of his fate: Barr, A.E.H.

Master of Jalna, The: De la Roche, Mazo

Master of life, A: Gibbs, Sir Philip

Master of life, The: Lighthall, W.D.

Master of man, The: Caine, Sir T.H. Hall

Master of men: Oppenheim, E. Phillips

Master of Merripit, The: Phillpotts, Eden

Master of none: Pertwee, Roland

Master of none: Street, A.G.

Master of our time, A: Grigson, Geoffrey

Master of silence, The: Bacheller, Irving

Master of the house, The: Hall, M.R.

Master of the house, The: Houghton, W.S.

Master of the inn, The: Herrick, Robert

Master of the isles, The: Carman, Bliss

Master of the magicians, The: Ward, E.S.

Master of the mill, The: Grove, F.P.

Master of the mine, The: Buchanan, R.W.

Master of the moose horn, The: Roberts, T.G.

Master of the revels: Marquis, Don

Master of Warlock, The: Eggleston, G.C.

Master poisoner, The: Hecht, Ben

Master revenge, The: Cody, J.A.

Master Rockafellar's voyage: Russell, W.C.

Master rogue, The: Phillips, D.G.

Master Sanguine: Brown, Ivor

Master spirit, A: Spofford, H.E.

Master Timothy's bookcase: Reynolds, G.

Master William Mitten: Longstreet, A.B.

Masterman Ready: Marryatt, Frederick

Masterpiece and the man, The: Gibbon, Monk

Masterpieces of figure painting: Newton, Eric

Masters, The: Snow, C.P.

Masters and men: Guedalla, Philip

Master's house, The: Thorpe, T.B.

Masters of modern French criticism, The: Babbitt, Irving

Masters of the Ukioye, The: Fenollosa, E.F.

Master's wife, The: Macphail, *Sir* Andrew

Master-spirits: Buchanan, R.W.

Masterton, and my unsentimental journey: Frankau, Gilbert

Mastif Whelp, with other ruff-Island-like currs fetcht from amongst the Antipodes, A: Goddard, William

Mast-ship, The: Ingraham, J.H.

Matador: Steen, Marguerite

Matador of the five towns: Bennett, Arnold

Match at mid-night, A: Rowley, William

Matchlock gun, The: Edmonds, W.D.

Matchmaker, The: Gibbons, Stella

Matchmaker, The: Wilder, Thornton

Matchmaker's arms: Dukes, Ashley

Mate Burke: Ingraham, J.H.

Mate in three: Peach, L. du Garde

Mate of the daylight, The: Jewett, S.O.

Mate of the "Easter Bell", The: Barr, A.E.H.

Mater: Mackaye, Percy

Mater coronata: Logan, J.D.

Mater Coronata: Stedman, E.C.

Materfamilias: Cambridge, Ada

Materia critica: Nathan, G.J.

Materialist conception, The: Prichard, K.S.

Materials for a description of Capri: Douglas, Norman

Mates: Ewart, E.A.

Mateship: Lawson, Henry

Mathematical principles of natural philosophy, The: Newton, *Sir* Isaac

Mathematical theory of relativity, The: Eddington, *Sir* A.S.

Mathematics for parents and teachers: Lodge, *Sir* Oliver

Matilda: Drayton, Michael

Matilda Montgomerie: Richardson, John

Mating call, The: Beach, R.E.

Mating of Lydia, The: Ward, M.A.

Mating season, The: Wodehouse, P.G.

Matins: Scollard, Clinton

Matins: Sherman, F.J.

Matins and vespers: Bowring, *Sir* John

Matisse, Picasso and Gertrude Stein: Stein, Gertrude

Matorni's vineyard: Oppenheim, E. Phillips

Matriarch, The: Stern, G.B.

Matrimonial openings: Jacobs, W.W.

Matrimonial speculations: Moodie, Susanna

Matrix: Wellesley, D.V.

Matrons, The: Percy, Thomas

Matter life and value: Joad, C.E.M.

Matter of life and death, A: Ridler, A.B.

Matthew Arnold: Brown, E.K.

Matthew Arnold: Saintsbury, George

Matthew Arnold: Trilling, Lionel

Matthew Arnold, a study: Chambers, *Sir* E.K.

Matthew Arnold, how to know him: Sherman, S.P.

Matthew Porter: Bradford, Gamaliel

Matthew Smith: Rothenstein, *Sir* John

Matthias at the door: Robinson, E.A.

Mattins and muttons: †Bede, Cuthbert

Maud: Tennyson, Alfred *Lord*

Maud and Cousin Bill: Tarkington, Booth

Maud Cherrill: Strong, L.A.G.

Maude: Rossetti, Christina

Maule's curse: Winters, Yvor

Mauleverer's millions: Reid, *Sir* Thomas

Mauretania: Sitwell, Sacheverell

Maurice Dering: Lawrence, G.A.

Maurice Guest: †Richardson, H.H.

Maurice Hewlett: Allen, J.L.

Maurice Maeterlinck: Thomas, E.E.P.

Maurice mystery: Cooke, J.E.

Maurice Tiernay, the soldier of fortune: Lever, C.J.

Maurice to Temple: Temple, William

Maurice's own idea: Malleson, Miles

Maurine: Wilcox, Ella Wheeler

Mauritius forever: Miller, Henry

Mausolaeum: Tate, Nahum

Mausoleum: Drummond of Hawthornden, William

Mausoleum, The: Theobald, Lewis

Mauve decade, The: Beer, T.

Maverick queen: Grey, Zane

Maw's vacation: Hough, Emerson

Max: Cecil, Lord David

Max and the white phagocytes: Miller, Henry

Max Beerbohm, a self-caricature: Beerbohm, *Sir* Max

Max Carrodos: Bramah, E.

Max Carrodos mysteries: Bramah, E.

Max Flambard: Dalley, J.B.

Max Hereford's dream: Lyall, Edna

Max Thornton: Glanville, Ernest

Maximilian: Masters, E.L.

Maxims by a man of the world: Payn, James

Maxims concerning patriotism: Berkeley, George

Maxims for revolutionists: Shaw, G.B.

Maxims of books and reading: Jackson, Holbrook

Maxims of Sir Morgan O'Doherty: Maginn, William

Maxims (33) found amongst the papers of the Great Almanzor: Savile, George

Maxwell: Hook, T.E.

Maxwell Drewitt: †Trafford, F.G.

May: Oliphant, Margaret

May and November correspondence, A: Hardy, A.S.

May Blossom: Belasco, David

May carols: De Vere, Aubrey Thomas

May Day: Garrick, David

May Day with the muses: Bloomfield, Robert

May Fair: Ainsworth, Harrison

Mayfair: Arlen, Michael

May Fair: Croly, George

May Martin: Thompson, D.P.

May Queen, The: Tennyson, Alfred *Lord*

May we come through?: Pertwee, Roland

May-Day: Chapman, George

May-Day: Emerson, R.W.

May-day in New York: Smith, Seba

Maydens dream, A: Greene, Robert

Mayfield deer, The: Van Doren, Mark

Mayflower, The: Stowe, Harriet Beecher

Mayflowers of Nova Scotia: Howe, Joseph

Mayor of Casterbridge, The: Hardy, Thomas

Mayor of Quinborough, The: Middleton, Thomas

Mayor of Troy, The: (†Q), Quiller-Couch, *Sir* Arthur

Mayor of Wind-Gap, The: Banim, Michael

Mayor on horseback, The: Oppenheim, E. Phillips

Maythorn story, The: Trease, Geoffrey

Mazeppa: Byron, George Gordon, *Lord*

Mazeppa: Payne, J.H.

McArone papers: Arnold, George

McMaster University, 1890–1940: Clarke, G.H.

McNeal–Sinclair debate on socialism: Sinclair, Upton

McTeague: †Norris, Frank

McVeys, The: Kirkland, Joseph

Me: Jacob, Naomi

Me: Saroyan, William

Me—again: Jacob, Naomi

Me an' th' son: †Rudd, Steele

Me and Frances: †Armstrong, Anthony

Me and Gus: Anthony, Frank S.

Me and Gus again: Anthony, Frank S.

Me and Harris: Pain, B.E.O.

Me and mine: Jones, Jack

Me and mine, you and yours: Jacob, Naomi

Me and my bike: Thomas, Dylan

Me and my diary: Jennings, Gertrude

Me and my doctors: Mais, S.P.B.

Me and Myn: Crockett, S.R.

Me and the Mediterranean: Jacob, Naomi

Me—and the swans: Jacob, Naomi

Me—in the kitchen: Jacob, Naomi

Me—in war time: Jacob, Naomi

Me—likes and dislikes: Jacob, Naomi

Me—looking back: Jacob, Naomi

Me—over there: Jacob, Naomi

Me—yesterday and today: Jacob, Naomi

Meadow blossoms: Alcott, Louisa M.

Meadow Brook: Holmes, M.J.

Meadow-grass: Brown, Alice

Meadowleigh: Manning, Anne

Meadows for ever, The: Blunden, Edmund

Meaning of art, The: Read, *Sir* Herbert

Meaning of beauty, The: Newton, Eric

Meaning of culture, The: Powys, John Cowper

Meaning of democracy, The: Brown, Ivor

Meaning of good, The: Dickinson, G.L.

Meaning of history, The: Harrison, Frederic

Meaning of Hitlerism, The: Steed, H.W.

Meaning of human history, The: Cohen, M.R.

Meaning of industrial freedom, The: Cole, G.D.H.

Meaning of life, The: Joad, C.E.M.

Meaning of Marx, The: Russell, Bertrand

Meaning of Marxism: Cole, G.D.H.

Meaning of meaning, The: Richards, I.A.

Meaning of murder, The: Brophy, John

Meaning of prestige, The: Nicolson, Hon. *Sir* Harold

Meaning of relativity, The: Einstein, Albert

Meaning of the glorious Koran, The: Pickthall, M.W.

Meaning of treason, The: †West, Rebecca

Meaning of truth, The: James, William

Meanings in Vedanta and Buddhism: Fausset, Hugh

Means to full employment, The: Cole, G.D.H.

Meanwhile; a packet of war letters: Benson, A.C.

Meanwhile, the picture of a lady: Wells, H.G.

Measure for measure: Shakespeare, William

Measure of a man, The: Barr, A.E.H.

Measure of a man, The: Duncan, Norman

Measure of dreams, The: Graves, Robert

Measure of man, The: Krutch, J.W.

Measure of my days, The: Millin, Sarah Gertrude

Measures and weights: Shabtis: Petrie, *Sir* William Flinders

Meat for mammon: Mitchell, Mary

Meat out of the eater: Wigglesworth, Michael

Mechanised muse, The: Kennedy, Margaret

Mechanism in thought and morals: Holmes, Oliver Wendell

Mechanism of nature, The: Andrade, E.N. da Costa

Memento: directed to all those that truly reverence the memory of King Charles the Martyr, A: L'Estrange, *Sir* Roger

Memnon: Binyon, Laurence

Memoir for the history of Connecticut, A: Wolcott, Roger

Memoir, in theology explained and defended: Dwight, Theodore

Memoir of a brother: Hughes, Thomas

Memoir of a map of the countries comprehended between the Black Sea and the Caspian: Ellis, George

Memoir of A.J. Butler: (†Q), Quiller-Couch, *Sir* Arthur

Memoir of Alfred Deakin, A: (†Elzevir), Murdoch, *Sir* W.L.F.

Memoir of Brigadier-General Gordon Shepard: Leslie, *Sir* J.R. Shane

Memoir of Cardinal Gasquet: Leslie, *Sir* J.R. Shane

Memoir of Daniel MacMillan: Hughes, Thomas

Memoir of David Scott: Scott, W.B.

Memoir of Dr. Samuel Gridley Howe: Howe, Julia Ward

Memoir of Edward, Lord Lytton: (†Owen Meredith), Lytton, E.R.B. *Earl*

Memoir of Henry Jacob Bigelow: Holmes, Oliver Wendell

Memoir of J.E.C. Bodley: Leslie, *Sir* J.R. Shane

Memoir of Jane Austen: Austen-Leigh, J.E.

Memoir of John Quincy Adams: Quincy, Josiah

Memoir of Joseph Curtis; a model man: Sedgwick, C.M.

Memoir of Lamb: Dyer, George

Memoir of Margaret and Henrietta Flower: Sigourney, L.H.

Memoir of Mrs. Harriet Newell Cook: Sigourney, L.H.

Memoir of Percy Bysshe Shelley, with new preface: Rossetti, W.M.

Memoir of Phebe P. Hammond: Sigourney, L.H.

Memoir of Richard Roberts Jones: Roscoe, William

Memoir of Thaddeus William Harris: Higginson, T.W.

Memoir of the Goddards of North Wilts, A: Jefferies, Richard

Memoir of the Honourable Albert Lawrence: Prescott, W.H.

Memoir of the life and character of John P. Emmet: Tucker, George

Memoir of the life of John Tulloch: Oliphant, Margaret

Memoir of the political life of the Right Hon. E. Burke, A: Croly, George

Memoir of the public services of William Henry Harrison of Ohio, A: Hall, James

Memoir of the Rt. Hon. J. Wilson: Bagehot, Walter

Memoir of Thomas Sadler: Morley, Henry

Memoir of William Forsyth: Miller, Hugh

Memoires for my grand-son: Evelyn, John

Memoires of the lives and actions of James and William Dukes of Hamilton and Castleherald, The: Burnet, Gilbert

Memoirs: Cumberland, Richard

Memoirs: Farjeon, Eleanor

Memoirs: Liddell Hart, B.

Memoirs: Ludlow, Edmund

Memoirs: Psalmanazar, George

Memoirs and adventures of Sir John Hepburn: Grant, James

Memoirs and adventures of Sir William Kirkaldy of Grange: Grant, James

Memoirs and Correspondence of Lyon Playfair: Reid, *Sir* Thomas

Memoirs and desultory writings: D'Alwis, James

Memoirs and friends: Benson, A.C.

Memoirs & portraits: Stevenson, R.L.

Memoirs and resolutions of Adam Graeme of Mossgray: Oliphant, Margaret

Memoirs by a celebrated literary and political character: Glover, Richard

Memoirs, letters and comic miscellanies in prose and verse: Smith, James

Memoirs of a Brahmin, The: Hockley, W.B.

Memoirs of a British agent: Lockhart, *Sir* Robert Bruce

Memoirs of a cavalier: Defoe, Daniel

Memoirs of a certain island adjacent to the kingdom of Utopia: Haywood, *Mrs.* Eliza

Memoirs of a femme de chambre, The: Blessington, Marguerite

Memoirs of a fox-hunting man: Sassoon, Siegfried

Memoirs of a Magdalen: Kelly, Hugh

Memoirs of a midget: De la Mare, Walter

Memoirs of a minister of France: Weyman, Stanley

Memoirs of a peeress: Gore, Catherine

Memoirs of a shy pornographer, The: Patchen, Kenneth

Memoirs of a space woman: Mitchison, Naomi

Memoirs of an aesthete: Acton, Harold

Memoirs of an American citizen, The: Herrick, Robert

Memoirs of an American lady: Grant, Anne

Memoirs of an infantry officer: Sassoon, Siegfried

Memoirs of an old parliamentarian: O'Connor, T.P.

Memoirs of Arlington, Vermont: Canfield, Dorothy

Memoirs of Arthur Hamilton: Benson, A.C.

Memoirs of Bartholomew Fair: Morley, Henry

Memoirs of Bryan Perdue: Holcroft, Thomas

Memoirs of Capt. John Creichton: Swift, Jonathan

Memoirs of Captain Rock: Moore, Thomas

Memoirs of celebrated women: James, G.P.R.

Memoirs of Constantine Dix, The: Pain, B.E.O.

Memoirs of Corporal Keeley: †Rudd, Steele

Memoirs of Dr. Burney: Burney, Fanny

Memoirs of great commanders: James, G.P.R.

Memoirs of Hecate County: Wilson, Edmund

Memoirs of Henry the Eighth of England: Herbert, H.W.

Memoirs of himself: Stevenson, R.L.

Memoirs of Ireland: Oldmixon, John

Memoirs of James, Marquis of Montrose: Grant, James

Memoirs of Joseph Grimaldi: Dickens, Charles

Memoirs of life and literature: Mallock, W.H.

Memoirs of Marau Taaroa, last Queen of Tahiti: Adams, H.B.

Memoirs of Margaret Fuller Ossoli: Fuller, Margaret

Memoirs of Mary: Gunning, *Mrs.* Susannah

Memoirs of Miss Sidney Bidulph: Sheridan, *Mrs.* Frances

Memoirs of Mr. C. J. Yellowplush and the diary of C. Jeames de la Pluche, Esq.: Thackeray, W.M.

Memoirs of Mrs. Anne Oldfield: Oldys, William

Memoirs of Mrs. Laetitia Boothby: Russell, W.C.

Memoirs of musick: North, Roger

Memoirs of my dead life: Moore, George

Memoirs of North-Britain: Oldmixon, John

Memoirs of Percy Bysshe Shelley: Peacock, Thomas Love

Memoirs of Richard Lovell Edgeworth: Edgeworth, Maria

Memoirs of Samuel Pepys: Scott, *Sir* Walter

Memoirs of several ladies of Great Britain: Amory, Thomas

Memoirs of Sherlock Holmes, The: Doyle, *Sir* Arthur Conan

Memoirs of Sir Walter Raleigh: Theobald, Lewis

Memoirs of Solar Pons, The: Derleth, A.W.

Memoirs of the affairs of Europe from the Peace of Utrecht: Russell, *Lord* John

Memoirs of the author of a vindication of the rights of women: Godwin, William

Memoirs of the Bobetes: Cary, Joyce

Memoirs of the Celts or Gauls: Ritson, Joseph

Memoirs of the Count de Montalembert: Oliphant, Margaret

Memoirs of the courts of Berlin, Dresden, etc.: Wraxall, *Sir* William

Memoirs of the Duke of Wellington: Phillips, Samuel

Memoirs of the family of Sackville: Collins, Arthur

Memoirs of the last ten years of the reign of George the Second: Walpole, Horace

Memoirs of the late Thomas Holcroft, written by himself and continued to the time of his death (by Hazlitt): Hazlitt, William

Memoirs of the life and writings of Robert Robinson: Dyer, George

Memoirs of the life of Colonel Hutchinson, Governor of Nottingham: Hutchinson, *Mrs.* Lucy

Memoirs of the life of Laurence Oliphant, and Alice Oliphant, his wife: Oliphant, Margaret

Memoirs of the life of Sir Walter Scott, Bart.: Lockhart, J.G.

Memoirs of the life of the Right Honourable Richard Brinsley Sheridan: Moore, Thomas

Memoirs of the life of William Wirt: Kennedy, J.P.

Memoirs of the press, historical and political, for thirty years past: Oldmixon, John

Memoirs of the reign of George the Second: Hervey, John

Memoirs of the reign of King George the third: Walpole, Horace

Memoirs of the Right Hon. Sir George Foster, The: Wallace, W.S.

Memoirs of Washington, by his adopted son: Custis, G.W.P.

Memoirs of what past in Christendom from 1672 to 1679: Temple, *Sir* William

Memoirs, 1749–1809: Hickey, William

Memoirs to 1795 written by himself. Continuation by his son: Priestley, Joseph

Memorable masque of the two honourable houses or Innes of Court, The: Chapman, George

Memorable providences: Mather, Cotton

Memoranda during the war: Whitman, Walt

Memoranda of the life of Jenny Lind: Willis, N.P.

Memorandum on resignation: Morley, John

Memorandum Walpoliana: Walpole, Horace

Memorial: Carman, Bliss

Memorial: Dodge, M.A.

Memorial, The: Isherwood, Christopher

Memorial and bibliographical sketches: Clarke, J.F.

Memorial containing travels through life or sundry incidents, A: Rush, Benjamin

Memorial of J.J. Gurney, A: Barton, Bernard

Memorial of Noah Porter: Bushnell, Horace

Memorial of the present deplorable state of New-England, A: Mather, Cotton

Memorial Tower, The: MacMechan, A.M.

Memorial volume of sacred poetry, A: Bowring, *Sir* John

Memoriall of all the English Monarchs, A: Taylor, John

Memorials of a quiet life: Hare, A.J.C.

Memorials of a residence on the Continent: Milnes, R.M.

Memorials of a tour in some parts of Greece; chiefly personal: Milnes, R.M.

Memorials of a tour on the continent, 1820: Wordsworth, William

Memorials of Coleorton: Wordsworth, William

Memorials of old Bridgehampton: Adams, J.T.

Memorials of Ray: Ray, John

Memorials of the Castle of Edinburgh: Grant, James

Memorie and rime: †Miller, Joaquin

Memories: Bowra, *Sir* Cecil

Memories: MacCarthy, *Sir* Desmond

Memories and adventures: Doyle, *Sir* Arthur Conan

Memories and experiences, The: Conway, M.D.

Memories and notes: (†Anthony Hope), Hawkins, Anthony Hope

Memories and studies: James, William

Memories and thoughts: Harrison, Frederic

Memories of a hundred years: Hale, E.E.

Memories of a misspent youth: Richards, Grant

Memories of a southern woman of letters: King, G.E.

Memories of childhood: Freeman, John

Memories of Christmas: Leacock, Stephen

Memories of Church Restoration: Hardy, Thomas

Memories of Dean Hole, The: Hole, S.R.

Memories of happy days: Green, Julian

Memories of London in the 'forties: Masson, David

Memories of my life: Galton, *Sir* Francis

Memories of the future: Knox, R.A.

Memories of two cities, Edinburgh and Aberdeen: Masson, David

Memory: De la Mare, Walter

Memory hold-the-door: Buchan, John

Memory of certain persons: Erskine, John

Memory of Moore, The: Fields, J.T.

Memory of Roswell Smith, A: Cable, G.W.

Memphis I: Petrie, *Sir* William Flinders

Men against the sea: Hall, J.N. and C.B. Nordhoff

Men and brethren: Cozzens, James Gould

Men and ghosts: Monkhouse, A.N.

Men and gods: Warner, Rex

Men and herring: Mitchison, Naomi

Men and machines: Chase, Stuart

Men and manners: Lathom, Francis

Men and memories: Rothenstein, *Sir* William

Men and the fields: Bell, Adrian

Men and wives: Compton-Burnett, Ivy

Men and women: Belasco, David

Men and women: Browning, Robert

Men and women: Caldwell, Erskine Preston

Men and women: Cobbold, Richard

Men and women of the French revolution: Gibbs, *Sir* Philip

Men are human: Palmer, E.V.

Men are unwise: Gow, Ronald

Men are unwise: Mannin, Ethel

Men at arms: Waugh, Evelyn

Men at high table: Bullett, Gerald

Men at odds, The: Rhys, Ernest

Men at work: Chase, Stuart

Men, books and birds: Hudson, W.H.

Men dislike women: Arlen, Michael

Men do not weep: Nichols, Beverley

Men, don't be selfish: Holmes, M.J.

Men I'm not married to: Parker, Dorothy

Men in blue glasses: Mais, S.P.B.

Men in darkness: Hanley, James

Men in the same boat: Beresford, J.D.

Men in white: Hodge, H.E.

Men in white: Kingsley, Sidney

Men like gods: Wells, H.G.

Men, maids, and mustard-pot: Frankau, Gilbert

Men must act: Mumford, Lewis

Men o' war: †Taffrail

Men of arms: Horgan, Paul

Men of capital: Gore, Catherine

Men of character: Jerrold, Douglas

Men of destiny: Lippmann, Walter

Men of earth: Massingham, Harold

Men of forty-eight: Lindsay, Jack

Men of invention and industry: Smiles, Samuel

Men of iron: Pyle, Howard

Men of letters of the British Isles: Sherman, S.P.

Men of might: Benson, A.C.

Men of Moss Hags, The: Crockett, S.R.

Men of Ness, The: Linklater, Eric

Men of our times: Stowe, Harriet Beecher

Men of stones: Warner, Rex

Men of the hills: Treece, Henry

Men of the last frontier: (†Grey Owl), Belaney, G.S.

Men of the mountain, The: Crockett, S.R.

Men of the outer islands: Beach, R.E.

Men of the R.A.F.: Rothenstein, *Sir* William

Men on a voyage: Millin, Sarah Gertrude

Men versus the man: Mencken, H.L.

Men were different: Leslie, *Sir* J.R.Shane

Men who explained miracles, The: Carr, J.D.

Men who made Australia, The: Lawson, Henry

Men who made the nation, The: Dos Passos, John

Men with the bark on: Remington, Frederic

Men without art: Lewis, P. Wyndham

Men without country: Hall, J.N. and C.B. Nordhoff

Men without wives: Drake-Brockman, H.

Men without women: Hemingway, Ernest

Men, women and boats: Crane, Stephen

Men, women and books: Hunt, Leigh

Men, women and emotions: Wilcox, Ella Wheeler

Men, women, and ghosts: Lowell, Amy

Men, women and ghosts: Ward, E.S.

Men, women and guns: †Sapper

Menace of Fascism, The: Strachey, John

Menace of German culture, The: Powys, John Cowper

Menace to our national defence, The: Angell, *Sir* Norman

Menaecmi: Warner, William

Menageries, The: Knight, Charles

Menander. The arbitration: Murray, George

Menander. The rape of the lock: Murray, George

Menaphon: Greene, Robert

Mencius on the mind: Richards, I.A.

Mendel: Cannan, Gilbert

Menders of the maimed: Keith, *Sir* Arthur

Mendicant rhymes: Housman, Laurence

Mending wall: Frost, Robert

Men's and women's wages: should they be equal?: Webb, Beatrice

Mens creatrix: Temple, William

Men's wives: Thackeray, W.M.

Mental efficiency: Bennett, Arnold

Mental portraits: Tuckerman, H.T.

Mental radio: Sinclair, Upton

Mentone, Cario, and Corfu: Woolson, C.F.

Mentor, The: Garland, Hamlin

Mentoria: Rowson, S.H.

Mephisto: Henley, W.E.

Mercedes: Aldrich, T.B.

Mercedes of Castile: Cooper, James Fenimore

Mercenary lover, The: Haywood, *Mrs*. Eliza

Merchandise: Bridges, Roy

Merchant Navy fights, The: Divine, A.D.

Merchant Navy film: Greenwood, Walter

Merchant of Venice, The: Shakespeare, William

Merchant of Yonkers, The: Wilder, Thornton

Merchants: Higginson, T.W.

Merchants from Cathay: Benét, William Rose

Merchants of wine: Waugh, Alec

Merciles beaute: Chaucer, Geoffrey

Mercurius Paed: Phillips, John

Mercurius rusticus: Wither, George

Mercurius Verax: Phillips, John

Mercury vindicated: Jonson, Ben

Mercy of Allah, The: Belloc, Hilaire

Mercy of God, The: Fausset, Hugh

Mercy Philbrick's choice: Jackson, H.H.

Mercy Warren: Brown, Alice

Merdhen, the manor and eyrie, and old landmarks and old laws: Martineau, Harriet

Mere accident, A: Moore, George

Mere chance, A: Cambridge, Ada

Mere Christianity: Lewis, C.S.

Mere literature: Wilson, Woodrow

Mere man and his problems, The: Sheldon, C.M.

Mère Marie of the Ursulines: Repplier, Agnes

Meredith: Blessington, Marguerite

Meredith: Lindsay, Jack

Meredith: McHenry, James

Meredith: Sassoon, Siegfried

Merely Mary Ann: Zangwill, Israel

Merie ballad called Christ's Kirk on the green, A: James I

Meriel Brede, secretary: Sladen, D.B.W.

Merivale Banks, The: Holmes, M.J.

Merivales, The: McCutcheon, G.B.

Merkland: Oliphant, Margaret

Merlin: Robinson, E.A.

Mermaid singing, The: Van Druten, John

Merope: Arnold, Matthew

Meropé: Hill, Aaron

Merrie and pleasant comedy, A: Rowley, William

Merrie dialogue betwixt the taker and mistaker, A: Breton, Nicholas

Merrileon Wise: Malleson, Miles

Merrill Moore: Untermeyer, Louis

Merrily we roll along: Kaufman, G.S.

Merry adventures of Robin Hood, The: Pyle, Howard

Merry chanter, The: Stockton, F.R.

Merry Dale: Hergesheimer, Joseph

Merry England: Ainsworth, Harrison

Merry hall: Nichols, Beverley

Merry heart, The: Swinnerton, Frank

Merry Hippo, The: Huxley, Elspeth, J.

Merry men, The: Stevenson, R.L.

Merry muse, The: Linklater, Eric

Merry tales: (†Mark Twain), Clemens, S.L.

Merry tales of the three wise men of Gotham, The: Paulding, J.K.

Merry widow welcome: Percy, Edward

Merry wives of Westminster, The: Lowndes, M.A.

Merry wives of Windsor, The: Shakespeare, William

Merry Zingara, The: Gilbert, *Sir* W.S.

Merry-garden: (†Q), Quiller-Couch, *Sir* Arthur

Merry-go-round, The: Maugham, Somerset

Merry-go-round, The: Van Vechten, Carl

Merry-go-round of song, A: Gale, Norman

Merry-Mount: Motley, J.L.

Merton of the movies: Connelly, Marc

Merton of the movies: Kaufman, G.S.

Mery jest how the sergeant would lerne to play the frere, A: More, *Sir* Thomas

Mery play betwene Johan Johan the husbande typ is wyfe & Syr Jhan the preest, A: Heywood, John

Mery play betwene the pardoner and the frere, the curate and neybour Pratte, A: Heywood, John

Mes souvenirs: Symons, Arthur

Mesa trail, The: Bedford-Jones, Henry

Mesmer, a monograph: Frankau, Gilbert

Mesmerists, The: Farjeon, B.L.

Mesolonghi capta: Murray, Gilbert

Message for Genevieve: Caldwell, Erskine Preston

Message from the sea, A: Collins, Wilkie

Message from the sea, A: Dickens, Charles

Message in code, the diary of Richard Rumbold, A: Plomer, W.C.F.

Message of peace, The: Church, Richard

Message of the bells, The: Van Loon, Hendrik

Message of the East, The: Coomaraswamy, A.K.

Message to Garcia, A: Hubbard, Elbert

Message to Hadrian: Trease, Geoffrey

Message to the Mother Church: Eddy, M.B.

Messalina: Deamer, Dulcie

Messalina of the suburbs: †Deiafield, E.M.

Messene redeemed: Lucas, F.L.

Messer Marco Polo: Byrne, Donn

Messiah: Carman, Bliss

Messiah, The: Montgomery, Robert

Messines: Cammaerts, Emile

Messrs. bat and ball: Gale, Norman

Metamorphosis of Pigmalions image, The: Marston, John

Metamorphosis of tabacco, The: Beaumont, *Sir* John

Metaphysicals and Milton, The: Tillyard, E.M.W.

Meteor: Behrman, S.N.

Meteorographica: Galton, *Sir* Francis

Method in the study of totemism: Lang, Andrew

Method of fluxions and infinite series, The: Newton, *Sir* Isaac

Method of freedom, The: Lippmann, Walter

Method of nature, The: Emerson, R.W.

Methodism and the new Catholicism: Pierce, Lorne

Methodist, The: Lloyd, Evan

Methods and aims in archaeology: Petrie, *Sir* William Flinders

Methods for improving the manufacture of Carolina indigo: Ledyard, John

Methods of ethics, The: Sidgwick, Henry

Methods of investigation: Webb, Beatrice

Methods of Lady Walderhurst, The: Burnett, Frances Hodgson

Methods of Mr. Sellyer, The: Leacock, Stephen

Methods of social study: Webb, Beatrice and Sidney Webb

Methods of study in natural history: Agassis, Jean

Methods of teaching rhetoric: Herrick, Robert

Methuselah's diary: Vachell, H.A.

Metri gratia, verse and prose: Guedalla, Philip

Metrical effusions: Barton, Bernard

Metrical legends of exalted characters: Baillie, Joanna

Metrical tales: Southey, Robert

Metrical tales and other poems: Lover, Samuel

Metrical visions: Cavendish, George

Metropolis, The: Sinclair, Upton

Metropolis coronata, the triumphes of ancient drapery in a second yeeres performance: Munday, Anthony

Mettle of the pasture, The: Allen, J.L.

Mexican guide, The: Janvier, T.A.

Mexican maze: Beals, Carleton

Mexico: Beals, Carleton

Mexico, a study of two Americas: Chase, Stuart

Mexico, and the life of the conqueror Hernando Cortes: Prescott, W.H.

Mexico I like, The: Dobie, J.F.

Meydum and Memphis: Petrie, *Sir* William Flinders

Mezentian gate, The: Eddison, Eric Rucker

Mezzanine: Benson, E.F.

Mezzotint: Mackenzie, *Sir* Compton

Mezzotints in modern music: Huneker, J.G.

M'Fingal: Trumbull, John

Mhudi: Plaatje, S.T.

Mi Amigo: Burnett, W.R.

Miami Woods: Gallagher, W.D.

Micah Clarke: Doyle, *Sir* Arthur Conan

Mice: Bullett, Gerald

Michael and his lost angel: Jones, H.A.

Michael and Mary: Milne, A.A.

Michael and Theodora: a Russian story: Barr, A.E.H.

Michael Angelo: Longfellow, H.W.

Michael Angelo: Lucas, E.V.

Michael Bonham: Simms, W.G.

Michael Bray: †Taffrail

Michael, brother of Jerry: London, Jack

Michael Drayton: Elton, Oliver

Michael Ernest Sadler: a memoir by his son: Sadleir, Michael

Michael Faraday: Bragg, *Sir* William

Michael McGrath, postmaster: †Connor, Ralph

Michael O'Halloran: Stratton-Porter, Gene

Michael Robartes and the dancer: Yeats, W.B.

Michael Scarlett: Cozzens, J.G.

Michaelmas terme: Middleton, Thomas

Michael's crag: Allen, Grant

Michael's evil deeds: Oppenheim, E. Phillips

Michael's wife: Frankau, Gilbert

Michel de Montaigne: Dowden, Edward

Mickey: De Selincourt, Aubrey

Mickle drede, The: Bottomley, Gordon

Micmac place names in the maritime provinces and Gaspe Peninsula: Rand, S.T.

Microcosm, The: Canning, George

Micro-cosmographie: Earle, John

Microcosmos: Davies, John

Microcosmus: Heylyn, Peter

Micro-cynicon: Middleton, Thomas

Mid American chants: Anderson, Sherwood

Midas: Lyly, John

Midas touch, The: Kennedy, Margaret

Mid-Atlantic: †Taffrail

Midcentury: Don Passos, John

Mid-channel: Lewisohn, Ludwig

Mid-Channel: Pinero, Sir A.W.

Middle East: Morton, H.V.

Middle East, a study in air power: Guedalla, Philip

Middle East archaeology: Woolley, Sir Leonard

Middle East diary: Coward, Noel

Middle generation, The: Beresford, J.D.

Middle kingdom, The: Morley, C.D.

Middle of the journey, The: Trilling, Lionel

Middle of the road, The: Gibbs, Sir Philip

Middle watch, The: (†Ian Hay), Beith, Sir John Hay

Middle years, The: James, Henry

Middle-aged man on the flying trapeze, The: Thurber, James

Middle-class: Millin, Sarah Gertrude

Middle-English vocabulary, A: Tolkien, J.R.R.

Middleman, The: Jones, H.A.

Middlemarch: †Eliot, George

Middlesex election, The: †Pindar, Peter

Middlesex Hospital, 1745–1948: Saunders, H.A.St.George

Middletown: a study in contemporary American culture: Lynd, R.S.

Middletown, in transition: Lynd, R.S.

Middy and the moors, The: Ballantyne, R.M.

Middy ashore, The: Bernard, W.B.

Midge, The: Bunner, H.C.

Midlander, The: Tarkington, Booth

Midnight: Green, Julian

Mid-night and daily thoughts: Killigrew, Sir William

Midnight and Percy Jones: Starrett, Vincent

Midnight at Baïae: Symonds, J.A.

Midnight bell, The: Hamilton, Patrick

Midnight bell, The: Lathom, Francis

Midnight court, The: †O'Connor, Frank

Midnight cry, A: Mather, Cotton

Midnight fantasy, A: Aldrich, T.B.

Midnight folk, The: Masefield, John

Midnight intruder, The: Hone, William

Midnight lace: Kantor, Mackinlay

Midnight on the desert: Priestley, J.B.

Midnight queen, The: Lippard, George

Midnight race, A: †Mrs. Partington

Mid-night thoughts: Killigrew, Sir William

Mid-Pacific: Hall, J.N.

Midshipmaid, The: (†Ian Hay), Beith, Sir John Hay

Midshipman, The: Ingraham, J.H.

Midsommer nights dreame, A: Shakespeare, William

Midstream: Connell, John

Midstream: my later life: Keller, Helen

Midsummer: Trowbridge, J.T.

Midsummer eve: Bottomley, Gordon

Midsummer eve: Drinkwater, John

Midsummer Eve: Hall, A.M.

Midsummer Eve: Russell, G.W.

Midsummer holiday, A: Swinburne, A.C.

Midsummer madness: Bax, Clifford

Midsummer medley for 1830, The: Smith, Horatio

Midsummer music: Graham, Stephen

Midsummer night: Masefield, John

Midsummer night, The: Williamson, Henry

Midsummer night madness: O'Faolain, Sean

Midsummer night's dream, A: Shakespeare, William

Mid-Victorian studies: Tillotson, Geoffrey

Midwinter: Buchan, John

Mightier than the sword: Ford, Ford Madox

Mighty and their fall, The: Compton-Burnett, Ivy

Mighty atom, The: †Corelli, Marie

Mighty men: Farjeon, Eleanor

Mighty men, from Achilles to Harold: Farjeon, Eleanor

Mignon: Cain, J.M.

Mignonette: (†Joseph Shearing), †Bowen, Marjorie

Migrations: Petrie, Sir William Flinders

Migrations: Scott, Evelyn

Mikado, The: Gilbert, Sir W.S.

Mike: Benson, E.F.

Mike: Wodehouse, P.G.

Mike and Psmith: Wodehouse, P.G.

Mike at Wrykyn: Wodehouse, P.G.

Mike Fletcher: Moore, George

Mike Howe, the bushranger of Van Diemen's land: Bonwick, James

Milan Grill Room, The: Oppenheim, E.Phillips

Mild and bitter: Herbert, *Sir* A.P.

Mild barbarian, A: Fawcett, Edgar

Mildensee: Royde-Smith, Naomi

Mildred: Holmes, M.J.

Mildred Arkell: Wood, Ellen

Mildred Pierce: Cain, J.M.

Mile-away murder: †Armstrong, Anthony

Miles Dixon: Cannan, Gilbert

Milesian chief, The: Maturin, C.R.

Milestones: Bennett, Arnold

Militarism, German and British: Hawkins, A.H.

Military and civil life of George Washington, The: Griswold, R.W.

Military antiquities respecting a history of the English army: Grose, Francis

Military discourse, A: Ralegh, *Sir* Walter

Milk for babes: Cotton, John

Milk of Paradise, The: Reid, Forrest

Mill Creek Irregulars, special detectives, The: Derleth, A.W.

Mill house, The: Bell, Adrian

Mill on the floss, The: †Eliot, George

Millbank: Holmes, M.J.

Miller of Martigné, The: Herbert, H.W.

Miller of Old Church, The: Glasgow, Ellen

Miller's daughter, The: Tennyson, Alfred *Lord*

Millicent's corner: Hannay, J.O.

Million, The: Hichens, R.S.

Million pound deposit, The: Oppenheim, E.Phillips

Millionaire of rough-and-ready, A: Harte, Bret

Millionairess, The: Shaw, G.B.

Million-dollar story, The: Wallace, Edgar

Millions: Poole, Ernest

Milly: Thompson, J.M.

Milly and Oily: Ward, M.A.

Milly Darrell: Braddon, M.E.

Milton: Belloc, Hilaire

Milton: Blake, William

Milton: Brooke, S.A.

Milton: Eliot, T.S.

Milton: Garnett, Richard

Milton: Macaulay, *Dame* Rose

Milton: Meredith, George

Milton: Pattison, Mark

Milton: Raleigh, *Sir* Walter

Milton: Tillyard, E.M.W.

Milton and his modern critics: Smith, L.L.P.

Milton and Wordsworth, prophets and poets: Grierson, *Sir* Herbert

Milton in the eighteenth century: Dowden, Edward

Miltonic setting, The: Tillyard, E.M.W.

Milton's correspondence and academic exercises: Tillyard, E.M.W.

Milton's God: Empson, William

Milton's prosody: Bridges, Robert

Milwaukee road, The: Derleth, A.W.

Mimic life: Ritchie, *Mrs.* A.C.M.

Mimshi Maiden, The: McCrae, Hugh

Mina: Fairfield, S.L.

Mince pie: Morley, C.D.

Mind and heart of Britain, The: Iyengar, K.R.Srinivasa

Mind and its workings, The: Joad, C.E.M.

Mind and matter: Joad, C.E.M.

Mind at the end of its tether: Wells, H.G.

Mind of light, The: Ghose, Sri Aurobindo

Mind of Mr. J.G.Reeder, The: Wallace, Edgar

Mind of the maker, The: Sayers, Dorothy

Mind of the race, The: Wells, H.G.

Mind reader The: Roberts, W. Adolphe

Mind readers, The: Allingham, Margery

"Mind the paint" girl, The: Pinero, *Sir* A.W.

Mind your language: Brown, Ivor

Mindes melodie, The: Montgomerie, Alexander

Mind's eye, The: Blunden, Edmund

Mind's eye, The: Brophy, John

"Mind-the-gates" girl, The: Jennings, Gertrude

Mine inheritance: Niven, F.J.

Mine own executioner: Balchin, Nigel

Mine own land: Mickle, A.D.

Mine own people: Kipling, Rudyard

Mine the harvest: Millay, E.St. Vincent

Mine with the iron door, The: Wright, H.B.

Mineralls, The: Marprelate, Martin

Miners and the Board, The: Cole, M.I.

Miner's right, The: †Boldrewood, Rolf

Minerva Britanna: or a garden of heroycal devises: Peacham, Henry

Ming Yellow: Marquand, J.P.

Mingled yarn, A: Tomlinson, H.M.

Mingo and other sketches in black and white: Harris, J.C.

Miniature, The: Phillpotts, Eden

Miniature history of the War, A: Ensor, *Sir* R.C.K.

Miniatures of French history: Belloc, Hilaire

Minick: Kaufman, G.S.

Minion, The: Sabatini, Rafael

Minions of the moon: Cawein, Madison and Eden Phillpotts

Minister of grace, A: Widdemer, Margaret

Minister's charge, The: Howells, W.D.

Ministers wife, The: Oliphant, Margaret

Minister's wooing, The: Stowe, Harriet Beecher

Ministry of fear, The: Greene, Graham

Ministry of water: †McDiarmid, Hugh

Minna and myself: Bodenheim, Maxwell and Ben Hecht

Minnesota and the Far West: Oliphant, Laurence

Minnie Maylow's story: Masefield, John

Minnie's Bishop: Hannay, J.O.

Minnow among Tritons: Potter, Stephen

Minor dialogues: Ridge, W.Pett

Minor morals for young people: Bowring, *Sir* John

Minor pleasures of life, The: Macaulay, *Dame* Rose

Minor poets of the Caroline period: Saintsbury, G.E.B.

Minor prophets, The: Pusey, E.B.

Minority report: De Voto, Bernard

Minority Report: Mencken, H.L.

Minority report: Rice, Elmer

Minos of Crete: Keyes, S.A.K.

Minster Church: Hawker, R.S.

Minstrel, The: Beattie, James

Minstrel boy, The: Strong, L.A.G.

Mint, The: Lawrence, T.E.

Mintage, The: Hubbard, Elbert

Minty Alley: James, C.L.R.

Minute for murder: Day-Lewis, C.

Minute particulars: Bishop, J. P.

Mirabeau: Calvert, G.H.

Miracle at Markham, The: Sheldon, C.M.

Miracle boy, The: Golding, Louis

Miracle in Forty-ninth Street: Hecht, Ben

Miracle in the rain: Hecht, Ben

Miracle man, The: Packard, F.L.

Miracle of Brean, The: Raymond, Ernest

Miracle of Coral Gables, The: Beach, R.E.

Miracle of the corn, The: Colum, Padraic

Miracle on Sinai: Sitwell, *Sir* Osbert

Miracle on Watling Street, The: Gow, Ronald

Miracle Plays: Our Lord's coming and childhood: Tynan, Katherine

Miracle songs of Jesus, The: Macdonald, W.P.

Miracles: Lewis, C.S.

Miracles by arrangement: Lindsay, Norman

Miracles of Our Lord, The: Macdonald, George

Miraculous horse, The: Bates, Ralph

Mirage: Masters, E.L.

Mirage water: Dunsany, E.J.

Miranda: Braddon, M. E.

Miranda Masters: Cournos, John

Miranda of the balcony: Mason, A.E.W.

Mirandola: Procter, B.W.

Miriam: Whittier, J.G.

Miriam Balestier: Fawcett, Edgar

Miriam Rozella: Farjeon, B.L.

Miriam's schooling: †Rutherford, Mark

Mirk Abbey: Payn, James

Mirour for magistrates of cyties, A: Whetstone, George

Mirror crack'd from side to side, The: Christie, Agatha

Mirror for witches, A: Forbes, Esther

Mirror in the roadway, The: †O'Connor, Frank

Mirror of faith, A: Neale, J.M.

Mirror of gesture, The: Coomaraswamy, A.K.

Mirror of Kong Ho: Bramah, E.

Mirror of man, The: Churchyard, Thomas

Mirror of silver, A: Bridges, Roy

Mirror of the months: Kaye-Smith, Shiela

Mirror of the sea, The: Conrad, Joseph

Mirror of the world, The (trn.): Caxton, William

Mirror of treue honnour exposing the life of Francis, Earl of Bedford, A: Whetstone, George

Mirror to France, A: Ford, Ford Madox

Mirrour for Magistrates, A: Sackville, Thomas

Mirrour of majestie, The: Peacham, Henry

Mirrour of mutabilitie, The: Munday, Anthony

Mirrour of vertue in worldly greatnes, The: Roper, William

Mirth and metre: Smedley, F.E.

Mirth and metre: Yates, E.H.

Mirthful haven: Tarkington, Booth

Mirum in modum: Davies, John

Mirza, The: Morier, J.J.

Misadventures of John Nicholson, The: Stevenson, R.L.

Misadventures of Sherlock Holmes: †Queen, Ellery

Misalliance: Shaw, G.B.

Miscellanea: Temple, *Sir* William

Miscellaneous antiquities: Walpole, Horace

Miscellaneous discourses concerning the dissolution and changes of the world: Ray, John

Miscellaneous lectures and reviews: Whately, Richard

Miscellaneous observations relating to education more especially as it respects the conduct of the mind: Priestley, Joseph

Miscellaneous pieces in verse and prose: Jenyns, Soame

Miscellaneous pieces relating to the Chinese: Percy, Thomas

Miscellaneous poems consisting of elegies, odes, pastorals, together with Calypso a masque: Cumberland, Richard

Miscellanies, aesthetic and literary: Coleridge, S.T.

Miscellanies in prose and verse: King, William

Miscellanies in prose and verse: Woolls, William

Miscellanies of the Philobiblon Society: Milnes, R.M.

Miscellanies, or Literary recreations: D'Israeli, Isaac

Miscellany of men, A: Chesterton, G.K.

Miscellany of sundry essayes, paradoxes: Osborne, Francis

Mischief in the lane: Derleth, A.W.

Mischief maker, The: Oppenheim, E.Phillips

Mischief's thanksgiving: Coolidge, Susan

Mischievous Brownie, The: Brazil, Angela

Mischmasch: †Carroll, Lewis

Misdoings of Charley Peace, The: Percy, Edward

Miser, The: Green, Paul

Miser, The: Malleson, Miles

Miser, The: Shadwell, Thomas

Miserable clerk, The: †Rudd, Steele

Miserie of Flaunders, The: Churchyard, Thomas

Miseries of Christmas, The: Riddell, *Mrs.* J.H.

Miseries of New York, The: Ingraham, J.H.

Miser's daughter, The: Ainsworth, Harrison

Miser's legacy, The: Maltby, H.F.

Miser's money: Phillpotts, Eden

Misfortunes of Elphin, The: Peacock, Thomas Love

Misfortunes of Peter Faber, The: Neal, J.C.

Misleading cases in common law: Herbert, *Sir* A.P.

Miss America: Turner, W.J.R.

Miss Armstrong's and other circumstances: Davidson, John

Miss Bellard's inspiration: Howells, W.D.

Miss Bendix: Royde-Smith, Naomi

Miss Betty: Stoker, Bram

Miss Bianca: Sharp, Margery

Miss Biddy Frobisher: Manning, Anne

Miss Billy: Porter, E.H.

Miss Billy—married: Porter, E.H.

Miss Billy's decision: Porter, E.H.

Miss Bobbie: Turner, E.S.

Miss Bouverie: Molesworth, *Mrs.*

Miss Bretherton: Ward, M.A.

Miss Brown: Lee, Vernon

Miss Brown of XXO: Oppenheim, E.Phillips

Miss Bunting: Thirkell, Angela

Miss Cayley's adventures: Allen, Grant

Miss Cherry-Blossom of Tokyo: Long, J.L.

Miss Civilization: Davis, R.H.

Miss Crespigny: Burnett, Frances Hodgson

Miss Defarge: Burnett, Frances Hodgson

Miss Eyre from Boston: Moulton, E.L.

Miss Gascoigne: Riddell, *Mrs.* J.H.

Miss Gilbert's career: Holland, J.G.

Miss Granby's secret: Farjeon, Eleanor

Miss Happiness and Miss Flower: Godden, Rumer

Miss Helyett: Belasco, David

Miss in her teens: Garrick, David

Miss Jacobsen's chance: Praed, *Mrs.* C.

Miss Jemima: De la Mare, Walter

Miss Lavington: Mottram, R.H.

Miss Linsey and Pa: Gibbons, Stella

Miss Lonelyhearts: †West, Nathaniel

"Miss Lou": Roe, E.P.

Miss Lucy in town: Fielding, Henry

Miss Ludington's sister: Bellamy, Edward

Miss Lulu Bett: Gale, Zona

Miss Mabel: Sherriff, R.C.

Miss MacKenzie: Trollope, Anthony

Miss Maitland's spy: Hannay, J.O.

Miss Mamma Aimee: Caldwell, Erskine Preston

Miss Mannering: Ridge, W.Pett

Miss Mapp: Benson, E.F.

Miss Marjoribanks: Oliphant, Margaret

Miss Marvel: Forbes, Esther

Miss Maxwell's affections: Pryce, Richard

Miss Mehetable's son: Aldrich, Thomas Bailey

Miss Mew: Sitwell, *Sir* Osbert

Miss Mouse and her boys: Molesworth, *Mrs.*

Miss Muff and Little Hungry: Warner, A.B.

Miss 1917: Wodehouse, P.G.

Miss Ogilvy finds herself: Hall, M.R.

Miss Oona McQuarrie: Smith, Alexander

Miss or Mrs.?: Collins, Wilkie

Miss Parson's adventure: Russell, W.C.

Miss Peter's special: Webb, Alice T.

Miss Pinkerton: Rinehart, Mary Roberts

Miss Polly Lopp: Read, O.P.

Miss Pym disposes: (†Josephine Tey), Mackintosh, Elizabeth

Miss Quillet: Baring-Gould, Sabine

Miss Ravenel's conversion from secession to loyalty: De Forest, John

Miss Robinson: Baker, Elizabeth

Miss Springtime: Wodehouse, P.G.

Miss Tassey: Baker, Elizabeth

Miss Tickletoby's lectures on English history: Thackeray, W.M.

Miss Tiller's vegetable garden: Warner, A.B.

Miss Tommy: Craik, *Mrs.* Dina

Miss Torrobin's experiment: Vachell, H.A.

Miss Tu: Lin Yu-T'ang

Miss Zilphia Gant: Faulkner, William

Missee Lee: Ransome, Arthur

Misselmah: Morier, J.J.

"Missing": Ward, M.A.

Missing angel, The: (†The Chiel), Cox, Erle

Missing answers to "An Englishwoman's love letters": The: Housman, Laurence

Missing aunt, The: Cole, G.D.H.

Missing Delora, The: Oppenheim, E.Phillips

Missing diplomats, The: Connolly, Cyril

Missing from home: Trease, Geoffrey

Missing hand, The: Hoffe, Monckton

Missing link, The: Dyson, E.G.

Missing masterpiece, The: Belloc, Hilaire

Missing million, The: Wallace, Edgar

Missing muse and other essays, The: Guedalla, Philip

Missing witness, The: Braddon, Mary Elizabeth

Mission and the man, The: Bedford-Jones, Henry

Mission of St. Philip Neri, The: Newman, J.H.

Mission of the Benedictine order, The: Newman, J.H.

Mission; or, Scenes in Africa, The: Marryat, Frederick

Mission that failed: Wallace, Edgar

Mission to Gelele, King of Dahome: Burton, *Sir* Richard

Missionaries to the Maoris, The: Anderson, J.C.

Missionary, The: Bowles, William

Missionary, The: Morgan, *Lady* Sydney

Missionary sketches: Smith, S.F.

Missionary travels and researches in South Africa: Livingstone, David

Missionary's memorial A: Barton, Bernard

Missioner, The: Oppenheim, E. Phillips

Mississippi Bubble, The: Hough, Emerson

Mississippi valley in the Civil War, The: Fiske, John

Mist of morning: MacKay, I.E.

Mist over Athelney: Trease, Geoffrey

Mistake, The: Vanbrugh, *Sir* John

Mistaken husband, The: Dryden, John

Mr. Absalom: Sullivan, Alan

Mr. Absalom Billingslea and other Georgia folk: Johnston, R.M.

Mr. Allen: Vachell, H.A.

Mr. Ambrose's letters on the rebellion: Kennedy, J.P.

Mr. Ames against time: Child, P.A.

Mr. and Mrs. Daventry: Harris, J.T.

Mr. and Mrs. Haddock abroad: Stewart, D.O.

Mr. and Mrs. Haddock in Paris, France: Stewart, D.O.

Mr. and Mrs. Nevill Tyson: Sinclair, May

Mr. and Mrs. Pennington: Young, Francis Brett

Mr. Anthony: Boyle, Roger

Mister Antonio: Tarkington, Booth

Mr. Apollo: Ford, Ford Madox

Mr. Arcularis: Aiken, Conrad

Mister Bosphorus and the muses: Ford, Ford Madox

Mr. Barrington: Bridges, Roy

Mr. Bazalgette's legacy: Merrick, Leonard

Mr. Belloc objects to "The outline of history": Wells, H.G.

Mr. Beluncle: Pritchett, V.S.

Mr. Benedict's lion: Edmonds, W.D.

Mr. Bennett and Mrs. Brown: Woolf, Virginia

Mr. Billingham the marquis and Madelon: Oppenheim, E. Phillips

Mr. Billy Downs and his likes: Johnston, R.M.

Mr. Bingle: McCutcheon, G.B.

Mr. Blake's walking-stick: Eggleston, Edward

Mr. Blettsworthy on Rampole Island: Wells, H.G.

Mr. Bolfry: †Bridie, James

Mr. Britling sees it through: Wells, H.G.

Mr. Brodrick's army: Churchill, *Sir* Winston

Mr. Brown's letters to a young man about town: Thackeray, W.M.

Mr. Budd (of Kennington, S.E.): Maltby, H.F.

Mr. Buffum: De Selincourt, Hugh

Mr. Byculla: Linklater, Eric

Mr. Campion and others: Allingham, Margery

Mister Caution—Mister Callaghan: †Cheyney, Peter

Mr. Charles, King of England: Drinkwater, John

Mr. Churchill: Guedalla, Philip

Mr. Clutterbucky's election: Belloc, Hilaire

Mr. Cohen takes a walk: Rinehart, Mary Roberts

Mr. C—n's discourse of freethinking: Swift, Jonathan

Mr. Cottons letter lately printed, examined and answered: Williams, Roger

Mr. Crewe's career: Churchill, Winston

Mr. Cronk's cases: Darlington, W.A.

Mr. Cupboard: Blackwood, Algernon

Mr. Darhy: Armstrong, M.D.

Mr. Digweed and Mr. Lumb: Phillpotts, Eden

Mr. Dooley in peace and in war: Dunne, Finley Peter

Mr. Dooley in the hearts of his countrymen: Dunne, Finley Peter

Mr. Dooley on making a will: Dunne, Finley Peter

Mr. Dooley says: Dunne, Finley Peter

Mr. Dooley's opinions: Dunne, Finley Peter

Mr. Dooley's philosophy: Dunne, Finley Peter

Mr. Dyson's speech to the freeholders on reform: Smith, Sydney

Mr. Emanuel: Golding, Louis

Mr. Eno, his birth, death and life: Munro, C.K.

Mr. Faint-heart: († Ian Hay), Beith, *Sir* John Hay

Mr. Faithful: Dunsany, E.J.M.D.P.

Mister Farebrother: Farjeon, B.L.

Mr. Faust: Ficke, Arthur Davison

Mr. Fleight: Ford, Ford Madox

Mr. Fortner's marital claims: Johnston, R.M.

Mr. Fortune's maggot: Warner, Sylvia Townsend

Mr. Fox: †Dane, Clemence

Mr. Gay's London: Herbert, *Sir* A.P.

Mr. Gilhooley: O'Flaherty, Liam

Mr. Gillie: †Bridie, James

Mr. Gladstone: Young, G.M.

Mr. Godly beside himself: Bullett, Gerald

Mr. Grantley's idea: Cooke, John Esten

Mr. Grex of Monte Carlo: Oppenheim, E.Phillips

Mr. Gurney and Mr. Slade: Deeping, Warwick

Mr. H.: Lamb, Charles

Mr. Hamish Gleave: Llewellyn, Richard

Mr. Hampdens speech: Denham, *Sir* John

Mr. Hides argument before the Lords: Clarendon, Edward Hyde

Mr. Hobbes considered in his loyalty, religion, reputation and manners: Hobbes, Thomas

Mr. Hodge and Mr. Hazard: Wylie, Elinor

Mr. Hogarth's will: Spence, C.H.

Mr. Howerson: Read, O.P.

Mr. Huffam: Walpole, *Sir* Hugh

Mr. Hurricane: Golding, Louis

Mr. Hutaf sees Hoboken in aquiline perspective: Morley, C.D.

Mr. Incoul's misadventure: Saltus, E.E.

Mr. Ingleside: Lucas, E.V.

Mr. Isaacs: Crawford, E. Marion

Mr. Jack Hamlin's meditation: Harte, Bret

Mr. January and Mrs. Ex: Akins, Zoë

Mr. J.G. Reeder returns: Wallace, Edgar

Mister Johnson: Cary, Joyce

Mr. Jorkens remembers Africa: Dunsany, E.J.M.D.P.

Mr. Justice Holmes and the Supreme Court: Frankfurter, Felix

Mr. Justice Maxwell: Wallace, Edgar

Mr. Justice Raffles: Hornung, E.W.

Mr. Kahn would like to know: Lippmann, Walter

Mr. Keegan's elopement: Churchill, Winston

Mr. Kettle and Mrs. Moon: Priestley, J.B.

Mr. Kinglake and the Quarterlys: Hayward, Abraham

Mr. Kingsley and Dr. Newman: a correspondence on the question whether Dr. Newman teaches that truth is no virtue: Newman, J.H.

Mr. Kris Kringle: a Christmas tale: Mitchell, S.W.

Mr. Laxworthy's adventures: Oppenheim, E.Phillips

Mr. Lazarus: O'Higgins, H.J.

Mr. Lessingham goes home: Oppenheim, E.Phillips

Mr. Littlejohn: Flavin, Martin

Mr. Locke's reply to the ...Bishop of Worcester's answer to his letter: Locke, John

Mr. Loveday's little outing: Waugh, Evelyn

Mr. Lucton's freedom: Young, Francis Brett

Mr. Macklin's reply to Mr. Garrick's answer: Macklin, Charles

Mr. Meeson's will: Haggard, *Sir* H.Rider

Mr. Midshipman Easy: Marryatt, Frederick

Mr. Midshipman Hornblower: Forester, C.S.

Mr. Mirakel: Oppenheim, E.Phillips

Mr. Misfortunate: †Bowen, Marjorie

Mr. Moffatt: Cobb, C.F.

Mr. Moon: Carman, Bliss

Mr. Moto is so sorry: Marquand, J.P.

Mr. Mulliner speaking: Wodehouse, P.G.

Mr. Munchausen: Bangs, J.K.

Mr. Nightingale's diary: Dickens, Charles

Mr. Norris changes trains: Isherwood, Christopher

Mr. Olim: Raymond, Ernest

Mr. Oram's story: De Selincourt, Aubrey

Mr. Pepys: Bax, Clifford

Mr. Perrin and Mr. Traill: Walpole, *Sir* Hugh

Mr. Petre: Belloc, Hilaire

Mr. Petunia: Gogarty, O. St. John

Mr. Pewter: Herbert, *Sir* A.P.

Mr. Pim: Milne, A.A.

Mr. Pim passes by: Milne, A.A.

Mr. Pisistratus Brown, M.P. in the highlands: Black, William

Mister Pitt: Gale, Zona

Mr. Prohack: Bennett, Arnold

Mr. Prudhomme at the International exhibition: Swinburne, A.C.

Mr. Punch's county songs: Lucas, E.V.

Mr. Punch's model music hall songs and dramas: †Anstey, F.

Mr. Punch's pocket Ibsen: †Anstey, F.

Mr. Punch's young reciter: †Anstey, F.

Mr.Rabbit at home: Harris, Joel Chandler

Mr. Romford's hounds: Surtees, R.S.

Mr. Roosevelt: Mackenzie, *Sir* Compton

Mr. Rowl: Broster, D.K.

Mr. Sampath: Narayan, R.K.

Mr. Scarborough's family: Trollope, Anthony

Mr. Sefton, murderer: Crofts, F.W.

Mr.Sheridan's umbrella:Strong, L.A.G.

Mr.Sidgwick's hedonism: Bradley, F.H.

Mr. Skeffington: Russell, E.M.

Mr. Smirke: Marvell, Andrew

Mr. Smith: Bromfield, Louis

Mr. Sponge's sporting tour: Surtees, R.S.

Mr. Standfast: Buchan, John

Mr. Stimpson and Mr. Gorse: Hamilton, Patrick

Mr. Sun and Mrs. Moon: Le Gallienne, Richard

Mr. Tangier's vacations: Hale, E.E.

Mr. Tasker's gods: Powys, T.F.

Mr. Teddy: Benson, E.F.

Mr. Tennyson and Mr. Browning: Dowden, Edward

Mr. Thackeray, Mr. Yates and the Garrick Club: Yates, E.H.

Mr. Thomas Coriat to his friends in England sendeth greetings: Coryate, Thomas

Mr. Tommy Dove: Deland, Margaret

Mr. Tyler's saints: †Bowen, Marjorie

Mr. Verdant Green married and done for: †Bede, Cuthbert

Mr. Waddington of Wyck: Sinclair, May

Mr. Waddy's return: Winthrop, Theodore

Mr. Washington: †Bowen, Marjorie

Mr. Weston's good wine: Powys, T.F.

Mr. Whistler's lecture on art: Swinburne, A.C.

Mr. White: Tarkington, Booth

Mr. William Shakespeare: His true chronicle histories of the life and death of King Lear and his three daughters: Shakespeare, William

Mr. Wilson's war: Dos Passos, John

Mr. Wingrave, millionaire: Oppenheim, E.Phillips

Mr. Witt's widow: (†Anthony Hope), Hawkins, Anthony Hope

Mr. Wray's cash box: Collins, Wilkie

Misticism in modern India:Sena, Kesava Chandra

Mistletoe child, The: Palmer, H.E.

Mistral: †Brand, Max

Mistress, The: Cowley, Abraham

Mistress and maid: Craik, *Mrs.* Dinah

Mistress Masham's repose: White, T.H.

Mistress Nell Gwyn: †Bowen, Marjorie

Mistress of mistresses: Eddison, Eric Rucker

Mistress of royalty, The: Pierce, Egan

Mistress of Shenstone, The: Barclay, F.L.

Mistress of the Manse, The: Holland, J.G.

Mistress Pat: Montgomery,L.M.

Mitch Miller: Masters, E.L.

Mithraic emblems: Campbell, Roy

Mithridates King of Pontus:Lee, Nathaniel

Mitre Court: Riddell, *Mrs*. J.H.

Mixed bag, A: Wren, P.C.

Mixed company: Shaw, Irwin

Mixed essays: Arnold, Matthew

Mixed farming and muddled thinking: Bateson, F.W.

Mixed grill, A: Phillpotts, Eden

Mixed grill: Ridge, W.P.

Mixed marriage: Ervine, St. John

Mixed pasture: Underhill, Evelyn

Mixed pickles: †Bell, Neil

Mixed sweets from Routledge's Annual: Wood, Ellen

Mixed vintage: Appel, Benjamin

Mixed vintages: Lucas, E.V.

Mixer, The: Wallace, Edgar

Mixt contemplations in better times: Fuller, Thomas

Mixture as before, The: Maugham, Somerset

Mixture of frailties, A: Davies, Robertson

Mizpah: Wilcox, E.W.

Mo Burdekin: Campion, Sarah

Mob, The: Galsworthy, John

Moby Dick: Melville, Herman

Moccasin maker, The: Johnson, E.P.

Moccasin Ranch, The: Garland, Hamlin

Moccasins of silence, The: Favenc, Ernest

Mock Beggar Hall: Graves, Robert

Mock doctor, The: Fielding, Henry

Mock-beggar, The: Kaye-Smith, Shiela

Mockers, The: Barlow, Jane

Mockery Gap: Powys, T.F.

Mocking is catching: Carey, Henry

Mock-mourners, The: Defoe, Daniel

Model memoirs and other sketches from simple to serious: Leacock, Stephen

Model men: Mayhew, Horace

Model women and children: Mayhew, Horace

Model of Christian Gray, The: Vachell, H.A.

Modern Aladdin, A: Pyle, Howard

Modern American novelists: Cournos, John

Modern and ancient roads in Eastern Asia Minor: Hogarth, D.G.

Modern Antaeus, A: Housman, Laurence

Modern antiques: O'Keeffe, John

Modern architects: Mumford, Lewis

Modern architecture: Wright, Frank Lloyd

Modern aristocracy or the bard's reception: Brydges, *Sir* Samuel Egerton

Modern Australian literature, 1900–1923: Palmer, Nettie

Modern British monarchy, The: Petrie, *Sir* Charles

Modern buccaneer, A: †Boldrewood, Rolf

Modern characteristics: Morley, John

Modern chivalry, The: Brackenridge, Hugh

Modern chivalry: Gore, Catherine

Modern Chivalry, or a new Orlando Furioso: Ainsworth, William H.

Modern chronicle, A: Churchill, Winston

Modern Columbus, A: Mais, S.P.B.

Modern comedy, A: Galsworthy, John

Modern democracy: Becker, C.L.

Modern development of the New World: Fiske, John

Modern Dick Whittington, A: Payn, James

Modern dilemma, The: Fausset, Hugh

Modern drama, The: Lewisohn, Ludwig

Modern drama in Europe: Jameson, Storm

Modern dramatists: Dukes, Ashley

Modern education superior to ancient: Mackenzie, Henry

Modern English fiction, a personal view: Bullett, Gerald

Modern English novel, The: Cross, W.L.

Modern English painters: Rothenstein, *Sir* John

Modern English usage: Fowler, H.W.

Modern Faust, A: Noel, R.B.W.

Modern fine gentleman, The: Jenyns, Soame

Modern fine lady, The: Jenyns, Soame

Modern foreign pictures in the Tate Gallery: Rothenstein, *Sir* John

Modern geography and history: Galt, John

Modern Greece: Hemans, *Mrs.* Felicia

Modern Griselda, The: Edgeworth, Maria

Modern hero, A: Bromfield, Louis

Modern history: Becker, C.L.

Modern history: Phillips, John

Modern husband, The: Fielding, Henry

Modern ideas of evolution as related to revelation and science: Dawson, *Sir* J.W.

Modern India: Dutt, R.P.

Modern instance, A: Howells, W.D.

Modern Italian poets: Howells, W.D.

Modern Japanese print: Michener, James

Modern languages at Oxford: Firth, *Sir* Charles

Modern literature of France: Reynolds, G.

Modern love: Meredith, George

Modern lover, A: Lawrence, D.H.

Modern lover, A: Moore, George

Modern lovers: Meynell, Viola

Modern man and maid, The: †Grand, Sarah

Modern medical treatment: Miller, Henry

Modern men and mummers: Pearson, Hesketh

Modern Mephistopheles, A: Alcott, Louisa M.

Modern Mephistopheles and a whisper in the dark, A: Alcott, Louisa M.

Modern miracle men: Beach, R.E.

Modern mythology: Lang, Andrew

Modern novel writing, or the elegant enthusiast: Beckford, William

Modern Orlando, The: Croly, George

Modern pagans: Sheldon, C.M.

Modern painters: Ruskin, John

Modern painting: Moore, George

Modern Plutarch, A: Cournos, John

Modern poetry: Macneice, Louis

Modern poetry and the tradition: Brooks, Cleanth

Modern prelude, A: Fausset, Hugh

Modern priestess of Isis: Leaf, Walter

Modern problems: Lodge, *Sir* Oliver

Modern Prometheus, The: Oppenheim, E. Phillips

Modern prose style: Dobrée, Bonamy

Modern "Rake's Progress", The: †West, Rebecca

Modern rhetoric: Brooks, Cleanth

Modern rhetoric, A: Warren, Robert Penn

Modern science in Bible lands: Dawson, *Sir* J.W.

Modern scientific ideas: Lodge, *Sir* Oliver

Modern short story, The: Bates, H.E.

Modern Socialism: Ensor, *Sir* R.C.K.

Modern society: Howe, Julia Ward

Modern states-man, The: Wither, George

Modern studies: Elton, Oliver

Modern symposium, A: Dickinson, Goldsworthy Lowes

Modern temper, The: Krutch, J.W.

Modern theories and forms of industrial organisation: Cole, G.D.H.

Modern tragedy, A: Bentley, Phyllis

Modern traveller, The: Belloc, Hilaire

Modern Utopia, A: Wells, H. G.

Modern Vanity Fair, A: Graham, Stephen

Modern views of electricity: Lodge, *Sir* Oliver

Modern views of matter: Lodge, *Sir* Oliver

Modern Vikings, The: Boyesen, H.H.

Modern warning, The: James, Henry

Modern writer, The: Anderson, Sherwood

Modernism in modern drama: Krutch, J.W.

Moderns, essays in literary criticism, The: Freeman, John

Modes and morals: Gerould, Katharine

Modes of thought: Whitehead, A.N.

Modest and free conference betwixt a conformist and a nonconformist, A: Burnet, Gilbert

Modest apology for my own conduct, A: Lyttelton, George *Baron*

Modest enquiry into ... paper currency, A: Franklin, Benjamin

Modest proposal for preventing the children of poor people from being a burthen to their parents, A: Swift, Jonathan

Modesta: Stern, G.B.

Modius Salium: Wood, Anthony à

Modred: Newbolt, *Sir* Henry

Mogg Megone: Whittier, J.G.

Mogreb-el-Acksa: Cunninghame Graham, Robert

Mogul tale, A: Inchbald, *Mrs.* Elizabeth

Mohamedan commentary in the Holy Bible, The: Ahmad Khan, *Sir* Saiyid

Mohawks: Braddon, M.E.

Mohocks, The: Gay, John

Mohun: Cooke, John Esten

Moira: Green, Julian

Moira of Green Hills: Lawson, Will

Mola Asinaria: Butler, Samuel

Moldy Warp the mole: Uttley, Alison

Molière: Palmer, J.L.

Molière: his life and his works: Matthews, J.B.

Moliere: the comic mask: Lewis, D.B.Wyndham

Molière-characters: Clarke, Charles Cowden

Moll Pitcher: Jones, J.S.

Moll Pitcher: Whittier, J.G.

Moll Pitcher, and the minstrel girl: Whittier, J.G.

Mollentrave on women: Sutro, Alfred

Mollie and the unwiseman: Bangs, J.K.

Mollie and the unwiseman a-broad: Bangs, J.K.

Molloy: Beckett, Samuel

Mollusc, The: Davies, H.H.

Molly Cottontail: Caldwell, Erskin Preston

Molly Mogg: Gay, John

Moloch: Praed, *Mrs.* C.

Molson family, The: Sandwell, B.K.

Moment, The: Woolf, Virginia

Moment after, The: Buchanan, R.B.

Moment in Peking: Lin Yu-T'ang

Moment of choice: Lindsay, Jack

Moment of time, A: Bates, H.E.

Moment of time, A: Hughes, R.A.W.

Moment of truth, The: Jameson, Storm

Moments en voyage: Mackaye, Percy

Moments of vision: Hardy, Thomas

Momus triumphans: Langbaine, Gerard

Monarch of dreams, The: Higginson, T.W.

Monarch of Mincing Lane: Black, William

Monarch of the glen, The: Mackenzie, *Sir* Compton

Monarch, the big bear of Tallac: Seton-Thompson, E.

Monarchick tragedies, The: Alexander, William

Monarchist, The: Jones, J.B.

Monarchy (Louis XIV): Belloc, Hilaire

Monarchy: Nicolson, Hon. *Sir* Harold

Monastery, The: Scott, *Sir* Walter

Monasticon Anglicanum: Dugdale, *Sir* William

Moncktons, The: Moodie, Susanna

Monday morning: Hamilton, Patrick

Monday night: Boyle, Kay

Monday or Tuesday: Woolf, Virginia

Money: Lytton, E.

Money and morals: Gill, Eric

Money doesn't matter: Jennings, Gertrude

Money for nothing: Wodehouse, P.G.

Money from Holme: (†Michael Innes), Stewart, J.I.M.

Money from home: Runyon, Damon

Money game, The: Angell, *Sir* Norman

Money: gold, silver, or bimetallism: (†Eli Perkins), Landon, Melville

Money in the bank: Wodehouse, P.G.

Money is an asse: Jordan, Thomas

Money, its present and future: Cole, G.D.H.

Money, land and transportation: Garland, Hamlin

Money, love and Kate: Porter, E.H.

Money magic: Garland, Hamlin

Money mad: Beach, R.E.

Money master, The: Parker, *Sir* H.G.

Money Moon, The: Farnol, J.J.

Money mystery, The: Angell, *Sir* Norman

Money pamphlets: Pound, Ezra

Money spinner, The: Pinero *Sir* A.W.

Money spinners, The: †Sinclair Murray

Money the mistress: Southern, Thomas

Money to grow on: Chase, Stuart

Money with menaces: Hamilton, Patrick

Money writes!: Sinclair, Upton

Money-box, The: Lynd, Robert

Moneychangers, The: Sinclair, Upton

Moneyed man, The: Smith, Horatio

Money-king, The: Saxe, J.G.

Money-lender, The: Gore, Catherine

Moneyman, The: Costain, T.B.

Moneys from Shylock: Rubenstein, Harold F.

Money-spinner, The: †Merriman, Seton

Monikins, The: Cooper, James Fenimore

Monitress Merle: Brazil, Angela

Monk, The: Lewis, M.G.

Monk and the hangman's daughter, The: Bierce, Ambrose

Monk and the miller's wife, The: Ramsay, Allan

Monk Knight of St. John, The: Richardson, John

Monk of Cruta, A: Oppenheim, E.Phillips

Monk of Fife, A: Lang, Andrew

Monkey: Waley, Arthur

Monkey-puzzle, The: Beresford, J.D.

Monkey's paw, The: Jacobs, W.W.

Monks are monks: Nathan, G.J.

Monk's Norton: Manning, Anne

Monks, nuns and monasteries: Sitwell, Sacheverell

Monks of St. Mark, The: Peacock, Thomas Love

Monks of Thelema, The: Besant, *Sir* Walter and James Rice

Monkshood: Phillpotts, Eden

Monnow: Benson, A.C.

Monody on Major André: Seward, Anna

Monody on the death of Gen. Cotesworth Pinckney: Simms, W.G.

Monody on the death of John Philip Kemble: Ainsworth, Harrison

Monody on the death of the Right Honourable R.B. Sheridan: Byron, George Gordon *Lord*

Monody on the death of Wendell Phillips, A: Aldrich, Thomas Bailey

Monody written at Matlock: Bowles, W.L.

Monogamy, a series of dramatic lyrics: Gould, Gerald

Monogram: Stern, G.B.

Monograph on the cirripedia, A: Darwin, Charles

Monographs. Personal and social: Milnes, R.M.

Monopoly: Morris, William

Monopoly versus property: Reade, Charles

Monsieur Beaucaire: Tarkington, Booth

Monsieur D'en Brochette: Bangs, J.K.

Monsieur d'Olive: Chapman, George

Monsieur Henri: Guiney, L.I.

Monsieur Judas: Hume, Fergus Wright

Monsieur Motte: King, G.E.

Monsieur Pichelmère: Baring-Gould, Sabine

Monsieur Thomas: Fletcher, John

Monster, The: Crane, Stephen

Monster, The: (†Harrington Hext), Phillpotts, Eden

Monster, The: Saltus, E.E.

Monstre Gai: Lewis, P. Wyndham

Monstrous regiment: Hollis, Christopher

Monstrous regiment of women, The: Ford, Ford Madox

Mont Blanc: Mayhew, Henry

Mont Saint Michel and Chartres: Adams, H.B.

Montalbert: Smith, Charlotte

Montcalm and Wolfe: Parkman, Francis

Montelion: Phillips, John

Montes the Matador: Harris, J.T.

Montessori mother, A: Canfield, Dorothy

Montezuma: Ingraham, J.H.

Montezuma and the conquest of Mexico: Eggleston, Edward

Montezuma's daughter: Haggard, *Sir* H. Rider

Montforts, The: †Mills, Martin

Month in England, A: Tuckerman, H.T.

Month in Gordon Square, A: Swinnerton, Frank

Month of the falling leaves, The: Marshall, Bruce

Month soon goes, A: Jameson, Storm

Months, The: Hosmer, W.H.C.

Months descriptive of the successive beauties of the year, The: Hunt, Leigh

Montreal after 250 years: Lighthall, W.D.

Montreal: seaport and city: Leacock, Stephen

Montrose: Buchan, John

Montrose: Wedgwood, C.V.

Montyon prizes, The: Kavanagh, Julia

Monument, The: Dennis, John

Monumental columne, erected to the living memory of the ever-glorious Henry, late Prince of Wales, A: Webster, John

Monumental poem in memory of Sir George Treby, A: Tate, Nahum

Monuments of Honor: Webster, John

Monuments of Sudanese Nubia, The: Breasted, J.H.

Mood without measure: Church, Richard

Moods: Alcott, Louisa M.

Moods and memories: Cawein, Madison

Moods, cadenced and declaimed: Dreiser, Theodore

Moods of Ginger Mick, The: Dennis, C.M.J.

Moods, songs & doggerels: Galsworthy, John

Mooltiki: Godden, Rumer

Moon, The: Squire, *Sir* J.C.

Moon, The: Thoreau, H.D.

Moon and sixpence, The: Maugham, Somerset

Moon endureth, The: Buchan, John

Moon for the misbegotten, A: O'Neill, Eugene

Moon in the yellow river, The: Johnston, W.D.

Moon is down, The: Steinbeck, John

Moon is feminine, The: †Dane, Clemence

Moon is shining bright as day, The: Nash, Ogden

Moon of desire: Prichard, K.S.

Moon of Israel: Haggard, *Sir* H. Rider

Moon of much gladness: Bramah, E.

Moon of the Caribbees, The: O'Neill, Eugene

Moon of the fourteenth night, The: Sladen, D.B.W.

Moon tenders, The: Derleth, A.W.

Moon worms, The: Lindsay, N.V.

Moonbeams from the larger lunacy: Leacock, Stephen

Moon-Calf: Dell, Floyd

Moondyne: O'Reilly, J.B.

Moon-face: London, Jack

Moonfleet: Falkner, John Meade

Moonflower, The: Nichols, Beverley

Moonhills: Vachell, H.A.

Moonlight, The: Cary, Joyce

Moonlight acre: Fitzgerald, R.D.

Moonlight is silver: †Dane, Clemence

Moonlit doorway, The: †Mackenzie, Kenneth

Moonlit way, The: Chambers, R.W.

Moonraking: Street, A.G.

Moon's farm: Read, *Sir* Herbert

Moons of grandeur: Benét, William Rose

Moonshine: Carman, Bliss

Moonshine: Roberts, T.G.

Moonshine and clover: Housman, Laurence

Moonshine and magic: Uttley, Alison

Moonstone, The: Collins, Wilkie

Moore versus Harris: Moore, George

Moorland cottage, The: Gaskell, *Mrs.* Elizabeth

Moorland idylls: Allen, Grant

Moors and the fens, The: †Trafford, F.G.

Moose-hunter, The: Neal, John

Mopsa the fairy: Ingelow, Jean

Moqu the wanderer: Colum, Padraic

Moral action and natural law in Kant, and some developments: Miller, E.M.

Moral alphabet, A: Belloc, Hilaire

Moral axioms in single couplets: Brydges, *Sir* Samuel Egerton

Moral basis of politics: Mitchison, Naomi

Moral courage: Mackenzie, *Sir* Compton

Moral crusader, The: Smith, Goldwin

Moral ending, A: Warner, Sylvia Townsend

Moral epistle, respectfully dedicated to Earl Stanhope: Landor, W.S.

Moral history of America's life struggle, The: †Nasby, Petroleum V.

Moral law and the highest good: Miller, E.M.

Moral obligation to be intelligent, The: Erskine, John

Moral philosophie of Doni, The: North, *Sir* Thomas

Moral pieces, in prose and verse: Sigourney, L.H.

Moral review of the revolutionary war, A: Judd, Sylvester

Moral sketches of prevailing opinions and manners: More, Hannah

Moral, social and professional duties of attorneys and solicitors, The: Warren, Samuel

Moral tales. By Lady—: Stevenson, J.H.

Moral tales for young people: Edgeworth, Maria

Moral uses of dark things: Bushnell, Horace

Moralist, The: Roberts, W. Adolphe

Moralities: Spence, Joseph

Morality of the profession of letters, The: Stevenson, R.L.

Morall fables of Esope: Henryson, Robert

Morals and dogma of freemasonry: Pike, Albert

Morals of Abou Adhem, The: †Nasby, Petroleum V.

Morals of chess, The: Franklin, Benjamin

Moran Chambers smiled: Oppenheim, E. Phillips

Moran of the Lady Letty: †Norris, Frank

Morando: Greene, Robert

Mord Em'ly: Ridge, W. Pett

Mordaunt: Moore, *Dr.* John

Mordred: Campbell, W.W.

Mordred: Robinson, E.A.

More: Beerbohm, *Sir* Max

More about Junius: Hayward, Abraham

More about me: Drinkwater, John

More about me: Jacob, Naomi

More "Bab" ballads: Gilbert, *Sir* W.S.

More beasts for worse children: Belloc, Hilaire

More bedtime stories: Moulton, E.L.

More biography: Bentley, E.C.

More books I like: Mais, S.P.B.

More books on the table: Gosse, *Sir* Edmund

More bye-words: Yonge, C.M.

More cricket songs: Gale, Norman R.

More dissemblers besides women: Middleton, Thomas

More echoes: Godley, A.D.

More educated Evans: Wallace, Edgar

More essays of love and virtue: Ellis, Havelock

More ever ready plays: Peach, L. du Garde

More for your garden: Sackville-West, Victoria

More from Methuselah: Vachell, H.A.

More ghost stories: James, M.R.

More harbours of memory: McFee, William

More Indian fairy stories: Anand, M.R.

More joy in heaven: Callaghan, M.E.

More knaves than one: Packard, F.L.

More lay thoughts of a Dean: Inge, W.R.

More leaves: Victoria, Queen of England

More lines from Deepwood: Bourinot, A.S.

More lives than one: Krutch, J.W.

More lyric odes to the Royal Academicians: †Pindar, Peter

More me and Gus: Anthony, Frank S.

More memories: thoughts about England spoken in America: Hole, Samuel Reynolds

More misleading cases: Herbert, *Sir* A.P.

More money: †Pindar, Peter,

More new Arabian nights: Stevenson, R.L.

More nice types: †Armstrong, Anthony and Raff

More nonsense pictures, rhymes, botany, etc.: Lear, Edward

More obiter dicta: Birrell, Augustine

More of us: Frankau, Gilbert

More opera nights: Newman, Ernest

More peers: Belloc, Hilaire

More people: Masters, E.L.

More poems: Housman, A.E.

More popular fallacies: Fowler, H.W.

More pricks than kicks: Beckett, Samuel

More reformation: Defoe, Daniel

More Rhodesian rhymes: Gouldsbury, H.C.

More short sixes: Bunner, H.C.

More short-ways with Dissenters: Defoe, Daniel

More songs from Vagabondia: Carman, Bliss

More spook stories: Benson, E.F.

More talk of Jane Austen: Kaye-Smith, Shiela and G.B. Stern

More than somewhat: Runyon, Damon

More than wife: Widdemer, Margaret

More lights on Yoga: Ghose, Sri Aurobindo

More tiny town tales: Logan, J.D.

More Tish: Rinehart, Mary Roberts

More trivia: Smith, L.L.P.

More verse and prose by the corn-law rhymer: Elliott, Ebenezer

More wanderings in London: Lucas, E.V.

More ways than one: Cowley, Mrs. Hannah

More women than men: Compton-Burnett, Ivy

More words ancient and modern: Weekley, Ernest

More work for the undertaker: Allingham, Margery

Moreover: (†Elzevir), Murdoch, Sir W.L.F.

Moreover, reflections on the game of cricket: De Selincourt, Hugh

Moreton Miles: Blocksidge, C.W.

Morgan Bible: Evans, Caradoc

Morgan's daughter: DeLisser, Herbert G.

Morgan's yard: Pryce, Richard

Morgesons, The: Stoddard, E.D.

Morley Ashton: Grant, James

Morley Ernstein: James, G.P.R.

Morley Roberts: the last eminent Victorian: Jameson, Storm

Mormons, The: Mayhew, Henry

Mormons and the silver mines: Bonwick, James

Mormons, or, life at Salt Lake City, The: English, Thomas Dunn

Morning: Riley, J.W.

Morning after the first night, The: Nathan, G.J.

Morning is near us, The: Glaspell, Susan

Morning journey: Hilton, James

Morning light: Tomlinson, H.M.

Morning, noon and night: Mackail, Denis

Morning, noon and night in London: Sitwell, Sacheverell

Morning ramble, The: Payne, Henry Nevil

Morning sacrifice: Cusack, E.D.

Morning song of Lord Zera, The: Aiken, Conrad

Morning sorrow: Rothenstein, Sir John

Morning star: Haggard, Sir H. Rider

Morning star, The: Williams, Emlyn

Morning tide: Gunn, Neil M.

Morning will come, The: Jacob, Naomi

Morning worship: Van Doren, Mark

Morning-glories: Alcott, Louisa M.

Morning-glory: Sassoon, Siegfried

Mornings in Florence: Ruskin, John

Mornings in Mexico: Lawrence, D.H.

Morning's war, The: Montague, C.E.

Moroccan mosaic: Mannin, Ethel

Morrell household calendar for 1936: Morley, C.D.

Morris Graeme: Ingraham, J.H.

Morris in the dance: Raymond, Ernest

Mortal antipathy, A: Holmes, Oliver Wendell

Mortal coils: Huxley, Aldous

Mortal image: Wylie, Elinor

Mortal storm, The: Bottome, Phyllis

Mortal strife: Powys, John Cowper

Mortal summer: Van Doren, Mark

Mortallone and Aunt Trinidad: (†Q), †Quiller-Couch, Sir Arthur

Mortals in the house, The: Dickens, Charles

Morte d'Arthur (prologue): Caxton, William

Mortgage o fa dream deferred: Hughes, J.L.

Mortgage on the hop-house roof, The: Tourgée, A.W.

Mortimer: Ingraham, J.H.

Mortimer Brice: Hichens, Robert

Mortimer touch: Linklater, Eric

Mortimeriados: Drayton, Michael

Mortomley's estate: Riddell, Mrs. J.H.

Morton's hope: Motley, J.L.

Morwyn: Powys, John Cowper

Mosada: Yeats, W.B.

Mosaic: Stern, G.B.

Mose Evans: Baker, W.M.

Moses: Rosenberg, Isaac

Moses: Untermeyer, Louis

Moses in red: Steffens, J.L.

Moses, Prince of Egypt: Fast, Howard M.

Moses' rock: †O'Connor, Frank

Mosquitoes: Faulkner, William

Moss and feather: Davies, W.H.

Moss Troopers, The: Crockett, S.R.

Mosses from an old manse: Hawthorne, Nathaniel

Most elegant and wittie epigrams of Sir John Harington, The: Harington, Sir John

Most exact discourse, how to trayne horses to amble, A: Markham, Gervase

Most excellent historie of the merchant of Venice, The: Shakespeare, William

Most famous historie of Mervine, The: Markham, Gervase

Most honorable tragedie of Sir Richard Grinvile, knight, The: Markham, Gervase

Most horrible, terrible, tollerable, termagant satyre, A: Taylor, John

Most important country, The: Connell, John

Most lamentable Romaine tragedie of Titus Andronicus, The: Shakespeare, William

Most likely to succeed: Dos Passos, John

Most of the game: Van Druten, J.W.

Most pleasaunt and excellent conceited comedie, of Syr John Falstaffe, and the merrie wives of Windsor, A: Shakespeare, William

Most secret: Carr, J.D.

Most secret: †Shute, Nevil

Most solemn epistle to the emperor of China, A: †Pindar, Peter

Most unfortunate day of my life, The: Edgeworth, Maria

"Most women…": Waugh, Alec

Moste excellent comedie of Alexander, Campaspe, and Diogenes, A: Lyly, John

Mostly Canallers: Edmonds, W.D.

Mostyn Stayne: Quinn, R.J.

Mote House Mystery, The: Vachell, H.A.

Moth, The: Cain, J.M.

Moth and rust: Cholmondeley, Mary

Moth and the flame, The: Fitch, Clyde William

Mother: Benson, E.F.

Mother, The: Buck, Pearl

Mother, The: Duncan, Norman

Mother, The: Ghose, Sri Aurobindo

Mother, The: Malleson, Miles

Mother, The: Mitchell, S.W.

Mother, The: Phillpotts, Eden

Mother, The: Royde-Smith, Naomi

Mother, The: Sitwell, Edith

Mother: Wister, Owen

Mother and child are doing well, The: Morton, J.M.

Mother and son: Compton-Burnett, Ivy

Mother and the father, The: Howells, W.D.

Mother Bombie: Lyly, John

Mother Carey's chickens: Crothers, Rachel

Mother Carey's chickens: Wiggin, K.D.

Mother colony of the Australias, The: Reid, *Sir* G.H.

Mother ditch: La Farge, Oliver

Mother Goose Land: Hall, J.N.

Mother knows best: Ferber, Edna

"Mother o' mine": Kipling, Rudyard

Mother of gold: Hough, Emerson

Mother of pearl: Herbert, *Sir* A.P.

Mother of the man, The: Phillpotts, Eden

Mother of us all, The: Stein, Gertrude

Mother tongue, The: Kittredge, G.L.

Mother, what is man?: Smith, Stevie

Mother-of-pearl: Jennings, Gertrude

Mothers, The: Adams, Arthur H.

Mothers, The: Fisher, V.A.

Mothers and children: Canfield, Dorothy

Mothers and daughters: Gore, Catherine

Mothers blessing, The: Breton, Nicholas

Mother's Day: Priestley, J.B.

Mother's little girl: Turner, E.S.

Mother's manual, The: Trollope, Frances

Mother's recompense, A: Aguilar, Grace

Mother's recompense, The: Wharton, Edith

Mothers to men: Gale, Zona

Moths: †Ouida

Motive: Lowndes, M.A.

Motley: †Bede, Cuthbert

Motley: Bengough, J.W.

Motley: De la Mare, Walter

Motley, A: Galsworthy, John

Motor-flight through France, A: Wharton, Edith

Mottled lizard, The: Huxley, Elspeth J.

Motto book, The: Hubbard, Elbert

Mouldy-Mowdiwart: Ramsay, Allan

Mt. Egmont: Baughan, B.E.

Mount Henneth: Bage, Robert

Mount Ida: Gibbon, Monk

Mount music: Somerville, Edith

Mount of olives, The: Vaughan, Henry

Mount Pleasant: Roscoe, William

Mount Royal: Braddon, M.E.

Mount Savage: Payne, J.H.

Mount Vernon on the Potomac: King, G.E.

Mount Zion: Betjeman, John

Mountain: Ervine, St. John

Mountain, The: Munro, C.K.

Mountain against mountain: Ficke, A.D.

Mountain bard, The: Hogg, James

Mountain beast, The: Gibbons, Stella

Mountain blood: Hergesheimer, Joseph

Mountain city: Sinclair, Upton

Mountain cloud: Barbeau, C.M.

Mountain Europa, A: Fox, John

Mountain flat: Mann, Leonard

Mountain interval: Frost, Robert

Mountain lovers: Gibson, Wilfred

Mountain lovers, The: †Macleod, Fiona

Mountain man: Fisher, V.A.

Mountain medicine: Guthrie, A.B.

Mountain of gold, The: †Winch, John

Mountain of magic, The: Nichols, Beverley

Mountain of the lovers, The: Hayne, P.H.

Mountain on the desert, The: Richter, Conrad

Mountain standard time: Horgan, Paul

Mountain tavern, The: O'Flaherty, Liam

Mountain time: De Voto, Bernard

Mountain town in France, A: Stevenson, R.L.

Mountaineers, The: Colman, George, *the younger*

Mountain-land: Chambers, R.W.

Mountains: Auden, W.H.

Mountains, The: White, S.E.

Mountains and lakes of Switzerland, The: Bray, Anna Eliza

Mountains and molehills: Cornford, Frances

Mountains of California, The: Muir, John

Mountains of the moon, The: Beresford, J.D.

Mountebanks, The: Gilbert, *Sir* W.S.

Mourner's vision, The: Donnelly, Ignatius Loyola

Mourning became Mrs. Spendlove: Gogarty, O. St. John

Mourning becomes Electra: O'Neill, Eugene

Mourning bride, The: Congreve, William

Mourning muse of Alexis, The: Congreve, William

Mourning poet, The: Brown, Thomas

Mourt's relation: Bradford, William

Mouse house: Godden, Rumer

Mouse is born, A: Loos, Anita

Mousetrap, The: Christie, Agatha

Mouse-trap, The: Howells, W.D.

Mousewife: Godden, Rumer

Mouthpiece, The: Wallace, Edgar

Movable feast: Hemingway, Ernest

Move the goods!: Chase, Stuart

Movements in European history: Lawrence, D.H.

Movements of the British Legion: Richardson, John

Moving finger, The: Christie, Agatha

Moving spirit in womanhood, The: Housman, Laurence

Moving tent, The: Graham, Stephen

Moyarra: an Australian legend: Rusden, G.W.

Moyses in a map of his miracles: Drayton, Michael

Moytura: Colum, Padraic

Mozart: Davenport, Marcia

Mozart: Sitwell, Sacheverell

Mozart: Turner, W.J.R.

Mozis Addums' new letters: Bagby, George William

For Mr. *read* Mister)

Mrs. Adis: Kaye-Smith, Shiela

Mrs. Albert Grundy: Frederic, Harold

Mrs. Ames: Benson, E.F.

Mrs. Annie Green: Read, O.P.

Mrs. Armytage: Gore, Catherine

Mrs. 'Arris goes to New York: Gallico, Paul

Mrs. 'Arris goes to Paris: Gallico, Paul

Mrs. Arthur: Oliphant, Margaret

Mrs. Balfame: Atherton, Gertrude

Mrs. Barr's short stories: Barr, A.E.H.

Mrs. Barry: Niven, F.J.

Mrs. Bligh: Broughton, Rhoda

Mrs. Caudle's curtain lectures: Jerrold, Douglas

Mrs. Cliff's yacht: Stockton, F.R.

Mrs. Craddock: Maugham, Somerset

Mrs. Curgenven of Curgenven: Baring-Gould, Sabine

Mrs. Dalloway: Woolf, Virginia

Mrs. Dane's defence: Jones, H.A.

Mrs. Dimmock's worries: Farjeon, B.L.

Mrs. Doratt: Erskine, John

Mrs. Dot: Maugham, Somerset

Mrs. Egg: Beer, T.

Mrs. Esmond's life: Bates, H.E.

Mrs. Falchion: Parker, *Sir* H.G.

Mrs. Farrell: Howells, W.D.

Mrs. Fischer's war: Temple, Joan

Mrs. Fisher, or the future of humour: Graves, Robert

Mrs. Fiske—her views on acting: Woollcott, A.H.

Mrs. Gailey: Kaye-Smith, Shiela

Mrs. Galer's business: Ridge, W.Pett

Mrs. Gamp: Dickens, Charles

Mrs. Gaskell: Lyall, Edna

Mrs. General Mucklestrap's four tall daughters: Sala, G.A.H.

Mrs. Gorringe's necklace: Davies, H.H.

Mrs. Grundy comes to tea: Peach, L.du Garde

Mrs. Grundy in Scotland: Muir, Willa

Mrs. Haliburton's troubles: Wood, Ellen

Mrs. Hallam's companion: Holmes, M.J.

Mrs. Harold Stagg: Grant, Robert

Mrs. Harter: †Delafield, E.M.

Mrs. Henry Sidgwick: Sidgwick, Ethel

Mrs. Kimber: Sitwell, *Sir* Osbert

Mrs. Lancelot: Hewlett, Maurice

Mrs. Leffingwell's boots: Thomas, Augustus

Mrs. Leicester's School: Lamb, Charles

Mrs. Lirriper's legacy: Dickens, Charles

Mrs. Lirriper's lodgings: Dickens, Charles

Mrs. Malone: Farjeon, Eleanor

Mrs. Marden: Hichens, Robert

Mrs. Markham's new history of England: Belloc, Hilaire

Mrs. Martin's man: Ervine, St. John

Mrs. Matthews: Trollope, Frances

Mrs. Maxon protests: (†Anthony Hope), Hawkins, Anthony Hope

Mrs. McGinty's dead: Christie, Agatha

Mrs. McThing: Chase, M.C.

Mrs. Merriam's scholars: Hale, E.E.

Mrs. Midnight's orations: Smart, Christopher

Mrs. Miller's aunt: Hannay, J.O.

Mrs. Moonlight: Levy, Benn W.

Mrs. Morton of Mexico: Ficke, A.D.

Mrs. Murphy: Pain, B.E.O.

Mrs. Nimble and Mr. Bumble: Uttley, Alison

Mrs. Oliver Cromwell: Irwin, Margaret

Mrs. Overtheway: Ewing, *Mrs.* Juliana Horatia

Mrs. Parkington: Bromfield, Louis

Mrs. Perkin's Ball: Thackeray, W.M.

Mrs. Pomeroy's reputation: Vachell, H.A.

Mrs. Pretty and the Premier: Adams, Arthur H.

Mrs. Raffles: Bangs, J.K.

Mrs. Rawleigh and Mrs. Paradock: †Bell, Neil

Mrs. Ritchie: Muir, Willa

Mrs. Rutherford's children: Warner, S.B., and A.B. Warner

Mrs. Sarah A. Ripley: Emerson, Ralph Waldo

Mrs. Siddons: Royde-Smith, Naomi

Mrs. Skagg's husbands: Harte, Bret

Mrs. Temperley: James, Henry

Mrs. Thrale of Streatham: Vulliamy, C.E.

Mrs. Tregaskiss: Praed, *Mrs.* C.

Mrs. Van Kleek: †Mordaunt, Elinor

Mrs.Warren's profession: Shaw, G.B.

Mrs. Warrender's profession: Cole, G.D.H.

Mrs. Waterbury's millenium: †Bridie, James

Mu'allakat: Blunt, Wilfred

Much ado about nothing: Shakespeare, William

Much darker days: Lang, Andrew

Much-admired song called the Drian-naun Don, A: Joyce, R.D.

Mud and purple: †O'Sullivan, Seumas

Mud and treacle: Levy, Benn W.

Mud lark, The: Stringer, A.J.A.

Mudfog papers, The: Dickens, Charles

Mufti: †Sapper

Mugby Junction: Dickens, Charles

Mughul administration: Sarkar, Y.J.

Mulatto: Hughes, J.L.

Mulberry bush: Farjeon, Eleanor

Mulberry bush, The: †Delafield, E.M.

Mulberry bush, The: Lynd, Sylvia

Mulberry garden, The: Sedley, *Sir* Charles

Mulberry leaves: Turnbull, S. C.P.

Mule on the minaret, The: Waugh, Alec

Mulgrave road, The: Bruce, Charles

Mulk Raj Anand: Lindsay, Jack

Mulliner nights: Wodehouse, P.G.

Mulliner omnibus: Wodehouse, P.G.

Mully of Mountown: King, William

Multabello road, The: Raymond, Ernest

Multiplex man: Van Loon, H.W.

Multitude and solitude: Masefield, John

Mumbudget: Simpson, H. de G.

Mummer's wife, A: Moore, George

Mummery: Cannan, Gilbert

Mummies and Moslems: Warner, C.D.

Mummy, The: Bernard, W.B.

Mundorum explicatio: Pordage, Samuel

Mundus muliebris: Evelyn, John

Munera Pulveris: Ruskin, John

Municipal history of Boston: Quincy, Josiah

Mural painting in the Boston public library: Fenollosa, E.F.

Murder at Crome House, The: Cole, G.D.H.

Murder at Government House: Huxley, Elspeth J.

Murder at Monte Carlo: Oppenheim, E.Phillips

Murder at the munition works: Cole, G.D.H.

Murder at the vicarage, The: Christie, Agatha

Murder by experts: †Queen, Ellery

Murder by nail: Farnol, J.J.

Murder by request: Nichols, Beverley

Murder for profit: Bolitho, William

Murder has been arranged, A: Williams, Emlyn

Murder in Earl's Court: (†Neil Gordon), Macdonell, A.G.

Murder in four parts: Cole, G.D.H.

Murder in Mesopotamia: Christie, Agatha

Murder in Peking: Starrett, Vincent

Murder in Sydney, A: Mann, Leonard

Murder in the bud: Bottome, Phyllis

Murder in the Cathedral: Eliot, T.S.

Murder in the Mews: Christie, Agatha

Murder in the submarine zone: †Carter Dickson

Murder intended: †Beeding, Francis

Murder is announced, A: Christie, Agatha

Murder is easy: Christie, Agatha

Murder most foul: Hannay, J.O.

Murder must advertise: Sayers, Dorothy

Murder of Delicia, The:†Corelli, Marie

Murder of Lidice, The: Millay, E.St.Vincent

Murder of Roger Ackroyd, The: Christie, Agatha

Murder of Sir Edmund Godfrey, The: Carr, J.D.

Murder on "B" deck: Starrett, Vincent

Murder on safari: Huxley, Elspeth J.

Murder on the links, The: Christie, Agatha

Murder on the Nile: Christie, Agatha

Murder on the Orient express: Christie, Agatha

Murder, piracy and treason: Postgate, Raymond

Murder stalks the Wakely family: Derleth, A.W.

Murderer is a fox: †Queen, Ellery

Murderers make mistakes: Crofts, F.W.

Murders and mysteries: Wallace, W.S.

Murders at Moon Dance: Guthrie, A.B.

Murders in the Rue Morgue, The: Poe, Edgar Allan

Murdi: Bercovici, Konrad

Murmurer, A: Breton, Nicholas

Murmurs of the stream: Parkes, *Sir* Henry

Murphy: Beckett, Samuel

Murphy's master: Payn, James

Murphy's Moa: Lawlor, P.A.

Murray's Berkshire architectural guide: Betjeman, John

Murray's Buckinghamshire architectural guide: Betjeman, John

Murvale Eastman, Christian socialist: Tourgée, A.W.

Muse in arms, The: Grenfell, J.H.

Muse in chains, The: Potter, Stephen

Muse in council, The: Drinkwater, John

Muse in exile, The: Watson, *Sir* J.W.

Muse unchained, The: Tillyard, E.M.W.

Muses elizium, The: Drayton, Michael

Muse's memorial of the earl of Oxford, The: Tate, Nahum

Muses mourning, The: Taylor, John

Muses sacrifice, The: Davies, John

Muses-teares for the losse of Henry, Prince of Wales, The: Davies, John

Musetta: Mottram, R.H.

Museum and English Journal of Education, The: Morley, John

Museum of cheats, The: Warner, Sylvia Townsend

Museum piece, A: Phillpotts, Eden

Museum pieces: Plomer, W.C.F.

Mushroom Town: †Onions, Oliver

Music: Swinburne, A.C.

Music, a short history: Turner, W.J.R.

Music after the great war: Van Vechten, Carl

Music and bad manners: Van Vechten, Carl

Music and its lovers: Lee, Vernon

Music and life: Turner, W.J.R.

Music and moonlight:O'Shaughnessy, A.W.E.

Music and poetry: Lanier, Sidney

Music at night: Huxley, Aldous

Music at night: Priestley, J.B.

Music cure, The: Shaw, G.B.

Music for Mohini: Bhattacharya, Bhabani

Music from behind the moon, The: Cabell, J.B.

Music in London: Shaw, G.B.

Music in the morning: Bell, Adrian

Music, lyrical and narrative poems: Freeman, John

Music makers: Peach, L. du Garde

Music master, The: Belasco, David

Music of poetry, The: Eliot, T.S.

Music of Spain, The: Van Vechten, Carl

Music of the earth, The: Carman, Bliss

Music of the heart, The: Langley, Noel

Music of the wild: Stratton-Porter, Gene

Musical century, The: Carey, Henry

Musical chair, A: Mackenzie, *Sir* Compton

Musical copyright: Hunt, Leigh

Musical critic's holiday, A:Newman, Ernest

Musical glasses, The: Gould, Gerald

Musical lady, The: Colman, George, *the elder*

Musical meanderings: Turner, W.J.R.

Musical motley, A: Newman, Ernest

Musical studies: Newman, Ernest

Musical tour, The: Dibdin, Charles

Musicall consort of heavenly harmonic, A: Churchyard, Thomas

Musicall gramarian, The: North, Roger

Music-mad: Hook, T.E.

Musings and memories: Raven, C.E.

Musings and prosings: Bayly, T.H.

Musings of Basava: Iyengar, K.R.Srinivasa

Musings over the Christian year: Yonge, Charlotte M.

Musk and amber: Mason, A.E.W.

Musket House: Roberts, T.G.

Mussulmane: Beckford, William

Must Britain travel the Moscow road?: Angell, *Sir* Norman

Must England's beauty perish?: Trevelyan, G.M.

Mustangs, The: Dobie, J.F.

Mustapha: Mallet, David

Mustard, pepper and salt: Uttley, Alison

Muster of arms, A: Raddall, T.H.

Mutations of the Phoenix: Read, *Sir* Herbert

Mutual flame, The: Knight, G.W.

Mute discourse: Stephens, J.B.

Mute singer, The: Ritchie, *Mrs.* Anne

Mutineer, The: †Becke, Louis

Mutiny!: Hall, J.N. and C.B. Nordhoff

Mutiny at Nore, The: Jerrold, Douglas

Mutiny in January: Van Doren, Carl

Mutiny of Madam Yes, The: Collins, Dale

Mutiny of the Elsinore, The: London, Jack

Mutiny on the Bounty: Hall, J.N. and C.B. Nordhoff

Mutius Scaevola: Ireland, W.H.

Mutton-birds and other birds: Guthrie-Smith, W.H.

My adventure in the Flying Scotsman: Phillpotts, Eden

My African journey: Churchill, *Sir* Winston

My Alpine Jubilee: Harrison, Frederic

My America: Adamic, Louis

My American: Gibbons, Stella

My Antonia: Cather, Willa

My apprenticeship: Webb, Beatrice

My army, O, my army!:Lawson, Henry

My aunt's rhinoceros: Fleming, Peter

My Aunt Margaret's mirror: Scott, *Sir* Walter

My Australia: †Eldershaw, M. Barnard

My Australian girlhood: Praed, *Mrs.* C.

My baseball diary: Farrell, James

My beautiful lady: Woolner, Thomas

My birds: Davies, W.H.

My bit of Dylon Thomas: Heppenstall, J.R.

My book to William C. Buskett: Field, Eugene

My boyhood: Burroughs, John

My boyhood days: Tagore, Sir R.

My brilliant career: Franklin, Miles

My brother Charles: †Bell, Neil

My brother Denys: Monsarrat, Nicholas

My brother Jonathan: Young, Francis Brett

My brother Tom: Ervine, St. John

My brother's face: Mukherji, D.G.

My brother's farm: Burroughs, John

My brother's keeper: Davenport, Marcia

My brother's keeper: Warner, A.B.

My career goes bung: Franklin, Miles

My Chinee cook: Stephens, J.B.

My city: Dreiser, Theodore

My confessional: Ellis, Havelock

My connection with the Atlas newspaper: Hildreth, Richard

My country and my people: Lin Yu-T'ang

My cousin, F. Marion Crawford: Elliott, M.H.

My cousin Rachel: Du Maurier, Daphne

My Danish sweetheart: Russell, W.C.

My dateless diary: Narayan, R.K.

My daughter Helen: Monkhouse, A.N.

My day in the wilderness: Jackson, H.H.

My days of anger: Farrell, James

My dear Cornelia: Sherman, S.P.

My dear Wells: Jones, H.A.

My desert friend: Hichens, Robert

My desire: Warner, S.B.

My Devon year: Phillpotts, Eden

My diaries: Blunt, Wilfred

"My Diary." The early years of my daughter Marianne: Gaskell, E.C.

My diary in America in the midst of war: Sala, G.A.H.

My discovery of England: Leacock, Stephen

My discovery of the West: Leacock, Stephen

My double and how he undid me: Hale, E.E.

My early life: Churchill, Sir Winston

My Europe: Lockhart, Sir Robert Bruce

My farm at Edgewood: Mitchell, D.G.

My father: a portrait of G.G. Coulton at home: Campion, Sarah

My Father and I: Linklater, Eric

My father and my father's friends: McCrae, Hugh

My father sits in the dark: Weidman, Jerome

My father's garden: Miller, Thomas

My father's house: Levin, Meyer

My favourite English poems: Masefield, John

My favourite murder: Bierce, Ambrose

My favourite novelist: Stockton, F.R.

My fellow devils: Hartley, L.P.

My fellow laborer and The wreck of the "Copeland": Haggard, Sir H. Rider

My first hundred years: Murray, Margaret

My first pantomime: Komai, Gonnosuké

My first play: Gregory, Lady Augusta

My first summer in the Sierra: Muir, John

My four weeks in France: Lardner, Ring

My friend Julia Lathrop: Addams, Jane

My friend Mr. Leakey: Haldane, J.B.S.

My friend, remember: Adams, Arthur H.

My friend Serafin: †Armstrong, Anthony

My friend the boss: Hale, E.E.

My friendly contemporaries: Garland, Hamlin

My friend's wife: Lang, J.

My garden: Davies, W.H.

My garden: Holtby, Winifred

My garden: Phillpotts, Eden

My garden of memories: Wiggin, K.D.

My glorious brothers: Fast, Howard M.

My guardian: a story of the Fen Country: Cambridge, Ada

My haunts and their frequenters: Yates, E.H.

My head! My head!: Graves, Robert

My heart and my flesh: Roberts, E.M.

My heart's in the Highlands: Saroyan, William

My heart's right there: Barclay, F.L.

My Hollywood diary: Wallace, Edgar

My Holy Satan: Fisher, V.A.

My husband's ghost: Morton, J.M.

My idealed John Bulleses: Markino, Yoshio

My Ireland: Dunsany, E.J.M.D.P.

My Ireland: O'Brien, Kate

My Irish year: Colum, Padraic

My island home: Hall, J.N.

My key of life, optimism: Keller, Helen

My ladies' sonnets: Le Gallienne, Richard

My Lady Clara: Robertson, T.W.

My lady dear, arise!: Mackaye, Percy

My Lady Ludlow: Gaskell, Mrs. Elizabeth

My lady Pokahontas: Cooke, J.E.

My lady Rotha: Weyman, Stanley

My lady wears a white cockade: Gow, Ronald

My lady's book: Gould, Gerald

My lady's hat: Hough, Emerson

My lady's plumes: Hough, Emerson

My Lady's slipper: Sigerson, Dora

My larger education: Washington, B.T.

My late wives: †Carter Dickson

My lattice: Scott, F.G.

My laughing philosopher: Phillpotts, Eden

My life: Harris, J.T.

My life: Maxwell, W.H.

My life. A record of events and opinions: Wallace, A.R.

My life and diet: Sinclair, Upton

My life and hard times: Thurber, James

My life and loves in Greenwich village: Bodenheim, Maxwell

My life and times: Jerome, Jerome K.

My life and times: Mackenzie, Sir Compton

My life as a teacher: Erskine, John

My life in art: Bemelmans, Ludwig

My life in the theatre: Hodge, H.E.

My life with the Eskimo: Stefansson, V.

My lifetime in letters: Sinclair, Upton

My lighthouse: Thaxter, C.L.

My literary life: Linton, Eliza

My literary passions: Howells, W.D.

My little bit: †Corelli, Marie

My little girl: Besant, Sir Walter and James Rice

My lives and how I lost them: Cullen, Countée

My long life: Sladen, D.B.W.

My Lord Duke: Hornung, E.W.

My Lord of Wrybourne: Farnol, J.J.

My love: Linton, Eliza

My love and I: Brown, Alice

My love must wait: Hill, Ernestine

My lyrical life: Massey, Gerald

My man Jeeves: Wodehouse, P.G.

My Mark Twain: Howells, W.D.

My master Gokhale: Sastri, Srinivasa

My memories and miseries as a schoolmaster: Leacock, Stephen

My memory of Gladstone: Smith, Goldwin

My miscellanies: Collins, Wilkie

My mortal enemy: Cather, Willa

My mother and I: Craik, Mrs. Dinah

My name is Aram: Saroyan, William

My name is legion: Morgan, Charles

My native Devon: Fortescue, Sir John

My native land: Adamic, Louis

My neighbours: Evans, Caradoc

My new home: Molesworth, Mrs.

My next bride: Boyle, Kay

My night-gown and slippers: Colman, George, the younger

My novel: Lytton, E.G.E.B. 1st Baron

My November guest: Frost, Robert

My old college, 1843–1943: Leacock, Stephen

My old Kentucky home: Foster, S.C.

My old man: Runyon, Damon

My one contribution to seventeenth century scholarship: Morley, C.D.

My only murder: Favenc, Ernest

My own fairy book: Lang, Andrew

My own master: Bell, Adrian

My own schooldays: Brazil, Angela

My own story: Trowbridge, J.T.

My people, stories of the peasantry of West Wales: Evans, Caradoc

My philosophical development: Russell, Bertrand

My philosophy: Lodge, Sir Oliver

My pilgrimage to the Wise Men of the East: Conway, M.D.

My place in the bazaar: Waugh, Alec

My Prague pig: Baring-Gould, Sabine

My Pretty and her little brother: Molesworth, Mrs.

My recollections and reflections: Markino, Yoshio

My record of music: Mackenzie, Sir Compton

My religion: Bennett, Arnold

My religion: Keller, Helen

My religious experience: Walpole, Sir Hugh

My remarkable uncle: Leacock, Stephen

My reminiscences: Reid, Sir G.H.

My reminiscences: Tagore, Sir R.

My rod my comfort: Lockhart, Sir Robert Bruce

My run home: †Boldrewood, Rolf

My San Francisco: Atherton, Gertrude

My school books: Van Loon, Hendrik

My schools and schoolmasters: Miller, Hugh

My Scotland: Macdonell, A.G.

My Scottish youth: Lockhart, Sir Robert Bruce

My sea: Noel, R.B.W.

My search for truth: Radhakrishan, Sarvepalli

My several worlds: Buck, Pearl

My share of the world: Browne, Frances

My shipmate Louise: Russell, W.C.

My shooting box: Herbert, H.W.

My shrubs: Phillpotts, Eden

My skirmish with Jolly Roger: Lawrence, D.H.

My son, my son!: Spring, Howard

My son Richard: Sladen, D.B.W.

My son's my son: Greenwood, Walter

My South Sea Island: Maugham, Somerset

My sporting days and nights: Golding, Louis

My star predominant: Knister, Raymond

My story: Caine, Sir T.H. Hall

My story: Rinehart, May Roberts

My story that I like best: Ferber, Edna

My strange rescue: Oxley, J.M.

My study windows: Lowell, J.R.

My summer in a garden: Warner, C.D.

My sundowner: Farrell, John

My talks with Dean Spanley: Dunsany, E.J.M.D.P.

My tattered loving: †Preedy, George

My ten years in a quandary and how they grew: Benchley, Robert

My theatre talks: Agate, J.E.

My third book: Moulton, E.L.

My thirty years out of the Senate: Smith, Seba

My travels: Chamier, Frederick

My tropic isle: Banfield, E.J.

My turn to make the tea: Dickens, Monica

My Uncle Jan: Wurdemann, Audrey

My uncle Silas: Bates, H.E.

My vagabondage: Vachell, H.A.

My vision of Canada: Deacon, W.A.

My visit to Fairview Villa: Leprohon, R.E.

My Wales: Davies, Rhys

My war with the United States: Bemelmans, Ludwig

My watch below: Russell, W.C.

My wife and I: Stowe, Harriet Beecher

My wife Ethel: Runyon, Damon

My winter garden: Thompson, Maurice

My witness: Winter, William

My wonderful wife: †Corelli, Marie

My world—and welcome to it: Thurber, James

My world as in my time: Newbolt, *Sir* Henry

My writing life: †Bell, Neil

My year in a log cabin: Howells, W.D.

My young master: Read, O.P.

Mycenaean tree and pillar cult, The: Evans, *Sir* A.J.

Myddleton Pomfret: Ainsworth, Harrison

Myopes, The: Pickthall, M.W.

Myrrour for magistrates, A: Skelton, John

Myrrour of Modestie, The: Greene, Robert

Myrtillo: Cibber, Colley

Myrtis: Sigourney, L.H.

Myrtle: †Hudson, Stephen

Myrtle bough,The: Benson,A.C.

Myself when young: Waugh, Alec

Mysteries and adventures:Doyⅼ Sir Arthur Conan

Mysteries of Ann, The: Brown, Alice

Mysteries of London: Reynolds, G.

Mysteries of the backwoods, The: Thorpe, T.B.

Mysteries of the Court of London, The: Reynolds, G.

Mysteries of the Court of Naples: Reynolds, G.

Mysteries of the pulpit: Lippard, George

Mysteries of the Riviera: Oppenheim, E.Phillips

Mysteries of Udolpho, The: Radcliffe, *Mrs*. Ann

Mysterious affair at Elsinore: (†Michael Innes), Stewart, J.I.M.

Mysterious affair at Styles, The: Christie, Agatha

Mysterious aviator,The: †Shute, Nevil

Mysterious freebooter, The: Lathom, Francis

Mysterious husband, The: Cumberland, Richard

Mysterious key, The: Alcott, Louisa M.

Mysterious marriage, The: Lee, Harriet

Mysterious mother, The: Walpole, Horace

Mysterious Mr. Bull, The: Lewis, P.Wyndham

Mysterious Mr. Quin, The: Christie, Agatha

Mysterious Mr. Sabin, The: Oppenheim, E.Phillips

Mysterious rider, The: Grey, Zane

Mysterious state-room, The: Ingraham, J.H.

Mysterious stranger, The: (†Mark Twain), Clemens, S.L.

Mysterious universe, The: Jeans, *Sir* James

Mysterious ways: Wren, P.C.

Mystery, The: Hodgson, Ralph

Mystery: Lathom, Francis

Mystery, The: White, S.E.

Mystery and tragedy: Moore, T.S.

Mystery at Geneva: Macaulay, *Dame* Rose

Mystery at Milford Haven: †Taffrail

Mystery cruise: †Taffrail

Mystery in Palace Gardens, The: Riddell, *Mrs*. J.H.

Mystery in the Channel: Crofts, F.W.

Mystery lady, The: Chambers, R.W.

Mystery mile: Allingham, Margery

Mystery of a hansom cab:Hume, Fergus Wright

Mystery of Alfred Doubt, The: Hay, William

Mystery of choice, The: Chambers, R.W.

Mystery of Cloomber, The: Doyle, *Sir* Arthur Conan

Mystery of Edwin Drood, The: Dickens, Charles

Mystery of Greenfingers:Priestley, J.B.

Mystery of Hamlet, King of Denmark, The: Mackaye, Percy

Mystery of iniquity unvailed, The: Burnet, Gilbert

Mystery of Keats, The: Murry, John Middleton

Mystery of M.Felix, The: Farjeon, B.L.

Mystery of Maata: Lawlor, P.A.

Mystery of Major Molineaux and human repetends: Clarke, Marcus

Mystery of Mary Stuart, The: Lang, Andrew

Mystery of Metropolisville,The: Eggleston, Edward

Mystery of Mirbridge, The: Payn, James

Mystery of Moorside Farm,The: Trease, Geoffrey

Mystery of Mr. Bernard Brown, The: Oppenheim, E.Phillips

Mystery of Mrs. Blencarrow, The: Oliphant, Margaret

Mystery of sacrifice, The: Underhill, Evelyn

Mystery of the blue train, The: Christie, Agatha

Mystery of the buried crosses, The: Garland, Hamlin

Mystery of the island, The: Kingsley, Henry

Mystery of the kingdom, The: Knox, R.A.

Mystery of the Laughlin Islands, The: †Becke, Louis

Mystery of the moated grange, The: Brazil, Angela

Mystery of the ocean star, The: Russell, W.C.

Mystery of the Royal Mail, The: Farjeon, B.L.

Mystery of the sea, The: Stoker, Bram

Mystery of the sleeping car express, The: Crofts, F.W.

Mystery of true faith: Sen, Keshub Chunder

Mystery of Witch-Face Mountain, The: †Craddock, C.E.

Mystery on Southampton Water: Crofts, F.W.

Mystery on the moors: Trease, Geoffrey

Mystery ranch: †Brand, Max

Mystery revealed, The: Goldsmith, Oliver

Mystery road, The: Oppenheim, E.Phillips

Mystery ships, trapping the U boats: Noyes, Alfred

Mystery woman, The: Praed, *Mrs.* C.

Mystic, The: Bailey, P.J.

Mystic events: Lathom, Francis

Mystic trees: †Field, Michael

Mystic way, The: Underhill, Evelyn

Mysticism: Underhill, Evelyn

Mysticism and logic: Russell, Bertrand

Mysticism and war: Underhill, Evelyn

Mysticism in English literature: Spurgeon, Caroline

Mysticism in modern India: Sen, Keshub Chunder

Mystics of the Church, The: Underhill, Evelyn

Myth and miracle: Knight, G.W.

Myth and romance: Cawein, Madison

Myth of rugged American individualism, The: Beard, C.A.

Myth of Shakespeare, A: Williams, Charles

Myth, ritual, and religion: Lang, Andrew

Myth Wawatam, The: Bedford-Jones, Henry

Mythologia ethica: Ayres, Philip

Mythology and the Renaissance tradition in English poetry: Bush, Douglas

Mythology and the romantic tradition in English poetry: Bush, Douglas

Myths and legends of the Polynesians: Anderson, J.C.

Myths and myth-makers: Fiske, John

Myths of the Hindus and Buddhists: Coomaraswamy, A.K.

Myths of the minstrel: Lewis, S.A.

Myths of the origin of fire: Frazer, *Sir* James

N

Naboth's vineyard: †Dane, Clemence

Naboth's vineyard: Somerville, Edith

Nada the lily: Haggard, *Sir* H. Rider

Nadine: Praed, *Mrs.* C.

Naggletons, The: Brooks, C.W.

Naiad, The: Pickthall, M.L.C.

Naked god, The: Fast, Howard M.

Naked heel: Speyer, *Mrs.* Leonora

Naked on roller skates: Bodenheim, Maxwell

Naked shingles: Isvaran, M.S.

Naked warriors: Read, *Sir* Herbert

Nakiketas: Sinclair, May

Namby-Pampy: Carey, Henry

Name and nature of poetry, The: Housman, A.E.

Name into word: Partridge, Eric

Name of action, The: Greene, Graham

Name of Garland: Ridge, W.Pett

Name this child: Partridge, Eric

Name to conjure with, A: Stern, G.B.

Nameless city, The: Hume, F.W.

Nameless places, The: Raymond, Ernest

Names and designations: Chapman, R.W.

Names and faces: Seymour, W.K.

Nanciebel: Black, William

Nancy: Broughton, Rhoda

Nancy: Carey, Henry

Nancy Flyer: a stagecoach epic, The: Poole, Ernest

Nancy Owlett: Phillpotts, Eden

Nansen: De Selincourt, Aubrey

Napoleon: Barton, Bernard

Napoleon: Belloc, Hilaire

Napoleon: Butterfield, Herbert

Napoleon: Trench, F.H.

Napoleon and his court: Forester, C.S.

Napoleon and his Marshals: Macdonell, A.G.

Napoleon and Palestine: Guedalla, Philip

Napoleon and the marshals of the empire: Griswold, R.W.

Napoleon and the spectre: Brontë, Charlotte

Napoleon Bonaparte: Fisher, H.A.L.

Napoleon crossing the Rockies: Mackaye, Percy

Napoleon fallen: Buchanan, R.B.

Napoleon in his own defence: Shorter, C.K.

Napoleon of Notting Hill, The: Chesterton, G.K.

Napoleon's fellow travellers: Shorter, C.K.

Naqada: Petrie, *Sir* William Flinders

Narcissus: Butler, Samuel

Narcissus: Meynell, Viola

Narcissus: Scott, Evelyn

Narcissus; a Belgian legend of Van Dyck: Whitlock, Brand

Narracong riddle, The: Derleth, A.W.

Narration, four lectures: Stein, Gertrude

Narrative of a second voyage in search of a N.W. Passage: Ross, *Sir* John

Narrative of all the robberies, escapes, etc. of John Shepphard, A: Defoe, Daniel

Narrative of an attempt to reach the North Pole 1827: Parry, *Sir* W.E.

Narrative of an expedition of five Americans into a land of wild animals: Kennedy, J.P.

Narrative of an expedition to the Zambesi and its tributaries: Livingstone, David

Narrative of an explorer in tropical South Africa: Galton, *Sir* Francis

Narrative of Arthur Gordon Pym, The: Poe, Edgar Allan

Narrative of facts relating to a prosecution for high treason, A: Holcroft, Thomas

Narrative of General Venables: Firth, *Sir* Charles

Narrative of James Williams: Whittier, J.G.

Narrative of the Canadian Red River exploring expedition of 1857: Hind, H.Y.

Narrative of the Earl of Elgin's mission to China and Japan: Oliphant, Laurence

Narrative of the late massacres, A: Franklin, Benjamin

Narrative of the miseries of New-England, A: Mather, Increase

Narrative of the travels and adventures of Monsieur Violet in California, Sonora and Western Texas: Marryatt, Frederick

Narrative of the Wairoan Massacre: Domett, Alfred

Narrative of travels on the Amazon and Rio Negro, A: Wallace, A.R.

Narrative pictures: Sitwell, Sacheverell

Narrative poems: Austin, Alfred

Narrative poems: D'Israeli, Isaac

Narrative poems on the female character: Mitford, Mary Russell

Narratives from criminal trials in Scotland: Burton, John Hill

Narratives of sorcery and magic: Wright, Thomas

Narrow corner, The: Maugham, Somerset

Narrow gate, The: Sheldon, C.M.

Narrow house, The: Scott, Evelyn

Narrow place, The: Muir, Edwin

Nasby of inflation: †Nasby, Petroleum V.

Nasby papers, The: (†Petroleum V. Nasby), Locke, D.R.

Nashes lenten stuffe, the praise of red herring: Nash, Thomas

Nasrin: Singh, Jogendra

Natalie: Burnett, Frances Hodgson

Natalie Masie and Pavilastukay: Masefield, John

Natasqua: Davis, R.B.H.

Nathalie: Kavanagh, Julia

Nathan Hale: Fitch, Clyde William

Nathaniel Hawthorne: Lathrop, G.P.

Nathaniel Hawthorne: Van Doren, Mark

Nathaniel Hawthorne: Woodberry, G.E.

Nathaniel Holmes Morison, 1815–1890: Morison, S.E.

Nathan's orchard: Huxley, Elspeth J.

Nation a family, A: Steele, *Sir* Richard

Nation of nations: Adamic, Louis

National airs: Moore, Thomas

National Apostasy: Keble, John

National ballads of Canada: Lanigan, G.T.

National bands: Kipling, Rudyard

National being, The: Russell, G.W.

National character, The: Bryant, *Sir* Arthur

National flag, The: Rajagopalachari, Chakravati

National gallery, A: †George, Daniel

National hymn, A: Crawford, F. Marion

National lyrics: Whittier, J.G.

National lyrics and songs for music: Hemans, *Mrs.* Felicia

National portraits: Palmer, E.V.

National tales: Hood, Thomas

National theatre, A: Barker, Harley Granville

National theatre: scheme and estimates, A: Archer, William

National training laboratories: Chase, Stuart

National value of art, The: Ghose, Sri Aurobindo

National Velvet: Bagnold, Enid

Nationalisation of health, The: Ellis, Havelock

Nationalising of business, The: Tarbell, Ida

Nationalism: Panikkar, K.M.

Nationalism: Tagore, *Sir* R.

Nationalist extra No. 1. Plutocracy or Nationalism: Bellamy, Edward

Nationality and race: Keith, *Sir* Arthur

Nationality and the League of Nations: Birrell, Augustine

Nationality and the war: Toynbee, A.J.

Nation-famous New York murders: Lewis, A.H.

Native African races and culture: Johnson, J.W.

Native American: Baker, Ray Stannard

Native American, A: Saroyan, William

Native argosy, A: Callaghan, M.E.

Native life in South Africa before and since the European war and the Boer rebellion: Plaatje, S.T.

Native moments: Moll, E.G.

Native of Winby, A: Jewett, Sarah O.

Native races of the pacific States, The: Bancroft, H.H.

Native son: Green, Paul

Native son: Wright, Richard

Natives of rock: Wescott, Glenway

Native's return, The: Adamic, Louis

Nativity: Campbell, Roy

Nativity: Sassoon, Siegfried

Natural genesis, The: Massey, Gerald

Natural history and antiquities of Selborne, The: White, Gilbert

Natural history and antiquities of the County of Surrey, The: Aubrey, John

Natural history letters from the Spectator: Massingham, Harold

Natural history of intellect: Emerson, Ralph Waldo

Natural history of the Ten Commandments, The: Seton-Thompson, E.

Natural history of Wiltshire, The: Aubrey, John

Natural history, the pleasure and purpose of observation: Grey of Fallodon, Edward

Natural house, The: Wright, Frank Lloyd

Natural inequality: Allen, Grant

Natural inheritance: Galton, *Sir* Francis

Natural religion and Christian theology: Raven, C.E.

Natural son, The: Cumberland, Richard

Natural theology: Chalmers, Thomas

Naturalism in English poetry: Brooke, Stopford

Naturalist in La Plata, The: Hudson, W.H.

Naturalist in Siluria, The: Reid, T.M.

Naturalist of souls, A: Bradford, Gamaliel

Naturalist's calendar, A: White, Gilbert

Naturalist's voyage, A: Darwin, Charles

Nature: Emerson, Ralph Waldo

Nature: addresses and lectures: Emerson, Ralph Waldo

Nature and art: Inchbald, *Mrs.* Elizabeth

Nature and art: Story, W.W.

Nature and authority of miracle, The: Ruskin, John

Nature and elements of poetry, The: Stedman, E.C.

Nature and human nature: Haliburton, T.C.

Nature and life: Whitehead, A.N.

Nature and the Bible: Dawson, *Sir* J.W.

Nature and the supernatural, as together constituting the one system of God: Bushnell, Horace

Nature fantasy in Australia: Chisholm, A.H.

Nature in American Literature: Foerster, Norman

Nature in Downland: Hudson, W.H.

Nature in English literature: Blunden, Edmund

Nature, Man and God: Temple, William

Nature near London: Jefferies, Richard

Nature of a crime, The: Conrad, Joseph

Nature of a crime, The: Ford, Ford Madox

Nature of capitalist crisis, The: Strachey, John

Nature of literary criticism, The: Elton, Oliver

Nature of love, The: Bates, H.E.

Nature of man, The: Blackmore, *Sir* R.D.

Nature of personality, The: Temple, William

Nature of the judicial process, The: Cardozo, B.N.

Nature of the physical world, The: Eddington, *Sir* A.S.

Nature of the social sciences in relation to objectives of instruction, The: Beard, C.A.

Nature poems: Davies, W.H.

Nature-notes and impressions: Cawein, Madison

Nature's serial story: Roe, E.P.

Nature-woman, The: Sinclair, Upton

Naucratia: Pye, H.J.

Naught to thirty-three: Bedford, Randolph

Naughty Anthony: Belasco, David

Naughty Nan: Long, J.L.

Naughty princess, The: †Armstrong, Anthony

Naukratis I: Petrie, *Sir* William Flinders

Naulahka: Kipling, Rudyard

Nautymobile, The: Mackenzie, *Sir* Compton

Naval history of the war, 1914–1918, A: Newbolt, *Sir* Henry

Naval occasions: †Bartimeus

Naval officer, The: Marryatt, Frederick

Naval pioneers of Australia, The: †Becke, Louis

Naval Service, The: Glascock, W.N.

Naval sketch book, The: Glascock, W.N.

Naval songs and ballads: Firth, *Sir* Charles

Naval stories: Leggett, William

Naval war of 1812, The: Forester, C.S.

Navies in exile: Divine, A.D.

Navigation and commerce: Evelyn, John

Navy: defense or portent? The: Beard, C.A.

Navy eternal: †Bartimeus

Navy in action, The: †Taffrail

Nazarene, The: Adams, Arthur H.

Nazarene, The: Calvert, G.H.

Nazarene, The: Lippard, George

Nazarene gospel restored, The: Graves, Robert

Nazareth: Housman, Laurence

Nazi and Nazarene: Knox, R.A.

Nazi massacres of the Jews and others: Temple, William

Neal Nelson: Ingraham, J.H.

Near a home: Channing, W.E.

Near and the far, The: Myers, L.H.

Near East, The: Hichens, R.S.

Near to nature's heart: Roe, E.P.

Nearer and dearer: †Bede, Cuthbert

Nearer East, The: Hogarth, D.G.

Nearer the grass roots: Anderson, Sherwood

Nearest neighbour, The: Browne, Frances

Nearly five million: Ridge, W. Pett

Neaste of waspes latelie found out and discovered in the Low Countries, A: Goddard, William

'Neath Austral skies: †Becke, Louis

Nebo the nailer: Baring-Gould, Sabine

Nebuly coat, The: Falkner, John Meade

Necessary angel, The: Stevens, Wallace

Necessity of atheism, The: Shelley, P.B.

Necessity of belief, The: Gill, Eric

Necessity of Communism, The: Murry, John Middleton

Necessity of pacificism, The: Murry, John Middleton

Necessity of poetry, The: Bridges, Robert

Neck or nothing: Garrick, David

Necromancer, The: Reynolds, G.

Ned Kelly: Stewart, D.A.

Ned McCobb's daughter: Howard, S.C.

Ned Musgrave: Hook, T.E.

Ned Myers: Cooper, James Fenimore

Ned of the Caribbees: Phillpotts, Eden

Nedra: McCutcheon, G.B.

Need and use of getting Irish literature into the English tongue, The: Brooke, Stopford A.

Neem is a lady, The: Isvaran, M.S.

Ne'er-do-weel, The: Gilbert, Sir W.S.

Ne'er-do-well, The: Beach, R.E.

Ne'er-do-well: †Yates, Dornford

Neglected genius: Ireland, W.H.

Neglected virtue: Hopkins, Charles

Negro Americans, what now?: Johnson, J.W.

Negro Christianized, The: Mather, Cotton

Negro mother, The: Hughes, J.L.

Negro question, The: Cable, George Washington

Negro: the Southerner's problem, The: Page, T.N.

Negrohead: Bridges, Roy

Nehru: Karaka, D.F.

Nehru–Jinnah correspondence, The: Nehru, J.

Neighbor Jackwood: Trowbridge, J.T.

Neighborhood stories: Gale, Zona

Neighborly poems: Riley, J.W.

Neighbors henceforth: Wister, Owen

Neighbor's wives, The: Trowbridge, J.T.

Neighbours, The: Gale, Zona

Neighbours: Gibson, Wilfred

Neighbours: Molesworth, Mrs.

Neighbours: Stead, R.J.C.

Neighbours on the green: Oliphant, Margaret

Neighing north, The: Dalton, A.C.

Neil and Tintinnabulum: Barrie, Sir J.M.

Neither out far nor in deep: Frost, Robert

Nell Gwyn: †Bowen, Marjorie

Nellie: Meredith, L.A.

Nelly Nawlan: Hall, Anna Maria

Nelly was a lady: Foster, S.C.

Nelly's hospital: Alcott, Louisa M.

Nelly's silver mine: Jackson, H.H.

Nelson: Pryce-Jones, A.P.

Nelson and the naval supremacy of England: Russell, W.C.

Nemesis: Thomas, Augustus

Nemesis of American business, The: Chase, Stuart

Neon wilderness: Algren, Nelson

Nepenthe: Darley, George

Neptunes triumph: Jonson, Ben

Neredi's embrace, The: MacMechan, A.M.

Nero: Bridges, Robert

Nero: Phillips, Stephen

Nero: Story, W.W.

Nero Caesar: Bolton, Edmund

Nervous man and man of nerve, The: Bernard, W.B.

Nest, The: Sedgwick, A.D.

Nest of simple folk, A: O'Faolain, Sean

Nesta: Molesworth, Mrs.

Nesta's new school: Brazil, Angela

Nests at Washington, The: Piatt, J.J.

Net, The: Beach, R.E.

Net for Venus, A: Garnett, David

Nether world, The: Gissing, George

Netherlands, The: Sitwell, Sacheverell

Netherlands displayed, The: †Bowen, Marjorie

Nets of love, The: Gibson, Wilfred

Nets to catch the wind: Wylie, Elinor

Netta (Hon. Mrs. Franklin): Gibbon, Monk

Nettles: Lawrence, D.H.

Neurotic America and the sex impulse, and some aspects of our national character: Dreiser, Theodore

Neurotic nightingale, The: Fisher, V.A.

Nevada: Grey, Zane

Never a dull moment: †Cheyney, Peter

Never ask the end: Paterson, Isabel

Never be a bookseller: Garnett, David

Never come back: †Lonsdale, Frederick

Never come the morning: Algren, Nelson

Never in vain: De Selincourt, Hugh

Never to forget: the battle of the Warsaw ghetto: Fast, Howard M.

Never too late: Thirkell, Angela

Never-fail Blake: Stringer, A.J.A.

Nevermore: †Boldrewood, Rolf

Nevertheless: Moore, M.C.

New Abelard, The: Buchanan, R.B.

New Adam, The: Untermeyer, Louis

New almanac for the Canadian True Blues, A: Mackenzie, W.L.

New American credo, The: Nathan, G.J.

New and easie institution of grammar, A: Taylor, Jeremy

New and improved grammar of the English tongue; for the use of schools, A: Hazlitt, William

New and old: Symonds, J.A.

New and original extravaganza entitled Dulcamara, A: Gilbert, *Sir* W.S.

New and true ghost story, A: Fields, James Thomas

New answer to an argument against a standing army, A: Prior, Matthew

New Apocalypse, The: Logan, J.D.

New approach to the Vedas, A: Coomaraswamy, A.K.

New Arabian nights: Stevenson, R.L.

New army in training, The: Kipling, Rudyard

New Athenian comedy, The: Settle, Elkanah

New Atlantis: Bacon, Francis

New atmosphere, A: Dodge, May Abigail

New background of science, The: Jeans, *Sir* James

New Bath Guide, The: Anstey, Christopher

New bats in old belfries: Betjeman, John

New bearings in English poetry: Leavis, F.R.

New Bedford of the past: Ricketson, Daniel

New bedtime stories: Moulton, E.L.

New beginnings and the record: Cole, G.D.H.

New belfry of Christ Church, The: †Carroll, Lewis

New boke about Shakespeare and Stratford-on-Avon, A: Halliwell, James Orchard

New boke of purgatory, A: Rastell, John

New book of days: Farjeon, Eleanor

New bottles for new wine: Huxley, *Sir* Julian

New bridge: Levin, Meyer

New brooms: Colman, George, *the elder*

New Canadian Loyalists, The: Gibbon, J.M.

New Candide, The: Cournos, John

New Canterbury tales: Hewlett, Maurice

New canto, A: Lamb, *Lady* Caroline

New cautionary tales: Belloc, Hilaire

New century history of the United States, The: Eggleston, Edward

New chapter in the life of Thutmose III, A: Breasted, J.H.

New characters (drawne to the life) of severall persons, in severall qualities: Webster, John

New chemistry, The: Andrade, E.N. da Costa

New child's guide to knowledge, The: Housman, Laurence

New chronicles of Rebecca: Wiggin, K.D.

New chum, The: Adams, Arthur H.

New chum: Masefield, John

New church doctrine, The: Carleton, William (McKendree)

New churches considered with respect to the opportunities they afford for the encouragement of painting: Haydon, Benjamin

New citizenship, The: Mackaye, Percy

New collected rhymes: Lang, Andrew

New collection of fairy tales, A: Brooke, Henry

New colour for the Canadian mosaic: Gibbon, J.M.

New Connecticut: Alcott, A.B.

New conscience and an ancient evil, A: Addams, Jane

New cosmopolis: Huneker, J.G.

New covenant, The: Cotton, John

New criticism, The: Ransom, J.C.

New day, The: Gilder, R.W.

New deal, A: Chase, Stuart

New deal for our universities, A: Iyengar, K.R. Srinivasa

New Deal in action, 1933–1939, The: Schlesinger, Arthur

New departure in the common schools of Quincey, The: Adams, C.F.

New description of Ireland, A: Rich, Barnabe

New dictionary of quotations on historical principles, A: Mencken, H.L.

New discourse of a stale subject, A: Harington, *Sir* John

New discoveries relating to the antiquities of man: Keith, *Sir* Arthur

New discovery of an old intreague, A: Defoe, Daniel

New dispensation, The: Sen, Keskub Chunder

New Disraeli, The: Meynell, Wilfred

New distemper, The: Quarles, Francis

New Dooley book: Dunne, Finley Peter

New droll, A: Jordan, Thomas

New earth: an experiment in colonialism: Huxley, Elspeth J.

New echoes: Cook, Eliza

New economic revolution, The: Cole, M.I.

New Elizabethans, The: Gibbs, *Sir* Philip

New empire, The: Panikkar, K.M.

New England: Coffin, Robert

New England boyhood, A: Hale, E.E.

New England girlhood outlined from memory, A: Larcom, Lucy

New England group, A: More, P.E.

New England history in ballads: Hale, E.E.

New England in the republic: Adams, J.T.

New England: Indian summer: Brooks, Van Wyck

New England legends: Spofford, H.E.

New England nun, A: Freeman, Mary

New England tale, A: Sedgwick, C.M.

New England tragedies, The: Longfellow, H.W.

New England tragedy, The: Longfellow, H.W.

New Englanders: Engle, Paul

New England's contributions to American civilization: Beals, Carleton

New Englands lamentation for Old Englands present errours: Shepard, Thomas

New Englands trials: Smith, John

New English Canaan, The: Morton, Thomas of Merry Mount

New English Dictionary on historical principles, A: Murray, Sir J.A.H.

New era in American poetry, The: Untermeyer, Louis

New essays and American impressions: Noyes, Alfred

New Europe, The: Toynbee, Arnold

New exodus, The: Frederic, Harold

New fables: Brooke, Henry

New facts regarding the life of Shakespeare: Collier, John Payne

New fiction, The: Traill, H.D.

New flag, The: Fuller, Henry Blake

New flower for children, A: Child, L.M.

New Forest, The: Smith, Horatio

New found land: MacLeish, Archibald

New France and New England: Fiske, John

New friends in Old Chester: Deland, Margaret

New (German) Testament, The: (†Anthony Hope), Hawkins, Anthony Hope

New girl at St. Chad's, The: Brazil, Angela

New ground of criticism, The: Calverton, V.F.

New Grub Street: Gissing, George

New guide to the English tongue, A: Godwin, William

New Gulliver, The: Pain, B.E.O.

New gun runners, The: (†Neil Gordon), Macdonell, A.G.

New Hampshire: Frost, Robert

New hangman, The: Housman, Laurence

New Harry and Lucy, The: Hale, E.E.

New harvest, The: Finlayson, Roderick

New Haven: Woodworth, Samuel

New hay at the old market: Colman, George, *the younger*

New hedonism, The: Allen, Grant

New Hesperides, The: Spingarn, J.E.

New history, The: Eggleston, Edward

New history for old: Pierce, Lorne

New hope: Suckow, Ruth

New hopes for a changing world: Russell, Bertrand

New house at Hardale: Trease, Geoffrey

New humanism, The: Housman, Laurence

New Humpty-Dumpty, The: Ford, Ford Madox

New idealism, The: Sinclair, May

New ideals in business: Tarbell, Ida

New ideals in healing: Baker, R.S.

New immortality, The: Dunne, J.W.

New imperative, The: Lippmann, Walter

New industrial unrest, The: Baker, R.S.

New inferno, The: Phillips, Stephen

New inne, or the light heart, The: Jonson, Ben

New interlude and a mery of the nature of the iiii elements, A: Rastell, John

New Jersey: Stockton, F.R.

New Jerusalem, The: Chesterton, G.K.

New June, The: Newbolt, Sir Henry

New King Arthur, The: Fawcett, Edgar

New lamps or old?: Halliwell, James Orchard

New land speaking: Canby, Henry Seidel

New Laokoon, The: Babbitt, Irving

New leaf mills: Howells, W.D.

New legends: Allen, Hervey

New leisure: Brighouse, Harold

New letter of notable contents, A: Harvey, Gabriel

New Leviathan, The: Collingwood, R.G.

New liberties for old: Becker, C.L.

New liberty pole – take care!: Freneau, Philip

New life, The: Blocksidge, C.W.

New life, A: Rice, Elmer

New light, The: Hicks, Granville

New light on the early history of the greater North-West: Thompson, David

New literary values: Daiches, David

New lives for old: Mead, Margaret

New lives for old: Snow, C.P.

New Lucian, The: Traill, H.D.

New Machiavelli, The: Wells, H.G.

New Magdalen, The: Collins, Wilkie

New man, The: Gibbs, Sir Philip

New men, The: Snow, C.P.

New methods of infantry training: Liddell Hart, B.

New Minnesinger, The: †Field, Michael

New mirror for travellers, The: Paulding, J.K.

New miscellany, A: Dyer, John

New moon, The: †Onions, Oliver

New moon, The: †Taffrail

New moon with the old, The: Smith, Dodie

New morning, The: Noyes, Alfred

New Nero, The: Fawcett, Edgar

New Nutcracker suite, The: Nash, Ogden

New opportunities in old professions: Sheldon, C.M.

New ordeal, The: Chesney, *Sir* George

New order, The: Prichard, K.S.

New Orleans sketches: Faulkner, William

New Orleans; the place and the people: King, G.E.

New outlook, A: Munshi, K.M.

New Pacific, The: Bancroft, H.H.

New Parsifal, The: Trevelyan, R.C.

New particulars regarding the works of Shakespeare: Collier, John Payne

New pastoral, The: Read, T.B.

New paths in genetics: Haldane, J.B.S.

New pathways in science: Eddington, *Sir* Arthur

New pattern for a tired world: Bromfield, Louis

New Paul and Virginia, The: Mallock, W.H.

New peerage, The: Lee, Harriet

New Penrod book, The: Tarkington, Booth

New pilgrimage and other poems, A: Blunt, Wilfred

New pilgrim's progress, A: Deakin, Alfred

New planet, The: Frankau, Pamela

New plot discovered: Heywood, Thomas

New poet: Allen, James Lane

New poetry of New England: Coffin, Robert

New poor, The: Jennings, Gertrude

New post, A: Davies, *Sir* John

New priest in Conception Bay, The: Lowell, Robert

New Priesthood, The: †Ouida

New primmer or methodical directions to attain the true spelling, reading, and writing of English, A: Pastorius, F.D.

New Prince Fortunatus, The: Black, William

New project for the regulation of the stage, A: Dennis, John

New providence, The: Mottram, R.H.

New provinces: Finch, R.D.C.

New provinces: Kennedy, Leo

New purchase, The: Hall, B.R.

New rambler, The: Morris, *Sir* Lewis

New rector, The: Weyman, Stanley

New Reform Bill, A: Webb, Beatrice

New reign, The: Smith, Sydney

New religion, The: Maltby, H.F.

New republic, The: Lippmann, Walter

New republic, or culture, faith and philosophy in an English country house, The: Mallock, W.H.

New revelation, The: Doyle, *Sir* Arthur Conan

New rich, The: Royde-Smith, Naomi

New road, The: Munro, Neil

New Rome, The: Buchanan, R.W.

New Samaria: Mitchell, S.W.

New Samhite, The: Sen, Kesava Chandra

New school at Scawdale, The: Brazil, Angela

New shepherd, The: Young, A.J.

New Sing Sing, The: Davis, R.H.

New sketch book, The: Darley, George

New song, A: Hughes, J.L.

New song of a young mans opinion of the difference between good and bad women, A: Wither, George

New song of the Bishop of London and the city churches, A: Squire, *Sir* J.C.

New Sonia Wayward, The: (†Michael Innes), Stewart, J.I.M.

New South, The: Grady, H.W.

New South Africa, The: Haggard, *Sir* H. Rider

New South Wales: Reid, *Sir* G.H.

New spirit, The: Ellis, Havelock

New spirit in literature, The: Nicolson, Hon. *Sir* Harold

New spirit of the age, A: Horne, R.H.

New Spoon River, The: Masters, E.L.

New star chamber, The: Masters, E.L.

New stone, bronze and early iron ages: Quennell, Marjorie

New studies in literature: Dowden, Edward

New study of English poetry, A: Newbolt, *Sir* Henry

New Swiss Family Robinson, The: Wister, Owen

New tales: Opie, Amelia

New teaching of history, The: Wells, H.G.

New testament, A: Anderson, Sherwood

New Testament commentary for English readers, A: Knox, R.A.

New Testament commentary II: Knox, R.A.

New Testament commentary III: Knox, R.A.

New Testament wordbook, A: Partridge, E.H.

New theory of evolution, A: Keith, *Sir* Arthur

New thought common sense and what life means to me: Wilcox, Ella Wheeler

New thought pastels: Wilcox, Ella Wheeler

New Timon, The: Lytton, E.G.E.B., *1st Baron*

New Timothy, The: Baker, W.M.

New translation of the Bible, A: Moffatt, James

New treasure seekers, The: Nesbit, E

New Veda: Sen, Keshub Chunder

New version of the psalms of David, A: Blackmore, *Sir* Richard

New version of the psalms of David, A: Tate, Nahum

New view of society, A: Owen, Robert

New viewpoints in American history: Schlesinger, A.M.

New views of Christianity: Brownson, Orestes

New voter's guide to party programmes, A: Holtby, Winifred

New voyage round the world, A: Dampier, William

New voyage round the world, A: Defoe, Daniel

New waggins of old tales by two wags: Bangs, J.K.

New way of life, A: Hichens, R.S.

New way of life, A: Strachey, John St. Loe

New way of gardening, The: (†Donald Barr), Barrett, C.L.

New way of making fowre-parts in counter-point, A: Campion, Thomas

New way to pay old debts, A: Massinger, Philip

New western front, The: Chase, Stuart

New wonder, A: Rowley, William

New World, The: Binyon, Laurence

New world, The: Bynner, Witter

New world, The: Masters, E.L.

New world ballads: Gibbon, J.M.

New world lyrics and ballads: Scott, D.C.

New world order, The: Wells, H.G.

New world for sold: Wells, H.G.

New writing in Europe: Lehmann, John

New Year letter: Auden, W.H.

New year verses: Freneau, Philip

New Year's Day: Gore, Catherine

New Year's Day (the 'seventies): Wharton, Edith

New Year's Eve, A: Barton, Bernard

New Year's Eve: Frank, Waldo

New Year's gift for sick children, A: Craik, *Mrs.* Dinah

New York: Cooper, James Fenimore

New York: Fawcett, Edgar

New York: Hanley, James

New York essays: Ford, Ford Madox

New York family, A: Fawcett, Edgar

New York is not America: Ford, Ford Madox

New York: its upper ten and lower million: Lippard, George

New York madness: Bodenheim, Maxwell

New York nights: Graham, Stephen

New York nocturnes: Stringer, A.J.A.

New York proclaimed: Pritchett, V.S.

New York with its pants down: Karaka, D.F.

New Zealand: Marsh, Ngaio Edith

New Zealand: Reeves, W.P.

New Zealand: a short history: Beaglehole, J.C.

New Zealand and the South Sea Islands: Vogel, *Sir* Julius

New Zealand and the statute of Westminster: Beaglehole, J.C.

New Zealand citizen, The: Mulgan, A.E.

New Zealand literature: McCormick, E.H.

New Zealand notables: Burdon, R.M.

New Zealand poems: Duggan, E.M.

New Zealand shipping company's pocket book: an interesting guide for passengers, The: Reeves, W.P.

New Zealand tragedy, A: Crofts, F.W.

New Zealand wars, The: Cowan, James

New Zealanders, The: Bolitho, H.H.

Newcomes, The: Thackeray, W.M.

Newdigate prize poem: Mallock, W.H.

Newe enterlude of vice conteyninge, the historye of Horestes with the cruell revengment of his fathers death, A: Pickering, John

Newer ideals of peace: Addams, Jane

Newer spirit, The: Calverton, C.F.

Newes, The: L'Estrange, *Sir* Roger

Newes from Graves-end: Dekker, Thomas

Newes from Hell: Dekker, Thomas

Newes from the new exchange: Nevile, Henry

New-found politicke, The: Florio, John

Newfoundland in 1842: Bonnycastle, *Sir* R.H.

Newfoundland verse: Pratt, E.J.

Newman: Tillotson, Geoffrey

Newman's Way: O'Faolain, Sean

Newmarket: Warton, Thomas

Newport: Lathrop, G.P.

Newport aquarelle, A: Elliot, M.H.

News from nowhere: Morris, William

News from Tartary: Fleming, Peter

News from the Duchy: (†Q), Quiller-Couch, *Sir* Arthur

News from the mountain: Church, Richard

News of England: Nichols, Beverley

News of the devil: Wolfe, Humbert

News of the night: Bird, R.M.

News of the Phoenix: Smith, A.J.M.

News of the world: Barker, George

Newspaper, The: Crabbe, George

Newspaper days, 1899–1906: Mencken, H.L.

Newtimber Lane: Raymond, Ernest

Newton Forster: Marryatt, Frederick

Newtonian system of philosophy adapted to the capacities of young gentlemen and ladies, The: Newbery, John

Newyeares guift presented to My Lady and M:rs the then Lady Katherine Stanhop now Countesse of Chesterfield, A: Massinger, Philip

New-Year's bargain, The: Coolidge, Susan

New-yeeres gift: presented at court from the Lady Parvula to the Lord Minimus, The: Heywood, Thomas

Next door house, The: Molesworth, *Mrs.*

Next door neighbours: Ridge, W.Pett

Next generation, The: Beresford, J.D.

Next Harvard: MacLeish, Archibald

Next religion, The: Zangwill, Israel

Next ten years in British social and economic policy, The: Cole, G.D.H.

Nexus: Miller, Henry

Niagara one hundred years ago: Carnochan, Janet

Niagara revisited: Howells, W.D.

Nice people: Crothers, Rachel

Nice types: †Armstrong, Anthony

Nicephorus: a tragedy of New Rome: Harrison, Frederic

Nicest girl in the school, The: Brazil, Angela

Nicholas Crabbe: (†Baron Corvo), Rolfe, Frederick

Nicholas Minturn: Holland, J.G.

Nick of the woods: Bird, R.M.

Nicky, son of Egg: Bullett, Gerald

Nicky-Nan, reservist: (†Q), Quiller-Couch, *Sir* Arthur

Nicodemus: Robinson, E.A.

Nicodemus: Young, A.J.

Nicola Silver: Turner, E.S.

Nicolette: Orczy, *Baroness*

Nietzsche: More, P.E.

Niger: the life of Mungo Park: †Gibbon, L.G.

Nigger heaven: Van Vechten, Carl

Nigger of the "Narcissus", The: Conrad, Joseph

Night: Campbell, W.W.

Night: Churchill, Charles

Night, a descriptive poem: Elliott, Ebenezer

Night among the horses, A: Barnes, Djuna

Night and day: Rosenberg, Isaac

Night and day: Woolf, Virginia

Night and death: White, J.B.

Night and morning: Lytton, E.G.E.B. *1st Baron*

Night and silence who is here?: Johnson, Pamela H.

Night at an inn, A: Dunsany, E.J.M.D.P.

Night at the Mocking Widow: †Carter Dickson

Night at the opera, A: Kaufman, G.S.

Night at the Vulcan: Marsh, Ngaio Edith

Night before, The: Robinson, E.A.

Night before Christmas, The: Moore, C.C.

Night cap and plume: †Preedy, George

Night fears: Hartley, L.P.

Night hawk: Stringer, A.J.A.

Night horseman, The: †Brand, Max

Night in Acadie, A: Chopin, Kate

Night in Alexandria, A: Lewisohn, Ludwig

Night in Bombay: Bromfield, Louis

Night in Cold Harbour, A: Kennedy, Margaret

Night in Montmartre, A: Malleson, Miles

Night is long, The: Millin, Sarah Gertrude

Night life of the gods, The: Smith, Thorne

Night music: Odets, Clifford

Night must fall: Williams, Emlyn

Night of errors: Rubenstein, Harold F.

Night of errors: (†Michael Innes), Stewart, J.I.M.

Night of Mr. H., The: Brighouse, Harold

Night of the party: Boyd, Martin

Night of the poor: Prokosch, Frederic

Night on a bald mountain: White, Patrick

Night operator, The: Packard, F.L.

Night over Taos: Anderson, Maxwell

Night rider: Warren, Robert Penn

Night thoughts: Wilson, Edmund

Night visitor, The: Bennett, Arnold

Night watches: Jacobs, W.W.

Night watches: Monkhouse, A.N.

Night wind, A: Bynner, Witter

Night-born, The: London, Jack

Night-comers, The: Ambler, Eric

Nightingale, The: Church, Richard

Nightingale, The: Hannay, Patrick

Nightingale, The: Robertson, T.W.

Nightingale, The: Thomas, Augustus

Nightingale, The: Wodehouse, P.G.

Nightingale House: Maltby, H.F.

Nightingale wood: Gibbons, Stella

Nightingales: Le Gallienne, Richard

Nightmare, The: Forester, C.S.

Nightmare Abbey: Peacock, Thomas Love

Nightmare at noon: Benét, Stephen Vincent

Nightmare has triplets, The: Cabell, James Branch

Nightmare town: Hammett, S.D.

Nightmares of eminent persons: Russell, Bertrand

Night-raven, The: Rowlands, Samuel

Nights abroad: Bercovici, Konrad

Nights of London, The: Morton, H.V.

Nights of love and laughter: Miller, Henry

Nights with Uncle Remus: Harris, J.C.

Night's works, A: Behrman, S.N.

Night-walker, The: Fletcher, John

Nightwatchman and other longshoremen, The: Jacobs, W.W.

Nightwood: Barnes, Djuna

Nikolai Gogol: Nabokov, Vladimir

Nil Admirari: †Pindar, Peter

Nile notes of a Howadji: Curtis, G.W.

Nimble rabbit, The: Brophy, John

Nimport: Bynner, E.L.

Nina: Griffith, Hubert

Nina Balatka: Trollope, Anthony

Nine bears, The: Wallace, Edgar

Nine bookes of various history: Heywood, Thomas

Nine bright shiners, The: Ridler, A.B.

Nine days of Dunkirk, The: †Divine, David

Nine days to Mukulla: Prokosch, Frederic

Nine days wonder, The: Masefield, John

Nine essays: Housman, A.E.

Nine little goslings: Coolidge, Susan

Nine of hearts: Farjeon, B.L.

Nine nines or novenas from a Chinese litany of old numbers: Belloc, Hilaire

Nine rivers from Jordan: Johnston, W.D.

Nine sharp and earlier: Farjeon, Herbert

Nine starlight tales: Uttley, Alison

Nine tailors, The: Sayers, Dorothy

Nine tales: De Selincourt, Hugh

Nine to six-thirty: Ridge, W. Pett

Nine unlikely tales: Nesbit, E.

Nine waxed faces, The: †Beeding, Francis

Nine wrong answers, The: Carr, J.D.

Ninepenny flute: Coppard, A.E.

Nineteen eighty-four: †Orwell, George

Nineteen stories: Greene, Graham

1914: Brooke, Rupert

Nineteen impressions: Beresford, J.D.

1919: Dos Passos, John

1939: Boyle, Kay

1925: Wallace, Edgar

Nineteen-forty: our finest hour: Mee, Arthur

Nineteenth century, The: Ellis, Havelock

Nineteenth century fiction: a bibliographical record: Sadleir, Michael

Nineteenth century painting: Rothenstein, Sir John

Nineteenth century questions: Clarke, J.F.

Ninety days' worth of Europe: Hale, E.E.

95 poems: Cummings, E.E.

Ninety-two days: Waugh, Evelyn

Nininger City: Donnelly, I.L.

Ninth avenue: Bodenheim, Maxwell

Ninth Earl, The: Besier, Rudolf

Ninth earl, The: Farnol, J.J.

Ninth vibration, The: Beck, Mrs. Lily

Ninth wave, The: Van Doren, Carl

Nipping or snipping of abuses, The: Taylor, John

Nisbet: Singh, Jogendra

Nixey's harlequin: Coppard, A.E.

Nix-nought-nothing: Mitchison, Naomi

No abolition of slavery: Boswell, James

No and yes: Eddy, M.B.

No anklet bells for her: Isvaran, M.S.

No armour: Dalley, J.B.

No barrier: Dark, Eleanor

No boats on Bannermere: Trease, Geoffrey

No boats on the river: Herbert, Sir A.P.

No cards: Gilbert, Sir W.S.

No castle in Spain: McFee, William

No common glory: †Pilgrim, David

No Crabb, no Christmas: Morley, C.D.

No cross no crown: Penn, William

No decency left: †Riding, Laura

No defence: Parker, Sir H.G.

No directions: Hanley, James

No dragon, no damsel: †Armstrong, Anthony

No earthly command: Calder-Marshall, Arthur

No easy way: Jacob, Naomi

No enemy: Ford, Ford Madox

No enemy (but himself): Hubbard, Elbert

No epitaph: Postgate, Raymond

No escape: Ercole, Velia

No escape: Davies, Rhys

No fine on fun: Herbert, Sir A.P.

No fury: †Beeding, Francis

No future for Luana: Derleth, A.W.

No greater love: Orczy, Baroness

No hero: Hornung, E.W.

No hero: Marquand, J.P.

No hero—this: Deeping, Warwick

No higher mountain: †Armstrong, Anthony

No highway: Sherriff, R.C.

No highway: †Shute, Nevil

No humour in my love: Bolitho, H.H.

No idle words: Brown, Ivor

No limit: Greenwood, Walter

No love: Garnett, David

No love lost: Howells, W.D.

No man's land: †Sapper

No man's street: Nichols, Beverley

No more gas: Hall, J.N. and C.B. Nordhoff

No more meadows: Dickens, Monica

No more mimosa: Mannin, Ethel

No more music: Lehmann, Rosamund

No more parades: Ford, Ford Madox

No mother to guide her: Loos, Anita

No name: Collins, Wilkie

No new thing: Mason, R.A.K.

No news: Frankau, Pamela

No news from Helen: Golding, Louis

No one will know: †Delafield, E.M.

No one's enemy but his own: Murphy, Arthur

No other man: Noyes, Alfred

No other tiger: Mason, A.E.W.

No other way: Besant, *Sir* Walter

No outspan: Reitz, Deneys

No painted plumage: Powys, T.F.

No pasaran!: Sinclair, Upton

No place like home: Nichols, Beverley

No place on earth: Cabell, James Branch

No plays of Japan, The: Waley, Arthur

No poems: Benchley, Robert

No price for freedom: Gibbs, Sir Philip

No quarter: Reid, T.M.

No quarter: Waugh, Alec

No quarter given: Horgan, Paul

No refuge but in truth: Smith, Goldwin

No retreat: Gregory, H.V.

No room at the inn: Ferber, Edna

No room at the inn: Temple, Joan

No Secrets Island: Sullivan, Alan

No servants: Jennings, Gertrude

No sign-posts in the sea: Sackville-West, V.

No sky: Balchin, Nigel

No son of mine: Stern, G.B.

No star is lost: Farrell, James

No such word: Pertwee, Roland

No swank: Anderson, Sherwood

No thanks: Cummings, E.E.

No. 13 Rue de Bon Diable: Hardy, A.S.

No thoroughfare: Collins, Wilkie

No thoroughfare: Dickens, Charles

No time for comedy: Behrman, S.N.

No time for cowards: Hesketh, Phoebe

No time like the present: Jameson, Storm

No traveller returns: Collier, John

No truce with time: Waugh, Alec

No villain need be: Fisher, V.A.

No way home: †Preedy, George

No whippinge nor trippinge: Breton, Nicholas

No wind of blame: Heyer, Georgette

No wit (help) like a womans: Middleton, Thomas

Noah: Mottram, R.H.

Noah an' Jonah an' Cap'n John Smith: Marquis, Don

Noah and the waters: Day-Lewis, C.

Nobby: Wallace, Edgar

Noble art of venerie or hunting, The: Turberville, George

Noble castle: Hollis, Christopher

Noble essences: Sitwell, *Sir* Osbert

Noble haul, A: Russell, W.C.

Noble heart, The: Lewes, G.H.

Noble in reason: Bentley, Phyllis

Noble jilt, The: Trollope, Anthony

Noble life, A: Craik, *Mrs.* Dinah

Noble peasant, The: Holcroft, Thomas

Noble purpose nobly won, A: Manning, Anne

Noble queen, A: Taylor, P.M.

Noble souldier, The: Dekker, Thomas

Noble souldier, The: Rowley, Samuel

Noble voice, The: Van Doren, Mark

Noblesse oblige: Agate, J.E.

Noblest frailty, The: Sadleir, Michael

Nobodaddy: MacLeish, Archibald

Nobody: Warner, S.B.

No-body, and some-body: Heywood, Thomas

Nobody lives forever: Burnett, W.R.

Nobody say a word: Van Doren, Mark

Nobody's fortune: Yates, E.H.

Nobody's in town: Ferber, Edna

Nobody's man: Oppenheim, E.Phillips

Nobody's son: Ingraham, J.H.

No'count boy, The: Green, Paul

Noctes ambrosianae of "Blackwood", The: Maginn, William

Noctes ambrosianae of "Blackwood", The: †North, Christopher, Lockhart, J.G. et al.

Nocturne: Swinnerton, Frank

Nocturne of remembered spring: Aiken, Conrad

Nocturnes—marines—Chevalet pieces: Whistler, James

Noel: Cannan, Gilbert

Noël: Longfellow, H.W.

Noemi: Baring-Gould, Sabine

Noh: Fenollosa, E.F.

Noise of history, The: Lehmann, John

Noise of their wings, The: Kantor, MacKinlay

Noisy Nora: Lofting, Hugh

Nollekens and his times: Smith, J.T.

Nomads and empire builders: Beals, Carleton

Nomad's land: Rinehart, Mary Roberts

Non sequitur: Coleridge, Mary

Non-combatants and others: Macaulay, *Dame* Rose

None are so blind: Wren, P.C.

None but the lonely heart: Llewellyn, Richard

None so pretty: Irwin, Margaret

None turn back: Jameson, Storm

Nones: Auden, W.H.

Nonesuch, The: Heyer, Georgette

Nonesuch century, The: Symons, A.J.A.

Nonesuch Coleridge, The: Potter, Stephen

Non-juror, The: Cibber, Colley

No-nose at the show: Lucas, E.V.

Nonparaeil, The: Smart, Christopher

Nonsence upon sence: Taylor, John

Nonsense novels: Leacock, Stephen

Nonsense of common-sense, The: Montagu, *Lady* Mary Wortley

Nonsense of it, The: Higginson, T.W.

Nonsense songs, stories, botany and alphabets: Lear, Edward

Nonsenseorship: Hecht, Ben and others

Nonsuch, land of water: Beebe, William

Non-violence in peace and war: Gandhi, M.K.

Noon wine: Porter, K.A.

No-one will ever know: Mottram, R.H.

Noontide branches: †Field, Michael

Noose: Llewellyn, Richard

Noose for Ned, A: Clune, Frank

Nor many waters: Waugh, Alec

Nor the years condemn: †Hyde, Robin

Nora Macarty: Aldrich, T.B.

Nordic twilight: Forster, E.M.

Norm: Christie, Agatha

Norma Ashe: Glaspell, Susan

Norman: Ingraham, J.H.

Norman church, The: Milne, A.A.

Norman Douglas: Tomlinson, H.M.

Norman Leslie: Fay, T.S.

Norman Maurice: Simms, W.G.

Norman's nugget: Oxley, J.M.

Norse tales: Thomas, E.E.P.

Norseland tales: Boyesen, H.H.

Norseman's pilgrimage, A: Boyesen, H.H.

North Africa and the desert: Woodberry, G.E.

North America: Trollope, Anthony

North American Indian portfolio: Catlin, George

North and south: Gaskell, *Mrs.* Elizabeth

North and South Devon: Pevsner, Nikolaus

North Briton, The: Churchill, Charles

North coast: Buchanan, R.W.

North coast: selected verse: Christesen, C.B.

North Eastern France: Hare, A.J.C.

North Italian painters of the Renaissance, The: Berensen, Bernhard

North of Boston: Frost, Robert

North of Grand Central: Marquand, J.P.

North of Rome: Church, Richard

North of Suez: McFee, William

North of the Danube: Caldwell, Erskine Preston

North of 36: Hough, Emerson

North overland with Franklin: Oxley, J.M.

North shore of Massachusetts, The: Grant, Robert

North shore watch, The: Woodberry, G.E.

North Western France: Hare, A.J.C.

North wind, The: Mackenzie, *Sir* Compton

Northanger Abbey: Austen, Jane

Northbridge Rectory: Thirkell, Angela

North-country chorister, The: Ritson, Joseph

Northcourt nonsense: Baring, Maurice

Northern antiquities: Percy, Thomas

Northern Atlantis, The: King, William

Northern Australia: (†Donald Barr), Barrett, C.L.

Northern element in English literature, The: Craigie, *Sir* W.A.

Northern garlands: Ritson, Joseph

Northern iron, The: Hannay, J.O.

Northern kingdom, The: Dawson, S.E.

Northern light, The: Cronin, A.J.

Northern light: Strong, L.A.G.

Northern lights: Parker, *Sir* H.G.

Northern neighbors: Grenfell, *Sir* W.T.

Northern Star, The: Hill, Aaron

Northern studies: Gosse, *Sir* Edmund

Northern trail, A: Blocksidge, C.W.

Northern travel: Taylor, Bayard

Northerners, The: Brighouse, Harold

Northing tramp, The: Wallace, Edgar

Northland lyrics: Roberts, T.G.

Northland songs: Gibbon, J.M.

Northward course of Empire, The: Stefansson, V.

North-ward hoe: Dekker, Thomas

Northwest passage: Roberts, Kenneth

North-west territory: Hind, H.Y.

Northwood: Hale, S.J.B.

Norwegian Odyssey: Mais, S.P.B.

Norwich victims, The: †Beeding, Francis

Nosce tepsum: Davies, *Sir* John

Nosegay and a similie for the reviewers a lyric epistle, A: Stevenson, J.H.

Nostromo: Conrad, Joseph

Not a bad show: †Beeding, Francis

Not a friend in the world: Sala, G.A.H.

Not a sparrow falls: †Bell, Neil

Not all in vain: Cambridge, Ada

Not all lies: Abbas, K.A.

Not angels quite: Dole, N.H.

Not at all jealous: Robertson, T.W.

Not by bread alone: Stefansson, V.

Not by the strange gods: Roberts, E.M.

Not counting the cost: †Tasma

Not enough tragedy: Gielgud, Val

Not for children: Rice, Elmer

Not George Washington: Wodehouse, P.G.

Not heaven: Frank, Waldo

Not I, but the wind: Lawrence, D.H.

Not in our stars: Bottome, Phyllis

Not in the calendar: Kennedy, Margaret

Not long for this world: Derleth, A.W.

Not on the screen: Fuller, H.B.

Not Paul but Jesus: Bentham, Jeremy

Not quite eighteen: Coolidge, Susan

Not quite true: Molesworth, *Mrs.*

Not so bad as we seem: Lytton, E.G.E.B. *1st Baron*

Not so deep as a well: Parker, Dorothy

Not that it matters: Milne, A.A.

Not under forty: Cather, Willa

Not waving but drowning: Smith, Stevie

Not wisely, but too well: Broughton, Rhoda

Not with thorns: (†Ennis Graham), Molesworth, *Mrs.*

Not without honour: Brittain, Vera

Not without laughter: Hughes, J.L.

Not wooed but won: Payn, James

Notable discovery of coosnage, A: Greene, Robert

Notable images of virtue: Day-Lewis, C.

Note in music, A: Lehmann, Rosamund

Note of hand, The: Cumberland, Richard

Note on Charlotte Brontë, A: Swinburne, A.C.

Note on experts, A: Wolfe, T.C.

Note on literary criticism, A: Farrell, James

Note on "Patience", A: Beerbohm, *Sir* Max

Note on the Muscovite Crusade: Swinburne, A.C.

Note on William Wordsworth, A: Browning, Elizabeth Barrett

Notebook on William Shakespeare, A: Sitwell, Edith

Note-books of night: Wilson, Edmund

Notes and elucidations to Henley's Lyra Heroica: Greg, W.W.

Notes and emendations to the text of Shakespeare's plays from early manuscript corrections in a copy of the folio in 1632: Collier, J.P.

Notes and fragments: Whitman, Walt

Notes and impressions: Reid, Forrest

Notes and lectures upon Shakespeare: Coleridge, S.T.

Notes and observations on pictures: Reynolds, *Sir* Joshua

Notes and observations on the Empress of Morocco: Shadwell, Thomas

Notes and observations on the Empress of Morocco revised: Settle, Elkanah

Notes and queries: †Machen, Arthur

Notes and sketches of New South Wales: Meredith, L.A.

Notes and sketches of the Paris exhibition: Sala, G.A.H.

Notes by an Oxford chiel: †Carroll, Lewis

Notes for a sea diary: Algren, Nelson

Notes for an autobiography: Van Vechten, Carl

Notes for poems: Plomer, W.C.F.

Notes from books in four essays: Taylor, *Sir* Henry

Notes from Calais base: Montague, C.E.

Notes from life, in six (prose) essays: Taylor, *Sir* Henry

Notes from my South Sea log: †Becke, Louis

Notes from the News: Payn, James

Notes of a camp-follower: Hornung, E.W.

Notes of a journey from Cornhill to Grand Cairo: Thackeray, W.M.

Notes of a journey through France and Italy: Hazlitt, William

Notes of a son and brother: James, Henry

Notes of conversation with Louis-Phillippe, at Claremont: Stanhope, P.H., *Earl*

Notes of conversations with the Duke of Wellington: Stanhope, P.H., *Earl*

Notes of eight years' travels and residence in Europe: Catlin, George

Notes on a cellar-book: Saintsbury, George

Notes on a collection of pictures by J.E.Millais: Lang, Andrew

Notes on a horse thief: Faulkner, William

Notes on Bermuda: Morley, C.D.

Notes on democracy: Mencken, H.L.

Notes on doctrinal and spiritual subjects: Faber, F.W.

Notes on Egyptian standard: Murray, Margaret

Notes on English etymology: Skeat, W.W.

Notes on English verse satire: Wolfe, Humbert

Notes on Joseph Conrad: Symons, Arthur

Notes on life and letters: Conrad, Joseph

Notes on Lord Chesterfield's works: Walpole, Horace

Notes on Malthus's political economy: Ricardo, David

Notes on men, women and books: Wilde, *Lady* J.F.

Notes on military writing for English-Canadian soldiers: Wallace, W.S.

Notes on novelists: James, Henry

Notes on poems and reviews: Swinburne, A.C.

Notes on prosody: Nabokov, Vladimir

Notes on railroad accidents: Adams, C.F.

Notes on Samuel Prout and William Hunt: Ruskin, John

Notes on sculptures in Rome and Florence: Shelley, P.B.

Notes on some of the principal pictures exhibited in the rooms of the Royal Academy: Ruskin, John

Notes on the construction of sheepfolds: Ruskin, John

Notes on the crisis: Lippmann, Walter

Notes on the district of Menteith: Cunninghame Graham, Robert

Notes on the establishment of a money unit: Jefferson, Thomas

Notes on the families of Truslow, Horler and Horley from English records: Adams, J.T.

Notes on the history of the Revels Office under the Tudors: Chambers, Sir E.K.

Notes on the liber studiorum of J.M.W. Turner: Brooke, S.A.

Notes on the mechanics of the poetic image: Winters, Yvor

Notes on the pictures and drawings on Mr. Alfred W. Hunt: Gosse, Sir Edmund

Notes on the poems of Alexander Pope: Walpole, Horace

Notes on the Royal Academy exhibition: Rossetti, W.M.

Notes on the Royal Academy exhibition: Swinburne, A.C.

Notes on the State of Virginia: Jefferson, Thomas

Notes on the Turner Gallery at Marlborough House: Ruskin, John

Notes on the verse drama: Hassall, Christopher

Notes on the Western states: Hall, James

Notes on Walt Whitman: Burroughs, John

Notes on witchcraft: Kittredge, G.L.

Notes to Goethe's poems: Boyd, James

Notes to the portraits at Woburn Abbey: Walpole, Horace

Notes to Whatley's principles of trade: Franklin, Benjamin

Notes toward a supreme fiction: Stevens, Wallace

Notes towards the definition of culture: Eliot, T.S.

Notes upon some of Shakespeare's plays: Kemble, F.A.

Nothing: Green, Henry

Nothing dies: Dunne, J.W.

Nothing is safe:† Delafield, E.M.

Nothing like leather: Monkhouse, A.N.

Nothing like leather: Pritchett, V.S.

Nothing new: Craik, *Mrs.* Dinah

Nothing serious: Pain, B.E.O.

Nothing serious: Wodehouse, P.G.

Nothing so strange: Hilton, James

Nothing to do with the war: †Armstrong, Anthony

Nothing to pay: Evans, Caradoc

Nothing to say: (†Q.K. Philander Doesticks P.B.), Thompson, Mortimer

Notice: Dreiser, Theodore

Notices of the most remarkable fires in Edinburgh: Chambers, Robert

Notions in garrison: Somerville, Edith

Notions of the Americans picked up by a travelling bachelor: Cooper, James Fenimore

Notorious Mrs. Ebbsmith, The: Pinero, Sir A.W.

Nottingham Castle: Bailey, P.J.

Notwithstanding: Cholmondeley, Mary

Noughts and crosses:(†Q), Quiller Couch, Sir Arthur

Nova Scarcity: MacMechan, A.M.

Nova Scotia: Willson, H.B.

Nova Scotia Chapbooks: MacMechan, A.M.

Nova Scotia-ness of Nova Scotia, The: MacMechan, A.M.

Novel, The: Crawford, Francis Marion

Novel and the modern world, The: Daiches, David

Novel notes: Jerome, Jerome K.

Novel of romantic beauty and nature and which looks like an engraving, A: Stein, Gertrude

Novel of tomorrow, The: Frank, Waldo

Novel of youth, A: Brittain, Vera

Novel on yellow paper: Smith, Stevie

Novel today, The: Allen, Walter Ernest

Novelette and other prose (1921–1931), A: Williams, W.C.

Novels and novelists: Mansfield, Katherine

Novels and plays of Saki, The: (†Saki), Munro, H.H.

Novels by eminent hands: Thackeray, W.M.

Novels of Benjamin Disraeli, The: Gosse, Sir Edmund

Novels of George Meredith, The: Sitwell, Sir Osbert

Novels, tales and sketches: Barrie, Sir J.M.

Novelty, The: Motteux, P.A.

Novelty and romancement: †Carroll, Lewis

November boughs: Whitman, Walt

November drear: Bridges, Robert

Novice of St. Dominick, The: Morgan, *Lady* Sydney

Novissima verba: last words: Harrison, Frederic

Novus Reformator Vapulans: Brown, Thomas

Now a stranger: Wolfe, Humbert

Now and then: Warren, Samuel

Now came still evening on: Vachell, H.A.

Now for a story:(Stephen Southwold), †Bell, Neil

Now for more stories!: (Stephen Southwold), †Bell, Neil

Now I lay me down to sleep: Bemelmans, Ludwig

Now in November: Johnson, J.W.

Now in wintry delights: Bridges, Robert

Now is the place: Layton, Irving

Now is time: Birney, Earle

Now on view: Brown, Ivor

Now sleeps the crimson petal: Bates, H.E.

Now that April's here: Callaghan, M.E.

Now that the gods are dead: Powys, L.C.

Now the sky: Van Doren, Mark

Now we are six: Milne, A.A.

Now with his love: Bishop, J.P.

Now you tell one: Hannay, J.O.

Now you've done it: Chase, M.C.

Nowadays: Dunsany, E.J.M.D.P.

Ntsukumbini, cattle thief: Brownlee, Frank

Nude with violin: Coward, Noel

Nugae antiquae: Harington, *Sir* John

Nugae canorae: Doughty, *Sir* A.G.

Nuggets and dust penned in California: Bierce, Ambrose

Nulma: Praed, *Mrs.* C.

Number 87:(†Harrington,Hext), Phillpotts, Eden

Number nine: Herbert, *Sir* A.P.

Number one: Dos Passos, John

Number one: Hall, A.M.

Number seventeen: Kingsley, Henry

Number six: Wallace, Edgar

Number twenty: Traill, H.D.

No. 26 Jayne street: Austin, Mary

Numbered chickens: Peach, L. du Garde

Numismata: Evelyn, John

Nunc dimittis: Housman, Laurence

Nun's curse, The: Riddell, *Mrs.* J.H.

Nuns in jeopardy: Boyd, Martin

Nuptial flight, The: Masters, E.L.

Nuptials, The: Ramsay, Allan

Nuptials of Britain's genius and fame, The: Dennis, John

Nuptials of Corbal, The: Sabatini, Rafael

Nurgahan: Singh, Jogendra

Nurse Cavell: Forester, C.S.

Nurse Heatherdale's story: Molesworth, *Mrs.*

Nursery, The: Phillpotts, Eden

Nursery in the nineties: Farjeon, Eleanor

Nursery noonings: Dodge, May Abigail

Nursery rhymes: Sackville-West, Victoria

Nursery rhymes of England, The: Halliwell, J.O.

Nursery rhymes of London town: Farjeon, Eleanor

Nursing home murder: Marsh, Ngaio Edith

Nut-cracker, The: Smart, Christopher

Nutmeg tree, The: Sharp, Margery

Nuts and nutcrackers: Lever, C.J.

Nuts and wine: Wodehouse, P.G.

Nuts in May: Skinner, C.O.

Nuts of knowledge, The: Russell, G.W.

Nydia: Boker, G.H.

Nye and Riley's railway guide: Riley, J.W. and E.W. Nye

Nye and Riley's wit and humor: Nye, E.W. (†Bill Nye) and J.W.Riley

Nylon pirates, The: Monsarrat, Nicholas

Nylon safari: Cloete, E.F.S.G.

Nymph and the lamp, The: Raddall, T.H.

Nymph and the nobleman, The: Sharp, Margery

Nymph in clover: Langley, Noel

Nymph of Tauris, The: †Pindar, Peter

Nyria: Praed, *Mrs.* C.

O

O.H.M.S.: Gow, Ronald

O! Absalom!: Spring, Howard

O death where is thy sting?: Monkhouse, A.N.

O dreams, O destinations: Bentley, Phyllis

O genteel Lady!: Forbes, Esther

O. Henryana: †Henry, O.

O lovely England: De la Mare, Walter

O Mistress Mine: Rattigan, Terence

O Pioneers!: Cather, Willa

O, shepherd, speak! Sinclair, Upton

O, these men, these men!: Thirkell, Angela

O to be a dragon: Moore, M.C.

Oak leaves and lavender: O'Casey, Sean

Oak Mot: Baker, W.M.

Oak openings, The: Cooper, James Fenimore

Oak settle, The: Brighouse, Harold

Oaken heart, The: Allingham, Margery

Oakfield plays: Steen, Marguerite

Oakleyites, The: Benson, E.F.

Oakshott Castle: Kingsley, Henry

Oath of allegiance, The: Ward, E.S.

Oatlands: O'Keeffe, John

Obedience of a Christen man, The: Tyndale, William

Oberland: Richardson, D.M.

Oberon: Barton, George

Oberon's horn: Morley, Henry

Obiter dicta: Birrell, Augustine

Obiter scripta: Harrison, Frederic

Obiter scripta: Santayana, George

Obituary of H.J. Huidekoper: Clarke, J.F.

Objections to the taxation of our American colonies considered, The: Jenyns, Soame

Objects of daily use: Petrie, *Sir* William Flinders

Oblation: Stephens, A.G.

Oblivion: Isvaran, M.S.

O'Briens and the O'Flahertys, The: Morgan, *Lady* Sydney

Observations: Beerbohm, *Sir* Max

Observations: Moore, M.C.

Observations and conjectures upon some passages of Shakespeare: Tyrwhitt, Thomas

Observations and reflections made in the course of a journey through France, Italy and Germany: Thrale, H.L.

Observations, anecdotes, and characters of books and men: Spence, Joseph

Observations by Mr. Dooley: Dunne, F.P.

Observations concerning princes and states: Quarles, Francis

Observations concerning the increase of mankind: Franklin, Benjamin

Observations concerning the scripture of oeconomy: Edwards, Jonathan

Observations, good or bad, stupid or clever, serious or jocular, on Esquire Foote's dramatic entertainment, intitled, The Minor: Boswell, James

Observations in the art of English poesie: Campion, Thomas

Observations made of the Low Countries: Germany, etc.: Ray, John

Observations of Henry, The: Jerome, Jerome K.

Observations of some specialities of divine providence in the life of Joseph Hall: Hall, Joseph

Observations on a late publication intituled "The present state of the nation": Burke, Edmund

Observations on a tour through Scotland and England: Dibdin, Charles

Observations on M. de Sorbier's voyage into England: Sprat, Thomas

Observations on Mr. Thelwall's letter to the editor of the Edinburgh Review: Jeffrey, *Lord* Francis

Observations on Paine's Rights of man: Adams, J.Q.

Observations on penal jurisprudence: Roscoe, William

Observations on several parts of Great Britain particularly the Highlands of Scotland: Gilpin, William

Observations on the causes and cure of smoky chimneys: Franklin, Benjamin

Observations on the conversion and Apostleship of St. Paul in a letter to Gilbert West: Lyttelton, George *Baron*

Observations on the duties of a physician, and the methods of improving medicine: Rush, Benjamin

Observations on the Fairy Queen: Warton, Thomas

Observations on the historie of King Charles: Heylyn, Peter

Observations on the importance of the American Revolution: Priestley, Joseph

Observations on the language of Chaucer: Child, F.J.

Observations on the language of Chaucer's Troilus: Kittredge, G.L.

Observations on the language of Gower's Confessio amantis: Child, F.J.

Observations on the life of Cicero: Lyttelton, George *Baron*

Observations on the mountains and lakes of Cumberland and Westmoreland: Gilpin, William

Observations on the mystery of print and the work of Johann Gutenberg: Van Loon, Hendrik

Observations on the plans by James Wyatt for Downing College: Hope, Thomas

Observations on the present state of the waste lands of Great Britain: Young, Arthur

Observations on the principles and methods of Infant Instruction: Alcott, A.B.

Observations on the River Wye relative chiefly to picturesque beauty: Gilpin, William

Observations on the Shakespeare forgeries at Bridgewater House: Halliwell, J.O.

Observations on the state of religion and literature in Spain: Bowring, *Sir* John

Observations on the three first volumes of the history of English poetry: Ritson, Joseph

Observations on the three first volumes of the history of English poetry (by Thomas Warton) in a letter to the author: Nichols, John

Observations on the twelfth article of war: Mallet, David

Observations on the 22. Stanza in the 9th canto of the second book of Spencers Faery Queen: Digby, *Sir* Kenelm

Observations on the western parts of England: Gilpin, William

Observations on the writings of the craftsman: Hervey, John

Observations relative to ... the Academy in Philadelphia: Franklin, Benjamin

Observations upon historie: Habington, William

Observations upon Religio Medici: Digby, *Sir* Kenelm

Observations upon the articles of peace with the Irish rebels: Milton, John

Observations upon the prophecies of Daniel: Newton, *Sir* Isaac

Observations upon the United Provinces of the Netherlands: Temple, *Sir* William

Observer, The: Cumberland, Richard

Obsession: Levin, Meyer

Obstinate virgin: Sullivan, Alan

Occasion of glory: Calder-Marshall, Arthur

Occasional letter from the farmer to the Freemen of Dublin: Brooke, Henry

Occasional offender, The: Stringer, A.J.A.

Occasional papers and reviews: Keble, John

Occasional pieces of poetry: Brainard, J.G.C.

Occasional prelude, An: Colman, George, *the elder*

Occasional prologue and epilogue to Othello, An: Smart, Christopher

Occasional sermons: Knox, R.A.

Occasional verses: Grant, Robert

Occasions: Jackson, Holbrook

Occasions and protests: Don Passos, John

Occasion's offspring: Stevenson, Matthew

Occultism and common-sense: Willson, H.B.

Occupation: writer: Graves, Robert

Ocean, The: Hanley, James

Ocean, The: Montgomery, James

Ocean: Young, Edward

Ocean free-lance, An: Russell, W.C.

Ocean to ocean: Grant, G.M.

Ocean tragedy, An: Russell, W.C.

Ocean tramp, An: McFee, William

Ocean waifs: Reid, T.M.

Oceola the seminole: Reid, T.M.

Octave of Claudius, The: Pain, B.E.O.

Octave of friends, An: Linton, Eliza

Octave to Mary, An: Tabb, J.B.

Octavia: Porter, Anna Maria

Octavius Brooks Frothingham and the new faith: Stedman, E.C.

October: Bridges, Robert

October blast: Yeats, W.B.

October vagabonds: Le Gallienne, Richard

Octopus, The: †Norris, Frank

Odatis: Morris, *Sir* Lewis

Odd—but even so: Wren, P.C.

Odd craft: Jacobs, W.W.

Odd fellow, The: Ingraham, J.H.

Odd man in: Strong, L.A.G.

Odd man out, The: Brighouse, Harold

Odd man out: Sherriff, R.C.

Odd man's story, An: Ascher, I.G.

Odd pairs: Housman, Laurence

Odd people: Reid, T.M.

Odd streaks, The: Pertwee, Roland

Odd women, The: Gissing, George

Odd-job man, The: †Onions, Oliver

Odds and ends: Collier, J.P.

Ode, An: Jenyns, Soame

Ode for Commonwealth Day: Evans, G.E.

Ode for his Majesty's birthday, An: Cibber, Colley

Ode for music, An: Sassoon, Siegfried

Ode for music: Warton, Thomas

Ode for musick (on St.Cecilia's Day): Pope, Alexander

Ode for the centenary of the death of Burns: Watson, *Sir* J.W.

Ode for the commemoration of the landing of Penn: Barker, J.N.

Ode for the Encaenia at Oxford: Keble, John

Ode for the inauguration of Franklin's statue: Fields, J.T.

Ode for the New Year, 1716: Rowe, Nicholas

Ode for the opening of the InternationalExhibition:Tennyson, Alfred *Lord*

Ode for the Thanksgiving Day: Prior, Matthew

Ode from Italy in time of war: Trench, F.H.

Ode from Ossian's poems: Hopkinson, Francis

Ode Gratulatoria Willelmo Cowper: Philips, John

Ode humbly inscrib'd to the Queen, An: Prior, Matthew

Ode in imitation of the second ode of the third book of Horace, An: Prior, Matthew

Ode in memory of the Rt. Honble. William Ewart Gladstone: Benson, A.C.

Ode (in the manner of Pindar) on the death of the Right Honourable William Earl Cowper, An: Philips, Ambrose

Ode inscribed to the Right Honourable the Earl of Sunderland at Windsor, An: Tickell, Thomas

Ode occasion'd by the death of Mr. Thomson: Collins, William

Ode, occasioned by His Excellency the Earl Stanhope's voyage to France, An: Tickell, Thomas

Ode occasioned by reading Mr. West's translation of Pindar, An: Warton, Joseph

Ode of Horace, An: Stevenson, R.L.

Ode of life, The: Morris, *Sir* Lewis

Ode of our times: Macartney, Frederick

Ode on a distant memory of Jane Eyre: Lang, Andrew

Ode on a distant prospect of Eton College: Gray, Thomas

Ode on General Elliott's return from Gibraltar: Seward, Anna

Ode on the anniversary of the King's birth: Shadwell, Thomas

Ode on the burial of King George the Fifth: Clarke, G.H.

Ode on the coronation of King Edward: Carman, Bliss

Ode on the day of the Coronation of King Edward VIII: Watson, *Sir* J.W.

Ode on the death of a favourite cat: Gray, Thomas

Ode on the death of Mr. Henry Purcell, An: Dryden, John

Ode on the death of the Duke of Wellington: Tennyson, Alfred *Lord*

Ode on the departing year: Coleridge, S.T.

Ode on the Diamond Jubilee of Confederation, An: MacDonald, W.P.

Ode on the French republic: Swinburne, A.C.

Ode on the institution of a Society in Liverpool for the encouragement of designing, An: Roscoe, William

Ode on the King's birth-day: Shadwell, Thomas

Ode on the marriage of H.R.H. the Duke of York and H.S.H. Princess Victoria Mary of Teck: Morris, *Sir* Lewis

Ode on the occasion of the laying of the foundation stone of the statue of Her Gracious Majesty the Queen: Halloran, Henry

Ode on the opening of the Colonial and Indian Exhibition: Tennyson, Alfred *Lord*

Ode on the opening of the Panama-Pacific International Exposition: Sterling, George

Ode on the Peace, An: Williams, H.M.

Ode on the popular superstitions of the Highlands of Scotland, An: Collins, William

Ode on the Royal visit to Canada: Clarke, G.H.

Ode on the spring: Gray, Thomas

Ode performed in the Senate-House at Cambridge: Gray, Thomas

Ode performed in the Senate-House, Cambridge: Kingsley, Charles

Ode performed in the Senate-House, Cambridge: Wordsworth, William

Ode recited at the commemoration of the living and dead soldiers of Harvard University: Lowell, J.R.

Ode to an informer, An: †Pindar, Peter

Ode to Dragon: More, Hannah

Ode to evening, An: Warton, Joseph

Ode to France: Morgan, Charles

Ode to Harvard, An: Bynner, Witter

Ode to his Majesty for the new year, An: Cibber, Colley

Ode to independence: Smollett, Tobias

Ode to Japan: Benson, A.C.

Ode to jurymen, An: †Pindar, Peter

Ode to Lafayette: Barker, J.N.

Ode to mankind, An: Carey, Henry

Ode to Mazzini: Swinburne, A.C.

Ode to my ass, An: †Pindar, Peter

Ode to Napoleon Buonaparte: Byron, George Gordon, *Lord*

Ode to peace: Williams, H.M.

Ode to superstition, An: Rogers, Samuel

Ode to the country gentlemen of England, An: Akenside, Mark

Ode to the Deity: Bowring, *Sir* John

Ode to the King, on his return from Ireland: Shadwell, Thomas

Ode to the late Thomas Edwards, Esq., An: Akenside, Mark

Ode to the livery of London, An: †Pindar, Peter

Ode to the memory of Charles Lamb: Wordsworth, William

Ode to the Mikado of Japan: Horne, R.H.

Ode to the Naiads of Fleet Ditch, An: Murphy, Arthur

Ode to the people of France, An: Roscoe, William

Ode to the right Honble the Earl of Lincoln, An: Bishop, Samuel

Ode to the Right Honourable the Earl of Huntingdon, An: Akenside, Mark

Ode to the right honourable the Earl of Northumberland on his being appointed Lord Lieutenant of Ireland: Smart, Christopher

Ode to tragedy, An: Boswell, James

Ode upon Her Majesty's birth-day, An: Tate, Nahum

Ode upon ode: †Pindar, Peter

Ode, upon the blessed Restoration: Cowley, Abraham

Ode upon the University of Dublin's foundation, An: Tate, Nahum

Ode, with a pastoral recitative on the marriage of the right Honourable James Earl of Weemyss, and Mrs. Janet Charteris, An: Ramsay, Allan

Odes: Gray, Thomas

Odes and addresses to great people: Hood, Thomas

Odes and eclogues: Dixon, R.W.

Odes for a curse-speaking Choir 1: Ottawar!: †Maurice, Furnley

Odes in contribution to the song of French history: Meredith, George

Odes in Ohio: Piatt, J.J.

Odes of importance: †Pindar, Peter

Odes on several descriptive and allegorical subjects: Collins, William

Odes on various subjects: Warton, Joseph

Odes to his Royal Highness the Prince Regent, His Imperial Majesty, the Emperor of Russia, and his Majesty the King of Prussia: Southey, Robert

Odes to Inns and out: †Pindar, Peter

Odes to Kien Long: †Pindar, Peter

Odes to Mr. Paine: †Pindar, Peter

Odes upon cash: Moore, Thomas

Odette D'Antrevernes: Firbank, Ronald

Odo, Count of Lingen: Brydges, *Sir* Samuel Egerton

O'Donnel: Morgan, *Lady* Sydney

O'Donoghue, The: Lever, C.J.

Odtaa: Masefield, John

Odysseus the wanderer: De Selincourt, Aubrey

Odyssey in English verse, The: Mackail, J.W.

Odyssey of a hero: Fisher, V.A.

Odyssey of a nice girl, The: Suckow, Ruth

Odyssey of Homer, The: Morris, William

Odyssey of Homer, The (trn.): Pope, A.

Oeconomy of charity, The: Trimmer, *Mrs.* Sarah

Oeconomy of love, The: Armstrong, John

Oedipus: Dryden, John

Oedipus: Lee, Nathaniel

Oedipus: Treece, Henry

Oedipus tyrannus: Shelley, P.B.

Of all things: Benchley, Robert

Of benevolence: Armstrong, John

Of bodies, and of man's soul: Digby, *Sir* Kenelm

Of Boston in New England: Bradford, William

Of demons and darkness: Collier, John

Of dramatick poesie, and essay: Dryden, John

Of education: Milton, John

Of Ellen Glasgow: Cabell, James Branch

Of English literature in the reign of Victoria, with a glance at the past: Morley, Henry

Of feigned comtemplative life: Wycliffe, John

Of gentylnes and nobylyte: a dialogue between the marchaunt, the knyght and the plowman: Rastell, John

Of human bondage: Maugham, Somerset

Of ideal time and choice: Stevens, Wallace

Of law and life and other things that matter: Frankfurter, Felix

Of law and men: Frankfurter, Felix

Of Lena Geyer: Davenport, Marcia

Of mice and men: Steinbeck,John

Of my things: Mickle, A.D.

Of one blood: Sheldon, C.M.

Of Parliamentary reform: Dobell, S.T.

Of Plymouth plantation: Bradford, William

Of population: Godwin, William

Of prelatical episcopacy: Milton, John

Of reading books: Lowes, J.L.

Of reformation touching church discipline in England: Milton, John

Of stage tyrants: Carey, Henry

Of the characters of women: Pope, Alexander

Of the friendship of Amis and Amile: Morris, William

Of the holiness of church-members: Cotton, John

Of the knowledge which maketh a wise man: Elyot, *Sir* Thomas

Of the Lady Mary: Waller, Edmund

Of the law terms: Spelman, *Sir* Henry

Of the lawes of ecclesiasticall politie: Hooker, Richard

Of the origin and progress of language: Monboddo, *Lord* J.B.

Of the Russe common wealth: Fletcher, Giles, *the elder*

Of the sacred order, and offices of episcopacy: Taylor, Jeremy

Of the true greatness of the Kingdom of Britain: Bacon, Francis

Of the use of riches: Pope, Alexander

Of the virgin and her sleeveless garment: Hoccleve, Thomas

Of thee I sing: Gershwin, Ira

Of thee I sing: Kaufman, G.S.

Of time and the river: Wolfe, T.C.

Of true greatness: Fielding, Henry

Of true religion, haeresie, schism, toleration, and what best means be used against the growth of Popery: Milton, John

Of verbal criticism: Mallet, David

Off Broadway: Anderson, Maxwell

Off for West Point: Sinclair, Upton

Off in a boat: Gunn, Neil

Off the arm: Marquis, Don

Off the deep end: Morley, C.D.

Off the gold coast: Maltby, H.F.

Off the record: (†Ian Hay), Beith, *Sir* John Hay

Off the record: Knox, R.A.

Off the rocks: Grenfell, *Sir* Wilfred

Off the Skelligs: Ingelow, Jean

Off to Philadelphia in the morning: Jones, Jack

Off trail in Nova Scotia: Bird, William

Off with her head: Cole, G.D.H.

Off with his head: Marsh, Ngaio Edith

Offer to the Clarendon Trustees, The: †Carroll, Lewis

Offering of swans, An: Gogarty, O. St.John

Office, The: Connell, John

Office and work of the Universities, The: Newman, J.H.

Office of justice for the peace in England, The: Beard, C.A.

Office of Lord High Steward of England, The: Ritson, Joseph

Officers and gentlemen: Waugh, Evelyn

Official account of the Noble Lord's bite and his dangerous condition: Hone, William

Official aptitude maximised—expense minimised: Bentham, Jeremy

Official history of Australia in the War of 1914–18, The: Bean, C.E.

Offshore light, The: Frankau, Pamela

Offshore wind, An: †Bartimeus

O'Flaherty, V.C.: Shaw, G.B.

O'Flaherty the great: Cournos, John

Ogburn story, The: Sherriff, R.C.

Oggechee cross-firings: Johnston, R.M.

Ogilvies, The: Craik, *Mrs.* Dinah

Ogre, The: Jones, H.A.

Ogre up-to-date, An: Turner, E.S.

Oh! Boy (Oh! Joy): Wodehouse, P.G.

Oh boys in brown: Turner, E.S.

Oh, Kay: Gershwin, Ira

Oh, Kay: Wodehouse, P.G.

Oh lady fair: Moore, Thomas

Oh! lady, lady!: Wodehouse, P.G.

Oh Millersville!: Hall, J.N.

Oh, money! money!: Porter, E.H.

Oh, shoot!: Beach, R.E.

Oh! Susanna: Foster, S.C.

Oh, these authors!: Jennings, Gertrude

Oh! to be in England: Bates, H.E.

Oh! to be in England: Mais, S.P.B.

Oh, what a plague is love!: Tynan, Katherine

Oh! you English: Karaka, D.F.

O'Haloran: McHenry, James

O'Hara: Maxwell, W.H.

O'Hara: Porter, Anna Maria

Ohio lady, The: Tarkington, Booth

Oil! (novel and play): Sinclair, Upton

Oithona: Brereton, John Le G.

Ojistoh: Johnson, E.P.

Okeepa, a religious ceremony and other customs of the Mandams: Catlin, George

Olaf Hjörward: Carman, Bliss

Old acquaintance: Fields, J.T.

Old acquaintance: Van Druten, J.W.

Old Adam, The: Bennett, Arnold

Old Admiral Death: Bridges, Roy

Old age pensions of the aged poor: Booth, Charles

Old and new masters: Lynd, Robert

Old and New Testament connected in the history of the Jews, The: Prideaux, Humphrey

Old and new World lyrics: Scollard, Clinton

Old and the new, The: Partridge, Eric

Old and young: Carman, Bliss

Old Argo, The: Strong, L.A.G.

Old bachelor, The: Wirt, William

Old Bank House, The: Thirkell, Angela

Old batchelour, The: Congreve, William

Old beauty and others: Cather, Willa

Old black Joe: Foster, S.C.

Old Blastus of Bandicoot: Franklin, Miles

Old boyhood: Rubenstein, Harold F.

Old brown book, The: (Stephen Southwold), †Bell, Neil

Old bunch: Levin, Meyer

Old Calabria: Douglas, Norman

Old California in picture and story: White, S.E.

Old Cambridge: Higginson, T.W.

Old captivity, An: †Shute, Nevil

Old caravan days: Catherwood, Mary

Old card, The: Pertwee, Roland

Old century, The: Sassoon, Siegfried

Old Chelsea Bun House, The: Manning, Anne

Old Chester days: Deland, Margaret

Old Chester secret, An: Deland, Margaret

Old Chester tales: Deland, Margaret

Old church, The: Hughes, Thomas

Old city manners: Lennox, Charlotte

Old Clinkers: O'Higgins, H.J.

Old clothesman, The: Holcroft, Thomas

Old contemporaries, The: Lucas, E.V.

Old Contemptibles, The: Ewart, E.A.

Old convent school in Paris, An: Coolidge, Susan

Old countess, The: Sedgwick, A.D.

Old country, The: Newbolt, Sir Henry

Old country house, An: Le Gallienne, Richard

Old country life: Baring-Gould, Sabine

Old couple, The: May, Thomas

Old Court: Ainsworth, Harrison

Old court suburb, The: Hunt, Leigh

Old Creole days: Cable, G.W.

Old crow: Brown, Alice

Old curiosity shop, The: Dickens, Charles

Old dark house, The: Priestley, J.B.

Old deal and the new, The: Beard, C.A.

Old debauchees, The: Fielding, Henry

Old Delabole: Phillpotts, Eden

Old dog Tray: Foster, S.C.

Old dominion, The: James, G.P.R.

Old dominion: her making and her manners, The: Page, T.N.

Old dovecote, The: Garnett, David

Old drama and the new, The: Archer, William

Old Ebenezer: Read, O.P.

Old England: Mottram, R.H.

Old English: Galsworthy, John

Old English home and its dependencies, An: Baring-Gould, Sabine

Old Erin Jucklin: Read, O.P.

Old familiar faces: Nicholson, Meredith

Old familiar faces: Watts-Dunton, W.T.

Old farmer and his almanack, The: Kittredge, G.L.

Old fashioned Christmas: Engle, Paul

Old fashioned fairy tales: Ewing, Mrs. Juliana Horatia

Old fashioned flowers: Sitwell, Sacheverell

Old fashioned folk: Smith, F.H.

Old fashioned girl, An: Alcott, Louisa M.

Old fires and profitable ghosts: (†Q), Quiller-Couch, Sir Arthur

Old flame, The: Herbert, Sir A.P.

Old fogy: Huneker, J.G.

Old folk of the centuries, The: Dunsany, E.J.M.D.P.

Old folks: Read, O.P.

Old folks at home, The: Foster, S.C.

Old folks at home, The: Harwood, H.M.

Old foolishness, The: Carroll, P.V.

Old French romances: Morris, William

Old friends: Bell, Clive

Old friends: Lang, Andrew

Old friends: Winter, William

Old friends and new: Jewett, S.O.

Old friends in fiction: Lynd, Robert

Old front line, The: Masefield, John

Old gang in the new gang, The: Lewis, P. Wyndham

Old garden, The: Cooke, R.T.

Old garden, The: Deland, Margaret

Old garden roses: Sitwell, Sacheverell

Old Garth: De Mille, James

Old gentleman of the black stock, The: Page, T.N.

Old Granny Sullivan: Neilson, J.S.

Old guard surrenders, The: Vachell, H.A.

Old hall, new hall: (†Michael Innes), Stewart, J.I.M.

Old helmet, The: Warner, S.B.

Old Hicks the guide: Webber, C.W.

Old homestead, The: †Rudd, Steele

Old house in the country, The: Reese, L.W.

Old house of Sudbury, The: Parsons, T.W.

Old huntsman, The: Sassoon, Siegfried

Old infant, The: Carleton, William (McKendree)

Old Joe: De la Mare, Walter

Old John: Brown, T.E.

Old judge, The: Haliburton, T.C.

Old June weather, The: Raymond, Ernest

Old junk: Tomlinson, H.M.

Old Kaskaskia: Catherwood, Mary

Old Kensington Palace: Dobson, H.A.

Old King Coal: Mais, S.P.B.

Old King's: MacMechan, A.M.

Old king's tale, The: Dunsany, E.J.M.D.P.

Old knight, The: Palmer, H.E.

Old ladies, The: Ackland, Rodney

Old ladies, The: Walpole, Sir Hugh

Old lady, The: Green, Anne

Old lady says "No"!, The: Johnston, W.D.

Old lady 31: Crothers, Rachel

Old lamps for new: Acton, Harold

Old lamps for new: Lucas, E.V.

Old lights in new chancels: Betjeman, John

Old lines in we-black-and-white: Smith, F.H.

Old lion, The: De la Mare, Walter

Old London merchant: Ainsworth, Harrison

Old Loopy: Morley, C.D.

Old love letters: Howard, B.C.

Old love stories retold: La Gallienne, Richard

Old Madame: Spofford, H.E.

Old maid, The: Akins, Zoë

Old maid, The: Brooke, Frances

Old maid, The: Murphy, Arthur

Old maids and burglars in Paradise: Ward, E.S.

Old maid's club, The: Zangwill, Israel

Old maid's love: Cannan, Gilbert

Old maid's paradise, An: Ward, E.S.

Old man, The: Faulkner, William

Old man, The: Wallace, Edgar

Old man in the corner, The: Orczy, Baroness

Old man and the sea, The: Hemingway, Ernest

Old man Minick: Ferber, Edna

Old man Murray: Lawson, Will

Old man of Edenton, The: Green, Paul

Old man of the stones, The: Mottram, R.H.

Old Man Savarin: Thomson, E.W.

Old Man Savarin stories: Thomson, E.W.

Old man taught wisdom, An: Fielding, Henry

Old mandarin, The: Morley, C.D.

Old manor house, The: Smith, Charlotte

Old man's diary, An: Collier, J.P.

Old man's folly, An: Dell, Floyd

Old mans lesson and a young mans love, An: Breton, Nicholas

Old man's love, An: Trollope, Anthony

Old man's road, The: Auden, W.H.

Old Margaret: Kingsley, Henry

Old Mark Langston: Johnston, R.M.

Old master, An: Jones, H.A.

Old master, An: Wilson, Woodrow

Old measures: Lighthall, W.D.

Old Melbourne memories: †Boldrewood, Rolf

Old men forget: Cooper, Duff

Old men of the sea, The: Mackenzie, Sir Compton

Old mischief: Deeping, Warwick

Old missionary, The: Hunter, Sir W.W.

Old Mr. Tredgold: Oliphant, Margaret

Old Mole: Cannan, Gilbert

Old mortality: Porter, K.A.

Old New York: Wharton, Edith

Old New Zealand: Maning, F.E.

Old nurse's stocking basket: Farjeon, Eleanor

Old oak chest, The: James, G.P.R.

Old order, The: Porter, K.A.

Old order changes, The: Mallock, W.H.

Old order changeth, The: White, W.A.

Old P.Q.: O'Higgins, H.J.

Old Park Road, The: Miller, Thomas

Old Paris: Brooke, S.A.

Old pastures: Colum, Padraic

Old Patch's Medley: †Bowen, Marjorie

Old Peabody pew, The: Wiggin, K.D.

Old people, The: Beresford, J.D.

Old people: Bolitho, H.H.

Old Peter's Russian tales: Ransome, Arthur

Old picture books: Pollard, A.W.

Old pincushion, The: Molesworth, Mrs.

Old Poor Law, The: Webb, Sidney and Beatrice Webb

Old portraits and modern sketches: Whittier, J.G.

Old Possum's book of practical cats: Eliot, T.S.

Old printer and the modern press, The: Knight, Charles

Old probabilities: †Billings, Josh

Old Province tales: MacMechan, A.M.

Old Province tales: Riddell, W.R.

Old Pybus: Deeping, Warwick

Old Quebec, the fortress of New France: Parker, Sir H.G.

Old Regime in Canada, The: Parkman, Francis

Old regimentals, The: Bernard, W.B.

Old reliable, The: Wodehouse, P.G.

Old Rialto Theatre, Hoboken, The: Morley, C.D.

Old road from Spain, The: Holme, Constance

Old road, The: Belloc, Hilaire

Old road to paradise, The: Widdemer, Margaret

Old roof-tree, The: Martin, C.E.

Old roses: Maltby, H.F.

Old sailors yarn: Farjeon, Eleanor

Old Saint Paul's: Ainsworth, Harrison

Old school day romances: Riley, J.W.

Old score, An: Gilbert, Sir W.S.

Old ships, The: Flecker, James Elroy

Old shrines and ivy: Winter, William

Old Soak, The: Marquis, Don

Old Soak and hail and farewell, The: Marquis, Don

Old Soak's history of the world, The: Marquis, Don

Old soldier: Niven, F.J.

Old South, The: Page, T.N.

Old Spookses' Pass, Malcolm's Katie: Crawford, I.V.

Old stag, The: Williamson, Henry

Old swimmin'-hole, The: Riley, J.W.

Old swords: Gielgud, Val

Old tales of a young country: Clarke, Marcus

Old Testament, a new translation, The: Moffat, James

Old Testament plays: Housman, Laurence

Old time gardens: Earle, A.M.

Old time before them, The: Phillpotts, Eden

Old times in middle Georgia: Johnston, R.M.

Old town by the sea, An: Aldrich, T.B.

Old trades and new knowledge: Bragg, Sir William

Old tree blossomed, The: Raymond, Ernest

Old Uncle Ned: Foster, S.C.

Old Vicarage, Grantchester, The: Brooke, Rupert

Old Virginia and her neighbours: Fiske, John

Old Wash Lucas: Green, Paul

Old Washington: Spofford, H.E.

Old Wellington days: Lawlor, P.A.

Old wine: Bottome, Phyllis

Old wine and new: Deeping, Warwick

Old wine in new bottles: †Mordaunt, Elinor

Old wives for new: Phillips, D.G.

Old wives tale, The: Peele, George

Old wives tales, The: Bennett, Arnold

Old woman and the cow, The: Anand, M.R.

Old woman remembers, The: Stringer, A.J.A.

Old world and the new, The: Trollope, Frances

Olde mad-cappes new gally-mawfry: Breton, Nicholas

Olde old very olde man, The: Taylor, John

Oldest inhabitant, The: Phillpotts, Eden

Oldest school in America, The: Grant, Robert

Old-fashioned roses: Riley, J.W.

Old-fashioned tales: Gale, Zona

Oldport days: Higginson, T.W.

Old-town folks: Stowe, Harriet Beecher

Ole George comes to tea: Ervine, St.John

Oleander River: Stern, G.B.

Olio, The: Grose, Francis

Olive: Craik, Mrs. Dinah

Olive branch, The: Carey, Mathew

Olive buds: Sigourney, L.H.

Olive fairy book, The: Lang, Andrew

Olive field, The: Bates, Ralph

Olive tree, The: Huxley, Aldous

Oliver Cromwell: Buchan, John

Oliver Cromwell: Drinkwater, John

Oliver Cromwell: Firth, Sir Charles

Oliver Cromwell: Harrison, Frederic

Oliver Cromwell: Morley, John

Oliver Cromwell: Smith, Horatio

Oliver Cromwell: Wedgwood, C.V.

Oliver Cromwell's letters and speeches: Carlyle, Thomas

Oliver Ellis: Grant, James

Oliver Goldsmith: Black, William

Oliver Goldsmith: Dobson, H.A.

Oliver Goldsmith: Thomas, Augustus

Oliver Newman: Southey, Robert

Oliver October: McCutcheon, G.B.

Oliver the wayward owl: Derleth, A.W.

Oliver Trenton, K.C.: Frankau, Gilbert

Oliver Twist: Dickens, Charles

Oliver Wiswell: Roberts, Kenneth

Oliver's bride: Oliphant, Margaret

Oliver's daughter: Church, Richard

Oliver's kind women: Gibbs, Sir Philip

Olivia: Molesworth, Mrs.

Olivia Delaplaine: Fawcett, Edgar

Olivia in India: Buchan, Anna

Olla Podrida: Marryatt, Frederick

Olney hymns: Cowper, William

Olor Iscanus: Vaughan, Henry

Olton pools: Drinkwater, John

Olympia: Murray, Gilbert

Olympian, The: Jennings, Gertrude

Olympian nights: Bangs, J.K.

Olympians, The: Hubbard, Elbert

Olympians, The: Priestley, J.B.

Olympus in an uproar: O'Keeffe, John

Omai: O'Keeffe, John

O'Malley of Shanganagh: Byrne, Donn

Omar Pasha: Reynolds, G.

Omar repentant: Le Gallienne, Richard

Omar, the tentmaker: Dole, N.H.

Ombra: Oliphant, Margaret

Omen, The: Galt, John

Omitted chapters of history, disclosed in the life and papers of Edmund Randolph: Conway, M.D.

Omnipresence of the Deity, The: Montgomery, Robert

Omnivorous years. 1774–76: Boswell, James

Omoo: Melville, Herman

On: Belloc, Hilaire

On a Chinese screen: Maugham, Somerset

On a dictum of Mr. Disraeli's: Birrell, Augustine

On a huge hill: Beresford, J.D.

On a rainy day: Canfield, Dorothy

On academies of art (more particularly the Royal Academy); and their pernicious effect on the genius of Europe: Hayden, B.R.

On active service, letters of G.B. Pollard: Pollard, A.W.

On actors and the art of acting: Lewes, G.H.

On an Australian farm: †Rudd, Steele

On an English screen: Agate, J.E.

On and off the cars: Sladen, D.B.W.

On any thing: Belloc, Hilaire

On approval: †Lonsdale, Frederick

On bail: Gilbert, *Sir* W.S.

On Baile's Strand: Yeats, W.B.

On beauty: Iyengar, K.R. Srinivasa

On becoming a writer: Brittain, Vera

On being creative: Babbitt, Irving

On being human: More, P.E.

On being ill: Woolf, Virginia

On biblomania: Carman, Bliss

On board Noah's Ark: Bemelmans, Ludwig

On board the Cumberland: Boker, G.H.

On British freedom: Bell, Clive

On Canadian poetry: Brown, E.K.

On catching colds: †Carroll, Lewis

On Christmas night: Denison, Merrill

On company's service: Ridge, W.Pett

On compromise: Morley, John

On concentration and suggestion in poetry: Colvin, *Sir* Sidney

On contemporary literature: Sherman, S.P.

On convocation: Stubbs, William

On Craig Dhu: Symons, Arthur

On creative writing: Engle, Paul

On descending into Hell: Buchanan, R.W.

On doing what one likes: Waugh, Alec

On dramatic method: Barker, Harley Granville

On education: Livingstone, *Sir* Richard

On education, especially in early childhood: Russell, Bertrand

On Emu Creek: †Rudd, Steele

On English composition: Kingsley, Charles

On English poetry: Graves, Robert

On English prose fiction as a rational amusement: Trollope, Anthony

On English translation: Knox, R.A.

On Englishing the Bible: Knox, R.A.

On everything: Belloc, Hilaire

On expression: Galsworthy, John

On fairy stories: Tolkien, J.R.R.

On foot in Devon: Williamson, Henry

On Forsyte's change: Galsworthy, John

On getting there: Knox, R.A.

On giving names to towns and streets: Clarke, J.F.

On guard: Gilbert, *Sir* W.S.

On Hamlet: Madariaga, Salvador de

On Heaven: Ford, F.M.

On Her Majesty's re-building the lodgings of the Black Prince: Tickell, Thomas

On heroes and hero-worship: Carlyle, Thomas

On His Grace the Duke of Marlborough: Wycherley, William

On His Majesty's service: Bridges, Roy

On home rule for Ireland: Arnold, Matthew

On Homer's poetry and on Virgil: Blake, William

On horseback: Warner, C.D.

On immortality: Grenfell, *Sir* Wilfred

On influence of books: Aldrich, T.B.

On John William Rizzo Hoppner born at Venice on 18 January, 1818: Byron, George Gordon, *Lord*

On liberty: Mill, John Stewart

On liberty and loyalty: Swinburne, A.C.

On literature today: Brooks, Van Wyck

On living in a revolution: Huxley, *Sir* Julian

On minding our manners in speech: Morley, C.D.

On Mr. Fechter's acting: Dickens, Charles

On modern poets: Winters, Yvor

On new shores: Bercovici, Konrad

On Newfound River: Page, T.N.

On nobility: Whitehead, William

On nothing: Belloc, Hilaire

On our selection: †Rudd, Steele

On Paddy's character of the Intelligencer: Swift, Jonathan

On picket duty: Alcott, Louisa M.

On poetry in drama: Barker, Harley Granville

On poetry: a rapsody: Swift, Jonathan

On poets and poetry: Eliot, T.S.

On political economy in connection with the moral state and moral prospects of Society: Chalmers, Thomas

On pride: Ramsey, Allan

On protection to agriculture: Ricardo, David

On Protestant education in Lower Canada: Dawson, *Sir* J.W.

On publishers and publishing: Pierce, Lorne

On races, species and their origin: Huxley, T.H.

On reading poetry: De Selincourt, Aubrey

On reading Shakespeare: Smith, Logan Pearsall

On receiving trivia from the author: Bridges, Robert

On sailing the sea: Belloc, Hilaire

On seeing the archers diverting themselves at the butts and rovers: Ramsay, Allan

On seeming to presume: Durrell, Lawrence

On some coins of Lycia: Warren, J.B.L.

On some influences of Christianity on National character: Church, Richard

On some large fossil horns: Percy, Thomas

On some supposed consequences of the doctrine of historical progress: Smith, Goldwin

On something: Belloc, Hilaire

On straw and other conceits: Lewis, D.B. Wyndham

On sunny shores: Scollard, Clinton

On ten plays of Shakespeare: Brooke, S.A.

On the advantages which have resulted from the establishment of the Board of Agriculture: Young, Arthur

On the art of reading: (†Q), Quiller-Couch, *Sir* Arthur

On the art of the theatre: Craig, *Sir* Gordon

On the art of writing: (†Q), Quiller-Couch, *Sir* Arthur

On the beach: †Shute, Nevil

On the birth-day of Washington: Brainard, J.G.C.

On the boiler: Yeats, W.B.

On the building of Springfield: Lindsay, Norman

On the choice of a profession: Stevenson, R.L.

On the comic writers of England: Clarke, Charles Cowden

On the conduct of the understanding: Montagu, Basil

On the conqueror of America shut up in Boston: Freneau, Philip

On the continent: Sitwell, *Sir* Osbert

On the course of collegiate education: Dawson, *Sir* J.W.

On the death of George, Duke of Albermarle: Flatman, Thomas

On the death of Mrs. Behn: Lee, Nathaniel

On the death of our late sovereign lord king Charles II: Flatman, Thomas

On the death of Rev. Dr. Sewell: Wheatley, Phillis

On the death of the illustrious Prince Rupert: Flatman, Thomas

On the death of Thomas, Earl of Ossory: Flatman, Thomas

On the deaths of Rev. John M'Gilchrist, John Brown, and John Henderson: Brown, *Dr.* John

On the edge: De la Mare, Walter

On the educational value of the natural history sciences: Huxley, T.H.

On the enforcement of law in cities: Whitlock, Brand

On the English family of Symonds: Symonds, J.A.

On the eternity of the Supreme Being: Smart, Christopher

On the fo'c'sle head: Russell, W.C.

On the frontier: Auden, W.H.

On the Frontier: Harte, Bret

On the frontier: Isherwood, Christopher

On the goodness of the Supreme Being: Smart, Christopher

On the herpetology of the Grand Duchy of Baden: Douglas, Norman

On the hill: Masefield, John

On the hiring line: O'Higgins, H.J.

On the husbandry of three celebrated British farmers: Young, Arthur

On the idea of comedy and the uses of the comic spirit: Meredith, George

On the immensity of the Supreme Being: Smart, Christopher

On the iron at Big Cloud: Packard, F.L.

On the late persecution of the Protestants in the South of France: Williams, H.M.

On the late Queen's death and his Majesty's accession to the throne: Young, Edward

On the liberty of the Press: Bentham, Jeremy

On the Makaloa mat: London, Jack

On the margin: Huxley, Aldous

On the meaning of life: Durant, W.J.

On the method of theoretical physics: Einstein, Albert

On the methods and results of ethnology: Huxley, T.H.

On the morning of Christ's nativity: Milton, John

On the Mother: Iyengar, K.R. Srinivasa

On the much lamented death of the Marquis of Tavistock: Anstey, Christopher

On the nature and means of early intellectual education: Alcott, A.B.

On the North-west skyline: Drake-Brockman, H.

On the nose: Morley, C.D.

On the old Athabaska trail: Burpee, Lawrence J.

On the old road: Ruskin, John

On the omniscience of the Supreme Being: Smart, Christopher

On the open range: Dobie, J.F.

On the origin and vicissitudes of literature, science and art: Roscoe, William

On the origin of species by means of natural selection: Darwin, Charles

On the place of Gilbert Keith Chesterton in English letters: Belloc, Hilaire

On the plantation: Harris, J.C.

On the poems of Henry Vaughan: Blunden, Edmund

On the poetry of Pope: Tillotson, Geoffrey

On the point: a summer idyl: Dole, N.H.

On the power of the Supreme Being: Smart, Christopher

On the present state of English pronunciation: Bridges, Robert

On the present state of Indian politics: Ahmad Khan, Sir Saiyid

On the present state of political parties in America: Oliphant, Laurence

On the prevention of war: Strachey, John

On the principles of classification in the animal kingdom: Agassis, Jean

On the progress of mankind and reform: Bancroft, George

On the Prometheus of Aeschylus: Coleridge, S.T.

On the racecourse: Gregory, Lady Augusta

On the relations between spoken and written language, with special reference to English: Bradley, Dr. Henry

On the responsibilities of employers: Helps, Sir Arthur

On the reverence due to the altar: Taylor, Jeremy

On the rocks: Shaw, G.B.

On the sacred memory of our late sovereign: Tate, Nahum

On the screen: Hichens, Robert

On the shelf: Morley, C.D.

On the shoe-string limited with Nye and Riley: (†Bill Nye), Nye, E.W.

On the shore: Halper, Albert

On the signs of the times: Barton, Bernard

On the Spanish Main: Masefield, John

On the spot: Wallace, Edgar

On the stage: Kemble, F.A.

On the stage and off: Jerome, Jerome K.

On the staircase: Swinnerton, Frank

On the stairs: Carman, Bliss

On the stairs: Fuller, H.B.

On the stream of travel: Hall, J.N.

On the study of Celtic literature: Arnold, Matthew

On the study of literature: Morley, John

On the subjection of women: Mill, John Stuart

On the threshold: Gibson, Wilfred

On the track: Lawson, Henry

On the trail: my reminiscences as a cowboy: Harris, J.T.

On the Trapanese origin of the Odyssey: Butler, Samuel

On the use of metaphor and "pathetic fallacy" in poetry: Noel, R.B.W.

On the various contrivances by which British and foreign orchids are fertilized by insects: Darwin, Charles

On the Veda: Ghose, Sri Aurobindo

On the vegetarian system of diet: Shelley, P.B.

On the wallaby: (†Donald Barr), Barrett, C.L.

On the war in North America: Young, Arthur

On the wing of occasions: Harris, J.C.

On the wisdom of America: Lin Yu-T'ang

On the wool track: Bean, C.E.

On the world's roof: Oxley, J.M.

On their Majesties Coronation: Lee, Nathaniel

On these I stand: Cullen, Countée

On tiptoe: White, S.E.

On to the bay: Kingston, G.A.

On toast: Ridge, W.Pett

On trail and rapid by dogsled and canoe: Cody, H.A.

On translating Homer: Arnold, Matthew

On translating Homer: last words: Arnold, Matthew

On translation: Belloc, Hilaire

On trial: Rice, Elmer

On two strings: Gale, Norman

On understanding women: Beard, Mary

On viol and flute: Gosse, Sir Edmund

On visiting bookshops: Morley, C.D.

On William Faulkner's The sound and the fury: Scott, Evelyn

On writing and writers: Raleigh, Sir Walter

On Yoga, II: Ghose, Sri Aurobindo

Once a hero: Brighouse, Harold

Once a week: Milne, A.A.

Once aboard the lugger: Hutchinson, Arthur

Once and future king, The: White, T.H.

Once around the block: Saroyan, William

Once in a lifetime: Kaufman, G.S.

Once in England: Raymond, Ernest

Once in the saddle: Rhodes, E.M.

Once is enough: †Lonsdale, Frederick

Once on a time: Milne, A.A.

Once there was a war: Steinbeck, John

Once there was music: Hodge, H.E.

Once upon a time: Crothers, Rachel

Once upon a time: Davis, R.H.

Once upon a time: Freeman, M.W.

Once upon a time: Knight, Charles

Once upon a time: Phillpotts, Eden

Once upon a time: (Stephen Southwold), †Bell, Neil

Once upon a time stories: (Stephen Southwold), †Bell, Neil

Ia, (†Q), Quiller-Couch, *Sir* Arthur

One and one and one: Untermeyer, Louis

One and the many, The: Gore-Booth, E.S.

One basket: Ferber, Edna

One before, The: Pain, B.E.O.

One billion wild horses: Chase, Stuart

One boy's Boston, 1887–1901: Morison, S.E.

One bright day: Buck, Pearl

One bull against the enemy of the Anglican race: (†Baron Corvo), Rolfe, Frederick

One came back: †Bell, Neil

One clear call: Sinclair, Upton

One day: Douglas, Norman

One day: Hubbard, Elbert

One day and another: Cawein, Madison

One day and another: Lucas, E.V.

One day awake: Monro, H.E.

One day in the history of the world: Saroyan, William

One fair woman, The: †Miller, Joaquin

One fault: Trollope, Frances

One foot in Eden: Muir, Edwin

One foot in fairyland: Farjeon, Eleanor

One fur coat: Macdonell, A.G.

One girl in the poster: Carman, Bliss

One good turn: De Selincourt, Aubrey

One good turn: Hale, E.E.

One hour: Courage, J.F.

One hundred and fifty (really 142) original letters between Dr. Edward Young and Mr. Samuel Richardson: Young, Edward

One hundred and five sonnets: Ascher, I.G.

One hundred and one ballads: Baring, Maurice

$106,000 blood money: Hammett, S.D.

One hundred and twenty-eight witnesses: Mottram, R.H.

One hundred and twenty-four sonnets from Dante, Petrarch and Camoens: Garnett, Richard

One hundred best books: Powys, John Cowper

One hundred days in Europe: Holmes, Oliver Wendell

100%, the story of a patriot: Sinclair, Upton

One hundred poems of Kabir: Underhill, Evelyn

One hundred representative New Zealand books: Anderson, J.C.

One hundred years ago: Hale, E.E.

One I knew the best of all, The: Burnett, Frances Hodgson

One increasing purpose: Hutchinson, Arthur

One kind and another: Pain, B.E.O.

One life: Rukeyser, Muriel

One life, one love: Braddon, M.E.

One little boy: De Selincourt, Hugh

One man in his time: Glasgow, Ellen

One man show: (†Michael Innes), Stewart, J.I.M.

One man's initiation: Dos Passos, John

One man's meat: White, E.B.

One man's view: Merrick, Leonard

£1,000,000 bank note, The: (†Mark Twain), Clemens, S.L.

One minute please: Benchley, Robert

One more flame: Mitchell, Mary

One more peep at the Royal Academy: †Pindar, Peter

One more river: Dukes, Ashley

One more river: Galsworthy, John

One more summer: De Selincourt, Aubrey

One o'clock: Lewis, M.G.

One of our brethren: Raymond, Ernest

One of our conquerors: Meredith, George

One of our girls: Howard, B.C.

One of ours: Cather, Willa

One of the best: †Bell, Neil

One of the crowd: Gibbs, *Sir* Philip

One of the six hundred: Grant, James

One of the Spicers: Baker, Elizabeth

One of the ten thousand: Graham, Stephen

One of the 28th: Henty, G.E.

One of the two: Sheldon, C.M.

One of them: Frankau, Gilbert

One of them: Lever, C.J.

One of those things: †Cheyney, Peter

One of those ways: Lowndes, M.A.

One of us: Frankau, Gilbert

One of us: Hicks, Granville

One of us: Poole, Ernest

One pair of feet: Dickens, Monica

One pair of hands: Dickens, Monica

One part love: Deutsch, Babette

One pound note, The: Lathom, Francis

One red rose for Christmas: Horgan, Paul

One score and ten: McCutcheon, G.B.

One small candle: Roberts, C.E.M.

One smoke: Austin, Mary

One thing and another: Phillpotts, Eden

One thing needful: Braddon, M.E.

1001 nights of Jean Macaque: Cloete, E.F.S.G.

One thousand beautiful things: Mee, Arthur

$1,000 a week: Farrell, James

One thousand famous things: Mee, Arthur

One thousand nights on a bed of stone: Abbas, K.A.

One thousand seven hundred and ninety-six: †Pindar, Peter

1 × 1: Cummings, E.E.

One too many, The: Linton, Eliza

One touch of Venus: Nash, Ogden

One touch of Venus: Perelman, S.J.

One tract more: Milnes, R.M.

One trip more: Manning, Anne

1/20 poems: Cummings, E.E.

One, two, buckle my shoe: Christie, Agatha

One way of living: †Bridie, James

One way ticket: Hughes, J.L.

One way to heaven: Cullen, Countée

One wild oat: Kantor, Mackinlay

One woman, The: Dixon, Thomas

One woman's life: Herrick, Robert

One year of grace: Gielgud, Val

One year of life: Roberts, C.E.M.

One year's reading for fun, 1942: Berenson, Bernhard

One-eyed moon, The: Steen, Marguerite

One-footed fairy, The: Brown, Alice

One-house farm: Coffin, Robert

O'Neill: Lytton, E.G.E.B. *1st Baron*

One's company: Fleming, Peter

One-upmanship: Potter, Stephen

One-way song: Lewis, P. Wyndham

Only a clod: Braddon, M.E.

Only a woman: Braddon, M.E.

Only an ensign: Grant, James

Only an inch from glory: Halper, Albert

Only child, An: †O'Connor, Frank

Only fade away: Marshall, Bruce

Only legend, The: Drinkwater, John

Only mugs work: Greenwood, Walter

Only natural: Trease, Geoffrey

Only one storm: Hicks, Granville

Only penitent, The: Powys, T.F.

Only the morning: Dalley, J.B.

Only the other day: Lucas, E.V.

Only toys: †Anstey, F.

Only yesterday: Bryant, *Sir* Arthur

Onslow family, The: Vulliamy, C.E.

Onward age, The: Read, T.B.

Onwards to victory: Churchill, *Sir* Winston

Op.1: Sayers, Dorothy

Opal fire: Praed, *Mrs.* C.

Opalescent parrot, The: Noyes, Alfred

Open air: Bell, Adrian

Open air, The: Jefferies, Richard

Open air drama, The: †Bridie, James

Open air plays: Brighouse, Harold

Open air pulpit, An: Knox, R.A.

Open boat, The: Crane, Stephen

Open boats: Noyes, Alfred

Open confession to a man from a woman: †Corelli, Marie

Open conspiracy, The: Wells, H.G.

Open country: Hewlett, Maurice

Open door, The: Housman, Laurence

Open door, The: Keller, Helen

Open door, The: Sutro, Alfred

Open door at home, The: Beard, C.A.

Open house: Deacon, W.A.

Open house: Priestley, J.B.

Open letter, An: Carman, Bliss

Open letters of an optimist: Walpole, *Sir* Hugh

Open letters to Jews and Christians: Cournos, John

Open letters to Lord Curzon: Dutt, R.C.

Open night, The: Lehmann, John

Open question, An: De Mille, James

Open road, The: Lucas, E.V.

Open sea, The: Masters, E.L.

Open secret, The: †Onions, Oliver

Open sky, The: Strong, L.A.G.

Open the door!: Sitwell, *Sir* Osbert

Open verdict, An: Braddon, M.E.

Open warfare: Gibbs, *Sir* Philip

Open water: Stringer, A.J.A.

Open windows: Mason, A.E.W.

Open Winkin: Farjeon, Eleanor

Openers of the gate, The: Beck, *Mrs.* Lily

Open-eyed conspiracy, An: Howells, W.D.

Opening a chestnut burr: Roe, E.P.

Opening night: Marsh, Ngaio Edith

Opening of the Crystal Palace considered in some of its relations to the prospects of art, The: Ruskin, John

Openings in the old trail: Harte, Bret

Opera, The: Brooks, C.W.S.

Opera, The: Gore, Catherine

Oper agoer, The: Mitchell, D.G.

Opera in Italy: Jacob, Naomi

Opera nights: Newman, Ernest

Opera of operas, The: Haywood, *Mrs.* Eliza

Opera Omnia: Selden, John

Operas and plays: Stein, Gertrude

"Operation Bootstrap" in Puerto Rico: Chase, Stuart

Operation heartbreak: Cooper, Duff

Operation M.O.: †Taffrail

Operation pax: (†Michael Innes), Stewart, J.I.M.

Operation thunderbolt: (†Michael Innes), Stewart, J.I.M.

Operation wild goose: Pertwee, Roland

Operette: Coward, Noel

Ophelia: Meynell, Viola

Opie Read in the Ozarts: Read, O.P.

Opie Read on golf: Read, O.P.

Opinion defied: Rich, Barnabe

Opinion of a cheerful Yankee: Bacheller, Irving

Opinions: †Henry, O.

Opinions and argument: Balfour, A.J.

Opinions of a philosopher, The: Grant, Robert

Opinions of Oliver Allston: Brooks, Van Wyck

Opinions of William Cobbett, The: Cole, G.D.H. and M.I. Cole

Opinions on the alarm of an invasion: Ralegh, *Sir* Walter

Opium question, The: Warren, Samuel

Opium War through Chinese eyes, The: Waley, Arthur

Opobalsamum Anglicanum: Wither, George

Oppidan, The: Leslie, *Sir* J.R. Shane

Opportunitie, The: Shirley, James

Opportunities: Warner, S.B.

Opposing self, The: Trilling, Lionel

Opposite neighbours: Molesworth, *Mrs.*

Opposition, The: Fielding, Henry

Opticks: Newton, *Sir* Isaac

Optimism: Keller, Helen

Optimist, The: †Delafield, E.M.

Optimist: Stephens, James

Optimist, The: Tuckerman, H.T.

Options: †Henry, O.

Opus posthumous: Stevens, Wallace

Opus 7: Warner, Sylvia Townsend

Oracles, The: Kennedy, Margaret

Oralloossa: Bird, R.M.

Orange blossoms: (†Joseph Shearing), †Bowen, Marjorie

Orange fairy book, The: Lang, Andrew

Orange girl, The: Besant, *Sir* Walter

Orange street: Mais, S.P.B.

Orange tree, The: Lynd, Robert

Orangeman, The: Ervine, St. John

Orara: Kendall, Henry

Oration at Lexington: Dana, R.H. *junior*

Oration, delivered at Leominster, An: Flint, Timothy

Oration delivered before the city government: Clarke, J.F.

Oration, delivered before the literary Societies of Dartmouth College, An: Emerson, Robert

Oration delivered before the Phi Beta Kappa Society at Cambridge, An: Emerson, Robert

Oration delivered before the Washington Benevolent Society, An: Dana, R.H. *senior*

Oration on the life and character of Gilbert Motier de Lafayette: Adams, J.Q.

Oration, on the occasion of celebrating the fortieth anniversary of the battle of Lake Erie: Calvert, G.H.

Orations and addresses: Bryant, W.C.

Orator, The: Wallace, Edgar

Orators, The: Auden, W.H.

Orchard, An: †Ouida

Orchard and vineyard: Sackville-West, Victoria

Orchard pavilion, The: Benson, A.C.

Orchard songs: Gale, Norman

Orchard walls, The: Hodge, H.E.

Orchard-land: Chambers, R.W.

Orchards: Deeping, Warwick

Orchard's Bay: Noyes, Alfred

Orchards of Ultima, Thule, The: MacMechan, A.M.

Orchestra: Davies, *Sir* John

Orchid, The: Grant, Robert

Ordeal: Collins, Dale

Ordeal: †Shute, Nevil

Ordeal, The: † Craddock, C.E.

Ordeal by innocence: Christie, Agatha

Ordeal in England: Gibbs, *Sir* Philip

Ordeal of Gilbert Pinfold, The: Waugh, Evelyn

Ordeal of Mansart: Dubois, William

Ordeal of Mark Twain, The: Brooks, Van Wyck

Ordeal of Richard Feverel, The: Meredith, George

Ordeal of this generation, the war, the League and the future, The: Murray, Gilbert

Order and progress: Harrison, Frederic

Order and solemnitie of the creation of Prince Henrie, Prince of Wales: Daniel, Samuel

Order of Chivalry, The: Morris, William

Order of chivalry or knighthood (trn.): Caxton, William

Order of good cheer, The: Gibbon, J.M.

Order of the Gospel, The: Mather, Increase

Order that the Churche in Denmarke doth use, The: Coverdale, Miles

Orders are orders: (†Ian Hay). Beith, *Sir* John Hay

Ordination addresses: Stubbs, William

Oregon idyll, An: †Miller, Joaquin

Oregon question, The: Gallatin, Albert

Orestes: La Gallienne, Richard

Orestes: Phillips, Stephen

Orestes: Theobald, Lewis

Orestes: Warren, J.B.L.

Orestes. A. Brownson: Schlesinger, Arthur

Organic architecture: Wright, Frank Lloyd

Organisation of thought, The: Whitehead, A.N.

Organised theatre, The: Ervine, St. John

Organization in daily life: Helps, *Sir* Arthur

Organized labour: Cole, G.D.H.

Oriel window, The: Molesworth, *Mrs.*

Orient express: Dos Passos, John

Orient express: Greene, Graham

Oriental acquaintance: De Forest, J.W.

Oriental Cairo: Sladen, D.B.W.

Oriental encounters: Starrett, Vincent

Oriental encounters, Palestine and Syria (1894–96): Pickthall, M.W.

Oriental forerunners of Byzantine painting: Breasted, J.H.

Oriental Institute of the University of Chicago, a beginning and a program, The: Breasted, J.H.

Oriental occupation of British Columbia: MacInnes, T.R.E.

Oriental tale, An: Morier, J.J.

Orientations: Maugham, Somerset

Origin and development of Religious belief: Baring-Gould, Sabine

Origin, causes and the object of the War, The: Fitzpatrick, *Sir* J.P.

Origin of evil: †Queen, Ellery

Origin of terms of human relationship, The: Lang, Andrew

Origin of the Festival of Saint-Jean-Baptiste: LeMoine, *Sir* J.M.

Origin of the West-Saxon kingdom: Young, G.M.

Origin of the world, The: Dawson, *Sir* J.W.

Origin, purpose and result of the Harrisburg convention, The: Ford, P.L.

Original belle, An: Roe, E.P.

Original letters, &c.: Lamb, Charles

Original letters and papers of state addressed to Oliver Cromwell: Milton, John

Original or Birth sin and the necessity of new birth unto life: Pattison, Mark

Original papers, containing the secret history of Great Britain from the Restoration to the accession of the House of Hanover: Macpherson, James

Original poems and other verse set to music: Howe, Julia

Original poetry: (†Victor and Cazire), Shelley, P.B.

Original, serious and religious poetry: Cobbold, Richard

Original songs for the rifle volunteers: Lover, Samuel

Original sonnets on various subjects: Seward, Anna

Original stories from real life: Wollstonecraft, Mary

Originales juridicales, or Historical memorials of the English laws, The: Dugdale, *Sir* William

Origins: Partridge, Eric

Origins of modern science, The: Butterfield, Herbert

Origins of religion, The: Lang, Andrew

Origins of the general theory of relativity, The: Einstein, Albert

Orion: Horne, R.H.

Orion and Sirius: Bonwick, James

Orissers, The: Myers, L.H.

Orkney and Shetland: Linklater, Eric

Orlandino: Edgeworth, Maria

Orlando: Woolf, Virginia

Orlando and Seraphina: Lathom, Francis

Orlando furioso in English heroical verse: Harington, *Sir* John

Orley Farm: Trollope, Anthony

Ormond: Brown, C.B.

Ormond: Flatman, Thomas

Ormond, or the debauchee: Lee, Sophia

Ornaments for the daughters of Zion: Mather, Cotton

Ornaments in jade: †Machen, Arthur

Ornithological biography: Audubon, J.J.

Oroonoko: Southern, Thomas

Orphan, The: Otway, Thomas

Orphan Aggie: O'Higgins, H.J.

Orphan angel, The: Wylie, Elinor

Orphan Dinah: Phillpotts, Eden

Orphan Island: Macaulay, *Dame* Rose

Orphan of China, The: Murphy, Arthur

Orphan of Pimlico, The: Thackeray, W.M.

Orphans: Oliphant, Margaret

Orphans in Gethsemane: Fisher, V.A.

Orphans of Elfholm, The: Browne, Frances

Orpheus: Rukeyser, Muriel

Orpheus: Turner, W.J.R.

Orpheus and Eurydice: Dennis, John

Orpheus and Eurydice: Henryson, Robert

Orpheus and Eurydice: King, William

Orpheus and Eurydice: Theobald, Lewis

Orpheus in Diloeryum: Sassoon, S.

Orpheus in Mayfair: Baring, Maurice

Orpheus in Thrace: Warren, J.B.L.

Orpheus, myths of the world: Colum, Padraic

Orthodoxy: Chesterton, G.K.

Orthodoxy: its truths and errors: Clarke, J.F.

Orts: Macdonald, George

O'Ruddy, The: Crane, Stephen

Orval: (†Owen Meredith), Lytton, E.R.B. *Earl*

Orville College: Wood, Ellen

Osbern and Ursyne: †Hobbes, John Oliver

Osbornes, The: Benson, E.F.

Oscar Wilde: Ransome, A.M.

Oscar Wilde: a present-time appraisal: Ervine, St.John

Oscar Wilde, a summing up: Douglas, *Lord* Alfred

Oscar Wilde and myself: Douglas, *Lord* Alfred

Oscar Wilde, his life and confessions: Harris, J.T.

Osireion at Abydos: Murray, Margaret

Ostrakoff jewels, The: Oppenheim, E. Phillips

Oswald Bastable: Nesbit, E.

Oswald Cray: Wood, Ellen

Othello: Shakespeare, William

Othello's occupation: Strong, L.A.G.

Other Americas, The: Guedalla, Philip

Other days: Winter, William

Other eyes than ours: Knox, R.A.

Other fellow, The: Smith, F.H.

Other girl, The: Thomas, Augustus

Other gods: Buck, Pearl

Other harmony, The: Sastri, Srinivasa

Other house, The: James, Henry

Other landscape, The: Gunn, Neil

Other lovers, The: Widdemer, Margaret

Other main-travelled roads: Garland, Hamlin

Other Mary, The: Marshall, Bruce

Other men's flowers: Wavell, A.P. *1st Earl*

Other Mrs. Jacobs, The: Praed, *Mrs.* C.

Other people's worlds: Mitchison, Naomi

Other person, The: Hume, F.W.

Other place, The: Priestley, J.B.

Other point of view, The: Drinkwater, John

Other provinces: Van Doren, Carl

Other Romilly, The: Oppenheim, E.Phillips

Other side, The: †Hudson, Stephen

Other side, The: Jameson, Storm

Other side, The: Vachell, H.A.

Other side of the hill, The: Liddell Hart, B.

Other times: Brighouse, Harold

Other times: Jerrold, Douglas

Other writings of Richard Henry Dana, Jr., The: Hart, James D.

Others to adorn: Gogarty, O. St.John

Otherwise Phyllis: Nicholson, Meredith

Otherworld, cadences: Flint, F.S.

Othmar: †Ouida

Otho: Neal, John

Ottawa lyrics: Bourinot, A.S.

Otterbury incident, The: Day-Lewis, C.

Ottilie: Lee, Vernon

Otto of the silver hand: Pyle, Howard

Ought women to learn the alphabet?: Higginson, T.W.

Oulita the serf: Helps, *Sir* Arthur

Our admirable Betty: Farnol, J.J.

Our adversary: Braddon, M.E.

Our African winter: Doyle, *Sir* Arthur Conan

Our America: Frank, Waldo

Our American adventure: Doyle, *Sir* Arthur Conan

Our arms in Zululand: Mitford, Bertram

Our army at Monterey: Thorpe, T.B.

Our army at the Front: Broun, Heywood

Our army on the Rio Grande: Thorpe, T.B.

Our battle ... being one man's answer to My Battle by Adolf Hitler: Van Loon, Hendrik

Our betters: Maugham, Somerset

Our bourgeois literature: Sinclair, Upton

Our business civilization: Adams, J.T.

Our case: Hollis, Christopher

Our casualty: Hannay, J.O.

Our Celtic heritage: Lindsay, Jack

Our century: Wilder, Thornton

Our Charley and what to do with him: Stowe, Harriet Beecher

Our children: Wood, Ellen

Our Christmas in a palace: Hale, E.E.

Our colonial story: Eggleston, G.C.

Our common birds: Grey of Fallodon, Edward *Lord*

Our common school system: Dodge, May Abigail

Our Countess: Maltby, H.F.

Our daily bread: Grove, F.P.

Our earth: Mackenzie, Kenneth

Our English cousins: Davis, R.H.

Our family affairs: Benson, E.F.

Our famous women: Stowe, Harriet Beecher

Our Fathers have told us: Ruskin, John

Our fellow men: Morton, H.V.

Our first century: Eggleston, G.C.

Our friend James Joyce: Colum, Padraic

Our friend the charlatan: Gissing, George

Our friends and all about them: Nesbit, Edith

Our gifted son: Baker, Dorothy

Our girls: Caine, *Sir* T.H. Hall

Our government: Cain, J.M.

Our great experiment in democracy: Becker, C.L.

Our hearts were young and gay: Skinner, C.O.

Our heritage of liberty: Leacock, Stephen

Our hero we're here!: Mackail, Denis

Our heroic themes: Boker, G.H.

Our house: Canby, H.S.

Our Irish theatre: Gregory, *Lady* Augusta

Our Italy: Warner, C.D.

Our Josephine: Read, O.P.

Our knowledge of the external world: Russell, Bertrand

Our lady: Sinclair, Upton

Our lady peace: Van Doren, Mark

Our land and land policy: George, Henry

Our life in the Swiss Highlands: Symonds, J.A.

Our little cave-man: Lindsay, Norman

Our Lord's coming and childhood: Tynan, Katherine

Our man in Havana: Greene, Graham

Our manifold nature: †Grand, Sarah

Our Marie: Jacob, Naomi

Our mess: Lever, C.J.

Our Mr. Dormer: Mottram, R.H.

Our Mr. Willis: Ridge, W.Pett

Our Mr. Wrenn: Lewis, H.S.

Our mutual friend: Dickens, Charles

Our nation: Commager, H.S.

Our national parks: Muir, John

Our nationalities: Bonwick, James

Our neighbour opposite: Burnett, Frances Hodgson

Our nervous system: Jennings, Gertrude

Our new crusade: Hale, E.E.

Our new prosperity: Baker, R.S.

Our new rector: †Bede, Cuthbert

Our new religion: Fisher, H.A.L.

Our new selection: †Rudd, Steele

Our Norland: Sangster, Charles

Our northern domain: Alaska, picturesque, historic and commercial: Dole, N.H.

Our old home: Hawthorne, Nathaniel

Our old Montreal: Gibbon, J.M.

Our old town: Miller, Thomas

Our old world background: Beard, C.A.

Our own little rebellion: Turner, H.G.

Our own lives: Jennings, Gertrude

Our partnership: Webb, Beatrice

Our present discontents: Inge, W.R.

Our recent actors: Marston, J.W.

Our salvation: Raven, C.E.

Our schools have kept us free: Commager, H.S.

Our search for a wilderness: Beebe, William

Our second American adventure: Doyle, *Sir* Arthur Conan

Our silver: Crawford, Francis Manon

Our street: Mackenzie, *Sir* Compton

Our street: Thackeray, W.M.

Our theatres in the nineties: Shaw, G.B.

Our time is gone: Hanley, James

Our town: Wilder, Thornton

Our uncle the traveller: Browne, Frances

Our Universe: Tagore, *Sir* Rabindranath

Our village: Mitford, Mary Russell

Our village today: Mais, S.P.B.

Our war aims: Steed, H.W.

Our wild flowers familiarly described and illustrated: Meredith, L.A.

Our women: Bennett, Arnold

Our wonderful selves: Pertwee, Roland

Our Yankee heritage: Beals, Carleton

Our year: Craik, *Mrs.* Dinah

Ours: Robertson, T.W.

Ourselves: Linton, Eliza

Ourselves and our neighbors: Moulton, E.L.

Ourselves to know: O'Hara, J.H.

Out at last: †Pindar, Peter

Out back: Lawson, Henry

Out of bondage: Robinson, R.E.

Out of doors: Hough, Emerson

Out of dust: Karaka, D.F.

Out of Erin: Stringer, A.J.A.

Out of great tribulation: Vachell, H.A.

Out of great tribulation: Wolfe, Humbert

Out of his head: Aldrich, T.B.

Out of India: Kipling, Rudyard

Out of my later years: Einstein, Albert

Out of silence: Ficke, A.D.

Out of soundings: Tomlinson, H.M.

Out of the blue: †Sapper

Out of the dark: Hesketh, Phoebe

Out of the dark: Keller, Helen

Out of the deep dark mould: Chattopadhyaya, Harindranath

Out of the depression—and after: Chase, Stuart

Out of the earth: Bromfield, Louis

Out of the East: Hearn, Lafcadio

Out of the flame: Sitwell, *Sir* Osbert

Out of the foam: Cooke, John

Out of the past: Postgate, Raymond

Out of the people: Priestley, J.B.

Out of the picture: Macneice, Louis

Out of the question: Howells, W.D.

Out of the ruins: Gibbs, *Sir* Philip

Out of the sea: Marquis, Don

Out of the silence: (†The Chiel), Cox, Erle

Out of the silent planet: Lewis, C.S.

Out of the South: Green, Paul

Out of the sunset sea: Tourgée, A.W.

Out of the whirlwind: Hassall, Christopher

Out of the whirlwind: Moffat, James

Out of the wilderness: MacDonald, W.P.

Out of the world and back: Young, A.J.

Out of work: Cole, G.D.H.

Out on the Pampas: Henty, G.E.

Out to win: Pertwee, Roland

Out trail, The: Rinehart, Mary Roberts

Outback marriage, An: (†The Banjo), Paterson, A.B.

Outbreak of war, The: Benson, E.F.

Outcast, The: Buchanan, R.W.

Outcast: Davies, H.H.

Outcast, The: Stephens, James

Outcast of the islands, An: Conrad, Joseph

Outcasts, The: Sitwell, Edith

Outcry, The: James, Henry

Outdoor omnibus, The: White, S.E.

Out-door papers: Higginson, T.W.

Outdoorland: Chambers, R.W.

Outdoors at Idlewood: Willis, N.P.

Outing with the Queen of Hearts, An: Tourgée, A.W.

Outland by Gordon Stairs: Austin, Mary

Outland piper, An: Davidson, D.G.

Outlanders: Imperial expansion in South Africa: Vulliamy, C.E.

Outlaw, The: †Brand, Max

Outlaw, The: Hall, A.M.

Outlaw, The: Hewlett, Maurice

Outlaw and lawmaker: Praed, *Mrs.* C.

Outlaw of the lowest planet: Patchen, Kenneth

Outlaw years, The: Coates, R.M.

Outlaws on Parnassus, The: Kennedy, Margaret

Outlaw's progress: Burdon, R.M.

Outlet, The: Adams, Andy

Outline of Australian literature, An: Green, H.M.

Outline of biography, An: Cross, W.L.

Outline of Canadian literature, An: Pierce, Lorne

Outline of European architecture, An: Pevsner, Nikolaus

Outline of marriage, The: Dell, Floyd

Outline of Mexican popular arts and crafts: Porter, K.A.

Outline of philosophy, An: Russell, Bertrand

Outline of philosophy, An: Watson, John

Outline of sanity, The: Chesterton, G.K.

Outline of the history of Ukiyo-ye, An: Fenollosa, E.F.

Outline of the rational system of society: Owen, Robert

Outline of the science of political economy, An: Senior, Nassau

Outlines and summaries: Foerster, Norman

Outlines in local colour: Matthews, J.B.

Outlines of a critical theory of ethics: Dewey, John

Outlines of a philosophy of art: Collingwood, R.G.

Outlines of comparative physiology: Agassis, Jean

Outlines of cosmic philosophy: Fiske, John

Outlines of European history: Breasted, J.H.

Outlines of general history: Colby, F.M.

Outlines of psychology: Royce, Josiah

Outlines of the early history of the East: Lytton, E.G.E.B. *1st Baron*

Outlines of the history of ethics: Sidgwick, Henry

Outlines of the history of religion: Ingram, J.K.

Outlines of the life of Shakespeare: Halliwell, J.O.

Outlook for Homo Sapiens, The: Wells, H.G.

Out-of-door Americans: Garland, Hamlin

Out-of-town places: Mitchell, D.G.

Outpost, The: Gibson, Wilfred

Outpost, The: (†Rann Daly), Palmer, E.V.

Outposts of mercy: Lucas, E.V.

Outrage in Manchukuo: Gielgud, Val

Outside, The: Glaspell, Susan

Outside Eden: Squire, *Sir* J.C.

Outside India: Abbas, K.A.

Outside information: Royde-Smith, Naomi

Outside looking in: Turnbull, S.C.P.

Outside the radius: Ridge, W. Pett

Outsider, The: Wright, Richard

Outsiders: an outline: Chambers, R.W.

Outspan, The: Fitzpatrick, *Sir* J.P.

Outspoken essays: Inge, W.R.

Outward bound: Morley, C.D.

Outward bound (novel and play): Vane, S.V.H.

Oveen's museum, The: Stockton, F.R.

Over!: De Selincourt, Hugh

Over a garden wall: Baker, Elizabeth

Over Bemerton's: Lucas, E.V.

Over prairie trails: Grove, F.P.

Over seventy: Wodehouse, P.G.

Over the Border: Hannay, J.O.

Over the border: Winter, William

Over the brazier: Graves, Robert

Over the bridge: Church, Richard

Over the footlights: Leacock, Stephen

Over the frontier: Smith, Stevie

Over the garden walls: Farjeon, Eleanor

Over the grass: Ogilvie, W.H.

Over the hills: Farnol, J.J.

Over the hills: Palmer, J.L.

Over the plum-pudding: Bangs, J.K.

Over the reefs: Gibbings, Robert

Over the river: Galsworthy, John

Over the Rocky mountains to Alaska: Stoddard, C.W.

Over the sliprails: Lawson, Henry

Over the straits: Meredith, L.A.

Over the teacups: Holmes, Oliver Wendell

Over the wall: Mottram, R.H.

Over the wall: Rubenstein, Harold F.

Over there: Bennett, Arnold

Over to Candleford: Thompson, Flora

Overdue: Russell, W.C.

Overlaid: Davies, Robertson

Overlander, The: Ogilvie, W.H.

Overlooked: Baring, Maurice

Overlooked: †Bartimeus

Overman, The: Sinclair, Upton

Overreacher, a study of Christopher Marlowe, The: Levin, Harry

Overruled: Shaw, G.B.

Overtones: Huneker, J.G.

Overture: Scott, F.R.

Overture, The: Sheridan, R.B.

Overture: Vane, S.V.H.

Overture: 1920: Bolitho, William

Overture to death: Marsh, Ngaio Edith

Overtures to death: Day-Lewis, C.

Overwhelming Saturday, An: Tarkington, Booth

Overworlds and Tura, The: Anderson, J.C.

Ovid's banquet of sence: Chapman, George

Ovid's Metamorphoses Englished: Sandys, George

Ovingdean Grange: Ainsworth, Harrison

Ovington's Bank: Weyman, Stanley

Owen D. Young: Tarbell, Ida

Owen Glendower: Powys, John Cowper

Owl, The: Heavysege, Charles

Owl in the attic, The: Thurber, James

Owl is abroad, The: Bridges, Roy

Owl of Athene, The: Phillpotts, Eden

Owl, the duck, and—Miss Rowe! Miss Rowe!, The: Powys, John Cowper

Owle, The: Drayton, Michael

Owl's clover: Stevens, Wallace

Own your own home: Lardner, Ring

Oxbow Wizard, The: Roberts, T.G.

Oxen, The: Hardy, Thomas

Oxen of the sun: Bacheller, Irving

Oxford: Lang, Andrew

Oxford: Montgomery, Robert

Oxford: Thomas, E.E.P.

Oxford: Tickell, Thomas

Oxford and her colleges: Smith, Goldwin

Oxford Blazers, The: Hassall, Christopher

Oxford book of nineteenth century verse (anth.): Hayward, J.D.

Oxford characters: Rothenstein, *Sir* William

Oxford companion to American literature, The: Hart, James D.

Oxford dictionary of English etymology, The: Onions, C.T.

Oxford drollery: Hicks, William "Captain"

Oxford from within: De Selincourt, Hugh

Oxford history of the American people, The: Morison, S.E.

Oxford history of the United States: Morison, S.E.

Oxford in the eighteenth century: Godley, A.D.

Oxford lectures on poetry: Bradley, A.C.

Oxford lectures on poetry: De Selincourt, Ernest

Oxford Movement, The: Church, Richard

Oxford Movement, The: Leslie, *Sir* J.R. Shane

Oxford Museum, The: Ruskin, John

Oxford studies: Pattison, Mark

Oxford tragedy, An: Masterman, *Sir* J.C.

Oxford Union, The: Hollis, Christopher

Oxford University chest, An: Betjeman, John

Oxonian in town, The: Colman, George, *the elder*

P

P.L.; or 30 Strand: Lemon, Mark

P.L.M. peoples, land falls, mountains: Wolfe, Humbert

P.R. Parliament, The: Wells, H.G.

Pa Maoris, The: Best, Elsdon

Pabo the priest: Baring-Gould, Sabine

Pacchiarotto: Browning, Robert

Pace that kills, The: Gould, Nathaniel

Pace that kills, The: Saltus, E.E.

Pacha of Many tales, The: Marryatt, Frederick

Pacific, The: (†Donald Barr), Barrett, C.L.

Pacific 1860: Coward, Noel

Pacific Parade: Clune, Frank

Pacific poems: †Miller, Joaquin

Pacific tales: †Becke, Louis

Pacific wonderland: (†Donald Barr), Barrett, C.L.

Pacificator, The: Defoe, Daniel

"Pacificus" letters: Hamilton, Alexander

Pacifist in trouble, A: Inge, W.R.

Pacifists, The: Jones, H.A.

Pack my bag: Green, Henry

Packet for Ezra Pound, A: Yeats, W.B.

Pactolus Prime: Tourgée, A.W.

Paddle-wheels away: Lawson, Will

Paddly pools: Malleson, Miles

Padlock, The: Bickerstaffe, Isaac

Padlocked: Beach, R.E.

Padre Ignacio: Wister, Owen

Padre in France, A: Hannay, J.O.

Padre of St.Jacobs, The: Graham, Stephen

Paduan pastoral, The: Hewlett, M.H.

Paean triumphall, A: Drayton, Michael

Pagan love: Gibbon, J.M.

Pagan papers: Grahame, Kenneth

Pagan poems: Moore, George

Pagan Review, The: †Macleod, Fiona

Pagan Spain: Wright, Richard

Paganini: Herbert, *Sir* A.P.

Pagan's pilgrimage, A: Powys, L.C.

Pagan's prayer, A: Carman, Bliss

Page, The: Craig, *Sir* Gordon

Pageant: †Lancaster, G.B.

Pageant, A: Rossetti, Christina

Pageant of England's life presented by her poets, A: Drinkwater, John

Pageant of life, A: Bradford, Gamaliel

Pageant of victory, A: Farnol, J.J.

Pages from a journal: †Rutherford, Mark

Pages from an old volume of life: Holmes, Oliver Wendell

Pages from an Oxford diary: More, P.E.

Pages from the past: Fisher, H.A.L.

Pages in waiting: Yates, E.H.

Pages in woman's life: Waugh, Alec

Pagoda, The: †Bowen, Marjorie

Paid, with thanks: (†Ian Hay), Beith, *Sir* John Hay

Paine of pleasure, The: Munday, Anthony

Pains and penalties: Housman, Laurence

Paintbox, The: Armstrong, M.D.

Painted angel: †Preedy, George

Painted caves, The: Grigson, Geoffrey

Painted clay: †Boake, Capel

Painted face, The: †Onions, Oliver

Painted fire: White, E.B.

Painted king, The: Davies, Rhys

Painted lath, The: Seymour, B.K.

Painted minx, The: Chambers, R.W.

Painted princess, The: Boyd, Martin

Painted shadows: Le Gallienne, Richard

Painted tigers: Isvaran, M.S.

Painted veil, The: Maugham, Somerset

Painted veils: Huneker, J.G.

Painters' holiday, A: Carman, Bliss

Painters of Japan, The: Morrison, Arthur

Painters of Quebec: Barbeau, C.M.

Painting and the Fine Arts: Hazlitt, William

Paintings of D.H.Lawrence, The: Lawrence, D.H.

Pair of blue eyes, A: Hardy, Thomas

Pair of knickerbockers, A: Phillpotts, Eden

Pair of lyric epistles to Lord Macartney and his ship, A: †Pindar, Peter

Pair of madcaps, A: Trowbridge, J.T.

Pair of patient lovers, A: Howells, W.D.

Pair of schoolgirls, A: Brazil, Angela

Paire of spy-knaves, A: Rowlands, Samuel

Paisley shawl, The: Niven, F.J.

Pal Joey (novel and play): O'Hara, J.H.

Palace and mosque at Ukhaider: Bell, Gertrude

Palace beautiful, The: (†Orpheus C.Kerr), Newell, R.H.

Palace in the garden, The: Molesworth, *Mrs.*

Palace of Apries, The: Petrie, *Sir* William Flinders

Palace of honour, The: Douglas, Gawin

Palace of Minos: Evans, *Sir* Arthur

Palace of pleasure beautified, The: Painter, William

Palace of truth, The: Gilbert, *Sir* W.S.

Palace plays: Housman, Laurence

Palace scenes: Housman, Laurence

Paladin, The: Vachell, H.A.

Paladins in Spain: Farjeon, Eleanor

Palamon and Arcite: Baring, Maurice

Pale ape, The: Shiel, M.P.

Pale blue nightgown, The: Golding, Louis

Pale fire: Nabokov, Vladimir

Pale horse, The: Christie, Agatha

Pale horse, pale rider: Porter, K.A.

Pale moon: Burnett, W.R.

Pale shade, The: Murray, Gilbert

Paleface: Lewis, P. Wyndham

Paleface and Redskin and other stories for boys and girls: †Anstey, F.

Palestine and Israel: Petrie, *Sir* William Flinders

Palestine campaigns, The: Wavell, A.P. *1st Earl*

Palestine plays: Housman, Laurence

Palette and plough: Robinson, E.S.L.

Palette knife, The: Morley, C.D.

Palfrey, The: Hunt, Leigh

Pali literature of Ceylon, The: Malalasekara, Gunapala

Palicio: Bridges, Robert

Palimpsest: Doolittle, Hilda

Palisades of fear, The: Bottrall, Ronald

Paliser case, The: Saltus, E.E.

Palladis tamia; wits treasury: Meres, Francis

Pallas and Venus: Prior, Matthew

Palm leaves: Milnes, R.M.

Palm Sunday to Easter: Temple, William

Palmerston: Guedalla, Philip

Palmetto-leaves: Stowe, Harriet Beecher

Palmy days: Thomas, Augustus

Palmyra: Peacock, Thomas Love

Palmyra: Ware, William

Palyse of honour, The: Douglas, Gavin

Pamela: Richardson, Samuel

Pamela's prodigy: Fitch, Clyde William

Pamela's spring song: Roberts, C.E.M.

Pamphlet against anthologies, A: Graves, Robert

Pamphlet against anthologies, A: Riding, Laura

Pamphlet poets, The: Millay, E. St.Vincent

Pamphlets and sketches: Lytton, E.G.E.B. *1st Baron*

Pamphlets for the people: Ingraham, J.H.

Pampines: Aldrich, T.B.

Pan America: Beals, Carleton

Pan and peacocks: Roberts, W. Adolphe

Pan and Syrinx: Theobald, Lewis

Pan and the twins: Phillpotts, Eden

Pan and the young shepherd: Hewlett, Maurice

Pan his Syrinx, or Pipe, compact of seven reedes: Warner, William

Pan in the parlour: Lindsay, Norman

Panacea: Tate, Nahum

Panama: Phillips, Stephen

Panama Canal Zone, The: Adams, C.F.

Pandora: Killigrew, *Sir* William

Pandora lifts the lid: Marquis, Don

Pandora lifts the lid: Morley, C.D.

Pandora's box: Mitchell, J.A.

Pandosto: Greene, Robert

Pandurang hari: Hockley, William Browne

Panegyric on the Reverend Dean Swift, A: Swift, Jonathan

Panegyric to Charles the Second, A: Evelyn, John

Panegyrical epistle to Mr. Thomas Snow, A: Gay, John

Panegyrick of King Charles, A: Wotton, *Sir* Henry

Panegyrick on Monck: Denham, *Sir* John

Panegyrick to Charles the Second, A: Flatman, Thomas

Panegyrick to His Majesty on his happy return, A: Fuller, Thomas

Panegyrick to the King's Most Excellent Majesty: Cotton, Charles

Panegyrike congratulatory delivered to the kings most excellent majesty: Daniel, Samuel

Panel, The: Ford, Ford Madox

Panels for the walls of heaven: Patchen, Kenneth

Paneros: Douglas, Norman

Pangolin, The: Moore, M.C.

Panic: MacLeish, Archibald

Panic in Box C: Carr, J.D.

Panic spring: Durrell, Lawrence

Panopticon, The: Bentham, Jeremy

Panopticon versus New South Wales, The: Bentham, Jeremy

Panorama: Bentley, Phyllis

Panorama, The: Whittier, J.G.

Pan's garden: Blackwood, Algernon

Pan's prophecy: Moore, T.S.

Pansie: Hawthorne, Nathaniel

Pansies: Lawrence, D.H.

Pansies for thoughts: MacKay, I.E.

Pansy Billings and Popsy: Jackson, H.H.

Pansy's wish: Aldrich, T.B.

Pantaloon: Toynbee, Philip

Panthea: Hoffe, Monckton

Panther, The: Bullett, Gerald A.

Pantomime: Stern, G.B.

Paolo and Francesca: Phillips, Stephen

Paolo Uccello: Pope-Hennessy, J.W.

Papa: Akins, Zoë

Papa la Fleur: Gale, Zona

Papa, you're crazy: Saroyan, William

Papal infallibility: Coulton, G.G.

Papal tyranny in the reign of King John: Cibber, Colley

Papa's war: Garnett, Edward

Paper cap, The: Barr, A.E.H.

Paper city, A: †Nasby, Petroleum V.

Paper houses: Plomer, W.C.F.

Paper money lyrics: Peacock, Thomas Love

Paper prison: Wren, P.C.

Paper thunderbolt, The: (†Michael Innes), Stewart, J.I.M.

Papers from Lilliput: Priestley, J.B.

Papers humorous and pathetic: Sala, G.A.H.

Papers on literature and art: Fuller, Margaret

Papers on public school education in England: Higgins, M.J.

Papistry stormed: Tennant, William

Pappe with a hatchet: Lyly, John

Para Handy: Munro, Neil

Parable against persecution, A: Franklin, Benjamin

Parable of the ten virgins, The: Shepard, Thomas

Parable of the water tank, The: Sinclair, Upton

Parable of the wicked mammon, The: Tyndale, William

Parables: Fletcher, John Gould

Parables from Nature: Gatty, Margaret

Parables of Our Lord and Saviour Jesus Christ, The: Smart, Christopher

Paracelsus: Browning, Robert

Parade with banners: Peattie, D.C.

Paradine case, The: Hichens, Robert

Paradise: Forbes, Esther

Paradise creek: Walmsley, Leo

Paradise enow: †Bridie, James

Paradise for sale: Gibbs, Sir Philip

Paradise lost: Milton, John

Paradise lost: Odets, Clifford

Paradise lost in our time: Bush, Douglas

Paradise of birds, The: Courthorpe, William John

Paradise place: Deeping, Warwick

Paradise regain'd: Milton, John

Paradisi in sole: Parkinson, John

Paradox of Scottish culture, The: Daiches, David

Paradoxes of legal science, The: Cardozo, B.N.

Paradoxes of Mr. Pond, The: Chesterton, G.K.

Paradoxes, problems: Donne, John

Paraenesis to the Prince, A: Alexander, William

Paragon, The: Pertwee, Roland

Parallel between Robert late Earle of Essex and George late Duke of Buckingham, A: Wotton, Sir Henry

Parallel, in the manner of Plutarch, A: Spence, Joseph

Paraphrase on part of the Book of Job, A: Young, Edward

Paraphrase on the book of Job, A: Blackmore, Sir R.D.

Paraphrase or poetical exposition of the thirteenth chapter of first book of St.Paul's Epistle to the Corinthians, A: Anstey, Christopher

Paraphrase upon the divine poems, A: Sandys, George

Paraphrase upon the psalmes, A: Sandys, George

Parasitaster: Marston, John

Parasite, The: Doyle, Sir Arthur Conan

Parasite, The: Mee, Arthur

Parasites, The: Du Maurier, Daphne

Parched earth: †Armstrong, Anthony

Pardners: Beach, R.E.

Pardoner's tale, The: †Bridie, James

Parent and child: Lodge, Sir Oliver

Parentator: Mather, Cotton

Parents and children: Compton-Burnett, Ivy

Parent's assistant, The: Edgeworth, Maria

Parents keep out: Nash, Ogden

Paris: Belloc, Hilaire

Paris: Green, Anne

Paris: Hare, A.J.C.

Paris: Liddell Hart, B.

Paris and Oenone: Binyon, Laurence

Paris and Helen: Turner, W.J.R.

Paris and the Parisians in 1835: Trollope, Frances

Paris and Vienne (trn.): Caxton, William

Paris bound: Barry, Philip

Paris calling: Golding, Louis

Paris, city of enchantment: Raymond, Ernest

Paris France: Stein, Gertrude

Paris herself again, in 1878–1879: Sala, G.A.H.

Paris in 1815: Croly, George

Paris in 1841: Gore, Catherine

Paris nights: Bennett, Arnold

Paris sketch book, The: Thackeray, W.M.

Parish, The: †Anstey, F.

Parish and the county, The: Webb, Sidney and Beatrice Webb

Parish priest and the life of prayer, The: Underhill, Evelyn

Parisian nights: Symons, Arthur

Parisians, The: Lytton, E.G.E.B. *Ist Baron*

Parisienne: Dukes, Ashley

Park wall, The: †Mordaunt, Elinor

Parker Pyne investigates: Christie, Agatha

Parlement of foules: Chaucer, Geoffrey

Parleyings with certain people of importance in their day: Browning, Robert

Parliament of bees, The: Day, John

Parliament of ladies, The: Nevile, Henry

Parliament of love, The: Massinger, Philip

Parliamentary government and the economic problems: Churchill, *Sir* Winston

Parliamentary government in England: Laski, Harold

Parliamentary letters: Bayly, Thomas Haynes

Parliamentary reform: Bagehot, Walter

Parlor, Bedlam, and Bath: Perelman, S.J.

Parlor car, The: Howells, W.D.

Parlor theatricals: Arnold, George

Parnassians personally encountered: Saltus, E.E.

Parnassus on wheels: Morley, C.D.

Parnell: Ervine, St. John

Parnell and his island: Moore, George

Parochial and Cathedral sermons: Pusey, E.B.

Parochial history of Bremhill: Bowles, W.L.

Parochial Sermons: Newman, J.H.

Parochial sermons: Pusey, E.B.

Parodies and reviews: Brown, Alice

Parodies regained: Knox, E.G.V.

Parody of a celebrated letter: Moore, Thomas

Parody outline of history, A: Stewart, D.O.

Parra Sastha: Carleton, William

Parricide, The: Reynolds, G.

Parrot, The: Haywood, *Mrs.* Eliza

Parrot, The: Sitwell, Sacheverell

Parrot and the—cat, The: Blackwood, Algernon

Parrot pie: Seymour, W.K.

Parrots of Australasia: (†Donald Barr), Barrett, C.L.

Parrot's training: Tagore, *Sir* R.

Parsley: Bemelmans, Ludwig

Parson Austen's daughter: Ashton, Helen

Parson Kelly: Lang, Andrew

Parson Kelly: Mason, A.E.W.

Parson's daughter, The: Hook, T.E.

Parson's horn-book, The: Lover, Samuel

Parson's pleasure: Morley, C.D.

Parson's progress, The: Mackenzie, *Sir* Compton

Part of a man's life: Higginson, T.W.

Part of King James his royall entertainment: Jonson, Ben

Part of the seventh epistle of the first book of Horace imitated: Swift, Jonathan

Part of the truth: Hicks, Granville

Part of the wonderful scene: Graham, Stephen

Part that is missing, The: Mottram, R.H.

Parterre, The: Meredith, L.A.

Parthenissa: Boyle, Roger

Partial portraits: James, Henry

Particular attention to the instruction of the young recommended in a discourse, A: Priestley, Joseph

Particular discourse concerning the great necessitie and manifolde comodyties that are likely to growe to this realme of Englande by the westerne discoveries lately attempted: Hakluyt, Richard

Parties in the United States: Adams, John Quincy

Parties of the play: Brown, Ivor

Parties, scenes from contemporary New York life: Van Vechten, Carl

Parting and a meeting, A: Howells, W.D.

Parting and the return, A: Bottomley, Gordon

Parting friends: Howells, W.D.

Parting of the ways, The: Mallock, W.H.

Partingtonian patchwork: (†*Mrs.* Partington), Shillaber, B.P.

Partisan, The: Simms, W.G.

Partisan leader, The: Tucker, N.B.

Partition of Europe, The: Guedalla, Philip

Partners: Deland, Margaret

Partners in crime: Christie, Agatha

Partnership: Baker, Elizabeth

Partnership, The: Bentley, Phyllis

Parts of a world: Stevens, Wallace

Parts of speech: Matthews, J.B.

Party: †Novello, Ivor

Party and patronage: Curtis, George William

Party dress, The: Hergesheimer, Joseph

Party going: Green, Henry

Party leaders: Baldwin, Joseph Clover

Party manners: Gielgud, Val

Party of Baccarat, A: Byrne, Donn

Party system, The: Belloc, Hilaire

Pasaphaë: Swinburne, A.C.

Pascal and other sermons: Church, Richard

Pascarel: †Ouida

Pasquil the playne: Elyot, *Sir* Thomas

Pasquils mistresse: Breton, Nicholas

Pasquils mad-cap and mad-cappes message: Breton, Nicholas

Pasquils passe and passeth not: Breton, Nicholas

Pasquin: Fielding, Henry

Pasquin: Steele, *Sir* Richard

Pass, The: White, S.E.

Passage, The: Palmer, E.V.

Passage of arms: Ambler, Eric

Passage of the sea, The: Fairfield, S.L.

Passage perilous, A: Jacob, Naomi

Passage to India, A: Forster, E.M.

Passage to India: Whitman, Walt

Passages from the diary of a late physician: Warren, Samuel

Passages from the diary of an early Methodist: Rowe, Richard

Passages in my autobiography: Morgan, *Lady* Sydney

Passages in the life of Mrs. Margaret Maitland: Oliphant, Margaret

Passages of a working life, with a prelude of early reminiscences: Knight, Charles

Passe Rose: Hardy, A.S.

Passenger to Teheran: Sackville-West, Victoria

Passers by: Galsworthy, John

Passers by: Oppenheim, E. Phillips

Passetyme of pleasure, The: Hawes, Stephen

Passing chapter, The: Leslie, *Sir* J.R. Shane

Passing cloud, The: Bernard, W.B.

Passing judgements: Nathan, G.J.

Passing of Chow-Chow, The: Rice, Elmer

Passing of Oul-I-But, The: Sullivan, Alan

Passing of the Essenes, The: Moore, George

Passing of the frontier, The: Hough, Emerson

Passing of the gods, The: Calverton, V.F.

Passing of the third floor back, The: Jerome, Jerome K.

Passing of Thomas, The: Janvier, T.A.

Passing world, A: Lowndes, M.A.

Passing-by: Baring, Maurice

Passion before death, A: Hanley, James

Passion in Rome, A: Callaghan, M.E.

Passion of Dido, The: Waller, Edmund

Passion of labour, The: Lynd, Robert

Passion of Sacco and Vanzetti, The: Fast, Howard M.

Passion, poison and petrifaction: Shaw, G.B.

Passionate centurie of love, The: Watson, Thomas

Passionate elopement, The: Mackenzie, *Sir* Compton

Passionate friends, The: Wells, H.G.

Passionate guest, The: Oppenheim, E. Phillips

Passionate heart, The: Gilmore, Mary

Passionate neatherd, The: Lindsay, Jack

Passionate pastoral, The: Lindsay, Jack

Passionate pilgrim, The: Bird, W.R.

Passionate pilgrim, A: James, Henry

Passionate pilgrime, The: Shakespeare, William

Passionate pilgrims, The: Palgrave, F.T.

Passionate Puritan, The: Mander, Jane

Passionate shepheard, The: Breton, Nicholas

Passionate shepherd to his love, The: Marlowe, Christopher

Passionate sightseer, The: Berenson, Bernhard

Passionate witch, The: Smith, Thorne

Passion-flowers: Howe, Julia Ward

Passions, The: Collins, William

Passions spin the plot: Fisher, V.A.

Passive obedience: Berkeley, George

Passport, Hoboken free state: Morley, C.D.

Passport to Hell: †Hyde, Robin

Past all dishonor: Cain, J.M.

Past and present: Carlyle, Thomas

Past and the future, The: Trevelyan, G.M.

Past meridian: Sigourney, L.H.

Past that lives today, The: Becker, C.L.

Past years: Lodge, *Sir* Oliver

Paste jewels: Bangs, J.K.

Pasteboard proclivities: Hubbard, Elbert

Pastel: Heyer, Georgette

Pastels and other rhymes: Baring, Maurice

Pastels under the Southern Cross: Woods, M.L.

Pastime of the people, The: Rastell, John

Pastime stories: Page, T.N.

Paston Carew, millionaire and miser: Linton, Eliza

Paston, George: Murray, John

Paston Letters, The: The Pastons

Pastor Fido: Settle, Elkanah

Pastoral: †Shute, Nevil

Pastoral cordial, A: Stevenson, J.H.

Pastoral in memory of the Duke of Ormond, A: Tate, Nahum

Pastoral New Zealand: Mulgan, A.E.

Pastoral poem on the victories at Schellenburgh and Blenheim, A: Oldmixon, John

Pastoral poetry and pastoral drama: Greg, W.W.

Pastoral puke, A: Stevenson, J.H.

Pastoral sermons, The: Knox, R.A.

Pastorall called the Arcadia, A: Shirley, James

Pastorals: Blunden, Edmund

Pastorals, epistles, odes and other original poems, with translations from Pindar, Anacreon and Sappho: Philips, Ambrose

Pastors and masters: Compton-Burnett, Ivy

Pastor's fire-side, The: Porter, Jane

Pastor's wife, The: Russell, E.M.

Pastures: Reese, L.W.

Pastures of heaven, The: Steinbeck, John

Pat of Silver Bush: Montgomery, L.M.

Patagonia, The: James, Henry

Patched cloak, The: Temple, Joan

Patches of sunlight: Dunsany, E.J.

Patchwork: Nichols, Beverley

Paterson: Williams, W.C.

Path and goal: Cambridge, Ada

Path by the window, The: Bell, Adrian

Path of a star, The: Duncan, S.J.

Path of glory, The: Peach, L. du Garde

Path of the just, The: Baring-Gould, Sabine

Path of the king, The: Buchan, John

Path to Rome, The: Belloc, Hilaire

Path to Sankoty, The: Carman, Bliss

Pathetic fallacy, The: Powys, L.C.

Pathetic odes: †Pindar, Peter

Pathfinder, The: Cooper, James Fenimore

Pathfinders of the great plains: Burpee, Lawrence J.

Pathos of distance, The: Huneker, J.G.

Paths of glory: Howard, S.C.

Paths of judgement: Sedgwick, A.D.

Paths to the present: Schlesinger, A.M.

Pathway, The: Williamson, Henry

Pathway of the sun, The: Timms, E.V.

Pathway to military practise, A: Rich, Barnabe

Pathway to the Holy Scripture, A: Tyndale, William

Patie and Roger: Ramsay, Allan

Patience: Gilbert, Sir W.S.

Patience: Warner, A.B.

Patience of a saint, The: Stern, G.B.

Patience Sparhawk and her times: Atherton, Gertrude

Patient Grissil: Dekker, Thomas

Patins: Heppenstall, J.R.

Patricia comes home: Strong, L.A.G.

Patricia Kemball: Linton, Eliza

Patrician, The: Galsworthy, John

Patrician and Parvenu: Poole, John

Patrician's daughter, The: Dickens, Charles

Patrician's daughter, The: Marston, J.W.

Patrick Butler for the defence: Carr, J.D.

Patrick engaged: †Armstrong, Anthony

Patrick helps: †Armstrong, Anthony

Patrick Henry and the frigate's keel: Fast, Howard M.

Patrick in Prussia: O'Keeffe, John

Patrick Shaw-Stewart: Knox, R.A.

Patrick undergraduate: †Armstrong, Anthony

Patrins to which is added an inquirendo into the wit and other good parts of his late Majesty, King Charles II: Guiney, L.I.

Patriot, The: Anstey, Christopher

Patriot, The: Buck, Pearl

Patriot, The: Johnson, Samuel

Patriot brothers, The: Halpine, C.G.

Patriotic gore: Wilson, Edmund

Patriotic lady: †Bowen, Marjorie

Patriotic schoolgirl, A: Brazil, Angela

Patriotic sketches of Ireland: Morgan, Lady Sydney

Patriotism and popular education: Jones, H.A.

Patriotism in literature: Drinkwater, John

Patriotism under three flags: Angell, Sir Norman

Patriots, The: Kingsley, Sidney

Patriots: Robinson, E.S.L.

Patriots and filibusters: Oliphant, Laurence

Patriots of Palestine, The: Yonge, C.M.

Patriot's progress, The: Williamson, Henry

Patrol of the Sun Dance trail, The: †Connor, Ralph

Patronage: Edgeworth, Maria

Pattering feet: Bourinot, A.S.

Pattern of a day: Hillyer, R.S.

Pattern of courtesy, The: Bullett, Gerald

Pattern of poetry, The: Seymour, W.K.

Paul and Christina: Barr, A.E.H.

Paul and Paulinism: Moffat, James

Paul Ardenheim, the Monk of Wissahikon: Lippard, George

Paul Clifford: Lytton, E.G.E.B. 1st Baron

Paul Deverell: Ingraham, J.H.

Paul Douglas: Sheldon, C.M.

Paul Faber, surgeon: Macdonald, George

Paul Fane: Willis, N.P.

Paul Felice: Monkhouse, A.N.

Paul Gauguin, his life and art: Fletcher, John Gould

Paul Gosslett's confessions in law and the civil service: Lever, C.J.

Paul Kelver: Jerome, Jerome K.

Paul Marchand: MacDonald, W.P.

Paul Nash: Rothenstein, Sir John

Paul Patoff: Crawford, F. Marion

Paul Perril, the merchant's son: Ingraham, J.H.

Paul Pry: Jerrold, Douglas

Paul Pry: Poole, John

Paul Ralston: Holmes, M.J.

Paul Redding: Read, T.B.

Paul Revere and the minute men: Canfield, Dorothy

Paul Revere and the world he lived in: Forbes, Esther

Paul the minstrel: Benson, A.C.

Paul Verlaine: Nicolson, Hon. Sir Harold

Paul Verlaine: Rothenstein, Sir William

Paulina: the story of an apple-butter pot: Johnson, J.W.

Pauline: Browning, Robert

Pauline: Stringer, A.J.A.

Pauline Pavlova: Aldrich, T.B.

Paul's letters to his kinsfolk: Scott, Sir Walter

Paul's wife: Sladen, D.B.W.

Paumanok: Morley, C.D.

Pauperism: Booth, Charles

Pausanias, the Spartan: Lytton, E.G.E.B. 1st Baron

Pause in the desert, A: La Farge, Oliver

Pavannes and divisions: Pound, Ezra

Paved with gold: Mayhew, Augustus Septimus

Pavements at Anderby: Holtby, Winifred

Pavilion of honour, The: †Preedy, George

Pavilion of women: Buck, Pearl

Pavilionstone: Dickens, Charles

Pawned: Packard, F.L.

Pawns: Drinkwater, John

Pawns count, The: Oppenheim, E. Phillips

Pay as you run: Graham, Stephen

Paycockes of Coggeshall, The: Power, Eileen

Paying guest, The: Gissing, George

Paying guests: Benson, E.F.

Payment deferred: Forester, C.S.

Payment of wages, The: Cole, G.D.H.

Peacable principles and true: Bunyan, John

Peace: Benson, A.C.

Peace: Bridges, Robert

Peace and bread in time of war: Addams, Jane

Peace and Dunkirk: Swift, Jonathan

Peace and India: Nehru, Jawaharlal

Peace and progress: Dole, N.H.

Peace and the Protestant Succession, The: Trevelyan, G.M.

Peace and war: Allingham, William

Peace at any price: Robertson, T.W.

Peace at eventide: Keller, Helen

Peace at once: Bell, Clive

Peace breaks out: Thirkell, Angela

Peace conference hints: Shaw, G.B.

Peace egg, The: Ewing, Mrs. Juliana Horatia

Peace in Friendship Village: Gale, Zona

Peace in our time: Coward, Noel

Peace in our time: †Onions, Oliver

Peace is our answer: Lindsay, Jack

Peace, it's wonderful: Saroyan, William

Peace like a river: Fisher, V.A.

Peace manoeuvres: Davies, R.H.

Peace of the Augustans, The: Saintsbury, George

Peace of the world, The: Wells, H.G.

Peace that was left, The: Cammaerts, Emile

Peace theories and the Balkan war: Angell, Sir Norman

Peace with honour: Milne, A.A.

Peace with Mexico: Gallatin, Albert

Peace with the dictators?: Angell, Sir Norman

Peaceful invasion: (†Ian Hay), Beith, Sir John Hay

Peacemaker, The: Forester, C.S.

Peace-maker, The: Middleton, Thomas

Peacemakers, The: McArthur, Peter

Peace-making: Nicolson, Hon. Sir Harold

Peace-tactics of Napoleon, 1806–1808, The: Butterfield, Herbert

Peacock brides: The: Bullett, Gerald

Peacock House: Phillpotts, Eden

Peacock pie: De la Mare, Walter

Peacock's holiday: Merivale, H.C.

Peak in Darien, The: Cobbe, Frances Power

Peal of bells, The: Lynd, Robert

Pearce Amerson's will: Johnston, R.M.

Pearl, The: Steinbeck, John

Pearl and the octopus: Stephens, A.G.

Pearl divers of Roncador reef, The: †Becke, Louis

Pearl fountain, The: Kavanagh, Julia

Pearl lagoon, The: Nordhoff, C.B.

Pearl of Orr's island, The: Stowe, Harriet Beecher

Pearl tree, The: Trevelyan, R.C.

Pearl-maiden: Haggard, Sir H. Rider

Pearls: Houghton, W.S.

Pearls and pebbles: Traill, C.P.

Pearls of the faith, or Islam's rosary: Arnold, Edwin

Pearly gates: Jennings, Gertrude

Pearly water, The: Gibbons, Stella

Peasant boy philosopher, The: Mayhew, Henry

Peasant life and rural conditions, c.1100 to c.1500: Power, Eileen

Peasantry of Bengal, The: Dutt, R.C.

Peasants: Bercovici, Konrad

Pebbles on the shore: Gardiner, A.G.

Peck of troubles, A: †George, Daniel

Peckover: Beresford, J.D.

Peculiar, a hero of the southern rebellion: Sargent, Epes

Peculiar: a tale of the great transition: Sargent, Epes

Peculiar treasure, A: Ferber, Edna

Pedagomania, or the gentle art of teaching: Bentley, Phyllis

Peder victorious: Rölvaag, O.E.

Pedlar and a Romish priest, A: Taylor, John

Pedlar's pack: †Onions, Oliver

Pedlar's pack, A: O'Reilly, D.P.

Pedro de Valdivia: Cunninghame Graham, R.B.

Peek's progress: †Bell, Neil

Peekshill, U.S.A.: Fast, Howard M.

Peep at the pixies, A: Bray, Anna Eliza

Peep behind the curtain, A: Garrick, David

Peep into the educational future, A: Canfield, Dorothy

Peep into the past, A: Beerbohm, *Sir* Max

Peeping Tom of Coventry: O'Keeffe, John

Peeps at people: Bangs, John Kendrick

Peep-show man, The: Colum, Padraic

Peer and the paper girl, The: Percy, Edward

Peer and the woman, The: Oppenheim, E. Phillips

Peerage of England, The: Collins, Arthur

Peers and parvenus: Gore, Catherine

Peg Woffington: Reade, Charles

Pegasus: Day-Lewis, C.

Peggy: Crothers, Rachel

Peggy O'Neal: Lewis, A.H.

Peirs Gaveston: Drayton, Michael

Pekinese national anthem, The: Lucas, E.V.

Pelagea: Coppard, A.E.

Pelayo: Ritchie, *Mrs.* Anne

Pelayo: Simms, W.G.

Pelham: Lytton, E.G.E.B. *1st Baron*

Pelican, The: Harwood, H.M.

Pelican Island: Divine, A.D.

Pelican island, The: Montgomery, James

Pelican walking: Stern, G.B.

Pelicans, The: †Delafield, E.M.

Pelopidas: Bird, R.M.

Pelorus Jack: Cowan, James

Pembroke: Freeman, Mary

Pemmican: Fisher, V.A.

Pemmican Pete: Mickle, A.D.

Pen and ink: Matthews, J.B.

Pen and the book, The: Besant, *Sir* Walter

Pen portraits and reviews: Shaw, G.B.

Pen to paper: Frankau, Pamela

Penalosa: Rhodes, E.M.

Penance of John Logan, The: Black, William

Penance of Portia James, The: †Tasma

Penang appointment: Collins, Norman

Pencilled fly-leaves: Piatt, J.J.

Pencillings: Murray, John Middleton

Pencillings by the way: Willis, N.P.

Pencraft: a plea for the older ways: Watson, *Sir* J.W.

Pender among the residents: Reid, Forrest

Pendulum, The: †Mordaunt, Elinor

Pendulum swing: Mitchell, Mary

Penelope: (†E.V.Cunningham) Fast, Howard M.

Penelope: Maugham, Somerset

Penelope: Mottley, John

Penelope: †Seranus

Penelope Brandling: Lee, Vernon

Penelope forgives: Baker, Elizabeth

Penelope of the "Polyantha": Wallace, Edgar

Penelope's English experiences: Wiggin, K.D.

Penelope's Irish experiences: Wiggin, K.D.

Penelope's man, the homing instinct: Erskine, John

Penelope's postscripts: Wiggin, K.D.

Penelope's progress: Wiggin, K.D.

Penelope's suitors: Bynner, E.L.

Penelopes web: Greene, Robert

Penetralia: Jephcott, S.W.

Penetration of Arabia, The: Hogarth, D.G.

Penguin Book of English Verse (anth.): Hayward, John

Penguin in the eyrie, A: Bolitho, H.H.

Penguin People, The: (†Donald Barr), Barrett, C.L.

Penhallow: Heyer, Georgette

Peninsula Place: Mackail, Denis

Penknife in my heart: Day-Lewis, C.

Pennsylvania: Royall, A.N.

Pennsylvania pilgrim, The: Whittier, J.G.

Penny Broadsheet: Mason, R.A.K.

Penny fiddle, The: Graves, Robert

Penny foolish: Sitwell, *Sir* Osbert

Penny for the lamp, A: †Onions, Oliver

Penny plain: Buchan, Anna

Penny Scot's treasure: Niven, F.J.

Penny Wheep: †McDiarmid, Hugh

Penny wise and book foolish: Starrett, Vincent

Pennycomequicks, The: Baring-Gould, Sabine

Penny-wise pound-foolish: Dekker, Thomas

Penrod: Tarkington, Booth

Penrod and Sam: Tarkington, Booth

Penrod, his complete story: Tarkington, Booth

Pens and pirates: Deacon, W.A.

Pension Beaurepas, The: James, Henry

Pentameron and Pentalogia, The: Landor, W.S.

Pentecost of calamity, The: Wister, Owen

Penthesilea: Binyon, Laurence

Penthesperon: Hassall, Christopher

Penthouse mystery, The: †Queen, Ellery

Penumbra: Isvaran, M.S.

Peonies and ponies: Acton, Harold

Peony: Buck, Pearl

People, The: Glaspell, Susan

People: Wallace, Edgar

People and houses: Suckow, Ruth

People and places: Mead, Margaret

People and things: Massingham, Harold

People and things: Nicolson, Hon. *Sir* Harold

People are curious: Hanley, James

People at sea: Priestley, J.B.

People behave like ballads: Coffin, Robert

People for whom Shakespeare wrote, The: Warner, C.D.

People I have met: Willis, N.P.

People in cages: Ashton, Helen

People in the South: Pryce-Jones, A.P.

People of destiny: Gibbs, *Sir* Philip

People of India, The: Taylor, P.M.

People of our class: Ervine, St. John

People of our neighbourhood, The: Freeman, Mary

People of South Africa, The: Millin, Sarah Gertrude

People of the abyss, The: London, Jack

People of the mist, The: Haggard, Sir H. Rider

People of the river: Wallace, Edgar

People, places and things: Payn, James

People talk, The: Appel, Benjamin

People, yes, The: Sandburg, Carl

People's album of London statues, The: Sitwell, *Sir* Osbert

People's atlas, The: Roberts, C.E.M.

People's court, The: Griffith, Hubert

People's front, The: Cole, G.D.H.

Peoples, houses and ships: †Mordaunt, Elinor

People's idea of God, The: Eddy, M.B.

People's lawyer, The: Jones, J.S.

People's man, A: Oppenheim, E. Phillips

People's palace, The: Sitwell, Sacheverell

People's presidential candidate, The: Hildreth, Richard

Pepaction: Burroughs, John

Pepita: Sackville-West, Victoria

Pepper and salt: Pyle, Howard

Pepper and salt: Vachell, H.A.

Pepper and sand: Williams, Emlyn

Pepys, his life and character: Drinkwater, John

Pequinillo: James, G.P.R.

Per amica silentia lunae: Yeats, W.B.

Per ardua: Saunders, H.A. St. George

Per ardua, 1914–1918: Baring, Maurice

Perch of the devil: Atherton, Gertrude

Perchance to dream: †Novello, Ivor

Percival and I: †Armstrong, Anthony

Percival at play: †Armstrong, Anthony

Percival Keene: Marryatt, Frederick

Percy: More, Hannah

Percy Bysshe Shelley: Swinburne, A.C.

Perdita: Brereton, John Le G.

Perdita: Wilcox, Ella Wheeler

Père Antoine's date palm: Aldrich, T.B.

Père Marquette: Repplier, Agnes

Père Raphaël: Cable, George Washington

Peregrine Bunce: Hook, T.E.

Peregrine Pickle (play): Reade, Charles

Peregrine's progress: Farnol, J.J.

Peregrine's saga, The: Williamson, Henry

Perelandra: Lewis, C.S.

Perennial: Gogarty, O. St. John

Perennial Philadelphians, The: Perelman, S.J.

Perennial philosophy, The: Huxley, Aldous

Perennial Shakespeare, The: Granville-Barker, *Sir* Harley

Perfect alibi, The: †Caudwell, Christopher

Perfect behavior: Stewart, D.O.

Perfect crime, The: †Queen, Ellery

Perfect cure, The: Houghton, W.S.

Perfect horseman, The: Markham, Gervase

Perfect little fool, A: Percy, Edward

Perfect salesman, The: Leacock, Stephen

Perfect treasure, A: Payn, James

Perfect Wagnerite, The: Shaw, G.B.

Perfect widow, The: Cannan, Gilbert

Perfect wife, The: Bottome, Phyllis

Perfect wife, The: Gibbings, Robert

Perfect woman, A: Hartley, L.P.

Perfect zoo: Farjeon, Eleanor

Perfection: Combe, William

Perfidious brother, The: Theobald, Lewis

Perfidy: Hecht, Ben

Perfidy of Captain Slyboots, The: Sala, G.A.H.

Perfite platforme of a hoppe garden, A: Scot, Reginald

Performing flea: Wodehouse, P.G.

Perfume of earth: Chattopadhyaya, H.

Perfume of the rainbow, The: Beck, *Mrs.* Lily

Perhaps I am: Bok, E.W.

Perhaps women: Anderson, Sherwood

Pericles: Mackenzie, *Sir* Compton

Pericles: Shakespeare, William

Pericles: Swinburne, A.C.

Pericles and Aspasia: Landor, W.S.

Pericles the Athenian: Warner, Rex

Peril at End House: Christie, Agatha

Peril in Peking: Starrett, Vincent

Peril of Richard Pardon, The: Farjeon, B.L.

Perilous adventures of Sir Bingo Walker, The: †Bridie, James

Perilous light, The: Gore-Booth, E.S.

Perilous pilgrimage: Treece, Henry

Perilous secret, A: Reade, Charles

Perils and adventures of Mr. William Thornley, The: Rowcroft, Charles

Perils and certain English prisoners, The: Dickens, Charles

Perils of Pearl Street, The: Green, Asa

Perimedes the blacksmith: Green, Robert

Period stuff: †Yates, Dornford

Peripatetic philosopher, The: Clarke, Marcus

Perishable goods: †Yates, Dornford

Perishable quality, The: Davies, Rhys

Perissa: Mais, S.P.B.

Perkin the peddlar: Farjeon, Eleanor

Perlycross: Blackmore, *Sir* R.D.

Permanence and change: Burke, Kenneth

Permanent horizon, The: Lewisohn, Ludwig

Perolla and Izadora: Cibber, Colley

Peronnik the fool: Moore, George

Perpervid: Davidson, John

Perpetua: Baring-Gould, Sabine

Perpetual curate, The: Oliphant, Margaret

Perpetual light: Benét, William Rose

Perpetual pessimist, The: †George, Daniel

Perplexed husband, The: Sutro, Alfred

Perplexed philosopher, A: George, Henry

Perplexity: Russell, W.C.

Persephone: Drinkwater, John

Persephone at Enna: Stringer, A.J.A.

Persephone in Hades: Pitter, Ruth

Persephone in winter: †Hyde, Robin

Perseus and Andromeda: Theobald, Lewis

Perseus in the wind: Stark, F.M.

Perseverance: Herbert, *Sir* A.P.

Persian critic, A: Pearson, Hesketh

Persian dawns, Egyptian nights: Mitchell, J.L.

Persian eclogues: Collins, William

Persian letters: Davidson, John

Persian love elegies: †Pindar, Peter

Persian painting: Anand, M.R.

Persian pearl, A: Darrow, C.S.

Persian tales (trn.): Philips, Ambrose

Persimmon tree, The: Barnard, M.

Persistence of poetry, The: Bynner, Witter

Person of evolution, The: Lighthall, W.D.

Person of quality's answer to Mr. Collier's letter, The: Dennis, John

Person, place and things: Shapiro, Karl

Person unknown, The: Maltby, H.F.

Personae: Pound, Ezra

Personal exposures: Beach, R.E.

Personal heresy, The: Lewis, C.S.

Personal heresy, The: Tillyard, E.M.W.

Personal history, adventures, experiences, and observations of David Copperfield the younger: Dickens, Charles

Personal idealism and mysticism: Inge, W.R.

Personal narrative of travels to the equinoctial regions of the new continent: Williams, H.M.

Personal note: Bruce, Charles

Personal pleasures: Macaulay, *Dame* Rose

Personal recollections of Joan of Arc: Clemens, Samuel Langhorne

Personal record: Green, Julian

Personal religion and the life of devotion: Inge, W.R.

Personal religion and the life of fellowship: Temple, William

Personal religion in Egypt: Petrie, *Sir* William Flinders

Personal remarks: Strong, L.A.G.

Personal reminiscences of Henry Irving: Stoker, Bram

Personal talk: †O'Sullivan, Seumas

Personalities and powers: Namier, *Sir* Lewis

Personality: Tagore, *Sir* R.

Personality plus: Ferber, Edna

Personally conducted: Stockton, F.R.

Persons and periods: Cole, G.D.H.

Persons and pictures from the histories of France and England: Herbert, H.W.

Persons and places: Santayana, George

Persons from Porlock: Starrett, Vincent

Persons unknown: Wallace, Edgar

"Perspectives": Chase, Stuart

Persuasion: Drinkwater, John

Persuasion: Austen, Jane

Persuasive to a Holy life, A: Ray, John

Peru: Prescott, W.H.

Peru: Williams, H.M.

Peter: Hardy, A.S.

Peter: Smith, F.H.

Peter Abelard: Waddell, Helen

Peter and his enemies: Jeffrey, *Lord* Francis

Peter and Paul: Rubenstein, Harold F.

Peter and Wendy: Barrie, *Sir* J.M.

Peter Ashley: Heyward, DuBose

Peter Bell: Wordsworth, William

Peter Budstone: Trowbridge, J.T.

Peter Duck: Ransome, Arthur

Peter Homunculus: Cannan, Gilbert

Peter Hurd: Horgan, Paul

Peter Ibbetson: Du Maurier, George

Peter Jackson, cigar merchant: Frankau, Gilbert

Peter kills the bear: Erskine, John

Peter Lavelle: Brophy, John

Peter Ottawa: Thomson, E.W.

Peter Pan in Kensington Gardens: Barrie, *Sir* J.M.

Peter Paragon: Palmer, J.L.

Peter Parley's universal history: Hawthorne, Nathaniel

Peter Pilgrim: Bird, R.M.

Peter Ploddy and other oddities: Neal, J.C.

Peter Pond, fur trader and adventurer: Innis, H.A.

Peter Porcupine: †Bowen, Marjorie

Peter Possum's portfolio: Rowe, Richard

Peter Rabbit's almanac: Potter, Helen Beatrix

Peter Ruff: Oppenheim, E. Phillips

Peter Rugg, the missing man: Austin, William

Peter Simple: Marryatt, Frederick

Peter Waring: Reid, Forrest

Peter Whiffle, his life and works: Van Vechten, Carl

Peterborough idea, The: Robinson, E.A.

Peterkin: Molesworth, *Mrs.*

Peter's letters to his kinsfolk: Lockhart, J.G.

Peter's pension: †Pindar, Peter

Peter's prophecy: †Pindar, Peter

Pethick-Lawrence: a portrait: Brittain, Vera

Petition to the House of Commons for the recall of Governor Fitzroy: Domett, Alfred

Petition to the King from the inhabitants of Pennsylvania, A: Dickinson, John

Petition to the King from the Stamp Act Congress, A: Dickinson, John

Petra, the Rock City of Edom: Murray, Margaret

Petrified forest, The: Sherwood, R.E.

Petruchio: Stern, G.B.

Petticoat government: Orczy, *Baroness*

Petticoat government: Trollope, Frances

Petticoats: Maltby, H.F.

Peveril of the Peak: Scott, *Sir* Walter

Ph.D's: Bacon, Leonard

Phaedra and Hippolitus: Smith, Edmund

Phaenomena quaedam Apocalyptica: Sewall, Samuel

Phaethon: Kingsley, Charles

Phantasies: a faerie romance for men and women: Macdonald, George

Phantasmagoria: †Carroll, Lewis

Phantasmion: Coleridge, Sara

Phantasms of the living: Myers, F.W.H.

Phantom death, The: Russell, W.C.

Phantom fortune: Braddon, M.E.

Phantom future, The: †Merriman, Seton

Phantom hour, The: Ghose, Sri Aurobindo

Phantom journal, The: Lucas, E.V.

Phantom lobster: Walmsley, Leo

Phantom lover, A: Lee, Vernon

Phantom public, The: Lippmann, Walter

Phantom regiment, The: Grant, James

Phantom rickshaw, The: Kipling, Rudyard

Phantom ship, The: Marryatt, Frederick

Phantom walls: Lodge, *Sir* Oliver

Phantom wires: Stringer, A.J.A.

Phantoms of the foot-bridge, The: †Craddock, C.E.

Pharais: †Macleod, Fiona

Pharisees and Publicans: Benson, E.F.

Pharmacopoeia Londinensis: Culpeper, Nicolas

Pharonnida: Chamberlayne, William

Pharos and Pharillon: Forster, E.M.

Phases of an inferior planet: Glasgow, Ellen

Phases of English poetry: Read, *Sir* Herbert

Phasian bird, The: Williamson, Henry

Phemie Keller: †Trafford, E.G.

Pheneas speaks: Doyle, *Sir* Arthur Conan

Phil and his friends: Trowbridge, J.T.

Philadelphia story, The: Barry, Philip

Philadelphia: the place and the people: Repplier, Agnes

Philander: Lennox, Charlotte

Philanderer, The: Shaw, G.B.

Philanderers, The: Mason, A.E.W.

Philaster: Settle, Elkanah

Philharmonic Society of New York, The: Huneker, J.G.

Philibert: Gratton, Thomas Colley

Philip: Church, Richard

Philip and Alexander of Macedon: Hogarth, D.G.

Philip and his wife: Deland, Margaret

Philip Augustus: James, G.P.R.

Philip goes forth: Kelly, G.E.

Philip Nolan's friends: Hale, E.E.

Philip of France and Marie de Méranie: Marston, J.W.

Philip Rollo: Grant, James

Philip the King: Masefield, John

Philip II of Spain: Gayarré, C.E.A.

Philip II of Spain: Petrie, *Sir* Charles

Philip van Artevelde: Taylor, *Sir* Henry

Philip Vernon: Mitchell, S.W.

Philippa: Molesworth, *Mrs.*

Philippa: Sedgwick, A.D.

Philistia: (†Cecil Power), Allen, Grant

Philistines, The: Johnson, Pamela H.

Phillida: Elliott, M.H.

Phillip of Australia: (†Eldershaw), M.Barnard

Phillis: Lodge, Thomas

Philo: an Evangeliad: Judd, Sylvester

Philocothonista: Heywood, Thomas

Philoctetes: Warren, J.B.L.

Philomela: Greene, Robert

Phil-O-Rum's canoe and Madeleine Verchères: Drummond, W.H.

Philosophaster: Burton, Robert

Philosophers at Court: Santayana, George

Philosophia pia: Glanvill, Joseph

Philosophical aspects of modern science: Joad, C.E.M.

Philosophical basis of religion, The: Watson, John

Philosophical discourse of earth, relating to the culture and improvement of it for vegetation, A: Evelyn, John

Philosophical enquiry into the origin of our ideas of the sublime and beautiful, A: Burke, Edmund

Philosophical essays: Ayer, A.J.

Philosophical essays: Russell, Bertrand

Philosophical essays concerning human understanding: Hume, David

Philosophical lectures: Coleridge, S.T.

Philosophical view of reform, A: Shelley, P.B.

Philosophies in little: Simpson, H. de G.

Philosophy: Joad, C.E.M.

Philosophy and civilization: Dewey, John

Philosophy and language: Ayer, A.J.

Philosophy and politics: Russell, Bertrand

Philosophy and the ordinary man: Samuel, Herbert *1st Viscount*

Philosophy and the social problem: Durant, W.J.

Philosophy for our times: Joad, C.E.M.

Philosophy 4: Wister, Owen

Philosophy: its scope and relations: Sidgwick, Henry

Philosophy of anarchism, The: Read, *Sir* Herbert

Philosophy of art, The: Ker, W.P.

Philosophy of Bergson, The: Russell, Bertrand

Philosophy of commonsense: Carey, Mathew

Philosophy of conflict, The: Ellis, Havelock

Philosophy of disenchantment, The: Saltus, E.E.

Philosophy of Friedrich Nietzsche, The: Mencken, H.L.

Philosophy of History, The: Collingwood, R.G.

Philosophy of immortality, A: Noel, R.B.W.

Philosophy of Kant, The: Sidgwick, Henry

Philosophy of Kant explained, The: Watson, John

Philosophy of limited editions, The: Le Gallienne, Richard

Philosophy of love, The: Glyn, Elinor

Philosophy of loyalty, The: Royce, Josiah

Philosophy of melancholy, The: Peacock, Thomas Love

Philosophy of modern art, The: Read, *Sir* Herbert

Philosophy of physical science, The: Eddington, *Sir* A.S.

Philosophy of Plotinus, The: Inge, W.R.

Philosophy of purpose, A: Lighthall, W.D.

Philosophy of Rabindranath Tagore, The: Radhakrishan, Sarvepalli

Philosophy of solitude, A: Powys, John Cowper

Philosophy of the plays of Shakespeare unfolded, The: Bacon, Delia Salter

Philosophy of the short story, The: Matthews, J.B.

Philosophy of the Upanishads, The: Radhakrishan, Sarvepalli

Philothea: Child, Lydia Maria

Phineas Finn: Trollope, Anthony

Phineas Quiddy: Poole, John

Phineas Redux: Trollope, Anthony

Phipps: Houghton, W.S.

Phoebe, junior: Oliphant, Margaret

Phoebe's guest house: Vachell, H.A.

Phoebe's mother: Meredith, L.A.

Phoenix: Abercrombie, Lascelles

Phoenix: Lawrence, D.H.

Phoenix, The: Middleton, Thomas

Phoenix: Wells, H.G.

Phoenix and the carpet, The: Nesbit, E.

Phoenix and the turtle, The: Shakespeare, William

Phoenix generation, The: Williamson, Henry

Phoenix' nest, The: Jenkins, Elizabeth

Phoenix of these late times, The: Heywood, Thomas

Phoenix rising: Steen, Marguerite

Phoenix too frequent, A: Fry, Christopher

Phoenixana: Derby, George Horatio

Phoenix-kind, The: Quennell, P.C.

Photographic pleasures popularly portrayed with pen and pencil: †Bede, Cuthbert

Photographs: †Carroll, Lewis

Phroso: (†Anthony Hope), Hawkins, Anthony Hope

Phylaster, or, love lyes a bleeding: Beaumont, Francis and John Fletcher

Phyllis: (†E.V.Cunningham), Fast, Howard M.

Phyllis of the Sierras, A: Harte, Bret

Phyllistrata: Roberts, C.E.M.

Physical and meteorological observations: Franklin, Benjamin

Physical basis of perception, The: Adrian, E.D. *1st Baron*

Physical configuration of the Australian continent: Favenc, Ernest

Physical education: Smiles, Samuel

Physical Force fallacy, The: Housman, Laurence

Physician, The: Jones, H.A.

Physician heal thyself: Phillpotts, Eden

Physics and experience: Russell, Bertrand

Physics and philosophy: Jeans, *Sir* James

Physics and politics: Bagehot, Walter

Physics for the modern world: Andrade, E.N. da Costa

Physiological aesthetics: Allen, Grant

Physiology of common life, The: Lewes, G.H.

Phytologia: Darwin, Erasmus

Piano quintet: Sackville-West, Edward

Piano-player and its music, The: Newman, Ernest

Piazza tales, The: Melville, Herman

Picaró: Nordhoff, C.B.

Piccadilly: Bennett, Arnold

Piccadilly: Oliphant, Laurence

Piccadilly Jim: Wodehouse, P.G.

Piccadilly lady, The: Hannay, J.O.

Piccadilly puzzle, The: Hume, F.W.

Piccaninnies: (†Donald Barr), Barrett, C.L.

Piccino: Burnett, Frances Hodgson

Pick and choose: †George, Daniel

Picked poems: Wilcox, Ella Wheeler

Picked up adrift: De Mille, James

Picked up in the streets: Rowe, Richard

Pickle for the knowing ones, A: Dexter, Timothy

Pickle the spy: Lang, Andrew

Pickled company, A: Belloc, Hilaire

Pick-me-up: Squire, *Sir* J.C.

Pickwick abroad: Reynolds, G.

Picnic, The: Boyd, Martin

Picnic, The: Green, Paul

Picnic races: Cusack, E.D.

Pictorial edition of the works of Shakespeare, The: Knight, Charles

Pictorial history of the American Indian, A: La Farge, Oliver

Pictorial reader, The: Sigourney, L.H.

Picts and Martyrs, The: Ransome, Arthur

Picturae Loquentes: Saltonstall, Wye

Picture, The: Baker, Elizabeth

Picture, The: Bowles, William Lisle

Picture, The: Massinger, Philip

Picture and text: James, Henry

Picture book history of the Jews: Fast, Howard M.

Picture of Dorian Gray, The: Wilde, Oscar

Picture of Scotland, The: Chambers, Robert

Picture of St. John, The: Taylor, Bayard

Picture of the desolated states, and the work of restoration, A: Trowbridge, J.T.

Picture show: Sassoon, Siegfried

Picture theatre advertising: Sargent, Epes

Picturebook, A: †O'Connor, Frank

Pictures: Whitman, Walt

Pictures and people: Royde-Smith, Naomi

Pictures and rhymes: †George, Daniel

Pictures and songs of home: Browne, Frances

Pictures at play: Lang, Andrew

Pictures at play by two art critics: Henley, W.E.

Pictures from Breughel: Williams, W.C.

Pictures from Italy: Dickens, Charles

Pictures from the life of Nelson: Russell, W.C.

Pictures, historical and biographical, drawn from English, Scottish and Irish history: Galt, John

Pictures in a theatre: Robinson, E.S.L.

Pictures in song: Scollard, Clinton

Pictures in the fire: Collier, John

Pictures in the hallway: O'Casey, Sean

Pictures of country life: Miller, Thomas

Pictures of life and of death: Patchen, Kenneth

Pictures of Old New Zealand: Cowan, James

Pictures of passions, fancies, and affections: Jordan, Thomas

Pictures of the floating world: Lowell, Amy

Pictures of the world at home and abroad: Ward, Robert Plumer

Pictures of wild animals: Seton-Thompson, E.

Picturesque California: Muir, John

Picturesque Quebec: LeMoine, *Sir* J.M.

Picturesque sketches of London past and present: Miller, Thomas

Picturesque views with poetical allusions: †Pindar, Peter

Pidgeon pie: Mitford, Nancy

Pie and the Patty-Pan, The: Potter, Helen Beatrix

Pie in the sky: Calder-Marshall, Arthur

Piece of my mind, A: Wilson, Edmund

Pieces of ancient popular poetry Ritson, Joseph

Pieces of eight: Le Gallienne, Richard

Pieces of hate: Broun, Heywood

Pied piper, The: Drinkwater, John

Pied piper, The: †Shute, Nevil

Pied Piper of Dipper Creek, The: Raddall, T.H.

Pied Piper of lovers: Durrell, Lawrence

Pier glass, The: Graves, Robert

Pierce Fenning: Ingraham, J.H.

Pierce Penilesse his supplication to the divell: Nash, Thomas

Pierced heart, The: Reid, T.M.

Pierces supererogation or a new prayse of the old asse: Harvey, Gabriel

Pierre: Melville, Herman

Pierre: Scott, D.C.

Pierre and his people: Parker, *Sir* H.G.

Pierre, the partisan: Herbert, H.W.

Pierrette cheats the publisher: Allen, C.R.

Pierrot in Australia: Adams, Arthur H.

Pierrot in town: Ashton, Helen

Pierrot of the minute, The: Dowson, E.C.

Pierrot wounded: Roberts, W. Adolphe

Piers Plainnes seaven yeres prentship: Chettle, Henry

Piers Plowman: Jusserand, Jean

Piet of Italy: Fairbridge, Dorothea

Pietas in Patriam: Mather, Cotton

Pietro Ghislerio: Crawford, F. Marion

Pietro of Siena: Phillips, Stephen

Pig in a poke, A: Davies, Rhys

Pigeon, The: Galsworthy, John

Pigeon pie, The: Yonge, Charlotte M.

Pigeon post: Ransome, Arthur

Pigs have wings: Wodehouse, P.G.

Pilgrim, The: Beaumont, Francis

Pilgrim, The: Dryden, John

Pilgrim, The: Johnstone, Charles

Pilgrim, The: Vanbrugh, *Sir* John

Pilgrim and the book, The: Mackaye, Percy

Pilgrim cottage: Roberts, C.E.M.

Pilgrim daughters, The: Pearson, Hesketh

Pilgrim fathers, The: Morison, S.E.

Pilgrim from Paddington: Royde-Smith, Naomi

Pilgrim hawk, The: Wescott, Glenway

Pilgrim of eternity, Byron, The: Drinkwater, John

Pilgrim of Glencoe, The: Campbell, Thomas

Pilgrim of the Apocalypse: Gregory, H.V.

Pilgrim on the earth, The: Green, Julian

Pilgrimage: Richardson, D.M.

Pilgrimage of Henry James, The: Brooks, Van Wyck

Pilgrims, The: Dole, N.H.

Pilgrims: Mannin, Ethel

Pilgrims in a foreign land: Evans, Caradoc

Pilgrim's joy: Cripps, A.S.

Pilgrims of adversity: McFee, William

Pilgrims of hope, The: Morris, William

Pilgrims of the night: Phillpotts, Eden

Pilgrims of the Rhine, The: Lytton, E.G.E.B. *1st Baron*

Pilgrims of the sun, The: Hogg, James

Pilgrims of the wild: (†Grey Owl), Belaney, G.S.

Pilgrim's progress: Brown, Alice

Pilgrim's progress, The: Bunyan, John

Pilgrim's regress, The: Lewis, C.S.

Pilgrim's progress, A: Nichols, Beverley

Pilgrim's progress to culture, The: Gibbs, *Sir* Philip

Pilgrim's rest: Young, Francis Brett

Pilgrim's way in New Zealand, A: Mulgan, A.E.

Pilgrim's way in South Africa, The: Fairbridge, Dorothea

Pilgrimage, The: Noguchi, Yone

Pilgrimage of Festus, The: Aiken, Conrad

Pilgrimage of freedom: Cournos, John

Pilgrimage of Grace: Cripps, A.S.

Pilgrimage of Mrs. Destinn, The: Mitchell, Mary

Pilgrimage of Peer, The: Mickle, A.D.

Pilgrimage to El-Medinah and Mecca: Burton, *Sir* Richard

Pilgrimage to Paradise, The: Breton, Nicholas

Pilkington's dictionary of painters: † Pindar, Peter

Pillar Mountain: †Brand, Max

Pillar of fire, The: Ingraham, H.H.

Pillars of society: Gardiner, A.G.

Pillars of the house, The: Yonge, Charlotte M.

Pillow fight, The: Monsarrat, Nicholas

Pillow-book of Sei Shonagon, The: Waley, Arthur

Pilot, The: Cooper, James Fenimore

Pilot at Swan Creek, The: †Connor, Ralph

Pilot Pete: Villiers, A.J.

Pimpernel and Rosemary: Orczy, *Baroness*

Pinch of prosperity, The: Vachell, H.A.

Pincher Martin, O.D.: †Taffrail

Pinckney's treaty: Bemis, S.F.

Pindar: Bowra, *Sir* Maurice

Pindari Carmina: Bowra, *Sir* Maurice

Pindariana: †Pindar, Peter

Pindaric poem to the Rev. Dr. Burnet, A: Behn, *Mrs.* Afra

Pindarick ode on the Union, A: Theobald, Lewis

Pindarick on the death of our late sovereign, A: Behn, *Mrs.* Afra

Pindarick poem on the happy coronation of his sacred Majesty James II, and his illus-

trious Consort Queen Mary: Behn, *Mrs.* Afra

Pindarique ode, humbly offer'd to the King on his taking Namure, A: Congreve, William

Pindarique ode on the victorious progress of Her Majesties arms, A: Congreve, William

Pindarique to their sacred majesties, James II and Queen Mary, A: Wilson, John

Pine needles: Warner, S.B.

Pine, rose and fleur de lis: †Seranus

Pines of Lory, The: Mitchell, J.A.

Ping-pong game, The: Saroyan, William

Pink and white tyranny: Stowe, Harriet Beecher

Pink church, The: Williams, W.C.

Pink front door, A: Gibbons, Stella

Pink furniture: Coppard, A.E.

Pink roses: Cannan, Gilbert

Pink string and sealing wax: Pertwee, Roland

Pink sugar: Buchan, Anna

Pinkertons ride again, The: Derleth, A.W.

Pinkney's garden: †Bell, Neil

Pin-money: Gore, Catherine

Pinorman: Aldington, Richard

Pins and pinnacles: Mander, Jane

Pioneer songs of Canada: Gibbon, J.M.

Pioneers, The: Cooper, James Fenimore

Pioneers, The: Prichard, K.S.

Pioneers! O Pioneers!: Saunders, H.A. St. George

Pioneers of France in the New World: Parkman, Francis

Pioneers of science: Lodge, *Sir* Oliver

Pioneers of the modern movement: Pevsner, Nikolaus

Pioneers on parade: Cusack, E.D.

Pioneers on parade: Franklin, Miles

Pip: (†Ian Hay), Beith, *Sir* John Hay

Pipe all hands: Tomlinson, H.M.

Pipe dream: Steinbeck, John

Pipe night: O'Hara, J.H.

Pipe of peace, The: Drinkwater, John

Pipefuls: Morley, C.D.

Piper of Hamelin, The: Buchanan, R.W.

Pipers and a dancer: Benson, Stella

Pipes o' Pan at Zekesbury: Riley, J.W.

Pipes of Pan: Carman, Bliss

Pipistrello: †Ouida

Pippa passes: Browning, Robert

Piracy: †Arlen, Michael

Pirate, The: Behrman, S.N.

Pirate, The: Scott, *Sir* Walter

Pirate and the three cutters, The: Marryatt, Frederick

Pirate chief, The: Ingraham, J.H.

Pirate city, The: Ballantyne, R.M.

Pirate ship, The: Munro, Neil

Pirates: †Taffrail

Pirates in the deep green sea: Linklater, Eric

Pirates of Penzance, The: Gilbert, *Sir* W.S.

Pirates of the spring: Reid, Forrest

Pisan cantos [74–84], The: Pound, Ezra

Pisgah-sight of Palestine, A: Fuller, Thomas

Pistols for two: Heyer, Georgette

Pistols for two: (†Owen Hatteras), Mencken, H.L. and G.J. Nathan

Pit, The: †Norris, Frank

Pit prop syndicate, The: Crofts, F.W.

Pitcairn's Island: Hall, J.N. and C.B. Nordhoff

Pitch lake: Mendes, Alfred

Pitiful wife, The: Jameson, Storm

Pitt and his statue: †Pindar, Peter

Pitter on cats: Pitter, Ruth

Pity of the world: †Mordaunt, Elinor

Pity the innocent: Mannin, Ethel

Pixies' plot: Phillpotts, Eden

Pizarro: Sheridan, R.B.

Place British Americans have won in history, The: Morgan, H.J.

Place called Estherville: Caldwell, Erskine Preston

Place in the city, A: Fast, Howard M.

Place names of Banks Peninsula: Anderson, J.C.

Place of art in a university, The: Read, *Sir* Herbert

Place of English literature in the modern university, The: Lee, *Sir* Sidney

Place of hawks: Derleth, A.W.

Place of man, the: Gupta, Nagendranath

Place of meaning in poetry, The: Daiches, David

Place of one's own, A: Sitwell, *Sir* Osbert

Place of science in modern civilization, The: Veblen, T.B.

Place of the damn'd, The: Swift, Jonathan

Place of the lion, The: Williams, Charles

Places: Belloc, Hilaire

Places of the mind: Grigson, Geoffrey

Placid Pug, and other rhymes, The: Douglas, *Lord* Alfred

Plague Court murders, The: †Carter Dickson

Plagued by the nightingale: Boyle, Kay

Plain and succinct narrative of the late riots and disturbances with an account of the commitment of Lord George Gordon to the Tower: Holcroft, Thomas

Plain case: Bottome, Phyllis

Plain dealer, The: Bickerstaffe, Isaac

Plain Jane: Herbert, *Sir* A.P.

Plain language from truthful James: Harte, Bret

Plain living: †Boldrewood, Rolf

Plain man and his wife, The: Bennett, Arnold

Plain man's guide to wine: Postgate, Raymond

Plain murder: Forester, C.S.

Plain or ringlets?: Surtees, R.S.

Plain sermons by contributors to the Tracts for the Times: Newman, J.H.

Plain song, 1914–1916: Phillpotts, Eden

Plain speaker, The: Hazlitt, William

Plain speaking: Craik, *Mrs.* Dinah

Plain tales from the hills: Kipling, Rudyard

Plain talks on familiar subjects: Holland, J.G.

Plain truth: Franklin, Benjamin

Plain truth of the Stratford-on-Avon controversy, The: †Corelli, Marie

Plain-dealer, The: Hill, Aaron

Plain-dealer, The: Wycherley, William

Plains of cement, The: Hamilton, Patrick

Plan for Britain, A: Cole, G.D.H.

Plan for democratic Britain, A: Cole, G.D.H.

Plan for settling the Western colonies: Franklin, Benjamin

Plan for the conduct of female education in boarding schools, A: Darwin, Erasmus

Plan of a dictionary of the English language, The: Johnson, Samuel

Plan of London County, The: Mumford, Lewis

Planchette: Sargent, Epes

Planet and glow-worm: Sitwell, Edith

Planetoid 127—and—the Sweizer pump: Wallace, Edgar

Planetomachia: Greene, Robert

Planning of the Elizabethan country house, The: Pevsner, Nikolaus

Plant and phantom: Macneice, Louis

Plant hunters, The: Reid, T.M.

Plantation pageants: Harris, Joel Chandler

Planter of the Old South, The: Johnston, R.M.

Planters manual, The: Cotton, Charles

Plaque with laurel: †Eldershaw, M. Barnard

Platkops children: Smith, Pauline

Platitudes in the making: Jackson, Holbrook

Plato and Christianity: Temple, William

Plato and his dialogues: Dickinson, G.L.

Plato and modern education: Livingstone, *Sir* Richard

Plato, and the other companions of Socrates: Grote, George

Plato and Platonism: Pater, Walter

Platonic friendship, A: Cambridge, Ada

Platonic tradition, The: Inge, W.R.

Platonica: More, Henry

Platonism: More, P.E.

Platonism and the spiritual life: Santayana, George

Platonism in the Italian poets: Santayana, George

Plato's mistake: Church, Richard

Plattner story, The: Wells, H.G.

Platypus, The: (†Donald Barr), Barrett, C.L.

Play: Robertson, T.W.

Play and profit in my garden: Roe, E.P.

Play hours with Pegasus: Herbert, *Sir* A.P.

Play in poetry: Untermeyer, Louis

Play of Everyman, The: Sterling, George

Play of love, a new and mery enterlude concerning pleasure and payne in love, A: Heywood, John

Play of "Saint George", The: Hardy, Thomas

Play of St. George, A: Masefield, John

Play of the wether, The: Heywood, John

Play parade: Coward, Noel

Play toward: a note on play production, A: Marsh, Ngaio Edith

Play with fire: Percy, Edward

Play-actress, The: Crockett, S.R.

Playback: Chandler, Raymond

Playbill: Rattigan, Terence

Playboy of the western world, The: Synge, J.M.

Playe called the foure P.P.: Heywood, John

Player king, The: Hassall, Christopher

Player Queen, The: Yates, W.B.

Playfair Cardus, The: Cardus, Neville

Playfellow, The: Hall, Anna Maria

Playfellow, The: Martineau, Harriet

Playgoers: Pinero, *Sir* A.W.

Playgoing: Agate, J.E.

Playground of Europe, The: Stephen, *Sir* Leslie

Playhouse and the play, The: Mackaye, Percy

Playing at peace: Wells, H.G.

Playing the game: Sladen, D.B.W.

Playing the mischief: De Forest, J.W.

Playing with fire: Barr, A.E.H.

Playing with fire: Grant, James

Playing with fire: Waugh, Alec

Playlets of the war: Shaw, G.B.

Play-making: a manual of craftsmanship: Archer, William

Plays, acting and music: Symons, Arthur

Plays and poems of William Shakespeare, The: Malone, Edmund

Plays and Puritans: Kingsley, Charles

Plays for earth and air: Dunsany, E.J.

Plays for my children: Carroll, P.V.

Plays for plain people: †Bridie, James

Plays for the classroom: Gow, Ronald

Plays for the meadow and the lawn: Brighouse, Harold

Plays for youth groups: Peach, Lawrence du Garde

Plays of gods and men: Dunsany, E.J.

Plays of near and far: Dunsany, E.J.

Plays of protest: Sinclair, Upton

Plays of the family Goodman: Peach, L. du Garde

Plays of the natural and the supernatural: Dreiser, Theodore

Plays of William Shakespeare, with the corrections and illustrations of various commentators, The: Johnson, Samuel

Plays out of time: Rubenstein, Harold F.

Plays: pleasant and unpleasant: Shaw, G.B.

Plays the thing, The: Wodehouse, P.G.

Playthings and parodies: Pain, B.E.O.

Playtime & company: Lucas, E.V.

Playtime in Russia: Griffith, H.F.

Play-time of the poor: Ward, M.A.

Playwright at work: Van Druten, John

Playwrights on playmaking: Matthews, J.B.

Plea for a wider use of artists and craftsmen, A: Rothenstein, *Sir* William

Plea for civilized Epirus, A: Reeves, W.P.

Plea for literature, A: Dawson, S.E.

Plea for prerogative, A: Taylor, John

Plea for pure democracy, A: Spence, C.H.

Plea for the abolition of tests in the University of Oxford, A: Smith, Goldwin

Plea for the constitution, A: Bentham, Jeremy

Plea for the Constitution of the U.S. of America wounded in the house of its guardians: Bancroft, George

Plea for the extension of University education in Canada: Dawson, *Sir* J.W.

Plea for the liberty of interpreting, A: Abercrombie, Lascelles

Plea for the poor, A: Woolman, John

Plea for the ragged schools of London, A: Browning, Elizabeth Barrett

Plea for the west, A: Beecher, Lyman

Plea defense of Richard Loeb and Nathan Leopold, on trial for murder: Darrow, C.S.

Plea of the Midsummer fairies, The: Hood, Thomas

Pleasance, The: MacMechan, A.M.

Pleasant comedie, called Summers last will and testament, A: Nash, Thomas

Pleasant comedie of Old Fortunatus, The: Dekker, Thomas

Pleasant comedie of Patient Grissill, The: Chettle, Henry

Pleasant comedy, called A mayden-head well lost, A: Heywood, Thomas

Pleasant conceited comedie, A: Heywood, Thomas

Pleasant conceited comedie called, Loves Labors lost, A: Shakespeare, William

Pleasant conceited historie, called The taming of a shrew, A: Shakespeare, William

Pleasant history of John Winchcomb, The: Deloney, Thomas

Pleasant husband, The: †Bowen, Marjorie

Pleasant Jim: †Brand, Max

Pleasant memories of pleasant lands: Sigourney, L.H.

Pleasant places: Hannay, J.O.

Pleasant Sally: Bromfield, Louis

Pleasant ways of St. Médard, The: King, G.E.

Pleasante conceited narrative of Panurge's fantastic ally, The: Lindsay, Jack

Please excuse me, Comrade: Collier, John

Please help Emily: Harwood, H.M.

Pleased to meet you: Morley, C.D.

Pleasure: Waugh, Alec

Pleasure of being oneself, The: Joad, C.E.M.

Pleasure of ruins: Macaulay, *Dame* Rose

Pleasure trove: Lucas, E.V.

Pleasures and speculations: De la Mare, Walter

Pleasures of a nonconformist, The: Lin Yu-T'ang

Pleasures of England, The: Ruskin, John

Pleasures of friendship, The: McHenry, James

Pleasures of hope, The: Campbell, Thomas

Pleasures of ignorance, The: Lynd, Robert

Pleasures of imagination, The: Akenside, Mark

Pleasures of literature, The: Powys, John Cowper

Pleasures of melancholy, The: Warton, Thomas

Pleasures of memory, The: Rogers, Samuel

Pleasures of philosophy, The: Durant, W.J.

Pleasures of poetry, The: Sitwell, Edith

Pleasures of princes, The (Book II of The English husbandman): Markham, Gervase

Pleasures of reading, The: Jackson, Holbrook

Plebeian, The: Steele, *Sir* Richard

Pledge of peace, The: Murry, John Middleton

Plexippus: Graves, Richard

Plexus: Miller, Henry

Plonk's party: †Armstrong, Anthony and Raff

Plot and no plot, A: Dennis, John

Plot and passion: Taylor, Tom

Plot in private life, A: Collins, Wilkie

Plot twenty-one: Ackland, Rodney

Plots, parables and fables: Turner, W.J.R.

Plough, The: Jacob, Naomi

Plough and the stars, The: O'Casey, Sean

Ploughman, The: White, Patrick

Ploughman of the moon: Service, Robert

Ploughman's progress, The: Kaye-Smith, Shiela

Ploughshare and pruning-hook: Housman, Laurence

Plowmen's clocks: Uttley, Alison

Pluck: †King, Basil

Pluck and luck: Benchley, Robert

Pluck the flower: Brophy, John

Plum pie: Wodehouse, P.G.

Plum pudding of divers ingredients: Morley, C.D.

Plum tree, The: Chase, M.E.

Plum tree, The: Phillips, D.G.

Plumb pudding, A: Carey, Mathew

Plumed serpent, The: Lawrence, D.H.

Plumed voice, The: Mann, Leonard

Plunge, The: Temple, Joan

Pluralistic universe, A: James, William

Plu-ri-bus-tah, a song that's-by-no-author: Thompsons, Mortimer N.

Plus fours: Vachell, H.A.

Plus ultra: Glanvill, Joseph

Plutocrat, The: Tarkington, Booth

Plymouth Rock and Ellis Island: Adamic, Louis

Pnin: Nabokov, Vladimir

Poached eggs and pearls: Jennings, Gertrude

Poacher, The: Bates, H.E.

Poacher's wife, The: Phillpotts, Eden

Pocahontas: Curtis, G.W.P.

Pocahontas: Eggleston, Edward

Pocahontas: Sigourney, L.H.

Pocahontas, or, the nonpareill of Virginia: Garnett, David

Pocket full of rye, A: Christie, Agatha

Pocket history of the second world war, The: Commager, H.S.

Pocket library of English literature, The: Saintsbury, G.E.B.

Pocket Oxford Dictionary of current English: Fowler, H.W.

Pocket-rifle, The: Trowbridge, J.T.

Podesta's daughter, The: Boker, George Henry

Poe as a literary critic: Cooke, John Esten

Poem address'd to the Quidnunc's at St. James's coffee house, A: Gay, John

Poem dedicated to the memory of ... Urian Oakes, A: Mather, Cotton

Poem dedicated to the memory of William Law, A: Blair, Robert

Poem delivered before the Phi beta kappa, A: Clarke, J.F.

Poem delivered before the Porter Rhetorical Society, A: Dana, R.H. *senior*

Poem delivered before the Society of United Brothers at Brown University: Willis, N.P.

Poem humbly addrest to the right honourable the earl of Portland on his Lordships return from his embassy in France, A: Oldmixon, John

Poem humbly dedicated to Catherine queen dowager, A: Behn, *Mrs.* Afra

Poem in imitation of Donaides, A: Mallet, David

Poem in praise of the Horn-book, A: Tickell, Thomas

Poem occasioned by His Majesty's voyage to Holland, A: Tate, Nahum

Poem, occasioned by the late discontents, A: Tate, Nahum

Poem of poems, The: Markham, Gervase

Poem on divine revelation, A: Brackenridge, H.H.

Poem on St. James's park, A: Waller, Edmund

Poem on the arrival of Queen Mary, A: Rymer, Thomas

Poem on the bill lately passed for regulating the slave trade, A: Williams, H.M.

Poem on the coronation of King James II and his Royal Consort Queen Mary, A: Phillips, John

Poem on the death of Frederick Prince of Wales, A: Falconer, William

Poem on the death of Mr. John Philips, A: Smith, Edmund

Poem, on the death of our late sovereign Lady Queen Mary, A: Cibber, Colley

Poem on the Last Day, A: Young, Edward

Poem on the late Civil War, A: Cowley, Abraham

Poem on the late promotion of several eminent persons, A: Tate, Nahum

Poem on the memorable fall of Chloe's P–s Pot, A: Philips, John

Poem, on the rising glory of America, A: Brackenridge, H.H.

Poem on the same subject, A: Howe, Joseph

Poem on the South Sea, A: Ramsay, Allan

Poem: sacred to the memory of George Washington, A: Alsop, Richard

Poem sacred to the Memory of Queen Anne, A: Tate, Nahum

Poem sacred to the memory of Sir Isaac Newton, A: Thomson, James

Poem, to His Excellency the Lord Privy-Seal, on the prospect of peace, A: Tickell, Thomas

Poem to Sir Roger L'Estrange, A: Behn, *Mrs.* Afra

Poem to the memory of John Cunningham: Fergusson, Robert

Poem to the memory of Lady Miller: Seward, Anna

Poem to the memory of Mr. Congreve, A: Thomson, James

Poem to the memory of the famous Archibald Pitcairn, A: Ramsay, Allan

Poem to the memory of the Right Honourable the Lord Talbot, the late Chancellor of Great Britain, A: Thomson, James

Poem upon tea, A: Motteux, P.A.

Poem upon the death of Queen Anne and the accession of King George, A: Dennis, John

Poem upon the late glorious successes of her Majesty's arms, A: Rowe, Nicholas

Poem-leaflets in remembrance of Marion Morse Mackaye: Mackaye, Percy

Poems (re-issued as Poems, Songs and Sonnets): Coleridge, Hartley

Poems (Poèmes). (Poems in English and French): Douglas, *Lord* Alfred

Poems (1904–1917): Gibson, Wilfred

Poems (chiefly in the Scottish dialect): McLachlan, Alexander

Poems, The: Jonson, Ben

Poems: a joking word: Riding, Laura

Poems about birds: Masisngham, Harold

Poems about God: Ransom, J.C.

Poems and Baudelaire flowers: Squire, *Sir* J.C.

Poems and fables: Trevelyan, R.C.

Poems and fancy: Hale, E.E.

Poems and inscriptions: Gilder, R.W.

Poems and lyrics of the joy of earth: Meredith, George

Poems and plays: Gogarty, O. St. John

Poems and portraits: Marquis, Don

Poems and recollections of the past: Hill, Fidelia

Poems and satires: Graves, Robert

Poems and songs: Kendall, Henry

Poems and translations in verse: Fuller, Thomas

Poems at white nights: Bottomley, Gordon

Poems before Congress: Browning, Elizabeth Barrett

Poems by Cheviot Tichburn: Ainsworth, Harrison

Poems, by Croaker, Croaker & Co., and Croaker, Jun.: Halleck, Fitz-Greene

Poems by Melanter: Blackmore, *Sir* R.D.

Poems by the way: Morris, William

Poems by two brothers: Tennyson, Frederick

Poems, chiefly in the Scottish dialect: Burns, Robert

Poems chiefly pastoral: Cunningham, John

Poems, consisting of odes and elegies: Dyer, George

Poems: descriptive, dramatic, legendary and contemplative: Simms, W.G.

Poems descriptive of rural life and scenery: Clare, John

Poems drunk and drowsy: Golding, Louis

Poems for a son with wings: Coffin, Robert

Poems for children: De la Mare, Walter

Poems for children: Hassall, Christopher

Poems for men: Runyon, Damon

Poems for our children: Hale, S.J.B.

Poems for people: Livesay, Dorothy

Poems for pictures: Ford, Ford Madox

Poems for speaking: Church, Richard

Poems for the sea: Sigourney, L.H.

Poems for young ladies: Goldsmith, Oliver

Poems from Bengali: Ghose, Sri Aurobindo

Poems from Eastern sources: Trench, R.C.

Poems from the Arabic and Persian: Landor, W.S.

Poems from the Chinese: Waley, Arthur

Poems from the Divan of Hafiz: Bell, Gertrude

Poems from the German: Garnett, Richard

Poems from the Greek anthology: Reid, Forrest

Poems from the mask: Mann, Leonard

Poems from the Port Hills: Baughan, B.E.

Poems from the Russian: Cornford, Frances

Poems grave and gay: Arnold, George

Poems grave and gay: Tabb, J.B.

Poems here at home: Riley, J.W.

Poems in burlesque: Dennis, John

Poems in English, Scotch, and Latin: Grahame, James

Poems in one volume: Squire, Sir J.C.

Poems in pencil: Bullett, Gerald

Poems in praise: Engle, Paul

Poems in Scots: Soutar, William

Poems in sunshine and firelight: Piatt, J.J.

Poems in the porch: Betjeman, John

Poems in wartime, 1940: Day-Lewis, C.

Poems lyrick and pastorall: odes, eglogs, The man in the Moone: Drayton, Michael

Poems; medley and Palestina: De Forest, J.W.

Poems, moral, elegant and pathetic and original sonnets: Williams, H.M.

Poems, narrative and lyrical: Motherwell, William

Poems new and old: Freeman, John

Poems new and old: Mottram, R.H.

Poems, odes, songs: Halloran, Henry

Poems, odes, songs, and other metrical effusions, The: Woodworth, Samuel

Poems of a Jew: Shapiro, Karl

Poems of adoration: †Field, Michael

Poems of conformity: Williams, Charles

Poems of dedication: Spender, Stephen

Poems of early and after years: Willis, N.P.

Poems of five decades: Eastman, Max

Poems of home and country: Smith, S.F.

Poems of home and travel: Taylor, Bayard

Poems of house and home: Piatt, J.J.

Poems of humor and protest: Patchen, Kenneth

Poems of impudence: Knox, E.V.

Poems of John Donne, The: Grierson, Sir H.J.C.

Poems of love: Ayres, Philip

Poems of love: Wilcox, Ella Wheeler

Poems of love and earth: Drinkwater, John

Poems of love and war: †Cheyney, Peter

Poems of many years: Milnes, R.M.

Poems of men and hours: Drinkwater, John

Poems of nature: Thoreau, H.D.

Poems of Ossian, The: Macpherson, James

Poems of our time: Church, Richard

Poems of passion: Wilcox, Ella Wheeler

Poems of passion: Willis, N.P.

Poems of people: Masters, E.L.

Poems of pleasure: Wilcox, Ella Wheeler

Poems of power: Wilcox, Ella Wheeler

Peoms of problems: Wilcox, Ella Wheeler

Poems of progress: Wilcox, Ella Wheeler

Poems of reflection: Wilcox, Ella Wheeler

Poems of religion and society: Adams, John Quincy

Poems of rural life in Common English: Barnes, William

Poems of rural life in the Dorset dialect: Barnes, William

Poems of rural life in the Dorset dialect. Third collection: Barnes, William

Poems of sentiment: Wilcox, Ella Wheeler

Poems of ten years, 1924–34: Wellesley, D.V.

Poems of the day and year: Tennyson, Frederick

Poems of the Midwest: Sandburg, Carl

Poems of the old days and the new: Ingelow, Jean

Poems of the Orient: Taylor, Bayard

Poems of the past and present: Hall, M.R.

Poems of the war: Boker, George Henry

Poems of the war and after: Brittain, Vera

Poems of thirty years: Bottomley, Gordon

Poems of Thomas Lord Vaux; Edward Earl of Oxford; Robert Earl of Essex; and Walter Earl of Essex, The: Oxford, Edward De Vere

Poems of two friends: Howells, W.D.

Poems of two friends: Piatt, J.J.

Poems of two wars: Squire, *Sir* J.C.

Poems of two years: Hassall, Christopher

Poems of various subjects: religious and moral: Wheatley, Phillis

Poems of West and East: Sackville-West, Victoria

Poems on interesting events in the reign of Edward III: Ritson, Joseph

Poems on most of the festivals of the Church: Boyle, Roger

Poems on several occasions: Cotton, Charles

Poems on several occasions: Haywood, *Mrs.* Eliza

Poems on several occasions: Mallet, David

Poems on several occasions, by a lady: Bury, *Lady* C.S.M.

Poems on several occasions, written in imitation of the manner of Anacreon: Oldmixon, John

Poems on slavery: Longfellow, H.W.

Poems on the abolition of the slave trade: Montgomery, James

Poems on the loss of St. Mary's Church, Cardiff: Montgomery, James

Poems on the war: Meynell, Alice

Poems on various subjects: Grant, Anne

Poems on various subjects. With introductory remarks on the present state of science and literature in France: Williams, H.M.

Poems, partly of rural life: Barnes, William

Poems: patriotic, religious, miscellaneous: Ryan, A.J.

Poems, religious and elegiac: Sigourney, L.H.

Poems: sacred and secular: Lang, J.D.

Poems: sacred, passionate, and humorous, The: Willis, N.P.

Poems, Scots and English: Buchan, John

Poems to paintings: †McDiarmid, Hugh

Poems to Vera: Sterling, George

Poems, with a memoir by his brother Derwent Coleridge: Coleridge, Hartley

Poems with the muses lookingglasse: and Amyntas: Randolph, Thomas

Poems with the tenth satyre of Juvenal Englished: Vaughan, Henry

Poems written chiefly at Bremhill: Bowles, W.L.

Poems written in discouragement: Yeats, W.B.

Poems written in the leisure hours of a journeyman mason: Miller, Hugh

Poem-scapes: Patchen, Kenneth

Poenamo: Campbell, *Sir* J.L.

Poesia religio: Mackaye, Percy

Poet, The: Nicholson, Meredith

Poet: a lying word: Riding, Laura

Poet and communication, The: Drinkwater, John

Poet and his age, The: Aldington, Richard

Poet and his master, The: Gilder, R.W.

Poet and nature, The: Cawein, Madison

Poet and the landscape, The: Young, A.J.

Poet and the lunatics, The: Chesterton, G.K.

Poet and tradition, The: Drinkwater, John

Poet as citizen, The:(†Q), Quiller-Couch, *Sir* Arthur

Poet at the breakfast-table, The: Holmes, Oliver Wendell

Poet Li Po, A.D. 701–762, The: Waley, Arthur

Poet, the fool and the faeries, The: Cawein, Madison

Poet to poet: Noguchi, Yone

Poetaster or the arraignment: Jonson, Ben

Poetic culture: Marston, J.W.

Poetic diction: Barfield, Owen

Poetic image, The: Day-Lewis, C.

Poetic mirror, The: Hogg, James

Poetic studies: Ward, E.S.

Poetic unreason: Graves, Robert

Poetical address to the Right Honourable Edmund Burke, A: Bowles, William Lisle

Poetical and congratulatory epistle to James Boswell Esq., A: †Pindar, Peter

Poetical decameron, The: Collier, John Payne

Poetical entertainer, The: Ward, Edward

Poetical epistle to a falling minister, A: †Pindar, Peter

Poetical epistle to Benjamin Count Rumford, A: †Pindar, Peter

Poetical epistle to Samuel Johnson, A: Murphy, Arthur

Poetical epistle to Sir Joshua Reynolds, Knt.: Combe, William

Poetical essay in manner of elegy on the lamented death of his late Majesty, A: Cunningham, John

Poetical essay on the existing state of things, A: Shelley, P.B.

Poetical meditations: Wolcott, Roger

Poetical quotations from Chaucer to Tennyson: Allibone, S.A.

Poetical reflections on a late poem, entituled Absalom and Achitophel: Buckingham, G.V.

Poetical remains: Hemans, *Mrs.* Felicia

Poetical serious and possibly impertinent epistle to the Pope, A: †Pindar, Peter

Poetical sketches: Blake, William

Poetical sketches of Scarborough: Combe, William

Poetical supplicating modest and affecting epistle to those literary colossuses the reviewers, A: †Pindar, Peter

Poetical tales by Sir Gregory Gander, Knt.: Ellis, George

Poetical translation of the fables of Phaedrus, A: Smart, Christopher

Poetical vagaries: Colman, George, *the younger*

Poetical varieties: Jordan, Thomas

Poetical works: Harte, Bret

Poetical works of the late Thomas Little, Esq., The: Moore, Thomas

Poetical works, with "A Cypresse Grove", The: Drummond of Hawthornden, William

Poeticall blossomes: Cowley, Abraham

Poetick sermon: To R—Y–Esq., The: Ramsay, Allan

Poetics of Aristotle, The: Pye, H.J.

Poetics, or a series of poems and disquisitions on poetry: Dyer, George

Poetry (a lecture given at the Queen's Hall, London): Masefield, John

Poetry and anarchism: Read, *Sir* Herbert

Poetry and Canada: Gustafson, Ralph

Poetry and career of Li Po, A.D. 701–762, The: Waley, Arthur

Poetry and contemporary speech: Abercrombie, Lascelles

Poetry and criticism: Sitwell, Edith

Poetry and dogma: Drinkwater, John

Poetry and drama (Theodore Spencer memorial lecture): Eliot, T.S.

Poetry and experience: MacLeish, Archibald

Poetry and Ireland: Johnson, Lionel Pigot

Poetry and Ireland: Yeats, W.B.

Poetry and modern life: Binyon, Laurence

Poetry and opinion: MacLeish, Archibald

Poetry and philosophy of George Meredith, The: Trevelyan, G.M.

Poetry and poets: Lowell, Amy

Poetry and politics: Wedgwood, C.V.

Poetry and prose of Donne: Hayward, J.D.

Poetry and religion: Spingarn, J.E.

Poetry and Renascence of wonder: Watts-Dunton, W.T.

Poetry and science: Blunden, Edmund

Poetry and the modern world: Daiches, David

Poetry and time: Newbolt, *Sir* Henry

Poetry as an universal nature: Marston, J.W.

Poetry as knowledge: Van Doren, Mark

Poetry at present: Williams, Charles

Poetry by the author of Gebir: Landor, W.S.

Poetry direct and oblique: Tullyard, E.M.W.

Poetry for children, entirely original: Lamb, Charles

Poetry for seamen: Sigourney, L.H.

Poetry for the people: Milnes, R.M.

Poetry for you: Day-Lewis, C.

Poetry handbook: Deutsch, Babette

Poetry harbinger: Fairburn, A.R.D.

Poetry in our time: Deutsch, Babette

Poetry in prose: De la Mare, Walter

Poetry, its appreciation and enjoyment: Untermeyer, Louis

Poetry, its music and meaning: Abercrombie, Lascelles

Poetry like the hawthorn: †McDiarmid, Hugh

Poetry militant: O'Dowd, B.P.

Poetry of Anna Matilda, The: Cowley, *Mrs*. Hannah

Poetry of architecture, The: Ruskin, John

Poetry of Byron: Nicolson, *Hon. Sir* Harold

Poetry of Dick Harris: Lawlor, P.A.

Poetry of exiles, A: Sladen, D.B.W.

Poetry of flowers and the flowers of poetry, The: Osgood, F.S.

Poetry of Iceland, The: Craigie, *Sir* William Alexander

Poetry of J.V.Cunningham, The: Winters, Yvor

Poetry of John Dryden, The: Van Doren, Mark

Poetry of life, The: Carman, Bliss

Poetry of nonsense, The: Cammaerts, Emile

Poetry of Robert Bridges, The: Smith, A.J.M.

Poetry of Robert Browning, The: Brooke, Stopford

Poetry of Sir Thomas Wyatt, The: Tillyard, E.M.W.

Poetry of the English speaking world: Aldington, Richard

Poetry of the Magyars: Bowring, *Sir* John

Poetry of the period, The: Austin, Alfred

Poetry of W.B. Yeats, The: Macneice, Louis

Poetry of W.B. Yeats, The: Winters, Yvor

Poetry recital, A: Stephens, James

Poetry: the problem of appreciation: Moll, E.G.

Poets, The: Wellesley, D.V.

Poet's alphabet, A: Davies, W.H.

Poets and poetry of America, The: Griswold, R.W.

Poets and poetry of Munster, The: Mangan, J.C.

Poets and prose writers of New South Wales, The: Barton, George

Poets and pundits: Fausset, Hugh

Poets and story-tellers: Cecil, *Lord* David

Poet's calendar, A: Davies, W.H.

Poet's circuits, The: Colum, Padraic

Poet's complaint of his muse, The: Otway, Thomas

Poets' corner, The: Beerbohm, *Sir* Max

Poet's defence, The: Bronowski, J.

Poet's diary, The: Austin, Alfred

Poet's enchiridion, The: Browning, Elizabeth Barrett

Poets eye, The: Lee, Vernon

Poets, farewell!: Wilson, Edmund

Poet's fate, The: Dyer, George

Poet's harvest home, A: Scott, W.B.

Poet's heart, The: Levy, Benn W.

Poet's home, A: Harpur, Charles

Poet's homes: Stoddard, R.H.

Poets in their pride: Grigson, G.E.H.

Poet's journal, The: Taylor, Bayard

Poet's notebook, A: Sitwell, Edith

Poet's portfolio, A: Montgomery, James

Poets of America: Stedman, E.C.

Poets of Greece, The: Arnold, Edwin

Poets of modern France, The: Lewisohn, Ludwig

Poets of the younger generation: Archer, William

Poet's pilgrimage, The: Collier, John Payne

Poet's pilgrimage, A: Davies, W.H.

Poet's pilgrimage to Waterloo, The: Southey, Robert

Poet's portfolio, A: Story, W.W.

Poet's progress, The: Cresswell, W.D.

Poet's pub: Linklater, Eric

Poet's quest: Mendes, Alfred

Poet's task, The: Day-Lewis, C.

Poet's walk, The: Meynell, Viola

Poet's youth, A: Woods, M.L.

Poganuc people: Stowe, Harriet Beecher

Point counter point: Huxley, Aldous

Point of no return: Marquand, J.P.

Point of Parliament: Herbert, Sir A.P.

Point of view, The: Iyengar, V.V. Srinivasa

Point of view, The: James, Henry

Point of view, The: Lawless, Emily

Point of view, The: Phillpotts, Eden

Point Valaine: Coward, Noel

Pointed roofs: Richardson, D.M.

Points of contact between revelation and natural science: Dawson, Sir J.W.

Points of friction: Repplier, Agnes

Points of honour: Boyd, Thomas

Points of my compass, The: White, E.B.

Points of view: Dickinson, G.L.

Points of view: Glyn, Elinor

Points of view: Repplier, Agnes

Points of view: Sherman, S.P.

Poirot investigates: Christie, Agatha

Poison belt, The: Doyle, Sir Arthur Conan

Poison in jest: Carr, J.D.

Poison in the garden suburb: Cole, G.D.H.

Poison Island: (†Q), Quiller-Couch, Sir Arthur

Poison ivy: †Cheyney, Peter

Poison pen: Llewellyn, Richard

Poison trail, The: †Armstrong, Anthony

Poisoned paradise, The: Service, Robert

Poisoners, The: †Preedy, George

Poland: Campbell, Thomas

Poland, Homer, and other poems: Aytoun, W.E.

Polar regions of the western continent explored, The: Snelling, W.J.

Poldekin: Tarkington, Booth

Polderoy papers, The: Vulliamy, C.E.

Pole star: White, S.E.

Police!!!: Chambers, R.W.

Police at the funeral: Allingham, Margery

Policeman's serenade: Herbert, Sir A.P.

Policewoman's love-hungry daughter, The: Hecht, Ben

Policy and passion: Praed, Mrs. C.

Policy of the Entente, 1904–1914: Russell, Bertrand

Polish bandit, The: Lathom, Francis

Polish tales: Gore, Catherine

Polite essays: Pound, Ezra

Polite farces for the drawing-room: Bennett, Arnold

Politeuphuia: Bodenham, John

Politian: an unfinished tragedy: Poe, Edgar Allan

Political and official papers: Kennedy, J.P.

Political and social doctrine of communism, The: Dutt, R.P.

Political and social growth of the United States, 1852–1933: Schlesinger, A.M.

Political and social history of U.S. 1829–1925: Schlesinger, A.M.

Political arithmetic: Young, Arthur

Political career of Richard Brinsley Sheridan: Sadleir, Michael

Political catechism, dedicated without permission to His Most Serene Highness Omar Bashan Dey, A: Hone, William

Political character of the working classes, The: Hutton, R.H.

Political characters of Shakespeare: Palmer, J.L.

Political conditions of allied success, The: Angell, Sir Norman

Political destiny of Canada, The: Smith, Goldwin

Political discourses: Hume, David

Political economy for the people: Tucker, George

Political economy of art, The: Ruskin, John

Political essays: Lowell, J.R.

Political essays, with sketches of public characters: Hazlitt, William

Political fables: Mather, Cotton

Political greenhouse, The: Connecticut Wits

Political greenhouse for the year 1798, The: Alsop, Richard

Political history of England, A: Fisher, H.A.L.

Political history of England: Pollard, A.F.

Political history of England, 1660–1702: Lodge, Sir Richard

Political history of the Devil, The: Defoe, Daniel

Political house that Jack built, The: Hone, William

Political ideals: Russell, Bertrand

Political institutions: Spencer, Herbert

Political litany, The: Hone, William

Political madhouse in America and nearer home, The: Shaw, G.B.

Political ode, A: Byron, George Gordon *Lord*

Political patterns in today's world: Brogan, *Sir* Denis

Political philosophy: Brougham, Henry

Political romance addressed to —, Esq. of York, A: Sterne, Laurence

Political scene, The: Lippmann, Walter

Political situation in Cape Colony, The: Schreiner, O.E.A.

Political thought from Locke to Bentham: Laski, Harold

Political unions: Fisher, H.A.L.

Political value of history, The: Lecky, W.E.

Politicians of today: Reid, *Sir* Thomas Wemyss

Politics and education: Harrison, Frederic

Politics and law in the United States: Brogan, *Sir* Denis

Politics and life: Drinkwater, John

Politics of the unpolitical, The: Read, *Sir* Herbert

Politics: the citizen's business: White, W.A.

Politician, The: Shirley, James

Poll degree from the third point of view, The: Stephen, *Sir* Leslie

Pollio: Mickle, William Julius

Polly: Gay, John

Polly Fulton: Marquand, J.P.

Polly Honeycombe: Colman, George, *the elder*

Polly Oliver: Coppard, A.E.

Polly Oliver's problem: Wiggin, K.D.

Pollyanna: Porter, E.H.

Pollyanna grows up: Porter, E.H.

Polonius: Fitzgerald, Edward

Poltergeists: Sitwell, Sacheverell

Polyhymnia describing the honourable triumph at tylt before her Majestie: Peele, George

Polymetis: Spence, Joseph

Polynesian voyagers: Best, Elsdon

Polyolbion: Drayton, Michael

Polyphemus: Austin, Alfred

Polyphemus: Trevelyan, R.C.

Pomander of verse, A: Nesbit, E.

Pomegranate, The: Roberts, W. Adolphe

Pomegranates: Campbell, Roy

Pomeroy Abbey: Wood, Ellen

Pomes Penyeach: Joyce, James

Pomfret Towers: Thirkell, Angela

Pommy Cow, The: Campion, Sarah

Pomona's travels: Stockton, F.R.

Pomp and circumstance: Coward, Noel

Pomp and circumstance: Hoffe, Monckton

Pomp of the Lavilettes, The: Parker, *Sir* H.G.

Pompeii: Hawker, R.S.

Pompeii: Macaulay, T.B. *Baron*

Pompey: †Orinda

Pompey's head: Basso, Hamilton

Pomps of Satan, The: Saltus, E.E.

Pongo and the bull: Belloc, Hilaire

Pongo papers and the Duke of Berwick, The: Douglas, *Lord* Alfred

Ponkapog papers: Aldrich, Thomas Bailey

Ponson case, The: Crofts, F.W.

Ponteach: Rogers, Robert

Pontiac and Bushy Run: Kirby, William

Pony tracks: Remington, Frederic

Poodle of Monsieur Gaillard, The: Janvier, T.A.

Poog and the caboose man: Mackaye, Percy

Poog's pasture: Mackaye, Percy

Pool in the desert, The: Duncan, S.J.

Pool of memory, The: Oppenheim, E. Phillips

Pool of Vishnu, The: Myers, L.H.

Pool of wisdom, The: Krishnamurti, Jiddu

Pools pilot: Herbert, *Sir* A.P.

Poo-poo and the dragons: Forester, C.S.

Poor Aubrey: Kelly, G.E.

Poor boys who became great: Smith, S.F.

Poor Caroline: Holtby, Winifred

Poor count's Christmas, The: Stockton, F.R.

Poor fellow: Riddell, *Mrs.* J.H.

Poor fool: Caldwell, Erskine Preston

Poor gentleman, The: Colman, George, *the younger*

Poor gentleman, A: Oliphant, Margaret

Poor gentlemen, The: (†Ian Hay), Beith, *Sir* John Hay

Poor incumbent, The: Gatty, *Mrs.* Margaret

Poor Jack: Cabell, James Branch

Poor Jack: Marryatt, Frederick

Poor John Fitch: Boyd, Thomas

Poor Judas Arts: Bagnold, Enid

Poor laws and pauper management: Bentham, Jeremy

Poor laws and paupers illustrated: Martineau, Harriet

Poor little Mookey: Hoffe, Monckton

Poor man, The: Benson, Stella

Poor man and his parish church, The: Hawker, R.S.

Poor man's tapestry, The: †Onions, Oliver

Poor men's music: Sitwell, Edith

Poor Miss Finch: Collins, Wilkie

Poor old competition: Chase, Stuart

Poor old Haymarket: Colman, George *the younger*

Poor parson, The: †Rudd, Steele

Poor people's Christmas: Noel, R.B.W.

Poor poems and rotten rhymes: Herbert, *Sir* A.P.

Poor poet and the beautiful lady, The: Mickle, A.D.

Poor Polly: Bridges, Robert

Poor relations: Mackenzie, *Sir* Compton

Poor relation's story, The: Dickens, Charles

Poor rich man, The: Sedgwick, C.M.

Poor Richard: Mackenzie, William

Poor Richard's almanack: Franklin, Benjamin

Poor scholar, The: Carleton, William

Poor scholar; a tale of progress, A: Allen, Charles R.

Poor shepherd, The: Gay, John

Poor Sir Edward: Hannay, J.O.

Poor sisters of Nazareth, The: Meynell, Alice

Poor soldier, The: O'Keeffe, John

Poor straws!: Jacob, Naomi

Poor Tom: Muir, Edwin

Poor Vulcan: Dibdin, Charles

Poor white: Anderson, Sherwood

Poor wise man, A: Rinehart, Mary Roberts

Poor young people: Sitwell, Edith, Osbert and Sacheverell

Poore douting Christian, The: Hooker, Thomas

Poorhouse, The: Hyde, Douglas

Popcorn: Skinner, C.O.

Pope: Strachey, Lytton

Pope and his patron, The: Trevelyan, *Sir* G.O.

Pope and human nature: Tillotson, Geoffrey

Pope and the Revolution, The: Newman, J.H.

Pope at home, The: Sladen, D.B.W.

Pope Jacynth: Lee, Vernon

Pope Joan: Reynolds, G.

Pope library, A: Wise, T.J.

Pope's epistles to several persons: Bateson, F.W.

Pope's Rape of the lock: Tillotson, Geoffrey

Popish kingdome, or reigne of Anti-christ, written by Thomas Naogeorgos, The: Googe, Barnabe

Poplar House Academy: Manning, Anne

Popo and Fifina: Hughes, J.L.

Poppies and mandragora: Saltus, E.E.

Popular and practical introduction to law studies, A: Warren, Samuel

Popular book: a history of America's literary taste, The: Hart, James D.

Popular education of France, with notices of that of Holland and Switzerland, The: Arnold, Matthew

Popular history of England, The: Knight, Charles

Popular history of the Mexican people, A: Bancroft, H.H.

Popular history of the United States, A: Bryant, W.C.

Popular member, The: Gore, Catherine

Popular rhymes of Scotland, The: Chambers, Robert

Popular schoolgirl, A: Brazil, Angela

Popular song: Sitwell, Edith

Popular songs of Ireland: Croker, T.C.

Popular tales: Edgeworth, Maria

Popular tales and sketches: Hall, Anna Maria

Popular theatre, The: Nathan, G.J.

Popular tribunals: Bancroft, H.H.

Popular verses: Lawson, Henry.

Porcelain lady, The: Niven, F.J.

Porch, The: Church, Richard

Porcupine's works: Cobbett, William

Porcupine, The: Robinson, E.A.

Porcupine's Gazette: Cobbett, William

Porcupiniad, The: Carey, Mathew

Porfirio Diaz, dictator of Mexico: Beals, Carleton

Porgy (novel and play): Heyward, DuBose

Porgy and Bess: Gershwin, Ira

Porius: Powys, John Cowper

Pornography and obscenity: Lawrence, D.H.

Porphyrion: Binyon, Laurence

Porridge poetry: Lofting, Hugh

Porro unum est necessarium: Sherman, S.P.

Port o' missing men: Wren, P.C.

Port of call: Peattie, D.C.

Port of missing men, The: Nicholson, Meredith

Port of Quebec, its annals, 1535–1900, The: LeMoine, *Sir* J.M.

Port Philip settlement: Bonwick, James

Port Said miscellany, A: McFee, William

Porta pietatis: Heywood, Thomas

Portage, Wisconsin, and other essays: Gale, Zona

Portal to Paradise: Roberts, C.E.M.

Portent, The: Macdonald, George

Porter of Bagdad, The: MacMechan, A.M.

Portfolio of Indian art: Coomaraswamy, A.K.

Portion of labor, The: Freeman, M.W.

Portland illustrated: Neal, John

Portrait, The: Colman, George, *the elder*

Portrait, The: (Hueffer), Ford, Ford Madox

Portrait, The: Swinburne, A.C.

Portrait gallery of the Crystal Palace, The: Phillips, Samuel

Portrait in a mirror: Morgan, Charles

Portrait in the Renaissance, The: Pope-Hennessy, J.W.

Portrait of a dictator, Francisco Solano Lopez: Cunninghame Graham, Robert Bontine

Portrait of a diplomatist: Nicolson, *Hon. Sir* Harold

Portrait of a dog: De la Roche, Mazo

Portrait of a genius but ...: Aldington, Richard

Portrait of a gentleman: Phillpotts, Eden

Portrait of a gentleman in slippers: Milne, A.A.

Portrait of a lady, The: James, Henry

Portrait of a man with red hair: Walpole, *Sir* Hugh

Portrait of a marriage: Buck, Pearl

Portrait of a play boy: Deeping, Warwick

Portrait of a rebel: Aldington, Richard

Portrait of a scholar, The: Chapman, R.W.

Portrait of a scoundrel: Phillpotts, Eden

Portrait of a village: Young, Francis Brett

Portrait of an American: Coffin, Robert

Portrait of an unknown lady: Brophy, John

Portrait of an unknown Victorian: Mottram, R.H.

Portrait of Canterbury: Church, Richard

Portrait of Clare: Young, Francis Brett

Portrait of Edith Wharton: Lubbock, Percy

Portrait of Europe: Madariaga, Salvador de

Portrait of General Gordon Meade, A: Bradford, Gamaliel

Portrait of George Moore in a study of his work, A: Freeman, John

Portrait of Gideon Power: †Bell, Neil

Portrait of Horace: Noyes, Alfred

Portrait of Mabel Dodge at the Villa Curonia: Stein, Gertrude

Portrait of Max: Behrman, S.N.

Portrait of Mr. W.H. Portland, The: Wilde, Oscar

Portrait of Socrates: Livingstone, Sir Richard

Portrait of the Abbot: Church, Richard

Portrait of the artist as a young dog: Thomas, Dylan

Portrait of the artist as a young man, A: Joyce, James

Portrait of Tiero: Akins, Zoë

Portrait-Royal: Tate, Nahum

Portraits: MacCarthy, Sir Desmond

Portraits and jewels of Mary Stuart: Lang, Andrew

Portraits and personalities: Bradford, Gamaliel

Portraits and prayers: Stein, Gertrude

Portraits and sketches: Gosse, Sir Edmund

Portraits and speculations: Ransome, Arthur

Portraits by inference: Wolfe, Humbert

Portraits from memory: Russell, Bertrand

Portraits in miniature: Strachey, Lytton

Portraits of American women: Bradford, Gamaliel

Portraits of people, of England Reclaimed: Sitwell, Sir Osbert

Portraits of places: James, Henry

Portraits of the princes and peoples of India: Eden, Emily

Portraits of women: Bradford, Gamaliel

Portreeve, The: Phillpotts, Eden

Portugal: Campbell, Roy

Portugal and Madeira: Sitwell, Sacheverell

Portuguese voyages to America in the fifteenth century: Morison, S.E.

Posie of gilloflowers, eche differing from other in colour and odeur, yet all sweete, A: Gifford, Humfrey

Position and prospects of the medical student, The: Holmes, Oliver Wendell

Position at noon: Linklater, Eric

Position of Peggy Harper, The: Merrick, Leonard

Positions wherein those circumstances be examined necessarie for the training up of children: Mulcaster, Richard

Positive man, The: O'Keeffe, John

Positive philosophy of August Comte freely translated and condensed, The: Martineau, Harriet

Possession: Bromfield, Louis

Possession: De la Roche, Mazo

Possession: Housman, Laurence

Possession: Millay, E. St. Vincent

Possible worlds: Haldane, J.B.S.

"Posson Jone": Cable, G.W.

Post D: Strachey, John

Post liminium: Johnson, L.P.

Post Office, The: Tagore, Sir R.

Post Office money orders: Dickens, Charles

Post Office went to war, The: (†Ian Hay), Beith, Sir John Hay

Post Victorian poetry: Palmer, H.E.

Postal Orders: Pertwee, Roland

Postal problem, A: †Carroll, Lewis

Postbag diversions: Lucas, E.V.

Poste with a madde packet of letters, A: Breton, Nicholas

Posthumous fragments of Margaret Nicholson: Shelley, P.B.

Posthumous papers of the Pickwick Club, The: Dickens, Charles

Posthumous works of the author of a vindication of the rights of women: Godwin, William

Postman always rings twice, The: Cain, James

Postman's horn: Bryant, Sir Arthur

Postmaster general, The: Belloc, Hilaire

Postmaster of Market Deighton, The: Oppenheim, E. Phillips

Post-mediaeval preachers: Baring-Gould, Sabine

Post-mortem: Coward, Noel

Post-prandial philosophy: Allen, Grant

Postscript of J.E.H. Macdonald, 1873–1932, A: Pierce, Lorne

Postscripts: †O. Henry

Postscripts: Priestley, J.B.

Postscripts to the royal and noble authors: Walpole, Horace

Postulates of English political economy, The: Bagehot, Walter

Post-war condition of Britain, The: Cole, G.D.H.

Post-war Europe, 1918–1937: Ghose, S.N.

Pot au feu: Pickthall, M.W.

Pot boiler, The: Sinclair, Upton

Pot boils, The: Jameson, Storm

Pot holes: Webster, E.C.

Pot of broth, The: Yeats, W.B.

Pot of earth, The: MacLeish, Archibald

Pot of gold, The: Freeman, Mary

Potable gold: Deutsch, Babette

Potato face: Sandburg, Carl

Potato patch, The: MacMechan, A.M.

Pot-boilers: Bell, Clive

Poteen: Deacon, W.A.

Potent philtre, A: Balestier, C.W.

Pothunters, The: Wodehouse, P.G.

Potiphar papers, The: Curtis, G.W.

Potiphar's wife: Arnold, Edwin

Potted fiction: Bangs, J.K.

Potterism: Macaulay, *Dame* Rose

Potter's field: Green, Paul

Potter's wheel, The: Hannay, J.O.

Potting shed, The: Greene, Graham

Pound wise: Sitwell, *Sir* Osbert

Poverty as an industrial problem: Tawney, R.H.

Powder and patch: Heyer, Georgette

Powder of sympathy, The: Morley, C.D.

Power: Fast, Howard M.

Power: Jacob, Naomi

Power: Russell, Bertrand

Power: Stringer, A.J.A.

Power and the glory, The: Greene, Graham

Power and the glory, The: Parker, *Sir* H.G.

Power in men: Cary, Joyce

Power of blackness: Hawthorne, Poe, Melville, The: Levin, Harry

Power of darkness, The: Anand, M.R.

Power of movement in plants, The: Darwin, Charles

Power of music, The: Hale, S.J.B.

Power of sympathy, The: Brown, W.H.

Power of the dead, The: Williamson, Henry

Power of words: Chase, Stuart

Power to kill, The: Hichens, Robert

Powerful drug, A: Barrie, *Sir* J.M.

Power-house, The: Appel, Benjamin

Powers behind the Prime Ministers, The: Petrie, *Sir* Charles

Powers of light, The: Mitchison, Naomi

Powers of the air, The: Moore, T.S.

Powers of the pen, The: Lloyd, Evan

Powers that be: Nichols, Beverley

Powhalan, a metrical romance in seven cantos: Smith, Seba

Powrring out of the seven vials, The: Cotton, John

Practical commentary ... upon the First Generall of John, A: Cotton, John

Practical criticism: Richards, I.A.

Practical discourse on hymn-singing, A: Bridges, Robert

Practical dowsing: Bell, A.

Practical economics: Cole, G.D.H.

Practical education: Edgeworth, Maria

Practical ethics: Samuel, Herbert *1st Viscount*

Practical ethics: Sidgwick, Henry

Practical mysticism: Underhill, Evelyn

Practical observations upon the education of the people: Brougham, Henry

Practical piety: More, Hannah

Practical plan for assimilating the English and American money, A: Bagehot, Walter

Practical plays for stage and classroom: Peach, Lawrence du Garde

Practical view of the prevailing religious system of professed Christians, A: Wilberforce, William

Practical wisdom of the Bible, The: Strachey, John St. Loe

Practice and theory of Bolshevism, The: Russell, Bertrand

Practice of optimism, The: Keller, Helen

Practised hand, The: Greenwood, Walter

Practyse of prelates, The: Tyndale, William

Praeterita: Ruskin, John

Praeterita: Warren, J.B.L.

Pragmatism: James, William

Prairie, The: Cooper, James Fenimore

Prairie born: Stead, R.J.C.

Prairie child, The: Stringer, A.J.A.

Prairie Christmas, A: Engle, Paul

Prairie folks: Garland, Hamlin

Prairie grove, A: Peattie, D.C.

Prairie mother, The: Stringer, A.J.A.

Prairie scout, The: Webber, C.W.

Prairie song and western story: Garland, Hamlin

Prairie songs: Garland, Hamlin

Prairie stories: Stringer, A.J.A.

Prairie wife, The: Stringer, A.J.A.

Praise and vertue of a jayle, and jaylers, The: Taylor, John

Praise of cleane linnen, The: Taylor, John

Praise of life: Binyon, Laurence

Prancing nigger: Firbank, Ronald

Prangmere Mess: †Armstrong, Anthony

Prater, The: Kelly, Hugh

Prater Violet: Isherwood, Christopher

Pray for the wanderer: O'Brien, Kate

Prayer: a child is born: Benét, Stephen Vincent

Prayer for little things: Farjeon, Eleanor

Prayer for my son, A: Walpole, *Sir* Hugh

Prayer for peace, The: Noyes, Alfred

Prayer for the living: Marshall, Bruce

Prayer of the reed, The: Carman, Bliss

Prayer-meeting, The: Green, Paul

Prayers and meditations: Johnson, Samuel

Prayers written at Vailima: Stevenson, R.L.

Preacher, The: Emerson, R.W.

Preacher of Cedar Mountain, The: Seton-Thompson, E.

Preacher's daughter, The: Barr, A.E.H.

Precaution: Cooper, James Fenimore

Precedence at Harvard college in the seventeenth century: Morison, S.E.

Precept and practice: Moodie, Susanna

Precepts and practice: Hook, T.E.

Precepts of Jesus: Roy, R.R.

Preciosa: Palgrave, F.T.

Precious bane: Webb, Mary

Precious blood, The: Faber, F.W.

Precious porcelain: †Bell, Neil

Precipitations: Scott, Evelyn

Predictions for the year 1708: Swift, Jonathan

Predilections: Moore, M.C.

Preface to a life: Gale, Zona

Preface ... to A midsommer nights dreame: Barker, Harley Granville

Preface to An abridgement of the Book of Common Prayer: Franklin, Benjamin

Preface to "Bartlett": Morley, C.D.

Preface to Logan's translation of Cicero's Cato Major: Franklin, Benjamin

Preface to logic, A: Cohen, M.R.

Preface ... to Love's labour's lost: Barker, Harley Granville

Preface ... to Macbeth: Barker, Harley Granville

Preface to morals, A: Lippmann, Walter

Preface to Paradise Lost, A: Lewis, C.S.

Preface to peace: Angell, Sir Norman

Preface to Pennsylvania Gazette: Franklin, Benjamin

Preface to politics, A: Lippmann, Walter

Preface to the B—p of S—r—m's introduction to the third volume of the history of the re-

formation of the Church of England, A: Swift, Jonathan

Preface ... to The Merchant of Venice: Barker, Harley Granville

Preface to the past: Cabell, James Branch

Preface to the Speech of Joseph Galloway, Esq.: Franklin, Benjamin

Preface to the tragedie of Cymbeline: Barker, Harley Granville

Preface to the tragedie of Julius Caesar: Barker, Harley Granville

Preface ... to the tragedie of King Lear: Barker, Harley Granville

Prefaces: Marquis, Don

Prefaces and essays: Saintsbury, George

Prefaces, biographical and critical, to the works of the English poets: Johnson, Samuel

Prefaces: lectures on art subjects: Suhrawardy, Shahid

Prefaces to Renaissance literature: Bush, Douglas

Prefaces to Shakespeare: Barker, Harley Granville

Prefect's uncle, A: Wodehouse, P.G.

Preferences: Macartney, Frederick

Preferment: Gore, Catherine

Prehistoric burials: Sassoon, Siegfried

Prehistoric Egypt: Petrie, Sir William Flinders

Prehistoric forerunners: Vulliamy, C.E.

Prejudices: Mencken, H.L.

Prelude: Aiken, Conrad

Prelude, A: Lawrence, D.H.

Prelude: Mansfield, Katherine

Prelude: Nichols, Beverley

Prelude, A: Sherman, F.J.

Prelude, The: Wordsworth, William

Prelude to a tragedy: Rubenstein, Harold F.

Prelude to adventure, The: Walpole, Sir Hugh

Prelude to Christopher: Dark, Eleanor

Prelude to death: †Mordaunt, Elinor

Prelude to independence: Schlesinger, A.M.

Prelude to jesting: Mitchell, Mary

Prelude to waking: †Brent of Bin Bin

Prelude to the locked chest by John Masefield: Bottomley, Gordon

Preludes: Meynell, Alice

Preludes and symphonies: Fletcher, John Gould

Preludes for Memnon: Aiken, Conrad

Preludes, 1921–1922: Drinkwater, John Gould

Preludes, sonnets and other verses: Logan, J.D.

Premier and the painter, The: Zangwill, Israel

Preparation to the Psalter, A: Wither, George

Pre-Raphaelite diaries and letters: Rossetti, W.M.

Pre-Raphaelite brotherhood, The: Ford, Ford Madox

Pre-Raphaelitism: Ruskin, John

Prerogative of parliaments, The: Ralegh, Sir Walter

Pre-Roman Britain: Massingham, Harold

Presage of victory: Freeman, John

Presbyterian child, The: Hergesheimer, Joseph

Presbyterian churches, The: Moffat, James

Presbyterians plea of merit, The: Swift, Jonathan

Presence and the power, The: †Bowen, Marjorie

Present age, The: Daiches, David

Present age from 1914, The: Muir, Edwin

Present and future of religion, The: Joad, C.E.M.

Present and the past, The: Compton-Burnett, Ivy

Present condition of Scottish arts and affairs, The: †McDiarmid, Hugh

Present condition of the free colored people of the United States: Clarke, J.F.

Present condition of the Northern States of the American Union, The: Trollope, Anthony

Present for the ladies, A: Tate, Nahum

Present from Margate, A: (†Ian Hay), Beith, *Sir* John Hay

Present from Margate, A: Mason, A.E.W.

Present hour, The: Mackaye, Percy

Present indicative: Coward, Noel

Present laughter: Coward, Noel

Present means and brief delineation of a free commonwealth, The: Milton, John

Present position of history, The: Trevelyan, G.M.

Present state of Europe, The: Phillips, John

Present state of music in France and Italy, The: Burney, *Dr.* Charles

Present state of music in Germany, the Netherlands, etc., The: Burney, *Dr.* Charles

Present state of New England, The: Mather, Cotton

Present state of the law: Brougham, Henry

Present state of wit, in a letter to a friend in the country, The: Gay, John

Present versus past: Traill, H.D.

Present without leave: Cresswell, W.D.

Presentation parlour: O'Brien, Kate

Present-day American stories: Hemingway, Ernest *and other writers*

Presenting Lily Mars: Tarkington, Booth

Presenting Moonshine: Collier, John

Presenting other people's children: Mitchison, Naomi

Presentment of the Grand-Jury of the county of the City of Dublin, The: Swift, Jonathan

Preservative agaynste deth, A: Elyot, *Sir* Thomas

Preserving Mr. Panmure: Pinero, *Sir* A.W.

President, The: Curtis, G.W.

President, The: Lewis, A.H.

Presidential agent, The: Sinclair, Upton

Presidential mission: Sinclair, Upton

Presidents in American history, The: Beard, C.A.

Presidents of America, The: Fiske, John

Press, The: Steed, H.W.

Press: a neglected factor in the history of the twentieth century, The: Innis, H.A.

Press and the organisation of society, The: Angell, *Sir* Norman

Press cuttings: Shaw, G.B.

Press the button: Hichens, Robert

Press the public wants, The: Martin, B.K.

Pressmen and governors: Miller, E.M.

Prester John: Buchan, John

Preston fight, or the insurrection of 1715: Ainsworth, Harrison

Presuppositions of critical history: Bradley, F.H.

Pretender, The: Service, Robert

Pretie and mery new enterlude: called the disobedient child, A: Ingelend, Thomas

Pretty book of pictures for little masters and misses, A: Newbery, John

Pretty druidess, The: Gilbert, *Sir* W.S.

Pretty lady, The: Bennett, Arnold

Pretty lessons in verse for good children: Coleridge, Sara

Pretty Mrs. Gaston: Cooke, J.E.

Pretty Polly: Coward, Noel

Pretty Polly, The: Russell, W.C.

Pretty Polly Pemberton: Burnett, Frances Hodgson

Pretty sinister: †Beeding, Francis

Pretty sister of José, The: Burnett, Frances Hodgson

Pretty story, A: Hopkinson, Francis

Pretty witty Nell: Bax, Clifford

Prevailing winds: Barnes, Margaret

Prevention of destitution, The: Webb, Beatrice and Sidney Webb

Previous convictions: Connolly, Cyril

Previous engagement, A: Howells, W.D.

Pre-war lady: Widdemer, Margaret

Priapus and the pool: Aiken, Conrad

Price I paid, The: Sinclair, Upton

Price is right, The: Weidman, Jerome

Price of blood, The: Pyle, Howard

Price of coal, The: Brighouse, Harold

Price of corn and wages of labour: Owen, Robert

Price of freedom, The: Mitchison, Naomi

Price of leadership, The: Murry, John Middleton

Price of liberty, The: Beals, Carleton

Price of love, The: Bennett, Arnold

Price of money, The: Sutro, Alfred

Price of revolution, The: Brogan, *Sir* Denis

Price of Thomas Scott, The: Baker, Elizabeth

Price she paid, The: Phillips, D.G.

Pride: Wellesley, D.V.

Pride and prejudice: Austen, Jane

Pride and prejudice: Squire, *Sir* J.C.

Pride of body: De Selincourt, Hugh

Pride of Eve, The: Deeping, Warwick

Pride of race in five panels: Farjeon, B.L.

Pride of sonnets, A: Morley, C.D.

Pride of Terrys, A: Steen, Marguerite

Pride's fancy: Raddall, T.H.

Priest dissected, The: Anstey, Christopher

Priest of the Ideal: Graham, Stephen

Priest to the temple, A: Herbert, George

Priestcraft distinguish'd from Christianity: Dennis, John

Priestess, The: Gibbons, Stella

Priestly life, The: Knox, R.A.

Prima Donna, The: Simms, W.G.

Primadonna, The: Crawford, F.Marion

Primavera: Phillips, Stephen

Prime Minister, The: Trollope, Anthony

Prime minister is dead, The: Simpson, H. de G.

Prime Ministers to the book: Pierce, Lorne

Prime of life, The: Brophy, John

Primer for America: Coffin, Robert

Primer for poets, A: Shapiro, Karl

Primer of Burns, A: Craigie, *Sir* W.A.

Primer of classical and English philology, A: Skeat, W.W.

Primer of combat: Boyle, Kate

Primer of economics, A: Chase, Stuart

Primer of English etymology, A: Skeat, W.W.

Primer of French literature, A: Saintsbury, George

Primer of historical French grammar, A: Weekley, Ernest

Primer to novels of George Meredith: Moffat, James

Primes and their neighbours, The: Johnston, R.M.

Primitive Christianity revived: Penn, William

Primitive heritage: Mead, Margaret

Primitive like an orb, A: Stevens, Wallace

Primitive Methodism and the new Catholicism: Pierce, Lorne

Primitive scenes and festivals: Sitwell, Sacheverell

Primitive song: Bowra, *Sir* Maurice

Primitive tradition recognised in Holy Scripture: Keble, John

Primitivism and decadence:Winters, Yvor

Primrose path, The: Nash, Ogden

Primrose path, The: Oliphant, Margaret

Primula: Garnett, Richard

Primula: †Preedy, George

Primulas and pansies: Grant, Robert

Prince, The: Ralegh, *Sir* Walter

Prince Absalom: Freeman, John

Prince Albert: Church, Richard

Prince and Betty, The: Wodehouse, P.G.

Prince and boatswain: Marquand, J.P.

Prince and heretic: †Bowen, Marjorie

Prince and Petronella, The: Brophy, John

Prince and the pauper, The: (†Mark Twain), Clemens, S.L.

Prince and the showgirl, The: Rattigan, Terence

Prince Arthur: Blackmore, *Sir* R.D.

Prince Caspian: Lewis, C.S.

Prince Charles Edward: Lang, Andrew

Prince Charlie: Mackenzie, *Sir* Compton

Prince Charlie and Flora: Gibbon, J.M.

Prince Charlie and his ladies: Mackenzie, *Sir* Compton

Prince China: Jacob, Naomi

Prince Consort, The: Fulford, Roger

Prince Deukalion: Taylor, Bayard

Prince Dorus: Lamb, Charles

Prince Hagen (novel and play): Sinclair, Upton

Prince Hempseed: †Hudson, Stephen

Prince Henries obsequies or mournefull elegies upon his death: Wither, George

Prince Hohenstiel-Schwangau, saviour of society: Browning, Robert

Prince in buckskin: Widdemer, Margaret

Prince in the heather: The: Linklater, Eric

Prince Isodore: Acton, Harold

Prince Jali: Myers, L.H.

Prince life: James, G.P.R.

Prince Little Boy: Mitchell, S.W.

Prince Lucifer: Austin, Alfred

Prince of Abissinia, The: Johnson, Samuel

Prince of Edur: Ghose, Sri Aurobindo

Prince of Graustark, The: McCutcheon, G.B.

Prince of illusion, The: Long, J.L.

Prince of India, The: Wallace, Lew

Prince of sinners, A: Oppenheim, E. Phillips

Prince of the blood, A: Payn, James

Prince of the captivity, A: Buchan, John

Prince of the fairy family, The: Hall, A.M.

Prince of the House of David, The: Ingraham, J.H.

Prince of the hundred soups, The: Lee, Vernon

Prince of Wales v. the Examiner, The: Hunt, Leigh

Prince of Wales's Garden Party, The: Riddell, *Mrs.* J.H.

Prince of Wales's library—the primer, The: Mayhew, Henry

Prince or somebody, The: Golding, Louis

Prince Otto: Stevenson, R.L.

Prince Prigio: Lang, Andrew

Prince Ricardo of Pantouflia: Lang, Andrew

Prince who hiccupped, The: †Armstrong, Anthony

Prince Zaleski: Shiel, M.P.

Princelye pleasures, at the courte at Kenelwoorth, The: Gascoigne, George

Prince's progress, The: Rossetti, Christina

Prince's quest, The: Watson, *Sir* J.W.

Princess, The: Gilbert, *Sir* W.S.

Princess, The: Lawrence, D.H.

Princess, The: Morgan, *Lady* Sydney

Princess, The: Tennyson, Alfred *Lord*

Princess Aline, The: Davis, R.H.

Princess and Curdie, The: Macdonald, George

Princess and the butterfly, The: Pinero, *Sir* A.W.

Princess and the goblin, The: Macdonald, George

Princess Badoura: Housman, Laurence

Princess by proxy: Pertwee, Roland

Princess Casamassima, The: James, Henry

Princess Ida: Gilbert, *Sir* W.S.

Princess marries the page, The: Millay, E. St. Vincent

Princess Napraxine: †Ouida

Princess Nobody, The: Lang, Andrew

Princess of Cleve, The: Lee, Nathaniel

Princess of Hanover, The: Woods, M.L.

Princess of the school, The: Brazil, Angela

Princess of the tower, The: Carman, Bliss

Princess of Thule, A: Black, William

Princess Penniless: Crockett, R.S.

Princess Priscilla's fortnight, The: Russell, E.M.

Princess September and the nightingale: Maugham, Somerset

Princess Sophia, The: Benson, E.F.

Princess Sunshine: Riddell, *Mrs.* J.H.

Princess Toto: Gilbert, *Sir* W.S.

Princess Zoubaroff, The: Firbank, Ronald

Princess's nose, The: Jones, H.A.

Princeton: Noyes, Alfred

Principalities and powers: Cammaerts, Emile

Principall navigations, voiages and discoveries of the English nation: Hakluyt, Richard

Principia mathematica: Russell, Bertrand

Principia mathematica: Whitehead, A.N.

Principia politica: Woolf, Leonard

Principle in art: Patmore, Coventry

Principle of relativity, The: Einstein, Albert

Principle of relativity, The: Whitehead, A.N.

Principles and practice of diplomacy, The: Panikkar, K.M.

Principles and purposes of nationalism: Bellamy, Edward

Principles in bio-physics: Richter, Conrad

Principles of alliance and federation contrasted, The: Miller, E.M.

Principles of art, The: Collingwood, R.G.

Principles of biography: Lee, *Sir* Sidney

Principles of biology: Spencer, Herbert

Principles of church reform: Arnold, Thomas

Principles of economic planning: Cole, G.D.H.

Principles of emendation in Shakespeare: Greg, W.W.

Principles of English prosody: Abercrombie, Lascelles

Principles of literary criticism: Abercrombie, Lascelles

Principles of literary criticism: Richards, I.A.

Principles of logic, The: Bradley, F.H.

Principles of mathematics, The: Russell, Bertrand

Principles of morality: Spencer, Herbert

Principles of nationalities, The: Zangwill, Israel

Principles of natural knowledge: Whitehead, A.N.

Principles of playmaking, The: Matthews, J.B.

Principles of pleading, The: Tucker, N.B.

Principles of political economy: Mill, John Stuart

Principles of political economy: Sidgwick, Henry

Principles of political economy and taxation: Ricardo, David

Principles of psychology, The: James, William

Principles of psychology: Spencer, Herbert

Principles of Shakespearian production: Knight, G.Wilson

Principles of social reconstruction: Russell, Bertrand

Principles of socialism, The: Cole, G.D.H.

Principles of sociology: Spencer, Herbert

Principles of success in literature, The: Lewes, G.H.

Principles of toleration, The: Mill, James

Principles of war: Belloc, Hilaire

Principles of zoology: Agassis, Jean

Prinsloo of Prinsloodorp: Blackburn, Douglas

Print of my remembrance, The: Thomas, Augustus

Printed copy of sermon preached ... on the death of George Adams Sampson, 1834: Emerson, R.W.

Printed expressly as a substitute for money: Lindsay, N.V.

Printers' and publishers' devices, 1485–1640: McKerrow, R.B.

Printer's devil: †Dane, Clemence, and H. de G. Simpson

Printing of books, The: Jackson, Holbrook

Prinvest – London: Gielgud, Val

Prior claim, A: Pye, H.J.

Priorsford: Buchan, Anna

Priscilla and Charybdis: Joad, C.E.M.

Priscilla runs away: Russell, E.M.

Priscilla's love-story: Spofford, H.E.

Prison amusements: Montgomery, James

Prison meditations: Bunyan, John

Prison-breakers, The: Wallace, Edgar

Prisoner, The: Beresford, J.D.

Prisoner, The: Brown, Alice

Prisoner at Laeken: King Leopold, legends and facts: Cammaerts, Emile

Prisoner at large, The: O'Keeffe, John

Prisoner in fairyland (the book that "Uncle Paul" wrote), A: Blackwood, Algernon

Prisoner in the opal, The: Mason, A.E.W.

Prisoner of Chillon, The: Byron, George Gordon, *Lord*.

Prisoner of grace: Cary, Joyce

Prisoner of Zenda, The: (†Anthony Hope), Hawkins, Anthony Hope

Prisoners and captives: †Merriman, Seton

Prisoner's base: Mitchell, Mary

Prisoners (Fast bound in misery and iron): Cholmondeley, Mary

Prisoners of conscience: Barr, A.E.H.

Prisoners of Hartling, The: Beresford, J.D.

Prisoners of Mainz, The: Waugh, Alec

Prisons: Huxley, Aldous

Privacity Agent and other modest proposals, The: Sandwell, B.K.

Privacy: Ayer, A.J.

Private Angelo: Linklater, Eric

Private anthology, A: Royde-Smith, Naomi

Private correspondence of *Sir* Benjamin Keene, K.B.: Lodge, *Sir* Richard

Private country: Durrell, Lawrence

Private dining room, The: Nash, Ogden

Private drafts: Durrell, Lawrence

Private enterprise: Ervine, St. John

Private enterprise: Thirkell, Angela

Private Gollantz: Jacob, Naomi

Private in the Guards: Graham, Stephen

Private life, The: James, Henry

Private life of an Indian prince: Anand, M.R.

Private life of Helen of Troy, The: Erskine, John

Private life of Mrs. Siddons, The: Royde-Smith, Naomi

Private life of Sherlock Holmes, The: Starrett, Vincent

Private life of the Gannets, The: Huxley, *Sir* Julian

Private lives: Coward, Noel

Private opinion: Pryce-Jones, A.P.

Private papers of Henry Ryecroft, The: Gissing, George

Private reader, The: Van Doren, Mark

Private road: Reid, Forrest

Private room, A: Pinero, *Sir* A.W.

Private room: Royde-Smith, Naomi

Private rooms: Priestley, J.B.

Private secretary, A: Chesney, *Sir* George

Private Selby: Wallace, Edgar

Private Timothy Fergus Clancy: Bird, W.R.

Private tutor, The: Bradford, Gamaliel

Private tutor, The: Montagu, Basil

Private view: De la Mare, Walter

Private worlds: Bottome, Phyllis

Privateer, The: (†Gordon Daviot), Mackintosh, Elizabeth

Privateer's-man, one hundred years ago, The: Marryatt, Frederick

Privilege: Sadleir, Michael

Privileged spectator: Mannin, Ethel

Privy Seal: Ford, Ford Madox

Prize cup, The: Trowbridge, J.T.

Prize money: Roberts, T.G.

Prize of life, The: Grenfell, *Sir* Wilfred

Prize tale: a New England sketch: Stowe, Harriet Beecher

Prize winner, The: Denison, Merrill

Pro patria: Scollard, Clinton

Pro Patria Australia: Gilmore, Mary

Pro Vere autumni lachrymae: Chapman, George

Probability, the foundation of eugenics: Galton, *Sir* Francis

Problem club, The: Pain, B.E.O.

Problem in Greek ethics, A: Symonds, J.A.

Problem in modern ethics, A: Symonds, J.A.

Problem of China, The: Russell, Bertrand

Problem of Christianity, The: Royce, Josiah

Problem of foreign policy, The: Murray, Gilbert

Problem of knowledge, The: Ayer, A.J.

Problem of pain, The: Lewis, C.S.

Problem of public schools, The: Tawney, R.H.

Problem of rebirth, The: Ghose, Sri Aurobindo

Problem of sovereignty, The: Laski, Harold

Problem of style, The: Murry, John Middleton

Problem of the fourth gospel, The: Clarke, J.F.

Problem of the green capsule, The: Carr, J.D.

Problem of the troublesome collaborator, The: Wells, H.G.

Problem of the wire cage, The: Carr, J.D.

Problems and perils of Socialism: Strachey, John St. Loe

Problems in Greek poetry: Bowra, *Sir* Maurice

Problems of contemporary history: Dutt, R.P.

Problems of Greater India: Panikkar, K.M.

Problems of Indian defence: Panikkar, K.M.

Problems of life and mind: Lewes, G.H.

Problems of men: Dewey, John

Problems of modern democracy: Godkin, E.L.

Problems of modern industry: Webb, Beatrice and Sidney Webb

Problems of peace: Murray, Gilbert

Problems of philosophy, The: Russell, Bertrand

Problems of relative growth: Huxley, *Sir* Julian

Problems of religion: Bullett, Gerald

Probus: Ware, William

Proceed, Sergeant Lamb: Graves, Robert

Proceedings and debates in the House of Commons in 1620, 1621: Tyrwhitt, Thomas

Proceedings on trial of J.H. Tooke for high treason: Tooke, John Horne

Process and reality: Whitehead, A.N.

Process of real freedom: Cary, Joyce

Procession, The: Steele, *Sir* Richard

Procession of flowers in Colorado, The: Jackson, H.H.

Procession of life, The: Vachell, H.A.

Processionals, The: †Mordaunt, Elinor

Proclamation of the gospel of beauty: Lindsay, N.V.

Prodigal, The: Church, Richard

Prodigal, The: McArthur, Peter

Prodigal father, The: Church, Richard

Prodigal parents, The: Lewis, H.S.

Prodigal son, The: Caine, *Sir* T.H. Hall

Prodigal son, The: Robinson, E.A.

Prodigal village, The: Bacheller, Irving

Prodigals and their inheritance, The: Oliphant, Margaret

Prodigals of Monte Carlo: Oppenheim, E. Phillips

Production, A: Craig, *Sir* Gordon

Prodwit's guide to writing: Vulliamy, C.E.

Professeur James de Mille: Stewart, George

Profession and principle: Moodie, Susanna

Professional patriots: Howard, S.C.

Professor, The: Benson, A.C.

Professor, The: Brontë, Charlotte

Professor, The: Gillette, William

Professor, The: Thackeray, W.M.

Professor, The: Warner, Rex

Professor at the breakfast-table, The: Holmes, Oliver Wendell

Professor Pressensee materialist and inventor: Cooke, J.E.

Professor's house, The: Cather, Willa

Professor's poison, The: (†Neil Gordon), Macdonell, A.G.

Profile House Gazette: Bangs, J.K.

Profiles from China: Tietjens, E.S.

Profiles from home: Tietjens, E.S.

Profit and loss: Barr, A.E.H.

Profit and the loss: Maltby, H.F.

Profitable meditations: Bunyan, John

Profiteers, The: Oppenheim, E. Phillips

Profits of authorship, The: †Carroll, Lewis

Profits of religion, The: Sinclair, Upton

Profligate, The: Pinero, *Sir* A.W.

Program for America, A: Durant, W.J.

Program for survival: Mumford, Lewis

Programme for progress, A: Strachey, John

Progress: Cunninghame Graham, Robert

Progress: Ervine, St. John

Progress: Munro, C.K.

Progress: a satirical poem: Saxe, J.G.

Progress and poverty: George, Henry

Progress and power: Becker, C.L.

Progress and prejudice: Gore, Catherine

Progress in literature: Abercrombie, Lascelles

Progress of dulness, The: Trumbull, John

Progress of gallantry, The: Graves, Richard

Progress of Julius, The: Du Maurier, Daphne

Progress of Kay, The: Bullett, Gerald

Progress of love, The: Lyttelton, George *Baron*

Progress of refinement, The: Pye, H.J.

Progress of reform, The: Curtis, G.W.

Progress of religious ideas, through successive ages, The: Child, L.M.

Progress of romance, The: Reeve, Clara

Progress of stories: Riding, Laura

Progress of the United States in population and wealth in fifty years: Tucker, George

Progress of wit, The: Hill, Aaron

Progress or revolution?: Smith, Goldwin

Progress, processions, and magnificant festivities, of King James the First, The: Nichols, John

Progressive geography for children: Croker, J.W.

Prohibition Aesop, The: Bengough, J.W.

Proi: Clarke, Marcus

Project for the advancement of religion and the reformation of manners, A: Swift, Jonathan

Projectors, The: Wilson, John

Prolegomena I: Pound, Ezra

Prolegomena for the Oxford Shakespeare: McKerrow, R.B.

Prologue: Bottomley, Gordon

Prologue, The: Canby, H.S.

Prologue for the Old Rialto Theatre, Hoboken, A: Morley, C.D.

Prologue spoken at Court before the Queen on Her Majesty's birthday: Prior, Matthew

Prologue spoken at Mithridates: Lee, Nathaniel

Prologue to American history, A: Morison, S.E.

Prologue to an unfinished lady: †Bridie, James

Prologue to Constantine the Great: Otway, Thomas

Prologue to his Majesty at the first play at the Cock-pit: Denham, *Sir* John

Prologue to King David: †Bridie, James

Prologue to the City-heiress: Otway, Thomas

Prologue to The orphan: Prior, Matthew

Prologue to the University of Oxford, The: Tickell, Thomas

Prolusiones academicae: Strachey, Lytton

Prom night: Kaufman, G.S.

Promenade: †Lancaster, G.B.

Promenades of an impressionist: Huneker, J.G.

Prometheus: Muir, Edwin

Prometheus: Swift, Jonathan

Prometheus and the Bolsheviks: Lehmann, John

Prometheus, the fire bringer: Horne, R.H.

Prometheus the firegiver: Bridges, Robert

Prometheus unbound: Shelley, P.B.

Prominent men of Canada: Adam, G.M.

Promise: Buck, Pearl

Promise: Sidgwick, Ethel

Promise, The: Steinbeck, John

Promise not to tell: Stern, G.B.

Promise of air, The: Blackwood, Algernon

Promise of power, The: Chase, Stuart

Promise of the bell, The: Repplier, Agnes

Promised Land, The: Parker, Sir H.G.

Promises of Alice, The: Deland, Margaret

Promises: poems: Warren, Robert Penn

Prompter, The: Hill, Aaron

Promus of Formularies and elegancies: Bacon, Francis

Pronunciation of English, The: Craigie, Sir W.A.

Proof, The: Winters, Yvor

Proof of the pudding, The: Nicholson, Meredith

Proof of victory: Mitchell, Mary

Proof palpable of immortality, The: Sargent, Epes

Proofs before pulping: Pain, B.E.O.

Propaganda's harvest: Martin, B.K.

Proper impropriety, A: Thomas, Augustus

Proper limitations of state interference, The: Leacock, Stephen

Proper objects of education, The: Priestley, Joseph

Proper Peter: Hoffe, Monckton

Proper place, The: Buchan, Anna

Proper sphere of government, The: Spencer, Herbert

Proper studies: Huxley, Aldous

Proper study of mankind: Chase, Stuart

Property: Tennyson, Alfred Lord

Property and progress: Mallock, W.H.

Prophecy and a plea, A: Bangs, J.K.

Prophecy of famine, The: Churchill, Charles

Prophecy of famine: Massingham, Harold

Prophecy of Queen Emma, The: Mickle, W.J.

Prophet, The: Taylor, Bayard

Prophet and fool: Golding, Louis

Prophet of Berkeley Square, The: Hichens, Robert

Prophet of joy, A: Bradford, Gamaliel

Prophet of the great smoky mountains, The: †Craddock, C.E.

Prophetess, The: Betterton, Thomas

Prophetic marriage, The: Deeping, Warwick

Prophets for the common reader: Chase, M.E.

Prophet's mantle, The: Nesbit, E.

Prophet's prayer, A: Carman, Bliss

Prophets, priests, and kings: Gardiner, A.G.

Proportions of the human figure, The: Story, W.W.

Proposal for correcting, improving and ascertaining the English tongue, A: Swift, Jonathan

Proposal for giving badges to the beggars in all the parishes of Dublin, A: Swift, Jonathan

Proposal for making an effectual provision for the poor, A: Fielding, Henry

Proposal for promoting useful knowledge, A: Franklin, Benjamin

Proposal for putting a speedy end to the war: Dennis, John

Proposal for putting reform to the vote throughout the Kingdom, A: Shelley, P.B.

Proposal for the better supplying of churches in our foreign plantations: Berkeley, George

Proposal for the restoration of public wealth and credit, A: Brooke, Henry

Proposal for the universal use of Irish manufacture, A: Swift, Jonathan

Proposal humbly offer'd to the P—t, for the more effectual preventing the further growth of Popery, A: Swift, Jonathan

Proposal under difficulties, A: Bangs, J.K.

Proposals for a Monmouth newspaper: Freneau, Philip

Proposals (for a new edition of Shakespeare): Malone, Edmund

Proposals for a translation of Homer's Iliad: Pope, Alexander

Proposals for an association of those philanthropists: Shelley, P.B.

Proposals for an economical and secure currency: Ricardo, David

Proposals for publishing a collection of trifles in verse: Clare, John

Proposals of Peggy, The: Peach, L. du Garde

Proposals relating to the education of youth in Pennsylvania: Franklin, Benjamin

Proposals touching the accomplishment of prophecies: Sewall, Samuel

Proposition: Cowley, Abraham

Proprietors of Peterborough, New Hampshire, The: Morison, S.E.

Props: Jacob, Naomi

Pros and cons, The: Jennings, Gertrude

Prose and poetry of Elinor Wylie, The: Benét, W.R.

Prose and verse: Lemon, Mark

Prose and verse: Moore, Thomas

Prose. By a poet: Montgomery, James

Prose fancies: Le Gallienne, Richard

Prose idylls, new and old: Kingsley, Charles

Prose keys to modern poetry: Shapiro, Karl

Prose literature, 1945–1950: Pryce-Jones, A.P.

Prose quotations from Socrates to Macaulay: Allibone, S.A.

Prose sketches and poems, written in the western country: Pike, Albert

Prose writers of America, The: Griswold, R.W.

Prose writers of Canada, The: Dawson, S.E.

Proser, The: Thackeray, W.M.

Proserpina: Ruskin, John

Proserpine and Midas: Shelley, Mary

Prosopopeia: Lodge, Thomas

Prosopopocia Britannica: Wither, George

Prospect, The: Moxon, Edward

Prospect, The: Thomson, James

Prospect before us, The: Dos Passos, John

Prospect of Britain, A: Young, A.J.

Prospect of death, A: Roscommon, D.W., *Earl of*

Prospect of flowers, A: Young, A.J.

Prospect of peace, The: Barlow, Joel

Prospect of plenty, The: Ramsay, Allan

Prospect of the most famous parts of the world, A: Speed, John

Prospector, The: †Connor, Ralph

Prospects of a golden age: Dos Passos, John

Prospects of industrial civilization, The: Russell, Bertrand

Prospectus of a school to be established at Round Hill: Bancroft, George

Prospectus of a work to be entitled Ogygian tales: Brooke, Henry

Prosperity, fact or myth: Chase, Stuart

Prospero's cell: Durrell, Lawrence

Protection of the treasures of art and history in war areas, The: Woolley, *Sir* Leonard

Protection or free trade: George, Henry

Protector, The: Wither, George

Protégée of Jack Hamlin's, A: Harte, Bret

Protest against law taxes, A: Bentham, Jeremy

Protest against the appointment of Benjamin Franklin: Dickinson, John

Protestant, The: Bray, A.E.

Protestatyon, The: †Marprelate, Martin

Proteus: †Lee, Vernon

Proteus redivivus: Head, Richard

Proteus and Amadeus: Blunt, Wilfred

Proteus and Amadeus: De Vere, Aubrey

Prothalamion: Toynbee, T.P.

Prothalamion or a spousall verse in honour of the double mariage of the Ladie Elizabeth and the Ladie Katherine Somerset: Spenser, Edmund

Proud and the free, The: Fast, Howard M.

Proud heaven: Mannin, Ethel

Proud riders: Davis, H.L.

Proud Rosalind: Farjeon, Eleanor

Proud servant, The: Irwin, Margaret

Proud sheriff: Rhodes, E.M.

Proud walkers, The: Vulliamy, C.E.

Proudhon: Brogan, *Sir* D.W.

Proust: Bell, Clive

Prouverbes, The: Lydgate, John

Provença: Pound, Ezra

Provence: Ford, Ford Madox

Proverbs: Chaucer, Geoffrey

Proverbs illustrated: Gatty, *Mrs.* Margaret

Proverbs of the noble Sir James Lopez de Mendoza, The: Googe, Barnabe

Providence: Mickle, W.J.

Providence: Smart, Christopher

Providence as manifested through Israel: Martineau, Harriet

Province House: MacMechan, A.M.

Provincetown plays, The: Dell, Floyd

Provincetown plays, The: Glaspell, Susan

Provincial American, The: Nicholson, Meredith

Provincial antiquities of Scotland: Scott, *Sir* Walter

Provincial glossary, A: Grose, Francis

Provincial lady, The: Malleson, Miles

Provincial lady goes further, The: †Delafield, E.M.

Provincial lady in America, The: †Delafield, E.M.

Provincial lady in London, The: †Delafield, E.M.

Provincial lady in war time, The: †Delafield, E.M.

Provincial lady omnibus, The: †Delafield, E.M.

Proving of Psyche, The: Fausset, Hugh

Provocations of Madame Palissy, The: Manning, Anne

Provok'd husband, The: Cibber, Colley

Provok'd wife, The: Vanbrugh, *Sir* John

Provost, The: Galt, John

Prowling through Papua: Clune, Frank

Prude, The: Haywood, *Mrs.* Eliza

Prudence Palfrey: Aldrich, T.B.

Prude's fall, The: Besier, Rudolf

Prude's progress, The: Phillpotts, Eden

Prue and I: Curtis, G.W.

Prufrock: Eliot, T.S.

Prunella: Granville-Barker, *Sir* Harley

Prunella: Housman, Laurence

Prunello: Mais, S.P.B.

Prune's progress: †Armstrong, Anthony and Raff

Prurient prude, The: Reade, Charles

Prussian officer, The: Lawrence, D.H.

Prussianism and its destruction: Angell, *Sir* Norman

Psalm of deaths, A: Mitchell, S.W.

Psalm of thanksgiving, A: Hopkinson, Francis

Psalms and hymns for public and private worship: Toplady, A.M.

Psalms and hymns for public worship: Croly, George

Psalms for the common reader: Chase, M.E.

Psalms of David imitated, The: Watts, Isaac

Psalms of David ... in metre, The: Hopkinson, Francis

Pseudo martyr: Donne, John

Pseudodoxia epidemica: Browne, *Sir* Thomas

Psmith in the City: Wodehouse, P.G.

Psmith, journalist: Wodehouse, P.G.

Psyche: Beaumont, Joseph

Psyche: DeLisser, Herbert G.

Psyche: Derleth, A.W.

Psyche: Shadwell, Thomas

Psyche's art: Alcott, Louisa M.

Psyche's task: Frazer, *Sir* James

Psychoanalysis and morality: Powys, John Cowper

Psychoanalysis and the unconscious: Lawrence, D.H.

Psychological and poetic approach to the study of Christ in the Fourth Gospel, A: Gore-Booth, E.S.

Psychology: Dewey, John

Psychology: briefer course: James, William

Psychology of sex: Ellis, Havelock

Psychometric experiments: Galton, *Sir* Francis

Ptarmigan: McIlwraith, J.N.

Pterodamozels, The: Trevelyan, R.C.

Pub on the pool, The: Divine, A.D.

Public and its government, The: Frankfurter, Felix

Public and its problems, The: Dewey, John

Public faces: Nicolson, *Hon. Sir* Harold

Public mind, its disorders: its exploitation, The: Angell, *Sir* Norman

Public opinion: Lippmann, Walter

Public opinion and foreign policy in the United States: Lippmann, Walter

Public papers of Woodrow Wilson, The: Raker, R.S.

Public philosophy: Lippmann, Walter

Public policy and the general welfare: Beard, C.A.

Public scandal, A: Hannay, J.O.

Public school and Civil Service reform, The: Curtis, G.W.

Public school in war time, A: Mais, S.P.B.

Public school life, boys, parents, masters: Waugh, Alec

Public School question, The: Smith, Goldwin

Public Schools and public needs: Coulton, G.G.

Public speaking: Bentley, Phyllis

Public speech: MacLeish, Archibald

Publick Advertisements: L'Estrange, *Sir* Roger

Publick employment and an active life prefer'd to solitude: Evelyn, John

Publick intelligence: L'Estrange, *Sir* Roger

Publick spirit of the Whigs, The: Swift, Jonathan

Publisher and his friends, A: Smiles, Samuel

Publishers and authors: Spedding, James

Puck: †Ouida

Puck and luck: Benchley, Robert

Puck of Pook's Hill: Kipling, Rudyard

Puck our Peke: Brown, Ivor

Pudding and dumpling burnt to pot: Carey, Henry

Pudgy Pete and Co.: Oppenheim, E. Phillips

Puffiad, The: Montgomery, Robert

Pugs and peacocks: Cannan, Gilbert

Pulpit and press: Eddy, M.B.

Pulpit in the grill room, A: Oppenheim, E. Phillips

Pulse of life, The: Lowndes, M.A.

Pulse of Oxford, The: Karaka, D.F.

Pulvis et umbra: Carman, Bliss

Punch: Aiken, Conrad

Punch and go: Galsworthy, John

Punch's complete letter writer: Jerrold, Douglas

Punch's letters to his son: Jerrold, Douglas

Punch's prize novelists: Thackeray, W.M.

Pupil of Aurelius, The: Black, William

Puppet show, The: Armstrong, M.D.

Puppet-booth, The: Fuller, H.B.

Puppets: †Novello, Ivor

Purcell papers, The: Le Fanu, J.S.

Purchase price, The: Hough, Emerson

Pure flame, The: Mannin, Ethel

Pure gold: Marston, J.W.

Pure gold: Rölvaag, O.E.

Pure poetry: Moore, George

Purely for pleasure: †Mordaunt, Elinor

Puritan, The: O'Flaherty, Liam

Puritan and Anglican: Dowden, Edward

Puritan and his daughter, The: Paulding, J.K.

Puritan and the Papist, The: Cowley, Abraham

Puritan bookshelf, A: Hart, James D.

Puritan in Babylon, A: White, W.A.

Puritan pronaos: Morison, S.E.

Puritan's guest, The: Holland, J.G.

Purple and fine linen: Fawcett, Edgar

Purple and fine women: Saltus, E.E.

Purple ball, The: Packard, F.L.

Purple bedroom, The: Phillpotts, Eden

Purple cloud, The: Shiel, M.P.

Purple dust: O'Casey, Sean

Purple East, The: Watson, *Sir* J.W.

Purple eyes: Long, J.L.

Purple island, The: Fletcher, Phineas

Purple land that England lost, The: Hudson, W.H.

Purple parasol, The: McCutcheon, G.B.

Purple plain, The: Bates, H.E.

Purse of coppers, A: O'Faolain, Sean

Pursuer, The: Golding, Louis

Pursuit (novel and play): Pertwee, Roland

Pursuit of Psyche: Turner, W.J.R.

Pursuit of knowledge, The: Leacock, Stephen

Pursuit of love: Mitford, Nancy

Pursuit of the house-boat, The: Bangs, J.K.

Pushcart at the curb, A: Dos Passos, John

Puss in boots: Drinkwater, John

Puss in Boots: Osgood, F.S.

Puss in the corner: Jennings, Gertrude

Puss-in-boots: Housman, Laurence

Pussy and doggy tales: Nesbit, E.

Put out more flags: Waugh, Evelyn

Put to the test: Braddon, M.E.

Put yourself in his place: Reade, Charles

Putman: Bannister, N.H.

Puzzle of Dickens's last plot, The: Lang, Andrew

Puzzled America: Anderson, Sherwood

Puzzled and pleased: Lathom, Francis

Pygmalion: Shaw, G.B.

Pygmalion: Woolner, Thomas

Pygmalion and Galatea: Gilbert, *Sir* W.S.

Pylgremage of the sowle, The: Lydgate, John

Pylon: Faulkner, William

Pyramid facts and fancies: Bonwick, James

Pyramids, The: Brooke, Rupert

Pyramids and temples of Gizeh: Petrie, *Sir* William Flinders

Pyrenees, The: Belloc, Hilaire

Pyrrhus, King of Epirus: Hopkins, Charles

Q

"Q": Leacock, Stephen

Quack, quack: Woolf, Leonard

Quack-doctor, The: Brooke, Henry

Quadrille: Coward, Noel

Quadrille: Swinnerton, Frank

Quadroon, The: Reid, T.M.

Quadroone, The: Ingraham, J.H.

Quadrupeds of North America, The: Audubon, J.J.

Quaenam fuerit mulierum apud veteres graecos conditio?: Smith, Goldwin

Quaeries wrote by Dr. J. Swift: Swift, Jonathan

Quaint companions: Merrick, Leonard

Quaint specimens: Knox, E.V.

Quake, quake, quake: Dehn, Paul

Quaker, The: Dibdin, Charles

Quaker city, The: Lippard, George

Quaker ladies: Carman, Bliss

Quakers past and present, The: Richardson, D.M.

Quality: Granville-Barker, Harley

Quality of mercy, The: Howells, W.D.

Quality Street: Barrie, *Sir* J. M.

Quare medicine: Green, Paul

Quarrels of authors: D'Israeli, Isaac

Quarry: Eberhart, Richard

Quarter: Maugham, Somerset

Quarter-centenary of the Battle of Gettysburg, The: Curtis, G.W.

Quarterly essays: Lytton, E.

Quartet: Nabokov, Vladimir

Quartet: Phillpotts, Eden

Quartet: Sheriff, R.C.

Quartet from The golden year: Eberhart, Richard

Quartet in Heaven: Kaye-Smith, Shiela

Quartette: Kipling, Rudyard

Quattrocentisteria: Hewlett, Maurice

Quebec: De la Roche, Mazo

Quebec: Willson, H.B.

Quebec of yester-year: Doughty, *Sir* A.G.

Quebec past and present... 1608–1876: LeMoine, *Sir* J.M.

Quebec under two flags: Doughty, *Sir* A.G.

Quebec, where ancient France lingers: Barbeau, C.M.

Queechy: Warner, S.B.

Queen and Mr. Gladstone, The: Guedalla, Philip

Queen and other poems, The: Garnett, Richard

Queen Elizabeth: Neale, J.E.

Queen Elizabeth: Williams, Charles

Queen Hynde: Hogg, James

Queen Lucia: Benson, E.F.

Queen Mab: Kavanagh, Julia

Queen Mab: Shelley, P.B.

Queen Mariamne: †Field, Michael

Queen Mary: Tennyson, Alfred *Lord*

Queen Mother and Rosamund, The: Swinburne, A.C.

Queen of Gothland, The: Trench, F.H.

Queen of hearts, The: Collins, Wilkie

Queen of love, The: Baring-Gould, Sabine

Queen of Scots: (†Gordon Daviot), Mackintosh, Elizabeth

Queen of seven swords, The: Chesterton, G.K.

Queen of Sheba, The: Aldrich, T.B.

Queen of Spades: Roe, E.P.

Queen of the air, The: Ruskin, John

Queen of the dawn: Haggard, Sir Henry Rider

Queen of the dormitory: Brazil, Angela

Queen of the Lakes, The: Reid, T.M.

Queen of the pirate isle, The: Harte, Bret

Queen of the swamp, The: Catherwood, Mary

Queen or the Pope? The: Warren, Samuel

Queen Phillippa's Golden Rule: Manning, Anne

Queen Sheba's ring: Haggard, Sir Henry Rider

Queen Silver-bell: Burnett, Frances Hodgson

Queen Titania: Boyesen, H.H.

Queen Victoria: Benson, E.F.

Queen Victoria: Fulford, Roger

Queen Victoria: Lee, Sir Sidney

Queen Victoria: Strachey, Lytton

Queen was in the parlour, The: Coward, Noel

Queen who flew, The: (Hueffer), Ford, Ford Madox

Queen Yseult: Swinburne, A.C.

Queene of Arragon, The: Habington, William

Queenes Arcadia, The: Daniel, Samuel

Queenhoo Hall: Strutt, Joseph

Queenie Hetherton: Holmes, M.J.

Queens: Rattigan, Terence

Queens and the hive, The: Sitwell, Edith

Queen's awards, The: †Queen, Ellery

Queen's birthday, The: Kirby, William

Queen's birthday, 1880: Le-Moine, Sir J.M.

Queen's budget opened, The: Hone, William

Queen's Bureau of Investigation: †Queen, Ellery

Queen's cadet, The: Grant, James

Queen's comedy, The: †Bridie, James

Queen's domain, The: Winter, William

Queen's enemies, The: Dunsany, E.J.M.D.P.

Queen's folly: Weyman, Stanley

Queen's house, The: Mackenzie, Sir Compton

Queen's husband, The: Sherwood, R.E.

Queen's justice, The: Arnold, Edwin

Queens majesties entertainment at Woodstock, The: Gascoigne, George

Queen's Maries, The: Whyte-Melville, G.J.

Queen's matrimonial ladder, The: Hone, William

Queen's pawn: Peach, L. du Garde

Queen's progress, The: Housman, Laurence

Queen's quair, The: Hewlett, Maurice

Queen's quorum: †Queen, Ellery

Queen's romance, A: Davidson, John

Queen's tact, The: Bolitho, H.H.

Queen's tragedy, The: Swinburne, A.C.

Queen's troth, The: Sladen, D.B.W.

Queen's twin, The: Jewett, S.O.

Queen's vigil, The: Gibson, Wilfred

Queen's wake, The: Hogg, James

Queen's wigs, The: Royde-Smith, Naomi

Queensland journey: Christesen, C.B.

Queensland, Queen of the North: Evans, G.E.

Queer book, A: Hogg, James

Queer fellow, The: Brophy, John

Queer fellows: Niven, F.J.

Queer little people: Stowe, Harriet Beecher

Queer partners: †Sinclair Murray

Queer things about Egypt: Sladen, D.B.W.

Queer things about Japan: Sladen, D.B.W.

Queery Leary nonsense: Lear, Edward

Quentin Durward: Scott, Sir Walter

Quentin Massys: Deakin, Alfred

Queries of highest consideration: Williams, Roger

Querist, The: Berkeley, George

Query upon query: Sterne, Laurence

Quest for certainty, The: Dewey, John

Quest for Corvo, The: Symons, A.J.A.

Quest for glory, The: †Bowen, Marjorie

Quest for song, A: Bangs, J.K.

Quest for winter sunshine, A: Oppenheim, E.Phillips

Quest of Quesnay, The: Tarkington, Booth

Quest of Sangraal, The: Hawker, R.S.

Quest of the face: Graham, Stephen

Quest of the fatal river, The: Machar, A.M.

Quest of the golden girl, The: Le Gallienne, Richard

Quest of the schooner Argus, The: Villiers, A.J.

Quest of the Silver Fleece, The: Dubois, William

Quest of Youth, The: Farnol, J.J.

Quest sinister: Mais, S.P.B.

Questing mind, The: Mickle, A.D.

Question, The: †Bowen, Marjorie

Question, The: Swinburne, A.C.

Question and answer, The: Belloc, Hilaire

Question of damages, A: Trowbridge, J.T.

Question of Hamlet, The: Levin, Harry

Question of memory, A: †Field, Michael

Question of our speech, The: James, Henry

Question of proof, A: Day-Lewis, C.

Question of queens: (†Michael Innes), Stewart, J.I.M.

Question of time, A: Atherton, Gertrude

Question of upbringing, A: Powell, Anthony

Questionable shapes: Howells, W.D.

Questionings on criticism and beauty: Balfour, A.J.

Questions about the nature and perpetuity of the seventh-day-Sabbath: Bunyan, John

Questions and answers for the Mendip and Sunday Schools: More, Hannah

Questions at issue: Gosse, *Sir* Edmund

Questions at the well, The: (†Fenil Haig), Ford, Ford Madox

Questions concerning liberty, necessity and chance, The: Hobbes, Thomas

Questions of our day: Ellis, Havelock

Questions on the customs, beliefs, and languages of savages: Frazer, *Sir* James

Quests: Vachell, H.A.

Quia pauper amavi: Pound, Ezra

Quick action: Chambers, R.W.

Quick and the dead, The: Bourinot, Arthur

Quick and the dead, The: Bradford, Gamaliel

Quick and the dead, The: Bullett, Gerald

Ouick service: Wodehouse, P.G.

Quicksands of Pactolus, The: Vachell, H.A.

Quid pro quo: Gore, Catherine

Quiet cities: Hergesheimer, Joseph

Quiet corner: Beresford, J.D.

Quiet corner: Vachell, H.A.

Quiet days in Clichy: Miller, Henry

Quiet gentleman, The: Heyer, Georgette

Quiet heart: Oliphant, Margaret

Quiet life, A: Burnett, Frances Hodgson

Quiet please: Cabell, James Branch

Quiet road, A: Reese, L.W.

Quiet shore, The: Raymond, Ernest

Quiet wedding: Rattigan, Terence

Quill's window: McCutcheon, G.B.

Quinney's (novel and play): Vachell, H.A.

Quinney's adventures: Vachell, H.A.

Quinney's for quality: Vachell, H.A.

Quintessence of Ibsenism, The: Shaw, G.B.

Quintrains of "Callander": MacDonald, W.P.

Quintus Servinton: Savery, Henry

Quinzaine for this Yule, A: Pound, Ezra

Quip for an upstart courtier, A: Greene, Robert

Quip modest, The: Ritson, Joseph

Quips and quiddits: Tabb, J.B.

Quisante: Hawkins, A.H.

Quite alone: Sala, G.A.H.

Quite early one morning: Thomas, Dylan

Quito Express: Bemelmans, Ludwig

Quits: Tautphoeus, Jemima *Baroness*

Quo musa tendis?: Stephen, J.K.

Quo vadimus: White, E.B.

Quorum: Bentley, Phyllis

Quota of seaweed: Basso, Hamilton

Quoth the raven: Lucas, E.V.

Qurneh: Petrie, *Sir* William Flinders

R

R.A.F. in Russia: Griffith, Hubert

R.A.F. occasions: Griffith, Hubert

R.C.Church in politics, The: Coulton, G.G.

R.F.C. alphabet: Baring, Maurice

R.F.C. H.Q. 1914–1918: Baring, Maurice

R.Holmes & Co.: Bangs, J.K.

R.J.'s mother: Deland, Margaret

R.L.Stevenson, a critical study: Swinnerton, Frank

R.O.F. The story of the Royal Ordnance Factories: (†Ian Hay), Beith, *Sir* John Hay

R. v R., being an account of the last years and the death of one Rembrandt Harmenszoon van Rijn: Van Loon, Hendrik

Rab and his friends: Brown, *Dr.* John

Rabbit in the air, notes from a diary kept while learning to handle an aeroplane, A: Garnett, David

Rabble in arms: Roberts, Kenneth

Rabelais: Besant, *Sir* Walter

Rabelais: Powys, John Cowper

Rabelais replies: Linklater, Eric

Rabindranath Tagore: Iyengar, K.R. Srinivasa

Rabindranath Tagore: Rhys, Ernest

Race: McFee, William

Race and politics in Kenya: Huxley, Elspeth J. and *Dame* M.F.Perham

Race for wealth, The: Riddell, *Mrs.* J.H.

Race of leaves, The: †Field, Michael

Race questions, provincialism and other American problems: Royce, Josiah

Race the sun: Collins, Dale

Rachel: Agate, J.E.

Rachel: Pratt, E.J.

Rachel Dene: Buchanan, R.W.

Rachel Dyer: Neal, John

Rachel Gray: Kavanagh, Julia

Rachel Ray: Trollope, Anthony

Rachel Rosing: Spring, Howard

Racial portraits: Petrie, *Sir* William Flinders

Racing rhymes: Gordon, A.L.

Racketeers, The: Hoffe, Monckton

Racketty-packetty house: Burnett, Frances Hodgson

Racundra's first cruise: Ransome, Arthur

Rada: Noyes, Alfred

Radical, The: Galt, John

Radical house that Jack built, The: Hone, William

Radical indictment!, A: Adams, H.B.

Radio plays: Peach, Lawrence du Garde

Radio theatre: Gielgud, Val

Rafael: Ingraham, J.H.

Raffles: further adventures of the amateur cracksman: Hornung, E.W.

Raft, The: Linklater, Eric

Raft in the Bush, The: Turner, E.S.

Rag, The: Monkhouse, A.N.

Rag bag, The: Willis, N.P.

Rage to live, A: O'Hara, J.H.

Ragged banners: Mannin, Ethel

Ragged lady: Howells, W.D.

Raging Turke, The: Goffe, Thomas

Ragnarok: Donnelly, I.L.

Rags of glory: Cloete, E.F.S.G.

Rahab: Frank, Waldo

Raid of the guerilla, The: †Craddock, C.E.

Raiderland: Crockett, S.R.

Raiders, The: Crockett, S.R.

Raiders of Spanish Peaks: Grey, Zane

Raigne of King Edward the third, The: Shakespeare, William

Railroads: their origin and problems: Adams, C.F.

Railway belle, The: Lemon, Mark

Railway children, The: Nesbit, E.

Railway man and his children, The: Oliphant, Margaret

Railway reform in Great Britain: Kipling, Rudyard

Railway station, The: Taylor, Tom

Rain before seven: De Voto, Bernard

Rain from heaven: Behrman, S.N.

Rain in the doorway: Smith, Thorne

Rain, rain, go to Spain: Lynd, Robert

Rain upon Godshill: Priestley, J.B.

Rainbow, The: Lawrence, D H.

Rainbow: Warner, Sylvia Townsend

Rainbow, The: Wirt, William

Rainbow and the rose, The: Nesbit, E.

Rainbow and the rose, The: †Shute, Nevil

Rainbow book of nature, The: Peattie, D.C.

Rainbow books, The: Mee, Arthur

Rainbow bridge, The: Livingstone, *Sir* Richard

Rainbow fish: Bates, Ralph

Rainbow in the sky: Untermeyer, Louis

Rainbow on the road: Forbes, Esther

Rainbow trail, The: Grey, Zane

Rainbow valley: Montgomery, L.M.

Rainbows and witches: Ogilvie, W.H.

Rainbow's end: Beach, R.E.

Rains came, The: Bromfield, Louis

Rainy June, A: †Ouida

Rajah Amar: Myers, L.H.

Rajani: songs of the night: Mukherji, D.G.

Rajayi's speeches: Rajagopalachari, Chakravati

Rajput painting: Coomaraswamy, A.K.

Rake and the hussy, The: Chambers, R.W.

Rakehelly man, The: Fairburn, A.R.D.

Rake's progress, The: †Bowen, Marjorie

Rake's progress—an opera, The: Auden, W.H.

Rakonitz chronicles, The: Stern, G.B.

Raleigh: Gosse, *Sir* Edmund

Ralki: Radhakrishan, Sarvepalli

Ralley cup, The: Green, Anne

Ralph Darnell: Taylor, P.M.

Ralph in the Bush: (†Donald Barr), Barrett, C.L.

Ralph Roister Doister: Udall, Nicholas

Ralph the bailiff: Braddon, M.E.

Ralph the Heir: Trollope, Anthony

Ralph Waldo Emerson: Alcott, A.B.

Ralph Waldo Emerson: Holmes, Oliver Wendell

Ralph Waldo Emerson: Woodberry, G.

Ralstons, The: Crawford, F. Marion

Ramayana: Rajagopalachari, Chakravati

Ramayana and the Mahabharata, The: Dutt, R.C.

Rambler, The: Johnson, Samuel

Rambler's harvest: (†Donald Barr), Barrett, C.L.

Rambles and reveries: Tuckerman, H.T.

Rambles beyond railways: Collins, Wilkie

Rambles in England and Ireland: Allingham, William

Rambles in Germany and Italy in 1840: Shelley, Mary

Rambles in India during twenty-four years, 1871–95: Dutt, R.C.

Rambles in Ireland: Lynd, Robert

Rambles in mission-fields: Smith, S.F.

Rambles in the Canadian forest: Traill, C.P.

Rambles round the zoo: (†Donald Barr), Barrett, C.L.

Rambling discourse, A: Galsworthy, John

Rambling recollections of a soldier of fortune: Maxwell, W.H.

Rambling sailor, The: Mew, Charlotte

Ramero: Ingraham, J.H.

Ramillies and the Union with Scotland: Trevelyan, G.M.

Ramona: Jackson, H.H.

Ramparts of virtue, The: Brophy, John

Ramsbottom letters, The: Hook, T.E.

Ramsey Milholland: Tarkington, Booth

Ran away to sea: Reid, T.M.

Rana, the hero of India: Mukherji, D.G.

Ranald Bannerman's boyhood: Macdonald, George

Ranch of the Beaver, The: Adams, Andy

Ranch of the golden flowers, The: Skinner, C.L.

Ranchero: White, S.E.

Rancher's revenge: †Brand, Max

Randall and the river of time: Forester, C.S.

Randall's thumb: Gilbert, Sir W.S.

Randolph: Austin, Alfred

Randolph: Neal, John

Random harvest: Hilton, James

Random itinerary, A: Davidson, John

Random rambles: Moulton, E.L.

Random records: Colman, George, the younger

Ranelagh House: Warton, Joseph

Range of intellectual conception is proportioned to the rank in animated life, The: Ruskin, John

Rangers, The: Thompson, D.P.

Ranolf and Amohia: Domett, Alfred

Ransom of red chief, The: †Henry, O.

Ranson's folly: Davis, Richard

Ranthorpe: Lewes, G.H.

Raoul Dufy: Stevens, Wallace

Rape of Lucrece, The: Heywood, Thomas

Rape of Proserpine, The: Theobald, Lewis

Rape of the belt, The: Levy, Benn W.

Rape of the lock, The: Pope, Alexander

Rape upon rape: Fielding, Henry

Rapid promotion: Maltby, H.F.

Rapid ramblings in Europe: Falkner, W.C.

Rapids, The: Sullivan, Alan

Rapids of Niagara, The: Warner, S.B.

Raptures: Davies, W.H.

Rare adventure, The: Fergusson, Sir Bernard

Rare books: Morley, C.D.

Rare luck: Ridge, W.Pett

Rare, vanishing and lost British birds: Hudson, W.H.

Rascals in paradise: Michener, J.A.

Rash act, The: Ford, Ford Madox

Rasselas: Johnson, Dr. Samuel

Rat, The: †Novello, Ivor

Rat trap, The: Coward, Noel

Rate for the job, The: Cole, M.I.

Rational religion: Smith, Goldwin

Rationale of evidence, The: Bentham, Jeremy

Rationale of punishment, The: Bentham, Jeremy

Ratnavali: Dutt, M.M.

Rat's castle: Bridges, Roy

Rats in the sacristy: Powys, L.C.

Rattlesnake, The: Sabatini, R.

Rat-trap, The: Heywood, Thomas

Rat-trap, The: Snelling, W.J.

Ravages of a carpet, The: Stowe, Harriet Beecher

Raven, The: Poe, Edgar Allen

Raven among the rocks: Mais, S.P.B.

Ravenna: Wilde, Oscar

Ravens almanacke foretelling of a plague, famine, and civill warre, The: Dekker, Thomas

Raven's brood: Benson, E.F.

Raven's nest, The: De Selincourt, Aubrey

Ravenshaw of Rietholme: Mitford, Bertram

Ravenshoe: Kingsley, Henry

Raw edge: Appel, Benjamin

Raw material: Bottome, Phyllis

Raw material: Canfield, Dorothy

Raw material: La Farge, Oliver

Rawdon's rood: Lawrence, D.H.

Raymond: Lodge, Sir Oliver

Raymond Roussel: Heppenstall, J.R.

Rayton: Roberts, T.G.

Razor's edge, The: Maugham, Somerset

Razzle dazzle: Saroyan, William

Re: an elephant up a tree: Van Loon, Hendrik

Reader, The: Steele, Sir Richard

Reader, here you'l plainly see Judgement perverted by these three; a priest, a judge, a patentee: Heywood, Thomas

Reader, I married him: Green, Anne

Reader is warned, The: †Carter Dickson

Reader over your shoulder, The: Graves, Robert

Reader's history of American literature, A: Higginson, T.W.

Readiana: comments on current events: Reade, Charles

Readie and easie way to establish a free commonwealth, The: Milton, John

Reading: Walpole, Sir Hugh

Reading a novel: Allen, Walter Ernest

Reading as usual: Forster, E.M.

Reading of books, The: Jackson, Holbrook

Reading of earth, A: Meredith, George

Reading of life, A: Meredith, George

Reading the spirit: Eberhart, Richard

Reading, writing and remembering: Lucas, E.V.

Readings: De la Mare, Walter

Readings from British drama: Nicoll, J.R.A.

Readings in American poetry: Griswold, R.W.

Readings in Crabbe's Tales of the Hall: Fitzgerald, Edward

Readings in English literature: Bullett, Gerald

Readings in jurisprudence and legal philosophy: Cohen, M.R.

Readings in natural philosophy: Clarke, Charles Cowden

Readings in Rabelais: Besant, Sir Walter

Readings in St. John's Gospel: Temple, William

Readings on poetry: Edgeworth, Maria

Ready-money, Mortiboy: Besant, Sir Walter and James Rice

Real bearings of the West India question: Higgins, M.J.

Real Charlotte, The: Somerville, E.

Real conversations: Archer, William

Real David Copperfield, The: Graves, Robert

Real dope, The: Lardner, Ring

Real issues, The: White, W.A.

Real life of Sebastian Knight, The: Nabokov, Vladimir

Real motive, The: Canfield, Dorothy

Real people: Beresford, J.D.

Real people: Wingfield, Shiela

Real presence and spirituall of Christ in the Blessed Sacrament, The: Taylor, Jeremy

Real property: Monro, H.E.

Real Russia, The: Prichard, K.S.

Real Sally, The: †Mordaunt, Elinor

Real soldiers of fortune: Davis, R.H.

Real Stanley Baldwin, The: Steed, H.W.

Real thing, The: James, Henry

Real Tripitka, The: Waley, Arthur

Real war, The: Liddell Hart, B.

Real woman, The: Hichens, Robert

Real world, The: Herrick, Robert

Realism in literature and art: Darrow, C.S.

Realities: Linton, Eliza

Realities of war: Gibbs, Sir Philip

Reality: Scott, D.C.

Reality of a spiritual world, The: Lodge, Sir Oliver

Really, my dear: Morley, C.D.

Realm of essence, The: Santayana, George

Realm of matter, The: Santayana, George

Realm of resemblance, The: Stevens, Wallace

Realm of spirit, The: Santayana, George

Realm of truth, The: Santayana, George

Realmah: Helps, Sir Arthur

Realms of day: De Selincourt, Hugh

Realms of silver: Mackenzie, Sir Compton

Reaped and bound: Mackenzie, Sir Compton

Reaping the whirlwind: Monkhouse, A.N.

Rear-Admiral William Branford Shubrick: Cooper, Susan Fenimore

Reason and beauty in the poetic mind: Williams, Charles

Reason and belief: Lodge, Sir Oliver

Reason and emotion in relation to conduct: De Zilwa, Lucien

Reason and law: Cohen, M.R.

Reason and nature: Cohen, M.R.

Reason and romanticism: Read, Sir Herbert

Reason and Sensuality: Lydgate, John

Reason and the result of Civil Service reform, The: Curtis, G.W.

Reason of church-government, The: Milton, John

Reason why, The: Glyn, Elinor

Reasonable man's peace, A: Wells, H.G.

Reasonable religion: Mather, Cotton

Reasonable shores, The: Stern, G.B.

Reasonableness of Christianity as delivered in the Scriptures, The: Locke, John

Reasons against the repealing the acts of Parliament concerning the Test: Burnet, Gilbert

Reasons and reasons: Moffatt, James

Reasons for a new edition of Shakespear's works: Collier, J.P.

Reasons for restoring some prayers and directions: Collier, Jeremy

Reasons for voting for Bryan: Higginson, T.W.

Reasons humbly offered to the Parliament of Ireland for repealing the Sacramental Test: Swift, Jonathan

Reasons of Mr. Bays changing his religion, The: Brown, Thomas

Reasons of Mr. Joseph Hains the player's conversion and re-conversion, The: Brown, Thomas

Reasons of the new convert's taking the oaths to the present Government, The: Brown, Thomas

Rebecca: Du Maurier, Daphne

Rebecca: Rowson, S.H.

Rebecca and Rowena: Thackeray, W.M.

Rebecca of Sunnybrook Farm: Wiggin, Kate

Rebecca's daughter: Thomas, Dylan

Rebel loyalist, The: †Connor, Ralph

Rebel of the family, The: Linton, Eliza

Rebel passion, The: Brittain, Vera

Rebel Queen, The: Besant, Sir Walter

Rebel rose, The: Praed, Mrs. C.

Rebel war clerk's diary at the Confederate States Capital, A: Jones, J.B.

Rebellion: Drinkwater, John

Rebellion: Mais, S.P.B.

Rebellion: its latent causes and their significance, The: Tuckerman, H.T.

Rebellion times in the Canadas: Lizars, Robina and K.M. Lizars

Rebellious heroine, A: Bangs, J.K.

Rebells anathematized: Taylor, John

Rebels, The: Child, L.M.

Rebels, The: Treece, Henry

Rebels: Vachell, H.A.

Rebel's recollections, A: Eggleston, G.C.

Rebound: Stewart, D.O.

Rebus written by a lady, A: Swift, Jonathan

Recalled to life: Allen, Grant

Re-captured rhymes: Traill, H.D.

Recent developments in the British labour movement: Cole, G.D.H.

Recent essays on the future of India: Nehru, Jawaharlal

Recent prose: Masefield, John

Recent Southern fiction: Porter, K.A.

Recessional: Kipling, Rudyard

Recipe for a magic childhood: Chase, M.E.

Reckless lady, The: Gibbs, *Sir* Philip

Reckoning, The: Chambers, R.W.

Recluse, The: Wordsworth, William

Recluse of Norway, The: Porter, Anna Maria

Recognition of Cuban independence: Adams, H.B.

Recollections: Morley, John

Recollections and private memoirs of Washington: Custis, G.W.P.

Recollections of a first visit to the Alps in August and September: Talfourd, *Sir* T.N.

Recollections of a literary life: Mitford, Mary Russell

Recollections of a tour made in Scotland: Wordsworth, Dorothy

Recollections of a varied life: Eggleston, G.C.

Recollections of an excursion to the monasteries of Alcobaça and Batalha: Beckford, William

Recollections of Christ's Hospital: Lamb, Charles

Recollections of D.G.Rossetti: Caine, *Sir* T.H.

Recollections of Europe: Cooper, James Fenimore

Recollections of foreign travel on life, literature and self-knowledge: Brydges, *Sir* S.E.

Recollections of Geoffrey Hamlyn, The: Kingsley, Henry

Recollections of the American war, 1812–24: Dunlop, William

Recollections of the Civil War: Elliott, M.H.

Recollections of the lakes: Meredith, L.A.

Recollections of the last days of Shelley and Byron: Trelawny, E.J.

Recollections of the last ten years: Flint, Timothy

Recollections of writers: Clarke, Charles Cowden

Recollections, personal and literary: Stoddard, R.H.

Recommendation of the study of the remains of Ancient Grecian and Roman architecture, sculpture and painting, A: Wilson, John

Reconstructed marriage, A: Barr, A.E.H.

Reconstruction in philosophy: Dewey, John

Reconstruction of religious thought in Islam, The: Iqbal, *Sir* Muhammad

Reconstruction of the Fabian Society: Wells, H.G.

Record guide, The: Sackville-West, Edward

Record of a girlhood: Kemble, Fanny

Record of America, The: Adams, J.T.

Record of conversations on the Gospels: Alcott, A.B.

Record of family faculties: Galton, *Sir* Francis

Recorder, The: Halleck, Fitz-Greene

Records of a family of engineers: Stevenson, R.L.

Records of later life: Kemble, Fanny

Records of love, The: Carey, Henry

Records of the Court of the Stationers' Company, 1576–1602: Greg, W.W.

Records of the English Bible: Pollard, A.W.

Records o the heart: Lewis, S.A.

Records of the Somerville family of Castlehaven and Drisbrane: Somerville, Edith

Records of the Western shore: Hawker, R.S.

Records of woman: Hemans, *Mrs.* Felicia

Recovery and faith: Radhakrishan, Sarvepalli

Recovery of belief, The: Joad, C.E.M.

Re-creation of Brian Kent, The: Wright, H.B.

Recreations: Sassoon, Siegfried

Recreations of an anthologist: Matthews, J.B.

Recreations of Christopher North, The: †North, Christopher

Recreations with the Muses: Alexander, William

Recrudescence of Madame Vic, The: Janvier, T.A.

Recruiting officer, The: Farquhar, George

Recruiting serjeant, The: Bickerstaffe, Isaac

Rector, The: Crothers, Rachel

Rector and the doctor's family, The: Oliphant, Margaret

Rector of Wyck, The: Sinclair, May

Rectorial address delivered at St. Andrews University, The: Barrie, *Sir* J.M.

Rectory children, The: Molesworth, *Mrs.*

Rectory umbrella and mischmasch, The: †Carroll, Lewis

Recuyell of the histories of Troy, The: Caxton, William

Red account, The: Gielgud, Val

Red aces: Wallace, Edgar

Red and white: Hale, E.E.

Red and white heather: Buchanan, R.W.

Red archives: Vulliamy, C.E.

Red as a rose is she: Broughton, Rhoda

Red axe, The: Crockett, S.R.

Red badge of courage, The: Crane, Stephen

Red Barbara: O'Flaherty, Liam

Red barn, The: Tarkington, Booth

Red beret, The: Saunders, H.A. St. George

Red, black, blond and olive: Wilson, Edmund

Red carpet for the sun, A: Layton, Irving

Red chapels of Banteai Srei, The: Sitwell, Sacheverell

Red city, The: Mitchell, S.W.

Red cloak flying: Widdemer, Margaret

Red cockade, The: Weyman, Stanley

Red comet: Trease, Geoffrey

Red cotton nightcap country: Browning, Robert

Red court farm, The: Wood, Ellen

Red cow and her friends, The: McArthur, Peter

Red Cross and the White, The: Saunders, H.A. St. George

Red Cross barge, The: Lowndes, M.A.

Red Cross girl, The: Davis, R.H.

Red Cross in France, The: Granville–Barker, Sir Harley

Red Cross Knight, The: Brontë, Charlotte

Red Danube, The: Marshall, Bruce

Red dawn, The: Dixon, Thomas

Red Dawson: Cronin, B.C.

Red deer: Jefferies, Richard

Red derelict, The: Mitford, Bertram

Red Eagle and the wars with the Greek Indians of Alabama: Eggleston, G.C.

Red eve: Haggard, Sir Henry Rider

Red fairy book, The: Lang, Andrew

Red feathers, The: Milne, A.A.

Red feathers, The: Roberts, T.G.

Red flag, The: Noel, R.B.W.

Red flag: Ridge, Lola

Red grange, The: Molesworth, Mrs.

Red gums: Esson, T.L.B.

Red haired man's wife, The: Carleton, William

Red Hall: Carleton, William

Red hand of Ulster, The: Hannay, J.O.

Red harvest: Hammett, S.D.

Red heart, The: Clune, Frank

Red hills, The: Davies, Rhys

Red house, The: Nesbit, E.

Red house mystery, The: Milne, A.A.

Red in the morning: †Yates, Dornford

Red knight, The: Young, Francis Brett

Red lamp, The: Rinehart, Mary Roberts

Red leaf, The: Hassall, Christopher

Red leaves and roses: Cawein, Madison

Red ledger, The: Packard, F.L.

Red letter nights: Agate, J.E.

Red letter Shakespeare: Chambers, Sir E.K.

Red light, The: Maltby, H.F.

Red man's luck: Skinner, C.L.

Red men and white: Wister, Owen

Red Morgan rides: Lawson, Will

Red notebook, The: Miller, Henry

Red Oleanders: Tagore, Sir R.

Red one, The: London, Jack

Red pagan, The: Stephens, A.G.

Red, papers on musical subjects: Van Vechten, Carl

Red path, The: Freeman, John

Red pen, The: Herbert, Sir A.P.

Red peony, The: Lin Yu-T'ang

Red Pirogue, The: Roberts, T.G.

Red pony, The: Steinbeck, John

Red poppies and white marble: Flavin, Martin

Red pottage: Cholmondeley, Mary

Red priest, The: Lewis, P. Wyndham

Red queen, white queen: Treece, Henry

Red ranger, The: Cody, H.A.

Red Redmaynes, The: Phillpotts, Eden

Red republic, The: Chambers, R.W.

Red riders, The: Page, T.N.

Red rock: Page, T.N.

Red rock wilderness: Huxley, Elspeth J.

Red room, The: Wells, H.G.

Red rose: Mannin, Ethel

Red roses for bronze: Doolittle, Hilda

Red roses for me: O'Casey, Sean

Red rover, The: Cooper, James Fenimore

Red saint, The: Deeping, Warwick

Red sand: Stribling, T.S.

Red settlement: Treece, Henry

Red Shoes ballet, The: Gibbon, Monk

Red sky at morning: Cusack, E.D.

Red sky at morning: Kennedy, Margaret

Red sky in the morning: Coffin, Robert

Red snow on Grand Pré: Mac-Mechan, A.M.

Red spider: Baring-Gould, Sabine

Red strangers, The: Huxley, Elspeth J.

Red Sunday: Griffith, Hubert

Red tapeworm, The: Mackenzie, Sir Compton

Red towers of Granada, The: Trease, Geoffrey

Red triangle, The: Morrison, Arthur

Red wall flower, A: Warner, S.B.

Red wax: Percy, Edward

Red west road, The: Lawson, Will

Red widow murders, The: †Carter Dickson

Red willows: Skinner, C.L.

Red wine and yellow hair: Patchen, Kenneth

Red wine of youth: Stringer, A.J.A.

Red wing, The: Ingraham, J.H.

Red-bird: Holmes, M.J.

Redburn: Melville, Herman

Redcliff: Phillpotts, Eden

Redeemed: Cunninghame Graham, Robert

Redeemer, The: Sassoon, Siegfried

Redemption: Blackmore, *Sir* R.D.

Redemption: Brooke, Henry

Redemption: Willson, H.B.

Redemption of Freetown, The: Sheldon, C.M.

Redgauntlet: Scott, *Sir* Walter

Redheaded outfield, The: Grey, Zane

Redheap: Lindsay, Norman

Rediscovered country, The: White, S.E.

Rediscovering America: Stearns, H.E.

Re-discovery of America, The: Frank, Waldo

Re-discovery of "loving mad Tom", The: Graves, Robert

Rediscovery of man: Frank, Waldo

Red-letter days in Applethorpe: Dodge, M.A.

Redmond, Count O'Hanlon: Carleton, William

Redruff: Seton-Thomson, E.

Redskins, The: Cooper, James Fenimore

Redwood: Sedgwick, C.M.

Reed Anthony: Adams, Andy

Reed of Pan, The: Benson, A.C.

Reeds shaken with the wind: Hawker, R.S.

Reef, The: Wharton, Edith

Reekiana: Chambers, Robert

Reeling earth, The: Millin, Sarah Gertrude

Re-enter Sir John: †Dane, Clemence and H. de G. Simpson

Referendum, The: Strachey, John St. Loe

Reflected glory: Kelly, G.E.

Reflection on our modern poesy, A: Phillips, John

Reflections and comments, 1865–1895: Godkin, E.L.

Reflections and memories: Squire, *Sir* J.C.

Reflections and reminiscences: Gupta, Nagendranath

Reflections at fifty: Farrell, James

Reflections concerning innate moral Principles:Bolingbroke, Henry St. John

Reflections critical and satyrical: Dennis, John

Reflections in a mirror: Morgan, Charles

Reflections of a married man, The: Grant, Robert

Reflections of a wondering Jew: Cohen, M.R.

Reflections of Ambrosine, The: Glyn, Elinor

Reflections on a Marine Venus: Durrell, Lawrence

Reflections on a paper intituled, His Majesty's reasons for withdrawing himself from Rochester: Burnet, Gilbert

Reflections on courtship and marriage: Franklin, Benjamin

Reflections on Dr. Swift's letter to the Earl of Oxford, about the English tongue:Oldmixon, John

Reflections on some of the late high-flown sermons: Phillips, John

Reflections on the causes that led to the formation of the Colonization Society: Carey, Mathew

Reflections on the death of a porcupine: Lawrence, D.H.

Reflections on the failure of socialism: Eastman, Max

Reflections on the golden bed: Anand, M.R.

Reflections on the present state of affairs at home and abroad: Young, Arthur

Reflections on the present system of banking: Carey, Mathew

Reflections on the Psalms: Lewis, C.S.

Reflections on the revolution in France: Burke, Edmund

Reflections on the revolution of our time: Laski, Harold

Reflections on the stage and Mr. Collier's defence of the short view: Oldmixon, John

Reflections on the subject of emigration from Europe: Carey, Mathew

Reflections suggested by the new theory of matter: Balfour, A.J.

Reflections upon Mons: King, William

Reflections upon our late and present proceedings in England: Sedley, *Sir* Charles

Reflections upon the education of children in charity schools: Trimmer, *Mrs.* Sarah

Reform: Montagu, Basil

Reformation, The: Durant, W.J.

Reformation: Traill, C.P.

Reformation of manners: Defoe, Daniel

Reformer, The: Sheldon, C.M.

Reformer exposing the vices of the age in several characters, The: Ward, Edward

Reformers of the nineteenth century: Grant, G.M.

Reformist's answer to the article entitled"State of Parties",The: Hunt, Leigh

Refuge from nightmare: Gould, Gerald

Refugee in America, The: Trollope, Frances

Refugees, The:Doyle, *Sir* Arthur Conan

Refusal, The: Cibber, Colley

Refutation of the libel on the memory of the late King of France, A: Williams, H.M.

Refutation of Deism, A: Shelley, P.B.

Regal and ecclesiastical antiquities of England, The: Strutt, Joseph

Regency Buck: Heyer, Georgette

Regeneration: an account of the social work of the Salvation Army: Haggard, *Sir* Henry Rider

Regent, The: Bennett, Arnold

Regicide, The: Smollett, Tobias

Regiment of women: †Dane, Clemence

Reginald: (†Saki), Munro, H.H.

Reginald Dalton: Lockhart, J.G.

Reginald Hetherege: Kingsley, Henry

Reginald in Russia: (†Saki), Munro, H.H.

Region cloud, The: Lubbock, Percy

Region of the summer stars, The: Williams, Charles

Register, The: Howells, W.D.

Registrum Sacrum Anglicanum: Stubbs, William

Regrets of a mountaineer: Stephen, *Sir* Leslie

Regular fellows I have met: Lardner, Ring

Rehabilitations: Lewis, C.S.

Rehearsal, The: Buckingham, G.V.

Rehearsal: Morley, C.D.

Rehearsal at Goatham, The: Gay, John

Rehearsal transpos'd, The: Marvell, Andrew

Rehearsals: Warren, J.B.L.

Reign of gilt, The: Phillips, D.G.

Reign of Henry VII, The: Pollard, A.F.

Reign of law, The: Allen, J.L.

Reign of Queen Victoria, The: Bolitho, H.H.

Reign of religion in contemporary philosophy, The: Radhakrishan, Sarvepalli

Reims revisited: Gosse, *Sir* Edmund

Reincarnations: Stephens, James

Rejected addresses: Smith, Horatio and James Smith

Rejected of men: Pyle, Howard

Rejected stone, The: Conway, M.D.

Rejoice in the Lamb: Smart, Christopher

Rejoinder to Prof. Weismann, A: Spencer, Herbert

Relapse, The: Vanbrugh, *Sir* John

Relation between Michael Angelo and Tintoret, The: Ruskin, John

Relation of a journey, A: Sandys, George

Relation of a Quaker, A: Denham, *Sir* John

Relation of fellow-feeling to sex, The: Housman, Laurence

Relation of Hans Sachs to the Decameron, The: MacMechan, A.M.

Relation of literature to life, The: Warner, C.D.

Relation of philosophy to science, The: Watson, John

Relation of the Alabama-Georgia dialect to the provincial dialects of Great Britain, The: Brooks, Cleanth

Relation of the kindergarten to the public school, The: Wiggin, Kate

Relation of the late royall entertainment given by the Lord Knowles, A: Campion, Thomas

Relation of the troubles which have hapned in New-England, A: Mather, Increase

Relation of the University and the technical college, The: Bragg, *Sir* Lawrence

Relations between poetry and painting, The: Stevens, Wallace

Relations of Lord Byron and Augusta Leigh, The: Trelawny, E.J.

Relations of Percy Bysshe Shelley with his two wives, Harriet and Mary, The: Trelawny, E.J.

Relationship between co-operation and trade unionism, The: Webb, Beatrice

Relative value of studies and accomplishments in the education of women, The: Hutton, R.H.

Relative values: Coward, Noel

Relativity: Lodge, *Sir* Oliver

Relativity: a popular exposition: Einstein, Albert

Relativity theory of protons and electrons: Eddington, *Sir* A.S.

Release of the soul, The: Cannan, Gilbert

Relentless city, The: Benson, E.F.

Relic, The: Hillyer, Robert

Relics and angels: Basso, Hamilton

Relicta: Munby, A.J.

Religio journalistici: Morley, C.D.

Religio laici: Dryden, John

Religio Medici: Browne, *Sir* Thomas

Religio Poetae: Patmore, Coventry

Religion, a criticism and a forecast: Dickinson, G.L.

Religion and conscience in Ancient Egypt: Petrie, *Sir* William Flinders

Religion and immortality: Dickinson, G.L.

Religion and love in Dante: Williams, Charles

Religion and philosophy: Collingwood, R.G.

Religion and science: Russell, Bertrand

Religion and society: Radhakrishan, Sarvepalli

Religion and the rise of capitalism: Tawney, R.H.

Religion in everyday life: Grenfell, *Sir* Wilfred

Religion in literature and religion in life: Brooke, S.A.

Religion in the making: Whitehead, A.N.

Religion of a Darwinist: Keith, *Sir* Arthur

Religion of a literary man, The: Le Gallienne, Richard

Religion of a sceptic, The: Powys, John Cowper

Religion of Ancient Egypt: Petrie, *Sir* William Flinders

Religion of ancient Scandinavia: Craigie, *Sir* W.A.

Religion of Man, The: Tagore, *Sir* R.

Religion of Plato, The: More, P.E.

Religion of solidarity, The: Bellamy, Edward

Religion of the good life: Zoroastrianism, The: Masani, *Sir* R.P.

Religion of the heart, The: Hunt, Leigh

Religion of war, The: Kipling, Rudyard

Religion we need, The: Radhakrishan, Sarvepalli

Religion without revelation: Huxley, *Sir* Julian

Religions of the world, The: Grant, G.M.

Religious advance towards rationalism,The:Housman,Laurence

Religious aspect of philosophy, The: Royce, Josiah

Religious basis of the forms of Indian society: Coomaraswamy, A.K.

Religious discourses: Scott, *Sir* Walter

Religious functions of comedy, The: Logan, J.D.

Religious interregnum, The: Bennett, Arnold

Religious life in Ancient Egypt: Petrie, *Sir* William Flinders

Religious poems: Stowe, H.B.

Religious problems of the nineteenth century: De Vere, Aubrey

Religious tendencies of the age, The: Lecky, W.E.

Reliquary, The: Barton, Bernard

Reliques of Ancient English poetry: Percy, Thomas

Reliques of Father Prout, The: Mahony, F.S.

Reliques of Irish poetry: Brooke, Charlotte

Reliquiae Bodleianae: Bodley, *Sir* Thomas

Reliquiae juveniles: Watts, Isaac

Reliquiae Spelmannianae: Spelman, *Sir* Henry

Reliquiae Wottonianae:Wotton, *Sir* Henry

Reluctant Madonna, The: Steen, Marguerite

Reluctant widow, The: Heyer, Georgette

Remaines of a greater worke, concerning Britaine: Camden, William

Remains of Gentilisme and Judaisme: Aubrey, John

Remains of Maynard Davis. Richardson, The: Simms, W.G.

Remains of the late learned and ingenious Dr. William King: King, William

Remaking of modern armies, The: Liddell Hart, B.

Remarkable history of Sir Thomas Upmore, Bart., M.P., The: Blackmore, *Sir* R.D.

Remarkable young man, The: Roberts, C.E.M.

Remarks and collections: Hearne, Thomas

Remarks and facts concerning American paper money: Franklin, Benjamin

Remarks at the centennial celebration of the Latin school: Emerson, R.W.

Remarks concerning the savages of North America: Franklin, Benjamin

Remarks, critical and illustrative, on the text and notes of the last edition of Shakespeare: Nichols, John

Remarks, critical and illustrative, on the text and notes of the last edition of Shakespeare: Ritson, Joseph

Remarks on a book, entitul'd Prince Arthur: Dennis, John

Remarks on a play, call'd The conscious lovers: Dennis,John

Remarks on forest scenery, and other woodland views: Gilpin, William

Remarks on Mr. Pope's Rape of the Lock: Dennis, John

Remarks on rural scenery: Smith, J.T.

Remarks on the character of George L. Stearns: Emerson, R.W.

Remarks on the history of England: Bolingbroke, Henry St. John

Remarks on the Oratorian Vocation: Newman, J.H.

Remarks on the speech of M.Dupont: More, Hannah

Remarks upon a late disingenuous discourse writ by one T.D.: Marvell, Andrew

Remarks upon an essay concerning humane understanding: Burnet, Thomas

Remarks upon Cato: Dennis, John

Remarks upon Mr. Pope's translation of Homer: Dennis, John

Remarks upon several passages in the preliminaries to the Dunciad: Dennis, John

Rembrandt: Lucas, E.V.

Remedie against sorrow and feare, A: Hooker, Richard

Remedy for duelling, The: Beecher, Lyman

Remember Mrs. Munch: Bullett, Gerald

Remember the Alamo: Barr, A.E.H.

Remember the Alamo!: Warren, Robert Penn

Remember to remember: Miller, Henry

Rememberings, 1895–1945: Mackaye, Percy

Remembrance: Massingham, Harold

Remembrance of the wel imployed life and godly end of George Gaskoigne esquire, A: Whetstone, George

Remembrance of the woorthie life of Sir Nicholas Bacon, A: Whetstone, George

Remembrance of things past: Ackland, Rodney

Remembrance Rock: Sandburg, Carl

Remembrance of Sir James Dier, A: Whetstone, George

Remembrance of the life of Thomas, Erle of Sussex, A: Whetstone, George

Remembrances: Gale, Norman

Remington sentence,The:Ridge, W.Pett

Reminiscences: Smith, Goldwin

Reminiscences and opinions, 1813–85: Doyle, *Sir* F.H.C.

Reminiscences, 1819–99: Howe, Julia

Reminiscences of a literary life: Dibdin, T.F.

Reminiscences of a South African pioneer: Scully, W.C.

Reminiscences of a visit to Quebec, July 1839: Kirby, William

Reminiscences of a workman's life: Dutt, R.C.

Reminiscences of Charles L. Eliot, artist: Thorpe, T.B.

Reminiscences of D.H.Lawrence: Murry, John Middleton

Reminiscences of Huxley from the Smithsonian report for 1900: Fiske, John

Reminiscences of Solar Pons, The: Derleth, A.W.

Reminiscences of the Evening Post: Bryant, W.C.

Reminiscences of the French war: Rogers, Robert

Reminiscences of the Impressionist painters: Moore, George

Reminiscences written for Miss Mary and Miss Agnes Berry: Walpole, Horace

Remnants: MacCarthy, *Sir* Desmond

Remonstrance, The: †Pindar, Peter

Remorse: Coleridge, S.T.

Remote people: Waugh, Evelyn

Removal of untouchability, The: Gandhi, M.K.

Remy de Gourmont: Aldington, Richard

Renaissance, The: Symonds, J.A.

Renaissance and English humanism, The: Bush, Douglas

Renaissance bronzes from the Samuel H.Kress collection: Pope-Hennessy, J.W.

Renaissance fancies and studies: †Lee, Vernon

Renaissance in India, The: Ghose, Sri Aurobindo

Renaissance in Italy: Symonds, J.A.

Renaissance of Modern Europe, The: Symonds, J.A.

Rena's experiment: Holmes, M.J.

Renascence: Millay, E.St.Vincent

Renascence of the English drama, The: Jones, H.A.

Rendezvous in a landscape: Derleth, A.W.

Rendition of Anthony Burns, The: Clarke, J.F.

Renegade: Lewisohn, Ludwig

Renegade poet, A: Thompson, Francis

Renegado, The: Massinger, Philip

Renewal of youth, The: Myers, F.W.H.

Renewal of youth, The: Russell, G.W.

Renny's daughter: De la Roche, Mazo

Renown at Stratford: Davies, Robertson

Renowned history of Giles Gingerbread, The: Newbery, John

Renshaw Fanning's quest: Mitford, Bertram

Rent day, The: Jerrold, Douglas

Rent in a cloud, A: Lever,C.J.

Rent, rings and houses: Cole, G.D.H.

Reorganization of the University of Oxford, The: Smith, Goldwin

Repealers, The: Blessington, Marguerite

Repent in haste: Marquand,J.P.

Repentance, The: Greene, Robert

Repentance of Magdalene Despar, The: Evans, G.E.

Reperusals and re-collections: Smith, L.L.P.

Replenishing Jessica: Bodenheim, Maxwell

Reply as true as steele to a swarme of sectaries, A: Taylor, John

Reply ... in behalf of the women of America, A: Stowe, Harriet Beecher

Reply to Lord Strangford's "Observations", A: Napier, *Sir* W.F.P.

Reply to Mr. Bosanquet's practical observations on the Bullion Committee: Ricardo, David

Reply to Mr. M.E.S.A.Hamilton's inquiry into the imputed Shakespeare forgeries: Collier, J.P.

Reply to the essay on population by the Rev. T.R.Malthus, A: Hazlitt, William

Reply to the observations of the Rev. Dr. Milles, on the ward robe account: Walpole, Horace

Reply to the speech of Joseph Galloway: Dickinson, John

Reply to various opponents, A: Napier, *Sir* W.F.P.

Replycacion agaynst certayne yong scolars, A: Skeltone John

Report and discourse of the affaires and state of Germany, The: Ascham, Roger

Report of a discourse concerning supreme power in affaires of religion, A: Hayward, *Sir* John

Report of a late practise enterprised by a Papist, The: Rich, Barnabe

Report of the Coroner's inquest on Jane Watson: Hone, William

Report of the County Chairman: Michener, J.A.

Report of the fight about the Iles of Açores, A: Ralegh, *Sir* Walter

Report on elementary education in Protestant Germany: Pattison, Mark

Report on experience: Mulgan, J.A.E.

Report on Fabian policy and resolutions: Shaw, G.B.

Report on Israel: Shaw, Irwin

Report on manufactures: Hamilton, Alexander

Report on manuscript lists in the archives relating to the United Empire loyalists: Campbell, W.W.

Report on public credit: Hamilton, Alexander

Report on Salvation Army colonies: Haggard,*Sir* Henry Rider

Report on the condition and needs of the Mission Indians of California: Jackson, H.H.

Report on the iron of Dodge and Washington counties: Percival, J.G.

Report on the pumic stone industry of the Lipari Islands, A: Douglas, Norman

Report on the relativity theory of gravitation: Eddington, *Sir* A.S.

Report to Saint Peter: Van Loon, Hendrik

Report to the Committee on the Poor Law: Owen, Robert

Reporter: Levin, Meyer

Reporter, The: Wallace, Edgar

Reporter for Lincoln, A: Tarbell, Ida

Reporting, editing and authorship: Jefferies, Richard

Reports on the excavations of the Palace of Knossos: Evans. *Sir* A.J.

Reports on the geology of Ceylon: Coomaraswamy, A.K.

Repose: Mottram, R.H.

Representative actors: Russell, W.C.

Representative men: Emerson, R.W.

Reprieve: Deeping, Warwick

Reprinted papers: Blunden, Edmund

Reprisal, The: Smollett, Tobias

Reprobation asserted: Bunyan, John

Reproof: Smollett, Tobias

Reptiles of Australia: (†Donald Barr), Barrett, C.L.

Repton School sermons: Temple, William

Republic, The: Cawein, Madison

Republic: conversations on fundamentals, The: Beard, C.A.

Republic of childhood, The: Wiggin, Kate

Republic of Plato, The: Richards, I.A.

Republican court, The: Griswold, R.W.

Republican letters: Clemens, S.L.

Republican superstitions as illustrated in the political history of America: Conway, M.D.

Republican tradition in Europe, The: Fisher, H.A.L.

Reputation: †Mordaunt, Elinor

Reputations: ten years after: Liddell Hart, B.

Requiem: †O'Sullivan, Seumas

Requiem: Wolfe, Humbert

Requiem, Edward the peace maker: Campbell, W.W.

Requiem for a nun: Faulkner, William

Requiem for a Wren: †Shute, Nevil

Res judicatae: Birrell, Augustine

Res literariae: Brydges, *Sir* S.E.

Rescue, The: Conrad, Joseph

Rescue, The: Sackville-West, Edward

Rescue, The: Sedgwick, A.D.

Rescuers, The: Sharp, Margery

Research magnificent, The: Wells, H.G.

Researches in Sinai: Petrie, *Sir* William Flinders

Resentment: Monkhouse, A.N.

Resentment: Waugh, Alec

Reservation and Catholicity: Coulton, G.G.

Residence in France, A: Cooper, James Fenimore

Resident women-students: †Carroll, Lewis

Resignation: Young, Edward

Resist not evil: Darrow, C.S.

Resolutions and declaration of rights adopted by the Stamp Act Congress, The: Dickinson, John

Resolves divine, morall, politicall: Feltham, Owen

Responsibilities: Yeats, W.B.

Responsibilities of the novelist, The: †Norris, Frank

Responsibility: Agate, J.E.

Respublica Anglicana: Wither, George

Rest and unrest: Thomas, E.E.P.

Rest cure, The: Jennings, Gertrude

Rest harrow: Hewlett, Maurice

Restituta: Brydges, *Sir* S.E.

Restless human hearts: Jefferies, Richard

Restless is the river: Derleth, A.W.

Restless sex, The: Chambers, R.W.

Restoration: Sidgwick, Ethel

Restoration comedy: Dobrée, Bonamy

Restoration of suffragan bishops, The: Newman, J.H.

Restoration of the works of art to Italy, The: Hemans, *Mrs.* Felicia

Restoration tragedy: Dobrée, Bonamy

Resurgam: Wilde, Oscar

Resurrection of Rome, The: Chesterton, G.K.

Resurrection of the dead, The: Bunyan, John

Retaliation: Goldsmith, Oliver

Retreat: Blunden, Edmund

Retreat, The: Reid, Forrest

Retreat for lay people, A: Knox, R.A.

Retreat for priests, A: Knox, R.A.

Retreat from glory: Lockhart, *Sir* Robert Bruce

Retreat in slow motion: Knox, R.A.

Retrogression: Watson, *Sir* J.W.

Retrospect: Boyd, Martin

Retrospect: Chapman, R.W.

Retrospect of flowers, A: Young, A.J.

Retrospect of scrutiny: Leavis, F.R.

Retrospect of western travel, A: Martineau, Harriet

Retrospection: Cumberland, Richard

Retrospection: Thrale, H.L.

Retrospection and introspection: Eddy, M.B.

Retrospections political and personal: Bancroft, H.H.

Retrospective adventures: Reid, Forrest

Retrospective reviews: Le Gallienne, Richard

Retrospects and prospects: descriptive and historical essays: Lanier, Sidney

Return, The: De la Mare, Walter

Return half, The: Van Druten, J.W.

Return I dare not: Kennedy, Margaret

Return journey: Seymour, Beatrice Kean

Return of a heroine: Steen, Marguerite

Return of Alcestis, The: Housman, Laurence

Return of Bulldog Drummond, The: †Sapper

Return of Don Quixote, The: Chesterton, G.K.

Return of Imry, The: Pertwee, Roland

Return of Kai-Lung: Bramah, E.

Return of Lanny Budd, The: Sinclair, Upton

Return of Long John Silver, The: Connell, John

Return of Peter Grimm, The: Belasco, David

Return of Robinson Crusoe, The: Treece Henry

Return of several ministers, The: Mather, Cotton

Return of Sherlock Holmes, The: Doyle, Sir Arthur Conan

Return of Solar Pons, The: Derleth, A.W.

Return of the brute: O'Flaherty, Liam

Return of the continental Op., The: Hammett, S.D.

Return of the druses, The: Browning, Robert

Return of the emigrant, The: De la Roche, Mazo

Return of the fugitives, The: Finlayson, Roderick

Return of the guards, The: Doyle, Sir F.H.C.

Return of the King, The: Tolkien, J.R.R.

Return of the native, The: Hardy, Thomas

Return of the O'Mahony, The: Frederic, Harold

Return of the petticoats, The: Deeping, Warwick

Return of the prodigal, The: Sinclair, May

Return of the scare-crow, The: Noyes, Alfred

Return of the soldier: Van Druten, J.W.

Return of the soldier, The: †West, Rebecca

Return of the traveller: Warner, Rex

Return of Ulysses, The: Bridges, Robert

Return to Burma: Fergusson, Sir Bernard

Return to Cheltenham: Ashton, Helen

Return to Coolami: Dark, Eleanor

Return to Danes Hill: Dukes, Ashley

Return to husbandry: Blunden, Edmund

Return to Jalna: De la Roche, Mazo

Return to Malaya: Lockhart, Sir Robert Bruce

Return to Paradise: Michener, J.A.

Return to philosophy: Joad, C.E.M.

Return to the cabbage, The: Gould, Gerald

Return to Tyassi: Levy, Benn W.

Return to yesterday: Ford, Ford Madox

Return to yesterday: Griffith, Hubert

Returned empty: Barclay, F.L.

Returning to emotion: Bodenheim, Maxwell

Reuben: Baughan, B.E.

Reuben and Rachel: Rowson, S.H.

Reuben Apsley: Smith, Horatio

Reunion all round: Knox, R.A.

Reunion in Vienna: Sherwood, R.E.

Rev. Annabel Lee, The: Buchanan, R.W.

Rev. Dean Swift's reasons against lowering the gold and silver coin, The: Swift, Jonathan

Rev. Joseph Cook, The: Fiske, John

Revaluation: tradition and development in English poetry: Leavis, F.R.

Revaluations, studies in biography: Abercrombie, Lascelles

Revanche: Rubenstein, Harold F.

Reveille in Washington: Leech, M.K.

Revelation: Deamer, Dulcie

Revelation of God, The: Temple, William

Revelation of Mr. Brightmans Revelation, A: Heywood, Thomas

Revelations of the dead alive: Banim, John

Revenge, The: Behn, Mrs. Afra

Revenge, The: Betterton, Thomas

Revenge, The: Chatterton, Thomas

Revenge: DeLisser, Herbert G.

Revenge: James, G.P.R.

Revenge, The: Young, Edward

Revenge for love, The: Lewis, P. Wyndham

Revenge of Bussy D'Ambois, The: Chapman, George

Revengeful mistress, The: Ayres, Philip

Revengers tragaedie, The: Tourneur, Cyril

Reverberator, The: James, Henry

Reverie: Aldington, Richard

Reverie, The: Johnstone, Charles

Reverie of policeman: Wolfe, Humbert

Reveries of a bachelor: Mitchell, D.G.

Reveries over childhood and youth: Yeats, W.B.

Reverses: a comedy drama: Clarke, Marcus

Reversible Santa Claus, A: Nicholson, Meredith

Reversion to type, A: †Delafield, E.M.

Review: Defoe, Daniel

Review, The: Colman, George, the younger

Review of Churchill's poems: Southey, Robert

Review of Dr. Hunter's Indian Musulmans: Ahmad Khan, Sir Saiyid

Review of English studies: Chapman, R.W.

Review of historical publications relating to Canada, 1896–1917/18: Wrong, G.M.

Review of the civil administration of Mesopotamia: Bell, G.M.

Review of the Constitution: Tooke, Home

Review of the eve of eternity: Clarke, Macdonald

Review of the French Revolution of 1848: Chamier, Frederick

Review of the reflections on the Prince of Orange's declaration, A: Burnet, Gilbert

Reviewer reviewed, The: Ward, R.P.

Reviewers reviewed: Ritchie, *Mrs.* Ann

Reviewing: Woolf, Virginia

Reviewing and criticism of books, The: Swinnerton, Frank

Reviews and discussions, literary, political and historical, not relating to Bacon: Spedding, James

Revised report of fourteen talks: Krishnamurti, Jiddu

Revision of the treaty, A: Keynes, John Maynard

Revolt in the desert: Lawrence, T.E.

Revolt of Boston, The: Herbert, H.W.

Revolt of Islam, The: Shelley, P.B.

Revolt of man, The: Besant, *Sir* Walter

Revolt of Tartarus, The: Heavysege, Charles

Revolt of the oyster, The: Marquis, Don

Revolt of the Protestants of the Cevennes, The: Bray, A.E.

Revolt of the sons, The: Lindsay, Jack

Revolution: Beresford, J.D.

Revolution: Burroughs, John

Revolution, The: Linklater, Eric

Revolution: London, Jack

Revolution and reaction in modern France: Dickinson, G.L.

Revolution by reason: Strachey, John

Revolution from 1789 to 1906: Postgate, Raymond

Revolution in New England justified, The: Sewall, Samuel

Revolution in Tanner's Lane, The: †Rutherford, Mark

Revolution in the mind and practice of the human race, The: Owen, Robert

Revolution in writing: Day-Lewis, C.

Revolutionary epick, The: Disraeli, Benjamin

Revolutionary New England: Adams, J.T.

Revolutionist's handbook, The: Shaw, G.B.

Revolutions of civilisation: Petrie, *Sir* William Flinders

Revolving lights: Richardson, D.M.

Revue: Nichols, Beverley

Reward of the faithfull, The: Fletcher, Giles, *the younger*

Rewards and fairies: Kipling, Rudyard

Rex Whistler: his life and his drawings: Whistler, Laurence

Rey Whistler: the Königsmark drawings: Whistler, Laurence

Reynard the fox: Caxton, William

Reynard the fox: Masefield, John

Rezánov: Atherton, Gertrude

Rhapsodies: Ireland, W.H.

Rhapsodist, The: Brown, C.B.

Rhapsody in red: Isvaran, M.S.

Rhapsody upon the marvellous: Cibber, Colley

Rhesus of Euripides, The: Murray, Gilbert

Rhetoric and English composition: Grierson, *Sir* Herbert

Rhetoric of motives: Burke, Kenneth

Rhine, The: Mayhew, Henry

Rhine and its castles, The: Gibbon, Monk

Rhinestones: Widdemer, Margaret

Rhoda Fleming: Meredith, George

Rhode Island's part in making America: Adams, J.T.

Rhodes: a life: Millin, Sarah Gertrude

Rhodes Memorial at Oxford, The: Watts-Dunton, W.T.

Rhododaphne: Peacock, Thomas Love

Rhododendron pie: Sharp, Margery

Rhondda roundabout (novel and play): Jones, Jack

Rhyme and punishment: Bacon, Leonard

Rhyme? and reason?: †Carroll, Lewis

Rhymed ruminations: Sassoon, Siegfried

Rhymes a la mode: Lang, Andrew

Rhymes and ballads for girls and boys: Coolidge, Susan

Rhymes for Everyman: Rhys, Ernest

Rhymes for middle years: Wellesley, D.V.

Rhymes for the young folk: Allingham, William

Rhymes from the mines: Dyson, E.G.

Rhymes of a Red-Cross man, The: Service, Robert

Rhymes of a rolling stone: Service, Robert

Rhymes of a roughneck: Service, Robert

Rhymes of a rounder: MacInnes, T.R.E.

Rhymes of childhood: Riley, J.W.

Rhymes of Darby and Joan: Fowler, H.W.

Rhymes of our planet: Carleton, William (McKendree)

Rhymes of the firing line: Runyon, Damon

Rhymes of the French régime: Bourinot, A.S.

Rhymes of travel, ballads and poems: Taylor, Bayard

Rhymes on the rules of the Cheshire Bowmen: Warburton, R.E.E.

Rhymes to be traded for bread: Lindsay, N.V.

Rhymes with reason: Meynell, Wilfred

Rhymes with reason and without: (†*Mrs.* Partington), Shillaber, B.H.

Rhyming chronicle of incidents and feelings, A: Ingelow, Jean

Rhyming picture guide to Ayot St. Lawrence: Shaw, G.B.

Rhythm in the novel: Brown, E.K.

Rhythm of Bernard de Morlaix on the celestial country, The: Neale, J.M.

Rhythm of education, The: Whitehead, A.N.

Rhythm of life, The: Meynell, Alice

Rib of the green umbrella: Mitchison, Naomi

Ribaldry of Greece: Lindsay, Jack

Ribaldry of Rome: Lindsay, Jack

Ribbon stories: Barker, M.A.

Ribbons and medals: †Traffrail

Rice: Abbas, K.A.

Riceyman steps: Bennett, Arnold

Rich and strange: Collins, Dale

Rich die hard, The: Nichols, Beverley

Rich house, The: Gibbons, Stella

Rich husband, The: Riddell, *Mrs.* J.H.

Rich land, poor land: Chase, Stuart

Rich man: Galt, John

Rich man's daughter, A Riddell, *Mrs.* J.H.

Rich man's daughter, A: Mottram, R.H.

Rich relatives: Mackenzie, *Sir* Compton

Rich wife, The: Niven, F.J.

Rich young man, The: Knox, R.A.

Richard Arbour: Payn, James

Richard Bruce: Sheldon, C.M.

Richard Cable, the lightshipman: Baring-Gould, Sabine

Richard Carvell: Churchill, Winston

Richard Coeur de Lion: Burgoyne, *Sir* John

Richard Coeur de Lion and Blondell: Brontë, Charlotte

Richard Croker: Lewis, A.H.

Richard Edney and the Governor's family: Judd, Sylvester

Richard Hartley, prospector: Blackburn, Douglas

Richard Henry Dana: Adams, C.F.

Richard Hurdis: Simms, W.G.

Richard Kurt: †Hudson, Stephen

Richard, Myrtle and I: †Hudson, Stephen

Richard of Bordeaux: (†Gordon Daviot), Mackintosh, Elizabeth

Richard Savage: Barrie, *Sir*J.M.

Richard Savage: Whitehead, Charles

Richard Steele: Dobson, H.A.

Richard Strauss: Newman, Ernest

Richard Strauss: Pryce-Jones, A.P.

Richard II: Shakespeare, William

Richard III: Shakespeare, William

Richard III and Macbeth: Caine, *Sir* T.Hall

Richard Triumphant: Ridge, W.Pett

Richard Wagner: Dole, N.H.

Riche his farewell to militarie profession: Rich, Barnabe

Richelieu: Belloc, Hilaire

Richelieu: James, G.P.R.

Richelieu: Lodge, *Sir* Richard

Richelieu: Lytton, E.G.E.B. *1st Baron*

Richelieu: a domestic tragedy: Payne, J.H.

Richelieu and the French monarchy: Wedgwood, C.V.

Richer dust, A: Jameson, Storm

Riches of Chaucer, The: Clarke, Charles Cowden

Richest man in Kansas, The: Sheldon, C.M.

Richmond: Masters, E.L.

Richmond Hill: Bannister, N.H.

Richmond on the Thames: Garnett, Richard

Richmond Park: Jennings, Gertrude

Richy and Sandy: Ramsay, Allan

Rickshawallah: Isvaran, M.S.

Ricquet with the tuft: Sidgwick, Ethel

Ridan the devil: †Becke, G.L.

Riddle, The: De la Mare, Walter

Riddle, The: Raleigh, *Sir* W.A.

Riddle by Dr. S—t, to my Lady Carteret, A: Swift, Jonathan

Riddle of a changing world, The: Gibbs, *Sir* Philip

Riddle of the sands, The: Childers, Erskine

Riddle of the tower, The: Beresford, J.D.

Riddle of this world, The: Ghose, Sri Aurobindo

Riddles in Scots: Soutar, William

Riddles unriddled: Wigglesworth, Michael

Ride from Hell, The: Palmer, H.E.

Ride from Milan, The: Swinburne, A.C.

Ride in the cab of the twentieth century limited, A: Morley, C.D.

Ride into danger: Treece, Henry

Ride on stranger: Tennant, Kylie

Ride through Kansas, A: Higginson, T.W.

Ride to Reims, The: Mackaye, Percy

Ride with me: Costain, T.B.

Riders in the chariot: White, P.V.M.

Riders of the purple sage: Grey, Zane

Riders to the sea: Synge, J.M.

Ridge of the white waters, The: Scully, W.C.

Ridiculous hat, The: Brophy, John

Riding recollections: Whyte-Melville, G.J.

Riding to Lithend, The: Bottomley, Gordon

Riding to the Tigris: Stark, Freya

Ridotto of Bath, The: Sheridan, R.B.

Rienzi: Mitford, Mary Russell

Rienzi, the last of the Roman tribunes: Lytton, E.G.E.B. *1st Baron*

Rievers: Faulkner, William

Rifle Rangers, The: Reid, T.M.

Rifle rule in Cuba: Odets, Clifford

Rifle-clubs: Tennyson, Alfred *Lord*

Rifleman Dodd: Forester, C.S.

Rift, A: Carman, Bliss

Rift in the lute, The: Langley, Noel

Rift in the lute, The: Linton, Eliza

Rift in the rock, The: Hall, A.M.

Rigby's romance: †Collins, Tom

Right age to marry, The: Maltby, H.F.

Right at last: Gaskell, *Mrs.* Elizabeth

Right divine of kings to govern wrong, The: Hone, William

Right excellent and famous historye of Promos and Cassandra, The: Whetstone, George

Right excelent and pleasant dialogue, betwene Mercury and an English souldier, A: Rich, Barnabe

Right ho, Jeeves: Wodehouse, P.G.

Right Honourable, The: Praed, *Mrs.* C.

Right honorable gentleman, The: Fulford, Roger

Rt. Hon. Sir Gilbert Parker, Bart., deceased: Kingston, G.A.

Right of precedence between physicians and civilians enquired into, The: Swift, Jonathan

Right of way, The, Parker, *Sir* H.G.

Right off the map: Montague, C.E.

Right place, The: Montague, C.E.

Right round the world: Sala, G.A.H.

Right Royal: Masefield, John

Right stuff, The: (†Ian Hay), Beith, *Sir* John Hay

Right to kiss, The: Roberts, C.E.M.

Right to marry, The: Herbert, *Sir* A.P.

Right way the safe way, The: Child, L.M.

Righted wrong, A: Yates, E.H.

Righteousness evangelicall describ'd, The: Taylor, Jeremy

Rightful heir, The: Lytton, E.G.E.B. *1st Baron*

Rights and duties of the Indian citizen: Sastri, Srinivasa

Rights of Great Britain asserted against the claims of America, The: Macpherson, James

Rights of kings, The: †Pindar, Peter

Rights of man, The: Wells, H.G.

Rights of man; being a answer to Mr. Burke's attack on the French Revolution: Paine, Thomas

Rights of the British Colonies asserted and proved, The: Otis, James

Rigmarole, rigmarole: Lindsay, N.V.

Rigordans, The: Percy, Edward

Rilla of Ingleside: Montgomery, L.M.

Rimeless numbers: Trevelyan, R.C.

Rinaldo: Dennis, John

Rinaldo: Hill, Aaron

Rind of earth: Derleth, A.W.

Ring and the book, The: Browning, Robert

Ring fence, The: Phillpotts, Eden

Ring for Jeeves: Wodehouse, P.G.

Ring of Amasis, The: (†Owen Meredith), Lytton, E.R.B. *Earl*

Ring of bells: Betjeman, John

Ring out, wild bells: Tennyson, Alfred *Lord*

Ring up the curtain: Maltby, H.F.

Ringan Gilhaize: Galt, John

Ringdove, The: Ingraham, J.H.

Ringer, The: Wallace, Edgar

Ringfield: †Seranus

Ringold Griffitt: Ingraham, J.H.

Rings on her fingers: Davies, Rhys

Rings on her fingers: Maltby, H.F.

Rings the bells of heaven: Coppard, A.E.

Ringside seats: Gerould, Katharine

Ringtime: Wodehouse, P.G.

Ringwood the Rover: Herbert, H.W.

Rio Grande: Thomas, Augustus

Rio Grande to Cape Horn: Beals, Carleton

Rio Grande's last race: (†The Banjo), Paterson, A.B.

Riot and conspiracy: Macklin, Charles

Rioters, The: Martineau, Harriet

Rip tide: Benét, W.R.

Rip Van Winkle: Mackaye, Percy

Rip Van Winkle goes to the play: Matthews, J.B.

Ripeness is all: Linklater, Eric

Ripostes: Pound, Ezra

Riqqeh: Petrie, *Sir* William Flinders

Riquet of the tuft: Brooke, S.A.

Riquette: Jennings, Gertrude

Rise and fall of Madam Coming Sir, The: Ward, Edward

Rise and fall of nineteenth century idealism, The: Jackson, Holbrook

Rise and fall of Stocks, The: Ramsay, Allan

Rise and fall of the Daily Herald: Dutt, R.P.

Rise and fall of the ex-socialist Government: Hollis, Christopher

Rise and progress of the English Commonwealth, The: Palgrave, *Sir* Francis

Rise of American civilization, The: Beard, Charles and Mary Beard

Rise of European Liberalism, The: Laski, Harold

Rise of Henry Morcar, The: Bentley, Phyllis

Rise of man and modern research, The: Breasted, J.H.

Rise of modern America, The: Schlesinger, Arthur

Rise of Silas Lapham, The: Howells, W.D.

Rise of the British dominion in India, The: Lyall, *Sir* Alfred C.

Rise of the city, The: Schlesinger, A.M.

Rise of the Dutch kingdom, 1795–1813, The: Van Loon, Hendrik

Rise of the Dutch republic, The: Motley, J.L.

Rise of the Empire, The: Besant, *Sir* Walter

Rise of the Greek epic, The: Murray, Gilbert

Rise of the Russian empire, The: (†Saki), Munro, H.H.

Rise of the Spanish American Empire, The: Madariaga, Salvador de

Rising gorge, The: Perelman, S.J.

Rising of the court, The: Lawson, Henry

Rising of the tide, The: Tarbell, Ida

Rising tide, The: Deland, Margaret

Rising tide: Lindsay, Jack

Rising village, The: Goldsmith, Oliver

Rite of passion, The: Williams, Charles

Rival beauties, The: Sheridan, R.B.

Rival fools, The: Cibber, Colley

Rival ladies, The: Dryden, John

Rival monster, The: Mackenzie, Sir Compton

Rival pastors, The: Powys, T.F.

Rival queans, The: Cibber, Colley

Rival queens, The: Holcroft, Thomas

Rival queens, The: Lee, Nathaniel

Rival sisters, The: Murphy, Arthur

Rivals, The: Griffin, Gerald

Rivals, The: Sheridan, R.B.

River, The: Godden, Rumer

River, The: Phillpotts, Eden

River Duddon, The: Wordsworth, William

River flows, The: Lucas, F.L.

River fury, The: Cody, H.A.

River line, The: Morgan, Charles

River of life, The: Strachey, John St. Loe

River of London, The: Belloc, Hilaire

River of pictures and peace, A: Baughan, B.E.

River of stars, The: Wallace, Edgar

River of unrest, The: Mitford, Bertram

River out of Eden: Jones, Jack

River War, The: Churchill, Sir Winston

River water: Carman, Bliss

Riverhead: Hillyer, Robert

River-land: Chambers, R.W.

River-man, The: White, S.E.

Rivermouth romance, A: Aldrich, T.B.

Rivers, The: Faulkner, William

Rivers among rocks: Gustafson, Ralph

Rivers of Damascus: Byrne, Donn

Rivers to cross: Pertwee, Roland

Rivers to the sea: Teasdale, Sara

Riverside nights: Herbert, Sir A.P.

Riverside walk, A: Todhunter, John

Rivet in grandfather's neck, The: Cabell, James Branch

Riviera girl, The: Wodehouse, P.G.

Riviera, new look and old, The: Mais, S.P.B.

Rivieras, The: Hare, A.J.C.

Rivingstone: Ingraham, J.H.

Rivington's confessions: Freneau, Philip

Rivington's last will and testament: Freneau, Philip

Road, The: Anand, M.R.

Road, The: Deeping, Warwick

Road, The: Dickens, Charles

Road, The: London, Jack

Road between, The: Farrell, James

Road from the Monument, The: Jameson, Storm

Road I knew, The: White, S.E.

Road in Tuscany, The: Hewlett, Maurice

Road of a naturalist, The: Peattie, D.C.

Road of the gods, The: Paterson, Isabel M.

Road round Ireland, The: Colum, Padraic

Road through the woods: Frankau, Pamela

Road to abundance, The: Eastman, Max

Road to Beersheba, The: Mannin, Ethel

Road to Castaly: Brown, Alice

Road to Downderry, The: Widdemer, Margaret

Road to Heaven, The: Beer, T.

Road to Labour unity: Dutt, R.P.

Road to Milltown, The: Perelman, S.J.

Road to Niklagard, The: Treece, Henry

Road to nowhere, The: Walsh, Maurice

Road to Oxiana, The: Byron, Robert

Road to Raebury, The: Brighouse, Harold

Road to Rome, The: Sherwood, R.E.

Road to ruin, The: Holcroft, Thomas

Road to ruin, The: Sassoon, Siegfried

Road to Stratford, The: †O'Connor, Frank

Road to the temple, The: Glaspell, Susan

Road to Tunis: Divine, A.D.

Road to understanding, The: Porter, E.H.

Road to Wigan Pier, The: †Orwell, George

Road to Xanadu, The: Lowes, J.L.

Road we are travelling, 1924–1942, The: Chase, Stuart

Roadmender, The: †Fairless, Michael

Roads of destiny: †Henry, O.

Roads to agreement: Chase, Stuart

Roads to freedom: socialism, anarchism and syndicalism: Russell, Bertrand

Roads to glory: Aldington, Richard

Roadside harp, A: Guiney, L.I.

Roadside meetings: Garland, Hamlin

Roadside poems for summer travellers: Larcom, Lucy

Roamer, The: Woodberry, G.E.

Roaming round Australia: Clune, Frank

Roaming round the Darling: Clune, Frank

Roan stallion: Jeffers, J.R.

Roaring, The: Lindsay, Jack

Roaring girle, The: Dekker, Thomas and Thomas Middleton

Roaring nineties, The: Prichard, K.S.

Roaring of the U.P. Trail, The: Grey, Zane

Roaring queen, The: Lewis, P. Wyndham

Roaring tower: Gibbons, Stella

Roast beef, medium, the business adventures of Emma McChesney: Ferber, Edna

Roast Leviathan: Untermeyer, Louis

Rob of the Bowl: Kennedy, J.P.

Rob Roy: Scott, *Sir* Walter

Rob Roy: Skinner, C.L.

Roba di Roma: Story, W.W.

Robber, The: Brooker, Bertram

Robber, The: James, G.P.R.

Robber bridegroom, The: Sidgwick, Ethel

Robber kitten, The: Ballantyne, R.M.

Robbers' roost: Grey, Zane

Robbery under arms: †Boldrewood, Rolf

Robbery under law: Waugh, Evelyn

Robert Ainsleigh: Braddon, M.E.

Robert and Helen: Jenkins, Elizabeth

Robert Ayres Landor: Partridge, Eric

Robert Bloomfield: a sketch of his life and writings: Rands, W.B.

Robert Bridges, a critical study: Young, Francis Brett

Robert Browning: Chesterton, G.K.

Robert Browning: Dowden, Edward

Robert Browning: personalia: Gosse, *Sir* Edmund

Robert Bruce: Reynolds, G.

Robert Burns: Curtis, G.W.

Robert Burns: Daiches, David

Robert Burns: Drinkwater, John

Robert Burns: Swinburne, A.C.

Robert Burns, a centenary song: Massey, Gerald

Robert Dick, baker of Thurso, geologist and botanist: Smiles, Samuel

Robert E. Lee: Drinkwater, John

Robert E. Lee: man and soldier: Page, T.N.

Robert E. Lee: the Southerner: Page, T.N.

Robert Elsmere: Ward, *Mrs.* Humphrey

Robert Emmett: Banister, N.H.

Robert Emmett: Guiney, L.I.

Robert Emmett: Postgate, Raymond

Robert Falconer: Macdonald, George

Robert Hardy's seven days: Sheldon, C.M.

Robert Herrick: Swinburne, A.C.

Robert Louis Stevenson: Brown, Alice

Robert Louis Stevenson: Chesterton, G.K.

Robert Louis Stevenson: Daiches, David

Robert Louis Stevenson: Le Gallienne, Richard

Robert Louis Stevenson: Raleigh, *Sir* W.A.

Robert Louis Stevenson: Stephen, *Sir* Leslie

Robert Macaire in England: Reynolds, G.

Robert, Nana and—me: Jacob, Naomi

Robert Norwood: Watson, A.D.

Robert Orange: †Hobbes, John Oliver

Robert Owen: Cole, G.D.H.

Robert Owen of New Lanark: Cole, M.I.

Robert Peckham: Baring, Maurice

Robert, Richy and Sandy: Ramsay, Allan

Robert Rueful: Fay, T.S.

Robert the Bruce: Linklater, Eric

Robert the devil: Gilbert, *Sir* W.S.

Roberts and the influences of his time: Cappon, James

Robert's wife: Ervine, St. John

Robertses on their travels, The: Trollope, Frances

Robespierre: Belloc, Hilaire

Robespierre: Croker, J.W.

Robin: Burnett, Frances Hodgson

Robin Hood: Noyes, Alfred

Robin Hood: Ritson, Joseph

Robin Hood: Southey, C.A. and Robert Southey

Robin Hood: Squire, *Sir* J.C.

Robin Hood and the pedlar: Drinkwater, John

Robin Hood's barn: Brown, Alice

Robin Hood's Bay: Doyle, *Sir* F.H.C.

Robin Linnet: Benson, E.F.

Robin Redbreast: Molesworth, *Mrs.*

Robinella: Wiggin, Kate

Robin's father: Besier, Rudolf

Robinson Crusoe's return: Pain, B.E.O.

Robinson Jeffers, a portrait: Adamic, Louis

Robinson Jeffers: the man and the artist: Sterling, George

Robson (the actor): Sala, G.A.H.

Roche-Blanche: Porter, Anna Maria

Rochester: Williams, Charles

Rochester, a conversation between Sir George Etherege and Mr. FitzJames: Dobrée, Bonamy

Rock, The: Eliot, T.S.

Rock ahead, The: Yates, E.H.

Rock and sand: Jacob, Naomi

Rock and the river, The: †Connor, Ralph

Rock of Rome, The: Knowles, J.S.

Rock pool, The: Connolly, Cyril

Rock Wagram: Saroyan, William

Rocke of regard, The: Whetstone, George

Rocket, The: Pinero, *Sir* A.W.

Rocket to the moon: Odets, Clifford

Rockets galore: Mackenzie, *Sir* Compton

Rocking chair, The: Klein, A.M.

Rocking horse, The: Morley, C.D.

Rocking horse journey: Vulliamy, C.E.

Rocklitz, The: †Preedy, George

Rocky fork: Catherwood, Mary

Rocky Mountains, The: (†Geoffrey Crayon), Irving, Washington

Rocky road, The: Brophy, John

Rocky road to Dublin, The: Stephens, James

Rococco: †Bowen, Marjorie

Rococo: Granville-Barker, *Sir* Harley

Rod and line: Ransome, Arthur

Rod for run-awayes, A: Dekker, Thomas

Rod of the Lone Patrol: Cody, H.A.

Rod, root and the flower, The: Patmore, Coventry

Roddy the rover: Carleton, William

Roden's corner: †Merriman, Seton

Roderick Hudson: James, Henry

Roderick, the last of the Goths: Southey, Robert

Roderigo of Bivar: Moore, T.S.

Rodman the boatsteerer: †Becke, Louis

Rodman the keeper: Woolson, C.F.

Rodmoor: Powys, John Cowper

Rodney Stone: Doyle, Sir Arthur Conan

Rodogune: Ghose, Sri Aurobindo

Rodolph: a fragment: Pinkney, E.C.

Rodolphe in Boston: Ingraham, J.H.

Rodomont: Bedford-Jones, Henry

Rodomonths infernal: Markham, Gervase

Roger Camerden: Bangs, J.K.

Roger Fry: Woolf, Virginia

Roger—not so jolly: †Bridie, James

Roger Sudden: Raddall, T.H.

Rogue elephant: Allen, Walter Ernest

Rogue Herries: Walpole, Sir Hugh

Rogue River feud: Grey, Zane

Rogues and vagabonds: Mackenzie, Sir Compton

Rogue's comedy, The: Jones, H.A.

Rogue's gallery: †Queen, Ellery

Rogue's haven: Bridges, Roy

Rogue's Island: Crockett, S.R.

Rogue's legacy: Deutsch, Babette

Rogue's life, A: Collins, Wilkie

Rogue's march, The: Hornung, E.W.

Rogue's moon, The: Chambers, R.W.

Rokeby: Scott, Sir Walter

Roland Blake: Mitchell, S.W.

Roland Cashel: Lever, C.J.

Roland for an Oliver, A: Carey, Mathew

Roland for an Oliver, A: Morton, Thomas

Roland Graeme: Knight, Machar, A.M.

Roland Yorke: Wood, Ellen

Rolf in the woods: Seton-Thompson, E.

Roll call, The: Mackaye, Percy

Roll of honour: Linklater, Eric

Roll river: Boyd, James

Roll sweet chariot: Green, Paul

Roll-call, The: Bennett, Arnold

Rolling down the Lachlan: Clune, Frank

Rolling down the Lea: Gogarty, O. St. John

Rolling in the dew: Mannin, Ethel

Rolling road, The: Ewart, E.A.

Rolling road, The: Strong, L.A.G.

Rolling stones: †Henry, O.

Roly-Poly Pudding, The: Potter, Helen Beatrix

Roma beata: Elliott, M.H.

Roman, The: Dobell, S.T.

Roman actor, The: Massinger, Philip

Roman and the Teuton, The: Kingsley, Charles

Roman antiquaries of Inveresk, The: Moir, D.M.

Roman Bartholow: Robinson, E.A.

Roman Britain: Collingwood, R.G.

Roman Britain: Quennell, Marjorie

Roman Britain and the English settlements: Collingwood, R.G.

Roman Ehnasya: Petrie, Sir William Flinders

Roman Eskdale: Collingwood, R.G.

Roman father, The: Whitehead, William

Roman forgeries: Traherne, Thomas

Roman fountain: Walpole, Sir Hugh

Roman hat mystery, The: †Queen, Ellery

Roman history from the foundation of the City of Rome to the destruction of the Western Empire, The: Goldsmith, Oliver

Roman holiday: Mais, S.P.B.

Roman holiday: Sinclair, Upton

Roman holidays and others: Howells, W.D.

Roman pictures: Lubbock, Percy

Roman portraits: Petrie, Sir William Flinders

Roman revenge, The: Hill, Aaron

Roman signal station on Castle Hill, The: Collingwood, R.G.

Roman singer, A: Crawford, F. Marion

Roman summer: Lewisohn, Ludwig

Roman traitor, The: Herbert, H.W.

Romance: Conrad, Joseph

Romance: Ford, Ford Madox

Romance: †Maurice, Furnley

Romance: Scott, Sir Walter

Romance and Jane Weston: Pryce, Richard

Romance and reality: Barr, A.E.H.

Romance and reality: Jackson, Holbrook

Romance and reality: Landon, L.E.M.

Romance and revery: Fawcett, Edgar

Romance in lavender, A: (Stephen Southwold), †Bell, Neil

Romance Island: Gale, Zona

Romance of a chalet, The: Praed, Mrs. C.

Romance of a Christmas card, The: Wiggin, Kate

Romance of a great port, The: Wallace, F.W.

Romance of a king's life, The: Jusserand, Jean

Romance of a midshipman: Russell, W.C.

Romance of a people, The: Fast, Howard M.

Romance of a plain man, The: Glasgow, Ellen

Romance of a station, The: Praed, Mrs. C.

Romance of an hour, The: Kelly, Hugh

Romance of an old-fashioned gentleman, The: Smith, F.H.

Romance of Antar, The: Tietjens, E.S.

Romance of business, The: Hubbard, Elbert

Romance of Canvas Town, A: †Boldrewood, Rolf

Romance of Casanova, The: Aldington, Richard

Romance of commerce, The: Oxley, J.M.

Romance of discovery, The: Van Loon, Hendrik

Romance of Dollard, The: Catherwood, Mary

Romance of empire, The: Gibbs, Sir Philip

Romance of forest and prairie life, The: Webber, C.W.

Romance of George Villiers, The: Gibbs, P.H.

Romance of his life, and other romances, The: Cholmondeley, Mary

Romance of Jenny Harlowe, The: Russell, W.C.

Romance of Judge Ketchum, The: Vachell, H.A.

Romance of Labrador, The: Grenfell, Sir Wilfred

Romance of Mademoiselle Aissé, The: Praed, Mrs. C.

Romance of names, The: Weekley, Ernest

Romance of nature, The: Meredith, L.A.

Romance of Niko Cheyne, The: Pertwee, Roland

Romance of old New York, A: Fawcett, Edgar

Romance of Rosy Ridge, The: Kantor, MacKinlay

Romance of Runnibene, The: †Rudd, Steele

Romance of the Canadian canoe, The: Gibbon, J.M.

Romance of the forest, The: Radcliffe, Mrs. Ann

Romance of the Hebrides, The: Lathom, Francis

Romance of the lost, A: MacInnes, T.R.E.

Romance of the moon, A: Mitchell, J.A.

Romance of the nineteenth century, A: Mallock, W.H.

Romance of the railroad, The: Hubbard, Elbert

Romance of the Republic, A: Child, L.M.

Romance of the sunny south, A: Ingraham, J.H.

Romance of the swag, The: Lawson, Henry

Romance of the wool trade: Bonwick, James

Romance of travel, The: Willis, N.P.

Romance of two worlds, A: †Corelli, Marie

Romance of Vienna, A: Trollope, Frances

Romance of war, The: Grant, James

Romance of Wastdale, A: Mason, A.E.W.

Romance of western history, The: Hall, James

Romance of Windsor Castle, The: Bolitho, H.H.

Romance of words, The: Weekley, Ernest

Romance of Zion Chapel, The: Le Gallienne, Richard

Romance to the rescue: Mackail, Denis

Romances: D'Israeli, Isaac

Romances of Old France: Le Gallienne, Richard

Romances of real life: Gore, Catherine

Romanism and truth: Coulton, G.G.

Romano Lavo-Lil: Borrow, George

Romans, The: Lindsay, Jack

Romans were here, The: Lindsay, Jack

Romantic, The: Lewisohn, Ludwig

Romantic, The: Sinclair, May

Romantic adventure: Glyn, Elinor

Romantic adventures of a milkmaid, The: Hardy, Thomas

Romantic age, The: Milne, A.A .

Romantic and unromantic poetry: Wolfe, Humbert

Romantic ballads and poems of phantasy: †Macleod, Fiona

Romantic ballet in lithographs of the time, The: Sitwell, Sacheverell

Romantic comedians, The: Glasgow, Ellen

Romantic farce, A: Davidson, John

Romantic history of Robin Hood, The: Pain, B.E.O.

Romantic imagination, The: Bowra, Sir Maurice

Romantic lady, The: Arlen, Michael

Romantic landscape: Dehn, Paul

Romantic movement in English poetry, The: Symons, Arthur

Romantic 'Nineties, The: (†Ishmael Dare), Jose, A.W.

Romantic nineties, The: Le Gallienne, Richard

Romantic poetry and fine arts: Blunden, Edmund

Romantic prince, The: Sabatini, Rafael

Romantic rebellion, The: Newton, Eric

Romantic tales: Craik, Mrs. Dinah M.

Romantic tales: Lewis, M.G.

Romantic tradition, The: Seymour, Beatrice Kean

Romantic young lady, A: Grant, Robert

Romanticism: Abercrombie, Lascelles

Romanticism comes of age: Barfield, Owen

Romantics, The: Rinehart, Mary Roberts

Romany cha: Bercovici, Konrad

Romany Mark, The: †Boake, Capel

Romany of the snows, A: Parker, Sir H.G.

Romany Rye: Borrow, George

Romany stain, The: Morley, C.D.

Romaunt of Manuel Pig-Tender, The: Cabell, James Branch

Romaunt of the Rose: Chaucer, Geoffrey

Rome: Thomson, James

Rome, and the early Christians: Ware, William

Rome and Venice: with other wanderings in Italy, 1866–1867: Sala, G.A.H.

Rome eternal: Horgan, Paul

Rome for sale: Lindsay, Jack

Rome haul: Edmonds, W.D.

Rome on the Euphrates: Stark, F.M.

Rome or death!: Austin, Alfred

Rome or death: Beals, Carleton

Romeo and Juliet: Shakespeare, William

Romeo in Moon Village: McCutcheon, G.B.

Römische Briefe vom Concil: Acton, John E.E.D.

Romish ecclesiastical history of late years, The: Steele, *Sir* Richard

Rommelle: Burnett, W.R.

Romola: †Eliot, George

Romulus the shepherd king: Payne, J.H.

Ronald Brunlees McKerrow: Greg, W.W.

Ronald Standish: †Sapper

Ronald's reason: Hall, A.M.

Rondeaux Parisiens: Swinburne, A.C.

Ronsard: Jusserand, Jean

Ronsard: Lewis, D.B. Wyndham

Roof, The: Galsworthy, John

Rook's garden, The: †Bede, Cuthbert

Rookwood: Ainsworth, William H.

Room, The: Stern, G.B.

Room forty-five: Howells, W.D.

Room in the tower, The: Benson, E.F.

Room of one's own, A: Woolf, Virginia

Room 24: Wallace, Edgar

Room upstairs, The: Dickens, Monica

Room with a view, A: Forster, E.M.

Room within, The: Church, Richard

Roome for a gentleman: Rich, Barnabe

Roosevelt and Hopkins: an intimate history: Sherwood, R.E.

Roosevelt and the Antinoe, The: Pratt, E.J.

Roosevelt and the New Deal: Brogan, *Sir* D.W.

Roosevelt: the story of a friendship, 1880–1919: Wister, Owen

Root and the flower, The: Myers, L.H.

Root of evil, The: Dixon, Thomas

Rootabaga country: Sandburg, Carl

Rootabaga pigeons: Sandburg, Carl

Rootabaga stories: Sandburg, Carl

Root-bound: Cooke, R.T.

Roots: Bynner, Witter

Roots: Jacob, Naomi

Roots go deep: Peach, L. du Garde

Roots of contemporary American architecture: Mumford, Lewis

Roots of the mountains, The: Morris, William

Rope: Hamilton, Patrick

Ropemakers of Plymouth, The: Morison, S.E.

Roper's Row: Deeping, Warwick

Ropes of sand: Warren, J.B.L.

Roping lions in the Grand Canyon: Grey, Zane

Rory and Bran: Dunsany, E.J.M.D.P.

Rory O'More: Lover, Samuel

Rosa Lambert: Reynolds, G.

Rosa: love sonnets to Mary Doyle: Harpur, Charles

Rosa Macleod: Brown, Alice

Rosalba: (†Olive Pratt Rayner), Allen, Grant

Rosalba's journal: Dobson, H.A.

Rosalie: Gershwin, Ira

Rosalie: Major, Charles

Rosalie: Wodehouse, P.G.

Rosalind and Helen: Shelley, P.B.

Rosalind at Red Gate: Nicholson, Meredith

Rosalynde: Lodge, Thomas

Rosalynde's lovers: Thompson, J.M.

Rosamond: Edgeworth, Maria

Rosamund: Addison, Joseph

Rosamund: Sterling, George

Rosamund, Queen of the Lombards: Swinburne, A.C.

Rosary, The: Barclay, F.L.

Rosary, A: Davidson, John

Rosary, The: Faber, F.W.

Rosary, The: Parsons, T.W.

Rosary in rhyme, The: Tabb, J.B.

Rosary of Pan, The: Stephen, A.M.

Rosary of renunciation, A: Logan, J.D.

Rosciad, The: Churchill, Charles

Rose Acre papers: Thomas, E.E.P.

Rose and Bottle, The: †O'Sullivan, Seumas

Rose and Crown: O'Casey, Sean

Rose and Crown, The: Priestley, J.B.

Rose and roof-tree: Lathrop, G.P.

Rose and Rose: Lucas, E.V.

Rose and Sylvie: Mannin, Ethel

Rose and the key, The: Le Fanu, Sheridan

Rose and the ring, The: Sidgewick, Ethel

Rose and the ring, The: Thackeray, W.M.

Rose, Blanche, and Violet: Lewes, G.H.

Rose Briar: Tarkington, Booth

Rose D'Albret: James, G.P.R.

Rose dawn, The: White, S.E.

Rose Deeprose: Kaye-Smith, Sheila

Rose family, The: Alcott, Louisa M.

Rose fancier's manual, The: Gore, Catherine

Rose Foster: Reynolds, G.

Rose in bloom: Alcott, Louisa M.

Rose in June, A: Oliphant, Margaret

Rose in the ring, The: McCutcheon, G.B.

Rose Island: Russell, W.C.

Rose leaves: Doughty, *Sir* A.G.

Rose leaves: Nesbit, Edith

Rose Lorraine: Kendall, Henry

Rose Mather: Holmes, M.J.

Rose o' the river: Wiggin, Kate

Rose of a hundred leaves, A: Barr, A.E.H.

Rose of a hundred years, Hamilton college, 1812–1912: Scollard, Clinton

Rose of China, The: Wodehouse, P.G.

Rose of Dutcher's Coolly: Garland, Henry

Rose of life, The: Braddon, M.E.

Rose of paradise, The: Pyle, Howard

Rose of Spadgers: Dennis, C.M.J.

Rose of the Rancho, The: Belasco, David

Rose of the wilderness: Crockett, S.R.

Rose of Wissahikon, The: Lippard, George

Rose of yesterday, A: Crawford, F. Marion

Rose of youth, The: †Mordaunt, Elinor

Rose: sketches in verse, The: Osgood, F.S.

Rose Timpson: Steen, Marguerite

Rosebud: Bemelmans, Ludwig

Rosebud from the garden of the Taj, A: McCrae, G.G.

Rose-garden husband, The: Widdemer, Margaret

Roselle of the north: Skinner, C.L.

Rosemary for remembrance: Bax, Clifford

Rosemary, that's for remembrance: †Mordaunt, Elinor

Rosencrantz and Guildenstern: Gilbert, Sir W.S.

Roses in December: †Mordaunt, Elinor

Roses of Monsieur Alphonse, The: Janvier, T.A.

Roseteague of the Heir of Treville Crewse: Bray, A.E.

Rosina: Brooke, Frances

Rosinante to the road again: Dos Passos, John

Rosine: Whyte-Melville, G.J.

Ross: Rattigan, Terence

Rossenal: Raymond, Ernest

Rosses, The: †O'Sullivan, Seumas

Rossetti: Benson, A.C.

Rossetti and Charles Wells: Watts-Dunton, W.T.

Rossetti and contemporary criticism: Ghose, S.N.

Rossetti and his circle: Beerbohm, Sir Max

Rossetti, his life and works: Waugh, Evelyn

Rossiad, The: Douglas, Lord Alfred

Ross-shire Buffs, The: Grant, James

Rosy: Molesworth, Mrs.

Rosy crucifixion, The: Miller, Henry

Rosy Trodd: Royde-Smith, Naomi

Rothelan: Galt, John

Rotters, The: Maltby, H.F.

Rotting Hill: Lewis, P. Wyndham

Rough draught of a new model at sea, A: Savile, George

Rough house, The: Marshall, Bruce

Rough justice: Braddon, M.E.

Rough justice: Montague, C.E.

Rough reformer, A: Glanville, Ernest

Rough rider, The: Carman, Bliss

Rough shaking, A: Macdonald, George

Rough shooting: Wren, P.C.

Rough sketches of Bath: Bayly, T.H.

Rough walk home, A: Bowes Lyon, Lilian

Rough water: Pertwee, Roland

Roughage: †George, Daniel

Rough-hewn: Canfield, Dorothy

Roughing it: (†Mark Twain), Clemens, S.L.

Roughing it in the bush: Moodie, Susanna

Roughneck, The: Service, Robert

Roumanian journey: Sitwell, Sacheverell

Round about a great estate: Jefferies, Richard

Round about England: Mais, S.P.B.

Round about rambles: Stockton, F.R.

Round Africa holiday: Mais, S.P.B.

Round Britain coach holiday: Mais, S.P.B.

Round dozen, A: Coolidge, Susan

Round dozen, The: Maugham, Somerset

Round Hill exhibition: Bancroft, George

Round table, The: Hunt, Leigh

Round table, The: Peacock, Thomas Love

Round table, The: Robinson, E.S.L.

Round table; a collection of essays on literature, men and manners, The: Hazlitt, William

Round the bend: †Shute, Nevil

Round the compass in Australia: Parker, Sir H.G.

Round the corner: Cannan, Gilbert

Round the fire stories: Doyle, Sir Arthur Conan

Round the galley fire: Russell, W.C.

Round the peat fire at Glenbrechy: †Bede, Cuthbert

Round the red lamp: Doyle, Sir Arthur Conan

Round the sofa: Gaskell, Mrs. Elizabeth

Round the world cruise holiday: Mais, S.P.B.

Round the world in any number of days: Baring, Maurice

Round up: Lardner, Ring

Roundabout, The: Priestley, J.B.

Roundabout journey, A: Warner, C.D.

Roundabout papers: Thackeray, W.M.

Roundabout rhymes: MacInnes, T.R.E.

Round-heads, The: Behn, Mrs. Afra

Rousseau: Morley, John

Rousseau: Vulliamy, C.E.

Rousseau and romanticism: Babbitt, Irving

Rout, The: Graves, Richard

Rout of Constantine de Sa de Noronha, The: Perera, Simon G.

Rout of the Amazons, The: Moore, T.S.

Rover, The: Behn, *Mrs.* Afra

Rover, The: Conrad, Joseph

Rover I would be, A: Lucas, E.V.

Roving angler, The: Palmer, H.E.

Roving critic, The: Van Doren, Carl

Roving east and roving west: Lucas, E.V.

Row in the house, A: Robertson, T.W.

Rowena and Rebecca: Thackeray, W.M.

Rowland for an Oliver, A: †Pindar, Peter

Rowland Massingham: Moodie, Susanna

Roxy: Eggleston, Edward

Royal Academy, 1895, The: Moore, George

Royal Army Service Corps, The: Fortescue, *Sir* J.W.

Royal books, The (prologue, epilogue): Caxton, William

Royal Canadian Institute Centennial Volume, 1849–1949, The: Wallace, W.S.

Royal convert, The: Rowe, Nicholas

Royal dream, The: Combe, William

Royal Dukes: Fulford, Roger

Royal Edinburgh: her saints, kings, prophets and poets: Oliphant, Margaret

Royal escape: Heyer, Georgette

Royal family, The: Ferber, Edna

Royal family, The: Kaufman, G.S.

Royal flush: Irwin, Margaret

Royal garland, The: Bickerstaffe, Isaac

Royal gentleman, A: Tourgée, A.W.

Royal George: Vulliamy, C.E.

Royal Georgie: Baring-Gould, Sabine

Royal heritage: Pertwee, Roland

Royal Highlanders, The: Grant, James

Royal jubilee, The: Hogg, James

Royal marine, The: Matthews, J.B.

Royal marriages and matrilineal descent: Murray, Margaret

Royal mischief, The: *Mrs.* Manley

Royal Netherlands Navy, The: Divine, A.D.

Royal progress: Bolitho, H.H.

Royal propaganda, A: Knight, G.W.

Royal regiment: Frankau, Gilbert

Royal Regiment, The: Grant, James

Royal runaway, The: Housman, Laurence

Royal Scots Fusiliers, The: Buchan, John

Royal shepherdess, The: Shadwell, Thomas

Royal street: Roberts, W. Adolphe

Royal tombs of the earliest dynasties: Petrie, *Sir* William Flinders

Royal tombs of the First Dynasty: Petrie, *Sir* William Flinders

Royal Tour and Weymouth amusements, The: †Pindar, Peter

Royal visit to Exeter, The: †Pindar, Peter

Royall king, and the loyall subject, The: Heywood, Thomas

Royall master, The: Shirley, James

Royals free: †Mordaunt, Elinor

Roycroft dictionary, The: Hubbard, Elbert

Roy's wife: Whyte-Melville, G.J.

Royston Gower: Miller, Thomas

Rubaiyat of Doc Sifers: Riley, J.W.

Rubáiyát of Omar Khayyám: Fitzgerald, Edward

Rubens, painter and diplomat: Cammaerts, Emile

Rubicon: Benson, E.F.

Rubies: Beck, *Mrs.* Lily

Ruby of Kishmoor, The: Pyle, Howard

Ruby ring, The: Molesworth, *Mrs.*

Ruby sword, The: Mitford Bertram

Rudd family, The: †Rudd, Steele

Rudder Grange: Stockton, F.R.

Ruddygore: Gilbert, *Sir* W.S.

Rude assignment: Lewis, P. Wyndham

Rude potato, The: Pitter, Ruth

Rudiments and rules of divine science: Eddy, M.B.

Rudiments of connoisseurship: study and criticism of Italian art: Berenson, Bernhard

Rudiments of English grammar, The: Priestley, Joseph

Rudiments of grammar, The: Shirley, James

Rudiments of Latin Prosody, The: Otis, James

Rudolph and Anima: Morley, C.D.

Rudyard Kipling: Palmer, J.L.

Rudyard Kipling: (†Michael Innes), Stewart, J.I.M.

Rudyard Kipling: a criticism: Le Gallienne, Richard

Rue: Housman, Laurence

Rue tree, The: Gilmore, Mary

Rueful mating, The: Stern, G.B.

Ruffino: †Ouida

Rufus: Church, Richard

Rugantino: Lewis, M.G.

Rugby, Tennessee: Hughes, Thomas

Rugger match, The: Squire, *Sir* J.C.

Ruggylug: Seton-Thompson, E.

Ruin, The: Sackville-West, Edward

"Ruin" of Jamaica, The: Hildreth, Richard

Ruined city, The: James, G.P.R.

Ruined city, The: †Shute, Nevil

Ruinous face, The: Hewlett, Maurice

Ruins and visions: Spender, Stephen

Ruins of Rome, The: Dyer, John

Ruint: Hughes, Hatcher

Rule a wife and have a wife: Fletcher, John and Francis Beaumont

Rule and exercises of holy living, The: Taylor, Jeremy

Rule and exercises of holy dying, The: Taylor, Jeremy

Rule of reason, The: Wilson, Thomas

Rule of three: Christie, Agatha

Rule of three, The: Coolidge, Susan

Rulers of kings: Atherton, Gertrude

Rulers of the Mediterranean, The: Davis, R.H.

Rulers of the South, The: Crawford, F.Marion

Rules and advices to the clergy of the diocese of Down and Connor: Taylor, Jeremy

Rules and regulations of an institution called Tranquillity commenced as an economical bank, The: Hone, William

Rules by which a great empire may be reduced to a small one: Franklin, Benjamin

Rules for a club: Franklin, Benjamin

Rules for drawing caricatures: Grose, Francis

Rules of the game, The: White, S.E.

Ruling passion, The: Riddell, Mrs. J.H.

Rumania under King Carol: Bolitho, H.H.

Rumbin galleries: Tarkington, Booth

Ruminator, The: Brydges, Sir S.E.

Rummy: Coppard, A.E.

Rumour, The: Munro, C.K.

Rumour and reflection; 1941:1944: Berensen, Bernhard

Rumour at nightfall: Greene, Graham

Run, sheep, run: Bodenheim, Maxwell

Run to earth: Braddon, M.E.

Runagates' Club, The: Buchan, John

Runaround: Appel, Benjamin

Runaway, The: Cowley, Mrs. Hannah

Runaway: Dell, Floyd

Runaway, The: Smith, Horatio

Runaway, The: Tagore, Sir R.

Runaway Browns, The: Bunner, H.C.

Runaways, The: Hannay, J.O.

Runaways, The: Phillpotts, Eden

Rungli-Rungliot: Godden, Rumer

Runner, The: †Connor, Ralph

Running deer: Trease, Geoffrey

Running man, The: †Armstrong, Anthony and Arnold Ridley

Running of the tide, The: Forbes, Esther

Running special: Packard, F.L.

Running the gauntlet: Yates, E.H.

Running the river: Eggleston, G.C.

Running water: Mason, A.E.W.

Rupert Brooke: Drinkwater, John

Rupert Brooke: Hassall, Christopher

Rupert Brooke and the intellectual imagination: De la Mare, Walter

Rupert Godwin: Braddon, M.E.

Rupert of Hentzau: (†Anthony Hope), Hawkins, Anthony Hope

Rupert of the Rhine: Fergusson, Sir Bernard

Rural calendar: Grahame, James

Rural Denmark: Haggard, Sir H. Rider

Rural economy: Young, Arthur

Rural education in New Mexico: Austin, Mary

Rural England: Haggard, Sir H. Rider

Rural hours: Cooper, Susan Fenimore

Rural letters and other records of thought at leisure: Willis, N.P.

Rural muse, The: Clare, John

Rural rides in the counties: Cobbett, William

Rural sports: Gay, John

Rural sports: Jones, J.B.

Rural studies: Mitchell, D.G.

Rural tales, ballads and songs: Bloomfield, Robert

Rus in urbe: Rice, Elmer

Ruse of the vanished woman, The: Gielgud, Val

Ruskin: Benson, A.C.

Ruskin: Livingstone, Sir Richard

Ruskin: Rossetti: Pre-Raphaelitism: Rossetti, W.M.

Ruskiniana: Ruskin, John

Ruskin's philosophy: Collingwood, R.G.

Ruskin's politics: Shaw, G.B.

Russell: James, G.P.R.

Russia: Eastman, Max

Russia: Swinburne, A.C.

Russia and the world: Graham, Stephen

Russia in division: Graham, Stephen

Russia in 1916: Graham, Stephen

Russia in the shadows: Wells, H.G.

Russian essays and stories: Baring, Maurice

Russian journal, A: Steinbeck, John

Russian journey: Priestley, J.B.

Russian shores of the Black Sea in the autumn of 1852, The: Oliphant, Laurence

Russians of the South, The: Brooks, C.W.S.

Rust of Rome, The: Deeping, Warwick

Rustic elegies: Sitwell, Edith

Rustic moralist, A: Inge, W.R.

Rustlers of Beacon Creek, The: †Brand, Max

Ruston Morley: Stephens, J.B.

Rusty sword, The: Riddell, Mrs. J.H.

Ruth: Gaskell, Mrs. Elizabeth

Ruth: Neale, J.M.

Ruth of St. Ronan's: Brazil, Angela

Ruth Whalley: Herbert, H.W.

Rutherford: Fawcett, Edgar

Rutherford and the nature of the atom: Andrade, E.N. da Costa

Ruy Blas: Gilbert, Sir W.S.

Ruysbroeck: Underhill, Evelyn

Ryder: Barnes, Djuna

Rye House plot, The: Reynolds, G.

Ryerson Poetry Chapbooks: Pierce, Lorne

Ryght delectable tratyse upon a goodly garlande or chapelet of laurell, A: Skelton, John

Ryght frutefull treatyse, intituled the myrrour of good maners, A: Barclay, Alexander

S

S.O.S. Ludlow: Hassall, Christopher

S.O.S. talks on unemployment: Mais, S.P.B.

S.P.E. Tracts: Craigie, Sir William Alexander

S.S. Glory, The: Niven, F.J.

S.S. San Pedro: Cozzens, J.G.

S. Srinivasa Iyengar: a decade of Indian politics: Iyengar, K.R. Srinivasa

Sabbath, The: Grahame, James

Sabbath at home, A: Manning, Anne

Sabbath Days: Barnes, William

Sabbath in Puritan New England, The: Earle, A.M.

Sabbath lyrics: Simms, W.G.

Sabbath thoughts and sacred communings: Aguilar, Grace

Sabbation: Trench, R.C.

Sabi Reserve, The: Cripps, A.S.

Sabina Zembra: Black, William

Sabishisa: Mannin, Ethel

Sable and purple: Watson, Sir J.W.

Sabrina Warham: Housman, Laurence

Sac Prairie people: Derleth, A.W.

Sack and destruction of the city of Columbia, S.C.: Simms, W.G.

Sackcloth into silk: Deeping, Warwick

Sacked city, The: †Preedy, George

Sacred and profane love: Sitwell, Sacheverell

Sacred and profane memories: Van Vechten, Carl

Sacred and secular: Gill, Eric

Sacred and profane love: Austin, Alfred

Sacred and profane love: Bennett, Arnold

Sacred anthology, The: Conway, Moncure Daniel

Sacred bullock, The: De la Roche, Mazo

Sacred dramas: More, Hannah

Sacred flame, The: Maugham, Somerset

Sacred fount, The: James, Henry

Sacred giraffe, The: Madariaga, Salvador de

Sacred Latin poetry, chiefly lyrical: Trench, R.C.

Sacred meditations in verse: Montgomery, Robert

Sacred memorie of the miracles wrought by Jesus Christ, A: Rowlands, Samuel

Sacred nugget, The: Farjeon, B.L.

Sacred place, The: Esson, T.L.B.

Sacred poetry of early religions: Church, Richard

Sacred river, The: Strong, L.A.G.

Sacred songs: Moore, Thomas

Sacred verses, with pictures: Williams, Isaac

Sacred wood, The: Eliot, T.S.

Sacrifice at Prato, A: Hewlett, Maurice

Sacrilege of Alan Kent: Caldwell, Erskine Preston

Sad and deplorable loving elegy to the memory of M. Richard Wyan, A: Taylor, John

Sad and solemne funerall, A: Churchyard, Thomas

Sad bird of the Adriatic, The: Tuckerman, H.T.

Sad Cypress: Christie, Agatha

Sad shepherd, The: Jonson, Ben

Sad variety, The: Day-Lewis, C.

Sad years, The: Sigerson, Dora

Sadak and Kalasrade: Mitford, Mary Russell

Saddles again: Ogilvie, W.H.

Sadducismus triumphatus: Glanvill, Joseph

Sadhana: Tagore, Sir R.

Sado: Plomer, W.C.F.

Safar Nameh: Bell, Gertrude

Safe amongst the pigs: Brighouse, Harold

Safe and sound: Hook, T.E.

Safe custody: †Yates, Dornford

Safe deposit, A: Hale, E.E.

Safety first: Fitzgerald, F. Scott

Safety match, A: (†Ian Hay), Beith, Sir John Hay

Safety pins: Morley, C.D.

Saffron and gold: Isvaran, M.S.

Saga Library, The: Morris, William

Saga of Indian sculpture: Munshi, K.M.

Saga of Pryderi, The: Griffith, Llewelyn

Sagacity: Benét, W.R.

Sagas of the sea: MacMechan, A.M.

Sagas of vaster Britain: Campbell, W.W.

Sage-brush stories: Niven, F.J.

Sagebrusher, The: Hough, Emerson

Sagusto: Roberts, C.E.M.

Said my philosopher: Mickle, A.D.

Said the cat to the dog: Armstrong, M.D.

Said the dog to the cat: Armstrong, M.D.

Said the fisherman: Pickthall, M.W.

Sail away: Coward, Noel

Sailing: De Selincourt, Aubrey

Sailing of the long ships, The: Newbolt, Sir Henry

Sailing ships: Bagnold, Enid

Sailing sunny seas: Wilcox, Ella Wheeler

Sailing to the seven seas: Chase, M.E.

Sailing tomorrow's seas: Treece, Henry

Sailor boy, The: Ireland, W.H.

Sailor of the Bremen: Shaw, Irwin

Sailors and Saints: Glascock, W.N.

Sailor's daughter, The: Cumberland, Richard

Sailor's friendship and a soldier's love, A: Porter, Anna Maria

Sailor's holiday: Linklater, Eric

Sailor's knots: Jacobs, W.W.

Sailor's language: Russell, W.C.

Sailors of fortune: McFee, William

Sailor's return, The: Garnett, David

Sailor's song: Hanley, James

Sailor's sweetheart, A: Russell, W.C.

Sailor's wedding, A: Carman, Bliss

Sailor's wisdom: McFee, William

Sails and mirage and other poems: Sterling, George

Sails of sunset: Roberts, C.E.M.

Saint Abe and his seven lovers: Buchanan, Robert Williams

St. Agnes' Eve: Tennyson, Alfred *Lord*

Saint and Mary Kate, The: †O'Connor, Frank

St. Andrews: Lang, Andrew

St. Augustine: †West, Rebecca

St. Bartholomew's eve: Newman, J.H.

St. Bernard and St. Francis: Coulton, G.G.

S. Catherine of Siena: Pollard, A.W.

St. Catherine's College: Brazil, Angela

St. Christopher's day: Armstrong, M.D.

St. Clair: Morgan, *Lady* Sydney

St. Clement's Eve: Taylor, *Sir* Henry

St. Elmo: Evans, A.J.

St. Eloy and the bear: †Bridie, James

St. Francis of Assisi: Chesterton, G.K.

St. Francis of Assisi: Massingham, Harold

St. Francis Poverello: Housman, Laurence

St. George and St. Michael: Macdonald, George

St. George and the dragon: Masefield, John

St. George and the dragons: Phillpotts, Eden

St. George at the Dragon: Spring, Howard

St. George's day: Davidson, John

St. George's day: Newbolt, *Sir* Henry

Saint Gervase of Plessy: Hewlett, Maurice

Saint Gregory's guest: Whittier, J.G.

St. Helena: Sherriff, R.C.

Saint Hercules: Armstrong, M.D.

St. Ignatius: Hollis, Christopher

St. Ignatius and the Company of Jesus: Derleth, A.W.

Saint Ignatius Loyola: Thompson, Francis

St. Irvyne: Shelley, P.B.

St. Ives: (†Q), Quiller-Couch, *Sir* Arthur

St. Ives: Stevenson, R.L.

Saint James's or the Court of Queen Anne: Ainsworth, Harrison

St. Jerome and the lion: Godden, Rumer

Saint Joan: Shaw, G.B.

Saint Joan of Arc: Sackville-West, Victoria

St. John in Patmos: Bowles, William Lisle

Saint John the Baptist: Myers, F.W.H.

St. Johns, The: Cabell, James Branch

Saint Johnson: Burnett, W.R.

St. Katherine of Ledbury: Masefield, John

St. Katherine's by the Tower: Besant, *Sir* Walter

Saint Katy the Virgin: Steinbeck, John

Saint Kavin: Carman, Bliss

St. Lawrence and the Saguenay, The: Sangster, Charles

Saint Lawrence basin, The: Dawson, S.E.

St. Leon: Godwin, William

St. Louis: Mackaye, Percy

St. Louis Street and its storied past: LeMoine, *Sir* J.M.

St. Louis woman: Cullen, Countée

St. Mark's rest: Ruskin, John

St. Martin's Eve: Wood, Ellen

St. Martin's summer: Dobrée, Bonamy

St. Martin's summer: Sabatini, Rafael

St. Mawr: Lawrence, D.H.

St. Michael and St. George: Priestley, J.B.

Saint Michael's gold: Bedford-Jones, Henry

St. Michael's Mount: Bowles, William Lisle

St. Patrick for Ireland: Shirley, James

St. Patrick's day: Sheridan, R.B.

St. Patrick's Eve: Lever, C.J.

St. Patrick's purgatory: Leslie, *Sir* J.R. Shane

St. Patrick's purgatory: Wright, Thomas

Saint Paul: Myers, F.W.H.

St. Paul and Protestantism: Arnold, Matthew

St. Paul's gospel: Knox, R.A.

Saint Perpetua, Martyr of Africa: Cripps, A.S.

Saint Peter relates an incident of the resurrection day: Johnson, J.W.

Saint Peter's chains: De Vere, Aubrey

S. Peters complaint and Saint Mary Magdalens funerall teares: Southwell, Robert

Saint Peters complaynt: Southwell, Robert

St. Ronan's Well: Scott, *Sir* Walter

St. Stephen's: Lytton, E.G.E.B. *1st Baron*

St. Thomas Aquinas: Chesterton, G.K.

St. Thomas of Canterbury: De Vere, Aubrey

St. Tom and the dragon: Turner, E.S.

St. Ursula's convent: Beckwith, J.C.

St. Vitus' Day: Graham, Stephen

Sainte-Beuve: Nicolson, Hon. *Sir* Harold

Saintmaker's Christmas Eve, The: Horgan, Paul

Saints and sinners: Bradford, Gamaliel

Saints and sinners: Jones, Henry Arthur

Saints dignitie and duty, The: Hooker, Thomas

Saints guide, The: Hooker, Thomas

Saints in Sussex: Kaye-Smith, Sheila

Saint's progress: Galsworthy, John

Saint's tragedy, The: Kingsley, Charles

Salámán and Absál: Fitzgerald, Edward

Salamanca wedding, The: Brown, Thomas

Salar the salmon: Williamson, Henry

Salathiel: Croly, George

Sale by auction: Peach, L. du Garde

Sale of Saint Thomas, The: Abercrombie, Lascelles

Salem Chapel: Oliphant, Margaret

Sally Dows: Harte, Bret

Sally go round the moon: Bates, H.E.

Sally Lunn: Walmsley, Leo

Sally Scarth: Jacob, Naomi

Salmagundi: Faulkner, William

Salmagundi:(†Geoffrey Crayon), Irving, Washington

Salmagundi: Paulding, J.K.

Salomé: Douglas, *Lord* Alfred

Salomé: Wilde, Oscar

Salome and the head: Nesbit, E.

Salsette and elephanta: Ruskin, John

Salt air: Higgins, F.R.

Salt marsh: Marriott, Anne

Salt seas and sailormen: Wallace, F.W.

Salt Water Ballads: Masefield, John

Salt water men, The: Schull, J.J.

Saltbush Bill, J.P.: (†The Banjo), Paterson, A.B.

Salted almonds and other tales: †Anstey, F.

Salted with fire: Macdonald, George

Salthaven: Jacobs, W.W.

Saltwater farm: Coffin, Robert

Salutation: Russell, G.W.

Salutation, The: Warner, Sylvia Townsend

Salutation to five: Leslie, *Sir* J.R. Shane

Salute from the fleet, A: Noyes, Alfred

Salute the King: Mee, Arthur

Salute to adventurers: Buchan, John

Salvage: Belasco, David

Salvage: Cronin, B.C.

Salvaging of civilisation, The: Wells, H.G.

Salvation on a string: Green, Paul

Salve Venetia: Crawford, F. Marion

Salvos: Frank, Waldo

Salzburg tales, The: Stead, C.E.

"Sam": Webber, C.W.

Sam Ego's House: Saroyan, William

Sam Lawson's Oldtown fireside stories: Stowe, Harriet Beecher

Sam. Ld. Bp. of Oxon his celebrated reasons for abrogating the Test, answered: Phillips, John

Sam Lovel's boy: Robinson, R.E.

Sam Lovel's camps: Robinson, R.E.

Sam Pig and Sally: Uttley, Alison

Sam Pig and the singing gate: Uttley, Alison

Sam Pig at the circus: Uttley, Alison

Sam Pig goes to market: Uttley, Alison

Sam Pig goes to the seaside: Uttley, Alison

Sam Pig in trouble: Uttley, Alison

Sam Pig story book, The: Uttley, Alison

Sam Slick's wise saws and modern instances: Haliburton, T.C.

Sam, the highest jumper of them all: Saroyan, William

Sam the sudden: Wodehouse, P.G.

Sambo and Snitch: Blackwood, Algernon

Same star, The: Lucas, E.V.

Samoa and its story: Cowan, James

Samor, Lord of the Bright City: Milman, H.H.

Samphire: Powys, John Cowper

Sampler, The: Church, Richard

Sampson's circus: Spring, Howard

Samson Agonistes: Milton, John

Samuel Boyd of Catchpole Square: Farjeon, B.L.

Samuel Butler: Cannan, Gilbert

Samuel Butler: Cole, G.D.H.

Samuel Butler: Joad, C.E.M.

Samuel Drummond: Boyd, Thomas

Samuel Johnson: Krutch, J.W.

Samuel Johnson: Stephen, *Sir* Leslie

Samuel Palmer: Grigson, Geoffrey

Samuel Pepys: Lubbock, Percy

Samuel Pepys, the man in the making: Bryant, *Sir* Arthur

Samuel Pepys, the saviour of the Navy: Bryant, *Sir* Arthur

Samuel Pepys, the years of peril: Bryant, *Sir* Arthur

Samuel Richardson: Dobson, Henry Austin

Samuel Richardson: Jeffrey, *Lord* Francis

Samuel Taylor Coleridge: Chambers, *Sir* E.K.

Samuel Taylor Coleridge: Fausset, Hugh

Samuel the kingmaker: Housman, Laurence

Samuel the seeker: Sinclair, Upton

San Cristobal de la Habana: Hergesheimer, Joseph

San Rosario ranch, The: Elliott, M.H.

Sanctions, a frivolity: Knox, R.A.

Sanctuaries for birds: Massingham, Harold

Sanctuary: Carman, Bliss

Sanctuary: Faulkner, William

Sanctuary: Mackaye, Percy

Sanctuary, The: Montgomery, Robert

Sanctuary: Wharton, Edith

Sand and shells: Hannay, James

Sandburrs: Lewis, A.H.

Sanders: Wallace, Edgar

Sanders of the river: Wallace, Edgar

Sandford Fleming, empire builder: Burpee, Lawrence J.

Sandhya: songs of twilight: Mukherji, D.G.

Sandi the kingmaker: Wallace, Edgar

Sandition: the Watsons: Lady Susan and other miscellanea: Austen, Jane

Sandoval: Beer, T.

Sands of fortune: †Sinclair Murray

Sandstone: Marriott, Anne

Sandwich Islands, The: Dana, R.H. *junior*

Sandy foundation shaken, The: Penn, William

Sandy's love affair: Crockett, S.R.

Sandy's selection: †Rudd, Steele

Sangamon, The: Masters, E.L.

Sangschaw: †McDiarmid, Hugh

Sanitary and social lectures and essays: Kingsley, Charles

Sanity of art, The: Shaw, G.B.

Sans merci: Lawrence, G.A.

Sanskrit citations in "The life divine": Ghose, Sri Aurobindo

Sant' Ilario: Crawford, F. Marion

Santa Barbara: †Ouida

Santa Claus: Cummings, E.E.

Santa Claus: Ingraham, J.H.

Santa Claus in summer: Mackenzie, *Sir* Compton

Santa Claus's partner: Page, T.N.

Santa Eulalia: La Farge, Oliver

Santa Fe: La Farge, Oliver

Santa Fé's partner: Janvier, T.A.

Santa Lucia: Austin, Mary

Santal: Firbank, Ronald

Santana, hero dog of France: Seton-Thompson, E.

Sapho and Phao: Lyly, John

Sappers at war: †Armstrong, Anthony

Sapphira and the slave girl: Cather, Willa

Sapphire, The: Mason, A.E.W.

Sappho: Carman, Bliss

Sappho: Durrell, Lawrence

Sappho: Lewis, S.A.

Sappho and Phaon: Mackaye, Percy

Sappho in Leucadia: Stringer, A.J.A.

Sappho in Levkas: Percy, W.A.

Sappho of Green Springs, A: Harte, Bret

Saqqara Mastabas: Murray, Margaret

Sara Crewe: Burnett, Frances Hodgson

Saraband for dead lovers: Simpson, H. de G.

Saracinesca: Crawford, F. Marion

Sarah: Brophy, John

Sarah Churchill, Duchess of Marlborough: Dobrée, Bonamy

Sarah de Berenger: Ingelow, Jean

Sarah Simon: Allen, Hervey

Sarah, the exemplary wife: Rowson, S.H.

Sarah's youth: Somerville, E.

Saratoga: Howard, B.C.

Saratoga in 1901: (†Eli Perkins), London, Melville

Saratoga trunk: Ferber, Edna

Sarchedon: Whyte-Melville, G.J.

Sard Harker: Masefield, John

Sardanapalus: Byron, George Gordon *Lord*

Sardonic arm, The: Bodenheim, Maxwell

Sargasso sea: Byrne, Donn

Sarmista: Dutt, M.M.

Sartor Resartus: Carlyle, Thomas

Sartoris: Faulkner, William

Sarvodaya: Gandhi, M.K.

Sassetta: Pope-Hennessy, J.W.

Satan: Montgomery, Robert

Satan absolved: Blunt, Wilfred

Satan as lightning: †King, Basil

Satan in search of a wife, and who danced at the wedding: Lamb, Charles

Satan in the suburbs: Russell, Bertrand

Satan, the waster: †Lee, Vernon

Satanella: Whyte-Melville, G.J.

Satanism and the world order: Murray, Gilbert

Satanstoe: Cooper, James Fenimore

Sati, a vindication of the Indian woman: Coomaraswamy, A.K.

Satin-wood box, The: Trowbridge, J.T.

Satire: Cannan, Gilbert

Satire and fiction: Lewis, P. Wyndham

Satire and humour: Cummings, E.E.

Satire on Colonel George Molle: Wentworth, W.C.

Satire on satirists, and admonition to detractors, A: Landor, W.S.

Satires and profanities: Thomson, James

Satires and satirists: Hannay, James

Satires of circumstance: Hardy, Thomas

Satirical poems: Sassoon, Siegfried

Satiro-mastix: Dekker, Thomas

Saturday and Sunday: Broadus, E.K.

Saturday life, A: Hall, M.R.

Saturday match, The: De Selincourt, Hugh

Saturday mornings: (†Elzevir), Murdoch, *Sir* W.L.F.

Saturday night: Green, Paul

Saturday night at the Crown: Greenwood, Walter

Saturday papers: Canby, Henry Seidel

Saturday songs: Traill, H.D.

Saturday's children: Anderson, Maxwell

Saturdee: Lindsay, Norman

Saturn over the water: Priestley, J.B.

Saturnine: Heppenstall, Rayner

Satyagraha in South Africa: Gandhi, M.H.

Satyagraha: non-violent resistance: Gandhi, M.K.

Satyameva Jayate: Rajagopala-chari, C.

Satyr against hypocrites, A: Phillips, John

Satyr against vertue, A: Old-ham, John

Satyr against wit, A: Black-more, Sir R.D.

Satyr to his muse: Shadwell, Thomas

Satyre: dedicated to his most excellent Majestie, A: Wither, George

Satyricall dialogue, or a sharp-lye-invective conference between Alexander the Great and that trulye woman-hater Diogynes, A: Goddard, William

Satyrs and sunlight: McCrae, Hugh

Satyrs upon the Jesuits: Old-ham, John

Saucy Arethusa, The: Chamier, Frederick

Sauk county: Derleth, A.W.

Saul: Brontë, Charlotte

Saul: Heavysege, Charles

Saunter through the West End, A: Hunt, Leigh

Saunterer's rewards: Lucas, E.V.

Saunterings: Warner, C.D.

Saurus: Phillpotts, Eden

Sausage, The: Gow, Ronald

Savage days, The: Toynbee, Philip

Savage holiday: Wright, Richard

Savage sanctuary: Spittel, R.L.

Saved by the enemy: (†Clarke Fitch), Sinclair, Upton

Savignys, The: †Lancaster, G.B.

Saving and spending: Cole, G.D.H.

Saving clause, The: †Sapper

Saviour of society: Swinburne, A.C.

Saviours: Dane, Clemence

Savitri—a legend and a symbol: Ghose, Sri Aurobindo

Savonarola: Austin, Alfred

Savonarola e il proire di San Marco: Landor, W.S.

Savonarola, Erasmus and other essays: Milman, H.H.

Savour of life, The: Bennett, Arnold

Savoy of London, The: Mackenzie, Sir Compton

Savrola: Churchill, Sir Winston

Saxe Holm's stories: Jackson, H.H.

Saxo Grammaticus: Weekley, Ernest

Say and seal: Warner, S.B. and A.B. Warner

Say au revoir but not goodbye: Shiel, M.P.

Say, is this the U.S.A.?: Caldwell, Erskine Preston

Say it with oil: Lardner, Ring

Say no to death: Cusack, E.D.

Say nothing: Hanley, James

Say now Shibboleth: Rhodes, E.M.

Say the word: Brown, Ivor

Saying your prayers: †Armstrong, Anthony

Sayings and doings: Hook, T.E.

Sayings of Christ, The: Mackail, J.W.

Sayings of Grandmamma, The: Glyn, Elinor

Sayings of the little ones: Sigourney, L.H.

Sayonora: Michener, J.A.

Scales of justice: Marsh, Ngaio Edith

Scallywag, The: Allen, Grant

Scallywag: (Stephen Southwold), †Bell, Neill

Scalp hunters, The: Reid, T.M.

Scamp's tragedy, The: Adams, Francis

Scandal at High Chimneys: Carr, J.D.

Scandal at school: Cole, G.D.H.

Scandal of Father Brown, The: Chesterton, G.K.

Scandal of Sophie Dawes, The: †Bowen, Marjorie

Scandal of spring: Boyd, Martin

Scandalmonger, The: White, T.H.

Scapegoat, The: Caine, Sir H. Hall

Scapegoat, The: Du Maurier, Daphne

Scapegoat, The: Frazer, Sir James

Scarabs: Petrie, Sir William Flinders

Scarabs in the Dublin Museum: Murray, Margaret

Scaramouch in Naxox: Davidson, John

Scaramouche: Sabatini, Rafael

Scaramouche the kingmaker: Sabatini, Rafael

Scarborough: Montgomery, Robert

Scarecrow, The: De la Mare, Walter

Scarecrow, The: Mackaye, Percy

Scarlet and Hyssop: Benson, E.F.

Scarlet boy, The: Calder-Marshall, Arthur

Scarlet car, The: Davis, R.H.

Scarlet feather: Ingraham, J.H.

Scarlet frontier, The: Timms, E.V.

Scarlet letter, The: Hawthorne, Nathaniel

Scarlet letter, The: Lathrop, G.P.

Scarlet letters: †Queen, Ellery

Scarlet Pimpernel, The: Orczy, Baroness

Scarlet Pimpernel looks at the world, The: Orczy, Baroness

Scarlet plague, The: London, Jack

Scarlet poppy, A: Spofford, H.E.

Scarlet shawl, The: Jefferies, Richard

Scarlet stripe, The: †Taffrail

Scarlet suit, The: Llewellyn, Richard

Scarlet sword, The: Bates, H.E.

Scarlet tanager, The: Trowbridge, J.T.

Scarlet tree, The: Sitwell, Sir Osbert

Scarronides: Cotton, Charles

Scarweather: Vulliamy, C.E.

Scattered scarlet: Ogilvie, W.H.

Scenario: Peach, L. du Garde

Scene: Craig, *Sir* Gordon

Scene is changed, The: Dukes, Ashley

Scenery and antiquities of Ireland, The: Willis, N.P.

Scenes and characters: Yonge, C.M.

Scenes and hymns of life: Hemans, *Mrs.* Felicia

Scenes and incidents in the western prairies: Gregg, Josiah

Scenes and legends of the north of Scotland: Miller, Hugh

Scenes and plays: Bottomley, Gordon

Scenes and portraits: Brooks, Van Wyck

Scenes and shadows of days departed: Bowles, William Lisle

Scenes and thoughts in Europe: Calvert, George Henry

Scenes from Italy's war: Trevelyan, G.M.

Scenes from scripture: Croly, George

Scenes from the Mesozoic and other drawings: Day, C.S.

Scenes in my native land: Sigourney, L.H.

Scenes of clerical life: †Eliot, George

Scenes of infancy: Leyden, John

Scenes that are brightest: Mottram, R.H.

Scent of hyacinths, A: Mannin, Ethel

Sceptic, The: Hemans, *Mrs.* Felicia

Sceptic, The: Moore, Thomas

Sceptical approach to religion, The: More, P.E.

Sceptical essays: Russell, Bertrand

Scepticism and animal faith: Santayana, George

Scepticisms: Aiken, Conrad

Sceptred flute, The: Naidu, Sarojini

Sceptres and crowns: Warner, S.B.

Scheherazade kept on talking: †Bridie, James

Schelling's transcendental idealism: Watson, John

Scheme for a new alphabet, A: Franklin, Benjamin

Scheme for the coalition of parties, A: Jenyns, Soame

Schemes: Wallace, Edgar

Schiller's life and writings: Carlyle, Thomas

Schirmer inheritance, The: Ambler, Eric

Schocks: Blackwood, Algernon

Scholar and the pedant, The: Kittredge, G.L.

Scholar errant: Burdon, R.M.

Scholar in America, The: Morison, S.E.

Scholar-friends,The:Lowell,J.R.

Scholar-gipsies: Buchan, John

Scholar's letters to a young lady, A: Child, F.J.

Scholemaster, The: Ascham, Roger

Schollers purgatory, The: Wither, George

School: Robertson, T.W.

School and playground: Pyle, Howard

School and society, The: Dewey, John

School at the turrets, The: Brazil, Angela

School by the sea, The: Brazil, Angela

School for ambassadors, The: Jusserand, Jean

School for arrogance, The: Holcroft, Thomas

School for fathers, The: Bickerstaffe, Isaac

School for greybeards, A: Cowley, *Mrs.* Hannah

School for grown children, A: Morton, Thomas

School for guardians, The: Murphy, Arthur

School for lovers, The: Whitehead, William

School for politics, The: Gayarré, C.E.A.

School for saints, The: †Hobbes, John Oliver

School for scandal, The: Sheridan, R.B.

School for spinsters: Pertwee, Roland

School for wives, The: Kelly, Hugh

School for wives, The: Malleson, Miles

School history of Georgia, A: †Arp, Bill

School history of Germany, A: Taylor, Bayard

School in American culture: Mead, Margaret

School in private: Toynbee, Philip

School in the forest, The: Brazil, Angela

School in the south, The: Brazil, Angela

School of charity, The: Underhill, Evelyn

School of reform, The: Morton, Thomas

School on the cliff, The: Brazil, Angela

School on the loch, The: Brazil, Angela

School on the moor, The: Brazil, Angela

School teaching and school reform: Lodge, *Sir* Oliver

School-boy, The: Cibber, Colley

School-boy, The: Holmes, Oliver Wendell

Schoolboy lyrics: Kipling, Rudyard

Schoolboy's apprentice, The: Lucas, E.V.

Schoolboy's story, The:Dickens, Charles

Schoole of complement, The: Shirley, James

Schoolgirl Kitty: Brazil, Angela

Schoolmaster, The: Benson, A.C.

Schoolmaster, The: De Selincourt, Aubrey

Schoolmaster's diary, A: Mais, S.P.B.

Schoolmaster's stories, The: Eggleston, Edward

Schoolmaster's tragedy, The: Adams, Francis

Schoolmistress, The: Pinero, *Sir* A.W.

School-mistress, The: Shenstone, William

Schoolroom window, The: O'Brien, Kate

Schools and universities on the Continent: Arnold, Matthew

Schools in the story of culture: Beard, C.A.

Schools of to-morrow: Dewey, John

Schools, school-books and schoolmasters: Hazlitt, W.C.

Schooner came to Atia, The: Finlayson, Roderick

Schubert: Bates, Ralph

Science: a poem: Hopkinson, Francis

Science advances: Haldane, J.B.S.

Science and a future life: Myers, F.W.H.

Science and culture: Huxley, T.H.

Science and English poetry: Bush, Douglas

Science and ethics: Haldane, J.B.S.

Science and everyday life: Haldane, J.B.S.

Science and faith: Bragg, *Sir* William

Science and government: Snow, C.P.

Science and health: Eddy, M.B.

Science and human progress: Lodge, *Sir* Oliver

Science and human values: Bronowski, J.

Science and immortality: Osler, *Sir* William

Science and music: Jeans, *Sir* James

Science and poetry: Richards, I.A.

Science and religion: Eddington, *Sir* Arthur Stanley

Science and religion, experience and interpretation: Raven, C.E.

Science and the modern world: Whitehead, A.N.

Science and the unseen world: Eddington, *Sir* Arthur Stanley

Science and the world mind: Wells, H.G.

Science: chemistry, physics, astronomy: Bronowski, J.

Science in Arcady: Allen, Grant

Science in peace and war: Haldane, J.B.S.

Science, liberty and peace: Huxley, Aldous

Science life and literature: Shiel, M.P.

Science, medicine and morals: Raven, C.E.

Science of English verse, The: Lanier, Sidney

Science of ethics: Stephen, *Sir* Leslie

Science of etymology, The: Skeat, W.W.

Science of fiction, The: Hardy, Thomas

Science of infantry tactics: Liddell Hart, B.

Science of life, The: Huxley, *Sir* Julian

Science of life, The: Wells, H.G.

Science of political economy, The: George, Henry

Science of rebellion: Kipling, Rudyard

Science, religion and the future: Raven, C.E.

Scientific basis of spiritualism, The: Sargent, Epes

Scientific lectures and essays: Kingsley, Charles

Scientific method in philosophy: Russell, Bertrand

Scientific outlook, The: Russell, Bertrand

Scientific religion: Oliphant, Laurence

Scientific research and social needs: Huxley, *Sir* Julian

Scientific spirit of the age, The: Cobbe, Frances Power

Scillaes metamorphosis: Lodge, Thomas

Scinde: Burton, *Sir* Richard

Sind revisited: Burton, *Sir* Richard

Scissors: Roberts, C.E.M.

Scoop: Waugh, Evelyn

Scopalomine in Africa: Scully, W.C.

Scope and method of economic science, The: Sidgewick, Henry

Scope of social anthropology, The: Frazer, *Sir* James

Score of famous composers, A: Dole, N.H.

Scorn of women: London, Jack

Scornful ladie, The: Beaumont, Francis and John Fletcher

Scot abroad, The: Burton, John Hill

Scotch: Lockhart, *Sir* Robert Bruce

Scotch reform, with a summary view of a plan for a judicatory: Bentham, Jeremy

Scoticisms: Beattie, James

Scotish poems: Douglas, Gawin

Scotish song: Ritson, Joseph

Scotland and the Commonwealth: Firth, *Sir* Charles

Scotland and the Protectorate: Firth, *Sir* Charles

Scotland illustrated by John C.Brown: Wilson, John

Scotland's lament: Barrie, *Sir* J.M.

Scots and their country: Muir, Edwin

Scot's Brigade, The: Grant, James

Scots in Canada: Gibbon, J.M.

Scots ode to the British antiquarians, A: Ramsay, Allan

Scots quair, A: †Gibbon, L.G.

Scots unbound: †McDiarmid, Hugh

Scots Wha Hae: history of the Royal Caledonian Society of Melbourne: Chisholm, A.H.

Scotsman in Canada, The: Campbell, W.W.

Scott and Haliburton: Logan, J.D.

Scott and Scotland: Muir, Edwin

Scotticisms: Hume, David

Scottish abbeys and social life: Coulton, G.G.

Scottish cavalier, The: Grant, James

Scottish chiefs, The: Porter, Jane

Scottish eccentrics: †McDiarmid, Hugh

Scottish historie of James the fourth, slaine at Flodden, The: Greene, Robert

Scottish islands, The: †McDiarmid, Hugh

Scottish journey: Muir, Edwin

Scottish pastorals, poems, songs, etc.: Hogg, James

Scottish scene: †Gibbon, L.G. and Hugh MacDiarmid

Scottish scene: †McDiarmid, Hugh and †L.G. Gibbon

Scottish sketches: Barr, A.E.H.

Scottish stories: Cunninghame Graham, R.B.

Scottish village, The: Cowley, *Mrs*. Hannah

Scott-King's modern Europe: Waugh, Evelyn

Scottsboro limited: Hughes, J.L.

Scourge for paper-persecutors, A: Davies, John

Scourge of folly, The: Davies, John

Scourge of villanie, The: Marston, John

Scourge stick, The: Praed, *Mrs*. C.

Scouring of the White Horse, The: Hughes, Thomas

Scouts of Empire: Burpee, Lawrence J.

Scowrers, The: Shadwell, Thomas

Scrap book, A: Saintsbury, George

Scraps: Jennings, Gertrude

Screens, The: Richards, I.A.

Screw loose, A: Warren J.B.L.

Screwtype letters, The: Lewis, C.S.

Scribbleomania: Ireland, W.H.

Scribbling lark, The: Williamson, Henry

Scriblers lash'd, The: Ramsay, Allan

Script of Jonathan Swift, The: Leslie, *Sir* J.R. Shane

Scripta Minoa: Evans, *Sir* A.J.

Scripture dictionary, A: Cruden, Alexander

Scripture idolatry: Higginson, T.W.

Scrolls from the Dead Sea, The: Wilson, Edmund

Scruffy: Gallico, Paul

Scudders, The: Bacheller, Irving

Sculler, rowing from Tiber to Thames, The: Taylor, John

Sculptura: Evelyn, John

Sculpture: Gill, Eric

Sculpture: Lytton, E.

Sculpture and the living model: Gill, Eric

Sculpture on machine-made buildings: Gill, Eric

Scuttleboom's treasure: Gow, Ronald

Scylla or Charybdis?: Broughton, Rhoda

Sea and lands: Arnold, Edwin

Sea and Sardinia: Lawrence, D.H.

Sea and sky: Brereton, John Le G.

Sea and Spinifex: Palmer, E.V.

Sea and Sussex: Kipling, Rudyard

Sea and the jungle, The: Tomlinson, H.M.

Sea and the wedding, The: Johnson, Pamela H.

Sea battle, A: Hannay, J.O.

Sea captain, The: Lytton, E.G.E.B. *1st Baron*

Sea escapes and adventures: †Taffrail

Sea garden by H.D.: Doolittle, Hilda

Sea hawk, The: Sabatini, Rafael

Sea horses, The: (Stephen Southwold), †Bell, Neill

Sea horses: Young, Francis Brett

Sea in ships, The: Villiers, A.J.

Sea is kind, The: Moore, T.S.

Sea lady, The: Wells, H.G.

Sea life in Nelson's time: Masefield, John

Sea lions, The: Cooper, James Fenimore

Sea loot: Divine, A.D.

Sea mystery, The: Crofts, F.W.

Sea of Cortez: Steinbeck, John

Sea of grass, The: Richter, Conrad

Sea queen, A: Russell, W.C.

Sea spray and smoke drift: Gordon, A.L.

Sea tower, The: Walpole, *Sir* Hugh

Sea turn and other matters, A: Aldrich, T.B.

Sea urchins: Jacobs, W.W.

Sea venturers of Britain: †Taffrail

Sea wall: Strong, L.A.G.

Sea warfare: Kipling, Rudyard

Sea whispers: Jacobs, W.W.

Sea without a haven, The: Broster, D.K.

Seaboard parish, The: Macdonald, George

Sea-change, A: Howells, W.D.

Sea-charm of Venice, The: Brooke, Stopford

Seacliff: De Forest, John William

Seacoast of Bohemia: Golding, Louis

Seacoast of Bohemia: Morley, C.D.

Sea-dogs of today: Villiers, A.J.

Seaford's snake: Mitford, Bertram

Seagull on the step: Boyle, Kay

Seal in the bedroom, The: Thurber, James

Sealed orders: Ward, E.S.

Seals, The: Gibbon, Monk

Sealskin cloak, The: †Boldrewood, Rolf

Sealskin trousers: Linklater, Eric

Seaman's friend: Dana, R.H. *junior*

Seamark, A: Carman, Bliss

Seamstress, The: Reynolds, G.

Seamy side, The: Besant, *Sir* Walter and James Rice

Seaports in the moon: Starrett, Vincent

Search, The: Krishnamurti, Jiddu

Search, The: Snow, C.P.

Search after happiness, A: More, Hannah

Search after happiness, The: Scott, *Sir* Walter

Search after Proserpine, The: De Vere, Aubrey

Search after sunrise: Brittain, Vera

Search for a background: Jacob, Naomi

Search for a soul: Bottome, Phyllis

Search for America, A: Grove, F.P.

Search for good sense, The: Lucas, F.L.

Search for money, A: Rowley, William

Search for Susie, The: Hannay, J.O.

Search for the Western sea, The: Burpee, Lawrence J.

Search party, The: Hannay, J.O.

Search relentless, The: Skinner, C.L.

Searching image, The: Dudek, Louis

Searching the net: Warren, J.B.L.

Search-light letters: Grant, Robert

Searchlights, The: Gibson, Wilfred

Searchlights: Vachell, H.A.

Searchlights and nightingales: Lynd, Robert

Seaside and the fireside, The: Longfellow, H.W.

Sea-side studies at Ilfracombe, Tenby, the Scilly Isles, and Jersey: Lewes, G.H.

Season, The: Austin, Alfred

Season and festival: Palmer, H.E.

Season at Sarsaparilla, The: White, Patrick

Season in Egypt: Petrie, *Sir* William Flinders

Season ticket, The: Haliburton, T.C.

Seasonable advice: Swift, Jonathan

Seasonable defence of preaching, A: Glanvill, Joseph

Seasonable memorial in some historical notes upon the liberties of the presse and pulpit, A: L'Estrange, *Sir* Roger

Seasonable recommendation and defence of reason in affairs of religion against infidelity, A: Glanvill, Joseph

Seasonably alarming and humiliating truths in a metrical version of certain select passages taken from the works of William Law: Byrom, John

Seasoned timber: Canfield, Dorothy

Seasons, The: Thomson, James

Seasons and the gardener, The: Bates, H.E.

Seat in the park, A: Pinero, *Sir* A.W.

Seat of the scornful: Carr, J.D.

Seatonian poems: Neale, J.M.

Seats of the mighty, The: Parker, *Sir* H.G.

Seaward: Hovey, Richard

Seaways: †Bartimeus

Sea-weeds, gathered at Aldborough: Barton, Bernard

Sea-wife: Anderson, Maxwell

Sea-wolf, The: London, Jack

Sebastian: Heppenstall, Rayner

Secession, coercion and civil war: Jones, J.B.

Secession, concession, or self-possession: which?: Clarke, J.F.

Second April: Millay, E. St. Vincent

Second Armada, The: Hayward, Abraham

Second booke of ayres by William Corkine, A: Donne, John

Second chapbook of rounds: Farjeon, Eleanor

Second characteristicks: Shaftesbury, Anthony Cooper *Earl of*

Second empire, The: Guedalla, Philip

Second front: Lindsay, Jack

Second funeral of Napoleon, The: Thackeray, W.M.

Second generation, The: Phillips, D.G.

Second growth: Akins, Zoë

Second harvest: Jacob, Naomi

Second hymn to Lenin: †McDiarmid, Hugh

Second innings: more autobiography: Cardus, Neville

Second journey through Persia, Armenia and Asia Minor to Constantinople: Morier, J.J.

Second jungle book: Kipling, Rudyard

Second key, The: Lowndes, M.A.

Second leaf, The: Riding, Laura

Second letter concerning toleration, A: Locke, John

Second letter to Archdeacon Singleton: Smith, Sydney

Second letter to Her Grace the Duchess of Devonshire, A: Combe, William

Second lie, The: MacKay, I.E.

Second Louisiana, The: Boker, G.H.

Second love: Trollope, Frances

Second man, The: Behrman, S.N.

Second marriage, The: Meynell, Viola

Second Mrs. Cornford, The: Seymour, Beatrice Kean

Second Mrs. Tanqueray, The: Pinero, *Sir* A.W.

Second musical entertainment perform'd on St. Cecilia's day, A: Oldham, John

Second Officer: †Taffrail

Second opportunity of Mr. Staplehurst: Ridge, W. Pett

Second overture: Anderson, Maxwell

Second part of Absalom and Achitophel, The: Tate, Nahum

Second part of conny-catching, The: Greene, Robert

Second part of Henrie the fourth, The: Shakespeare, William

Second part of If you know not me you know no bodie, The: Heywood, Thomas

Second part of the dissuasive from popery, The: Taylor, Jeremy

Second part of the honest whore, The: Dekker, Thomas

Second part of the rover, The: Behn, *Mrs.* Afra

Second parte of the confutacion of Tyndale answered, The: More, *Sir* Thomas

Second parte to the mothers blessing, A: Markham, Gervase

Second person singular, The: Meynell, Alice

Second reflections in a mirror: Morgan, Charles

Second satire, The: Pope, Alexander

Second scrap book, A: Saintsbury, George

Second scroll, The: Klein, A.M.

Second series: Harris, James Thomas

Second sight: Gunn, Neil

Second son, The: Aldrich, Thomas Bailey

Second son, The: Oliphant, Margaret

Second string: (†Anthony Hope) Hawkins, Anthony Hope

Second strings: Godley, Alfred Denis

Second things of life, The: Moffatt, James

Second thoughts: Broughton, Rhoda

Second thoughts of an idle fellow, The: Jerome, Jerome K.

Second threshold: Barry, Philip

Second to none: Grant, James

Second tome of the Travailes and adventures of Don Simonides, The: Rich, Barnabe

Second tour of Doctor Syntax, The: Combe, William

Second travels of an Irish Gentleman in search of a religion: White, J.B.

Second tree from the corner, The: White, E.B.

Second vindication of the reasonableness of Christianity, A: Locke, John

Second voyage of Christopher Columbus from Cadiz to Hispaniola, The: Morison, S.E.

Second voyage round the world, A: Cook, James

Second world, The: Blackmur, R.P.

Second World War, The: Churchill, *Sir* Winston

Second World War, The: Cooper, Alfred Duff

Second youth: Deeping, Warwick

Second youth of Theodora Desanges, The: Linton, Eliza

Second-story man, The: Sinclair, Upton

Secret, The: Binyon, Laurence

Secret, The: Ficke, A.D.

Secret, The: Milne, A.A.

Secret, The: Oppenheim, E. Phillips

Secret adversary, The: Christie, Agatha

Secret agent, The: Conrad, Joseph

Secret agent X-9: Hammett, S.D.

Secret bargain and the Ulster Plot: Kipling, Rudyard

Secret battle, The: Herbert, *Sir* A.P.

Secret bird, The: Muir, D.C.A.

Secret city, The: Walpole, *Sir* Hugh

Secret diary of William Byrd of Westover, The: Byrd, William

Secret dispatch, The: Grant, James

Secret dream, The: Priestley, J.B.

Secret fiord, The: Trease, Geofrey

Secret front, The: Gallico, Paul

Secret garden, The: Burnett, Frances Hodgson

Secret glory, The: †Machen, Arthur

Secret harbour: White, S.E.

Secret history and memoirs of the barracks of Ireland, The: Brooke, Henry

Secret history of Arius and Odolphus, The: Cibber, Colley

Secret history of Europe, The: Oldmixon, John

Secret history of the American revolution: Van Doren, Carl

Secret history of the Calves-Head Clubb, The: Ward, Edward

Secret history of the English occupation of Egypt, The: Blunt, Wilfred

Secret history of the Mongols, The: Waley, Arthur

Secret house, The: Wallace, Edgar

Secret information: Hichens, Robert

Secret inheritance, A: Farjeon, B.L.

Secret journey, The: Hanley, James

Secret key, The: Evans, G.E.

Secret kingdom, The: Greenwood, Walter

Secret kingdom, The: Seymour, W.K.

Secret life, The: Granville-Barker, *Sir* Harley

Secret life of Miss Lottinger, The: †Bell, Neil

Secret lives: Benson, E.F.

Secret love: Dryden, John

Secret memoirs of Count Tadasu Hayashi, G.C.V.O., The: Hayashi, Tadasu, *Viscount*

Secret name, The. The Soviet record 1917–1958: Lin Yu T'ang

Secret of Coconut Island, The: (†Donald Barr), Barrett, C.L.

Secret of Chimneys, The: Christie, Agatha

Secret of death, with some collected poems, The: Arnold, Edwin

Secret of Dr. Kildare, The: †Brand, Max

Secret of Father Brown, The: Chesterton, G.K.

Secret of Kyriels, The: Nesbit, E.

Secret of Narcisse, The: Gosse, *Sir* Edmund

Secret of Pooduck Island, The: Noyes, Alfred

Secret of serenity, The: Canfield, Dorothy

Secret of the Australian desert, The: Favenc, Ernest

Secret of the border castle, The: Brazil, Angela

Secret of the castle, The: Jennings, Gertrude

Secret of the clan, The: Brown, Alice

Secret of the Lebombo, A: Mitford, Bertram

Secret of the sea, A: Matthews, J.B.

Secret of the sea, The: Turner, E.S.

Secret of the totem, The: Lang, Andrew

Secret places of the heart, The: Wells, H.G.

Secret police, The: Lang, J.

Secret power, The: †Corelli, Marie

Secret river, The: Macaulay, *Dame* Rose

Secret river, The: Rawlings, Marjorie

Secret rose, The: Yeats, W.B.

Secret sanctuary, The: Deeping, Warwick

Secret service: Gillette, William

Secret service operator 13: Chambers, R.W.

Secret services: Frankau, Gilbert

Secret session speeches: Churchill, *Sir* Winston

Secret son, The: Kaye-Smith, Sheila

Secret springs, The: O'Higgins, H.J.

Secret stair, The: Bottome, Phyllis

Secret trail, The: †Armstrong, Anthony

Secret vanguard: (†Michael Innes), Stewart, J.I.M.

Secret veld, The: Slater, F.C.

Secret water: Ransome, Arthur

Secret way, The: Gale, Zona

Secret woman, The: Phillpotts, Eden

Secretary of the Royal Society of Canada, The: Davin, N.F.

Secretary to Bayne, M.P.: Ridge, W.Pett

Secretly armed: Bottome, Phyllis

Secrets: Besier, Rudolf

Secrets: Davies, W.H.

Secrets at Roseladies, The: Catherwood, Mary

Secrets of the self, The: Iqbal, Sir Muhammad

Secrets of the south, The: Jephcott, S.W.

Secrets of the Vatican, The: Sladen, D.B.W.

Secrets worth knowing: Morton, Thomas

Sectarian, The: Picken, Andrew

Section: Rock-drill: Pound, Ezra

Security: Brown, Ivor

Sedge fire: Moll, E.G.

Sedment, I, II: Petrie, Sir William Flinders

Seducers in Ecuador: Sackville-West, Victoria

Seduction: Holcroft, Thomas

See England first: Mais, S.P.B.

See Naples and die: Rice, Elmer

See you in the morning: Patchen, Kenneth

See you later: Wodehouse, P.G.

Seed and the sower, The: Van der Post, Laurens

Seed of Adam, The: Williams, Charles

Seeds in the wind: Soutar, William

Seeds of enchantment, The: Frankau, Gilbert

Seeds of time: Drinkwater, John

Seedtime: Palmer, E.V.

Seein' reason: Pertwee, Roland

Seeing and knowing: Berenson, Bernhard

Seeing is believing: †Carter Dickson

Seeing life: †Bowen, Marjorie

Seeing life: Oppenheim, E.Phillips

Seeing Soviet Russia: Griffith, Hubert

Seeing things at night: Broun, Heywood

Seek and find: Rossetti,Christina

Seekers, The: Bates, H.E.

Seekers, The: Dickinson, Goldsworthy Lowes

Seen and the unseen at Stratford-on-Avon, The: Howells, W.D.

Seen and unseen: Noguchi, Yone

Seen dimly before dawn: Balchin, Nigel

Seen in Germany: Baker, R.S.

Seen in the Hadhramaut: Stark, Freya

Seen unknown: Jacob, Naomi

Seer, The: Hunt, Leigh

"See-saw": Stern, G.B.

Seeta: Taylor, P.M.

Seething pot, The: Hannay, J.O.

Seffy: Long, J.L.

Segregation: Warren, Robert Penn

Seized by a shadow: Sladen, D.B.W.

Sejanus his fall: Jonson, Ben

Selbys, The: Green, Anne

Select and rare Scottish melodies: Hogg, James

Select biographies: Cromwell and Bunyan: Southey, Robert

Select charters and other illustrations of English constitutional history to the reign of Edward the First: Stubbs, William

Select collection of English songs, A: Ritson, Joseph

Select conversations with an uncle: Wells, H.G.

Select documents, 1789–1875: Cole, G.D.H.

Select epigrams from the Greek anthology: Mackail, J.W.

Select letters of Major Jack Downing, The: Smith, Seba

Select poems: Barnes, William

Select second husband for Sir Thomas Overburie's wife, now a matchless widow, A: Davies, John

Select stories: Kipling, Rudyard

Selected criticism; prose and poetry: Bogan, Louise

Selected essays: (†Alpha of the Plough), Gardiner, A.G.

Selected essays: Hayward, Abraham

Selected examples of Indian art: Coomaraswamy, A.K.

Selected lyrical poems: Church, Richard

Selected poems: Smith, Stevie

Selected poems: Spender, Stephen

Selected prejudices: Mencken, H.L.

Selected warriors: †Armstrong, Anthony

Selection of German Hebrew melodies, A: Hogg, James

Selections from prattle: Bierce, Ambrose

Selections from the Anti-Jacobin: Canning, George

Selections from the correspondence of the First Lord Acton: Figgis J.N. and R.V. Laurence

Selections from the Kur-án: Lane, Edward William

Selections from the poetical literature of the West: Gallagher, W.D.

Selections in Augustan booklet: Palmer, H.E.

Self: Gore, Catherine

Self: Nichols, Beverley

Self and self-management: Bennett, Arnold

Self condemned: Lewis, P. Wyndham

Self indulgence: Bury, Lady C.S.M.

Self-communion: Brontë, Anne

Self-culture: Clarke, J.F.

Self-doomed: Farjeon, B.L.

Self-government in industry: Cole, G.D.H.

Self-help: Smiles, Samuel

Self-portrait: Frankau, Gilbert

Self's the man: Davidson, John

Self-selected essays: Priestley, J.B.

Self-sufficiency: Lippmann, Walter

Selina is older: Kaye-Smith, Sheila

Selling of Joseph, The: Sewall, Samuel

Selmin of Selmingfold: Mitford, Bertram

Selvaggio: Manning, Anne

Sembal: Cannan, Gilbert

Semeiotica Uranica: Culpeper, Nicolas

Semi-attached couple, The: Eden, Emily

Semi-centennial: Bacon, Leonard

Semi-centennial celebration of the inauguration of Washington. Ode: Bryant, W.C.

Semi-detached house, The: Eden, Emily

Semmes of the Alabama: Roberts, W. Adolphe

Sen trew vertew encressis dignytee: James I

Senator North: Atherton, Gertrude

Send for Dr. O'Grady: Hannay, J.O.

Send round the hat: Lawson, Henry

Seneca and Elizabethan tragedy: Lucas, F.L.

Senilities: Graves, Richard

Senior partner, The: Riddell, *Mrs.* J.H.

Sensation novel, A: Gilbert, *Sir* W.S.

Sensational tales: Clarke, Marcus

Sense and sensation: Taylor, Tom

Sense and sensibility: Austen, Jane

Sense of beauty, The: Santayana, George

Sense of glory, The: Read, *Sir* Herbert

Sense of humor, The: Eastman, Max

Sense of quality: study and criticism of Italian art, The: Berenson, Bernhard

Sense of reality, A: Greene, Graham

Sense of the past, The: James, Henry

Senses and the soul, and moral sentiment in Religion, The: Emerson, Ralph Waldo

Sensory integration: Adrian, E.D. *1st Baron*

Sensus communis: an essay on the freedom of wit and humour: Shaftesbury, Anthony Ashley Cooper, *Earl of*

Sentence deferred: Derleth, A.W.

Sentences and paragraphs: Davidson, John

Sentences and thinking: Foerster, Norman

Sentiment of rationality, The: James, William

Sentiment of the sword, The: Burton, *Sir* Richard

Sentimental dialogue between an English Lady of quality and an Irish gentleman, A: Stevenson, J.H.

Sentimental journey through France and Italy, A: Sterne, Laurence and J.H. Stevenson

Sentimental Tommy: Barrie, *Sir* J.M.

Sentimental traveller, The: †Lee, Vernon

Sentimentalist, The: Collins, Dale

Sentiments of a true patriot, The: Bowles, W. L.

Separate lives: Palmer, E.V.

Separate tables: Rattigan, Terence

Separation, The: Bury, *Lady* C.S.M.

September: Swinnerton, Frank

September tide: Du Maurier, Daphne

Septimius Felton: Hawthorne, Nathaniel

Sepulchral monuments of Italy, The: Ruskin, John

Sequel, The: Russell, W.C.

Sequel to Don Juan: Reynolds, G.

Sequel to Oh lady fair: Moore, Thomas

Sequence, The: Glyn, Elinor

Sequences: Sassoon, Siegfried

Sequences, hymns and other ecclesiastical verses: Neale, J.M.

Sequestered shrine, The: Mackaye. Percy

Seraphim, The: Browning, Elizabeth Barrett

Serbski Pesme: (†Owen Meredith), Lytton, E. R. B. *Earl*

Serena Blandish or the difficulty of getting married: Bagnold, Enid

Serenade: Cain, James

Sergeant Lamb of the ninth: Graves, Robert

Sergeant Lamb's America: Graves, Robert

Sergeant Michael Cassidy: †Sapper

Sergeant Poppett and Policeman James: Blackwood, Algernon

Sergeant Shakespeare: Cooper, Alfred Duff

Sergeant Sir Peter: Wallace, Edgar

Serial universe: Dunne, J.W.

Series of essays on the life of Mohamed, A: Ahmad Khan, *Sir* Saiyid

Series of lectures on the science of government, A: Tucker, N.B.

Series of sermons on the epistle and gospel for each Sunday in the year, A: Williams, Isaac

Serious and patheticall contemplation of the mercies of God, A: Traherne, Thomas

Serious and useful scheme, to make an hospital for incurables, A: Swift, Jonathan

Serious poem upon William Wood, brasier, tinker, hardware-man, coiner, counterfeiter, founder and esquire, A: Swift, Jonathan

Serious reflections during the life and surprising adventures of Robinson Crusoe: Defoe, Daniel

Serious wooing, The: †Hobbes, John Oliver

Sermon, delivered in Leominster, A: Flint, Timothy

Sermon of commemoration of the Lady Danvers, A: Donne, John

Sermon of valediction: Donne, John

Sermon on Acts i. 8: Donne, John

Sermon on Judges XX.15: Donne, John

Sermon on military duty, A: Belknap, Jeremy

Sermon on Mr. H. Raine's charity, A: Bishop, Samuel

Sermon on Psalm 38 v. 9: Donne, John

Sermon on religious charity, A: Smith, Sydney

Sermon [on St John, xi, 25, 26], A: Johnson, Samuel

Sermon preached at the consecration of two Archbishops and ten Bishops, A: Taylor, Jeremy

Sermon preached at the funerall of Sr. George Dalston, A: Taylor, Jeremy

Sermon preached at the opening of the Parliament of Ireland, A: Taylor, Jeremy

Sermon preached before the incorporated society of the propagation of the Gospel in foreign parts, A: Berkeley, George

Sermon preached in Christ-Church, Dublin: at the funeral of the Archbishop of Armagh: with a narrative of his whole life, A: Taylor, Jeremy

Sermon preached in Saint Maries Church in Oxford, A: Taylor, Jeremy

Sermon preached May 11th, 1808, A: Flint, Timothy

Sermon preached to the King's Mtie, A: Donne, John

Sermon upon the conduct to be observed by the Established Church towards Catholics and other dissenters, A: Smith, Sydney

Sermons: Churchill, Charles

Sermons: Maturin, C.R.

Sermons academical and occasional: Keble, John

Sermons and soda water: O'Hara, J.H.

Sermons bearing on subjects of the day: Newman, J.H.

Sermons chiefly on the interpretation of Scripture: Arnold, Thomas

Sermons, chiefly on the Theory of Religious Belief, preached before the University of Oxford: Newman, J.H.

Sermons chiefly upon practical subjects: Bishop, Samuel

Sermons for sailors: Kingsley, Charles

Sermons for the Christian year: Keble, John

Sermons for the new life: Bushnell, Horace

Sermons for the Times: Kingsley, Charles

Sermons of Mr. Yorick, The: Sterne, Laurence

Sermons of theism, atheism, and the popular theology: Parker, Theodore

Sermons on living subjects: Bushnell, Horace

Sermons on national subjects: Kingsley, Charles

Sermons on various subjects: Whately, Richard

Sermons on various subjects (includes some hymns): Watts, Isaac

Sermons out of Church: Craik, Mrs. Dinah

Sermons preached at Trinity Chapel, Brighton: Robertson, F.W.

Sermons preached before the University of Oxford: Pusey, E.B.

Sermons preached upon several occasions: Barrow, Isaac

Sermons to gentlemen upon temperance and exercise: Rush, Benjamin

Sermons to the clergy: Dodge, May Abigail

Serpent, The: Gunn, Neil

Serpent and the rope, The: Rao, Raja

Serpent in the wilderness, The: Masters, E.L.

Serpent of Division, The: Lydgate, John

Servant girl question, The: Spofford, H.E.

Servant of reality, A: Bottome, Phyllis

Servant of the County: Cole, M.I.

Servant of the king, A: Warner, A.B.

Servant of the public, A: (†Anthony Hope), Hawkins, Anthony Hope

Servants of the future: Mitchell, Mary

Servian popular poetry: Bowring, Sir John

Service: Smith, Dodie

Service, The: Thoreau, H.D.

Service for two: Flavin, Martin

Service of prayer for use in wartime, A: Underhill, Evelyn

Service with a smile: Wodehouse, P.G.

Servile state, The: Belloc, Hilaire

Serving at mass: Gill, Eric

Sesame and lilies: Ruskin, John

Set in authority: Duncan, S.J.

Set of eight songs, A: Hopkinson, Francis

Set of glees, A: Moore, Thomas

Set of six, A: Conrad, Joseph

Set of the sails, The: Villiers, A.J.

Set with green herbs: †Bowen, Marjorie

Seth's brother's wife: Frederic, Harold

Settlement of the trouble between Mr. Thring and Mr. Wells: Wells, H.G.

Settler, The: Kipling, Rudyard

Settlers and pioneers: Cowan, James

Settlers and sunbirds: Slater, F.C.

Settlers in Canada, The: Marryatt, Frederick

Settlers in Kenya: Huxley, Elspeth J.

Settlers of Karossa Creek, The: †Becke, Louis

Settlers of the marsh: Grove, F.P.

Settons, The: Buchan, Anna

Seven ages of Washington, The: Wister, Owen

Seven ages of woman, The: Mackenzie, *Sir* Compton

Seven arms, The: Strong, L.A.G.

Seven Bobsworth: Beresford, J.D.

Seven by seven: Bates, H.E.

Seven centuries of verse: Smith, A.J.M.

Seven conundrums, The: Oppenheim, E.Phillips

Seven days: Rinehart, Mary Roberts

Seven days, The: Williams, Isaac

Seven days in new Crete: Graves, Robert

Seven days of the sun, The: Turner, W.J.R.

Seven deadly sinnes of London, The: Dekker, Thomas

Seven deadly sins, The: †Bowen, Marjorie

Seven deadly sins, The: O'Dowd, B.P.

Seven dials mystery, The: Christie, Agatha

Seven discourses delivered in the Royal Academy by the President: Reynolds, *Sir* Joshua

Seven Emus: Herbert, A.F.X.

Seven English cities: Howells, W.D.

Seven for a secret: Webb, Mary

Seven hills, The: De Mille, James

Seven Kings of England: Trease, Geoffrey

Seven lamps of architecture, The: Ruskin, John

Seven lectures on Shakespeare and Milton: Coleridge, S.T.

Seven lectures on the law and history of copyright in books: Birrell, Augustine

Seven little Australians: Turner, E.S.

Seven men: Beerbohm, *Sir* Max

Seven men came back: Deeping, Warwick

Seven modern comedies: Dunsany, E.J.M.D.P.

Seven noble lives: Gupta, Nagendranath

Seven of diamonds,The: †Brand, Max

Seven pillars of wisdom: Lawrence, T.E.

7 p.m.: Van Doren, Mark

Seven poor men of Sydney: Stead, C.E.

Seven Queens of England, The: Trease, Geoffrey

Seven seas: Kipling, Rudyard

Seven sins, The: Wurdemann, Audrey

Seven sisters, The: Prokosch, Frederic

Seven sleepers, The: †Beeding, Francis

Seven sleepers, The: Van Doren, Mark

Seven sleepers of Ephesus: Coleridge, M.E.

Seven sonnets and a psalm of Montreal: Butler, Samuel

Seven sons of Mammon, The: Sala, G.A.H.

Seven Spanish cities, and the way to them: Hale, E.E.

Seven stabs: (†Neil Gordon), Macdonell, A.G.M

Seven stages: Trease, Geoffrey

Seven streams, The: Deeping, Warwick

Seven summers: Anand, M.R.

Seven suspects: (†Michael Innes), Stewart, J.I.M.

Seven tales: Blocksidge, C.W.

Seven tales and Alexander: Bates, H.E.

Seven tales. By seven authors: Hall, Anna Maria

Seven tales by seven authors: Smedley, F.E.

Seven things: Carman, Bliss

Seven thunders, The: Millin, Sarah Gertrude

Seven torches of character, The: †King, Basil

Seven types of ambiguity: Empson, William

Seven unpublished poems to Alice Meynell: Patmore, Coventry

Seven virtues and G.K.Chesterton, The: Cammaerts, Emile

Seven who fled, The: Prokosch, Frederic

Seven who waited, The: Derleth, A.W.

Seven winters: Bowen, E.D.C.

Seven wise men, The: Crockett, S.R.

Seven years: Kavanagh, Julia

Seven years' harvest: Canby, H.S.

Sevenoaks: Holland, J.G.

Seventeen: Tarkington, Booth

Seventeen hundred and ninety-one: Murphy, Arthur

Seventeen lectures on the study of medieval and modern history: Stubbs, William

1764: Lindsay, Jack

Seventeen sonnets: Gibbon, Monk

Seventeenth century literature: Wedgwood, C.V.

Seventeenth century poetry (anth.): Hayward, John

Seventeenth century studies: a contribution to the history of English poetry: Gosse, *Sir* Edmund

Seventh Bowl, The: †Bell, Neil

Seventh hill, The: Hillyer, Robert

Seventh man, The: †Brand, Max

Seventh report from the select committee of the House of Assembly of Upper Canada on grievances, The: Mackenzie, W.L.

Seventh sense, The: Roberts, Kenneth

Seventy fathom treasure: Divine, A.D.

Seventy five: Bates, H.E.

Seventy North: †Taffrail

Seventy times seven: Stern, G.B.

Seventy years in archaeology: Petrie, *Sir* William Flinders

Seventy-six: Neal, John

Several letters, written by a noble lord to a young man at the University: Shaftesbury, Anthony Cooper,*Earl of*

Several observations: Grigson, Geoffrey

Several reasons proving that inoculating the small pox is a lawful practice: Mather, Increase

Severed head, A: Priestley, J.B.

Seward and the Declaration of Paris: Adams, C.F.

Sex and Christianity: McFarlane, John Clare

Sex and temperament in three primitive societies: Mead, Margaret

Sex expression in literature: Calverton, V.F.

Sex locked out: Lawrence, D.H.

Sextains: †Baylebridge, W.

Sexual inversion: Ellis, Havelock

Sexual inversion: Symonds, J.A.

Sh-h-h…here comes the censor!: Deacon, W.A.

Shabby genteel story, A: Thackeray, W.M.

Shabby summer: Deeping, Warwick

Shabby tiger: Spring, Howard

Shack-locker, The: Wallace, F.W.

Shades of Eton: Lubbock, Percy

Shadow, The: Bedford-Jones, Henry

Shadow, The: Farnol, J.J.

Shadow, The: Gunn, Neil

Shadow, The: Maltby, H.F.

Shadow, The: Phillpotts, Eden

Shadow, The: Stringer, A.J.A.

Shadow and flame: Lindsay, Jack

Shadow and substance: Carroll, P.V.

Shadow between his shoulder blades, The: Harris, J.C.

Shadow factory, The: Ridler, A.B.

Shadow flies, The: Macaulay, *Dame* R.

Shadow garden, The: Cawein, Madison

Shadow in the glass: Derleth, A.W.

Shadow line, The: Conrad, Joseph

Shadow of a crime, The: Caine, *Sir* T.Hall

Shadow of a dream, The: Howells, W.D.

Shadow of a great light, The: Sladen, D.B.W.

Shadow of a gunman, The: O'Casey, Sean

Shadow of a sorcerer, The: Gibbons, Stella

Shadow of Ashlydyat: Wood, Ellen

Shadow of Cain, The: Sitwell, Edith

Shadow of life, The: Sedgwick, A.D.

Shadow of night, The: Chapman, George

Shadow of night: Derleth, A.W.

Shadow of Spain, The: Trease, Geoffrey

Shadow of the dial, The: Bierce, Ambrose

Shadow of the East, The: Hull, Ethel M.

Shadow of the glen, The: Synge, J.M.

Shadow of the hawk: Trease, Geoffrey

Shadow of the hawk: Scott, Evelyn

Shadow of the long knives: Boyd, Thomas

Shadow of the obelisk, The: Parsow, T.W.

Shadow of the rope, The: Hornung, E.W.

Shadow of the sword, The: Buchanan, R.W.

Shadow of the unseen, The: Pain, B.E.O.

Shadow of the vine: Nichols, Beverley

Shadow of the wall, The: Coleridge, Mary

Shadow on Mockways: †Bowen, Marjorie

Shadow passes, A: Phillpotts, Eden

Shadow riders, The: Paterson, Isabel M.

Shadow verses: Bradford, Gamaliel

Shadow world, The: Garland, Hamlin

Shadowed hour, The: Erskine, John

Shadowed victory: Stringer, A.J.A.

Shadowings: Hearn, Lafcadio

Shadows mystery, The: Cronin, B.C.

Shadows of ecstasy: Williams, Charles

Shadows of Shasta: †Miller, Joaquin

Shadows of the old booksellers: Knight, Charles

Shadows of the stage: Winter, William

Shadows of yesterday: †Bowen, Marjorie

Shadows on the down: Noyes, Alfred

Shadows on the rock: Cather, Willa

Shadows on the snow: Farjeon, B.L.

Shadowy paths: Palmer, Nettie

Shadowy third, The: Glasgow, Ellen

Shadowy third, The: Vachell, H.A.

Shadowy waters, The: Yeats, W.B.

Shaftesbury: Traill, H.D.

Shagganappi, The: Johnson, E.P.

Shaggy dog story, The: Partridge, Eric

Shair, The: Ghose, Kashiprosad

Shake hands and come out fighting: Strong, L.A.G.

Shaken by the wind: Frankau, Pamela

Shaker lover, The: Thompson, D.P.

Shakespear illustrated: Lennox, Charlotte

Shakespeare: Bax, Clifford

Shakespeare: Brown, Ivor

Shakespeare: Calvert, G.H.

Shakespeare: Chambers, *Sir* E.K.

Shakespeare: Dowden, Edward

Shakespeare: Drinkwater, John

Shakespeare: Hazlitt, William

Shakespeare: Murry, John Middleton

Shakespeare: Raleigh, *Sir* W.A.

Shakespeare: Rubenstein, Harold F.

Shakespeare: Saintsbury, George

Shakespeare: Swinburne, A.C.

Shakespeare: Van Doren, Mark

Shakespeare and Hawaii: Morley, C.D.

Shakespeare and his forerunners: Lanier, Sidney

Shakespeare and his love: Harris, J.T.

Shakespeare and his world: Brown, Ivor

Shakespeare and the modern stage: Lee, *Sir* Sidney

Shakespeare and the spiritual life: Masefield, John

Shakespeare and the stoicism of Seneca: Eliot, T.S.

Shakespeare and Tolstoy: Knight, G.W.

Shakespeare as dramatist: Squire, *Sir* J.C.

Shakespeare, Bacon and the great unknown: Lang, Andrew

Shakespeare characters: Clarke, Charles Cowden

Shakespeare first folio, The: Greg, W.W.

Shakespeare for schools: Mais, S.P.B.

Shakespeare for young players: Davies, Robertson

Shakespeare glossary, A: Onions, C.T.

Shakespeare in France: Jusserand, Jean

Shakespeare in Harlem: Hughes, J.L.

Shakespeare in his time: Brown, Ivor

Shakespeare murders, The: (†Neil Gordon), Macdonell, A.C.

Shakespeare on the stage: Winter, William

Shakespeare personally: Masson, David

Shakespeare Tercentenary ode: Bridges, Robert

Shakespeare, the man: Smith, Goldwin

Shakespeare: the poet and his background: Quennell, P.C.

Shakespeare to Hardy: Blunden, Edmund

Shakespearean facsimiles: Halliwell-Phillipps, J.O.

Shakespearean gleanings: Chambers, *Sir* E.K.

Shakespearean tragedy: Bradley, A.C.

Shakespeares and the birthplace, The: Brown, Ivor

Shakespeare's bawdy: Partridge, Eric

Shakespeare's boy actors: Davies, Robertson

Shakespeare's Christmas: (†Q), Quiller-Couch, *Sir* Arthur

Shakespeare's earlier editors: McKerrow, R.B.

Shakespeare's England: Lee, *Sir* Sidney

Shakespeare's England: Raleigh, *Sir* Walter A.

Shakespeare's England: Winter, William

Shakespeare's English: Bradley, *Dr.* Henry

Shakespeare's fight with the pirates: Pollard, A.W.

Shakespeare's folios and quartos: Pollard, A.W.

Shakespeare's hand in the play of Sir Thomas More: Pollard, A.W.

Shakespeare's hand in the play of Sir Thomas More: Wilson, John Dover

Shakespeare's happy comedies: Wilson, John Dover

Shakespeare's history plays: Tillyard, E.M.W.

Shakespeare's imagery and what it tells us: Spurgeon, Caroline

Shakespeare's King Henry the Fifth: Lee, *Sir* Sidney

Shakespeare's last plays: Tillyard, E.M.W.

Shakespeare's legacy: Barrie, *Sir* J.M.

Shakespeare's politics: Knights, L.C.

Shakespeare's problem plays: Tillyard, E.M.W.

Shakespeare's sonnets: an introduction for historians and others: Wilson, John Dover

Shakespeare's sonnets never before interpreted: Massey, Gerald

Shakespeare's sonnets reconsidered: Butler, Samuel

Shakespeare's workmanship: Quiller-Couch, *Sir* Arthur

Shakespearian Tempest, The: Knight, G.W.

Shakespeariana: Halliwell, J.O

Shakespere: Kittredge, G.L.

Shakespere as a playwright: Matthews, J.B.

Shakespere's predecessors: Symonds, J.A.

Shall I win her?: Grant, James

Shall we deflate some more?: Lippmann, Walter

Shall we join the ladies?: Barrie, *Sir* J.M.

Shallow end, The: (†Ian Hay), Beith, *Sir* John Hay

Sham education: Shaw, G.B.

Shame of Motley, The: Sabatini, Rafael

Shame of the cities, The: Steffens, Lincoln

Shame the devil: O'Flaherty, Liam

Shamed life: Monkhouse, A.N.

Shameful harvest: Street, A.G.

Shammer shamm'd, The: L'Estrange, *Sir* Roger

Shamrocks: Tynan, Katherine

Shandon Bells: Black, William

Shandygaff: Morley, C.D.

Shanghai Jim: Packard, F.L.

Shannon's way: Cronin, A.J.

Shantykeeper's daughter, The: Palmer, E.V.

Shape of things to come, The: Wells, H.G.

Shapes and shadows: Cawein, Madison

Shapes and stories: Grigson, G.E.H.

Shapes of clay: Bierce, Ambrose

Shapes of sleep, The: Priestley, J.B.

Shaping men and women: Sherman, S.P.

Sharps and flats: Field, Eugene

Shattered glass: Bromfield, Louis

Shaving of Shagpat, The: Meredith, George

Shaw: Joad, C.E.M.

Shaw: MacCarthy, *Sir* Desmond

Shaw Neilson: Devaney, J.M.

She: Haggard, *Sir* H. Rider

She always caught the post: Royde-Smith, Naomi

She and Allan: Haggard, *Sir* H. Rider

She and I: Frankau, Pamela

She died a lady: †Carter Dickson

She dwelt with beauty: Lowndes, M.A.

She fell among thieves: †Yates, Dornford

She Gallant, The: O'Keeffe, John

She had to do something: O'Faolain, Sean

She knew three brothers: Widdemer, Margaret

She painted her face: †Yates, Dornford

She-shanties: Herbert, *Sir* A.P.

She stoops to conquer: Goldsmith, Oliver

She was no lady: Ervine, St. John

She was young and he was old: (†Ennis Graham), (Molesworth, *Mrs.*)

She wou'd and she wou'd not: Cibber, Colley

She wou'd if she cou'd: Etherege, *Sir* George

She would be a soldier: Noah, M.M.

Sheaf, A: Galsworthy, John

Sheaf gleaned in French fields, A: Dutt, Toru

Sheaf of blue bells, A: Orczy, *Baroness*

Sheaf of stories, A: Coolidge, Susan

Sheaf of studies, A: Chambers, *Sir* E.K.

Sheaf of verse bound for the fair, A: Tuckerman, H.T.

Sheaf of verses, A: Hall, M.R.

Sheaf of winter lyrics, A: Campbell, W.W.

Shearer's colt, The: (†The Banjo), Paterson, A.B.

Sheaves: Benson, E.F.

Sheaves: Tagore, *Sir* Rabindranath

Sheba Lane: Drake-Brockman, H.

Sheepfold, The: Housman, Laurence

Sheepfold Hill: Aiken, Conrad

Sheep's head and Babylon: †Bowen, Marjorie

Sheepstor: Baring-Gould, Sabine

Sheik, The: Hull, E.M.

Sheila: Coleman, H.J.

Sheila Vedder: Barr, A.E.H.

Sheila's mystery: Molesworth, *Mrs.*

Shelbourne, The: Bowen, E.D.C.

Shelburne essays: More, P.E.

Shell country book, The: Grigson, G.E.H.

Shelley: Blunden, Edmund

Shelley: Carman, Bliss

Shelley: Symonds, J.A.

Shelley: Thompson, Francis

Shelley: Thomson, James

Shelley and Calderon: Madariaga, Salvador de

Shelley and Lord Beaconsfield: Garnett, Richard

Shelley in 1892: Gosse, *Sir* Edmund

Shelley in Italy: Lehmann, J.F.

Shelley library, A: Wise, T.J.

Shelley's centenary: Watson, *Sir* J.W.

Shells: Peach, L. du Garde

Shells: Wilcox, E.W.

Shells by a stream: Blunden, Edmund

Sheltered life, The: Glasgow, E.A.G.

Shenandoa: Scollard, Clinton

Shenandoah: Howard, B.C.

Shepheardes calender, The: Spenser, Edmund

Shepheards hunting, The: Wither, George

Shepheards oracles, The: Quarles, Francis

Shepheards pipe: Browne, William

Shepherd, A: Broun, Heywood

Shepherd, The: Blunden, Edmund

Shepherd of eternity, The: Gore-Booth, E.S.

Shepherd of Guadaloupe, The: Grey, Zane

Shepherd of the hills, The: Wright, H.B.

Shepherd of the sun: Appel, Benjamin

Shepherd singing ragtime: Golding, Louis

Shepherdess, The: Meynell, Alice

Shepherd's artifice, The: Dibdin, Charles

Shepherd's calendar, The: Clare, John

Shepherd's country: Massingham, Harold

Shepherd's farm: Bell, Adrian

Shepherds in sackcloth: Kaye-Smith, S.

Shepherd's life, A: Hudson, W.H.

Shepherd's week, The: Gay, John

Sheppard Lee: Bird, R.M.

Shepper new-founder, The: White, S.E.

Sheppey: Maugham, Somerset

Sheridan: Darlington, W.A.

Sheridan: Oliphant, Margaret

Sheridan, a military narrative: Hergesheimer, Joseph

Sheridan's ride: Read, T.B.

Sherlock Holmes: Gillette, William

Sherlockiana: Beerbohm, *Sir* Max

Sherman: Guiney, L.I.

Sherman: soldier, realist, American: Liddell Hart, B.

Sherods, The: McCutcheon, G.B.

Sherry: McCutcheon, G.B.

Sherston's progress: Sassoon, S.

Sherwood Anderson & other famous Creoles: Faulkner, William

Sherwood, or, Robin Hood and the three kings: Noyes, Alfred

Shetland plan, The: †Taffrail

Shewing-up of Blanco Posnet, The: Shaw, G.B.

Shield of Achilles, The: Auden, W.H.

Shield of Achilles, The: Gregory, Horace

Shield of love, The: Farjeon, B.L.

Shield of the valiant, The: Derleth, A.W.

Shifting of the fire, The: Ford, Ford Madox

Shilling, A: Taylor, John

Shilling book of beauty, The: †Bede, Cuthbert

Shilling for candles, A: (†Tey Josephine), Mackintosh, Elizabeth

Shilling for my thoughts, A: Chesterton, G.K.

Shingled honeymoon, The: Maltby, H.F.

Shingle-short: Baughan, B.E.

Shining and free: Stern, G.B.

Shining ferry: (†Q), Quiller-Couch, *Sir* Arthur

Shining pyramid,The: †Machen, Arthur

Shining river, The: Slater, F.C.

Shining ship, The: MacKay, I.E.

Shining with Shiner: Lee, J.A.

Ship, The: Ervine, St.John

Ship, The: Forester, C.S.

Ship, The: Russell, W.C.

Ship beautiful, The: Allen, C.R.

Ship chandler, The: Sala, G.A.H.

Ship in the desert, The: †Miller, Joaquin

Ship of death, The: Lawrence, D.H.

Ship of fools: Porter, Katherine Anne

Ship of solace, A: †Mordaunt, Elinor

Ship of souls, The: Hough, Emerson

Ship of stars, The: (†Q), Quiller-Couch, *Sir* Arthur

Ship of the line, A: Forester, C.S.

Ship that died of shame, The: Monsarrat, Nicholas

Ship to shore: McFee, William

Shipmates: †Taffrail

Shipping industry: Kipling, Rudyard

Ships adventure, The: Russell, W.C.

Ships and how they sailed the seven seas (5000 B.C.–A.D. 1935): Van Loon, Hendrik

Ships and sealing- wax: Hannay, J.O.

Ship's company: Jacobs, W.W.

Ships in the bay!: Broster, D.K.

Shipwreck, The: Falconer, William

Shipwreck: Stewart, D.A.

Shirley: Brontë, Charlotte

Shirley: (†E.V.Cunningham) Fast, Howard M.

Shirley Sanz: Pritchett, V.S.

Shivaji: Dutt, R.C.

Shivaji and his times: Sarkar, Y.J.

Shivering shocks: †Dane, Clemence

Shoal water: †Yates, Dornford

Shoe and stocking stories: †Mordaunt, Elinor

Shoemakers holiday, The: Dekker, Thomas

Shoes of fortune, The: Munro, Neil

Shoes of happiness, The: Markham, Edwin

Shoot, The: Graves, Robert

Shooting: Pye, H.J.

Shooting an elephant: †Orwell, George

Shops and companies of London: Mayhew, Henry

Shops and houses: Swinnerton, Frank

Shore acres: Herne, J.A.

Shores of light, The: Wilson, Edmund

Shorn!: Grant, Robert

Short account of a late short administration, A: Burke, Edmund

Short account of Algiers, A: Carey, Mathew

Short account of canteens in the British Army, The: Fortescue, *Sir* John

Short account of the malignant fever lately prevalent in Philadelphia, A: Carey, Mathew

Short and sweet: Bates, H.E.

Short answer to a whole litter of libels, A: L'Estrange, *Sir* Roger

Short catechism, A: Shepard, Thomas

Short catechism for the institution of young persons in the Christian religion, A: Taylor, Jeremy

Short character of His Ex. T.E. of W(harton), A: Swift, Jonathan

Short circuits: Leacock, Stephen

Short cruises: Jacobs, W.W.

Short discourse upon the reasonableness of men's having a religion, A: Buckingham, G.V.

Short flights: Nicholson, Meredith

Short histories of the literature of the world: Gosse, *Sir* Edmund

Short history of American foreign policy and diplomacy, A: Bemis, S.F.

Short history of Australasia, A: (†Ishmael Dare), Jose, A.W.

Short history of culture: Lindsay, Jack

Short history of culture from prehistory to the Renascence, A: Lindsay, Jack

Short history of England, A: Chesterton, G.K.

Short history of English literature, A: Saintsbury, George

Short history of French literature, A: Saintsbury, George

Short history of modern English literature, A: Gosse, *Sir* Edmund

Short history of New England, The: Mather, Cotton

Short history of Scotland, A: Lang, Andrew

Short history of the British working class movement, 1789–1925, A: Cole, G.D.H.

Short history of the Canterbury College, University of New Zealand, A: Hight, James

Short history of the City of Philadelphia, A: Coolidge, Susan

Short history of the Great War, A: Pollard, A.F.

Short history of the life and writings of Alain René Le Sage, A: Saintsbury, George

Short history of the Montagu-Puffins, A: Vulliamy, C.E.

Short history of the Opposition during the last session of Parliament, A: Macpherson, James

Short journal and itinerary journals of George Fox, The: Fox, George

Short life of Napoleon Bonaparte, A: Tarbell, Ida

Short poems for short people: Fawcett, Edgar

Short ramble through some parts of France and Italy, A: Armstrong, John

Short reign and a merry one, A: Poole, John

Short reign of Pippin IV, The: Steinbeck, John

Short rule of good life, A: Southwell, Robert

Short shipments: †Mordaunt, Elinor

Short sixes: Bunner, H.C.

Short statement of facts relating to the history, manners, customs, language, and literature of the Micmac tribe of Indians, A: Rand, S.T.

Short stories of Saki, The: (†Saki), Munro, H.H.

Short story, The: Canby, H.S.

Short story,The: O'Faolain, Sean

Short story, The: Pain, B.E.O.

Short story in English, The: Canby, H.S.

Short studies of American authors: Higginson, T.W.

Short survey of Ireland truely discovering who hath armed that people with disobedience, A: Rich, Barnabe

Short takes: Runyon, Damon

Short talks with the dead: Belloc, Hilaire

Short title catalogue of English books (1475–1640), A: Pollard, A.W.

Short turns: Benefield, Barry

Short view of Russia, A: Keynes, John Maynard

Short view of the English stage, A: Agate, J.E.

Short view of the immorality and profaneness of the English stage, A: Collier, Jeremy

Short view of the late troubles in England, A: Dugdale, *Sir* William

Short view of the life and death of George Villiers Duke of Buckingham, A: Wotton, *Sir* Henry

Short view of the life and reign of King Charles, A: Heylyn,Peter

Short view of the State of Ireland, A: Swift, Jonathan

Short view of tragedy, A: Rymer, Thomas

Short vindication of The Relapse and The Provok'd Wife, from immorality and prophaneness, A: Vanbrugh, *Sir* John

Short way with authors, A: Cannan, Gilbert

Shortened history of England, A: Trevelyan, G.M.

Shorter history of England, A: Belloc, Hilaire

Shortest night, The: Stern, G.B.

Shortest-way with Dissenters, The: Defoe, Daniel

Short-stop, The: Grey, Zane

Shorty Bill: †Sapper

Shoshonee valley, The: Flint, Timothy

Shot in the dark, A: Garnett, David

Shot in the park, A: Plomer, W.C.F.

Shot with crimson: McCutcheon, G.B.

Should women vote?: Higginson, T.W.

Shoulder of Shasta, The: Stoker, Bram

Shoulders of Atlas, The: Freeman, M.W.

Shout of the King, The: Raymond, Ernest

Shouts and murmurs: Woollcott, A.H.

Show, The: Galsworthy, John

Show boat: Ferber, Edna

Show folks, The: Egan, Pierce

Show must go on, The: Rice, Elmer

Show piece, The: Tarkington, Booth

Show-off, The: Kelly, G.E.

Shred of evidence, A: Sherriff, R.C.

Shrewsbury: Weyman, Stanley

Shri Hasha of Kanauj: Panikkar, K.M.

Shrimp and the anemone, The: Hartley, L.P.

Shrines and cities of France and Italy: Underhill, Evelyn

Shropshire: Betjeman, John

Shropshire: Hare, A.J.C.

Shropshire lad, A: Housman, A.E.

Shroud my body down: Green, Paul

Shrouding, The: Kennedy, Leo

Shut your mouth: Catlin, George

Shuttle, The: Burnett, Frances Hodgson

Shy plutocrat, The: Oppenheim, E.Phillips

Shylock of the river: Hume, F.W.

Shylock reasons with Mr. Chesterton: Wolfe, Humbert

Shyp of folys of the worlde, The: Barclay, Alexander

Si Mihi!: Fowler, H.W.

Siamese twin mystery, The: †Queen, Ellery

Siamese twins, The: Lytton, E.G.E.B. *1st Baron*

Sibyl: Calvert, G.H.

Sibylline leaves: Coleridge, S.T.

Sicelides a piscatory: Fletcher, Phineas

Sicilian idyll, A: Todhunter, John

Sicilian idyll and Judith, A: Moore, T.S.

Sicilian marriage, A: Sladen, D.B.W.

Sicilian noon: Golding, Louis

Sicilian romance, A: Radcliffe, *Mrs.* Ann

Sicilian story, A: Proctor, B.W.

Sicilian Vespers, The: Runciman, *Sir* Steven

Sicily in shadow and in sun: Elliott, M.H.

Sicily: the new winter resort: Sladen, D.B.W.

Sick heart river: Buchan, John

Sick stockrider, The: Gordon, A.L.

Sickert: Rothenstein, *Sir* John

Sickness of an acquisitive society, The: Tawney, R.H.

Siddharta, man of peace: Chattopadhyaya, Harindranath

Side of the angels, The: †King, Basil

Side show of the Southern side of the War, A: †Arp, Bill

Side street: Farrell, J.T.

Sidelights on new London and Newer York: Chesterton, G.K.

Sidelights on relativity: Einstein, Albert

Sidero-thriambos: Munday, Anthony

Side-walk studies: Dobson, H.A.

Sidney: Deland, Margaret

Sidney Clifton: Fay, T.S.

Siege at Peking, The: Fleming, Peter

Siege of Acre, The: Cowley, *Mrs*. Hannah

Siege of Aquileia, The: Home, John

Siege of Babylon, The: Pordage, Samuel

Siege of Constantinople, The: Fairfield, S.L.

Siege of Constantinople, The: Payne, H.N.

Siege of Copenhagen, The: Grahame, James

Siege of Corinth, The: Byron, George Gordon *Lord*

Siege of London, The: James, Henry

Siege of Meaux, The: Pye, H.J.

Siege of Monterey, The: Falkner, W.C.

Siege of pleasure, The: Hamilton, Patrick

Siege of Quebec and the battle of the Plains of Abraham, The: Doughty, *Sir* A.G.

Siege of Sinope, The: Brooke, Frances

Siege of the seven suitors, The: Nicholson, Meredith

Siege of Thebes, The: Lydgate, John

Siege of Tripoli, The: Noah, M.M.

Siege of Troy, The: Settle, Elkanah

Siege of Valencia, a dramatick poem, The: Hemans, *Mrs*. Felicia

Siegfried: Baring-Gould, Sabine

Siegfried's journey, 1916–1920: Sassoon, S.

Sienese codex of the Divine Comedy, A: Pope-Hennessy, J.W.

Sienese painter of the Franciscan legend, A: Berenson, Bernhard

Sienese quattrocento painting: Pope-Hennessy, J.W.

Sierra: Bates, Ralph

Sigh no more: Coward, Noel

Sighes at the contemporary deaths of the Countesse of Cleaveland and the Mistresse Cicily Killegrue: Quarles, Francis

Sight and song: †Field, Michael

Sight unseen: Rinehart, Mary Roberts

Sights and thoughts in foreign churches and among foreign peoples: Faber, F.W.

Sigiriya graffiti: Paranavitana, S.

Sign at six, The: White, S.E.

Sign of fear: Derleth, A.W.

Sign of four, The: Doyle, *Sir* Arthur Conan

Sign of the fish, The: Quennell, P.C.

Sign of the prophet Jonah, The: †Bridie, James

Sign of the spider, The: Mitford, Bertram

Sign talk dictionary: Seton-Thompson, E.

Signa: †Ouida

Signa severa: Knox, R.A.

Signal Boys: Eggleston, G.C.

Signal thirty two: Kantor, Mackinlay

Signalling without wires: Lodge, *Sir* Oliver

Signature: Scott, F.R.

Significance of Indian art, The: Ghose, Sri Aurobindo

Significance of Sinclair Lewis, The: Sherman, S.P.

Signpost: Livesay, Dorothy

Signpost to poetry: Wolfe, Humbert

Signs and seasons: Burroughs, John

Signs and wonders: Beresford, J.D.

Signs of change: Morris, William

Signs of the times: Lucas, E.V.

Sikhism: Panikkar, Kavalam M.

Silas Crockett: Chase, M.E.

Silas Marner: †Eliot, George

Silas Strong: Bacheller, Irving

Silas Timberman: Fast, Howard M.

Silcote of Silcotes: Kingsley, Henry

Silence: Freeman, Mary

Silence farm: †Macleod, Fiona

Silence for the murderer: Crofts, F.W.

Silence observed: (†Michael Innes), Stewart, J.I.M.

Silence of history: Farrell, J.T.

Silence of the sea, The: Belloc, Hilaire

Silent duchess, The: Green, Anne

Silent grow the guns: Kantor, Mackinlay

Silent isle, The: Benson, A.C.

Silent land, The: O'Dowd, B.P.

Silent man, The: †Miller, Joaquin

Silent miaow, The: Gallico, Paul

Silent murders, The: (†Neil Gordon), Macdonell, A.G.

Silent partner, The: Ward, E.S.

Silent places, The: White, S.E.

Silent Sam: O'Higgins, H.J.

Silent Scot, frontier scout: Skinner, C.L.

Silent sea, The: Martin, C.E.

Silent south, The: Cable, G.W.

Silent storms: Poole, Ernest

Silent tragedy, A: Riddell, *Mrs*. J.H.

Silent voices, The: Tennyson, Alfred *Lord*

Silent war, The: Mitchell, J.A.

Silent witness, A: Yates, E.H.

Silent wooing, A: Galsworthy, John

Silent zone, The: Dalton, A.C.

Silenus: Woolner, Thomas

Silex Scintillans: sacred poems and private ejaculations: Vaughan, Henry

Silhouettes: Gosse, *Sir* Edmund

Silhouettes: Symons, Arthur

Silhouettes of American life: Davis, Rebecca

Silk hat soldier, The: Le Gallienne, Richard

Silken secret, The: Trease, Geoffrey

Silver Acre, The: Carleton, William

Silver age, The: Heywood, Thomas

Silver arrow, The: Hubbard, Elbert

Silver Blimp, The: Walmsley, Leo

Silver bottle, The: Ingraham, J.H.

Silver box, The: Galsworthy, John

Silver branch, The: Deamer, Dulcie

Silver casket, The: Bax, Clifford

Silver cat, The: Wolfe, Humbert

Silver chair, The: Lewis, C.S.

Silver chalice, The: Costain, T.B.

Silver Christ, The: †Ouida

Silver circus tales: Coppard, A.E.

Silver cord, The: Brooks, C.W.S.

Silver cord, The: Howard, S.C.

Silver curlew, The: Farjeon, Eleanor

Silver darlings, The: Gunn, Neil

Silver domino, The: †Corelli, Marie

Silver eagle, The: Burnett, W.R.

Silver fields: Robinson, R.E.

Silver flute, The: Webster, M.M.

Silver fox, The: Somerville, E.

Silver guard: Trease, Geoffrey

Silver horde, The: Beach, R.E.

Silver king, The: Jones, H.A.

Silver Ley: Bell, Adrian

Silver lining, The: Brighouse, Harold

Silver linings: Bray, Adrian

Silver medal, The: Trowbridge, J.T.

Silver pitchers: Alcott, Louisa M.

Silver poppy, The: Stringer, A.J.A.

Silver sand: Crockett, S.R.

Silver sand and snow: Farjeon, Eleanor

Silver shell, The: Chase, M.E.

Silver ship of Mexico, The: Ingraham, J.H.

Silver skull, The: Crockett, S.R.

Silver spoon, The: Galsworthy, John

Silver stair, The: Williams, Charles

Silver stallion, The: Cabell, James Branch

Silver star, The: Bedford, Randolph

Silver store, The: Baring-Gould, Sabine

Silver stream: Herbert, Sir A.P.

Silver tassie, The: O'Casey, Sean

Silver thorn, The: Walpole, Sir Hugh

Silver tip: †Brand, Max

Silver tongues (anth.): Hayward, John

Silver trumpet, The: Barfield, Owen

Silver trumpet, The: Cloete, E.F.S.G.

Silver wedding: Hodgson, Ralph

Silverado squatters, The: Stevenson, R.L.

Silver-gilt standard, The: Hannay, J.O.

Silverland: Lawrence, G.A.

Silverton's: Molesworth, Mrs.

Silvia: Kavanagh, Julia

Silvia: Lillo, George

Simba: White, S.E.

Similitudes: Larcom, Lucy

Simon Dale: †Bell, Neil

Simon Dale: Hawkins, A.H.

Simon Girty: Boyd, Thomas

Simon learns to live: Mitchell, Mary

Simon the Coldheart: Heyer, Georgette

Simonetta Perkins: Hartley, L.P.

Simpkins plot, The: Hannay, J.O.

Simple adventures of a memsahib, The: Duncan, S.J.

Simple art of murder, The: Chandler, Raymond

Simple case for socialism, The: Cole, G.D.H.

Simple cobler of Aggawam in America, The: Ward, Nathaniel

Simple honourable man, A: Richter, Conrad

Simple life: Balchin, Nigel

Simple life limited, The: Ford, Ford Madox

Simple on a soap-box: Lee, J.A.

Simple Peter Cradd: Oppenheim, E.Phillips

Simple Simon: Mitchell, Mary

Simple Simon Smith: Collins, Dale

Simple speaks his mind: Hughes, J.L.

Simple stakes a claim: Hughes, J.L.

Simple story, A: Inchbald, Mrs. Elizabeth

Simple takes a wife: Hughes, J.L.

Simple tales: Opie, Amelia

Simples: Call, F.O.

Simpleton, A: Reade, Charles

Simpleton of the Unexpected Isles, The: Shaw, G.B.

Simplicity and Tolstoy: Chesterton, G.K.

Simplicity Jones: Armstrong, M.D.

Simply heavenly: Hughes, J.L.

Simpson: †Mordaunt, Elinor

Simpson: Sackville-West, Edward

Simpson and Co. New York: Poole, John

Sin: Kaye-Smith, Sheila

Sin eater, The: †Macleod, Fiona

Sin of David, The: Phillips, Stephen

Sin of William Jackson, The: Orczy, Baroness

Sin of witchcraft: Kipling, Rudyard

Sin that was his, The: Packard, F.L.

Sinbad the sailor: Mackaye, Percy

Sinbad the soldier: Wren, P.C.

Sinbada: †Mordaunt, Elinor

Since Cezanne: Bell, Clive

Since fifty: Rothenstein, Sir William

Since Ibsen: Nathan, G.J.

Since Lenin died: Eastman, Max

Since then: Gibbs, Sir Philip

Since then: Glover, Denis

Sincere convert, The: Shepard, Thomas

Sincerely, Willis Wayde: Marquand, J.P.

Sincerity: Deeping, Warwick

Sincerity, a story of our time: Erskine, John

Sinclair – Astor letters: Sinclair, Upton

Sinclair Lewis, a biographical sketch: Van Doren, Carl

Sinclair Lewis, our own Diogenes: Parrington, V.L.

Sinclair Lewis's Dodsworth: Howard, S.C.

Sindh, and the races that inhabit the valley of the Indus: Burton, *Sir* Richard

Sinecurist's creed, The: Hone, William

Sinews of peace, The: Churchill, *Sir* Winston

Sinews of war, The: Bennett, Arnold

Sinews of war, The: Phillpotts, Eden

Sinfire: Fawcett, Edgar

Sinful woman: Cain, James

Sing for your supper: Farjeon, Eleanor

Sing for your supper: Frankau, Pamela

Sing high! Sing low!: Sitwell, *Sir* Osbert

Singer from the sea, A: Barr, A.E.H.

Singing crow, The: Crane, Nathalia

Singing garden, The: Dennis, C.M.J.

Singing guns: †Brand, Max

Singing heart, The: Allen, C.R.

Singing heart, The: Scollard, Clinton

Singing in the shrouds: Marsh, Ngaio Edith

Singing in the wilderness: Peattie, D.C.

Singing jailbirds: Sinclair, Upton

Singing mouse stories, The: Hough, Emerson

Singing of psalmes a gospel-ordinance: Cotton, John

Singing sands, The: (†Tey Josephine), Mackintosh, Elizabeth

Singing season, The: Paterson, Isabel M.

Singing silence, The: Logan, J.D.

Singing wells, The: Pertwee, Roland

Singing winds: Bercovici, Konrad

Singing wood, The: Widdemer, Margaret

Single flame, A: Boyd, Martin

Single heart, The: Jameson, Storm

Single heart and double face: Reade, Charles

Single hound, The. Poems of a lifetime: Dickinson, Emily Elizabeth

Single man, A: Davies, H.H.

Single man, A: Isherwood, C.

Single star, The: Roberts, W. Adolphe

Singleton Fontenoy: Hannay, James

Sings and wings: Wolfe, Humbert

Sings Harry: Glover, Denis

Sing-song: Rossetti, Christina

Singsongs of the war: Hewlett, Maurice

Singular life, A: Ward, E.S.

Singular preference, The: Quennell, P.C.

Singularly deluded: †Grand, Sarah

Sinister errand: †Cheyney, Peter

Sinister man, The: Wallace, Edgar

Sinister sex, The: Hecht, Ben

Sinister street: Mackenzie, *Sir* Compton

Sink or swim: Strong, L.A.G.

Sinners beware: Oppenheim, E.Phillips

Sinner's comedy, The: †Hobbes, John Oliver

Sinners guyde, The: Meres, Francis

Sinners in the hands of an angry God: Edwards, Jonathan

Sins of the father, The: Dixon, Thomas

Sins of the government, sins of the nation: Barbauld, *Mrs.* A.L.

Sip! Swallow!: Herbert, *Sir* A.P.

Sir Adam disappeared: Oppenheim, E.Phillips

Sir Andrew Wylie, of that ilk: Galt, John

Sir Anthony Love: Southern, Thomas

Sir Arthur Nicolson, bart.; first Lord Carnock: Nicolson, Hon. *Sir* Harold

Sir Bob: Madariaga, Salvador de

Sir Brook Fossbrooke: Lever, C.J.

Sir Charles Danvers: Cholmondeley, Mary

Sir Charles Firth and Master Hugh Peter: Morison, S.E.

Sir Donald MacLean: Cowan, James

Sir Edward Carson and the Ulster movement: Ervine, St. John

Sir Edward Seaward's narrative of his shipwreck: Porter, Jane

Sir Eldred of the Bower: More, Hannah

Sir Evelyn Ruggles-Brise: Leslie, *Sir* J.R. Shane

Sir Francis Drake: Benson, E.F.

Sir Frank Lockwood: Birrell, Augustine

Sir Frederick Haldimand: McIlwraith, J.N.

Sir George Alexander and the St. James' Theatre: Mason, A.E.W.

Sir George Goldie, founder of Nigeria: Wellesley, D.V.

Sir George Mackenzie, King's Advocate: Lang, Andrew

Sir George of Almack's: Maltby, H.F.

Sir George Otto Trevelyan: a memoir: Trevelyan, G.M.

Sir George Tressady: Ward, *Mrs.* Humphrey

Sir Gibbie: Macdonald, George

Sir Gregory Nonsence his newes from no place: Taylor, John

Sir Harry Hotspur of Humblethwaite: Trollope, Anthony

Sir Harry Wildair: Farquhar, George

Sir Henry Clinton's invitation to the refugees: Freneau, Philip

Sir Henry Lee: Chambers, *Sir* E.K.

Sir Henry Morgan: buccaneer and governor: Roberts, W. Adolphe

Sir Henry Raeburn and his works: Brown, *Dr.* John

Sir Hornbook: Peacock, Thomas Love

Sir Hugh the heron: Rossetti, Dante Gabriel

Sir Isumbras at the ford: Broster, D.K.

Sir J.H. Meiring Beck: Scully, W.C.

Sir James Le Moine: Kirby, William

Sir Jasper Carew, his life and experiences: Lever, C.J.

Sir Jasper's tenant: Braddon, M.E.

Sir John Chiverton: Ainsworth, Harrison

Sir John Constantine: (†Q), Quiller-Couch, Sir Arthur

Sir John Denham: Dobrée, Bonamy

Sir John Dering: Farnol, J.J.

Sir John Macdonald: Wallace, W.S.

Sir John Magill's last journey: Crofts, F.W.

Sir John Piers: Betjeman, John

Sir John Vanbrugh: Whistler, Laurence

Sir Joseph Banks and the emperor of Morocco: †Pindar, Peter

Sir Joseph Banks, Bart., an appreciation: Mackaness, George

Sir Joseph Banks: his relations with Australia: Mackaness, George

Sir Joshua Reynolds as a portrait painter: Collins, J.C.

Sir Kenelm reads in bed: Morley, C.D.

Sir Lancelot: Faber, F.W.

Sir Leslie Stephen as a biographer: Thompson, Francis

Sir Limpidus: Pickthall, M.W.

Sir Martin Mar-all: Dryden, John

Sir Martin Mar-people his coller of esses: Davies, *Sir* John

Sir Nigel: Doyle, *Sir* Arthur Conan

Sir Patient Fancy: Behn, *Mrs.* Afra

Sir Percival: Shorthouse, J.H.

Sir Percy hits back: Orczy, *Baroness*

Sir Philip Sidney: Symonds, J.A.

Sir Philip Sidney, his honourable life, his valiant death and true vertues: Whetstone, George

Sir Pompey and Madame Juno: Armstrong, M.D.

Sir Proteus: Peacock, Thomas Love

Sir Pulteney: Lucas, E.V.

Sir Ralph Esher: Hunt, Leigh

Sir Ralph Willoughby: Brydges, *Sir* S.E.

Sir Richard Whittington: Besant, *Sir* Walter and James Rice

Sir Robert Sherley: Middleton, Thomas

Sir Robert's fortune: Oliphant, Margaret

Sir Rohan's ghost: Spofford, H.E.

"... 'Sir', she said": Waugh, Alec

Sir Theodore Broughton: James, G.P.R.

Sir Theodore's guest: Allen, Grant

Sir Thomas Beecham: a portrait: Cardus, Neville

Sir Thomas Browne: Gosse, *Sir* Edmund

Sir Thomas Malory: Kittredge, G.L.

Sir Thomas More: Munday, Anthony

Sir Thomas More: Southey, Robert

Sir Thomas Overbury: Rowlands, Samuel

Sir Thomas Wyatt and some collected studies: Chambers, *Sir* E.K.

Sir Toady Crusoe: Crockett, S.R.

Sir Tom: Oliphant, Margaret

Sir Walter Raleigh: Buchan, John

Sir Walter Raleigh: Thoreau, H.D.

Sir Walter Raleigh, captain and adventurer: Trease, Geoffrey

Sir Walter Raleigh in the Tower: Johnson, L.P.

Sir Walter Scott: Buchan, John

Sir Walter Scott: Cecil, *Lord* David

Sir Walter Scott: Hutton, R.H.

Sir Walter Scott: Lang, Andrew

Sir Walter Scott: Pope-Hennessy, *Dame* Una

Sir Walter Scott: Saintsbury, George

Sir Walter Scott and the border minstrelsy: Lang, Andrew

Sir Walter Scott, Bart.: Grierson, *Sir* Herbert

Sir Wilfried Laurier: McArthur, Peter

Sirdar's oath, The: Mitford, Bertram

Siren land: Douglas, Norman

Siren song: Herbert, *Sir* A.P.

Sirens, The: Binyon, Laurence

Sirens wake, The: Dunsany, E.J.M.D.P.

Sirocco: Bates, Ralph

Sissinghurst: Sackville-West, Victoria

Sister, The: Lennox, Charlotte

Sister Anne: Potter, Helen Beatrix

Sister Benvenuta and the Christ Child: †Lee, Vernon

Sister Carrie: Dreiser, Theodore

Sister Jane: Harris, J.C.

Sister Louise: Whyte-Melville, G.J.

Sister Sorrow: Praed, *Mrs.* C.

Sister Sue: Porter, E.H.

Sister Teresa: Moore, George

Sister to Esau, A: Barr, A.E.H.

Sisters, The: Cambridge, Ada

Sisters, The: De Vere, Aubrey

Sisters, The: Swinburne, A.C.

Sisters Brontë, The: Oliphant, Margaret

Sister's bye-hours, A: Ingelow, Jean

Sister's gift, A: Manning, Anne

Sisters of St. Clara, The: Fairfield, S.L.

Sisters tragedy, The: Aldrich, T.B.

Sisters' tragedy, The: Hughes, R.A.W.

Sisters-in-law, The: Atherton, Gertrude

Sister-songs: Thompson, Francis

Sistine eve, The: Mackaye, Percy

Sisyphus: Trevelyan, R.C.

Sittaford mystery, The: Christie, Agatha

Sitting on a fence: †Armstrong, Anthony

Sitter on the rail, The: Mackay, Jessie

Sitting on the world: Broun, Heywood

Sitting pretty: Wodehouse, P.G.

Situation, The: Curtis, G.W.

Siva Ratri: Isvaran, M.S.

Six Australian poets: Moore, T.I.

Six books of metamorphoses. Ovid. (trn.) Caxton, William

Six British battles: Belloc, Hilaire

Six British soldiers: Fortescue, Sir John

Six common things: Benson, E.F.

Six criminal women: Jenkins, Elizabeth

Six cushions, The: Yonge, Charlotte M.

Six days: Glyn, Elinor

Six days' grace: Burnett, W.R.

Six essays on Johnson: Raleigh, Sir Walter A.

Six fantasies: Brighouse, Harold

Six French poets: Lowell, Amy

Six golden angels: †Brand, Max

Six great Englishmen: De Selincourt, Aubrey

Six great explorers: Divine, A.D.

Six great novelists: Allen, Walter Ernest

Six great playwrights: De Selincourt, Aubrey

Six great poets: De Selincourt, Aubrey

Six great sailors: Divine, A.D.

Six great thinkers: De Selincourt, Aubrey

Six hour shift, A: McFee, William

Six letters, addressed to the working people of England: Cobbett, William

Six London plays: Rubenstein, Harold F.

Six men of Dorset: Greenwood, Walter

Six men of Dorset: Malleson, Miles

Six months tour through the North of England: Young, Arthur

Six new plays: Shirley, James

Six nonlectures: Cummings, E.E.

Six o'clock and after: De Selincourt, Aubrey

Six of Calais, The: Shaw, G.B.

Six of one by half a dozen of the other: Hale, E.E.

Six plays of Eugene O'Neill: Mickle, A.D.

Six poems. Illustrative of engravings by H.R.H. the Princess Elizabeth: Combe, William

Six poems on Bruges: Binyon, Laurence

Six political discourses founded on the scripture: Brackenridge, H.H.

Six portraits of Sir Rabindranath Tagore: Rothenstein, Sir William

Six proud walkers, The: †Beeding, Francis

Six Proust reconstructions: Johnson, Pamela H.

Six queer things, The: †Caudwell, Christopher

Six sermons of the errors of the Roman Catholic Church: Maturin, C.R.

Six sermons on intemperance: Beecher, Lyman

Six Star Ranch: Porter, E.H.

Six stories written in the first person singular: Maugham, Somerset

Six tales of Brock the Badger: Uttley, Alison

Six tales of Sam Pig: Uttley, Alison

Six tales of the four pigs: Uttley, Alison

Six television stories: Blackwood, Algernon

Six temples at Thebes: Petrie, Sir William Flinders

Six thousand and one nights: Darlington, W.A.

Six to one: Bellamy, Edward

Six to sixteen: Ewing, Mrs. Juliana Horatia

Six trees: Freeman, M.W.

Six weeks in Russia: Ransome, Arthur

Six weeks' tour through the Southern Counties of England and Wales: Young, Arthur

Six who were left in a shoe: Colum, Padraic

Six years ago: Grant, James

Sixes and sevens: †Henry, O.

Sixteen dead men and other poems of Easter Week: Sigerson, Dora

1649: Lindsay, Jack

16 rue Cortambert: Green, Anne

Sixteen self sketches: Shaw, G.B.

Sixth Beatitude, The: Hall, M.R.

Sixth column, The: Fleming, Peter

Sixth floor: Ackland, Rodney

Sixth heaven, The: Hartley, L.P.

Sixth of October, The: Hichens, Robert

Sixty Jane: Long, J.L.

Sixty seconds: Bodenheim, Maxwell

Sixty years in journalism: Dafoe, J.W.

Sixty years of living architecture: Wright, Frank Lloyd

Sixty years of Victorian literature: Shorter, C.K.

Sixty-four, ninety-four!: Mottram, R.H.

69 Birnam Road: Ridge, W.Pett

Sixty-three poems: Gibson, Wilfred

Skeeters Kirby: Masters, E.L.

Skeleton clock, another adventure of Sir Henry Merryvale, The: Carr, J.D.

Skeleton in the clock, The: †Carter Dickson

Skerrett: O'Flaherty, Liam

Sketch book of Geoffrey Crayon, Gent, The:(†Geoffrey Crayon), Irving, Washington

Sketch for a self-portrait: Berenson, Bernhard

Sketch of a sinner: Swinnerton, Frank

Sketch of an overland route to British Columbia, A: Hind, H.Y.

Sketch of Connecticut, forty years since: Sigourney, L.H.

Sketch of fashion, The: Gore, Catherine

Sketch of new Utilitarianism: Lighthall, W.D.

Sketch of old England, A: Paulding, J.K.

Sketch of our political condition, A: Moore, C.C.

Sketch of the campaign of Count a Suwarrow Ryminski: Porter, Jane

Sketch of the history of the Champlain Society, A: Wallace, W.S.

Sketch of the history of the doctrine of the atonement, A: Clarke, J.F.

Sketch of the history of the Edinburgh Theatre Royal: Chambers, Robert

Sketch of the language and literature of Holland: Bowring, Sir John

Sketch of the late battle of the Wind Mill, near Prescott: Richardson, John

Sketch of the life and character of Rutherford B. Hayes: Howells, W.D.

Sketch of the life and character of the late Lord Kinneder: Scott, Sir Walter

Sketch of the life of John Gilbert, A: Winter, William

Sketch of the life of John Howard Payne: Fay, T.S.

Sketch of the life of Oliver Wendell Holmes: Frankfurter, Felix

Sketch of the old parish burying ground of Windsor, Nova Scotia: Hind, H.Y.

Sketch of the origin and history of the Granville Street Baptist Church, A: Saunders, E.M.

Sketches among the poor: Gaskell, Mrs. Elizabeth

Sketches and essays: Hazlitt, William

Sketches and studies in Italy and Greece: Symonds, J.A.

Sketches by "Boz": Dickens, Charles

Sketches from Cambridge: Stephens, Sir Leslie

Sketches from Nine Sharp: Farjeon, Herbert

Sketches from Normandy: (†Louis Becke), Becke, G.L.

Sketches from real life: Child, L.M.

Sketches from spread it abroad: Farjeon, Herbert

Sketches from the Little Revue: Farjeon, Herbert

Sketches in criticism: Brooks, Van Wyck

Sketches in Holland and Scandinavia: Hare, A.J.C.

Sketches in Italy and Greece: Symonds, J.A.

Sketches in lavender, blue and green: Jerome, Jerome K.

Sketches in London: Grant, James

Sketches in the Deccan: Taylor, P.M.

Sketches of American character: Hale, S.J.B.

Sketches of Canada and the United States: Mackenzie, W.L.

Sketches of celebrated Canadians and persons connected with Canada: Morgan, H. J.

Sketches of character and tales founded on fact: Thomas, F.W.

Sketches of Claymore: Thomas, F.W.

Sketches of eighteenth century America: Crèvecœur, Michel-Guillaume Jean de

Sketches of eminent statesmen and writers: Hayward, Abraham

Sketches of English character: Gore, Catherine

Sketches of European capitals: Ware, William

Sketches of history in six sermons: Godwin, William

Sketches of history, life and manners in the United States: Royall, A.N.

Sketches of history, life, and manners in the West: Hall, James

Sketches of Irish character: Hall, A.M.

Sketches of moral and mental philosophy: Chalmers, Thomas

Sketches of Switzerland: Cooper, James Fenimore

Sketches of the life and character of Patrick Henry: Wirt, William

Sketches of the lives of the brothers Everett: Hale, E.E.

Sketches of the natural history of Ceylon: Tennent, Sir J.E.

Sketches of the poetical literature of the past half-century: Moir, D.M.

Sketches of the principal picture-galleries in England: Hazlitt, William

Sketches of the sixties: (†Mark Twain), Clemens, S.L.

Sketches of the state of manners and opinions in the French Republic: Williams, H.M.

Sketches of young couples: Dickens, Charles

Sketches of young gentlemen: Dickens, Charles

Sketches on various subjects, moral, literary and political: Pye, H.J.

Sketches: or essays on various subjects: Armstrong, John

Skiddle: Fairbridge, Dorothea

Skies of Europe: Prokosch, Frederic

Skin and bones: Smith, Thorne

Skin for skin: Powys, L.C.

Skin game, The: Galsworthy, John

Skin o' my tooth: Orczy, Baroness

Skin of our teeth, The: Wilder, Thornton

Skin-deep: Royde-Smith, Naomi

Skippers of Nancy Gloucester, The: Mackaye, Percy

Skipper's wooing, The: Jacobs, W.W.

Skirmishes and sketches: Dodge, M.A.

Skookum Chuck: White, S.E.

Skotlands Rimur (Icelandic Ballads on the Gowrie Conspiracy): Craigie, Sir W.A.

Skull of Swift, The: Leslie, Sir J.R. Shane

Sky and the forest, The: Forester, C.S.

Sky high to Shanghai: Clune, Frank

Sky line: what Wright had wrought, The: Mumford, Lewis

Sky lines and wood smoke: Clark, C.B.

Sky pilot, The: †Connor, Ralph

Sky Pilot in No Man's Land, The: †Connor, Ralph

Skye high: Pearson, Hesketh

Skylark, The: Hodgson, Ralph

Skylight one: Aiken, Conrad

Sky-line, The: MacMechan, A.M.

Skyline riders, The: Lawson, Henry

Skylines and horizons: Heyward, DuBose

Skyscrapers: Namier, *Sir* Lewis

Slabs of the sunburnt West: Sandburg, Carl

Slack water: Divine, A.D.

Slade: Deeping, Warwick

Slanderers, The: Deeping, Warwick

Slanders, The: Pertwee, Roland

Slane's long shots: Oppenheim, E.Phillips

Slang: Partridge, Eric

Slang today and yesterday: Partridge, Eric

Slap at slop and the Bridge St. Gang, A: Hone, William

Slap-band boys, The: Brazil, Angela

Slaughter of the innocents, The: Saroyan, William

Slave, The: Hichens, Robert

Slave, The: Hildreth, Richard

Slave, The: Morton, Thomas

Slave girl of Agra: an Indian historical romance, The: Dutt, R.C.

Slave king, The: Ingraham, J.H.

Slave labor in manufactures: Carey, Mathew

Slave of the lamp, The: †Merriman, Seton

Slavery: More, Hannah

Slavery in America: Simms, W.G.

Slavery in the United States: Clarke, J.F.

Slavery in the United States: Paulding, J.K.

Slavery the mere pretext for rebellion; not its cause: Kennedy, J.P.

Slaves in Algiers: Rowson, S. H.

Slaves of solitude, The: Hamilton, Patrick

Slaves of the lamp: Frankau, Pamela

Slaves of the lamp: Webster, M.M.

Slayer of souls, The: Chambers, R.W

Sleep in peace: Bentley, Phyllis

Sleep of prisoners, A: Fry, Christopher

Sleepers awake: Patchen, Kenneth

Sleeping Bacchus, The: Saunders, H.A. St.George

Sleeping beauty, The: Le Gallienne, Richard

Sleeping beauty, The: (†Q), Quiller-Couch, *Sir* Arthur

Sleeping beauty, The: Sitwell, Edith

Sleeping Beauty Pantomime, A: Jennings, Gertrude

Sleeping car, The: Howells, W.D.

Sleeping clergyman, A: †Bridie, James

Sleeping fires: Atherton, Gertrude

Sleeping fires: Gissing, George

Sleeping fury, The: Armstrong, M.D.

Sleeping fury, The: Bogan, Louise

Sleeping prince, The: Rattigan, Terence

Sleeping sphinx, The: Carr, J.D.

Sleepless moon, The: Bates, H.E.

Slide rule: †Shute, Nevil

Slight case of murder, A: Runyon, Damon

Slight irritations: Knox, E.V.

Slippery ladder, The: Ridge, W.Pett

Slocombe dies: Strong, L.A.G.

Slow dawning: Dark, Eleanor

Slow Joe: †Brand, Max

Slow night, The: Hassall, Christopher

Slow wall: Speyer, *Mrs.* Leonora

Slowcoach, The: Lucas, E.V.

Slower Judas, The: Stern, G. B.

Small bachelor, The: Wodehouse, P.G.

Small back room, The: Balchin, Nigel

Small beer: Bemelmans, Ludwig

Small boy, A: James, Henry

Small dark man, The: Walsh, Maurice

Small farmer, The: Massingham, Harold

Small house at Allington, The: Trollope, Anthony

Small house over the water, The: Lemon, Mark

Small miracle: Gallico, Paul

Small moments: Church, Richard

Small room with large windows, A: Curnow, T.A.M.

Small stir, A: †Bridie, James

Small tableaux: Tennyson, Charles

Small talk: Nicolson, Hon. *Sir* Harold

Small things: Deland, Margaret

Small town: Hicks, Granville

Small war on Murray Hill: Sherwood, R.E.

Smallways rub along: †Bell, Neil

Smaragda's lover: Turner, W.J.R.

Smart set, The: Fitch, Clyde William

Smarty's party: Kelly, G.E.

Smile and the tear, The: Somerville, E.

Smile at the foot of the ladder: Miller, Henry

Smiler with the knife, The: Day-Lewis, C.

Smiles, Samuel: Murray, John

Smiling Charlie: †Brand, Max

Smire, an acceptance in the third person: Cabell, James Branch

Smirt, an urbane nightmare: Cabell, James Branch

Smith: Davidson, John

Smith: Deeping, Warwick

Smith: Maugham, Somerset

Smith, a sylvan interlude: Cabell, James Branch

Smith administration: Kipling, Rudyard

Smith and Jones: Monsarrat, Nicholas

Smith and the Pharaohs: Haggard, *Sir* Henry Rider

Smith of Smiths, The: Pearson, Hesketh

Smithfield reserved: Brown, Ivor

Smithy: Wallace, Edgar

Smithy and the Hun: Wallace, Edgar

Smithy's friend Nobby: Wallace, Edgar

Smoke and steel: Sandburg, Carl

Smoke and sword: Wren, P.C.

Smoke bellew: London, Jack

Smoke of battle: Chambers, R.W.

Smoke rings: Stern, G.B.

Smoke screens: Brighouse, Harold

Smoke-eaters, The: O'Higgins, H.J.

Smoked glass: (†Orpheus C. Kerr), Newell, R.H.

Smoking car, The: Howells, W.D.

Smoking flax, The: Stead, R.J.C.

Smoking mountain: Boyle, Kay

Smoky cell: Wallace, Edgar

Smoky days: Thomson, E.W.

Smollett: his life and a selection from his writings: Chambers, Robert

Smuggler, The: Banim, John

Smuggler, The: James, G.P.R.

Smuggler Jack: Peach, L. du Garde

Smugglers' cave, The: Hannay, J.O.

Smugglers' cave, The: Molesworth, *Mrs*.

Smugglers, chronicles of the last raiders of Solway, The: Crockett, S.R.

Smugglers of the Clone, The: Crockett, S.R.

Snake in the grass, The: Armstrong, M.D.

Snake-bite: Hichens, Robert

Snakes' pass, The: Stoker, Bram

Snapdragon: Ewing, *Mrs*. Juliana Horatia

Snare, The (novel and play): Sabatini, Rafael

Snare of strength, The: Bedford, Randolph

Snare of the fowler, The: Bullett, Gerald

Snared nightingale: Trease, Geoffrey

Snarleyow or, the dog fiend: Marryatt, Frederick

Snell's folly: Beresford, D.J.

Snickerty Nick: Bynner, Witter

Snooty baronet: Lewis, P. Wyndham

Snow for Christmas: Starrett, Vincent

Snow goose, The: Gallico, Paul

Snow man, The: Housman, Laurence

Snow poems: Wolfe, Humbert

Snow storm, The: Gore, Catherine

Snowbound: Stoker, Bram

Snow-bound: Whittier, J.G.

Snow-bound at Eagle's: Harte, Bret

Snowdrop: a New Year gift for children, The: Osgood, F.S.

Snowflake: Gallico, Paul

Snowflakes and sunbeams: Ballantyne, R.M.

Snowflakes and sunbeams: Campbell, W.W.

Snow-image and other twicetold tales, The: Hawthorne, Nathaniel

Snows of Helicon, The: Tomlinson, H.M.

Snows of Kilimanjaro: Hemingway, Ernest

Snug and Serena count twelve: Uttley, Alison

Snug and Serena go to town: Uttley, Alison

Snug harbour: Jacobs, W.W.

So-big: Ferber, Edna

So brief the spring: Greenwood, Walter

So disdained: †Shute, Nevil

So far and no father: Harwood, H.M.

So far have I travelled: Wellesley, D.V.

So great a man: †Pilgrim, David

So here cometh [sic] white hyacinths: Hubbard, Elbert

So here then cometh Pig-Pen Pete: Hubbard, Elbert

So immortal a flower: Roberts, C.E.M.

So keep going to the sun: Lindsay, N.V.

So little time: Marquand, J.P.

So long, Mick: Brereton, John Le G.

So long to learn: Masefield, John

So lovers dream: Waugh, Alec

So many hungers: Bhattacharya, B.

So many loves: Walmsley, Leo

So many ways: Cawein, Madison

So much good: Frankau, Gilbert

So much to record: Bird, W.R.

So perish the roses: †Bell, Neil

So Tiberius: Mannin, Ethel

So well remembered: Hilton, James

So wild the heart: Trease, Geoffrey

Soames and the flag: Galsworthy, John

Soap behind the ears: Skinner, C.O.

Sober advice from Horace: Pope, Alexander

Sober truth: Sitwell, *Sir* Osbert

Sociable plover, A: Linklater, Eric

Social climbers, The: Wilson, Romer

Social compact, The: Adams, J.Q.

Social convenience, A: Harwood, H.M.

Social credit: Pound, Ezra

Social credit: Strachey, John

Social credit and the Labour Party: Muir, Edwin

Social equality: Mallock, W.H.

Social foundations of post-war building, The: Mumford, Lewis

Social history and literature: Tawney, R.H.

Social justice and the stations of the cross: Gill, Eric

Social life in Ancient Egypt: Petrie, *Sir* William Flinders

Social life in Britain from the Conquest to the Reformation: Coulton, G.G.

Social life in old Virginia: Page, T.N.

Social origins: Lang, Andrew

Social pictorial satire: Du Maurier, George

Social planning for Canada: Underhill, F.H.

Social pressure: Helps, *Sir* Arthur

Social principles and society: Gill, Eric

Social problem as seen from the view point of trade unionism, capital, and socialism, The: Sinclair, Upton

Social problems: George, Henry

Social reform and birth control: Chesterton, G.K.

Social register, The: Loos, Anita

Social rights and duties: Stephen, *Sir* Leslie

Social secretary, The: Phillips, D.G.

Social sketches: Higgins, Matthew James

Social statics: Spencer, Herbert

Social strugglers: Boyesen, H.H.

Social study, the people of South Africa: Millin, Sarah Gertrude

Social theory: Cole, G.D.H.

Social upheaval, A: Ascher, I.G.

Socialism: Owen, Robert

Socialism and art: Squire, *Sir* J.C.

Socialism and co-operation: Woolf, Leonard

Socialism and national minimum: Webb, Beatrice

Socialism and superior brains: Shaw, G.B.

Socialism and the family: Wells, H.G.

Socialism and the living wage: Dutt, R.P.

Socialism and the scientific motive: Wells, H.G.

Socialism: for and against: Besant, *Mrs.* Annie

Socialism for millionaires: Shaw, G.B.

Socialism in England: Webb, Sidney

Socialism in evolution: Cole, G.D.H.

Socialism in New Zealand: Lee, J.A.

Socialism: its growth and outcome: Morris, William

Socialism: principles and outlook: Shaw, G.B.

Socialist and Labour Movement in England, Germany and France: Steed, H.W.

Socialist economics: Cole, G.D.H.

Socialist thought: Cole, G.D.H.

Society: Robertson, T.W.

Society and solitude: Emerson, Ralph Waldo

Society for pure English: Bridges, Robert, R.W. Chapman *and others*

Society in America: Martineau, Harriet

Society in Rome under the Caesars: Inge, W.R.

Society of authors, The: Besant, *Sir* Walter

Socrates: Bax, Clifford

Socrates: Mitchison, Naomi

Socrates and Athenian society in his age: Godley, A.D.

Socrates asks why: Linklater, Eric

Soft answers: Aldington, Richard

Soft side, The: James, Henry

Soft spot, The: Hutchinson, Arthur

Sojourner, The: Rawlings, Marjorie

Soldier, The: Aiken, Conrad

Soldier and a scholar, A: Swift, Jonathan

Soldier and death, The: Ransome, Arthur

Soldier from Virginia, A: †Bowen, Marjorie

Soldier monk, A: (†Ensign Clarke Fitch): Sinclair, Upton

Soldier of fortune, The: Warren, J.B.L.

Soldier of humour, A: Lewis, P. Wyndham

Soldier of life, A: De Selincourt, Hugh

Soldier of Valley Forge: Roberts, T.G.

Soldier's art, The: Powell, A.D.

Soldiers bathing: Prince, F.T.

Soldier's bride, The: Hall, James

Soldiers immortal: Muir, D.C.A.

Soldiers of fortune: Davis, R.H.

Soldiers of misfortune: Wren, P.C.

Soldier's orphan, The: Moodie, Susanna

Soldiers' pay: Faulkner, William

Soldiers' peaches, The: Cloete, E.F.S.G.

Soldier's return, The: Hook, T.E.

Soldiers three: Kipling, Rudyard

Soldier's wife: Reynolds, G.

Soldiers wind: Hanley, James

Soldier's women: Herbert, A.F.X.

Solemn boy: Bolitho, H.H.

Solemn dirge, sacred to the memory of Frederic, Prince of Wales, A: Smart, Christopher

Solemn epistle to Mrs. Clarke, A: †Pindar, Peter

Solemne passion of the soules love, A: Breton, Nicholas

Solid gold Cadillac, The: Kaufman, G.S.

Solid mandala, The: White, Patrick

Soliloquies in England and later soliloquies: Santayana, George

Soliloquies in song: Austin, Alfred

Soliloquy: Shaftesbury, Anthony Ashley Cooper, *Earl of*

Soliloquy of a hermit, The: Powys, T.F.

Solitary, The: Whitehead, Charles

Solitary hours: Southey, C.A.

Solitary hunter, The: Palliser, John

Solitary man, The: Church, Richard

Solitary rambles and adventures of a hunter in the prairies: Palliser, John

Solitary summer, The: Russell, E.M.

Solitary war, A: Williamson, Henry

Solitary warrior, The: Ruskin, John

Solitary way, The: Soutar, William

Solitude: Gale, Norman R.

Solitude: Sackville-West, Victoria

Solo singing: Newman, Ernest

Solomon and Balkis: Freeman, John

Solomon and Solomonic literature: Conway, Moncure Daniel

Solomon in all his glory: Lynd, Robert

Solomon Isaacs: Farjeon, B.L.

Solomon, my son!: Erskine, John

Solomons recantation, entituled Ecclesiastes, paraphrased: Quarles, Francis

Solomon's Temple spiritualiz'd: Bunyan, John

Solstice: Jeffers, J.R.

Solstices: Macneice, Louis

Solway ford and other poems: Gibson, Wilfred

Some account of a journey across the Alps in a letter to a friend: Hayward, Abraham

Some account of Horace his behaviour in Cambridge: King, William.

Some account of ... innoculating ...the small pox: Mather, Cotton

Some account of Mrs. Clarida Singlehart: Manning, Anne

Some account of my cousin Nicholas: Barham, R.H.

Some account of...small-pox: Franklin, Benjamin

Some account of the capture of the ship "Aurora": Freneau, Philip

Some account of the life and writings of Charles Cotton, Esq.: Oldys, William

Some account of the Pennsylvania hospital: Franklin, Benjamin

Some account of the school for the liberal education of boys: Bancroft, George

Some advice humbly offer'd to the members of the October Club, in a letter from a person of honour: Swift, Jonathan

Some American people: Caldwell, Erskine Preston

Some are more human than others: Smith, Stevie

Some arguments against enlarging the power of bishops in letting of leases: Swift, Jonathan

Some articles on the depreciation of silver and on topics connected with it: Bagehot, Walter

Some aspects and problems of London publishing between 1550 and 1650: Greg, W.W.

Some aspects of Asiatic history: Lyall, Sir Alfred C.

Some aspects of Maori myth and religion: Best, Elsdon

Some aspects of modern poetry: Noyes, Alfred

Some aspects of South Australian life: Spence, C.H.

Some aspects of travel: Kipling, Rudyard

Some authors: Raleigh, Sir Walter A.

Some birds of the countryside: Massingham, Harold

Some books I like: Mais, S.P.B.

Some Canadian noms-de-plume identified: Scadding, Henry

Some cautions to those who are to chuse members to serve in Parliament: Savile, George

Some Chinese ghosts: Hearn, Lafcadio

Some cities and San Francisco: Bancroft, H.H.

Some comparative values: Fowler, H.W.

Some considerations humbly offered to the Right Honourable the Lord-Mayor, in the choice of recorder: Swift, Jonathan

Some considerations of the consequences of the lowering of interest, and raising the value of money: Locke, John

Some considerations on the bills of credit: Mather, Cotton

Some considerations on the keeping of Negroes: Woolman, John

Some contemporary American poets: Fletcher, John Gould

Some contemporary poets: Monro, H.E.

Some cycles of Cathay: White, W.A.

Some days with Washington: Van Doren, Carl

Some discourses, sermons and remains: Glanvill, Joseph

Some distinguished Americans: O'Higgins, H.J.

Some diversions of a man of letters: Gosse, Sir Edmund

Some do not: Ford, Ford Madox

Some early impressions: Stephen, Sir Leslie

Some early legislation and legislators in Upper Canada: Riddell, W.R.

Some early recollections of Liverpool: Birrell, Augustine

Some eighteenth-century byways: Buchan, John

Some emotions and a moral: †Hobbes, John Oliver

Some enquiry into the causes which have obstructed the advance of historical painting for the last seventy years in England: Haydon, Benjamin Robert

Some Essex verses: Cripps, A.S.

Some everyday folk—and Dawn: Franklin, Miles

Some every-day folks: Phillpotts, Eden

Some experiences of an Irish R.M.: Somerville, Edith

Some fallacies: (†Elzevir), Murdoch, Sir W.L.F.

Some few hints in defence of dramatic entertainments: Ramsay, Allan

Some flowers: Sackville-West, Victoria

Some free thoughts upon the present state of affairs: Swift, Jonathan

Some fruits of solitude: Penn, William

Some further adventures of an Irish R.M.: Somerville, Edith

Some Gospel-truths opened according to the Scriptures: Bunyan, John

Some happenings: Vachell, H.A.

Some hints on pattern-designing: Morris, William

Some historical remarks concerning the Collegiate School of Connecticut in New Haven: Johnson, Samuel

Some I knew well: Bax, Clifford

Some important truths about conversion: Mather, Increase

Some impressions of my elders: Ervine, St. John

Some Irish yesterdays: Somerville, Edith

Some Japanese artists: Noguchi, Yone

Some ladies in haste: Chambers, R.W.

Some lapsed names in Canadian local nomenclature: Scadding, Henry

Some later verses: Harte, Bret

Some limericks: Douglas, Norman

Some literary aspects of France in the War: Gosse, *Sir* Edmund

Some literary recollections: Payn, James

Some loose stones: Knox, R. A.

Some lost works of Cotton Mather: Kittredge, G.L.

Some love letters: Field, Eugene

Some loves and a life: Praed, *Mrs.* C.

Some memorable yesterdays: Bhattacharya, B.

Some memories of W.B. Yeats: Masefield, John

Some modern authors: Mais, S.P.B.

Some modern British authors: Church, Richard

Some modern difficulties: Baring-Gould, Sabine

Some modern French poets: a commentary, with specimens: Flint, F.S.

Some moonshine tales: Uttley, Alison

Some mythical elements in English literature: Tillyard, E. M. W.

Some new pieces never before publisht: Oldham, John

Some news: Marshall, Bruce

Some notes on H.P. Lovecraft: Derleth, A.W.

Some notes on the currency problem: Adams, J. T.

Some notes towards an essay on the beginnings of American dramatic literature, 1606–1789: Ford, Paul Leicester

Some notices of the life and writings of Fitz-Greene Hallek: Bryant, W.C.

Some observations on imperial problems: Miller, E.M.

Some observations on the art of narrative: Bentley, Phyllis

Some observations upon a paper, relating to Wood's halfpence: Swift, Jonathan

Some of my Bush friends in Tasmania: Meredith, L.A.

Some of us: Cabell, James Branch

Some old portraits: Tarkington, Booth

Some others and myself: Suckow, Ruth

Some passages in the life of Major Gahagan: Thackeray, W.M.

Some passages in the life of Mr. Adam Blair: Lockhart, John Gibson

Some passages in the life of William Thom: Kennedy, J.P.

Some passages of the life and death of John Earl of Rochester: Burnet, Gilbert

Some people: Nicolson, Hon. *Sir* Harold

Some persons unknown: Hornung, E.W.

Some phases of imperial preference in policy: Miller, E.M.

Some poems: Auden, W.H.

Some popular fallacies about vivisection: †Carroll, Lewis

Some private views being essays from the Nineteenth Century Review with some occasional articles from the Times: Payn, James

Some problems of philosophy: James, William

Some queries upon the demand of the Presbyterians to have the sacramental test repealed at this session of the Parliament: Swift, Jonathan

Some reasons against the bill for settling the tyth of hemp, flax, &c: Swift, Jonathan

Some reasons to prove that no person is obliged by his principles, as a Whig to oppose Her Majesty or her present ministry: Swift, Jonathan

Some recollections of Newport artists: Elliott, M.H.

Some reflections on his Majesty's proclamation of the twelfth of February: Burnet, Gilbert

Some relations between political and economic theory: Cole, G.D.H.

Some religious elements in English literature: Macaulay, *Dame* Rose

Some remarks on the Barrier Treaty: Swift, Jonathan

Some remarks on the tale of a tub: King, William

Some remarks upon a pamphlet, entitl'd, [A letter to the seven lords of the committee, appointed to examine Gregg]: Swift, Jonathan

Some reminiscences: Conrad, Joseph

Some roots of English poetry: Hillyer, Robert

Some Shakespearean themes: Knights, L.C.

Some soldier poets: Moore, T.S.

Some sources of human history: Petrie, *Sir* William Flinders

Some talk about animals and their masters: Helps, *Sir* Arthur

Some talk of Alexander: †Bridie, James

Some tasks for education: Livingstone, *Sir* Richard

Some things worth knowing: Chase, Stuart

Some thoughts concerning education: Locke, John

Some thoughts concerning the present revival of religion in New England: Edwards, Jonathan

Some thoughts on the economics of public education: Tawney, R.H.

Some thoughts on the tillage of Ireland: Swift, Jonathan

Some thoughts on university education: Livingstone, *Sir* Richard

Some thoughts upon the liberty and the rights of Englishmen: Montagu, Basil

Some trust in chariots: Jones, Jack

Some turns of thought in modern philosophy: Santayana, George

Some unpublished letters of Horace Walpole: Walpole, *Sir* Spencer

Some verses to Germans: Masefield, John

Some versions of pastoral: Empson, William

Some war impressions: Farnol, J.J.

Some Winchester letters: Johnson, Lionel Pigot

Some women's hearts: Moulton, E.L.

Some world far from ours: Warner, Sylvia Townsend

Somebody at the door: Postgate, Raymond

Somebody else: Lathrop, G.P.

Somebody in boots: Algren, Nelson

Somebody knows: Van Druten, J.W.

Somebody's luggage: Dickens, Charles

Somebody's neighbours: Cooke, Rose Terry

Somebody's rocking my dreamboat: Langley, Noel

Someday I'll find you: Widdemer, Margaret

Somehow good: De Morgan, W.F.

Someone in the dark: Derleth, A.W.

Someone puts a pineapple together: Stevens, Wallace

Someone waiting: Williams, Emlyn

Somerset essays: Powys, L.C.

Somerset Maugham: Brophy, John

Something about a well: Brown, *Dr.* John

Something about Eve: Cabell, James Branch

Something about words: Weekley, Ernest

Something childish: Mansfield, Katherine

Something fishy: Wodehouse, P.G.

Something for every body: Hall, B.R.

Something for nothing: Uttley, Alison

Something for tokens: Macartney, Frederick

Something fresh: Wodehouse, P.G.

Something in common: Hughes, J.L.

Something in my heart: Greenwood, Walter

Something light: Sharp, Margery

Something more about the soldier's orphan: Moodie, Susanna

Something more important: Maltby, H.F.

Something near: Derleth, A.W.

Something occurred: Farjeon, B.L.

Something of myself for my friends known and unknown: Kipling, Rudyard

Something old, something new: Canfield, Dorothy

Something to hide: Monsarrat, Nicholas

Something to talk about: Phillpotts, Eden

Something wrong: Nesbit, E.

Sometime: Herrick, Robert

Somewhere in France: Davis, R.H.

Somnath, the shrine eternal: Munshi, K.M.

Son at the front, A: Wharton, Edith

Son of a hundred kings: Costain, T.B.

Son of a tinker: Walsh, Maurice

Son of Adam, The: Chattopadhyaya, Harindranath

Son of Apple: Walsh, Maurice

Son of Hagar, A: Caine *Sir* Henry Hall

Son of his father, The: Oliphant, Margaret

Son of his father, A: Wright, H.B.

Song of Italy, A: Swinburne, A.C.

Son of Mother India answers, A: Mukherji, D.G.

Son of old Harry, A: Tourgée, A.W.

Son of perdition, The: Cozzens, James Gould

Son of Richard Carden, The: †Bell, Neil

Son of Royal Langbrith, The: Howells, W.D.

Son of the gods: Beach, R.E.

Son of the gods, A: Bierce, Ambrose

Son of the hawk: Raddall, T.H.

Son of the middle border, A: Garland, Hamlin

Son of the morning: Frankau, Gilbert

Son of the people, A: Orczy, *Baroness*

Son of the soil, A: Merivale, H.C.

Son of the soil, A: Oliphant, Margaret

Son of the state, A: Ridge, W. Pett

Son of the sun, A: London, Jack

Son of the swordmaker: Read, O.P.

Son of the wolf, The: London, Jack

Son of woman: the story of D.H.Lawrence: Murry, John Middleton

Sonata: Erskine, John

Song: Gibson, Wilfred

Song and idea: Eberhart, Richard

Song and its fountains: Russell, G.W.

Song and story: Fawcett, Edgar

Song for American freedom, A: Dickinson, John

Song for December, A: Bates, H.E.

Song for New Year's day, The: Tate, Nahum

Song for St. Caecilia's day, A: Flatman, Thomas

Song for St. Cecilia's day, A: Dryden, John

Song for Simeon, A: Eliot, T.S.

Song for the ter-centenary of Lake Champlain: Scollard, Clinton

Song from the Persian: Aldrich, T.B.

Song in September: Gale, Norman R.

Song in the meadow: Roberts, E.M.

Song in the wilderness: Green, P.E.

Song o' the South: Blocksidge, C.W.

Song of a falling world: Lindsay, Jack

Song of a sailor man: Phillpotts, Eden

Song of a single note, A: Barr, A.E.H.

Song of brotherhood, The: Brereton, John Le G.

Song of darkness and light, A: Bridges, Robert

Song of Hiawatha, The: Longfellow, H.W.

Song of honour, The: Hodgson, Ralph

Song of Igor's campaign, The: Nabokov, Vladimir

Song of India: Clune, Frank

Song of Lambert, The: De la Roche, Mazo

Song of life, The: Davies, W.H.

Song of life, The: Krishnamurti, J.

Song of Los, The: Blake, William

Song of love, The: Davies, W.H.

Song of mother love, A: Cross, Zora

Song of Renny, The: Hewlett, Maurice

Song of sixpence, A: (†Ian Hay), Beith, *Sir* John Hay

Song of sixpence, A: Cronin, A.J.

Song of Solomon newly translated from the original Hebrew, The: Percy, Thomas

Song of songs, The: Davies, Rhys

Song of songs, The: Golding, Louis

Song of speed, A: Henley, W.E.

Song of the Anderson Cavalry: Boker, G.H.

Song of the battle of the Nile, The: Bowles, William Lisle

Song of the Cardinal, The: Stratton-Porter, Gene

Song of the cold, The: Sitwell, Edith

Song of the Dardanelles: Lawson, Henry

Song of the drums, The: Dukes, Ashley

Song of the English, The: Kipling, Rudyard

Song of the gypsymaiden: Isvaran, M.S.

Song of the lark, The: Cather, Willa

Song of the militant romance, The: Lewis, P.Wyndham

Song of the plow, The: Hewlett, Maurice

Song of the prairie land: Macdonald, W.P.

Song of the rebel, The: Cooke, John Esten

Song of the sandwich, The: Wilcox, Ella Wheeler

Song of the shirt, The: Hood, Thomas

Song of the soldiers: Hardy, Thomas

Song of the stone wall, The: Keller, Helen

Song of the sun: Rhys, Ernest

Song of the sword, The: Henley, W.E.

Song of the tide, A: Raymond, Ernest

Song of the Undertow, The: Macdonald, W.P.

Song of the Vermonters, The: Whittier, J.G.

Song of the wave, The: Lodge, G.C.

Song of the women: Kipling, Rudyard

Song of welcome in honour of His Excellency, the Marquis of Lansdowne, Governor-General of Canada: †Seranus

Song on the wind: Nichols, Beverley

Song story of Francesco and Beatrice, The: Doughty, *Sir* A.G.

Song through space: White, T.C.

Song to David, A: Smart, Christopher

Song without words: the story of Felix Mendelssohn: Erskine, John

Songes and sonettes: Surrey, Henry Howard, *Earl*

Songs after Lincoln: Horgan, Paul

Songs America sings, The: Van Loon, Hendrik

Songs and ballads: Bayly, Thomas Haynes

Songs and ballads for manufacturers: Neale, J.M.

Songs and ballads for the people: Neale, J.M.

Songs and carols: Dalton, A.C.

Songs and glees: Moore, Thomas

Songs and incantations: Turner, W.J.R.

Songs and meditations: Hewlett, Maurice

Songs and odes: Dixon, R.W.

Songs and satires: Masters, E.L.

Songs and slang of the British soldier: Partridge, Eric

Songs and slang of the British soldier, 1914–18: Brophy, John

Songs and sonnets: Coleman, H.J.

Songs and sonnets, Smith: L.L.P.

Songs and verses on sporting subjects: Warburton, R.E.E.

Songs at the start: Guiney, L.I.

Songs, ballads and other poems: Bayly, Thomas Haynes

Songs before sunrise: Swinburne, A.C.

Songs for a little house: Morley, C.D.

Songs for a medium voice: Symons, Arthur

Songs for Christmas festival: Higginson, R.W.

Songs for Eve: MacLeish, Archibald

Songs for little people: Gale, Norman R.

Songs from a southern shore: Scollard, Clinton

Songs from books: Kipling, Rudyard

Songs from Connacht: Colum, Padraic

Songs from London: Ford, Ford Madox

Songs from prison: Gandhi, M.K.

Songs from Punch: Farjeon, Eleanor

Songs from the clay: Stephens, James

Songs from the mountains: Kendall, Henry

Songs from Southern Seas: O'Reilly, J.B.

Songs from Vagabondia: Carman, Bliss

Songs from Vagabondia: Hovey, Richard

Songs in Jack the gyant queller, The: Brooke, Henry

Songs in many keys: Holmes, Oliver Wendell

Songs in the common chord: Barr, A.E.H.

Songs late and early: Kaye-Smith, Sheila

Songs, legends and ballads: O'Reilly, J.B.

Songs now first collected: Hogg, James

Songs of a day: Mackaye, Percy

Songs of a Savoyard: Gilbert, *Sir* W.S.

Songs of a Semite: Lazarus, Emma

Songs of a sentimental bloke, The: Dennis, C.M.J.

Songs of a Sourdough: Service, Robert

Songs of a sun-lover: Service, Robert

Songs of a Syrian lover: Scollard, Clinton

Songs of a worker: O'Shaughnessy, A.W.E.

Songs of action: Doyle, *Sir* Arthur Conan

Songs of Annette: Allen, Hervey

Songs of Bluenose: Cody, H.A.

Songs of Britain: Morris, *Sir* Lewis

Songs of chaos: Read, *Sir* Herbert

Songs of cheer: Bangs, J.K.

Songs of childhood: De la Mare, Walter

Songs of doubt and dream: Fawcett, Edgar

Songs of England: Austin, Alfred

Songs of fair weather: Thompson, Maurice

Songs of far-away lands: †Miller, Joaquin

Songs of feast, field and fray: Lawrence, G.A.

Songs of heroic days: O'Hagan, Thomas

Songs of Innocence: Blake, William

Songs of Italy: †Miller, Joaquin

Songs of Jamaica: McKay, Claude

Songs of joy: Davies, W.H.

Songs of Killarney: Graves, Alfred Percival

Songs of labor: Whittier, J.G.

Songs of loss: Hewlett, Maurice

Songs of love and death: Ghose, Manmohan

Songs of love and empire: Nesbit, E.

Songs of love and labor: †Seranus

Songs of love and life: Cross, Zora

Songs of many seasons, 1862–1874: Holmes, Oliver Wendell

Songs of memory and hope: Newbolt, *Sir* Henry

Songs of mourning: Campion, Thomas

Songs of night: Young, A.J.

Songs of Oriel: Leslie, *Sir* J.R. Shane

Songs of peace: Ledwidge, Francis

Songs of Robert Bridges: Young, Francis Brett

Songs of salvation, sin and satire: Palmer, H.E.

Songs of shadow-of-a-leaf: Noyes, Alfred

Songs of summer: Stoddard, R.H.

Songs of summer lands: †Miller, Joaquin

Songs of sunrise lands: Scollard, Clinton

Songs of three counties: Hall, M.R.

Songs of the affections: Hemans, *Mrs.* Felicia

Songs of the army of the night: Adams, Francis

Songs of the bat: Lucas, E.V.

Songs of the class 1829: Holmes, Oliver Wendell

Songs of the coast dwellers: Skinner, C.L.

Songs of the field: Ledwidge, Francis

Songs of the Gael: Graves, Alfred Percival

Songs of the heights and deeps: Noel, R.B.W.

Songs of the makers of Canada: Logan, J.D.

Songs of the Mexican seas: †Miller, Joaquin

Songs of the Old Testament, The: Wither, George

Songs of the prairie: Stead, R.J.C.

Songs of the road: Doyle, *Sir* Arthur Conan

Songs of the Saguenay: Bailey, A.G.

Songs of the sea: Sargent, Epes

Songs of the sea nymphs: Miller, Thomas

Songs of the settlement: O'Hagan, Thomas

Songs of the Sierras: †Miller, Joaquin

Songs of the silent word: Ward, E.S.

Songs of the soul: †Miller, Joaquin

Songs of the South: O'Hara, J.B.

Songs of the south country: Belloc, Hilaire

Songs of the spring tides: Swinburne, A.C.

Songs of the sun-lands: †Miller, Joaquin

Songs of the trawlers: Noyes, Alfred

Songs of Trafalgar: Croker, John Wilson

Songs of travel: Stevenson, R.L.

Songs of two: Hardy, A.S.

Songs of two centuries: Carleton, William (McKendree)

Songs of two nations: Swinburne, A.C.

Songs of two seasons: Nesbit, Edith

Songs of two worlds: Morris, *Sir* Lewis

Songs of Vidyapati: Ghose, Sri Aurobindo

Songs of youth: Kipling, Rudyard

Songs of Zion: Montgomery, James

Songs out of Egypt: Scollard, Clinton

Songs out of exile: Gouldsbury, H.C.

Songs to Myrtilla: Ghose, Sri Aurobindo

Songs unsung: Anderson, J.C.

Songs unsung: Morris, *Sir* Lewis

Songs we sing, The: Van Loon, Hendrik

Songs, with bibliography, The. Ed. J.C.Dick: Burns, Robert

Songs without clothes: Gill, Eric

Songs without music: Michael, J.L.

Songs without notes: Morris, *Sir* Lewis

Song-tide: Marston, P.B.

Son-in-law, The: O'Keeffe, John

Sonnet XLIV of Michelangelo Buonarroti: Bridges, Robert

Sonnets, a sequence on profane love: Boker, G.H.

Sonnets and canzonets: Alcott, A.B.

Sonnets and fugitive pieces: Tennyson, Charles

Sonnets and Innuptam: Moloney, Patrick

Sonnets and other poems: Hayne, P.H.

Sonnets and other poems, with a versification of the six bards of Ossian: Brydges, *Sir* S.E.

Sonnets and rondels: O'Hara, J.B.

Sonnets and songs by Proteus: Blunt, Wilfred

Sonate and verse: Belloc, Hilaire

Sonnets for youth: Call, F.O.

Sonnets from Antan: Cabell, James Branch

Sonnets from nature: Phillpotts, Eden

Sonnets in memory of my mother: Bourinot, A.S.

Sonnets of a portrait-painter: Ficke, A.D.

Sonnets of good cheer: Masefield, John

Sonnets of M. A. Buonarotti and T. Campanella, The: Symonds, J.A.

Sonnets of Shakespeare, The: Donnelly, Ignatius Loyola

Sonnets of sorrow and triumph: Wilcox, Ella Wheeler

Sonnets on the death of Browning: Swinburne, A.C.

Sonnets on the death of the Duke of Wellington: Evans, Sebastian

Sonnets on the war: Dobell, S.T.

Sonnets on the War: Smith, Alexander

Sonnets to a red-haired lady: Marquis, Don

Sonnets to an imaginary Madonna: Fisher, V.A.

Sonnets to Craig: Sterling, George

Sonnets to Duse: Teasdale, Sara

Sonnets to the unknown soldier: Stewart, D.A.

Sonnets, with folk songs from the Spanish: Ellis, Havelock

Sons: Buck, Pearl

Sons and daughters: Oliphant, Margaret

Sons and fathers: Monkhouse, A.N.

Sons and lovers: Lawrence, D.H.

Sons and soldiers: Shaw, Irwin

Sons o' man: †Lancaster, G.B.

Sons of fire: Braddon, Mary Elizabeth

Sons of light: Blunden, Edmund Charles

Sons of Mrs. Aab, The: Millin, Sarah Gertrude

Sons of the Emerald Isle, The: Mackenzie, W.L.

Sons of the fathers: Halper, Albert

Sons of the Martian: Peattie, D.C.

Sons of the Mistral: Campbell, Roy

Sons of the morning: Phillpotts, Eden

Sons of the other: Gibbs, *Sir* Philip

Sons of the Puritans: Marquis, Don

Sons of the sheik: Hull, Ethel M.

Sons of the sword: Woods, M.L.

Sons of the swordmaker: Walsh, Maurice

Sooner or later: Brooks, Charles William Shirley

Sooner or later: Glyn, Elinor

Sophia: Ervine, St. John

Sophia: Lennox, Charlotte

Sophia: Weyman, Stanley

Sophisticates, The: Atherton, Gertrude

Sophoclean tragedy: Bowra, *Sir* Maurice

Sophocles' King Oedipus: Yeats, W.B.

Sophocles. Oedipus at Colonnus: Murray, George

Sophocles. Oedipus, king of Thebes: Murray, George

Sophocles. The Antigone: Murray, George

Sophocles. The wife of Hercules and the Trachinian women: Murray, George

Sophonisba: Lee, Nathaniel

Sophro the wise: Binyon, Laurence

Sophy, The: Denham, *Sir* John

Sophy Cassmajor: Sharp, Margery

Sophy of Kravonia: (†Anthony Hope), Hawkins, Anthony Hope

Soprano: Crawford, F. Marion

Sorcerer, The: Gilbert, *Sir* W.S.

Sorcerer's apprentice, The: Huxley, Elspeth J.

Sorcerer's son, The: Johnson, Josephine

Sorceress, The: Oliphant, Margaret

Sordello: Browning, Robert

Sorority house: Chase, M.C.

Sorrell and son: Deeping, Warwick

Sorrow in sunlight: Firbank, Ronald

Sorrow of war: Golding, Louis

Sorrowes joy: Fletcher, Giles, *the younger*

Sorrowful princess, The: Gore-Booth, E.S.

Sorrowfull verses made on the death of our most soveraigne Lady Queene Elizabeth my gracious mistresse: Churchyard, Thomas

Sorrows and joys of a New Zealand naturalist: Guthrie-Smith, W.H.

Sorrows of gentility, The: Jewsbury, Geraldine

Sorrows of Satan, The: †Corelli, Marie

Sorrows of Switzerland, The: Bowles, William Lisle

Sorry you've been troubled: †Cheyney, Peter

Sort of ecstasy, A: Smith, A.J.M.

Sort of traitors, A: Balchin, Nigel

Sort-of-prince, The: Brighouse, Harold

Sospiri di Roma: †Macleod, Fiona

Sot-weed factor, The: Cook, Ebenezer

Soul, The: Brooks, Van Wyck

Soul and body of John Brown: Rukeyser, Muriel

Soul from the sword: Bridges, Roy

Soul of a bishop, The: Wells, H.G.

Soul of China, The: Waley, Arthur

Soul of Countess Adrian, The: Praed, *Mrs.* C.

Soul of Kol Nikon: Farjeon, Eleanor

Soul of Lilith, The: †Corelli, Marie

Soul of London, The: Ford, Ford Madox

Soul of man, The: Wilde, Oscar

Soul of Marshall Gilles de Raix, The: Lewis, D.B. Wyndham

Soul of Melicent, The: Cabell, James Branch

Soul of Nyria, The: Praed, *Mrs.* C.

Soul of Samuel Pepys, The: Bradford, Gamaliel

Soul of Spain, The: Ellis, Havelock

Soul of Susan Yellam, The: Vachell, H.A.

Soul of the city receives the gift of the Holy Spirit, The: Lindsay, Norman

Soul of the street, The: Duncan, Norman

Soul of war, The: Gibbs, *Sir* Philip

Souldiers accidence, The: Markham, Gervase

Souldiers exercise, The: Markham, Gervase

Souldiers fortune, The: Otway, Thomas

Souldiers grammar, The: Markham, Gervase

Souldiers wishe to Britons welfare, A: Rich, Barnabe

Soules effectuall calling to Christ, The: Hooker, Thomas

Soules exaltation, The: Hooker, Thomas

Soules harmony, The: Breton, Nicholas

Soules humiliation, The: Hooker, Thomas

Soules immortal crowne devided into seaven dayes workes, The: Breton, Nicholas

Soules implantation, The: Hooker, Thomas

Soules ingrafting into Christ, The: Hooker, Thomas

Soules preparation for Christ, The: Hooker, Thomas

Soul's destroyer, The: Davies, W.H.

Soul's inheritance, The: Lodge, G.C.

Souls of Black Fold, The: Dubois, William

Souls of passage: Barr, A.E.H.

Souls on Fifth: Granville-Barker, *Sir* Harley

Soul's quest, The: Scott, F.G.

Soul's tragedy, A: Browning, Robert

Sound and the fury, The: Faulkner, William

Sound barrier, The: Rattigan, Terence

Sound beleever, The: Shepard, Thomas

Sound of a city: Farrell, J.T.

Sound of Bow bells, The: Weidman, Jerome

Sound of the sea: Walmsley, Leo

Sound of the trumpet, The: Millin, Sarah Gertrude

Sound wagon, The: Stribling, T.S.

Sounding brass: Mannin, Ethel

Soundings from the Atlantic: Holmes, Oliver Wendell

Sounds and sweet airs: Todhunter, John

Sour grapes: Williams, W.C.

Source, The: Michener, James

Source book of Greek science, A: Cohen, M.R.

Sources for a biography of Shakespeare: Chambers, *Sir* E.K.

Sources of bigotry in the United States: Myers, Gustavus

Sources of modern art: Pevsner, Nikolaus

Sources of religious insight, The: Royce, Josiah

Sources of the early Chinese novel: Buck, Pearl

South: a tour of its battlefields and ruined cities, The: Trowbridge, J.T.

South Africa: Kipling, Rudyard

South Africa: Millin, Sarah Gertrude

South Africa: Trollope, Anthony

South Africa a century ago: Barnard, *Lady* Anne

South African forces in France, The: Buchan, John

South African gold fields, The: Glanville, Ernest

South African opposition, 1939–1945, The: Roberts, Michael

South American holiday: Mais, S.P.B.

South American journey: Frank, Waldo

South and east: Masefield, John

South Carolina in the Revolutionary War: Simms, W.G.

South coast: selected verse: Christesen, C.B.

South country, The: Thomas, E.E.P.

South Eastern France: Hare, A.J.C.

South London: Besant, *Sir* Walter

South moon under: Rawlings, Marjorie

South of Rio Grande: †Brand, Max

South Riding: Holtby, Winifred

South Sea Bubble, The: Ainsworth, Harrison

South Sea Bubble: Coward, Noel

South sea bubble, A: Pertwee, Roland

South Sea tales: London, Jack

South star: Fletcher, John Gould

South to Cadiz: Tomlinson, H.M.

South to Samarkand: Mannin, Ethel

South to Sicily: O'Faolain, Sean

South Vancouver past and present: Lewis, A.H.

South Wales coast: Rhys, Ernest

South Western France: Hare, A.J.C.

South wind: Douglas, Norman

South wind, The: Mackenzie, *Sir* Compton

South wind, The: Palmer, Nettie

Southennan: Galt, John

Southern Baroque art: Sitwell, Sacheverell

Southern cross, The: Esson, T.L.B.

Southern cross, The: Green, Paul

Southern flight, A: Scollard, Clinton

Southern gates of Arabia, The: Stark, Freya

Southern marches, The: Massingham, Harold

Southern passages and pictures: Simms, W.G.

Southern rambles: Mais, S.P.B.

Southern soldier stories: Eggleston, G.C.

Southern songs: Blocksidge, C.W.

Southern steel: Cusack, E.D.

Southern struggle for pure government, The: Cable, George Washington

Southern tour: Royall, A.N.

Southern writers in the modern world: Davidson, Donald

Southerner, The: Dixon, Thomas

Southey: Dowden, Edward

South-sea idylls: Stoddard, C.W.

South-Sea sisters, The: Horne, Richard Henry

Southward ho!: Jackson, Holbrook

Southward Ho!: Simms, W.G.

Southward journey: Sutherland, H.G.

Southways: Caldwell, Erskine Preston

South-west, The: Ingraham, J.H.

Souvenir: Dell, Floyd

Souvenir from Qam, A: Connelly, Marc

Souvenir of "Back to Beaufort": O'Dowd, B.P.

Souvenir of France's Day: Stephens, A.G.

Souvenir of Vancouver, A: Dalton, A.C.

Souvenirs of France: Kipling, Rudyard

Sovereign flower, The: Knight, G.W.

Sovereignty and goodness of God, The: Rowlandson, M.W.

Sovereignty of character, The: Watson, A.D.

Sovereignty of ideals, The: Watson, A.D.

Soviet attitudes toward authority: Mead, Margaret

Soviet Communism—a new civilisation?: Webb, Beatrice and Sidney Webb

Soviet genetics and world science: Huxley, *Sir* Julian

Soviet Russia: Nehru, Jawaharlal

Soviet Russia after ten years: Chase, Stuart

Sowers, The: †Merriman, Seton

Sowing, The: Hough, Emerson

Sowing: Woolf, Leonard

Sowing and reaping: Washington, B.T.

Sowing the wind: Linton, Eliza

Sow's ear, The: Cronin, B.C.

Space, time and gravitation: Eddington, *Sir* Arthur

Spadework: Woolley, *Sir* Leonard

Spaewife, The: Galt, John

Spagnolette: a poetic drama, The: Lazarus, Emma

Spain: Auden, W.H.

Spain: Hale, E.E.

Spain: Madariaga, Salvador de

Spain: Sitwell, Sacheverell

Spain and her daughters: O'Hagan, Thomas

Spain 1939: four poems: Bronowski, J.

Spain under Charles the Second: Stanhope, Philip Stanhope *Earl*

Spanglers and tingles, The (the vival belles): Jones, J.B.

Spanish armada, The: Sladen, D.B.W.

Spanish barber, The: Manning, Anne

Spanish Baroque art: Sitwell, Sacheverell

Spanish bayonet: Benét, S.V.

Spanish bride, The: Heyer, Georgette

Spanish Cape mystery: †Queen, Ellery

Spanish caravel, The: Bullett, Gerald

Spanish character: Babbitt, Irving

Spanish circus (1788–1808): Armstrong, M.D.

Spanish conquest in America and its relation to the history of slavery, The: Helps, *Sir* Arthur

Spanish Curate, The: Beaumont, Francis

Spanish drama, The: Lewes, G.H.

Spanish earth, The: Hemingway, Ernest

Spanish farm, The: Mottram, R.H.

Spanish folksongs: Madariaga, Salvador de

Spanish fryar, The: Dryden, John

Spanish galleon, The: Ingraham, J.H.

Spanish gardener, The: Cronin, A.J.

Spanish gipsie, The: Middleton, Thomas

Spanish gold: Hannay, J.O.

Spanish gypsy, The: †Eliot, George

Spanish heroine, The: Falkner, W.C.

Spanish holiday: Mais, S.P.B.

Spanish husband, The: Payne, J.H.

Spanish jade, The: Hewlett, Maurice

Spanish journey: Sutherland, H.G.

Spanish lady: Walsh, Maurice

Spanish lady, The: Woods, M.L.

Spanish Main and Tavern, The: Lindsay, Jack

Spanish Maine: Wren, P.C.

Spanish marriage, The: Simpson, H. de G.

Spanish masquerado, The: Greene, Robert

Spanish match, The: Ainsworth, Harrison

Spanish papers: (†Geoffrey Crayon), Irving, Washington

Spanish Peggy: Catherwood, Mary

Spanish pistol, The: Macdonell, A.G.

Spanish Royal House, The: Petrie, *Sir* Charles

Spanish sketches: Field, *Baron*

Spanish student, The: Longfellow, H.W.

Spanish temper, The: Pritchett, V.S.

Spanish virgin, The: Pritchett, V.S.

Spanish vistas: Lathrop, G.P.

Spark, The (the 'sixties): Wharton, Edith

Sparke of friendship, A: Churchyard, Thomas

Sparkenbroke: Morgan, Charles

Sparkles for bright eyes: Alcott, Louisa M.

Sparkling cyanide: Christie, Agatha

Sparks fly upward: La Farge, Oliver

Sparks from a flint: Lucas, E.V.

Spartacus: Fast, Howard M.

Spartacus: Mitchell, J.L.

Spartacus: Moodie, Susanna

Spartan dame, The: Southern, Thomas

Spartan manual, The: Ritson, Joseph

Spats' fact'ry: Dyson, E.G.

Speak for England: Agate, J.E.

Speak, memory: Nabokov, Vladimir

Speak to the earth: Young, A.J.

Speaking for myself: White, S.E.

Speaking for Scotland: †McDiarmid, Hugh

Speaking generally: Wavell, A.P. *1st Earl*

Speaking likenesses: Rossetti, Christina

Speaking personally: (†Elzevir), Murdoch, *Sir* W.L.F.

Speaking rather seriously: Ridge, W. Pett

Speaking tree, The: Rukeyser, Muriel

Speaking turns: Pertwee, Roland

Spear head: Brophy, John

Spears against us: Roberts, C.E.M.

Special delivery: Cabell, James Branch

Special delivery: Gielgud, Val

Special messenger: Chambers, R.W.

Special performances: Ridge, W. Pett

Special theory of relativity: Einstein, Albert

Specimen chapter from Kennebec, A: Coffin, Robert

Specimen days and collect: Whitman, Walt

Specimen hunters, The: Oxley, J.M.

Specimen of a history of Oxfordshire: Warton, Thomas

Specimens: †Miller, Joaquin

Specimens of a bibliography: Lang, Andrew

Specimens of an improved metrical translation of the Psalms of David: Lang, J.D.

Specimens of Anglo-Saxon prose and poetry: Craigie, *Sir* William Alexander

Specimens of early English metrical romances: Ellis, George

Specimens of early English poets: Ellis, George

Specimens of English prose style from Malory to Macaulay: Saintsbury, G.E.B.

Specimens of Icelandic Rimur: Craigie, *Sir* William Alexander

Specimens of the British critics by Christopher North: Wilson, John

Specimens of the British poets: Campbell, Thomas

Specimens of the Polish poets: Bowring, *Sir* John

Specimens of the Russian poets: Bowring, *Sir* John

Specimens of the table-talk: Coleridge, S.T.

Speckledy Hen, The: Uttley, Alison

Speckled bird, A: Evans, A.J.

Spectra: Bynner, Witter

Spectra: Ficke, Arthur Davidson

Spectre, The: Pye, H.J.

Spectre of power, A: †Craddock, C.E.

Spectre of the forest, The: McHenry, James

Spectre steamer, The: Ingraham, J.H.

Speculation and the reform of the New York stock exchange: Adams, J.T.

Speculation, or a defence of mankind: Anstey, Christopher

Speculative dialogues: Abercrombie, Lascelles

Speculative instruments: Richards, I.A.

Speculum animae: Inge, W.R.

Speculum mentis: Collingwood, R.G.

Speech against prelates innovations: Waller, Edmund

Speech, at Middleton, in the fifth district: Dana, R.H. *junior*

Speech [at the] Artists' Benevolent Institution: Kipling, Rudyard

Speech at the Guildhall in Bristol upon his Parliamentary conduct: Burke, Edmund

Speech at the Taunton reform meeting: Smith, Sydney

Speech delivered in the House of Commons on moving for leave to bring in a Bill to consolidate the law relating to copyright: Talfourd, *Sir* T.N.

Speech for the defendent in the prosecution of the Queen v. Moxon for the publication of Shelley's works: Talfourd, *Sir* T.N.

Speech, 4 July 1643: Waller, Edmund

Speech in opening the impeachment of Warren Hastings: Burke, Edmund

Speech in the House of Commons, May 8, 1818, on the education of the poor, The: Brougham, H.P.

Speech of Edmund Burke, Esq.; on American taxation: Burke, Edmund

Speech of Lord Dundreary on the Great Hippocampus question: Kingsley, Charles

Speech of Mr. Tucker, of Virginia, on the restriction of slavery in Missouri: Tucker, George

Speech on the education of the poor, House of Commons, June 29, 1820, The: Brougham, H.P.

Speeches (1880–1905) on fiscal reform: Balfour, A.J.

Speeches and writings: Gandhi, M.K.

Speeches in commemoration of William Morris: Drinkwater, John

Speeches in commemoration of William Morris: Jackson, Holbrook

Speeches in stirring times and letters to a son: Dana, R.H. *junior*

Speeches on army reform: Trevelyan, *Sir* G.O.

Speeches on foreign affairs, 1904–14: Grey of Fallodon, Edward *Lord*

Speeches on the County Franchise: Trevelyan, *Sir* G.O.

Speeches relating to the Labouring classes: Shaftesbury, Anthony Ashley Cooper, *Earl of*

Speeches upon questions relating to public rights: Brougham, Henry Peter

Speed the plough: Morton, Thomas

Speed the plough: Neale, J.M.

Speed the plough: Robinson, E.S.L.

Spell, The: Brontë, Charlotte

Spell for old bones: Linklater, Eric

Spell of Acadia, The: Call, F.O.

Spell of French Canada, The: Call, F.O.

Spell of London, The: Morton, H.V.

Spell of Switzerland, The: Dole, N.H.

Spell of the Yukon, The: Service, Robert

Spella Ho: Bates, H.E.

Spelling book, A: Cobbett, William

Spelling of yesterday and the spelling of today, The: Matthews, J.B.

Spell-land: Kaye-Smith, Sheila

Spendthrift, The: Ainsworth, Harrison

Spenlove in Arcady: McFee, William

Spenser: Church, Richard

Sphere of glass, The: Lehmann, John

Sphinx, The: Bayldon, Arthur

Sphinx, The: Mackaye, Percy

Sphinx: Swift, Jonathan

Sphinx, The: Wilde, Oscar

Sphinx of Eaglehawk, The: †Boldrewood, Rolf

Sphinx's children, The: Cooke, Rose Terry

Spice of life: †Bell, Neil

Spice woman's basket, The:

Spicewood: Reese, L.W.

Spider: Steen, Marguerite

Spider and the flie, The: Heywood, John

Spider boy: Van Vechten, Carl

Spider strides: (†Michael Innes), Stewart, J.I.M.

Spider's palace, The: Hughes, R.A.W.

Spider's web: Christie, Agatha

Spies in amber: †Armstrong, Anthony

Spike: Clark, Charles Badger

Spikenard: Housman, Laurence

Spillikins: Hannay, J.O.

Spillway: Barnes, Djuna

Spindrift: Flavin, Martin

Spindrift: Mitchison, Naomi

Spinner of the years, The: Bentley, Phyllis

Spinners, The: Phillpotts, Eden

Spinners' book of fiction, The: Atherton, Gertrude

Spinning-wheel stories: Alcott, Louisa M.

Spinster, The: Steele, *Sir* Richard

Spinster: in defence of the woollen manufactures, The: Steele, *Sir* Richard

Spinsters in jeopardy: Marsh, Ngaio Edith

Spinsters of Lavender Lane, The: Peach, L. du Garde

Spirit and origin of Christian Monasticism, The: Hannay, J.O.

Spirit and the flesh: Buck, Pearl

Spirit in Man, The: Bushnell, Horace

Spirit in prison, A: Hichens, Robert

Spirit Lake: Kantor, Mackinlay

Spirit levels: Morley, C.D.

Spirit of an Illinois town and the little Renault, The: Catherwood, Mary

Spirit of conservatism, The: Bryant, *Sir* Arthur

Spirit of discovery, The: Bowles, William Lisle

Spirit of Japanese art, The: Noguchi, Yone

Spirit of Japanese poetry, The: Noguchi, Yone

Spirit of Judaism, The: Aguilar, Grace

Spirit of love, The: Fausset, Hugh

Spirit of love, The: McLachlan, Alexander

Spirit of man, The: Grenfell, Julian

Spirit of modern German literature, The: Lewisohn, Ludwig

Spirit of modern philosophy, The: Royce, Josiah

Spirit of Parsifal Robinson, The: Rubinstein, Harold F.

Spirit of peers and people, The: Horne, R.H.

Spirit of place, The: Meynell, Alice

Spirit of prayer, The: More, Hannah

Spirit of revolt, The: Gibbs, Sir Philip

Spirit of romance, The: Pound, Ezra

Spirit of Rome, The: †Lee, Vernon

Spirit of '76, The: Becker, C.L.

Spirit of seventy-six, The: Commager, H.S.

Spirit of society, The: Brownell, William C.

Spirit of Sweetwater, The: Garland, Hamlin

Spirit of the age, The: Hazlitt, William

Spirit of the border: Grey, Zane

Spirit of the Border, The: Grey, Zane

Spirit of the Litany of the Church of England, The: Cobbold, Richard

Spirit of the party, The: Brooke, Henry

Spirit of the people, The: Ford, Ford Madox

Spirit of time, The: Hichens, Robert

Spirit of youth and the city streets, The: Addams, Jane

Spirit rises, A: Warner, Sylvia Townsend

Spirit watches, The: Pitter, Ruth

Spirit-rapper, The: Brownson, Orestes

Spirits of the corn and of the wild: Frazer, Sir James

Spiritual adventures: Symons, Arthur

Spiritual Aeneid, A: Knox, R.A.

Spiritual and mental concepts of the Maoris: Best, Elsdon

Spiritual authority and temporal power: Coomaraswamy, A.K.

Spiritual autopsies: Mencken, H.L.

Spiritual conferences: Faber, F.W.

Spiritual life, The: Underhill, Evelyn

Spiritual milk for Boston babes in either England: Cotton, John

Spiritual progress: Sen, Keshub Chunder

Spiritual propine of a pastour to his people, A: Melville, James

Spiritual Quixote, The: Graves, Richard

Spiritual unrest, The: Baker, R.S.

Spiritual vampirism: Webber, C.W.

Spiritualist's reader, The: Doyle, Sir Arthur Conan

Spiritualized happiness-theory: Lighthall, W.D.

Spite of heaven, The: †Onions, Oliver

Spitfire, The: Chamier, Frederick

Spleen, The: Colman, George, the elder

Spleen, The: Green, Matthew

Spleen, The: Winchilsea, A.F.

Splendid brother: Ridge, W. Pett

Splendid fairing, The: Holme, Constance

Splendid shilling, The: Philips, John

Splendid silence, The: Sullivan, Alan

Splendid sin, A: Allen, Grant

Splendid spur, The: (†Q), Quiller-Couch, Sir Arthur

Splendid village, The: Elliott, Ebenezer

Splendour in the grass: Wurdemann, Audrey

Splendour of Asia, The: Beck, Mrs. Lily

Splendour that was Egypt, The: Murray, Margaret

Splendours and miseries: Sitwell, Sacheverell

Splintered sword, The: Treece, Henry

Spoil of office, A: Garland, Hamlin

Spoiled child, The: Bickerstaffe, Isaac

Spoilers, The: Beach, R.E.

Spoils of Poynton, The: James, Henry

Spoils of time, The: Gibbs, Sir Philip

Spokesman's secretary, The: Sinclair, Upton

Spook stories: Benson, E.F.

Spoon River anthology: Masters, E.L.

Sport of chance, The: †Macleod, Fiona

Sport of Gods: Cournos, John

Sport of Kings, The: (†Ian Hay), Beith, Sir John

Sport royal: (†Anthony Hope), Hawkins, Anthony Hope

Sporting anecdotes: Egan, Pierce

Sporting annual, The: Gould, Nathaniel

Sporting blood: †Queen, Ellery

Sporting life and other trifles, The: Lynd, Robert

Sporting rights and the inner man: Brighouse, Harold

Sporting verse: Gordon, A.L.

Sports and pastimes of merry England: Miller, Thomas

Sports and pastimes of the people of England, The: Strutt, Joseph

Sportsman's country: Peattie, D.C.

Sportsman's dictionary, The: Pye, H.J.

Sportswoman's love letters, A: Housman, Laurence

Spot: Jennings, Gertrude

Spotted horses: Faulkner, William

Spouter, The: Murphy, Arthur

Spoyle of Antwerpe, The: Gascoigne, George

Spragge's canyon: Vachell, H.A.

Sprays of Shamrock: Scollard, Clinton

Spreading dawn, The: †King, Basil

Spreading the news: Gregory, *Lady* Augusta

Sprig muslin: Heyer, Georgette

Sprigs of Laurel: O'Keeffe, John

Spring: Kirby, William

Spring: Thomson, James

Spring and all: Williams, W.C.

Spring birth: Van Doren, Mark

Spring cleaning, The: Burnett, Frances Hodgson

Spring cleaning: †Lonsdale, Frederick

Spring comedies: Barker, M.A.

Spring concert, The: Tarkington, Booth

Spring dance: Barry, Philip

Spring days: Moore, George

Spring fever: Wodehouse, P.G.

Spring glory: Wren, P.C.

Spring in Bloomsbury: Brighouse, Harold

Spring in New Hampshire: McKay, Claude

Spring in Sicily: Quennell, P.C.

Spring in Ultima Thule: MacMechan, A.M.

Spring in winter: Chattopadhyaya, Harindranath

Spring journey, The: Pryce-Jones, A.P.

Spring morning: Cornford, Francis

Spring of alkion, The: Haggard, *Sir* Henry Rider

Spring of joy, The: Webb, Mary

Spring of youth: Griffith, L.C.

Spring, 1600: Williams, Emlyn

Spring song, The: Bates, H.E.

Spring song, The: Reid, Forrest

Spring song and other stories: Cary, Joyce

Spring sowing: O'Flaherty, Liam

Spring thunder: Van Doren, Mark

Spring tide: Priestley, J.B.

Springboard: Macneice, Louis

Springhaven: Blackmore, *Sir* R.D.

Springs of Helicon, The: Mackail, J.W.

Springtime: Tarkington, Booth

Springtime and harvest: a romance: Sinclair, Upton

Springtime for Henry: Levy, Benn W.

Spur of morning: Mulgan, A.E.

Spur of the moment, The: (†Elzevir), Murdoch, *Sir* W.L.F.

Spur to smite, A: †Lancaster, G.B.

Spy, The: Cooper, James Fenimore

Spy, The: Sinclair, Upton

Spy master, The: Oppenheim, E.Phillips

Spy of Napoleon, A: Orczy, *Baroness*

Spy paramount, The: Oppenheim, E.Phillips

Spy upon the conjurer, A: Haywood, *Mrs*. Eliza

Spyglass: Davidson, Donald

Squanders of Castle Squander, The: Carleton, Williams

Square circle, The: Mackail, Denis

Square egg, The:(†Saki), Munro, H.H.

Square emerald, The: Wallace, Edgar

Square peg, The: Masefield, John

Squawky: Potter, Stephen

Squeaker, The: Wallace, Edgar

Squibob papers, The: Derby, G.H.

Squire, The: Bagnold, Enid

Squire, The: Pinero, *Sir* A.W.

Squire and the parson, The: Jenyns, Soame

Squire Arden: Oliphant, Margaret

Squire of Alsatia, The: Shadwell, Thomas

Squire of Sandel-side, The: Barr, A.E.H.

Squire speaks: Mason, R.A.K.

Squirrel goes skating: Uttley, Alison

Squirrel inn, The: Stockton, F.R.

Squirrel, the hare and the Little Grey Rabbit, The: Uttley, Alison

Squirrel-cage, The: Canfield, Dorothy

Squirrels and other furbearers: Burroughs, John

Sri Aurobindo: Iyengar, K.R. Srinivasa

Stabbed in the dark: Linton, Eliza

Stadt Huys of new Amsterdam, The: Earle, A.M.

Staff at Simson's, The: Niven, F.J.

Staffordshire pottery figures: Read, *Sir* Herbert

Stag, The: Nichols, Beverley

Stage coach, The: Motteux, P.A.

Stage defended from Scripture, The: Dennis, John

Stage door: Kaufman, George

Stage for poetry, A: Bottomley, Gordon

Stage life of Mary Anderson, The: Winter, William

Stage play, A: Gilbert, *Sir* W.S.

Stage struck: Akins, Zoe

Stage-coach, The: Farquhar, George

Stage-coach, The: Montgomery, Robert

Stage-coach and tavern days: Earle, A.M.

Stageland: Jerome, Jerome, K.

Stained radiance: Mitchell, J.L.

Staircase, The: Abercrombie, Lascelles

Stairs of sand: Grey, Zane

Stairs that kept on going down, The: Mackenzie, *Sir* Compton

Stairway of surprise, The: Benét, W.R.

Stakes of diplomacy, The: Lippmann, Walter

Stalin: an impartial study: Graham, Stephen

Stalin–Wells talk: Wells, H.G.

Stalin's Russia and the crisis in socialism: Eastman, Max

Stalking horse: Gielgud, Val

Stalking horse, The: Sabatini, Rafael

Stalky and Co.: Kipling, Rudyard

Stallion: Steen, Marguerite

Stamboul train: Greene, Graham

Stampede: White, S.E.

Stand at ease: (†Ian Hay), Beith, *Sir* John Hay

Stand fast, Craig Royston!: Black, William

Stand still like the hummingbird: Miller, Henry

Standard bearer, The: Crockett, S.R.

Standard history of the war, The: Wallace, Edgar

Standard of Liberty, The: Brackenridge, H.H.

Standards: Brownell, William

Standing room only: Greenwood, Walter

Standing the test: Oxley, J.M.

Stane Street, The: Belloc, Hilaire

Stanley Baldwin: Bryant, *Sir* Arthur

Stanley Baldwin: Young, G.M.

Stanley Brereton: Ainsworth, Harrison

Stanley Buxton: Galt, John

Stanley Spencer: Newton, Eric

Stans puer ad mensam: Lydgate, John

Stanzas to the memory of the late king: Hemans, *Mrs.* Felicia

Stanzas to Tolstoy: Trench, F.H.

Stanzas: written to be sung at the funeral of Henry D. Thoreau: Emerson, R.W.

Staple of news, The: Jonson, Ben

Star, The: O'Connor, T.P.

Star begotten: Wells, H.G.

Star Chamber, The: Ainsworth, Harrison

Star in a mist: Stringer, A.J.A.

Star in the East, The: Oliphant, Laurence

Star of Araby, The: Markham, Edwin

Star of Attéghéi, The: Browne, Frances

Star of Bethlehem, The: Nesbit, Edith

Star of Empire, The: Reid, T.M.

Star of Seville, The: Kemble, Fanny

Star out of Jacob, The: Warner, A.B.

Star over Bethlehem: Christie, Agatha

Star quality: Coward, Noel

Star rover, The: London, Jack

Star spangled manner, The: Nichols, Beverley

Star spangled Virgin: Heyward, DuBose

Star turns red, The: O'Casey, Sean

Star woman, The: Bedford-Jones, Henry

Star-born, The: Williamson, Henry

Starbrace: Kaye-Smith, Sheila

Starbucks, The: Read, O.P.

Stark Munro letters, The: Doyle, *Sir* Arthur Conan

Starlight window, The: Brighouse, Harold

Starlings, The: †Bridie, James

Starlit dome, The: Knight, G.W.

Starry adventure: Austin, Mary

Starry floor: Farjeon, Eleanor

Starry harness: Benét, W.R.

Stars, The: Field, Eugene

Stars: Jeffers, J.R.

Stars and atoms: Eddington, *Sir* A.S.

Stars are dark, The: †Cheyney, Peter

Stars are still here, The: White, S.E.

Stars bow down, The: (†Gordon Daviot), Mackintosh, Elizabeth

Stars in their courses, The: Jeans, *Sir* James

Stars look down, The: Cronin, A.J.

Stars, the world, and the women, The: Davies, Rhys

Stars to-night: Teasdale, Sara

Start from somewhere else: Gogarty, O.St.John

Start in life, A: Trowbridge, J.T.

Start of the road, The: Erskine, John

Starvecrow Farm: Weyman, Stanley

Starved Rock: Masters, E.L.

Starvel tragedy, The: Crofts, F.W.

Star-wagon, The: Anderson, Maxwell

Stat nominis umbra: †Junius

State and the doctor, The: Webb, Beatrice and Sidney Webb

State children in Australia: Spence, C.H.

State: elements of historical and practical politics, The: Wilson, Woodrow

State experiments in Australia and New Zealand: Reeves, W.P.

State in peace and war, The: Watson, John

State in theory and practice, The: Laski, Harold

State of Christendom, The: Wotton, *Sir* Henry

State of France, The: Evelyn, John

State of innocence, The: Dryden, John

State of mind of Mr. Sherwood, The: Royde-Smith, Naomi

State of the case between the Lord Chamberlain of His Majesty's Household and the Governor of the Royal Company of Comedians, The: Steele, *Sir* Richard

State of the expedition from Canada as laid before the House of Commons, The: Burgoyne, *Sir* John

State of the nation: Dos Passos, John

State versus Elinor Norton, The: Rinehart, Mary Roberts

Statecraft of Machiavelli, The: Butterfield, Herbert

Statesman's manual, The: Coleridge, S.T.

Statement, A: Boyle, Kay

Statement: Fay, T.S.

Statement of a recent affair in Philadelphia, A: Herbert, H.W.

Statement of the provision for the poor in America and Europe: Senior, Nassau

States through Irish eyes, The: Somerville, E.

Statesman, The: Taylor, *Sir* Henry

Statesmen of the Commonwealth: Forster, John

Station, The: Byron, Robert

Station amusements in New Zealand: Barker, M.A.

Station ballads, The: Wright, D.M.

Station life in New Zealand: Barker, M.A.

Station YYY: Tarkington, Booth

Statistical account of Upper Canada: Gourlay, R.F.

Statistical, historical and political description of the colony of New South Wales: Wentworth, W.C.

Statistical sketches of Upper Canada, for the use of emigrants: Dunlop, William

Statistics of the West: Hall, James

Statue, The: Bennett, Arnold

Statue, The, Phillpotts, Eden

Statue in the wood, The: Pryce, Richard

Statue's daughter, The: †O'Connor, Frank

Statues in the block, The: O'Reilly, J.B.

Status of the Jews in Egypt: Petrie, *Sir* William Flinders

Statutory authorities: Webb, Sidney and Beatrice Webb

Staying with relations: Macaulay, *Dame* Rose

St*ckt*n Jubilee, The: Ritson, Joseph

Steadfast: (†Elzevir), Murdoch, *Sir* W.L.F.

Steadfast man; a life of St.Patrick, The: Gallico, Paul

Steadfast prince, The: Trench, R.C.

Steadfast, the story of a saint and a sinner: Cooke, R.S.

Steady as you go: †Bartimeus

Stealing of the mare: Blunt, Wilfred

Steam Raft: Catlin, George

Steamboat, The: Galt, John

Steam-packet, The: Reynolds, G.

Steel belt: Ingraham, J.H.

Steel of empire: Gibbon, J.M.

Steep places, The: Angell, *Sir* Norman

Steep trails: Muir, John

Steeple bush: Frost, Robert

Steeplejack: Huneker, J.G.

Steichen, the photographer: Sandburg, Carl

Steinway collection of paintings, The: Huneker, J.G.

Stele glas, The: Gascoigne, George

Stella Fregelius: Haggard, *Sir* Henry Rider

Stellar movements and the structure of the universe: Eddington, *Sir* A.S.

Stemming the tide: Churchill, *Sir* Winston

Step by step: Churchill, *Sir* Winston

Step on the green light: Brogan, *Sir* D.W.

Step to Stir-Bitch-Fair, A: Ward, Edward

Stephania: †Field, Michael

Stephania: Story, W.W.

Stephen Austin: Father of Texas: Beals, Carleton

Stephen Caldrick: Robertson, T.W.

Stephen Decatur and the suppression of piracy on the Mediterranean: †Arp, Bill

Stephen Escott: Lewisohn, Ludwig

Stephen Foster story, The: Green, Paul

Stephen Hero: Joyce, James

Stephen Leacock: McArthur, Peter

Stephen, M.D.: Warner, S.B.

Stephen Moralis: †Shute, Nevil

Stephen Vincent Benét: my brother Steve: Benét, W.R.

Stepmother, The: James, G.P.R.

Stepmother, The: Milne, A.A.

Steppin heavenward: Aldington, Richard

Stepping-stones to happiness: Spofford, H.E.

Steps: Graves, Robert

Steps of belief: Clarke, J.F.

Steps of honor, The: †King, Basil

Steps to immaturity: Potter, Stephen

Steps to Parnassus: Squire, *Sir* J.C.

Steps to the Temple: Crashaw, Richard

Stepson, The: Armstrong, M.D.

Stepsons of France: Wren, P.C.

Stepsons of light: Rhodes, E.M.

Sterne: Traill, H.D.

Steward, The: Wallace, Edgar

Stickeen: Muir, John

Stickit minister and some common men, The: Crockett, S.R.

Stickit Minister's wooing, The: Crockett, S.R.

Sticks and stones: Mumford, Lewis

Stiff upper lip: Durrell, Lawrence

Stiff upper lip, Jeeves: Wodehouse, P.G.

Stifled laughter: Hay, William

Still alarm, The: Kaufman, G.S.

Still centre, The: Spender, Stephen

Still dead: Knox, R.A.

Still glides the stream: Thompson, Flora

Still house of O'Darrow, The: Bacheller, Irving

Still is the summer night: Derleth, A.W.

Still life: Murray, John Middleton

Still life: Pratt, E.J.

Still more misleading cases: Herbert, *Sir* A.P.

Still more sporting adventure!, A: Knox, R.A.

Still rebels, still Yankees: Davidson, Donald

Still she wished for company: Irwin, Margaret

Still small voice: Derleth, A.W.

Still water tragedy, The: Aldrich, T.B.

Still waters: Thomas, Augustus

Still waters run deep: Taylor, Tom

Stimuli: Knox, R.A.

Stingaree: Hornung, E.W.

Stinging nettles: †Bowen, Marjorie

Stir: Carman, Bliss

Stocking our selection: †Rudd, Steele

Stoic, The: Dreiser, Theodore

Stoic, Christian and Humanist: Murray, Gilbert

Stoker, The: Brighouse, Harold

Stoker Bush: Hanley, James

Stoker Haslett: Hanley, James

Stokeshill place: Gore, Catherine

Stokesley secret, The: Yonge, Charlotte M.

Stokin': Lawson, Will

Stolen bacillus, The: Wells, H.G.

Stolen bride, The: †Bowen, Marjorie

Stolen child, The: Galt, John

Stolen idols: Oppenheim, E. Phillips

Stolen march, The: †Yates, Dornford

Stolen moments: Parkes, Sir Henry

Stolen or strayed: Collins, Dale

Stolen rolls, The: Hoffe, Monckton

Stolen treasure: Pyle, Howard

Stolen voyage, The: Turner, E.S.

Stolen white elephant, The: (†Mark Twain), Clemens, S.L.

Stone implements of the Maoris, The: Best, Elsdon

Stone of chastity, The: Sharp, Margery

Stone trees: Freeman, John

Stone-age of Mt. Carmel human fossil remains: Keith, Sir Arthur

Stonefolds, The: Gibson, Wilfred

Stonehenge: Petrie, Sir William Flinders

Stones, The: Tagore, Sir Rabindranath

Stones awake, The: Beals, Carleton

Stones broken from the rocks: Hawker, R.S.

Stones of Venice, The: Ruskin, John

Stonewall Jackson and the old Stonewall Brigade: Cooke, J.E.

Stony Creek: Kirby, William

Stony limits: †McDiarmid, Hugh

Stooping lady, The: Hewlett, Maurice

Stooping Venus: Marshall, Bruce

Stop press: (†Michael Innes), Stewart, J.I.M.

Stopover: Tokyo: Marquand, J.P.

Stops of various quills: Howells, W.D.

Store, The: Stribling, T.S.

Store of ladies: Golding, Louis

Storied Halifax: MacMechan, A.M.

Stories about our dogs: Stowe, Harriet Beecher

Stories after nature: Wells, C.J.

Stories and interludes: Pain, B.E.O.

Stories and sketches: Payn, James

Stories, essays and poems: Belloc, Hilaire

Stories for boys: Davis, R.H.

Stories for children from the history of England: Croker, J.W.

Stories for children in illustration of the Lord's Prayer: Molesworth, Mrs.

Stories for the middle ranks of society: More, Hannah

Stories from Boccaccio: Payn, James

Stories from Holy Writ: Waddell, Helen

Stories from Louisiana history: King, G.E.

Stories from 1001 afternoons in New York: Hecht, Ben

Stories from the Bible: De la Mare, Walter

Stories from the history of Italy: Manning, Anne

Stories from the history of the Caliph Haroun al Raschid: Manning, Anne

Stories from the Italian poets: Hunt, Leigh

Stories in grey: Pain, B.E.O.

Stories in light and shadow: Harte, Bret

Stories in the dark: Pain, B.E.O.

Stories in verse: Hunt, Leigh

Stories of American life by American writers: Mitford, Mary Russell

Stories of Australia in the early days: Clarke, Marcus

Stories of Georgia: Harris, J.C.

Stories of Indiana: Thompson, Maurice

Stories of Irish peasantry: Hall, A.M.

Stories of life and love: Barr, A.E.H.

Stories of Michael Robartes and his friends: Yeats, W.B.

Stories of new France: Machar, A.M.

Stories of New Jersey: Stockton, F.R.

Stories of Ohio: Howells, W.D.

Stories of old New Spain: Janvier, T.A.

Stories of peace and war: Remington, Frederic

Stories of Red Hanraham: Yeats, W.B.

Stories of the Canadian forest: Traill, C.P.

Stories of the Cherokee hills: Thompson, J.M.

Stories of the governess, The: Hall, A.M.

Stories of the great operas: Newman, Ernest

Stories of the old Dominion from the settlement to the end of the Revolution: Cooke, J.E.

Stories of the sea: Marryatt, Frederick

Stories of the Sierras: Harte, Bret

Stories of the Spanish Main: Stockton, F.R.

Stories of the three burglars, The: Stockton, F.R.

Stories of the wild life: White, S.E.

Stories of venial sin: O'Hara, J.H.

Stories of Vinegar Hill: Warner, A.B.

Stories of Waterloo: Maxwell, W.H.

Stories old and new: †O'Connor, Frank

Stories revived: James, Henry

Stories to study: Galt, John

Stories told at twilight: Moulton, E.L.

Stories told to children: †Fairless, Michael

Stories Toto told me: (†Baron Corvo), Rolfe, Frederick

Stories with a moral, humorous and descriptive of Southern life: Longstreet, A.B.

Stories with a vengeance: Sala, G.A.H.

Stories without tears: Pain, B.E.O.

Stories without women: Byrne, Donn

Storm, The: Defoe, Daniel

Storm, The: Drinkwater, John

Storm: Munro, C.K.

Storm and echo: Prokosch, Frederic

Storm at midnight: Taylor, Tom

Storm at sea: Lindsay, Jack

Storm centre, The: †Craddock, C.E.

Storm cloud of the nineteenth century, The: Ruskin, John

Storm in a teacup: †Bridie, James

Storm in a teacup: Phillpotts, Eden

Storm king banner: Cody, H. A.

Storm music: †Yates, Dornford

Storm of time: Dark, Eleanor

Storm operation: Anderson, Maxwell

Storm over the land: Sandburg, Carl

Storm song: Johnston, W.D.

Stormalong: Ewart, E.A.

Stormalong: Villiers, A.J.

Stormbury: Phillpotts, Eden

Stormy violence, The: Lindsay, Jack

Stormy waters: Buchanan, R.W.

Story and song of Earl Roderick, The: Sigerson, Dora

Story and the fable, The: Muir, Edwin

Story brought by Brigit, The: Gregory, *Lady* Augusta

Story for strangers, A: Connelly, Marc

Story girl, The: Montgomery, L.M.

Story hour, The: Wiggin, Kate

Story of a baby, The: Turner, E.S.

Story of a bad boy, The: Aldrich, T.B.

Story of a Belgian dog, The: Morley, C.D.

Story of a child, The: Deland, Margaret

Story of a famous old Jewish firm, The: Thomson, James

Story of a feather, The: Jerrold, Douglas

Story of a fierce bad rabbit, The: Potter, Helen Beatrix

Story of a Labrador doctor, The: Grenfell, *Sir* Wilfred

Story of a literary career, The: Wilcox, Ella Wheeler

Story of a mine, The: Harte, Bret

Story of a New York House, The: Bunner, H.C.

Story of a New Zealand river, The: Mander, Jane

Story of a Norfolk farm, The: Williamson, Henry

Story of a novel, The: Wolfe, T.C.

Story of a play, The: Howells, W.D.

Story of a red deer, The: Fortescue, *Sir* John

Story of a round-house, The: Masefield, John

Story of a royal favourite, The: Gore, Catherine

Story of a short life, The: Ewing, *Mrs*. Juliana Horatia

Story of a spring morning, The: Molesworth, *Mrs*.

Story of a story, The: Matthews, J.B.

Story of a thousand, The: Tourgée, A.W.

Story of a wonder man, The: Lardner, Ring

Story of a year, The: Molesworth, *Mrs*.

Story of a year, 1848, The: Postgate, Raymond

Story of Aaron, The: Harris, J.C.

Story of Acadia, The: Hannay, James

Story of Achilles, The: Leaf, Walter

Story of Al Raoui, The: Beckford, William

Story of America, The: Van Loon, Hendrik

Story of an African farm, The: Schreiner, Olive

Story of an American farm: Hodge, H.E.

Story of an untold love, The: Ford, P.L.

Story of Avis, The: Ward, E. S.

Story of Balladeadro, The: McCrae, G.G.

Story of Barbara, The: Braddon, M.E.

Story of Bessie Costrel, The: Ward, M.A.

Story of Boon, The: Jackson, H.H.

Story of California, The: White, S.E.

Story of Canada, The: Creighton, D.G.

Story of Charles Strange, The: Wood, Ellen

Story of Chicago, The: Kirkland, Joseph

Story of civilization: Becker, C.L.

Story of civilization, The: Durant, W.J.

Story of civilization, The: Joad, C.E.M.

Story of Columbus, The: Trowbridge, J.T.

Story of courage, A: Lathrop, G.P.

Story of David, The: Peach, L. du Garde

Story of Dr. Dolittle, The: Lofting, Hugh

Story of Dr. Wassell, The: Hilton, James

Story of doom, A: Ingelow, Jean

Story of Duciehurst, The:†Craddock, C.E.

Story of electromagnetism, The: Bragg, *Sir* William

Story of Elizabeth Gould, The: Chisholm, A.H.

Story of Elizabeth Tudor, The: Irwin, Margaret

Story of England: makers of the realm, The: Bryant, *Sir* Arthur

Story of English literature, The: Broadus, E.K.

Story of Enriquez, The: Harte, Bret

Story of Esther Costello, The: Monsarrat, Nicholas

Story of Eudocia and her brothers, The: Dixon, R.W.

Story of Fabian Socialism, The: Cole, M.I.

Story of Forget-me-not and Lily of the valley, The: Baring, Maurice

Story of Francis Cludde, The: Weyman, Stanley

Story of Fuzzypeg the hedgehog, The: Uttley, Alison

Story of ginger cubes, The: Morley, C.D.

Story of holly and ivy, The: Godden, Rumer

Story of Huey P. Long, The: Beals, Carleton

Story of Indian civilization, The: Joad, C.E.M.

Story of Ireland, The: O'Faolain, Sean

Story of Irving Berlin, The: Woollcott, A.H.

Story of Ivy, The: Lowndes, *Mrs*. Belloc

Story of Jack Ballister's fortunes, The: Pyle, Howard

Story of Jesus Christ, The: Ward, E.S.

Story of Joan of Arc, The: Lang, Andrew

Story of Keats and Shelley, The: Raymond, Ernest

Story of Keedon Bluffs, The: †Craddock, C.E.

Story of Kennett, The: Taylor, Bayard

Story of King Alfred, The: Besant, *Sir* Walter

Story of King Arthur and his knights, The: Pyle, Howard

Story of Laura Secord, The: Wallace, W.S.

Story of Leon Barrentz, The: †Bell, Neil

Story of Lola Gregg, The: Fast, Howard M.

Story of Louie, The: †Onions, Oliver

Story of Louisiana, The: Thompson, Maurice

Story of Lowry Maen, The: Colum, Padraic

Story of mankind, The: Van Loon, Hendrik

Story of Marco, The: Porter, E.H.

Story of Margaret Catchpole, The: Barton, George

Story of Marie Powell, wife to Mr. Milton, The: Graves, Robert

Story of Massachusetts, The: Hale, E.E.

Story of Mhow Court-martial: Higgins, M.J.

Story of Miss Moppet, The: Potter, Helen Beatrix

Story of Mona Sheehy, The: Dunsany, Edward Plunkett, *Baron*

Story of money, The: Angell, *Sir* Norman

Story of Mount Desert Island, Maine, The: Morison, S.E.

Story of Mrs. Tubbs, The: Lofting, Hugh

Story of my boyhood and youth, The: Muir, John

Story of my experiments with truth, The: Gandhi, M.K.

Story of my heart, The: Jefferies, Richard

Story of my life: Belasco, David

Story of my life, The: Darrow, C.S.

Story of my life, The: Hare, A.J.C.

Story of my life, The: Keller, Helen

Story of my life, The: Taylor, P.M.

Story of Nefrekepta from a demotic papyrus, The: Murray, Gilbert

Story of Norway, The: Boyesen, H.H.

Story of old Fort Loudon, The: †Craddock, C.E.

Story of old Kingston, The: Machar, A.M.

Story of One-Ear, The: Sullivan, Alan

Story of Oriental philosophy, The: Beck, *Mrs*. Lily

Story of Ossian, The: Masefield, John

Story of Oxford, The: Mais, S.P.B.

Story of Patsy, The: Wiggin, Kate

Story of Paul Jones, The: Lewis, A.H.

Story of philosophy, The: Durant, W.J.

Story of Psyche, A: Griffin, Gerald

Story of Ragged Robyn, The: †Onions, Oliver

Story of Rimini: Hunt, Leigh

Story of sea warfare, The: Divine, A.D.

Story of seven young goslings, The: Housman, Laurence

Story of Sigurd, The: Peach, L. du Garde

Story of Sigurd the Volsung and the fall of the Niblungs, The: Morris, William

Story of Sir Launcelot and his companions, The: Pyle, Howard

Story of slavery, The: Washington, B.T.

Story of Sonny Sahib, The: Duncan, S.J.

Story of sugar, The: Strong, L.A.G.

Story of the Bible, The: Van Loon, Hendrik

Story of the champions of the Round Table, The: Pyle, Howard

Story of the Count de Chambord, The: Sala, G.A.H.

Story of the cowboy, The: Hough, Emerson

Story of the discontented little elephant, The: Somerville, Edith

Story of the Durham miners: Webb, Sidney

Story of the Gadsbys, The: Kipling, Rudyard

Story of the glittering plain, The: Morris, William

Story of the Grail, The: Pyle, Howard

Story of the great fire in St. John, N.B., The: Stewart, George

Story of the guns, The: Tennent, *Sir* J.E.

Story of the gypsies: Bercovici, Konrad

Story of the injured lady, The: Swift, Jonathan

Story of the Irish citizen army, The: O'Casey, Sean

Story of the Jewish way of life, The: Levin, Meyer

Story of the King's highway, The: Webb, Sidney and Beatrice Webb

Story of the Malakand field forces, The: Churchill, *Sir* Winston

Story of the negro, The: Washington, B.T.

Story of the Normans, The: Jewett, S.O.

Story of the old colony of New Plymouth, The: Morison, S.E.

Story of the outlaw, The: Hough, Emerson

Story of the Oxfordshire and Buckinghamshire Light Infantry, the old 43rd and 52nd Regiments, The: Newbolt, *Sir* Henry

Story of the second world war, The: Commager, H.S.

Story of the siren, The: Forster, E.M.

Story of the synagogue, The: Levin, Meyer

Story of the Temple and its associations, The: †Bowen, Marjorie

Story of the tower, The: Wright, Frank Lloyd

Story of the treasure-seekers, The: Nesbit, E.

Story of the Yale university press told by a friend, The: Day, Clarence

Story of their days, The: Niven, F.J.

Story of Thyrza, The: Brown, Alice

Story of Toad Lane, The: Chase, Stuart

Story of Tonty, The: Catherwood, Mary

Story of two from an old Dutch town, A: Lowell, Robert

Story of two noble lives, Charlotte, Countess Canning, and Louisa, Marchioness of Waterford, The: Hare, A.J.C.

Story of Utopias, The: Mumford, Lewis

Story of Valentine and his brother, The: Oliphant, Margaret

Story of Venus and Tannhäuser, The: Beardsley, Aubrey

Story of Vimy-Ridge, The: Bird, W.R.

Story of Viteau, The: Stockton, F.R.

Story of Waitstill Baxter, The: Wiggin, Kate

Story of Wales, The: Davies, Rhys

Story of Wilbur the hat, The: Van Loon, Hendrik

Story shop, The: Molesworth, *Mrs.*

Story teller's pack, A: Stockton, F.R.

Story teller's story, A: Anderson, Sherwood

Story to tell, A: Fleming, Peter

Story without a name, The: Stringer, A.J.A.

Story without a tail, A: Maginn, William

Story-book only: McCrae, Hugh

Story-teller forty years in London, A: Ridge, W.Pett

Story-teller's holiday, A: Moore, George

Story-tellers of Britain: Peach, L. du Garde

Strabane of the Mulberry Hills: Hay, William

Strabo on the Troad: Leaf, Walter

Stradella: Crawford, F.Marion

Strafford: Browning, Robert

Strafford: Sterling, John

Strafford: Traill, H.D.

Strafford: Wedgwood, C.V.

Straight deal, A: Wister, Owen

Straight road, The: Pickthall, M.L.C.

Strait gate, The: Bunyan, John

Strait of Anian, The: Birney, Earle

Strange adventure of James Shervinton, The: †Becke, Louis

Strange adventures of a houseboat: Black, William

Strange adventures of a Phaeton, The: Black, William

Strange adventures of Captain Dangerous, The: Sala, G.A.H.

Strange attraction, The: Mander, Jane

Strange beginning· Jacob, Naomi

Strange boarders of Palace Crescent, The: Oppenheim, E.Phillips

Strange but true: Miller, Hugh

Strange case of Dr. Jekyll and Mr. Hyde: Stevenson, R.L.

Strange case of Lucille Clery, The: †Shearing, Joseph

Strange case of Miss Annie Spragg, The: Bromfield, Louis

Strange case of Mr. Jocelyn Thew, The: Oppenheim, E.Phillips

Strange case of Mr. Pelham, The: †Armstrong, Anthony

Strange countess, The: Wallace, Edgar

Strange elopement, A: Russell, W.C.

Strange enchantment, A: Farjeon, B.L.

Strange fortune of two excellent princes, The: Breton, Nicholas

Strange fruit: Bottome, Phyllis

Strange fugitive: Callaghan, M.E.

Strange gentleman, The: Dickens, Charles

Strange glory: Myers, L.H.

Strange histories: Deloney, Thomas

Strange holiness: Coffin, Robert

Strange horse-race, A: Dekker, Thomas

Strange interlude: O'Neill, Eugene

Strange journey: Chattopadhyaya, Harindranath

Strange journeys of Colonel Polders, The: Dunsany, E.J.M.D.P.

Strange life of Charles Waterton, The: Aldington, Richard

Strange lover, The: Dunsany, E.J.M.D.P.

Strange manuscript found in a copper cylinder, A: De Mille, James

Strange meetings: Monro, H.E.

Strange melody: †Bell, Neil

Strange moon: Stribling, T.S.

Strange necessity, The: †West, Rebecca

Strange new world: Chrisholm, A.H.

Strange newes of the intercepting certaine letters: Nash, Thomas

Strange news out of divers countries: Breton, Nicholas

Strange orchestra: Ackland, Rodney

Strange rendezvous: Fairburn, A.R.D.

Strange rival: Beresford, J.D.

Strange river, The: Green, Julian

Strange roads: †Machen, Arthur

Strange stories: Allen, Grant

Strange stories: Blackwood, Algernon

Strange stories from history: Eggleston, G.C.

Strange story, A: Lytton, E.G.E.B. *1st Baron*

Strange survivals: Baring-Gould, Sabine

Strange true stories of Louisiana: Cable, G.W.

Strange vanguard, The: Bennett, Arnold

Strange victory: Teasdale, Sara

Strange visitation of Josiah McNason, The: †Corelli, Marie

Strange voyage, A: Russell, W.C.

Strange waters: Sterling, George

Strange woman's daughter, A: Walsh, Maurice

Strange world, A: Braddon, M.E.

Strange yesterday: Fast, Howard M.

Stranger, A: Walpole, *Sir* Hugh

Stranger, The: Mottram, R.H.

Stranger at Coney Island: Fearing, Kenneth

Stranger from the Tonto: Grey, Zane

Stranger from up-along, The: Roberts, T.G.

Stranger in Lowell, The: Whittier, J.G.

Stranger in Spain, A: Morton, H.V.

Stranger on the island, The: Whitlock, Brand

Stranger prince, The: Irwin, Margaret

Strangers and brothers: Snow, C.P.

Strangers and pilgrims: Braddon, M.E.

Strangers and wayfarers: Jewett, S.O.

Strangers' banquet, The: Byrne, Donn

Strangers' friend, The: Lawson, Henry

Stranger's gate, The: Oppenheim, E. Phillips

Strangers to freedom: †Bowen, Marjorie

Strangled cry, The: Strachey, John

Stratagems and spoils: White, W.A.

Strategy and compromise: Morison, S.E.

Strategy of culture, The: Innis, H.A.

Strategy of indirect approach, The: Liddell Hart, B.

Stratford-on-Avon, from the earliest times to the death of William Shakespeare: Lee, *Sir* Sidney

Stratford-upon-Avon: Mee, Arthur

Stratford-upon-Avon, report on future development: Abercrombie, Lascelles

Strathern or life at home and abroad: Blessington, Marguerite

Strathmore: Marston, J.W.

Strathmore: †Ouida

Straunge and wonderfull adventures of Don Simonides, The: Rich, Barnabe

Straw without bricks: †Delafield, E.M.

Strawberry handkerchief, The: Barr, A.E.H.

Strawberry Hill accounts: Walpole, Horace

Strawberry roan: Street, A.G.

Strawberry time: Mottram, R.H.

Straws and prayer-books: Cabell, J.B.

Straws in amber: Jacob, Naomi

Stray birds: Tagore, *Sir* R.

Stray lamb, The: Smith, Thorne

Stray thoughts: Ridge, W.P.

Stray-aways: Somerville, E.

Strayed reveller, The: Arnold, Matthew

Streak, The: †Brand, Max

Stream of life, The: Huxley, *Sir* Julian

Stream that stood still, The: Nichols, Beverley

Streamline: Herbert, *Sir* A.P.

Streamlines: Morley, C.D.

Streams of ocean: De Selincourt, Aubrey

Street angel, The: Hoffe, Monckton

Street called straight, The: †King, Basil

Street dust: †Ouida

Street haunting: Woolf, Virginia

Street I know, The: Stearns, H.E.

Street in Petra, A: Murray, Margaret

Street in Suffolk, A: Bell, Adrian

Street of adventure, The: Gibbs, *Sir* Philip

Street of dreams, The: Seymour, W.K.

Street of seven stars, The: Rinehart, Mary Roberts

Street of the eye, The: Bullett, Gerald

Street of the Gazelle, The: Deamer, Dulcie

Street scene: Rice, Elmer

Street singer, The: †Lonsdale, Frederick

Street songs: Sitwell, Edith

Streets, The: Hichens, Robert

Streets in the moon: MacLeish, Archibald

Streets of Ascolan, The: Chambers, R.W.

Streets of London, The: Darlington, W.A.

Streets of night: Dos Passos, John

Strength of the hills, The: Finch, R.D.C.

Strength of the strong, The: London, Jack

Stretton: Kingsley, Henry

Stricken deer, The: Cecil, *Lord* David

Stricklands, The: Monkhouse, A.N.

Strict joy: Stephens, James

Strictly business: †Henry, O.

Strictly from hunger: Perelman, S.J.

Strictly personal: Maugham, Somerset

Strictures on the modern system of female education: More, Hannah

Strife: Galsworthy, John

Strike at Arlingford, The: Moore, George

Strike up the band: Gershwin, Ira

Striking hours, The: Phillpotts, Eden

String of pearls, The: James, G.P.R.

Strings, my Lord, are false, The: Carroll, P.V.

Stroke of business, A: Morrison, Arthur

Strolling saint, The: Sabatini, Rafael

Strong city, The: Noyes, Alfred

Strong girl, A: Powys, T.F.

Strong hearts: Cable, G.W.

Strong Mac: Crockett, S.R.

Strong poison: Sayers, Dorothy

Strongest plume, The: De Selincourt, Hugh

Stronghold, The: Church, Richard

Stronghold, The: Levin, Myer

Structure and distribution of coral reefs, The: Darwin, Charles

Structure of animal life, The: Agassis, J.L.R.

Structure of complex words, The: Empson, William

Structure of politics at the accession of George III, The: Namier, Sir Lewis

Structure of the novel, The: Muir, Edwin

Struggle for fame, A: Riddell, Mrs. J.H.

Struggle for freedom, The: (†Elzevir), Murdoch, Sir W.L.F.

Struggle for immortality, The: Ward, E.S.

Struggle for independence, The: Becker, C.L.

Struggle for national education, The: Morley, John

Struggle for self-government, The: Steffens, J.L.

Struggle of the modern, The: Spender, Stephen

Struggles of a book against excessive taxation, The: Knight, Charles

Struggles of Brown, Jones and Robinson by one of the firm, The: Trollope, Anthony

Stuart Little: White, E.B.

Stuart masques and the Renaissance stage: Nicoll, J.R.A.

Stuarts, The: Petrie, Sir Charles

Stubble before the wind: Praed, Mrs. C.

Stubborn tree, A: Powys, T.F.

Stubborness of Geraldine, The: Fitch, C.W.

Stubb's calendar: Thackeray, W.M.

Stucco house, The: Cannan, Gilbert

Student, The: Lytton, E.G.E.B. *1st Baron*

Student's manual of the history of India, A: Taylor, P.M.

Student's modern Europe: Lodge, Sir Richard

Student's notes to an anthology of modern verse: Bullett, Gerald

Student's pastime, A: Skeat, W.W.

Student's quarter, The: Thackeray, W.M.

Studies and illustrations of the writings of Shakespeare: Knight, Charles

Studies for stories: Ingelow, Jean

Studies French and English: Lucas, F.L.

Studies from life: Craik, Mrs. D.M.

Studies from life: De Selincourt, Hugh

Studies green and gray: Newbolt, Sir Henry

Studies in a dying culture: †Caudwell, Christopher

Studies in animal life: Lewes, G.H.

Studies in biography: Walpole, Sir Spencer

Studies in class structure: Cole, G.D.H.

Studies in classic American literature: Lawrence, D.H.

Studies in conduct: Morley, John

Studies in early French poetry: Besant, Sir Walter

Studies in early Victorian literature: Harrison, Frederic

Studies in eighteenth century diplomacy: Lodge, Sir Richard

Studies in German literature: Taylor, Bayard

Studies in history and politics: Fisher, H.A.L.

Studies in humanism: Mackail, J.W.

Studies in idealism: Fausset, Hugh

Studies in Keats: Murry, John Middleton

Studies in Keats, new and old: Murry, John Middleton

Studies in law and politics: Laski, Harold

Studies in letters and life: Woodberry, G.E.

Studies in literature: Dowden, Edward

Studies in literature: Morley, John

Studies in literature: (†Q), Quiller-Couch, Sir Arthur

Studies in literature and history: Lyall, Sir Alfred

Studies in logical theory: Dewey, John

Studies in love and in terror: Lowndes, Mrs. Belloc

Studies in mediaeval painting: Berenson, Bernhard

Studies in Medieval thought: Coulton, G.G.

Studies in metaphyiscal poetry: Van Doren, Mark

Studies in Milton: Tillyard, E.M.W.

Studies in Mughul India: Sarkar, Y.J.

Studies in Napoleonic statesmanship: Fisher, H.A.L.

Studies in New Zealand scenery: Baughan, B.E.

Studies in Parliament: Hutton, R.H.

Studies in patriotism: McFee, William

Studies in Pauline eschatology, and its background: Pratt, E.J.

Studies in philosophy and science: Cohen, M.R.

Studies in poetry: Brooke, S.A.

Studies in poetry and criticism: Collins, J.C.

Studies in poetry: critical: O'Hagan, Thomas

Studies in prose and poetry: Swinburne, A.C.

Studies in prose and verse: Symons, Arthur

Studies in rhyme: Parkes, *Sir* Henry

Studies in Russia: Hare, A.J.C.

Studies in seven arts: Symons, Arthur

Studies in Shakespeare: Collins, J.C.

Studies in Shakespeare: Nicoll, J.R.A.

Studies in song: Swinburne, A.C.

Studies in spiritual history: †Macleod, Fiona

Studies in stanzas: (†Orpheus C. Kerr), Newell, R.H.

Studies in strange souls: Symons, Arthur

Studies in the contemporary theatre: Palmer, J.L.

Studies in the Elizabethan drama: Symons, Arthur

Studies in the history of the Renaissance: Pater, Walter

Studies in the literature of Northern Europe: Gosse, *Sir* Edmund

Studies in the minimum wage: Tawney, R.H.

Studies in the psychology of sex: Ellis, Havelock

Studies in the South and West: Warner, C.D.

Studies in the spirit and truth of Christianity: Temple, William

Studies in the text of Matthew Arnold's prose works: Brown, E.K.

Studies in two literatures: Symons, Arthur

Studies in verse: Warren, J.B.L.

Studies in wives: Lowndes, *Mrs.* Belloc

Studies in words: Lewis, C.S.

Studies in world economics: Cole, G.D.H.

Studies, literary and social: Johnston, R.M.

Studies: military and diplomatic: Adams, C.F.

Studies, new and old: Cobbe, Frances Power

Studies of a biographer: Stephen, *Sir* Leslie

Studies of a litterateur: Woodberry, G.E.

Studies of contemporary superstition: Mallock, W.H.

Studies of English mystics: Inge, W.R.

Studies of English poets: Mackail, J.W.

Studies of good and evil: Royce, Josiah

Studies of plant life in Canada: Traill, C.P.

Studies of religious dualism: More, P.E.

Studies of sensation and event: Jones, Ebenezer

Studies of the eighteenth century in Italy: †Lee, Vernon

Studies of the Greek poets: Symonds, J.A.

Studies of the stage: Matthews, J.B.

Studies on modern painters: Symons, Arthur

Studies on Thackeray: Hannay, James

Studies, scientific and social: Wallace, A.R.

Studio winter number: Coulton, G.G.

Studs Lonigan, a trilogy: Farrell, James

Study and criticism of Italian art, The: Berenson, Bernhard

Study and stage: a year book of criticism: Archer, William

Study in King Lear: Stringer, A.J.A.

Study in scarlet, A: Doyle, *Sir* Arthur Conan

Study in temptations, A: †Hobbes, John Oliver

Study of American English, The: Craigie, *Sir* W.A.

Study of Ben Jonson, A: Swinburne, A.C.

Study of British genius, A: Ellis, Havelock

Study of Clough, Arnold, Rossetti and Morris, A: Brooke, S.A.

Study of drama, The: Granville-Barker, *Sir* Harley

Study of English literature, The: Collins, John

Study of English literature, The: Lee, *Sir* Sidney

Study of Gawain and the green knight, A: Kittredge, G.L.

Study of George Orwell, A: Hollis, Christopher

Study of Hawthorne, A: Lathrop, G.P.

Study of history, The: Smith, Goldwin

Study of history, A: Toynbee, Arnold

Study of Justin Martyr, The: Trench, R.C.

Study of Les Misérables, A: Swinburne, A.C.

Study of Literature, A: Daiches, David

Study of Oscar Wilde, A: Symons, Arthur

Study of poetry, The: De Selincourt, Ernest

Study of St. Paul, A: Baring-Gould, Sabine

Study of Shakespeare, A: Swinburne, A.C.

Study of Shelley, A: Edgar, O.P.

Study of Shelley, A: Todhunter, John

Study of sociology, The: Spencer, Herbert

Study of the Commedia dell' Arte, A: Nicoll, J.R.A.

Study of the drama, A: Matthews, J.B.

Study of the short story, A: Canby, H.S.

Study of Thomas Hardy, A: Symons, Arthur

Study of versification, A: Matthews, J.B.

Study of Victor Hugo, A: Swinburne, A.C.

Study of Wagner, A: Newman, Ernest

Study of Walter Pater, A: Symons, Arthur

Study with critical and explanatory notes of Alfred Tennyson's poem "The Princess", A: Dawson, S.E.

Stuff and nonsense: De la Mare, Walter

Stuff of dreams, The: Uttley, Alison

Stuffed owl, The: Lewis, D.B. Wyndham

Stultifera Navis: Ireland, W.H.

Stumble on the threshold, A: Payn, James

Stumbling shepherd, The: Cody, H.A.

Stumbling-blocks: Dodge, M.A.

Stupa in Ceylon, The: Paranavitana, Senerat

Stupidity's harvest: Mitchell, Mary

Stuyvesant: Belasco, David

Style: Lucas, F.L.

Style: Raleigh, *Sir* Walter A.

Styrbiorn the strong: Eddison, Eric Rucker

Styrian Lake, The: Faber, F.W.

Subjection to Christ: Shepard, Thomas

Subjects for painters: †Pindar, Peter

Subjects joy for the Parliament, The: Taylor, John

Sublime failures: Leslie, *Sir* J.R.Shane

Sublime tobacco: Mackenzie, *Sir* Compton

Submarine and anti-submarine: Newbolt, *Sir* Henry

Substance of faith, The: Lodge, *Sir* Oliver

Substance that is poetry: Coffin, Robert

Substitute for war, A: Mackaye, Percy

Subtle knot, The: Lindsay, Jack

Suburb: Monkhouse, A.N.

Suburban sage, The: Bunner, H.C.

Suburban sketches: Howells, W.D.

Subway, The: Rice, Elmer

Subway circus: Saroyan, William

Success: Cunninghame Graham, Robert

Success: Milne, A.A.

Success to the Mayor: Mottram, R.H.

Success with small fruits: Roe, E.P.

Succession: Sidgwick, Ethel

Successor, The: Pryce, Richard

Successors of Mary the First, The: Eard, W.S.

Successors of Spenser, The: De Selincourt, Hugh

Successward: a young man's book for young men: Bok, E.W.

Such a charming young man: Akins, Zoë

Such a good man: Besant, *Sir* Walter and James Rice

Such a nice young man, Maltby, H.F.

Such an enmity: Pertwee, Roland

Such as they are: Higginson, T.W.

Such counsels you gave to me: Jeffers, J.R.

Such divinity: Trease, Geoffrey

Such is life: †Collins, Tom

Such is my beloved: Callaghan, M.E.

Such men are dangerous: Dukes, Ashley

Such pleasure: Boyd, Martin

Such, such were the joys: †Orwell, George

Such things are: Inchbald, *Mrs.* Elizabeth

Suddaine turne of fortunes wheale, The: Taylor, John

Sudden death: Crofts, F.W.

Sue: A play in three acts: Harte, Bret

Sue Verney: Lindsay, Jack

Suez-cide!!: Jefferies, Richard

Sufficiency of Holy Scriptures for the salvation of man, The: Pattison, Mark

Suffield Case, The: Stephens, A.G.

Suffolk harvest, A: Bell, Adrian

Sugar for the horse: Bates, H.E.

Sugar islands, The: Waugh, Alec

Suggestions on academical organisation with special reference to Oxford: Pattison, Mark

Suggestions on behalf of the Church Missionary Society: Newman, John Henry

Suggestions on popular education: Senior, Nassau

Suggestions towards the future government of India: Martineau, Harriet

Suicide or murder?: Fisher, V.A.

Suitable child, The: Duncan, Norman

Suite in three keys: Coward, Noel

Suki: a little tiger: Huxley, Elspeth

Sullen lovers, The: Shadwell, Thomas

Sullivan county sketches, The: Crane, Stephen

Sullivan's Bay: Bridges, Roy

Sultan, The: Bickerstaffe, Isaac

Sultan and the lady, The: Linklater, Eric

Sultan Stork: Thackeray, W.M.

Sumerians, The: Woolley, *Sir* Leonard

Summa totalis: Davies, John

Summarie of Englyshe chronicles, A: Stow, John

Summary of the duties of a Justice of the Peace out of sessions: Pye, H.J.

Summary of wisedome, The: Benlowes, Edward

Summary view of the rights of British America, A: Jefferson, Thomas

Summer: Thomson, James

Summer: Thoreau, H.D.

Summer: Wharton, Edith

Summer and winter in the two Sicilies, A: Kavanagh, Julia

Summer Christmas, A: Sladen, D.B.W.

Summer cloud, The: Noguchi, Yone

Summer clouds: Phillpotts, Eden

Summer cruise in the Mediterranean: Willis, N.P.

Summer cruising in the South seas: Stoddard, C.W.

Summer day, A: Deland, Margaret

Summer day's dream: Priestley, J.B.

Summer evening tale, A: Ainsworth, Harrison

Summer fête, The: Moore, Thomas

Summer flowers: Glover, Denis

Summer game, The: Cardus, Neville

Summer half: Thirkell, Angela

Summer harvest: Drinkwater, John

Summer holiday: Kaye-Smith, Sheila

Summer holiday: Royde-Smith, Naomi

Summer in a canon, A: Wiggin, Kate

Summer in Arcady: Allen, J.L.

Summer in Italy: O'Faolain, Sean

Summer in Paris, The: Callaghan, M.E.

Summer in Scotland: Brown, Ivor

Summer in Skye, A: Smith, Alexander

Summer intrigue, The: Swinnerton, Frank

Summer islands: Douglas, Norman

Summer leaves: Mackail, Denis

Summer lightning: Wodehouse, P.G.

Summer moonshine: Wodehouse, P.G.

Summer never ends: Frank, Waldo

Summer of life: Seymour, Beatrice Kean

Summer of love: Kilmer, Joyce

Summer on the lakes in 1845: Fuller, Margaret

Summer recollection, A: Adams, Sarah

Summer rest: Dodge, M.A.

Summer schools of philosophy at Mt. Desert: Mitchell, J.A.

Summer stories for boys and girls: Molesworth, Mrs.

Summer stories from the Argosy: Wood, Ellen

Summer storm: Swinnerton, Frank

Summer story, A: Read, T.B.

Summer tempest: (†Margaret Gregory), Ercole, Velia

Summer to decide, A: Johnson, Pamela H.

Summer tourist, The: Braddon, M.E.

Summer will show: Warner, Sylvia Townsend

Summer wreath, A: Praed, Mrs. C.

Summer's fancy, A: Blunden, Edmund

Summer's lease: Rothenstein, Sir John

Summer's play: Stern, G.B.

Summer's tale, The: Cumberland, Richard

Summertime: Mackail, Denis

Summing up, The: Maugham, Somerset

Summing-up on Russia: Graham, Stephen

Summit and chasm: Palmer, H.E.

Summit of the years, The: Burroughs, John

Summoned by bells: Betjeman, John

Summons, The: Mason, A.E.W.

Summons to the free, A: Benét, S.V.

Sun: Lawrence, D.H.

Sun, The: Galsworthy, John

Sun, The: O'Connor, T.P.

Sun across the sky: Dark, Eleanor

Sun also rises, The: Hemingway, Ernest

Sun and cloud on river and sea: (†Ishmael Dare), Jose, A.W.

Sun and saddle leather: Clark, C.B.

Sun and shadow in Spain: Elliott, M.H.

Sun circle: Gunn, Neil

Sun cure, The: Noyes, Alfred

Sun cured: Morley, C.D.

Sun dial time: Marquis, Don

Sun dials and roses of yesterday: Earle, A.M.

Sun do more, The: Hughes, J.L.

Sun field, The: Broun, Heywood

Sun Hawk, The: Chambers, R.W.

Sun hunting: Roberts, Kenneth

Sun in Capricorn: Basso, Hamilton

Sun in capricorn, The: Sackville-West, Edward

Sun in exile: Cusack, E.D.

Sun in my hands, The: Cusack, E.D.

Sun in Scorpio, The: Sharp, Margery

Sun in the sands, The: Williamson, Henry

Sun is my undoing, The: Steen, Marguerite

Sun king, The: Mitford, Nancy

Sun on the water: Strong, L.A.G.

Sun orchids: Stewart, Douglas

Sun puppy book, The: (†Donald Barr), Barrett, C.L.

Sun shall greet them, The: †Rame, David

Sun virgin, The: Dixon, Thomas

Sun zoo book, The: (†Donald Barr), Barrett, C.L.

Sunbridge girls at Six Star Ranch, The: Porter, E.H.

Sunburnt South, The: Slater, F.C.

Sunday: Narayan, R.K.

Sunday after the war: Miller, Henry

Sunday mornings: Squire, Sir J.C.

Sunday school conventions and institutes: Eggleston, Edward

Sunday school stories: Hale, E.E.

Sunday Sun, The: O'Connor, T.P.

Sunday under three heads: Dickens, Charles

Sundays: Oliphant, Margaret

Sundering flood, The: Morris, William

Sunderland capture: Bacon, Leonard

Sundown Leflare: Remington, Frederic

Sundry creditors: Balchin, Nigel

Sundry great gentlemen: †Bowen, Marjorie

Sunken garden, The: Crane, Nathalia

Sunken garden, The: De la Mare, Walter

Sunlight in New Granada: McFee, William

Sunlight on the lawn: Nichols, Beverley

Sunlight sonata, The: †Bridie, James

Sunlit Carribean: Waugh, Alec

Sunlit land, Queensland, The: (†Donald Barr), Barrett, C.L.

Sunne in aries, The: Middleton, Thomas

Sunny memories of foreign lands: Stowe, Harriet Beecher

Sunny side, The: Milne, A.A.

Sunny south, The: Ingraham, J.H.

Sunny stories and some shady ones: Payn, James

Sunrise: Black, William

Sunrise for Peter: Bird, W.R.

Sunrise in Italy: Morley, Henry

Sunrise to sunset: Bell, Adrian

Sun's darling, The: Dekker, Thomas

Sun's-darling, The: Ford, John

Sunset and evening star: O'Casey, Sean

Sunset gun: Parker, Dorothy

Sunset pass: Grey, Zane

Sunset song: †Gibbon, L.G.

Sunset touch, A: Spring, Howard

Sunset trail, The: Lewis, A.H.

Sunshine, a story about the city of New York: Bemelmans, Ludwig

Sunshine and the dry-fly: Dunne, J.W.

Sunshine family, The: Turner, E.S.

Sunshine sisters: †Novello, Ivor

Sunshine sketches of a little town: Leacock, Stephen

Sun-up: Ridge, Lola

Sunward: Golding, Louis

Superbiae Flagellum: Taylor, John

Superficial journey through Tokyo and Peking, A: Quennell, P.C.

Superhuman antagonists, The: Watson, Sir J.W.

Superintendent Wakley's mistake: Cole, G.D.H.

Superintendent Wilson's holiday: Cole, G.D.H.

Superman, The: Ghose, Sri Aurobindo

Supermanship: Potter, Stephen

Supernaturalism of New England, The: Whittier, J.G.

Superpersonalism: Lighthall, W.D.

Supers and supermen: Guedalla, Philip

Superstition corner: Kaye-Smith, Sheila

Superstition of divorce, The: Chesterton, G.K.

Superstitions of the sceptic, The: Chesterton, G.K.

Supper, The: Binyon, Laurence

Supper for the dead: Green, Paul

Supper of the Lorde, The: Tyndale, William

Supplement to the course of sermons for the whole year, A: Taylor, Jeremy

Supplement to the edition of Shakespeare published in 1778 by Johnson and Steevens, A: Malone, Edmund

Supplement to the historic doubts on the life and reign of King Richard III: Walpole, Horace

Supplementary chapter to The Bible in Spain, A: Borrow, George

Supplication for Miss Carteret in the smallpox: Philips, Ambrose

Supplication in contemplation of side tailes and muzzled faces, A: Lindsay, Sir David

Supplication of the Black Aberdeen: Kipling, Rudyard

Supply at Saint Agatha's, The: Ward, E.S.

Supplycacyon of soulys, The: More, Sir Thomas

Suppressed desires: Glaspell, Susan

Suppressed poem, A: Sassoon, Siegfried

Supramental manifestation upon earth, The: Ghose, Sri Aurobindo

Supreme Court and the Constitution, The, Beard, C.A.

Supreme Court, independent or controlled? The: Lippmann, Walter

Sure hand of God: Caldwell, Erskine Preston

Surest way to the greatest honour, The: Mather, Increase

Surf skief, The: Ingraham, J.H.

Surfeit of Lampreys: Marsh, Ngaio Edith

Surgeon of Paris, The: Jones, J.S.

Surgeon's secret, The: Russell, W.C.

Surly Tim: Burnett, Frances Hodgson

Surnames: Weekley, Ernest

Surplus population: Cobbett, William

Surprise for the bagpipe player, A: Patchen, Kenneth

Surprised by joy: Lewis, C.S.

Surprising adventures of Sir Toady Lion with those of General Napoleon Smith, The: Crockett, S.R.

Surrender of Calais, The: Colman, George, the younger

Surrender of Santiago, The: †Norris, Frank

Surry of Eagle's-nest: Cooke, J.E.

Survay of London, A: Stow, John

Survey, A: Beerbohm, Sir Max

Survey, 1830–1880: Elton, Oliver

Survey of and a blue-print for Utopia, A: Mannin, Ethel

Survey of English literature, A: Elton, Oliver

Survey of experimental philosophy considered in its present state of improvement, A: Goldsmith, Oliver

Survey of Indian history, A: Panikkar, K.M.

Survey of modernist poetry, A: Graves, Robert

Survey of modernist poetry, A: Riding, Laura

Survey of the ancient world: Breasted, J.H.

Survey of the antiquities of the City of Oxford: Wood, Anthony à

Survey of the Lake District: Martineau, Harriet

Survey of the principal repositories of the public records: Hallam, Henry

Survey of the summe of Church-discipline, A: Hooker, Thomas

Survey, 1730–1780: Elton, Oliver

Survival, The: Bottome, Phyllis

Survival and new arrivals: Belloc, Hilaire

Survival of man, The: Lodge, *Sir* Oliver

Survival of the fittest, The: Squire, *Sir* J.C.

Survivor, The: Oppenheim, E. Phillips

Survivors, The: Shaw, Irwin

Susan: Munby, A.J.

Susan and god: Crothers, Rachel

Susan Crowther: Jacob, Naomi

Susan Drummond: Riddell, *Mrs.* J.H.

Susan Lennox: her fall and rise: Phillips, D.G.

Susan Prouleigh: DeLisser, Herbert G.

Susan Spray: Kaye-Smith, S.

Susan Warner: Warner, A.B.

Susanna and Sue: Wiggin, Kate

Susannah and the Elders: †Bridie, James

Susan's escort: Hale, E.E.

Susie: Maltby, H.F.

Susie's career: Hichens, Robert

Suspect: Percy, Edward

Suspended judgements: Powys, John Cowper

Suspense: Conrad, Joseph

Suspense: †Merriman, Seton

Suspicion of Herod, The: Crashaw, Richard

Suspicious characters: Sayers, Dorothy

Sussex: Hare, A.J.C.

Sussex: Mais, S.P.B.

Sussex alphabet: Farjeon, Eleanor

Sussex gorse: Kaye-Smith, Sheila

Susy: a story of the plains: Harte, Bret

Sut Lovingood: Harris, G.W.

Sut Lovingood travels with old Abe Lincoln: Harris, G.W.

Sutherland as it was and is: Miller, Hugh

Suttee of Safa, The: Deamer, Dulcie

Suvla John: Deeping, Warwick

Suwanee river: Read, O.P.

Suwarron gold: Cowan, James

Suzanne and I: Mickle, A.D.

Swags up!: Brereton, John Le G.

Swallow: Haggard, *Sir* Henry Rider

Swallow Barn: Kennedy, J.P.

Swallow dive, The: Lynd, Sylvia

Swallow flights: Moulton, E.L.

Swallowdale: Ransome, Arthur

Swallowing the anchor: McFee, William

Swallows and Amazons: Ransome, Arthur

Swami and his friends: Narayan, R.K.

Swan, The: Steen, Marguerite

Swan and her friends, A: Lucas, E.V.

Swan Creek blizzard, The: †Connor, Ralph

Swan of Lichfield, The: Pearson, Hesketh

Swan of Usk, The: Ashton, Helen

Swan song: Galsworthy, John

Swan song and other Kulapati's letters: Munshi, K.M.

Swank: Pertwee, Roland

Swan's egg, The: Hall, A.M.

Swans fly over, The: Uttley, Alison

Swan's road: Mitchison, Naomi

Swarme of sectaries, A: Taylor, John

Swayne family, The: Palmer, E.V.

Swear by the night: Crane, Nathalia

Swear not at all: Bentham, Jeremy

Swearers-bank, The: Swift, Jonathan

Sweeney Agonistes: Eliot, T.S.

Sweeney in the trees: Saroyan, William

Sweep of lute-strings, A: Macartney, Frederick

Sweet and sour: O'Hara, J.H.

Sweet and twenties, The: Nichols, Beverley

Sweet and twenty: Dell, Floyd

Sweet Beulah land: Finlayson, Roderick

Sweet content: Molesworth, *Mrs.*

Sweet Cork of thee: Gibbings, Robert

Sweet cry of hounds, The: Somerville, E.

Sweet danger: Allingham, Margery

Sweet danger: Wilcox, Ella Wheeler

Sweet Genevieve: Derleth, A.W.

Sweet Kitty Bellairs: Belasco, David

Sweet land of Michigan: Derleth, A.W.

Sweet lavender: Nesbit, Edith

Sweet Lavender: Pinero, *Sir* A.W.

Sweet morn of Judas' day: Llewellyn, Richard

Sweet Nancy: Buchanan, R.W.

Sweet of the year, The: Massingham, Harold

Sweet story of old, The: †Stretton, Hesba

Sweet Thames run softly: Gibbings, Robert

Sweet Thursday: Steinbeck, John

Sweet waters: Nicolson, *Sir* Harold

Sweet Will: Jones, H.A.

Sweet witch: †Llewellyn, Richard

Sweetacres: Street, A.G.

Sweetheart Manette: Thompson, J.M.

Sweetheart mine: Brereton, John Le G.

Sweetheart travellers: Crockett, S.R.

Sweethearts: Gilbert, *Sir* W.S.

Sweethearts at home: Crockett, S.R.

Swell looking girl: Caldwell, Erskine Preston

Swept channels: †Taffrail

Swete and devoute sermon of Holy Saynte Ciprian of the mortalite of man, A: Elyot, *Sir* Thomas

Swift: Stephen, *Sir* Leslie

Swift: Van Doren, Carl

Swift shadow, The: Strong, L.A.G.

Swift's Gulliver's travels, etc.: Hayward, J.D.

Swift's selected prose: Hayward, J.D.

Swinburne: Drinkwater, John

Swinburne: Gosse, *Sir* Edmund

Swinburne: Grierson, *Sir* Herbert

Swinburne: Nicolson, *Sir* Harold

Swinburne: Thomas, E.E.P.

Swinburne: Treece, Henry

Swinburne: Woodberry, G.E.

Swinburne and Baudelaire: Nicolson, *Sir* Harold

Swinburne: personal recollections: Gosse, *Sir* Edmund

Swinburne's poems and ballads: Rossetti, W.M.

Swing, brother, swing: Marsh, Ngaio Edith

Swing the appearances: Barfield, Owen

Swingin' round the cirkle: †Nasby, Petroleum V.

Swinging flesh, The: Layton, Irving

Swiss emigrant's return, The: Brontë, Charlotte

Swiss enchantment: Gibbon, Monk

Swiss family Manhattan: Morley, C.D.

Swiss family Perelman, The: Perelman, S.J.

Swiss summer, The: Gibbons, Stella

Switchback, The: †Bridie, James

Swollen-headed William: Lucas, E.V.

Swoop, The: Wodehouse, P.G.

Sword and gown: Lawrence, G.A.

Sword and roses: Hergesheimer, Joseph

Sword and the distaff, The: Simms, W.G.

Sword and the pen, The: Alcott, A.B.

Sword and the sickle, The: Anand, M.R.

Sword blades and poppy seed: Lowell, Amy

Sword decides, The: †Bowen, Marjorie

Sword in the desert, A: Palmer, H.E.

Sword in the stone, The: White, T.H.

Sword of Brigadier-General Richard Montgomery, The: LeMoine, *Sir* J.M.

Sword of honour: Waugh, Evelyn

Sword of Islam, The: Sabatini, Rafael

Sword of justice, The: GoreBooth, E.S.

Sword of pain, The: Evans, G.E.

Sword of Robert E. Lee: Ryan, A.J.

Sword of the spirit, The: Tawney, R.H.

Sword of Welleran, The: Dunsany, Edward Plunkett, *Baron*

Sword of wood, The: Chesterton, G.K.

Sword of youth, The: Allen. J.L.

Swords: Howard, S.C.

Swords and flutes: Seymour, W.K.

Swords and ploughshares: Drinkwater, John

Syamali: Tagore, *Sir* Rabindranath

Sybaris and other homes: Hale, E.E.

Sybil: Disraeli, Benjamin

Sybil Knox: Hale, E.E.

Sybil's book: Barker, M.A.

Sybil's second love: Kavanagh, Julia

Sycamores, The: Whittier, J.G.

Sydney book, The: Barnard, M.

Sydney Goodsir Smith: †McDiarmid, Hugh

Sydney or the Bush: DrakeBrockman, H.

Sydney Smith: Bullett, Gerald

Sydney Sovereign, A: †Tasma

Sydneyside Syxon, A: †Boldrewood, Rolf

Sylva: Evelyn, John

Sylva poetica: Fletcher, Phineas

Sylva sylvarum: Bacon, Francis

Sylvan secrets, in bird-songs and books: Thompson, Maurice

Sylvan wanderer, The: Brydges, *Sir* S.E.

Sylvester: Heyer, Georgette

Sylvia: (†E.V. Cunningham), Fast, Howard M.

Sylvia: Read, T.R.

Sylvia: Darley, George

Sylvia: Sinclair, Upton

Sylvia and Michael: Mackenzie, *Sir* Compton

Sylvia's lovers: Gaskell, *Mrs.* Elizabeth

Sylvia's marriage: Sinclair, Upton

Sylvie and Bruno: †Carroll, Lewis

Sylvie and Bruno concluded: †Carroll, Lewis

Symbol and the saint, The: Field, Eugene

Symbolism: Whitehead, A.N.

Symbolism and fiction: Levin, Harry

Symbolist movement in literature: Symons, Arthur

Sympathy: Quennell, P.C.

Symphony in two flats: †Novello, Ivor

Sympneumata: Oliphant, Laurence

Symptoms of being 35: Lardner, Ring

Synge and the Ireland of his time: Yeats, W.B.

Synopsis of the birds of America, A: Audubon, J.J.

Synthesis of Yoga, The: Ghose, Sri Aurobindo

Syr P.S. His Astrophel and Stella: Daniel, Samuel

Syr P.S. His Astrophel and Stella: Sidney, *Sir* Philip

Syr Thomas Mores answere to the poysoned booke which W. Tyndale hath named the souper of the Lorde: More, *Sir* Thomas

Syracusan medallions: Evans, *Sir* A.J.

Syria and Egypt: Petrie, *Sir* William Flinders

Syrian travel and Syrian tribes: Noel, R.B.W.

Syrlin: †Ouida

System of logic, ratiocinative and inductive, A: Mill, John Stuart

System of national education, A: Ghose, Sri Aurobindo

System of synthetic philosophy: first principles, A: Spencer, Herbert

Syzgies and Lanrick: †Carroll, Lewis

T

T.E.Ellis, M.P.: Griffith, Llewelyn

T.E.Lawrence: in Arabia and after: Liddell Hart, B.

T.E.Lawrence; the genius of friendship: Williamson, Henry

T.E.Lawrence to his biographer: Graves, Robert

T.E. Lawrence to his biographers: Liddell Hart, B.

T. Harris dissected: Colman, George, *the elder*

T.S.Eliot: Dikter i Urval: Bottrall, Ronald

T.Tembarom: Burnett, Frances Hodgson

T.T.T.Wells: Jefferies, Richard

TVA: Adventure in planning: Huxley, *Sir* Julian

Table book, The: Hone, William

Table d'hôte: Ridge, W.Pett

Table near the band, A: Milne, A.A.

Table of the springs of action, A: Bentham, Jeremy

Table talk: Cowper, William

Table talk: Hazlitt, William

Table talk: Hunt, Leigh

Table talk of Samuel Marchbanks, The: Davies, Robertson

Tables of English literature: Morley, Henry

Tables of the law, The: Yeats, W.B.

Tables shewing the descent of the Crown of England: Ritson, Joseph

Tables turned, The: Morris, William

Table-talk: Alcott, A.B.

Table-talk: Selden, John

Tablets: Alcott, A.B.

Tabloid news: Bromfield, Louis

Taboo: Cabell, James Branch

Taboo in literature, The: Cabell, James Branch

Tabs: †Novello, Ivor

Tacey Cromwell: Richter, Conrad

Tactics and strategy of the Great Duke of Marlborough, The: Belloc, Hilaire

Tadpole Hall: Ashton, Helen

Taffy: Evans, Caradoc

Tails with a twist: Douglas, *Lord* Alfred

Tainted money: Carleton, William (McKendree)

Take away the darkness: Bynner, Witter

Take back your freedom: Ginsbury, Norman

Take courage: Bentley, Phyllis

Take it crooked: †Beeding, Francis

Take it easy: Runyon, Damon

Take it to bed: Lewis, D.B. Wyndham

Take them, stranger: Deutsch, Babette

Take three tenses: Godden, Rumer

Take two at bedtime: Allingham, Margery

Taken alive: Roe, E.P.

Taken at the flood: Braddon, Mary Elizabeth

Taken at the flood: Christie, Agatha

Taken by the hand: Buchan, Anna

Taken care of: Sitwell, Edith

Taken from life: Beresford, J. D.

Taken from the enemy: Newbolt, *Sir* Henry

Taking of Helen, The: Masefield, John

Taking of the Gry, The: Masefield, John

Taking of Toll, The: Coomaraswamy, A.K.

Talba, The: Bray, Anna Eliza

Talbot Harland: Ainsworth, William H.

Tale: Davies, Rhys

Tale book, The: Hall, Anna Maria

Tale for midnight, A: Prokosch, Frederic

Tale of a lonely parish, A: Crawford, F. Marion

Tale of a nun, The: Housman, Laurence

Tale of a shipwreck, The: Hall, J.N.

Tale of a town and an enchanted sea, The: Martyn, Edward

Tale of a tub, A: Jonson, Ben

Tale of a tub, A: Swift, Jonathan

Tale of Balen, A: Swinburne, A.C.

Tale of Benjamin Bunny, The: Potter, Helen Beatrix

Tale of Beowulf, The: Morris, William

Tale of Chicago, The: Masters, E.L.

Tale of Chloe, The: Meredith, George

Tale of eternity, A: Massey, Gerald

Tale of Genji, The: Waley, Arthur

Tale of Gloucester, The: Potter, Helen Beatrix

Tale of Jemima Puddle-Duck, The: Potter, Helen Beatrix

Tale of Johnny Town-Mouse, The: Potter, Helen Beatrix

Tale of Jonathas, The: Hoccleve (or Occleve), Thomas

Tale of King Florus, The: Morris, William

Tale of little Pig Robinson, The: Potter, Helen Beatrix

Tale of Mr. Jeremy Fisher, The: Potter, Helen Beatrix

Tale of Mr. Tod, The: Potter, Helen Beatrix

Tale of Mrs. Tiggy-Winkle, The: Potter, Helen Beatrix

Tale of Mrs. Tittlemouse, The: Potter, Helen Beatrix

Tale of mystery, A: Holcroft, Thomas

Tale of old Japan, A: Noyes, Alfred

Tale of Paraguay, A: Southey, Robert

Tale of Peter Rabbit, The: Potter, Helen Beatrix

Tale of Pigling Bland, The: Potter, Helen Beatrix

Tale of Squirrel Nutkin, The: Potter, Helen Beatrix

Tale of Rosamund Gray and Old Blind Margaret, A: Lamb, Charles

Tale of Timmy Tiptoes, The: Potter, Helen Beatrix

Tale of Tom Kitten, The: Potter, Helen Beatrix

Tale of the Emperor Coustans, The: Morris, William

Tale of the Flopsy Bunnies, The: Potter, Helen Beatrix

Tale of the House of the Wolfings, A: Morris, William

Tale of the land of Green Ginger, The: Langley, Noel

Tale of the ten, The: Russell, W.C.

Tale of three bonnets, A: Ramsay, Allan

Tale of three lions, A: Haggard, Sir H. Rider

Tale of Tiddley Winks, The: Gilmore, Mary

Tale of Tom Tiddler, The: Farjeon, Eleanor

Tale of Troy, A: Masefield, John

Tale of true love, A: Austin, Alfred

Tale of twenty five hours, A: Matthews, J.B.

Tale of two bad mice, The: Potter, Helen Beatrix

Tale of two cities, A: Dickens, Charles

Tale of two glimps, A: Bemelmans, Ludwig

Tale of two tunnels, A: Russell, W.C.

Tale of valor: Fisher, V.A.

Tale of young lovers, A: Roberts, C.E.M.

Tale that is told, A: Niven, F.J.

Tales about temperaments: †Hobbes, John Oliver

Tales and fables: †Pindar, Peter

Tales and fantasies: Stevenson, R.L.

Tales and historic scenes in verse: Hemans, Mrs. Felicia

Tales and novelettes: Knowles, James Sheridan

Tales and sketches: Disraeli, Benjamin

Tales and sketches: Miller, Hugh

Tales and sketches: by a country schoolmaster: Leggett, William

Tales and sketches of the West of Scotland: Picken, Andrew

Tales and stories from Spenser's Faery Queene: Royde-Smith, Naomi

Tales before midnight: Benét, S.V.

Tales by the O'Hara family: Banim, John

Tales for a godchild: Mackail, Denis

Tales for Christmas Eve: Broughton, Rhoda

Tales for fifteen: Cooper, James Fenimore

Tales from a far riding: †Onions, Oliver

Tales from a rolltop desk: Morley, C.D.

Tales from British history: Aguilar, Grace

Tales from Chaucer in prose: Clarke, Charles Cowden

Tales from five chimneys: Pickthall, M.W.

Tales from Greenery Street: Mackail, Denis

Tales from Shakespear, designed for the use of young persons: Lamb, Charles

Tales from the telling house: Blackmore, Sir R.D.

Tales from the Veldt: Glanville, Ernest

Tales from two hemispheres: Boyesen, H.H.

Tales in verse: Crabbe, George

Tales my father taught me: Sitwell, Sir Osbert

Tales of a Devon village: Williamson, Henry

Tales of a dying race: Grace, A.A.

Tales of a fairy court: Lang, Andrew

Tales of a grandfather: Scott, Sir Walter

Tales of a tar: Glascock, W.N.

Tales of a time and place: King, G.E.

Tales of a traveller: (†Geoffrey Crayon), Irving, Washington

Tales of a wayside inn: Longfellow, H.W.

Tales of a woman's trials: Hall, Anna Maria

Tales of all countries: Trollope, Anthony

Tales of an empty cabin: (†Grey Owl), Belaney, G.S.

Tales of Barnegat, The: Smith, F.H.

Tales of Chicago streets: Hecht, Ben

Tales of college life: †Bede, Cuthbert

Tales of fantasy and fact: Matthews, J.B.

Tales of faraway folk: Deutsch, Babette

Tales of fashionable life: Edgeworth, Maria

Tales of fishes: Grey, Zane

Tales of fishing virgin seas: Grey, Zane

Tales of forest folk: (Stephen Southwold), †Bell, Neil

Tales of four pigs and Brock the badger: Uttley, Alison

Tales of fresh-water fishing: Grey, Zane

Tales of hearsay: Conrad, Joseph

Tales of Hoffmann, The: Gibbon, Monk

Tales of Ireland: Carleton, William

Tales of Jo Egg, The: (Stephen Southwold), †Bell, Neil

Tales of John Oliver Hobbes, The: †Hobbes, John Oliver

Tales of lonely trails: Grey, Zane

Tales of mean streets: Morrison, Arthur

Tales of men and ghosts: Wharton, Edith

Tales of moorland and estuary: Williamson, Henry

Tales of my landlord: Scott, Sir Walter

Tales of my neighbourhood: Griffin, Gerald

Tales of mystery and revenge: Langley, Noel

Tales of Old China: Lin Yu-T'ang

Tales of old travel re-narrated: Kingsley, Henry

Tales of old-time Texas: Dobie, J.F.

Tales of Orris: Ingelow, Jean

Tales of pity on fishing, shooting and hunting: Porter, Anna Maria

Tales of real life: Opie, Amelia

Tales of St. Austin's: Wodehouse, P.G.

Tales of soldiers and civilians: Bierce, Ambrose

Tales of Southern rivers: Grey, Zane

Tales of space and time: Wells, H.G.

Tales of swordfish and tuna: Grey, Zane

Tales of Tahitian waters: Grey, Zane

Tales of Tasmania: Rowcroft, Charles

Tales of terror: Lewis, Matthew Gregory

Tales of terror: Scott, *Sir* Walter

Tales of the angler's Eldorado, N.Z.: Grey, Zane

Tales of the Argonauts: Harte, Bret

Tales of the Border: Hall, James

Tales of the Broad Acres: Jacob, Naomi,

Tales of the Colonies: Rowcroft, Charles

Tales of the Colony: Turner, H.G.

Tales of the convict system: †Warung, Price

Tales of the Crusaders: Scott, *Sir* Walter

Tales of the early ages: Smith, Horatio

Tales of the early days: †Warung, Price

Tales of the enchanted islands of the Atlantic: Higginson, T.W.

Tales of the factories: Southey, C.A.

Tales of the fish patrol: London, Jack

Tales of the five towns: Bennett, Arnold

Tales of the good woman: Paulding, J.K.

Tales of the Great St. Bernard: Croly, George

Tales of the Great War: Newbolt, *Sir* Henry

Tales of the grotesque and arabesque: Poe, Edgar Allen

Tales of the hall: Crabbe, George

Tales of the heart: Opie, Amelia

Tales of the home folks in peace and war: Harris, Joel Chandler

Tales of the Hoy: †Pindar, Peter

Tales of the Isle of Death, Norfolk Island: †Warung, Price

Tales of the jazz age: Fitzgerald, F. Scott

Tales of the Labrador: Grenfell, *Sir* Wilfred

Tales of the long bow, The: Chesterton, G.K.

Tales of the Maori Bush: Cowan, James

Tales of the Maori coast: Cowan, James

Tales of the Mermaid tavern: Noyes, Alfred

Tales of the Munster festivals: Griffin, Gerald

Tales of the Mustangs: Dobie, J.F.

Tales of the Northwest: Snelling, W.J.

Tales of the old regime: †Warung, Price

Tales of the Pemberton family for the use of children: Opie, Amelia

Tales of the Puritans: Bacon, Delia Salter

Tales of the sea: MacMechan, A.M.

Tales of the South Pacific: Michener, J.A.

Tales of the southern border: Webber, C.W.

Tales of the tenements: Phillpotts, Eden

Tales of the trade: Kipling, Rudyard

Tales of the trains: Lever, C.J.

Tales of the uncanny and the supernatural: Blackwood, Algernon

Tales of the West Riding: Bentley, Phyllis

Tales of three cities: James, Henry

Tales of three hemispheres: Dunsany, Edward Plunkett, *Baron*

Tales of trail and town: Harte, Bret

Tales of travel in the north of Europe: Snelling, W.J.

Tales of travel west of the Mississippi: Snelling, W.J.

Tales of two people: Hawkins, Anthony Hope

Tales of unrest: Conrad, Joseph

Tales of war: Dunsany, Edward Plunkett, *Baron*

Tales of wonder: Dunsany, Edward Plunkett, *Baron*

Tales of wonder: Lewis, Matthew Gregory

Tales out of school: Stockton, F.R.

Tales out of school: Trease, Geoffrey

Tales quaint and queer: (Stephen Southwold), †Bell, Neil

Tales round a winter hearth: Porter, Jane, and Anna Maria Porter

Tales told by Simpson: Sinclair, May

Tales told in the twilight: Molesworth, *Mrs.*

Taliesin: Hovey, Richard

Taliessin through Logres: Williams, Charles

Talifer: Robinson, E.A.

Talisman ring, The: Heyer, Georgette

Talk about Russia with Nasha Scott: Buck, Pearl

Talk about Shakespeare: Calvert, George Henry

Talk of the town, The: Payn, James

Talk to teachers on psychology: James, William

Talkers, The: Chambers, R.W.

Talking: Priestley, J.B.

Talking Bronco: Campbell, Roy

Talking horse and other tales, The: †Anstey, F.

Talking it over: Palmer, Nettie

Talking oak, The: Tennyson, Alfred *Lord*

Talking of Dick Whittington: Pearson, Hesketh

Talking of Jane Austen: Kaye-Smith, Sheila and G.B. Stern

Talking of music: Cardus, Neville

Talking to India: Forster, E.M.

Talks about wireless: Lodge, *Sir* Oliver

Talks in a free country: Inge, W.R.

Talks in China: Tagore, *Sir* R.

Talks on nationalism: Bellamy, Edward

Talks to boys, talks to girls: Mee, Arthur

Talks to the Joneses: Holland, J.G.

Talks with Nehru (by Norman Cousins): Nehru, J.

Tall hunter: Fast, Howard M.

Tall men, The: Davidson, D.G.

Tall ship on other naval occasions: †Bartimeus

Tall tales of the Kentucky Mountains: Mackaye, Percy

Tallahassee girl, A: Thompson, Maurice

Tallement des Réaux: Gosse, *Sir* Edmund

Talley method, The: Behrman, S.N.

Talleyrand: Cooper, Alfred Duff

Tally Ho!: †Miller, Joaquin

Tam: Wallace, Edgar

Tam o' the Scots: Wallace, Edgar

Tamar: Jeffers, J.R.

Tamarisk Town: Kaye-Smith, Sheila

Tambour: Raddall, T.H.

Tambourine, trumpet and drum: Kaye-Smith, Sheila

Tamburines to glory: Hughes, J.L.

Tambourlaine the Great: Marlowe, Christopher

Tamerlane: Poe, Edgar Allen

Tamerlane: Rowe, Nicholas

Tamerton church tower: Patmore, Coventry

Taming of the frontier, The: De Voto, Bernard

Taming of the Shrew, The: Shakespeare, William

Tampico: Hergesheimer, Joseph

Tamplin's tales of his family: Pain, B.E.O.

Tamworth Reading Room, The: Newman, J.H.

Tancred: Disraeli, Benjamin

Tancred and Sigismunda: Thomson, James

Tangled miracle, The: Brooker, Bertram

Tangled skein, The: Orczy, *Baroness*

Tangled tale, A: †Carroll, Lewis

Tangled talk: Rands, W.B.

Tangled threads, The: Porter, E.H.

Tangled web, A: Day-Lewis, C.

Tangled web, A: Montgomery, L.M.

Tanglewood tales for girls and boys: Hawthorne, Nathaniel

Tanis I: Petrie, *Sir* William Flinders

Tanis II: Petrie, *Sir* William Flinders

Tanks, The: Liddell Hart, B.

Tanks are coming, The: Lee, J.A.

Tannhäuser: (†Owen Meredith), Lytton, E.R.B. *Earl*

Tantalus: Emerson, Ralph Waldo

Tante: Sedgwick, A.D.

Tâo: Bailey, A.G.

Taos pueblo: Austin, Mary

Tapestry, The: Beresford, J.D.

Tapestry, The: Bridges, Robert

Tapestry in gray: Flavin, Martin

Tapestry room, The: Molesworth, *Mrs.*

Tappan's burro: Grey, Zane

Taps at reveille: Fitzgerald, F. Scott

Tapster's tapestry: Coppard, A.E.

Tapu of Banderah, The: †Becke, Louis

Taquisara: Crawford, F. Marion

Tar, a midwest childhood: Anderson, Sherwood

Tara: Taylor, P.M.

Tar-baby: Harris, Joel Chandler

Tarboe: Parker, *Sir* H.G.

Tardy George: Boker, George Henry

Target Island: Brophy, John

Tariff or budget: Garvin, J.L.

Tarka the otter: Williamson, Henry

Tarkhan I: Petrie, *Sir* William Flinders

Tarkhan II: Petrie, *Sir* William Flinders

Tarpaulin muster, A: Masefield, John

Tarr: Lewis, P. Wyndham

Tarriff in our times, The: Tarbell, Ida

Tarry at home travels: Hale, E.E.

Tarry knight: Allen, C.R.

Tartana: Ramsay, Allan

Tartans of the clans of Scotland, The: Grant, James

Tartuffe: Malleson, Miles

Task, The: Cowper, William

Task for coastal command: Bolitho, H.H.

Task of social hygiene, The: Ellis, Havelock

Tasker Jevons: Sinclair, May

Tasman and New Zealand: McCormick, E.H.

Tasmanian friends and foes: Meredith, L.A.

Tasmanian lily, The: Bonwick, James

Tasmanian memory of 1834 in five scenes: Meredith, L.A.

Tassel-gentle: Frankau, Pamela

Tasso and Leonora: Manning, Anne

Taste: Armstrong, John

Taste of glory of Robert Gray: Beals, Carleton

Tate Gallery, The: Rothenstein, *Sir* John

Tatter of scarlet, A: Crockett, S.R.

Tatter'd loving: Bottome, Phyllis

Tatterdemalion: Galsworthy, John

Tattle-tales of Cupid: Ford, Paul Leicester

Tattooed countess, The: Van Vechten, Carl

Taurine Provence: Campbell, Roy

Tavern, The: Steen, Marguerite

Tavern Knight, The: Sabatini, Rafael

Taxation no tyranny: Johnson, Samuel

Taxation of foreign income, The: Buchan, John

Taxi: †Armstrong, Anthony

Taylor anecdote book, The: Thorpe, T.B.

Taylor on Thame Isis: Taylor, John

Taylors arithmetike: Taylor, John

Taylors farewell to the tower-bottles: Taylor, John

Taylors goose: Taylor, John

Taylors motto: et habeo, et careo, et curo: Taylor, John

Taylors pastorall: Taylor, John

Taylors revenge: Taylor, John

Te Whanga-nui-a-tara: Best, Elsdon

Tea at the Abbey: Vulliamy, C.E.

Tea from China: Wallace, F.W.

Tea table, The: Haywood, *Mrs.* Eliza

Tea with Mrs. Goodman: Toynbee, Philip

Teach yourself local government: Golding, Louis

Teacher: Keller, Helen

Teacher of Dante, A: Dole, N.H.

Teacher of the violin, A: Shorthouse, J.H.

Teacher's manual accompanying the Breasted-Huth ancient history maps, A: Breasted, J.H.

Teaching, a science: the teacher an artist: Hall, B.R.

Teaching and the spirit of research: Lowes, J.L.

Teaching from the chair and at the bedside: Holmes, Oliver Wendell

Teaching of English, The: Palmer, H.E.

Teaching of the old boy, The: MacInnes, T.R.E.

Teacup terrace: Marshall, Bruce

Team bells woke me: Davis, H.L.

Tear in the cup, The: Read, O.P.

Tears of the beloved, The: Markham, Gervase

Teares on the death of Meliades: Drummond of Hawthornden, William

Tears and smiles: Barker, James Nelson

Tears and smiles: †Pindar, Peter

Tears and triumph: O'Reilly, D.P.

Tears of Amaryllis for Amyntas, The: Congreve, William

Tears of fancie, The: Watson, Thomas

Tears of St. Margaret, The: †Pindar, Peter

Tears of Scotland, The: Smollett, Tobias

Tears of the muses, The: Hill, Aaron

Tea-table talk: Jerome, Jerome K.

Technics and civilization: Mumford, Lewis

Technique of the photoplay, The: Sargent, Epes

Technocracy: Chase, Stuart

Technology: Bronowski, J.

Tecumseh: Mair, Charles

Tecumseh and Richardson: Richardson, John

Tecumseh and the Shawnee prophet: Eggleston, Edward

Tedious and brief: †Bridie, James

Teeftallow: Stribling, T.S.

Teeth of the lion, The: Patchen, Kenneth

Teilhard de Chardin, scientist and seer: Raven, C.E.

Tekeli: Hook, T.E.

Teleology of the outer consciousness, The: Lighthall, W.D.

Telescope, The: Sherriff, R.C.

Tell el Armarna: Petrie, *Sir* William Flinders

Tell England: Raymond, Ernest

Tell me a story: Canfield, Dorothy

Tell me a story: (†Ennis Graham), Molesworth, *Mrs.*

Tell me another: (Stephen Southwold), †Bell, Neil

Tell the people: Buck, Pearl

Teller, The: Westcott, E.N.

Temora: Macpherson, James

Temper, or domestic scenes: Opie, Amelia

Temperamental journey, The: Belasco, David

Temperamental people: Rinehart, Mary Roberts

Tempers, The: Williams, W.C.

Tempest, The: Dryden, John

Tempest, The: Shadwell, Thomas

Tempest, The: Shakespeare, William

Tempest and sunshine: Holmes, M.J.

Tempest-tost: Davies, Robertson

Temple, The: Herbert, George

Temple, The: Waley, Arthur

Temple and tomb in India: Deakin, Alfred

Temple beau, The: Fielding, Henry

Temple House: Stoddard, E.D.

Temple of fame, The: Pope, Alexander

Temple of glass, The: Lydgate, John

Temple of love, The: Motteux, P.A.

Temple of nature, The: Darwin, Erasmus

Temple on the hill, The: Brereton, John Le G.

Temple talks: Krishnamurti, Jiddu

Temple tower: †Sapper

Temples of Lower Nubia, The: Breasted, J.H.

Tempo of modern life, The: Adams, J.T.

Temporal power: †Corelli, Marie

Temporary gentleman, A: Maltby, H.F.

Temptation: Bale, John

Temptation of Tavernake, The: Oppenheim, E. Phillips

Temptation and atonement: Gore, Catherine

Temptation of the Friar Gonsol, The: Field, Eugene

Tempter, The: Jones, Henry Arthur

Ten burnt offerings: Macneice, Louis

Ten candlelight tales: Uttley, Alison

Ten Commandments in the animal world, The: Seton-Thompson, E.

Ten composers: Cardus, Neville

Ten creeks run: †Brent of Bin Bin

Ten days of Christmas: Stern, G.B.

Ten days' wonder: †Queen, Ellery

Ten fascinating women: Jenkins, Elizabeth

Ten great religions, The: Clarke, J.F.

Ten holy horrors, The: †Beeding, Francis

Ten little Niggers: Christie, Agatha

Ten minute alibi: †Armstrong, Anthony

Ten minute stories: Blackwood, Algernon

Ten minutes' tension: Pertwee, Roland

Ten more plays of Shakespeare: Brooke, Stopford

Ten North Frederick: O'Hara, J.H.

Ten novels and their authors: Maugham, W.S.

Ten o'clock: Whistler, James

Ten old men: (Stephen Southwold), †Bell, Neil

Ten reasons for repealing the test act: Swift, Jonathan

Ten saints: Farjeon, Eleanor

Ten tales: Bierce, Ambrose

Ten tales of Tim Rabbit: Uttley, Alison

Ten teacups, The: †Carter Dickson

Ten theophanies, The: (†George F.Harrington), Baker, W.M.

Ten thousand a year: Warren, Samuel

Ten times one is ten: Hale, E.E.

Ten wicked men: Timms, E.V.

Ten years after: Gibbs, *Sir* Philip

Ten years ago: Mottram, R.H.

Ten years' digging: Petrie, *Sir* William Flinders

Ten years tenant, The: Besant, *Sir* Walter and James Rice

Tenant farmer: Caldwell, Erskine Preston

Tenant of Wildfell Hall, The: Brontë, Anne

Tenants: James, Henry

Tenants of Malory, The: Le Fanu, Sheridan

Tendencies in modern American poetry: Lowell, Amy

Tendency of history, The: Adams, H.B.

Tender and true: Spence, C.H.

Tender buttons, objects, food, rooms: Stein, Gertrude

Tender husband, The: Steele, *Sir* Richard

Tender is the night: Fitzgerald, F. Scott

Tender only to one: Smith, Stevie

Tender passion, The: Griffith, Hubert

Tendrils: Hawker, Robert Stephen

Ten-minute tales: Bullett, Gerald W.

Ten-minute tales: (Stephen Southwold), †Bell, Neil

Tennessean, The: Royall, A.N.

Tennessee judge, A: Read, O.P.

Tennessee: the new river; Civil war to TVA, The: Davidson, Donald

Tennessee: the old river, frontier to secession, The: Davidson, Donald

Tennyson: Brooke, Stopford

Tennyson: Garnett, Richard

Tennyson: Lucas, F.L.

Tennyson: Lyall, *Sir* Alfred

Tennyson: Noyes, Alfred

Tennyson: Wolfe, Humbert

Tennyson, a modern portrait: Fausset, Hugh

Tennyson as prophet: Myers, F.W.H.

Tennyson, aspects of his life, character and poetry: Nicolson, *Sir* Harold

Tennyson, Ruskin, Mill; and other literary estimates: Harrison, Frederic

Tennyson's two brothers: Nicolson, *Sir* Harold

Tenor, The: Shapiro, Karl

Tension: †Delafield, E.M.

Tent, The: O'Flaherty, Liam

Tent on the beach, The: Whittier, J.G.

Tent show summer: Derleth, A.W.

Tentamen: Hook, T.E.

Tenth island, The: Willson, H.B.

Tenth man, The: Maugham, Somerset

Tenth muse, The: Read, *Sir* Herbert

Tenth muse, The: Thomas, E.E.P.

Tenth muse, and other poems, The: Arnold, Edwin

Tenth muse lately sprung up in America, The: Bradstreet, Anne

Tenth satyr of Juvenal, The: Shadwell, Thomas

Tenting tonight: Rinehart, Mary Roberts

Tents of Israel: Stern, G.B.

Tents of Shem, The: Allen, Grant

Tents of the Arabs, The: Dunsany, Edward Plunkett, *Baron*

Tents of trouble: Runyon, Damon

Tenure of kings and magistrates, The: Milton, John

Teraminta: Carey, Henry

Tercentenary of Izaak Walton, The: Lang Andrew

Tercentennial history of Harvard University: Morison, S.E.

Terence O'Shaughnessy's first attempt to get married: Maxwell, W.H.

Teresa: O'Faolain, Sean

Teresa of Avila: O'Brien, Kate

Teresa of Watling Street: Bennett, Arnold

Terminations: James, Henry

Terrace in Capri: Golding, Louis

Terrace in the sun: Roberts, C.E.M.

Terrae filius: Colman, George, *the elder*

Terrible battell betweene time and death, A: Rowlands, Samuel

Terrible crystal, The: †McDiarmid, Hugh

Terrible day, A: Garnett, David

Terrible hobby of Sir Joseph Londe, bt., The: Oppenheim, E.P.

Terrible inheritance, A: Allen, Grant

Terrible people, The: Wallace, Edgar

Terrible temptation, A: Reade, Charles

Terriford mystery, The: Lowndes, *Mrs.* Belloc

Terror, The: †Machen, Arthur

Terror, The: Wallace, Edgar

Terror in Russia?: Sinclair, Upton

Terror in the Thames: Divine, A.D.

Terror keep: Wallace, Edgar

Terror of St. Trinians, The: Lewis, D.B. Wyndham

Terrorist, The: O'Flaherty, Liam

Terrors of the night, The: Nash, Thomas

Terry's trials and triumphs: Oxley, J.M.

Tess of the D'Urbervilles: Hardy, Thomas

Tessa [and] the trader's wife: †Becke, Louis

Test me!: Pertwee, Roland

Test of the news, A: Lippmann, Walter

Test to destruction, A: Williamson, Henry

Testament: Wright, Frank Lloyd

Testament of a critic: Nathan, G.J.

Testament of a man forbid, The: Davidson, John

Testament of a prime minister, The: Davidson, John

Testament of a vivisector, The: Davidson, John

Testament of an empire-builder, The: Davidson, John

Testament of beauty, The: Bridges, Robert

Testament of Cressid, The: Henryson, Robert

Testament of experience: Brittain, Vera

Testament of friendship: Brittain, Vera

Testament of Joad, The: Joad, C.E.M.

Testament of light, The: Bullett, Gerald

Testament of love: Usk, Thomas

Testament of love: Wurdemann, Audrey

Testament of Stephen Fane, The: †Bell, Neil

Testament of W.Tracie, esquier, expounded, The: Tyndale, William

Testament of youth: Brittain, Vera

Testcase for humanity: Einstein, Albert

Testimony: Higginson, T.W.

Testimony against several prophane and superstitious customs, A: Mather, Increase

Testimony of the Holy Scriptures respecting wine and strong drink, The: Dawson, *Sir* J.W.

Testimony of the suns, The: Bierce, Ambrose

Testimony of the suns, The: Sterling, George

Tetrachordon: Milton, John

Texan in England, A: Dobie, J.F.

Texan ranger, The: Ingraham, J.H.

Texan virago, The: Webber, C.W.

Texas matchmaker, A: Adams, Andy

Text-book of biology: Wells, H.G.

Texts and pretexts: Huxley, Aldous

Thackeray: Brown, *Dr.* John

Thackeray: Trollope, Anthony

Thackeray the novelist: Tillotson, Geoffrey

Thackerays in India, The: Hunter, *Sir* William Wilson

Thaddeus of Warsaw: Porter, Jane

Thalaba the destroyer: Southey, Robert

Thalia Rediviva: Vaughan, Henry

Thames, The: Besant, *Sir* Walter

Thames, The: Herbert, *Sir* A.P.

Thamyris: Trevelyan, R.C.

Thanatos: a modern symposium: Toynbee, Philip

Thane of Fife, The: Tennant, William

Thank Heaven fasting: †Delafield, E.M.

Thank you, Jeeves: Wodehouse, P.G.

Thank you, Mr. Moto: Marquand, J.P.

Thankful Blossom: Harte, Bret

Thankful retribution, A: Wither, George

Thankless child: Swinnerton, Frank

Thanks before going: Masefield, John

Thanks to Sanderson: Ridge, W.Pett

Thanksgiving ode, January 18, 1816: Wordsworth, William

Thanksgiving retrospect, A: Wiggin, Kate

That bad man: Steed, H.W.

That Betty: Spofford, H.E.

That boy of Norcott's: Lever, C.J.

That brute Simmons: Morrison, Arthur

That Christmas in Peace Haven: Grenfell, *Sir* Wilfred

That fellow Perceval: Green, Anne

That fortune: Warner, C.D.

That girl: Turner, E.S.

That great Lucifer: Irwin, Margaret

That hideous strength: Lewis, C.S.

That kind of man: Beresford, J.D.

That lady: O'Brien, Kate

That lass O'Lowries: Burnett, Frances Hodgson

That little cutty: Oliphant, Margaret

That printer of Udell's: Wright, H.B.

That royal hour: Bercovici, Konrad

That very Mab: Lang, Andrew

That was yesterday: Jameson, Storm

That which hath been: Fairbridge, Dorothea

That which is hidden: Hichens, Robert

That wild lie: Jacob, Naomi

That winter night: Buchanan, R.W.

Thatched roof, A: Nichols, Beverley

That's me all over: Skinner, C.O.

Thealma and Clearchus: Chalkhill, John

Theaters of Paris, The: Matthews, J.B.

Theatre: Maugham, Somerset

Theatre, The: Rubenstein, Harold F.

Theatre, The: Steele, *Sir* Richard

Theatre advancing, The: Craig, Gordon

Theatre and dramatic theory: Nicoll, J.R.A.

Theatre in England, The: Taylor, Tom

Theatre in my time, The: Ervine, St. John

Theatre in the fifties, The: Nathan, G.J.

Theatre (1954–1955): Brown, Ivor

Theatre (1956): Brown, Ivor

Theatre of ideas, The: Jones, H.A.

Theatre of the Empire of Great Britain, The: Speed, John

Theatre of the moment, The: Nathan, G.J.

Theatre outlook: Priestley, J.B.

Theatre Royal: Kaufman, G.S.

Theatre, the drama, the girls, The: Nathan, G.J.

Theatre through its stage door, The: Belasco, David

Theatrical candidates, The: Garrick, David

Theatrical figures in porcelain: Sitwell, Sacheverell

Theatrical recorder, The: Holcroft, Thomas

Theatrical world, The: Archer, William

Theatricals: two comedies: James, Henry

Theatrocrat, The: Davidson, John

Theatrum botanicum: Parkinson, John

Theatrum poetarum: Phillips, Edward

Theft: London, Jack

Their blood is strong: Steinbeck, John

Their child: Herrick, Robert

Their father's god: Rölvaag, O.E.

Their happiest Christmas: Lyall, Edna

Their hour upon the stage: Agate, J E.

Their Majesties: Bolitho, H.H.

Their name liveth: (†Ian Hay), Beith, *Sir* John Hay

Their pilgrimage: Warner, C.D.

Their seven stars unseen: Mudie, I.M.

Their shining eldorado: Huxley, Elspeth J.

Their silver wedding journey: Howells, W.D.

Their spirit: Grant, Robert

Their wedding journey: Howells, W.D.

Their yesterdays: Wright, H.B.

Theirs be the guilt: Sinclair, Upton

Theism and humanism: Balfour, A.J.

Theism and thought: Balfour, A.J.

Thelma: †Corelli, Marie

Theme and variations: Church, Richard

Theme and variations: Stephens, James

Theme is freedom, The: Dos Passos, John

Themes and variations: Huxley, Aldous

Themes in French culture: Mead, Margaret

Then and now: Maugham, Somerset

Then shall the dust return: Green, Julian

Then there were three: Farjeon, Eleanor

Then we shall hear singing: Jameson, Storm

"Theo": Burnett, Frances Hodgson

Theodora Phranza: Neale, J.M.

Theodore: Ingraham, J.H.

Theodore and Co.: Harwood, H.M.

Theodore & Co.: †Novello, Ivor

Theodore Hook: Lockhart, John Gibson

Theodore Parker: Commager, H.S.

Theodore Parker, an anthology: Commager, H.S.

Theodore Parker and his theology: Clarke, J.F.

Theodore Parker: Yankee crusader: Commager, H.S.

Theodosius: Lee, Nathaniel

Theodric: Campbell, Thomas

Theological and miscellaneous works: Priestley, Joseph

Theology in the English poets: Brooke, Stopford

Theology of the Gospels: Moffat, James

Theophanies: Underhill, Evelyn

Theophano: the crusade of the tenth century: Harrison, Frederic

Theophila: Benlowes, Edward

Theophile: Swinburne, A.C.

Theopolis Americana: Mather, Cotton

Theories and forms of political organisation: Cole, G.D.H.

Theory and practice in international relations: Madariaga, Salvador de

Theory and practice of socialism, The: Strachey, John

Theory of business enterprise, The: Veblen, T.B.

Theory of drama, The: Nicoll, J.R.A.

Theory of flight: Rukeyser, Muriel

Theory of money and banks investigated, The: Tucker, George

Theory of moral sentiments, The: Smith, Adam

Theory of morals: Hildreth, Richard

Theory of poetry, The: Abercrombie, Lascelles

Theory of population: Spencer, Herbert

Theory of spiritual progress, A: White, W.A.

Theory of the earth, The: Burnet, Thomas

Theory of the leisure class, The: Veblen, T.B.

Theory of vision, The: Berkeley, George

There and back: Macdonald, George

There came both mist and snow: (†Michael Innes), Stewart, J.I.M.

There go the ships: MacMechan, A.M.

There is no armour: Spring, Howard

There is no hurry: Hall, Anna Maria

There is no natural religion: Blake, William

There lay the city: Karaka, D. F.

There shall be no night: Sherwood, R.E.

There was a jolly miller: Mottram, R.H.

There was a little girl: Longfellow, H.W.

There was a man in our town: Hicks, Granville

There was a ship: Le Gallienne, Richard

There was an old man: Phillpotts, Eden

There was an old woman: Phillpotts, Eden

There was an old woman: †Queen, Ellery

There was once a man: (†Orpheus C.Kerr), Newell, R.H.

There were two pirates: Cabell, James Branch

There will be bread and love: Coffin, Robert

There'll always be an England: Mais, S.P.B.

There's a birdie in the cage: O'Faolain, Sean

There's a horse in my tree: Langley, Noel

There's a porpoise close behind us: Langley, Noel

There's always Juliet: Van Druten, J.W.

There's trouble brewing: Day-Lewis, C.

Theresa Marchmont: Gore, Catherine

Theron and Aspasio: Hervey, James

Thesaurus incantatus: †Machen, Arthur

These are the maritimes: Bird, William

These bars of flesh: Stribling, T.S.

These charming people (novel and play): Arlen, Michael

These foolish things: Sadleir, Michael

These generations: †Mordaunt, Elinor

These I have loved: Mais, S.P.B.

These I would choose: Waugh, Alexander

These liberties: Knox, E.V.

These little ones: Nesbit, E.

These lovers fled away: Spring, Howard

These Lynnekers: Beresford, J.D.

These many years: Matthews, J.B.

These mortals: Harwood, H.M.

These mortals: Irwin, Margaret

These old shades: Heyer, Georgette

These people, those books: Smith, Dodie

These pretty things: Jennings, Gertrude

These restless heads: Cabell, James Branch

These splendid ships: †Divine, David

These tears of fire: Turnbull, S.C.P.

These 13: Faulkner, William

These thousand hills: Guthrie, A.B.

These times: Untermeyer, Louis

These twain: Bennett, Arnold

These were actors: Agate, J.E.

These were thy merchants: Bridges, Roy

Theses Sabbaticae: Shepard, Thomas

Theseus, Medea and lyrics: Moore, T.S.

Thespis: Gilbert, *Sir* W.S.

Thespis: Kelly, Hugh

They: Kipling, Rudyard

"They" and Brushwood Boy: Kipling, Rudyard

They and I: Jerome, Jerome K.

They are returning: Pratt, E.J.

They asked for a paper: Lewis, C.S.

They blocked the Suez Canal: Divine, A.D.

They brought their women: Ferber, Edna

They burned the books: Benét, S.V.

They call me carpenter: Sinclair, Upton

They came to a city: Priestley, J.B.

They came to Baghdad: Christie, Agatha

They could do no other: Phillpotts, Eden

They do it with mirrors: Christie, Agatha

They fought with what they had: Edmonds, W.D.

They found him dead: Heyer, Georgette

They had a horse: Edmonds, W.D.

They hanged my saintly Billy: Graves, Robert

They keep riding down all the time: Patchen, Kenneth

They knew what they wanted: Howard, S.C.

They left the land: Jacob, Naomi

They never came back: Mee, Arthur

They never come back: Plomer, W.C.F.

They never say when: †Cheyney, Peter

They of the high trails: Garland, Hamlin

They seek a country: Young, Francis Brett

They shall inherit the earth: Callaghan, M.E.

They stooped to folly: Glasgow, Ellen

They that go down: Steen, Marguerite

"They that walk in darkness": Zangwill, Israel

They walk in the city: Priestley, J.B.

They wanted to live: Roberts, C.E.M.

They went: Douglas, Norman

They went to Portugal: Macaulay, *Dame* Rose

They went to the island: Strong, L.A.G.

They were defeated: Macaulay, *Dame* Rose

They were seven: Phillpotts, Eden

They were still dancing: Waugh, Evelyn

They winter abroad: White, T.H.

They wouldn't be chessmen: Mason, A.E.W.

Thicker than water: Payn, James

Thief, The: Mayhew, Henry

Thief for the night, A: Wodehouse, P.G.

Thief in the night, A: Hornung, E.W.

Thief in the night, The: Spofford, H.E.

Thief of the moon: Slessor, Kenneth

Thief of virtue, The: Phillpotts, Eden

Thin ghost and others, A: James, M.R.

Thin ice: Mackenzie, *Sir* Compton

Thin man, The: Hammett, S.D.

Thine enemy: Gibbs, *Sir* Philip

Thing at their heels, The: (†Harrington Hext), Phillpotts, Eden

Thing of beauty, A: Cronin, A.J.

Thing to be explained, A: Housman, Laurence

Thing to love, A: Huxley, Elspeth J.

Things as they are: Godwin, William

Things as they are: Horgan, Paul

Things as they are: Stein, Gertrude

Things I have seen and people I have known: Sala, G.A.H.

Things men do, The: Davies, Rhys

Things near and far: †Machen, Arthur

Things new and old: Beerbohm, *Sir* Max

Things new and old: Inge, W.R.

Things one hears: Lynd, Robert

Things past: Sadleir, Michael

Things past redress: Birrell, Augustine

Things remembered: Hardy, A.S.

Things seen: Steevens, George Warrington

Things that annoy me: Knox, E.V.

Things that are Caesar's: Carroll, P.V.

Things that have interested me: Bennett, Arnold

Things to come: Murry, John Middleton

Things we are, The: Murry, John Middleton

Things we'd like to know: Hoffe, Monckton

Things which belong, The: Holme, Constance

Things which have interested me: Bennett, Arnold

Things worth while: Higginson, T.W.

Think fast, Mr. Moto: Marquand, J.P.

Think of the earth: Brooker, Bertram

Think of tomorrow: Monsarrat, Nicholas

Think—or be damned: Penton, B.C.

Thinking aloud: Street, A.G.

Thinking and meaning: Ayer, A.J.

Thinking it over: Pearson, Hesketh

Thinking of living: Graham, Stephen

Thinking reed, The: †West, Rebecca

Third and fourth booke of ayres, The: Campion, Thomas

Third angel, The: Weidman, Jerome

Third bullet, The: Carr, J.D.

Third bullet, The: †Carter Dickson

Third circle, The: †Norris, Frank

Third class at Miss Kaye's, The: Brazil, Angela

Third dialogue, A: Bradford, William

Third estate, The: †Bowen, Marjorie

Third hunger: Coffin, Robert

Third letter for toleration, A: Locke, John

Third letter to Archdeacon Singleton: Smith, Sydney

Third man, The: Greene, Graham

Third Mary Stuart, The: †Bowen, Marjorie

Third Miss St. Quentin, The: Molesworth, *Mrs.*

Third spring, The: Moore, T.I.

Third tour of Doctor Syntax, The: Combe, William

Third violet, The: Crane, Stephen

Third way, The: Cloete, E.F.S.G.

Third window, The: Sedgwick, A.D.

Thirde and last part of conny-catching, The: Greene, Robert

Thirst: O'Neill, Eugene

13 clocks, The: Thurber, James

Thirteen for luck: Christie, Agatha

Thirteen letters ... to John Covel: Newton, *Sir* Isaac

Thirteen o'clock: Benét, S.V.

—13 Piccadilly: †Bell, Neil

Thirteen problems, The: Christie, Agatha

Thirteen stories: Cunninghame Graham, Robert

Thirteen such years: Waugh, Alec

Thirteen travellers, The: Walpole, *Sir* Hugh

Thirteen ways home: Nesbit, E.

Thirteen worthies: Powys, L.C.

Thirteen years after: Bird, W.R.

Thirteen years in England and America: Noguchi, Yone

Thirteenth Caesar, The: Sitwell, Sacheverell

Thirteenth disciple, The: Mitchell, J.L.

Thirteenth district, The: Whitlock, Brand

Thirteenth resolution, The: Sheldon, C.M.

Thirty Canadian V.C.'s: Roberts, T.G.

Thirty clocks strike the hour: Sackville-West, Victoria

Thirty million gas masks: Campion, Sarah

Thirty personalities and a self-portrait: Lewis, P. Wyndham

Thirty pieces of silver: Fast, Howard M.

Thirty strange stories: Wells, H.G.

Thirty tales: Bates, H.E.

Thirty tales and sketches: Cunninghame Graham, Robert

$30,000 bequest, The: (†Mark Twain), Clemens, S.L.

Thirty thousand on the hook: Grey, Zane

Thirty years: Craik, *Mrs.* Dinah

Thirty years: Marquand, J.P.

Thirty years of wit: (†Eli Perkins), Landon, Melville

Thirty Years' War, The: Wedgwood, C.V.

Thirty-first of June, The: Priestley, J.B.

39 East: Crothers, Rachel

Thirty-nine steps, The: Buchan, John

Thirty-one poems: Young, A.J.

Thirty-seven conclusions of Lollards: Wycliffe, John

This above all: Sherriff, R.C.

This age of ours: Mickle, A.D.

This and that: Molesworth, *Mrs.*

This and that and the other: Belloc, Hilaire

This bed thy centre: Johnson, Pamela H.

This blessed plot: Pearson, Hesketh

This blind rose: Wolfe, Humbert

This body the earth: Green, Paul

This brunette prefers work: Loos, Anita

This charming green hat fair: Pain, B.E.O.

This dark will lighten: Mason, R.A.K.

This declaration: Green, Paul

This earth: Faulkner, William

This England: Chase, M.E.

This England: Wallace, Edgar

This fiction business: Bedford-Jones, Henry

This fine-pretty world: Mackaye, Percy

This freedom: Hutchinson, Arthur

This green earth: Bourinot, A.S.

This green mortality: Lavater, Louis

This happy breed: Coward, Noel

This have and have-not business: Angell, *Sir* Norman

This hectic age: Cross, Zora

This house is haunted: Bridges, Roy

This inconstancy: Pertwee, Roland

This India: Karaka, D.F.

This insubstantial pageant: Gibbon, Monk

This is Aucassin and Nicolette: Thomson, E.W.

This is Australia: Mudie, I.M.

This is impossible: Hamilton, Patrick

This is New York: Sherwood, R.E.

This is Nova Scotia: Bird, W.R.

This is Rome: Morton, H.V.

This is Russia: Griffith, Hubert

This is Simpson's: Denison, Merrill

This is the end: Benson, Stella

This is the Holy Land: Morton, H.V.

This is the school-room: Monsarrat, Nicholas

This is your century: Trease, Geoffrey

This is your day: Untermeyer, Louis

This is your wife: Greenwood, Walter

This isn't the end: Widdemer, Margaret

This land, these people: Fast, Howard M.

This life we live: †Gregory, Margaret, (Velia Ercole)

This little world: Young, Francis Brett

This mad ideal: Dell, Floyd

This man and this woman: Farrell, James

This man is dangerous: †Cheyney, Peter

This measure: Adams, Leonie

This misery of boots: Wells, H.G.

This modern poetry: Deutsch, Babette

This mortal coil: Allen, Grant

This music crept by me upon the waters: MacLeish, Archibald

This nettle danger: Gibbs, *Sir* Philip

This other Eden: Knox, E.V.

This our divine pain: Barfield, Owen

This passion called love: Glyn, Elinor

This people: Lewisohn, Ludwig

This picture and that: Matthews, J.B.

This plot of earth: Massingham, Harold

This porcelain clay: Jacob, Naomi

This proud heart: Buck, Pearl

This publican: †Yates, Dornford

This room and this gin and these sandwiches: Wilson, Edmund

This Russian business: Brown, E.T.

This sceptred isle: Knight, G.W.

This shining woman: †Preedy, George

This side of paradise: Fitzgerald, F. Scott

This simian world: Day, C.S.

This son of Vulcan: Besant, *Sir* Walter and James Rice

This sorry scheme: Marshall, Bruce

This stage of fools: Merrick, Leonard

This strange adventure: Rinehart, Mary Roberts

This, that and the other: Moulton, E.L.

This time for love: †Bell, Neil

This troubled world: Drinkwater, John

This troublesome world: Barker, M.A.

This unknown island: Mais, S.P.B.

This very earth: Caldwell, Erskine Preston

This vital flesh: †Baylebridge, W.

This wanderer: Golding, Louis

This was a man: Coward, Noel

This was a man: Mannin, Ethel

This was England: Vachell, H.A.

This was my Newport: Elliott, M.H.

This way to heaven: Evans, Caradoc

This way to paradise: Huxley, Aldous

This woman business: Levy, Benn W.

This wound: Derleth, A.W.

This year, next year: De la Mare, Walter

Thistle and the pen: Linklater, Eric

Thistledown: Winter, William

Thistledown and thunder: Bolitho, H.H.

Tho. Wyatis translatyon of Plutarckes boke of the quyete of mynde: Wyatt, *Sir* Thomas

Thomas à Becket: Darley, George

Thomas and Sally: Bickerstaffe, Isaac

Thomas Bewick and his pupils: Dobson, Henry Austin

Thomas Carlyle: Conway, Moncure Daniel

Thomas Chalmers, preacher, philosopher, and statesman: Oliphant, Margaret

Thomas Chandler Haliburton: Logan, J.D.

Thomas Cranmer of Canterbury: Williams, Charles

Thomas Edwards: Griffith, Llewelyn

Thomas Girtin: Binyon, Laurence

Thomas Gray: Benson, A.C.

Thomas Hardy: Abercrombie, Lascelles

Thomas Hardy: Blunden, Edmund

Thomas Hardy: Tomlinson, H.M.

Thomas Hardy from serial to novel: Chase, M.E.

Thomas Henry: Ridge, W. Pett

Thomas Henry Huxley as a man of letters: Huxley, Aldous

Thomas Jefferson; the making of a President: Dos Passos, John

Thomas Jefferson, the serene citizen from Monticello: Van Loon, Hendrik

Thomas Love Peacock: Priestley, J.B.

Thomas More: Hollis, Christopher

Thomas Muskerry: Colum, Padraic

Thomas Nabbes: Swinburne, A.C.

Thomas of Reading: Deloney, Thomas

Thomas Paine: Conway, Moncure Daniel

Thomas Paine, author-soldier of the American revolution: Lippard, George

Thomas Pownall: Lighthall, W.D.

Thomas Stevenson civil engineer: Stevenson, R.L.

Thomas—Thomas—Anvil—Thomas: Coffin, Robert

Thomas Wilson, a discourse of usury: Tawney, R.H.

Thomas Wingfold, curate: Macdonald, George

Thomas Wolfe: Johnson, Pamela H.

Thomas Wolfe as I knew him: Fisher, V.A.

Thomasheen James: Walsh, Maurice

Thomasina: Gallico, Paul

Thomyris, Queen of Scythia: Motteux, P.A.

Thor, with angels: Fry, Christopher

Thoreau: Canby, Henry Seidel

Thoreau: Channing, William Ellery

Thoreau: Dreiser, Theodore

Thoreau: Stewart, George

Thoreau Macdonald: Pierce, Lorne

Thoreau's last letter: Robinson, E.A.

Thorgils of Treadholt: Hewlett, Maurice

Thorley Weir: Benson, E.F.

Thorn in her flesh: Phillpotts, Eden

Thorn in the flesh, A: Broughton, Rhoda

Thorn in the flesh, A: Wiggin, Kate

Thorofare: Morley, C.D.

Thorough good cook, The: Sala, G.A.H.

Thoroughfares: Gibson, Wilfred

Those ancient lands: Golding, Louis

Those barren leaves: Huxley, Aldous

Those days: an autobiography: Bentley, E.C.

Those delightful Americans: Duncan, S.J.

Those folk of Bulboro: Wallace, Edgar

Those foreigners: Postgate, Raymond

Those not elect: Adams, Leonie

Those other days: Oppenheim, E. Phillips

Those United States: Bennett, Arnold

Those were the days: Sitwell, *Sir* Osbert

Thou and the other one: Barr, A.E.H.

Thou art the man: Braddon, Mary Elizabeth

Thou shalt not kill: Lowndes, *Mrs.* Belloc

Thou shell of death: Day-Lewis, C.

Though life us do part: Ward, E.S.

Thought and word: Allingham, William

Thought relics: Tagore, *Sir* R.

Thoughts: a series of sonnets: Harpur, Charles

Thoughts after Lambeth: Eliot, T.S.

Thoughts and adventures: Churchill, *Sir* Winston

Thoughts and aphorisms: Ghose, Sri Aurobindo

Thoughts and details on scarcity: Burke, Edmund

Thoughts and glimpses: Ghose, Sri Aurobindo

Thoughts in past years: Williams, Isaac

Thoughts in prose and verse: Phillpotts, Eden

Thoughts in the cloister and the crowd: Helps, *Sir* Arthur

Thoughts in the wilderness: Priestley, J.B.

Thoughts in wartime: Temple, William

Thoughts, moods and ideals: Lighthall, W.D.

Thoughts occasioned by Dr. Parr's Spital sermon: Godwin, William

Thoughts of my cats: Marshall, Bruce

Thoughts on African colonization: Garrison, W.L.

Thoughts on art, philosophy and religion: Dobell, S.T.

Thoughts on education: Burnet, Gilbert

Thoughts on great mysteries: Faber, F.W.

Thoughts on laughter: Montagu, Basil

Thoughts on man, his nature, productions and discourses: Godwin, William

Thoughts on Parliamentary Reform: Jenyns, Soame

Thoughts on parliamentary reform: Mill, John Stewart

Thoughts on penitentiaries and prison discipline: Carey, Mathew

Thoughts on some problems of the day: Temple, William

Thoughts on South Africa: Schreiner, Oliver

Thoughts on the cause of the present discontents: Burke, Edmund

Thoughts on the causes and consequences of the present high price of provisions: Jenyns, Soame

Thoughts on the Divine love: Temple, William

Thoughts on the education of character: Livingstone, Sir Richard

Thoughts on the education of her daughters: Wollstonecraft, Mary

Thoughts on the effects of the British Government on the State of India: Tennant, William

Thoughts on the importance of the manners of the great to general society: More, Hannah

Thoughts on the late transactions respecting Falkland's Islands: Johnson, Samuel

Thoughts on the poets: Tuckerman, H.T.

Thoughts on the relative value of fresco and oil painting, as applied to the architectural decorations of the Houses of Parliament: Haydon, Benjamin

Thoughts on the war: Murray, Gilbert

Thoughts on things: †Armstrong, Anthony

Thoughts on war: Liddell Hart, B.

Thoughts upon female education: Rush, Benjamin

Thoughts upon government: Helps, Sir Arthur

Thoughts upon the aristocracy of England: Brougham, Henry

Thoughts without words: Day, C.S.

Thousand and one afternoons in Chicago, A: Hecht, Ben

Thousand and one churches, The: Bell, Gertrude

Thousand and one nights, The: Lane, Edward

$1,000 a week: Farrell, James

Thousand for Sicily: Trease, Geoffrey

Thousand islands, The: Machar, A.M.

Thousand mile walk to the Gulf, A: Muir, John

Thousand years ago, A: Mackaye, Percy

Thousandth woman, The: Hornung, E.W.

Thrasymachus: Joad, C.E.M.

Thread of gold, The: Benson, A.C.

Thread of scarlet, A: Marshall, Bruce

Three: Frankau, Pamela

Three: Kantor, Mackinlay

Three academic pieces: Stevens, Wallace

Three act tragedy: Christie, Agatha

Three against the world: Kaye-Smith, Sheila

Three arrows: Young, E.R.

Three asses in the Pyrenees: Walmsley, Leo

Three Australian three-act plays: Cusack, E.D.

Three birds: Maltby, H.F.

Three black Pennys, The: Hergesheimer, Joseph

Three book types: Gill, Eric

Three books of song: Longfellow, H.W.

Three Brontës, The: Sinclair, May

Three brothers, The: Bannister, N.H.

Three brothers, The: Muir, Edwin

Three brothers, The: Oliphant, Margaret

Three brothers, The: Phillpotts, Eden

Three by candlelight: (Stephen Southwold), †Bell, Neil

Three came to Ville Marie: Sullivan, Alan

Three cards and a widow: Percy, Edward

Three centuries of Canadian nursing: Gibbon, J.M.

Three centuries of Harvard, 1636–1936: Morison, S.E.

Three clerks, The: Trollope, Anthony

Three coffins, The: Carr, J.D.

Three comrades of Jesus: Watson, A.D.

Three corvettes: Monsarrat, Nicholas

Three couriers, The: Mackenzie, Sir Compton

Three cousins, The: Trollope, Frances

Three days: Macaulay, Dame Rose

Three dialogues between Hylas and Philonous: Berkeley, George

Three dialogues on the amusements of clergymen: Gilpin, William

Three Edwards: Costain, T.B.

Three eighteenth century figures: Dobrée, Bonamy

Three elephant power: (†The Banjo), Paterson, A.B.

Three English women in America: Pope-Hennessy, Dame Una

Three Englishmen: Frankau, Gilbert

Three episodes in Massachusetts history: Adams, C.F.

Three eras of modern poetry: Sitwell, Edith

Three essays in method: Berenson, Bernhard

Three essays on America: Brooks, Van Wyck

Three essays: on picturesque beauty; on picturesque travel; and on sketching landscape: Gilpin, William

Three essays on religion: Mill, John Stuart

Three experimental imprints: Allen, Hervey

Three fantasies: Pain, B.E.O.

Three fates, The: Crawford, F. Marion

Three feathers: Black, William

Three fevers: Walmsley, Leo

Three fishers, The: †Beeding, Francis

Three flights up: Howard, S.C.

Three Fredericton poets: writers of the University of New Brunswick and the New Dominion: Pierce, Lorne

Three French moralists, and the gallantry of France: Gosse, *Sir* Edmund

Three friends: Bridges, Robert

Three friends, The: Collins, Norman

Three generations: Elliott, M.H.

Three gentlemen, The: Mason, A.E.W.

Three go back: Mitchell, J.L.

Three golden hairs, The: Sidgwick, Ethel

Three grains of spirituall frankincense: Wither, George

Three great sanctuaries of Tuscany: Vallombrosa, Camaldoli, Laverna, The: Bury, *Lady* C.S.M.

Three green bottles: De Selincourt, Aubrey

Three Gringos in Venezuela and Central America: Davis, R.H.

Three Guineas: Woolf, Virginia

Three heroines of New England romance: Guiney, L.I.

Three hills, The: Squire, *Sir* J.C.

Three histories: Behn, *Mrs.* Afra

Three homes: Robinson, E.S.L.

Three hostages, The: Buchan, John

Three hours: Hale, S.J.B.

Three hours after marriage: Gay, John

Three houses: Thirkell, Angela

Three hundred games and pastimes: Lucas, E.V.

Three hundredth anniversary of Shakespeare's birth: Courthorpe, William John

Three hunting songs: Warburton, R.E.E.

Three hymns to Lenin: †McDiarmid, Hugh

Three impostors, The: †Machen, Arthur

Three Irish bardic tales: Todhunter, John

Three jolly gentlemen: Golding, Louis

Three just men, The: Wallace, Edgar

Three kingdoms: Jameson, Storm

Three kings, The: Grigson, Geoffrey

Three kings, The: Lawson, Will

Three knaves, The: Phillpotts, Eden

Three laws: Bale, John

Three laws of politics, The: Collingwood, R.G.

Three lectures delivered at the Royal Institution, on the Ancien Régime: Kingsley, Charles

Three lectures upon animal life: Rush, Benjamin

Three letters to Nikai Tikonov: Lindsay, Jack

Three letters to the editor of the "Cornhill Magazine" on public education: Higgins, Matthew James

Three letters, written in Spain, to D. Francisco Riguelme: Landor, W.S.

Three little dramas for marionettes (trn.): Sutro, Alfred

Three little kittens: Ballantyne, R.M.

Three little maids: Turner, E.S.

Three little spades: Warner, A.B.

Three lives, stories of the good Anna, Melanctha and the gentle Lena: Stein, Gertrude

Three lovers, The: Swinnerton, Frank

Three loves: Cronin, A.J.

Three lyric songs: Clarke, G.H.

Three maidens, The: Phillpotts, Eden

Three marriages: †Delafield, E.M.

Three Marys, The: Niven, F.J

Three men: Colum, Padraic

Three men and Jennie: Jacob, Naomi

Three men die: Millin, Sarah Gertrude

Three men in a boat: Jerome, Jerome K.

Three men in new suits: Priestley, J.B.

Three men on the Bummel: Jerome, Jerome K.

Three men's war: Mottram, R.H.

Three Miss Kings, The: Cambridge, Ada

Three moneths observations of the Low-Countries: Feltham, Owen

Three mulla-mulgars, The: De la Mare, Walter

Three musketeers, The: Wodehouse, P.G.

Three Northern love stories: (trn.): Morris, William

Three notable stories: Hardy, Thomas

Three notelets on Shakespeare: Thoms, W.J.

Three oak mystery, The: Wallace, Edgar

Three of a kind: Cain, James

Three of a kind: †Shute, Nevil

Three of them: Doyle, *Sir* Arthur Conan

Three of us, The: Crothers, Rachel

Three old brothers: †O'Connor, Frank

Three operettas. Music by Oscar Weil: Bunner, H.C.

Three pair of heels: †Bell, Neil

Three papers presented to the Royal Society against Dr. Wallis: Hobbes, Thomas

Three partners: Harte, Bret

Three paths, The: Kavanagh, Julia

Three pearls, The: Fortescue, *Sir* John

Three personal records of the war: Mottram, R.H.

Three personal records of the war: Partridge, Eric

Three persons: Macphail, *Sir* Andrew

Three Phi Beta Kappa addresses: Adams, C.F.

Three philosophical poets: Santayana, George

Three pigeons, The: †Armstrong, Anthony

Three pirates of Penzance: Rinehart, Mary Roberts

Three plays: The garbage man; Airways inc; Fortune heights: Dos Passos, John

Three plays without words: Rice, Elmer

Three Premiers of Nova Scotia: Saunders, E.M.

Three pretty men: Cannan, Gilbert

Three problems for Solar Pons: Derleth, A.W.

Three proper, and wittie, familiar letters: Harvey, Gabriel

Three proper, and wittie, familiar letters: Spenser, Edmund

Three reliques of ancient western poetry: Wilson, Edmund

Three resurrections and the triumph of Maeve, The: Gore-Booth, E.S.

Three rooms: Deeping, Warwick

Three score and ten: Barr, A.E.H.

Three score and ten: Waugh, Alec

Three scouts, The: Trowbridge, J.T.

Three sea songs: MacMechan, A.M.

Three sisters, The: Sinclair, May

Three soldiers: Dos Passos, John

Three sorrows of story-telling and ballads of St. Columkille, The: Hyde, Douglas

Three speeches in favour of a measure for an extension of copyright: Talfourd, Sir T.N.

Three stalwarts: Drums along the Mohawk; Rome haul; and Erie Water: Edmonds, W.D.

Three statues of St. Germain: Mackaye, Percy

Three stories and ten poems: Hemingway, Ernest

Three strange lovers: Calverton, V.F.

Three strangers, The: Lee, Harriet

Three sunsets: †Carroll, Lewis

Three tales of Hamlet: Heppenstall, Rayner

Three tales of Venice: (†Baron Corvo), Rolfe, Frederick

Three taps, The: Knox, R.A.

Three taverns, The: Robinson, E.A.

Three terms at Uplands: Brazil, Angela

Three things: Glyn, Elinor

Three things: Yeats, W.B.

Three times dead: Braddon, Mary Elizabeth

Three times three: Saroyan, William

Three times tried: Farjeon, B.L.

Three tours of Dr. Syntax, The: Combe, William

Three tracts relating to Spanish and Portuguese affairs: Bentham, Jeremy

Three villages: Howells, W.D.

Three voices of poetry, The: Eliot, T.S.

Three voyages of Martin Frobisher: Stefansson, V.

Three warnings to John Bull: Thrale, H.L.

Three wayfarers, The: Hardy, Thomas

Three ways home: Kaye-Smith, Sheila

Three ways of thought in Ancient China: Waley, Arthur

Three weeks: Glyn, Elinor

Three weeks in politics: Bangs, John Kendrick

Three who died: Derleth, A.W.

Three wives: Seymour, Beatrice Kean

Three wizards and a witch: Riddell, Mrs. J.H.

Three women: Wilcox, Ella Wheeler

Three women and Mr. Frank Cardwell: Ridge, W.Pett

Three wonder plays: Gregory, Lady Augusta

Three wonders of this age, The: Heywood, Thomas

Three worlds: Van Doren, Carl

Three years in Europe, 1868 to 1871: Dutt, R.C.

Three years, 1924–1927: Mencken, H.L.

Three-coloured pencil, The: Mais, S.P.B.

Threefold cord, A: Macdonald, George

Threefold cord: philosophy, science, religion, A: Samuel, Herbert, 1st Viscount

Three-quarter length portrait of Michael Arlen: Sitwell, Sir Osbert

Three-quarter length portrait of Viscountess Wimborne, A: Sitwell, Sir Osbert

Threescore: Calvert, George Henry

Threiplauds of Fingask, The: Chambers, Robert

Threnodia Augustalis: Dryden, John

Threnodia Augustalis: Goldsmith, Oliver

Threshing day, A: Bates, H.E.

Threshold of Atrides, The: Warren, J.B.L.

Thrice a stranger: Brittain, Vera

Thrice the brindled cat hath mew'd: Davies, Robertson

Thrift: Smiles, Samuel

Thrill of tradition, The: Moffatt, James

Throne of David, The: Ingraham, J.H.

Throstle, The: Tennyson, Alfred Lord

Through a glass darkly: Phillpotts, Eden

Through Afro-America: an English reading of the race problem: Archer, William

Through all the changing scenes of life: Baring-Gould, Sabine

Through another gate: Bridges, Roy

Through Bosnia, etc.: Evans, Sir A.J.

Through Connemara in a governess cart: Somerville, E.

Through eyes of youth: Roberts, C.E.M.

Through flood and flame: Baring-Gould, Sabine

Through Glacier Park: Rinehart, Mary Roberts

Through lands of the Bible: Morton, H.V.

Through literature to life: Raymond, Ernest

Through Mashonaland with pick and pen: Fitzpatrick, Sir J.P.

Through nature to God: Fiske, John

Through one administration: Burnett, Frances Hodgson

Through Russian Central Asia: Graham, Stephen

Through space and time: Jeans, *Sir* James

Through the crack: Blackwood, Algernon

Through the eye of the needle: Howells, W.D.

Through the fog of war: Liddell Hart, B.

Through the fourth wall: Darlington, W.A.

Through the long night: Linton, Eliza

Through the Mackenzie basin: Mair, Charles

Through the magic door: Doyle, *Sir* Arthur Conan

Through the Menin gate: Mottram, R.H.

Through the postern gate: Barclay, F.L.

Through the storm: Gibbs, *Sir* Philip

Through the Torii: Noguchi, Yone

Through the twilight: Carman, Bliss

Through the wheat: Boyd, Thomas

Through the wilderness: Massingham, Harold

Through the woods: Bates, H.E.

Through the Zulu country: Mitford, Bertram

Through thirty years: Steed, H.W.

Through wintry terrors: Sigerson, Dora

Throwback, The: Lewis, A.H.

Thrush and the jay, The: Lynd, Sylvia

Thucydides: Livingstone, *Sir* Richard

Thumping legacy, The: Morton, J.M.

Thunder mountain: Grey, Zane

Thunder of new wings, The: De la Roche, Mazo

Thunder of Valmy: Trease, Geoffrey

Thunder on the left: Morley, C.D.

Thunder underground: Lindsay, Jack

Thunderbolt, The: Pinero, *Sir* A.W.

Thunderer, The: Beck, *Mrs.* Lily

Thundering herd, The: Grey, Zane

Thunderstorm: Stern, G.B.

Thursday afternoons: Dickens, Monica

Thursday evening: Morley, C.D.

Thursdays and Fridays: Agate, J.E.

Thurso's landing: Jeffers, J.R.

Thus far and no further: Godden, Rumer

Thus her tale: De la Mare, Walter

Thus to revisit: Ford, Ford Madox

Thy first begotten: †Bell, Neil

Thy neighbour's wife: O'Flaherty, Liam

Thy rod and thy staff: Benson, A.C.

Thy servant a dog: Kipling, Rudyard

Thyra Varrick: Barr, A.E.H.

Thyrza: Gissing, George

Tiberius: Adams, Francis

Tiburon: Tennant, Kylie

Ticket-of-leave man, The: Taylor, Tom

Tickless time: Glaspell, Susan

Tick-tock tales: (Stephen Southwold), †Bell, Neil

Ticky: Gibbons, Stella

Ticonderoga: James, G.P.R.

Tidal creek: Finlayson, Roderick

Tid'apa: Frankau, Gilbert

Tiddledywink tales: Bangs, John Kendrick

Tiddledywink's poetry book, The: Bangs, John Kendrick

Tide of life, The: Kirkconnell, Watson

Tide of love, The: O'Hagan, Thomas

Tide of time, The: Masters, E.L.

Tidefall: Raddall, T.H.

Tidemarks: Tomlinson, H.M.

Tides: Drinkwater, John

Tidings: Carman, Bliss

Tidstankar: Wells, H.G.

Tie that binds, The: Porter, E.H.

Tiger: †Brand, Max

Tiger: Bynner, Witter

Tiger claws: Packard, F.L.

Tiger hunter, The: Reid, T.M.

Tiger in the house, The: Van Vechten, Carl

Tiger in the smoke, The: Allingham, Margery

Tiger joy: Benét, S.V.

Tiger who walks alone, The: Skinner, C.L.

Tiger-lilies: Lanier, Sidney

Tiger's cub, A: Phillpotts, Eden

Tigress in Prothero, A: Swinnerton, Frank

Tigress on the hearth, The: Sharp, Margery

Tilbury Nego: Whyte-Melville, G.J.

Tilda: Van Doren, Mark

Till death do us part: Carr, J.D.

Till I end my song: Gibbings, Robert

Till the day I die: Odets, Clifford

Till we have faces: Lewis, C.S.

Tilly of Bloomsbury: (†Ian Hay), Beith, *Sir* John Hay

Tillyloss scandal, A: Barrie, *Sir* J.M.

Tilted cart, The: Gilmore, Mary

Tim Rabbit and company: Uttley, Alison

Tim Rabbit's dozen: Uttley, Alison

Timbal Gulch trail: †Brand, Max

Timber; or Discoveries: Jonson, Ben

Timber wolves: Cronin, B.C.

Timbuctoo: Hallam, Arthur Henry

Timbuctoo: Tennyson, Alfred *Lord*

Time and chance: Connell, John

Time and chance: Hubbard, Elbert

Time and change: Burroughs, John

Time and eternity: Cannan, Gilbert

Time and memory: Lucas, F.L.

Time and the business: Jones, Jack

Time and the Conways: Priestley, J.B.

Time and the gods: Dunsany, Edward Plunkett, *Baron*

Time and the hour: Spring, Howard

Time and the woman: Pryce, Richard

Time and tide by Weare and Tyne: Ruskin, John

Time and time again: Hilton, James

Time and western man: Lewis, P.Wyndham

Time before this, The: Monsarrat, Nicholas

Time enough later: Tennant, Kylie

Time exposures (†Search light): Frank, Waldo

Time flies: Rossetti, Christina

Time importuned: Warner, Sylvia Townsend

Time in Rome, A: Bowen, E.D.C.

Time in the rock: Aiken, Conrad

Time is not yet ripe, The: Esson, T.L.B.

Time is ripe, The: Greenwood, Walter

Time machine, The: Wells, H.G.

Time marches on: Rinehart, Mary Roberts

Time must have a stop: Huxley, Aldous

Time of fortune, A: Appel, Benjamin

Time of hope: Snow, C.P.

Time of man, The: Roberts, E.M.

Time of the assassins, The: Miller, Henry

Time of your life, The: Saroyan, William

Time piece: Jacob, Naomi

Time poets, The: Heming, William

Time stands: Seymour, W.K.

Time to act, A: MacLeish, Archibald

Time to be going: Mottram, R.H.

Time to dance, A: Day-Lewis, C.

Time to heal: Deeping, Warwick

Time to keep, A: Sutherland, H.G.

Time to laugh, A: Davies, Rhys

Time to live: Lindsay, Jack

Time to speak, A: MacLeish, Archibald

Time vindicated: Jonson, Ben

Time with a gift of tears: Bax, Clifford

Time works wonders: Jerrold, Douglas

Timeless land, The: Dark, Eleanor

Timeless quest, The: Hassall, Christopher

Timeless serpent, The: Fulford, R.T.B.

Timeless travellers, The: MacKay, I.E.

Timeless world: Holcroft, M.H.

Timely caution, A: Wither, George

Times, The: Churchill, Charles

Times, The: Pinero, *Sir* A.W.

Times, The: Saxe, J.G.

Times and tendencies: Repplier, Agnes

Time's increase: Mottram, R.H.

Time's joke: Dunsany, Edward Plunkett, *Baron*

Time's laughingstocks: Hardy, Thomas

Times of Melville and Whitman, The: Brooks, Van Wyck

Times of men are in the hand of God, The: Mather, Increase

Times on the American War, The: Stephen, *Sir* Leslie

Time's rocket: †O'Connor, Frank

Timoleon: Melville, Herman

Timon of Athens: Shakespeare, William

Timotheus, the future of the theatre: Dobrée, Bonamy

Timothy: Palmer, J.L.

Timothy Dexter revisited: Marquand, J.P.

Timothy Titcomb's testimony against wine: Holland, J.G.

Timothy's angels: Benet, W.R.

Timothy's quest: Wiggin, Kate

Timour the Tartar!: Brooks, C.W.S.

Timour the Tartar: Lewis, Matthew Gregory

Tin trumpet, The: Smith, Horatio

Tin wedding: Leech, M.K.

Ting-a-ling: Stockton, F.R.

Tinker, tailor: Herbert, *Sir* A.P.

Tinker's leave: Baring, Maurice

Tinker's wedding, The: Synge, J.M.

Tinkham brother's tide-mill, The: Trowbridge, J.T.

Tinkle of bells, A: Riley, J.W.

Tinkling cymbals: Fawcett, Edgar

Tinsel Eden: Mannin, Ethel

Tinted Venus, The: †Anstey, F.

Tintoretto: Newton, Eric

Tiny: Ward, E.S.

Tiny Carteret: †Sapper

Tiny garments: Skinner, C.O.

Tiny house, The: Turner, E.S.

Tiny Luttrell: Hornung, E.W.

Tiny town tales: Logan, J.D.

Tinykin's transformations: Lemon, Mark

Tip on a dead jockey: Shaw, Irwin

Tip toes: Gershwin, Ira

Tippoo Sultaun: Taylor, P.M.

Tired church members: Warner, A.B.

Tired petitioner, The: Wither, George

Tiresias: Tennyson, Alfred *Lord*

Tiresias: Woolner, Thomas

Tis merrie when gossips meete: Rowlands, Samuel

Tis pitty shees a whore: Ford, John

Tis well it's no worse: Bickerstaffe, Isaac

Tish: Rinehart, Mary Roberts

Tish plays the game: Rinehart, Mary Roberts

Tish, the chronicle of her escapades: Rinehart, Mary Roberts

Titan, The: Dreiser, Theodore

Titania: Cripps, A.S.

Titanic, The: Pratt, E.J.

Titans, The: Doughty, C.M.

Titans: Pratt, E.J.

Titcomb's letters to young people, single and married: Holland, J.G.

Tithe barn, The: Powys, T.F.

Tithe-proctor, The: Carleton, William

Tithes too hot to be touched: Spelman, *Sir* Henry

Title, The: Bennett, Arnold

Title clear: Duncan, S.J.

Title-mart, The: Churchill, Winston

Tito and his people: Fast, Howard M.

Titus Andronicus: Shakespeare, William

Titus and Berenice: Otway, Thomas

Titus the toad: Kirkconnell, Watson

Tiverton tales: Brown, Alice

T—l—nd's invitation to dismal, to dine with the Calves-head Club: Swift, Jonathan

To a Chicadee: Carman, Bliss

To a friend in the wilderness: Fairburn, A.R.D.

To a girl dancing: Sterling, George

To a god unknown: Steinbeck, John

To a lady on her passion for old china: Gay, John

To a young gentleman in love: Prior, Matthew

To a young wretch: Frost, Robert

To any dead officer (who left school for the army in 1914): Sassoon, Siegfried

To arms!: Lindsay, Jack

To awaken Pegasus: Dunsany, Edward Plunkett, *Baron*

To be a farmer's boy: Street, A.G.

To be a pilgrim: Cary, Joyce

To be read at dusk: Dickens, Charles

To be recited to Flossie on her birthday: Williams, W.C.

To be taken with salt: McArthur, Peter

To bed at noon: Gielgud, Val

To bed at noon: †Shearing, Joseph

To Bobchen Haas: Stein, Gertrude

To call her mine: Besant, *Sir* Walter

To catch a spy: Ambler, Eric

To Christopher Duke of Albemarle, on his voyage to Jamaica: Behn, *Mrs.* Afra

To circumjack Cencrastus: †McDiarmid, Hugh

To Corona: †Cheyney, Peter

To Cuba and back: Dana, R.H. *junior*

To Doctor D—l—y on the libels writ against him: Swift, Jonathan

To Elia: Clare, John

To God: from the wearynations: †Maurice, Furnley

To H.R.H. Princess Beatrice: Tennyson, Alfred *Lord*

To have and have not: Hemingway, Ernest

To have or to be—take your choice: Van Loon, Hendrik

To have the honour: Milne, A.A.

To hell, with Crabb Robinson: Mottram, R.H.

To Hell, with culture: Read, *Sir* Herbert

To him that hath: †Connor, Ralph

To his excellence Richard Earle of Arran: Wilson, John

To His Grace, the Arch-Bishop of Dublin: Swift, Jonathan

To his sacred Majesty: Dryden, John

To his sonne, upon his Minerva: Massinger, Philip

To kill a cat: Pertwee, Roland

To Leda: Moore, T.S.

To leeward: Crawford, F. Marion

To let: Galsworthy, John

To London Town: Morrison, Arthur

To love and be wise: (†Tey Josephine), Mackintosh, Elizabeth

To love and to cherish: Bird, W.R.

To M. Gabriell Harvey: Spenser, Edmund

To M(argaret) B(urne) J(ones): Wilde, Oscar

To marry or not to marry: Inchbald, *Mrs.* Elizabeth

To meet the McGregors: Linklater, Eric

To meet the sun: Fitzgerald, R.D.

To Miss Georgiana, youngest daughter of Lord Carteret: Philips, Ambrose

To Miss Margaret Pulteney, daughter of Daniel Pulteney, Esq.: Philips, Ambrose

To Mr. Frederic Villiers: Daley, Victor

To Mr. Law: Ramsay, Allan

To my honourable freinde Sir Francis Foljambe knight and baronet: Massinger, Philip

To my Lady Morton: Waller, Edmund

To my Lord Chancellor: Dryden, John

To my mother: Sassoon, Siegfried

To my sister!: Gordon, A.L.

To my sons: Wright, H.B.

To nature: Blunden, Edmund

To "Our Club": Boker, George Henry

To paint is to love again: Miller, Henry

To provident landlords and capitalists: Shaw, G.B.

To Quito and back: Hecht, Ben

To race again: Green, Anne

To right the wrong: Lyall, Edna

To Rosemounde: Chaucer, Geoffrey

To sea, to sea: †Mordaunt, Elinor

To see ourselves: †Delafield, E.M.

To Shakespeare after three hundred years: Hardy, Thomas

To Sir Godfrey Kneller, at his country seat: Tickell, Thomas

To step aside: Coward, Noel

To Stratford with love: Monsarrat, Nicholas

To teach the senators wisdom: Masterman, *Sir* J.C.

To tell you the truth: Merrick, Leonard

To the bitter end: Braddon, Mary Elizabeth

To the Canadian mothers: Scott, D.C.

To the chapel perilous: Mitchison, Naomi

To the chief of police at Los Angeles: Sinclair, Upton

To the Duke on his return: Lee, Nathaniel

To the electors of London University, general election 1923: Wells, H.G.

To the end of the trail: Hovey, Richard

To the exequies of the Honourable Sir Antonye Alexander Knight: Drummond of Hawthornden, William

To the Finland station: Wilson, Edmund

To the Freelands tulip at Christmas: Colum, Padraic

To the frozen south: Villiers, A.J.

To the Honourable Duncan Forbes of Culloden: Ramsay, Allan

To the Honourable Miss Carteret: Philips, Ambrose

To the Indies: Forester, C.S.

To the Isles of Spice: Clune, Frank

To the King, an ode on his Majesty's arrival in Holland: Prior, Matthew

To the King, upon his Majesties happy return: Waller, Edmund

To the King's Most Excellent Majesty: Wheatley, Phillis

To the ladies: Connelly, Marc

To the ladies: Kaufman, G.S.

To the last man: Grey, Zane

To the lighthouse: Woolf, Virginia

To the Majestie of King James: Drayton, Michael

To the memory of George Duke of Buckingham: Behn, *Mrs.* Afra

To the memory of a lady lately deceased: Lyttelton, George *Baron*

To the most beautiful Scots ladies: Ramsay, Allan

To the North: Bowen, E.D.C.

To the one I love best: Bemelmans, Ludwig

To the Parliament of the Commonwealth: Wither, George

To the pious memory of the accomplisht young lady Mrs. Anne Killigrew: Dryden, John

To the Prince and Princess of Orange upon their marriage: Lee, Nathaniel

To the public: Blake, William

To the public danger: Hamilton, Patrick

To the quayside: Golding, Louis

To the Queen: Wordsworth, William

To the Queen, upon her Majesty's birthday: Waller, Edmund

To the Queen's taste: †Queen, Ellery

To the red rose: Sassoon, Siegfried

To the Right Honourable Mr. Harley, wounded by Guiscard: Prior, Matthew

To the rough riders: Bangs, John Kendrick

To the sister of Charles Lamb: Landor, W.S.

To the students: Gandhi, M.K.

To the sweet singer of Israel: Lindsay, N.V.

To the United States Senate: Lindsay, N.V.

To the University of Cambridge in New England: Wheatley, Phillis

To the unknown god: Murry, John Middleton

To the wood no more: Raymond, Ernest

To Themis: Blunden, Edmund

To think of tea!: Repplier, Agnes

To Verhaeren: Seymour, W.K.

To W.T.W.D.: Swinburne, A.C.

To wake the dead: Carr, J.D.

To whom else: Graves, Robert

To whom it may concern: Farrell, James

To whom we belong: Hodge, H.E.

To you, Mr. Chips: Hilton, James

Toad: Cronin, B.C.

Toad of Toad Hall: Milne, A.A.

Tobacco and alcohol: Fiske, John

Tobacco Road: Caldwell, Erskine Preston

Tobias and the angel: †Bridie, James

Tobit transplanted: Benson, Stella

Tobruk to Turkey: Clune, Frank

Toby and the nighttime: Horgan, Paul

Toby Shad: †Taffrail

Tocsin of revolt, The: Matthews, J.B.

Tocsin of social life, The: Stewart, John

Today and forever: Buck, Pearl

Today and yesterday: Young, G.M.

Today is Friday: Hemingway, Ernest

Today is mine: †Bowen, Marjorie

Together: Douglas, Norman

Together: Herrick, Robert

Together and apart: Kennedy, Margaret

Toilers of Babylon: Farjeon, B.L.

Toilers of the field, The: Jefferies, Richard

Toilers of the hills: Fisher, V.A.

Toinette: Tourgée, A.W.

Tokefield papers: Swinnerton, Frank

Tol'able David: Hergesheimer, Joseph

Told: Mackenzie, *Sir* Compton

Told after supper: Jerome, Jerome K.

Told again: De la Mare, Walter

Told at the Plume: Phillpotts, Eden

Told by an idiot: Macaulay, *Dame* Rose

Told by Uncle Remus: Harris, J.C.

Told in the twilight: Wood, Ellen

Tolerance: Van Loon, Hendrik

Toll of the Bush, The: Satchell, William

Toll of the tides, The: Roberts, T.G.

Toll-gate, The: Heyer, Georgette

Tolstoy: Garnett, Edward

Tolstoy, the inner drama: Fausset, Hugh

Tom: Cummings, E.E.

Tom Akerley: Roberts, T.G.

Tom Bailey's adventures: Aldrich, Thomas Bailey

Tom Bowling: Chamier, Frederick

Tom Brown at Oxford: Hughes, Thomas

Tom Brown's school days: Hughes, Thomas

Tom Cobb: Gilbert, *Sir* W.S.

Tom Crib's memorial to Congress: Moore, Thomas

Tom Cringle's Log: Scott, Michael

Tom Gerrard: †Becke, Louis

Tom Grogan: Smith, F.H.

Tom Moody's tales: Lemon, Mark

Tom o' Bedlam and his song: †Machen, Arthur

Tom Paine: Pearson, Hesketh

Tom Paulding: Matthews, J.B.

Tom Sawyer abroad: (†Mark Twain), Clemens, S.L.

Tom Sawyer, detective: (†Mark Twain), Clemens, S.L.

Tom Thumb: Fielding, Henry

Tom Tiddler's ground: De la Mare, Walter

Tom Tiddler's ground: Dickens, Charles

Tom Wallis: †Becke, Louis

Tom Whipple: Edmonds, W.D.

Tomaso's fortune: †Merriman, Seton

Tomb of T'sin, The: Wallace, Edgar

Tomb of two brothers: Murray, Margaret

Tombs of Knossos: Evans, *Sir* A.J.

Tombs of the courtiers: Petrie, *Sir* William Flinders

Tommy and Co.: Jerome, Jerome K.

Tommy and Grizel: Barrie, *Sir* J.M.

Tommy Gallagher's crusade: Farrell, James

Tommy the Hawker and Snifter his boy: Dyson, E.G.

Tommy, Tilly and Mrs. Tubbs: Lofting, Hugh

Tommy Trot's visit to Santa Claus: Page, T.N.

Tomorrow: Brereton, John Le G.

Tomorrow: Mackaye, Percy

Tomorrow: Peach, L.du Garde

Tomorrow: Webster, M.M.

Tomorrow and tomorrow: Barry, Philip

Tomorrow and tomorrow: †Eldershaw, M.Barnard

Tomorrow is a revealing: Bowes-Lyon, Lilian

Tomorrow is ours: Abbas, K.A.

Tomorrow morning, Faustus!: Richards, I.A.

Tomorrow to fresh woods: Davies, Rhys

Tomorrow we shall be free: Connell, John

Tomorrow will be different: †George, Daniel

Tomorrowland: Bangs, John Kendrick

Tomorrow's another day: Burnett, W.R.

Tomorrow's tide: Bruce, Charles

Tomorrow's trade: Chase, Stuart

Tom's a-cold: Collier, John

Tongue in your head, A: Strong, L.A.G.

Tongues of conscience: Hichens, Robert

Tongues of fire: Blackwood, Algernon

Tongues of the Monte: Dobie, J.F.

To-night at eight-thirty: Coward, Noel

Tonks: a New Zealand yarn: Church, H.N.W.

Tonnewonte: Beckwith, J.C.

Tono-Bungay: Wells, H.G.

Tontine: Costain, T.B.

Tony: †Hudson, Stephen

Tony and the wonderful door: Fast, Howard M.

Tony Butler: Lever, C.J.

Tony Lumpkin in town: O'Keeffe, John

Too: Molesworth, *Mrs.*

Too clever by half: Lang, J.

Too clever for love: Greenwood, Walter

Too dear for my possessing: Johnson, Pamela Hansford

Too early to tell: Weidman, Jerome

Too fat to light: Beach, R.E.

Too many ghosts: Gallico, Paul

Too many people: Priestley, J.B.

Too much alike: Lang, J.

Too much alone: Trafford, *Mrs.* H., and F.G.Trafford

Too much Bluebeard: Jennings, Gertrude

Too much business: Chase, M.C.

Too much college: Leacock, Stephen

Too much Johnson: Gillette, William

Too much love of living: Hichens, R.S.

Too old to rat: Lawson, Henry

Too true to be good: Shaw, G.B.

Too young to marry: Flavin, Martin

Tooloona: Stringer, A.J.A.

Tools and weapons: Petrie, *Sir* William Flinders

Tooth-ache, The: Mayhew, Horace

Top speed: Ridge, W. Pett

Topaze: Levy, Benn W.

Toper's End: Cole, G.D.H.

Top-floor killer: Roberts, W. Adolphe

Topographer, The: Brydges, *Sir* Samuel Egerton

Topographical miscellanies, Brydges: *Sir* Samuel Egerton

Topper: Smith, Thorne

Topper takes a trip: Smith, Thorne

Topside: Priestley, J.B.

Topsy M.P.: Herbert, *Sir* A.P.

Topsy omnibus: Herbert, *Sir* A.P.

Topsy Turvy: Herbert, *Sir* A.P.

Topsyturvydom: Gilbert, *Sir* W.S.

Tor hill, The: Smith, Horatio

Torch, The: Dixon, Thomas

Torch, The: Phillpotts, Eden

Torch, The: Woodberry, G.E.

Torch-bearer, The: Fairbridge, Dorothea

Torch-bearers, The: Kelly, G.E.

Torch-bearers, The: Noyes, Alfred

Torches through the Bush: †Connor, Ralph

Toro of the Little People: Walmsley, Leo

Toronto of old: Scadding, Henry

Toronto, old and new: Adam, G.M.

Toronto, past and present: Scadding, Henry

Toronto's first germ: Scadding, Henry

Torquemada: Fast, Howard M.

Torquemada and the Spanish Inquisition: Sabatini, Rafael

Torrent, The: Robinson, E.A.

Torrents of spring, The: Hemingway, Ernest

Tortest: Willis, N.P.

Tortilla flat: Steinbeck, John

Tortoise and the hare, The: Jenkins, Elizabeth

Tortoises: Lawrence, D.H.

Tortoises, terrapins and turtles: Lear, Edward

Tortoiseshell cat, The: Royde-Smith, Naomi

Tory lover, The: Jewett, S.O.

Tory Quaker, The: Ward, Edward

Totem poles: Barbeau, C.M.

Totem poles of the Gitskan, Upper Skeena River, British Columbia: Barbeau, C.M.

Totemica: Frazer, *Sir* James

Totemism: Frazer, *Sir* James

Totemism and exogamy: Frazer, *Sir* James

Touch and go: Lawrence, D.H.

Touch of Abner, The: Cody, H.A.

Touch of nutmeg, A: Collier, John

Touch of the dragon, A: Basso, J.H.

Touch of the poet, A: O'Neill, Eugene

Touch wood: Smith, Dodie

Touching the Orient: Sitwell, Sacheverell

Touchstone, The: Wharton, Edith

Touchstone of fortune, The: Major, Charles

Tough at the top: Herbert, *Sir* A.P.

Toulemonde: Morley, C.D.

Tour in 1867: †Carroll, Lewis

Tour in Ireland, A: Young, Arthur

Tour in Scotland: (†Geoffrey Crayon), Irving, Washington

Tour in Scotland, A: Pennant, Thomas

Tour in Scotland and voyage to the Hebrides, A: Pennant, Thomas

Tour in Switzerland, A: Williams, H.M.

Tour in Tartan-land, A: †Bede, Cuthbert

Tour of Dr. Syntax, The: Combe, William

Tour of duty: Dos Passos, John

Tour of Europe and Asia, A: Galt, John

Tour of H.R.H. The Prince of Wales through British America and the United States, The: Morgan, H.J.

Tour thro' the whole island of Great Britain, A: Defoe, Daniel

Tour through France, A: Wraxall, *Sir* Nathaniel William

Tourist in Africa, A: Waugh, Evelyn

Tourists accommodated: Canfield, Dorothy

Tourist's guide to Ireland, A: O'Flaherty, Liam

Tourist's note-book, The: LeMoine, *Sir* J.M.

Tourmalin's time cheques: †Anstey, F.

Toward Stendhal: Levin, Harry

Toward the bonne entente: Pierce, Lorne

Toward the flame: Allen, Hervey

Toward the gulf: Masters, E.L.

Towards a better life: Burke, Kenneth

Towards a new theatre: Craig, Gordon

Towards a personal Armageddon: Treece, Henry

Towards a Socialist agriculture: Bateson, F.W.

Towards an appreciation of Literature: †O'Connor, Frank

Towards an appreciation of the theatre: Robinson, E.S.L.

Towards an enduring peace: Bourne, Randolph

Towards Balzac: Levin, Harry

Towards discipleship: Krishnamurti, Jiddu

Towards fidelity: Fausset, Hugh

Towards Social Democracy?: Webb, Sidney

Towards standards: Foerster, Norman

Towards the goal: Ward, *Mrs.* Humphrey

Towards the last spike: Pratt, E.J.

Towards the stars: Marson, Una

Towards universal man: Tagore, *Sir* R.

Towards world government: Russell, Bertrand

Towards zero: Christie, Agatha

Tower, The: Steen, Marguerite

Tower, The: Yeats, W.B.

Tower Hill: Ainsworth, Harrison

Tower of Babel, The: Austin, Alfred

Tower of darkness: †Bell, Neil

Tower of flame, The: Beach, R.E.

Tower of ivory: Atherton, Gertrude

Tower of ivory: MacLeish, Archibald

Tower of London, The: Ainsworth, Harrison

Tower of oblivion, The: †Onions, Oliver

Tower of Taddeo, The: †Ouida

Tower of the dream, The: Harpur, Charles

Tower of the mirrors, The: †Lee, Vernon

Tower on the Tor: Rowe, Richard

Towers of Trebizond, The: Macaulay, *Dame* Rose

Towing-path Bess: Pryce, Richard

Town, The: Faulkner, William

Town, The: Hunt, Leigh

Town: Jackson, Holbrook

Town, The: Richter, Conrad

Town and country: Morton, Thomas

Town and country: Trollope, Frances

Town and country sermons: Kingsley, Charles

Town and forest: Manning, Anne

Town before you, The: Cowley, *Mrs.* Hannah

Town down the river, The: Robinson, E.A.

Town eclogues: Montagu, *Lady* Mary Wortley

Town geology: Kingsley, Charles

Town in bloom, The: Smith, Dodie

Town like Alice, A: †Shute, Nevil

Town major of Miraucourt, The: Priestley, J.B.

Town of the cascades, The: Banim, Michael

Town talk: Steele, *Sir* Richard

Town that would have a pageant, The: Peach, L. du Garde

Town traveller, The: Gissing, George

Town-fopp, The: Behn, *Mrs.* Afra

Townsend to Lichfield: Cabell, James Branch

Townsman, The: Buck, Pearl

Toxin: †Ouida

Toxophilus: Ascham, Roger

Toy cart, The: Symons, Arthur

Toyland: O'Shaughnessy, A.W.E.

Toys of death, The: Cole, G.D.H.

Toys of peace, The: Munro, H.H.

Tracer of lost persons, The: Chambers, R.W.

Tracings of Iceland and the Faroe Islands: Chambers, Robert

Tracings of the North of Europe: Chambers, Robert

Track to highway: Mulgan, A.E.

Tracks we tread, The: †Lancaster, G.B.

Tract on monetary reform, A: Keynes, John Maynard

Tract upon health for cottage circulation, A: Morley, Henry

Tractor and the corn goddess, The: Anand, M.R.

Tracts for priests and people: Hughes, Thomas

Tracts for Sunday school teachers: Eggleston, Edward

Tracts for the times: Dodge, May Abigail

Tracts for the Times: Keble, John

Tracts for the times: Newman, J.H.

Tracts for the Times, Pusey, E. B.

Tracts for today: Conway, Moncure Daniel

Tracts of Mr. Thomas Hobbs of Malmesbury: Hobbes, Thomas

Tracts, theological and ecclesiastical: Newman, J.H.

Tracy diamonds, The: Holmes, M.J.

Tracy's ambition: Griffin, Gerald

Tracy's tiger: Saroyan, William

Trade malice: Reade, Charles

Trade unionism and munitions: Cole, G.D.H.

Trade unionism in war time: Cole, G.D.H.

Trade unionism on the railways: Cole, G.D.H.

Trader in Cannibal land, A: Cowan, James

Traders' dream: Mottram, R.H.

Trades' Unions and strikes: Knight, Charles

Trading: Warner, S.B.

Tradition and design in the Iliad: Bowra, *Sir* Maurice

Tradition and dream: Allen, Walter Ernest

Tradition and Hugh Walpole: †Dane, Clemence

Tradition and re-action in modern poetry: Binyon, Laurence

Tradition of war, The: Bourne, R.S.

Traditionary stories of old families and legendary illustrations of family history: Picken, Andrew

Traditions of Edinburgh: Chambers, Robert

Trafalgar Day: †Dane, Clemence

Traffics and discoveries: Kipling, Rudyard

Tragedie of Chabot Admirall of France, The: Chapman, George

Tragedie of Chabot admirall of France, The: Shirley, James

Tragedie of Cleopatra Queen of Aegypt, The: May, Thomas

Tragedie of Darius, The: Alexander, William

Tragedie of Dido Queene of Carthage, The: Marlowe, Christopher

Tragedie of Gorboduc, The: Sackville, Thomas

Tragedie of Hamlet, The: Macdonald, George

Tragedie of King Richard the second, The: Shakespeare, William

Tragedie of Orestes, The: Goffe, Thomas

Tragedie of Philotas: Daniel, Samuel

Tragedies of Maddelen, Agamemnon, Lady Macbeth, Antonia and Clytemnestra, The: Galt, John

Tragedies of the last age, The: Rymer, Thomas

Tragedy behind the curtain, The: Bayldon, Arthur

Tragedy called all's lost by lust, A: Rowley, William

Tragedy in relation to Aristotle's Poetics: Lucas, F.L.

Tragedy of Albertus Wallenstein, The: Glapthorne, Henry

Tragedy of Antigone, the Theban princesse, The: May, Thomas

Tragedy of Chrononhotonthol’gos, The: Carey, Henry

Tragedy of Coriolanus, The: Shakespeare, William

Tragedy of Count Alarcos, The: Disraeli, Benjamin

Tragedy of Featherstone, The: Farjeon, B.L.

Tragedy of Hoffman or a revenge for a father, The: Chettle, Henry

Tragedy of Ida Noble, The: Russell, W.C.

Tragedy of Jane Shore, The: Rowe, Nicholas

Tragedy of Julia Agrippina, Empresse of Rome, The: May, Thomas

Tragedy of King Richard the II, The: Theobald, Lewis

Tragedy of King Richard the third, The: Shakespeare, William

Tragedy of King Saul, The: Boyle, Roger

Tragedy of Macbeth, The: Shakespeare, William

Tragedy of Mustapha, The: Grenville, *Sir* Fulke

Tragedy of Mustapha, son of Solyman the Magnificent, The: Boyle, Roger

Tragedy of Nan, The: Masefield, John

Tragedy of Nero, The: Lee, Nathaniel

Tragedy of pardon, The: †Field, Michael

Tragedy of Pompey the Great, The: Masefield, John

Tragedy of Portugal, The: Gibbs, *Sir* Philip

Tragedy of Pudd'nhead Wilson, The: (†Mark Twain), Clemens, S.L.

Tragedy of Russia, The: Durant, W.J.

Tragedy of Sophonisba, The: Thomson, James

Tragedy of superstition, The: Barker, James Nelson

Tragedy of the Caesars, The: Baring-Gould, Sabine

Tragedy of the Dutchesse of Malfy, The: Webster, John

Tragedy of the Korosko, The: Doyle, *Sir* Arthur Conan

Tragedy of the Lady Jane Grey, The: Rowe, Nicholas

Tragedy of the late most reverende father David, The: Lindsay, *Sir* David

Tragedy of the pyramids, The: Sladen, D.B.W.

Tragedy of Thierry King of France: Fletcher, John

Tragedy of Thierry King of France, and his brother Theodoret, The: Beaumont, Francis

Tragedy of waste, The: Chase, Stuart

Tragedy of X, The: (†Barnaby Ross), †Queen, Ellery

Tragedy of Y, The: (†Barnaby Ross), †Queen, Ellery

Tragedy of Z, The: (†Barnaby Ross), †Queen, Ellery

Tragedy of Zara, The: Hill, Aaron

Tragic America: Dreiser, Theodore

Tragic bride, The: Young, Francis Brett

Tragic comedians, The: Meredith, George

Tragic ground: Caldwell, Erskine Preston

Tragic Mary, The: †Field, Michael

Tragic mothers: Moore, T.S.

Tragic muse, The: †Bridie, James

Tragic muse, The: Griffith, Hubert

Tragic muse, The: James, Henry

Tragical historie of Hamlet Prince of Denmarke, The: Shakespeare, William

Tragical history of King Richard III: Cibber, Colley

Tragicall history of D. Faustus, The: Marlowe, Christopher

Tragicall legend of Robert, Duke of Normandy, The: Drayton, Michael

Tragi-comedy: called, match mee in London, A: Dekker, Thomas

Tragi-comedy of Joan of Hedington, The: King, William

Tragi-coomodie, called the witch, A: Middleton, Thomas

Tragoedy of Othello, the Moore of Venice, The: Shakespeare, William

Trail blazers of the air: Tennant, Kylie

Trail book, The: Austin, Mary

Trail driver, The: Grey, Zane

Trail of an artist-naturalist: Seton-Thompson, E.

Trail of Cthulhu, The: Derleth, A.W.

Trail of fear, The: †Armstrong, Anthony

Trail of '98, The: Service, Robert

Trail of the black king; The: †Armstrong, Anthony

Trail of the bugles, The: Carman, Bliss

Trail of the golden horn, The: Cody, H.A.

Trail of the goldseekers, The: Garland, Hamlin

Trail of the hawk, The: Lewis, H.S.

Trail of the Lonesome Pine, The: Fox, John

Trail of the Lotto, The: †Armstrong, Anthony

Trail of the sandhill stag: Seton-Thompson, E.

Trail of the shadow, The: Bedford-Jones, Henry

Trail of the sword, The: Parker, *Sir* H.G.

Trail of the tide, The: Herbin, J.F.

Trailin'!: Brand, Max

Trail-makers of the middle border: Garland, Hamlin

Trails and trials in physiology: Hill, A.V.

Train of powder, A: †West, Rebecca

Training of children, The: Jackson, H.H.

Training of the sea, The: Sullivan, Alan

Training the Airmen: Roberts, C.E.M.

Traitor, The: Combe, William

Traitor, The: Dixon, Thomas

Traitors, The: Oppenheim, E. Phillips

Traitor's gate, The: Wallace, Edgar

Traitor's purse: Allingham, Margery

Traits and stories of the Irish Peasantry: Carleton, William

Traits and travesties, social and political: Oliphant, Laurence

Traits and trials of early life: Landon, L.E.M.

Traits of American life: Hale, S.J.B.

Traits of the Aborigines of America: Sigourney, L.H.

Traits of travel: Gratton, Thomas Colley

Tramp abroad, A: (†Mark Twain), Clemens, S.L.

Tramping Methodist, The: Kaye-Smith, Sheila

Tramping with a poet in the Rockies: Graham, Stephen

Trampling of the lilies, The: Sabatini, Rafael

Tramp's excuse, The: Lindsay, N.V.

Tramp's sketches, A: Graham, Stephen

Transaction of hearts, A: Saltus, E.E.

Transactioneer, The: King, William

Transactions of Lord Louis Lewis, The: Pertwee, Roland

Transatlantic episode: Jones, Jack

Trans-Atlantic historical solidarity: Adams, C.F.

Transatlantic sketches: James, Henry

Trans-Caucasian Campaign of the Turkish Army under Omar Pasha, The: Oliphant, Laurence

Trans-Caucasian Provinces the proper field of operation for a Christian army, The: Oliphant, Laurence

Transcendent and multiplied rebellion and treason, discovered, by the lawes of the land: Clarendon, Edward Hyde *Earl of*

Transcripts and studies: Dowden, Edward

Transfiguration of life, The: Clarke, J.F.

Transformation of nature in art, The: Coomaraswamy, A.K.

Transformations of man, The: Mumford, Lewis

Transformed metamorphosis, The: Tourneur, Cyril

Transgressor, The: Green, Julian

Transient quest, A: Saltus, E.E.

Transients, The: Van Doren, Mark

Transit of civilization from England to America in the seventeenth century, The: Eggleston, Edward

Transit of the red dragon, The: Phillpotts, Eden

Transit of Venus, The: Harwood, H.M.

Transition: Durant, W.J.

Transition: Durrell, Lawrence

Transition: Muir, Edwin

Transitional poem: Day-Lewis, C.

Translation of a savage, The: Parker, *Sir* H.G.

Translation of certaine psalmes into English verse, The: Bacon, Francis

Translation of Manon Lescaut: Waddell, Helen

Translation of the New Testament: Knox, R.A.

Translation of the Old Testament: Knox, R.A.

Translations and fragments: Rusden, G.W.

Translations and tomfooleries: Shaw, G.B.

Translations from the Chinese: Morley, C.D.

Transmigration of the seven Brahmans, The: Thoreau, H.D.

Transparent sea, The: Dudek, Louis

Transparent tree, The: Van Doren, Mark

Transplanted, The: Niven, F.J.

Transplanted: Whitlock, Brand

Transport to summer: Stevens, Wallace

Transposition: Lewis, C.S.

Transvaal from within, The: Fitzpatrick, *Sir* J.P.

Trap, The: Dukes, Ashley

Trap, The: Richardson, D.M.

Trash dedicated without respect to J. Halse, Esq. M.P. Penzance: Praed, W.M.

Traulus: Swift, Jonathan

Travail of gold: Benson, E.F.

Travailes of the three English brothers, Sir Thomas, Sir Anthony, Mr. Robert Shirley, The: Day, John

Travel in New Zealand: Cowan, James

Travel light: Mitchison, Naomi

Travel tales of Mr. Joseph Jorkens, The: Dunsany, Edward Plunkett, *Baron*

Traveler, The: Connelly, Marc

Traveler at forty, A: Dreiser, Theodore

Traveler from Altruria, A: Howells, W.D.

Travelers, The: Tarkington, Booth

Traveling with the innocents abroad: (†Mark Twain), Clemens, S.L.

Traveller, The: De la Mare, Walter

Traveller, The: Goldsmith, Oliver

Traveller in Italy: Morton, H.V.

Traveller in little things, A: Hudson, W.H.

Traveller in Rome, A: Morton, H.V.

Traveller in the fur cloak, The: Weyman, Stanley

Traveller in time, A: Uttley, Alison

Traveller in war-time, A: Churchill, Winston

Traveller returns, A: †Dane, Clemence

Travellers, The: Sedgwick, C.M.

Travellers: Strong, L.A.G.

Travellers and outlaws: Higginson, T.W.

Traveller's luck: Lucas, E.V.

Traveller's pack: †Mordaunt, Elinor

Traveller's prelude: Stark, Freya

Traveller's samples: †O'Connor, Frank

Travelling about over new and old ground: Barker, M.A.

Travelling companions, The: †Anstey, F.

Travelling companions: James, Henry

Travelling grave, The: Hartley, L.P.

Travelling home: Cornford, Frances

Travelling sketches: Trollope, Anthony

Travelling thirds, The: Atherton, Gertrude

Travels and adventures in Canada and the Indian Territories, between the years 1760 and 1776: Henry, Alexander

Travels and researches of eminent English missionaries: Picken, Andrew

Travels and travellers: Trollope, Frances

Travels, compiled by Cedric H. Glover: Burney, *Dr.* Charles

Travels during the years 1787–1790: Young, Arthur

Travels from Hamburg through Westphalia: Holcroft, Thomas

Travels in Africa: Park, Mungo

Travels in America by George Fibbleton: Green, Asa

Travels in Arabia Deserta: Doughty, C.M.

Travels in China: Barrow, *Sir* John

Travels in England, France, Spain and the Barbary States: Noah, M.M.

Travels in Greece and Russia: Taylor, Bayard

Travels in London: Thackeray, W.M.

Travels in Philadelphia: Morley, C.D.

Travels in South Kensington: Conway, Moncure Daniel

Travels in two democracies: Wilson, Edmund

Travels in West Africa: Kingsley, Mary

Travels into several remote nations of the world. In four parts. By Lemuel Gulliver, first a surgeon and then a Captain of several ships: Swift Jonathan

Travels into the interior of South Africa: Barrow, *Sir* John

Travels of a Republican Radical in search of hot water: Wells, H.G.

Travels of an alchemist, The: Waley, Arthur

Travels of an Irish gentleman in search of a religion: Moore, Thomas

Travels through France and Italy: Smollett, Tobias

Travels through North and South Carolina, Georgia, East and West Florida: Bartram, William

Travels to discover the source of the Nile: Bruce, James

Travels to Italy, 1654–8: Reresby, *Sir* John

Travels with a donkey in the Cévennes: Stevenson, R.L.

Travels with Charley: in search of America: Steinbeck, John

Traytor, The: Shirley, James

Tread the green grass: Green, Paul

Treading the winepress: †Connor, Ralph

Treason in the egg: Strong, L.A.G.

Treasure: MacKay, I.E.

Treasure house of Belgium, The: Cammaerts, Emile

Treasure house of Martin Hews, The: Oppenheim, E. Phillips

Treasure in the forest, The: Wells, H.G.

Treasure Island: Stevenson, R.L.

Treasure of Heaven, The: †Corelli, Marie

Treasure of Ho, The: Beck, *Mrs.* Lily

Treasure of the humble, The: Sutro, Alfred

Treasure of the lake: Haggard, *Sir* H. Rider

Treasure of the seas, The: De Mille, James

Treasure of the Tropics, The: Cronin, B.C.

Treasure on Pelican: Priestley, J.B.

Treasure trail: Niven, F.J.

Treasure trail: Pertwee, Roland

Treasure trove: Lover, Samuel

Treasurer's report, The: Benchley, Robert

Treasures of the snow, The: Bourinot, A.S.

Treasures of the snow, The: Kaye-Smith, Sheila

Treasures of Typhon, The: Phillpotts, Eden

Treasury of birdlore, A: Krutch, J.W.

Treasury of poems, A: Chattopadhyaya, Harindranath

Treasury of sacred song, The: Palgrave, F.T.

Treasury of seventeenth century verse, A: Massingham, Harold

Treat 'em rough: Lardner, Ring

Treatise concerning religious affections, A: Edwards, Jonathan

Treatise concerning the principles of human knowledge, A: Berkeley, George

Treatise concerning the state of departed souls, A: Dennis, John

Treatise of civil power in ecclesiastical causes, A: Milton, John

Treatise of human nature, A: Hume, David

Treatise of Miraclis pleyinge: Wycliffe, John

Treatise of the plague, A: Lodge, Thomas

Treatise of the system of the world, A: Newton, *Sir* Isaac

Treatise of union of England and Scotland, A: Hayward, *Sir* John

Treatise on ancient armour and weapons, A: Grose, Francis

Treatise on the Astrolabe: Chaucer, Geoffrey

Treatise on money, A: Keynes, John Maynard

Treatise on probability, A: Keynes, John Maynard

Treatise on right and wrong: Mencken, H.L.

Treatise on the art of war, A: Boyle, Roger

Treatise on the education of children and youth, A: Watts, Isaac

Treatise on the gods: Mencken, H.L.

Treatise on universal algebra, A: Whitehead, A.N.

Treatises of 1. The liberty of prophesying. 2. Prayer ex tempore. 3. Episcopacie: Taylor, Jeremy

Trebizond: Vijayatunga, J.

Tree, The: Bates, H.E.

Tree, The: (†Grey Owl), Belaney, G.S.

Tree of bitter fruit, The: Gouldsbury, H.C.

Tree of good and evil, The: Samuel, Herbert *1st Viscount*

Tree of healing, The: Moffatt, James

Tree of heaven, The: Chambers, R.W.

Tree of heaven, The: Raymond, Ernest

Tree of heaven, The: Sinclair, May

Tree of idleness, The: Durrell, Lawrence

Tree of laughing bells, The: Lindsay, N.V.

Tree of life, The: Fletcher, John Gould

Tree of life, The: Massingham, Harold

Tree of man, The: White, P.V.M.

Tree of resurrection, The: Brown, A.A.

Tree that didn't get trimmed, The: Morley, C.D.

Tree that sat down, The: Nichols, Beverley

Tree with a bird in it, A: Widdemer, Margaret

Trees: Kilmer, Joyce

Trees: Monro, H.E.

Trees, The: Richter, Conrad

Trefoil, The: Benson, A.C.

Trek, The: Slater, F.C.

Trelawney of Trelawne: Bray, Anna Eliza

Trelawney with Shelley and Byron: †Miller, Joaquin

Trelawny of the Wells: Pinero, Sir A.W.

Tremaine: Ward, Robert

Trembling of a leaf, The: Maugham, Somerset

Trembling of the veil, The: Yeats, W.B.

Tremendous trifles: Chesterton, G.K.

Tremordyn Cliff: Trollope, Frances

Tremulous string, The: Gibbon, Monk

Trending into Maine: Roberts, Kenneth

Trent, The: Roberts, C.E.M.

Trent intervenes: Bentley, E.C.

Trenton Falls: Willis, N.P.

Trent's last case: Bentley, E.C.

Trent's own case: Bentley, E.C.

Trent's Trust: Harte, Bret

Trespass: Williams, Emlyn

Trespasser, The: Lawrence, D.H.

Trespasser, The: Parker, Sir H.G.

Trespasses: Percy, Edward

Trevanion: Marston, J.W.

Trevanion: Smith, Horatio

Trevannion: Strong, L.A.G.

Trevlyn Hold: Wood, Ellen

Trial, The: Yonge, Charlotte M.

Trial and error: Strong, L.A.G.

Trial by jury: Gilbert, Sir W.S.

Trial by jury, The: Hook, T.E.

Trial by terror: Gallico, Paul

Trial of a city: Birney, Earle

Trial of a judge: Spender, Stephen

Trial of a poet: Shapiro, Karl

Trial of Charles I, The: Wedgwood, C.V.

Trial of Eugene Debs, The: Eastman, Max

Trial of Jeanne d'Arc, The: Garnett, Edward

Trial of Jesus, The: Masefield, John

Trial of the Hon. George Gordon, The: Holcroft, Thomas

Trial of Theodore Parker, for the misdemeanor of a speech in Faneuil Hall against kidnapping, The: Parker, Theodore

Trial of Thomas Cranmer, The: Ridler, A.B.

Trial without jury: Payne, J.H.

Triall by armes: Hergesheimer, Joseph

Trials and other tribulations: Runyon, Damon

Trials of domestic life: Bray, Anna Eliza

Trials of Margaret Lyndsay, The: Wilson, John

Trials of the heart: Bray, Anna Eliza

Trials of the human heart: Rowson, S.H.

Trials of Topsy, The: Herbert, Sir A.P.

Triangle, A: Baring, Maurice

Triangles of life: Lawson, Henry

Tribe that lost its head, The: Monsarrat, Nicholas

Tribes and temples: La Farge, Oliver

Tribune Primer: Field, Eugene

Tribute and Circe, The: Doolittle, Hilda

Tribute for Harriet: Thirkell, Angela

Tribute to Freud: Doolittle, Hilda

Tribute to Judge Sprague, A: Dana, R.H. junior

Tribute to the angels: Doolittle, Hilda

Tricke to catch the old-one, A: Middleton, Thomas

Tricks and traps of horse dealers, The: †Forester, Frank

Tricks of the trade: Squire, Sir J.C.

Tri-color, The: Simms, W.G.

Tricolour, The: Sigerson, Dora

Tricotrin: †Ouida

Trifler, The: Masters, E.L.

Triflers, The: Graves, Richard

Trifles: Glaspell, Susan

Trilby: Du Maurier, George

Trimblerigg: Housman, Laurence

Trimmed lamp, The: †Henry, O.

Trimming of Thomas Nash gentleman, The: Harvey, Gabriel

Trincolax: Sladen, D.B.W.

Trinity: Bridges, Roy

Trinity bells: Barr, A.E.H.

Trinity College, Cambridge: Trevelyan, G.M.

Trinity Town: Collins, Norman

Trio: Baker, Dorothy

Trio: Bentley, Phyllis

Trio: Maugham, Somerset

Trio from Rio, The: Mickle, A.D.

Triolets: Baring, Maurice

Trip to Barbary, by a roundabout route, A: Sala, G.A.H.

Trip to Bath, A: Sheridan, Mrs. Frances

Trip to Cuba, A: Howe, Julia Ward

Trip to England, A: Smith, Goldwin

Trip to England, The: Winter, William

Trip to Hawaii, A: Stoddard, C.W.

Trip to Jamaica, A: Ward, Edward

Trip to Kissingen, A: Taylor, Tom

Trip to London, The: Davies, Rhys

Trip to New-England, A: Ward, Edward

Trip to New York, A: Turner, W.J.R.

Trip to Parnassus, A: Rowson, S.H.

Trip to Scarborough, A: Sheridan, R.B.

Trip to Scotland, A: Whitehead, William

Trip to the North-east of Lake Tiberias, A: Oliphant, Laurence

Triple fugue: Sitwell, *Sir* Osbert

Triple thinkers, The: Wilson, Edmund

Tripod for homeward incense: Macartney, Frederick

Tristan and Isolde, restoring Palamede: Erskine, John

Tristan and Isolt: Masefield, John

Tristan and Iseult: Symons, Arthur

Tristan of Blent: (†Anthony Hope), Hawkins, Anthony Hope

Tristia: †Pindar, Peter

Tristram: Robinson, E.A.

Tristram: Swinburne, A.C.

Tritheism charged upon Dr. Sherlock's new notion of the Trinity: South, Robert

Tritons: Bynner, Edwin Lassetter

Triumph: Niven, F.J.

Triumph, The: Tate, Nahum

Triumph in the West: Bryant, *Sir* Arthur

Triumph of beautie, The: Shirley, James

Triumph of Bohemia, The: Sterling, George

Triumph of fashion, The: Pye, H.J.

Triumph of Gloriana, The: Swinburne, A.C.

Triumph of Hilary Blachland, The: Mitford, Bertram

Triumph of music, The: Cawein, Madison

Triumph of Palmerston, The: Martin, B.K.

Triumph of peace, The: Shirley, James

Triumph of peace, The: Tate, Nahum

Triumph of the egg, The: Anderson, Sherwood

Triumph of the machine, The: Lawrence, D.H.

Triumph of the Orwell, The: Barton, Bernard

Triumph of the Philistines, The: Jones, H.A.

Triumph of the Scarlet Pimpernel, The: Orczy, *Baroness*

Triumph of Tim, The: Vachell, H.A.

Triumph of time, The: Jameson, Storm

Triumph of union, The: Tate, Nahum

Triumph of woman, The: Rowcroft, Charles

Triumphal march: Eliot, T.S.

Triumphant beast, The: †Bowen, Marjorie

Triumphant Squalitone: Delisser, Herbert G.

Triumphes of re-united Britannia, The: Munday, Anthony

Triumphs of health and prosperity, The: Middleton, Thomas

Triumphs of integrity, The: Middleton, Thomas

Triumphs of Isis, The: Warton, Thomas

Triumphs of love and antiquity, The: Middleton, Thomas

Triumphs of the Cross, The: Neale, J.M.

Triumphs of the golden fleece, The: Munday, Anthony

Triumphs of the reformed religion in America, The: Mather, Cotton

Triumphs of Truth, The: Middleton, Thomas

Triumphs over death, The: Southwell, Robert

Trivia: Gay, John

Trivia: Smith, L.L.P.

Trivial breath: Wylie, Elinor

Trivium amoris: Todhunter, John

Trixy: Ward, E.S.

Troia Britanica: Heywood, Thomas

Troia-nova triumphans: Dekker, Thomas

Troilus and Cressida: Dryden, John

Troilus and Cressida: Hassall, Christopher

Troilus and Cressida: Shakespeare, William

Troilus and Criseyde: Chaucer, Geoffrey

Trojan ending, A: Riding, Laura

Trojan horse, The: MacLeish, Archibald

Trojan horse, The: Morley, C.D.

Trojan women of Euripides, The: Murray, Gilbert

Troll garden, The: Cather, Willa

Trollope: a bibliography: Sadleir, Michael

Trollope: a commentary: Sadleir, Michael

Trooper Peter Halket of Mashonaland: Schreiner, Olive

Trooper to the Southern Cross: Thirkell, Angela

Trophy of arms, A: Pitter, Ruth

Tropic days: Banfield, E.J.

Tropic heat: †Mordaunt, Elinor

Tropic of Cancer: Miller, Henry

Tropic of Capricorn: Miller, Henry

Tropic reveries: Marson, Una

Tropical Australia: (†Donald Barr), Barrett, C.L.

Tropical nature: Wallace, A.R.

Tropical winter: Hergesheimer, Joseph

Trottolino: †Ouida

Troubadour, The: Landon, L.E.M.

Troubadour, The: Sigerson, Dora

Trouble at number seven, The: Bullett, Gerald

Trouble for Lucia: Benson, E.F.

Trouble in July: Caldwell, Erskine Preston

Trouble in the glen: Walsh, Maurice

Trouble is my business: Chandler, Raymond

Trouble trail: †Brand, Max

Trouble with tigers, The: Saroyan, William

Troubled air, The: Shaw, Irwin

Troubled heart and how it is comforted at last, A: Stoddard, C.W.

Troubled island: Hughes, J.L.

Troubled star: De Voto, Bernard

Troublesome reigne and lamentable death of Edward the second, King of England, The: Marlowe, Christopher

Troy: Wolfe, Humbert

Troy, a study in Homeric geography: Leaf, Walter

Troy chimneys: Kennedy, Margaret

Troy Park: Sitwell, Edith

Truants, The: Mason, A.E.W.

Truce, The: Ingraham, J.H.

Truce of God, The: Rinehart, Mary Roberts

True: Lathrop, G.P.

True and a kinde excuse in defence of that booke, intituled a newe description of Irelande, A: Rich, Barnabe

True and false society: Morris, William

True and genuine account of the life and actions of Jonathan Wild, A: Defoe, Daniel

True and pathetic history of Desbarollda, the waltzing mouse, The: Langley, Noel

True bear stories: †Miller, Joaquin

True book about castles, The: Treece, Henry

True born Irishman, The: Macklin, Charles

True character of Mr. Pope and his writings, A: Dennis, John

True Cross, The: Whyte-Melville, G.J.

True description of his majesties royall ship, built this yeare, 1637, at Wooll-witch in Kent, A: Heywood, Thomas

True description of unthankfulnesse, A: Breton, Nicholas

True discourse of the two infamous upstart prophets: Heywood, Thomas

True discription of a royall masque, The: Daniel, Samuel

True eyes and the whirlwind: Bedford, Randolph

True faith, by an Indian Theist: Sen, Kesava Chandra

True George Washington, The: Ford, Paul Leicester

True grace: Edwards, Jonathan

True harvest: Bourinot, A.S.

True heart, The: Warner, Sylvia Townsend

True history of Joshua Davidson, The: Linton, Eliza

True history of Shakespeare's sonnets, The: Douglas, *Lord* Alfred

True impartial history and wars of the Kingdom of Ireland, The: Shirley, James

True lawe of free monarchies, The: James VI of Scotland

True love: Monkhouse, A.N.

True loving sorrow attired in a robe of griefe upon the funeral of the Duke of Richmond and Lennox: Taylor, John

True nature of imposture fully display'd in the life of Mahomet, The: Prideaux, Humphrey

True patriot, The: Fielding, Henry

True radical programme, The: Shaw, G.B.

True relation of the apparation of one Mrs. Veal, A: Defoe, Daniel

True relation of the lives and deaths of the two most famous English pyrats, Purser and Clinton, A: Heywood, Thomas

True relation of ... Virginia, A: Smith, John

True report of a late practise enterprized by a Papist, The: Rich, Barnabe

True reporte of the prosperous successe which God gave unto our souldiours in Ireland, The: Munday, Anthony

True state of the differences, A: Colman, George, *the elder*

True stories from history and biography: Hawthorne, Nathaniel

True story, A: †Hudson, Stephen

True story and the recent carnival of crime, A:(†MarkTwain), Clemens, S.L.

True story of Dick Whittington, The: Sitwell, *Sir* Osbert

True tales of an old shellback: (Stephen Southwold), †Bell, Neil

True Tilda: Quiller-Couch, *Sir* A.

True tragedie of Richard Duke of York, The: Shakespeare, William

True tragedy of Rienzi, Tribune of Rome, The: Todhunter, John

True traveller, The: Davies, W.H.

True travellers, a tramps opera: Davies, W.H.

True travels, adventures, and observations of Captaine John Smith, The: Smith, John

True voice of feeling, The: Read, *Sir* Herbert

True widow, The: Shadwell, Thomas

True woman, The: Munro, C.K.

True woman, A: Orczy, *Baroness*

True womanhood: Neal, John

True words for brave men: Kingsley, Charles

True-born Englishman, The: Defoe, Daniel

Trumpet, The: Thomas, E.E.P.

Trumpet and the swan, The: †Bowen, Marjorie

Trumpet in the dust, The: Holme, Constance

Trumpet of jubilee, The: Lewisohn, Ludwig

Trumpet shall sound, The: Tomlinson, H.M.

Trumpet voluntary: Stern, G.B.

Trumpet-major, The: Hardy, Thomas

Trumpets at Rome: †Bowen, Marjorie

Trumpets from Montparnasse: Gibbings, Robert

Trumpets in the West: Trease, Geoffrey

Trumps: Curtis, George William

Trunk crime: Percy, Edward

Trust the people: Houghton, W.S.

Trustee from the toolroom, The: †Shute, Nevil

Trusty knaves, The: Rhodes, E.M.

Truth: Chaucer, Geoffrey

Truth, The: Fitch, Clyde

Truth: Sterling, George

Truth: a New Year's gift for scribblers: Snelling, W.J.

Truth about an author, The: Bennett, Arnold

Truth about Blayds, The: Milne, A.A.

Truth about Los Angeles, The: Adamic, Louis

Truth about lovers, The: Widdemer, Margaret

Truth about my father, The: †Bell, Neil

Truth about Soviet Russia, The: Webb, Sidney and Beatrice Webb

Truth about the Khilafat, The: Ahmad Khan, *Sir* Saiyid

Truth about Tristram Varick, The: Saltus, E.E.

Truth and falsehood in religion: Inge, W.R.

Truth and opinion: Wedgewood, C.V.

Truth game, The: †Novello, Ivor

Truth is God: Gandhi, M.K.

Truth is not sober: Holtby, Winifred

Truth of our times, The: Peacham, Henry

Truths and fictions of the Middle Ages: Palgrave, *Sir* Francis

Truth's triumph in the gracious preservation of the King: Taylor, John

Truxton King: McCutcheon, G.B.

Try anything once: Clune, Frank

Try anything twice: †Cheyney, Peter

Try it again: Priestley, J.B.

Try nothing twice: Clune, Frank

Tryal of the cause of the Roman Catholics: Brooke, Henry

Trying patient, A: Payn, James

Tryphena: Phillpotts, Eden

Tryphon: Boyle, Roger

Trysting place, The: Tarkington, Booth

Tryumphs of honour and industry, The: Middleton, Thomas

Tubal Cain: Hergesheimer, Joseph

Tubber Derg: Carleton, William

Tubus historicus: an historicall perspective: Ralegh, *Sir* Walter

Tudor economic documents: Tawney, R.H.

Tuesday afternoon: Strong, L.A.G.

Tuhoe, the children of the mist: Best, Elsdon

Tuileries, The: Gore, Catherine

Tulips and chimneys: Cummings, E.E.

Tully of old age and of friendship: Caxton, William

Tumbled house: Seymour, Beatrice Kean

Tumble-down Dick: Fielding, Henry

Tumbledown Dick: Spring, Howard

Tumbling in the hay: Gogarty, O.St. John

Tumult in the North: †Preedy, George

Tumultuous shore: Ficke, Arthur

Tunnel, The: Richardson, D.M.

Tunnel from Calais: Divine, A.D.

Tunnel-trench: Griffith, Hubert

Tura and the fairies: Anderson, J.C.

Turbott Wolfe: Plomer, William

Turbulent duchess, The: Orczy, *Baroness*

Turbulent tales: Sabatini, Rafael

Turgenev: Garnett, Edward

"Turk": Read, O.P.

Turk and no Turk, A: Colman, George, *the younger*

Turkey: Toynbee, Arnold

Turkey and the Turk, The: Chesterton, G.K.

Turkey egg, A: Read, O.P.

Turkey in Europe: Eliot, *Sir* Charles

Turkey in the straw: Kantor, Mackinlay

Turmoil, The: Tarkington, Booth

Turn again tales: Housman, Laurence

Turn away no more: Campion, Sarah

Turn back the leaves: †Delafield, E.M.

Turn back the river: Hardy, W.G.

Turn of the balance, The: Whitlock, Brand

Turn of the road, The: †Bartimeus

Turn of the screw, The: James, Henry

Turn of the tide, The: Bryant, *Sir* Arthur

Turn of the tide, The: Porter, E.H.

Turn of the tide, The: Tomlinson, H.M.

Turn of the year, The: Grove, F.P.

Turn the key softly: Brophy, John

Turn West: Turn East: Canby, Henry Seidel

Turnabout: Smith, Thorne

Turner: Rothenstein, *Sir* John

Turning of Griggsby, The: Bacheller, Irving

Turning path, The: Bottrall, Ronald

Turning things over: Lucas, E.V.

Turning wheels: Cloete, E.F.

Turning wind, A: Rukeyser, Muriel

Turnpike house, The: Hume, F.W.

Turnpike sailor, The: Russell, W.C.

Turns and movies: Aiken, Conrad

Turns of fortune: Hall, Anna Maria

Turnstile, The: Mason, A.E.W.

Turret, The: Sharp, Margery

Turtle and the sparrow, The: Prior, Matthew

Turtles of Tasman, The: London, Jack

Turvey: Birney, Earle

Tuscan cities: Howells, W.D.

Tussock land: Adams, Arthur H.

Tutira: the story of a New Zealand sheep station: Guthrie-Smith, W.H.

Tutor's story, The: Kingsley, Charles

'Twas all for the best: Bird, R.M.

'Twas in Trafalgar Bay: Besant, *Sir* Walter and James Rice

Tweedles: Tarkington, Booth

'Tween snow and fire: Mitford, Bertram

Twelfth night: Shakespeare, William

Twelfth of August, The: More, Hannah

Twelfth-day gift, The: Newbery, John

Twelve adventurers, The: Brontë, Charlotte

Twelve against the gods: Bolitho, William

Twelve ancestral signs in the Billings' Zodiac gallery: †Billings, Josh

Twelve conclusions of Lollards: Wycliffe, John

Twelve days: Sackville-West, Victoria

Twelve disguises: †Beeding, Francis

$1200 a year: Ferber, Edna

Twelve idyls and other poems: Abercrombie, Lascelles

Twelve Japanese painters: Ficke, Arthur

Twelve medieval ghost stories: James, M.R.

Twelve men: Dreiser, Theodore

Twelve miles from a lemon: Dodge, May Abigail

Twelve million black voices: Wright, Richard

Twelve moneths, The: Stevenson, Matthew

Twelve months: Powys, L.C.

Twelve months in a curatorship: †Carroll, Lewis

Twelve noon: Church, Richard

Twelve portraits: Rothenstein, Sir William

Twelve profitable sonnets: Mac-Mechan, A.M.

Twelve seasons: Krutch, J.W.

Twelve stories and a dream: Wells, H.G.

Twelve tales: Allen, Grant

Twelve tales: Frankau, Gilbert

12.30 from Croydon, The: Crofts, F.W.

Twelve tiny tales: Molesworth, Mrs.

Twelve tracts or sermons by Purvey: Wycliffe, John

Twelve types: Chesterton, G.K.

Twelve unprofitable sonnets: MacMechan, A.M.

Twenties fanfrolics and after: Lindsay, Jack

Twentieth century: Hecht, Ben

Twentieth century Canadian poetry: Birney, Earle

Twentieth century harlequinade: Sitwell, Dame Edith, and Sir Osbert Sitwell

20th Century Psalter: Church, Richard

Twentieth door, The: Sheldon, C.M.

Twentieth plane, The: Watson, A.D.

Twenty: Benson, Stella

Twenty bath-tub ballads: Service, Robert

Twenty centuries of travel: Power, Eileen

Twenty good stories: Read, O. P.

Twenty lessons in reading and writing prose: Davidson, Donald

Twenty notches: †Brand, Max

Twenty o'clock: Hubbard, Elbert

Twenty one golden rules to depress agriculture: Carey, Mathew

Twenty poems: Kipling, Rudyard

Twenty poems less: Riding, Laura

20,000 leagues under the sea: Benchley, Robert

Twenty thousand streets under the sky: Hamilton, Patrick

Twenty three poems: Seymour, W.K.

Twenty years at Hull House: Addams, Jane

Twenty years of my life: Sladen, D.B.W.

XXVIII sermons preached at Golden Grove: Taylor, Jeremy

Twenty-five: Nichols, Beverley

Twenty-five Chinese poems: Bax, Clifford

Twenty-five nudes engraved: Gill, Eric

XXV sermons preached at Golden Grove: Taylor, Jeremy

Twenty-five years, 1892–1916: Grey of Fallodon, Edward

XXIV elegies: Fletcher, John Gould

Twenty-four hours: Bromfield, Louis

Twenty-four portraits: Rothenstein, Sir William

Twenty-one stories: Greene, Graham

Twenty-one years' work, 1865–1886: Besant, Sir Walter

27 stories: Buck, Pearl

XXVI sermons: Donne, John

Twenty-three and a half hours' leave: Rinehart, Mary Roberts

Twenty-three selected poems: Gibson, Wilfred

XXII and X. XXXII ballades in blue china: Lang, Andrew

XXII ballades in blue china: Lang, Andrew

Twice a year: Bourne, Randolph

Twice have the trumpets sounded: Davies, Robertson

Twice required: Millay, E.St. Vincent

Twice round the clock: Sala, G.A.H.

Twice round the London clock: Graham, Stephen

Twice thirty: Bok, E.W.

Twice-told tales: Hawthorne, Nathaniel

Twig is bent, The: †Boake, Capel

Twilight: Frost, Robert

Twilight grey: Vachell, H.A.

Twilight in Italy: Lawrence, D.H.

Twilight land: Pyle, Howard

Twilight litanies: Logan, J.D.

Twilight of liberty: Kirkconnell, Watson

Twilight of magic, The: Lofting, Hugh

Twilight of the Gods, The: Garnett, Richard

Twilight on the Floods: Steen, Marguerite

Twilight people, The: †O'Sullivan, Seumas

Twilight sleep: Wharton, Edith

Twilight songs: Tynan, Katherine

Twilight tales: (Stephen Southwold), †Bell, Neil

Twin adventures, The: Saroyan, William

Twin roses: Ritchie, Mrs. A.C.M.

Twin sombreros: Grey, Zane

Twin tales: Stringer, A.J.A.

Twinkle, twinkle little star: Clarke, Marcus

Twin-rivals, The: Farquhar, George

Twins, The: Browning, Elizabeth Barrett

Twins of Table Mountain, The: Harte, Bret

Twister, The: Wallace, Edgar

Twixt cup and lip: Linton, Eliza

'Twixt eagle and dove: Lucas, E.V.

Twixt earth and stars: Hall, M.R.

Twixt land and sea: Conrad, Joseph

'Twixt shadow and shine: Clarke, Marcus

Two addresses to the freeholders of Westmoreland: Wordsworth, William

Two admirals, The: Cooper, James Fenimore

Two and twenty years ago: Dunlop, William

Two aristocracies, The: Gore, Catherine

Two awheel and some others afoot in Australia: (†Ishmael Dare), Jose, A.W.

Two baronets, The: Bury, *Lady* C.S.M.

Two Biddicut boys: Trowbridge, J.T.

Two bird lovers in Mexico: Beebe, William

Two bites at a cherry: Aldrich, T.B.

Two black sheep: Deeping, Warwick

Two blind countries, The: Macaulay, *Dame* Rose

Two bookes of ayres: Campion, Thomas

Two bouquets, The: Farjeon, Herbert

Two boy tramps: Oxley, J.M.

Two brothers: Pollard, A.W.

Two brothers: Toynbee, T.P.

Two bucks without hair: Millin, Sarah Gertrude

Two by tricks: Yates, E.H.

Two by two: Garnett, David

Two captains, The: Russell, W.C.

Two carnations, The: †Bowen, Marjorie

Two centuries of costume in America: Earle, A.M.

Two cheers for democracy: Forster, E.M.

Two Christmas poems: Noyes, Alfred

Two congratulatory poems to their Majesties: Behn, *Mrs.* Afra

Two consolations: Jeffers, J.R.

Two cultures and the scientific revolution, The: Snow, C.P.

Two cultures? The significance of C.P. Snow: Leavis, F.R.

Two destinies, The: Collins, Wilkie

Two destinies, The: Doyle, *Sir* Francis

Two dissertations: Edwards, Jonathan

Two Elizabethan stage abridgements: Greg, W.W.

Two epistles: Gay, John

Two epistles to Mr. Pope, concerning the authors of the age: Young, Edward

Two essays: Hume, David

Two essays on Conrad: Galsworthy, John

Two essays on scripture miracles and on ecclesiastical: Newman, J.H.

Two excursions into reality: Durrell, Lawrence

Two farmers, The: Trimmer, *Mrs.* Sarah

Two feet from Heaven: Wren, P.C.

Two fishers: Palmer, H.E.

Two flights up: Rinehart, Mary Roberts

Two foemen: Palmer, H.E.

Two fools: Hannay, J.O.

Two for the river: Hartley, L.P.

Two forewords: Kipling, Rudyard

Two fragments of ghost stories: Gaskell, *Mrs.* Elizabeth

Two friends, The: Blessington, Marguerite

Two friends, The: Hall, Anna Maria

Two frontier churches: Carnochan, Janet

Two frontiers, The: Fletcher, John Gould

Two games: MacMechan, A.M.

Two generals, The: Fitzgerald, Edward

Two generations: Grove, F.P.

Two generations: Niven, F.J.

Two generations: Sitwell, *Sir* Osbert

Two gentlemen and a lady: Woollcott, A.H.

Two gentlemen in bonds: Ransom, J.C.

Two gentlemen of Rome: Raymond, Ernest

Two gentlemen of Soho: Herbert, *Sir* A.P.

Two gentlemen of Verona, The: Shakespeare, William

Two gentlemen of Virginia: Eggleston, G.C.

Two girls: Coolidge, Susan

Two gray tourists: Johnston, R.M.

Two guardians, The: Yonge, Charlotte

Two (hitherto unpublished) poems: Stein, Gertrude

CCXI sociable letters: Newcastle, Margaret, *Duchess of*

221 B: Studies in Sherlock Holmes: Starrett, Vincent

Two hundred epigrammes: Heywood, John

Two imitations of Chaucer: Prior, Matthew

Two immigrants: Mackaye, Percy

Two in a train: Deeping, Warwick

Two in Italy: Elliott, M.H.

Two internationals, The: Dutt, R.P.

Two Jacks, The: Bird, W.R.

Two jungle books, The: Kipling, Rudyard

Two kisses, a tale of a very modern courtship, The: †Onions, Oliver

Two knights, The: Swinburne, A.C.

Two Lake poets: Wise, T.J.

Two lamps, The: Hecht, Ben

Two laughters, The: (†Elzevir), Murdoch, *Sir* W.L.F.

Two leaves and a bud: Anand, M.R.

Two lectures on architecture: Wright, F.L.

Two lectures on population: Senior, Nassau

Two lectures on the present state and prospects of historical study: Stubbs, William

Two legs and four: †Armstrong, Anthony

Two letters addressed to a member of the present Parliament: Burke, Edmund

Two letters on cow-keeping: Martineau, Harriet

Two letters on the conduct of our domestick parties: Burke, Edmund

Two letters on the tea-tax: Dickinson, John

Two letters to Earl Camden: Canning, George

Two letters to Joseph Conrad: Wells, H.G.

Two letters to Mr. Le Clerc: Newton, *Sir* Isaac

Two letters to the Right Honourable Lord Byron: Bowles, William Lisle

Two lilies: Kavanagh, Julia

Two little confederates: Page, T.N.

Two little pilgrims' progress: Burnett, Frances Hodgson

Two little savages: Seton-Thompson, E.

Two little scamps and a puppy: Brazil, Angela

Two little waifs: Molesworth, *Mrs.*

Two little wooden shoes: †Ouida

Two logs crossing: Edmonds, W.D.

Two lovely beasts: O'Flaherty, Liam

Two loves and a life: Reade, Charles

Two lyric epistles on Margery the cook maid to the Critical Review: Stevenson, J.H.

Two lyric epistles: one to my cousin Shandy on his coming to Town and the other to the grown Gentlewomen the Misses of ***: Stevenson, J.H.

Two Mackenzies, The: Ridge, W.Pett

Two magics, The: James, Henry

Two marriages: Craik, *Mrs.* Dinah

Two marshals, The: Guedalla, Philip

Two Marys, The: Oliphant, Margaret

Two men: Stoddard, E.D.

Two men of Sandy Bar: Harte, Bret

Two mentors, The: Reeve, Clara

Two minstrels: Palmer, H.E.

Two Mrs. Scudamores, The: Oliphant, Margaret

Two nations: Hollis, Christopher

Two noble kinsmen, The: Fletcher, John and William Shakespeare

Two of a kind: Calder-Marshall, Arthur

Two of them: Barrie, *Sir* J.M.

Two of them together, The: Cripps, A.S.

Two offenders: †Ouida

Two old friends: Sheldon, C.M.

Two old men's tales of love and war: McCrae, G.G.

Two on a tower: Hardy, Thomas

Two on an island: Rice, Elmer

Two or three graces: Huxley, Aldous

Two other very commendable letters: Spenser, Edmund

Two other, very commendable letters, of the same mens writing: Harvey, Gabriel

Two Pasquins: Steele, *Sir* Richard

Two paths, The: Ruskin, John

Two people: Milne, A.A.

Two phases of criticism, historical and aesthetic: Woodberry, G.E.

Two pioneers of romanticism: Joseph and Thomas Warton: Gosse, *Sir* Edmund

Two plays for dancers: Yeats, W.B.

Two poems: an incident and an epilogue: Bok, E.W.

Two poems for Christmas: Patchen, Kenneth

Two prima donnas, The: Sala, G.A.H.

Two princes of Persia, The: Porter, Jane

Two prisoners: Page, T.N.

Two proper prides: Traill, H.D.

Two quiet lives: Cecil, *Lord* David

Two revolutions, The: Lockhart, *Sir* Robert Bruce

Two rivulets: Whitman, Walt

Two saplings, The: De la Roche, Mazo

Two scamps: Hannay, J.O.

Two sermons preached in the Church of S. Aloysius, Oxford: Newman, J.H.

Two shall be born: Roberts, T.G.

Two sides of a question: Sinclair, May

Two sides of a story: Lathrop, G.P.

Two sides of the face: (†Q), Quiller-Couch, *Sir* Arthur

Two sides of the river, The: Morris, William

Two sisters, The: Bates, H.E.

Two sisters: Tagore, *Sir* R.

Two slatterns and a king: Millay, E.St.Vincent

Two sons-in-law, The: Payne, J.H.

Two springs, The: Somerville, William

Two stolen dolls: Packard, F.L.

Two stories: a fragmentary poem: Farrell, John

Two stories of the seen and unseen: Oliphant, Margaret

Two strangers: Oliphant, Margaret

Two studies in integrity: Mannin, Ethel

Two sunshine house sonnets: Carman, Bliss

Two surplices, The: Cambridge, Ada

Two thieves, The: Powys, T.F.

2,500 years of Buddhism: Malalasekara, Gunapala

Two to one: Colman, George, *the younger*

Two too many: MacKay, I.E.

Two towers, The: Tolkien, J.R.R.

Two tramps in mud-time: Frost, Robert

Two treatises: Digby, *Sir* Kenelm

Two treatises of government: Locke, John

Two treatises on the quadrature of curves: Newton, *Sir* Isaac

Two under the Indian sun: Godden, Rumer

Two valleys: Fast, Howard M.

Two Vanrevels, The: Tarkington, Booth

Two virtues, The: Sutro, Alfred

Two visits to Denmark: 1872, 1874: Gosse, *Sir* Edmund

Two voices, The: English, Thomas Dunn

Two weeks in another town: Shaw, Irwin

Two wives, The: Swinnerton, Frank

Two women, The: †Henry, O.

Two women: Woolson, C. F.

Two worlds: Gilder, R. W.

Two worlds: an Edinburgh Jewish childhood: Daiches, David

Two worlds and their ways: Compton-Burnett, Ivy

Two worlds for memory: Noyes, Alfred

Two years: O'Flaherty, Liam

Two years ago: Kingsley, Charles

Two years before the mast: Dana, R.H. *junior*

Two years in the French West Indies: Hearn, Lafcadio

Twoo bookes of Francis Bacon of the proficience and advancement of learning divine and humane, The: Bacon, Francis

Two-party system in English Constitutional history, The: Trevelyan, G.M.

Twopence coloured: Hamilton, Patrick

Twos and threes: Stern, G.B.

'Twould puzzle a conjuror: Poole, John

Two-way passage: Adamic, Louis

Twymans, The: Newbolt, *Sir* Henry

Tylney Hall: Hood, Thomas

Tyopa: Glanville, Ernest

Typee: Melville, Herman

Types of American character: Bradford, Gamaliel

Types of Canadian women: Morgan, H.J.

Types of Christian saintliness: Inge, W.R.

Typewriter girl, The: (†Olive Pratt Rayner), Allen, Grant

Typhoon: Conrad, Joseph

Typographical antiquities of Great Britain, The: Dibdin, Thomas Frognall

Typography: Jackson, Holbrook

Tyrannick love: Dryden, John

Tyranny of the ark, The: Garland, Hamlin

Tyranny of words, The: Chase, Stuart

Tyrant, The: Sabatini, Rafael

Tyro, The: Lewis, P.Wyndham

Tyrone Power: Winter, William

Tyrrell's bookshop: Quinn, R.J.

U

U 97: Forester, C.S.

U.E., The: Kirby, William

U.P. Trail, The: Grey, Zane

U.S. foreign policy: shield of the republic: Lippmann, Walter

U.S. 1: Rukeyser, Muriel

U.S. vs Susan B.Anthony, The: Denison, Merrill

U.S. war aims: Lippmann, Walter

U.S.A.: Dos Passos, John

U.S.A.: an outline: Brogan, *Sir* Denis

Ubi ecclesia: Chesterton, G.K.

U-Boat in the Hebrides: Divine, A.D.

Ugly Anna: Coppard, A.E.

Ugly birds without wings, The: †McDiarmid, Hugh

Ugly dachshund, The: Stern, G.B.

Ugly story of Miss Wetherby, The: Pryce, Richard

Ugo Bassi: Wilde, *Lady* J.F.

Ukridge: Wodehouse, P.G.

Uleg Beg: Bacon, Leonard

Ulenspiegel: Dukes, Ashley

Ulick and Soracha: Moore, George

Ulric: Fay, T.S.

Ulster: Kipling, Rudyard

Ultima Thule: Burton, *Sir* Richard

Ultima Thule: Longfellow, H.W.

Ultima Thule: †Richardson, H.H.

Ultima Thule: Stefansson, V.

Ultimate laws of physiology, The: Spencer, Herbert

Ultimate Viking, The: Linklater, Eric

Ultra-crepidarius: Hunt, Leigh

Ultramarine: Lowry, M.B.

Ulysses: Joyce, James

Ulysses: Phillips, Stephen

Ulysses: Rowe, Nicholas

Ulysses S.Grant: Wister, Owen

Ulysses S.Grant, his life and character: Garland, Hamlin

Ulysses: scenes and studies in many lands: Palgrave, W.G.

Ulysses too many, A: Jameson, Storm

Ulysses upon Ajax: Harington, *Sir* John

Umbra: Pound, Ezra

Umbrellas: Baker, Elizabeth

Una and the Red Cross knight: Royde-Smith, Naomi

Unacknowledged legislator, The: Dobrée, Bonamy

Unarmed victory: Russell, Bertrand

Unattainable, The: Maugham, Somerset

Unbearable Bassington, The: Munro, H.H.

Unbeleevers preparing for Christ, The: Hooker, Thomas

Unbidden guest, The: Hornung, E.W.

Unborn tomorrow: Frankau, Gilbert

Uncanny country: Baughan, B.E.

Uncanny stories: Sinclair, May

Uncanny tales: Crawford, F. Marion

Uncanny tales: (†Ennis Graham), Molesworth, *Mrs.*

Uncelestial city, The: Wolfe, Humbert

Uncensored: Rattigan, Terence

Uncertain glory, The: Marshall, Bruce

Uncertain trumpet, The: Hutchinson, Arthur

Uncertainties of Indian finance, The: Hunter, *Sir* William

Unchanging quest: Gibbs, *Sir* Philip

Uncharted way, The: Churchill, Winston

Unclassed, The: Gissing, George

Unclay: Powys, T.F.

Uncle and Aunt: Coolidge, Susan

Uncle Anyhow: Sutro, Alfred

Uncle Ben's whale: Edmonds, W.D.

Uncle Bernac: Doyle, *Sir* Arthur Conan

Uncle Dottery: Powys, T.F.

Uncle dynamite: Wodehouse, P.G.

Uncle Fred in the springtime: Wodehouse, P.G.

Uncle Horace: Hall, A.M.

Uncle Jack: Besant, *Sir* Walter

Uncle Jimmy: Gale, Zona

Uncle Joe's monopoly: Eggleston, Edward

Uncle John: Whyte-Melville, G.J.

Uncle Lionel: Mais, S.P.B.

Uncle Lisha's outing: Robinson, R.E.

Uncle Lisha's shop: life in a corner of Yankee-land: Robinson, R.E.

Uncle of an angel, The: Janvier, T.A.

Uncle Peel: Bacheller, Irving

Uncle Piper of Piper's Hill: †Tasma

Uncle Remus and Brer Rabbit: Harris, Joel Chandler

Uncle Remus and his friends: Harris, Joel Chandler

Uncle Remus and the little boy: Harris, Joel Chandler

Uncle Remus: his songs and his sayings: Harris, Joel Chandler

Uncle Remus returns: Harris, Joel Chandler

Uncle Robert's airship: Jennings, Gertrude

Uncle Sam in the eyes of his family: Erskine, John

Uncle Sam trustee: Bangs, J.K.

Uncle Sam Ward and his circle: Elliott, M.H.

Uncle Sam's emancipation: Stowe, Harriet Beecher

Uncle Sam's money box: Hall, A.M.

Uncle Samson: Nichols, Beverley

Uncle Silas: Le Fanu, Sheridan

Uncle Stephen: Reid, Forrest

Uncle Tom Andy Bill: Major, Charles

Uncle Tom Pudd: Housman, Laurence

Uncle Tom's Cabin: Stowe, Harriet Beecher

Uncle Tom's children: Wright, Richard

Uncle Walter: Trollope, Frances

Uncloseted skeleton: An, Bynner, E.L.

Unclouded summer: Waugh, Alec

Uncommercial traveller, The: Dickens, Charles

Uncommon danger: Ambler, Eric

Uncommon law: Herbert, *Sir* A.P.

Unconditional surrender: Waugh, Evelyn

Unconditioned songs: †Maurice, Furnley

Unconquered, The: Maugham, Somerset

Unconquered isle, The: (†Ian Hay), Beith, *Sir* John Hay

Unconscious Beethoven, The: Newman, Ernest

Unconscious memory: Butler, Samuel

Unconsidered trifles: Mackenzie, *Sir* Compton

Uncrowned King, The: Orczy, *Baroness*

Uncrowned king, The: Wright, H.B.

Undefeated, The: Mitchell, Mary

Under a colored cap: O'Casey, Sean

Under a thatched roof: Hall, J.N.

Under an elm-tree: Morris, William

Under arms: Doughty, C.M.

Under black banner: Trease, Geoffrey

Under Capricorn: Simpson, H. de G.

Under dispute: Repplier, Agnes

Under dog, The: Smith, F.H.

Under Drake's flag: Henty, George

Under glimpses: MacCarthy, *Sir* Denis

Under groove, The: Stringer, A.J.A.

Under London: Gielgud, Val

Under love's rule: Braddon, M.E.

Under Milk Wood: Thomas, Dylan

Under my elm: Baker, R.S.

Under new management: Jacob, Naomi

Under one roof: Cholmondeley, Mary

Under one roof: Payn, James

Under sail in the last of the clippers: Wallace, F.W.

Under sealed orders: Allen, Grant

Under sealed orders: †Bartimeus

Under sealed orders: Cody, H.A.

Under Spokane's brocaded sun: Lindsay, N.V.

Under summer skies: Scollard, Clinton

Under the apple-trees: Burroughs, John

Under the cliff: Grigson, Geoffrey

Under the crust: Page, T.N.

Under the Deodars: Kipling, Rudyard

Under the evening lamp: Stoddard, R.H.

Under the fifth rib: Joad, C.E.M.

Under the greenwood tree: Hardy, Thomas

Under the hill: Beardsley, Aubrey

Under the lilacs: Alcott, Louisa M.

Under the Long Barrow: Palmer, J.L.

Under the maples: Burroughs, John

Under the microscope: Swinburne, A.C.

Under the northern lights: Sullivan, Alan

Under the pylon: Brighouse, Harold

Under the red dragon: Grant, James

Under the red ensign: Tomlinson, H.M.

Under the red flag: Braddon, M.E.

Under the red robe: Weyman, Stanley

Under the Redwoods: Harte, Bret

Under the rose: Davies, Rhys

Under the skin: Bottome, Phyllis

Under the skull and bones: Gow, Ronald

Under the skylights: Fuller, H.B.

Under the sun: Bourinot, A.S.

Under the sun: Sala, G.A.H.

Under the sun: a Jamaica comedy: DeLisser, Herbert G.

Under the sunset: Stoker, Bram

Under the Tonto Rim: Grey, Zane

Under the tree: Roberts, E.M.

Under the volcano: Lowry, M.B.

Under the wheel: Garland, Hamlin

Under the Wilgas: Gilmore, Mary

Under the willows: Lowell, J.R.

Under tropic skies: †Becke, Louis,

Under two flags: †Ouida

Under two skies: Hornung, E.W.

Under Western eyes: Conrad, Joseph

Under which king: Niven, F.J.

Under which Lord?: Linton, Eliza

Underbrush: Fields, J.T.

Undercliff: Eberhart, Richard

Undercurrent, The: Grant, Robert

Underdog: Burnett, W.R.

Undergraduate sonnets: Swinburne, A.C.

Undergrowth: Young, Francis Brett

Under-London: Graham, Stephen

Underneath the bough: †Field, Michael

Understanding drama: Brooks, Cleanth

Understanding fiction: Brooks, Cleanth

Understanding Germany, the only way to end war: Eastman, Max

Understanding poetry: Brooks, Cleanth

Understood Betsey: Canfield, Dorothy

Understudies: Freeman, M.W.

Undertaker's garland, The: Bishop, J.P.

Undertaker's garland, The: Wilson, Edmund

Undertones: Buchanan, R.W.

Undertones: Cawein, Madison

Undertones of war: Blunden, Edmund

Under-woods: Jonson, Ben

Underwoods: Stevenson, R.L.

Undesirable governess, The: Crawford, F. Marion

Undine: Schreiner, Olive

Undiscoverables, The: Bates, Ralph

Undiscovered country, The: Howells, W.D.

Undiscovered Russia: Graham, Stephen

Undreamed of shores: Harris, J.T.

Undying fire, The: Wells, H.G.

Uneasy money: Wodehouse, P.G.

Uneasy terms: †Cheyney, Peter

Unemployment: Gill, Eric

Unemployment, a study syllabus: Cole, G.D.H.

Unemployment and adult education: Chase, Stuart

Unemployment and industrial maintenance: Cole, G.D.H.

Unexpected guest, The: Christie, Agatha

Unexpected guests, The: Howells, W.D.

Unexpected island, The: Lin Yu-T'ang

Unexplored fields of Canadian literature: Pierce, Lorne

Unfaithful wife, The: Royde-Smith, Naomi

Unfinished autobiography, An: Fisher, H.A.L.

Unfinished autobiography, An: Murray, Gilbert

Unfinished business: Erskine, John

Unfinished cathedral: Stribling, T.S.

Unfinished clue, The: Heyer, Georgette

Unfinished journey: Jones, Jack

Unfinished portrait: (†Mary Westmacott) Christie, Agatha

Unfinished road, The: Beresford, J.D.

Unfinished victory: Bryant, Sir Arthur

Unforgettable unforgotten: Buchan, Anna

Unforgotten years: Smith, L.L.P.

Unfortunate man, The: Chamier, Frederick

Unfortunate traveller, The: Nash, Thomas

Unfulfilled, The: Hardy, W.G.

Ungardeners, The: Turner, E.S.

Ungava: Ballantyne, R.M.

Unguarded gates: Aldrich, T.B.

Unhandsome corpse: Campion, Sarah

Unhappy far-off things: Dunsany, Edward Plunkett, Baron

Unheroic North, The: Denison, Merrill

Unhistorical pastoral, An: Davidson, John

Unholy estate, The: Sladen, D.B.W.

Unholy trinity: Gill, Eric

Unholy wish, The: Wood, Ellen

Unicorn: Steen, Marguerite

Unicorn from the stars, The: Gregory, Lady Augusta

Unicorn from the Stars, The: Yeats, W.B.

Unicorn murders, The: †Carter Dickson

Unicorns: Huneker, J.G.

Uniform of glory, The: Wren, P.C.

Uninhabited house, The: Riddell, *Mrs.* J.H.

Uninvited, The: Fairbridge, Dorothea

Union, The: Fitzpatrick, *Sir* J.P.

Union Bible companion, The: Allibone, S.A.

Union officer in the reconstruction, A: De Forest, J.W.

Union portraits: Bradford, Gamaliel

Union square: Halper, Albert

Union Steamship Co.'s edition of Glanville's Guide to South Africa, The: Glanville, Ernest

Unique Hamlet, The: Starrett, Vincent

Uniqueness of Man, The: Huxley, *Sir* Julian

Unit in the social studies: Michener, J.A.

Unitarians and the future: Ward, *Mrs.* Humphrey

United Empire Loyalists, The: Wallace, W.S.

United Empire Loyalists of Canada, The: Kirby, William

United States: an experiment in democracy, The: Becker, C.L.

United States and Canada, The: Wrong, G.M.

United States and the abortive armed neutrality of 1794, The: Bemis, S.F.

United States and the war, The: Murray, Gilbert

United States as a world power, 1900–1950, The: Bemis, S.F.

United States in world affairs, The: Lippmann, Walter

Unity: Beresford, J.D.

Unity of art, The: Ruskin, John

Unity of good: Eddy, M.B.

Unity of India, The: Nehru, J.

Unity of Italy: Dana, R.H. *junior*

Universal arithmetick: Newton, *Sir* Isaac

Universal beauty: Brooke, Henry

Universal dictionary of the marine, An: Falconer, William

Universal English shorthand, The: Byrom, John

Universal gallant, The: Fielding, Henry

Universal hymn: Bailey, P.J.

Universal prayer, A: Montgomery, Robert

Universal suffrage and Napoleon the third: Oliphant, Laurence

Universality of Christ, The: Temple, William

Universe around us, The: Jeans, *Sir* James

Universe of light, The: Bragg, *Sir* William

Universities, The: Wright, Thomas

University and Anglican sermons: Knox, R.A.

University and education today, The: Butterfield, Herbert

University College, London, 1828–1878: Morley, Henry

University Hall: opening address: Ward, *Mrs.* Humphrey

University of Illinois in retrospect, The: Van Doren, Mark

University of London election: Wells, H.G.

University of New Zealand, The: Beaglehole, J.C.

University of the state of New York, The: Curtis, G.W.

Unjust judge, The: Hall, A.M.

Unjust steward, The: Oliphant, Margaret

Unkind word, The: Craik, *Mrs.* D.M.

Unknowable, The: Santayana, George

Unknown, The: Lathom, Francis

Unknown, The: Maugham, Somerset

Unknown Ajax, The: Heyer, Georgette

Unknown assailant: Hamilton, Patrick

Unknown Cornwall: Vulliamy, C.E.

Unknown country, An: Craik, *Mrs.* D.M.

Unknown Devon: Peach, L. Du Garde

Unknown Eros, The: Patmore, Coventry

Unknown God, The: Noyes, Alfred

Unknown goddess, The: Wolfe, Humbert

Unknown known, The: Moore, T.S.

Unknown land, An: Samuel, Herbert *1st Viscount*

Unknown lover, The: Gosse, *Sir* Edmund

Unknown to history: Yonge, Charlotte M.

Unknown warrior, The: Palmer, H.E.

Unknown wrestler, The: Cody, H.A.

Unleavened bread: Grant, Robert

Unless I marry: Stern, G.B.

Unlit lamp, The: Hall, M.R.

Unlovely sin, The: Hecht, Ben

Unlucky number, The: Phillpotts, Eden

Unmade in heaven: Bradford, Gamaliel

Unmarried father, An: Dell, Floyd

Unnamed lake, The: Scott, F.G.

Unnatural death: Sayers, Dorothy

Unnaturall combat, The: Massinger, Philip

Unobstructed universe, The: White, S.E.

Unofficial despatches: Wallace, Edgar

Unpardonable liar, An: Parker, *Sir* H.G.

Unpleasant visitors, The: Mackenzie, *Sir* Compton

Unpleasantness at the Bellona Club, The: Sayers, Dorothy

Unpopular essays: Russell, Bertrand

Unpopular opinions: Sayers, Dorothy

Unpractised heart, The: Strong, L.A.G.

Unprofessional essays: Murry, John Middleton

Unprofessional tale. †Normyx: Douglas, Norman

Unpublished letters: Arnold, Matthew

Unpublished orations: Fiske, John

Unquiet field, An: Seymour, Beatrice Kean

Unquiet grave, The: Connolly, Cyril

Unquiet spirit, The: Steen, Marguerite

Unravelled knots: Orczy, *Baroness*

Unreality: †Bartimeus

Unrelenting struggle, The: Churchill, *Sir* Winston

Unreliable history: Baring, Maurice

Unrest: Deeping, Warwick

Unreturning, The: Carman, Bliss

Unseen assassins, The: Angell, *Sir* Norman

Unseen friend, The: Larcom, Lucy

Unseen kings: Gore-Booth, E.S.

Unseen life of New York: Beebe, William

Unseen witness, The: Kantor, Mackinlay

Unseen world, The: Fiske, John

Unsentimental journey through Cornwall, An: Craik, *Mrs.* D.M.

Unsocial Socialist, An: Shaw, G.B.

Unsolved problems in woman suffrage: Higginson, T.W.

Unspeakable gentleman, The: Marquand, J.P.

Unspeakable Skipton, The: Johnson, Pamela Hansford

Unspoken sermons: Macdonald, George

Unspoken thoughts: Cambridge, Ada

Unsuspected chasm: (†Michael Innes), Stewart, J.I.M.

Untamed, The: †Brand, Max

Untamed America: Mackaye, Percy

Untidy gnome, The: Gibbons, Stella

Until the day break: Bromfield, Louis

Untilled field, The: Moore, George

Untimely papers: Bourne, R.S.

Unto Caesar: Orczy, *Baroness*

Unto such glory: Green, Paul

Unto the third generation: Shiel, M.P.

Unto this last: Ruskin, John

Untold adventures of Santa Claus, The: Nash, Ogden

Untouchable: Anand, M.R.

Untrodden ways: Massingham, Harold

Untutored townsman's invasion of the country, The: Joad, C.E.M.

Unum Necessarium: Taylor, Jeremy

Unvanquished: Fast, Howard M.

Unvanquished, The: Faulkner, William

Unveiled: Seymour, B.K.

Unwelcome man, The: Frank, Waldo

Up among the ice-floes: Oxley, J.M.

Up and down: Benson, E.F.

Up and down the house: Warner, A.B.

Up and down the London streets: Lemon, Mark

Up and out: Powys, John Cowper

Up at the hills: Taylor, Tom

Up at the villa: Maugham, Somerset

Up country: Peattie, D.C.

Up from nowhere: Tarkington, Booth

Up from slavery: Washington, B.T.

Up hill, down dale: Phillpotts, Eden

Up in the hills: Dunsany, Edward Plunkett, *Baron*

Up, into the singing mountain: Llewellyn, Richard

Up North: (†Donald Barr), Barrett, C.L.

Up side streets: Ridge, W.Pett

Up stream: Lewisohn, Ludwig

Up Terrapin river: Read, O.P.

Up the country: †Brent of Bin Bin

Up the country: Eden, Emily

Up the hill and over: MacKay, I.E.

Up the ladder of gold: Oppenheim, E. Phillips

Up the rebels: Hannay, J.O.

Up the Rhine: Hood, Thomas

Up the trail from Texas: Dobie, J.F.

Up to her chamber window: Aldrich, T.B.

Up to Mametz: Griffith, Llewelyn

Up to midnight: Meredith, George

Up-along and down-along: Phillpotts, Eden

Upanishads for the lay reader: Rajagopalachari, Chakravati

Upas tree, The: Barclay, F.L.

Upbuilders: Steffens, Lincoln

Upholsterer, The: Murphy, Arthur

Uplands: Chase, M.E.

Uplands of dream: Saltus, E. E.

Upon her Majesty's new buildings: Waller, Edmund

Upon the marriage of the Prince of Orange with the Lady Mary: Oldham, John

Upon this rock: Cammaerts, Emile

Upper berth, The: Crawford, F. Marion

Upper Canada sketches: Riddell, W.R.

Upper Rhine, The: Mayhew, Henry

Uprooted: Whitlock, Brand

Ups and downs: †Boldrewood, Rolf

Ups and downs: Hale, E.E.

Upside-down: Mackail, Denis

Up-to-date primer, The: Bengough, J.W.

Upton letters, The: Benson, A.C.

Upton Sinclair: Dell, Floyd

Upward anguish, The: Wolfe, Humbert

Ur excavations: Woolley, *Sir* Leonard

Ur of the Chaldees: Woolley, *Sir* Leonard

Urania: Pitter, Ruth

Urania: Spencer, W.R.

Urania: a rhymed lesson: Holmes, Oliver Wendell

Urbanities: Lucas, E.V.

Urchin Moor: Royde-Smith, Naomi

Urgent hangman, The: †Cheyney, Peter

Uriah on the hill: Powys, T.F.

Uriconium: Wright, Thomas

Uriel: Mackaye, Percy

Urith: Baring-Gould, Sabine

Urlyn the harper: Gibson, Wilfred

Ursa Major: Doctor Johnson and his friends: Vulliamy, C.E.

"Us" an old fashioned story: Molesworth, *Mrs.*

Usage and abusage: Partridge, Eric

Use of drama, The: Barker, Harley Granville-

Use of man, The: Dunsany, Edward Plunkett, *Baron*

Use of poetry and the use criticism, The: Eliot, T.S.

Use of riches, A: (†Michael Innes), Stewart, J.I.M.

Useful knowledge Useful knowledge Useful knowledge: Stein, Gertrude

Useful miscellanies, King: William

Useful transactions in philosophy: King, William

Useful work versus useless toil: Morris, William

Usefulness of the stage, The: Dennis, John

Uses of diversity, The: Chesterton, G.K.

Ushant: Aiken, Conrad

Usurper, The: McHenry, James

Ut pictura poesis!: Colman, George, *the elder*

Utamaro: Noguchi, Yone

Uther and Igraine: Deeping, Warwick

Utilitarianism: Mill, John Stuart

Utopia: Gilbert, *Sir* W.S.

Utopia of usurpers: Chesterton, G.K.

Uttermost farthing, The: Lowndes, *Mrs.* Belloc

V

V-E Day: Brown, A.A.

V.I.P.'s, The: Rattigan, Terence

V-Letter: Shapiro, Karl

V.V.: Alcott, Louisa M.

Vacant country, The: Wells, H.G.

Vacation of the Kelwyns, The: Howells, W.D.

Vacation rambles: Hughes, Thomas

Vacation rambles and thoughts: Talfourd, *Sir* T.N.

Vacation song: Millay, E. St. Vincent

Vacation tourists: Galton, *Sir* Francis

Vachel Lindsay, a poet in America: Masters, E.L.

Vagabond in the Caucasus, A: Graham, Stephen

Vagabond tales: Boyesen, H.H.

Vagabondiana: Smith, J.T.

Vagabonds, The: Carman, Bliss

Vagabonds, The: Trowbridge, J.T.

Vagabonds, The: Woods, M.L.

Vagabunduli Libellus: Symonds, J.A.

Vagaries vindicated: Colman, George, *the younger*

Vagrant memories: Winter, William

Vailima letters: Stevenson, R.L.

Vain fortune: Moore, George

Vain oblations: Gerould, Katherine

Vain pursuit: Richards, Grant

Vainglory: Firbank, Ronald

Val D'Arno: Ruskin, John

Vale: Inge, W.R.

Vale: Russell, G.W.

Vale of cedars, The: Aguilar, Grace

Vale of shadows, The: Scollard, Clinton

Vale of tempe, The: Cawein, Madison

Valedictory: Kantor, MacKinlay

Valentin: Kingsley, Henry

Valentine: Richards, Grant

Valentine impromptu, A: Carman, Bliss

Valentine McClutchy: Carleton, William

Valentine verses: Cobbold, Richard

Valentine's Eve: Opie, Amelia

Valentinian: Beaumont, Francis

Valentinian: Rochester, John Wilmot, *Earl of*

Valerie: an autobiography: Marryatt, Frederick

Valerie French: †Yates, Dornford

Valerie Upton: Sedgwick, A.D.

Valerius: (†Gordon Daviot), Mackintosh, Elizabeth

Valerius: Lockhart, J.G.

Valet's tragedy, The: Lang, Andrew

Valiant dust: Gerould, Katherine

Valiant dust: Wren, P.C.

Valiant is the word for Carrie: Benefield, Barry

Valiant ladies: Bax, Clifford

Valiant one, The: Crothers, Rachel

Valiant runaways, The: Atherton, Gertrude

Valiant woman, The: Kaye-Smith, Sheila

Valley captives, The: Macaulay, *Dame* Rose

Valley Forge: Anderson, Maxwell

Valley of bones, The: Powell, Anthony

Valley of decision: Davenport, Marcia

Valley of decision, The: Wharton, Edith

Valley of democracy, The: Nicholson, Meredith

Valley of fear, The: Doyle, *Sir* Arthur Conan

Valley of ghosts, The: Wallace, Edgar

Valley of Shenandoah, The: Tucker, George

Valley of stars, The: (†Wallace Dixon), Cronin, B.C.

Valley of the Humber, 1615–1913, The: Lizars, K.M.

Valley of the kings, The: Pickthall, M.W.

Valley of the moon, The: Lewis, H.S.

Valley of the moon, The: London, Jack

Valley of the shadow, The: Robinson, E.A.

Valley of the wild horses: Grey, Zane

Valley of thunder: Beach, R.E.

Valley of vision, The: Fisher, V.A.

Valley vultures: †Brand, Max

Valleys beyond, The: Timms, E.V.

Valleys of the assassins, The: Stark, Freya

Vallombrosa: Story, W.W.

Valmouth: Firbank, Ronald

Valour: Deeping, Warwick

Valperga: Shelley, Mary

Valse des fleurs: Sitwell, Sacheverell

Values for survival: Mumford, Lewis

Values of the vote: Eastman, Max

Vampire, The: Kipling, Rudyard

Vampire, The: Palmer, H.E.

Van Am!: Bangs, J.K.

Van Bibber and others: Davis, R.H.

Van Der Decken: Belasco, David

Van Dyck: Lucas, E.V.

Van lords: Royde-Smith, Naomi

Van Zorn: Robinson, E.A.

Vanderlyn's kingdom: (†Michael Innes), Stewart, J.I.M.

Vandover and the brute: †Norris, Frank

Vane sisters, The: Nabokov, Vladimir

Vane's story: Thomson, James

Vanessa: Walpole, Sir Hugh

Vanessa and her correspondence with Swift: Swift, Jonathan

Vanished Arcadia, A: Cunninghame Graham, R.B.

Vanished fleets: Villiers, A.J.

Vanished messenger, The: Oppenheim, E. Phillips

Vanished supremacies: Namier, Sir Lewis

Vanished trails: Spittel, R.L.

Vanished tribes, The: Devaney, J.M.

Vanishing American, The: Grey, Zane

Vanishing gift, The: †Corelli, Marie

Vanishing hero, The: O'Faolain, Sean

Vanishing points: Brown, Alice

Vanishing roads: Le Gallienne, Richard

Vanitas: †Lee, Vernon

Vanities and verities: Mottram, R.H.

Vanity Fair: Pryce-Jones, A.P.

Vanity Fair: Thackeray, W.M.

Vanity girl, The: Mackenzie, Sir Compton

Vanity of dogmatizing, The: Glanvill, Joseph

Vanity of human wishes, The: Johnson, Samuel

Vanity row: Burnett, W.R.

Vanity Square: Saltus, E.E.

Vanity under the sun: Collins, Dale

Vanneck: Grant, Robert

'Vantage striker: Simpson, H. de G.

Vaquero of the brush country, A: Dobie, J.F.

Varia: Repplier, Agnes

Variable winds at Jalna: De la Roche, Mazo

Variants in the first quarto of King Lear, The: Greg, W.W.

Variation of animals and plants under domestication, The: Darwin, Charles

Variation of public opinion, The: Crabbe, George

Variation on a theme: Collier, John

Variation on a theme: Rattigan, Terence

Variations: Huneker, J.G.

Variations on a time theme: Muir, Edwin

Variations on the theme of music: Turner, W.J.R.

Varieties of religious experience, The: James, William

Variety: †Grand, Sarah

Variety: Whitehead, William

Variety lane: Lucas, E.V.

Variety of people, A: Marquis, Don

Variety of things, A: Beerbohm, Sir Max

Variety of ways: Dobrée, Bonamy

Various scientific papers on crystal structure: Bragg, Sir Lawrence

Various views of human nature: Moore, Dr. John

Varsity story, The: Callaghan, M.E.

Vasavadutta: Ghose, Sri Aurobindo

Vasconselos: Simms, W.G.

Vashti: Evans, Sir A.J.

Vassal affair, The: †West, Rebecca

Vassall Morton: Parkman, Francis

Vathek: Beckford, William

Vaticinium causale: Wither, George

Vats of tyre, The: Bridges, Roy

Vaurien: D'Israeli, Isaac

Vee Boers, The: Reid, T.M.

Vegetable kingdom, The: Colum, Padraic

Vegetable, or, from president to postman, The: Fitzgerald, F. Scott

Vehement flame, The: Deland, Margaret

Veil, The: De la Mare, Walter

Veil of the temple, The: Mallock, W.H.

Veiled delight, The: †Bowen, Marjorie

Veiled lady, The: Smith, F.H.

Veiled women: Pickthall, M.W.

Veils: Hichens, Robert

Vein of iron: Glasgow, Ellen

Velasco: Sargent, Epes

Velasquez: Lucas, E.V.

Veld Patriarch: Slater, F.C.

Veldt official, A: Mitford, Bertram

Veldt vendetta, A: Mitford, Bertram

Veld verse: Fairbridge, K.O.

Velvet glove, The: †Merriman, Seton

Velvet Johnnie: †Cheyney, Peter

Velvet studies: Wedgwood, C.V.

Vence: Peattie, D.C.

Vendetta: †Corelli, Marie

Vendetta, The: Parker, Sir H.G.

Vendetta of the desert, A: Scully, W.C.

Venetia: Disraeli, Benjamin

Venetia: Heyer, Georgette

Venetian blinds: Mannin, Ethel

Venetian bracelet, The: Landon, L.E.M.

Venetian glass nephew, The: Wylie, Elinor

Venetian life: Howells, W.D.

Venetian lovers: Gibbs, *Sir* Philip

Venetian masque: Sabatini, Raphael

Venetian painters of the Renaissance: Berenson, Bernhard

Venetian painting in America—the fifteenth century: Berenson, Bernhard

Venetian Trelawny: Reynolds, G.

Venetians, The: Braddon, M.E.

Vengeance of Noel Brassard, The: Carman, Bliss

Vengeance of the gang, The: Gow, Ronald

Vengeance of the gods, The: Warner, Rex

Veni Creator!: Wolfe, Humbert

Venice: Domett, Alfred

Venice: Hare, A.J.C.

Venice: Sullivan, Alan

Venice of today: Smith, F.H.

Venice preserv'd: Otway, Thomas

Venkataramani—writer and thinker: Isvaran, M.S.

Venoni: Lewis, M.G.

Ventilations: Pearson, Hesketh

Venture: Eastman, Max

Venture in 1777, A: Mitchell, S.W.

Venture to the interior: Van der Post, Laurens

Ventures, The: Dehn, Paul

Ventures into verse: Mencken, H.L.

Venus and Adonis: Cibber, Colley

Venus and Adonis: Shakespeare, William

Venus and Anchises: Fletcher, Phineas

Venus half-castle: Mann, Leonard

Venus in the kitchen: Douglas, Norman

Venus invisible: Crane, Nathalai

Venus observed: Fry, Christopher

Venus of Milo: Sill, E.R.

Venus over Lannery: Armstrong, M.D.

Venus rising from the sea: Bennett, Arnold

Venusberg: Powell, Anthony

Vera: Russell, E.M.

Vera: Wilde, Oscar

Vera the medium: Davis, R.H.

Veracity: Livingstone, Sir Richard

Veranilda: Gissing, G.R.

Verbena Camellia Stephanotis: Besant, *Sir* Walter

Verbum Sempiternae: Taylor, John

Verdict: Christie, Agatha

Verdict of Bridlegoose, The: Powys, L.C.

Verdict of the sea, The: Sullivan, Alan

Verdict of twelve: Postgate, Raymond

Verdict on India: Nichols, Beverley

Verdun Belle: Woollcott, A.H.

Vere of Ours: Grant, James

Verena in the midst: Lucas, E.V.

Vérendrye: Stephen, A.M.

Verge, The: Glaspell, Susan

Vergil: MacMechan, A.M.

Vergilius: Bacheller, Irving

Vermeer of Delft: Lucas, E.V.

Vermeer the magical: Lucas, E.V.

Vermilion boat, The: Ghose, S.N.

Vermilion gate, The: Lin Yu-T'ang

Vermilion box, The: Lucas, E.V.

Vermont: a study of independence: Robinson, R.E.

Vermont summer homes: Canfield, Dorothy

Vermont tradition: Canfield, Dorothy

Vernal walk, The: Elliott, Ebenezer

Verner's pride: Wood, Ellen

Vernon's aunt: Duncan, S.J.

Verona: Ruskin, John

Veronica: Munro, C.K.

Verry merry wherry-ferry-voyage, A: Taylor, John

Versailles treaty and after, The: Baker, R.S.

Versatilities: (†Orpheus C. Kerr), Newell, R.H.

Verse in bloom: Gale, Norman

Verse of Hilaire Belloc: Belloc, Hilaire

Verses: Belloc, Hilaire

Verses addressed to her two nephews on St. Helen's Day: Williams, H.M.

Verses and ditties made at the coronation of Queen Anne: Udall, Nicholas

Verses and reverses: Meynell, Wilfred

Verses and sonnets: Belloc, Hilaire

Verses by two undergraduates: Brooks, Van Wyck

Verses by two undergraduates: Wheelock, J.H.

Verses composed at the request of Jane Wallis Penfold: Wordsworth, William

Verses dedicated to her mother: Rossetti, C.G.

Verses for children (The blue bells on the lea, Mother's birthday review, and A soldier's children): Ewing, *Mrs.* Juliana

Verses for Mrs. Daniel: Bridges, Robert

Verses for penitents: Newman, J.H.

Verses from Glenarvon: Lamb, *Lady* Caroline

Verses from 1929 on: Nash, Ogden

Verses humbly address'd to Sir Thomas Hanmer: Collins, William

Verses humbly presented to the King, at his arrival in Holland: Prior, Matthew

Verses in peace and war: Leslie, *Sir* J.R. Shane

Verses lately written: Cowley, Abraham

Verses new and old: Galsworthy, John

Verses of a V.A.D.: Brittain, Vera

Verses of other days: Hayward, Abraham

Verses of the sea: Pratt, E.J.

Verses on religious subjects: Newman, J.H.

Verses on Sir Joshua Reynolds's painted window at New College, Oxford: Warton, Thomas

Verses on the Benevolent Institution of the Philanthropic Society: Bowles, William Lisle

Verses on the death of D. Swift: Swift, Jonathan

Verses on the death of Lady Anson: Mallet, David

Verses on the death of P. B. Shelley: Barton, Bernard

Verses on the late unanimous resolutions to support the constitution: Brydges, *Sir* Samuel Egerton

Verses on various subjects written in the vicinity of Stoke Park: Pye, H. J.

Verses, popular and humorous: Lawson, Henry

Verses presented to the Prince of Orange: Mallet, David

Verses sacred and profane: †O'Sullivan, Seumas

Verses spoken to the Lady Henrietta-Cavendish Holles Harley, in the library of St. John's College, Cambridge: Prior, Matthew

Verses to John Howard Esq.: Bowles, William Lisle

Verses to order: Godley, A. D.

Verses to the memory of Garrick spoken as a monody: Sheridan, R. B.

Verses to the memory of Mr. Pelham: Cibber, Colley

Verses to the memory of Richard Reynolds: Montgomery, James

Verses to the people of England: Whitehead, William

Verses written in India: Lyall, *Sir* Alfred

Verses written in Westminster Abbey, after the funeral of Charles James Fox: Rogers, Samuel

Verses written while we lived in tents: Howitt, Richard

Version of Ossian's address to the sun, A: Byron, George Gordon *Lord*

Versions from Hafiz: Leaf, Walter

Versus: Nash, Ogden

Versus inopes rerum, nugaquae Canorae: Jenyns, Soame

Vertue of the Masse, The: Lydgate, John

Very good, Jeeves: Wodehouse, P. G.

Very heaven: Muir, D. C. A.

Very house, The: De la Roche, Mazo

Very strange, but very true: Lathom, Francis

Very woman, A: Massinger, Philip

Very young and quite another story: Ingelow, Jean

Very young couple, A: Farjeon, B. L.

Vespers: Milne, A. A.

Vespers in Vienna: Marshall, Bruce

Vespers of Palermo: Hemans, *Mrs.* Felicia

Vesprie Towers: Watts-Dunton, W. T.

Vessels departing: Williams, Emlyn

Vestal fire: Mackenzie, *Sir* Compton

Vested interests: Veblen, T. B.

Vestiges of the natural history of creation: Chambers, Robert

Vestigia retrorsum: Munby, A. J.

Veteran and his pipe, The: Tourgée, A. W.

Via Borealis: Scott, D. C.

Via Crucis: Crawford, F. Marion

Via intelligentiae: Taylor, Jeremy

Viaduct murder, The: Knox, R. A.

Via-Media of the Anglican Church, The: Newman, J. H.

Vicar of Bullhampton, The: Trollope, Anthony

Vicar of Dunkerly Briggs, The: Golding, Louis

Vicar of Morwenstow, The: Baring-Gould, Sabine

Vicar of the marches, The: Scollard, Clinton

Vicar of Wakefield, The: Goldsmith, Oliver

Vicar of Wakefield, The: Housman, Laurence

Vicar of Wrexhill, The: Trollope, Frances

Vicarious sacrifice, The: Bushnell, Horace

Vicarious years, The: Van Druten, John

Vicar's daughter, The: Macdonald, George

Vicar's experiments, The: Vulliamy, C. E.

Vicar's guest, The: Cambridge, Ada

Vicar's walk: Vachell, H. A.

Vice and luxury public mischiefs: Dennis, John

Vice versa: †Anstey, F.

Viceroy Sarah: Ginsbury, Norman

Vicissitudes of a life, The: James, G. P. R.

Vicissitudes of Evangeline, The: Glyn, Elinor

Victim, The: Dixon, Thomas

Victim, The: Tennyson, Alfred *Lord*

Victim of circumstance, A: Gissing, George

Victims of Society, The: Blessington, Marguerite

Victor Daley: Stephens, A. G.

Victor Hugo: Cappon, James

Victor Ollnee's discipline: Garland, Hamlin

Victoria: Austin, Alfred

Victoria: Rowson, S. H.

Victoria: a pig in a pram: Chase, M. E.

Victoria and Albert: Housman, Laurence

Victoria and Disraeli: Bolitho, H. H.

Victoria County Centennial history: Kirkconnell, Watson

Victoria four-thirty: Roberts, C. E. M.

Victoria of England: Sitwell, Edith

Victoria, Queen and Empress: Arnold, Edwin

Victoria Regina: Housman, Laurence

Victoria, the widow and her son: Bolitho, H. H.

Victoria University College: Beaglehole, J. C.

Victoria Victrix: Whitehead, Charles

Victorian age, The: Inge, W. R.

Victorian age in literature, The: Chesterton, G. K.

Victorian age of English literature, The: Oliphant, Margaret

Victorian England: Young, G.M.

Victorian era, The: Murdoch, *Sir* W.L.F.

Victorian house, The: Child, P.A.

Victorian ode for Jubilee Day: Thompson, Francis

Victorian Order of Nurses for Canada, The: Gibbon, J.M.

Victorian panorama: Quennell, Peter

Victorian peep-show: Armstrong, M.D.

Victorian poetry: Drinkwater, John

Victorian poets: Stedman, E.C.

Victorian prose masters: Brownell, William C.

Victorian schoolmaster, A: Coulton, G.G.

Victorian village, A: Reese, L.W.

Victoriana: Sitwell, *Sir* Osbert

Victorians, The: Petrie, *Sir* Charles

Victorians and after, The: Dobrée, Bonamy

Victories of love, The: Patmore, Coventry

Victories of the British armies, The: Maxwell, W.H.

Victorious defeat, A: Balestier, C.W.

Victorious Troy: Masefield, John

Victors, beware: Madariaga, Salvador de

Victors of peace—Florence Nightingale, Pasteur, Father Damien: (†Q), Quiller-Couch, *Sir* Arthur

Victory: Churchill, Winston

Victory: Conrad, Joseph

Victory and death of Lord Viscount Nelson, The: Cumberland, Richard

Victory at Valmy: Trease, Geoffrey

Victory for the slain: Lofting, Hugh

Victory in the Pacific: Morison, S.E.

Vida: Crockett, S.R.

Vidyapati: Coomaraswamy, A.K.

Vienna: Spender, Stephen

Vienna and the Austrians: Trollope, Frances

View from a blind I, The: Barker, George

View from here, The: Coates, R.M.

View from Pompey's head, The: Basso, Hamilton

View from the Parsonage, The: Kaye-Smith, Sheila

View from this window, The: Whistler, Laurence

View of certain military matters, A: Savile, *Sir* Henry

View of Lord Bolingbroke's philosophy in four letters to a friend, A: Warburton, William

View of society and manners in Italy, A: Moore, *Dr.* John

View of society in France, Switzerland, etc., A: Moore, *Dr.* John

View of sundry examples, A: Munday, Anthony

View of the controversy between Great Britian and her colonies, A: Seabury, Samuel

View of the English stage, A: Hazlitt, William

View of the general tenour of the New Testament regarding the nature of Jesus Christ, A: Baillie, Joanna

View of the hard labour bill: Bentham, Jeremy

View of the internal evidence of the Christian religion, A: Jenyns, Soame

View of the present state of Ireland, A: Spenser, Edmund

View of the state of Europe during the Middle Ages: Hallam, Henry

View over the park: Snow, C.P.

Views afoot: Taylor, Bayard

Views and opinions: †Ouida

Views and opinions: Rands, W.B.

Views and reviews: Ellis, Havelock

Views and reviews: Ghose, Sri Aurobindo

Views and reviews: James, Henry

Views and reviews; essays in appreciation (art): Henley, W.E.

Views and reviews; essays in appreciation (literature): Henley, W.E.

Views and reviews in American literature, history and fiction, The: Simms, W.G.

Views and vagabonds: Macaulay, *Dame* Rose

Views in Rome and its environs: Lear, Edward

Views of Attica: Warner, Rex

Views of the Ionian islands: Lear, Edward

Views of the public debt: Gallatin, Albert

"Vigil": Mackay, Jessie

Vigil: Williams, Emlyn

Vigil of a nation, The: Lin Yu-T'ang

Vigil of faith, The: Hoffman, C.F.

Vigil of Venus, The: (†Q), Quiller-Couch, *Sir* Arthur

Vigils: Sassoon, Siegfried

Vignettes from nature: Allen, Grant

Vignettes of Manhattan: Matthews, J.B.

Viking blood, The: Wallace, F.W.

Viking heart, The: Salverson, L.G.

Viking's dawn: Treece, Henry

Viking's sunset: Treece, Henry

Vikings of today: Grenfell, *Sir* Wilfred

Vile bodies: Waugh, Evelyn

Villa anodyne: Frankau, Pamela

Villa Claudia, The: Mitchell, J.A.

Villa Rubein: (†John Sinjohn) Galsworthy, John

Village, The: Anand, M.R.

Village, The: Crabbe, George

Village Anglicum: Spelman, *Sir* Henry

Village, are you ready yet not yet, A: Stein, Gertrude

Village at war: †Armstrong, Anthony

Village band, The: Dole, N.H.

Village bells: Manning, Anne

Village book, The: Williamson, Henry

Village Casanova: †Bell, Neil

Village commune, A: †Ouida

Village coquettes, The: Dickens, Charles

Village daybook: Derleth, A.W.

Village doctor, The: Kaye-Smith, Sheila

Village garland, The: Hall, Anna Maria

Village green, The: Miller, Thomas

Village improvement parade, The: Lindsay, N.V.

Village in a valley, A: Nichols, Beverley

Village in the jungle, The: Woolf, Leonard

Village inn, The: Herbert, H.W.

Village magazine, The: Lindsay, N.V.

Village merchant, The: Freneau, Philip

Village minstrel, The: Clare, John

Village of Mariendorpt, The: Porter, A.M.

Village of souls, The: Child, P.A.

Village patriarch, The: Elliott, Ebenezer

Village politics: (†Will Chip), More, Hannah

Village sermons preached at Whatley: Church, Richard

Village street, The: †Brand, Max

Village tragedy, A: Woods, M.L.

Village verse book, The: Bowles, William Lisle

Village watch-tower, The: Wiggin, Kate

Village wife's lament, The: Hewlett, Maurice

Village wooing, The: Shaw, G.B.

Village year: Derleth, A.W.

Villare Cantianum: Philipot, Thomas

Villette: Brontë, Charlotte

Vindication of His Excellency the Lord C—t, A: Swift, Jonathan

Vindication of Isaac Bickerstaff Esq., A: Swift, Jonathan

Vindication of Lord Byron, A: Austin, Alfred

Vindication of natural diet, A: Shelley, P.B.

Vindication of natural society, A: Burke, Edmund

Vindication of providence, A: Young, Edward

Vindication of some passages in the fifteenth and sixteenth chapters of the history of the decline and fall of the Roman Empire, A: Gibbon, Edward

Vindication of the appendix to the poems called Rowley's, A: Tyrwhitt, Thomas

Vindication of the British colonies, A: Otis, James

Vindication of the Church and State of Scotland, A: Burnet, Gilbert

Vindication of the conduct of the House of Representatives, A: Otis, James

Vindication of the government of the New-England churches, A: Wise, John

Vindication of the reasonableness of Christianity, from Mr. Edward's reflections, A: Locke, John

Vindication of the rights of men in a letter to Edmund Burke, A: Wollstonecraft, Mary

Vindication of the rights of woman, A: Wollstonecraft, Mary

Vindiciae Ecclesiae Anglicanae: Southey, Robert

Vindiciae Hibernicae: Carey, Mathew

Vindiciae Wykehamicae: Bowles, William Lisle

Vindictive man, The: Holcroft, Thomas

Vinedresser, The: Moore, T.S.

Vineyard, The: †Hobbes, John Oliver

Vinland the good: †Shute, Nevil

Vintage: Benson, E.F.

Vintage London: Betjeman, John

Vintage murder: Marsh, Ngaio Edith

Viola Gwynne: McCutcheon, G.B.

Violante: †Preedy, George

Violet, The: Brontë, Charlotte

Violet fairy book, The: Lang, Andrew

Violet Jermyn: Grant, James

Violet Moses: Merrick, Leonard

Viper of Milan, The: †Bowen, Marjorie

Viper's progress: Mitchell, Mary

Virgidemiarum: Hall, Joseph

Virgil: Woodberry, G.E.

Virgin: Vachell, H.A.

Virgin and the gipsy, The: Lawrence, D.H.

Virgin in judgement, The: Phillpotts, Eden

Virgin Martir, The: Massinger, Philip and Thomas Dekker

Virgin of the sun, The: Haggard, Sir H. Rider

Virgin prophetesse, The: Settle, Elkanah

Virgin Spain: Frank, Waldo

Virgin widow, The: Quarles, Francis

Virgin widow, The: Taylor, Sir Henry

Virgin with the laughing child, The: Pope-Hennessy, J.W.

Virginia: Brooke, Frances

Virginia: Cooke, John Esten

Virginia: Glasgow, Ellen

Virginia Bohemians, The: Cooke, John Esten

Virginia comedians, The: Cooke, John Esten

Virginia of Elk Creek Valley: Chase, M.E.

Virginia Woolf: Daiches, David

Virginia Woolf: Forster, E.M.

Virginia Woolf: a critical study: Holtby, Winifred

Virginian, The: Wister, Owen

Virginians, The: Thackeray, W.M.

Virginians are coming again, The: Lindsay, N.V.

Virginians in Texas, The: Baker, W.M.

Virginibus puerisque: Stevenson, R.L.

Virginius: Knowles, James Sheridan

Virgins character, The: Massinger, Philip

Virtue of the shoe, The: Bangs, J.K.

Virtues of Sid Hamet the magician's rod, The: Swift, Jonathan

Virtuoso, The: Shadwell, Thomas

Virtuous girl, A: Bodenheim, Maxwell

Virtuous knight, The: Sherwood, R.E.

Virtuous woman, A: Muir, D.C.A.

Viscosity and plasticity: Andrade, E.N. da Costa

Visibility good: Lucas, E.V.

Vision, The: Beckford, William

Vision, The: Cary, Henry

Vision, The: Defoe, Daniel

Vision: Pickthall, M.L.C.

Vision, A: Yeats, W.B.

Vision, concerning his late pretended Highness, Cromwell the wicked, A: Cowley, Abraham

Vision of William, concerning Piers Plowman: Langland, William

Vision of William concerning Piers Plowman, The: Skeat, W.W.

Vision of bags, A: Swinburne, A.C.

Vision of beasts and gods, A: Barker, George

Vision of Columbus, The: Barlow, Joel

Vision of Cortes, Cain and other poems, The: Simms, W.G.

Vision of Don Roderick, The: Scott, *Sir* Walter

Vision of Echard, The: Whittier, J.G.

Vision of Er, The: Doyle, *Sir* Francis

Vision of future India, A: Masani, *Sir* R.P.

Vision of Giorgione, A: Bottomley, Gordon

Vision of Heaven, A: Montgomery, Robert

Vision of Hell, A: Montgomery, Robert

Vision of judgement, The: Byron, George Gordon *Lord*

Vision of judgement, A: Southey, Robert

Vision of Mons. Chamillard concerning the Battle of Ramilies, The: Phillips, John

Vision of saints, A: Morris, *Sir* Lewis

Vision of Sappho, A: Carman, Bliss

Vision of Sir Launfal, The: Lowell, J.R.

Vision of the mermaids, A: Hopkins, Gerard Manley

Vision of the three T's, The: †Carroll, Lewis

Vision of the 12 goddesses, The: Daniel, Samuel

Vision splendid, The: Broster, D.K.

Visionaries: Huneker, J.G.

Visioning, The: Glaspell, Susan

Visions and beliefs in the West of Ireland: Gregory, *Lady* Augusta

Visions, and revisions: Powys, John Cowper

Visions of England, The: Palgrave, F.T.

Visions of the daughters of Albion: Blake, William

Visions of the evening: Fletcher, John Gould

Visit India with me: Mukherji, D.G.

Visit of Brother Ives, The: Raymond, Ernest

Visit of the Princess: Mottram, R.H.

Visit to America, A: Macdonell, A.G.

Visit to America: Nehru, Jawaharlal

Visit to India, China, and Japan in the year 1853, A: Taylor, Bayard

Visit to Italy, A: Trollope, Frances

Visit to Japan, A: Tagore, *Sir* R.

Visit to London: Lucas, E.V.

Visit to Penmorten, The: Courage, J.F.

Visit to the museum, A: Nabokov, Vladimir

Visit to three fronts, A: Doyle, *Sir* Arthur Conan

Visitations: Macneice, Louis

Visiting the caves: Plomer, William

Visitor, The: Monsarrat, Nicholas

Visitor's handbook to Rosslyn and Hawthornden, The: †Bede, Cuthbert

Visits of Elizabeth, The: Glyn, Elinor

Vistas: †Macleod, Fiona

Vistas of history: Morison, S.E.

Vistas of New York: Matthews, J.B.

Visvakarma: Coomaraswamy, A.K.

Vital center: the politics of freedom, The: Schlesinger, Arthur

Vital flame, The: Mackenzie, *Sir* Compton

Vital lies: †Lee, Vernon

Vital message, The: Doyle, *Sir* Arthur Conan

Vital peace, a study of risks: Steed, H.W.

"Vital spark" and her queer crew, The: Munro, Neil

Vitas patrum: Caxton, William

Vittoria: Meredith, George

Viva: Cummings, E.E.

Vive Leroy: Ford, Ford Madox

Vive moi!: O'Faolain, Sean

Vivia Perpetua: Adams, Sarah

Vivian Bertram: Reynolds, G.

Vivian Grey: Disraeli, Benjamin

Viviparous quadrupeds of North America, The: Audubon, John James

Vixen: Braddon, Mary Elizabeth

Vixen: Seton-Thompson, E.

Vizier of the two-horned Alexander, The: Stockton, F.R.

Viziers of Bassora, The: Ghose, Sri Aurobindo

Vizier's son, The: Hockley, William Browne

Vkiyoye primitives, The: Noguchi, Yone

Vocal miscellany: Moore, Thomas

Vocal parts of an entertainment called Apollo and Daphne: Theobald, Lewis

Vocal parts of an entertainment call'd Merlin, The: Theobald, Lewis

Voice, The: Deland, Margaret

Voice from the attic, A: Davies, Robertson

Voice from the dark, A: Phillpotts, Eden

Voice from the minaret, The: Hichens, Robert

Voice from the Nile, A: Thomson, James

Voice from the place of S. Morwenna, A: ˌHawker, Robert Stephen

Voice from the South, A: Longstreet, A.B.

Voice of Asia, The: Michener, J.A.

Voice of Bugle Ann, The: Kantor, Mackinlay

Voice of desire, The: †Baylebridge, W.

Voice of flowers, The: Sigourney, L.H.

Voice of Jerusalem, The: Zangwill, Israel

Voice of the city, The: †Henry, O.

Voice of the coyote, The: Dobie, J.F.

Voice of the desert, The: Krutch, J.W.

Voice of the flags, The: Carleton, William (McKendree)

Voice of the forest: McCrae, Hugh

Voice of the people, The: Glasgow, Ellen

Voice of the street, The: Poole, Ernest

Voice of the turtle, The: Van Druten, John

Voice of the valley, The: Noguchi, Yone

Voice of Wales, The: Griffith, Llewelyn

Voice on the wind, A: Cawein, Madison

Voice outside, The: Jennings, Gertrude

Voice said "Good night", A: Pertwee, Roland

Voices and visions: Fawcett, Edgar

Voices and visions: Scollard, Clinton

Voices from the dust: Farnol, J.J.

Voices from the hearth: Ascher, I.G.

Voices in the house: Buck, Pearl

Voices of a summer day: Shaw, Irwin

Voices of Africa: Scully, W.C.

Voices of freedom: Whittier, J.G.

Voices of freedom and lyrics of love: Massey, Gerald

Voices of the desert: Favenc, Ernest

Voices of the night: Longfellow, H.W.

Voices of the stones: Russell, G.W.

Volcano: Roberts, C.E.M.

Volga boatman, The: Bercovici, Konrad

Volpone: Jonson, Ben

Voltaire: Aldington, Richard

Voltaire: Morley, John

Voltaire: Noyes, Alfred

Voltaire: Vulliamy, C.E.

Voltaire, a biographical fantasy: Riding, Laura

Voltaire, a lecture: Darrow, C.S.

Voltaire in love: Mitford, Nancy

Voltaire in the shades: Mickle, W.J.

Voltaire, Montesquieu and Rousseau in England: Collins, John Churton

Volume from the life of Herbert Barclay, A: Calvert, George Henry

Volumes in folio: Le Gallienne, Richard

Volunteers: Rowson, S.H.

Volunteers, The: Shadwell, Thomas

Volunteer's adventures, A: De Forest, John William

Völuspa: Coomaraswamy, A.K.

Vortex, The: Coward, Noel

Voss: White, P.V.M.

Vote on war, A: Sheldon, C.M.

Votes for women: Fulford, Roger

Votive tablets: Blunden, Edmund

Votum Perenne: Shadwell, Thomas

Vow of the peacock, The: Landon, L.E.M.

Vox Clamantis: Ayres, Philip

Vox Pacifica: Wither, George

Voyage, The: Fairburn, A.R.D.

Voyage, The: Morgan, Charles

Voyage, The: Muir, Edwin

Voyage, The: Murry, John Middleton

Voyage, The: Woolls, William

Voyage at anchor, A: Russell, W.C.

Voyage home, The: Jameson, Storm

Voyage in the southern and antarctic regions, 1839–1843: Ross, Sir J.C.

Voyage of Autoleon, The: Bacon, Leonard

Voyage of Captain Bart: Erskine, John

Voyage of Captain Popanilla, The: Disraeli, Benjamin

Voyage of Columbus, The: Rogers, Samuel

Voyage of consolation, The: Duncan, S.J.

Voyage of discovery for exploring Baffin's Bay and a N.W. Passage, A: Ross, Sir John

Voyage of Ithobal, The: Arnold, Edwin

Voyage of the dawn-treader, The: Lewis, C.S.

Voyage of the Hu ruhui, The: Cresswell, W.D.

Voyage of the Pamir: Villiers, A.J.

Voyage on a pan of ice, A: Grenfell, Sir Wilfred

Voyage out, The: Woolf, Virginia

Voyage to Boston, A: Freneau, Philip

Voyage to Cochin-China: Barrow, Sir John

Voyage to Madera, Barbadoes, etc., A: Sloane, Sir Hans

Voyage to Pagany, A: Williams, W.C.

Voyage to Purilia, A: Rice, Elmer

Voyage to the Cape, A: Russell, W.C.

Voyage to the moon, A: Tucker, George

Voyage to the Pacific Ocean, A: Cook, James

Voyage towards the South Pole and round the world, A: Cook, James

Voyagers, The: Colum, Padraic

Voyages: Cook, James

Voyages and adventures of Captain Barth, The: Ayres, Philip

Voyages and descriptions: Dampier, William

Voyages and discoveries of the companions of Columbus:

(†Geoffrey Crayon), Irving, Washington

Voyages and travels in the years 1809, 1810 and 1811: Galt, John

Voyages from Montreal in the years 1789 and 1793: Mackenzie, Alexander

Voyages of discovery and research within the Artic Regions: Barrow, *Sir* John

Voyages of Dr. Dolittle, The: Lofting, Hugh

Voyageur, The: Drummond, W.H.

Vulgar streak, The: Lewis, P. Wyndham

Vulgar verses: Munby, A.J.

Vulgarity in literature: Huxley, Aldous

Vulnerable: a tale with cards: Collins, Dale

Vultures, The: †Merriman, Secton,

Vyasa and Valmiki: Ghose, Sri Aurobindo

W

W.B.Yeats, a critical study: Reid, Forrest

W.B.Yeats: a memoir: Gogarty, O. St. John

W.D. dinner: Baring, Maurice

W.E.A. and adult education, The: Tawney, R.H.

W.E. Ford, a biography: Beresford, J.D.

W.E. Henley: Connell, John (Henry Robertson)

W.G. Grace: Bax, Clifford

Wabash arch, The: Thompson, J.M.

Wacousta: Richardson, John

Wag-by-Wall: Potter, Helen Beatrix

Wager, A: Mitchell, S.W.

Wager of battle: Herbert, H.W.

Wages of virtue, The: Wren, P.C.

Waggoner, The: Blunden, Edmund

Waggoner, The: Wordsworth, William

Wagner: Newman, Ernest

Wagner: Turner, W.J.R.

Wagner as man and artist: Newman, Ernest

Wagner nights: Newman, Ernest

Wagner the Werewolf: Reynolds, G.

Wagoner of the Alleghanies,The: Read, T.B.

Waif, A: Carman, Bliss

Waif of the Plains, A: Harte, Bret

Waif woman, The: Stevenson, R.L.

Waifs and strays: †Henry, O.

Waifs and Strays of natural history: Gatty, Margaret

Waif's progress, A: Broughton, Rhoda

Wait for the end: Lemon, Mark

Wait for the stroke!: Iyengar, V.V. Srinivasa

Waiting at the church: Lonsdale, Frederick

Waiting for daylight: Tomlinson, H.M.

Waiting for Gillian: Balchin, Nigel

Waiting for Godot: Beckett, Samuel

Waiting for Lefty: Odets, Clifford

Waiting for the bus: Jennings, Gertrude

Waiting for the Mahatma: Narayan, R.K.

Waiting for the verdict: Davis, R.B.H.

Waiting for winter: O'Hara, J.H.

Waiting hills: Holcroft, M.H.

Waiting in the wings: Coward, Noel

Waiting race, A: Yates, E.H.

Wake of the raiders, The: Divine, A.D.

Wake robin: Burroughs, John

Wake up, Jonathan: Hughes, Hatcher

Wake up, Jonathan: Rice, Elmer

Wakefield: Mackaye, Percy

Wakefield's course: De la Roche, Mazo

Walden: Thoreau, H.D.

Walden west: Derleth, A.W.

Waldenses, The: De Vere, A.T.

Waldo Trench and others; stories of Americans in Italy: Fuller, H.B.

Wales: Thomas, E.E.P.

Wales England wed: Rhys, Ernest

Wales in colour: Griffith, Llewelyn

Walk in the wilderness, A: Hanley, James

Walk on the wild side, A: Algren, Nelson

Walk with God, The: Howe, Julia Ward

Walker, London: Barrie, *Sir* J.M.

Walking at week-ends: Mais, S.P.B.

Walking doll, The: (†Orpheus C.Kerr), Newell, R.H.

Walking in England: Trease, Geoffrey

Walking in Somerset: Mais, S.P.B.

Walking shadows: Noyes, Alfred

Walking statue, The: Hill, Aaron

Walks from Eden: Warner, S.B.

Walks in Edinburgh: Chambers, Robert

Walks in London: Hare, A.J.C.

Walks in Rome: Hare, A.J.C.

Walks of Islington and Hogsdon, The: Jordan, Thomas

Wall, The: Cournos, John

Wall, The: Hanley, James

Wall, The: Rinehart, Mary Roberts

Wall of partition, The: Barclay, F.L.

Wallace: the Hero of Scotland: Reynolds, G.

Wallace's invocation to Bruce: Hemans, *Mrs.* Felicia

Walled city, The: Huxley, Elspeth J.

Walled in: Ward, E.S.

Wallenstein: Coleridge, S.T.

Wallet of Kai-Lung, The: Bramah, E.

Wallet of time, The: Winter, William

Walls do not fall, The: Doolittle, Hilda

Walls of glass: Bottome, Phyllis

Walls of Jericho, The: Sutro, Alfred

Wally for queen!: Sinclair, Upton

Wally Wanderoon and his storytelling machine: Harris, J.C.

Walpole: Lytton, E.

Walpole: Morley, John

Walsh Colville: Porter, A.M.

Walsingham, the gamester: Chamier, Frederick

Walt: Morley, C.D.

Walt Whitman: Canby, H.S.

Walt Whitman: Le Gallienne, Richard

Walt Whitman: Thomson, James

Walt Whitman: a study: Symonds, J.A.

Walt Whitman, a study and a selection: Bullett, Gerald

Walt Whitman; builder for America: Deutsch, Babette

Walt Whitman: the poet: Van Doren, Mark

Walter Colyton: Smith, Horatio

Walter de la Mare, a critical study: Reid, Forrest

Walter Gibbs, the young boss: Thomson, E.W.

Walter J. Phillips, R.C.A.: Scott, D.C.

Walter Pater: Benso. A.C.

Walter Pater: Thomas, E.E.P.

Walter Savage Landor: Forster, John

Walter Scott: Pearson, Hesketh

Walter Sickert: a conversation: Woolf, Virginia

Walter Woolfe: English, T.D.

Walter's word: Payn, James

Waltham: Picken, Andrew

Waltham: an American revolutionary tale: McHenry, James

Waltz: Byron, George Gordon, *Lord*

Waltz invention, The: Nabokov, Vladimir

Wampum and old gold: Allen, Hervey

Wan Lee: The Pagan: Harte, Bret

Wanda: †Ouida

Wander light: Raymond, Ernest

Wanderer, The: Burney, Frances

Wanderer, The: Channing, W.E.

Wanderer, The: (†Owen Meredith), Lytton, E.R.B. *Earl*

Wanderer among pictures, A: Lucas, E.V.

Wanderer in Florence, A: Lucas, E.V.

Wanderer in Holland, A: Lucas, E.V.

Wanderer in Japan, A: Blunden, Edmund

Wanderer in London, A: Lucas, E.V.

Wanderer in Paris, A: Lucas, E.V.

Wanderer in Rome, A: Lucas, E.V.

Wanderer in Syria, The: Curtis, G.W.

Wanderer in Venice, A: Lucas, E.V.

Wanderer of Liverpool, The: Masefield, John

Wanderer of Switzerland, The: Montgomery, James

Wanderer of the wasteland: Grey, Zane

Wanderers: Munro, C.K.

Wanderers: Winter, William

Wanderer's necklace, The: Haggard, *Sir* H. Rider

Wanderer's song: Symons, Arthur

Wanderer's way, A: Raven, C.E.

Wandering and diversions: Lucas, E.V.

Wandering ghosts: Crawford, F. Marion

Wandering Heath: (†Q), Quiller-Couch, *Sir* Arthur

Wandering heir, The: Reade, Charles

Wandering Jew, The: Buchanan, R.W.

Wandering Jew, The: Conway, M.D.

Wandering Jew, The: Shelley, P.B.

Wandering Jew, or the travels and observations of Hareach the Prolonged, The: Galt, John

Wandering minstrel, The: Mayhew, Henry

Wandering recollections of a somewhat busy life: Neal, John

Wandering scholar, The: Hogarth, D.G.

Wandering scholar in the Levant, A: Hogarth, D.G.

Wandering scholars, The: Waddell, Helen

Wandering songs: Dunsany, Edward Plunkett, *Baron*

Wandering stars: †Dane, Clemence

Wandering words: Arnold, Edwin

Wanderings: Herrick, Robert

Wanderings: Symons, Arthur

Wanderings in India: Lang, J.

Wanderings in South America, the North West of the United States and the Antilles: Waterton, Charles

Wanderings in Spain: Hare, A.J.C.

Wanderings in the Highlands and Islands: Maxwell, W.H.

Wanderings in three continents: Burton, *Sir* Richard

Wanderings in West Africa: Burton, *Sir* Richard

Wanderings of a spiritualist, The: Doyle, *Sir* Arthur Conan

Wanderings of an antiquary: Wright, Thomas

Wanderings of Oisin, The: Yeats, W.B.

Wanderings of our fat contributor: Thackeray, W.M.

Wanderings of Wenamen, The: Lindsay, Jack

Wanglers, The: Maltby, H.F.

Wanted—a chaperon: Ford, P.L.

Wanted a match maker: Ford, P.L.

Wanton Mally: Tarkington, Booth

War: Long, J.L.

War: Robertson, T.W.

War: Wallace, Edgar

War abolished: one way to permanent peace: Krishnamurti, Jiddu

War aims: Angell, *Sir* Norman

War and after, The: Lodge, *Sir* Oliver

War and Arcadia: Mitford, Bertram

War and civilisation: Toynbee, Arnold

War and common sense: Wells, H.G.

War and culture, The: Powys, J.C.

War and democracy, The: Wilson, J.D.

War and Elizabeth, The: Ward, *Mrs.* Humphrey

War and liberty, The: Samuel, Herbert *1st Viscount*

War and literature, The: Hardy, Thomas

War and love: Aldington, Richard

War and self-determination: Ghose, Sri Aurobindo

War and the Arme Blanche: Childers, Erskine

War and the Christian: Raven, C.E.

War and the Christian faith: †Machen, Arthur

War and the European Revolution in relation to history, The: Trevelyan, G.M.

War and the future: Wells, H.G.

War and the nations, The: Newbolt, *Sir* Henry

War and the way out, The: Dickinson, G.L.

War books: Tomlinson, H.M.

War bulletin number five: Lindsay, N.V.

War bulletin number one: Lindsay, N.V.

War bulletin number three: Lindsay, N.V.

War bulletin number two: Lindsay, N.V.

War dance and the fire-fly dance, The: Seton-Thompson, E.

War debts and reparations: Cole, G.D.H.

War diaries: Millin, Sarah Gertrude

War dog: Treece, Henry

War for peace, The: Woolf, Leonard

War for the world, The: Zangwill, Israel

War God, The: Zangwill, Israel

War in heaven: Williams, Charles

War in outline, 1914–1918, The: Liddell Hart, B.

War in Samoa: Stevenson, R.L.

War in South Africa, The: Doyle, *Sir* Arthur Conan

War in the air: Garnett, David

War in the air, The: Raleigh, *Sir* W.A.

War in the air, The: Wells, H.G.

War in the blood: Madariaga, Salvador de

War in the mountains: Kipling, Rudyard

War in the Strand: Bolitho, H.H.

War is kind: Crane, Stephen

War is war: Archer, William

War: its nature, cause and cure: Dickinson, G.L.

War lords, The: Gardiner, A.G.

War lyrics: Campbell, W.W.

War nurse: †West, Rebecca

War of 1870, The: Acton, John

War of 1812: Richardson, John E.E.D.

War of Independence, The: Fiske, John

War of the classes: London, Jack

War of the standards, The: Tourgée, A.W.

War of the worlds, The: Wells, H.G.

War paint and rouge: Chambers, R.W.

War path, The: Jones, J.B.

War poems: Dunsany, E.J.

War poems, The: Sassoon, S.

War poets: Blunden, Edmund

War-songs for freemen: Child, F.J.

War speeches: Churchill, *Sir* Winston

War story, A: Aldington, Richard

War that will end war, The: Wells, H.G.

War—the offspring of fear: Russell, Bertrand

War to the knife: †Boldrewood, Rolf

War trail, The: Reid, T.M.

War voices and memories: Scollard, Clinton

War waits: Massey, Gerald

Waratah rhymes for young Australia: Meredith, L.A.

Ward of the Golden Gate, A: Harte, Bret

Ward of Thorpe Combe, The: Trollope, Frances

Warden, The: Trollope, Anthony

Warden of the smoke and bells: Llewellyn, Richard

Warfare in England: Belloc, Hilaire

Warfarings: Clarke, G.H.

Warleigh of the Fatal Oak: Bray, A.E.

Warming pan, The: Jacobs, W.W.

Warning for swearers, A: Taylor, John

Warning for wantons, A: Mitchell, Mary

Warning Hill: Marquand, J.P.

Warning to the curious, A: James, M.R.

Warnings of history: Munshi, K.M.

Warren Hastings: Lyall, *Sir* Alfred C.

Warrens of Virginia, The: Eggleston, G.C.

Warres of Pompey and Caesar, The: Chapman, George

Warres, warres, warres: Dekker, Thomas

Warrigal Joe: (†Donald Barr), Barrett, C.L.

Warriors at ease: †Armstrong, Anthony

Warriors at war: †Armstrong, Anthony

Warrior's return, The: Opie, Amelia

Warriors still at ease: †Armstrong, Anthony

Wars I have seen: Stein, Gertrude

Wars of the elements, The: Ward, Edward

Wartime billeting: Cole, M.I.

Wartime letters to peace lovers: Brittain, Vera

War-time silhouettes: †Hudson, Stephen

Warwhoop: Kantor, Mackinlay

Warwick woodlands, The: Herbert, H.W.

Warwickshire Avon, The: (†Q), Quiller-Couch, Sir Arthur

War-workers, The: †Delafield, E.M.

Was Europe a success?: Krutch, J.W.

Was it right to forgive?: Barr, A.E.H.

Was there love once?: Raymond, Ernest

Washdirt: Devaney, J.M.

Washer of the ford, The: †Macleod, Fiona

Washerwoman's child, The: Uttley, Alison

Washington and Betsy Ross: Mackaye, Percy

Washington and his generals: Lippard, George

Washington and his men: Lippard, George

Washington and its romance: Page, T.N.

Washington and the generals of the American revolution: Griswold, R.W.

Washington and the hope of peace: Wells, H.G.

Washington and the theatre: Ford, P.L.

Washington Bible class, A: Dodge, M.A.

Washington, in 1868: (†Mark Twain), Clemens, S.L.

Washington Irving: Curtis, G.W.

Washington Irving: Warner, C.D.

Washington Square: James, Henry

Washington, the man who made us: Mackaye, Percy

Washington the nation-builder: Markham, Edwin

Washington to Petrograd—via Rome: Eastman, Max

Washoe Giant in San Francisco: (†Mark Twain), Clemens, S.L.

Wasp, The: Roberts, T.G.

Wasps: Evans, Caradoc

Wasp's honey: Howitt, Richard

Waste: Herrick, Robert

Waste and the machine age: Chase, Stuart

Waste land, The: Eliot, T.S.

Wasters, The: Adams, Arthur H.

Wat Tyler: Southey, Robert

Wat Tyler M.P.: Sala, G.A.H.

Watch and ward: James, Henry

Watch below: McFee, William

Watch for the dawn: Cloete, Stuart

Watch the end: Miller, Thomas

Watch this space: Herbert, Sir A.P.

Watch your thirst: Wister, Owen

Watcher and other weird stories, The: Le Fanu, Sheridan

Watcher by the threshold, The: Buchan, John

Watchers, The: Mason, A.E.W.

Watchers of the sky: Noyes, Alfred

Watchers of twilight: Stringer, A.J.A·

Watching a play: Munro, C.K.

Watchmaker's wife, The: Stockton, F.R.

Watch-woord to Englande, A: Munday, Anthony

Water beetle, The: Mitford, Nancy

Water buffalo children: Buck, Pearl

Water gipsies, The: Herbert, Sir A.P.

Water into gold: Hill, Ernestine

Water of life, The: Bunyan, John

Water of life, The: Kingsley, Charles

Water of the wondrous isles, The: Morris, William

Water on the brain: Mackenzie, Sir Compton

Water unlimited: Roberts, Kenneth

Water-babies, The: Kingsley, Charles

Water-cormorant his complaint, The: Taylor, John

Watercress girl, The: Bates, H.E.

Water-cresses: Alcott, Louisa M.

Water-drops: Sigourney, L.H.

Waterfront: Brophy, John

Waterhole, The: Moll, E.G.

Waterlily fires: Rukesyer, Muriel

Waterloo Bridge: Sherwood, R.E.

Waterman, The: Dibdin, Charles

Water-music: Squire, Sir J.C.

Water-rat's picnic: Uttley, Alison

Waters of Caney Fork, The: Read, O.P.

Waters of Edera, The: †Ouida

Waters of Jordan, The: Vachell, H.A.

Waters of Kronos, The: Richter, Conrad

Waters of Walla: Phillpotts, Eden

Watershed, The: Calder-Marshall, Arthur

Watersprings: Benson, A.C.

Waterway: Dark, Eleanor

Water-witch, The: Cooper, James Fenimore

Watery maze: the story of combined operations, The: Fergusson, Sir Bernard

Watlings for worth: Vachell, H.A.

Watlington Hill: Mitford, Mary Russell

Watsons, The: Austen, Jane

Watt: Beckett, Samuel

Watter's Mou': Stoker, Bram

Wattlefold, The: †Field, Michael

Waugh in Abyssinia: Waugh, Evelyn

Wau-nan-gee: Richardson, John

Wave, The: Scott, Evelyn

Wave, an Egyptian aftermath, The: Blackwood, Algernon

Wave of life, A: Fitch, C.W.

Wavell: portrait of a soldier: Fergusson, *Sir* Bernard

Wavell, scholar and soldier: Connell, John

Waverley: Scott, *Sir* Walter

Waves, The: Woolf, Virginia

Wax works murder, The: Carr, J.D.

Way according to Laotzu, The: Bynner, Witter

Way and its power, The: Waley, Arthur

Way beyond, The: Farnol, J.J.

Way down east: Smith, Seba

Way home, The: †King, Basil

Way home, The: †Richardson, H.H.

Way it worked out, The: Stern, G.B.

Way lies west, The: Griffith, Llewelyn

Way of a maid, The: Tynan, Katherine

Way of a man, The: Dixon, Thomas

Way of a man, The: Hough, Emerson

Way of all flesh, The: Butler, Samuel

Way of ambition, The: Hichens, Robert

Way of an Indian, The: Remington, Frederic

Way of Congregational churches cleared, The: Cotton, John

Way of life, The: Cotton, John

Way of Ecben, The: Cabell, James Branch

Way of love, A: Courage, J.F.

Way of Martha and the way of Mary, The: Graham, Stephen

Way of my world, The: Brown, Ivor

Way of power, The: Beck, *Mrs.* Lily

Way of sailing a ship, The: Monsarrat, Nicholas

Way of stars, The: Beck, *Mrs.* Lily

Way of the churches of Christ in New-England, The: Cotton, John

Way of the gods, The: Long, J.L.

Way of the Scarlet Pimpernel, The: Orczy, *Baroness*

Way of the sea, The: Duncan, Norman

Way of the spirit, The: Haggard, *Sir* H. Rider

Way of the world, The: Congreve, William

Way of the world, The: Hall, A.M.

Way of these women, The: Oppenheim, E.Phillips

Way out, A: Frost, Robert

Way out, The: Hough, Emerson

Way out, The: Rajagopalachari, Chakravati

Way out: what lies ahead for America, The: Sinclair, Upton

Way the ball bounces, The: Lindsay, Jack

Way the world is going, The: Wells, H.G.

Way things are, The: †Delafield, E.M.

Way things go, The: †Lonsdale, Frederick

Way things happen, The: †Dane, Clemence

Way things happen, The: De Selincourt, Hugh

Way through the wood, A: Balchin, Nigel

Way to a horse, The: Squire, *Sir* J.C.

Way to beauty, The: Rubenstein, Harold F.

Way to blessedness, The: Fletcher, Phineas

Way to get married, The: Morton, Thomas

Way to get wealth, A: Markham, Gervase

Way to keep him, The: Murphy, Arthur

Way to peace, The: Deland, Margaret

Way to peace, The: Gould, Gerald

Way to prosperity, The: Mather, Cotton

Way to Santiago, The: Calder-Marshall, Arthur

Way to social peace, A: Steed, H.W.

Way to the house of Santa Claus, The: Burnett, Frances Hodgson

Way to the present, The: Van Druten, J.W.

Way to the stars: Rattigan, Terence

Way to the West and the lives of three early Americans, The: Hough, Emerson

Way to wealth, The: Franklin, Benjamin

Way to world peace, The: Wells, H.G.

Way we live now, The: Trollope, Anthony

Way west, The: Guthrie, A.B.

Wayfarer in Hungary, A: Hannay, J.O.

Wayfaring: Meynell, Alice

Wayfaring men: Lyall, Edna

Wayne at Stony Point: Scollard, Clinton

Ways and means: Colman, George, *the younger*

Ways and means: Housman, Laurence

Ways and means: †Maurice, Furnley

Ways of escape: Gibbs, *Sir* Philip

Ways of life, The: Oliphant, Margaret

Ways of the hour, The: Cooper, James Fenimore

Ways of white folk, The: Hughes, J.L.

Ways of women The: Tarbell, Ida

Wayside courtships: Garland, Hamlin

Wayside gleams: Salverson, L.G.

Wayside lute, A: Reese, L.W.

Wayward bus, The: Steinbeck, John

Wayward man, The: Ervine, St. John

Wayward saint, The: Carroll, P.V.

Wayzgoose, The: Campbell, Roy

W—ds—r prophecy, The: Swift, Jonathan

We accept with pleasure: De Voto, Bernard

We and our neighbors: Stowe, Harriet Beecher

We and the world: Ewing, *Mrs.* Juliana

We are betrayed: Fisher, V.A.

We are leaving: Caldwell, Erskine Preston

We are living: Caldwell, Erskine Preston

We are not alone: Hilton, James

We are the living: Caldwell, Erskine Preston

We aren't so dumb: Hollis, . Christopher

We bereaved: Keller, Helen

We can't afford it!: Brougham, Henry

We can't be as bad as all that: Jones, H.A.

We didn't mean to go to sea: Ransome, Arthur

We Europeans: Huxley, *Sir* Julian

We fly by night: Colman, George, *the younger*

We have been warned: Mitchison, Naomi

We Kaytons: †Rudd, Steele

We keep going: †Armstrong, Anthony

We moderns: Muir, Edwin

We never die: Karaka, D.F.

We, people of America: Sinclair, Upton

We proudly present: †Novello, Ivor

We shall eat and drink again: Golding, Louis

We shall ne'er be younger: Percy, Edward

We shall return: Lindsay, Jack

We shall see!: Wallace, Edgar

We, the accused: Raymond, Ernest

We, the people: Rice, Elmer

We two: Lyall, Edna

We wander through the West: Mais, S.P.B.

We were there at the battle for Bataan: Appel, Benjamin

We were there in the Klondike Gold rush: Appel, Benjamin

We were there with Cortes and Montezuma: Appel, Benjamin

We who are playing tonight: Lindsay, N.V.

Weak spot, The: Kelly, G.E.

Weak woman, A: Davies, W.H.

Weaker sex, The: Pinero, *Sir* A.W.

Weaker vessel, The: Benson, E.F.

Weald of Kent and Sussex: Kaye-Smith, Sheila

Weald of youth, The: Sassoon, Siegfried

Wearieswa': Swinburne, A.C.

Wearing of the gray: Cooke, J.E.

Weary blues, The: Hughes, J.L.

Weather at Tregulla, The: Gibbons, Stella

Weather in the streets, The: Lehmann, Rosamund

Weathercock, The: Uttley, Alison

Weathergoose woo!: Mackaye, Percy

Weavers, The: Parker, *Sir* H.G.

Weavers and weft: Braddon, M.E.

Web, The: Hough, Emerson

Web and the rock, The: Wolfe, Thomas

Web of circumstance, The: De Zilwa, Lucien

Web of life, The: Gibson, Wilfred

Web of life, The: Herrick, Robert

Web of traitors: Trease, Geoffrey

Webbs in perspective, The: Tawney, R.H.

Webster's poker book: Connelly, Marc

Wedding, The: Mackail, Denis

Wedding, The: Shirley, James

Wedding bouquet: ballet, A: Stein, Gertrude

Wedding day: Boyle, Kay

Wedding day, The: Inchbald, · *Mrs.* Elizabeth

Wedding gift, The: Raddall, T.H.

Wedding guest, The: Barrie, *Sir* J.M.

Wedding guest, The: Jones, H.A.

Wedding journey, The: Edmonds, W.D.

Wedding march, The: Gilbert, *Sir* W.S.

Wedding morn, A: Kaye-Smith, Sheila

Wedding of the rose and the lotus, The: Lindsay, N.V.

Wedding presents: Cannan, Gilbert

Wedding song: Mackaye, Percy

Wedding-day, The: Fielding, Henry

Wedge, The: Williams, W.C.

Wednesday's children: †Hyde, Robin

Wee dog: Mickle, A.D.

Wee Willie Winkie: Kipling, Rudyard

Weeds, a story of women shifting for themselves: Sladen, D.B.W.

Weeds and wildflowers: Lytton, E.G.E.B. *1st Baron*

Weeds of witchery: Bayly, T.H.

Week in Hepsidam, A: Bagby, G.W.

Week of darkness, The: Manning, Anne

Week on the Concord and Merrimack Rivers, A: Thoreau, H.D.

Weekend in Paris: †Bell, Neil

Week-end Wodehouse: Wodehouse, P.G.

Week-ends in England: Mais, S.P.B.

Weekly comedy, The: Ward, Edward

Weeping ferry: Woods, M.L.

Weeping willow, The: Sigourney, L.H.

Weepings and wailings: Squire, *Sir* J.C.

Weighed and wanting: Macdonald, George

Weight of the evidence: (†Michael Innes), Stewart, J.I.M.

Weir of Hermiston, The: Stevenson, R.L.

Weird o' it, The: Shiel, M.P.

Weird of Deadly Hollow, The: Mitford, Bertram

Weird of the wanderer, The: (†Baron Corvo), Rolfe, Frederick

Weird stories: Riddell, *Mrs.* J.H.

Weismannism once more: Spencer, Herbert

Welch harper, The: Knowles, J.S.

Welchman's hose: Graves, Robert

Welcome: Deutsch, Babette

Welcome home!: Bemelmans, Ludwig

Welcome to Alexandra, A: Tennyson, Alfred *Lord*

Welcome to our city: Wolfe, Thomas

Welcome to Prince Albert, A: Hawker, R.S.

Welcome to the city: Shaw, Irwin

Welded: O'Neill, Eugene

Well and the shallows, The: Chesterton, G.K.

Well, anyhow...: Herbert, *Sir* A.P.

Well at the world's end, The: Gunn, Neil

Well at world's end, The: Morris, William

Well caught: †Armstrong, Anthony

We'll gather lilacs: †Novello, Ivor

Well of loneliness, The: Hall, Radclyffe

Well of the saints, The: Synge, J.M.

We'll shift our ground: Blunden, Edmund

Well wrought urn, The: Brooks, Cleanth

Well-beloved, The: Hardy, Thomas

Well-born workman, The: Reade, Charles

Wellington: Aldington, Richard

Wellington: Fortescue, *Sir* John

Wellington: a reassessment: Petrie, *Sir* Charles

Wells brothers, the young cattle kings: Adams, Andy

Wells of Beersheba, The: Davison, F.D.

Wells of St. Mary's, The: Sherriff, R.C.

Well-to-do Arthur: Ridge, W. Pett

Well-worn roads: Smith, F.H.

Welsh, The: Griffith, Llewelyn

Welsh and their country, The: Griffith, Llewelyn

Welsh melodies: Hemans, *Mrs.* Felicia

Welsh opera, The: Fielding, Henry

Welsh rabbit, The: (Stephen Southwold), †Bell, Neil

Welsh sonata, The: Hanley, James

Wendell Phillips: Higginson, T.W.

Wendell Phillips: Woodberry, G.E.

Wept of Wish-ton-Wish, The: Cooper, James Fenimore

We're all low people there: Phillips, Samuel

We're going through: Moore, T.I.

Were human sacrifices in use among the Romans?: Macaulay, Thomas *Baron*

Were you ever a child: Dell, Floyd

We're not going to do nothing: Day-Lewis, C.

Werner: Byron, George Gordon, *Lord*

Wessex poems: Hardy, Thomas

Wessex tales: Hardy, Thomas

Wessex wins: Street, A.G.

West country pilgrimage, A: Phillpotts, Eden

West country sketch book, A: Phillpotts, Eden

West from a car-window, The: Davis, R.H.

West Indian, The: Cumberland, Richard

West Indies, The: Montgomery, James

West Indies and the Spanish Main, The: Trollope, Anthony

West is West: Rhodes, E.M.

West: its commerce and navigation, The: Hall, James

West: its soil, surface, and productions, The: Hall, James

West Lawn and the Rector of St. Marks, The: Holmes, M.J.

West of midnight: Engle, Paul

West of morning: Derleth, A.W.

West of the Pecos: Grey, Zane

West pier, The: Hamilton, Patrick

West Point colors: Warner, A.B.

West Sussex: Lucas, E.V.

West to North: Mackenzie, *Sir* Compton

West wind, The: Church, H.N.W.

West wind, The: Mackenzie, *Sir* Compton

West wind drift: McCutcheon, G.B.

West with the sun: Cloete, E.F.S.G.

Westcotes, The: (†Q), Quiller-Couch, *Sir* Arthur

Western Australia, its past history, its present trade, etc.: Favenc, Ernest

Western Flanders: Binyon, Laurence

Western front, The: Montague, C.E.

Western Germany: Gibbon, Monk

Western home, The: Sigourney, L.H.

Western idyll: Kirkconnell, Watson

Western intellectual tradition from Leonardo to Hegel, The: Bronowski, J.

Western journal, A: Wolfe, Thomas

Western Mediterranean, 1942–45: †Taffrail

Western merchant, The: Jones, J.B.

Western political tradition, The: Tawney, R.H.

Western question in Greece and Turkey, The: Toynbee, Arnold

Western Star: Benét, S.V.

Western track, The: Bayldon, Arthur

Western union: Grey, Zane

Western unity and the Common Market: Lippman, Walter

Western wind, A: White, T.H.

Western windows: Piatt, J.J.

Westerners, The: White, S.E.

Westing: Sandwell, B.K.

Westminster: Besant, *Sir* Walter

Westminster Alice, The: Munro, H.H.

Westminster Hall: †Pilgrim, David

Westminster Hall: Saunders, H.A. St. George

Westminster sermons: Kingsley, Charles

Westover manuscripts: Byrd, William

Westover of Wanalah: Eggleston, G.C.

Westrow revived: Wither, George

West-running Brook: Frost, Robert

Westward Ho!: Kingsley, Charles

Westward Ho!: Paulding, J.K.

West-ward hoe: Dekker, Thomas

Westward march of American settlement, The: Garland, Hamlin

Westward passage: Barnes, Margaret

Westward rock, The: Strong, L.A.G.

Westways: Mitchell, S.W.

Westwood: Gibbons, Stella

Westwoods: Farjeon, Eleanor

Wet days at Edgewood: Mitchell, D.G.

Wet Flanders plain, The: Williamson, Henry

Wet magic: Nesbit, E.

Wet parade, The: Sinclair, Upton

Wet wit and dry humour: Leacock, Stephen

Wetherall affair, The: De Forest, J.W.

Wetherbys, The: Lang, J.

Weymouth Sands: Powys, John Cowper

Whalers of the midnight sun: Villiers, A.J.

Whaling in the frozen south: Villiers, A.J.

Whare Kohanga, The: Best, Elsdon

What a husband should do: Griffith, Hubert

What a life!: Lucas, E.V.

What a word: Herbert, *Sir* A.P.

What America means to me: Buck, Pearl

What, and why, and when to read: Markham, Edwin

What are masterpieces: Stein, Gertrude

What are we to do?: Strachey, John

What are years: Moore, M.C.

What are you going to do about Alf?: Miller, Henry

What are you going to do about it?: Huxley, Aldous

What became of Anna Bolton: Bromfield, Louis

What became of the slaves on a Georgia plantation?: (†Q.K. Philander Doesticks), Thompson, M.N.

What books do for Mankind: Cole, E.W.

What can be done about America's economic troubles?: Sinclair, Upton

What can Jesus Christ do with me: Grenfell, *Sir* Wilfred

What can she do?: Roe, E.P.

What career?: Hale, E.E.

What cheer!: Russell, W.C.

What Christ means to me: Grenfell, *Sir* Wilfred

What Christmas is as we grow older: Dickens, Charles

What classical education means: Cappon, James

What dare I think?: Huxley, *Sir* Julian

What did her husband say?: Maltby, H.F.

What did it mean?: Thirkell, Angela

What did Jesus really teach?: Sheldon, C.M.

What Dooley says: Dunne, F.P.

What dreams may come: Atherton, Gertrude

What dreams may come: Beresford, J.D.

What d'ye call it, The: Gay, John

What d'you know?: Munro, Neil

What everybody wants: Greenwood, Walter

What everybody wants to know about money: Cole, G.D.H.

What far kingdom: Bourinot, A.S.

What Farrar saw: Hanley, James

What God means to me: Sinclair, Upton

What grandmother did not know: Canfield, Dorothy

What happened at Quasi: Eggleston, G.C.

What happened at Hazelwood: (†Michael Innes), Stewart, J.I.M.

What happened on the boat: Thirkell, Angela

What happened to the Corbetts?: †Shute, Nevil

What happens in Hamlet: Wilson, John Dover

What hath a man?: Millin, Sarah Gertrude

What he cost her: Payn, James

What I believe: Beresford, J.D.

What I believe: Forster, E.M.

What I believe: Russell, Bertrand

What I have had: Brighouse, Harold

What I really wrote about the War: Shaw, G.B.

What I saw and heard in Panama: Elliott, M.H.

What I saw in America: Chesterton, G.K.

What I saw in Germany: Gardiner, A.G.

What I think: Vijayatunga, Jinadasa

What is a classic?: Eliot, T.S.

What is a play?: Brown, Ivor

What is American literature?: Van Doren, Carl

What is beneficial employment?: Tawney, R.H.

What is capital?: Jones, H.A.

What is coming?: Wells, H.G.

What is England doing?: Noyes, Alfred

What is happiness?: Armstrong, M.D.

What it is to be young: Bridie, James

What is love?: †Delafield, E.M.

What is man?: (†Mark Twain), Clemens, S.L.

What is materialism?: Stephen, *Sir* Leslie

What is music: Erskine, John

What is of Faith as to everlasting punishment?: Pusey, E.B.

What is of obligation for a Catholic to believe concerning the inspiration of the Canonical Scriptures: Newman, J.H.

What is poetry?: Wheelock, J.H.

What is sensation?: Lewes, G.H.

What is she?: Mackaye, Percy

What is she?: Smith, Charlotte

What is socialism and culture?: Sinclair, Upton

What is this Jewish heritage?: Lewisohn, Ludwig

What is this socialism?: Cole, G.D.H.

What is "womanly"?: Housman, Laurence

What it is to be young: †Bridie, James

What it's all about: White, W.A.

What Katy did: Coolidge, Susan

What Katy did at school: Coolidge, Susan

What Katy did next: Coolidge, Susan

What lack I yet?: Powys, T.F.

What life means to me: Grenfell, Sir Wilfred

What life means to me: Sinclair, Upton

What Maisie knew: James, Henry

What Marx really meant: Cole, G.D.H.

What me befell: Jusserand, Jean

What medicine can do for law: Cardozo, B.N.

What might happen: Maltby, H.F.

What might have been expected: Stockton, F.R.

What next?: Mackail, Denis

What next, baby?: Macdonell, A.G.

What no woman knows: †Bell, Neil

What not: Macaulay, Dame Rose

What o'clock tales: Housman, Laurence

What of it?: Lardner, Ring

What peace to the wicked?: Wither, George

What really happened (novel and play): Lowndes, Mrs. Belloc

What say they?: †Bridie, James

What Shakespeare is not: O'Hagan, Thomas

What shall we do now?: Lucas, E.V.

What she could: Warner, S.B.

What should be done—now: Wells, H.G.

What some men don't know: Maltby, H.F.

What the Church means to me: Grenfell, Sir Wilfred

What the League of Nations has done and is doing: Nitobe, Inazo

What the Mexican conference really means: Austin, Mary

What the new census means: Chase, Stuart

What the public wants: Bennett, Arnold

What the public wants: Palmer, H.E.

What the war means to us: Hough, Emerson

"What then, does Dr. Newman mean?": Kingsley, Charles

What they think: Crothers, Rachel

What think ye of Christ: Dodge, M.A.

What think ye of Christ?: Raven, C.E.

What time collects: Farrell, J.T.

What Timmy did: Lowndes, Mrs. Belloc

What to do with the B.B.C.: Postgate, Raymond

What to read on economic problems of today and tomorrow: Cole, G.D.H.

What to read on English economic history: Cole, G.D.H.

What to read on the evolution of music: Newman, Ernest

What to see in Britain: Mais, S.P.B.

What to teach and how to teach it: Mayhew, Henry

What to wear?: Ward, E.S.

What we must all come to: Murphy, Arthur

What will he do with it?: Lytton, E.G.E.B. 1st Baron

What will the world say?: Lemon, Mark

What will you do with Jesus Christ: Grenfell, Sir Wilfred

What Wilson did at Paris: Baker, R.S.

What women won in Wisconsin: Gale, Zona

What you ought to know about your baby: Mencken, H.L.

What you will: Marston, John

Whatever love is: Chambers, R.W.

What's become of Waring: Powell, Anthony

What's bred in the bone: Allen, Grant

What's bred in the bone: Brighouse, Harold

What's in it for me?: Weidman, Jerome

What's mine's mine: Macdonald, George

What's o'clock: Lowell, Amy

What's the use of books: Sinclair, Upton

What's to come: Jacob, Naomi

What's wrong with drama?: Rubenstein, Harold F.

What's wrong with the world: Chesterton, G.K.

What's your name: Adamic, Louis

What's-his-name: McCutcheon, G.B.

Whaup o' the Rede: Ogilvie, W.H.

Wheel, The: Housman, Laurence

Wheel of fire, The: Knight, G.W.

Wheel of fortune, The: Cumberland, Richard

Wheel of fortune, The: Gibbs, Sir Philip

Wheel of life, The: Glasgow, Ellen

Wheel of time, The: James, Henry

Wheel stood still, The: Vachell, H.A.

Wheels: Sitwell, Edith

Wheels and butterflies: Yeats, W.B.

Wheels of chance, The: Wells, H.G.

Wheels of the machine, The: Sheldon, C.M.

Wheels of time, The: Barclay, Florence

Wheels within wheels: Waugh, Alec

Wheel-tracks: Somerville, E.

When a feller needs a friend: O'Higgins, H.J.

When a man marries: Rinehart, Mary Roberts

When a man's a man: Wright, H.B.

When all is done: Uttley, Alison

When all the woods are green: Mitchell, S.W.

When blood is their argument: Ford, Ford Madox

When boyhood dreams come true: Farrell, James

When Carruthers laughed: †Sapper

When churchyards yawn: Maltby, H.F.

When Cobb and Co. was King: Lawson, Will

When democracy builds: Wright, Frank Lloyd

When did they meet again?: Brighouse, Harold

When dreams come true: Saltus, E.E.

When George was king: Johnson, E.P.

When ghost meets ghost: De Morgan, W.F.

When God dropped in: Collins, Dale

When God laughs: London, Jack

When I am dead: Austin, Mary

When I grow rich: Sidgwick, Ethel

When I was a child: Markino, Yoshio

When I was a little girl: Gale, Zona

When I was King: Lawson, Henry

When I was very young: Milne, A.A.

When I weekly knew: Hardy, Thomas

When knighthood was in flower: Major, Charles

When ladies meet: Crothers, Rachel

When Lincoln died: Thomson, E.W.

When love flies out of the window: Merrick, Leonard

When men grew tall: Lewis, A.H.

When Mr. Punch was young: Allen, C.R.

When my girl comes home: Pritchett, V.S.

When no man pursueth: Lowndes, *Mrs.* Belloc

When Shady Avenue was Shady Lane: Allen, Hervey

When sorrows come: Vachell, H.A.

When sparrows fall: Salverson, L.G.

When the battle was fought: †Craddock, C.E.

When the bells rang: †Armstrong, Anthony and Bruce Graeme

When the Blackfleet went south: Young, E.R.

When the bough breaks: Mitchison, Naomi

When the crash comes: Nichols, Beverley

When the devil was well: Stevenson, R.L.

When the gangs came to London: Wallace, Edgar

When the going was good: Waugh, Evelyn

When the green woods laugh: Bates, H.E.

When the Jack hollers: Hughes, J.L.

When the sleeper wakes: Wells, H.G.

When the stuffed prophets quarrel: Lindsay, N.V.

When the tide runs out: †Winch, John

When the turtles sing: Marquis, Don

When the whippoorwill: Rawlings, Marjorie

When the wicked man: Ford, Ford Madox

When the wind blows: Steen, Marguerite

When the world shook: Haggard, *Sir* H. Rider

When they love: Baring, Maurice

When thou wast naked: Powys, T.F.

When Valmond came to Pontiac: Parker, *Sir* H.G.

When we are married: Priestley, J.B.

When we become men: Mitchison, Naomi

When we came out: Hicks, Granville

When we were here together: Patchen, Kenneth

When we were very young: Milne, A.A.

When West was West: Wister, Owen

When William came: (†Saki), Munro, H.H.

When you see me, you know me: Rowley, Samuel

When you think of me: Caldwell, Erskine Preston

Where am I?: Mackail, Denis

Where angels dared to tread: Calverton, V.F.

Where angels fear to tread: Forster, E.M.

Where are the dead?: Belloc, Hilaire

Where did everybody go?: Langley, Noel

Where do we go from here?: Sayers, Dorothy

Where fancy beckons: Vachell, H.A.

Where fear was: a book about fear: Benson, A.C.

Where go you lovely Maggie: Aldrich, T.B.

Where love and friendship dwelt: Lowndes, *Mrs.* Belloc

Where love lies deepest: Ashford, Daisy

Where man belongs: Massingham, Harold

Where the blue begins: Morley, C.D.

Where the clocks chime twice: Waugh, Alec

Where the cross is made: O'Neill, Eugene

Where the dead men lie: Boake, Barcroft

Where the forest murmurs: †Macleod, Fiona

Where the laborers are few: Deland, M.W.C.

Where the sun never sets: Weidman, Jerome

Where the white Sambur roams: Spittel, R.L.

Where the wind goes: Devaney, J.M.

Where there is nothing: Yeats, W.B.

Where there's a will: Rinehart, Mary Poberts

Where there's a will there's a way: Morton, J.M.

Wherefore and the why, The: Herbert, *Sir* A.P.

Where's the money coming from?: Chase, Stuart

Whether a dove or seagull: Warner, Sylvia

Which I never: Strong, L.A.G.

Which is the man?: Cowley, *Mrs*. Hannah

Which: Lord Bўron or Lord Bўron, a bet: Sutro, Alfred

Which sister?: Russell, W.C.

Which way to peace?: Russell, Bertrand

Whig Historians: Fisher, H.A.L.

Whig interpretation of history, The: Butterfield, Herbert

Whig Party, 1807–1812, The: Roberts, Michael

While freedom lives: Davison, F.D.

While golden sleep doth reign: Farjeon, B.L.

While Paris laughed: Merrick, Leonard

While rivers run: Walsh, Maurice

While Rome burns: Woollcott, Alexander

While the billy boils: Lawson, Henry

While the heart beats young: Riley, J.W.

While the sirens slept: Dunsany, Edward Plunkett, *Baron*

While the sun shines: Rattigan, Terence

While you wait: †Armstrong, Anthony

Whilomville: Crane, Stephen

Whim and its consequences, A: James, G.P.R.

Whims and oddities: Hood, Thomas

Whimsicalities: Hood, Thomas

Whin: Gibson, Wilfred

Whip for an ape; A: Lyly, John

Whipper whipt, The: Quarles, Francis

Whipperginny: Graves, Robert

Whipping boy, The: Monsarrat, Nicholas

Whippingham papers, The: Swinburne, A.C.

Whirl asunder, A: Atherton, Gertrude

Whirligigs: †Henry, O

Whirlpool, The: Gissing, George

Whirlwind, The: Phillpotts, Eden

Whiskers and Co.: Jennings, Gertrude

Whiskers will not be worn: †Armstrong, Anthony and Raff

Whisky galore: Mackenzie, *Sir* Compton

Whisky and Scotland: Gunn, Neil

Whisper in the gloom, The: Day-Lewis, C.

Whisper to a bride: Sigourney, L.H.

Whisperer, The: Hall, A.M.

Whispering gallery, The: Lehmann, John

Whispering lane, The: Hume, F.W.

Whispering leaves in Grosvenor Square, 1936–37: Yoshida, Yuki

Whispering Lodge: †Sinclair Murray

Whispers about women: Merrick, Leonard

Whistle, The: Franklin, Benjamin

Whistler v. Ruskin. Art and art critics:Whistler,James McNeill

Whistling cat: Chambers, R.W.

Whistling chambermaid, The: Royde-Smith, Naomi

Whistling maid, The: Rhys, Ernest

White and the gold: Costain, T.B.

White April: Reese, L.W.

White Australia: Bedford, Randolph

White blackbird, The: Young, A.J.

White blackbird, and Portrait, The: Robinson, E.S.L.

White blackfellows: (†Donald Barr), Barrett, C.L.

White blackmail: Percy, Edward

White buildings: Crane, Hart

White camel: Phillpotts, Eden

White canoe, The:Sullivan,Alan

White carnation, The: Sherriff, R.C.

White chief, The: Reid, T.M.

White cockade, The: Grant, James

White cockade, The: Gregory, *Lady* Augusta

White company, The: Doyle, *Sir* Arthur Conan

White cry, The: Stewart, D.A.

White deer, The: Thurber,James

White divel, The: Webster, John

White doe of Rylstone, The: Wordsworth, William

White dresses: Green, Paul

White eagles: Gielgud, Val

White eagles overSerbia:Durrell, Lawrence

White face: Wallace, Edgar

White faced pacer, The: Neal, John

White Fang: London, Jack

White feather, The: Wodehouse, P.G.

White gate, The: Chase, M.E.

White Gate, The: Deeping, Warwick

White gauntlet, The: Reid, T.M.

White goddess, The: Graves, Robert

White gold: Cronin, B.C.

White guard, The: Ackland, Rodney

White gull, The: Carman, Bliss

White hand and the black, The: Mitford, Bertram

White hands: Stringer, A.J.A.

White hare, The: Bowes-Lyon, Lilian

White Heather: Black, William

White Hecatomb, The: Scully, W.C.

White heron, A: Jewett, S.O.

White Hoods, The: Bray, A.E.

White horse and red lion: Agate, J.E.

White horse of the Peppers, The: Lover, Samuel

White horses of Vienna, The: Boyle, Kay

White hour, The: Gunn, Neil M.

White House, The: Braddon, M.E.

White islander, The: Catherwood, Mary

White jacket: Melville, Herman

White ladies of Worcester, The: Barclay, Florence

White lady, The: Reynolds, G.

White leader, The: Skinner, C.L.

White lies: Reade, Charles

White man's saga: Linklater, Eric

White magic: Phillips, D.G.

White magic: White, S.E.

White man, listen!: Wright, Richard

White man's country: Lord Delamare and the making of Kenya: Huxley, Elspeth J.

White man's foot, The: Allen, Grant

White mice, The: Davis, R.H.

White moll, The: Packard, F.L.

White monkey, The: Galsworthy, John

White morning, The: Atherton, Gertrude

White mule: Williams, W.C.

White narcissus: Knister, Raymond

White oxen, The: Burke, Kenneth

White paternoster, The: Powys, T.F.

White peacock, The: Lawrence, D.H.

White people, The: Burnett, Frances Hodgson

White pilgrim, The: Merivale, H.C.

White plumes of Navarre, The: Crockett, S.R.

White Pope, The: Crockett, S.R.

White Priory murders, The: †Carter Dickson

White prophet, The: Caine, Sir T.Hall

White rabbit, The: Marshall, Bruce

White rajah, The: Monsarrat, Nicholas

White rajahs, The: Runciman, Sir Steven

White rat, The: Barker, M.A.

White robe, The: Cabell, James Branch

White roof-tree, A: Turner, E.S.

White rose, The: Whyte-Melville, G.J.

White rose and red: Buchanan, R.W.

White rose of Memphis, The: Falkner, W.C.

White sail, The: Guiney, L.I.

White sand and grey sand: Gibbons, Stella

White sheep of the family, The: (†Ian Hay), Beith, Sir John Hay

White sheep of the family, The: Peach, L. du Garde

White shield, The: Mitford, Bertram

White sister, The: Crawford, F.Marion

White sparrow, The: Colum, Padraic

White Squaw and the Yellow Chief, The: Reid, T.M.

White steed, The: Carroll, P.V.

White umbrella in Mexico, A: Smith, F.H.

White wampum, The: Johnson, E.P.

White wand, The: Hartley, L.P.

White wedding, The: Shiel, M.P.

White widow, The: Bottomley, Gordon

White wife, The: †Bede, Cuthbert

White wings: Barry, Philip

White wings: Black, William

White witch of Rosehall, The: DeLisser, Herbert G.

White wolf: †Brand, Max

White wolf, The: (†Q), Quiller-Couch, Sir Arthur

White wool, etc.: Jacob, Naomi

Whiteboy, The: Hall, A.M.

White-footed deer, The: Bryant, W.C.

White-hall: Hopkins, Charles

Whitehall: Maginn, William

Whitehall: Timms, E.V.

Whiteheaded boy, The: Robinson, E.S.L.

Whiteladies: Oliphant, Margaret

Whiteladies: Young, Francis Brett

Whiteoak brothers, Jalna, The: De la Roche, Mazo

Whiteoak harvest: De la Roche, Mazo

Whiteoak heritage: De la Roche, Mazo

Whiteoaks: De la Roche, Mazo

Whiteoaks of Jalna: De la Roche, Mazo

Whitewash: Vachell, H.A.

Whitewashing Julia: Jones, H.A.

Whither painting?: Rothenstein, Sir William

Whither the theatre?: Bax, Clifford

Whitman: Masters, E.L.

Whitman a study: Burroughs, John

Whitman, a study: Fausset, Hugh

Whitman's self-reliance: Burroughs, John

Who dies?: Mais, S.P.B.

Who fears to speak of Ninety-eight?: Ingram, J.K.

Who goes sailing?: Connell, John

Who goes there!: Chambers, R.W.

Who is he?: Vachell, H.A.

Who is my neighbour?: Ridler, A.B.

Who is Sylvia?: Rattigan, Terence

Who killed Cock Robin?: (†Harrington Hext) Phillpotts, Eden

Who killed Cock Robin?: Sitwell, Sir Osbert

Who killed Diana?: (†Harrington Hext), Phillpotts, Eden

Who killed Joe's baby: Sheldon, C.M.

Who killed Marie Westhoven: (†Eric North), Cronin, B.C.

Who lifted the lid off of hell?: Hubbard, Elbert

Who lost an American: Algren, Nelson

Who pays?: Mitchell, Mary

Who rides on a tiger: Lowndes, Mrs. Belloc

Who walks in fear: †Bell, Neil

Who wants a guinea?: Colman, George, the younger

Who wants war?: Prichard, K.S.

Who was lost and is found: Oliphant, Margaret

Who was Sarah Findlay?: Barrie, *Sir* J.M. and †Mark Twain

Who was the mother of Franklin's son?: Ford, P.L.

Who would have daughters?: Steen, Marguerite

Whole art of husbandrie, The: Markham, Gervase

Whole crew of kind gossips all met to be merry, A: Rowlands, Samuel

Whole family, The: Bangs, J.K.

Whole hog book, The: Bengough, J.W.

Whole of the story, The: Bentley, Phyllis

Whole town's talking, The: Loos, Anita

Whole Voyald, The: Saroyan, William

Whole works of Homer, The (trn.): Chapman, George

Whom God hath joined: Bennett, Arnold

Whom God hath sundered: †Onions, Oliver

Whom to marry and how to get married: Mayhew, Augustus Septimus

Whore of Babylon, The: Dekker, Thomas

Whoroscope: Beckett, Samuel

Who's afraid?: Engle, Paul

Who's there within?: Golding, Louis

Who's Who?: Wodehouse, P.G.

Whose body: Sayers, Dorothy

Whosoever shall offend: Crawford, F.Marion

Why a world centre of industry at San Francisco Bay: Bancroft, H.H.

Why be a mud turtle?: White, S.E.

Why Britain fights: Tawney, R.H.

Why Britain is at war: Nicolson, Hon. *Sir* Harold

Why didn't they ask Evans?: Christie, Agatha

Why do I write?: Greene, Graham

Why do I write?: Pritchett, V.S.

Why does nobody collect me?: Benchley, Robert

Why don't they cheer?: Stead, R.J.C.

Why don't we learn from history? Liddell Hart, B.

Why Europe leaves home: Roberts, Kenneth

Why exhibit works of art: Coomaraswamy, A.K.

Why Frau Frohmann raised her prices: Trollope, Anthony

Why freedom matters: Angell, *Sir* Norman

Why I am for Harding: Bangs, J.K.

Why I am not a Christian: Russell, Bertrand

Why I believe in personal immortality: Lodge, *Sir* Oliver

Why I believe in poverty as the richest experience that can come to a boy: Bok, E.W.

Why I don't write plays: Hardy, Thomas

Why Italy is with the Allies: (†Anthony Hope), Hawkins, Anthony Hope

Why Miss Ann Maria Simmons never married: Freeman, M.W.

Why North Queensland wants separation: Stephens, A.G.

Why not?: Widdemer, Margaret

Why not grow young?: Service, Robert

Why shoot a butler?: Heyer, Georgette

Why so, Socrates?: Richards, I.A.

Why stop learning: Canfield, Dorothy

Why war?: Einstein, Albert

Why war?: Joad, C.E.M.

Why was I killed?: Warner, Rex

Why Waterloo?: Herbert, *Sir* A.P.

Why we had to go to war: Mee, Arthur

Why we should read: Mais, S.P.B.

Why you should be a socialist: Strachey, John

Whym Chow, flame of love: †Field, Michael

Wicked marquis, The: Oppenheim, E.Phillips

Wicked water: Kantor, Mackinlay

Wicked world, The: Gilbert, *Sir* W.S.

Wickford Point: Marquand, J.P.

Wickham and the Armada: Treece, Henry

Wickhamses, The: Ridge, W. Pett

Wicklow gold mines, The: O'Keeffe, John

Wicklow mountains, The: O'Keeffe, John

Widdershins: †Onions, Oliver

Widdow, The: Beaumont, Francis

Widdow, The: Fletcher, John

Widdow, The: Middleton, Thomas

Widow Ranter, The: Behn, *Mrs.* Afra

Widdowes teares, The: Chapman, George

Wide fields: Green, Paul

Wide horizon: Roberts, C.E.M.

Wide is the gate: Sinclair, Upton

Wide, wide world, The: Warner, S.B.

Widecombe fair: Phillpotts, Eden

Wider hope, The: De Quincey, Thomas

Widow Barnaby, The: Trollope, Frances

Widow Barony, The: Burnett, W.R.

Widow bewitch'd, The: Mottley, John

Widow garland, The: Phillpotts, Eden

Widow Guthrie: Johnston, R.M.

Widow in the bye street, The: Masefield, John

Widow in Thrums, A: Barrie, *Sir* J.M.

Widow married, The: Trollope, Frances

Widow, nun and courtesan: Lin Yu-T'ang

Widow of Delphi, The: Cumberland, Richard

Widow of Heardingas, The: Percy, Edward

Widower indeed, A: Broughton, Rhoda

Widowers' houses: Shaw, G.B.

Widowing of Mrs. Holroyd, The: Lawrence, D.H.

Widow's cruise, The: Day-Lewis, C.

Widow's cruise, The: Temple, Joan

Widow's marriage, The: Boker, G.H.

Widow's son, The: Woodworth, Samuel

Widow's tale, A: Barton, Bernard

Widow's tale, A: Oliphant, Margaret

Widow's tale, The: Southey, C.A.

Widow's vow, The: Inchbald, *Mrs.* Elizabeth

Wieland: Brown, C.B.

Wife, The: Belasco, David

Wife, The: Knowles, J.S.

Wife apparent: †Yates, Dornford

Wife for a month, A: Beaumont, Francis

Wife now the widdow of Sir Thomas Overbury, A: Donne, John

Wife now the widdow of Sir Thomas Overbury, A: Overbury, *Sir* Thomas

Wife of a million, The: Lathom, Francis

Wife of Bath, The: Gay, John

Wife of Elias, The: Phillpotts, Eden

Wife of his youth, The: Chestnutt, C.W.

Wife of Sir Isaac Harman, The: Wells, H.G.

Wife to be lett, A: Haywood, *Mrs.* Eliza

Wife traders, The: Stringer, A.J.A.

Wife without a smile, A: Pinero, *Sir* A.W.

Wife's portrait, The: Marston, J.W.

Wigs on the green: Mitford, Nancy

Wigwam, The: Brooks, C.W.S.

Wigwam and the cabin, The: Simms, W.G.

Wil of wit, wits wil, or wils wit: Breton, Nicholas

Wilbur, the trusting whippoor-will: Derleth, A.W.

Wild animal play for children, The: Seton-Thompson, E.

Wild animal ways: Seton-Thompson, E.

Wild animals: White, S.E.

Wild animals at home: Seton-Thompson, E.

Wild animals I have known: Seton-Thompson, E.

Wild apples: Bruce, Charles

Wild apples: Gogarty, O. St. John

Wild bird's nest, The: †O'Connor, Frank

Wild body, The: Lewis, P. Wyndham

Wild Ceylon: Spittel, R.L.

Wild cherry: Reese, L.W.

Wild Colonial boys: Clune, Frank

Wild colonial girl, The: Stephens, A.G.

Wild country: Bromfield, Louis

Wild Decembers: †Dane, Clemence

Wild deer of Exmoor, The: Williamson, Henry

Wild earth: Colum, Padraic

Wild Eelin: Black, William

Wild elephant and the method of capturing and training it in Ceylon, The: Tennent, *Sir* J.E.

Wild flag, The: White, E.B.

Wild flowers: Bloomfield, Robert

Wild fruit: Phillpotts, Eden

Wild gallant, The: Dryden, John

Wild garden: Carman, Bliss

Wild geese, The: Weyman, Stanley

Wild geese calling: White, S.E.

Wild geese overhead: Gunn, Neil

Wild girl of Nebraska, The: Webber, C.W.

Wild goose chase, The: Warner, Rex

Wild goslings: Benét, W.R.

Wild grapes: Bottome, Phyllis

Wild green earth, The: Fergusson, *Sir* Bernard

Wild honey: Niven, F.J.

Wild honey: Uttley, Alison

Wild honey from various thyme: †Field, Michael

Wild Horse Mesa: Grey, Zane

Wild huntress, The: Reid, T.M.

Wild huntsman, The: (†Geoffrey Crayon), Irving, Washington

Wild Irish boy, The: Maturin, C.R.

Wild Irish girl, The: Morgan, *Lady* Sydney

Wild is the river: Bromfield, Louis

Wild justice: Hannay, J.O.

Wild Justice: Woods, M.L.

Wild Knight, The: Chesterton, G.K.

Wild life in a southern county: Jefferies, Richard

Wild life in Australia: (†Donald Barr), Barrett, C.L.

Wild life in Southern seas: †Becke, Louis

Wild notes from the lyre of a native minstrel: Tompson, Charles

Wild oats: O'Keeffe, John

Wild oats of Han, The: Prichard, K.S.

Wild olive, The: †King, Basil

Wild oranges: Hergesheimer, Joseph

Wild palms, The: Faulkner, William

Wild pastures: Beach, R.E.

Wild planet, The: (†Elzevir), Murdoch, *Sir* W.L.F.

Wild rose, A: Dickinson, G.L.

Wild roses of Cape Ann: Larcom, Lucy

Wild scenes and song birds: Webber, C.W.

Wild scenes and wild hunters of the world: Webber, C.W.

Wild scenes in the forest and prairie: Hoffman, C.F.

Wild Southern scenes: Jones, J.B.

Wild sports of the West: Maxwell, W.H.

Wild strawberries: Thirkell, Angela

Wild swan, The: Gilmore, Mary

Wild swan, The: O'Flaherty, Liam

Wild swans, The: Mannin, Ethel

Wild swans at Coole, The: Yeats, W.B.

Wild tulip, The: Lucas, F.L.

Wild Wales: Borrow, George

Wild western scenes: Jones, J.B.

Wild white boy: Spittel, R.L.

Wild white man, The: O'Hara, J.B.

Wild white man and the blacks of Victoria, The: Bonwick, James

Wild youth: Parker, Sir H.G.

Wildash: Ingraham, J.H.

Wildbird, The: Ingraham, J.H.

Wilde v. Whistler: Whistler, James

Wilderness, The: McHenry, James

Wilderness: Warren, Robert Penn

Wilderness and the war path, The: Hall, James

Wilderness clearing: Edmonds, W.D.

Wilderness of monkeys, A: Niven, F.J.

Wilderness of Zin, The: Lawrence, T.E.

Wilderness of Zin, The: Woolley, Sir Leonard

Wilderness trek: Grey, Zane

Wildfire: Grey, Zane

Wild-goose chase, The: Beaumont, Francis

Wildness road: Green, Paul

Wildwood: Johnson, J.W.

Wilfred Cumbermede: Macdonald, George

Wilful our premeditated: Crofts, F.W.

Wilhemina in London: Pain, B.E.O.

Will Denbigh, nobleman: Craik, Mrs. D.M.

Will he marry her?: Lang, J.

Will of song, The: Mackaye, Percy

Will of the people, The: Boker, G.H.

Will Shakespeare: †Dane, Clemence

Will socialism destroy the home: Wells, H.G.

Will Terril: Ingraham, J.H.

Will to believe, The: James, William

Will Warburton: Gissing, George

Willa Cather: Brown, E.K.

Willa Cather: Daiches, David

Willard Gibbs: Rukeyser, Muriel

Willey House, The: Parsons, T.W.

William Allair: Wood, Ellen

William and Dorothy: Ashton, Helen

William and Margaret: Mallet, David

William Barnes: Grigson, Geoffrey

William Black, novelist: Reid, Sir T.W.

William Blake: Chesterton, G.K.

William Blake: Murry, John Middleton

William Blake: Nicoll, Allardyce

William Blake: Swinburne, A.C.

William Blake: Symons, Arthur

William Blake, creative will and the poetic image: Lindsay, Jack

William Blake, painter and poet: Garnett, Richard

William Brown of Oregon: †Miller, Joaquin

"William, by the Grace of God—": †Bowen, Marjorie

William Caxton: Jackson, Holbrook

William Caxton: Knight, Charles

William Charles Macready: Archer, William

William Cobbett: Chesterton, G.K.

William Cobbett: Cole, G.D.H.

William Congreve: Dobrée, Bonamy

William Cowper: Cecil, Lord David

William Cowper: Fausset, Hugh

William Crowe, 1745–1829: Blunden, Edmund

William Dampier: Russell, W.C.

William Faulkner: Brooks, Cleanth

William Greenwood: MacMechan, A.M.

William Hazlitt: Birrell, Augustine

William Hemminge's elegy on Randolph's finger: Heming, William

William Hickling Prescott, 1796–1859: Morison, S.E.

William Hogarth: †Bowen, Marjorie

William Hogarth: Dobson, H.A.

William Hogarth: Sala, G.A.H.

William Holman Hunt: Meynell, Alice

William James: Royce, Josiah

William Johnson Fox: Garnett, Richard

William Kirby: Pierce, Lorne

William Kirby: Riddell, W.R.

William Laud, sometime Archbishop of Canterbury: Benson, A.C.

William Morris: Drinkwater, John

William Morris: Noyes, Alfred

William Morris as I knew him: Shaw, G.B.

William Morris, craftsman-socialist: Jackson, Holbrook

William Nicholson: Steen, Marguerite

William Penn: Vulliamy, C.E.

William Penn, Quaker and pioneer: Dobrée, Bonamy

William, Prince of Orange: †Bowen, Marjorie

William Rothenstein: Beerbohm, Sir Max

William Shakespeare: Chambers, Sir E.K.

William Shakespeare: Knight, Charles

William Shakespeare: Masefield, John

William Shakespeare: a study of facts and problems: Chambers, Sir E.K.

William Shakespeare, pedagogue and poacher: Garnett, Richard

William Shakespeare. The histories: Knights, L.C.

William Shakespeare: two poems: Prince, F.T.

William Tell: Knowles, J.S.

William Tell told again: Wodehouse, P.G.

William the Conqueror: Belloc, Hilaire

William the Conqueror: Costain, T.B.

William the Silent: Harrison, Frederic

William the silent: Squire, *Sir* J.C.

William the Silent: Wedgwood, C.V.

William III: Traill, H.D.

William III and the revolution of 1688: †Bowen, Marjorie

William Thomas Arnold: Montague, C.E.

William Thomas Arnold, journalist and historian: Ward, *Mrs.* Humphrey

William Vaughn Moody—twenty years after: Mackaye, Percy

William West Skiles: Cooper, S.F.

William Wetmore story and his friends: James, Henry

William's other Anne: Brown, Ivor

Willing horse, The: (†Ian Hay), Beith, *Sir* John Hay

Willing to die: Le Fanu, Sheridan

Will-o'-the-Wisp: Orczy, *Baroness*

Willoughby's, The: Brown, Alice

Willow and leather: Lucas, E.V.

Willow brook: Warner, S.B.

Willow cabin, The: Frankau, Pamela

Willows, The: Blackwood, Algernon

Willow's forge: Kaye-Smith, Sheila

Will's wonder book: Alcott, Louisa M.

Willy Reilly and his dear Cooleen Bawn: Carleton, William

Wilmay: Pain, B.E.O.

Wilmot and Tilley: Hannay, James

Wilson and some others: Cole, G.D.H.

Wilton Harvey: Sedgwick, C.M.

Wiltshire essays: Hewlett, Maurice

Winchester: Mee, Arthur

Winchester house: Green, Anne

Wind among the reeds, The: Yeats, W.B.

Wind and the rain, The: Hodge, H.E.

Wind and the sand, The: Glover, Denis

Wind and the whirlwind, The: Blunt, Wilfred

Wind between the worlds, The: Brown, Alice

Wind bloweth, The: Byrne, Donn

Wind blows over, The: De la Mare, Walter

Wind in his fists: Bottome, Phyllis

Wind in the elms: Derleth, A.W.

Wind in the rose-bush, The: Freeman, Mary

Wind in the trees, The: Tynan, Katherine

Wind in the willows, The: Grahame, Kenneth

Wind is rising, The: Tomlinson, H.M.

Wind o' the moors: Peach, L. du Garde

Wind of destiny, The: Hardy, A.S.

Wind of freedom, The: Mackenzie, *Sir* Compton

Wind of heaven, The: Williams, Emlyn

Wind on the heath: Jacob, Naomi

Wind on the moon, The: Linklater, Eric

Wind our enemy, The: Marriott, Anne

Wind over Wisconsin: Derleth, A.W.

Wind ship, The: Villiers, A.J.

Wind song: Sandburg, C.A.

Windfall: Brophy, John

Windfall, The: †Craddock, C.E.

Windfall: Sherriff, R.C.

Windfalls: Gardiner, A.G.

Windfalls: O'Casey, Sean

Windfalls: Trevelyan, R.C.

Windfall's eve: Lucas, E.V.

Windflower, A: Carman, Bliss

Winding lane, The: Gibbs, *Sir* Philip

Winding road: †Bell, Neil

Winding stair, The: Mason, A.E.W.

Winding stair, The: Yeats, W.B.

Windless cabins: Van Doren, Mark

Windlestraws: Bottome, Phyllis

Windlestraws: Prichard, K.S.

Windmills: Cannan, Gilbert

Window, The: Tennyson, Alfred *Lord*

Window at the White Cat, The: Rinehart, Mary Roberts

Window gazer, The: MacKay, I.E.

Window in prison and prison-land, A: Nehru, Jawaharlal

Window in the wall, The: Knox, R.A.

Window on a hill, A: Church, Richard

Window seat, The: Mottram, R.H.

Windows: Galsworthy, John

Windows of night: Williams, Charles

Windows on a vanished time: Bullett, Gerald

Winds of autumn: (†Margaret Gregory), Ercole, Velia

Winds of chance, The: Beach, R.E.

Winds of doctrine: Santayana, George

Winds of God, The: Bacheller, Irving

Winds of heaven, The: Dickens, Monica

Winds of morning: Davis, H.L.

Winds of the day: Spring, Howard

Windsor Castle: Ainsworth, Harrison

Windsor Castle: Thomas, E.E.P.

Windsor Castle in a monument to our late Sovereign K. Charles II: Otway, Thomas

Windsor tapestry: Mackenzie, *Sir* Compton

Windsor-Forest, to the Right Honourable George Lord Lansdown: Pope, Alexander

Windswept: Chase, M.E.

Wind-voices: Marston, P.B.

Windy McPherson's son: Anderson, Sherwood

Wine: Gay, John

Wine and roses: Daley, Victor

Wine for Gospel wantons: Shepard, Thomas

Wine from these grapes: Millay, E. St. Vincent

Wine is poured, The: Seymour, Beatrice Kean

Wine of choice: Behrman, S. N.

Wine of Good Hope, †Rame, David

Wine of the country: Basso, Hamilton

Wine of the Puritans, The: Brooks, Van Wyck

Wine of wizardry, A: Sterling, George

Wine women and song: Symonds, J.A.

Wine, women and waiters: Frankau, Gilbert

Winefred: Baring-Gould, Sabine

Wine-press, The: Noyes, Alfred

Winesburg, Ohio: Anderson, Sherwood

Wing of the wild bird, The: Watson, A.D.

Wing of the wind, The: Ingraham, J.H.

Wing-and-wing, The: Cooper, James Fenimore

Winged chariot: De la Mare, Walter

Winged destiny, The: †Macleod, Fiona

Winged horse, The: Frankau, Pamela

Winged lion, The: De Mille, James

Winged seeds: Prichard, K.S.

Winged trees, The: †Bowen, Marjorie

Winged victory, The: †Grand, Sarah

Winged victory: Mackaye, Percy

Wingless victory, The: Anderson, Maxwell

Wings and the child: Nesbit, E.

Wings for to fly: Green, Paul

Wings of adventure, The: Gibbs, Sir Philip

Wings of death: Tagore, Sir R.

Wings of night, The: Raddall, T.H.

Wings of the dove, The: James, Henry

Wings of the morning: Virtue, Vivian

Wings of tomorrow: Turnbull, S.C.P.

Wings over the Atlantic: Divine, A.D.

Winifred Mount: Pryce, Richard

Winkles, The: Jones, J.B.

Winner, The: Mottram, R.H.

Winner take nothing: Hemingway, Ernest

Winners, The: Housman, Laurence

Winnie-the-Pooh: Milne, A.A.

Winning his spurs: Henty, G.A.

Winning lady, The: Freeman, Mary

Winning of Barbara Worth, The: Wright, H.B.

Winning of Lucia, The: Barr, A.E.H.

Winnowed verse: Lawson, Henry

Winnowed wisdom: Leacock, Stephen

Winnowing-fan, The: Binyon, Laurence

Winona of Camp Karonya: Widdemer, Margaret

Winona of the camp fire: Widdemer, Margaret

Winona on her own: Widdemer, Margaret

Winona's dreams come true: Widdemer, Margaret

Winona's war farm: Widdemer, Margaret

Winona's way: Widdemer, Margaret

Winslow boy, The: Rattigan, Terence

Winsome Winnie: Leacock, Stephen

Winston affair, The: Fast, Howard M.

Winston Churchill, the writer: Connell, John

Winstonburg line, The: Sitwell, Sir Osbert

Winter: Thomson, James

Winter: Thoreau, H.D.

Winter alone, The: Scott, Evelyn

Winter diary, A: Van Doren, Mark

Winter evening tales: Barr, A.E.H.

Winter evenings: Hall, James

Winter garden, The: Galsworthy, John

Winter harvest: Young, A.J.

Winter holiday, A: Carman, Bliss

Winter holiday: Ransome, Arthur

Winter in Arabia, A: Stark, Freya

Winter in Beech Street, A: Wilson, Edmund

Winter in London: Brown, Ivor

Winter in Mentone, A: Hare, A.J.C.

Winter in the air: Warner, Sylvia Townsend

Winter in the West, A: Hoffman, C.F.

Winter journey: Odets, Clifford

Winter miscellany, A: Wolfe, Humbert

Winter nights: Blunden, Edmund

Winter of discontent: Frankau, Gilbert

Winter of our discontent, The: Steinbeck, John

Winter orchard: Johnson, J.W.

Winter pilgrimage, A: Haggard, Sir H. Rider

Winter solstice: Bullett, Gerald

Winter solstice, The: Monro, H.E.

Winter song: Hanley, James

Winter sports holiday: Mais, S.P.B.

Winter sports in Switzerland: Benson, E.F.

Winter sunshine: Burroughs, John

Winter the huntsman: Sitwell, Sir Osbert

Winter words: Hardy, Thomas

Winter-meditations: Mather, Cotton

Winters, The: Jenkins, Elizabeth

Winters of content: Sitwell, Sir Osbert

Winter's tale, The: Shakespeare, William

Winterset: Anderson, Maxwell

Wintersmoon: Walpole, Sir Hugh

Winthropi Justa: Mather, Cotton

Wintry bough, The: Percy, Edward

Winwood: Ingraham, J.H.

Wire devils, The: Packard, F.L.

Wire tappers, The: Stringer, A.J.A.

Wisconsin earth, a Sac prairie sampler: Derleth, A.W.

Wisconsin in their bones: Derleth, A.W.

Wisconsin plays: Gale, Zona

Wisconsin, river of a thousand isles, The: Derleth, A.W.

Wisdom and destiny: Sutro, Alfred

Wisdom for the wise: Herbert, *Sir* A.P.

Wisdom of China, The: Lin Yu-T'ang

Wisdom of China and India, The: Lin Yu-T'ang

Wisdom of Confucius, The: Lin Yu-T'ang

Wisdom of Father Brown, The: Chesterton, G.K.

Wisdom of fools, The: Deland, Margaret

Wisdom of God manifested in the works of the creation, The: Ray, John

Wisdom of the desert, The: Hannay, J.O.

Wisdom of the Egyptians: Petrie, *Sir* William Flinders

Wisdom of the fields, The: Massingham, Harold

Wisdom of the heart, The: Miller, Henry

Wisdom of the simple, The: Holme, Constance

Wisdom of the West: Russell, Bertrand

Wisdom of the wise, The: †Hobbes, John Oliver

Wisdom on the hire system: Lucas, E.V.

Wisdom tooth, The: Connelly, Marc

Wisdom while you wait: Lucas, E.V.

Wisdome of Solomon paraphrased, The: Middleton, Thomas

Wisdom's daughter: Haggard, *Sir* H. Rider

Wisdom's gate: Barnes, Margaret

Wise and the foolish virgins, The: Steen, Marguerite

Wise have not spoken, The: Carroll, P.V.

Wise owl's story: Uttley, Alison

Wise virgins, The: Woolf, Leonard

Wise, witty, eloquent kings of the platform and pulpit: (†Eli Perkins), Landon, Melville

Wise woman, The: Macdonald, George

Wise woman of Inverness, The: Black, William

Wise-woman of Hogsdon, The: Heywood, Thomas

Wish to goodness!: Housman, Laurence

Wish you were here: Calder-Marshall, Arthur

Wishes limited: Darlington, W.A.

Wishing princess, The: Brazil, Angela

Wishing-cap papers, The: Hunt, Leigh

Wishing-ring man, The: Widdemer, Margaret

Wish-shop, The: Brighouse, Harold

Wisteria Cottage: Coates, R.M.

Wit and humor of the age: (†Eli Perkins), Landon, Melville

Wit and humour: Brooks, C.W.S.

Wit and humour: Hunt, Leigh

Wit, humor and pathos: Landon, Melville de Lancey

Wit in a constable: Glapthorne, Henry

Wit with-out money: Beaumont, Francis and John Fletcher

Witch, The: Williams, Charles

Witch cult in Western Europe: Murray, Margaret

Witch doctor, The: Devaney, J.M.

Witch in the wood, The: White, T.H.

Witch of Edmonton, The: Dekker, Thomas

Witch of Edmonton, The: Ford, John

Witch of Edmonton a known true story, The: Rowley, William

Witch of Methryn, The: †Llewellyn, Richard

Witch of Prague, The: Crawford, F. Marion

Witch of Ramoth, The: Van Doren, Mark

Witch of the low-tide, etc., The: Carr, J.D.

Witch Perkins: Scott, Evelyn

Witch stories: Linton, Eliza

Witch trial at Mount Holly, A: Franklin, Benjamin

Witch wolf, The: Harris, Joel Chandler

Witch wood: Buchan, John

Witchcraft: Williams, Charles

Witchcraft in Old and New England: Kittredge, G.L.

Witchery of archery, The: Thompson, Maurice

Witches brew, The: Pratt, E.J.

Witches of New York, The: Thompson, M.N.

Witching Hill: Hornung, E.W.

Witching hour, The: Thomas, Augustus

Witching of Elspie, The: Scott, D.C.

Witch's cauldron: Phillpotts, Eden

Witch's daughter, The: Brighouse, Harold

Witch's head, The: Haggard, *Sir* H. Rider

With a silken thread: Linton, Eliza

With all John's love: Lowndes, *Mrs.* Belloc

With Americans of past and present days: Jusserand, Jean

With both armies in South Africa: Davis, R.H.

With Clive in India: Henty, G.A.

With Eastern eyes: Poole, Ernest

With edged tools: †Merriman, Seton

With folded wings: White, S.E.

With Gauge & Swallow, attorneys: Tourgée, A.W.

With harp and crown: Besant, *Sir* Walter and James Rice

With hey, ho: Cournos, John

With Kitchener in the Sudan: Henty, G.A.

With love and irony: Lin Yu-T'ang

With love from Rachel: Sullivan, Alan

With many voices: Europe talks about America: Appel, Benjamin

With much love: Green, Anne

With my friends: Matthews, J.B.

With Number Three, surgical and medical, and new poems: Kipling, Rudyard

With poor emigrants to America: Graham, Stephen

With reed and lyre: Scollard, Clinton

With Roberts to Pretoria: Henty, G.A.

With Rogers on the frontier: Oxley, J.M.

With Sa'di in the garden, or, the book of love: Arnold, Edwin

With staff and scrip: O'Hagan, Thomas

With the allies: Davis, R.H.

With the Allies to Pekin: Henty, G.A.

With the band: Chambers, R.W.

With the eyes of youth: Black, William

With the Flagship of the South: Bean, C.E.

With the fourteenth army: Karaka, D.F.

With the French in France and Salonika: Davis, R.H.

With the Guards to Mexico: Fleming, Peter

With the immortals: Crawford, F. Marion

With the living voice: Masefield, John

With the night mail: Kipling, Rudyard

With the procession: Fuller, Henry Blake

With the Russian pilgrims to Jerusalem: Graham, Stephen

With the Turk in wartime: Pickthall, M.W.

With the wild geese: Lawless, Emily

With the wits: More, P.E.

With trumpet and drum: Field, Eugene

With wings as eagles: Benét, William Rose

Withered nosegay, A: Coward, Noel

Withered root, The: Davies, Rhys

Withering fires: †Bowen, Marjorie

Within and without: Macdonald, George

Within four walls: Gibson, Wilfred

Within the bubble: (†Joseph Shearing), †Bowen, Marjorie

Within the Capes: Pyle, Howard

Within the cup: Bottome, Phyllis

Within the gates: O'Casey, Sean

Within the gates: Ward, E.S.

Within the maze: Wood, Ellen

Within the precincts: Oliphant, Margaret

Within the rim: James, Henry

Within the tides: Conrad, Joseph

Within this present: Barnes, Margaret Campbell

Without a home: Roe, E.P.

Without apology: Douglas, Lord Alfred

Without armour: Hilton, James

Without love: Barry, Philip

Without my cloak: O'Brien, Kate

Without prejudice: Zangwill, Israel

Without the city wall: Bolitho, H.H.

Without witness: †Armstrong, Anthony and Harold Simpson

Witness for the defence, The: Mason, A.E.W.

Witness for the prosecution: Christie, Agatha

Witness of Canon Welcome, The: Raymond, Ernest

Witness tree, A: Frost, Robert

Wits, The: Kirkman, Francis

Wits Bedlam where is had whipping-cheer to cure the mad: Davies, John

Wits miserie, and the worlds madnesse: Lodge, Thomas

Wits paraphras'd, The: Stevenson Matthew

Wits private wealth stored with choice commodities: Breton, Nicholas

Wits Trenchmour in a conference had betwixt a Scholler and an Angler: Breton, Nicholas

Wittes pilgrimage through a world of amorous sonnets: Davies, John

Wittie faire one, The: Shirley, James

Witts reactions: Herbert, George

Wives: Bradford, Gamaliel

Wives and daughters: Gaskell, Mrs. Elizabeth

Wives and husbands: Hall, Anna Maria

Wives as they were and maids as they are: Inchbald, Mrs. Elizabeth

Wives excuse, The: Southern, Thomas

Wives in exile: †Macleod, Fiona

Wives of the prophet, The: Read, O.P.

Wizard, The: Haggard, Sir H. Rider

Wizard bird, The: Millin, Sarah Gertrude

Wizard's mask, The: Chattopadhyaya, H.

Wizard's son, The: Oliphant, Margaret

Wolcott Balestier: Gosse, Sir Edmund

Wolf Solent: Powys, John Cowper

Wolf woman, The: Stringer, A.J.A.

Wolfe of Badenoch, The: Lauder, Sir Thomas Dick

Wolfenburg: Black, William

Wolfer, The: Niven, F.J.

Wolfert's roost: (†Geoffrey Crayon), Irving, Washington

Wolf's-bane rhymes: Powys, John Cowper

Wolf-tracker, The: Grey, Zane

Wolfville: Lewis, A.H.

Wolfville days: Lewis, A.H.

Wolfville folks: Lewis, A.H.

Wolfville nights: Lewis, A.H.

Wolsey: Pollard, A.F.

Wolves of God, The: Blackwood, Algernon

Wolves were in the sledge, The: Gibbons, Stella

Woman, A: Davies, Rhys

Woman: Morgan, Lady Sydney

Woman: Watson, A.D.

Woman among savages, A: Simpson, H. de G.

Woman among women, The: Davies, Rhys

Woman and her master: Morgan, *Lady* Sydney

Woman and her wishes: Higginson, T.W.

Woman and labour: Schreiner, Olive

Woman and the man: Buchanan, R.B.

Woman as world builders: Dell, Floyd

Woman at dusk, A: Stringer, A.J.A.

Woman at the door, The: Deeping, Warwick

Woman at the mill, The: Davison, F.D.

Woman clothed with sun, The: Lucas, F.L.

Woman from nowhere, The: Brophy, John

Woman from Sicily, The: Swinnerton, Frank

Woman from the East, The: Wallace, Edgar

Woman hater, The: Beaumont, John and John Fletcher

Woman hater, A: Reade, Charles

Woman in ambush: Beach, R.E.

Woman in armour, A: Catherwood, Mary

Woman in exile, A: Vachell, H.A.

Woman in France during the eighteenth century: Kavanagh, Julia

Woman in sacred history: Stowe, Harriet Beecher

Woman in sunshine, A: Swinnerton, Frank

Woman in the back seat, The: Steen, Marguerite

Woman in the case, The: Fitch, Clyde William

Woman in the dark: Hammett, S.D.

Woman in the hall, The: Stern, G.B.

Woman in the moone, The: Lyly, John

Woman in the nineteenth century: Fuller, Margaret

Woman in the picture: De Voto, Bernard

Woman in the rain, The: Stringer, A.J.A.

Woman in white, The: Collins, Wilkie

Woman is a weather-cocke, A: Field, Nathaniel

Woman kilde with kindnesse, A: Heywood, Thomas

Woman of Andros, The: Wilder, Thornton

Woman of genius, A: Austin, Mary

Woman of honor, A: Bunner, Henry Cuyler

Woman of Knockaloe, The: Caine, *Sir* Henry Hall

Woman of my life, The: Bemelmans, Ludwig

Woman of no importance, A: Wilde, Oscar

Woman of the Shee, A: Byrne, Donn

Woman of the world, The: Gore, Catherine

Woman of the world, A: Wilcox, Ella Wheeler

Woman on her way, A: Van Druten, J.W.

Woman on the beast, The: Simpson, H. de G.

Woman or suffragette?: †Corelli, Marie

Woman suffrage and sentiment: Eastman, Max

Woman suffrage tracts: Curtis, George William

Woman tamer, The: Esson, T.L.B.

Woman, the angel of life: Montgomery, Robert

Woman thou gavest me, The: Caine, *Sir* Henry Hall

Woman unashamed, A: Engle, Paul

Woman ventures, A: Phillips, D.G.

Woman who couldn't die, The: Stringer, A.J.A.

Woman who dared, The: Sargent, Epes

Woman who did, The: Allen, Grant

Woman who had imagination, The: Bates, H.E.

Woman who rode away, The: Lawrence, D.H.

Woman who stole everything, The: Bennett, Arnold

Woman who went to Hell, The: Sigerson, Dora

Woman with the fan, The: Hichens, Robert

Woman within, The: Glasgow, Ellen

Woman-captain, The: Shadwell, Thomas

Womankind in Western Europe from the earliest times to the seventeenth century: Wright, Thomas

Womanly noblesse: Chaucer, Geoffrey

Woman's exile, A: Carman, Bliss

Woman's friendship: Aguilar, Grace

Woman's honor: Glaspell, Susan

Woman's influence, A: Jennings, Gertrude

Woman's kingdom, The: Craik, *Mrs.* Dinah

Woman's reason, A: Howells, W.D.

Woman's record: Hale, S.J.B.

Woman's reliquary, A: Dowden, Edward

Woman's revenge: Payne, J.H.

Woman's story, A: Hall, Anna Maria

Woman's thoughts about women, A: Craik, *Mrs.* Dinah

Woman's vengeance, A: Payn, James

Woman's war, A: Deeping, Warwick

Woman's will, A: Burnett, Frances Hodgson

Woman's wit: Cibber, Colley

Woman's wrongs: Dodge, May Abigail

Women: Maturin, C.R.

Women: Tarkington, Booth

Women against men: Jameson, Storm

Women also dream: Mannin, Ethel

Women: an enquiry: Muir, Willa

Women and a changing civilisation: Holtby, Winifred

Women and children: De Selincourt, Hugh

Women and children last: Nichols, Beverley

Women and men: Ford, Ford Madox

Women and men: Higginson, T.W.

Women and social justice: Gandhi, M.K.

Women and the Factory Acts: Webb, Beatrice

Women and the revolution: Mannin, Ethel

Women and Thomas Harrow: Marquand, J.P.

Women are like that: †Delafield, E.M.

Women as force in history: Beard, Mary

Women as they are: Gore, Catherine

Women at Oxford, The: Brittain, Vera

Women at Point Sur, The: Jeffers, J.R.

Women at war: Percy, Edward

Women beware women: Middleton, Thomas

Women in love: Lawrence, D.H.

Women in love: Sutro, Alfred

Women in the citizenships of yesterday, today and tomorrow: Beard, Mary

Women must weep: Fawcett, Edgar

Women must work: Aldington, Richard

Women of Christianity exemplary for acts of piety and charity: Kavanagh, Julia

Women of Israel, The: Aguilar, Grace

Women of New Zealand, The: Simpson, Helen

Women of Shakespeare, The: Harris, J.T.

Women of the Bible: Morton, H.V.

Women of the horizon, The: Frankau, Gilbert

Women of to-day: Cole, M.I.

Women, work in modern England: Brittain, Vera

Womenkind: Gibson, Wilfred

Women's comedy, The: Simpson, Helen

Women's conquest of New York, The: Janvier, T.A.

Women's side, The: †Dane, Clemence

Women's suffrage; the reform against nature: Bushnell, Horace

Women's work in municipalities: Beard, Mary

Won by a head: Austin, Alfred

Won by waiting: Lyall, Edna

Won in Western Canada: Oxley, J.M.

Wonder, The: Beresford, J.D.

Wonder box, The: Mee, Arthur

Wonder child, The: Turner, E.S.

Wonder clock, The: Pyle, Howard

Wonder hat, The: Hecht, Ben

Wonder hero: Priestley, J.B.

Wonder night, The: Binyon, Laurence

Wonder of a kingdome, The: Dekker, Thomas

Wonder of all the wonders, The: Swift, Jonathan

Wonder of this age, The: Heywood, Thomas

Wonder of women, The: Marston, John

Wonder-book for girls and boys, A: Hawthorne, Nathaniel

Wonderful adventures of Paul Punyan, The: Untermeyer, Louis

Wonderful century, The: Wallace, A.R.

Wonderful garden, The: Nesbit, E.

Wonderful knight: Farjeon, Eleanor

Wonderful life [of Christ], The: †Stretton, Hesba

Wonderful O, The: Thurber, James

Wonderful outings: Knox, E.V.

Wonderful strange and miraculous astrologicall prognostication, A: Nash, Thomas

Wonderful visit, The: Ervine, St.John

Wonderful visit, The: Wells, H.G.

Wonderful wonder of all wonders, The: Swift, Jonathan

Wonderful works of God commemorated, The: Mather, Cotton

Wonderful year: Mee, Arthur

Wonderful yeare, The: Dekker, Thomas

Wonderings. Between one and six years: Masefield, John

Wonderland of the North, The: Cross, Zora

Wonders of Herodotus: Farjeon, Eleanor

Wonders of science, The: Mayhew, Henry

Wonders of the Arctic world, The: Sargent, Epes

Wonders of the invisible world, The: Mather, Cotton

Wonders of the little world, The: Wanley, Nathaniel

Wonders of the peake, The: Cotton, Charles

Wonders worth the hearing: Breton, Nicholas

Wonder-worker of Padua, The: Stoddard, C.W.

Wondrous tale of Alroy and the rise of Iskander, The: Disraeli, Benjamin

Wood and stone: Powys, John Cowper

Wood and the trees, The: Mitchell, Mary

Wood beyond the world, The: Morris, William

Wood fire in No.3, The: Smith, F.H.

Wood magic: Jefferies, Richard

Wood pigeons and Mary, The: Molesworth, *Mrs.*

Woodbridge record: Mitchell, D.G.

Woodcarver's wife, The: Pickthall, M.L.C.

Woodcraft manual for boys (for girls), The: Seton-Thompson, E.

Woodcuts: Stephens, A.G.

Woodcuts and some words: Craig, Gordon

Wooden horse, The: Walpole, *Sir* Hugh

Wooden Pegasus, The: Sitwell, Edith

Wooden ships and iron men: Wallace, F.W.

Wooden spoon, The: Griffith, Llewelyn

Wooden world dissected in character of a ship of war, The: Ward, Edward

Woodie Thorpe's pilgrimage: Trowbridge, J.T.

Woodland life, The: Thomas, E.E.P.

Woodland tales: Seton-Thompson, E.

Woodlanders, The: Hardy, Thomas

Woodman, The: Channing, William Ellery

Woodman, The: James, G.P.R.

Wood-myth and fable: Seton-Thompson, E.

Woodnymph: Phillpotts, Eden

Woodrow Wilson: White, W.A.

Woodrow Wilson and world settlement: Baker, Ray Stannard

Woodshed, The: Heppenstall, J.Rayner

Woodsmoke: Young, Francis Brett

Woodstock: La Gallienne, Richard

Woodstock: Scott, Sir Walter

Wooing of Artemis, The: Todhunter, John

Wooing of Malkatoon, The: Wallace, Lew

Wool trade in English medieval history, The: Power, Eileen

Wool-gathering: Dodge, May Abigail

Worcester account, The: Behrman, S.N.

Worcester Carson League, The: Higginson, T.W.

Word and the will, The: Payn, James

Word at St.Kavins, The: Carman, Bliss

Word for his sponsor, A: Hall, J.N.

Word for the Navy, A: Swinburne, A.C.

Word from Wales: Griffith, Llewelyn

Word in edgeways, A: Brown, Ivor

Word in your ear, A: Brown, Ivor

Word of comfort to a melancholy country, A: Wise, John

Word of Gideon, The: Jones, H.A.

Word of honour: †Sapper

Word of love, The: Engle, Paul

Word of mouth: Weidman, Jerome

Word of Satan in the Bible, The: Adamic, Louis

Word of the sorceress, The: Mitford, Bertram

Word over all: Day-Lewis, C.

Word to Caesar: Trease, Geoffrey

Word to New England, A: Bradford, William

Word to New Plymouth, A: Bradford, William

Word to the public, A: Lytton, E.G.E.B. 1st Baron

Word to the wise, A: Berkeley, George

Word to the wise, A: Kelly, Hugh

Word-links: †Carroll, Lewis

Words: Stead, R.J.C.

Words ancient and modern: Weekley, Ernest

Words and idioms: Smith, L.L.P.

Words and names: Weekley, Ernest

Words and their ways in English speech: Kittredge, G.L.

Words and thoughts: Marquis, Don

Words at war, words at peace: Partridge, Eric

Words by request: Hassall, Christopher

Words for a musical entertainment on the taking of Namur: Motteux, P.A.

Words for music: Yeats, W.B.

Words for the hour: Howe, Julia Ward

Words in our time: Brown, Ivor

Words in season: Brown, Ivor

Words of advice to schoolboys: Kingsley, Charles

Words on the air: Steed, H.W.

Words upon the window pane, The: Yeats, W.B.

Words, words, words!: Partridge, Eric

Wordsworth: Calvert, G.H.

Wordsworth: Myers, F.W.H.

Wordsworth: Raleigh, Sir Walter A.

Wordsworth: Read, Sir Herbert

Wordsworth: a re-interpretation: Bateson, F.W.

Wordsworthian and other studies: De Selincourt, Ernest

Wordsworth's grave: Watson, Sir J.W.

Work: Alcott, Louisa M.

Work and culture: Gill, Eric

Work and leisure: Gill, Eric

Work and play: Bushnell, Horace

Work and property: Gill, Eric

Work for the idle hands: Craik, Mrs. Dinah

Work for the winter: Bell, Julian

Work of art: Lewis, H.S.

Work of Henry Ospovat, The: †Onions, Oliver

Work of Rex Whistler, The: Whistler, Laurence

Work of Robert Nathan, The: Bromfield, Louis

Work of St.Francis: Kantor, Mackinlay

Work over: Neale, J.M.

Work suspended: Waugh, Evelyn

Work, wealth and happiness of mankind, The: Wells, H.G.

Worke for armorours: Dekker, Thomas

Worker in sandalwood, The: Pickthall, M.L.C.

Worker's control in the Russian mining industry: Strachey, John

Workers in the dawn: Gissing, George

Worker's International, The: Postgate, Raymond

Workes of a young wyt trust up with a fardell of pretie fancies, The: Breton, Nicholas

Workes of Geffrey Chaucer, with divers addicions, whiche were never in printe before, The: Stow, John

Workes of Lucius Annaeus Seneca, The: Lodge, Thomas

Working bullocks: Prichard, K.S.

Working men's homes: Hale, E.E.

Working novelist, The: Pritchett, V.S.

Working of Dyarchy: Panikkar, K.M.

Working with the hands: Washington, B.T.

Working-man's companion, The: Knight, Charles

Workmen's earnings, strikes and savings: Smiles, Samuel

Works and days: †Field, Michael

Works manager today, The: Webb, Sidney

Works of Cheviot Tichburn, The: Ainsworth, Harrison

Works of Father Prout, The: Mahony, F.S.

Works of Frances Hodgkins: McCormick, E.H.

Works of Machiavelli, The: Nevile, Henry

Works of Ossian, The: Macpherson, James

Works of F. Rabelais, M.D., The: Urquhart, Sir Thomas

Works of Shakespear in six volumes collated and corrected, The: Pope, A.

Works of Shakespeare, The: Theobald, Lewis

Works of Shakespeare, with a memoir and essay on his genius, The: Proctor, B.W.

Workshop organization: Cole, G.D.H.

World a mask, The: Boker, G.H.

World after the Peace Conference, The: Toynbee, Arnold

World ahead, A: Lindsay, Jack

World and Africa, The: Dubois, William

World and the artist, The: Drinkwater, John

World and the individual, The: Royce, Josiah

World and the West, The: Toynbee, Arnold

World as I see it, The: Einstein, Albert

World as it goes, The: Combe, William

World at auction, The: †Field, Michael

World at my shoulder, The: Tietjens, E.S.

World at Westminster, The: Moore, Thomas

World before the flood, The: Montgomery, James

World before them, The: Moodie, Susanna

World blackout: Millin, Sarah Gertrude

World brain: Wells, H.G.

World conflict in its relation to American democracy, The: Lippmann, Walter

World crisis, The: Churchill, Sir Winston

World decision, The: Herrick, Robert

World divided is a world lost, A: Van Loon, Hendrik

World does not move, The: Tarkington, Booth

World drama: Nicoll, Allardyce

World enough and time: Warren, Robert Penn

World for sale, The: Parker, Sir H.G.

World I knew, The: Golding, Louis

World I live in, The: Keller, Helen

World I never made, A: Farrell, James

World in a village, The: O'Keeffe, John

World in bud, The: Bullett, Gerald

World in false face, The: Nathan, G.J.

World in his arms, The: Beach, R.E.

World in the Church, The: †Trafford, F.G.

World in the crucible, The: Parker, Sir H.G.

World in the evening, The: Isherwood, Christopher

World in the moon, The: Settle, Elkanah

World in transition: Cole, G.D.H.

World is round, The: Stein, Gertrude

World is yours, The: †Lancaster, G.B.

World, its debts and the rich men, The: Wells, H.G.

World my wilderness, The: Macauley, Dame Rose

World of animals, The: Krutch, J.W.

World of chance, The: Howells, W.D.

World of dreams, The: Ellis, Havelock

World of fiction: De Voto, Bernard

World of Gilbert and Sullivan, The: Darlington, W.A.

World of H.G. Wells, The: Brooks, Van Wyck

World of Harlequin, The: Nicoll, Allardyce

World of Homer, The: Lang, Andrew

World of James McNeill Whistler, The: Gregory, Horace

World of labour, The: Cole, G.D.H.

World of light, The: Huxley, Aldous

World of love, A: Bowen, E.D.C.

World of men, The: Palmer, E.V.

World of sex, The: Miller, Henry

World of sound, The: Bragg, Sir William

World of today, The: Becker, C.L.

World of Washington Irving, The: Brooks, Van Wyck

World of William Clissold, The: Wells, H.G.

World of words, The: Partridge, Eric

World over, The: Wharton, Edith

World owes me a living, The: Rhys, J.L.

World politics: Dutt, R.P.

World set free, The: Wells, H.G.

World so wide: Lewis, H.S.

World, the flesh and Father Smith, The: Marshall, Bruce

World to play with, The: Dukes, Ashley

World to win, A: Sinclair, Upton

World turns slowly round, The: Mottram, R.H.

World under snow: Broster, D.K.

World voices: Wilcox, Ella Wheeler

World we live in: Bromfield, Louis

World we make, The: Kingsley, Sidney

World we saw, The: Munshi, K.M.

World well lost, The: Linton, Eliza

World went mad, The: Brophy, John

World went very well then, The: Besant, *Sir* Walter

World within a war, A: Read, *Sir* Herbert

World within world: Spender, Stephen

World without end: Frankau, Gilbert

World without end: Massingham, Harold

Worlde of wordes, Italian and English, A: Florio, John

Worldes hydrographical discription, The: Davys, John

Worldlings, The: Merrick, Leonard

Worlds and I, The: Wilcox, Ella Wheeler

Worlds apart: Barfield, Owen

World's bane, The: Bentley, Phyllis

World's body, The: Ransom, J.C.

World's design, The: Madariaga, Salvador de

World's desire, The: Haggard, *Sir* H. Rider

World's desire, The: Lang, Andrew

World's end, The: Jefferies, Richard

World's End: Johnson, Pamela H.

World's end: Sinclair, Upton

World's great snare, The: Oppenheim, E. Phillips

World's highway, The: Angell, *Sir* Norman

World's Lincoln, The: Drinkwater, John

Worlds not realized: Gatty, Margaret

Worlds of color: Dubois, William

World's own, The: Howe, Julia Ward

World's pilgrim, The: Gore-Booth, E.S.

World's room, The: Whistler, Laurence

Worlds within worlds: Benson, Stella

World's wonder: †Bowen, Marjorie

Worleys: Reese, L.W.

Worm of death, The: Day-Lewis, C.

Worm of Spindlestonheugh, The: Swinburne, A.C.

Worm ourobouras, The: Eddison, Eric Rucker

Wormwood: †Corelli, Marie

Worn earth: Engle, Paul

Worn thimble, The: Hall, Anna Maria

Worship: Underhill, Evelyn

Worship of nature, The: Frazer, *Sir* James

Worshipper of the image, The: Le Gallienne, Richard

Worst Christmas story, The: Morley, C.D.

Worsted man, The: Bangs, J.K.

Worth of a penny, The: Peacham, Henry

Worth of a woman, The: Phillips, D.G.

Worth while: Wren, P.C.

Worthiness of Wales, The: Churchyard, Thomas

Worthy communicant, The: Taylor, Jeremy

Worthy tract of Paulus Jovius, The: Daniel, Samuel

Worzel-Flummery: Milne, A.A.

Would you kill him?: Lathrop, G.P.

Would-be-goods, The: Nesbit, E.

Wound and the bow, The: Wilson, Edmund

Wounded allies' relief committee, The: Bennett, Arnold

Wounded bird, The: Freeman, John

Wounded name, The: Broster, D.K.

Wounded souls: Gibbs, *Sir* Philip

Wounds in the rain: Crane, Stephen

Wounds of Civill War, The: Lodge, Thomas

Wrack at tidesend: Sitwell, *Sir* Osbert

Wraith of the red swan, The: Carman, Bliss

Wrath to come, The: Oppenheim, E. Phillips

Wreath, A: Blocksidge, C.W.

Wreath, 1894–1914, The: Hewlett, Maurice

Wreath for Margery, A: Gregory, H.V.

Wreath for Rivera: Marsh, Ngaio Edith

Wreath for San Gemignano, A: Aldington, Richard

Wreath for the enemy, A: Frankau, Pamela

Wreath of wild flowers from New England, A: Osgood, F.S.

Wreck, The: Tagore, *Sir* R.

Wreck of the Golden Mary, The: Dickens, Charles

Wreck of the "Grosvenor", The: Russell, W.C.

Wreck of the Northern Belle, The: Arnold, Edwin

Wreck of the Red Bird, The: Eggleston, G.C.

Wrecked in port: Yates, E.H.

Wrecker, The: Stevenson, R.L.

Wreckers of Sable Island, The: Oxley, J.M.

Wren, The: Tarkington, Booth

Wrestling Jacob: †Bowen, Marjorie

Wrist-watch castaways, The: Ewart, E.A.

Writ for libel: Pearson, Hesketh

Writ in barracks: Wallace, Edgar

Writ in sand: Cunninghame Graham, Robert

Write it right: Bierce, Ambrose

Writer and absolute, The: Lewis, P. Wyndham

Writer and his world, The: Morgan, Charles

Writer in America, The: Brooks, Van Wyck

Writer's diary, A: Woolf, Virginia

Writers on writing: Allen, Walter Ernest
Writer's notebook, A: Maugham, Somerset
Writer's notes on his trade, A: Montague, C.E.
Writer's point of view, The: Maugham, W.S.
Writer's recollections, A: Ward, *Mrs.* Humphrey
Writer's situation: Jameson, Storm
Writer's trade, The: Strong, L.A.G.
Writing aloud: Beresford, J.D.
Writing and thinking: Foerster, Norman
Writing fiction: Derleth, A.W.
Writing for money: De Voto, Bernard
Writing in America: Caldwell, Erskine Preston

Writing is work: Rinehart, Mary Roberts
Writing of English, The: Mais, S.P.B.
Writing of fiction, The: Wharton, Edith
Writing of history, The: Jusserand, Jean
Writing on the wall, The: Lindsay, Jack
Writings, The: Wister, Owen
Writings and buildings: Wright, Frank Lloyd
Wrong box, The: Stevenson, R.L.
Wrong envelope, The: (†Ennis Graham), Molesworth, *Mrs.*
Wrong foot foremost: Strong, L.A.G.
Wrong shadow, The: Brighouse, Harold
Wrong side out: Russell, W.C.

Wrongs of Africa, The: Roscoe, William
Wrongs of woman, The: Wollstonecraft, Mary
Wuthering Heights: Brontë, Emily
Wyandotté: Cooper, James Fenimore
Wych Hazel: Warner, S.B. and A.B. Warner
Wylder's hand: Le Fanu, Sheridan
Wyllard's weird: Braddon, Mary Elizabeth
Wyndham Lewis: Newton, Eric
Wyndham Towers: Aldrich, T.B.
Wyoming: Grey, Zane
Wytty and wytless: Heywood, John
Wyvern mystery, The: Le Fanu, Sheridan

X

X at Oberammergau: Wolfe, Humbert
X = 0: Drinkwater, John
XYZ: Colman, George, *the younger*

Xaîpe: Cummings, E.E.
Xerxes: Cibber, Colley
Ximena: Cibber, Colley
Ximena: Taylor, Bayard
Xingu: Wharton, Edith

X Rays: Dodge, M.A.
X-Rays and crystal structure: Bragg, *Sir* Laurence
X-Rays and crystal structure: Bragg, *Sir* William

Y

Yaksas: Coomaraswamy, A.K.
Yale University: Benét, S.V.
Yama and Yami: Isvaran, M.S.
Yankee among the nullifiers, A: Green, Asa
Yankee coast: Coffin, Robert
Yankee Doodle: Grant, Robert
Yankee fantasies: Mackaye, Percy
Yankee from the west, A: Read, O.P.
Yankee in Canada, A: Thoreau, H.D.
Yankee yarns and Yankee letters: Haliburton, T.C.

Yankey in London, The: Tyler, Royall
Yard, The: Vachell, H.A.
Yarn of Old Harbour town, The: Russell, W.C.
Yarrow revisited: Wordsworth, William
Yates pride, The: Freeman, Mary
Yattendon hymnal, The: Bridges, Robert
Ye belle alliance: Sala, G.A.H.
Ye fearful saints!: Housman, Laurence
Ye Field of ye Clothe of Golde: Sala, G.A.H.

Ye olden blue laws: Myers, Gustavus
Year: a glimpse from a watchtower, The: Dunsany, Edward Plunkett, *Baron*
Year at Margarets, The: †Armstrong, Anthony
Year Bearer's people, The: La Farge, Oliver
Year before last: Boyle, Kay
Year from a reporter's notebook, A: Davis, R.H.
Year in the country, A: Uttley, Alison
Year in, year out: Milne, A.A.
Year more or less, A: Joad, C.E.M.

Year nine, The: Manning, Anne

Year of consolation, A: Kemble, Fanny

Year of decision: De Voto, Bernard

Year of delight, The: Widdemer, Margaret

Year of my life, A: Street, A.G.

Year of prophesying, A: Wells, H.G.

Year of shame, The: Watson, Sir J.W.

Year of sorrow, The: Spencer, William Robert

Year of space: Linklater, Eric

Year of the world, The: Scott, W.B.

Year of Trafalgar, The: Newbolt, Sir Henry

Year that the locust..., A: Hutchinson, Arthur

Year with Bisshe-Bantam, A: Phillpotts, Eden

Year worth living, A: (†George F. Harrington), Baker, W.M.

Year-book of daily recreation and information concerning remarkable men and manners, times and seasons, The: Hone, William

Yearling, The: Rawlings, Marjorie

Years, The: Woolf, Virginia

Years between, The: Du Maurier, Daphne

Years between, The: Kipling, Rudyard

Year's end: Johnson, J.W.

Year's housekeeping in South Africa, A: Barker, M.A.

Years in a mirror: Gielgud, Val

Year's journey through Central and Eastern Arabia, A: Palgrave, W.G.

Year's letters, A: Swinburne, A.C.

Year's life, A: Lowell, J.R.

Years of endurance, The: Bryant, Sir Arthur

Years of grace: Barnes, Margaret Campbell

Years of love, The: Widdemer, Margaret

Years of my youth: Howells, W.D.

Years of plenty: Brown, Ivor

Years of the locust: Gielgud, Val

Years of victory: Bryant, Sir Arthur

Year's residence in the United States of America, A: Cobbett, William

Years with Rose, The: Thurber, James

Year's work in Civil-Service reform, The: Curtis, George William

Yeast, a problem: Kingsley, Charles

Yehuda: Levin, Meyer

Yellow Book, The: Beardsley, Aubrey

Yellow chief, The: Reid, T.M.

Yellow crayon, The: Oppenheim, E. Phillips

Yellow danger, The: Shiel, M.P.

Yellow fairy book, The: Lang, Andrew

Yellow flag, The: Yates, E.H.

Yellow frigate, The: Grant, James

Yellow gentians and blue: Gale, Zona

Yellow god, The: Haggard, Sir H. Rider

Yellow jack: Howard, S.C.

Yellow mask, The: Wallace, Edgar

Yellow placard, The: Lynd, Sylvia

Yellow poppy, The: Broster, D.K.

Yellow sands: Phillpotts, Eden

Yellow snake, The: Wallace, Edgar

Yellow tapers for Paris: Marshall, Bruce

Yellow ticket, The: Harris, J.T.

Yellow-maned lion, The: Glanville, Ernest

Yellowplush correspondence, The: Thackeray, W.M.

Yellowplush papers: Thackeray, W.M.

Yemassee, The: Simms, W.G.

Yeoman's hospital: Ashton, Helen

Yeomen of the Guard, The: Gilbert, Sir W.S.

Yes, Mrs. Williams: Williams, C.W.

Yes, my darling daughter: Ackland, Rodney

Yesterdailies: †Armstrong, Anthony

Yesterday: Hichens, Roben

Yesterday and long ago: (Stephen Southwold), †Bell, Neil

Yesterday is dead: Cloete, Stuart

Yesterday's burdens: Coates, R.M.

Yesterdays with authors: Fields, J.T.

Yet again: Beerbohm, Sir Max

Yet I ride the little horse: Temple, Joan

Yet other waters: Farrell, James

Yieger's cabinet: Webber, C.W.

Yoga and its objects, The: Ghose, Sri Aurobindo

Yoga explained: Yeats-Brown, Francis

Yoga, the way of self-fulfilment: Viljayatunga, Jinadasa

Yogic Sadhan: Ghose, Sri Aurobindo

Yoke of life, The: Grove, F.P.

Yoke of thunder, The: Coffin, Robert

Yolanda: Jacob, Naomi

Yolanda, maid of Burgundy: Major, Charles

Yolande: Black, William

Yollop: McCutcheon, G.B.

Yonnondio: Hosmer, W.H.C.

York: Mee, Arthur

York road, The: Reese, L.W.

Yorke, the adventurer: †Becke, Louis

Yorkshire garland, The: Ritson, Joseph

Yorkshire oddities, incidents and strange events: Baring-Gould, Sabine

Yorkshire West Riding: Pevsner, Nikolaus

Yorktown and Appomattox: Bagby, G.W.

Yosemite, The: Muir, John

Yosemite: Sterling, George

You; a personal message: Bok, E.W.

You and I: Barry, Philip

You and the refugee: Angell, *Sir* Norman

You can always duck: †Cheyney, Peter

You can call it a day: †Cheyney, Peter

You can't be too careful: Wells, H.G.

You can't get there from here: Nash, Ogden

You can't go home again: Wolfe, Thomas

You can't have it back: Mottram, R.H.

You can't hit a woman: †Cheyney, Peter

You can't keep the change: †Cheyney, Peter

You can't take it with you: Kaufman, G.S.

You, emperors and others: Warren, Robert Penn

You Han, flying boy of China: Buck, Pearl

You have a point there: Partridge, Eric

You have seen their faces: Caldwell, Erskine Preston

You know me Al: Lardner, Ring

You know what people are: Lucas, E.V.

You make your own life: Pritchett, V.S.

You never can tell: Shaw, G.B.

You never know, do you?: Coppard, A.E.

You never know your luck: Parker, *Sir* H.G.

You who have dreams: Anderson, Maxwell

You'd be surprised: †Cheyney, Peter

Youma: Hearn, Lafcadio

Young admiral, The: Shirley, James

Young adventure: Benét, S.V.

Young Alaskans, The: Hough, Emerson

Young Alaskans in the far North: Hough, Emerson

Young Alaskans in the Rockies, The: Hough, Emerson

Young Alaskans on the Missouri, The: Hough, Emerson

Young Alaskans on the trail, The: Hough, Emerson

Young Alexander the Great, The: Mitchison, Naomi

Young Alfred the Great, The: Mitchison, Naomi

Young America: Halleck, Fitz-Greene

Young Americans abroad: Hale, E.E.

Young Americans in the Orient: Hale, E.E.

Young Ames: Edmonds, W.D.

Young anarchy: Gibbs, *Sir* Philip

Young Archimedes: Huxley, Aldous

Young Art and old Hector: Gunn, Neil

Young artist, The: Ingraham, J.H.

Young B. Franklin: Mayhew, Henry

Young Bess: Irwin, Margaret

Young blood: Hornung, E.W.

Young Brontes, The: Bentley, Phyllis

Young Caesar, The: Warner, Rex

Young Carthaginian, The: Henry, G.A.

Young Cosima, The: †Richardson, H.H.

Young Countess, The: Trollope, Frances

Young desire it, The: †Mackenzie, Seaforth

Young Diana, The: †Corelli, Marie

Young Dr. Kildare: †Brand, Max

Young Duchess, The: Reynolds, G.

Young Duke, The: Disraeli, Benjamin

Young Earnest: Cannan, Gilbert

Young emigrants, The: Sedgewick, *Mrs.* S.A.L.

Young Emmanuel: Jacob, Naomi

Young emperor William II of Germany, The: Frederic, Harold

Young enchanted, The: Walpole, *Sir* Hugh

Young enthusiasts: Jenkins, Elizabeth

Young Felix: Swinnerton, Frank

Young folk's centennial rhymes: Carleton, William (McKendree)

Young folks' history of Russia: Dole, N.H.

Young folks' history of the United States: Higginson, T.W.

Young forester, The: Grey, Zane

Young foresters, The: Browne, Frances

Young Franc-tireurs, The: Henty, G.A.

Young genius, The: Ingraham, J.H.

Young Gerard: Farjeon, Eleanor

Young girl's life, A: Farjeon, B.L.

Young girl's wooing, A: Roe, E.P.

Young guard, The: Hornung, E.W.

Young Harry Tremayne: Pertwee, Roland

Young have secrets, The: Courage, J.F.

Young Heaven: Malleson, Miles

Young heiress, The: Trollope, Frances

Young idea, The: Coward, Noel

Young idea, The: Swinnerton, Frank

Young immigrants, The: Lardner, Ring

Young India: Gandhi, M.K.

Young Jägers, The: Reid, T.M.

Young Joe, and other boys: Trowbridge, J.T.

Young John Bull: Lathom, Francis

Young king, The: Behn, *Mrs.* Afra

Young king, The: Binyon, Laurence

Young laird and Edinburgh Katie, The: Ramsay, Allan

Young lion hunter, The: Grey, Zane

Young lions, The: Shaw, Irwin

Young lives: Le Gallienne, Richard

Young Livingstones, The: Mackail, Denis

Young Lonigan, a boyhood in Chicago streets: Farrell, James

Young love: Trollope, Frances

Young love, variations on a theme: Erskine, John

Young Lovell, The: Ford, Ford Madox

Young Lucretia: Freeman, Mary

Young Madame Conti: Griffith, Hubert

Young Madame Conti: Levy, Benn W.

Young man, The: Potter, Stephen

Young man comes to London, A: Arlen, Michael

Young man from the South, A: Robinson, E.S.L.

Young man in a hurry, A: Chambers, R.W.

Young man in business, The: Bok, E.W.

Young man Washington, The: Morison, S.E.

Young man with a horn: Baker, Dorothy

Young manhood of Studs Lonigan, The: Farrell, James

Young man's account of his conversion from Calvinism, A: Judd, Sylvester

Young man's fancies: Mottram, R.H.

Young man's fancy, A: Bell, Adrian

Young man's girl, The: Chambers, R.W.

Young man's year, A: (†Anthony Hope), Hawkins, Anthony Hope

Young master of Ayson Hall, The: Stockton, F.R.

Young matriarch, The: Stern, G.B.

Young Melbourne, The: Cecil, Lord David

Young men and the old, The: Cloete, Stuart

Young men are coming, The: Shiel, M.P.

Young men in love: †Arlen, Michael

Young men in spats: Wodehouse, P.G.

Young mischief and the perfect pair: De Selincourt, Hugh

Young Mistley: †Merriman, Seton

Young mountaineers, The: †Craddock, C.E.

Young Mrs. Cruse: Meynell, Viola

Young Mrs. Greeley: Tarkington, Booth

Young Mrs. Jardine: Craik, Mrs. Dinah

Young Mrs. Winthrop: Howard, B.C.

Young Musgrave: Oliphant, Margaret

Young Nick and Old Nick: Crockett, S.R.

Young people, The: Beresford, J.D.

Young people of Shakespeare's dramas, The: Barr, A.E.H.

Young people's pride: Benét, S.V.

Young person in pink, The: Jennings, Gertrude

Young Philip Madison: Williamson, Henry

Young physician, The: Young, Francis Brett

Young pitcher, The: Grey, Zane

Young pretender, The: Allen, C.R.

Young Quaker, The: O'Keeffe, John

Young Renny: De la Roche, Mazo

Young revolutionist, The: Buck, Pearl

Young Robin Brand detective: Crofts, F.W.

Young seigneur, The: Lighthall, W.D.

Young soldier hearts of France: Machar, A.M.

Young stagers, The: Wren, P.C.

Young surveyor, The: Trowbridge, J.T.

Young Tom: Reid, Forrest

Young traveller in England and Wales, The: Trease, Geoffrey

Young traveller in Greece, The: Trease, Geoffrey

Young traveller in India and Pakistan, The: Trease, Geoffrey

Young 'un: De Selincourt, Hugh

Young visitors, The: Ashford, Daisy

Young voyageurs, The: Reid, T.M.

Young Washington at Mt. Vernon: Mackaye, Percy

Young woman citizen, The: Austin, Mary

Young women out of love: Arlen, Michael

Young Woodley (novel and play): Van Druten, J.W.

Young woodsman, The: Oxley, J.M.

Young writer, The: Trease, Geoffrey

Younger brother, The: Behn, Mrs. Afra

Younger brother, The: Dibdin, Charles

Younger generation, The: Houghton, W.S.

Younger quire, The: Untermeyer, Louis

Younger set, The: Chambers, R.W.

Younger son, The: Belasco, David

Younger sons: Drake-Brockman, H.

Younger Venus, The: Royde-Smith, Naomi

Youngest, The: Barry, Philip

Youngest camel: Boyle, Kay

Youngest drama, The: Dukes, Ashley

Youngest girl in the fifth, The: Brazil, Angela

Youngest of three, The: Maltby, H.F.

Your amiable uncle: letters to his nephews: Tarkington, Booth

Your daughter Iris: Weidman, Jerome

Your deal my lovely: †Cheyney, Peter

Your England: Lockhart, Sir Robert Bruce

Your fiery furnace: Green, Paul

Your five gallants: Middleton, Thomas

Your humble servant: Tarkington, Booth

Your million dollars...: Sinclair, Upton

Your money's worth: Chase, Stuart

Your turn, Mr. Moto: Marquand, J.P.

You're only young once: Widdemer, Margaret

Yours, A.Lincoln: Horgan, Paul

Yours and mine: Warner, A.B.

Yours ever, Sam Pig: Uttley, Alison

Yours unfaithfully: Malleson, Miles

Yourself and your body: Grenfell, *Sir* Wilfred

Youth: Conrad, Joseph

Youth: Malleson, Miles

Youth: Rosenberg, Isaac

Youth after the war: Mais, S.P.B.

Youth and life: Bourne, Randolph

Youth and sensibility: Fausset, Hugh

Youth and the bright Medusa: Cather, Willa

Youth at the helm: Griffith, Hubert

Youth be damned!: Willson, H.B.

Youth goes west: Knister, Raymond

Youth in architecture: Mumford, Lewis

Youth in the air: Carman, Bliss

Youth of beauty: Roberts, C.E.M.

Youth of Jefferson, The: Cooke, John Esten

Youth of Parnassus, The: Morley, C.D.

Youth of Parnassus, The: Smith, L.L.P.

Youth of Washington, The: Mitchell, S.W.

Youth rides out: Seymour, Beatrice Kean

Youthful impostor, The: Reynolds, G.

Youth's encounter: Mackenzie, *Sir* C.

Yuan Mei: eighteenth century Chinese poet: Waley, Arthur

Yule tree, The: Carman, Bliss

Yuletide in a younger world: Hardy, Thomas

Yvernelle: †Norris, Frank

Z

Zaca adventure: Beebe, William

Zachary Phips: Bynner, Edwin Lassetter

Zadoc pine: Bunner, Henry Cuyler

Zaidee: Oliphant, Margaret

Zanoni: Lytton, E.G.E.B. *1st Baron*

Zanzibar: Burton, *Sir* Richard

Zapolya: Coleridge, S.T.

Zara, or, the girl of the period: English, Thomas Dunn

Zastrozzi: Shelley, P.B.

Zeal of thy house, The: Sayers, Dorothy

Zelanto: Munday, Anthony

Zelda Dameron: Nicholson, Meredith

Zella sees herself: †Delafield, E.M.

Zeluco: Moore, *Dr.* John

Zen Buddhism and its relation to art: Waley, Arthur

Zenana, The: Hockley, William Browne

Zenana, The: Landon, L.E.M.

Zenobia: Murphy, Arthur

Zenobia: Ware, William

Zenon the martyr: Cobbold, Richard

Zeph: Jackson, H.H.

Zephaniah Doolittle: English, Thomas Dunn

Zephyr book of English verse, The: Bottrall, Ronald

Zeppelin nights: Ford, Ford Madox

Zéro: Praed, *Mrs.* C.

Ziegfeld follies: Gershwin, Ira

Ziggurat and its surroundings, The: Woolley, *Sir* Leonard

Zigzag journey through Mexico, A: Reid, T.M.

Zigzags in France: Lucas, E.V.

Zillah: Smith, Horatio

Zimri: Hawkesworth, John

Zincali, The: Borrow, George

Zinzendorff: Sigourney, L.H.

Zisha: †Corelli, Marie

Zodiake of life: Googe, Barnabe

Zoe: the history of two lives: Jewsbury, Geraldine

Zohrab the hostage: Morier, J.J.

Zone police, The: Davis, R.H.

Zoo, The: Arlen, Michael

Zoo, The: Gibbings, Robert

Zoo: Macneice, Louis

Zoonomia: Darwin, Erasmus

Zorinski: Morton, Thomas

Zoroaster: Crawford, F. Marion

'Zouri's Christmas: Tourgée, A.W.

Zuleika Dobson or an Oxford love story: Beerbohm, *Sir* Max

Zuriel's grandchild: Riddell, *Mrs.* J.H.

Zury, the meanest man in Spring County: Kirkland, Joseph